1991
Florida
Statistical Abstract

Anne H. Shermyen, Editor
Susan S. Floyd, Managing Editor
Gayle H. Thompson, Production Supervisor
Dorothy A. Evans, Desktop Publishing Supervisor

Twenty-fifth Edition

Bureau of Economic and Business Research
College of Business Administration
University of Florida

University Press of Florida
Gainesville Tallahassee Tampa Boca Raton
Pensacola Orlando Miami Jacksonville
1991

UNIVERSITY OF FLORIDA

John V. Lombardi, President

COLLEGE OF BUSINESS ADMINISTRATION

John Kraft, Dean

BUREAU OF ECONOMIC AND BUSINESS RESEARCH

Stanley K. Smith, Director and
Population Program Director
Anne H. Shermyen, Associate Director Research
Programs/Services
Carol Taylor West, Forecasting Program Director
Barbara A. Bickart, Survey Program Director
David A. Denslow, Research Economist

University Press of Florida is the scholarly publishing agency for the
State University System of Florida, comprised of Florida A&M University
(Tallahassee), Florida Atlantic University (Boca Raton), Florida
International University (Miami), Florida State University (Tallahassee),
University of Central Florida (Orlando), University of Florida (Gainesville),
University of North Florida (Jacksonville), University of South Florida (Tampa),
University of West Florida (Pensacola).

Order books from University Press of Florida
15 N.W. 15th Street
Gainesville, FL 32611
1-800-226-3822

ISBN 0-8130-1085-3 and ISBN 0-8130-1086-1 (pbk.)
ISSN 0071-6022

Printed in the United States of America on acid-free paper

Cover photograph is of a sunrise over the Atlantic at Hutchinson Island,
Martin County and is courtesy of the Stuart/Martin County
Chamber of Commerce and the Dobens family, in memory
of the photographer, Chuck Dobens.

PREFACE

The twenty-fifth edition of the *Florida Statistical Abstract* continues a tradition of providing comprehensive and timely statistics about the social, economic and political organization of Florida. The purpose of the *Florida Statistical Abstract* is twofold; it serves as a convenient volume for statistical reference and as a guide to other statistical publications and sources. This volume includes a selection of data collected by public and private entities. Agencies of the State of Florida and the Federal Government contribute the majority of data.

Every effort is made to publish the most up-to-date figures possible, however, these data cover a wide range of activities reported for different time periods, so uniformity is impossible. Each table title states the time period for data shown in the table and exceptions are footnoted. Source notes are given at the bottom of each table. Data not available in publications but obtained from an agency are identified in the source notes as "unpublished data." Usually more statistical detail and more comprehensive discussion of methods and definitions exist in the source than can be included in the *Abstract*. Often an issuing agency has additional or updated data available after the *Abstract* goes to press. Suggestions for locating sources and additional information are in the Appendix.

Statistics in this edition are generally for the most recent year or period available by the summer of 1991. Each year all tables are reviewed: new tables of current interest are added, continuing series are updated or revised to reflect changes in source definitions or methods, and less timely data are eliminated. Some tables of "benchmark" data, although not timely, are repeated. The reader is encouraged to use tables in earlier editions, particularly for census data. At the back of this edition is an index of census tables appearing in previous editions.

Organization of the *Florida Statistical Abstract*. The *Abstract* is organized around five divisions each of which is subdivided into sections. Table numbers correspond to the section numbers. The first division (Sections 1.00 through 7.00) generally includes tables presenting data on characteristics of the population: number of people, housing, health, education, income, employment, and welfare. The next three divisions covering Sections 9.00 through 23.00, (Section 8.00 presents data on geography and the environment), primarily refer to establishments engaged in economic, social, and political activities.

Establishments are classified according to the Standard Industrial Classification (SIC) system in most sources. Developed by the U.S. Office of Management and Budget, the system is described in the *Standard Industrial Classification Manual* which was published in updated form in 1987. The *Manual* defines an establishment as "an economic unit generally at a single physical location where business is conducted, or where services or industrial operations are performed." An establishment is not necessarily identical with an enterprise or company which may consist of more than one establishment. Both profit-making and not-for-profit organizations are included as well as agencies of the federal, state, and local governments. Major industry divisions are assigned two-digit codes: 01 through 99; subdivisions are classified by three- and four-digit codes. (See the Glossary, "Industrial Classification System, Standard," for more discussion.)

The last division of the *Abstract* contains tables of a comparative nature: economic and social trends. Time series showing the fluctuations of such major economic indicators as prices and employment are included in Section 24.00. Selected statistics of the economic, social, and physical environments of Florida, other Sunbelt and populous states comprise Section 25.00.

Changes in this edition. New tables present data covering workers' compensation injuries and cost by industry, solid waste disposal, State Student Assessment Test (SSAT) scores, hurricanes, water rates, new home loans, phosphate reserves, Florida Consumer Confidence Index, adult congregate living facilities and selected service industries from the 1987 Census of Service

Industries. Data introduced in the state comparisons include Medicaid payments, hazardous waste sites, teenage mothers, adults under correctional supervision, lottery tickey sales per capita and Hispanic elected officials. All population tables (Section 1.00) have been updated with data from the 1990 Census of Population. Many tables in other sections are revised and reflect new data items. Most changes relating to specific tables and sources are discussed in notes to the tables or in the Appendix.

Abstract diskettes. *Abstract* tables are available on microcomputer diskette. To order diskettes please contact the Bureau of Economic and Business Research, 221 Matherly Hall, Gainesville, Florida, 32611-2017, (904) 392-0171.

Bureau of Economic and Business Research. The Bureau's mission is twofold: (1) to produce, collect, analyze and disseminate economic and demographic data on Florida; and (2) conduct and publish findings of applied research on topics relating to the state's on-going economic growth and development. The Bureau's activities are organized around four research programs: forecasting, population, survey, and local government studies.

Acknowledgements. Many members of the Bureau shared in the preparation of this edition of the *Abstract* but the key personnel were: managing editor, Susan Floyd; production supervisor, Gayle Thompson; and desktop publishing supervisor, Dorothy Evans. Susan acted as our vigilant project manager, collecting sources and reviewing continuing series for changes, setting up and monitoring table production and reviewing the index. Gayle, new to the position in the spring, quickly mastered development of the spreadsheet tables and supervised the student assistants. She made useful suggestions for table changes and developed new education tables in Section 4.00. Dorothy Evans made final table corrections, page layouts, and assisted in proofing. This edition marks the twentieth volume that Dorothy has carefully shepherded through production.

Carol McLarty, information specialist, worked around her telephone calls to help research and contact data sources, obtain copyright permission from private firms and review the index. She updated the index of census tables and was primary proofreader. Robyn Richards backed up data entry and word processing and helped proof the final index with Janet Fletcher and Janet Rose. Student assistants Astra Cuidad-Real, Sheena Newsom and Lisa Stone are to be commended for their careful work in entering most of the data, checking errors and proofing. Wendy Glasser prepared *Abstract* diskettes for distribution and before leaving helped to train Gayle for her new position. Janet Galvez provided data from the BEBR Data Base. Ravi Bayya provided computing support to obtain data from the BEBR Population Program and other sources. Raymond Major and Chris McCarty supplied data from the Florida Consumer Attitude Survey. Clinton Collins was the computer network manager. Ann Pierce supervised Leslie Bogart and Mohini Wettasinghe in preparing the cover. The clerical staff assisted with promotional mailing. The University Press of Florida coordinated the printing and distribution.

Jan Coyne, cartographer for the Geography Department, prepared the maps and section divider graphics. These were adapted from the *Florida Graphic Atlas*, a companion publication to the *Abstract* and prepared under the editorship of Dr. John Dunkle. Please call the Geography Department Cartographic Laboratory at (904) 392-0494 to order or to obtain information about the *Atlas*.

We are always pleased to receive suggestions for improving the coverage and presentation of data in the *Florida Statistical Abstract.*

Anne H. Shermyen
Editor

Gainesville, Florida
September 1991

CONTENTS

Counties and Standard Metropolitan Statistical Areas
Prior to January 1983

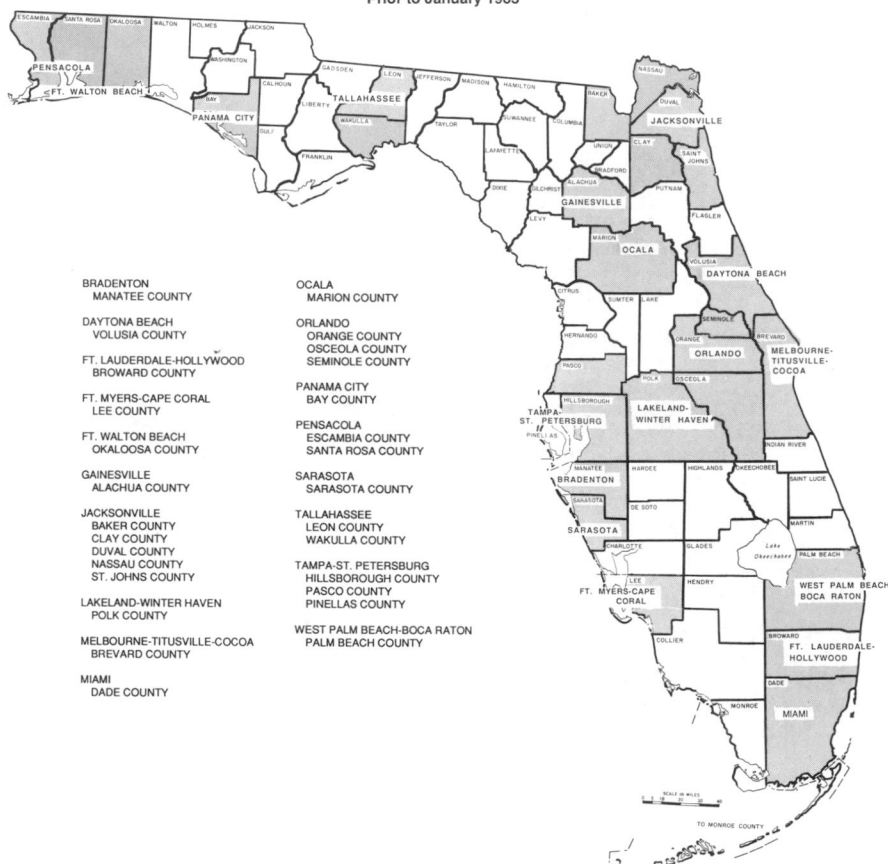

BRADENTON
  MANATEE COUNTY

DAYTONA BEACH
  VOLUSIA COUNTY

FT. LAUDERDALE-HOLLYWOOD
  BROWARD COUNTY

FT. MYERS-CAPE CORAL
  LEE COUNTY

FT. WALTON BEACH
  OKALOOSA COUNTY

GAINESVILLE
  ALACHUA COUNTY

JACKSONVILLE
  BAKER COUNTY
  CLAY COUNTY
  DUVAL COUNTY
  NASSAU COUNTY
  ST. JOHNS COUNTY

LAKELAND-WINTER HAVEN
  POLK COUNTY

MELBOURNE-TITUSVILLE-COCOA
  BREVARD COUNTY

MIAMI
  DADE COUNTY

OCALA
  MARION COUNTY

ORLANDO
  ORANGE COUNTY
  OSCEOLA COUNTY
  SEMINOLE COUNTY

PANAMA CITY
  BAY COUNTY

PENSACOLA
  ESCAMBIA COUNTY
  SANTA ROSA COUNTY

SARASOTA
  SARASOTA COUNTY

TALLAHASSEE
  LEON COUNTY
  WAKULLA COUNTY

TAMPA-ST. PETERSBURG
  HILLSBOROUGH COUNTY
  PASCO COUNTY
  PINELLAS COUNTY

WEST PALM BEACH-BOCA RATON
  PALM BEACH COUNTY

Counties and Metropolitan Statistical Areas

Effective June 30, 1990

BRADENTON MSA
  MANATEE COUNTY

DAYTONA BEACH MSA
  VOLUSIA COUNTY

FT. LAUDERDALE-HOLLYWOOD-
POMPANO BEACH PMSA*
  BROWARD COUNTY

FT. MYERS-CAPE CORAL MSA
  LEE COUNTY

FT. PIERCE MSA
  MARTIN COUNTY
  ST. LUCIE COUNTY

FT. WALTON BEACH MSA
  OKALOOSA COUNTY

GAINESVILLE MSA
  ALACHUA COUNTY
  BRADFORD COUNTY

JACKSONVILLE MSA
  CLAY COUNTY
  DUVAL COUNTY
  NASSAU COUNTY
  ST. JOHNS COUNTY

LAKELAND-WINTER HAVEN MSA
  POLK COUNTY

MELBOURNE-TITUSVILLE-PALM
BAY MSA
  BREVARD COUNTY

MIAMI-HIALEAH PMSA*
  DADE COUNTY

NAPLES MSA
  COLLIER COUNTY

OCALA MSA
  MARION COUNTY

ORLANDO MSA
  ORANGE COUNTY
  OSCEOLA COUNTY
  SEMINOLE COUNTY

PANAMA CITY MSA
  BAY COUNTY

PENSACOLA MSA
  ESCAMBIA COUNTY
  SANTA ROSA COUNTY

SARASOTA MSA
  SARASOTA COUNTY

TALLAHASSEE MSA
  GADSDEN COUNTY
  LEON COUNTY

TAMPA-ST. PETERSBURG-
CLEARWATER MSA
  HERNANDO COUNTY
  HILLSBOROUGH COUNTY
  PASCO COUNTY
  PINELLAS COUNTY

WEST PALM BEACH-BOCA RATON-
DELRAY BEACH MSA
  PALM BEACH COUNTY

* MIAMI-FT. LAUDERDALE CMSA

POPULATION

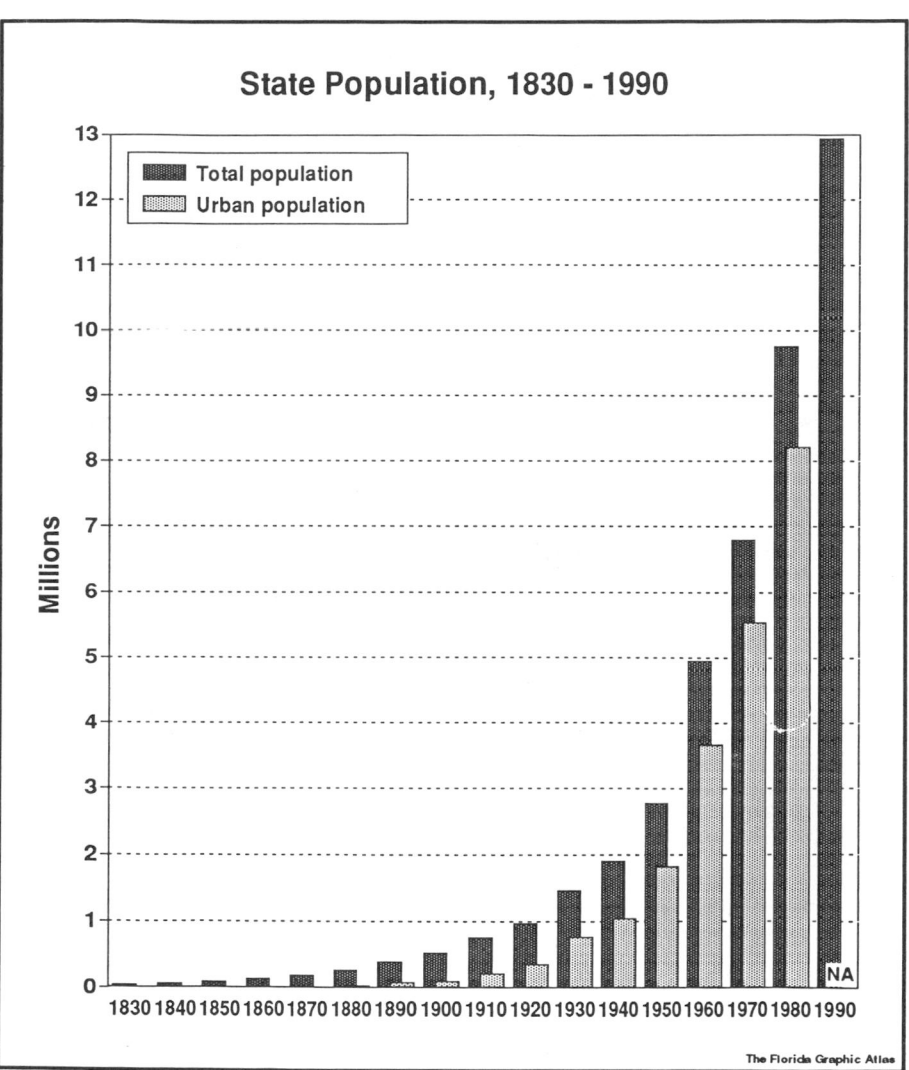

State Population, 1830 - 1990

Millions

■ Total population
▧ Urban population

1830 1840 1850 1860 1870 1880 1890 1900 1910 1920 1930 1940 1950 1960 1970 1980 1990

NA

The Florida Graphic Atlas

Source: Table 1.10

SECTION 1.00
POPULATION

TABLES LISTED BY MAJOR HEADINGS

Table 1.10. POPULATION: CENSUS COUNTS AND URBAN AND RURAL POPULATION IN FLORIDA
CENSUS YEARS 1830 TO 1990

Census year and date	Total population — Number	Change from preceding census — Number	Change from preceding census — Percentage	Urban population — Number	Urban population — Percentage of total	Rural population — Number	Rural population — Percentage of total
Previous urban definition 1/							
1830 (June 1)	34,730	(X)	(X)	0	0.0	34,730	100.0
1840 (June 1)	54,477	19,747	56.9	0	0.0	54,477	100.0
1850 (June 1)	87,445	32,968	60.5	0	0.0	87,445	100.0
1860 (June 1)	140,424	52,979	60.6	5,708	4.1	134,716	95.9
1870 (June 1)	187,748	47,324	33.7	15,275	8.1	172,473	91.9
1880 (June 1)	269,493	81,745	43.5	26,947	10.0	242,546	90.0
1890 (June 1)	391,422	121,929	45.2	77,358	19.8	314,064	80.2
1900 (June 1)	528,542	137,120	35.0	107,031	20.3	421,511	79.7
1910 (April 15)	752,619	224,077	42.4	219,080	29.1	533,539	70.9
1920 (January 1)	968,470	215,851	28.7	353,515	36.5	614,955	63.5
1930 (April 1)	1,468,211	499,741	51.6	759,778	51.7	708,433	48.3
1940 (April 1)	1,897,414	429,203	29.2	1,045,791	55.1	851,623	44.9
1950 (April 1)	2,771,305	873,891	46.1	1,566,788	56.5	1,204,517	43.5
1960 (April 1)	4,951,560	2,180,255	78.7	3,077,989	62.2	1,873,571	37.8
Current urban definition 2/							
1950 (April 1)	2,771,305	873,891	46.1	1,813,890	65.5	957,415	34.5
1960 (April 1)	4,951,560	2,180,255	78.7	3,661,383	73.9	1,290,177	26.1
1970 (April 1)	6,791,418	1,839,858	37.2	5,544,551	81.7	1,244,892	18.3
1980 (April 1)	9,746,324	2,954,906	43.5	8,212,385	84.3	1,533,939	15.7
1990 (April 1)	12,937,926	3,191,602	32.8	(NA)	(NA)	(NA)	(NA)

(X) Not applicable.

(NA) Not available.

1/ Figures have been adjusted to constitute a substantially consistent series based on incorporated places of 2,500 or more persons with additional areas defined as urban under special rules.

2/ The current urban definition defines the urban population as all persons living in urbanized areas and in places of 2,500 or more persons outside urbanized areas. An urbanized area comprises an incorporated place and adjacent densely settled surrounding area that together have a minimum population of 50,000. Population not classified as urban constitutes the rural population. Rural classification need not imply farm residence or a sparsely settled area because a small city is rural as long as it is outside an urbanized area and has fewer than 2,500 persons.

Source: U.S., Department of Commerce, Bureau of the Census, *1980 Census of Population: Number of Inhabitants, Florida.* PC80-1-A11 and University of Florida, Bureau of Economic and Business Research, Population Program, *Florida Population: Census Summary, 1990.*

Florida Statistical Abstract 1991

Table 1.12. POPULATION: CENSUS COUNTS, APRIL 1, 1980 AND 1990 IN FLORIDA, OTHER
STATES, AND THE UNITED STATES

State	1980 (1,000)	1990 (1,000)	Percentage change 1980 to 1990	State	1980 (1,000)	1990 (1,000)	Percentage change 1980 to 1990
Florida	9,746	12,938	32.8	Missouri	4,917	5,117	4.1
				Montana	787	799	1.6
Alabama	3,894	4,041	3.8	Nebraska	1,570	1,578	0.6
Alaska	402	550	36.9	Nevada	800	1,202	50.1
Arizona	2,718	3,665	34.8	New Hampshire	921	1,109	20.5
Arkansas	2,286	2,351	2.8	New Jersey	7,365	7,730	5.0
California	23,668	29,760	25.7	New Mexico	1,303	1,515	16.3
Colorado	2,890	3,294	14.0	New York	17,558	17,990	2.5
Connecticut	3,108	3,287	5.8	North Carolina	5,882	6,629	12.7
Delaware	594	666	12.1	North Dakota	653	639	-2.1
District of Columbia	638	607	-4.9	Ohio	10,798	10,847	0.5
				Oklahoma	3,025	3,146	4.0
Georgia	5,463	6,478	18.6	Oregon	2,633	2,842	8.0
Hawaii	965	1,108	14.9	Pennsylvania	11,864	11,882	0.2
Idaho	944	1,007	6.7	Rhode Island	947	1,003	6.0
Illinois	11,427	11,431	0.0	South Carolina	3,122	3,487	11.7
Indiana	5,490	5,544	1.0	South Dakota	691	696	0.8
Iowa	2,914	2,777	-4.7	Tennessee	4,591	4,877	6.2
Kansas	2,364	2,478	4.8	Texas	14,229	16,987	19.4
Kentucky	3,661	3,685	0.7	Utah	1,461	1,723	17.9
Louisiana	4,206	4,220	0.3	Vermont	511	563	10.0
Maine	1,125	1,228	9.2	Virginia	5,347	6,187	15.7
Maryland	4,217	4,781	13.4	Washington	4,132	4,867	17.8
Massachusetts	5,737	6,016	4.9	West Virginia	1,950	1,793	-8.0
Michigan	9,262	9,295	0.4	Wisconsin	4,706	4,892	4.0
Minnesota	4,076	4,375	7.3	Wyoming	470	454	-3.4
Mississippi	2,521	2,573	2.1	United States	226,546	248,710	9.8

Source: University of Florida, Bureau of Economic and Business Research, Population Program, *Florida Population: Census Summary, 1990.*

Florida Statistical Abstract 1991

Table 1.20. POPULATION: CENSUS COUNTS, APRIL 1, 1980 AND 1990, AND ESTIMATES, APRIL 1, 1979 THROUGH 1989, IN THE STATE AND COUNTIES OF FLORIDA

(in thousands, rounded to hundreds)

County	Census 1980	Census 1990	Estimates 1979	1981	1982	1983	1984	1985	1986	1987	1988	1989
Florida	9,747.0	12,937.9	9,448.5	10,138.2	10,430.2	10,678.7	10,982.5	11,322.3	11,654.1	12,000.2	12,327.6	12,650.9
Alachua	151.4	181.6	148.2	154.5	158.7	160.8	165.5	169.2	171.5	173.9	176.1	179.1
Baker	15.3	18.5	14.9	15.8	16.0	16.4	16.8	16.9	17.2	17.5	17.8	18.1
Bay	97.7	127.0	94.4	100.2	103.9	106.7	110.7	116.5	120.1	122.5	124.4	125.8
Bradford	20.0	22.5	19.5	20.0	20.6	22.6	22.4	22.6	22.3	22.8	23.0	23.0
Brevard	273.0	399.0	264.3	284.2	297.8	308.6	319.5	334.8	349.7	363.0	376.3	388.4
Broward	1,018.3	1,255.5	988.1	1,049.7	1,069.0	1,082.5	1,100.8	1,124.8	1,147.9	1,176.8	1,206.7	1,232.5
Calhoun	9.3	11.0	8.9	9.4	9.4	9.4	9.4	9.6	9.7	9.8	10.1	10.8
Charlotte	58.5	111.0	54.9	62.1	67.9	71.5	75.6	80.7	85.7	91.4	97.0	103.2
Citrus	54.7	93.5	50.8	59.4	62.8	65.3	68.8	72.7	77.5	81.7	85.9	90.4
Clay	67.1	106.0	63.3	69.8	72.7	75.6	80.6	86.0	89.7	95.7	98.5	103.0
Collier	86.0	152.1	79.7	92.3	99.5	105.0	110.2	115.9	122.0	127.7	135.3	143.7
Columbia	35.4	42.6	34.4	35.9	36.9	37.7	38.3	38.9	39.6	40.4	41.1	41.9
Dade	1,625.5	1,937.1	1,597.4	1,718.5	1,736.3	1,750.0	1,768.7	1,789.3	1,815.6	1,846.8	1,879.1	1,908.9
De Soto	19.0	23.9	18.6	19.5	20.1	20.6	21.0	21.5	22.0	22.4	22.9	23.5
Dixie	7.8	10.6	7.7	7.9	8.3	8.9	9.0	9.2	9.4	9.6	9.8	10.2
Duval	571.0	673.0	571.3	578.7	583.9	592.2	605.0	619.1	633.7	645.9	656.4	663.4
Escambia	233.8	262.8	232.2	238.3	241.8	244.9	249.1	253.3	256.9	259.0	260.4	261.6
Flagler	10.9	28.7	9.9	12.3	13.3	14.3	15.4	17.0	18.5	20.5	23.1	26.0
Franklin	7.7	9.0	7.7	7.8	8.0	8.1	8.4	8.5	8.6	8.6	8.7	8.8
Gadsden	41.7	41.1	41.1	41.7	41.7	41.7	41.6	41.4	41.3	41.4	41.4	41.1
Gilchrist	5.8	9.7	5.6	6.4	6.8	7.3	7.2	7.5	7.7	7.9	8.5	9.1
Glades	6.0	7.6	6.0	6.1	6.2	6.4	6.5	6.8	6.9	7.1	7.2	7.3
Gulf	10.7	11.5	10.6	10.7	10.7	10.9	10.9	11.0	11.1	11.2	11.2	11.3

See footnote at end of table.

Continued . . .

Table 1.20. POPULATION: CENSUS COUNTS, APRIL 1, 1980 AND 1990, AND ESTIMATES, APRIL 1, 1979 THROUGH 1989, IN THE STATE AND COUNTIES OF FLORIDA (Continued)

(in thousands, rounded to hundreds)

County	Census		Estimates									
	1980	1990	1979	1981	1982	1983	1984	1985	1986	1987	1988	1989
Hamilton	8.8	10.9	8.8	8.8	8.9	9.0	9.1	9.2	9.4	9.5	10.1	10.6
Hardee	20.4	19.5	19.3	20.3	20.3	20.3	20.2	20.2	20.1	20.0	19.9	19.7
Hendry	18.6	25.8	18.1	19.4	20.1	20.7	21.5	22.4	23.3	24.0	24.8	25.3
Hernando	44.5	101.1	39.3	49.4	53.9	58.5	64.0	70.2	76.5	83.4	90.5	95.5
Highlands	47.5	68.4	46.3	50.3	52.3	53.5	55.5	57.5	59.4	62.1	64.3	66.4
Hillsborough	646.9	834.1	630.8	663.9	682.6	698.9	721.4	747.4	769.2	792.2	809.5	822.6
Holmes	14.7	15.8	14.5	14.8	14.9	15.0	15.0	15.0	15.1	15.1	15.2	15.5
Indian River	59.9	90.2	56.8	63.3	67.2	69.9	72.8	75.0	77.7	80.2	83.7	86.8
Jackson	39.2	41.4	39.1	39.5	40.1	40.3	40.3	40.7	40.6	41.2	41.2	41.2
Jefferson	10.7	11.3	10.6	10.8	10.9	11.0	11.0	11.1	11.1	11.2	11.2	11.3
Lafayette	4.0	5.6	4.0	4.0	4.1	4.2	4.4	4.5	4.7	5.1	5.2	5.4
Lake	104.9	152.1	99.2	108.6	112.9	116.9	121.3	126.5	131.2	137.2	141.0	146.5
Lee	205.3	335.1	192.7	216.8	233.0	243.9	260.2	273.7	286.7	300.6	312.3	325.4
Leon	148.7	192.5	142.2	152.7	156.5	159.5	163.0	166.9	169.7	174.4	178.9	187.5
Levy	19.9	25.9	19.8	20.5	21.2	21.8	22.2	22.6	23.3	23.8	24.5	25.3
Liberty	4.3	5.6	4.2	4.3	4.4	4.4	4.5	4.5	4.6	4.6	4.7	4.7
Madison	14.9	16.6	14.8	15.0	15.0	15.1	15.2	15.3	15.3	15.4	15.4	15.8
Manatee	148.4	211.7	142.8	156.0	162.9	169.0	173.9	180.1	186.1	193.5	199.7	205.7
Marion	122.5	194.8	114.5	130.0	136.3	143.5	149.2	158.9	167.1	174.2	180.9	188.1
Martin	64.0	100.9	60.6	67.7	71.6	74.4	78.0	80.9	84.2	88.3	92.0	96.2
Monroe	63.2	78.0	64.0	64.5	66.0	67.2	68.7	69.9	71.4	73.1	75.5	76.8
Nassau	32.9	43.9	32.4	33.8	35.2	36.1	37.2	38.6	39.8	41.2	42.1	43.5
Okaloosa	109.9	143.8	108.6	113.4	117.2	121.4	125.5	130.6	134.9	137.5	139.8	141.6
Okeechobee	20.3	29.6	19.9	21.3	22.5	23.0	24.0	24.9	26.1	27.3	28.1	28.9

See footnote at end of table.

Continued . . .

Table 1.20. POPULATION: CENSUS COUNTS, APRIL 1, 1980 AND 1990, AND ESTIMATES, APRIL 1, 1979 THROUGH 1989, IN THE STATE AND COUNTIES OF FLORIDA (Continued)

(in thousands, rounded to hundreds)

County	Census 1980	Census 1990	1979	1981	1982	1983	Estimates 1984	1985	1986	1987	1988	1989
Orange	470.9	677.5	460.6	484.5	498.8	513.5	533.8	556.4	577.9	602.8	622.3	652.4
Osceola	49.3	107.7	46.5	55.4	60.5	64.4	70.1	77.4	82.2	87.6	95.2	101.0
Palm Beach	576.8	863.5	542.7	618.4	647.8	667.2	695.2	723.3	753.7	784.8	817.5	841.5
Pasco	193.7	281.1	178.0	204.9	213.4	221.8	229.2	237.6	249.1	258.2	267.0	274.4
Pinellas	728.5	851.7	714.7	746.0	758.2	771.2	786.0	801.3	814.4	825.7	834.0	844.6
Polk	321.7	405.4	311.8	329.8	339.3	346.7	355.0	365.0	374.1	383.0	391.6	399.0
Putnam	50.5	65.1	49.7	51.5	53.3	55.0	56.2	57.7	59.5	61.0	62.3	63.9
St. Johns	51.3	83.8	48.7	53.8	57.2	60.6	64.1	68.2	72.1	74.2	78.3	82.0
St. Lucie	87.2	150.2	82.8	95.2	101.3	106.7	110.7	116.5	122.9	129.5	136.3	144.1
Santa Rosa	56.0	81.6	54.6	58.2	59.8	62.6	65.2	67.3	70.2	73.3	75.6	79.1
Sarasota	202.3	277.8	193.5	211.3	220.3	229.2	236.7	244.1	251.1	258.1	264.3	271.4
Seminole	179.8	287.5	168.0	187.3	194.3	202.1	213.9	226.3	238.1	251.4	264.7	277.3
Sumter	24.3	31.6	22.1	24.8	25.4	26.0	26.8	27.6	28.6	29.3	29.8	30.9
Suwannee	22.3	26.8	21.7	23.1	23.5	23.7	24.1	24.5	25.0	25.3	25.7	26.3
Taylor	16.5	17.1	16.2	16.7	16.8	16.9	17.0	17.1	17.1	17.2	17.2	17.2
Union	10.2	10.3	10.6	10.1	11.3	10.6	10.5	10.6	10.4	10.6	10.1	10.3
Volusia	258.8	370.7	248.1	269.2	278.1	286.5	296.7	308.4	321.1	333.6	347.6	360.2
Wakulla	10.9	14.2	10.5	10.9	11.2	11.4	12.2	12.7	12.9	13.2	13.5	13.8
Walton	21.3	27.8	20.6	21.7	22.2	22.9	23.9	25.0	25.5	26.2	26.6	27.1
Washington	14.5	16.9	14.3	14.8	15.0	15.1	15.3	15.6	15.8	16.3	16.5	16.8

Note: These are revised intercensal estimates that incorporate the effects of 1990 census counts, all revisions to 1980 census counts, and any changes that may have occurred in the underlying base data.

Source: University of Florida, Bureau of Economic and Business Research, Population Program, *Florida Population: Census Summary, 1990*, and *Special Population Reports*, May 1991. Census data from U.S. Bureau of the Census.

Table 1.31. POPULATION: CENSUS COUNTS IN THE STATE, COUNTIES, AND MUNICIPALITIES
OF FLORIDA, APRIL 1, 1980 AND 1990

Area	1980	1990	Area	1980	1990
Florida	9,746,961	12,937,926	Brevard (Continued)		
Incorporated	5,245,606	6,404,550	Palm Bay	18,560	62,632
Unincorporated	4,501,355	6,533,376	Palm Shores	77	210
			Rockledge	11,877	16,023
Alachua	151,369	181,596	Satellite Beach	9,163	9,889
Alachua	3,561	4,529	Titusville	31,910	39,394
Archer	1,230	1,372	West Melbourne	5,078	8,399
Gainesville	81,371	84,770	Unincorporated	103,318	149,560
Hawthorne	1,303	1,305			
High Springs	2,491	3,144	Broward	1,018,257	1,255,488
LaCrosse	170	122	Coconut Creek	6,288	27,485
Micanopy	737	612	Cooper City	10,140	20,791
Newberry	1,826	1,644	Coral Springs	37,349	79,443
Waldo	993	1,017	Dania	11,811	13,024
Unincorporated	57,687	83,081	Davie	20,515	47,217
			Deerfield Beach	39,193	46,325
Baker	15,289	18,486	Ft. Lauderdale	153,279	149,377
Glen St. Mary	462	480	Hacienda Village	126	A/
Macclenny	3,851	3,966	Hallandale	36,460	30,996
Unincorporated	10,976	14,040	Hillsboro Beach	1,554	1,748
			Hollywood	121,323	121,697
Bay	97,740	126,994	Lauderdale-by-the-Sea	2,639	2,990
Callaway	7,154	12,253	Lauderdale Lakes	25,426	27,341
Cedar Grove	1,104	1,479	Lauderhill	37,271	49,708
Lynn Haven	6,239	9,298	Lazy Lake Village	31	33
Mexico Beach	632	992	Lighthouse Point	11,488	10,378
Panama City	33,346	34,378	Margate	35,900	42,985
Panama City Beach	2,148	4,051	Miramar	32,813	40,663
Parker	4,298	4,598	North Lauderdale	18,479	26,506
Springfield	7,220	8,715	Oakland Park	23,035	26,326
Unincorporated	35,599	51,230	Parkland	545	3,558
			Pembroke Park	5,326	4,933
Bradford	20,023	22,515	Pembroke Pines	35,776	65,452
Brooker	429	312	Plantation	48,501	66,692
Hampton	466	296	Pompano Beach	52,618	72,411
Lawtey	692	676	Sea Ranch Lakes	584	619
Starke	5,306	5,226	Sunrise	39,681	64,407
Unincorporated	13,130	16,005	Tamarac	29,376	44,822
			Wilton Manors	12,742	11,804
Brevard	272,959	398,978	Unincorporated	167,988	155,757
Cape Canaveral	5,733	8,014			
Cocoa	16,096	17,722	Calhoun	9,294	11,011
Cocoa Beach	10,926	12,123	Altha	478	497
Indialantic	2,883	2,844	Blountstown	2,632	2,404
Indian Harbour Beach	5,967	6,933	Unincorporated	6,184	8,110
Malabar	1,118	1,977			
Melbourne	46,536	59,646	Charlotte	58,460	110,975
Melbourne Beach	2,713	3,021	Punta Gorda	6,797	10,747
Melbourne Village	1,004	591	Unincorporated	51,663	100,228

See footnotes at end of table.   Continued . . .

Table 1.31. POPULATION: CENSUS COUNTS IN THE STATE, COUNTIES, AND MUNICIPALITIES
OF FLORIDA, APRIL 1, 1980 AND 1990 (Continued)

Area	1980	1990	Area	1980	1990
Citrus	54,703	93,515	De Soto	19,039	23,865
Crystal River	2,778	4,044	Arcadia	6,002	6,488
Inverness	4,095	5,797	Unincorporated	13,037	17,377
Unincorporated	47,830	83,674			
			Dixie	7,751	10,585
Clay	67,052	105,986	Cross City	2,154	2,041
Green Cove Springs	4,154	4,497	Horseshoe Beach	304	252
Keystone Heights	1,056	1,315	Unincorporated	5,293	8,292
Orange Park	8,766	9,488			
Penney Farms	630	609	Duval	571,003	672,971
Unincorporated	52,446	90,077	Atlantic Beach	7,847	11,636
			Baldwin	1,526	1,450
			Jacksonville	540,920	635,230
Collier	85,971	152,099	Jacksonville Beach	15,462	17,839
Everglades	524	321	Neptune Beach	5,248	6,816
Naples	17,581	19,505			
Unincorporated	67,866	132,273	Escambia	233,794	262,798
			Century	495	1,989
Columbia	35,399	42,613	Pensacola	57,619	58,165
Ft. White	386	268	Unincorporated	175,680	202,644
Lake City	9,257	10,005			
Unincorporated	25,756	32,340	Flagler	10,913	28,701
			Beverly Beach	217	312
Dade	1,625,509	1,937,094	Bunnell	1,816	1,873
Bal Harbour	2,973	3,045	Flagler Beach	2,208	3,820
Bay Harbor Islands	4,869	4,703	Marineland (part)	8	21
Biscayne Park	3,088	3,068	Painters Hill	40	A/
Coral Gables	43,241	40,091	Unincorporated	6,624	22,675
El Portal	2,055	2,457			
Florida City	6,174	5,806	Franklin	7,661	8,967
Golden Beach	612	774	Apalachicola	2,565	2,602
Hialeah	145,254	188,004	Carrabelle	1,304	1,200
Hialeah Gardens	2,700	7,713	Unincorporated	3,792	5,165
Homestead	20,668	26,866			
Indian Creek Village	103	44	Gadsden	41,674	41,105
Islandia	12	13	Chattahoochee	5,332	4,382
Medley	537	663	Greensboro	562	586
Miami	346,865	358,548	Gretna	1,448	1,981
Miami Beach	96,298	92,639	Havana	2,782	1,654
Miami Shores	9,244	10,084	Midway	0	852
Miami Springs	12,350	13,268	Quincy	8,591	7,444
North Bay	4,920	5,383	Unincorporated	22,959	24,206
North Miami	42,566	49,998			
North Miami Beach	36,553	35,359	Gilchrist	5,767	9,667
Opa-Locka	14,460	15,283	Bell	227	267
Pennsuco	15	A/	Fanning Springs (part)	164	230
South Miami	10,944	10,404	Trenton	1,131	1,287
Surfside	3,763	4,108	Unincorporated	4,245	7,883
Sweetwater	8,251	13,909			
Virginia Gardens	2,098	2,212	Glades	5,992	7,591
West Miami	6,076	5,727	Moore Haven	1,250	1,432
Unincorporated	798,820	1,036,925	Unincorporated	4,742	6,159

    See footnotes at end of table.   Continued . . .

Florida Statistical Abstract 1991

Table 1.31.   POPULATION: CENSUS COUNTS IN THE STATE, COUNTIES, AND MUNICIPALITIES
OF FLORIDA, APRIL 1, 1980 AND 1990 (Continued)

Area	1980	1990	Area	1980	1990
Gulf	10,658	11,504	Indian River (Continued)		
Port St. Joe	4,027	4,044	Sebastian	2,831	10,205
Ward Ridge	104	A/	Vero Beach	16,176	17,350
Wewahitchka	1,742	1,779	Unincorporated	38,455	58,186
Unincorporated	4,785	5,681			
			Jackson	39,154	41,375
Hamilton	8,761	10,930	Alford	548	472
Jasper	2,093	2,099	Bascom	134	90
Jennings	749	712	Campbellton	336	202
White Springs	781	704	Cottondale	1,056	900
Unincorporated	5,138	7,415	Graceville	2,918	2,675
			Grand Ridge	591	536
Hardee	20,357	19,499	Greenwood	577	474
Bowling Green	2,310	1,836	Jacob City	0	261
Wauchula	2,986	3,253	Malone	897	765
Zolfo Springs	1,495	1,219	Marianna	7,006	6,292
Unincorporated	13,566	13,191	Sneads	1,690	1,746
			Unincorporated	23,401	26,962
Hendry	18,599	25,773	Jefferson	10,703	11,296
Clewiston	5,219	6,085	Monticello	2,994	2,573
La Belle	2,287	2,703	Unincorporated	7,709	8,723
Unincorporated	11,093	16,985			
			Lafayette	4,035	5,578
Hernando	44,469	101,115	Mayo	891	917
Brooksville	5,582	7,440	Unincorporated	3,144	4,661
Weeki Wachee	8	53			
Unincorporated	38,879	93,622	Lake	104,870	152,104
			Astatula	755	981
Highlands	47,526	68,432	Clermont	5,461	6,910
Avon Park	8,026	8,042	Eustis	9,453	12,967
Lake Placid	963	1,158	Fruitland Park	2,259	2,754
Sebring	8,736	8,900	Groveland	1,992	2,300
Unincorporated	29,801	50,332	Howey-in-the-Hills	626	724
			Lady Lake	1,193	8,071
Hillsborough	646,939	834,054	Leesburg	13,191	14,903
Plant City	19,270	22,754	Mascotte	1,112	1,761
Tampa	271,577	280,015	Minneola	851	1,515
Temple Terrace	11,097	16,444	Montverde	397	890
Unincorporated	344,995	514,841	Mount Dora	5,883	7,196
			Tavares	4,398	7,383
Holmes	14,723	15,778	Umatilla	1,872	2,350
Bonifay	2,534	2,612	Unincorporated	55,427	81,399
Esto	304	253			
Noma	113	207	Lee	205,266	335,113
Ponce de Leon	454	406	Cape Coral	32,103	74,991
Westville	343	257	Ft. Myers	36,638	45,206
Unincorporated	10,975	12,043	Sanibel	3,363	5,468
			Unincorporated	133,162	209,448
Indian River	59,896	90,208			
Fellsmere	1,161	2,179	Leon	148,655	192,493
Indian River Shores	1,254	2,278	Tallahassee	81,548	124,773
Orchid	19	10	Unincorporated	67,107	67,720

See footnotes at end of table.   Continued . . .

Florida Statistical Abstract 1991

Table 1.31. POPULATION: CENSUS COUNTS, IN THE STATE, COUNTIES, AND MUNICIPALITIES
OF FLORIDA, APRIL 1, 1980 AND 1990 (Continued)

Area	1980	1990	Area	1980	1990
Levy	19,870	25,923	Nassau	32,894	43,941
Bronson	853	875	Callahan	869	946
Cedar Key	700	668	Fernandina Beach	7,224	8,765
Chiefland	1,986	1,917	Hilliard	1,869	1,751
Fanning Springs (part)	150	263	Unincorporated	22,932	32,479
Inglis	1,173	1,241			
Otter Creek	167	136	Okaloosa	109,920	143,776
Williston	2,240	2,179	Cinco Bayou	202	322
Yankeetown	600	635	Crestview	7,617	9,886
Unincorporated	12,001	18,009	Destin	0	8,080
			Ft. Walton Beach	20,829	21,471
			Laurel Hill	610	543
Liberty	4,260	5,569	Mary Esther	3,530	4,139
Bristol	1,044	937	Niceville	8,543	10,507
Unincorporated	3,216	4,632	Shalimar	390	341
			Valparaiso	6,142	4,672
Madison	14,894	16,569	Unincorporated	62,057	83,815
Greenville	1,096	950			
Lee	297	306	Okeechobee	20,264	29,627
Madison	3,487	3,345	Okeechobee	4,225	4,943
Unincorporated	10,014	11,968	Unincorporated	16,039	24,684
Manatee	148,445	211,707	Orange	470,865	677,491
Anna Maria	1,537	1,744	Apopka	6,019	13,512
Bradenton	30,228	43,779	Bay Lake	74	B/
Bradenton Beach	1,595	1,657	Belle Isle	2,848	5,272
Holmes Beach	4,023	4,810	Eatonville	2,185	2,170
Longboat Key (part)	2,460	2,544	Edgewood	1,034	1,062
Palmetto	8,637	9,268	Lake Buena Vista	98	1,776
Unincorporated	99,965	147,905	Maitland	8,763	9,110
			Oakland	658	700
Marion	122,488	194,833	Ocoee	7,803	12,778
Belleview	1,913	2,666	Orlando	128,291	164,693
Dunnellon	1,427	1,624	Windermere	1,302	1,371
McIntosh	404	411	Winter Garden	6,789	9,745
Ocala	37,170	42,045	Winter Park	22,339	22,242
Reddick	657	554	Unincorporated	282,662	433,060
Unincorporated	80,917	147,533			
			Osceola	49,287	107,728
Martin	64,014	100,900	Kissimmee	15,487	30,050
Jupiter Island	364	549	St. Cloud	7,840	12,453
Ocean Breeze Park	469	519	Unincorporated	25,960	65,225
Sewalls Point	1,187	1,588			
Stuart	9,467	11,936	Palm Beach	576,758	863,518
Unincorporated	52,527	86,308	Atlantis	1,325	1,653
			Belle Glade	16,535	16,177
Monroe	63,188	78,024	Boca Raton	49,447	61,492
Key Colony Beach	977	977	Boynton Beach	35,624	46,194
Key West	24,382	24,832	Briny Breezes	387	400
Layton	88	183	Cloud Lake	160	121
Unincorporated	37,741	52,032	Delray Beach	34,329	47,181

See footnotes at end of table.   Continued . . .

Florida Statistical Abstract 1991

Table 1.31. POPULATION: CENSUS COUNTS IN THE STATE, COUNTIES, AND MUNICIPALITIES
   OF FLORIDA, APRIL 1, 1980 AND 1990 (Continued)

Area	1980	1990	Area	1980	1990
Palm Beach (Continued)			**Pinellas** (Continued)		
Glen Ridge	235	207	Kenneth City	4,344	4,462
Golf Village	110	234	Largo	57,958	65,674
Golfview	210	153	Madeira Beach	4,520	4,225
Greenacres City	8,780	18,683	North Redington Beach	1,156	1,135
Gulf Stream	475	690	Oldsmar	2,608	8,361
Haverhill	1,249	1,058	Pinellas Park	32,811	43,426
Highland Beach	2,030	3,209	Redington Beach	1,708	1,626
Hypoluxo	573	830	Redington Shores	2,142	2,366
Juno Beach	1,142	2,121	Safety Harbor	6,461	15,124
Jupiter	9,868	24,986	St. Petersburg	238,647	238,629
Jupiter Inlet Colony	378	405	St. Petersburg Beach	9,354	9,200
Lake Clarke Shores	3,174	3,364	Seminole	4,586	9,251
Lake Park	6,909	6,704	South Pasadena	4,188	5,644
Lake Worth	27,048	28,564	Tarpon Springs	13,251	17,906
Lantana	8,048	8,392	Treasure Island	6,316	7,266
Manalapan	329	312	Unincorporated	199,309	259,247
Mangonia Park	1,419	1,453			
North Palm Beach	11,344	11,343	**Polk**	321,652	405,382
Ocean Ridge	1,355	1,570	Auburndale	6,501	8,858
Pahokee	6,346	6,822	Bartow	14,780	14,716
Palm Beach	9,729	9,814	Davenport	1,509	1,529
Palm Beach Gardens	14,407	22,965	Dundee	2,227	2,335
Palm Beach Shores	1,232	1,040	Eagle Lake	1,678	1,758
Palm Springs	8,166	9,763	Ft. Meade	5,546	4,976
Riviera Beach	26,489	27,639	Frostproof	2,995	2,808
Royal Palm Beach	3,423	14,589	Haines City	10,799	11,683
South Bay	3,886	3,558	Highland Park	184	155
South Palm Beach	1,304	1,480	Hillcrest Heights	177	221
Tequesta Village	3,685	4,499	Lake Alfred	3,134	3,622
West Palm Beach	63,305	67,643	Lake Hamilton	1,552	1,128
Unincorporated	212,303	406,210	Lake Wales	8,466	9,670
			Lakeland	47,406	70,576
Pasco	193,661	281,131	Mulberry	2,932	2,988
Dade City	4,923	5,663	Polk City	576	1,439
New Port Richey	11,196	14,044	Winter Haven	21,119	24,725
Port Richey	2,165	2,523	Unincorporated	190,071	242,195
St. Leo	899	1,009			
San Antonio	529	776	**Putnam**	50,549	65,070
Zephyrhills	5,742	8,220	Crescent City	1,722	1,859
Unincorporated	168,207	248,926	Interlachen	848	1,160
			Palatka	10,175	10,201
Pinellas	728,531	851,659	Pomona Park	791	663
Belleair	3,673	3,968	Welaka	492	533
Belleair Beach	1,643	2,070	Unincorporated	36,521	50,654
Belleair Bluffs	2,522	2,128			
Belleair Shore	80	60	**St. Johns**	51,303	83,829
Clearwater	85,170	98,784	Hastings	636	595
Dunedin	30,203	34,012	Marineland (part)	23	0
Gulfport	11,180	11,727	St. Augustine	11,985	11,692
Indian Rocks Beach	3,717	3,963	St. Augustine Beach	1,289	3,657
Indian Shores	984	1,405	Unincorporated	37,370	67,885

See footnotes at end of table.   Continued . . .

Florida Statistical Abstract 1991

Table 1.31. POPULATION: CENSUS COUNTS IN THE STATE, COUNTIES, AND MUNICIPALITIES
OF FLORIDA, APRIL 1, 1980 AND 1990 (Continued)

Area	1980	1990	Area	1980	1990
St. Lucie	87,182	150,171	Taylor (Continued)		
Ft. Pierce	33,802	36,830	Unincorporated	8,278	9,960
Port St. Lucie	14,690	55,866			
St. Lucie Village	593	584	Union	10,166	10,252
Unincorporated	38,097	56,891	Lake Butler	1,830	2,116
			Raiford	259	198
Santa Rosa	55,988	81,608	Worthington Springs	220	178
Gulf Breeze	5,478	5,530	Unincorporated	7,857	7,760
Jay	633	666			
Milton	7,206	7,216	Volusia	258,762	370,712
Unincorporated	42,671	68,196	Daytona Beach	54,176	61,921
			Daytona Beach Shores	1,324	2,335
Sarasota	202,251	277,776	Deland	15,354	16,491
Longboat Key (part)	2,383	3,393	Edgewater	6,726	15,337
North Port	6,205	11,973	Holly Hill	9,953	11,141
Sarasota	48,868	50,961	Lake Helen	2,047	2,344
Venice	12,153	16,922	New Smyrna Beach	13,557	16,543
Unincorporated	132,642	194,527	Oak Hill	938	917
			Orange City	2,795	5,347
Seminole	179,752	287,529	Ormond Beach	21,438	29,721
Altamonte Springs	21,105	34,879	Pierson	1,085	2,988
Casselberry	15,247	18,911	Ponce Inlet	1,003	1,704
Lake Mary	2,853	5,929	Port Orange	18,756	35,317
Longwood	10,029	13,316	South Daytona	11,252	12,482
Oviedo	3,074	11,114	Unincorporated	98,358	156,124
Sanford	23,176	32,387			
Winter Springs	10,475	22,151	Wakulla	10,887	14,202
Unincorporated	93,793	148,842	St. Marks	286	307
			Sopchoppy	444	367
Sumter	24,272	31,577	Unincorporated	10,157	13,528
Bushnell	983	1,998			
Center Hill	751	735	Walton	21,300	27,760
Coleman	1,022	857	DeFuniak Springs	5,563	5,120
Webster	856	746	Freeport	669	843
Wildwood	2,665	3,421	Paxton	659	600
Unincorporated	17,995	23,820	Unincorporated	14,409	21,197
Suwannee	22,287	26,780	Washington	14,509	16,919
Branford	622	670	Caryville	633	631
Live Oak	6,732	6,332	Chipley	3,330	3,866
Unincorporated	14,933	19,778	Ebro	233	255
			Vernon	885	778
Taylor	16,532	17,111	Wausau	347	313
Perry	8,254	7,151	Unincorporated	9,081	11,076

A/ Included in unincorporated.
B/ Population not yet determined.

Source: University of Florida, Bureau of Economic and Business Research, Population Program, *Florida Population: Census Summary, 1990*. Data from U.S. Bureau of
the Census.

Table 1.34. POPULATION: CENSUS COUNTS, APRIL 1, 1980 AND 1990, BY AGE, RACE, AND SEX IN FLORIDA

Age	All races			White			Black 1/		
	Total	Male	Female	Total	Male	Female	Total	Male	Female
1980									
All ages	9,746,324	4,675,626	5,070,698	8,319,448	3,999,052	4,320,396	1,346,801	639,227	707,574
0-14	1,876,774	958,454	918,320	1,444,440	740,342	704,098	412,068	207,863	204,205
15-24	1,622,767	815,703	807,064	1,321,271	670,818	650,453	287,140	137,738	149,402
25-44	2,450,189	1,200,503	1,249,686	2,076,435	1,027,817	1,048,618	344,175	159,469	184,706
45-64	2,109,021	972,606	1,136,415	1,895,378	875,757	1,019,621	202,285	91,971	110,314
65 and over	1,687,573	728,360	959,213	1,581,924	684,318	897,606	101,133	42,186	58,947
1990									
All ages	12,937,926	6,261,719	6,676,207	10,749,285	5,208,238	5,541,047	1,759,534	839,189	920,345
0-14	2,412,069	1,234,719	1,177,350	1,791,893	920,389	871,504	515,304	260,740	254,564
15-24	1,669,825	851,917	817,908	1,287,008	660,626	626,382	302,018	148,064	153,954
25-44	3,927,400	1,958,352	1,969,048	3,217,653	1,620,833	1,596,820	553,029	259,971	293,058
45-64	2,559,201	1,207,541	1,351,660	2,233,546	1,057,092	1,176,454	259,358	119,287	140,071
65 and over	2,369,431	1,009,190	1,360,241	2,219,185	949,298	1,269,887	129,825	51,127	78,698

1/ "Black" reflects the self-identification of respondents in the 1980 census.
Note: Due to adjustments made by the U.S. Bureau of the Census, the 1980 race data are different from those published in earlier Abstracts.

Source: U.S., Bureau of the Census, 1980 Census of Population and Housing, unpublished data, and 1990 Census of Population and Housing, Summary Tape File 1-A.

Florida Statistical Abstract 1991

Table 1.35. POPULATION: CENSUS COUNTS BY SEX AND AGE GROUP IN THE STATE AND COUNTIES OF FLORIDA, APRIL 1, 1990

County	Total	Sex		Age					
		Male	Female	0-14	15-24	25-44	45-64	65 and over	18 and over
Florida	12,937,926	6,261,719	6,676,207	2,412,069	1,669,825	3,927,400	2,559,201	2,369,431	10,071,689
Alachua	181,596	89,128	92,468	33,674	45,733	58,915	26,364	16,910	142,081
Baker	18,486	9,655	8,831	4,677	2,849	6,236	3,248	1,476	12,855
Bay	126,994	62,562	64,432	27,046	17,789	41,058	25,842	15,259	94,745
Bradford	22,515	12,429	10,086	4,503	3,027	7,821	4,440	2,724	17,109
Brevard	398,978	197,163	201,815	74,075	48,299	124,289	85,933	66,382	311,524
Broward	1,255,488	601,177	654,311	216,955	142,145	401,128	234,520	260,740	998,870
Calhoun	11,011	5,704	5,307	2,397	1,626	3,243	2,149	1,596	8,140
Charlotte	110,975	53,512	57,463	14,437	9,320	23,376	26,353	37,489	93,687
Citrus	93,515	44,711	48,804	13,677	7,965	19,818	22,772	29,283	77,049
Clay	105,986	52,272	53,714	25,234	15,452	36,078	20,238	8,984	75,452
Collier	152,099	75,386	76,713	25,748	16,450	41,751	33,567	34,583	121,759
Columbia	42,613	20,940	21,673	9,923	5,898	12,505	8,633	5,654	30,712
Dade	1,937,094	928,411	1,008,683	391,630	270,256	609,719	394,683	270,806	1,469,084
De Soto	23,865	12,316	11,549	4,648	3,234	6,595	4,765	4,623	18,199
Dixie	10,585	5,484	5,101	2,182	1,320	2,973	2,550	1,560	7,997
Duval	672,971	328,737	344,234	148,683	101,792	233,334	117,368	71,794	498,625
Escambia	262,798	127,599	135,199	55,922	42,194	82,052	51,335	31,295	196,418
Flagler	28,701	13,756	14,945	4,582	2,677	6,718	7,379	7,345	23,222
Franklin	8,967	4,378	4,589	1,775	1,070	2,336	2,172	1,614	6,814
Gadsden	41,105	19,535	21,570	10,108	6,160	12,169	7,483	5,185	28,941
Gilchrist	9,667	5,108	4,559	1,987	1,745	2,592	2,011	1,332	7,245
Glades	7,591	3,848	3,743	1,531	858	1,825	1,887	1,490	5,735

Continued . . .

See footnote at end of table.

Table 1.35. POPULATION: CENSUS COUNTS BY SEX AND AGE GROUP IN THE STATE AND COUNTIES OF FLORIDA, APRIL 1, 1990 (Continued)

County	Total	Sex		Age					
		Male	Female	0-14	15-24	25-44	45-64	65 and over	18 and over
Gulf	11,504	5,779	5,725	2,311	1,561	3,215	2,657	1,760	8,681
Hamilton	10,930	5,727	5,203	2,559	1,828	3,383	1,915	1,245	7,774
Hardee	19,499	9,885	9,614	4,760	2,872	5,170	3,735	2,962	13,811
Hendry	25,773	13,058	12,715	6,786	3,965	7,410	4,787	2,825	17,695
Hernando	101,115	48,483	52,632	15,452	9,203	21,565	23,847	31,048	82,467
Highlands	68,432	32,462	35,970	10,757	5,978	13,877	14,923	22,897	55,614
Hillsborough	834,054	406,217	427,837	170,480	120,985	284,369	156,087	102,133	631,780
Holmes	15,778	8,008	7,770	3,181	2,241	4,512	3,370	2,474	11,857
Indian River	90,208	43,578	46,630	14,684	8,996	22,435	19,501	24,592	72,722
Jackson	41,375	20,982	20,393	8,215	6,637	12,156	8,197	6,170	31,096
Jefferson	11,296	5,401	5,895	2,738	1,547	3,196	2,141	1,674	8,028
Lafayette	5,578	3,214	2,364	1,120	878	1,903	1,069	608	4,198
Lake	152,104	72,929	79,175	25,335	15,260	36,018	33,705	41,786	121,841
Lee	335,113	161,917	173,196	55,628	34,570	89,226	72,686	83,003	269,543
Leon	192,493	92,601	99,892	36,446	46,188	64,877	29,178	15,804	149,368
Levy	25,923	12,397	13,526	5,238	3,078	6,822	5,869	4,916	19,644
Liberty	5,569	3,172	2,397	1,096	870	1,917	1,059	627	4,221
Madison	16,569	8,488	8,081	3,763	2,574	4,832	3,059	2,341	12,009
Manatee	211,707	100,147	111,560	34,455	21,514	54,455	41,875	59,408	171,091
Marion	194,833	93,813	101,020	36,260	21,883	51,088	42,413	43,189	151,741
Martin	100,900	49,522	51,378	14,858	9,679	26,589	22,084	27,690	83,162
Monroe	78,024	40,976	37,048	11,678	7,945	27,362	18,583	12,456	64,469
Nassau	43,941	21,735	22,206	9,814	6,123	14,181	9,359	4,464	32,037

See footnote at end of table.

Continued . . .

Table 1.35. POPULATION: CENSUS COUNTS BY SEX AND AGE GROUP IN THE STATE AND COUNTIES OF FLORIDA, APRIL 1, 1990
(Continued)

County	Total	Sex		Age					
		Male	Female	0-14	15-24	25-44	45-64	65 and over	18 and over
Okaloosa	143,776	72,763	71,013	31,611	21,475	49,402	27,969	13,319	106,461
Okeechobee	29,627	15,142	14,485	6,650	4,096	8,044	6,030	4,807	21,577
Orange	677,491	336,061	341,430	137,092	110,292	239,987	118,086	72,034	516,005
Osceola	107,728	52,716	55,012	22,929	15,023	34,158	20,653	14,965	80,579
Palm Beach	863,518	414,538	448,980	144,256	90,205	253,892	164,925	210,240	693,965
Pasco	281,131	133,220	147,911	42,189	26,832	63,817	57,470	90,823	230,908
Pinellas	851,659	397,563	454,096	126,538	88,716	242,382	172,355	221,668	700,203
Polk	405,382	196,590	208,792	81,717	53,124	112,905	82,393	75,243	307,640
Putnam	65,070	31,739	33,331	13,809	7,940	17,248	14,340	11,733	48,528
St. Johns	83,829	40,665	43,164	15,624	10,589	25,990	17,835	13,791	65,196
St. Lucie	150,171	73,443	76,728	29,487	16,563	42,211	30,376	31,534	115,549
Santa Rosa	81,608	40,644	40,964	18,721	10,994	27,351	16,783	7,759	59,434
Sarasota	277,776	130,050	147,726	36,476	24,402	66,790	60,700	89,408	234,065
Seminole	287,529	140,587	146,942	60,693	39,743	102,490	54,903	29,700	214,622
Sumter	31,577	15,857	15,720	5,837	3,900	7,754	7,020	7,066	24,572
Suwannee	26,780	12,939	13,841	5,771	3,573	7,077	5,837	4,522	19,682
Taylor	17,111	8,301	8,810	3,972	2,355	4,934	3,577	2,273	12,288
Union	10,252	6,339	3,913	2,200	1,357	4,233	1,697	765	7,617
Volusia	370,712	179,481	191,231	61,273	46,973	102,992	75,109	84,365	297,689
Wakulla	14,202	6,948	7,254	3,310	1,867	4,458	2,918	1,649	10,182
Walton	27,760	13,637	14,123	5,451	3,291	7,756	6,677	4,585	21,166
Washington	16,919	8,194	8,725	3,455	2,281	4,440	3,757	2,986	12,649

Note: Detail may not add to totals because of rounding.

Source: U.S. Bureau of the Census, *1990 Census of Population and Housing,* Summary Tape File 1-A.

Florida Statistical Abstract 1991

Table 1.36. POPULATION: CENSUS COUNTS, APRIL 1, 1980 AND 1990, OF PERSONS
AGED 65 AND OVER IN THE STATE AND COUNTIES OF FLORIDA

| | Persons 65 years of age and over | | | | Percentage change, 1980-90 | |
County	April 1 1980	April 1 1990	Percentage of total population 1980	1990	65 years and over	Total population
Florida	1,687,573	2,369,431	17.3	18.3	40.4	32.7
Alachua	10,747	16,910	7.1	9.3	57.3	20.0
Baker	1,340	1,476	8.8	8.0	10.1	20.9
Bay	9,257	15,259	9.5	12.0	64.8	29.9
Bradford	2,085	2,724	10.4	12.1	30.6	12.4
Brevard	34,666	66,382	12.7	16.6	91.5	46.2
Broward	223,682	260,740	22.0	20.8	16.6	23.3
Calhoun	1,425	1,596	15.3	14.5	12.0	18.5
Charlotte	19,855	37,489	34.0	33.8	88.8	89.8
Citrus	15,870	29,283	29.0	31.3	84.5	71.0
Clay	4,931	8,984	7.4	8.5	82.2	58.1
Collier	16,390	34,583	19.1	22.7	111.0	76.9
Columbia	3,595	5,654	10.2	13.3	57.3	20.4
Dade	255,286	270,806	15.7	14.0	6.1	19.2
De Soto	3,089	4,623	16.2	19.4	49.7	25.3
Dixie	937	1,560	12.1	14.7	66.5	36.6
Duval	55,163	71,794	9.7	10.7	30.1	17.9
Escambia	20,747	31,295	8.9	11.9	50.8	12.4
Flagler	2,003	7,345	18.4	25.6	266.7	163.0
Franklin	1,145	1,614	14.9	18.0	41.0	17.0
Gadsden	5,025	5,185	12.1	12.6	3.2	-1.4
Gilchrist	634	1,332	11.0	13.8	110.1	67.6
Glades	881	1,490	14.7	19.6	69.1	26.7
Gulf	1,209	1,760	11.3	15.3	45.6	7.9
Hamilton	1,159	1,245	13.2	11.4	7.4	24.8
Hardee	2,204	2,962	11.4	15.2	34.4	-4.2
Hendry	1,600	2,825	8.6	11.0	76.6	38.6
Hernando	10,853	31,048	24.4	30.7	186.1	127.4
Highlands	12,527	22,897	26.4	33.5	82.8	44.0
Hillsborough	74,313	102,133	11.5	12.2	37.4	28.9
Holmes	2,126	2,474	14.4	15.7	16.4	7.2
Indian River	12,180	24,592	20.3	27.3	101.9	50.6
Jackson	5,430	6,170	13.9	14.9	13.6	5.7
Jefferson	1,418	1,674	13.2	14.8	18.1	5.5

See footnote at end of table.   Continued . . .

Table 1.36. POPULATION: CENSUS COUNTS, APRIL 1, 1980 AND 1990, OF PERSONS
AGED 65 AND OVER IN THE STATE AND COUNTIES OF FLORIDA (Continued)

County	Persons 65 years of age and over				Percentage change, 1980-90	
	April 1 1980	April 1 1990	Percentage of total population 1980	1990	65 years and over	Total population
Lafayette	491	608	12.2	10.9	23.8	38.2
Lake	26,640	41,786	25.4	27.5	56.9	45.0
Lee	45,871	83,003	22.3	24.8	80.9	63.3
Leon	9,764	15,804	6.6	8.2	61.9	29.5
Levy	3,103	4,916	15.6	19.0	58.4	30.5
Liberty	516	627	12.1	11.3	21.5	30.7
Madison	2,119	2,341	14.2	14.1	10.5	11.2
Manatee	40,156	59,408	27.1	28.1	47.9	42.6
Marion	20,899	43,189	17.1	22.2	106.7	59.1
Martin	15,654	27,690	24.5	27.4	76.9	57.6
Monroe	8,927	12,456	14.1	16.0	39.5	23.5
Nassau	2,549	4,464	7.7	10.2	75.1	33.6
Okaloosa	6,373	13,319	5.8	9.3	109.0	30.8
Okeechobee	2,451	4,807	12.1	16.2	96.1	46.2
Orange	50,007	72,034	10.6	10.6	44.0	43.9
Osceola	8,749	14,965	17.8	13.9	71.0	118.6
Palm Beach	134,452	210,240	23.3	24.3	56.4	49.7
Pasco	59,437	90,823	30.7	32.3	52.8	45.2
Pinellas	202,825	221,668	27.8	26.0	9.3	16.9
Polk	46,033	75,243	14.3	18.6	63.5	26.0
Putnam	7,659	11,733	15.2	18.0	53.2	28.7
St. Johns	7,501	13,791	14.6	16.5	83.9	63.4
St. Lucie	14,797	31,534	17.0	21.0	113.1	72.3
Santa Rosa	4,072	7,759	7.3	9.5	90.5	45.8
Sarasota	60,609	89,408	30.0	32.2	47.5	37.3
Seminole	17,616	29,700	9.8	10.3	68.6	60.0
Sumter	4,054	7,066	16.7	22.4	74.3	30.1
Suwannee	3,105	4,522	13.9	16.9	45.6	20.2
Taylor	2,095	2,273	12.7	13.3	8.5	3.5
Union	609	765	6.0	7.5	25.6	0.8
Volusia	57,794	84,365	22.3	22.8	46.0	43.3
Wakulla	1,225	1,649	11.3	11.6	34.6	30.4
Walton	3,395	4,585	15.9	16.5	35.1	30.3
Washington	2,254	2,986	15.5	17.6	32.5	16.6

Note: Detail may not add to totals because of rounding.
Source: University of Florida, Bureau of Economic and Business Research, Population Program, *Population Studies*, August 1991. Volume 24. Bulletin No. 97-98.

Table 1.37. POPULATION PROJECTIONS: CENSUS COUNTS, APRIL 1, 1990, AND PROJECTIONS
APRIL 1, 1995, 2000, 2005, AND 2010, BY AGE AND SEX IN FLORIDA

Age	Census 1990	Projections 1995	2000	2005	2010
Total	12,937,926	14,451,779	15,728,426	16,946,345	18,096,562
0-4	934,556	990,735	982,660	1,004,660	1,065,334
5-9	814,118	982,996	1,020,203	1,003,659	1,020,725
10-14	737,063	885,196	1,028,446	1,056,456	1,033,560
15-19	799,279	807,953	947,883	1,073,244	1,092,215
20-24	857,379	856,065	860,919	989,240	1,088,514
25-29	1,052,106	911,360	885,127	888,784	1,011,448
30-34	1,048,148	1,111,805	966,567	927,619	930,898
35-39	957,428	1,126,956	1,168,653	1,020,085	972,082
40-44	840,970	1,042,390	1,205,744	1,238,449	1,082,915
45-49	697,323	924,955	1,121,369	1,288,066	1,312,761
50-54	585,439	761,139	998,596	1,194,993	1,362,807
55-59	588,552	655,908	837,943	1,095,136	1,292,608
60-64	669,241	680,372	746,719	945,720	1,227,121
65-69	741,225	756,844	750,853	822,194	1,031,684
70-74	619,598	737,919	746,450	739,803	806,868
75-79	485,393	559,713	661,306	674,757	665,203
80-84	299,999	380,425	437,585	526,844	536,405
85 and over	210,110	279,048	361,403	456,636	563,414
Male	6,264,222	6,992,523	7,599,041	8,172,968	8,714,525
0-4	478,776	504,494	500,372	511,562	542,446
5-9	416,447	502,412	519,320	510,853	519,435
10-14	377,241	453,141	525,984	538,641	526,831
15-19	410,413	411,659	483,108	546,717	554,873
20-24	434,821	440,818	441,515	507,136	557,764
25-29	530,513	461,263	452,709	453,501	515,771
30-34	524,188	558,908	487,367	471,118	472,073
35-39	475,078	557,159	580,824	508,113	486,884
40-44	414,292	513,830	592,310	611,383	535,569
45-49	339,471	451,150	547,426	627,629	643,088
50-54	279,966	363,362	477,704	572,992	653,156
55-59	275,935	304,205	388,736	510,053	603,955
60-64	303,475	311,741	339,797	431,674	562,594
65-69	333,477	345,198	344,788	376,362	473,367
70-74	276,309	327,758	335,230	334,935	364,470
75-79	206,089	239,595	281,570	290,881	289,045
80-84	117,603	150,752	175,101	209,829	216,108
85 and over	70,128	95,078	125,180	159,589	197,096

See footnote at end of table.   Continued . . .

Florida Statistical Abstract 1991

Table 1.37. POPULATION PROJECTIONS: CENSUS COUNTS, APRIL 1, 1990, AND PROJECTIONS
  APRIL 1, 1995, 2000, 2005, AND 2010, BY AGE AND SEX IN FLORIDA (Continued)

Age	Census 1990	Projections 1995	2000	2005	2010
Female	6,673,704	7,459,256	8,129,385	8,773,377	9,382,037
0-4	455,779	486,241	482,288	493,098	522,888
5-9	397,671	480,584	500,883	492,806	501,290
10-14	359,822	432,055	502,462	517,815	506,729
15-19	388,866	396,294	464,775	526,527	537,342
20-24	422,558	415,247	419,404	482,104	530,750
25-29	521,593	450,097	432,418	435,283	495,677
30-34	523,960	552,897	479,200	456,501	458,825
35-39	482,350	569,797	587,829	511,972	485,198
40-44	426,678	528,560	613,434	627,066	547,346
45-49	357,852	473,805	573,943	660,437	669,673
50-54	305,473	397,777	520,892	622,001	709,651
55-59	312,617	351,703	449,207	585,083	688,653
60-64	365,766	368,631	406,922	514,046	664,527
65-69	407,748	411,646	406,065	445,832	558,317
70-74	343,290	410,161	411,220	404,868	442,398
75-79	279,304	320,118	379,736	383,876	376,158
80-84	182,396	229,673	262,484	317,015	320,297
85 and over	139,982	183,970	236,223	297,047	366,318

  Note: Medium projections are shown. High and low projections are available from
the Bureau of Economic and Business Research, University of Florida.

  Source: University of Florida, Bureau of Economic and Business Research, Population Program, unpublished data.

Florida Statistical Abstract 1991

Table 1.40. POPULATION PROJECTIONS: CENSUS COUNTS, APRIL 1, 1990, AND PROJECTIONS, APRIL 1, 1995 AND 2000, BY SEX IN THE STATE AND COUNTIES OF FLORIDA

County	Census 1990			Projections 1995			2000		
	Total	Male	Female	Total	Male	Female	Total	Male	Female
Florida	12,937,926	6,264,222	6,673,704	14,451,779	6,992,523	7,459,256	15,728,426	7,599,041	8,129,385
Alachua	181,596	89,135	92,461	197,235	97,062	100,173	210,148	103,418	106,730
Baker	18,486	9,653	8,833	20,006	10,473	9,533	21,314	11,151	10,163
Bay	126,994	62,577	64,417	139,224	67,089	72,135	149,368	70,880	78,488
Bradford	22,515	12,423	10,092	23,523	13,066	10,457	24,490	13,795	10,695
Brevard	398,978	197,209	201,769	457,059	226,290	230,769	506,726	251,042	255,684
Broward	1,255,488	601,492	653,996	1,377,992	663,278	714,714	1,479,652	713,965	765,687
Calhoun	11,011	5,703	5,308	11,646	5,986	5,660	12,147	6,194	5,953
Charlotte	110,975	53,531	57,444	136,032	65,184	70,848	157,921	75,232	82,689
Citrus	93,515	44,728	48,787	112,750	53,443	59,307	129,485	60,772	68,713
Clay	105,986	52,288	53,698	124,971	61,578	63,393	141,383	69,588	71,795
Collier	152,099	75,397	76,702	184,127	91,092	93,035	212,031	104,513	107,518
Columbia	42,613	20,954	21,659	46,255	22,880	23,375	49,247	24,510	24,737
Dade	1,937,094	928,890	1,008,204	2,083,555	995,988	1,087,567	2,201,836	1,050,364	1,151,472
De Soto	23,865	12,315	11,550	26,078	13,494	12,584	27,902	14,420	13,482
Dixie	10,585	5,483	5,102	11,670	6,280	5,390	12,641	6,911	5,730
Duval	672,971	328,851	344,120	718,175	349,541	368,634	754,124	365,825	388,299
Escambia	262,798	127,644	135,154	274,298	133,486	140,812	282,764	137,483	145,281
Flagler	28,701	13,758	14,943	37,778	17,761	20,017	45,792	21,041	24,751
Franklin	8,967	4,379	4,588	9,459	4,697	4,762	9,839	4,947	4,892
Gadsden	41,105	19,554	21,551	41,676	20,065	21,611	42,412	20,540	21,872
Gilchrist	9,667	5,105	4,562	11,489	6,136	5,353	13,079	7,044	6,035

Continued . . .

Florida Statistical Abstract 1991

Table 1.40. POPULATION PROJECTIONS: CENSUS COUNTS, APRIL 1, 1990, AND PROJECTIONS, APRIL 1, 1995 AND 2000, BY SEX IN THE STATE AND COUNTIES OF FLORIDA (Continued)

County	Census 1990			1995			Projections 2000		
	Total	Male	Female	Total	Male	Female	Total	Male	Female
Glades	7,591	3,850	3,741	8,295	4,058	4,237	8,884	4,227	4,657
Gulf	11,504	5,781	5,723	11,886	5,855	6,031	12,142	5,893	6,249
Hamilton	10,930	5,725	5,205	11,687	6,129	5,558	12,223	6,391	5,832
Hardee	19,499	9,890	9,609	19,863	10,024	9,839	20,234	10,172	10,062
Hendry	25,773	13,056	12,717	28,767	14,864	13,903	31,279	16,294	14,985
Hernando	101,115	48,502	52,613	128,112	61,360	66,752	151,827	72,509	79,318
Highlands	68,432	32,471	35,961	78,377	37,137	41,240	86,887	41,116	45,771
Hillsborough	834,054	406,388	427,666	917,670	445,302	472,368	987,241	477,184	510,057
Holmes	15,778	8,007	7,771	16,076	8,198	7,878	16,234	8,317	7,917
Indian River	90,208	43,590	46,618	104,826	51,280	53,546	117,402	57,914	59,488
Jackson	41,375	20,985	20,390	42,400	21,885	20,515	43,012	22,515	20,497
Jefferson	11,296	5,401	5,895	11,621	5,431	6,190	11,836	5,440	6,396
Lafayette	5,578	3,212	2,366	6,204	3,567	2,637	6,676	3,833	2,843
Lake	152,104	72,953	79,151	174,998	83,642	91,356	194,624	92,674	101,950
Lee	335,113	161,983	173,13υ	395,359	190,602	204,757	447,466	214,678	232,788
Leon	192,493	92,642	99,851	211,917	102,459	109,458	228,235	110,655	117,580
Levy	25,923	12,400	13,523	28,938	13,805	15,133	31,483	14,963	16,520
Liberty	5,569	3,169	2,400	5,830	3,341	2,489	6,046	3,496	2,550
Madison	16,569	8,491	8,078	16,836	8,729	8,107	17,027	8,960	8,067
Manatee	211,707	100,204	111,503	241,099	114,470	126,629	266,168	126,542	139,626
Marion	194,833	93,854	100,979	229,090	110,221	118,869	258,681	124,227	134,454
Martin	100,900	49,535	51,365	119,090	59,035	60,055	134,836	67,309	67,527
Monroe	78,024	40,968	37,056	84,497	44,315	40,182	89,785	46,875	42,910
Nassau	43,941	21,742	22,199	48,918	24,332	24,586	53,107	26,466	26,641

Continued . . .

Florida Statistical Abstract 1991

Table 1.40. POPULATION PROJECTIONS: CENSUS COUNTS, APRIL 1, 1990, AND PROJECTIONS, APRIL 1, 1995 AND 2000, BY SEX
IN THE STATE AND COUNTIES OF FLORIDA (Continued)

County	Census 1990			Projections 1995			2000		
	Total	Male	Female	Total	Male	Female	Total	Male	Female
Okaloosa	143,776	72,766	71,010	158,087	79,641	78,446	169,981	85,433	84,548
Okeechobee	29,627	15,149	14,478	33,951	17,531	16,420	37,650	19,663	17,987
Orange	677,491	336,147	341,344	778,484	384,092	394,392	864,990	424,249	440,741
Osceola	107,728	52,736	54,992	134,916	65,325	69,591	158,770	76,062	82,708
Palm Beach	863,518	414,742	448,776	997,889	480,263	517,626	1,113,237	535,904	577,333
Pasco	281,131	133,285	147,846	324,966	153,603	171,363	362,601	170,540	192,061
Pinellas	851,659	397,764	453,895	907,992	424,618	483,374	952,685	445,586	507,099
Polk	405,382	196,682	208,700	444,706	217,878	226,828	477,326	235,334	241,992
Putnam	65,070	31,752	33,318	71,888	35,036	36,852	77,589	37,801	39,788
St. Johns	83,829	40,677	43,152	98,962	47,529	51,433	112,046	53,447	58,599
St. Lucie	150,171	73,468	76,703	180,106	87,399	92,707	206,121	99,394	106,727
Santa Rosa	81,608	40,659	40,949	93,669	46,959	46,710	103,993	52,337	51,656
Sarasota	277,776	130,112	147,664	313,518	146,208	167,310	343,831	159,716	184,115
Seminole	287,529	140,642	146,887	341,767	167,168	174,599	388,789	190,043	198,746
Sumter	31,577	15,858	15,719	35,286	17,450	17,836	38,421	18,570	19,851
Suwannee	26,780	12,942	13,838	29,042	14,238	14,804	30,889	15,222	15,667
Taylor	17,111	8,305	8,806	17,458	8,542	8,916	17,649	8,693	8,956
Union	10,252	6,333	3,919	11,170	6,983	4,187	11,581	7,176	4,405
Volusia	370,712	179,544	191,168	425,887	205,700	220,187	473,133	227,857	245,276
Wakulla	14,202	6,948	7,254	15,793	7,734	8,059	17,136	8,385	8,751
Walton	27,760	13,644	14,116	30,783	15,099	15,684	33,314	16,350	16,964
Washington	16,919	8,198	8,721	18,105	8,617	9,488	19,058	8,994	10,064

Source: University of Florida, Bureau of Economic and Business Research, Population Program, *Population Studies*,
September 1991, Volume 24 No. 3-4. Bulletin No. 97-98.

Florida Statistical Abstract 1991

Table 1.41. POPULATION PROJECTIONS: CENSUS COUNTS, APRIL 1, 1990, AND PROJECTIONS, APRIL 1, 1995 AND 2000, BY AGE IN THE STATE AND COUNTIES OF FLORIDA

County	Census 1990			Projections 1995			2000		
	0-24	25-64	65 and over	0-24	25-64	65 and over	0-24	25-64	65 and over
Florida	4,142,394	6,439,207	2,356,325	4,522,945	7,214,885	2,713,949	4,840,111	7,930,718	2,957,597
Alachua	80,049	84,725	16,822	86,513	90,902	19,820	91,243	97,024	21,881
Baker	7,618	9,403	1,466	8,438	9,802	1,766	8,791	10,471	2,052
Bay	45,467	66,363	15,164	49,408	71,675	18,141	52,176	76,826	20,366
Bradford	7,628	12,177	2,709	8,171	12,342	3,010	8,426	12,949	3,115
Brevard	124,299	208,677	66,002	138,711	237,215	81,133	150,217	263,757	92,752
Broward	365,006	631,254	259,227	392,058	708,272	277,662	415,841	773,410	290,401
Calhoun	4,075	5,350	1,586	4,106	5,893	1,647	4,057	6,471	1,619
Charlotte	24,152	49,476	37,347	29,165	58,504	48,363	32,884	68,167	56,870
Citrus	22,000	42,351	29,164	25,878	50,578	36,294	29,132	58,955	41,398
Clay	41,215	55,845	8,926	45,806	67,415	11,750	49,830	76,679	14,874
Collier	42,894	74,806	34,399	50,723	89,471	43,933	57,854	103,250	50,927
Columbia	16,033	20,963	5,618	17,449	22,860	5,946	18,302	25,027	5,918
Dade	671,581	996,411	269,101	707,366	1,078,011	298,178	738,203	1,149,373	314,260
De Soto	7,998	11,273	4,594	8,593	12,411	5,074	8,861	13,795	5,246
Dixie	3,552	5,481	1,552	3,981	5,928	1,761	4,255	6,427	1,959
Duval	254,072	347,604	71,294	263,535	371,726	82,914	272,326	391,727	90,071
Escambia	99,391	132,307	31,100	101,361	138,905	34,032	103,249	143,942	35,573
Flagler	7,375	14,011	7,315	9,132	17,146	11,500	10,292	20,082	15,418
Franklin	2,886	4,476	1,605	3,083	4,735	1,641	3,192	4,956	1,691
Gadsden	16,475	19,481	5,149	16,034	20,258	5,384	15,614	21,223	5,575
Gilchrist	3,774	4,569	1,324	4,186	5,655	1,648	4,473	6,717	1,889

Continued . . .

Table 1.41. POPULATION PROJECTIONS: CENSUS COUNTS, APRIL 1, 1990, AND PROJECTIONS, APRIL 1, 1995 AND 2000, BY AGE IN THE STATE AND COUNTIES OF FLORIDA (Continued)

County	Census 1990			Projections 1995			2000		
	0-24	25-64	65 and over	0-24	25-64	65 and over	0-24	25-64	65 and over
Glades	2,425	3,684	1,482	2,742	3,919	1,634	2,995	4,303	1,586
Gulf	3,921	5,832	1,751	3,973	6,055	1,858	3,989	6,335	1,818
Hamilton	4,438	5,256	1,237	4,654	5,586	1,447	4,771	5,900	1,552
Hardee	7,731	8,826	2,942	8,042	8,675	3,146	8,238	8,963	3,033
Hendry	10,898	12,072	2,803	11,898	13,713	3,156	12,680	15,113	3,486
Hernando	25,057	45,142	30,917	30,436	54,822	42,854	34,672	65,056	52,099
Highlands	17,014	28,625	22,793	20,292	31,753	26,332	22,894	35,758	28,235
Hillsborough	295,615	436,955	101,484	320,112	479,702	117,856	340,283	517,829	129,129
Holmes	5,489	7,828	2,461	5,567	7,897	2,612	5,379	8,210	2,645
Indian River	24,063	41,673	24,472	27,593	48,375	28,858	30,077	55,774	31,551
Jackson	15,016	20,222	6,137	15,860	20,177	6,363	15,770	20,965	6,277
Jefferson	4,341	5,292	1,663	4,313	5,328	1,980	4,325	5,410	2,101
Lafayette	2,020	2,953	605	2,110	3,350	744	2,075	3,701	900
Lake	41,260	69,264	41,580	47,015	77,722	50,261	51,923	86,744	55,957
Lee	91,731	160,814	82,568	107,253	189,144	98,962	121,209	216,366	109,891
Leon	83,326	93,447	15,720	90,117	103,233	18,567	96,176	111,402	20,657
Levy	8,438	12,597	4,888	8,974	14,227	5,737	9,302	15,859	6,322
Liberty	1,988	2,957	624	2,139	2,968	723	2,173	3,090	783
Madison	6,423	7,822	2,324	6,582	8,012	2,242	6,677	8,282	2,068
Manatee	56,924	95,688	59,096	64,776	109,518	66,805	71,765	123,242	71,161
Marion	59,060	92,822	42,951	67,399	108,682	53,009	74,587	124,158	59,936
Martin	24,946	48,389	27,565	30,100	56,164	32,826	34,338	63,956	36,542
Monroe	19,971	45,657	12,396	21,256	49,340	13,901	22,170	53,231	14,384
Nassau	16,161	23,345	4,435	17,885	26,017	5,016	19,149	28,598	5,360

Continued . . .

Table 1.41. POPULATION PROJECTIONS: CENSUS COUNTS, APRIL 1, 1990, AND PROJECTIONS, APRIL 1, 1995 AND 2000, BY AGE IN THE STATE AND COUNTIES OF FLORIDA (Continued)

County	Census 1990			Projections 1995			Projections 2000		
	0-24	25-64	65 and over	0-24	25-64	65 and over	0-24	25-64	65 and over
Okaloosa	53,824	76,720	13,232	58,606	84,018	15,463	62,528	89,545	17,908
Okeechobee	10,903	13,950	4,774	12,890	15,413	5,648	14,367	17,252	6,031
Orange	250,658	355,251	71,582	279,019	407,984	91,481	304,810	452,332	107,848
Osceola	38,492	54,367	14,869	46,155	67,946	20,815	52,450	80,229	26,091
Palm Beach	238,541	415,929	209,047	274,340	484,735	238,814	304,911	548,873	259,453
Pasco	70,169	120,567	90,395	77,083	142,698	105,185	83,060	162,811	116,730
Pinellas	218,719	412,308	220,632	228,948	446,681	232,363	237,344	477,546	237,795
Polk	136,845	193,758	74,779	148,644	214,543	81,519	157,660	236,092	83,574
Putnam	22,067	31,339	11,664	23,442	34,315	14,131	24,689	37,316	15,584
St. Johns	26,600	43,511	13,717	30,861	50,634	17,467	34,224	57,732	20,090
St. Lucie	46,828	72,003	31,340	55,779	85,800	38,527	62,820	100,044	43,257
Santa Rosa	30,146	43,752	7,709	33,614	50,300	9,755	36,076	56,129	11,788
Sarasota	61,905	126,824	89,047	69,561	144,453	99,504	75,519	162,816	105,496
Seminole	101,811	156,195	29,523	115,129	189,304	37,334	126,597	217,938	44,254
Sumter	9,875	14,674	7,029	10,585	16,034	8,667	11,067	17,662	9,692
Suwannee	9,459	12,823	4,497	10,154	13,994	4,894	10,548	15,219	5,122
Taylor	6,419	8,435	2,257	6,068	8,732	2,658	5,689	9,046	2,914
Union	3,604	5,888	760	3,942	6,337	891	3,968	6,581	1,032
Volusia	109,807	176,961	83,944	121,539	204,921	99,427	132,069	231,488	109,576
Wakulla	5,245	7,317	1,640	5,999	7,826	1,968	6,413	8,546	2,177
Walton	8,869	14,330	4,561	9,688	15,585	5,510	10,095	17,044	6,175
Washington	5,812	8,138	2,969	6,114	8,549	3,442	6,372	9,004	3,682

Source: University of Florida, Bureau of Economic and Business Research, Population Program, *Population Studies*, September 1991, Volume 24 No. 3-4. Bulletin No. 97-98.

Table 1.42. POPULATION PROJECTIONS: CENSUS COUNTS, APRIL 1, 1990, AND PROJECTIONS, APRIL 1, 1995 AND 2000, BY RACE IN THE STATE AND COUNTIES OF FLORIDA

(rounded to thousands)

County	Census 1990			Projections 1995			Projections 2000		
	Total	White	Black	Total	White	Black	Total	White	Black
Florida	12,938	10,926	1,808	14,452	12,132	2,062	15,728	13,111	2,300
Alachua	182	142	35	197	153	38	210	162	41
Baker	18	16	3	20	17	3	21	18	3
Bay	127	110	14	139	120	15	149	128	17
Bradford	23	18	5	24	18	5	24	19	6
Brevard	399	360	32	457	411	37	507	453	42
Broward	1,255	1,037	198	1,378	1,129	223	1,480	1,201	248
Calhoun	11	9	2	12	10	2	12	10	2
Charlotte	111	106	4	136	129	5	158	150	7
Citrus	94	91	2	113	109	3	129	125	4
Clay	106	98	6	125	116	6	141	131	7
Collier	152	143	7	184	172	10	212	197	13
Columbia	43	35	8	46	38	8	49	41	8
Dade	1,937	1,480	421	2,084	1,553	486	2,202	1,602	545
De Soto	24	20	4	26	21	5	28	22	5
Dixie	11	10	1	12	10	1	13	11	1
Duval	673	493	165	718	520	180	754	540	193
Escambia	263	202	53	274	210	55	283	216	57
Flagler	29	26	2	38	34	3	46	41	4
Franklin	9	8	1	9	8	1	10	8	2
Gadsden	41	17	24	42	17	24	42	18	24
Gilchrist	10	9	1	11	10	1	13	12	1

Continued . . .

Florida Statistical Abstract 1991

Table 1.42. POPULATION PROJECTIONS: CENSUS COUNTS, APRIL 1, 1990, AND PROJECTIONS, APRIL 1, 1995 AND 2000, BY RACE IN THE STATE AND COUNTIES OF FLORIDA (Continued)

(rounded to thousands)

County	Census 1990			Projections 1995			2000		
	Total	White	Black	Total	White	Black	Total	White	Black
Glades	8	6	1	8	7	1	9	7	1
Gulf	12	9	2	12	10	2	12	10	2
Hamilton	11	7	4	12	7	5	12	7	5
Hardee	19	18	1	20	18	1	20	19	1
Hendry	26	20	5	29	23	5	31	25	5
Hernando	101	97	4	128	122	5	152	145	6
Highlands	68	61	7	78	69	9	87	76	10
Hillsborough	834	706	114	918	773	126	987	826	138
Holmes	16	15	1	16	15	1	16	15	1
Indian River	90	82	8	105	95	9	117	107	10
Jackson	41	30	11	42	31	11	43	31	12
Jefferson	11	6	5	12	7	5	12	7	5
Lafayette	6	5	1	6	5	1	7	6	1
Lake	152	137	14	175	156	18	195	172	21
Lee	335	310	23	395	364	27	447	410	32
Leon	192	142	47	212	154	54	228	163	60
Levy	26	22	3	29	25	3	31	28	3
Liberty	6	5	1	6	5	1	6	5	1
Madison	17	10	7	17	9	7	17	9	8
Manatee	212	193	17	241	220	19	266	242	21
Marion	195	168	25	229	196	30	259	220	36
Martin	101	94	6	119	110	8	135	124	9
Monroe	78	73	4	84	79	5	90	83	5
Nassau	44	39	5	49	43	5	53	47	6

Continued . . .

Florida Statistical Abstract 1991

Table 1.42. POPULATION PROJECTIONS: CENSUS COUNTS, APRIL 1, 1990, AND PROJECTIONS, APRIL 1, 1995 AND 2000, BY RACE IN THE STATE AND COUNTIES OF FLORIDA (Continued)

(rounded to thousands)

County	Census 1990			Projections 1995			2000		
	Total	White	Black	Total	White	Black	Total	White	Black
Okaloosa	144	126	13	158	138	15	170	147	16
Okeechobee	30	27	2	34	30	3	38	33	3
Orange	677	554	107	778	624	131	865	679	154
Osceola	108	99	6	135	124	8	159	145	10
Palm Beach	864	742	111	998	855	129	1,113	948	147
Pasco	281	273	6	325	315	7	363	351	8
Pinellas	852	773	67	908	822	72	953	859	76
Polk	405	346	56	445	377	62	477	403	69
Putnam	65	53	12	72	58	13	78	62	14
St. Johns	84	76	7	99	89	9	112	100	11
St. Lucie	150	124	25	180	147	31	206	165	38
Santa Rosa	82	77	3	94	89	3	104	99	3
Sarasota	278	264	12	314	296	15	344	324	17
Seminole	288	257	25	342	306	28	389	348	31
Sumter	32	26	5	35	29	6	38	31	7
Suwannee	27	23	4	29	24	4	31	26	5
Taylor	17	14	3	17	14	4	18	13	4
Union	10	8	2	11	8	3	12	9	3
Volusia	371	333	34	426	381	40	473	420	46
Wakulla	14	12	2	16	13	2	17	14	3
Walton	28	25	2	31	28	2	33	30	2
Washington	17	14	2	18	15	3	19	16	3

Source: University of Florida, Bureau of Economic and Business Research, Population Program, *Population Studies*, September 1991, Volume 24 No. 3-4. Bulletin No. 97-98.

Florida Statistical Abstract 1991

Table 1.65. POPULATION: CENSUS COUNTS IN THE STATE AND METROPOLITAN AREAS OF FLORIDA, APRIL 1, 1960 THROUGH 1990

Metropolitan area	1960	1970	1980	1990	Percentage change 1970-1980	1980 1990
Florida	4,951,560	6,791,418	9,746,961	12,937,926	43.5	32.7
Metropolitan areas, total	4,467,733	6,213,151	8,884,433	11,754,090	43.0	32.3
Bradenton	69,168	97,115	148,445	211,707	52.9	42.6
Daytona Beach	125,319	169,487	258,762	370,712	52.7	43.3
Ft. Lauderdale-Hollywood-Pompano Beach	333,946	620,100	1,018,257	1,255,488	64.2	23.3
Ft. Myers-Cape Coral	54,539	105,216	205,266	335,113	95.1	63.3
Ft. Pierce	56,226	78,871	151,196	251,071	91.7	66.1
Martin County	16,932	28,035	64,014	100,900	128.3	57.6
St. Lucie County	39,294	50,836	87,182	150,171	71.5	72.3
Ft. Walton Beach	61,175	88,187	109,920	143,776	24.6	30.8
Gainesville	86,520	119,389	171,392	204,111	43.6	19.1
Alachua County	74,074	104,764	151,369	181,596	44.5	20.0
Bradford County	12,446	14,625	20,023	22,515	36.9	12.4
Jacksonville	522,169	612,585	722,252	906,727	17.9	25.5
Clay County	19,535	32,059	67,052	105,986	109.2	58.1
Duval County	455,411	528,865	571,003	672,971	8.0	17.9
Nassau County	17,189	20,626	32,894	43,941	59.5	33.6
St. Johns County	30,034	31,035	51,303	83,829	65.3	63.4
Lakeland-Winter Haven	195,139	228,515	321,652	405,382	40.8	26.0
Melbourne-Titusville-Palm Bay	111,435	230,006	272,959	398,978	18.7	46.2
Miami-Hialeah	935,047	1,267,792	1,625,509	1,937,094	28.2	19.2
Naples	15,753	38,040	85,971	152,099	126.0	76.9
Ocala	51,616	69,030	122,488	194,833	77.4	59.1
Orlando	337,516	453,270	699,904	1,072,748	54.4	53.3
Orange County	263,540	344,311	470,865	677,491	36.8	43.9
Osceola County	19,029	25,267	49,287	107,728	95.1	118.6
Seminole County	54,947	83,692	179,752	287,529	114.8	60.0
Panama City	67,131	75,283	97,740	126,994	29.8	29.9
Pensacola	203,376	243,075	289,782	344,406	19.2	18.9
Escambia County	173,829	205,334	233,794	262,798	13.9	12.4
Santa Rosa County	29,547	37,741	55,988	81,608	48.3	45.8
Sarasota	76,895	120,413	202,251	277,776	68.0	37.3
Tallahassee	116,214	142,231	190,329	233,598	33.8	22.7
Gadsden County	41,989	39,184	41,674	41,105	6.4	-1.4
Leon County	74,225	103,047	148,655	192,493	44.3	29.5
Tampa-St. Petersburg-Clearwater	820,443	1,105,553	1,613,600	2,067,959	46.0	28.2
Hernando County	11,205	17,004	44,469	101,115	161.5	127.4
Hillsborough County	397,788	490,265	646,939	834,054	32.0	28.9
Pasco County	36,785	75,955	193,661	281,131	155.0	45.2
Pinellas County	374,665	522,329	728,531	851,659	39.5	16.9
West Palm Beach-Boca Raton-Delray Beach	228,106	348,993	576,758	863,518	65.3	49.7

Note: Data are for Metropolitan Statistical Areas (MSAs) and for Primary Metropolitan Statistical Areas (PMSAs) defined as of June 30, 1990. See Glossary for definitions and map at the front of the book for area boundaries.

Source: University of Florida, Bureau of Economic and Business Research, Population Program, *Florida Population: Census Summary, 1990*. Data from U.S. Bureau of the Census.

Table 1.66. POPULATION: CENSUS COUNTS IN THE STATE, COMPREHENSIVE PLANNING
DISTRICTS, AND COUNTIES OF FLORIDA, APRIL 1, 1970, 1980, AND 1990

District and county	1970	1980	1990	Percentage change 1970 to 1980	1980 to 1990
Florida	6,791,418	9,746,961	12,937,936	43.5	32.7
District 1	444,805	547,974	675,633	23.2	23.3
Bay	75,283	97,740	126,994	29.8	29.9
Escambia	205,334	233,794	262,798	13.9	12.4
Holmes	10,720	14,723	15,778	37.3	7.2
Okaloosa	88,187	109,920	143,776	24.6	30.8
Santa Rosa	37,741	55,988	81,608	48.3	45.8
Walton	16,087	21,300	27,760	32.4	30.3
Washington	11,453	14,509	16,919	26.7	16.6
District 2	219,915	282,946	337,522	28.7	19.3
Calhoun	7,624	9,294	11,011	21.9	18.5
Franklin	7,065	7,661	8,967	8.4	17.0
Gadsden	39,184	41,674	41,105	6.4	-1.4
Gulf	10,096	10,658	11,504	5.6	7.9
Jackson	34,434	39,154	41,375	13.7	5.7
Jefferson	8,778	10,703	11,296	21.9	5.5
Leon	103,047	148,655	192,493	44.3	29.5
Liberty	3,379	4,260	5,569	26.1	30.7
Wakulla	6,308	10,887	14,202	72.6	30.4
District 3	215,142	296,984	354,196	38.0	19.3
Alachua	104,764	151,369	181,596	44.5	20.0
Bradford	14,625	20,023	22,515	36.9	12.4
Columbia	25,250	35,399	42,613	40.2	20.4
Dixie	5,480	7,751	10,585	41.4	36.6
Gilchrist	3,551	5,767	9,667	62.4	67.6
Hamilton	7,787	8,761	10,930	12.5	24.8
Lafayette	2,892	4,035	5,578	39.5	38.2
Madison	13,481	14,894	16,569	10.5	11.2
Suwannee	15,559	22,287	26,780	43.2	20.2
Taylor	13,641	16,532	17,111	21.2	3.5
Union	8,112	10,166	10,252	25.3	0.8
District 4	662,705	799,003	1,018,984	20.6	27.5
Baker	9,242	15,289	18,486	65.4	20.9
Clay	32,059	67,052	105,986	109.2	58.1
Duval	528,865	571,003	672,971	8.0	17.9
Flagler	4,454	10,913	28,701	145.0	163.0
Nassau	20,626	32,894	43,941	59.5	33.6
Putnam	36,424	50,549	65,070	38.8	28.7
St. Johns	31,035	51,303	83,829	65.3	63.4
District 5	132,825	265,802	446,963	100.1	68.2
Citrus	19,196	54,703	93,515	185.0	71.0
Hernando	17,004	44,469	101,115	161.5	127.4
Levy	12,756	19,870	25,923	55.8	30.5

See footnote at end of table.   Continued . . .

Florida Statistical Abstract 1991

Planning Districts

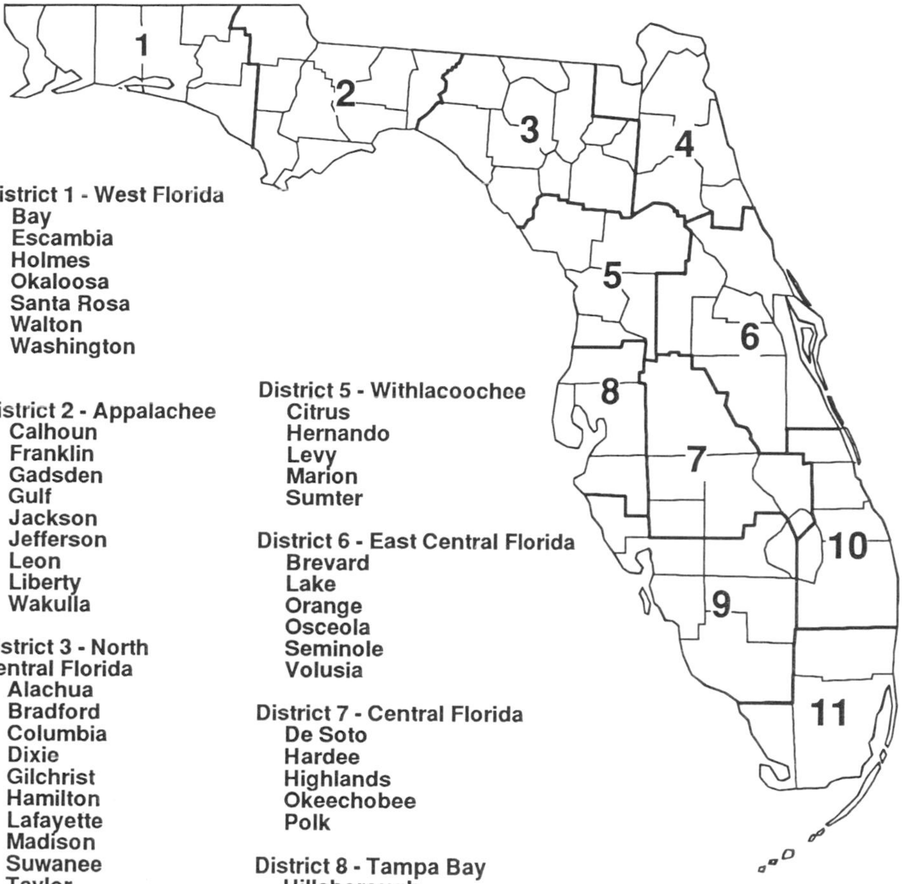

District 1 - West Florida
Bay
Escambia
Holmes
Okaloosa
Santa Rosa
Walton
Washington

District 2 - Appalachee
Calhoun
Franklin
Gadsden
Gulf
Jackson
Jefferson
Leon
Liberty
Wakulla

District 3 - North Central Florida
Alachua
Bradford
Columbia
Dixie
Gilchrist
Hamilton
Lafayette
Madison
Suwanee
Taylor
Union

District 4 - Northeast Florida
Baker
Clay
Duval
Flagler
Nassau
Putnam
St. Johns

District 5 - Withlacoochee
Citrus
Hernando
Levy
Marion
Sumter

District 6 - East Central Florida
Brevard
Lake
Orange
Osceola
Seminole
Volusia

District 7 - Central Florida
De Soto
Hardee
Highlands
Okeechobee
Polk

District 8 - Tampa Bay
Hillsborough
Manatee
Pasco
Pinellas

District 9 - Southwest Florida
Charlotte
Collier
Glades
Hendry
Lee
Sarasota

District 10 - Treasure Coast
Indian River
Martin
Palm Beach
St. Lucie

District 11 - South Florida
Broward
Dade
Monroe

Table 1.66. POPULATION: CENSUS COUNTS IN THE STATE, COMPREHENSIVE PLANNING
DISTRICTS, AND COUNTIES OF FLORIDA, APRIL 1, 1970, 1980, AND 1990
(Continued)

District				Percentage change	
and county	1970	1980	1990	1970 to 1980	1980 to 1990
District 5 (Continued)					
Marion	69,030	122,488	194,833	77.4	59.1
Sumter	14,839	24,272	31,577	63.6	30.1
District 6	922,068	1,336,495	1,994,542	44.9	49.2
Brevard	230,006	272,959	398,978	18.7	46.2
Lake	69,305	104,870	152,104	51.3	45.0
Orange	344,311	470,865	677,491	36.8	43.9
Osceola	25,267	49,287	107,728	95.1	118.6
Seminole	83,692	179,752	287,529	114.8	60.0
Volusia	169,487	258,762	370,712	52.7	43.3
District 7	297,204	428,838	546,805	44.3	27.5
De Soto	13,060	19,039	23,865	45.8	25.3
Hardee	14,889	20,357	19,499	36.7	-4.2
Highlands	29,507	47,526	68,432	61.1	44.0
Okeechobee	11,233	20,264	29,627	80.4	46.2
Polk	228,515	321,652	405,382	40.8	26.0
District 8	1,185,664	1,717,576	2,178,551	44.9	26.8
Hillsborough	490,265	646,939	834,054	32.0	28.9
Manatee	97,115	148,445	211,707	52.9	42.6
Pasco	75,955	193,661	281,131	155.0	45.2
Pinellas	522,329	728,531	851,659	39.5	16.9
District 9	306,756	576,539	909,327	87.9	57.7
Charlotte	27,559	58,460	110,975	112.1	89.8
Collier	38,040	85,971	152,099	126.0	76.9
Glades	3,669	5,992	7,591	63.3	26.7
Hendry	11,859	18,599	25,773	56.8	38.6
Lee	105,216	205,266	335,113	95.1	63.3
Sarasota	120,413	202,251	277,776	68.0	37.3
District 10	463,856	787,850	1,204,797	69.8	52.9
Indian River	35,992	59,896	90,208	66.4	50.6
Martin	28,035	64,014	100,900	128.3	57.6
Palm Beach	348,993	576,758	863,518	65.3	49.7
St. Lucie	50,836	87,182	150,171	71.5	72.3
District 11	1,940,478	2,706,954	3,270,606	39.5	20.8
Broward	620,100	1,018,257	1,255,488	64.2	23.3
Dade	1,267,792	1,625,509	1,937,094	28.2	19.2
Monroe	52,586	63,188	78,024	20.2	23.5

Note: Data are for planning district boundaries as defined in May 1984. See map
at the front of the book. 1980 census counts include all adjustments through
December 30, 1990 made to the numbers originally published by the U.S. Bureau of the
Census. Therefore, 1980 census numbers for some counties may differ from those
published previously in *Abstract*.

Source: University of Florida, Bureau of Economic and Business Research, Population Program, *Florida Population: Census Summary, 1990*. Data from U.S. Bureau of
the Census.

Table 1.67. POPULATION: CENSUS COUNTS IN THE STATE, DEPARTMENT OF HEALTH AND REHABILITATIVE SERVICES DISTRICTS, AND COUNTIES OF FLORIDA, APRIL 1, 1970, 1980, AND 1990

District and county	1970	1980	1990	Percentage change 1970 to 1980	Percentage change 1980 to 1990
Florida	6,791,418	9,746,961	12,937,926	43.5	32.7
District 1	347,349	421,002	515,942	21.2	22.6
Escambia	205,334	233,794	262,798	13.9	12.4
Okaloosa	88,187	109,920	143,776	24.6	30.8
Santa Rosa	37,741	55,988	81,608	48.3	45.8
Walton	16,087	21,300	27,760	32.4	30.3
District 2	344,493	441,344	530,893	28.1	20.3
Bay	75,283	97,740	126,994	29.8	29.9
Calhoun	7,624	9,294	11,011	21.9	18.5
Franklin	7,065	7,661	8,967	8.4	17.0
Gadsden	39,184	41,674	41,105	6.4	-1.4
Gulf	10,096	10,658	11,504	5.6	7.9
Holmes	10,720	14,723	15,778	37.3	7.2
Jackson	34,434	39,154	41,375	13.7	5.7
Jefferson	8,778	10,703	11,296	21.9	5.5
Leon	103,047	148,655	192,493	44.3	29.5
Liberty	3,379	4,260	5,569	26.1	30.7
Madison	13,481	14,894	16,569	10.5	11.2
Taylor	13,641	16,532	17,111	21.2	3.5
Wakulla	6,308	10,887	14,202	72.6	30.4
Washington	11,453	14,509	16,919	26.7	16.6
District 3	426,574	686,779	984,653	61.0	43.4
Alachua	104,764	151,369	181,596	44.5	20.0
Bradford	14,625	20,023	22,515	36.9	12.4
Citrus	19,196	54,703	93,515	185.0	71.0
Columbia	25,250	35,399	42,613	40.2	20.4
Dixie	5,480	7,751	10,585	41.4	36.6
Gilchrist	3,551	5,767	9,667	62.4	67.6
Hamilton	7,787	8,761	10,930	12.5	24.8
Hernando	17,004	44,469	101,115	161.5	127.4
Lafayette	2,892	4,035	5,578	39.5	38.2
Lake	69,305	104,870	152,104	51.3	45.0
Levy	12,756	19,870	25,923	55.8	30.5
Marion	69,030	122,488	194,833	77.4	59.1
Putnam	36,424	50,549	65,070	38.8	28.7
Sumter	14,839	24,272	31,577	63.6	30.1
Suwannee	15,559	22,287	26,780	43.2	20.2
Union	8,112	10,166	10,252	25.3	0.8
District 4	795,768	1,007,216	1,324,626	26.6	31.5
Baker	9,242	15,289	18,486	65.4	20.9
Clay	32,059	67,052	105,986	109.2	58.1
Duval	528,865	571,003	672,971	8.0	17.9
Flagler	4,454	10,913	28,701	145.0	163.0
Nassau	20,626	32,894	43,941	59.5	33.6

See footnote at end of table. Continued . . .

Florida Statistical Abstract 1991

Table 1.67. POPULATION: CENSUS COUNTS IN THE STATE, DEPARTMENT OF HEALTH AND
REHABILITATIVE SERVICES DISTRICTS, AND COUNTIES OF FLORIDA, APRIL 1, 1970,
1980, AND 1990 (Continued)

District				Percentage change	
and county	1970	1980	1990	1970 to 1980	1980 to 1990
District 4 (Cont.)					
St. Johns	31,035	51,303	83,829	65.3	63.4
Volusia	169,487	258,762	370,712	52.7	43.3
District 5	598,284	922,192	1,132,790	54.1	22.8
Pasco	75,955	193,661	281,131	155.0	45.2
Pinellas	522,329	728,531	851,659	39.5	16.9
District 6	587,380	795,384	1,045,761	35.4	31.5
Hillsborough	490,265	646,939	834,054	32.0	28.9
Manatee	97,115	148,445	211,707	52.9	42.6
District 7	683,276	972,863	1,471,726	42.4	51.3
Brevard	230,006	272,959	398,978	18.7	46.2
Orange	344,311	470,865	677,491	36.8	43.9
Osceola	25,267	49,287	107,728	95.1	118.6
Seminole	83,692	179,752	287,529	114.8	60.0
District 8	592,727	985,113	1,426,505	66.2	44.8
Charlotte	27,559	58,460	110,975	112.1	89.8
Collier	38,040	85,971	152,099	126.0	76.9
De Soto	13,060	19,039	23,865	45.8	25.3
Glades	3,669	5,992	7,591	63.3	26.7
Hardee	14,889	20,357	19,499	36.7	-4.2
Hendry	11,859	18,599	25,773	56.8	38.6
Highlands	29,507	47,526	68,432	61.1	44.0
Lee	105,216	205,266	335,113	95.1	63.3
Polk	228,515	321,652	405,382	40.8	26.0
Sarasota	120,413	202,251	277,776	68.0	37.3
District 9	475,089	808,114	1,234,424	70.1	52.8
Indian River	35,992	59,896	90,208	66.4	50.6
Martin	28,035	64,014	100,900	128.3	57.6
Okeechobee	11,233	20,264	29,627	80.4	46.2
Palm Beach	348,993	576,758	863,518	65.3	49.7
St. Lucie	50,836	87,182	150,171	71.5	72.3
District 10	620,100	1,018,257	1,255,488	64.2	23.3
Broward	620,100	1,018,257	1,255,488	64.2	23.3
District 11	1,320,378	1,688,697	2,015,118	27.9	19.3
Dade	1,267,792	1,625,509	1,937,094	28.2	19.2
Monroe	52,586	63,188	78,024	20.2	23.5

Note: 1980 census counts include all adjustments through December 1990 made to
the numbers originally published by the U.S. Bureau of the Census. Therefore, 1980
census numbers for some counties may differ from those published previously in
Abstract. See map of districts in Section 7.00.

Source: University of Florida, Bureau of Economic and Business Research, Population Program, *Florida Population: Census Summary, 1990*. Data from U.S. Bureau of
the Census.

Florida Statistical Abstract 1991

Table 1.69. POPULATION: CENSUS COUNTS, APRIL 1, 1970, 1980, AND 1990, IN THE 35
MOST POPULOUS CITIES IN FLORIDA, 1990

City	Total population			Rank			Per-centage change 1980 to 1990
	1970	1980	1990	1970	1980	1990	1990
Jacksonville	504,265	540,920	635,230	1	1	1	17.4
Miami	334,859	346,865	358,548	2	2	2	3.4
Tampa	277,714	271,577	280,015	3	3	3	3.1
St. Petersburg	216,159	238,647	238,629	4	4	4	0.0
Hialeah	102,452	145,254	188,004	7	6	5	29.4
Orlando	99,006	128,291	164,693	8	7	6	28.4
Ft. Lauderdale	139,590	153,279	149,377	5	5	7	-2.5
Tallahassee	72,624	81,548	124,773	10	11	8	53.0
Hollywood	106,873	121,323	121,697	6	8	9	0.3
Clearwater	52,074	85,170	98,784	14	10	10	16.0
Miami Beach	87,072	96,298	92,639	9	9	11	-3.8
Gainesville	64,510	81,371	84,770	11	12	12	4.2
Coral Springs	1,489	37,349	79,443	220	27	13	112.7
Cape Coral	A/	32,103	74,991	A/	41	14	133.6
Pompano Beach	38,587	52,618	72,411	20	17	15	37.6
Lakeland	42,803	47,406	70,576	16	21	16	48.9
West Palm Beach	57,375	63,305	67,643	13	13	17	6.9
Plantation	23,523	48,501	66,692	33	20	18	37.5
Largo	24,230	57,958	65,674	29	14	19	13.3
Pembroke Pines	15,496	35,776	65,452	49	34	20	82.9
Sunrise	7,403	39,681	64,407	88	25	21	62.3
Palm Bay	7,176	18,560	62,632	92	61	22	237.5
Daytona Beach	45,327	54,176	61,921	15	16	23	14.3
Boca Raton	28,506	49,447	61,492	27	18	24	24.4
Melbourne	40,236	46,536	59,646	19	22	25	28.2
Pensacola	59,507	57,619	58,165	12	15	26	0.9
Port St. Lucie	330	14,690	55,866	336	72	27	280.3
Sarasota	40,237	48,868	50,961	18	19	28	4.3
North Miami	34,767	42,566	49,998	21	24	29	17.5
Lauderhill	8,465	37,271	49,708	79	28	30	33.4
Davie	5,859	20,515	47,217	110	58	31	130.2
Delray Beach	19,915	34,329	47,181	40	36	32	37.4
Deerfield Beach	16,662	39,193	46,325	44	26	33	18.2
Boynton Beach	18,115	35,624	46,194	41	35	34	29.7
Ft. Myers	27,351	36,638	45,206	28	30	35	23.4

A/ Not incorporated in 1970.
Note: Changes in city populations include the effects of annexations. 1980
census counts include all adjustments through December 1990 made by the U.S. Bureau
of the Census. Therefore, 1980 census numbers for some cities may differ from those
published previously in *Abstract*.
Source: University of Florida, Bureau of Economic and Business Research, Population Program, *Florida Population: Census Summary, 1990*. Data from U.S. Bureau of
the Census.

Table 1.72.   POPULATION: COMPONENTS OF CHANGE IN THE STATE AND COUNTIES OF FLORIDA
APRIL 1, 1980 TO APRIL 1, 1990

			Population change 1980 to 1990	Components of change			
				Natural increase 1/		Net migration	
County	Total population			Number	Per- centage	Number	Per- centage
	1980	1990					
Florida	9,746,961	12,937,926	3,190,965	420,867	13.2	2,770,098	86.8
Alachua	151,369	181,596	30,227	15,013	49.7	15,214	50.3
Baker	15,289	18,486	3,197	1,699	53.1	1,498	46.9
Bay	97,740	126,994	29,254	9,672	33.1	19,582	66.9
Bradford	20,023	22,515	2,492	1,228	49.3	1,264	50.7
Brevard	272,959	398,978	126,019	15,498	12.3	110,521	87.7
Broward	1,018,257	1,255,488	237,231	13,138	5.5	224,093	94.5
Calhoun	9,294	11,011	1,717	354	20.6	1,363	79.4
Charlotte	58,460	110,975	52,515	-5,093	0.0	57,608	100.0
Citrus	54,703	93,515	38,812	-3,814	0.0	42,626	100.0
Clay	67,052	105,986	38,934	7,336	18.8	31,598	81.2
Collier	85,971	152,099	66,128	5,290	8.0	60,838	92.0
Columbia	35,399	42,613	7,214	2,853	39.5	4,361	60.5
Dade	1,625,509	1,937,094	311,585	105,181	33.8	206,404	66.2
De Soto	19,039	23,865	4,826	1,056	21.9	3,770	78.1
Dixie	7,751	10,585	2,834	516	18.2	2,318	81.8
Duval	571,003	672,971	101,968	61,260	60.1	40,708	39.9
Escambia	233,794	262,798	29,004	21,987	75.8	7,017	24.2
Flagler	10,913	28,701	17,788	-33	0.0	17,821	100.0
Franklin	7,661	8,967	1,306	302	23.1	1,004	76.9
Gadsden	41,674	41,105	-569	3,827	0.0	-4,396	100.0
Gilchrist	5,767	9,667	3,900	397	10.2	3,503	89.8
Glades	5,992	7,591	1,599	71	4.4	1,528	95.6
Gulf	10,658	11,504	846	451	53.3	395	46.7
Hamilton	8,761	10,930	2,169	642	29.6	1,528	70.4
Hardee	20,357	19,499	-858	2,109	0.0	-2,967	100.0
Hendry	18,599	25,773	7,174	3,035	42.3	4,139	57.7
Hernando	44,469	101,115	56,646	-2,428	0.0	59,074	100.0
Highlands	47,526	68,432	20,906	-1,206	0.0	22,112	100.0
Hillsborough	646,939	834,054	187,115	55,387	29.6	131,728	70.4
Holmes	14,723	15,778	1,055	99	9.4	956	90.6
Indian River	59,896	90,208	30,312	426	1.4	29,886	98.6
Jackson	39,154	41,375	2,221	1,047	47.1	1,174	52.9
Jefferson	10,703	11,296	593	670	100.0	-77	0.0
Lafayette	4,035	5,578	1,543	178	11.5	1,365	88.5
Lake	104,870	152,104	47,234	-754	0.0	47,988	100.0
Lee	205,266	335,113	129,847	3,761	2.9	126,086	97.1

See footnotes at end of table.   Continued . . .

Florida Statistical Abstract 1991

Table 1.72. POPULATION: COMPONENTS OF CHANGE IN THE STATE AND COUNTIES OF FLORIDA
APRIL 1, 1980 TO APRIL 1, 1990 (Continued)

				Components of change			
				Natural			
			Population	increase 1/		Net migration	
	Total population		change		Per-		Per-
County	1980	1990	1980 to 1990	Number	centage	Number	centage
Leon	148,655	192,493	43,838	14,875	33.9	28,963	66.1
Levy	19,870	25,923	6,053	463	7.7	5,590	92.3
Liberty	4,260	5,569	1,309	196	14.9	1,113	85.1
Madison	14,894	16,569	1,675	880	52.5	795	47.5
Manatee	148,445	211,707	63,262	-1,775	0.0	65,037	100.0
Marion	122,488	194,833	72,345	5,251	7.3	67,094	92.7
Martin	64,014	100,900	36,886	-210	0.0	37,096	100.0
Monroe	63,188	78,024	14,836	3,080	20.8	11,756	79.2
Nassau	32,894	43,941	11,047	3,536	32.0	7,511	68.0
Okaloosa	109,920	143,776	33,856	15,125	44.7	18,731	55.3
Okeechobee	20,264	29,627	9,363	2,228	23.8	7,135	76.2
Orange	470,865	677,491	206,626	47,320	22.9	159,306	77.1
Osceola	49,287	107,728	58,441	4,493	7.7	53,948	92.3
Palm Beach	576,758	863,518	286,760	12,131	4.2	274,629	95.8
Pasco	193,661	281,131	87,470	-12,026	0.0	99,496	100.0
Pinellas	728,531	851,659	123,128	-36,750	0.0	159,878	100.0
Polk	321,652	405,382	83,730	19,738	23.6	63,992	76.4
Putnam	50,549	65,070	14,521	2,128	14.7	12,393	85.3
St. Johns	51,303	83,829	32,526	2,222	6.8	30,304	93.2
St. Lucie	87,182	150,171	62,989	6,076	9.6	56,913	90.4
Santa Rosa	55,988	81,608	25,620	6,534	25.5	19,086	74.5
Sarasota	202,251	277,776	75,525	-12,447	0.0	87,972	100.0
Seminole	179,752	287,529	107,777	16,201	15.0	91,576	85.0
Sumter	24,272	31,577	7,305	569	7.8	6,736	92.2
Suwannee	22,287	26,780	4,493	607	13.5	3,886	86.5
Taylor	16,532	17,111	579	1,062	100.0	-483	0.0
Union	10,166	10,252	86	482	100.0	-396	0.0
Volusia	258,762	370,712	111,950	-3,780	0.0	115,730	100.0
Wakulla	10,887	14,202	3,315	753	22.7	2,562	77.3
Walton	21,300	27,760	6,460	537	8.3	5,923	91.7
Washington	14,509	16,919	2,410	211	8.8	2,199	91.2

1/ Births minus deaths.
Note: Vital statistics data for persons of unreported residence are included
only in the entries for the state. For this reason, natural increase and net
migration columns will not add to their state totals. 1980 census counts include
all adjustments through December 1990, made to the numbers originally published by
the U.S. Bureau of the Census. Therefore, 1980 census numbers for some counties may
differ from those published previously in *Abstract*.
Source: University of Florida, Bureau of Economic and Business Research, Population Program, *Florida Population: Census Summary, 1990*. Data from U.S. Bureau of
the Census.

Florida Statistical Abstract 1991

Table 1.75. POPULATION: CENSUS COUNTS, RANK, PERCENTAGE DISTRIBUTION, LAND AREA AND DENSITY IN THE STATE AND COUNTIES OF FLORIDA, APRIL 1, 1990

					Density	
		Estimate		Land	Persons	
		Rank	Per-	area 1/	per	Rank
		in	centage	(square	square	in
County	Number	state	of state	miles)	mile	state
Florida	12,937,926	(X)	100.00	54,157	239	(X)
Dade	1,937,094	1	14.97	1,955	991	3
Broward	1,255,488	2	9.70	1,211	1,037	2
Palm Beach	863,518	3	6.67	1,993	433	9
Pinellas	851,659	4	6.58	280	3,042	1
Hillsborough	834,054	5	6.45	1,053	792	6
Orange	677,491	6	5.24	910	744	7
Duval	672,971	7	5.20	776	867	5
Polk	405,382	8	3.13	1,823	222	18
Brevard	398,978	9	3.08	995	401	11
Volusia	370,712	10	2.87	1,113	333	14
Lee	335,113	11	2.59	803	417	10
Seminole	287,529	12	2.22	298	965	4
Pasco	281,131	13	2.17	738	381	13
Sarasota	277,776	14	2.15	573	485	8
Escambia	262,798	15	2.03	661	398	12
Manatee	211,707	16	1.64	747	283	16
Marion	194,833	17	1.51	1,610	121	30
Leon	192,493	18	1.49	676	285	15
Alachua	181,596	19	1.40	902	201	20
Lake	152,104	20	1.18	954	159	26
Collier	152,099	21	1.18	1,994	76	36
St. Lucie	150,171	22	1.16	581	258	17
Okaloosa	143,776	23	1.11	936	154	27
Bay	126,994	24	0.98	758	168	24
Charlotte	110,975	25	0.86	690	161	25
Osceola	107,728	26	0.83	1,350	80	32
Clay	105,986	27	0.82	592	179	23
Hernando	101,115	28	0.78	477	212	19
Martin	100,900	29	0.78	555	182	21
Citrus	93,515	30	0.72	629	149	28
Indian River	90,208	31	0.70	497	182	22
St. Johns	83,829	32	0.65	617	136	29
Santa Rosa	81,608	33	0.63	1,024	80	33
Monroe	78,024	34	0.60	1,034	75	37
Highlands	68,432	35	0.53	1,029	67	39

See footnotes at end of table.   Continued . . .

Florida Statistical Abstract 1991

Table 1.75. POPULATION: CENSUS COUNTS, RANK, PERCENTAGE DISTRIBUTION, LAND AREA
AND DENSITY IN THE STATE AND COUNTIES OF FLORIDA, APRIL 1, 1990 (Continued)

County	Number	Estimate Rank in state	Per- centage of state	Land area 1/ (square miles)	Density Persons per square mile	Rank in state
Putnam	65,070	36	0.50	733	89	31
Nassau	43,941	37	0.34	649	68	38
Columbia	42,613	38	0.33	797	53	42
Jackson	41,375	39	0.32	942	44	43
Gadsden	41,105	40	0.32	518	79	34
Sumter	31,577	41	0.24	561	56	41
Okeechobee	29,627	42	0.23	771	38	46
Flagler	28,701	43	0.22	491	58	40
Walton	27,760	44	0.21	1,066	26	53
Suwannee	26,780	45	0.21	690	39	45
Levy	25,923	46	0.20	1,100	24	55
Hendry	25,773	47	0.20	1,163	22	57
DeSoto	23,865	48	0.18	636	38	47
Bradford	22,515	49	0.17	293	77	35
Hardee	19,499	50	0.15	637	31	50
Baker	18,486	51	0.14	585	32	49
Taylor	17,111	52	0.13	1,058	16	63
Washington	16,919	53	0.13	590	29	51
Madison	16,569	54	0.13	710	23	56
Holmes	15,778	55	0.12	488	32	48
Wakulla	14,202	56	0.11	601	24	54
Gulf	11,504	57	0.09	559	21	59
Jefferson	11,296	58	0.09	609	19	61
Calhoun	11,011	59	0.09	568	19	60
Hamilton	10,930	60	0.08	517	21	58
Dixie	10,585	61	0.08	701	15	64
Union	10,252	62	0.08	246	42	44
Gilchrist	9,667	63	0.07	354	27	52
Franklin	8,967	64	0.07	545	16	62
Glades	7,591	65	0.06	763	10	66
Lafayette	5,578	66	0.04	545	10	65
Liberty	5,569	67	0.04	837	7	67

(X) Not applicable.

1/ Land area figures represent the total area in the counties in 1990 and are not
adjusted for lands which cannot be developed (government-owned parks or reserves) or
are uninhabitable (swamps or marshes).

Source: University of Florida, Bureau of Economic and Business Research, Population Program, *Florida Population: Census Summary, 1990.* Data from U.S. Bureau of
the Census.

Florida Statistical Abstract 1991

Table 1.80. INMATES AND PATIENTS: ESTIMATED NUMBER RESIDING IN FEDERAL AND STATE GOVERNMENT-OPERATED INSTITUTIONS AND CONSIDERED NONRESIDENTS OF THE LOCAL AREA FOR REVENUE-SHARING PURPOSES IN THE STATE, COUNTIES, AND MUNICIPALITIES OF FLORIDA, APRIL 1, 1990

County or city	Inmates and patients
Florida	55,690
Alachua	1,765
Gainesville	1,368
Unincorporated	397
Baker unincorporated	1,669
Bay	89
Panama City	44
Unincorporated	45
Bradford unincorporated	3,201
Brevard	1,116
Titusville	42
Unincorporated	1,074
Broward	1,447
Ft. Lauderdale	145
Pembroke Pines	539
Pompano Beach	27
Unincorporated	736
Calhoun unincorporated	793
Charlotte unincorporated	1,295
Collier unincorporated	68
Columbia	436
Lake City	436
Dade	5,360
Miami	2,480
North Miami	151
Unincorporated	2,729
De Soto unincorporated	1,651
Dixie unincorporated	1,064
Duval	458
Jacksonville	458
Escambia	204
Pensacola	40
Unincorporated	164
Gadsden	1,855
Chatahoochee	1,720
Quincy	135
Gilchrist unincorporated	615
Gulf unincorporated	226
Hamilton unincorporated	924
Hendry unincorporated	1,171
Hernando unincorporated	90
Highlands unincorporated	115
Hillsborough	1,346
Tampa	872
Unincorporated	474
Holmes unincorporated	793
Indian River unincorporated	257
Jackson	2,346
Marianna	195
Unincorporated	2,151
Lafayette unincorporated	747
Lake unincorporated	553
Lee	518
Cape Coral	24
Ft. Myers	83
Unincorporated	411
Leon	1,551
Tallahassee	1,364
Leon (continued)	
Unincorporated	187
Levy unincorporated	174
Liberty unincorporated	913
Madison unincorporated	1,078
Manatee	139
Bradenton	139
Marion	2,491
Ocala	72
Unincorporated	2,419
Martin	1,366
Stuart	1,342
Monroe	80
Key West	28
Unincorporated	52
Nassau	43
Fernandina Beach	43
Okaloosa unincorporated	1,408
Okeechobee unincorporated	164
Orange	1,442
Eatonville	64
Winter Park	48
Unincorporated	1,330
Osceola unincorporated	53
Palm Beach	1,674
Boca Raton	293
Lantana	125
West Palm Beach	1,248
Pasco unincorporated	572
Pinellas	1,666
Clearwater	79
St. Petersburg	207
Unincorporated	1,380
Polk	2,667
Bartow	118
Unincorporated	2,549
Putnam unincorporated	319
St. Lucie unincorporated	102
Santa Rosa	211
Milton	54
Unincorporated	157
Sarasota unincorporated	8
Seminole	169
Sanford	41
Unincorporated	128
Sumter unincorporated	1,060
Union unincorporated	2,614
Volusia	1,554
Daytona Beach	50
Holly Hill	7
Unincorporated	1,497
Washington unincorporated	0

Source: University of Florida, Bureau of Economic and Business Research, Population Program, unpublished data.

Table 1.83. POPULATION PROJECTIONS: CENSUS COUNTS, APRIL 1, 1990, AND PROJECTIONS SPECIFIED YEARS APRIL 1, 1995 THROUGH 2020, IN THE STATE AND COMPREHENSIVE PLANNING DISTRICTS OF FLORIDA

Comprehensive Planning District	Census 1990 (1,000)	Projections (1,000)					
		1995	2000	2005	2010	2015	2020
Florida	12,937.9						
Low		13,846.5	14,613.4	15,361.7	16,078.1	16,810.1	17,479.1
Medium		14,451.8	15,728.4	16,946.4	18,096.6	19,230.4	20,260.2
High		14,971.3	16,765.2	18,457.4	20,043.7	21,579.3	22,968.0
District 1	675.6						
Low		682.8	678.8	666.5	646.4	619.3	584.4
Medium		730.3	774.8	816.9	856.5	895.9	931.0
High		779.1	885.4	997.5	1,114.9	1,238.8	1,366.8
District 2	337.5						
Low		336.6	330.7	320.6	306.8	289.5	268.4
Medium		362.3	382.6	401.9	420.1	438.1	454.2
High		388.4	441.3	496.6	554.8	616.0	679.5
District 3	354.2						
Low		359.8	359.7	355.5	347.6	336.6	322.4
Medium		382.6	405.5	426.6	446.6	465.9	483.6
High		406.2	459.3	513.6	570.5	629.9	690.7
District 4	1,019.0						
Low		1,049.0	1,057.1	1,049.3	1,026.1	989.0	936.8
Medium		1,120.8	1,205.3	1,286.1	1,362.2	1,437.1	1,505.1
High		1,194.6	1,376.7	1,570.1	1,774.4	1,991.5	2,217.3
District 5	447.0						
Low		482.9	496.1	492.2	471.6	435.6	383.4
Medium		534.2	609.9	682.4	751.2	818.9	880.9
High		586.7	735.3	897.8	1,073.0	1,262.6	1,462.9
District 6	1,994.5						
Low		2,129.8	2,192.2	2,201.7	2,159.1	2,069.7	1,928.7
Medium		2,313.2	2,587.0	2,849.0	3,097.5	3,341.8	3,565.2
High		2,501.0	3,031.0	3,601.3	4,209.6	4,861.5	5,542.9
District 7	546.8						
Low		557.6	556.0	545.6	526.6	499.7	464.2
Medium		603.1	650.0	694.8	737.2	779.0	817.0
High		649.5	756.0	868.9	988.2	1,114.6	1,245.8
District 8	2,178.6						
Low		2,237.3	2,252.1	2,236.6	2,190.8	2,118.4	2,015.8
Medium		2,391.8	2,568.7	2,737.4	2,896.5	3,053.5	3,195.2
High		2,550.9	2,933.9	3,339.0	3,764.7	4,214.8	4,680.4
District 9	909.3						
Low		969.1	989.1	979.6	941.2	876.3	783.1
Medium		1,066.1	1,201.4	1,330.8	1,453.3	1,574.0	1,684.3
High		1,165.3	1,436.4	1,730.7	2,047.0	2,387.9	2,746.6
District 10	1,204.8						
Low		1,288.0	1,325.4	1,329.6	1,301.1	1,242.8	1,152.4
Medium		1,401.9	1,571.5	1,733.9	1,887.8	2,039.2	2,177.7
High		1,518.6	1,847.5	2,202.2	2,580.6	2,986.6	3,411.2
District 11	3,270.6						
Low		3,372.2	3,426.3	3,450.2	3,443.9	3,411.9	3,348.9
Medium		3,546.1	3,771.3	3,985.8	4,187.6	4,386.9	4,565.8
High		3,727.0	4,187.7	4,667.8	5,165.9	5,686.6	6,219.4

Note: Rounded to hundreds. See footnote on methodology on Table 1.84.
Source: University of Florida, Bureau of Economic and Business Research, Population Program, *Population Studies*, July 1991, Volume 24, No. 2. Bulletin No. 96.

Table 1.84. POPULATION PROJECTIONS: CENSUS COUNTS APRIL 1, 1990, AND PROJECTIONS
APRIL 1, 1995, 2000, 2005, 2010, 2015, AND 2020, IN THE STATE AND
COUNTIES OF FLORIDA

(in thousands, rounded to hundreds)

County	Census 1990	Projections					
		1995	2000	2005	2010	2015	2020
Florida	12,937.9						
Low		13,846.5	14,613.4	15,361.7	16,078.1	16,810.1	17,479.1
Medium		14,451.8	15,728.4	16,946.4	18,096.6	19,230.4	20,260.2
High		14,971.3	16,765.2	18,457.4	20,043.7	21,579.3	22,968.0
Alachua	181.6						
Low		187.6	190.9	192.6	192.5	191.0	187.7
Medium		197.2	210.1	222.5	234.1	245.6	255.9
High		207.3	233.3	260.5	288.8	318.3	348.6
Baker	18.5						
Low		18.4	18.1	17.4	16.5	15.3	13.9
Medium		20.0	21.3	22.5	23.5	24.6	25.6
High		21.6	25.0	28.4	31.9	35.7	39.7
Bay	127.0						
Low		128.9	128.2	125.5	121.0	114.8	106.8
Medium		139.2	149.4	159.0	168.1	177.1	185.3
High		149.8	173.4	198.4	224.7	252.6	281.5
Bradford	22.5						
Low		21.7	20.8	19.3	17.7	16.0	14.2
Medium		23.5	24.5	24.9	25.3	25.7	26.1
High		25.4	28.7	31.5	34.4	37.4	40.4
Brevard	399.0						
Low		423.2	434.8	437.4	431.2	417.1	394.1
Medium		457.1	506.7	554.2	599.2	643.5	683.9
High		491.8	588.3	691.4	800.8	917.5	1,039.1
Broward	1,255.5						
Low		1,310.4	1,344.3	1,364.7	1,371.8	1,367.4	1,349.3
Medium		1,378.0	1,479.7	1,576.6	1,668.0	1,758.2	1,839.6
High		1,448.3	1,643.0	1,846.4	2,057.7	2,279.1	2,505.8
Calhoun	11.0						
Low		10.7	10.3	9.7	9.0	8.2	7.4
Medium		11.7	12.2	12.5	12.9	13.2	13.5
High		12.6	14.2	15.8	17.5	19.2	21.0
Charlotte	111.0						
Low		122.6	127.5	127.5	122.5	113.1	98.9
Medium		136.0	157.9	178.8	198.6	218.1	236.0
High		149.8	191.3	236.7	285.9	339.3	395.7
Citrus	93.5						
Low		101.6	104.6	103.7	99.1	91.1	79.4
Medium		112.8	129.5	145.5	160.7	175.7	189.4
High		124.2	156.9	192.7	231.3	273.3	317.6
Clay	106.0						
Low		112.6	114.2	112.0	106.1	96.8	83.9
Medium		125.0	141.4	157.1	172.0	186.6	200.1
High		137.6	171.3	208.0	247.5	290.3	335.4
Collier	152.1						
Low		165.9	171.2	170.2	162.9	149.9	130.8
Medium		184.1	212.0	238.8	264.1	289.1	312.0
High		202.7	256.8	316.1	380.2	449.6	523.0

See footnote at end of table.   Continued . . .

Florida Statistical Abstract 1991

Table 1.84. POPULATION PROJECTIONS: CENSUS COUNTS APRIL 1, 1990, AND PROJECTIONS
   APRIL 1, 1995, 2000, 2005, 2010, 2015, AND 2020, IN THE STATE AND
   COUNTIES OF FLORIDA (Continued)

(in thousands, rounded to hundreds)

County	Census 1990	Projections 1995	2000	2005	2010	2015	2020
Columbia	42.6						
Low		44.0	44.7	45.1	45.0	44.6	43.8
Medium		46.3	49.2	52.1	54.8	57.4	59.8
High		48.6	54.7	61.0	67.6	74.4	81.4
Dade	1,937.1						
Low		1,981.4	2,000.4	2,003.4	1,990.2	1,963.4	1,920.1
Medium		2,083.6	2,201.8	2,314.4	2,420.0	2,524.5	2,617.8
High		2,189.9	2,445.0	2,710.4	2,985.4	3,272.4	3,565.9
De Soto	23.9						
Low		23.5	22.5	21.1	19.3	17.1	14.4
Medium		26.1	27.9	29.6	31.3	32.9	34.4
High		28.7	33.8	39.2	45.0	51.2	57.6
Dixie	10.6						
Low		10.5	10.2	9.6	8.8	7.8	6.6
Medium		11.7	12.6	13.5	14.3	15.0	15.7
High		12.9	15.3	17.8	20.5	23.4	26.4
Duval	673.0						
Low		682.9	685.1	682.4	674.6	662.6	645.5
Medium		718.2	754.1	788.3	820.3	852.0	880.1
High		754.8	837.4	923.2	1,011.9	1,104.4	1,198.9
Escambia	262.8						
Low		260.8	256.9	251.7	245.2	237.6	228.7
Medium		274.3	282.8	290.7	298.1	305.5	311.8
High		288.3	314.0	340.5	367.8	396.0	424.7
Flagler	28.7						
Low		34.0	37.0	38.1	37.5	35.2	31.3
Medium		37.8	45.8	53.5	60.8	68.0	74.6
High		41.6	55.5	70.8	87.5	105.7	125.1
Franklin	9.0						
Low		8.7	8.3	7.9	7.4	6.8	6.1
Medium		9.5	9.8	10.2	10.5	10.9	11.2
High		10.2	11.5	12.9	14.3	15.8	17.3
Gadsden	41.1						
Low		39.6	38.2	36.5	34.8	33.0	31.2
Medium		41.7	42.4	42.9	43.5	44.0	44.5
High		43.8	46.7	49.4	52.2	55.0	57.9
Gilchrist	9.7						
Low		10.1	10.0	9.5	8.5	7.1	5.4
Medium		11.5	13.1	14.5	15.9	17.2	18.4
High		12.9	16.4	20.1	24.2	28.6	33.2
Glades	7.6						
Low		7.5	7.2	6.7	6.1	5.4	4.6
Medium		8.3	8.9	9.4	10.0	10.5	11.0
High		9.1	10.8	12.5	14.3	16.3	18.4
Gulf	11.5						
Low		10.9	10.3	9.6	8.8	8.0	7.1
Medium		11.9	12.1	12.4	12.6	12.8	13.0
High		12.8	14.2	15.6	17.1	18.6	20.2

See footnote at end of table.   Continued . . .

Florida Statistical Abstract 1991

Table 1.84. POPULATION PROJECTIONS: CENSUS COUNTS APRIL 1, 1990, AND PROJECTIONS
    APRIL 1, 1995, 2000, 2005, 2010, 2015, AND 2020, IN THE STATE AND
    COUNTIES OF FLORIDA (Continued)

(in thousands, rounded to hundreds)

County	Census 1990	Projections					
		1995	2000	2005	2010	2015	2020
Hamilton	10.9						
Low		10.8	10.4	9.8	9.1	8.3	7.5
Medium		11.7	12.2	12.6	13.0	13.4	13.8
High		12.6	14.3	16.0	17.7	19.5	21.3
Hardee	19.5						
Low		18.3	17.0	15.7	14.3	12.8	11.3
Medium		19.9	20.2	20.6	21.0	21.3	21.7
High		21.5	23.5	25.5	27.7	29.9	32.1
Hendry	25.8						
Low		26.6	26.8	26.5	25.7	24.5	22.9
Medium		28.8	31.3	33.6	35.7	37.9	39.8
High		31.0	36.3	41.9	47.8	54.0	60.5
Hernando	101.1						
Low		115.4	122.6	124.4	121.0	112.7	99.3
Medium		128.1	151.8	174.6	196.2	217.4	237.0
High		141.1	183.9	231.1	282.4	338.2	397.3
Highlands	68.4						
Low		72.6	74.6	75.0	73.9	71.5	67.6
Medium		78.4	86.9	95.0	102.7	110.3	117.2
High		84.3	100.9	118.5	137.3	157.3	178.1
Hillsborough	834.1						
Low		849.7	847.1	831.6	803.2	763.5	711.0
Medium		917.7	987.2	1,053.6	1,116.2	1,177.9	1,233.7
High		987.5	1,146.1	1,314.4	1,491.7	1,679.6	1,874.5
Holmes	15.8						
Low		14.8	13.8	12.6	11.4	10.2	8.9
Medium		16.1	16.2	16.3	16.3	16.3	16.3
High		17.4	19.0	20.5	22.1	23.7	25.3
Indian River	90.2						
Low		94.4	94.8	92.3	86.9	78.8	68.0
Medium		104.8	117.4	129.4	140.8	152.1	162.3
High		115.4	142.2	171.4	202.7	236.5	272.1
Jackson	41.4						
Low		40.3	39.1	37.7	36.3	34.7	33.0
Medium		42.4	43.0	43.6	44.1	44.6	45.0
High		44.6	47.8	51.0	54.4	57.8	61.3
Jefferson	11.3						
Low		10.7	10.0	9.3	8.5	7.7	6.8
Medium		11.6	11.8	12.0	12.2	12.4	12.5
High		12.6	13.9	15.2	16.6	18.0	19.4
Lafayette	5.6						
Low		5.6	5.4	5.0	4.6	4.0	3.4
Medium		6.2	6.7	7.0	7.4	7.7	8.0
High		6.8	8.1	9.3	10.6	12.0	13.4
Lake	152.1						
Low		162.0	167.0	168.4	166.4	161.2	152.5
Medium		175.0	194.6	213.4	231.2	248.7	264.6
High		188.3	225.9	266.2	309.0	354.6	402.1

See footnote at end of table.   Continued . . .

Table 1.84.   POPULATION PROJECTIONS: CENSUS COUNTS APRIL 1, 1990, AND PROJECTIONS
         APRIL 1, 1995, 2000, 2005, 2010, 2015, AND 2020, IN THE STATE AND
         COUNTIES OF FLORIDA (Continued)

(in thousands, rounded to hundreds)

County	Census 1990	Projections 1995	2000	2005	2010	2015	2020
Lee	335.1						
Low		356.2	361.4	354.5	336.0	306.5	265.6
Medium		395.4	447.5	497.4	544.7	591.2	633.8
High		435.3	542.0	658.4	783.9	919.6	1,062.6
Leon	192.5						
Low		196.2	195.8	192.4	186.0	177.0	164.9
Medium		211.9	228.2	243.8	258.5	273.1	286.2
High		228.0	264.9	304.2	345.5	389.3	434.9
Levy	25.9						
Low		26.8	27.0	26.8	26.1	24.9	23.3
Medium		28.9	31.5	33.9	36.2	38.5	40.5
High		31.1	36.5	42.3	48.4	54.8	61.6
Liberty	5.6						
Low		5.3	4.9	4.4	3.9	3.3	2.7
Medium		5.8	6.0	6.1	6.2	6.3	6.4
High		6.4	7.3	8.1	9.0	9.9	10.8
Madison	16.6						
Low		15.5	14.4	13.2	12.0	10.7	9.4
Medium		16.8	17.0	17.1	17.2	17.2	17.3
High		18.2	19.9	21.6	23.3	25.0	26.8
Manatee	211.7						
Low		223.2	228.4	229.0	225.1	217.2	204.9
Medium		241.1	266.2	290.1	312.8	335.1	355.5
High		259.4	309.0	361.9	418.1	477.9	540.1
Marion	194.8						
Low		206.4	208.9	204.6	193.6	176.4	152.8
Medium		229.1	258.7	287.0	313.9	340.3	364.5
High		252.3	313.4	380.0	451.8	529.3	611.1
Martin	100.9						
Low		107.3	108.9	106.9	101.3	92.4	80.1
Medium		119.1	134.8	149.9	164.2	178.2	191.1
High		131.1	163.3	198.5	236.3	277.3	320.4
Monroe	78.0						
Low		80.4	81.6	82.1	81.9	81.1	79.5
Medium		84.5	89.8	94.8	99.6	104.2	108.4
High		88.8	99.7	111.0	122.8	135.1	147.7
Nassau	43.9						
Low		45.3	45.6	45.1	43.8	41.9	39.2
Medium		48.9	53.1	57.1	60.9	64.6	68.0
High		52.6	61.7	71.2	81.4	92.1	103.3
Okaloosa	143.8						
Low		146.4	145.9	143.1	138.2	131.3	122.2
Medium		158.1	170.0	181.3	192.0	202.6	212.1
High		170.1	197.3	226.2	256.6	288.9	322.3
Okeechobee	29.6						
Low		31.4	32.3	32.5	32.1	31.0	29.3
Medium		34.0	37.7	41.2	44.5	47.8	50.9
High		36.5	43.7	51.4	59.5	68.2	77.3

See footnote at end of table.   Continued . . .

Florida Statistical Abstract 1991

Table 1.84. POPULATION PROJECTIONS: CENSUS COUNTS APRIL 1, 1990, AND PROJECTIONS
APRIL 1, 1995, 2000, 2005, 2010, 2015, AND 2020, IN THE STATE AND
COUNTIES OF FLORIDA (Continued)

(in thousands, rounded to hundreds)

County	Census 1990	Projections					
		1995	2000	2005	2010	2015	2020
Orange	677.5						
Low		720.8	742.2	748.0	738.4	715.0	676.4
Medium		778.5	865.0	947.7	1,026.1	1,103.2	1,173.7
High		837.7	1,004.2	1,182.3	1,371.3	1,573.1	1,783.2
Osceola	107.7						
Low		121.6	128.2	129.5	125.4	116.5	102.4
Medium		134.9	158.8	181.6	203.4	224.7	244.3
High		148.6	192.3	240.5	292.7	349.5	409.6
Palm Beach	863.5						
Low		924.0	955.2	965.7	955.8	927.5	878.9
Medium		997.9	1,113.2	1,223.6	1,328.1	1,431.0	1,525.0
High		1,073.8	1,292.3	1,526.4	1,775.0	2,040.5	2,317.0
Pasco	281.1						
Low		300.9	311.1	314.6	311.4	302.2	286.4
Medium		325.0	362.6	398.6	432.7	466.3	496.9
High		349.7	420.9	497.3	578.3	664.8	755.0
Pinellas	851.7						
Low		863.5	865.5	861.4	851.1	835.5	813.5
Medium		908.0	952.7	995.1	1,034.8	1,074.2	1,109.1
High		954.3	1,057.9	1,165.4	1,276.6	1,392.5	1,510.8
Polk	405.4						
Low		411.8	409.6	401.3	387.0	367.3	341.6
Medium		444.7	477.3	508.4	537.7	566.7	592.8
High		478.5	554.1	634.3	718.7	808.0	900.7
Putnam	65.1						
Low		66.6	66.6	65.5	63.4	60.4	56.4
Medium		71.9	77.6	83.0	88.2	93.2	97.8
High		77.4	90.1	103.6	117.8	132.9	148.6
St. Johns	83.8						
Low		89.2	90.5	88.8	84.2	76.8	66.6
Medium		99.0	112.0	124.6	136.5	148.1	158.9
High		109.0	135.7	164.9	196.4	230.4	266.3
St. Lucie	150.2						
Low		162.3	166.5	164.7	157.1	144.1	125.4
Medium		180.1	206.1	231.0	254.7	277.9	299.3
High		198.3	249.7	305.9	366.6	432.3	501.7
Santa Rosa	81.6						
Low		86.7	89.2	89.9	88.7	85.8	81.2
Medium		93.7	104.0	113.9	123.2	132.4	140.8
High		100.8	120.7	142.1	164.7	188.8	214.0
Sarasota	277.8						
Low		290.3	295.0	294.2	288.0	276.9	260.3
Medium		313.5	343.8	372.8	400.2	427.2	451.7
High		337.4	399.2	465.1	534.9	609.1	686.4
Seminole	287.5						
Low		307.9	314.0	309.3	293.9	268.9	233.5
Medium		341.8	388.8	433.8	476.5	518.5	557.0
High		376.3	471.0	574.3	685.9	806.6	933.9

See footnote at end of table.

Continued . . .

Florida Statistical Abstract 1991

Table 1.84. POPULATION PROJECTIONS: CENSUS COUNTS APRIL 1, 1990, AND PROJECTIONS
    APRIL 1, 1995, 2000, 2005, 2010, 2015, AND 2020, IN THE STATE AND
    COUNTIES OF FLORIDA (Continued)

(in thousands, rounded to hundreds)

County	Census 1990	Projections 1995	2000	2005	2010	2015	2020
Sumter	31.6						
Low		32.7	33.0	32.7	31.8	30.5	28.6
Medium		35.3	38.4	41.4	44.2	47.0	49.5
High		38.0	44.6	51.7	59.1	67.0	75.3
Suwannee	26.8						
Low		27.6	28.1	28.3	28.2	27.9	27.4
Medium		29.0	30.9	32.6	34.3	35.9	37.4
High		30.5	34.3	38.2	42.3	46.6	50.9
Taylor	17.1						
Low		16.1	15.0	13.8	12.6	11.3	9.9
Medium		17.5	17.6	17.8	18.0	18.1	18.2
High		18.9	20.7	22.5	24.4	26.3	28.2
Union	10.3						
Low		10.3	9.8	9.3	8.6	7.9	7.1
Medium		11.2	11.6	12.0	12.3	12.7	13.0
High		12.1	13.6	15.1	16.7	18.4	20.1
Volusia	370.7						
Low		394.3	406.0	409.1	403.8	391.0	369.8
Medium		425.9	473.1	518.3	561.1	603.2	641.7
High		458.3	549.3	646.6	749.9	860.2	975.0
Wakulla	14.2						
Low		14.2	13.8	13.1	12.1	10.8	9.2
Medium		15.8	17.1	18.4	19.6	20.8	21.9
High		17.4	20.8	24.4	28.2	32.4	36.7
Walton	27.8						
Low		28.5	28.6	28.2	27.4	26.1	24.4
Medium		30.8	33.3	35.7	38.0	40.3	42.3
High		33.1	38.7	44.6	50.8	57.4	64.3
Washington	16.9						
Low		16.7	16.2	15.5	14.5	13.5	12.2
Medium		18.1	19.1	20.0	20.8	21.7	22.4
High		19.6	22.3	25.2	28.2	31.4	34.7

Note: The medium projection is the one we believe is most likely to provide an
accurate forecast of future population. The high and low projections indicate the
range in which future populations are likely to fall. They do not represent
absolute limits to growth; for any county, the future population may be above the
high projection or below the low projection. If future distributions of errors are
similar to past distributions, however, future populations will fall between high
and low projections in approximately two-thirds of Florida's counties. For a
detailed description of projection methodology, see the source.

Source: University of Florida, Bureau of Economic and Business Research, Population Program, *Population Studies*, July 1991, Volume 24, No. 2. Bulletin No. 96.

Florida Statistical Abstract 1991

Table 1.85. VETERANS: NUMBER BY AGE IN THE STATE AND COUNTIES OF FLORIDA
    MARCH 31, 1991

County	Total	17-24	25-34	35-44	45-54	55-64	65-74	75 and over
Florida	1,548,140	13,720	124,380	255,660	245,960	351,330	427,730	129,450
Alachua	20,270	120	3,090	5,590	3,400	3,710	3,540	810
Baker	1,660	30	210	360	340	360	260	90
Bay	15,260	160	1,450	2,930	3,110	3,690	3,230	660
Bradford	3,130	40	390	580	520	680	690	240
Brevard	63,880	550	5,640	9,700	10,460	16,050	17,500	3,990
Broward	143,710	1,020	9,570	25,850	25,690	31,240	36,290	14,040
Calhoun	680	20	70	110	150	170	130	40
Charlotte	19,080	110	710	1,530	1,580	4,190	8,920	2,040
Citrus	19,090	190	640	2,020	1,830	4,080	8,190	2,140
Clay	14,860	150	1,310	3,200	3,500	3,430	2,660	600
Collier	18,050	80	1,050	2,590	2,800	3,840	5,580	2,100
Columbia	4,570	60	460	900	850	1,180	980	140
Dade	151,320	1,500	13,150	23,560	22,700	37,700	42,000	10,700
De Soto	2,230	30	210	280	370	520	650	190
Dixie	1,410	10	100	240	230	280	410	130
Duval	81,650	920	8,480	17,730	14,060	17,260	19,280	3,920
Escambia	34,950	460	3,680	6,910	6,000	7,830	8,270	1,800
Flagler	3,970	20	290	550	570	660	1,510	380
Franklin	880	10	60	110	170	240	250	50
Gadsden	3,180	70	380	550	440	730	830	170
Gilchrist	890	10	70	120	180	230	200	80
Glades	810	0	60	100	120	220	160	150
Gulf	1,060	10	90	170	220	330	130	120
Hamilton	690	20	90	120	110	140	120	70
Hardee	1,880	20	130	230	320	510	520	140
Hendry	2,160	20	260	360	390	590	440	90
Hernando	16,570	130	980	1,730	2,160	3,240	5,840	2,480
Highlands	9,290	90	500	920	1,050	2,170	3,500	1,060
Hillsborough	98,940	900	9,760	20,370	18,300	22,470	21,650	5,510
Holmes	1,520	20	120	230	290	430	400	40
Indian River	11,820	120	780	1,620	1,670	2,540	3,630	1,470
Jackson	3,720	90	350	630	700	980	640	320
Jefferson	900	10	90	140	120	270	190	90

    See footnote at end of table.   Continued . . .

Florida Statistical Abstract 1991

Table 1.85. VETERANS: NUMBER BY AGE IN THE STATE AND COUNTIES OF FLORIDA
    MARCH 31, 1991 (Continued)

County	Total	17-24	25-34	35-44	45-54	55-64	65-74	75 and over
Lafayette	380	0	40	80	80	110	60	0
Lake	18,740	150	1,410	2,500	2,660	4,240	5,110	2,670
Lee	42,600	300	2,820	6,120	6,410	8,860	12,930	5,170
Leon	20,420	150	2,460	5,060	4,120	4,020	3,860	760
Levy	3,080	30	270	480	490	820	850	140
Liberty	550	0	50	90	110	110	160	20
Madison	1,150	20	160	190	230	270	200	90
Manatee	25,660	210	1,740	3,110	3,180	6,090	8,420	2,920
Marion	25,440	240	2,080	3,920	3,820	5,630	7,400	2,370
Martin	13,880	110	820	1,970	1,970	2,940	4,210	1,850
Monroe	12,990	100	680	2,030	1,940	2,580	4,400	1,260
Nassau	5,600	50	620	1,020	1,100	1,440	1,170	220
Okaloosa	21,400	220	1,910	3,710	4,430	5,640	4,740	750
Okeechobee	3,330	70	230	540	600	770	760	370
Orange	80,160	670	7,750	15,740	13,840	18,300	19,390	4,460
Osceola	12,370	140	1,250	2,350	2,640	2,790	2,170	1,050
Palm Beach	104,500	830	7,440	16,790	16,970	22,380	28,270	11,830
Pasco	44,250	310	1,840	4,040	4,280	10,350	19,110	4,320
Pinellas	125,050	970	7,900	15,200	15,550	29,210	41,530	14,700
Polk	42,450	420	4,120	7,870	7,590	10,250	9,820	2,390
Putnam	8,000	90	690	1,160	1,150	1,870	2,370	670
St. Johns	11,620	90	830	1,980	1,820	2,790	3,160	960
St. Lucie	16,420	170	1,310	2,910	2,310	3,650	4,710	1,370
Santa Rosa	8,810	100	1,000	1,810	1,810	2,110	1,650	340
Sarasota	41,490	230	2,060	4,350	4,370	9,570	15,820	5,090
Seminole	38,810	390	3,030	7,710	8,140	8,970	9,010	1,550
Sumter	3,890	60	290	480	570	920	1,080	470
Suwannee	2,480	30	240	590	440	590	420	170
Taylor	1,880	30	230	350	320	500	340	120
Union	1,160	50	250	250	240	180	210	0
Volusia	48,380	420	3,980	7,930	7,050	9,770	14,110	5,120
Wakulla	1,690	20	150	480	310	380	290	60
Walton	3,830	40	360	560	720	910	1,040	210
Washington	1,600	20	150	260	300	360	370	130

Note: Detail may not add to totals because of rounding.

Source: U.S., Veterans Administration, *Veteran Population, March 31, 1991.*

Florida Statistical Abstract 1991

Table 1.87. VETERANS: ESTIMATED NUMBER OF VETERANS IN CIVIL LIFE IN FLORIDA AND
THE UNITED STATES BY PERIOD OF SERVICE, MARCH 31, 1990

(rounded to thousands)

Area	Total veterans	War veterans								Peacetime veterans Service between Korea and Vietnam
					Korea		Vietnam			
		Total	World War I	World War II	Total	No service in World War II	Total	No service in Korea	Post-Vietnam era	
Florida	1,541	1,229	7	649	291	206	428	366	153	133
United States	26,878	20,663	90	8,954	4,820	3,943	8,266	7,676	2,957	2,931

Source: U.S., Veterans Administration, *Veteran Population, March 31, 1990*.

Table 1.90. IMMIGRANTS: NUMBER ADMITTED BY SPECIFIED AREA OF BIRTH AND RESIDENCE
IN FLORIDA AND THE UNITED STATES, 1989

Area of birth	Florida	United States	Area of birth	Florida	United States
Europe	4,092	82,891	North America (Cont.)		
United Kingdom	1,248	14,090	Caribbean	17,185	88,932
Asia	6,811	312,149	Cuba	6,527	10,046
Phillipines	1,218	57,034	Haiti	3,222	13,658
North America	28,681	607,398	Central America	6,742	101,034
Canada	1,985	12,151	South America	7,987	58,926
Mexico	2,751	405,172	Africa	803	25,166

Table 1.91. IMMIGRANTS: NUMBER ADMITTED BY COUNTRY OF BIRTH AND INTENDED RESIDENCE
IN MIAMI-HIALEAH METROPOLITAN AREA AND OTHER SPECIFIED METROPOLITAN AREAS, 1989

Country of birth	Total admitted 1/	Metropolitan area of intended residence					
		Miami-Hialeah, FL	New York NY	Los Angeles-Long Beach, CA	Chicago IL	San Francisco, CA	Washington, DC-VA MD-VA
Total 2/	1,090,924	24,569	116,598	262,805	60,336	22,754	26,695
Mexico	405,172	435	1,599	149,827	32,541	3,800	330
El Salvador	57,878	558	2,009	32,693	480	2,349	4,408
Philippines	57,034	209	2,717	10,516	3,040	3,611	1,131
Vietnam	37,739	44	782	3,936	595	991	1,652
Korea	34,222	55	3,336	6,385	1,384	384	1,854
Mainland China	32,272	127	9,983	3,749	874	3,500	753
India	31,175	106	3,216	1,559	2,951	268	1,199
Dominican Republic	26,723	823	15,778	50	73	6	207
Jamaica	24,523	1,971	11,156	342	353	13	749

1/ Includes other metropolitan areas not shown separately.
2/ Includes other countries not shown separately.
Source for Tables 1.90 and 1.91: U.S., Department of Commerce, Bureau of the
Census, *Statistical Abstract of the United States, 1991*.

Florida Statistical Abstract 1991

HOUSING

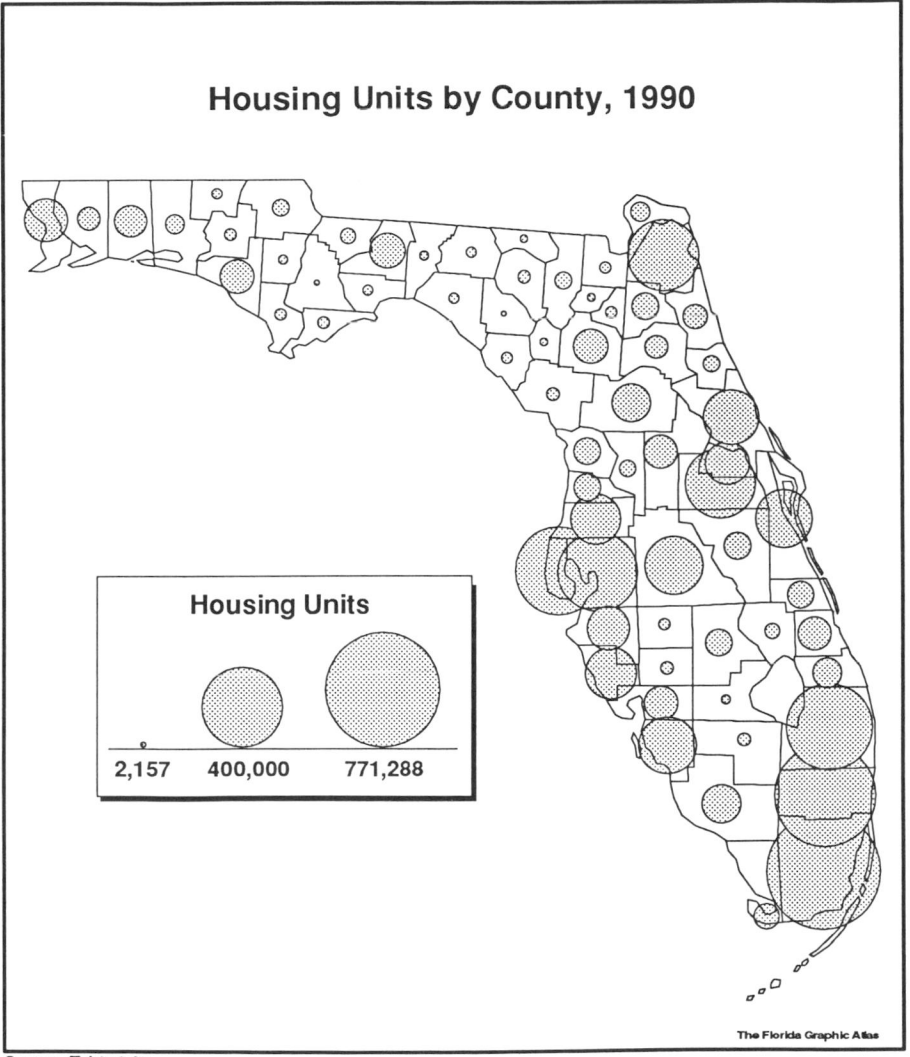

Housing Units by County, 1990

Housing Units

2,157   400,000   771,288

The Florida Graphic Atlas

Source: Table 2.01

Table 2.01. HOUSING UNITS: TOTAL, VACANT, AND OCCUPIED UNITS AND VACANCY RATES
   IN THE STATE AND COUNTIES OF FLORIDA, 1990

County	Total units	Vacant units Total	Vacant units Seasonal or recre- ational use 1/	Vacancy rate 2/ Home- owner	Vacancy rate 2/ Rental	Occupied units 3/ Owner	Occupied units 3/ Renter
Florida	6,100,262	965,393	417,670	3.4	12.4	3,452,160	1,682,709
Alachua	79,022	7,764	468	3.1	10.3	38,525	32,733
Baker	5,975	421	66	1.3	8.5	4,405	1,149
Bay	65,999	17,061	6,528	3.4	30.4	32,075	16,863
Bradford	8,099	906	143	2.3	12.3	5,542	1,651
Brevard	185,150	23,785	8,737	3.3	12.2	111,742	49,623
Broward	628,660	100,218	52,387	3.0	11.4	359,570	168,872
Calhoun	4,468	675	177	1.9	12.0	3,011	782
Charlotte	64,641	16,208	10,863	3.0	14.5	38,559	9,874
Citrus	49,854	9,281	5,302	3.8	12.5	33,761	6,812
Clay	40,249	3,586	964	2.6	8.7	26,895	9,768
Collier	94,165	32,462	22,588	6.6	16.5	43,319	18,384
Columbia	17,818	2,207	361	1.9	13.6	11,509	4,102
Dade	771,288	78,933	19,062	2.8	9.1	375,912	316,443
De Soto	10,310	2,088	931	3.8	13.3	6,084	2,138
Dixie	6,445	2,529	1,629	4.4	24.3	3,235	681
Duval	284,673	27,428	738	2.8	12.6	159,444	97,801
Escambia	112,230	13,622	2,159	3.3	13.3	63,835	34,773
Flagler	15,215	3,335	1,607	4.9	10.0	9,090	2,790
Franklin	5,891	2,263	1,308	5 2	40.1	2,921	707
Gadsden	14,859	1,454	196	1.6	9.3	10,131	3,274
Gilchrist	4,071	787	299	2.3	13.9	2,806	478
Glades	4,624	1,739	1,327	4.6	14.0	2,256	629
Gulf	6,339	2,015	1,190	4.6	31.6	3,396	928
Hamilton	4,119	631	90	1.3	14.7	2,657	831
Hardee	7,941	1,550	664	1.6	15.5	4,844	1,547
Hendry	9,945	1,543	366	3.0	15.0	5,947	2,455
Hernando	50,018	7,718	3,925	3.3	13.2	35,760	6,540
Highlands	40,114	10,570	6,215	4.9	20.0	23,055	6,489
Hillsborough	367,740	42,868	6,188	3.6	13.5	204,966	119,906
Holmes	6,785	985	160	2.4	12.6	4,687	1,113
Indian River	47,128	9,071	4,749	4.2	11.9	28,561	9,496
Jackson	16,320	1,855	371	1.4	8.7	11,142	3,323
Jefferson	4,395	413	52	1.3	11.5	3,055	927
Lafayette	2,266	545	169	1.8	9.3	1,389	332
Lake	75,707	12,091	6,055	3.2	12.2	49,839	13,777
Lee	189,051	48,927	31,408	4.8	15.8	101,093	39,031

See footnotes at end of table.   Continued . . .

Table 2.01. HOUSING UNITS: TOTAL, VACANT, AND OCCUPIED UNITS AND VACANCY RATES
     IN THE STATE AND COUNTIES OF FLORIDA, 1990 (Continued)

County	Total units	Vacant units Total	Seasonal or recre- ational use 1/	Vacancy rate 2/ Home- owner	Rental	Occupied units 3/ Owner	Renter
Leon	81,325	6,497	376	1.8	9.9	42,561	32,267
Levy	12,307	2,228	1,135	3.0	10.4	8,248	1,831
Liberty	2,157	451	268	1.2	11.1	1,378	328
Madison	6,275	753	171	1.4	8.7	4,196	1,326
Manatee	115,245	24,185	14,669	3.7	11.8	64,574	26,486
Marion	94,567	16,390	6,952	3.8	12.6	59,112	19,065
Martin	54,199	11,177	6,900	4.2	11.4	33,079	9,943
Monroe	46,215	12,632	7,928	4.3	13.6	20,854	12,729
Nassau	18,726	2,534	844	1.8	20.8	12,715	3,477
Okaloosa	62,569	9,256	3,345	2.9	13.3	33,154	20,159
Okeechobee	13,266	3,052	1,475	4.0	15.3	7,397	2,817
Orange	282,686	27,834	4,575	3.0	10.7	151,062	103,790
Osceola	47,959	8,809	3,982	3.4	14.3	25,730	13,420
Palm Beach	461,665	96,107	51,593	3.8	12.8	262,894	102,664
Pasco	148,965	27,291	14,058	4.1	14.6	98,384	23,290
Pinellas	458,341	77,706	33,932	3.9	13.8	263,388	117,247
Polk	186,225	30,256	13,130	3.3	12.6	109,885	46,084
Putnam	31,840	6,770	3,483	3.1	12.7	19,800	5,270
St. Johns	40,712	7,286	2,858	3.6	19.2	23,517	9,909
St. Lucie	73,843	15,669	6,607	4.9	17.7	41,807	16,367
Santa Rosa	32,831	2,931	349	2.8	9.8	22,521	7,379
Sarasota	157,055	31,562	19,683	3.1	14.0	95,598	29,895
Seminole	117,845	10,188	1,400	3.1	10.7	72,003	35,654
Sumter	15,298	3,179	1,506	4.2	13.1	9,707	2,412
Suwannee	11,699	1,665	369	2.1	12.0	7,950	2,084
Taylor	7,908	1,507	570	2.3	16.1	5,027	1,374
Union	2,975	317	29	1.8	11.2	1,857	801
Volusia	180,972	27,556	11,269	4.0	13.5	110,359	43,057
Wakulla	6,587	1,377	737	2.8	16.5	4,347	863
Walton	18,728	7,434	3,618	6.0	43.4	8,850	2,444
Washington	7,703	1,260	417	1.8	11.7	5,188	1,255

1/ Vacant units intended for use only in certain seasons, for recreational or
other occasional use throughout the year.

2/ Percentage relationship of vacant units for sale to total homeowner inventory
or for rent to total rental inventory.

3/ Usual place of residence of the person or group of persons living in the unit
at the time of the census innumeration.

Source: U.S., Department of Commerce, Bureau of the Census, *1990 Census of
Housing*, Summary Tape File 1A.

Table 2.05. HOUSEHOLDS AND AVERAGE HOUSEHOLD SIZE: CENSUS COUNTS, APRIL 1, 1970
1980, AND 1990, IN THE STATE AND COUNTIES OF FLORIDA

County	Households 1970	1980	1990	Percentage change 1980-90	Average household size 1970	1980	1990	Percentage change 1980-90
Florida	2,284,786	3,744,254	5,134,869	37.1	2.90	2.55	2.46	-3.5
Alachua	31,115	54,607	71,258	30.5	3.06	2.60	2.40	-7.7
Baker	2,229	4,243	5,554	30.9	3.62	3.22	3.00	-6.8
Bay	23,403	34,754	48,938	40.8	3.18	2.76	2.54	-8.0
Bradford	4,058	6,297	7,193	14.2	3.26	2.87	2.68	-6.6
Brevard	68,560	101,783	161,365	58.5	3.30	2.64	2.43	-8.0
Broward	222,563	417,517	528,442	26.6	2.76	2.42	2.35	-2.9
Calhoun	2,393	3,221	3,793	17.8	3.18	2.84	2.64	-7.0
Charlotte	11,668	25,922	48,433	86.8	2.35	2.25	2.23	-0.9
Citrus	7,358	22,985	40,573	76.5	2.59	2.36	2.27	-3.8
Clay	9,396	21,646	36,663	69.4	3.35	3.06	2.86	-6.5
Collier	13,012	33,966	61,703	81.7	2.88	2.49	2.41	-3.2
Columbia	7,669	12,183	15,611	28.1	3.24	2.87	2.67	-7.0
Dade	428,026	609,830	692,355	13.5	2.91	2.63	2.75	4.6
De Soto	3,761	6,256	8,222	31.4	3.03	2.76	2.62	-5.1
Dixie	1,708	2,663	3,916	47.1	3.19	2.76	2.56	-7.2
Duval	161,666	208,351	257,245	23.5	3.14	2.69	2.54	-5.6
Escambia	60,387	81,067	98,608	21.6	3.25	2.79	2.57	-7.9
Flagler	1,488	4,359	11,880	172.5	2.96	2.49	2.40	-3.6
Franklin	2,429	2,765	3,628	31.2	2.91	2.73	2.42	-11.4
Gadsden	9,066	12,092	13,405	10.9	3.73	3.24	2.90	-10.5
Gilchrist	1,146	2,006	3,284	63.7	3.10	2.82	2.65	-6.0
Glades	1,115	2,224	2,885	29.7	3.24	2.69	2.57	-4.5
Gulf	3,001	3,683	4,324	17.4	3.36	2.89	2.56	-11.4
Hamilton	2,353	2,904	3,488	20.1	3.26	2.99	2.81	-6.0
Hardee	4,368	6,253	6,391	2.2	3.36	3.05	2.95	-3.3
Hendry	3,617	5,959	8,402	41.0	3.26	3.06	2.99	-2.3
Hernando	6,084	17,735	42,300	138.5	2.77	2.48	2.37	-4.4
Highlands	10,468	18,960	29,544	55.8	2.78	2.43	2.28	-6.2
Hillsborough	158,750	237,943	324,872	36.5	3.02	2.66	2.51	-5.6
Holmes	3,550	5,244	5,800	10.6	3.00	2.79	2.56	-8.2
Indian River	12,325	23,331	38,057	63.1	2.90	2.49	2.33	-6.4
Jackson	10,295	13,332	14,465	8.5	3.10	2.76	2.56	-7.2
Jefferson	2,481	3,486	3,982	14.2	3.50	3.04	2.79	-8.2

Continued . . .

Table 2.05.   HOUSEHOLDS AND AVERAGE HOUSEHOLD SIZE: CENSUS COUNTS, APRIL 1, 1970
    1980, AND 1990, IN THE STATE AND COUNTIES OF FLORIDA (Continued)

County	Households				Average household size			
	1970	1980	1990	Per-centage change 1980-90	1970	1980	1990	Per-centage change 1980-90
Lafayette	955	1,413	1,721	21.8	3.03	2.86	2.74	-4.2
Lake	24,621	41,650	63,616	52.7	2.77	2.47	2.35	-4.9
Lee	37,313	82,509	140,124	69.8	2.77	2.46	2.35	-4.5
Leon	31,022	54,103	74,828	38.3	3.03	2.57	2.43	-5.4
Levy	4,175	7,267	10,079	38.7	3.04	2.70	2.52	-6.7
Liberty	1,064	1,485	1,706	14.9	3.17	2.82	2.69	-4.6
Madison	4,000	4,977	5,522	11.0	3.29	2.98	2.75	-7.7
Manatee	38,488	61,998	91,060	46.9	2.50	2.36	2.29	-3.0
Marion	22,317	45,458	78,177	72.0	3.03	2.64	2.44	-7.6
Martin	10,122	25,863	43,022	66.3	2.72	2.40	2.28	-5.0
Monroe	16,827	26,340	33,583	27.5	2.89	2.34	2.24	-4.3
Nassau	6,018	10,976	16,192	47.5	3.42	2.98	2.68	-10.1
Okaloosa	24,915	37,538	53,313	42.0	3.38	2.84	2.60	-8.5
Okeechobee	3,178	6,981	10,214	46.3	3.34	2.85	2.75	-3.5
Orange	108,645	170,754	254,852	49.3	3.07	2.67	2.56	-4.1
Osceola	9,092	18,615	39,150	110.3	2.74	2.60	2.68	3.1
Palm Beach	123,347	234,339	365,558	56.0	2.78	2.42	2.32	-4.1
Pasco	30,361	81,346	121,674	49.6	2.46	2.34	2.26	-3.4
Pinellas	211,301	319,527	380,635	19.1	2.43	2.25	2.18	-3.1
Polk	73,024	114,394	155,969	36.3	3.05	2.70	2.53	-6.3
Putnam	11,494	18,397	25,070	36.3	3.12	2.72	2.55	-6.3
St. Johns	10,004	18,623	33,426	79.5	2.93	2.65	2.44	-7.9
St. Lucie	16,847	32,506	58,174	79.0	2.98	2.65	2.54	-4.2
Santa Rosa	10,846	18,595	29,900	60.8	3.34	2.94	2.68	-8.8
Sarasota	48,634	88,739	125,493	41.4	2.44	2.25	2.18	-3.1
Seminole	25,757	63,247	107,657	70.2	3.23	2.82	2.64	-6.4
Sumter	4,627	8,582	12,119	41.2	3.05	2.68	2.46	-8.2
Suwannee	4,855	7,739	10,034	29.7	3.16	2.84	2.61	-8.1
Taylor	4,227	5,826	6,401	9.9	3.22	2.83	2.67	-5.7
Union	1,639	2,119	2,658	25.4	3.25	2.95	2.91	-1.4
Volusia	62,747	105,773	153,416	45.0	2.62	2.39	2.33	-2.5
Wakulla	1,926	3,730	5,210	39.7	3.26	2.89	2.70	-6.6
Walton	5,270	8,043	11,294	40.4	3.05	2.64	2.44	-7.6
Washington	3,620	5,235	6,443	23.1	3.14	2.75	2.55	-7.3

    Source: University of Florida, Bureau of Economic and Business Research, Popula-
tion Program, *Population Studies*, April 1991.   Volume 24, No. 1.   Bulletin No. 95.

Florida Statistical Abstract 1991

Table 2.08.   HOUSING UNITS: SPECIFIED CHARACTERISTICS OF THE HOUSING INVENTORY
    IN THE MIAMI-FT. LAUDERDALE METROPOLITAN STATISTICAL AREA (MSA), 1986, AND
    TAMPA-ST.PETERSBURG MSA, 1985

(in thousands)

Unit characteristics	Miami-Ft. Lauderdale	Tampa-St. Petersburg
Housing units, total	1,405.9	971.9
Seasonal	42.8	44.0
Year-round	1,363.1	927.9
Owner-occupied	721.9	550.3
Renter-occupied	434.0	234.7
Vacant	207.3	142.9
For rent	66.3	49.6
For sale	28.4	25.4
Mobile home	33.2	119.6
Units in structure		
1, detached	572.9	552.0
1, attached	112.1	35.9
2 to 4	122.2	82.8
5 to 9	72.4	56.0
10 to 19	91.2	50.3
20 to 49	170.8	37.8
50 or more	231.0	37.6
Year structure built		
1985 to 1989	52.5	30.9
1980 to 1984	134.0	134.5
1975 to 1979	253.2	213.2
1970 to 1974	266.5	190.7
1960 to 1969	303.8	194.1
1950 to 1959	234.0	118.9
1940 to 1949	86.9	43.1
1939 or earlier	74.9	46.4
Median year built	1970	1972
Collective ownership		
Cooperatives	17.0	10.4
Condominiums	344.4	102.7
Number of rooms		
1 to 2	63.0	17.9
3 to 4	620.4	359.6
5 to 6	470.7	436.2
7 to 8	221.9	136.8
9 or more	30.0	21.5
Median number of rooms	4.6	4.9
Median number of bedrooms	2.1	2.2
Size of unit (square feet)		
Less than 500	10.3	20.9
500 to 749	21.8	51.7
750 to 999	37.1	89.1
1,000 to 1,499	175.1	241.7

See footnotes at end of table.   Continued . . .

Table 2.08. HOUSING UNITS: SPECIFIED CHARACTERISTICS OF THE HOUSING INVENTORY
IN THE MIAMI-FT. LAUDERDALE METROPOLITAN STATISTICAL AREA (MSA), 1986, AND
TAMPA-ST.PETERSBURG MSA, 1985 (Continued)

(in thousands)

Unit characteristics	Miami-Ft. Lauderdale	Tampa-St. Petersburg
Size of unit (square feet) (Continued)		
1,500 to 1,999	143.6	129.5
2,000 to 2,499	76.6	63.2
2,500 to 2,999	29.4	24.5
3,000 or more	65.3	18.4
Median size of unit	1,623	1,327
Lot size (acres)		
Less than 1/8	68.1	76.1
1/8 up to 1/4	269.8	219.2
1/4 up to 1/2	85.8	89.4
1/2 up to 1	24.2	29.5
1 or more	17.8	53.5
Median lot size	0.20	0.22
Description of neighborhood 1/		
Single-family detached houses	747.4	678.1
Single-family attached or 1 to 3 story multiunit	605.5	300.2
4 to 6 story multiunit	221.0	34.0
7 stories or more multiunit	125.4	17.9
Mobile homes	38.6	148.2
Residential parking lots	148.4	138.9
Commercial, institutional, or industrial	257.7	124.0
Body of water	146.9	132.3
Open space, park, woods, farm, or ranch	104.8	224.0
4+ lane highway, railroad, or airport	85.5	(NA)
Monthly housing costs 2/		
Less than $200	141.2	209.8
$200 to $299	152.5	133.1
$300 to $399	176.7	137.4
$400 to $499	170.8	108.7
$500 to $599	152.7	72.0
$600 to $699	94.9	37.8
$700 to $799	67.7	24.1
$800 to $999	95.4	26.8
$1,000 to $1,249	31.6	11.2
$1,250 or more	44.3	19.2
No cash rent	17.9	12.1
Median monthly costs (dollars) 3/	451	337
Value of owner housing units 4/		
Less than $10,000	17.5	19.2
$10,000 to $19,999	12.3	32.9
$20,000 to $29,999	19.7	34.1
$30,000 to $39,999	42.1	61.7
$40,000 to $49,999	75.8	96.8

See footnotes at end of table.

Continued . . .

Florida Statistical Abstract 1991

Table 2.08. HOUSING UNITS: SPECIFIED CHARACTERISTICS OF THE HOUSING INVENTORY
IN THE MIAMI-FT. LAUDERDALE METROPOLITAN STATISTICAL AREA (MSA), 1986, AND
TAMPA-ST.PETERSBURG MSA, 1985 (Continued)

(in thousands)

Unit characteristics	Miami-Ft. Lauderdale	Tampa-St. Petersburg
Value of owner housing units 4/ (Continued)		
$50,000 to $59,999	103.1	73.9
$60,000 to $69,999	116.6	78.4
$70,000 to $79,999	96.5	48.8
$80,000 to $99,999	110.1	63.8
$100,000 to $119,999	47.6	25.9
$120,000 to $149,999	40.6	19.9
$150,000 to $199,999	42.0	17.5
$200,000 to $249,999	19.0	10.6
$250,000 to $299,999	12.7	5.8
$300,000 or more	14.8	5.0
Time shared units	0.4	0.2
Median value of unit (dollars)	69,832	57,099
Annual taxes paid per $1,000 value		
Less than $5	89.8	263.4
$5 to $9	303.5	229.6
$10 to $14	242.4	64.1
$15 to $19	76.4	13.6
$20 to $24	26.9	3.8
$25 or more	31.4	20.1
Median taxes paid per 1,000 value (dollars)	10	6

(NA) Not available.
1/ Includes area within 300 feet surrounding unit. Figures may not add to total
because more than one category may apply to unit.
2/ Includes rent on vacant units.
3/ Excludes no cash rent.
4/ Sales price for units for sale; purchase price for units sold but not yet
occupied.

Source: U.S., Department of Commerce, Bureau of the Census and U.S., Department
of Housing and Urban Development, Office of Policy Development and Research, *American Housing Survey for the Miami-Ft. Lauderdale Metropolitan Area in 1986* and
American Housing Survey for the Tampa-St.Petersburg Metropolitan Area in 1985. H-
170-86-28 and H-170-85-62.

Florida Statistical Abstract 1991

Table 2.20. HOMES FOR THE AGING: NUMBER OF HOMES AND NUMBER OF UNITS FOR HOMES WHICH ARE MEMBERS OF THE FLORIDA ASSOCIATION OF HOMES FOR THE AGING (FAHA) BY FAHA DISTRICT IN FLORIDA, 1991

City	Homes	Number of-- Residen-tial units	Nursing beds	City	Homes	Number of-- Residen-tial units	Nursing beds
Florida	197	34,843	6,715	District 6 (Cont.)			
District 1	38	5,679	1,062	Hialeah	2	300	0
Atlantic Beach	1	346	42	Hollywood	1	200	0
Dowling Park	1	286	107	Lauderhill	1	46	0
Ft. Walton Beach	1	95	0	Miami	6	1,187	514
Gainesville	2	327	0	Miami Beach	2	351	0
Jacksonville	19	2,831	572	Miami Springs	1	50	269
Jacksonville Beach	1	199	0	North Miami	1	79	0
Keystone Heights	1	89	0	Opa Locka	1	113	0
Macclenny	1	0	68	Pembroke Pines	1	0	85
Marianna	2	124	0	Plantation	1	329	60
Palatka	1	76	0	Pompano Beach	3	860	144
Penney Farms	1	291	40	District 7	15	3,113	914
Pensacola	2	439	90	Boca Raton	2	1,008	180
Ponte Vedra Beach	1	259	30	Delray Beach	4	982	214
Tallahassee	4	317	113	Juno Beach	1	301	60
District 2	20	3,795	481	Lake Worth	2	268	60
Apopka	1	90	0	West Palm Beach	6	554	400
Fern Park	1	176	0	District 8	11	1,660	280
Leesburg	1	235	60	Cocoa	1	150	0
Longwood	1	242	60	Melbourne	4	688	0
Mt. Dora	1	120	0	Merritt Island	1	158	96
Orlando	10	1,815	180	Palm Bay	1	66	0
Sanford	1	158	0	Rockledge	1	0	100
Winter Park	4	959	181	Vero Beach	2	448	84
District 3	16	2,713	397	West Melbourne	1	150	0
Largo	1	400	0	District 9	11	1,975	326
Pinellas Park	2	195	0	Clearwater	4	711	246
St. Petersburg	11	1,938	277	Dunedin	1	386	0
Seminole	1	0	120	Lecanto	1	48	0
South Pasadena	1	180	0	New Port Richey	2	224	0
District 4	16	2,688	150	Palm Harbor	1	380	80
Tampa	16	2,688	150	Port Richey	1	136	0
District 5	21	4,283	1,018	Tarpon Springs	1	90	0
Bradenton	4	548	93	District 10	10	2,034	595
Cape Coral	1	231	60	Davenport	1	69	60
Ft. Myers	2	1,027	240	Kissimmee	1	861	170
Lehigh Acres	1	80	0	Lakeland	5	901	245
Naples	2	683	46	Plant City	1	75	0
Port Charlotte	3	290	224	Sebring	1	60	120
Sarasota	6	946	295	Winter Haven	1	68	0
Venice	2	478	60	District 11	12	2,018	360
District 6	27	4,885	1,132	Daytona Beach	5	460	120
Coral Springs	1	432	0	Deland	4	676	60
Deerfield Beach	2	262	60	Holly Hill	1	300	60
Ft. Lauderdale	3	556	0	Orange City	1	510	120
Hallandale	1	120	0	Port Orange	1	72	0

Note: Include personal care units, cluster homes, adult congregate living facility units and/or assisted living units. Excludes homes in construction.

Source: Florida Association of Homes for the Aging, *1991 Directory of Members.*

Florida Statistical Abstract 1991

Table 2.21. ADULT CONGREGATE LIVING FACILITIES: NUMBER AND CAPACITY OF FACILITIES
IN THE STATE AND COUNTIES OF FLORIDA, JANUARY 1991

County	Number of facilities 1/	Capacity	County	Number of facilities 1/	Capacity
Florida	1,503	63,687	Lafayette	1	12
			Lake	22	849
Alachua	13	1,025	Lee	31	1,730
Baker	1	11	Leon	5	325
Bay	11	370	Levy	1	64
Bradford	3	28	Liberty	3	88
Brevard	16	1,031	Madison	2	83
Broward	150	7,767	Manatee	34	1,848
Calhoun	5	74	Marion	24	892
Charlotte	24	801	Martin	4	67
Citrus	18	848	Monroe	2	32
Clay	5	64	Nassau	1	60
Collier	6	1,213	Okaloosa	3	132
Columbia	7	127	Okeechobee	1	20
Dade	245	7,635	Orange	67	1,121
De Soto	0	0	Osceola	7	240
Dixie	1	15	Palm Beach	68	3,561
Duval	48	2,130	Pasco	41	2,790
Escambia	28	1,277	Pinellas	272	8,960
Flagler	0	0	Polk	36	1,937
Franklin	1	40	Putnam	11	327
Gadsden	2	29	St. Johns	6	201
Gilchrist	2	29	St. Lucie	7	73
Glades	0	0	Santa Rosa	4	99
Gulf	1	11	Sarasota	57	3,234
Hamilton	2	28	Seminole	18	840
Hardee	3	43	Sumter	1	7
Hendry	2	50	Suwannee	4	72
Hernando	6	719	Taylor	0	0
Highlands	11	536	Union	0	0
Hillsborough	78	4,294	Volusia	55	3,294
Holmes	1	30	Wakulla	1	24
Indian River	7	114	Walton	2	75
Jackson	5	119	Washington	8	103
Jefferson	2	69			

1/ Facilities licensed by the Florida Department of Health and Rehabilitative
Services and in operation as of January 29, 1991.

Source: State of Florida, Department of Health and Rehabilitative Services,
Directory of Adult Congregate Living Facilities, 1991.

Florida Statistical Abstract 1991

Table 2.30. PUBLIC LODGING: LICENSED LODGINGS, APARTMENTS, ROOMING HOUSES, RENTAL CONDOMINIUMS, AND TRANSIENT APARTMENTS IN THE STATE AND COUNTIES OF FLORIDA, FISCAL YEAR 1990-91

County	Total licensed lodgings 1/		Apartment buildings		Rooming houses		Rental condominiums		Transient apartment buildings 2/	
	Number	Units	Number	Units	Number	Units	Number	Units	Number	Units
Florida	29,183	1,133,067	16,889	715,727	772	9,524	2,077	45,068	4,652	26,740
Alachua	389	20,651	325	17,023	10	83	0	0	8	202
Baker	5	166	2	59	0	0	0	0	0	0
Bay	797	18,210	79	3,853	1	1	124	4,058	374	1,043
Bradford	31	801	13	372	1	2	0	0	2	17
Brevard	529	28,513	285	17,433	16	167	58	1,348	54	1,262
Broward	3,837	122,273	2,748	86,800	42	427	43	1,467	469	4,908
Calhoun	5	115	2	88	0	0	0	0	0	0
Charlotte	139	3,291	24	1,115	0	0	35	632	42	271
Citrus	79	1,854	36	777	6	52	1	9	10	68
Clay	51	4,841	35	3,906	3	19	1	50	3	7
Collier	202	10,346	95	3,807	3	52	23	860	10	78
Columbia	86	3,060	46	1,059	6	67	0	0	4	123
Dade	7,002	214,271	6,254	157,661	160	1,837	20	2,742	15	25
De Soto	21	350	11	168	3	35	0	0	2	16
Dixie	12	177	1	32	2	13	0	0	1	7
Duval	821	68,942	645	56,208	39	444	6	47	5	58
Escambia	886	15,281	98	9,416	2	35	562	985	157	286
Flagler	48	767	7	78	3	15	17	188	7	9
Franklin	280	866	3	54	2	8	5	123	253	284
Gadsden	22	647	12	532	0	0	0	0	4	21
Gilchrist	2	52	1	24	0	0	0	0	0	0
Glades	17	271	0	0	3	14	2	30	2	9

See footnotes at end of table.

Continued . . .

Table 2.30. PUBLIC LODGING: LICENSED LODGINGS, APARTMENTS, ROOMING HOUSES, RENTAL CONDOMINIUMS, AND TRANSIENT APARTMENTS IN THE STATE AND COUNTIES OF FLORIDA, FISCAL YEAR 1990-91 (Continued)

County	Total licensed lodgings 1/		Apartment buildings		Rooming houses		Rental condominiums		Transient apartment buildings 2/	
	Number	Units	Number	Units	Number	Units	Number	Units	Number	Units
Gulf	155	438	3	113	1	12	0	0	145	236
Hamilton	16	489	6	107	0	0	0	0	0	0
Hardee	19	264	9	136	2	13	0	0	5	70
Hendry	43	747	19	223	3	50	2	120	3	13
Hernando	36	1,287	16	763	4	41	1	4	4	28
Highlands	132	2,926	57	1,207	6	52	2	32	43	659
Hillsborough	961	85,830	732	69,802	37	510	1	237	32	448
Holmes	7	247	1	31	0	0	0	0	0	0
Indian River	115	3,223	64	1,293	2	18	6	396	11	116
Jackson	21	824	10	343	0	0	0	0	1	10
Jefferson	13	279	6	147	0	0	0	0	0	0
Lafayette	3	51	1	36	1	9	0	0	0	0
Lake	163	5,588	93	3,133	8	104	1	87	7	59
Lee	529	21,116	236	9,752	6	44	60	2,526	57	621
Leon	351	21,722	289	16,405	5	718	0	0	4	60
Levy	48	674	9	191	9	63	6	95	5	26
Liberty	1	10	0	0	0	0	0	0	0	0
Madison	11	394	7	249	0	0	0	0	1	29
Manatee	558	14,070	139	9,073	12	68	99	1,150	235	773
Marion	190	7,596	86	3,749	16	93	0	0	12	80
Martin	97	2,798	55	1,158	6	38	1	30	8	362
Monroe	365	9,918	125	1,811	29	287	9	225	27	389
Nassau	124	2,862	16	558	0	0	31	1,068	46	56
Okaloosa	461	10,612	95	3,008	1	24	261	3,040	47	239

Continued . . .

See footnotes at end of table.

Table 2.30. PUBLIC LODGING: LICENSED LODGINGS, APARTMENTS, ROOMING HOUSES, RENTAL CONDOMINIUMS, AND TRANSIENT APARTMENTS IN THE STATE AND COUNTIES OF FLORIDA, FISCAL YEAR 1990-91 (Continued)

County	Total licensed lodgings 1/		Apartment buildings		Rooming houses		Rental condominiums		Transient apartment buildings 2/	
	Number	Units	Number	Units	Number	Units	Number	Units	Number	Units
Okeechobee	18	397	2	74	0	0	0	0	6	60
Orange	964	120,818	595	62,921	51	527	22	2,697	92	1,815
Osceola	1,366	30,441	85	6,651	9	107	153	2,064	993	1,519
Palm Beach	1,467	58,466	1,032	39,440	92	1,580	16	578	97	1,331
Pasco	142	8,409	81	5,851	4	44	1	550	14	142
Pinellas	2,240	82,466	1,111	54,146	46	551	126	4,267	500	4,538
Polk	575	21,035	317	11,664	47	633	7	1,207	88	1,139
Putnam	47	1,207	16	681	9	67	1	29	1	10
St. Johns	200	8,455	52	2,546	15	86	53	2,010	5	45
St. Lucie	157	4,813	59	1,272	18	249	8	909	34	289
Santa Rosa	215	2,174	34	1,160	0	0	37	166	132	151
Sarasota	677	16,542	202	7,388	13	106	115	3,920	258	1,307
Seminole	160	25,732	124	22,633	4	30	1	2	1	6
Sumter	21	822	6	161	0	0	0	0	6	33
Suwannee	19	469	7	197	0	0	0	0	4	19
Taylor	40	833	7	282	1	12	0	0	7	25
Union	2	80	2	80	0	0	0	0	0	0
Volusia	846	36,508	353	14,632	12	113	102	3,391	42	580
Wakulla	12	181	0	0	0	0	2	30	2	2
Walton	327	3,343	5	153	1	4	56	1,699	254	760
Washington	8	166	3	42	0	0	0	0	1	1

1/ Includes hotels and motels shown separately in Table 19.60.
2/ Apartments which rent for six months or less.

Source: State of Florida, Department of Business Regulation, Division of Hotels and Restaurants, *Master File Statistics: Public Lodging and Food Service Establishments,* Fiscal Year July 1990 through June 1991.

Table 2.36. MOBILE HOME AND RECREATIONAL VEHICLE TAGS: NUMBER SOLD IN THE STATE
AND COUNTIES OF FLORIDA, FISCAL YEAR 1989-90

County	Mobile homes 1/	Real property 2/	Recreational vehicles	County	Mobile homes 1/	Real property 2/	Recreational vehicles
Florida	544,367	49,921	230,939	Lafayette	122	63	120
				Lake	18,885	3,454	6,697
Alachua	5,252	191	2,364	Lee	26,034	2,114	11,633
Baker	769	254	418	Leon	5,964	564	2,488
Bay	4,691	563	2,932	Levy	726	847	751
Bradford	1,489	235	675	Liberty	167	84	100
Brevard	13,349	1,758	8,802	Madison	1,027	284	223
Broward	23,389	485	10,327	Manatee	25,016	1,191	6,246
Calhoun	113	65	123	Marion	16,960	2,444	5,925
Charlotte	8,648	1,339	3,327	Martin	5,375	514	2,515
Citrus	3,764	2,470	3,622	Monroe	1,995	678	2,869
Clay	2,273	1,052	1,995	Nassau	3,334	701	921
Collier	6,810	539	3,383	Okaloosa	2,244	199	2,350
Columbia	1,977	551	886	Okeechobee	2,181	818	2,160
Dade	14,387	224	10,112	Orange	18,281	379	9,909
De Soto	2,363	315	1,352	Osceola	7,602	705	3,434
Dixie	170	283	349	Palm Beach	16,301	704	7,595
Duval	18,352	1,293	8,679	Pasco	22,031	3,000	12,574
Escambia	4,104	542	4,572	Pinellas	59,166	1,843	14,921
Flagler	1,137	196	1,369	Polk	44,593	2,933	12,514
Franklin	144	66	180	Putnam	4,256	1,380	2,088
Gadsden	1,063	380	315	St. Johns	3,480	256	1,833
Gilchrist	830	294	320	St. Lucie	14,276	599	3,363
Glades	316	190	172	Santa Rosa	1,565	423	1,709
Gulf	177	95	206	Sarasota	22,060	1,245	7,078
Hamilton	372	109	173	Seminole	4,690	182	3,829
Hardee	752	420	793	Sumter	2,691	669	1,670
Hendry	2,911	373	905	Suwannee	3,243	691	676
Hernando	4,167	1,475	2,994	Taylor	944	281	466
Highlands	8,204	853	4,050	Union	544	299	136
Hillsborough	39,131	1,179	14,492	Volusia	23,654	953	7,879
Holmes	551	148	177	Wakulla	782	281	320
Indian River	9,240	163	2,122	Walton	629	223	362
Jackson	1,280	250	622	Washington	372	145	253
Jefferson	512	88	157	Office agency	490	337	367

1/ Includes military mobile homes.
2/ Tags sold to mobile home owners who also own the land on which the mobile home
stands. A real property tag is bought only once, not annually.

Source: State of Florida, Department of Highway Safety and Motor Vehicles, Division of Motor Vehicles, *Tags and Revenue, July 1, 1989 through June 30, 1990.*

Florida Statistical Abstract 1991

VITAL STATISTICS
AND HEALTH

**Reported Adult Cases of AIDS,
January 1, 1980 - June 30, 1991**

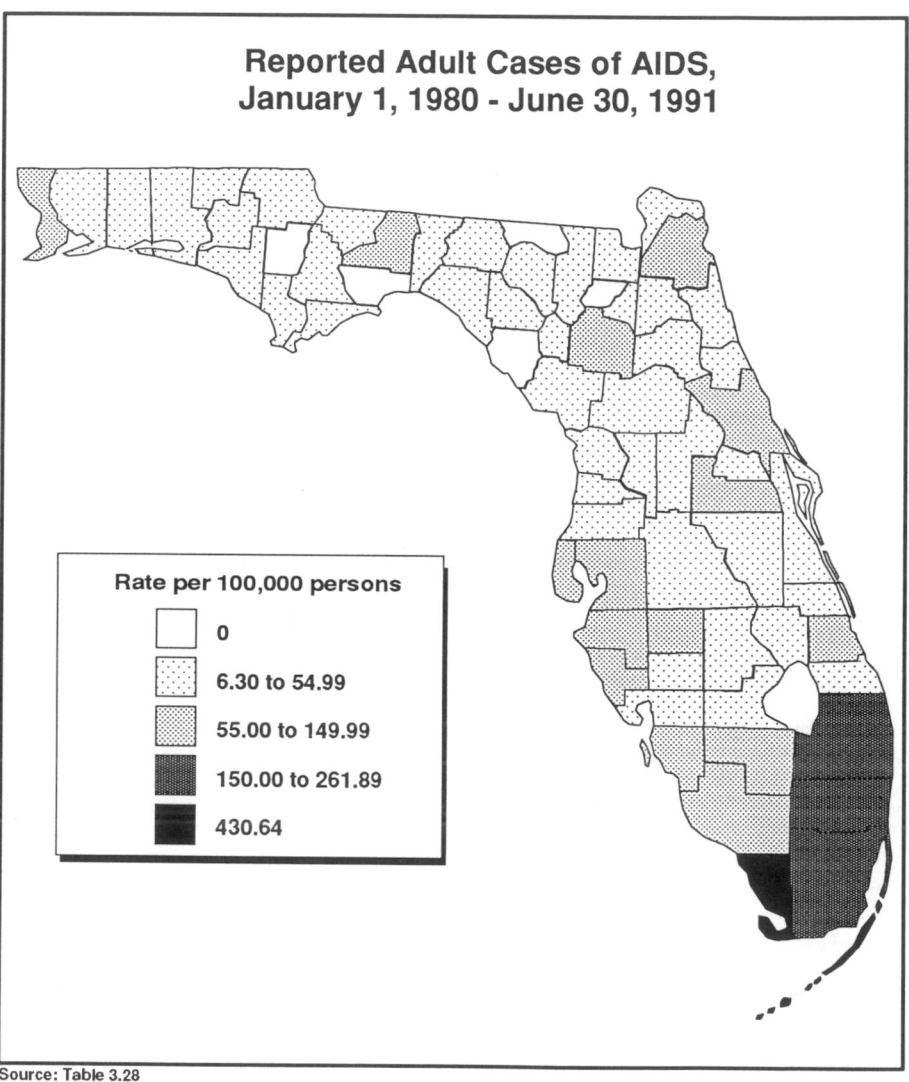

Rate per 100,000 persons

	0
	6.30 to 54.99
	55.00 to 149.99
	150.00 to 261.89
	430.64

Source: Table 3.28

SECTION 3.00
VITAL STATISTICS AND HEALTH

TABLES LISTED BY MAJOR HEADINGS

Table 3.01. BIRTH AND DEATH RATES: RATES PER 1,000 POPULATION BY RACE IN FLORIDA AND THE UNITED STATES, 1975 THROUGH 1990

	Resident live birth rates						Resident death rates					
	Total		White		Black and other races		Total		White		Black and other races	
Year	Flor-ida	U.S.	Flor-ida	U.S.	Flor-ida	U.S.	Flor-ida	U.S.	Flor-ida	U.S.	Flor-ida	U.S.
1975	12.2	14.6	10.7	13.6	20.1	20.7	10.1	8.8	10.5	8.9	7.8	8.8
1976	11.9	14.6	10.4	13.6	20.1	19.2	10.2	8.8	10.7	9.0	7.6	7.5
1977	12.3	15.1	10.7	14.1	20.9	19.7	10.2	8.6	10.7	8.7	7.7	7.3
1978	12.3	15.0	10.6	14.0	21.1	19.5	10.3	8.7	10.9	8.8	7.3	7.1
1979	12.7	15.6	11.1	14.5	21.3	19.8	10.3	8.5	10.9	8.7	7.4	6.9
1980	13.4	15.9	11.6	14.9	23.1	22.1	10.7	8.8	11.2	8.9	7.5	8.8
1981	13.6	15.8	11.8	14.8	22.9	21.6	10.7	8.6	11.3	8.8	7.4	8.4
1982	13.8	15.9	12.1	14.9	22.7	21.4	10.4	8.5	11.1	8.7	6.8	8.2
1983	14.0	15.5	12.1	14.6	25.3	20.9	10.6	8.6	11.1	8.8	7.9	8.3
1984	14.1	15.5	12.3	14.5	24.7	20.8	10.4	8.6	10.9	8.9	7.8	8.3
1985	14.4	15.8	12.5	14.8	25.3	21.1	10.6	8.7	11.0	9.0	7.8	8.5
1986	14.2	15.6	12.4	14.5	24.6	21.2	10.4	8.7	10.9	9.0	7.8	8.5
1987	14.4	15.7	12.6	14.5	24.6	21.6	10.5	8.7	11.0	9.0	7.9	8.6
1988	14.8	15.9	12.9	14.7	25.4	22.2	10.5	8.8	11.0	9.1	7.8	8.7
1989	14.8	(NA)	12.9	(NA)	24.9	(NA)	10.3	8.7	10.8	8.9	7.6	8.5
1990	15.0	(NA)	13.0	(NA)	25.2	(NA)	10.1	(NA)	10.6	(NA)	7.4	(NA)

(NA) Not available.

Note: Some data are revised; 1990 Florida and 1989 U.S. data are preliminary.

Source: U.S., Department of Commerce, Bureau of the Census, *Statistical Abstract of the United States, 1991*, annual editions and State of Florida, Department of Health and Rehabilitative Services, Office of Vital Statistics, *Vital News*, March 1991.

Table 3.02. RESIDENT LIVE BIRTHS: NUMBER OF BIRTHS BY AGE OF MOTHER IN FLORIDA 1985 THROUGH 1990

Age of mother	1985	1986	1987	1988	1989 A/	1990 B/
All ages	163,732	167,628	175,072	183,998	192,887	198,018
Less than 15	670	665	666	714	729	762
15	1,407	1,505	1,449	1,614	1,551	1,658
16	2,709	2,891	3,021	3,052	3,249	3,131
17	4,348	4,423	4,546	5,119	5,275	5,168
18	6,139	6,140	6,230	6,640	7,439	7,509
19	8,017	7,902	7,940	8,335	9,069	9,609
20-24	52,310	51,741	51,809	52,210	52,458	52,829
25-29	50,557	52,037	54,779	57,065	59,336	60,013
30-34	27,739	29,690	32,580	35,524	38,018	40,721
35-39	8,638	9,328	10,440	11,894	13,435	14,303
40-44	1,147	1,213	1,519	1,733	1,958	2,193
45 years and over	41	68	72	69	77	75
Age not stated	10	25	21	29	293	47
Less than 19 years, number	15,273	15,624	15,912	17,139	18,243	18,228
Percentage of total	9.3	9.3	9.1	9.3	9.5	9.2

A/ Revised. B/ Provisional.

Source: State of Florida, Department of Health and Rehabilitative Services, Public Health Statistics Section, *Florida Vital Statistics, 1989*, and *Vital News*, March 1991.

Florida Statistical Abstract 1991

Table 3.07.   ABORTIONS: REPORTED TERMINATIONS OF PREGNANCY IN FLORIDA, 1976 THROUGH
   1989

Year	Induced abor- tions 1/	Total resident births 2/	Total known pregnancies 3/		Abortion rate per 100 pregnancies
			Number	Rate per 100 women aged 15-44	
1976	37,340	105,829	143,169	8.0	26.1
1977	42,177	112,064	154,241	8.3	27.3
1978	43,884	114,561	158,445	8.2	27.7
1979	56,152	121,145	178,540	9.6	31.5
1980	61,659	131,811	194,825	7.2	31.6
1981	67,802	138,521	207,822	(NA)	32.6
1982	49,424	144,500	195,529	8.8	25.5
1983	43,477	149,062	194,135	(NA)	22.6
1984	50,507	155,344	207,442	9.0	24.5
1985	53,011	163,732	218,315	9.2	24.3
1986	50,262	167,628	219,491	9.0	22.9
1987	51,201	175,072	227,891	9.0	22.5
1988	65,153	183,998	250,889	9.5	26.0
1989	62,626	192,887	257,315	9.5	24.3

(NA) Not available.
1/ Abortions have been legal in Florida since April 1972.
2/ Includes live births and stillbirths of 20 weeks or more gestation.
3/ Includes induced abortions, total resident births, and total reported resident
fetal deaths.
Note: Some data are revised.

Table 3.08.   RESIDENT INFANT DEATHS: NUMBER AND RATE BY RACE IN FLORIDA, 1977
   THROUGH 1990

Year	Number of deaths			Mortality rate per 1,000 live births		
	Total	White	Black and other races	Total	White	Black and other races
1977	1,717	983	733	15.5	12.1	24.5
1978	1,592	958	634	14.0	11.6	20.4
1979	1,809	1,091	716	14.9	12.3	22.1
1980	1,915	1,135	779	14.5	11.9	21.5
1981	1,847	1,055	792	13.3	10.4	21.1
1982	1,855	1,074	779	12.9	10.5	21.1
1983	1,815	1,085	728	12.1	9.8	18.5
1984	1,681	984	696	10.9	8.5	17.8
1985	1,846	1,128	718	11.3	9.3	17.2
1986	1,844	1,093	750	11.0	8.8	17.7
1987	1,849	1,036	810	10.6	7.9	18.2
1988	1,949	1,167	782	10.6	8.6	16.4
1989	1,899	1,141	756	9.8	8.0	15.2
1990 A/	1,925	1,136	787	9.7	7.7	15.4

A/ Provisional.
Note: Some data are revised.
   Source for Tables 3.07 and 3.08:   State of Florida, Department of Health and
Rehabilitative Services, Public Health Statistics Section, *Florida Vital Statistics,*
1989, and unpublished data.

Florida Statistical Abstract 1991

Table 3.09. RESIDENT LIVE BIRTHS AND RESIDENT DEATHS: TOTAL NUMBER, 1989 AND 1990
AND NUMBER BY RACE, 1990, IN THE STATE AND COUNTIES OF FLORIDA

County	Number of births 1989	Number of births, 1990 Total 1/	White	Black and other races	Number of deaths 1989	Number of deaths, 1990 Total 1/	White	Black and other races
Florida	192,887	198,018	146,770	51,150	132,037	133,855	118,807	15,004
Alachua 2/	2,798	2,738	1,735	1,002	1,188	1,209	894	315
Baker 2/	315	285	239	46	149	139	120	19
Bay	2,075	2,042	1,649	392	1,037	1,081	950	130
Bradford	358	339	258	81	225	209	176	33
Brevard	5,373	5,669	4,797	872	3,408	3,605	3,379	224
Broward	17,930	18,660	12,800	5,838	14,314	14,352	13,082	1,265
Calhoun	150	158	132	26	112	127	111	16
Charlotte	1,000	1,063	991	72	1,529	1,576	1,541	34
Citrus	928	898	845	53	1,353	1,357	1,329	27
Clay	1,580	1,648	1,469	179	647	706	668	38
Collier	2,201	2,486	2,187	299	1,519	1,509	1,439	68
Columbia	670	681	503	177	391	404	328	76
Dade	33,330	34,423	22,734	11,672	18,704	18,191	14,978	3,206
De Soto 2/	411	402	311	91	280	253	224	29
Dixie	183	137	119	17	101	100	94	5
Duval	12,892	12,878	8,438	4,437	5,586	5,626	4,046	1,580
Escambia	4,478	4,469	2,940	1,529	2,224	2,178	1,668	510
Flagler	304	301	252	49	290	312	284	28
Franklin	130	104	92	12	122	111	95	16
Gadsden 2/	814	792	250	542	409	417	179	238
Gilchrist	143	127	112	15	76	122	120	2
Glades	86	91	64	27	80	84	76	8
Gulf	184	145	113	32	111	118	94	24
Hamilton	180	144	65	79	94	104	71	33
Hardee	476	448	414	34	194	190	174	16
Hendry	586	603	456	147	229	214	168	46
Hernando	966	991	884	107	1,287	1,378	1,340	37
Highlands	865	852	638	214	943	994	930	64
Hillsborough	14,012	14,394	10,914	3,458	7,020	7,157	6,204	952
Holmes	176	149	135	14	162	195	184	11
Indian River	1,021	1,107	895	212	1,032	1,052	975	76
Jackson	526	457	286	171	432	450	326	124
Jefferson	189	197	84	113	135	129	76	53
Lafayette	66	68	59	9	33	39	38	1
Lake	2,022	1,990	1,563	427	2,012	2,072	1,934	138

See footnotes at end of table.   Continued . . .

Table 3.09.   RESIDENT LIVE BIRTHS AND RESIDENT DEATHS: TOTAL NUMBER, 1989 AND 1990
AND NUMBER BY RACE, 1990, IN THE STATE AND COUNTIES OF FLORIDA (Continued)

County	Number of births 1989	Number of births, 1990 Total 1/	White	Black and other races	Number of deaths 1989	Number of deaths, 1990 Total 1/	White	Black and other races
Lee	4,296	4,518	3,833	685	3,647	3,742	3,564	176
Leon 2/	2,697	2,763	1,715	1,046	1,052	1,126	796	330
Levy	363	357	295	62	342	369	312	57
Liberty	84	66	59	7	54	40	38	2
Madison	297	228	87	141	176	182	118	64
Manatee	2,847	2,873	2,365	505	2,704	2,767	2,619	148
Marion	2,771	2,759	2,089	670	2,245	2,201	1,929	270
Martin	1,271	1,330	1,016	314	1,151	1,205	1,161	44
Monroe	968	1,006	864	141	707	657	620	36
Nassau	736	696	598	98	330	364	300	61
Okaloosa	2,458	2,466	2,001	465	889	920	840	78
Okeechobee	548	564	502	62	319	301	274	27
Orange	11,331	12,014	8,714	3,293	4,778	4,765	4,040	724
Osceola	1,706	1,886	1,681	203	912	872	820	51
Palm Beach	12,685	12,890	9,319	3,567	9,821	10,044	9,099	944
Pasco	3,048	3,033	2,865	166	4,078	4,232	4,180	52
Pinellas	10,024	10,417	8,348	2,067	12,130	12,122	11,532	590
Polk	⏴ 6,296	6,464	5,020	1,440	3,953	4,284	3,788	493
Putnam	910	1,029	726	303	731	795	665	130
St. Johns	1,092	1,158	960	198	822	817	722	94
St. Lucie	2,291	2,364	1,653	710	1,531	1,555	1,327	228
Santa Rosa	1,279	1,301	1,192	109	536	546	516	30
Sarasota	2,718	2,808	2,409	399	3,867	4,058	3,910	146
Seminole	4,203	4,375	3,594	779	1,823	1,901	1,679	222
Sumter	443	430	287	143	374	414	370	44
Suwannee	334	343	253	90	312	372	315	57
Taylor	306	285	205	80	169	192	151	41
Union 2/	137	132	105	27	81	86	62	24
Volusia	4,568	4,754	3,962	792	4,458	4,512	4,196	314
Wakulla	215	197	158	39	118	153	128	25
Walton	345	353	308	45	296	300	268	32
Washington	202	223	164	59	203	201	173	28

1/ Unknown race included in total only.
2/ Large institutional population.
Note: Data are for births and deaths occurring to residents of the specified
area regardless of place of occurrence.   1989 data are revised; 1990 data are
provisional.

Source: State of Florida, Department of Health and Rehabilitative Services,
Public Health Statistics Section, *Florida Vital Statistics, 1989*, and *Vital News*,
March 1991.

Florida Statistical Abstract 1991

Table 3.10. RESIDENT LIVE BIRTHS AND RESIDENT DEATHS: RATES, 1984-86 AVERAGE AND
1989, AND BY RACE, 1989, IN THE STATE AND COUNTIES OF FLORIDA

| | Birth rate per 1,000 population | | | | Death rate per 1,000 population | | | |
| | | 1989 | | | | 1989 | | |
County	1984-86 average	Total	White	Black and other races	1984-86 average	Total	White	Black and other races
Florida	14.3	15.0	13.1	25.3	10.5	10.3	10.8	7.6
Alachua 1/	14.8	14.9	12.0	25.0	6.2	6.3	5.9	7.7
Baker 1/	17.2	16.4	15.7	20.0	6.6	7.7	7.9	7.2
Bay	15.9	14.9	13.8	22.4	7.5	7.5	7.5	7.2
Bradford 1/	14.2	14.6	14.5	14.7	8.9	9.2	10.0	6.0
Brevard	13.2	13.2	12.5	20.0	8.6	8.4	8.7	5.8
Broward	12.8	14.5	11.4	33.1	11.5	11.5	12.2	7.3
Calhoun	14.5	13.9	12.7	21.4	12.2	10.3	10.3	10.7
Charlotte	8.5	10.1	9.8	17.7	15.1	15.4	15.6	8.7
Citrus	10.1	10.2	10.0	16.5	15.4	14.8	15.1	7.1
Clay	15.2	15.0	13.7	35.9	6.7	6.2	6.2	5.0
Collier	14.0	15.5	14.2	34.4	9.8	10.7	10.9	8.3
Columbia	16.4	15.6	13.9	24.0	9.1	9.1	8.7	11.1
Dade	16.0	17.8	15.4	25.4	9.8	10.0	10.8	7.3
De Soto 1/	15.9	17.1	16.4	20.1	11.1	11.7	12.5	8.0
Dixie	14.6	17.4	16.6	25.0	8.8	9.6	9.9	7.0
Duval	18.5	18.5	16.8	23.1	8.6	8.0	7.7	9.0
Escambia	15.9	15.4	13.1	23.9	7.6	7.7	7.6	7.8
Flagler	10.7	13.0	11.1	38.7	10.7	12.4	12.1	16.0
Franklin	16.7	14.9	13.2	22.5	12.1	13.9	13.2	16.7
Gadsden 1/	16.4	17.3	13.1	20.4	8.8	8.7	9.0	8.4
Gilchrist	17.1	19.0	18.5	24.6	11.3	10.1	10.7	1.9
Glades	10.2	11.1	9.5	18.8	9.7	10.3	10.8	8.3
Gulf	12.7	14.7	12.7	23.6	10.1	8.9	8.9	9.0
Hamilton	18.8	17.8	12.9	25.9	10.7	9.3	9.3	9.3
Hardee	18.0	21.0	20.3	28.6	8.0	8.5	7.7	16.7
Hendry	22.0	22.2	20.6	28.5	7.7	8.7	8.4	9.6
Hernando	9.6	10.3	9.7	25.5	13.6	13.8	14.0	9.3
Highlands	11.8	12.5	10.8	23.9	14.1	13.6	14.3	8.8
Hillsborough	16.0	16.4	14.7	26.5	8.6	8.2	8.3	7.8
Holmes	11.9	10.1	9.7	28.9	10.9	9.3	8.9	28.9
Indian River	11.8	11.1	9.9	22.2	11.7	11.2	11.6	8.4
Jackson	12.3	11.8	10.9	14.1	10.4	9.7	9.8	9.6
Jefferson	16.2	15.2	10.6	22.1	9.6	10.9	10.2	11.9
Lafayette	11.4	12.5	9.7	58.4	8.8	6.3	5.8	13.0
Lake	12.5	13.8	12.4	24.2	13.4	13.7	14.5	8.2

See footnotes at end of table.

Continued . . .

Florida Statistical Abstract 1991

Table 3.10. RESIDENT LIVE BIRTHS AND RESIDENT DEATHS: RATES, 1984-86 AVERAGE AND
1989, AND BY RACE, 1989, IN THE STATE AND COUNTIES OF FLORIDA (Continued)

| County | Birth rate per 1,000 population | | | | Death rate per 1,000 population | | | |
| | | 1989 | | | | 1989 | | |
	1984-86 average	Total	White	Black and other races	1984-86 average	Total	White	Black and other races
Lee	12.7	13.2	12.2	25.9	11.5	11.2	11.5	7.4
Leon 1/	14.4	14.5	12.2	20.4	5.6	5.6	5.8	5.3
Levy	14.0	14.5	12.4	29.2	12.8	13.6	13.1	17.1
Liberty	14.1	17.4	16.1	26.0	10.0	11.2	11.1	11.4
Madison	17.6	18.5	15.5	22.4	10.7	11.0	12.2	9.4
Manatee	13.5	14.7	13.3	30.6	14.7	14.0	14.5	8.5
Marion	14.4	14.4	12.9	23.4	11.3	11.7	12.2	8.5
Martin	11.8	13.2	10.9	41.3	12.5	11.9	12.4	6.6
Monroe	13.6	12.2	11.6	20.9	9.0	8.9	8.9	8.9
Nassau	15.4	15.4	15.2	16.6	6.6	6.9	6.9	7.0
Okaloosa	16.9	15.3	14.2	22.6	5.6	5.5	5.9	2.8
Okeechobee	18.0	18.2	17.8	21.2	10.7	10.6	10.7	9.8
Orange	16.2	17.4	15.6	25.7	7.8	7.3	7.7	5.7
Osceola	15.2	16.8	16.0	28.6	8.9	9.0	9.0	8.3
Palm Beach	13.4	14.5	12.2	29.7	11.9	11.2	11.7	8.2
Pasco	10.0	11.1	10.8	22.1	15.4	14.8	15.1	5.6
Pinellas	10.9	11.7	10.4	25.6	15.4	14.2	14.8	7.9
Polk	15.1	15.3	14.1	21.7	9.9	9.6	9.9	7.8
Putnam	14.9	14.7	12.1	25.4	11.1	11.8	11.8	11.8
St. Johns	13.2	12.8	12.4	16.2	10.0	9.7	9.7	9.3
St. Lucie	15.7	16.1	13.6	26.3	10.4	10.7	11.4	8.2
Santa Rosa	17.5	18.7	18.0	31.6	6.7	7.8	7.9	6.7
Sarasota	10.0	10.3	9.4	24.1	15.1	14.6	15.0	8.4
Seminole	13.6	14.9	13.7	25.9	6.8	6.4	6.3	7.9
Sumter	13.4	14.3	12.7	21.6	11.7	12.1	13.1	7.7
Suwannee	13.4	12.2	11.1	17.6	11.8	11.4	11.7	10.1
Taylor	16.2	16.0	15.1	18.5	10.4	8.8	9.0	8.4
Union 1/	12.5	13.2	17.6	5.5	7.4	7.8	9.6	4.8
Volusia	12.1	12.7	11.7	20.3	13.2	12.4	12.9	8.0
Wakulla	12.8	14.6	13.7	19.4	7.8	8.0	8.0	8.1
Walton	12.5	11.7	11.5	14.2	9.8	10.1	10.0	10.4
Washington	13.0	12.4	11.8	15.6	11.5	12.5	12.4	12.6

1/ Large institutional population in county.
    Note: Data are for births and deaths occurring to residents of the specified
area regardless of place of occurrence.

    Source: State of Florida, Department of Health and Rehabilitative Services,
Public Health Statistics Section, *Florida Vital Statistics, 1989.*

Table 3.17. RESIDENT DEATHS: NUMBER OF DEATHS BY CAUSE IN FLORIDA, 1988, 1989, AND
    1990

Cause of death and international list number	1988	1989	1990
All causes	131,358	132,249	133,855
Intestinal infectious diseases, 001-009	21	27	26
Tuberculosis, 010-018	142	146	138
Meningococcal infection, 036	16	10	10
Septicemia, 038	1,010	943	917
Human immunodeficiency virus (HIV), 042-044	1,419	2,003	2,232
Herpes zoster and simplex, 053-054	17	16	19
Viral hepatitis, 070	87	118	110
Syphilis, 090-097	10	9	14
Mycoses, 110-118	97	122	115
Late effects--tuberculosis, 137	14	12	12
Other infectious and parasitic diseases, 020-139	245	268	271
Malignant neoplasm (cancer), 140-208	31,035	32,281	33,444
Neoplasm not specified malignant, 210-239	466	497	486
Diabetes mellitus, 250	2,071	2,722	2,870
Nutritional deficiencies, 260-269	155	152	146
Anemias, 280-285	245	270	234
Alcohol psychosis, dependence, abuse, 291, 303, 3050	376	328	416
Meningitis, 320-322	54	53	48
Parkinson's disease, 332	393	471	493
Motor neurone disease, 3352	209	198	188
Major cardiovascular diseases, 390-448	59,050	57,584	57,122
Phlebitis and thrombophlebitis, 451	87	86	77
Venous embolism and thrombosis, 452-453	19	25	13
Other circulatory diseases, 454-459	120	97	119
Pneumonia and influenza, 480-487	3,284	3,143	3,391
Chronic obstructive lung disease and allied conditions, 490-496	5,240	5,391	5,580
Pulmonary fibrosis and other alveular pneumopathy, 515-516	341	431	434
Ulcer of stomach and duodenum, 531-533	364	364	339
Hernia and intestinal obstruction, 550-553, 560	280	288	324
Diverticula of intestine, 562	154	172	191
Chronic liver disease and cirrhosis, 571	1,633	1,727	1,649
Cholelithiasis, other gallbladder diseases, 574-575	143	167	167
Diseases of pancreas, 577	183	172	167
Nephritis, nephrosis, renal failure, 580-589	1,367	1,193	1,263
Infections of kidney, 590	77	69	54
Maternal causes, 630-676	14	16	13
Congenital anomalies, 740-759	630	636	655
Perinatal conditions, 760-779	929	956	918
Symptoms, signs, ill-defined condition, 780-799	2,923	2,605	2,803
All other diseases, 240-739	7,615	7,836	7,884
Accidental injury and poisoning, 800-949	5,156	5,054	4,951
Suicide, 950-959	1,948	1,962	1,932
Homicide, 960-978	1,640	1,555	1,542
Other injury and poisoning, 980-999	79	74	81

    Source: State of Florida, Department of Health and Rehabilitative **Services,**
Public Health Statistics Section, *Vital News*, March 1991, and previous **edition.**

Florida Statistical Abstract 1991

Table 3.18. ACCIDENTAL DEATHS: NUMBER OF DEATHS DUE TO ACCIDENTS WHICH OCCURRED
IN FLORIDA BY RACE AND SEX AND BY TYPE OF ACCIDENT, 1989

Cause of accident	Total	White Male	White Female	Black and other races Male	Black and other races Female	Total	White Male	White Female	Black and other races Male	Black and other races Female
						Rate per 100,000 population				
Total	5,460	3,098	1,485	635	235	42.5	58.9	26.4	67.3	23.0
Motor vehicle	3,103	1,789	855	325	128	24.2	34.0	15.2	34.4	12.6
Falls	602	312	243	39	8	4.7	5.9	4.3	4.1	0.8
Drownings	448	275	65	98	10	3.5	5.2	1.2	10.4	1.0
Poisoning	293	155	75	42	21	2.3	2.9	1.3	4.5	2.1
Suffocations	219	98	82	24	14	1.7	1.9	1.5	2.5	1.4
Fire/flame	172	62	54	34	21	1.3	1.2	1.0	3.6	2.1
Medicosurgical	100	42	45	5	8	0.8	0.8	0.8	0.5	0.8
Air/space transport	70	65	3	1	1	0.5	1.2	0.1	0.1	0.1
Struck by object	52	36	6	9	1	0.4	0.7	0.1	1.0	0.1
Electric current	48	39	1	7	1	0.4	0.7	0.0	0.7	0.1
Firearms/explosives	46	34	2	8	2	0.4	0.6	0.0	0.8	0.2
Machinery	35	27	1	7	0	0.3	0.5	0.0	0.7	0.0
Railway	31	22	3	4	2	0.2	0.4	0.1	0.4	0.2
Water transport 1/	31	23	7	1	0	0.2	0.4	0.1	0.1	0.0
Excessive cold	26	6	1	12	7	0.2	0.1	0.0	1.3	0.7
Excessive heat	11	5	2	4	0	0.1	0.1	0.0	0.4	0.0
Other road vehicle	9	4	4	1	0	0.1	0.1	0.1	0.1	0.0
Venomous animals and plants	9	8	0	0	1	0.1	0.2	0.0	0.0	0.1
Lightning	9	6	3	0	0	0.1	0.1	0.1	0.0	0.0
Other injury caused by animals	8	5	2	1	0	0.1	0.1	0.1	0.1	0.0
Cutting and piercing instruments	8	4	0	3	1	0.1	0.1	0.0	0.3	0.1
All other	130	80	31	10	9	1.0	1.5	0.6	1.1	0.9

1/ Except drownings.

Table 3.19. SUICIDE: RESIDENT SUICIDE DEATHS BY RACE AND SEX AND SUICIDE RATES PER
100,000 POPULATION IN FLORIDA, 1984 THROUGH 1989

Year	Total suicide deaths 1/ Number	Total suicide deaths 1/ Rate	White Male	White Female	Black and other races Male	Black and other races Female
1984	1,824	16.5	1,315	430	70	9
1985	1,854	16.3	1,367	390	77	20
1986	1,959	16.7	1,380	481	80	18
1987	2,005	16.5	1,446	445	95	19
1988	2,065	16.5	1,499	444	104	18
1989	2,083	16.2	1,497	461	108	16

1/ Unknown race included in total only.
Source for Tables 3.18 and 3.19: State of Florida, Department of Health and
Rehabilitative Services, Public Health Statistics Section, *Florida Vital Statistics*,
1989.

Florida Statistical Abstract 1991

Table 3.27. MORBIDITY: REPORTED CASES OF SPECIFIED NOTIFIABLE DISEASES IN FLORIDA
1986 THROUGH 1990

Disease	1986	1987	1988	1989	1990
Amebiasis	41	62	55	68	33
Campylobacteriosis	1,543	1,662	1,934	1,771	1,775
Encephalitis					
Primary	(NA)	16	16	5	2
Post-infectious	10	6	4	4	8
St. Louis	(NA)	(NA)	(NA)	(NA)	223
Other, including unspecified	34	26	27	19	29
Giardiasis	1,647	1,673	1,747	1,655	1,696
Gonorrhea	67,443	62,944	60,714	50,055	(NA)
Hepatitis					
A	1,268	729	742	1,190	657
B	1,659	1,563	1,480	1,016	896
Associated with blood or					
blood products	72	57	40	42	11
Not associated with blood or					
blood products	171	98	92	79	62
Unspecified	172	100	76	78	33
Influenza (confirmed)	396	420	439	268	(NA)
Legionnaires' Disease	38	27	17	16	16
Malaria	49	39	39	67	55
Measles (Rubeola)	400	125	170	322	603
Meningitis					
Aseptic	713	665	618	794	739
Meningococcal	102	117	122	99	106
Other bacterial	345	334	294	287	207
Meningococcemia	(NA)	(NA)	39	23	29
Mumps	62	67	43	65	198
Pertussis	82	53	72	95	59
Rabies	183	111	184	190	82
Rubella (excluding congenital)	12	10	3	21	17
Salmonellosis	3,159	2,960	2,435	2,597	2,563
Shigellosis	800	818	1,995	1,946	1,630
Syphilis (all stages)	4,344	7,440	8,378	7,092	(NA)
Tuberculosis 1/	1,478	1,586	1,668	1,703	(NA)
Typhoid fever	10	16	19	15	33
Vibrio (all species)	(NA)	(NA)	28	30	57

(NA) Not available.
1/ Includes new and reactivated cases.

Source: State of Florida, Department of Health and Rehabilitative Services,
Health Program Office, *Report of Selected Communicable Diseases (Conditions),
Florida, 1989 Cumulative Report*, previous editions and unpublished data.

Florida Statistical Abstract 1991

Table 3.28. MORBIDITY: REPORTED ADULT CASES OF ACQUIRED IMMUNO-DEFICIENCY
SYNDROME (AIDS), JUNE 30, 1991, AND CUMULATIVE CASES, JANUARY 1, 1980
THROUGH JUNE 30, 1991, IN THE STATE AND COUNTIES OF FLORIDA

County	Number of diag-nosed cases 1991	Cumulative cases 1980-91 Number	Per-cent-age of total	Rate per 100,000 popula-tion 1/	County	Number of diag-nosed cases 1991	Cumulative cases 1980-91 Number	Per-cent-age of total	Rate per 100,000 popula-tion 1/
Florida	1,305	16,484	100.0	127.4	Jefferson	0	4	0.0	35.4
Unknown	0	13	0.1	(X)	Lafayette	0	1	0.0	17.9
DOC 2/	18	346	2.1	(X)	Lake	3	31	0.2	20.4
Alachua	11	108	0.7	59.5	Lee	23	393	2.4	117.3
Baker	0	8	0.0	43.3	Leon	12	121	0.7	62.9
Bay	3	49	0.3	38.6	Levy	0	5	0.0	19.3
Bradford	1	5	0.0	22.2	Liberty	1	1	0.0	18.0
Brevard	18	213	1.3	53.4	Madison	0	5	0.0	30.2
Broward	260	2,923	17.7	232.8	Manatee	22	129	0.8	60.9
Calhoun	0	0	0.0	0.0	Marion	3	96	0.6	49.3
Charlotte	4	38	0.2	34.2	Martin	0	55	0.3	54.5
Citrus	1	20	0.1	21.4	Monroe	27	336	2.0	430.6
Clay	1	29	0.2	27.4	Nassau	2	12	0.1	27.3
Collier	16	132	0.8	86.8	Okaloosa	2	29	0.2	20.2
Columbia	1	13	0.1	30.5	Okeechobee	0	11	0.1	37.1
Dade	330	5,073	30.8	261.9	Orange	78	769	4.7	113.5
De Soto	0	10	0.1	41.9	Osceola	6	54	0.3	50.1
Dixie	0	0	0.0	0.0	Palm Beach	140	1,548	9.4	179.3
Duval	63	769	4.7	114.3	Pasco	11	138	0.8	49.1
Escambia	23	184	1.1	70.0	Pinellas	57	726	4.4	85.2
Flagler	0	7	0.0	24.4	Polk	21	208	1.3	51.3
Franklin	0	1	0.0	11.2	Putnam	3	17	0.1	26.1
Gadsden	1	16	0.1	38.9	St. Johns	2	45	0.3	53.7
Gilchrist	0	1	0.0	10.3	St. Lucie	10	157	1.0	104.5
Glades	0	2	0.0	26.3	Santa Rosa	2	10	0.1	12.3
Gulf	0	1	0.0	8.7	Sarasota	19	201	1.2	72.4
Hamilton	0	0	0.0	0.0	Seminole	11	119	0.7	41.4
Hardee	2	14	0.1	71.8	Sumter	0	2	0.0	6.3
Hendry	4	31	0.2	120.3	Suwannee	2	8	0.0	29.9
Hernando	2	20	0.1	19.8	Taylor	0	6	0.0	35.1
Highlands	3	16	0.1	23.4	Union	0	2	0.0	0.0
Hillsborough	60	899	5.5	107.8	Volusia	19	240	1.5	64.7
Holmes	1	3	0.0	19.0	Wakulla	0	0	0.0	0.0
Indian River	5	42	0.3	46.6	Walton	1	6	0.0	21.6
Jackson	0	10	0.1	24.2	Washington	0	3	0.0	17.7

(X) Not applicable.
1/ Based on population census counts as of April 1, 1990.
2/ Department of Corrections.
Note: Data are reported by county of residence at data of diagnosis.
Source: State of Florida, Department of Health and Rehabilitative Services, AIDS
Program, *The Florida HIV/AIDS Surveillance Report*, June-July 1991. Number 82-83.

Florida Statistical Abstract 1991

Table 3.32. MARRIAGES AND ANNULMENTS AND DISSOLUTIONS OF MARRIAGE: NUMBER
   PERFORMED OR GRANTED IN THE STATE AND COUNTIES OF FLORIDA, 1987 THROUGH
   1989

County of	Marriages 1/			Annulments and dissolutions of marriage		
occurrence	1987	1988	1989	1987	1988	1989
Florida	136,492	138,072	137,892	79,465	78,708	79,810
Alachua	1,682	1,696	1,690	1,060	973	1,040
Baker	215	246	250	137	119	155
Bay	1,866	1,784	1,895	1,150	1,146	1,036
Bradford	308	310	268	142	188	176
Brevard	4,133	4,117	4,105	2,314	2,213	2,408
Broward	11,826	11,878	11,631	6,848	7,016	6,846
Calhoun	144	147	131	61	70	70
Charlotte	899	909	945	330	446	416
Citrus	849	900	885	420	430	459
Clay	1,061	1,141	1,137	581	780	845
Collier	1,458	1,593	1,711	771	823	933
Columbia	463	513	548	289	271	348
Dade	21,902	21,384	20,836	14,172	12,743	12,596
De Soto	290	291	264	148	120	159
Dixie	134	137	125	70	71	64
Duval	7,691	7,735	7,641	5,786	5,593	5,816
Escambia	3,709	3,796	3,901	1,926	2,079	2,083
Flagler	186	224	232	131	126	113
Franklin	138	155	146	58	68	69
Gadsden	393	444	369	117	194	155
Gilchrist	86	98	100	41	42	51
Glades	74	63	70	14	14	14
Gulf	170	166	171	87	62	87
Hamilton	145	116	148	67	46	72
Hardee	261	271	242	124	135	163
Hendry	372	357	355	322	250	209
Hernando	720	769	817	395	383	440
Highlands	624	676	684	352	392	344
Hillsborough	9,337	9,018	8,974	5,931	5,936	6,084
Holmes	237	206	211	111	130	142
Indian River	848	978	921	557	525	606
Jackson	454	471	524	264	274	281
Jefferson	178	159	189	388	429	371

See footnote at end of table.   Continued . . .

Florida Statistical Abstract 1991

Table 3.32. MARRIAGES AND ANNULMENTS AND DISSOLUTIONS OF MARRIAGE: NUMBER
PERFORMED OR GRANTED IN THE STATE AND COUNTIES OF FLORIDA, 1987 THROUGH
1989 (Continued)

County of	Marriages 1/			Annulments and dissolutions of marriage		
occurrence	1987	1988	1989	1987	1988	1989
Lafayette	49	56	48	30	21	28
Lake	1,522	1,520	1,466	984	1,069	973
Lee	3,225	3,492	3,498	1,901	1,914	1,875
Leon	1,849	1,912	1,821	1,096	1,016	1,073
Levy	284	325	285	115	112	103
Liberty	75	73	81	12	0	27
Madison	147	164	168	71	82	87
Manatee	1,885	1,900	1,985	1,117	1,167	1,169
Marion	2,037	2,137	1,991	1,264	1,173	1,316
Martin	956	1,034	1,018	508	597	572
Monroe	1,356	1,524	1,685	461	395	450
Nassau	401	470	483	296	309	323
Okaloosa	2,025	2,071	2,115	1,180	1,121	1,052
Okeechobee	377	383	392	198	206	217
Orange	8,512	8,564	8,816	4,112	3,972	4,212
Osceola	1,258	1,246	1,453	714	766	789
Palm Beach	7,693	7,926	8,164	4,301	4,286	4,344
Pasco	2,216	2,234	2,137	1,245	1,316	1,304
Pinellas	8,953	9,080	8,815	4,700	4,792	4,560
Polk	4,753	4,668	4,667	2,632	2,733	2,822
Putnam	647	633	654	383	420	374
St. Johns	1,157	1,206	1,256	392	410	442
St. Lucie	1,220	1,292	1,310	674	602	683
Santa Rosa	840	859	886	405	467	496
Sarasota	2,594	2,641	2,699	1,458	1,474	1,545
Seminole	2,272	2,440	2,367	1,313	1,234	1,345
Sumter	347	338	287	205	209	169
Suwannee	330	330	330	149	156	176
Taylor	263	227	237	103	94	92
Union	110	128	115	62	43	62
Volusia	3,522	3,690	3,694	1,871	2,018	2,037
Wakulla	173	194	216	64	84	91
Walton	310	326	328	178	232	224
Washington	276	234	302	107	131	127

1/ State total includes a few marriages performed out of state but recorded in
Florida.

Source: State of Florida, Department of Health and Rehabilitative Services,
Public Health Statistics Section, *Florida Vital Statistics, 1989*, and previous
editions.

EDUCATION

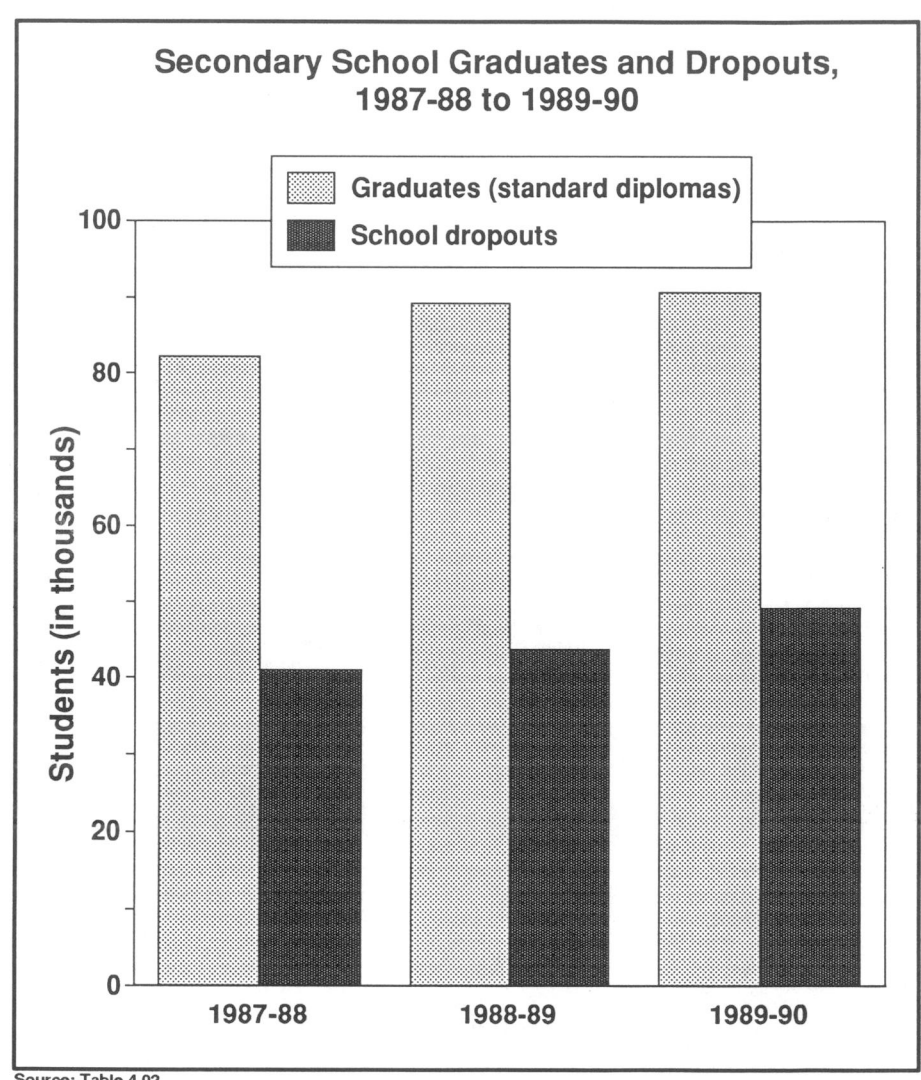

Secondary School Graduates and Dropouts, 1987-88 to 1989-90

Legend:
- Graduates (standard diplomas)
- School dropouts

Y-axis: Students (in thousands)

X-axis: 1987-88, 1988-89, 1989-90

Source: Table 4.02

SECTION 4.00
EDUCATION

TABLES LISTED BY MAJOR HEADINGS

Table 4.02. PUBLIC ELEMENTARY AND SECONDARY SCHOOLS: SPECIFIED STUDENT DATA
    IN FLORIDA, 1986-87 THROUGH 1989-90

Item	1986-87	1987-88	1988-89	1989-90	Percentage change since 1986-87
Student membership	1,607,320	1,664,563	1,720,927	1,789,944	11.36
Prekindergarten	4,287	5,939	8,317	14,399	235.88
Kindergarten	134,732	145,384	153,775	158,907	17.94
Grade 1	133,743	143,854	152,910	161,358	20.65
Grade 2	123,061	130,833	141,231	151,198	22.86
Grade 3	117,387	127,904	136,582	146,938	25.17
Grade 4	117,394	121,543	132,484	141,804	20.79
Grade 5	114,901	120,423	124,849	136,746	19.01
Grade 6	118,947	119,972	126,533	130,095	9.37
Grade 7	130,072	127,935	127,685	133,782	2.85
Grade 8	126,414	128,022	127,642	128,219	1.43
Grade 9	145,470	142,661	144,212	145,734	0.18
Grade 10	136,424	135,106	130,428	132,000	-3.24
Grade 11	114,825	117,910	114,621	112,125	-2.35
Grade 12	89,663	97,077	99,658	96,639	7.78
Graduates (standard diplomas)	(NA)	82,184	89,206	90,759	(NA)
Membership in selected programs for exceptional students	(NA)	228,362	247,335	262,168	(NA)
Mentally handicapped					
Educable	14,828	15,148	15,733	16,496	11.25
Trainable	5,233	5,543	5,943	6,198	18.44
Specific learning disability	64,786	71,530	63,194	84,267	30.07
Emotionally handicapped	16,330	17,127	18,257	18,847	15.41
Speech/language and hearing	54,162	57,217	78,286	66,351	22.50
Profoundly handicapped	4,963	5,408	6,079	6,745	35.91
Gifted	47,463	51,123	53,972	57,042	20.18
Other exceptionalities	4,820	5,266	5,871	6,222	29.09
School dropouts	(NA)	40,989	43,795	49,198	(NA)
Nonpromotions	(NA)	123,304	111,328	109,581	(NA)
Suspensions (out of school)	(NA)	127,063	133,607	142,895	(NA)
Suspensions (in school)	(NA)	87,982	119,828	122,549	(NA)
Corporal punishment	(NA)	103,647	84,495	65,060	(NA)
Expulsions	(NA)	911	1,060	993	(NA)
Students referred to alternative education programs for disciplinary reasons	(NA)	29,611	11,931	9,908	(NA)
Students referred to courts/juvenile authorities	(NA)	3,001	4,219	4,673	(NA)

(NA) Not available.

Source: State of Florida, Department of Education, Division of Public Schools,
Profiles of Florida School Districts, 1989-90, Student and Staff Data.

Table 4.05.　PUBLIC SCHOOLS:　SPECIFIED CHARACTERISTICS IN FLORIDA, SCHOOL YEARS
　　　　　1967-68 THROUGH 1989-90

School year	Resident population 1/ Total	Aged 5-17	Fall member-ship 2/	Public high school graduates 3/	Instruc-tional personnel
1967-68	6,433,000	1,505,772	1,298,025	66,199	60,739
1969-70	6,789,443	1,607,862	1,408,067	71,900	69,895
1971-72	7,120,026	1,654,540	1,460,375	78,572	74,945
1973-74	7,845,092	1,731,021	1,529,958	84,098	82,689
1975-76	8,485,230	1,779,797	1,547,316	88,932	82,327
1977-78	8,717,334	1,762,371	1,530,207	91,412	84,829
1979-80	9,245,231	1,800,331	1,502,846	87,826	84,623
1980-81	9,739,992	1,876,269	1,508,125	88,755	87,891
1981-82	10,375,332	1,998,658	1,485,593	89,199	88,912
1982-83	10,591,701	2,040,338	1,482,270	86,871	89,898
1983-84	10,891,701	1,724,795	1,492,366	85,908	90,348
1984-85	10,930,389	1,752,422	1,520,975	81,140	94,048
1985-86	11,287,932	1,675,790	1,559,507	81,508	97,139
1986-87	11,549,831	1,667,636	1,603,033	83,692	100,498
1987-88	12,043,618	1,688,627	1,664,563	90,792	104,848
1988-89	12,417,608	1,695,383	1,720,927	92,449	109,865
1989-90	13,152,691	1,700,468	1,789,925	(NA)	114,501

	Average instructional salary 4/ (dollars)	Number of schools	Assessed valuation of property ($1,000)	Total expenditure all purposes ($1,000)	Current expense per pupil 5/ (dollars)
1967-68	7,563.26	1,955	28,956,948	832,849	564.47
1969-70	8,900.12	1,910	32,229,726	1,179,713	728.20
1971-72	9,434.99	1,921	42,203,040	1,415,405	871.28
1973-74	10,963.96	1,983	58,970,326	1,734,642	1,053.74
1975-76	12,337.67	2,043	98,472,027	2,386,061	1,271.00
1977-78	13,541.17	2,179	117,824,205	2,725,308	1,491.00
1979-80	14,149.02	2,302	147,170,490	3,316,050	1,832.00
1980-81	15,404.90	2,345	147,965,109	3,755,837	2,058.00
1981-82	16,779.52	2,347	193,536,278	4,133,541	2,283.00
1982-83	18,351.76	2,350	226,683,285	4,521,420	2,463.00
1983-84	19,449.12	2,284	243,385,858	4,950,393	2,676.00
1984-85	20,836.47	2,304	266,774,135	5,461,194	2,964.00
1985-86	22,250.08	2,296	323,579,927	6,103,747	3,205.00
1986-87	23,733.76	2,400	353,683,447	6,909,814	3,423.00
1987-88	25,198.00	2,675	378,703,589	7,643,660	3,679.00
1988-89	26,974.00	2,552	411,786,114	8,793,842	3,964.00
1989-90	(NA)	(NA)	(NA)	(NA)	(NA)

(NA) Not available.
　1/ Population figures for noncensus years are mid-year estimates.　1985-86 through 1989-90 population breakdowns are for aged 15-24.
　2/ Membership data prior to 1973-74 based on average daily membership; data for 1973-74 to present are based on fall membership survey.
　3/ Regular day school only; excludes state/university schools and adult programs.
　4/ Includes teachers and other instructional personnel.
　5/ Per pupil expense through 1973-74 based on average daily attendance; 1974-75 through present, on full-time equivalent student count.
　Source:　State of Florida, Department of Education, Division of Public Schools, *Profiles of Florida School Districts, 1989-90, Student and Staff Data.*

Florida Statistical Abstract 1991

Table 4.20. PUBLIC ELEMENTARY AND SECONDARY SCHOOLS: PUPIL MEMBERSHIP IN GRADES
PREKINDERGARTEN THROUGH TWELVE BY RACE OR ETHNIC GROUP IN THE STATE AND
COUNTIES OF FLORIDA, FALL 1990

		Percentage of membership			
County	Total	White non-hispanic	Black non-hispanic	His-panic 1/	Asian/ Pacific Islander	American Indian/ Alaskan native
Florida	1,861,592	61.89	24.03	12.40	1.51	0.17
K-12 only	1,841,408	62.15	23.78	12.39	1.52	0.17
Alachua	26,387	61.84	34.19	2.04	1.78	0.15
Baker	4,256	83.06	16.66	0.12	0.14	0.02
Bay	21,875	80.95	15.67	0.93	2.20	0.26
Bradford	4,166	77.53	21.29	0.72	0.26	0.19
Brevard	56,639	81.81	14.00	2.33	1.69	0.17
Broward	161,101	56.77	31.70	9.22	2.05	0.27
Calhoun	2,181	81.89	17.33	0.37	0.14	0.28
Charlotte	13,030	89.46	7.17	2.07	1.16	0.14
Citrus	11,697	92.93	4.63	1.45	0.73	0.27
Clay	21,933	89.50	7.24	1.46	1.70	0.10
Collier	20,878	68.70	9.00	21.53	0.40	0.36
Columbia	8,106	73.34	25.02	0.79	0.74	0.11
Dade	292,411	18.99	33.27	46.50	1.20	0.04
De Soto	3,896	68.99	22.02	8.03	0.80	0.15
Dixie	1,957	89.32	10.12	0.31	0.26	0.00
Duval	111,149	59.26	36.61	1.62	2.39	0.12
Escambia	43,091	64.97	31.34	0.65	2.83	0.20
Flagler	4,012	79.41	15.53	3.41	1.55	0.10
Franklin	1,577	80.85	18.20	0.51	0.38	0.06
Gadsden	8,554	11.83	85.20	2.84	0.12	0.01
Gilchrist	1,793	93.25	6.25	0.39	0.11	0.00
Glades	902	58.43	30.38	9.53	0.44	1.22
Gulf	2,191	76.72	22.59	0.23	0.27	0.18
Hamilton	2,320	49.53	48.19	2.07	0.13	0.09
Hardee	4,412	57.77	9.68	31.87	0.45	0.23
Hendry	5,724	54.79	22.27	21.31	0.37	1.26
Hernando	12,861	87.52	8.15	3.34	0.75	0.24
Highlands	9,248	69.78	21.23	7.93	0.65	0.42
Hillsborough	123,462	64.43	21.54	12.09	1.64	0.29
Holmes	3,476	96.66	2.33	0.55	0.40	0.06
Indian River	11,838	77.09	18.31	3.71	0.63	0.25
Jackson	7,784	66.82	32.67	0.33	0.15	0.03
Jefferson	2,101	32.89	66.63	0.43	0.05	0.00
Lafayette	1,084	86.99	11.53	1.48	0.00	0.00
Lake	21,065	77.86	17.98	3.51	0.54	0.11

See footnotes at end of table.   Continued . . .

Florida Statistical Abstract 1991

Table 4.20. PUBLIC ELEMENTARY AND SECONDARY SCHOOLS: PUPIL MEMBERSHIP IN GRADES
PREKINDERGARTEN THROUGH TWELVE BY RACE OR ETHNIC GROUP IN THE STATE AND
COUNTIES OF FLORIDA, FALL 1990 (Continued)

		Percentage of membership			
County	Total	White non-hispanic	Black non-hispanic	His-panic 1/	Asian/ Pacific Islander	American Indian/ Alaskan native
Lee	43,240	76.88	14.65	7.55	0.81	0.11
Leon	27,241	62.09	35.57	0.93	1.31	0.09
Levy	4,787	78.15	19.45	1.94	0.36	0.10
Liberty	1,195	85.52	12.22	2.01	0.25	0.00
Madison	3,257	45.38	54.25	0.09	0.21	0.06
Manatee	26,326	75.12	16.24	7.78	0.81	0.05
Marion	29,577	74.30	21.49	3.44	0.61	0.16
Martin	11,808	79.60	13.20	6.08	1.03	0.08
Monroe	8,285	74.89	10.84	12.96	1.11	0.19
Nassau	8,586	83.25	16.31	0.21	0.19	0.05
Okaloosa	26,140	82.38	12.19	2.29	2.92	0.23
Okeechobee	5,963	74.48	9.39	13.65	0.40	2.08
Orange	102,672	60.31	25.71	11.12	2.69	0.17
Osceola	19,570	71.26	8.66	17.63	2.21	0.24
Palm Beach	105,712	60.71	26.87	10.60	1.59	0.23
Pasco	33,891	90.86	4.28	3.83	0.88	0.15
Pinellas	94,364	78.42	18.05	1.35	2.08	0.09
Polk	65,218	72.09	22.33	4.63	0.75	0.20
Putnam	11,972	66.05	29.65	3.58	0.58	0.13
St. Johns	12,080	82.97	15.24	1.02	0.68	0.09
St. Lucie	22,224	64.08	31.52	3.59	0.69	0.12
Santa Rosa	15,741	92.03	5.69	0.71	1.25	0.32
Sarasota	27,888	85.45	11.02	2.53	0.97	0.03
Seminole	49,027	77.17	13.54	6.87	2.28	0.14
Sumter	5,112	69.23	28.01	2.25	0.33	0.18
Suwannee	5,462	78.98	20.40	0.42	0.16	0.04
Taylor	3,812	75.97	23.45	0.18	0.18	0.21
Union	1,875	79.15	19.68	0.75	0.43	0.00
Volusia	48,403	78.71	15.50	4.81	0.88	0.10
Wakulla	3,404	82.73	16.77	0.21	0.18	0.12
Walton	4,320	86.23	12.27	0.49	0.76	0.25
Washington	3,283	74.02	24.25	1.28	0.40	0.06

K-12 Kindergarten through 12th grade; no prekindergarten.
1/ A person of Mexican, Puerto Rican, Cuban, Central or South American, or other
Spanish culture or origin, regardless of race.

Source: State of Florida, Department of Education, Division of Public Schools,
MIS Statistical Brief: Membership in Florida Public Schools, Fall 1990.

Florida Statistical Abstract 1991

Table 4.24. PUBLIC AND NONPUBLIC SCHOOLS: MEMBERSHIP BY GRADE IN FLORIDA, SCHOOL
    YEARS 1988-89 AND 1989-90

| | Public schools | | Nonpublic schools | | Nonpublic as a percentage of total membership | |
Grade	1988-89	1989-90	1988-89	1989-90	1988-89	1989-90
Prekindergarten	8,317	20,184	59,833	57,321	87.80	73.96
Kindergarten	153,773	163,209	26,454	26,302	14.68	13.88
First	152,910	165,375	19,942	19,698	11.54	10.64
Second	141,231	159,653	17,211	17,483	10.86	9.87
Third	136,584	155,946	15,666	15,881	10.29	9.24
Fourth	132,484	150,965	14,084	14,686	9.61	8.87
Fifth	124,848	144,778	13,116	13,474	9.51	8.51
Sixth	126,533	139,866	14,234	14,279	10.11	9.26
Seventh	127,685	136,337	13,563	14,264	9.60	9.47
Eighth	127,642	133,621	12,583	12,726	8.97	8.70
Ninth	144,216	148,396	11,154	11,188	7.18	7.01
Tenth	130,426	134,193	10,103	10,500	7.19	7.26
Eleventh	114,622	114,293	9,624	9,528	7.75	7.69
Twelfth	99,659	94,776	9,770	9,263	8.93	8.90
Prekindergarten through twelfth	1,720,930	1,861,592	247,337	246,593	12.57	11.70
Kindergarten through twelfth	1,712,613	1,841,408	187,504	189,272	9.87	9.32

Note: Students enrolled in exceptional education and alternative programs are
included in both totals. Excluded from both are nonacademic/nontechnical, after
school, summer, correspondence, and adult programs.
    Source: State of Florida, Department of Education, Division of Public Schools
and Office of Private Education Services, *MIS Statistical Brief: Membership in
Florida Public Schools, Fall 1990* and *Characteristics of Nonpublic Schools in
Florida, 1989-90*, and previous editions.

Table 4.25. NATIONAL SCHOOL LUNCH PROGRAM: PUPILS PARTICIPATING AND COST TO THE
    FEDERAL GOVERNMENT IN FLORIDA AND THE UNITED STATES, 1980, 1987, 1988, AND
    1989

Item	1980	1987	1988	1989
Florida				
Pupils participating (thousands)	1,055	1,031	1,053	1,089
Federal cost (millions of dollars)	102	124	131	141
United States				
Pupils participating (thousands)	26,384	23,869	24,060	24,189
Federal cost (millions of dollars)	2,200	2,679	2,800	2,900

Note: Data are for the month in which most pupils participated nationwide. Data
covers public and private elementary and secondary schools and residential child
care institutions.
    Source: U.S., Department of Commerce, Bureau of the Census, *Statistical Abstract
of the United States, 1991.*

Florida Statistical Abstract 1991

Table 4.26. NONPUBLIC SCHOOLS: NUMBER OF SCHOOLS AND MEMBERSHIP IN NONPUBLIC
   SCHOOLS IN THE STATE AND COUNTIES OF FLORIDA, SCHOOL YEARS 1988-89 AND
   1989-90

| County | Number of schools | | Membership | | |
	1988-89	1989-90	1988-89	1989-90	Percentage change
Florida	1,455	1,427	197,695	197,804	0.1
Alachua	24	20	1,680	1,763	4.9
Baker	0	0	0	0	0.0
Bay	13	11	1,334	1,227	-8.0
Bradford	1	1	9	14	55.6
Brevard	37	34	4,655	4,575	-1.7
Broward	134	128	23,256	23,073	-0.8
Calhoun	0	0	0	0	0.0
Charlotte	5	4	701	627	-10.6
Citrus	8	8	550	568	3.3
Clay	10	11	1,070	1,083	1.2
Collier	11	11	1,302	1,246	-4.3
Columbia	2	2	165	151	-8.5
Dade	362	353	46,726	46,478	-0.5
De Soto	4	3	153	112	-26.8
Dixie	1	1	11	14	27.3
Duval	73	78	13,673	14,530	6.3
Escambia	21	23	4,712	4,878	3.5
Flagler	0	0	0	0	0.0
Franklin	2	2	51	77	51.0
Gadsden	5	4	679	679	0.0
Gilchrist	1	3	38	72	89.5
Glades	0	0	0	0	0.0
Gulf	1	1	86	91	5.8
Hamilton	0	0	0	0	0.0
Hardee	0	0	0	0	0.0
Hendry	2	2	112	125	11.6
Hernando	6	6	665	757	13.8
Highlands	7	7	451	501	11.1
Hillsborough	107	106	15,872	16,436	3.6
Holmes	1	1	1	1	0.0
Indian River	9	10	1,156	1,235	6.8
Jackson	1	1	31	27	-12.9
Jefferson	1	1	350	327	-6.6
Lafayette	0	0	0	0	0.0
Lake	17	16	1,295	1,271	-1.9
Lee	30	33	3,318	3,391	2.2

See footnote at end of table.   Continued . . .

Florida Statistical Abstract 1991

Table 4.26. NONPUBLIC SCHOOLS: NUMBER OF SCHOOLS AND MEMBERSHIP IN NONPUBLIC
  SCHOOLS IN THE STATE AND COUNTIES OF FLORIDA, SCHOOL YEARS 1988-89 AND
  1989-90 (Continued)

County	Number of schools 1988-89	Number of schools 1989-90	Membership 1988-89	Membership 1989-90	Percentage change
Leon	25	25	3,452	3,539	2.5
Levy	6	6	126	142	12.7
Liberty	0	0	0	0	0.0
Madison	1	1	85	83	-2.4
Manatee	15	17	2,074	2,106	1.5
Marion	20	23	2,742	2,883	5.1
Martin	9	9	1,307	1,404	7.4
Monroe	7	7	541	545	0.7
Nassau	8	10	301	311	3.3
Okaloosa	6	7	702	712	1.4
Okeechobee	2	1	64	44	-31.3
Orange	78	71	11,154	11,266	1.0
Osceola	6	5	338	244	-27.8
Palm Beach	92	86	16,270	15,589	-4.2
Pasco	17	19	1,220	1,239	1.6
Pinellas	88	88	13,458	13,552	0.7
Polk	28	28	4,308	3,884	-9.8
Putnam	9	9	377	361	-4.2
St. Johns	12	12	945	881	-6.8
St. Lucie	12	12	1,675	1,739	3.8
Santa Rosa	3	2	215	160	-25.6
Sarasota	27	25	3,126	3,072	-1.7
Seminole	38	34	4,348	4,255	-2.1
Sumter	1	1	72	102	41.7
Suwannee	4	4	168	268	59.5
Taylor	4	3	58	21	-63.8
Union	1	0	24	0	-100.0
Volusia	38	39	4,407	4,053	-8.0
Wakulla	0	0	0	0	0.0
Walton	2	2	36	20	-44.4
Washington	0	0	0	0	0.0

Note: Number of nonpublic schools includes nonpublic kindergarten and private
households who have incorporated to teach children at home. Caution should be
exercised in comparing these data to prior years due to changes in reporting
practices.

Source: State of Florida, Department of Education, Office of Nonpublic Schools,
Characteristics of Nonpublic Schools in Florida, 1989-90, and previous edition.

Table 4.27. PUBLIC SCHOOLS: NUMBER OF SCHOOLS AND MEMBERSHIP IN PUBLIC
SCHOOLS IN THE STATE AND COUNTIES OF FLORIDA, SCHOOL YEARS 1988-89
AND 1989-90

	Number of schools		Membership 1/		
County	1988-89	1989-90	1988-89	1989-90	Percentage change
Florida	2,591	2,694	1,712,610	1,775,545	3.7
Alachua	40	40	24,403	25,178	3.2
Baker	7	7	3,976	4,100	3.1
Bay	32	32	21,180	21,125	-0.3
Bradford	8	10	4,008	4,105	2.4
Brevard	74	75	51,336	53,647	4.5
Broward	184	183	142,021	149,336	5.2
Calhoun	6	6	2,097	2,129	1.5
Charlotte	20	21	10,933	11,760	7.6
Citrus	18	19	10,407	10,957	5.3
Clay	24	25	20,351	20,972	3.1
Collier	33	33	17,997	19,260	7.0
Columbia	11	12	7,875	7,984	1.4
Dade	319	352	265,732	278,789	4.9
De Soto	11	11	3,913	3,751	-4.1
Dixie	4	4	1,756	1,820	3.6
Duval	147	156	104,434	106,425	1.9
Escambia	69	69	41,769	41,730	-0.1
Flagler	5	6	3,327	3,733	12.2
Franklin	5	5	1,477	1,486	0.6
Gadsden	16	16	8,392	8,321	-0.8
Gilchrist	3	4	1,713	1,830	6.8
Glades	3	4	835	860	3.0
Gulf	6	6	2,237	2,204	-1.5
Hamilton	7	7	2,307	2,332	1.1
Hardee	8	8	4,087	4,225	3.4
Hendry	13	12	5,515	5,555	0.7
Hernando	17	18	11,348	12,031	6.0
Highlands	15	15	8,418	8,781	4.3
Hillsborough	177	183	118,343	119,786	1.2
Holmes	9	8	3,219	3,161	-1.8
Indian River	20	20	10,718	11,190	4.4
Jackson	17	17	7,505	7,523	0.2
Jefferson	5	5	2,104	2,054	-2.4
Lafayette	2	3	1,010	1,053	4.3
Lake	43	44	19,801	20,321	2.6
Lee	62	63	39,195	41,058	4.8

See footnote at end of table. Continued . . .

Florida Statistical Abstract 1991

Table 4.27. PUBLIC SCHOOLS: NUMBER OF SCHOOLS AND MEMBERSHIP IN PUBLIC
SCHOOLS IN THE STATE AND COUNTIES OF FLORIDA, SCHOOL YEARS 1988-89
AND 1989-90 (Continued)

County	Number of schools		Membership 1/		Percentage
	1988-89	1989-90	1988-89	1989-90	change
Leon	46	46	25,625	26,466	3.3
Levy	11	13	4,523	4,635	2.5
Liberty	4	4	1,048	1,049	0.1
Madison	7	7	3,159	3,136	-0.7
Manatee	51	54	24,482	25,197	2.9
Marion	36	39	27,194	27,985	2.9
Martin	25	26	11,007	11,320	2.8
Monroe	17	17	7,669	7,893	2.9
Nassau	16	17	8,222	8,376	1.9
Okaloosa	36	36	24,920	25,416	2.0
Okeechobee	12	11	5,484	5,604	2.2
Orange	140	148	91,558	96,915	5.9
Osceola	21	21	15,927	17,876	12.2
Palm Beach	129	139	95,208	99,666	4.7
Pasco	46	47	31,526	32,460	3.0
Pinellas	141	144	90,447	92,108	1.8
Polk	117	124	62,352	63,890	2.5
Putnam	20	18	11,424	11,546	1.1
St. Johns	15	15	10,771	11,497	6.7
St. Lucie	27	28	19,563	21,039	7.5
Santa Rosa	27	28	14,044	15,084	7.4
Sarasota	38	39	26,498	27,122	2.4
Seminole	46	46	44,709	46,613	4.3
Sumter	11	11	4,918	5,053	2.7
Suwannee	6	7	5,177	5,220	0.8
Taylor	7	8	3,501	3,612	3.2
Union	4	4	1,794	1,844	2.8
Volusia	70	73	43,834	46,003	4.9
Wakulla	6	6	2,913	3,043	4.5
Walton	10	10	4,270	4,174	-2.2
Washington	9	9	3,107	3,131	0.8

1/ Based on K-12 fall membership survey.

Source: State of Florida, Department of Education, Division of Public Schools,
Profiles of Florida School Districts, 1989-90, Student and Staff Data, and previous
edition.

Table 4.50. HIGHER EDUCATION: LOCATION AND ENROLLMENT OF SELECTED COLLEGES AND
UNIVERSITIES IN FLORIDA, APRIL 15, 1990

School 1/	City	County	Enroll-ment 2/
Art Institute of Ft. Lauderdale	Ft. Lauderdale	Broward	1,893
Barry University	Miami	Dade	5,238
Bethune Cookman College	Daytona Beach	Volusia	1,860
Brevard Community College	Cocoa	Brevard	12,375
Broward Community College	Ft. Lauderdale	Broward	21,682
Caribbean Center for Advanced Studies/Miami Institute of Psychology	Miami	Dade	204
Central Florida Community College	Ocala	Marion	3,995
Chipola Junior College	Marianna	Jackson	1,922
Clearwater Christian College	Clearwater	Pinellas	353
College of Boca Raton	Boca Raton	Palm Beach	1,137
Daytona Beach Community College	Daytona Beach	Volusia	9,365
Eckerd College	St. Petersburg	Pinellas	1,293
Edison Community College	Ft. Myers	Lee	7,249
Edwards Waters College	Jacksonville	Duval	597
Embry-Riddle Aeronautical University	Bunnell	Flagler	10,766
Flagler Career Institute, Jacksonville	Jacksonville	Duval	248
Miami Campus	Miami	Dade	441
Flagler College	St. Augustine	St. Johns	1,201
Florida A & M University	Tallahassee	Leon	6,396
Florida Atlantic University	Boca Raton	Palm Beach	11,325
Florida Baptist Theological College	Graceville	Jackson	368
Florida Bible College	Kissimmee	Osceola	139
Florida Christian College, Incorporated	Kissimmee	Osceola	123
Florida College	Temple Terrace	Hillsborough	379
Florida Community College at Jacksonville	Jacksonville	Duval	16,778
Florida Institute of Technology	Melbourne	Brevard	6,254
Florida International University	Miami	Dade	18,128
Florida Keys Community College	Key West	Monroe	1,840
Florida Memorial College	Miami	Dade	1,962
Florida Southern College	Lakeland	Polk	2,670
Florida State University	Tallahassee	Leon	25,907
Ft. Lauderdale College	Ft. Lauderdale	Broward	60
Gulf Coast Community College	Panama City	Bay	5,149
Hillsborough Community College	Tampa	Hillsborough	15,573
Hobe Sound Bible College	Hobe Sound	Martin	202
Indian River Community College	Ft. Pierce	St. Lucie	9,483
International Fine Arts College	Miami	Dade	446
ITT Technical Institute	Tampa	Hillsborough	531
Jacksonville University	Jacksonville	Duval	2,347
Jones College	Lakeland	Polk	178
Jacksonville	Jacksonville	Duval	1,573
Keiser Institute of Technology	Ft. Lauderdale	Broward	104
Lake City Community College	Lake City	Columbia	1,893
Lake-Sumter Community College	Leesburg	Lake	2,078
Liberty Christian College	Pensacola	Escambia	284
Manatee Community College	Bradenton	Manatee	7,874
Miami Christian College	Miami	Dade	166
Miami-Dade Community College	Miami	Dade	43,880
National Education Center			
Bauder College Campus	Ft. Lauderdale	Broward	1,201
Tampa Technical Institute Campus	Tampa	Hillsborough	1,566

See footnotes at end of table.   Continued . . .

Florida Statistical Abstract 1991

Table 4.50. HIGHER EDUCATION: LOCATION AND ENROLLMENT OF SELECTED COLLEGES AND
    UNIVERSITIES IN FLORIDA, APRIL 15, 1990 (Continued)

School 1/	City	County	Enroll-ment 2/
National Education Center (Continued)			
Bauder College Miami	Miami	Dade	104
New England Institute of Technology	West Palm Beach	Palm Beach	580
North Florida Junior College	Madison	Madison	1,220
Nova University	Ft. Lauderdale	Broward	8,763
Okaloosa-Walton Junior College	Niceville	Okaloosa	5,270
Orlando College	Orlando	Orange	838
Palm Beach Atlantic College	West Palm Beach	Palm Beach	1,139
Palm Beach Community College	Lake Worth	Palm Beach	13,121
Pasco Hernando Community College	Dade City	Pasco	3,973
Pensacola Junior College	Pensacola	Escambia	10,866
Phillips Junior College	Melbourne	Brevard	239
Polk Community College	Winter Haven	Polk	5,879
Prospect Hall College	Hollywood	Broward	216
Ringling School of Art and Design	Sarasota	Sarasota	483
Rollins College	Winter Park	Orange	3,738
St. John Vianney College Seminary	Miami	Dade	64
St. Johns River Community College	Palatka	Putnam	2,453
St. Leo College	St. Leo	Pasco	5,772
St. Petersburg Junior College	St. Petersburg	Pinellas	18,870
St. Thomas of Villanova University	Miami	Dade	3,363
St. Vincent De Paul Regional Seminary	Boynton Beach	Palm Beach	99
Santa Fe Community College	Gainesville	Alachua	9,633
Seminole Community College	Sanford	Seminole	6,996
South Florida Community College	Avon Park	Highlands	1,308
Southeastern Academy	Kissimmee	Osceola	203
Southeastern College Assemblies of God	Lakeland	Polk	1,155
Southeastern College of Osteopathic Medicine	North Miami Beach	Dade	375
Spurgeon Baptist Bible College	Mulberry	Polk	57
Stetson University	Deland	Volusia	2,974
Tallahassee Community College	Tallahassee	Leon	7,264
Talmudic College of Florida	Miami Beach	Dade	94
Tampa College	Tampa	Hillsborough	1,635
Troy State University-Florida Region	Ft. Walton Beach	Okaloosa	(NA)
United Electronics Institute of Florida	Tampa	Hillsborough	498
University of Central Florida	Orlando	Orange	18,342
University of Florida	Gainesville	Alachua	33,282
University of Miami	Coral Gables	Dade	13,828
University of North Florida	Jacksonville	Duval	7,162
University of Sarasota	Sarasota	Sarasota	194
University of South Florida	Tampa	Hillsborough	29,912
University of Tampa	Tampa	Hillsborough	2,401
University of West Florida	Pensacola	Escambia	7,095
Valencia Community College	Orlando	Orange	14,840
Warner Southern College	Lake Wales	Polk	363
Webber College	Babson Park	Polk	265

(NA) Not available.
    1/ Includes institutions accredited at the college level by an agency recognized
by the U.S. Secretary of Education.   2/ Includes undergraduate, graduate, first-
professional, and unclassified students, both full- and part-time.
    Source: U.S., Department of Education, National Center for Education Statistics,
Office of Educational Research and Improvement, *1989-90 Directory of Postsecondary
Institutions: Volume I, 4-Year and 2-Year*.

Table 4.53. HIGHER EDUCATION: ENROLLMENT IN UNIVERSITIES OF THE STATE UNIVERSITY
SYSTEM OF FLORIDA BY LEVEL, SEX, RACE, AND STATUS, FALL 1989

Sex and race	Educational and general		Health or medical center and veterinarian medicine		IFAS	
	Under-graduate	Graduate	Under-graduate	Graduate	Under-grad-uate	Grad-uate
Part-time 1/						
Total	50,419	12,415	300	874	146	194
Sex						
Female	28,300	6,694	264	524	65	67
Male	22,119	5,721	36	350	81	127
Not reported	0	0	0	0	0	0
Race						
Asian	1,153	206	3	28	2	3
Black	3,447	533	15	21	11	6
Hispanic	5,983	810	10	50	5	3
American Indian or Alaskan native	64	25	0	0	1	1
White	38,231	10,202	266	761	116	137
Other	602	639	6	14	11	44
Not reported	939	0	0	0	0	0
Full-time 2/						
Total	89,094	11,227	992	1,537	676	437
Sex						
Female	46,780	5,020	772	767	305	133
Male	42,314	6,207	220	770	371	304
Not reported	0	0	0	0	0	0
Race						
Asian	2,337	165	40	77	17	6
Black	10,423	655	49	83	93	10
Hispanic	7,167	547	62	121	32	19
American Indian or Alaskan native	100	26	1	4	0	1
White	66,944	7,914	826	1,169	485	229
Other	2,032	1,919	14	82	46	172
Not reported	91	1	0	1	3	0

IFAS Institute of Food and Agricultural Sciences.
1/ Includes undergraduates enrolled for fewer than 12 hours and graduate students enrolled for fewer than 9 hours.
2/ Includes undergraduates enrolled for 12 or more hours and graduate students enrolled for 9 or more hours.
Note: Unclassified students are counted as undergraduates. Data are from the student data course file enrollment report, Fall 1989. Staff waivers are excluded.

Source: State of Florida, State University System, Board of Regents, *Fact Book, 1989-90.*

Table 4.54. HIGHER EDUCATION: TOTAL HEADCOUNT ENROLLMENT IN THE UNIVERSITIES
OF THE STATE UNIVERSITY SYSTEM OF FLORIDA, FALL 1982 THROUGH 1989

University	1982	1983	1984	1985
Educational and general, total	130,437	135,525	139,715	141,785
University of Florida	30,957	31,908	32,436	32,651
Florida State University	21,739	21,267	21,351	21,474
Florida A & M University	4,435	4,894	5,187	4,919
University of South Florida	25,130	26,172	26,501	26,733
Florida Atlantic University	9,464	9,388	10,695	10,465
University of West Florida	5,245	5,922	6,010	6,150
University of Central Florida	14,239	15,648	15,853	16,447
Florida International University	13,786	14,868	15,800	16,613
University of North Florida	5,442	5,458	5,882	6,333
Special units, total 1/	4,635	4,920	4,890	4,907
University of Florida				
Institute of Food and Agricultural Science	1,584	1,524	1,471	1,451
Health Center and Veterinary Medicine	2,525	2,608	2,638	2,639
University of South Florida				
Medical Center	526	788	781	817

University	1986	1987	1988	1989
Educational and general, total	144,076	146,967	153,093	163,155
University of Florida	31,687	31,151	31,370	31,481
Florida State University	22,912	23,485	25,555	27,582
Florida A & M University	5,240	5,743	6,247	7,182
University of South Florida	27,946	28,392	28,621	30,255
Florida Atlantic University	10,705	11,082	11,361	11,629
University of West Florida	6,107	6,645	7,017	7,631
University of Central Florida	16,530	17,398	18,158	20,084
Florida International University	16,403	16,313	17,703	19,767
University of North Florida	6,546	6,758	7,061	7,544
Special units, total 1/	4,864	4,828	4,926	5,156
University of Florida				
Institute of Food and Agricultural Science	1,406	1,349	1,354	1,453
Health Center and Veterinary Medicine	2,598	2,599	2,642	2,747
University of South Florida				
Medical Center	860	880	930	956

1/ Includes medical professionals.
Note: Data are from the student data course file enrollment reports.

Source: State of Florida, State University System, Board of Regents, *Fact Book 1989-90.*

Florida Statistical Abstract 1991

Table 4.60. PUBLIC COMMUNITY COLLEGES: COLLEGE LEVEL HEADCOUNT ENROLLMENT BY
OBJECTIVE STATUS AND INSTITUTION IN FLORIDA, 1988-89

Community college	Total	Advanced and pro-fessional	Voca-tional (credit)	Adult general	Community instruc-tional services	Other 1/
					Other objectives	
Total	964,366	175,584	271,760	135,224	55,656	326,142
Brevard	62,141	8,309	28,537	10,958	1,883	12,454
Broward	99,833	10,733	16,474	7,541	6,118	58,967
Central Florida	13,424	3,348	6,747	1,202	120	2,007
Chipola	10,508	1,621	3,542	798	0	4,547
Daytona Beach	35,788	5,623	9,594	7,770	2,232	10,569
Edison	25,463	3,772	5,334	1,465	2,388	12,504
Florida Community College at Jacksonville	84,038	10,264	29,883	22,340	1,382	20,169
Florida Keys	10,549	711	3,378	69	97	6,294
Gulf Coast	18,252	3,663	6,136	1,494	897	6,062
Hillsborough	35,051	11,190	7,979	4,550	685	10,647
Indian River	53,443	3,839	19,183	9,585	0	20,836
Lake City	4,801	1,458	1,863	821	175	484
Lake Sumter	6,584	1,241	1,421	533	499	2,890
Manatee	16,856	7,989	2,107	715	1,947	4,098
Miami-Dade	102,724	19,631	17,246	22,422	12,132	31,293
North Florida	2,910	403	1,175	693	142	497
Okaloosa-Walton	18,073	4,360	2,455	2,778	39	8,441
Palm Beach	54,994	8,203	16,569	3,486	781	25,955
Pasco-Hernando	16,516	2,183	4,806	922	0	8,605
Pensacola	43,149	9,657	8,538	8,345	3,076	13,533
Polk	30,442	3,479	11,539	1,390	63	13,971
St. Johns River	4,398	1,861	755	1,136	0	646
St. Petersburg	60,435	14,067	15,581	4,223	8,854	17,710
Santa Fe	29,893	9,066	4,894	3,186	10,326	2,421
Seminole	31,508	5,350	9,770	7,144	1,598	7,646
South Florida	14,832	1,398	2,116	3,229	171	7,918
Tallahassee	15,253	8,651	2,738	1,679	13	2,172
Valencia	62,508	13,514	31,400	4,750	38	12,806

1/ Includes lifelong learning.
Note: Data are revised.
Source: State of Florida, Department of Education, Division of Community
Colleges, *Report for Florida Community Colleges: The Fact Book 1989-90.*

Table 4.61. PUBLIC COMMUNITY COLLEGES: TRANSFER STUDENTS FROM FLORIDA COMMUNITY
COLLEGES TO FLORIDA UNIVERSITIES BY SEX AND UNIVERSITY, FALL 1988 AND 1989

	1988			1989		
Institution	Total	Male	Female	Total	Male	Female
State University System, total	54,118	24,348	29,770	59,294	26,204	33,090
Florida Agricultural and						
Mechanical University	734	369	365	812	405	407
Florida Atlantic University	5,673	2,356	3,317	5,713	2,331	3,382
Florida International University	8,470	3,490	4,980	9,524	3,786	5,738
Florida State University	7,381	3,517	3,864	8,799	4,120	4,679
University of Central Florida	9,820	4,705	5,115	11,363	5,348	6,015
University of Florida	6,167	3,288	2,879	6,161	3,285	2,876
University of North Florida	3,274	1,311	1,963	3,638	1,490	2,148
University of South Florida	9,395	4,032	5,363	9,883	4,095	5,788
University of West Florida	3,204	1,280	1,924	3,401	1,344	2,057

Table 4.62. PUBLIC COMMUNITY COLLEGES: TRANSFER STUDENTS FROM FLORIDA COMMUNITY
COLLEGES TO FLORIDA UNIVERSITIES BY RACE AND UNIVERSITY, FALL 1989

	Transfer students						
Institution	Total	White	Black	His-panic	Ameri-can Indian	Asian	Other 1/
State University System, total	59,294	46,062	3,359	7,196	83	1,478	1,116
Florida Agricultural and							
Mechanical University	812	275	465	38	1	21	12
Florida Atlantic University	5,713	4,689	301	380	3	172	168
Florida International University	9,524	3,360	813	4,772	11	235	333
Florida State University	8,799	7,928	326	382	16	95	52
University of Central Florida	11,363	9,685	466	568	21	400	223
University of Florida	6,161	5,139	213	432	6	178	193
University of North Florida	3,638	3,229	227	67	4	94	17
University of South Florida	9,883	8,663	366	518	13	215	108
University of West Florida	3,401	3,094	182	39	8	68	10

1/ Includes students classified as nonresident aliens and unclassified students.

Source for Tables 4.61 and 4.62: State of Florida, Department of Education,
State Board of Community Colleges, *Articulation*, Fall 1989.

Florida Statistical Abstract 1991

Table 4.75. PUBLIC HIGH SCHOOL TESTING: STATE STUDENT ASSESSMENT TEST, PART I
   (SSAT-I), GRADE 10 COMPOSITE SCORES IN THE STATE AND COUNTIES OF FLORIDA
   1987 THROUGH 1990

County	Reading				Writing				Mathematics			
	1987	1988	1989	1990	1987	1988	1989	1990	1987	1988	1989	1990
Florida	89	89	89	92	85	87	86	93	89	89	88	87
Alachua	90	91	91	94	87	88	89	94	90	89	90	88
Baker	85	86	84	92	83	85	85	96	91	92	84	90
Bay	90	90	89	94	86	89	88	95	91	90	88	87
Bradford	86	82	77	85	85	82	78	87	93	88	80	80
Brevard	92	91	91	93	89	90	89	95	90	89	87	86
Broward	91	91	90	93	88	90	89	95	90	90	89	89
Calhoun	93	89	89	96	91	93	91	96	97	97	93	96
Charlotte	94	92	93	95	90	90	90	95	92	93	91	89
Citrus	94	92	93	95	88	92	92	95	93	93	93	90
Clay	94	94	91	95	90	93	88	96	92	93	90	91
Collier	89	88	88	92	85	87	88	93	90	91	90	86
Columbia	88	88	85	93	87	87	83	94	90	88	85	86
Dade	85	85	84	87	78	81	81	88	86	85	85	82
De Soto	88	90	90	93	81	84	86	92	89	90	89	87
Dixie	84	81	80	90	82	82	77	90	92	89	81	81
Duval	89	90	88	93	82	86	86	93	89	90	87	88
Escambia	91	91	90	93	85	88	88	94	90	90	89	87
Flagler	88	89	88	94	82	85	87	94	90	87	86	85
Franklin	81	84	87	88	75	84	86	91	74	85	91	77
Gadsden	79	82	78	79	80	84	78	88	88	87	83	80
Gilchrist	92	92	83	94	86	89	81	95	88	86	79	87
Glades	78	83	85	89	77	81	82	88	84	87	86	76
Gulf	89	88	87	93	88	90	86	92	93	91	88	83
Hamilton	78	83	78	87	82	84	81	91	85	92	84	89
Hardee	90	87	86	91	86	90	86	94	94	94	90	90
Hendry	81	85	83	84	78	84	85	91	88	89	87	84
Hernando	93	93	92	95	88	90	89	95	92	94	91	87
Highlands	90	88	87	89	85	87	85	91	88	89	86	81
Hillsborough	88	89	89	94	84	87	87	95	88	88	88	89
Holmes	87	89	89	90	85	89	88	90	91	91	91	87
Indian River	89	89	86	90	86	89	87	93	90	89	86	84
Jackson	88	87	85	92	85	87	84	93	93	93	90	89
Jefferson	77	80	73	83	73	78	72	88	77	77	74	77
Lafayette	87	79	80	94	82	80	80	95	91	87	94	94
Lake	90	92	90	94	87	90	88	95	92	93	89	88
Lee	90	90	90	92	85	87	85	94	87	86	85	83
Leon	91	92	90	95	87	90	87	95	92	92	91	90

See footnotes at end of table.   Continued . . .

Florida Statistical Abstract 1991

Table 4.75. PUBLIC HIGH SCHOOL TESTING: STATE STUDENT ASSESSMENT TEST, PART I
(SSAT-I), GRADE 10 COMPOSITE SCORES IN THE STATE AND COUNTIES OF FLORIDA
1987 THROUGH 1990 (Continued)

County	Reading				Writing				Mathematics			
	1987	1988	1989	1990	1987	1988	1989	1990	1987	1988	1989	1990
Levy	89	88	89	93	87	86	87	94	93	91	92	87
Liberty	87	83	86	87	81	86	84	91	90	89	90	84
Madison	80	78	81	87	81	77	81	92	88	88	88	83
Manatee	91	90	90	93	89	89	89	94	90	91	90	88
Marion	88	88	88	92	83	86	86	93	89	88	88	87
Martin	91	92	91	94	87	90	90	95	89	90	89	88
Monroe	90	91	93	95	89	93	92	96	91	93	93	90
Nassau	88	88	90	94	83	85	88	96	89	86	89	89
Okaloosa	92	92	91	95	91	93	91	96	93	93	93	90
Okeechobee	89	90	88	93	83	90	89	94	92	93	92	93
Orange	91	90	90	93	86	88	88	94	90	90	89	87
Osceola	90	89	88	92	85	87	86	93	85	86	84	84
Palm Beach	90	89	88	92	84	86	86	93	89	89	89	88
Pasco	90	90	89	91	85	88	87	94	89	87	86	84
Pinellas	91	90	90	93	84	88	86	95	87	88	87	88
Polk	87	85	85	89	82	84	84	91	88	86	86	85
Putnam	88	88	87	92	84	90	87	96	92	94	92	90
St. Johns	92	91	92	95	87	88	89	95	87	89	90	87
St. Lucie	86	85	84	90	83	83	82	93	90	86	84	84
Santa Rosa	91	91	91	95	88	89	91	95	90	88	89	87
Sarasota	94	93	94	95	90	91	91	96	92	92	92	89
Seminole	94	93	93	95	91	92	91	95	93	92	92	90
Sumter	87	88	88	93	84	88	86	94	93	92	91	89
Suwannee	86	90	87	91	84	88	83	94	87	90	88	87
Taylor	87	84	86	89	88	85	84	93	89	86	87	83
Union	90	89	91	93	88	88	89	93	93	94	90	91
Volusia	90	90	90	93	86	88	87	95	92	91	89	88
Wakulla	86	89	92	95	83	90	95	96	92	95	96	93
Walton	91	90	89	93	92	92	88	94	93	91	89	90
Washington	88	85	84	92	85	87	87	94	92	90	86	86
Laboratory 1/	93	93	94	95	86	87	89	93	91	87	91	87

1/ Schools funded through and administered by the state university system.
    Note: Average percentage of students, grade 10, mastering specified performance
standards within each section of the SSAT-I. SSAT-I measures student mastery of
Minimum Student Performance Standards that should be acquired by beginning of grade
eleven. Mastery of the standards is required for high school graduation in Florida.

    Source: State of Florida, Department of Education, Division of Public Schools,
State, District, and Regional Report of Statewide Assessment Results, March 1990.
MIS Series 90-18, and previous editions.

Florida Statistical Abstract 1991

Table 4.76. PUBLIC HIGH SCHOOL TESTING: PERCENTAGE PASSING THE STATE STUDENT
   ASSESSMENT TEST, PART II (SSAT-II), IN THE STATE AND COUNTIES OF FLORIDA
   1987 THROUGH 1990

County	Communications				Mathematics			
	1987	1988	1989	1990	1987	1988	1989	1990
Florida	88	88	85	87	82	80	76	78
Alachua	91	93	90	93	85	83	80	81
Baker	87	83	80	88	83	78	73	82
Bay	87	91	86	90	83	79	69	78
Bradford	87	81	71	79	92	79	57	67
Brevard	92	91	88	90	86	81	79	81
Broward	90	91	88	90	84	84	80	82
Calhoun	93	97	90	92	96	98	89	93
Charlotte	92	92	90	88	90	87	85	83
Citrus	91	97	96	95	95	96	93	96
Clay	95	95	88	91	88	88	80	79
Collier	87	88	86	88	85	83	83	80
Columbia	89	89	84	91	80	79	69	84
Dade	80	78	76	76	73	69	66	65
De Soto	91	91	90	87	79	73	79	79
Dixie	87	82	85	84	83	83	69	79
Duval	89	89	86	88	83	79	74	75
Escambia	90	90	85	87	83	80	75	75
Flagler	89	91	91	95	85	76	81	77
Franklin	78	85	88	86	65	73	83	63
Gadsden	89	90	81	79	79	76	64	64
Gilchrist	89	91	78	90	78	78	62	80
Glades	82	86	86	78	82	73	67	57
Gulf	97	91	91	91	95	87	86	81
Hamilton	79	77	79	79	72	81	70	74
Hardee	94	92	88	87	91	89	84	84
Hendry	84	87	86	84	76	81	77	73
Hernando	92	94	89	93	87	87	78	79
Highlands	87	89	84	83	82	80	75	70
Hillsborough	85	90	89	93	80	79	78	84
Holmes	87	88	90	83	88	86	81	77
Indian River	87	87	79	82	80	78	71	72
Jackson	90	90	84	88	86	83	79	78
Jefferson	88	82	65	73	87	76	63	67
Lafayette	79	74	88	99	83	74	81	88
Lake	90	93	87	89	89	89	79	80
Lee	87	88	84	86	79	74	69	73
Leon	90	92	86	91	85	86	79	81

See footnotes at end of table.   Continued . . .

Florida Statistical Abstract 1991

Table 4.76. PUBLIC HIGH SCHOOL TESTING: PERCENTAGE PASSING THE STATE STUDENT
     ASSESSMENT TEST, PART II (SSAT-II), IN THE STATE AND COUNTIES OF FLORIDA
     1987 THROUGH 1990 (Continued)

County	Communications				Mathematics			
	1987	1988	1989	1990	1987	1988	1989	1990
Levy	89	91	86	88	84	80	79	74
Liberty	90	79	67	80	90	84	76	62
Madison	89	91	85	88	84	82	77	76
Manatee	91	90	88	91	89	83	82	77
Marion	85	87	85	88	82	80	77	78
Martin	90	90	87	88	83	86	79	81
Monroe	90	91	91	90	90	91	91	86
Nassau	87	86	86	91	82	75	78	76
Okaloosa	92	91	90	91	90	86	86	81
Okeechobee	89	90	83	88	91	91	89	90
Orange	92	91	91	92	89	84	81	82
Osceola	87	91	86	89	79	77	73	78
Palm Beach	88	88	85	88	83	82	79	83
Pasco	87	89	85	88	83	78	74	73
Pinellas	88	88	84	89	79	77	74	78
Polk	87	86	84	86	83	78	80	80
Putnam	89	92	89	91	85	85	83	80
St. Johns	91	92	93	92	83	83	82	78
St. Lucie	86	87	79	88	80	74	71	72
Santa Rosa	90	89	90	91	83	77	76	77
Sarasota	93	92	91	92	91	87	85	83
Seminole	93	92	92	93	90	86	86	86
Sumter	89	89	86	87	86	84	84	84
Suwannee	82	88	78	84	78	82	77	80
Taylor	86	84	78	83	71	77	63	72
Union	92	92	86	97	86	85	64	85
Volusia	90	90	88	91	89	85	82	84
Wakulla	86	95	94	94	91	94	95	89
Walton	94	94	85	88	82	80	78	80
Washington	93	91	85	91	86	78	72	80
Laboratory 1/	92	91	91	92	90	76	76	79

1/ Schools funded through and administered by the state university system.
     Note: Data are for grade 10. SSAT-II measures the application of the Minimum
Student Performance Standards tested in the SSAT-I to everyday life situations.
Passing the SSAT-II is a requirement for high school graduation in Florida.

     Source: State of Florida, Department of Education, Division of Public Schools,
State, District, and Regional Report of Statewide Assessment Results, March 1990.
MIS Series 90-18, and previous editions.

Table 4.82. PUBLIC HIGH SCHOOL GRADUATES: GRADUATES BY TYPE OF DIPLOMA, 1990, AND BY TYPE OF POST-SECONDARY INSTITUTION ENTERED, 1990-91, IN THE STATE AND COUNTIES OF FLORIDA

| | 1990 graduates receiving | | Total graduates continuing education | | Graduates entering-- | | | | Out-of-state colleges and universities | Technical trade and other | |
	Standard diplomas	Special diplomas	Number	Percentage	Florida community colleges Public	Florida community colleges Private	Florida colleges and universities Public	Florida colleges and universities Private		In-state	Out-of-state
County											
Florida	88,934	1,856	59,181	65.2	30,697	525	12,053	3,158	8,232	3,277	1,239
Alachua	1,256	24	1,008	78.8	523	10	206	48	178	17	26
Baker	180	16	84	42.9	72	0	9	0	0	3	0
Bay	1,120	9	802	71.0	504	3	116	12	24	12	131
Bradford	211	5	111	51.4	89	0	10	0	7	1	4
Brevard	2,958	51	1,963	65.2	1,122	5	373	82	259	34	88
Broward	7,220	118	5,572	75.9	2,519	46	1,290	381	901	371	64
Calhoun	108	3	57	51.4	43	0	5	0	7	1	1
Charlotte	672	17	486	70.5	177	0	102	24	92	80	11
Citrus	601	11	264	43.1	119	7	58	13	36	29	2
Clay	1,305	20	797	60.2	482	7	135	18	74	77	4
Collier	998	8	687	68.3	264	5	130	56	160	59	13
Columbia	404	13	174	41.7	136	0	13	4	15	3	3
Dade	13,411	160	9,849	72.6	5,837	19	1,639	580	1,285	467	22
De Soto	160	8	75	44.6	44	1	11	2	12	5	0
Dixie	89	0	27	30.3	24	0	1	1	0	1	0
Duval	4,788	174	2,714	54.7	1,287	0	706	229	416	76	0
Escambia	2,223	98	1,089	46.9	462	1	288	17	244	50	27
Flagler	196	3	151	75.9	68	8	20	10	33	12	0
Franklin	83	5	33	37.5	18	7	3	0	2	3	0
Gadsden	400	24	141	33.3	48	0	54	6	12	21	0
Gilchrist	101	0	35	34.7	30	0	3	0	0	2	0
Glades	42	2	29	65.9	20	0	1	0	3	5	0
Gulf	154	2	114	73.1	56	0	9	4	10	32	3
Hamilton	151	9	69	43.1	41	0	10	1	12	1	4
Hardee	180	13	109	56.5	54	2	24	5	14	9	1
Hendry	239	5	146	59.8	84	0	20	12	8	9	13
Hernando	595	14	360	59.1	213	12	51	14	30	39	1
Highlands	423	23	307	68.8	196	3	53	9	22	21	3
Hillsborough	6,187	62	3,711	59.4	1,552	127	1,117	230	532	2	151
Holmes	179	9	86	45.7	59	0	1	0	17	6	3
Indian River	568	2	345	60.5	193	0	65	16	55	3	13
Jackson	436	18	278	61.2	194	0	32	5	37	3	7
Jefferson	94	10	99	95.2	38	0	15	5	3	11	27
Lafayette	59	3	30	48.4	22	0	1	1	0	6	0
Lake	1,015	58	636	59.3	310	11	117	32	76	88	2

See footnote at end of table.

Continued . . .

Table 4.82. PUBLIC HIGH SCHOOL GRADUATES: GRADUATES BY TYPE OF DIPLOMA, 1990, AND
BY TYPE OF POST-SECONDARY INSTITUTION ENTERED, 1990-91, IN THE STATE AND
COUNTIES OF FLORIDA (Continued)

| | 1990 graduates receiving | | Total graduates continuing education | | Graduates entering-- | | | | | | |
| | | | | | Florida community colleges | | Florida colleges and universities | | Out-of-state colleges and universities | Technical trade and other | |
County	Stan-dard dip-lomas	Spe-cial dip-lomas	Num-ber	Per-cent-age	Pub-lic	Pri-vate	Pub-lic	Pri-vate		In-state	Out-of-state
Lee	2,119	45	1,432	66.2	763	2	234	79	197	121	36
Leon	1,369	28	906	64.9	442	10	281	52	104	17	0
Levy	235	12	107	43.3	74	0	23	1	4	5	0
Liberty	53	6	19	32.2	17	0	0	0	1	0	1
Madison	148	1	72	48.3	53	0	10	4	3	0	2
Manatee	1,180	30	627	51.8	355	4	98	14	95	58	3
Marion	1,404	59	906	61.9	597	9	108	21	85	29	57
Martin	645	5	342	52.6	160	6	101	12	52	9	2
Monroe	419	9	209	48.8	102	1	50	9	40	5	2
Nassau	376	8	190	49.5	119	0	18	15	25	10	3
Okaloosa	1,508	21	975	63.8	482	9	181	11	252	25	15
Okeechobee	255	9	107	40.5	71	4	13	1	7	7	4
Orange	4,866	118	3,688	74.0	1,532	73	1,011	267	424	347	34
Osceola	668	8	299	44.2	129	7	44	18	40	37	24
Palm Beach	4,811	74	3,502	71.7	1,681	7	696	163	547	193	215
Pasco	1,564	29	827	51.9	419	30	180	39	68	84	7
Pinellas	5,050	102	3,531	68.5	1,938	8	661	156	518	235	15
Polk	3,058	82	1,967	62.6	1,081	15	297	108	224	200	42
Putnam	509	22	340	64.0	205	0	26	11	19	75	4
St. Johns	490	21	293	57.3	138	2	48	21	35	49	0
St. Lucie	689	14	336	47.8	173	0	118	11	30	2	2
Santa Rosa	862	22	563	63.7	303	0	123	4	120	7	6
Sarasota	1,478	42	1,058	69.6	476	12	192	68	243	50	17
Seminole	2,698	19	2,133	78.5	1,033	40	551	104	301	21	83
Sumter	254	9	103	39.2	64	0	20	9	3	7	0
Suwannee	285	12	127	42.8	100	0	10	6	8	1	2
Taylor	180	0	90	50.0	68	0	13	0	5	2	2
Union	75	5	33	41.3	26	0	5	0	2	0	0
Volusia	2,268	34	1,708	74.2	1,030	11	225	125	174	112	31
Wakulla	143	2	56	38.6	35	1	14	0	6	0	0
Walton	199	5	110	53.9	65	0	3	10	21	5	6
Washington	270	6	87	31.5	66	0	11	2	3	5	0

Note: Data were obtained from the 1990 fall student survey, ESE 269. Because
some high schools do not have a formal follow-up program for graduates, it was
necessary for the principal or guidance couselor to prepare estimates for some of
the items included. Figures include twelfth grade graduates from adult centers and
exceptional and gifted schools.
Source: State of Florida, Department of Education, Division of Public Schools,
MIS Statistical Brief: Florida Public High School Graduates, 1990. Series 90-12B.

Florida Statistical Abstract 1991

INCOME AND WEALTH

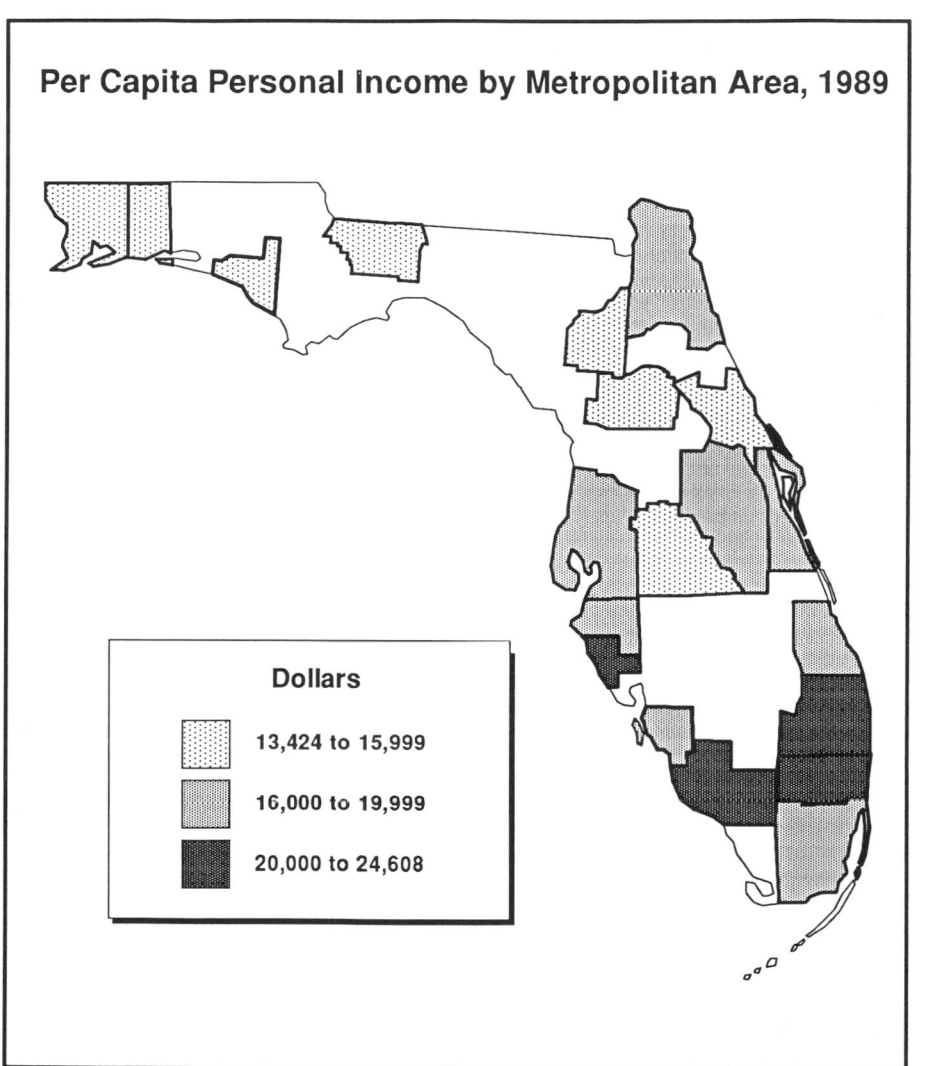

Per Capita Personal Income by Metropolitan Area, 1989

Dollars

13,424 to 15,999

16,000 to 19,999

20,000 to 24,608

Source: Table 5.11

TABLES LISTED BY MAJOR HEADINGS

SECTION 5.00
INCOME AND WEALTH (CONTINUED)

TABLES LISTED BY MAJOR HEADINGS

Table 5.01. INDIVIDUAL INCOME TAX RETURNS: SPECIFIED INCOME, DEDUCTION, AND TAX
   ITEMS IN FLORIDA AND THE UNITED STATES, 1989

(amounts in thousands of dollars, except where indicated)

Item	Florida	United States
All returns	5,970,839	113,242,080
Number of exemptions 1/	12,972,987	244,351,038
Adjusted gross income	169,688,335	3,250,669,292
Salaries and wages, number of returns	4,752,691	95,374,189
Amount	110,066,825	2,451,493,264
Interest income, number of returns	3,502,161	70,190,273
Amount	17,286,456	219,055,532
Dividends, number of returns	1,316,861	23,112,757
Amount	7,246,028	80,080,288
Net capital gain (less loss), number of returns	862,967	12,991,868
Amount	12,700,493	143,433,451
Taxable pensions, number of returns	1,052,932	16,698,852
Amount	10,982,789	145,966,450
Unemployment compensation, number of returns	190,349	7,023,685
Amount	337,168	12,325,280
Number of sole proprietorship returns	753,343	14,149,144
Number of farm returns (Schedule F)	34,811	2,026,428
Total itemized deductions, number of returns	1,544,586	33,014,609
Amount	19,786,065	442,391,630
Average (whole dollars)	12,809	13,400
Taxable income, number of returns	4,798,471	92,610,860
Amount	116,522,150	2,176,335,173
Total tax liability, number of returns	4,888,055	94,081,688
Amount	25,034,769	453,493,931
Average (whole dollars)	5,121	4,820
Earned income credit, number of returns	697,369	11,918,403
Amount	404,053	6,695,917
Excess earned income credit 2/		
Number of returns	494,586	8,349,978
Amount	283,859	4,710,515
Overpayment, number of returns	4,034,984	78,447,846
Amount	3,660,044	72,781,284
Tax due at time of filing, number of returns	1,491,560	27,576,665
Amount	3,997,373	58,663,779

1/ Includes exemptions for age and blindness.
2/ Represents the refundable portion of the credit and equals the amount in excess of total tax liability, including any advance earned income credit payments for those returns which had such an excess.
Note: Data are estimates based on samples and are preliminary.

Source: U.S., Department of the Treasury, Internal Revenue Service, *Statistics of Income: SOI Bulletin*, Spring 1991.

Florida Statistical Abstract 1991

Table 5.02. INDIVIDUAL INCOME TAXES: RETURNS, ADJUSTED GROSS INCOME, EXEMPTIONS
AND INCOME TAX IN FLORIDA AND THE UNITED STATES, 1979 THROUGH 1989

					Amount ($1,000,000)			
	Number (1,000)				Adjusted gross		Total income	
	Returns		Exemptions 1/		income		tax	
Year	Florida	United States	Florida	United States	Florida	United States	Florida	United States
1979	3,901	(NA)	9,418	(NA)	56,849	(NA)	8,570	(NA)
1980	4,159	93,902	10,013	227,925	67,126	1,613,731	10,852	250,341
1981	4,334	(NA)	10,512	(NA)	75,735	(NA)	9,335	(NA)
1982	4,460	(NA)	10,892	(NA)	81,118	(NA)	12,573	(NA)
1983	4,645	(NA)	(NA)	(NA)	89,972	(NA)	13,365	(NA)
1984	4,906	(NA)	11,595	(NA)	101,265	(NA)	15,842	(NA)
1985	5,113	101,660	12,030	244,180	110,593	2,305,951	17,310	325,710
1986	5,301	(NA)	12,413	(NA)	123,771	(NA)	20,901	(NA)
1987	5,533	106,996	12,473	217,495	140,279	2,773,824	20,737	369,203
1988	5,760	109,708	12,559	221,884	159,547	3,083,020	23,849	412,870
1989	5,971	113,242	12,973	244,351	169,688	3,250,669	25,035	453,494

(NA) Not available.
1/ Includes exemptions for age and blindness.
Note: Includes taxable and nontaxable returns. All figures are estimates based
on samples. 1989 data are preliminary.

Source: U.S., Department of the Treasury, Internal Revenue Service, *Statistics
of Income: SOI Bulletin*, Spring 1991.

Table 5.03. FAMILY INCOME: PERCENTAGE DISTRIBUTION OF ANNUAL INCOME BY INCOME
CATEGORY AND HOUSEHOLD SIZE IN FLORIDA, 1990

Income category	Total house- holds	Household size					
		1	2	3	4	5	6 or more
Less than $10,000	4.0	1.7	1.3	0.4	0.3	0.1	0.1
$10,000 to $14,999	5.7	1.9	2.2	0.8	0.5	0.2	0.1
$15,000 to $19,999	9.8	2.9	3.8	1.5	1.0	0.5	0.2
$20,000 to $24,999	13.5	3.0	5.7	1.9	1.6	1.0	0.3
$25,000 to $34,999	23.8	4.5	9.3	4.1	3.6	1.7	0.6
$35,000 to $44,999	16.3	2.2	6.1	3.1	3.4	1.1	0.4
$45,000 or more	26.9	2.1	9.7	6.1	6.1	2.3	0.7

Note: Distribution of family income is based on telephone surveys with sample
size of approximately 500 Florida households. The surveys are conducted nine months
a year and the monthly results have been pooled to develop the annual frequency
distributions.

Source: University of Florida, Bureau of Economic and Business Research, Survey
Program, unpublished data.

Florida Statistical Abstract 1991

Table 5.05. PERSONAL INCOME: TOTAL AND PER CAPITA PERSONAL INCOME IN FLORIDA
   OTHER SUNBELT STATES, OTHER POPULOUS STATES, AND THE UNITED STATES, 1988
   THROUGH 1990

| | Total personal income ($1,000,000) | | | | Per capita personal income (amounts in dollars) | | | |
| | | | | Per-cent-age change 1989- | | | 1990 | |
State	1988	1989	1990	1990	1988	1989	Amount	Rank among states
			Sunbelt states					
Florida	204,479	224,410	240,459	7.2	16,572	17,710	18,586	19
Alabama	52,772	56,287	59,907	6.4	12,862	13,668	14,826	44
Arizona	52,370	56,353	59,732	6.0	15,034	15,846	16,297	34
Arkansas	29,195	31,261	33,423	6.9	12,187	12,995	14,218	47
California	533,116	576,433	618,850	7.4	18,823	19,834	20,795	7
Georgia	96,823	103,339	109,765	6.2	15,274	16,057	16,944	30
Louisiana	54,006	56,636	60,730	7.2	12,255	12,926	14,391	45
Mississippi	29,073	30,942	32,770	5.9	11,095	11,804	12,735	50
New Mexico	18,789	20,165	21,556	6.9	12,444	13,196	14,228	46
North Carolina	92,886	100,418	107,403	7.0	14,314	15,283	16,203	35
Oklahoma	43,032	45,614	48,581	6.5	13,307	14,147	15,444	38
South Carolina	44,924	47,905	52,646	9.9	12,967	13,641	15,099	42
Tennessee	68,203	72,757	77,052	5.9	13,926	14,728	15,798	37
Texas	245,652	263,610	284,678	8.0	14,592	15,515	16,759	32
Virginia	106,619	115,762	122,178	5.5	17,731	18,985	19,746	12
			Other populous states					
Illinois	204,693	220,021	232,071	5.5	17,626	18,873	20,303	9
Indiana	82,239	88,499	93,494	5.6	14,794	15,824	16,864	31
Massachusetts	123,447	131,473	136,226	3.6	20,958	22,234	22,642	3
Michigan	151,995	162,610	170,534	4.9	16,450	17,535	18,346	20
New Jersey	171,763	183,622	193,008	5.1	22,256	23,736	24,968	2
New York	347,942	373,682	395,336	5.8	19,428	20,818	21,975	4
Ohio	168,343	179,381	189,537	5.7	15,494	16,446	17,473	24
Pennsylvania	194,678	209,393	221,850	5.9	16,225	17,392	18,672	18
United States	4,058,181	4,367,401	4,647,055	6.4	16,511	17,594	18,685	(X)

(X) Not applicable.
Note: Data for 1988 and 1989 are revised; 1990 are preliminary.

   Source: U.S., Department of Commerce, Bureau of Economic Analysis, *Survey of
Current Business*, April 1991.

Florida Statistical Abstract 1991

Table 5.08. PERSONAL INCOME: TOTAL AND PER CAPITA DISPOSABLE PERSONAL INCOME
   IN FLORIDA, OTHER SUNBELT STATES, OTHER POPULOUS STATES, AND THE
   UNITED STATES, 1984 THROUGH 1990

State	Total (million dollars)							Percentage change 1989- 1990
	1984	1985	1986	1987	1988	1989	1990	
Sunbelt states								
Florida	124,279	135,557	146,668	159,299	175,223	191,494	205,210	7.2
Alabama	34,844	36,593	39,365	41,715	45,302	48,086	51,174	6.4
Arizona	32,179	35,609	38,720	41,915	45,447	48,610	51,509	6.0
Arkansas	20,127	21,635	22,748	23,750	25,574	27,273	29,152	6.9
California	335,105	361,967	387,009	413,088	452,228	484,898	520,625	7.4
Georgia	58,010	63,013	69,483	74,728	81,893	86,675	92,102	6.3
Louisiana	42,610	44,103	44,941	44,850	47,637	49,744	53,278	7.1
Mississippi	20,012	20,940	22,156	23,277	25,155	26,691	28,226	5.8
New Mexico	12,783	14,053	14,717	15,341	16,179	17,356	18,549	6.9
North Carolina	58,693	61,892	67,422	72,508	79,706	85,835	91,693	6.8
Oklahoma	32,967	32,695	33,281	33,243	35,430	37,350	39,710	6.3
South Carolina	28,995	30,729	32,914	35,344	38,657	40,990	45,044	9.9
Tennessee	44,235	46,701	50,763	54,851	60,040	63,666	67,361	5.8
Texas	177,326	190,620	196,658	200,567	214,594	229,361	247,629	8.0
Virginia	65,146	70,045	76,295	82,327	90,366	97,524	103,124	5.7
Other populous states								
Illinois	139,042	146,348	154,318	161,541	176,078	187,793	197,834	5.3
Indiana	56,201	58,655	62,210	65,956	70,660	75,479	79,879	5.8
Massachusetts	74,449	79,649	85,641	93,448	104,555	110,552	114,173	3.3
Michigan	100,991	107,933	115,450	120,121	129,520	137,690	144,589	5.0
New Jersey	105,953	113,608	120,621	131,641	146,547	155,789	163,891	5.2
New York	219,711	231,039	246,376	260,446	287,165	305,827	325,600	6.5
Ohio	116,194	121,796	127,987	133,886	144,816	153,433	162,079	5.6
Pennsylvania	130,600	138,599	146,877	154,197	167,632	179,799	190,523	6.0
United States 1/	2,662	2,832	3,008	3,184	3,468	3,710	3,949	6.4

See footnotes at end of table.   Continued . . .

Florida Statistical Abstract 1991

Table 5.08. PERSONAL INCOME: TOTAL AND PER CAPITA DISPOSABLE PERSONAL INCOME
   IN FLORIDA, OTHER SUNBELT STATES, OTHER POPULOUS STATES, AND THE
   UNITED STATES, 1984 THROUGH 1990 (Continued)

							1990	
								Rank among
State	1984	1985	1986	1987	1988	1989	Amount	states
Sunbelt states								
Florida	11,244	11,924	12,547	13,249	14,201	15,113	15,861	18
Alabama	8,730	9,099	9,718	10,214	11,042	11,676	12,665	43
Arizona	10,540	11,264	11,801	12,339	13,047	13,669	14,053	34
Arkansas	8,578	9,168	9,593	9,944	10,675	11,337	12,401	46
California	13,000	13,734	14,334	14,937	15,967	16,684	17,494	8
Georgia	9,925	10,544	11,388	11,998	12,919	13,468	14,217	33
Louisiana	9,550	9,835	9,991	10,082	10,809	11,353	12,625	44
Mississippi	7,700	8,011	8,442	8,870	9,599	10,182	10,969	50
New Mexico	8,962	9,690	9,963	10,255	10,716	11,358	12,243	48
North Carolina	9,516	9,889	10,655	11,311	12,283	13,063	13,833	36
Oklahoma	9,928	9,864	10,073	10,169	10,956	11,584	12,624	45
South Carolina	8,794	9,214	9,734	10,317	11,158	11,672	12,919	41
Tennessee	9,356	9,797	10,574	11,296	12,259	12,888	13,811	37
Texas	11,028	11,639	11,790	11,954	12,747	13,499	14,578	29
Virginia	11,561	12,280	13,159	13,917	15,028	15,994	16,667	11
Other populous states								
Illinois	12,064	12,683	13,356	13,944	15,162	16,109	17,307	9
Indiana	10,234	10,664	11,303	11,925	12,711	13,496	14,408	31
Massachusetts	12,847	13,677	14,677	15,957	17,751	18,696	18,977	4
Michigan	11,147	11,876	12,627	13,049	14,018	14,848	15,555	20
New Jersey	14,094	15,012	15,818	17,152	18,988	20,138	21,201	2
New York	12,394	13,003	13,836	14,601	16,035	17,037	18,098	7
Ohio	10,788	11,304	11,874	12,378	13,329	14,067	14,942	24
Pennsylvania	10,982	11,681	12,346	12,911	13,971	14,934	16,035	16
United States	11,257	11,863	12,474	13,081	14,109	14,945	15,878	(X)

Per capita (amounts in dollars)

(X) Not applicable.
1/ In hundred million dollars.
    Note: Disposable personal income is equal to total personal income less personal
tax and nontax payments. Personal taxes are tax payments by persons (except
personal contributions to social insurance) and include income, estate and gift, and
personal property taxes. Nontaxes include passport fees, fines and penalties,
donations, and tuitions and fees paid to government schools and hospitals. 1984
through 1989 data are revised; 1990 data are preliminary.

    Source: U.S., Department of Commerce, Bureau of Economic Analysis, *Survey of
Current Business*, April 1991.

Florida Statistical Abstract 1991

Table 5.09. PERSONAL INCOME: TOTAL AMOUNT ON A PLACE-OF-RESIDENCE BASIS IN THE STATE AND COUNTIES OF FLORIDA, 1979 THROUGH 1989

(in millions, rounded to thousands of dollars)

County	1979	1980	1981	1982	1983	1984	1985	1986	1987	1988	1989
Florida	82,565.5	96,078.1	110,295.8	118,530.3	130,641.3	143,926.3	158,411.4	171,115.7	187,065.4	204,478.7	224,410.3
Alachua	1,008.3	1,154.4	1,320.6	1,452.3	1,583.8	1,766.8	1,952.1	2,098.5	2,288.5	2,493.1	2,735.8
Baker	84.3	94.8	103.7	118.7	129.2	148.0	159.9	175.4	190.4	205.0	221.5
Bay	674.8	771.7	879.1	960.3	1,055.5	1,177.7	1,295.9	1,400.0	1,489.8	1,6-5.7	1,747.3
Bradford	104.2	118.5	132.4	146.5	159.7	176.4	191.1	202.4	210.1	226.6	250.3
Brevard	2,254.8	2,695.8	3,110.2	3,398.7	3,771.3	4,227.6	4,716.1	5,037.2	5,486.4	5,992.1	6,618.4
Broward	10,406.0	12,193.4	14,150.1	14,862.0	16,239.0	17,720.5	19,227.0	20,440.4	22,219.5	24,244.0	26,469.9
Calhoun	47.8	49.4	53.3	54.6	58.3	62.6	67.8	73.1	77.8	89.3	96.3
Charlotte	476.8	572.3	673.1	721.2	814.5	932.2	1,073.0	1,187.3	1,330.2	1,463.5	1,670.3
Citrus	315.9	385.6	466.3	519.0	588.6	707.3	823.5	907.7	994.6	1,079.7	1,213.9
Clay	511.4	608.4	706.7	784.7	895.9	1,011.7	1,144.3	1,273.8	1,389.9	1,520.7	1,658.0
Collier	916.6	1,071.7	1,311.5	1,419.2	1,600.0	1,787.9	2,028.2	2,281.6	2,686.5	2,979.0	3,413.0
Columbia	223.9	252.6	282.8	306.1	330.4	360.6	384.0	407.5	431.7	470.8	509.8
Dade	14,691.7	16,807.7	18,678.1	19,794.0	21,016.1	22,686.6	24,257.2	25,717.0	27,952.2	30,481.5	32,963.6
De Soto	128.5	144.2	148.1	153.3	165.3	178.0	192.5	207.8	224.2	250.8	270.7
Dixie	38.2	44.0	49.4	54.3	62.5	65.8	70.8	76.5	83.2	92.3	103.4
Duval	4,629.9	5,213.3	5,871.5	6,408.6	6,901.5	7,643.5	8,305.7	8,913.1	9,601.1	10,315.3	11,056.2
Escambia	1,682.4	1,880.5	2,154.5	2,317.8	2,513.8	2,716.4	2,902.5	3,102.0	3,287.3	3,518.5	3,793.2
Flagler	79.4	93.9	114.8	125.0	146.3	170.0	200.9	227.2	269.8	308.9	348.4
Franklin	41.8	47.0	50.1	51.7	58.5	62.7	71.3	78.2	81.9	94.4	103.1
Gadsden	203.1	227.3	247.9	265.0	292.6	316.5	338.4	374.1	405.6	442.4	483.5
Gilchrist	38.9	42.6	48.0	54.5	60.9	66.4	73.5	78.3	83.9	92.3	100.5

See footnote at end of table.

Continued . . .

Table 5.09. PERSONAL INCOME: TOTAL AMOUNT ON A PLACE-OF-RESIDENCE BASIS IN THE STATE AND COUNTIES OF FLORIDA, 1979 THROUGH 1989 (Continued)

(in millions, rounded to thousands of dollars)

County	1979	1980	1981	1982	1983	1984	1985	1986	1987	1988	1989
Glades	28.4	35.1	37.5	41.5	52.7	49.4	54.0	56.5	53.5	57.7	60.7
Gulf	70.0	72.0	80.9	86.3	93.0	99.6	104.4	114.2	119.1	128.1	135.7
Hamilton	52.1	57.7	65.2	66.3	66.5	76.2	78.7	83.0	87.7	97.5	106.5
Hardee	145.4	169.8	166.2	166.8	183.5	189.1	203.4	211.8	223.6	254.5	266.1
Hendry	156.7	193.1	196.7	222.4	279.9	256.9	267.2	280.8	299.6	340.7	356.9
Hernando	285.4	348.9	423.9	473.1	573.8	664.1	804.2	918.9	1,030.9	1,136.4	1,281.0
Highlands	348.9	411.2	445.0	488.7	544.0	592.5	669.3	738.7	793.2	877.9	963.9
Hillsborough	4,830.9	5,593.9	6,410.5	7,000.7	7,740.2	8,628.8	9,497.0	10,298.2	11,213.7	12,283.2	13,402.1
Holmes	72.9	79.8	94.8	100.6	108.1	122.5	126.8	136.9	143.1	154.7	170.7
Indian River	583.0	683.8	823.0	857.1	944.5	1,064.1	1,219.7	1,318.8	1,498.7	1,658.8	1,880.8
Jackson	221.9	234.1	273.0	284.5	298.9	329.7	355.3	374.3	409.1	442.0	480.7
Jefferson	63.8	69.5	74.0	78.2	83.1	90.3	98.8	107.6	113.7	123.4	129.0
Lafayette	24.4	26.6	35.3	38.1	38.5	46.5	49.0	56.2	57.0	59.7	66.8
Lake	879.9	1,052.4	1,143.6	1,220.7	1,446.0	1,581.7	1,782.9	1,947.7	2,134.5	2,366.0	2,600.4
Lee	1,760.8	2,105.5	2,487.8	2,649.3	2,983.7	3,350.8	3,813.3	4,237.5	4,743.6	5,209.6	5,858.2
Leon	1,061.0	1,213.5	1,379.7	1,490.2	1,636.8	1,785.5	1,949.4	2,171.3	2,407.8	2,665.8	2,942.5
Levy	116.8	131.1	152.4	161.2	179.0	193.7	210.5	229.7	248.0	265.6	291.5
Liberty	22.1	25.2	28.4	31.1	35.3	39.3	41.2	44.3	46.7	50.4	55.9
Madison	85.5	88.2	100.2	102.5	109.5	119.4	127.2	137.2	146.4	159.8	173.9
Manatee	1,285.6	1,522.7	1,766.1	1,914.1	2,153.7	2,323.9	2,528.0	2,718.5	2,921.6	3,164.0	3,529.7
Marion	772.3	926.9	1,081.3	1,203.5	1,347.8	1,506.1	1,712.2	1,894.2	2,091.0	2,278.6	2,524.6
Martin	650.8	812.2	969.2	1,063.3	1,190.4	1,341.2	1,539.4	1,707.6	1,939.7	2,143.4	2,393.7
Monroe	510.1	568.3	647.7	689.5	750.7	823.8	931.9	1,052.7	1,175.2	1,279.2	1,418.3
Nassau	247.2	288.4	331.3	353.4	391.9	445.6	499.2	556.5	621.6	666.0	721.4

See footnote at end of table.

Continued . . .

Table 5.09. PERSONAL INCOME: TOTAL AMOUNT ON A PLACE-OF-RESIDENCE BASIS IN THE STATE AND COUNTIES OF FLORIDA, 1979 THROUGH 1989 (Continued)

(In millions, rounded to thousands of dollars)

County	1979	1980	1981	1982	1983	1984	1985	1986	1987	1988	1989
Okaloosa	777.2	874.0	1,021.2	1,121.2	1,251.6	1,376.4	1,511.6	1,651.2	1,813.5	1,953.8	2,124.2
Okeechobee	121.1	147.4	168.9	178.8	192.2	213.6	246.7	275.4	296.8	318.0	346.9
Orange	3,823.8	4,431.2	5,090.2	5,594.4	6,303.2	7,010.5	7,782.6	8,536.7	9,419.6	10,383.8	11,409.3
Osceola	353.8	432.0	508.2	565.5	738.8	873.9	1,042.1	1,169.3	1,303.3	1,470.4	1,661.9
Palm Beach	6,256.3	7,469.7	8,947.6	9,635.9	10,935.0	12,249.3	13,970.8	15,219.0	17,000.9	18,610.9	20,707.4
Pasco	1,281.9	1,562.5	1,817.8	1,970.9	2,212.8	2,443.2	2,703.0	2,957.1	3,163.7	3,446.4	3,769.6
Pinellas	6,663.9	7,710.5	8,895.2	9,593.1	10,710.0	11,775.3	12,857.5	13,661.8	14,665.7	15,928.9	17,554.0
Polk	2,499.2	2,924.6	3,177.4	3,279.1	3,538.6	3,825.8	4,130.5	4,412.1	4,774.5	5,294.4	5,767.8
Putnam	290.6	331.9	391.7	436.0	467.9	495.9	546.0	594.6	623.6	671.2	719.2
St. Johns	414.8	485.8	577.9	636.1	733.0	834.0	961.6	1,096.5	1,240.6	1,356.9	1,528.2
St. Lucie	661.5	819.5	937.5	1,007.6	1,129.1	1,168.1	1,279.6	1,400.0	1,552.6	1,746.3	1,913.6
Santa Rosa	381.1	433.7	502.4	553.9	612.0	681.2	738.7	797.8	882.4	955.0	1,030.8
Sarasota	2,181.0	2,526.0	2,983.5	3,148.0	3,535.5	3,953.3	4,410.9	4,776.1	5,267.1	5,739.7	6,401.6
Seminole	1,429.5	1,729.1	2,020.6	2,295.2	2,423.1	2,709.6	3,004.5	3,396.8	3,788.8	4,214.4	4,633.8
Sumter	136.6	155.6	175.1	188.5	213.7	234.0	259.9	284.2	310.7	336.9	372.6
Suwannee	127.6	140.5	165.8	179.2	189.4	214.7	223.5	248.2	255.6	280.5	306.7
Taylor	103.2	117.7	137.0	149.2	156.2	166.4	175.2	189.9	194.8	210.7	227.3
Union	42.0	44.8	52.2	57.3	61.6	68.7	72.4	79.4	86.2	91.8	97.5
Volusia	1,929.1	2,276.3	2,638.2	2,842.8	3,180.1	3,499.9	3,887.9	4,215.8	4,588.5	5,027.4	5,553.0
Wakulla	59.7	68.7	76.8	83.0	91.3	98.9	110.1	122.7	134.5	151.6	167.0
Walton	116.1	129.7	147.7	159.1	177.5	199.7	219.1	237.5	245.4	270.8	298.2
Washington	81.0	88.0	96.9	104.9	113.8	128.1	133.4	141.2	152.9	163.4	181.7

Note: Some data are revised.

Source: U.S., Department of Commerce, Bureau of Economic Analysis, unpublished data.

Table 5.10. PERSONAL INCOME: PER CAPITA AMOUNTS ON A PLACE-OF-RESIDENCE BASIS IN THE UNITED STATES AND THE STATE AND COUNTIES OF FLORIDA, 1979 THROUGH 1989

(rounded to dollars)

County	1979	1980	1981	1982	1983	1984	1985	1986	1987	1988	1989
United States	9,033	9,919	10,949	11,482	12,100	13,116	13,899	14,597	15,425	16,510	17,592
Florida	8,718	9,764	10,820	11,318	12,149	13,029	13,939	14,639	15,559	16,577	17,715
Alachua	6,905	7,576	8,462	9,031	9,625	10,461	11,240	11,875	12,695	13,631	14,719
Baker	5,595	6,150	6,522	7,299	7,711	8,725	9,248	9,871	10,497	11,046	11,670
Bay	6,920	7,844	8,730	9,210	9,892	10,681	11,306	11,721	12,094	12,875	13,524
Bradford	5,413	5,874	6,400	6,740	6,879	7,523	8,003	8,367	8,547	9,172	10,029
Brevard	8,572	9,766	10,807	11,230	11,953	12,797	13,570	13,944	14,673	15,432	16,445
Broward	10,549	11,890	13,447	13,874	14,937	16,095	17,164	17,947	19,101	20,425	21,898
Calhoun	5,260	5,297	5,672	5,861	6,127	6,537	7,006	7,559	7,923	8,726	9,243
Charlotte	8,621	9,632	10,661	10,694	11,522	12,426	13,501	14,073	14,832	15,416	16,600
Citrus	6,125	6,907	7,744	8,120	8,600	9,694	10,684	10,985	11,375	11,793	12,559
Clay	7,948	8,969	9,981	10,604	11,614	12,311	13,066	13,851	14,409	15,138	15,785
Collier	11,193	12,238	13,986	14,108	15,190	16,043	17,318	18,465	20,547	21,504	23,322
Columbia	6,493	7,078	7,693	8,170	8,667	9,184	9,547	9,936	10,415	11,187	11,947
Dade	9,272	10,238	10,968	11,559	12,201	13,115	13,905	14,577	15,643	16,808	17,963
De Soto	6,928	7,522	7,531	7,587	8,053	8,463	8,997	9,555	10,046	11,055	11,712
Dixie	5,147	5,633	6,146	6,441	6,989	7,234	7,641	7,995	8,334	8,954	9,690
Duval	8,251	9,089	10,074	10,851	11,430	12,446	13,182	13,766	14,479	15,317	16,074
Escambia	7,200	7,981	8,887	9,339	9,927	10,493	11,039	11,480	11,907	12,633	13,375
Flagler	7,610	8,378	9,269	9,488	10,332	10,955	11,885	12,144	12,947	13,296	13,506
Franklin	5,530	6,111	6,443	6,529	7,304	7,558	8,621	9,454	9,768	11,147	12,100
Gadsden	4,969	5,429	5,829	6,182	6,750	7,251	7,627	8,342	8,894	9,651	10,445
Gilchrist	6,829	7,236	7,555	8,151	8,978	9,440	10,145	10,744	11,392	12,094	12,947

See footnote at end of table.

Continued . . .

Table 5.10. PERSONAL INCOME: PER CAPITA AMOUNTS ON A PLACE-OF-RESIDENCE BASIS IN THE UNITED STATES AND THE STATE AND COUNTIES OF FLORIDA, 1979 THROUGH 1989 (Continued)

(rounded to dollars)

County	1979	1980	1981	1982	1983	1984	1985	1986	1987	1988	1989
Glades	4,828	5,833	6,105	6,582	8,300	7,428	7,958	8,369	7,794	8,380	8,776
Gulf	6,649	6,748	7,561	7,844	8,337	8,736	8,880	9,562	9,806	10,374	10,824
Hamilton	5,901	6,558	7,271	7,298	7,301	8,194	8,427	8,959	9,284	9,971	10,733
Hardee	7,511	8,302	7,997	7,949	8,813	9,038	9,611	9,763	10,250	11,695	12,128
Hendry	8,748	10,240	9,900	10,818	13,082	11,656	11,816	11,976	12,267	13,560	13,728
Hernando	7,036	7,621	8,326	8,467	9,377	9,761	10,751	11,414	11,842	12,113	12,676
Highlands	7,613	8,538	8,791	9,250	9,977	10,455	11,363	12,090	12,354	13,199	13,932
Hillsborough	7,567	8,582	9,568	10,191	10,930	11,815	12,584	13,276	14,091	15,070	16,044
Holmes	4,831	5,380	6,210	6,455	6,906	7,755	7,986	8,511	8,809	9,286	10,096
Indian River	10,067	11,247	12,807	12,582	13,230	14,174	15,690	16,291	17,944	19,090	20,880
Jackson	5,616	5,951	6,829	7,075	7,423	8,089	8,587	9,013	9,621	10,388	11,205
Jefferson	6,056	6,455	6,735	6,946	7,301	7,738	8,531	9,235	9,618	10,278	10,628
Lafayette	6,161	6,578	8,619	9,122	9,011	10,503	10,961	11,662	10,820	11,003	11,554
Lake	8,669	9,936	10,405	10,729	12,212	12,793	13,910	14,820	15,484	16,648	17,698
Lee	9,143	10,119	11,369	11,479	12,353	13,132	14,290	15,075	16,017	16,852	18,063
Leon	7,459	8,097	8,937	9,418	10,113	10,752	11,484	12,572	13,556	14,585	15,724
Levy	6,055	6,516	7,243	7,291	7,881	8,286	8,705	9,199	9,720	10,165	10,884
Liberty	5,269	5,916	6,657	7,137	7,782	8,719	9,178	9,640	9,955	10,983	12,110
Madison	5,771	5,901	6,613	6,726	7,140	7,731	8,224	8,791	9,317	10,110	10,934
Manatee	8,951	10,150	11,317	11,866	13,015	13,705	14,477	15,210	15,986	16,927	18,482
Marion	6,556	7,450	8,198	8,642	9,105	9,691	10,392	10,897	11,463	12,003	12,699
Martin	10,647	12,499	14,106	14,600	15,658	16,888	18,573	19,627	21,107	22,371	23,832
Monroe	7,898	8,917	9,844	10,285	11,010	11,758	13,116	14,414	15,666	16,636	17,986
Nassau	7,586	8,698	9,696	9,928	10,763	11,713	12,528	13,329	14,241	14,731	15,316

Continued . . .

See footnote at end of table.

Table 5.10. PERSONAL INCOME: PER CAPITA AMOUNTS ON A PLACE-OF-RESIDENCE BASIS IN THE UNITED STATES AND COUNTIES OF FLORIDA, 1979 THROUGH 1989 (Continued)

(rounded to dollars)

County	1979	1980	1981	1982	1983	1984	1985	1986	1987	1988	1989
Okaloosa	6,981	7,881	8,911	9,443	10,049	10,605	11,189	11,731	12,409	12,974	13,619
Okeechobee	6,072	7,150	7,682	7,668	8,077	8,611	9,478	9,985	10,365	10,711	11,193
Orange	8,272	9,340	10,439	11,144	12,136	13,038	14,023	14,848	15,849	16,980	18,083
Osceola	7,617	8,540	9,130	9,458	11,459	12,413	13,579	14,685	15,421	16,390	17,596
Palm Beach	11,356	12,753	14,422	14,922	16,378	17,662	19,288	20,191	21,636	22,739	24,319
Pasco	6,950	7,951	8,761	9,085	9,848	10,628	11,395	11,888	12,281	12,995	13,710
Pinellas	9,387	10,524	11,900	12,639	13,819	14,896	15,995	16,873	17,976	19,402	21,255
Polk	7,992	9,020	9,515	9,600	10,150	10,691	11,212	11,684	12,352	13,377	14,246
Putnam	5,888	6,531	7,566	8,120	8,372	8,638	9,303	9,857	9,951	10,756	11,304
St. Johns	8,528	9,340	10,558	11,091	12,201	13,083	14,161	15,291	16,608	17,318	18,436
St. Lucie	8,058	9,215	9,814	9,919	10,589	10,439	11,056	11,405	11,999	12,841	13,349
Santa Rosa	6,866	7,676	8,595	9,259	9,955	10,720	11,306	11,870	12,650	13,370	14,023
Sarasota	11,185	12,362	14,057	14,318	15,431	16,698	18,117	19,160	20,639	22,023	24,039
Seminole	8,375	9,495	10,573	11,496	11,480	12,273	13,011	13,766	14,665	15,614	16,316
Sumter	5,856	6,356	6,940	7,228	7,926	8,379	8,952	9,423	10,069	10,689	11,517
Suwannee	5,690	6,246	7,134	7,499	7,746	8,564	8,782	9,530	9,670	10,441	11,225
Taylor	6,154	7,067	8,002	8,549	8,844	9,287	9,635	10,210	10,273	11,016	11,700
Union	3,983	4,402	5,108	5,210	5,725	6,427	6,773	7,566	8,158	8,811	9,452
Volusia	7,704	8,706	9,709	10,082	10,909	11,646	12,509	13,074	13,702	14,432	15,364
Wakulla	5,707	6,286	6,951	7,216	7,576	7,818	8,395	9,166	9,842	10,659	11,438
Walton	5,705	6,046	6,699	6,929	7,491	8,067	8,461	8,820	8,856	9,573	10,245
Washington	5,627	6,034	6,515	6,913	7,349	8,154	8,451	8,893	9,397	10,181	10,741

Note: Some data are revised.

Source: U.S., Department of Commerce, Bureau of Economic Analysis, unpublished data.

Table 5.11.   PERSONAL INCOME: TOTAL AND PER CAPITA AMOUNTS ON A PLACE-OF-RESIDENCE
BASIS IN THE STATE AND METROPOLITAN AREAS OF FLORIDA, 1987, 1988, AND 1989

Metropolitan area	Total personal income ($1,000,000)			Per capita personal income (dollars)		
	1987	1988	1989	1987	1988	1989
Florida	187,065.4	204,478.7	224,410.3	15,589	16,587	17,739
Bradenton	2,921.6	3,164.0	3,529.7	15,096	15,846	17,159
Daytona Beach	4,588.5	5,027.4	5,553.0	13,753	14,462	15,418
Ft. Lauderdale-Hollywood-						
Pompano Beach	22,219.5	24,244.0	26,469.9	18,881	20,091	21,477
Ft. Myers-Cape Coral	4,743.6	5,209.6	5,858.2	15,779	16,680	18,004
Ft. Pierce	3,492.3	3,889.7	4,307.2	16,036	17,044	17,924
Martin County	1,939.7	2,143.4	2,393.7	21,964	23,309	24,878
St. Lucie County	1,552.6	1,746.3	1,913.6	11,993	12,815	13,280
Ft. Walton Beach	1,813.5	1,953.8	2,124.2	13,185	13,974	14,999
Gainesville	2,498.7	2,719.7	2,986.1	12,701	13,661	14,777
Alachua County	2,288.5	2,493.1	2,735.8	13,161	14,161	15,279
Bradford County	210.1	226.6	250.3	9,199	9,836	10,876
Jacksonville	12,853.2	13,868.9	14,963.8	14,998	15,844	16,776
Clay County	1,389.9	1,520.7	1,658.0	14,520	15,435	16,094
Duval County	9,601.1	10,315.3	11,056.2	14,864	15,715	16,665
Nassau County	621.6	666.0	721.4	15,100	15,871	16,584
St. Johns County	1,240.6	1,366.9	1,528.2	16,720	17,451	18,634
Lakeland-Winter Haven	4,774.5	5,294.4	5,767.8	12,466	13,519	14,455
Melbourne-Titusville-						
Palm Bay	5,486.4	5,992.1	6,618.4	15,113	15,922	17,041
Miami-Hialeah	27,952.2	30,481.5	32,963.6	15,136	16,221	17,268
Naples	2,686.5	2,979.0	3,413.0	21,032	22,016	23,742
Ocala	2,091.0	2,278.6	2,524.6	12,004	12,599	13,424
Orlando	14,511.7	16,069.1	17,705.0	15,408	16,361	17,178
Orange County	9,419.6	10,383.8	11,409.3	15,625	16,686	17,488
Osceola County	1,303.3	1,470.9	1,661.9	14,887	15,450	16,459
Seminole County	3,788.8	4,214.4	4,633.8	15,070	15,924	16,709
Panama City	1,489.8	1,615.7	1,747.3	12,159	12,987	13,888
Pensacola	4,169.7	4,473.5	4,823.9	12,551	13,311	14,159
Escambia County	3,287.3	3,518.5	3,793.2	12,694	13,510	14,500
Santa Rosa County	882.4	955.0	1,030.8	12,044	12,628	13,033
Sarasota	5,267.1	5,739.7	6,401.6	20,407	21,718	23,587
Tallahassee	2,813.4	3,108.2	3,426.0	13,035	14,109	14,990
Gadsden County	405.6	442.4	483.5	9,797	10,678	11,770
Leon County	2,407.8	2,665.8	2,942.5	13,804	14,903	15,696
Tampa-St. Petersburg-						
Clearwater	30,074.0	32,794.8	36,006.7	15,348	16,389	17,675
Hernando County	1,030.9	1,136.4	1,281.0	12,363	12,551	13,410
Hillsborough County	11,213.7	12,283.2	13,402.1	14,154	15,174	16,292
Pasco County	3,163.7	3,446.4	3,769.6	12,251	12,909	13,739
Pinellas County	14,665.7	15,928.9	17,554.0	17,762	19,100	20,783
West Palm Beach-Boca						
Raton-Delray Beach	17,000.9	18,610.9	20,707.4	21,662	22,765	24,608

Note: Data for Metropolitan Statistical Areas (MSAs) and Primary Metropolitan
Statisitcal Areas (PMSAs) defined as of June 30, 1989.   See Glossary for definitions
and map at the front of the book for area boundaries.   Data for 1987 and 1988 are
revised.
    Source: U.S., Department of Commerce, Bureau of Economic Analysis, unpublished
data.

Florida Statistical Abstract 1991

Table 5.12. PERSONAL INCOME: PER CAPITA AMOUNTS BY TYPE IN THE UNITED STATES AND THE STATE AND COUNTIES OF FLORIDA 1988 AND 1989

(rounded to dollars)

| County | 1988 | | | | | | 1989 | | | | | |
| | | | Transfer payments | | | | | | Transfer payments | | | |
	Total personal income	Nonfarm personal income	Income mainte- nance 1/	Unem- ploy- ment insur- ance	Retire- ment and other	Dividends interest and rent	Total personal income	Nonfarm personal income	Income mainte- nance 1/	Unem- ploy- ment insur- ance	Retire- ment and other	Dividends interest and rent
United States	16,475	16,279	204	56	1,275	2,706	17,555	17,349	218	60	1,346	3,078
Florida	16,587	16,378	122	27	1,572	3,964	17,739	17,545	136	30	1,657	4,547
Alachua	14,161	14,054	161	14	1,099	2,129	15,279	15,163	181	17	1,189	2,458
Baker	11,520	10,966	152	26	903	810	12,206	11,633	166	28	988	937
Bay	12,987	12,981	134	39	1,605	1,887	13,883	13,883	156	44	1,731	2,193
Bradford	9,836	9,547	172	13	1,128	1,045	10,876	10,495	194	14	1,231	1,231
Brevard	15,922	15,865	78	26	1,855	2,934	17,041	16,994	89	30	1,976	3,341
Broward	20,091	20,061	62	30	1,589	5,609	21,477	21,450	74	37	1,675	6,466
Calhoun	8,804	8,550	335	36	1,215	1,081	8,916	8,782	338	31	1,235	1,200
Charlotte	15,092	14,969	43	11	2,701	5,823	16,186	16,086	50	13	2,848	6,456
Citrus	12,572	12,531	86	31	2,587	4,181	13,422	13,386	99	34	2,632	4,694
Clay	15,435	15,360	53	19	1,447	1,621	16,094	16,026	59	21	1,433	1,816
Collier	22,016	21,535	72	18	1,896	9,425	23,742	23,187	77	18	1,921	10,452
Columbia	11,461	11,312	196	31	1,373	1,449	12,154	12,002	220	34	1,441	1,673
Dade	16,221	16,137	236	36	990	3,254	17,268	17,180	259	40	1,025	3,765
De Soto	10,958	10,285	171	12	1,539	1,956	11,505	11,006	189	15	1,600	2,252
Dixie	9,382	9,240	311	23	1,237	1,260	10,128	10,000	303	24	1,496	1,445
Duval	15,715	15,694	150	28	1,237	1,990	16,665	16,645	170	29	1,338	2,310
Escambia	13,510	13,497	192	23	1,678	1,798	14,500	14,496	219	21	1,803	2,098
Flagler	13,370	13,010	70	17	2,366	3,421	13,408	13,013	80	21	2,400	3,588
Franklin	10,819	10,819	477	25	1,382	2,013	11,715	11,715	385	28	1,486	2,354
Gadsden	10,678	10,068	346	17	1,066	1,176	11,770	11,138	391	19	1,170	1,395
Gilchrist	10,829	9,176	132	20	1,204	1,471	11,033	9,595	141	20	1,256	1,635
Glades	8,059	5,824	120	38	782	1,584	8,297	6,320	141	35	840	1,836
Gulf	11,402	11,402	273	29	1,409	1,298	12,039	12,039	270	32	1,565	1,523

Continued . . .

See footnotes at end of table.

Table 5.12. PERSONAL INCOME: PER CAPITA AMOUNTS BY TYPE IN THE UNITED STATES AND THE STATE AND COUNTIES OF FLORIDA 1988 AND 1989 (Continued)

(rounded to dollars)

County	1988 Total personal income	1988 Nonfarm personal income	1988 Transfer payments Income mainte-nance 1/	1988 Transfer payments Unem-ploy-ment insur-ance	1988 Transfer payments Retire-ment and other	1988 Dividends interest and rent	1989 Total personal income	1989 Nonfarm personal income	1989 Transfer payments Income mainte-nance 1/	1989 Transfer payments Unem-ploy-ment insur-ance	1989 Transfer payments Retire-ment and other	1989 Dividends interest and rent
Hamilton	9,687	9,407	334	23	1,041	868	10,015	9,798	349	17	1,103	973
Hardee	12,814	10,170	238	22	1,010	1,939	13,542	11,387	261	32	1,143	2,318
Hendry	13,742	10,244	184	54	872	1,776	14,122	11,079	207	52	930	2,059
Hernando	12,551	12,393	85	23	2,605	3,262	13,410	13,272	100	24	2,677	3,658
Highlands	13,656	12,470	111	21	2,267	4,217	14,517	13,554	129	23	2,422	4,826
Hillsborough	15,174	14,953	132	30	1,181	2,217	16,292	16,077	149	32	1,250	2,563
Holmes	10,165	9,614	297	21	1,360	1,254	10,985	10,357	325	18	1,440	1,451
Indian River	19,829	19,171	67	33	2,332	8,018	21,666	21,144	72	32	2,501	9,103
Jackson	10,732	10,420	238	22	1,275	1,291	11,663	11,383	258	19	1,396	1,521
Jefferson	10,977	9,564	334	11	1,138	1,391	11,443	10,496	364	13	1,255	1,641
Lafayette	11,392	8,299	150	12	1,173	1,333	12,440	9,049	174	23	1,343	1,548
Lake	16,784	15,352	97	22	2,254	4,488	17,752	16,542	111	27	2,381	5,099
Lee	16,680	16,523	72	14	1,997	5,338	18,004	17,846	80	15	2,102	6,041
Leon	14,903	14,891	109	14	1,073	1,907	15,696	15,689	117	15	1,121	2,133
Levy	10,832	10,416	216	25	1,438	2,034	11,537	11,110	225	20	1,546	2,338
Liberty	10,685	10,637	255	20	1,191	989	11,834	11,806	276	0	1,337	1,167
Madison	10,380	9,995	384	26	1,147	1,666	11,028	10,685	404	23	1,232	1,922
Manatee	15,846	15,342	78	16	1,921	5,000	17,159	16,640	88	18	2,031	5,723
Marion	12,599	12,432	138	21	1,874	2,822	13,424	13,293	153	21	2,005	3,206
Martin	23,309	22,427	55	23	2,187	9,042	24,878	24,130	64	30	2,268	10,180
Monroe	16,951	16,951	74	10	1,245	5,702	18,472	18,472	82	11	1,300	6,589
Nassau	15,817	15,739	108	38	1,047	1,735	16,584	16,500	116	26	1,131	1,982
Okaloosa	13,974	13,964	86	22	1,983	1,953	14,999	14,992	101	23	2,142	2,261
Okeechobee	11,335	10,379	126	25	1,483	1,839	11,988	11,173	140	28	1,597	2,108
Orange	16,686	16,373	97	24	1,215	2,421	17,488	17,207	109	26	1,261	2,712

See footnotes at end of table.

Continued . . .

Table 5.12. PERSONAL INCOME: PER CAPITA AMOUNTS BY TYPE IN THE UNITED STATES AND THE STATE AND COUNTIES OF FLORIDA 1988 AND 1989 (Continued)

(rounded to dollars)

	1988		Transfer payments				1989		Transfer payments			
County	Total personal income	Nonfarm personal income	Income mainte- nance 1/	Unem- ploy- ment insur- ance	Retire- ment and other	Dividends interest and rent	Total personal income	Nonfarm personal income	Income mainte- nance 1/	Unem- ploy- ment insur- ance	Retire- ment and other	Dividends interest and rent
Osceola	15,450	15,161	60	18	1,222	2,151	16,459	16,247	72	25	1,264	2,396
Palm Beach	22,765	22,381	66	33	1,788	8,593	24,608	24,226	74	40	1,901	9,843
Pasco	12,909	12,731	81	20	2,349	3,587	13,739	13,586	93	23	2,324	4,116
Pinellas	19,100	19,083	78	24	2,081	5,450	20,783	20,768	88	25	2,267	6,336
Polk	13,519	12,948	121	38	1,500	2,643	14,455	13,987	135	40	1,571	3,054
Putnam	10,778	10,484	227	30	1,681	1,650	11,252	10,963	256	27	1,713	1,899
St. Johns	17,451	17,087	96	23	1,558	3,672	18,634	18,222	106	24	1,636	4,129
St. Lucie	12,815	12,215	129	44	1,767	2,795	13,280	12,827	140	52	1,839	3,116
Santa Rosa	12,628	12,564	122	26	1,491	1,590	13,033	12,997	132	22	1,529	1,782
Sarasota	21,718	21,666	48	16	2,822	9,210	23,587	23,543	54	16	2,908	10,562
Seminole	15,924	15,843	58	26	1,119	1,942	16,709	16,629	65	31	1,155	2,169
Sumter	11,287	10,772	196	25	1,959	1,999	12,042	11,471	218	24	2,094	2,281
Suwannee	10,912	10,325	211	21	1,528	1,788	11,642	10,959	236	24	1,618	2,069
Taylor	12,261	12,176	213	37	1,244	1,258	13,247	13,165	249	44	1,341	1,488
Union	9,109	8,572	154	10	882	725	9,422	8,772	162	9	904	836
Volusia	14,462	14,268	92	23	2,040	3,875	15,418	15,238	100	26	2,103	4,407
Wakulla	11,215	11,153	209	15	1,161	1,126	12,111	12,054	220	13	1,236	1,305
Walton	10,177	10,081	193	31	1,680	1,526	10,993	10,910	206	27	1,751	1,765
Washington	10,262	9,819	286	28	1,619	1,438	10,834	10,464	307	35	1,697	1,669

1/ Includes supplemental security income payments, payments to families with dependent children (AFDC), general assistance payments, food stamp payments, and other assistance payments, including emergency assistance.

Note: These data were derived by dividing each type of income by the total population of the area, not just the segment of the population receiving that particular type of income. Per capita is computed using Bureau of Economic and Business Research *Estimates of Population* for 1988 and 1989.

Source: U.S., Department of Commerce, Bureau of Economic Analysis, unpublished data.

Table 5.13. PERSONAL INCOME: DERIVATION OF PERSONAL INCOME ON A PLACE-OF-RESIDENCE
BASIS IN THE STATE AND METROPOLITAN AREAS OF FLORIDA, 1989

(rounded to millions of dollars)

Metroplitan area	Total earn- ings by place of work 1/	Less personal contri- butions to social security	Plus resi- dence adjust- ment 2/	Plus dividends interest and rent	Plus transfer payments	Personal income by place of residence
Florida	139,479	8,291	-144	57,524	35,843	224,410
Bradenton	1,676	105	135	1,177	647	3,530
Daytona Beach	2,737	173	207	1,587	1,194	5,553
Ft. Lauderdale-Hollywood- Pompano Beach	13,482	844	2,211	7,970	3,652	26,470
Ft. Myers-Cape Coral	3,000	188	48	1,966	1,032	5,858
Ft. Pierce	2,148	129	137	1,429	722	4,307
Ft. Walton Beach	1,512	85	-72	320	449	2,124
Gainesville	2,214	100	-90	468	493	2,986
Jacksonville	11,395	666	-58	2,144	2,148	14,964
Lakeland-Winter Haven	3,908	229	-145	1,218	1,015	5,768
Melbourne-Titusville- Palm Bay	4,428	268	34	1,297	1,127	6,618
Miami-Hialeah	24,862	1,445	-2,374	7,187	4,734	32,964
Naples	1,667	99	-48	1,503	391	3,413
Ocala	1,381	87	55	603	572	2,525
Orlando	14,315	829	-559	2,613	2,165	17,705
Panama City	1,204	69	-28	276	364	1,747
Pensacola	3,335	190	4	690	985	4,824
Sarasota	2,775	188	-200	2,867	1,148	6,402
Tallahassee	2,744	114	-144	457	483	3,426
Tampa-St. Petersburg- Clearwater	22,029	1,374	66	8,938	6,347	36,007
West Palm Beach-Boca Raton-Delray Beach	10,630	644	-116	8,282	2,555	20,707

1/ Consists of wage and salary disbursements, other labor income, and proprietors' income.

2/ An estimate of the net gain or loss to an area because of commuting from place
of residence to place of work. Some persons earn income in the area in which they
live; others earn income outside that area.

Note: Data are for Metropolitan Statistical Areas (MSAs) and Primary Metropolitan Statistical Areas (PMSAs) defined as of June 30, 1989. See Glossary for
definitions and map at the front of the book for area boundaries.

Source: U.S., Department of Commerce, Bureau of Economic Analysis, unpublished
data.

Florida Statistical Abstract 1991

Table 5.14. PERSONAL INCOME: DERIVATION OF PERSONAL INCOME ON A PLACE-OF-RESIDENCE
BASIS IN THE UNITED STATES AND THE STATE AND COUNTIES OF FLORIDA, 1988 AND
1989

(rounded to millions of dollars)

County	Total earnings by place of work 1/	Less personal contri- butions to social security	Plus resi- dence adjust- ment 2/	Plus dividends interest and rent	Plus transfer payments	Personal income by place of residence
			1988 A/			
United States	2,997,734	193,383	-581	666,458	587,953	4,058,181
Florida	130,895	7,428	-134	48,863	32,282	204,479
Alachua	1,945	85	-128	375	387	2,493
Baker	94	3	66	14	34	205
Bay	1,146	63	-29	235	327	1,616
Bradford	110	5	48	24	50	227
Brevard	4,086	238	25	1,104	1,015	5,992
Broward	12,839	759	2,100	6,768	3,297	24,244
Calhoun	52	3	3	11	26	89
Charlotte	547	37	19	565	370	1,463
Citrus	440	30	-2	359	312	1,080
Clay	542	30	640	160	209	1,521
Collier	1,470	84	-38	1,275	356	2,979
Columbia	279	14	45	60	102	471
Dade	23,784	1,333	-2,257	6,115	4,172	30,482
De Soto	137	6	13	45	62	251
Dixie	49	2	8	12	25	92
Duval	9,404	535	-1,315	1,306	1,456	10,315
Escambia	2,742	151	-263	468	722	3,519
Flagler	152	9	15	79	72	309
Franklin	48	3	6	18	26	94
Gadsden	275	11	30	49	100	442
Gilchrist	44	1	17	13	20	92
Glades	35	1	1	11	12	58
Gulf	89	5	0	15	30	128
Hamilton	114	6	-43	9	24	98
Hardee	154	6	28	39	40	255
Hendry	244	8	18	44	43	341
Hernando	411	28	141	295	317	1,136
Highlands	417	23	-5	271	217	878
Hillsborough	10,406	577	-1,052	1,795	1,712	12,283
Holmes	65	3	32	19	42	155
Indian River	760	44	-10	671	282	1,659
Jackson	258	12	25	53	118	442
Jefferson	61	3	24	16	26	123
Lafayette	34	1	10	7	10	60

See footnotes at end of table.

Continued . . .

Table 5.14. PERSONAL INCOME: DERIVATION OF PERSONAL INCOME ON A PLACE-OF-RESIDENCE
BASIS IN THE UNITED STATES AND THE STATE AND COUNTIES OF FLORIDA, 1988 AND
1989 (Continued)

(rounded to millions of dollars)

County	Total earnings by place of work 1/	Less personal contri- butions to social security	Plus resi- dence adjust- ment 2/	Plus dividends interest and rent	Plus transfer payments	Personal income by place of residence
			1988 A/	(Continued)		
Lake	1,129	59	202	633	461	2,366
Lee	2,734	162	44	1,667	926	5,210
Leon	2,245	90	-163	341	333	2,666
Levy	114	6	45	50	63	266
Liberty	22	1	9	5	16	50
Madison	88	5	12	26	40	160
Manatee	1,536	90	136	998	584	3,164
Marion	1,284	76	51	510	510	2,279
Martin	973	55	111	831	284	2,143
Monroe	747	41	-13	430	155	1,279
Nassau	300	16	229	73	80	666
Okaloosa	1,419	78	-67	273	407	1,954
Okeechobee	159	8	46	52	69	318
Orange	10,361	579	-2,194	1,507	1,289	10,384
Osceola	682	38	428	205	194	1,471
Palm Beach	10,022	579	-148	7,025	2,291	18,611
Pasco	1,288	90	360	958	930	3,446
Pinellas	8,505	527	608	4,545	2,799	15,929
Polk	3,669	202	-137	1,035	930	5,294
Putnam	373	21	40	103	176	671
St. Johns	543	30	371	288	195	1,367
St. Lucie	1,021	56	36	381	364	1,746
Santa Rosa	413	23	269	120	175	955
Sarasota	2,602	165	-188	2,434	1,057	5,740
Seminole	2,077	117	1,272	514	469	4,214
Sumter	146	8	46	60	94	337
Suwannee	156	8	16	46	70	281
Taylor	154	9	2	22	41	211
Union	77	2	-7	7	17	92
Volusia	2,551	151	188	1,347	1,093	5,027
Wakulla	57	3	54	15	29	152
Walton	126	7	34	41	78	271
Washington	91	4	5	24	53	169

See footnotes at end of table.   Continued . . .

Table 5.14. PERSONAL INCOME: DERIVATION OF PERSONAL INCOME ON A PLACE-OF-RESIDENCE
   BASIS IN THE UNITED STATES AND THE STATE AND COUNTIES OF FLORIDA, 1988 AND
   1989 (Continued)

(rounded to millions of dollars)

County	Total earnings by place of work 1/	Less personal contri- butions to social security	Plus resi- dence adjust- ment 2/	Plus dividends interest and rent	Plus transfer payments	Personal income by place of residence
			1989			
United States	3,177,124	212,117	-587	765,847	637,134	4,367,401
Florida	139,479	8,291	-144	57,524	35,843	224,410
Alachua	2,094	95	-141	440	438	2,736
Baker	100	4	69	17	38	221
Bay	1,204	69	-28	276	364	1,747
Bradford	121	5	51	28	55	250
Brevard	4,428	268	34	1,297	1,127	6,618
Broward	13,482	844	2,211	7,970	3,652	26,470
Calhoun	54	3	3	13	29	96
Charlotte	611	44	18	666	419	1,670
Citrus	488	36	-4	424	342	1,214
Clay	585	34	698	187	222	1,658
Collier	1,667	99	-48	1,503	391	3,413
Columbia	296	16	47	70	112	510
Dade	24,862	1,445	-2,374	7,187	4,734	32,964
De Soto	143	7	13	53	68	271
Dixie	56	3	8	15	28	103
Duval	9,888	579	-1,402	1,532	1,617	11,056
Escambia	2,894	164	-279	549	794	3,793
Flagler	166	10	16	93	83	348
Franklin	51	3	6	21	28	103
Gadsden	289	12	36	57	113	483
Gilchrist	47	2	18	15	23	101
Glades	35	1	1	13	13	61
Gulf	90	5	0	17	34	136
Hamilton	126	7	-50	10	27	106
Hardee	153	7	29	46	45	266
Hendry	249	9	16	52	48	357
Hernando	448	33	164	349	352	1,281
Highlands	433	27	-6	320	243	964
Hillsborough	11,162	640	-1,110	2,108	1,882	13,402
Holmes	71	4	34	23	46	171
Indian River	847	53	-20	790	316	1,881
Jackson	271	14	28	63	133	481
Jefferson	59	3	25	19	29	129
Lafayette	37	1	10	8	12	67
Lake	1,188	69	221	747	513	2,600
Lee	3,000	188	48	1,966	1,032	5,858
Leon	2,455	102	-181	400	370	2,943

See footnotes at end of table.   Continued . . .

Florida Statistical Abstract 1991

Table 5.14. PERSONAL INCOME: DERIVATION OF PERSONAL INCOME ON A PLACE-OF-RESIDENCE
BASIS IN THE UNITED STATES AND THE STATE AND COUNTIES OF FLORIDA, 1988 AND
1989 (Continued)

(rounded to millions of dollars)

County	Total earnings by place of work 1/	Less personal contri- butions to social security	Plus resi- dence adjust- ment 2/	Plus dividends interest and rent	Plus transfer payments	Personal income by place of residence
		1989 (Continued)				
Levy	124	7	45	59	71	292
Liberty	28	1	7	6	17	56
Madison	92	5	12	30	44	174
Manatee	1,676	105	135	1,177	647	3,530
Marion	1,381	87	55	603	572	2,525
Martin	1,054	64	110	979	314	2,394
Monroe	805	46	-15	506	169	1,418
Nassau	325	18	238	86	90	721
Okaloosa	1,512	85	-72	320	449	2,124
Okeechobee	168	9	49	61	79	347
Orange	11,300	651	-2,439	1,769	1,430	11,409
Osceola	761	45	487	242	217	1,662
Palm Beach	10,630	644	-116	8,282	2,555	20,707
Pasco	1,379	106	382	1,129	985	3,770
Pinellas	9,040	594	629	5,351	3,128	17,554
Polk	3,908	229	-145	1,218	1,015	5,768
Putnam	384	22	46	121	190	719
St. Johns	598	35	408	339	218	1,528
St. Lucie	1,094	64	27	449	408	1,914
Santa Rosa	441	26	283	141	191	1,031
Sarasota	2,775	188	-200	2,867	1,148	6,402
Seminole	2,255	133	1,392	602	518	4,634
Sumter	155	9	53	71	104	373
Suwannee	167	9	16	55	78	307
Taylor	163	10	2	26	46	227
Union	80	3	-6	9	18	97
Volusia	2,737	173	207	1,587	1,194	5,553
Wakulla	62	4	58	18	32	167
Walton	141	9	34	48	84	298
Washington	94	5	6	28	58	182

Δ/ Revised.
1/ Consists of wage and salary disbursements, other labor income, and proprietors' income.
2/ An estimate of the net gain or loss to an area because of commuting from place
of residence to place of work. Some persons earn income in the area in which they
live; others earn income outside that area.

Source: U.S., Department of Commerce, Bureau of Economic Analysis, unpublished
data.

Florida Statistical Abstract 1991

Table 5.20. PERSONAL INCOME: TOTAL EARNINGS ON A PLACE-OF-WORK BASIS AND PERCENTAGE DISTRIBUTION BY TYPE AND MAJOR INDUSTRIAL SOURCE IN FLORIDA, OTHER SUNBELT STATES, OTHER POPULOUS STATES, AND THE UNITED STATES, 1989

(income in millions of dollars)

Item	Florida	Sunbelt States										
		Alabama	Arizona	Ar-kansas	Cali-for-nia 1/	Georgia	Loui-siana	Mis-sis-sippi	New Mexico	North Caro-lina 1/	Okla-homa	South Caro-lina 1/
Earnings by place of work	139,457	40,867	39,223	21,894	430,008	79,862	40,348	21,360	14,134	77,418	31,647	36,294
Percentage distribution by type of income												
Wage and salary disbursements	81.4	80.2	82.9	74.6	79.6	81.9	78.9	77.1	80.7	81.4	75.7	83.0
Other labor income	7.1	7.9	7.1	7.6	7.6	7.7	8.2	7.6	7.5	7.3	7.4	7.6
Proprietors income	11.4	11.9	10.0	17.8	12.8	10.4	12.9	15.3	11.8	11.4	16.9	9.4
Percentage distribution by industrial source of income												
Farm	1.7	2.4	1.5	6.5	1.8	1.7	1.5	3.6	2.3	2.2	3.6	1.2
Manufacturing	10.7	23.9	15.5	23.7	18.0	18.3	14.4	24.9	7.8	27.7	15.3	27.1
Mining	0.4	1.3	1.4	0.7	0.5	0.4	5.3	0.8	3.8	0.3	5.4	0.2
Construction	7.2	5.4	7.0	5.3	6.7	5.9	6.5	4.8	6.4	6.5	4.9	6.9
Wholesale trade	6.5	5.7	5.5	5.1	6.4	9.4	5.8	5.0	4.3	6.3	5.6	4.5
Retail trade	12.3	9.1	11.1	10.1	9.5	9.8	9.6	9.9	10.6	10.1	9.8	10.2
Finance, insurance, and real estate	7.6	4.5	7.0	4.4	7.4	6.6	5.1	4.6	4.3	4.6	4.9	4.5
Transportation, communications and public utilities	6.4	7.2	6.2	9.0	5.8	8.8	8.6	7.1	7.4	6.7	7.8	5.9
Services	30.1	20.8	26.2	19.5	28.1	21.9	25.6	18.8	26.1	18.7	22.4	18.7
Other industries 2/	1.0	0.4	0.8	0.6	0.9	0.4	0.6	0.5	0.5	0.5	0.4	0.5
Government	16.0	19.3	17.8	15.2	15.0	16.6	17.1	20.0	26.6	16.4	19.8	20.2

See footnotes at end of table.

Continued . . .

Table 5.20. PERSONAL INCOME: TOTAL EARNINGS ON A PLACE-OF-WORK BASIS AND PERCENTAGE DISTRIBUTION BY TYPE AND MAJOR INDUSTRIAL SOURCE IN FLORIDA, OTHER SUNBELT STATES, OTHER POPULOUS STATES, AND THE UNITED STATES, 1989 (Continued)

(income in millions of dollars)

Item	Sunbelt states (Continued)					Other populous states						United States 1/
	Ten-nessee	Texas	Vir-ginia	Illi-nois	Indi-ana	Massa-chu-setts	Mich-igan	New Jersey	New York	Ohio	Penn-syl-vania	
Earnings by place of work	55,216	197,289	82,548	162,519	65,259	97,843	118,863	121,767	282,024	130,277	146,234	3,177,852
Percentage distribution by type of income												
Wage and salary disbursements	79.6	79.2	83.8	80.2	80.7	82.1	82.8	82.7	82.4	82.9	80.2	80.7
Other labor income	7.7	7.9	7.1	7.8	8.3	7.5	9.2	7.6	6.8	7.9	8.3	7.6
Proprietors income	12.7	12.9	9.2	12.0	10.9	10.4	8.0	9.7	10.9	9.2	11.5	11.7
Percentage distribution by industrial source of income												
Farm	1.2	1.6	0.8	1.4	1.8	0.2	0.7	0.2	0.3	0.7	0.7	1.6
Manufacturing	24.2	16.1	14.6	20.5	32.5	20.2	34.1	19.5	14.8	29.9	22.9	19.7
Mining	0.5	4.1	0.9	0.6	0.6	0.2	0.4	0.2	0.2	0.6	0.9	1.0
Construction	6.2	6.3	7.8	6.0	6.1	6.2	4.9	6.5	5.1	5.3	6.5	6.2
Wholesale trade	6.8	7.1	5.4	8.2	5.5	7.1	5.9	9.0	6.8	6.4	6.3	6.5
Retail trade	10.2	9.8	9.3	8.8	9.4	9.6	8.9	9.1	7.5	9.3	9.5	9.5
Finance, insurance, and real estate	5.2	6.8	5.4	8.5	4.7	7.9	4.4	7.1	14.3	5.2	6.2	7.0
Transportation, communications and public utilities	7.3	7.5	6.9	7.2	6.9	4.8	5.1	7.6	6.0	5.9	6.6	6.6
Services	23.5	24.3	24.5	26.0	19.4	31.4	22.2	26.8	29.4	23.3	27.4	25.5
Other industries 2/	0.4	0.5	0.5	0.4	0.4	0.6	0.3	0.4	0.3	0.4	0.4	0.6
Government	14.6	16.0	23.9	12.2	12.7	11.9	13.1	13.5	15.2	13.0	12.6	15.7

1/ 1989 estimates of protectors' income and of rental income of persons reflect the uninsured losses caused by Hurricane Hugo and by the Loma Prieta earthquake. 2/ Includes agricultural services, forestry, fisheries, and other.
Note: Data differ from figures on other income tables because of revisions made after publication of these numbers.
Source: U.S., Department of Commerce, Bureau of Economic Analysis, Survey of Current Business, August 1990.

Florida Statistical Abstract 1991

Table 5.21. PERSONAL INCOME: AMOUNTS BY MAJOR SOURCE IN THE METROPOLITAN AND NONMETROPOLITAN AREAS OF FLORIDA, THE SOUTHEAST, AND THE UNITED STATES, 1988 AND 1989

(rounded to millions of dollars)

Item	Total	Florida Metro-politan areas	Non-metro-politan areas	Total	Southeast Metro-politan areas	Non-metro-politan areas	Total	United States Metro-politan areas	Non-metro-politan areas
			Income by place of residence, 1988 A/						
Total personal income	204,479	189,515	14,964	848,795	615,501	233,294	4,058,181	3,350,581	707,600
Nonfarm personal income	201,900	187,659	14,241	835,998	611,152	224,846	4,009,918	3,332,520	677,398
Farm personal income	2,579	1,856	723	12,797	4,350	8,448	48,263	18,061	30,202
Derivation of personal income									
Total earnings by place of work	130,895	123,383	7,512	610,542	459,925	150,617	2,997,734	2,550,233	447,501
Less: Personal contributions for social insurance	7,428	7,025	403	36,507	27,395	9,112	193,383	165,453	27,930
Plus: Adjustment for resi-dence	-134	-893	759	3,840	-7,596	11,437	-581	-35,833	35,252
Equals: Net earnings by place of residence	123,333	115,465	7,868	577,875	424,934	152,942	2,803,770	2,348,947	454,823
Plus: Dividends, interest, and rent	48,863	45,023	3,841	138,421	104,447	33,974	666,458	547,027	119,431
Plus: Transfer payments	32,282	29,027	3,255	132,499	86,121	46,379	587,953	454,608	133,345
			Earnings by place of work, 1988 A/						
Components of earnings									
Wages and salaries	106,392	100,991	5,401	493,526	379,848	113,678	2,422,580	2,094,316	328,264
Other labor income	9,293	8,802	491	45,210	34,162	11,048	225,323	193,378	31,945
Proprietors' income	15,210	13,590	1,620	71,807	45,915	25,892	349,831	262,539	87,292
Farm	2,059	1,456	602	10,857	3,598	7,259	39,340	13,750	25,590
Nonfarm	13,151	12,133	1,018	60,950	42,317	18,633	310,491	248,789	61,702

See footnotes at end of table.

Continued . . .

Table 5.21. PERSONAL INCOME: AMOUNTS BY MAJOR SOURCE IN THE METROPOLITAN AND NONMETROPOLITAN AREAS OF FLORIDA, THE SOUTHEAST, AND THE UNITED STATES, 1988 AND 1989 (Continued)

(rounded to millions of dollars)

Item	Florida Total	Florida Metropolitan areas	Florida Non-metropolitan areas	Southeast Total	Southeast Metropolitan areas	Southeast Non-metropolitan areas	United States Total	United States Metropolitan areas	United States Non-metropolitan areas
Earnings by industry									
Earnings by place of work, 1988 A/ (Continued)									
Farm	2,579	1,856	723	12,797	4,350	8,448	48,263	18,061	30,202
Nonfarm	128,316	121,526	6,789	597,745	455,575	142,170	2,949,471	2,532,172	417,299
Private	107,918	102,588	5,329	491,025	375,029	115,996	2,484,564	2,147,595	336,969
Agricultural services 1/	1,307	B/ 1,079	B/ 219	3,639	B/ 2,400	B/ 1,080	17,820	13,386	4,434
Mining	547	B/ 481	(D)	8,181	B/ 3,400	B/ 4,398	32,222	19,163	13,059
Construction	10,008	9,398	B/ 588	41,442	B/ 32,196	B/ 9,058	191,060	162,290	28,770
Manufacturing	14,551	13,704	847	118,627	76,611	B/ 42,003	604,294	500,456	103,838
Nondurable goods	5,192	4,725	(D)	59,008	B/ 35,837	B/ 22,059	224,227	178,579	45,648
Durable goods	9,359	8,979	B/ 371	59,619	B/ 40,500	B/ 18,310	380,067	321,876	58,191
Transportation and public utilities	8,834	8,352	482	45,015	B/ 35,414	B/ 8,759	201,691	171,314	30,377
Wholesale trade	8,350	B/ 8,145	B/ 188	37,806	B/ 32,355	B/ 5,255	193,843	176,589	17,254
Retail trade	16,241	15,258	983	63,845	48,575	15,271	286,591	241,124	45,467
Finance, insurance and real estate	10,582	10,264	B/ 318	35,627	B/ 31,048	B/ 4,542	220,570	206,073	14,497
Services	37,498	35,865	1,633	136,841	112,804	23,480	736,473	657,202	79,271
Government and government enterprises	20,398	18,938	1,460	106,720	80,546	26,174	464,907	384,576	80,331
Federal, civilian	3,521	3,370	151	23,262	19,566	3,695	97,005	85,244	11,761
Federal, military	2,523	2,430	93	15,800	12,905	2,895	43,181	36,215	6,966
State and local	14,354	13,138	1,216	67,659	48,075	19,584	324,721	263,117	61,604

See footnotes at end of table.

Continued . . .

Table 5.21. PERSONAL INCOME: AMOUNTS BY MAJOR SOURCE IN THE METROPOLITAN AND NONMETROPOLITAN AREAS OF FLORIDA, THE SOUTHEAST, AND THE UNITED STATES, 1988 AND 1989 (Continued)

(rounded to millions of dollars)

Item	Florida			Southeast			United States		
	Total	Metro-politan areas	Non-metro-politan areas	Total	Metro-politan areas	Non-metro-politan areas	Total	Metro-politan areas	Non-metro-politan areas
	Income by place of residence, 1989								
Total personal income	224,410	207,897	16,513	914,325	664,744	249,581	4,367,401	3,606,280	761,121
Nonfarm personal income	221,961	206,101	15,860	901,737	660,414	241,323	4,316,147	3,587,586	728,561
Farm personal income	2,449	1,797	652	12,589	4,330	8,258	51,254	18,694	32,560
Derivation of personal income									
Total earnings by place of work	139,479	131,441	8,038	647,284	488,309	158,975	3,177,124	2,702,365	474,759
Less: Personal contributions for social insurance	8,291	7,824	467	40,227	30,098	10,130	212,117	181,051	31,066
Plus: Adjustment for residence	-144	-936	792	4,367	-7,554	11,921	-587	-37,102	36,515
Equals: Net earnings by place of residence	131,044	122,681	8,362	611,424	450,657	160,767	2,964,420	2,484,213	480,207
Plus: Dividends, interest, and rent	57,524	52,992	4,532	159,535	120,594	38,941	765,847	628,495	137,352
Plus: Transfer payments	35,843	32,224	3,618	143,366	93,493	49,873	637,134	493,572	143,562
	Earnings by place of work, 1989								
Components of earnings									
Wages and salaries	113,517	107,632	5,885	523,116	402,840	120,275	2,562,601	2,215,363	347,238
Other labor income	9,983	9,440	543	48,618	36,711	11,907	241,622	207,242	34,380
Proprietors' income	15,979	14,369	1,610	75,550	48,757	26,793	372,901	279,760	93,141
Farm	1,922	1,391	531	10,617	3,568	7,049	42,219	14,310	27,909
Nonfarm	14,057	12,978	1,079	64,934	45,189	19,744	330,682	265,450	65,232

See footnotes at end of table.

Continued . . .

Table 5.21. PERSONAL INCOME: AMOUNTS BY MAJOR SOURCE IN THE METROPOLITAN AND NONMETROPOLITAN AREAS OF FLORIDA, THE SOUTHEAST, AND THE UNITED STATES, 1988 AND 1989 (Continued)

(rounded to millions of dollars)

Earnings by place of work, 1989 (Continued)

Item	Florida			Southeast			United States		
	Total	Metro-politan areas	Non-metro-politan areas	Total	Metro-politan areas	Non-metro-politan areas	Total	Metro-politan areas	Non-metro-politan areas
Earnings by industry									
Farm	2,449	1,797	652	12,589	4,330	8,258	51,254	18,694	32,560
Nonfarm	137,030	129,645	7,385	634,696	483,978	150,717	3,125,870	2,683,671	442,199
Private	114,768	108,991	5,777	520,350	397,481	122,869	2,628,329	2,271,638	356,691
Agricultural services 1/	1,394	B/ 1,159	B/ 229	3,846	B/ 2,595	B/ 1,174	18,821	14,189	4,632
Mining	574	B/ 518	(D)	8,236	B/ 3,399	B/ 4,453	32,556	19,183	13,373
Construction	10,092	9,469	B/ 600	42,138	32,675	B/ 9,277	197,097	167,515	29,582
Manufacturing	14,966	14,054	912	123,331	B/ 79,155	B/ 44,174	625,534	516,763	108,771
Nondurable goods	5,448	4,948	(D)	61,659	B/ 37,264	B/ 23,302	232,631	184,871	47,760
Durable goods	9,519	9,106	B/ 399	61,672	B/ 41,750	B/ 19,220	392,903	331,892	61,011
Transportation and public utilities	8,907	8,404	504	46,814	36,754	B/ 9,175	210,714	178,883	31,831
Wholesale trade	9,012	B/ 8,779	B/ 219	40,775	34,340	B/ 5,766	208,020	189,302	18,718
Retail trade	17,227	16,165	1,062	67,051	50,993	16,057	301,737	253,795	47,942
Finance, insurance and real estate	10,594	10,273	B/ 321	36,343	31,563	B/ 4,650	223,983	209,336	14,647
Services	42,001	40,149	1,852	151,816	125,171	B/ 26,066	809,867	722,673	87,194
Government and government enterprises	22,262	20,654	1,608	114,346	86,498	27,848	497,541	412,033	85,508
Federal, civilian	3,803	3,640	163	24,571	20,764	3,807	102,688	90,405	12,283
Federal, military	2,705	2,608	97	16,414	13,443	2,971	44,641	37,418	7,223
State and local	15,754	14,406	1,348	73,361	52,291	21,070	350,212	284,210	66,002

(D) Data withheld to avoid disclosure of information about individual firms.
B/ Revised. B/ This estimate constitutes the major portion of the true estimate.
1/ Includes forestry, fisheries, and other. "Other" includes wages and salaries of U.S. residents employed by foreign embassies, consulates, and international organizations in the United States.
Source: U.S., Department of Commerce, Bureau of Economic Analysis, unpublished data.

Table 5.23.   PERSONAL INCOME: AMOUNTS BY MAJOR SOURCE IN FLORIDA, FOURTH QUARTER
1989 THROUGH FOURTH QUARTER 1990

(rounded to millions of dollars)

Item	Fourth quarter 1989	1990 First quarter	Second quarter	Third quarter	Fourth quarter
Income by place of residence					
Total personal income	230,272	235,643	239,401	242,816	243,976
Nonfarm personal income	228,082	233,214	237,325	240,438	242,098
Farm personal income	2,190	2,430	2,076	2,378	1,878
Derivation of total personal income					
Total earnings by place of work	142,159	145,829	148,432	150,324	149,934
Less personal contributions for social insurance	8,466	8,802	8,833	9,006	8,986
Plus adjustment for residence	-150	-157	-163	-164	-163
Equals net earnings by place of residence	133,542	136,870	139,437	141,154	140,786
Plus dividends, interest, and rent	59,560	59,967	60,785	61,906	62,382
Plus transfer payments	37,169	38,806	39,179	39,756	40,808
State unemployment benefits	374	436	495	497	614
Other transfer payments	36,795	38,370	38,685	39,259	40,194
Earnings by place of work					
Components of earnings					
Wages and salaries	115,922	118,622	121,185	122,432	122,365
Other labor income	10,245	10,561	10,729	10,820	10,905
Proprietors' income	15,992	16,646	16,519	17,072	16,663
Farm	1,657	1,894	1,530	1,828	1,320
Nonfarm	14,335	14,752	14,988	15,245	15,344
Earnings by industry					
Farm	2,190	2,430	2,076	2,378	1,878
Nonfarm	139,968	143,400	146,356	147,946	148,056
Private	116,807	119,544	121,474	123,387	123,162
Agricultural services, forestry, and fisheries, and other 1/	1,414	1,422	1,322	1,409	1,379
Mining	560	571	570	618	669
Construction	9,969	10,187	10,009	9,792	9,094
Manufacturing	14,985	15,424	15,284	15,605	15,487
Nondurable goods	5,541	5,579	5,630	5,665	5,748
Durable goods	9,445	9,844	9,655	9,941	9,739
Transportation and public utilities	8,950	9,420	9,809	9,775	9,749
Wholesale trade	9,221	9,247	9,504	9,454	9,422
Retail trade	17,520	17,817	18,081	17,981	17,811
Finance, insurance, and real estate	10,710	10,794	10,995	11,283	11,255
Services	43,478	44,661	45,900	47,470	48,296
Government and government enterprises	23,162	23,856	24,882	24,559	24,895
Federal, civilian	3,869	4,002	4,243	4,176	4,139
Federal, military	2,741	2,864	2,851	2,847	2,878
State and local	16,552	16,990	17,787	17,536	17,878

1/ Includes wages and salaries of U.S. residents employed by foreign embassies,
consulates, and international organizations in the United States.
   Note: Seasonally adjusted at annual rates. Data reported in April 1991.
   Source: U.S., Department of Commerce, Bureau of Economic Analysis, unpublished
data.

Florida Statistical Abstract 1991

Table 5.26.   PERSONAL INCOME: TOTAL EARNINGS ON PLACE-OF-WORK BASIS BY MAJOR
TYPE OF INCOME IN THE STATE AND COUNTIES OF FLORIDA, 1988 AND 1989

(rounded to thousands of dollars)

County	Total earnings	Wage and salary disbursements	Other labor income	Proprietors income Total	Farm	Nonfarm 1/
			1988 A/			
Florida	130,894,576	106,391,533	9,293,136	15,209,907	2,058,602	13,151,305
Alachua	1,944,722	1,627,894	131,602	185,226	15,368	169,858
Baker	93,500	68,537	6,469	18,494	7,926	10,568
Bay	1,145,869	933,515	72,660	139,694	476	139,218
Bradford	110,163	83,864	6,891	19,408	6,159	13,249
Brevard	4,085,617	3,463,961	312,829	308,827	18,072	290,755
Broward	12,838,917	10,614,289	913,190	1,311,438	27,206	1,284,232
Calhoun	51,917	35,529	3,254	13,134	2,079	11,055
Charlotte	547,066	408,958	36,230	101,878	9,434	92,444
Citrus	440,351	331,430	33,445	75,476	3,056	72,420
Clay	542,166	414,635	38,911	88,620	4,829	83,791
Collier	1,469,939	1,093,549	92,636	283,754	54,958	228,796
Columbia	279,194	224,124	20,577	34,493	5,075	29,418
Dade	23,784,197	19,797,847	1,739,169	2,247,181	125,799	2,121,382
De Soto	137,445	102,665	8,596	26,184	9,635	16,549
Dixie	48,644	36,528	3,537	8,579	1,184	7,395
Duval	9,403,545	8,196,230	681,182	526,133	10,144	515,989
Escambia	2,742,392	2,304,360	188,107	249,925	2,509	247,416
Flagler	151,647	117,025	11,370	23,252	7,181	16,071
Franklin	47,593	29,759	2,685	15,149	0	15,149
Gadsden	274,585	213,404	18,656	42,525	18,512	24,013
Gilchrist	44,170	23,645	2,026	18,499	12,418	6,081
Glades	34,523	17,922	1,655	14,946	11,670	3,276
Gulf	88,640	72,042	8,628	7,970	0	7,970
Hamilton	114,200	95,582	11,514	7,104	2,151	4,953
Hardee	153,756	86,321	7,280	60,155	44,106	16,049
Hendry	243,524	133,313	12,357	97,854	76,483	21,371
Hernando	410,992	304,417	27,495	79,080	12,056	67,024
Highlands	417,044	274,584	24,398	118,062	65,431	52,631
Hillsborough	10,405,657	8,726,121	771,957	907,579	147,196	760,383
Holmes	65,309	43,035	3,695	18,579	7,312	11,267
Indian River	759,720	565,048	49,140	145,532	48,041	97,491
Jackson	258,327	203,263	18,081	36,983	10,156	26,827
Jefferson	61,381	43,540	3,922	13,919	8,270	5,649
Lafayette	33,507	14,504	1,288	17,715	15,027	2,688
Lake	1,129,490	739,358	68,260	321,872	172,149	149,723

See footnotes at end of table.   Continued . . .

Florida Statistical Abstract 1991

Table 5.26. PERSONAL INCOME: TOTAL EARNINGS ON PLACE-OF-WORK BASIS BY MAJOR
   TYPE OF INCOME IN THE STATE AND COUNTIES OF FLORIDA, 1988 AND 1989
   (Continued)

(rounded to thousands of dollars)

County	Total earnings	Wage and salary dis- bursements	Other labor income	Proprietors income Total	Farm	Nonfarm 1/
			1988 A/ (Continued)			
Lee	2,734,352	2,141,805	186,775	405,772	35,862	369,910
Leon	2,244,758	1,927,107	145,626	172,025	1,361	170,664
Levy	113,892	76,288	7,058	30,546	9,178	21,368
Liberty	22,392	16,528	1,656	4,208	131	4,077
Madison	87,684	65,158	6,684	15,842	3,059	12,783
Manatee	1,535,823	1,160,139	109,381	266,303	84,072	182,231
Marion	1,283,507	1,005,618	96,441	181,448	17,129	164,319
Martin	973,039	713,256	65,837	193,946	70,320	123,626
Monroe	747,479	575,609	40,676	131,194	0	131,194
Nassau	300,384	238,536	21,709	40,139	1,950	38,189
Okaloosa	1,419,160	1,216,073	78,996	124,091	965	123,126
Okeechobee	159,250	109,337	9,184	40,729	16,085	24,644
Orange	10,361,005	8,724,601	780,531	855,873	154,234	701,639
Osceola	681,987	531,878	45,939	104,170	21,527	82,643
Palm Beach	10,021,890	8,048,420	719,476	1,253,994	190,528	1,063,466
Pasco	1,288,214	949,626	86,299	252,289	40,979	211,310
Pinellas	8,504,625	6,634,393	583,936	1,286,296	11,939	1,274,357
Polk	3,668,718	2,832,750	263,527	572,441	198,633	373,808
Putnam	372,870	288,350	28,963	55,557	15,372	40,185
St. Johns	542,525	403,182	36,376	102,967	24,695	78,272
St. Lucie	1,021,400	765,394	69,160	186,846	69,611	117,235
Santa Rosa	413,135	325,056	25,179	62,900	3,691	59,209
Sarasota	2,601,714	2,036,672	176,527	388,515	11,566	376,949
Seminole	2,076,696	1,585,493	143,663	347,540	17,312	330,228
Sumter	145,705	102,545	9,568	33,592	13,046	20,546
Suwannee	156,234	110,925	10,795	34,514	11,854	22,660
Taylor	154,373	127,603	14,073	12,697	1,220	11,477
Union	76,777	61,377	4,925	10,475	5,115	5,360
Volusia	2,550,833	1,976,472	171,800	402,561	56,540	346,021
Wakulla	57,081	40,633	4,387	12,061	745	11,316
Walton	125,984	94,721	8,652	22,611	1,649	20,962
Washington	91,381	65,190	5,645	20,546	6,166	14,380

See footnotes at end of table.   Continued . . .

Table 5.26. PERSONAL INCOME: TOTAL EARNINGS ON PLACE-OF-WORK BASIS BY MAJOR
TYPE OF INCOME IN THE STATE AND COUNTIES OF FLORIDA, 1988 AND 1989
(Continued)

(rounded to thousands of dollars)

County	Total earnings	Wage and salary dis-bursements	Other labor income	Proprietors income Total	Farm	Nonfarm 1/
			1989			
Florida	139,478,956	113,516,715	9,983,162	15,979,079	1,922,134	14,056,945
Alachua	2,093,502	1,748,464	143,206	201,832	17,254	184,578
Baker	100,200	73,229	7,093	19,878	8,408	11,470
Bay	1,203,994	976,127	78,082	149,785	338	149,447
Bradford	120,971	90,735	7,566	22,670	8,274	14,396
Brevard	4,427,657	3,762,565	337,897	327,195	15,035	312,160
Broward	13,481,745	11,117,660	967,985	1,396,100	24,730	1,371,370
Calhoun	54,236	38,166	3,513	12,557	971	11,586
Charlotte	610,654	464,866	41,187	104,601	7,842	96,759
Citrus	488,054	370,748	37,903	79,403	2,776	76,627
Clay	584,744	449,353	42,050	93,341	4,443	88,898
Collier	1,666,727	1,254,136	106,903	305,688	69,401	236,287
Columbia	296,110	237,181	22,457	36,472	5,360	31,112
Dade	24,862,193	20,612,031	1,802,509	2,447,653	136,273	2,311,380
De Soto	143,114	109,913	9,511	23,690	5,885	17,805
Dixie	56,094	42,628	4,318	9,148	1,108	8,040
Duval	9,887,674	8,592,364	725,828	569,482	9,530	559,952
Escambia	2,893,818	2,415,080	203,146	275,592	204	275,388
Flagler	166,019	127,778	12,379	25,862	9,103	16,759
Franklin	51,421	32,410	2,958	16,053	0	16,053
Gadsden	288,675	224,495	20,105	44,075	18,930	25,145
Gilchrist	46,751	26,584	2,345	17,822	11,418	6,404
Glades	34,537	19,278	1,818	13,441	10,038	3,403
Gulf	90,094	73,192	8,767	8,135	0	8,135
Hamilton	126,240	106,434	12,972	6,834	1,633	5,201
Hardee	152,899	93,898	8,000	51,001	33,931	17,070
Hendry	249,482	146,296	13,924	89,262	66,454	22,808
Hernando	448,169	336,292	30,530	81,347	10,918	70,429
Highlands	432,988	297,309	26,959	108,720	53,117	55,603
Hillsborough	11,161,518	9,358,268	833,259	969,991	145,172	824,819
Holmes	71,471	46,586	4,135	20,750	8,653	12,097
Indian River	847,064	650,605	57,714	138,745	38,315	100,430
Jackson	270,698	214,105	19,474	37,119	8,759	28,360
Jefferson	59,489	42,156	3,772	13,561	7,489	6,072
Lafayette	37,304	16,025	1,449	19,830	17,010	2,820
Lake	1,188,285	805,538	75,390	307,357	147,309	160,048

See footnotes at end of table.   Continued . . .

Table 5.26. PERSONAL INCOME: TOTAL EARNINGS ON PLACE-OF-WORK BASIS BY MAJOR
    TYPE OF INCOME IN THE STATE AND COUNTIES OF FLORIDA, 1988 AND 1989
    (Continued)

(rounded to thousands of dollars)

County	Total earnings	Wage and salary dis- bursements	Other labor income	Proprietors income Total	Farm	Nonfarm 1/
		1989 (Continued)				
Lee	2,999,617	2,361,513	208,887	429,217	37,857	391,360
Leon	2,455,367	2,105,425	162,231	187,711	603	187,108
Levy	124,078	84,126	7,877	32,075	9,801	22,274
Liberty	27,873	21,383	2,115	4,375	B/	4,342
Madison	92,391	69,269	6,893	16,229	2,470	13,759
Manatee	1,675,766	1,271,945	120,087	283,734	89,760	193,974
Marion	1,380,829	1,087,805	105,767	187,257	11,409	175,848
Martin	1,054,212	794,027	74,011	186,174	61,020	125,154
Monroe	805,087	619,505	44,914	140,668	0	140,668
Nassau	325,257	257,885	23,840	43,532	2,327	41,205
Okaloosa	1,511,782	1,291,759	86,651	133,372	543	132,829
Okeechobee	167,944	118,736	10,217	38,991	12,622	26,369
Orange	11,300,348	9,566,110	857,530	876,708	142,719	733,989
Osceola	760,514	605,011	52,461	103,042	15,391	87,651
Palm Beach	10,630,170	8,555,710	766,254	1,308,206	194,651	1,113,555
Pasco	1,379,011	1,025,857	93,030	260,124	35,716	224,408
Pinellas	9,040,322	7,052,700	625,373	1,362,249	10,796	1,351,453
Polk	3,907,791	3,053,983	287,426	566,382	161,910	404,472
Putnam	384,499	296,424	29,861	58,214	15,518	42,696
St. Johns	597,724	443,195	40,752	113,777	29,910	83,867
St. Lucie	1,093,613	839,092	76,588	177,933	53,036	124,897
Santa Rosa	440,714	348,099	27,335	65,280	1,746	63,534
Sarasota	2,774,777	2,181,958	188,810	404,009	9,978	394,031
Seminole	2,254,601	1,723,030	156,132	375,439	17,872	357,567
Sumter	155,389	107,104	10,417	37,868	15,359	22,509
Suwannee	166,866	116,664	11,415	38,787	14,685	24,102
Taylor	163,161	134,533	15,012	13,616	1,170	12,446
Union	79,943	62,365	5,235	12,343	6,421	5,922
Volusia	2,737,395	2,129,129	187,958	420,308	53,641	366,667
Wakulla	62,492	44,994	4,836	12,662	704	11,958
Walton	140,541	107,160	10,217	23,164	1,348	21,816
Washington	94,291	67,724	5,926	20,641	5,037	15,604

A/ Revised.
B/ Less than $50,000.
1/ Excludes limited partners.
  Source: U.S., Department of Commerce, Bureau of Economic Analysis, unpublished
data.

Table 5.30. PERSONAL INCOME: TOTAL EARNINGS ON A PLACE-OF-WORK BASIS IN THE FARM AND NONFARM SECTORS IN THE STATE AND COUNTIES OF FLORIDA, 1988 AND 1989

(rounded to thousands of dollars)

County	Total earnings	Farm income	Nonfarm Total	Private 1/	Government and government enterprises Total	Federal Civilian	Military	State and local
				1988 A/				
Florida	130,894,576	2,578,918	128,315,658	107,917,510	20,398,148	3,520,909	2,522,921	14,354,318
Alachua	1,944,722	18,850	1,925,872	1,202,153	723,719	93,740	6,685	623,294
Baker	93,500	9,869	83,631	37,741	45,890	1,324	242	44,324
Bay	1,145,869	682	1,145,187	788,545	356,642	97,996	122,695	135,951
Bradford	110,163	6,659	103,504	59,756	43,748	1,021	323	42,404
Brevard	4,085,617	21,404	4,064,213	3,436,895	627,318	194,667	103,282	329,369
Broward	12,838,917	36,076	12,802,841	11,258,527	1,544,314	181,708	17,705	1,344,901
Calhoun	51,917	2,572	49,345	34,475	14,870	1,006	134	13,730
Charlotte	547,066	11,871	535,195	469,003	66,192	6,843	1,241	58,108
Citrus	440,351	3,518	436,833	368,781	68,052	4,402	1,198	62,452
Clay	542,166	7,349	534,817	454,978	79,839	9,361	1,281	69,197
Collier	1,469,939	65,054	1,404,885	1,268,569	136,316	14,753	1,811	119,752
Columbia	279,194	6,113	273,081	188,997	84,084	26,883	699	56,502
Dade	23,784,197	157,397	23,626,800	20,349,986	3,276,814	632,754	167,745	2,476,315
De Soto	137,445	15,404	122,041	72,290	49,751	1,365	296	48,090
Dixie	48,644	1,398	47,246	31,786	15,460	1,029	135	14,296
Duval	9,403,545	13,887	9,389,658	7,452,912	1,936,746	458,825	730,255	747,666
Escambia	2,742,392	3,363	2,739,029	1,878,488	860,541	310,711	264,207	285,623
Flagler	151,647	8,315	143,332	124,661	18,671	1,899	304	16,468
Franklin	47,593	0	47,593	36,053	11,540	1,150	111	10,279
Gadsden	274,585	25,282	249,303	136,747	112,556	3,451	702	108,403
Gilchrist	44,170	14,091	30,079	15,836	14,243	542	99	13,602

See footnotes at end of table.

Continued . . .

Table 5.30. PERSONAL INCOME: TOTAL EARNINGS ON A PLACE-OF-WORK BASIS IN THE FARM AND NONFARM SECTORS IN THE STATE AND COUNTIES OF FLORIDA, 1988 AND 1989 (Continued)

(rounded to thousands of dollars)

County	Total earnings	Farm income	Nonfarm Total	Private 1/	Government and government enterprises Total	Federal Civilian	Military	State and local
				1988 A/ (Continued)				
Glades	34,523	16,009	18,514	12,306	6,208	316	90	5,802
Gulf	88,640	0	88,640	75,228	13,412	516	161	12,735
Hamilton	114,200	2,812	111,388	90,490	20,898	677	128	20,093
Hardee	153,756	52,519	101,237	76,473	24,764	1,447	285	23,032
Hendry	243,524	86,722	156,802	117,212	39,590	2,908	329	36,353
Hernando	410,992	14,306	396,686	323,268	73,418	6,559	1,227	65,632
Highlands	417,044	76,230	340,814	272,077	68,737	7,925	4,884	55,928
Hillsborough	10,405,657	178,892	10,226,765	8,707,306	1,519,459	313,669	191,515	1,014,275
Holmes	65,309	8,392	56,917	37,798	19,119	1,458	218	17,443
Indian River	759,720	55,113	704,607	619,150	85,457	10,412	1,136	73,909
Jackson	258,327	12,869	245,458	153,685	91,773	9,092	1,070	81,611
Jefferson	61,381	11,387	49,994	38,244	11,750	916	157	10,677
Lafayette	33,507	16,208	17,299	7,575	9,724	362	71	9,291
Lake	1,129,490	201,909	927,581	786,920	140,661	12,299	4,130	124,232
Lee	2,734,352	49,111	2,685,241	2,322,074	363,167	40,187	4,946	318,034
Leon	2,244,758	2,169	2,242,589	1,313,979	928,610	47,410	8,444	872,756
Levy	113,892	10,196	103,696	78,001	25,695	1,740	817	23,138
Liberty	22,392	224	22,168	15,908	6,260	1,026	60	5,174
Madison	87,684	5,928	81,756	62,821	18,935	1,280	206	17,449
Manatee	1,535,823	100,734	1,435,089	1,249,975	185,114	17,090	3,147	164,877
Marion	1,283,507	30,292	1,253,215	1,057,272	195,943	15,197	2,511	178,235
Martin	973,039	81,166	891,873	807,930	83,943	7,549	1,545	74,849
Monroe	747,479	0	747,479	547,582	199,897	34,823	71,060	94,014

See footnotes at end of table.

Continued . . .

Table 5.30. PERSONAL INCOME: TOTAL EARNINGS ON A PLACE-OF-WORK BASIS IN THE FARM AND NONFARM SECTORS IN THE STATE AND COUNTIES OF FLORIDA, 1988 AND 1989 (Continued)

(rounded to thousands of dollars)

County	Total earnings	Farm income	Nonfarm Total	Private 1/	Government and government enterprises Total	Federal Civilian	Military	State and local
				1988 A/ (Continued)				
Nassau	300,384	3,272	297,112	227,412	69,700	30,931	591	38,178
Okaloosa	1,419,160	1,439	1,417,721	790,112	627,609	159,990	351,111	116,508
Okeechobee	159,250	26,848	132,402	105,871	26,531	2,175	388	23,968
Orange	10,361,005	194,567	10,166,438	8,893,158	1,273,280	235,605	311,110	726,565
Osceola	681,987	27,445	654,542	568,959	85,583	5,770	1,173	78,640
Palm Beach	10,021,890	313,520	9,708,370	8,692,572	1,015,798	123,272	12,802	879,724
Pasco	1,288,214	47,430	1,240,784	1,065,753	175,031	16,976	3,468	154,587
Pinellas	8,504,625	14,229	8,490,396	7,582,843	907,553	187,016	31,340	689,197
Polk	3,668,718	223,803	3,444,915	3,003,556	441,359	39,895	5,670	395,794
Putnam	372,870	18,352	354,518	283,783	70,735	4,634	816	65,285
St. Johns	542,525	28,461	514,064	429,200	84,864	10,035	1,844	72,985
St. Lucie	1,021,400	81,763	939,637	790,264	149,373	13,472	3,032	132,869
Santa Rosa	413,135	4,796	408,339	269,355	138,984	17,863	63,571	57,550
Sarasota	2,601,714	13,712	2,588,002	2,299,100	288,902	32,934	3,771	252,197
Seminole	2,076,696	21,517	2,055,179	1,824,679	230,500	17,319	3,521	209,660
Sumter	145,705	15,371	130,334	98,003	32,331	1,733	412	30,186
Suwannee	156,234	15,094	141,140	113,626	27,514	2,326	352	24,836
Taylor	154,373	1,453	152,920	133,437	19,483	1,066	250	18,167
Union	76,777	5,410	71,367	30,749	40,618	524	136	39,958
Volusia	2,550,833	67,407	2,483,426	2,081,750	401,676	32,591	6,977	362,108
Wakulla	57,081	833	56,248	42,678	13,570	1,354	186	12,030
Walton	125,984	2,542	123,442	97,701	25,741	1,965	895	22,881
Washington	91,381	7,312	84,069	52,496	31,573	1,175	218	30,180

See footnotes at end of table.

Continued . . .

Table 5.30. PERSONAL INCOME: TOTAL EARNINGS ON A PLACE-OF-WORK BASIS IN THE FARM AND NONFARM SECTORS IN THE STATE AND COUNTIES OF FLORIDA, 1988 AND 1989 (Continued)

(rounded to thousands of dollars)

1989

County	Total earnings	Farm income	Nonfarm					
			Total	Private 1/	Government and government enterprises			
					Total	Federal		State and local
						Civilian	Military	
Florida	139,478,956	2,449,076	137,029,880	114,768,012	22,261,868	3,803,067	2,704,687	15,754,114
Alachua	2,093,502	20,723	2,072,779	1,287,359	785,420	100,297	7,419	677,704
Baker	100,200	10,389	89,811	40,482	49,329	1,522	248	47,559
Bay	1,203,994	533	1,203,461	823,480	379,981	104,335	127,580	148,066
Bradford	120,971	8,760	112,211	62,957	49,254	1,139	327	47,788
Brevard	4,427,657	18,278	4,409,379	3,719,811	689,568	220,558	103,923	365,087
Broward	13,481,745	33,487	13,448,258	11,876,881	1,571,377	197,008	17,907	1,356,462
Calhoun	54,236	1,454	52,782	35,549	17,233	1,078	136	16,019
Charlotte	610,654	10,320	600,334	520,762	79,572	7,229	1,318	71,025
Citrus	488,054	3,209	484,845	409,378	75,467	4,778	1,267	69,422
Clay	584,744	7,023	577,721	487,834	89,887	9,971	1,388	78,528
Collier	1,666,727	79,786	1,586,941	1,428,917	158,024	16,080	1,917	140,027
Columbia	296,110	6,371	289,739	199,143	90,596	28,193	582	61,821
Dade	24,862,193	167,823	24,694,370	21,126,597	3,567,773	673,329	174,213	2,720,231
De Soto	143,114	11,742	131,372	76,396	54,976	1,411	302	53,263
Dixie	56,094	1,312	54,782	37,090	17,692	1,117	140	16,435
Duval	9,887,674	13,260	9,874,414	7,761,351	2,113,063	501,366	811,014	800,683
Escambia	2,893,818	1,069	2,892,749	1,970,670	922,079	335,501	280,334	306,244
Flagler	166,019	10,262	155,757	132,089	23,668	2,256	1,424	19,988
Franklin	51,421	0	51,421	39,308	12,113	1,041	111	10,961
Gadsden	288,675	25,933	262,742	142,894	119,848	3,475	723	115,650
Gilchrist	46,751	13,105	33,646	17,612	16,034	485	102	15,447
Glades	34,537	14,465	20,072	13,249	6,823	305	90	6,428

See footnotes at end of table.

Continued . . .

Table 5.30. PERSONAL INCOME: TOTAL EARNINGS ON A PLACE-OF-WORK BASIS IN THE FARM AND NONFARM SECTORS IN THE STATE AND COUNTIES OF FLORIDA, 1988 AND 1989 (Continued)

(rounded to thousands of dollars)

County	Total earnings	Farm income	Nonfarm Total	Private 1/	Government and government enterprises Total	Federal Civilian	Military	State and local
				1989 (Continued)				
Gulf	90,094	0	90,094	75,400	14,694	623	163	13,908
Hamilton	126,240	2,303	123,937	101,069	22,868	725	130	22,013
Hardee	152,899	42,363	110,536	83,933	26,603	1,522	288	24,793
Hendry	249,482	76,908	172,574	129,979	42,595	3,092	341	39,162
Hernando	448,169	13,108	435,061	353,524	81,537	6,797	1,324	73,416
Highlands	432,988	63,930	369,058	292,513	76,545	8,539	5,558	62,448
Hillsborough	11,161,518	177,140	10,984,378	9,313,996	1,670,382	341,241	198,406	1,130,735
Holmes	71,471	9,765	61,706	40,430	21,276	1,501	221	19,554
Indian River	847,064	45,332	801,732	706,024	95,708	10,837	1,180	83,691
Jackson	270,698	11,542	259,156	159,028	100,128	12,642	1,173	86,313
Jefferson	59,489	10,676	48,813	35,790	13,023	961	159	11,903
Lafayette	37,304	18,204	19,100	8,674	10,426	417	76	9,933
Lake	1,188,285	177,281	1,011,004	854,247	156,757	13,127	4,089	139,541
Lee	2,999,617	51,542	2,948,075	2,536,125	411,950	43,562	5,162	363,226
Leon	2,455,367	1,381	2,453,986	1,439,869	1,014,117	50,653	8,202	955,262
Levy	124,078	10,792	113,286	84,637	28,649	1,823	892	25,934
Liberty	27,873	130	27,743	17,411	10,332	1,076	60	9,196
Madison	92,391	5,406	86,985	62,684	24,301	1,407	208	22,686
Manatee	1,675,766	106,707	1,569,059	1,366,481	202,578	17,398	3,153	182,027
Marion	1,380,829	24,569	1,356,260	1,135,628	220,632	16,175	2,654	201,803
Martin	1,054,212	71,964	982,248	890,355	91,893	8,028	1,601	82,264
Monroe	805,087	0	805,087	593,119	211,968	37,415	72,601	101,952
Nassau	325,257	3,660	321,597	245,149	76,448	33,090	617	42,741
Okaloosa	1,511,782	1,008	1,510,774	834,211	676,563	174,670	370,671	131,222

See footnotes at end of table.

Continued . . .

Table 5.30. PERSONAL INCOME: TOTAL EARNINGS ON A PLACE-OF-WORK BASIS IN THE FARM AND NONFARM SECTORS IN THE STATE AND COUNTIES OF FLORIDA, 1988 AND 1989 (Continued)

(rounded to thousands of dollars)

County	Total earnings	Farm income	Nonfarm Total	Private 1/	Government and government enterprises Total	Federal Civilian	Federal Military	State and local
				1989 (Continued)				
Okeechobee	167,944	23,597	144,347	115,528	28,819	2,189	406	26,224
Orange	11,300,348	183,688	11,116,660	9,692,705	1,423,955	257,645	340,100	826,210
Osceola	760,514	21,352	739,162	638,371	100,791	6,542	1,238	93,011
Palm Beach	10,630,170	321,564	10,308,606	9,163,296	1,145,310	132,899	13,176	999,235
Pasco	1,379,011	41,922	1,337,089	1,147,346	189,743	17,575	3,605	168,563
Pinellas	9,040,322	13,001	9,027,321	8,047,328	979,993	196,008	35,601	748,384
Polk	3,907,791	186,753	3,721,038	3,238,289	482,749	41,969	5,744	435,036
Putnam	384,499	18,489	366,010	287,316	78,694	4,673	833	73,188
St. Johns	597,724	33,750	563,974	471,387	92,587	10,212	1,944	80,431
St. Lucie	1,093,613	65,320	1,028,293	861,649	166,644	14,204	3,154	149,286
Santa Rosa	440,714	2,858	437,856	284,734	153,122	19,395	69,859	63,868
Sarasota	2,774,777	12,077	2,762,700	2,437,184	325,516	34,961	4,028	286,527
Seminole	2,254,601	22,064	2,232,537	1,978,014	254,523	19,897	3,713	230,913
Sumter	155,389	17,677	137,712	102,301	35,411	1,831	424	33,156
Suwannee	166,866	18,001	148,865	119,324	29,541	2,454	358	26,729
Taylor	163,161	1,399	161,762	140,770	20,992	1,087	255	19,650
Union	79,943	6,721	73,222	33,675	39,547	544	135	38,868
Volusia	2,737,395	64,589	2,672,806	2,226,351	446,455	34,207	7,182	405,066
Wakulla	62,492	790	61,702	46,825	14,877	1,477	191	13,209
Walton	140,541	2,251	138,290	110,167	28,123	2,166	1,126	24,831
Washington	94,291	6,198	88,093	55,367	32,726	1,337	221	31,168

A/ Revised.
1/ See Table 5.34 for private nonfarm income by industrial source.
Source: U.S., Department of Commerce, Bureau of Economic Analysis, unpublished data.

Table 5.33. PERSONAL INCOME: PRIVATE NONFARM EARNINGS ON A PLACE-OF-WORK BASIS BY INDUSTRIAL SOU.... IN FLORIDA 1984 THROUGH 1989

(rounded to thousands of dollars)

Item	1984	1985	1986	1987	1988	1989	Percentage change 1984-1989
Agricultural services, forestry, fisheries, and other 1/	795,492	912,505	1,004,651	1,162,258	1,306,810	1,393,775	75.2
Agricultural services	730,861	793,136	844,857	1,033,300	1,151,634	1,236,301	69.2
Forestry	28,414	20,899	10,764	17,394	(D)	15,518	-45.4
Fisheries	34,773	96,934	147,393	109,723	139,201	139,917	302.4
Other 1/	1,444	1,536	1,637	1,841	(D)	2,039	41.2
Mining	627,993	824,005	421,108	413,091	547,189	574,292	-8.6
Coal mining	4,760	4,600	4,530	2,440	2,894	(D)	(D)
Oil and gas extraction	387,290	580,934	184,216	185,732	290,738	299,780	-22.6
Metal mining	12,407	13,467	12,919	13,780	14,032	(D)	(D)
Nonmetallic minerals, except fuels	223,536	225,004	219,443	211,139	239,525	255,954	14.5
Construction	7,507,541	8,187,207	8,894,304	9,220,033	10,007,504	10,092,400	34.4
General building contractors	2,356,254	2,523,417	2,793,914	2,813,253	3,023,949	2,919,049	23.9
Heavy construction contractors	1,067,755	1,142,950	1,210,568	1,271,720	1,412,961	1,449,471	35.7
Special trade contractors	4,083,532	4,520,840	4,889,822	5,135,060	5,570,594	5,723,880	40.2
Manufacturing	11,146,846	12,004,866	12,709,676	13,533,353	14,551,318	14,966,319	34.3
Nondurable goods	4,071,118	4,281,636	4,499,115	4,787,375	5,191,822	5,447,782	33.8
Food and kindred products	1,010,402	1,041,478	1,099,012	1,132,928	1,206,181	1,276,894	26.4
Textile mill products	34,952	33,820	38,987	59,156	66,406	95,718	173.9
Apparel and other textile products	375,656	365,207	386,122	416,421	452,375	463,492	23.4
Paper and allied products	429,138	448,351	454,701	470,868	495,463	526,221	22.6
Printing and publishing	1,045,800	1,194,614	1,317,184	1,452,378	1,607,950	1,675,434	60.2
Chemicals and allied products	756,112	774,476	768,465	765,058	816,752	836,620	10.6
Petroleum and coal products	51,996	54,853	62,913	65,212	62,912	60,840	17.0
Tobacco manufactures	37,314	34,232	29,872	30,139	29,217	29,268	-21.6

See footnotes at end of table.

Continued . . .

Table 5.33. PERSONAL INCOME: PRIVATE NONFARM EARNINGS ON A PLACE-OF-WORK BASIS BY INDUSTRIAL SOURCE IN FLORIDA 1984 THROUGH 1989 (Continued)

(rounded to thousands of dollars)

Item	1984	1985	1986	1987	1988	1989	Percentage change 1984-1989
Manufacturing (Continued)							
Nondurable goods (Continued)							
Rubber and miscellaneous plastics products	291,845	301,165	312,696	363,703	421,435	446,586	53.0
Leather and leather products	37,903	33,440	29,163	31,512	33,131	36,709	-3.2
Durable goods	7,075,728	7,723,230	8,210,561	8,745,978	9,359,496	9,518,537	34.5
Lumber and wood products	474,189	499,296	526,397	558,816	577,717	566,034	19.4
Furniture and fixtures	202,031	221,978	240,839	266,801	293,294	288,408	42.8
Primary metal industries	128,388	130,295	135,884	149,563	160,111	176,205	37.2
Fabricated metal products	742,375	788,830	830,129	882,337	894,464	880,172	18.6
Machinery, except electrical	1,167,680	1,281,524	1,300,920	1,302,817	1,394,790	1,387,467	18.8
Electric and electronic equipment	1,822,530	2,004,473	2,080,899	2,192,476	2,388,569	2,495,092	36.9
Transportation equipment, except motor vehicles	1,487,345	1,676,421	1,867,516	2,048,005	2,190,510	2,212,338	48.7
Motor vehicles and equipment	81,675	93,290	111,365	130,968	145,768	164,097	100.9
Stone, clay, and glass products	539,093	549,433	600,336	651,633	689,439	695,834	29.1
Instruments and related products	268,439	305,262	330,957	364,546	403,934	435,339	62.2
Miscellaneous manufacturing industries	161,983	172,428	185,319	198,016	220,900	217,551	34.3
Transportation and public utilities	7,021,709	7,427,372	7,881,529	8,456,741	8,834,188	8,907,457	26.9
Railroad transportation	357,320	329,523	310,799	293,166	322,064	323,340	-9.5
Trucking and warehousing	1,258,051	1,310,400	1,457,396	1,605,009	1,802,247	1,917,315	52.4
Water transportation	277,598	294,144	291,449	330,943	376,449	393,215	41.6
Other transportation	1,746,964	1,884,201	2,052,307	2,258,261	2,265,153	2,162,723	23.8
Local and interurban passenger transit	149,200	152,588	176,125	201,830	218,484	246,972	65.5
Transportation by air	1,318,210	1,421,952	1,520,029	1,655,306	1,586,389	1,397,664	6.0
Pipelines, except natural gas	1,727	1,793	1,753	2,114	2,077	2,331	35.0
Transportation services	277,827	307,868	354,400	399,011	458,203	515,756	85.6

Continued . . .

See footnotes at end of table.

Table 5.33. PERSONAL INCOME: PRIVATE NONFARM EARNINGS ON A PLACE-OF-WORK BASIS BY INDUSTRIAL SOURCE IN FLORIDA 1984 THROUGH 1989 (Continued)

(rounded to thousands of dollars)

Item	1984	1985	1986	1987	1988	1989	Percentage change 1984-1989
Transportation and public utilities (Continued)							
Communication	2,267,310	2,354,366	2,346,467	2,483,572	2,508,772	2,465,608	8.7
Electric, gas, and sanitary services	1,114,466	1,254,738	1,423,111	1,485,790	1,559,503	1,645,256	47.6
Wholesale trade	5,594,975	6,232,523	6,615,110	7,440,770	8,349,544	9,011,995	61.1
Retail trade	11,283,640	12,363,306	13,521,956	14,798,993	16,240,984	17,226,768	52.7
Building materials and farm equipment	622,259	691,264	714,165	782,552	843,514	882,403	41.8
General merchandise store	1,289,500	1,393,241	1,488,380	1,648,774	1,677,470	1,772,628	37.5
Food stores	1,812,332	1,920,822	2,052,752	2,239,691	2,497,825	2,687,539	48.3
Automotive dealers and service stations	2,095,479	2,360,064	2,513,477	2,759,583	2,997,181	3,018,632	44.1
Apparel and accessory stores	525,253	565,537	602,852	668,481	719,182	769,122	46.4
Furniture and home furnishings stores	730,101	846,551	912,942	994,700	1,090,412	1,188,414	62.8
Eating and drinking places	2,552,074	2,831,989	3,240,864	3,592,946	3,921,019	4,236,825	66.0
Miscellaneous retail stores	1,656,642	1,753,838	1,996,524	2,112,266	2,494,381	2,671,205	61.2
Finance, insurance, and real estate	6,335,641	7,155,252	8,179,497	10,814,230	10,582,345	10,593,697	67.2
Banking and credit agencies	2,271,306	2,539,948	2,925,379	3,220,491	3,470,317	3,597,401	58.4
Other finance, insurance, and real estate	4,064,335	4,615,304	5,254,118	7,593,739	7,112,028	6,996,296	72.1
Security and commodity brokers, and services	711,510	907,847	1,118,721	1,360,218	1,398,531	1,369,842	92.5
Insurance carriers	1,139,916	1,283,766	1,464,114	1,630,664	1,797,535	1,936,312	69.9
Insurance agents, brokers, and services	826,732	924,561	1,111,945	1,267,927	1,441,159	1,536,347	85.8
Real estate	962,193	877,672	909,851	2,350,737	2,092,887	1,943,993	102.0
Combined real estate, insurance, etc.	3,484	7,108	11,759	13,859	993	-4,901	-240.7
Holding and other investment companies	420,500	614,350	637,728	970,334	380,923	214,703	-48.9

See footnotes at end of table.

Continued . . .

Table 5.33. PERSONAL INCOME: PRIVATE NONFARM EARNINGS ON A PLACE-OF-WORK BASIS BY INDUSTRIAL SOURCE IN FLORIDA 1984 THROUGH 1989 (Continued)

(rounded to thousands of dollars)

Item	1984	1985	1986	1987	1988	1989	Percentage change 1984-1989
Services	23,019,285	25,688,429	29,281,416	33,315,744	37,497,628	42,001,309	82.5
Hotels and other lodging places	1,266,797	1,375,894	1,561,140	1,789,388	1,968,491	2,114,586	66.9
Personal services	847,628	1,027,074	1,146,669	1,237,059	1,419,011	1,581,252	86.6
Private households	640,737	659,369	672,983	688,585	744,234	796,606	24.3
Business services	3,611,150	4,117,219	4,694,554	5,391,894	6,163,074	7,202,848	99.5
Auto repair, services, and garages	935,640	1,042,718	1,150,895	1,243,669	1,354,398	1,460,414	56.1
Miscellaneous repair services	473,029	450,190	519,994	556,340	612,947	688,449	45.5
Amusement and recreation services	1,049,214	1,133,502	1,262,711	1,423,987	1,546,642	1,821,823	73.6
Motion pictures	71,369	81,756	89,613	98,901	108,419	128,337	79.8
Health services	7,175,136	7,930,718	8,709,543	10,268,433	11,574,255	12,893,655	79.7
Legal services	1,913,393	2,186,068	2,535,778	2,987,953	3,306,936	3,497,483	82.8
Educational services	610,967	678,193	730,274	813,038	914,501	996,503	63.1
Social services	472,929	541,820	623,595	725,273	857,090	984,853	108.2
Museums, botanical, zoological gardens	7,410	8,917	10,411	11,535	13,791	15,969	115.5
Membership organizations	874,894	916,212	997,086	1,107,429	1,272,726	1,393,591	59.3
Miscellaneous services	3,068,992	3,538,779	4,576,170	4,972,260	5,641,113	6,424,940	109.4
Government and government enterprises	14,362,563	15,680,936	16,991,646	18,704,757	20,398,148	22,261,868	55.0
Federal, civilian	2,671,917	2,882,433	2,932,650	3,187,731	3,520,909	3,803,067	42.3
Military	2,043,403	2,216,416	2,395,653	2,493,326	2,522,921	2,704,687	32.4
State and local	9,647,243	10,582,087	11,663,343	13,023,700	14,354,318	15,754,114	63.3

(D) Data withheld to avoid disclosure of information about individual industries.
1/ Includes wages and salaries of U.S. residents employed by foreign embassies, consulates and international organizations in the United States.
Note: Some data are revised.

Source: U.S., Department of Commerce, Bureau of Economic Analysis, unpublished data.

Florida Statistical Abstract 1991

Table 5.34. PERSONAL INCOME: PRIVATE NONFARM EARNINGS ON A PLACE-OF-WORK BASIS BY MAJOR INDUSTRIAL SOURCE IN THE STATE AND COUNTIES OF FLORIDA, 1988 AND 1989

(rounded to thousands of dollars)

1988

County	Total private nonfarm earnings	Manufacturing	Mining	Contract construction	Wholesale trade	Retail trade	Finance insurance and real estate	Transportation, communication and public utilities	Services	Other private industry 1/
Florida	107,917,510	14,551,318	547,189	10,007,504	8,349,544	16,240,984	10,582,345	8,834,188	37,497,628	1,306,810
Alachua	1,202,153	124,623	3,138	104,281	53,219	211,150	89,155	54,181	552,040	10,366
Baker	37,741	6,267	A/	2,719	753	7,986	2,163	11,060	6,513	255
Bay	788,545	94,887	842	86,577	35,150	174,348	54,359	58,450	270,922	13,010
Bradford	59,756	10,238	1,466	4,434	1,264	13,894	3,048	4,884	19,998	530
Brevard	3,436,895	990,135	7,149	267,619	97,012	422,582	124,452	180,541	1,323,332	24,073
Broward	11,258,527	1,312,790	52,226	1,111,661	879,223	1,778,202	1,221,273	767,956	4,046,511	88,685
Calhoun	34,475	6,095	(D)	3,154	(D)	6,561	895	6,931	8,670	802
Charlotte	469,003	14,499	3,825	83,999	10,110	89,321	39,732	27,761	192,243	7,513
Citrus	368,781	14,239	2,484	53,956	6,187	67,158	22,304	81,166	116,433	4,854
Clay	454,978	41,872	15,579	69,003	28,813	95,544	22,663	40,083	136,342	5,079
Collier	1,268,569	51,175	14,799	207,283	56,375	214,278	120,593	61,636	497,618	44,812
Columbia	188,997	36,931	256	20,495	14,322	42,191	8,454	15,181	50,252	915
Dade	20,349,986	2,079,224	65,037	1,208,494	2,149,701	2,676,807	2,244,474	2,594,081	7,220,215	111,953
De Soto	72,290	8,025	506	7,094	2,919	13,267	4,189	4,751	21,373	10,166
Dixie	31,786	13,274	(D)	2,429	(D)	5,996	575	2,283	5,627	985
Duval	7,452,912	879,721	16,781	634,975	838,010	960,944	1,096,788	824,756	2,155,847	45,039
Escambia	1,878,488	308,724	3,638	190,730	118,872	290,191	109,416	163,199	685,414	8,324
Flagler	124,661	33,019	531	17,482	1,554	17,593	17,426	4,903	29,157	2,996
Franklin	36,053	2,614	57	1,679	5,054	6,042	1,570	2,134	10,305	6,598
Gadsden	136,747	34,071	(D)	14,752	(D)	21,165	5,998	10,924	27,372	2,081
Gilchrist	15,836	1,796	A/	1,921	786	2,474	915	2,500	4,778	639

Continued . . .

See footnotes at end of table.

Table 5.34. PERSONAL INCOME: PRIVATE NONFARM EARNINGS ON A PLACE-OF-WORK BASIS BY MAJOR INDUSTRIAL SOURCE IN THE STATE AND COUNTIES OF FLORIDA, 1988 AND 1989 (Continued)

(rounded to thousands of dollars)

1988 (Continued)

County	Total private nonfarm earnings	Manufacturing	Mining	Contract construction	Wholesale trade	Retail trade	Finance insurance and real estate	Transportation, communication and public utilities	Services	Other private industry 1/
Glades	12,306	274	(D)	613	223	1,475	(D)	3,103	2,217	3,130
Gulf	75,228	42,766	A/	2,534	737	5,217	2,211	11,095	10,140	493
Hamilton	90,490	73,888	A/	1,742	517	4,787	747	3,507	4,882	408
Hardee	76,473	5,432	(D)	(D)	5,957	12,117	4,279	6,089	22,717	10,792
Hendry	117,212	27,720	1,971	13,215	3,497	18,409	4,638	6,200	22,921	18,641
Hernando	323,268	20,033	(D)	51,235	11,109	55,888	20,561	26,824	117,149	(D)
Highlands	272,077	24,931	1,373	33,169	9,588	61,868	19,373	18,521	88,169	15,085
Hillsborough	8,707,306	1,001,228	10,592	767,566	1,073,517	1,136,223	944,431	843,438	2,852,493	77,818
Holmes	37,798	9,330	55	1,740	1,219	7,324	1,626	2,769	13,570	165
Indian River	619,150	60,769	5,080	88,455	15,481	108,417	45,917	15,983	242,121	36,927
Jackson	153,685	34,378	547	11,870	13,105	33,695	10,826	14,145	33,742	1,377
Jefferson	38,244	5,014	61	3,420	2,316	5,880	2,383	7,708	10,162	1,300
Lafayette	7,575	1,928	A/	843	422	1,005	(D)	795	1,696	(D)
Lake	786,920	106,566	9,481	85,470	38,156	139,664	53,883	73,945	233,322	46,433
Lee	2,322,074	130,770	13,633	359,335	120,740	458,171	199,439	153,171	844,659	42,156
Leon	1,313,979	64,523	1,849	122,737	84,275	228,274	124,228	79,165	602,964	5,964
Levy	78,001	7,347	3,650	12,622	3,700	15,770	4,398	8,980	18,571	2,963
Liberty	15,908	4,547	A/	1,679	76	1,632	382	2,309	5,237	A/
Madison	62,821	25,087	59	1,787	2,322	9,417	1,978	6,231	14,969	971
Manatee	1,249,975	268,411	5,728	98,961	48,910	223,667	75,625	57,576	439,171	31,926
Marion	1,057,272	220,037	5,119	116,127	93,854	189,663	66,181	51,004	288,390	26,837
Martin	807,930	103,829	6,119	142,205	23,036	135,283	72,290	43,075	259,558	22,535
Monroe	547,582	11,611	3,554	55,898	17,833	131,327	29,116	41,276	226,981	29,986

See footnotes at end of table.

Continued . . .

Table 5.34. PERSONAL INCOME: PRIVATE NONFARM EARNINGS ON A PLACE-OF-WORK BASIS BY MAJOR INDUSTRIAL SOURCE IN THE STATE AND COUNTIES OF FLORIDA, 1988 AND 1989 (Continued)

(rounded to thousands of dollars)

1988 (Continued)

County	Total private nonfarm earnings	Manufacturing	Mining	Contract construction	Wholesale trade	Retail trade	Finance insurance and real estate	Transportation, communication and public utilities	Services	Other private industry 1/
Nassau	227,412	69,234	381	24,514	6,581	36,007	7,823	13,913	58,942	10,017
Okaloosa	790,112	115,157	1,059	72,183	23,630	157,621	64,995	49,522	293,854	12,091
Okeechobee	105,871	6,460	299	12,882	6,334	24,230	6,615	8,339	37,642	3,070
Orange	8,893,158	1,424,398	9,937	776,918	765,312	1,086,027	789,526	713,020	3,260,606	67,414
Osceola	568,959	63,064	564	74,896	21,416	130,578	27,386	14,844	229,222	6,989
Palm Beach	8,692,572	1,374,118	48,170	884,449	571,027	1,229,570	880,035	437,697	3,119,977	147,529
Pasco	1,065,753	81,605	4,417	152,243	40,701	213,912	67,430	81,941	399,908	23,596
Pinellas	7,582,843	1,288,326	24,948	642,197	410,406	1,187,409	1,067,187	343,097	2,565,696	53,577
Polk	3,003,556	583,870	127,547	244,314	197,698	501,334	178,997	204,206	890,927	74,663
Putnam	283,783	103,556	2,564	29,841	5,901	45,949	10,794	24,240	57,069	3,869
St. Johns	429,200	59,359	1,903	38,435	20,073	84,687	21,816	18,374	169,236	5,317
St. Lucie	790,264	52,758	3,626	102,932	38,267	143,983	56,247	90,798	249,768	51,885
Santa Rosa	269,355	47,100	6,973	33,993	8,497	41,119	10,687	29,629	88,132	3,225
Sarasota	2,299,100	215,930	17,889	299,918	104,051	425,143	208,041	112,574	894,078	21,476
Seminole	1,824,679	291,243	3,122	252,614	134,796	320,789	142,018	110,006	550,684	19,407
Sumter	98,003	13,682	(D)	6,699	3,582	19,015	3,124	22,771	24,258	(D)
Suwannee	113,626	21,140	384	10,811	5,517	25,348	7,069	14,905	26,823	1,629
Taylor	133,437	69,992	(D)	(D)	4,582	15,510	3,322	4,029	18,565	1,839
Union	30,749	11,161	(D)	1,055	381	3,419	967	5,634	7,805	(D)
Volusia	2,081,750	291,478	6,917	240,566	89,633	413,563	147,063	117,786	753,812	20,932
Wakulla	42,678	18,022	55	2,740	679	5,818	1,251	2,310	9,484	2,319
Walton	97,701	16,819	333	8,719	1,802	19,435	3,698	9,431	36,283	1,181
Washington	52,496	8,157	74	5,361	2,805	7,651	869	8,872	18,094	613

See footnotes at end of table.

Continued . . .

Table 5.34. PERSONAL INCOME: PRIVATE NONFARM EARNINGS ON A PLACE-OF-WORK BASIS BY MAJOR INDUSTRIAL SOURCE IN THE STATE AND COUNTIES OF FLORIDA, 1988 AND 1989 (Continued)

(rounded to thousands of dollars)

1989

County	Total private nonfarm earnings	Manufacturing	Mining	Contract construction	Wholesale trade	Retail trade	Finance insurance and real estate	Transportation, communication and public utilities	Services	Other private industry 1/
Florida	114,768,012	14,966,319	574,292	10,092,400	9,011,995	17,226,768	10,593,697	8,907,457	42,001,309	1,393,775
Alachua	1,287,359	129,858	3,186	107,051	60,032	215,967	91,087	56,163	613,370	10,645
Baker	40,482	6,872	A/	2,249	792	9,279	2,230	11,804	7,147	82
Bay	823,480	99,617	882	82,664	36,668	177,633	54,591	59,406	299,494	12,525
Bradford	62,957	10,886	(D)	4,760	1,305	15,783	3,281	4,639	20,522	(D)
Brevard	3,719,811	1,055,882	7,457	269,158	109,926	459,971	126,641	133,312	1,532,550	24,914
Broward	11,876,881	1,325,922	51,148	1,104,412	976,003	1,884,252	1,193,220	766,614	4,481,400	93,910
Calhoun	35,549	5,259	A/	3,318	1,242	7,046	908	7,191	9,761	801
Charlotte	520,762	17,164	4,028	88,882	11,240	106,340	38,791	29,779	216,542	7,996
Citrus	409,378	15,565	2,735	54,078	7,110	72,020	21,865	94,054	136,461	5,490
Clay	487,834	40,542	17,452	69,625	24,729	110,143	22,011	39,782	157,720	5,830
Collier	1,428,917	60,190	15,797	236,504	66,762	240,649	125,506	61,659	570,742	51,108
Columbia	199,143	37,035	146	19,303	16,403	45,649	9,648	15,908	54,114	937
Dade	21,126,597	2,110,993	61,745	1,189,997	2,301,240	2,792,685	2,213,978	2,399,977	7,939,984	115,998
De Soto	76,396	7,226	642	8,218	3,028	14,931	4,028	4,753	23,952	9,618
Dixie	37,090	17,243	(D)	2,752	(D)	6,417	544	2,154	6,280	1,052
Duval	7,761,351	910,947	15,492	625,806	839,992	980,112	1,165,035	867,311	2,308,155	48,501
Escambia	1,970,670	311,731	4,333	190,430	125,116	299,176	109,892	173,452	748,400	8,140
Flagler	132,089	31,226	661	17,756	1,676	19,709	15,293	5,362	37,091	3,315
Franklin	39,308	2,808	61	1,615	5,959	6,402	1,621	2,266	11,864	6,712
Gadsden	142,894	35,895	(D)	14,652	(D)	23,255	5,524	9,776	30,477	2,877
Gilchrist	17,612	1,878	A/	2,090	896	2,741	884	2,538	5,842	714
Glades	13,249	262	(D)	617	419	1,887	(D)	3,301	2,025	3,383

See footnotes at end of table.

Continued . . .

Table 5.34. PERSONAL INCOME: PRIVATE NONFARM EARNINGS ON A PLACE-OF-WORK BASIS BY MAJOR INDUSTRIAL SOURCE IN THE STATE AND COUNTIES OF FLORIDA, 1988 AND 1989 (Continued)

(rounded to thousands of dollars)

1989 (Continued)

County	Total private nonfarm earnings	Manufacturing	Mining	Contract construction	Wholesale trade	Retail trade	Finance insurance and real estate	Transportation, communication and public utilities	Services	Other private industry 1/
Gulf	75,400	42,285	A/	2,380	794	5,509	2,436	10,576	10,715	667
Hamilton	101,069	82,804	A/	2,187	438	5,191	710	3,471	5,788	467
Hardee	83,933	5,485	(D)	(D)	6,199	13,816	4,177	6,482	26,468	11,562
Hendry	129,979	30,097	2,040	15,448	4,055	19,256	4,951	6,724	25,069	22,339
Hernando	353,524	21,388	14,288	49,660	12,400	62,054	19,370	29,138	137,867	7,359
Highlands	292,513	27,340	1,563	33,711	10,706	66,178	18,612	19,042	99,647	15,714
Hillsborough	9,313,996	1,035,152	11,697	728,700	1,187,990	1,197,321	972,803	874,470	3,227,319	78,544
Holmes	40,430	9,797	63	1,993	1,330	7,809	1,795	2,464	15,104	75
Indian River	706,024	78,240	5,332	96,429	30,937	118,932	46,944	16,076	273,428	39,706
Jackson	159,028	36,560	587	9,462	14,199	33,672	11,627	13,884	37,245	1,832
Jefferson	35,790	5,031	65	2,949	1,725	6,319	2,381	4,974	10,916	1,430
Lafayette	8,674	2,361	A/	689	590	1,158	(D)	775	2,081	(D)
Lake	854,247	-16,956	11,238	88,536	40,110	147,297	55,246	76,182	270,268	48,414
Lee	2,536,125	-142,525	14,414	385,301	137,382	493,243	207,826	158,385	952,351	44,698
Leon	1,439,869	70,225	1,983	129,459	89,775	247,142	130,563	86,938	677,403	6,381
Levy	84,637	8,138	(D)	12,269	3,937	18,138	4,528	9,161	22,429	(D)
Liberty	17,411	5,188	A/	1,978	57	1,898	464	2,251	5,525	A/
Madison	62,684	21,258	63	1,925	2,255	10,967	2,112	6,625	16,563	916
Manatee	1,366,481	288,986	7,955	101,230	54,428	231,724	71,062	56,723	517,794	36,579
Marion	1,135,628	230,507	5,027	118,169	107,349	196,517	66,982	54,429	332,885	23,763
Martin	890,355	103,013	6,607	155,641	27,146	150,195	70,132	50,039	302,909	24,673
Monroe	593,119	12,314	3,835	57,705	18,310	138,406	31,869	45,461	254,567	30,652
Nassau	245,149	70,120	406	28,279	8,247	37,633	7,605	16,217	64,559	12,083
Okaloosa	834,211	112,299	1,223	76,875	24,993	161,604	57,747	53,448	333,667	12,355
Okeechobee	115,528	7,687	163	14,037	6,530	26,645	5,782	8,429	43,395	2,860

See footnotes at end of table.

Continued . . .

Table 5.34. PERSONAL INCOME: PRIVATE NONFARM EARNINGS ON A PLACE-OF-WORK BASIS BY MAJOR INDUSTRIAL SOURCE IN THE STATE AND COUNTIES OF FLORIDA, 1988 AND 1989 (Continued)

(rounded to thousands of dollars)

1989 (Continued)

County	Total private nonfarm earnings	Manufac- turing	Mining	Contract con- struction	Wholesale trade	Retail trade	Finance insurance and real estate	Transporta- tion, com- munication and public utilities	Services	Other private indus- try 1/
Orange	9,692,705	1,437,188	11,266	781,576	828,481	1,195,670	808,802	780,382	3,773,681	75,659
Osceola	638,371	66,509	591	83,929	22,714	151,050	31,125	15,812	259,003	7,638
Palm Beach	9,163,296	1,325,514	50,561	894,706	581,856	1,300,347	859,628	486,266	3,505,733	158,685
Pasco	1,147,346	86,820	4,666	147,916	43,246	234,746	66,240	85,954	452,089	25,669
Pinellas	8,047,328	1,358,215	26,093	633,320	459,087	1,238,015	1,049,725	364,107	2,860,591	58,175
Polk	3,238,289	604,662	139,464	256,709	222,184	542,351	190,501	217,119	986,515	78,784
Putnam	287,316	107,856	2,680	21,689	6,996	47,403	10,741	22,308	63,638	4,005
St. Johns	471,387	74,054	2,056	40,054	24,736	90,497	21,470	20,451	192,292	5,777
St. Lucie	861,649	55,624	3,623	105,640	42,020	153,025	58,326	98,785	286,716	57,890
Santa Rosa	284,734	50,794	8,062	34,071	10,050	42,000	10,351	29,325	96,865	3,216
Sarasota	2,437,184	218,694	19,318	317,419	106,692	457,361	183,486	113,285	997,523	23,406
Seminole	1,978,014	301,263	3,471	262,095	149,919	343,070	142,608	115,391	640,205	19,992
Sumter	102,301	15,169	(D)	6,613	3,712	21,020	2,411	20,816	27,752	(D)
Suwannee	119,324	20,584	390	11,623	6,035	27,716	7,367	14,988	28,733	1,888
Taylor	140,770	72,017	(D)	(D)	4,289	15,678	3,721	4,282	20,962	1,893
Union	33,675	11,974	(D)	1,548	528	2,791	1,034	6,038	9,330	(D)
Volusia	2,226,351	308,384	7,414	243,000	96,464	439,425	135,478	124,762	848,387	23,037
Wakulla	46,825	19,794	59	2,955	1,186	6,214	1,273	2,331	10,676	2,337
Walton	110,167	20,510	330	8,265	2,265	20,105	3,989	12,814	40,399	1,490
Washington	55,367	9,937	79	4,306	3,071	7,613	704	8,716	20,364	577

(D) Data withheld to avoid disclosure of information about individual industries.
A/ Less than $50,000.
1/ Includes agricultural services, forestry, fisheries, and other.
Note: 1988 data are revised.

Source: U.S., Department of Commerce, Bureau of Economic Analysis, unpublished data.

Table 5.38.   PERSONAL INCOME: TRANSFER PAYMENTS BY TYPE IN FLORIDA, 1988 AND 1989

(rounded to thousands of dollars)

Type of transfer payment	1988 A/	1989
Total personal income by place of residence	204,478,700	224,410,300
Total transfer payments	32,282,463	35,842,756
Percentage of personal income	15.79	15.97
Government payments to individuals	30,379,699	33,789,138
Retirement and disability insurance benefit payments	19,383,745	20,965,797
Old age, survivors, and disability insurance payments	13,942,522	15,163,703
Railroad retirement and disability payments	330,930	352,149
Federal civilian employee retirement payments	2,140,873	2,252,191
Military retirement payments	2,002,973	2,137,030
State and local government employee retirement payments	822,903	905,224
Workers' compensation payments (federal and state)	112,910	125,063
Other government disability insurance and retirement payments	30,634	30,437
Unemployment insurance benefit payments	337,277	381,613
State unemployment insurance compensation	326,916	373,097
Unemployment Compensation for Federal Civilian Employees (UCFE)	2,924	2,650
Unemployment Compensation for Railroad Employees	1,201	1,404
Unemployment Compensation for Veterans (UCX)	4,719	3,936
Other unemployment compensation	1,517	526
Federal education and training assistance payments (excluding veterans)	247,843	263,412
Income maintenance benefit payments	1,507,958	1,720,806
Supplemental Security Income (SSI) payments	551,514	597,181
Aid to Families with Dependent Children (AFDC)	333,661	382,794
Food stamps	413,339	486,977
Other income maintenance	209,444	253,854
Veterans' benefit payments	1,220,799	1,273,192
Veterans' pensions and compensation	1,067,191	1,122,830
Educational assistance to veterans, dependents, and survivors	36,363	35,328
Veterans' life insurance benefit payments	114,462	111,107
Other assistance to veterans	2,783	3,927
Other payments to individuals	9,341	10,827
Business payments to individuals	1,090,608	1,179,021
Payments to nonprofit institutions	812,156	874,597
Federal government payments	205,552	207,470
State and local government payments	252,758	274,921
Business payments (corporate gifts)	353,846	392,206

A/ Revised.

Source: U.S., Department of Commerce, Bureau of Economic Analysis, unpublished data.

Florida Statistical Abstract 1991

Table 5.39. PERSONAL INCOME: TRANSFER PAYMENTS IN THE STATE AND COUNTIES
  OF FLORIDA, 1987, 1988, AND 1989

	1987 A/		1988 A/		1989	
County	Amount ($1,000)	As a percentage of total personal income	Amount ($1,000)	As a percentage of total personal income	Amount ($1,000)	As a percentage of total personal income
Florida	29,721,761	15.9	32,282,463	15.8	35,842,756	16.0
Alachua	350,281	15.3	386,506	15.5	438,118	16.0
Baker	31,531	16.6	33,663	16.4	38,496	17.4
Bay	300,097	20.1	326,879	20.2	364,344	20.9
Bradford	46,176	22.0	49,507	21.8	54,868	21.9
Brevard	967,669	17.6	1,014,840	16.9	1,126,607	17.0
Broward	2,998,114	13.5	3,296,748	13.6	3,651,898	13.8
Calhoun	23,055	29.6	25,931	29.0	28,695	29.8
Charlotte	346,961	26.1	369,760	25.3	419,307	25.1
Citrus	291,180	29.3	312,333	28.9	341,813	28.2
Clay	192,199	13.8	209,434	13.8	222,142	13.4
Collier	324,147	12.1	356,223	12.0	390,720	11.4
Columbia	91,236	21.1	101,800	21.6	112,234	22.0
Dade	3,741,458	13.4	4,171,921	13.7	4,733,930	14.4
De Soto	55,792	24.9	61,571	24.5	68,021	25.1
Dixie	21,569	25.9	25,447	27.6	27,651	26.7
Duval	1,337,659	13.9	1,455,655	14.1	1,617,159	14.6
Escambia	668,430	20.3	721,624	20.5	793,982	20.9
Flagler	65,512	24.3	72,183	23.4	83,010	23.8
Franklin	21,848	26.7	26,211	27.8	27,952	27.1
Gadsden	90,218	22.2	99,920	22.6	113,163	23.4
Gilchrist	18,363	21.9	20,259	21.9	22,986	22.9
Glades	10,075	18.8	11,553	20.0	12,565	20.7
Gulf	27,709	23.3	30,298	23.6	33,982	25.0
Hamilton	20,740	23.6	23,545	24.1	26,522	24.9
Hardee	37,781	16.9	40,137	15.8	45,179	17..
Hendry	38,905	13.0	43,443	12.7	48,478	13.6
Hernando	301,831	29.3	316,827	27.9	352,007	27.5
Highlands	208,399	26.3	217,299	24.8	242,659	25.2
Hillsborough	1,573,686	14.0	1,712,328	13.9	1,882,451	14.0
Holmes	38,874	27.2	41,852	27.1	46,438	27.2
Indian River	266,714	17.8	282,488	17.0	316,343	16.8
Jackson	109,777	26.8	117,777	26.6	132,887	27.6
Jefferson	23,882	21.0	25,520	20.7	28,628	22.2
Lafayette	9,815	17.2	10,206	17.1	12,005	18.0
Lake	438,907	20.6	461,440	19.5	513,440	19.7

See footnote at end of table.   Continued . . .

Table 5.39. PERSONAL INCOME: TRANSFER PAYMENTS IN THE STATE AND COUNTIES
OF FLORIDA, 1987, 1988, AND 1989 (Continued)

	1987 A/		1988 A/		1989	
County	Amount ($1,000)	As a per-centage of total personal income	Amount ($1,000)	As a per-centage of total personal income	Amount ($1,000)	As a per-centage of total personal income
Lee	888,743	18.7	926,254	17.8	1,032,392	17.6
Leon	305,442	12.7	332,591	12.5	370,297	12.6
Levy	59,890	24.1	63,274	23.8	70,557	24.2
Liberty	14,702	31.5	16,055	31.9	17,345	31.0
Madison	37,094	25.3	39,541	24.7	44,228	25.4
Manatee	555,004	19.0	584,031	18.5	646,728	18.3
Marion	478,342	22.9	509,626	22.4	572,444	22.7
Martin	262,061	13.5	283,747	13.2	314,362	13.1
Monroe	146,291	12.4	155,252	12.1	168,836	11.9
Nassau	72,692	11.7	80,191	12.0	90,222	12.5
Okaloosa	375,932	20.7	406,905	20.8	448,986	21.1
Okeechobee	70,320	23.7	68,947	21.7	78,732	22.7
Orange	1,195,787	12.7	1,289,108	12.4	1,430,129	12.5
Osceola	180,386	13.8	193,980	13.2	217,359	13.1
Palm Beach	2,142,243	12.6	2,291,194	12.3	2,554,952	12.3
Pasco	881,687	27.9	930,352	27.0	985,208	26.1
Pinellas	2,579,103	17.6	2,798,545	17.6	3,127,596	17.8
Polk	844,398	17.7	929,768	17.6	1,015,122	17.6
Putnam	159,752	25.6	175,996	26.2	189,599	26.4
St. Johns	176,489	14.2	195,337	14.3	218,176	14.3
St. Lucie	329,739	21.2	363,868	20.8	407,699	21.3
Santa Rosa	155,169	17.6	175,280	18.4	191,362	18.6
Sarasota	965,827	18.3	1,056,692	18.4	1,147,784	17.9
Seminole	427,118	11.3	468,599	11.1	517,989	11.2
Sumter	87,606	28.2	93,867	27.9	103,589	27.8
Suwannee	62,704	24.5	70,386	25.1	78,377	25.6
Taylor	37,758	19.4	41,234	19.6	45,814	20.2
Union	14,750	17.1	16,561	18.0	17,977	18.4
Volusia	983,509	21.4	1,092,681	21.7	1,194,080	21.5
Wakulla	24,308	18.1	28,762	19.0	31,805	19.0
Walton	69,587	28.4	77,603	28.7	83,854	28.1
Washington	46,738	30.6	53,108	31.3	58,476	32.2

A/ Revised.

Source: U.S., Department of Commerce, Bureau of Economic Analysis, unpublished
data.

Florida Statistical Abstract 1991

Table 5.45. MONEY INCOME: ESTIMATED PER CAPITA AMOUNTS IN THE STATE, COUNTIES
AND MUNICIPALITIES OF FLORIDA, 1979 AND 1987

(in dollars)

Area	1979	1987	Percentage change	Area	1979	1987	Percentage change
Florida	7,260	12,456	71.6	Brevard (Continued)			
				Satellite Beach	8,873	15,100	70.2
Alachua	6,094	10,928	79.3	Titusville	7,001	12,026	71.8
Alachua	5,156	9,446	83.2	West Melbourne	7,072	12,501	76.8
Archer	5,097	8,420	65.2				
Gainesville	6,150	10,603	72.4	Broward	8,621	14,914	73.0
Hawthorne	3,949	6,895	74.6	Coconut Creek	9,864	17,246	74.8
High Springs	4,822	8,301	72.1	Cooper City	8,924	16,136	80.8
LaCrosse	4,264	7,315	71.6	Coral Springs	8,928	16,468	84.5
Micanopy	5,374	9,548	77.7	Dania	6,609	11,228	69.9
Newberry	4,174	7,544	80.7	Davie	7,845	13,747	75.2
Waldo	4,199	7,028	67.4	Deerfield Beach	7,872	13,878	76.3
				Ft. Lauderdale	9,752	16,692	71.2
Baker	4,727	8,033	69.9	Hallendale	10,047	16,260	61.8
Glen St. Mary	5,021	8,450	68.3	Hillsboro Beach	18,952	30,260	59.7
Macclenny	5,209	8,905	71.0	Hollywood	8,727	14,633	67.7
				Lauderdale-by-			
Bay	5,968	9,689	62.3	the-sea	13,858	23,104	66.7
Callaway	5,755	9,045	57.2	Lauderdale Lakes	7,456	12,734	70.8
Cedar Grove	5,172	8,796	70.1	Lauderhill	8,627	14,419	67.1
Lynn Haven	5,890	9,501	61.3	Lazy Lake	8,621	14,914	73.0
Mexico Beach	7,345	12,540	70.7	Lighthouse Point	12,146	21,949	80.7
Panama City	5,937	9,519	60.3	Margate	7,430	12,671	70.5
Panama City Beach	7,221	11,325	56.8	Miramar	7,830	13,051	66.7
Parker	6,403	10,019	56.5	North Lauderdale	7,225	12,935	79.0
Springfield	4,409	6,953	57.7	Oakland Park	8,559	14,898	74.1
				Parkland	11,232	21,628	92.6
Bradford	4,813	7,892	64.0	Pembroke Park	7,461	12,739	70.7
Brooker	4,536	7,533	66.1	Pembroke Pines	8,956	14,854	65.9
Hampton	4,518	6,714	48.6	Plantation	10,494	19,313	84.0
Lawtey	4,511	7,494	66.1	Pompano Beach	9,245	15,927	72.3
Starke	4,812	8,048	67.2	Sea Ranch Lakes	15,841	30,259	91.0
				Sunrise	7,727	13,355	72.8
Brevard	7,448	12,775	71.5	Tamarac	8,979	15,512	72.8
Cape Canaveral	8,477	14,021	65.4	Wilton Manors	8,685	15,115	74.0
Cocoa	5,988	10,330	72.5				
Cocoa Beach	10,595	18,376	73.4	Calhoun	4,710	7,815	65.9
Indialantic	11,051	18,596	68.3	Altha	3,814	6,784	77.9
Indian Harbour				Blountstown	5,342	8,983	68.2
Beach	8,917	15,627	75.2				
Malabar	7,714	13,416	73.9	Charlotte	7,547	12,554	66.3
Melbourne	6,430	11,482	78.6	Punta Gorda	10,045	18,019	79.4
Melbourne Beach	11,685	20,874	78.6				
Melbourne Village	9,410	17,031	81.0	Citrus	6,055	10,487	73.2
Palm Bay	7,099	11,370	60.2	Crystal River	6,170	10,105	63.8
Palm Shores	7,448	12,775	71.5	Inverness	5,907	9,678	63.8
Rockledge	7,335	12,724	73.5				

See footnote at end of table.

Continued . . .

Florida Statistical Abstract 1991

Table 5.45.   MONEY INCOME: ESTIMATED PER CAPITA AMOUNTS IN THE STATE, COUNTIES
AND MUNICIPALITIES OF FLORIDA, 1979 AND 1987 (Continued)

(in dollars)

Area	1979	1987	Per- cent- age change	Area	1979	1987	Per- cent- age change
Clay	6,741	11,556	71.4	Dixie	4,690	7,334	56.4
Green Cove Springs	4,662	7,798	67.3	Cross City	4,021	6,162	53.2
Keystone Heights	7,065	11,626	64.6	Horseshoe Beach	5,127	7,450	45.3
Orange Park	8,203	13,849	68.8				
Penney Farms	6,485	11,727	80.8	Duval	6,822	11,614	70.2
				Atlantic Beach	7,374	12,445	68.8
Collier	9,424	16,466	74.7	Baldwin	4,707	7,437	58.0
Everglades	5,170	10,087	95.1	Jacksonville	6,767	11,514	70.1
Naples	16,942	30,627	80.8	Jacksonville Beach	7,554	13,072	73.0
				Neptune Beach	10,093	17,034	68.8
Columbia	5,702	9,213	61.6				
Ft. White	2,792	4,567	63.6	Escambia	6,183	10,316	66.8
Lake City	5,992	9,392	56.7	Century	4,489	7,976	77.7
				Pensacola	6,881	11,560	68.0
Dade	7,722	12,401	60.6				
Bal Harbour	25,412	42,221	66.1	Flagler	6,920	11,529	66.6
Bay Harbor Islands	17,189	26,282	52.9	Beverly Beach	6,641	11,142	67.8
Biscayne Park	8,957	14,201	58.5	Bunnell	4,182	6,473	54.8
Coral Gables	12,900	24,297	88.3	Flagler Beach	7,780	13,229	70.0
El Portal	9,354	15,010	60.5	Marineland (part)	6,920	11,529	66.6
Florida City	4,105	6,557	59.7				
Golden Beach	18,017	26,297	46.0	Franklin	4,653	7,648	64.4
Hialeah	5,915	8,927	50.9	Apalachicola	4,230	6,889	62.9
Hialeah Gardens	8,262	13,169	59.4	Carrabelle	5,124	8,127	58.6
Homestead	5,507	8,979	63.0				
Indian Creek	19,100	30,512	59.7	Gadsden	4,172	6,990	67.5
Islandia	0	0	0.0	Chattahoochee	3,871	6,426	66.0
Medley	8,902	14,456	62.4	Greensboro	4,410	7,274	64.9
Miami	6,084	9,830	61.6	Gretna	2,930	4,434	51.3
Miami Beach	8,904	13,638	53.2	Havana	3,990	6,810	70.7
Miami Shores	13,026	20,280	55.7	Midway	2,798	4,854	73.5
Miami Springs	10,244	15,544	51.7	Quincy	5,211	8,269	58.7
North Bay Village	10,912	17,056	56.3				
North Miami	8,738	13,671	56.5	Gilchrist	4,804	8,743	82.0
North Miami Beach	8,070	13,788	70.9	Bell	3,837	6,778	76.6
Opa-Locka	4,628	7,404	60.0	Fanning Springs			
South Miami	9,201	14,520	57.8	(part)	4,133	7,325	77.2
Surfside	10,451	15,965	52.8	Trenton	4,683	8,120	73.4
Sweetwater	4,955	7,908	59.6				
Virginia Gardens	9,233	14,751	59.8	Glades	4,615	7,667	66.1
West Miami	7,652	12,156	58.9	Moore Haven	5,379	9,701	80.3
De Soto	4,913	8,139	65.7	Gulf	4,932	8,153	65.3
Arcadia	4,715	8,110	72.0	Port St. Joe	5,311	8,960	68.7
				Wewahitchka	4,507	6,752	49.8

See footnote at end of table.   Continued . . .

Florida Statistical Abstract 1991

Table 5.45. MONEY INCOME: ESTIMATED PER CAPITA AMOUNTS IN THE STATE, COUNTIES
    AND MUNICIPALITIES OF FLORIDA, 1979 AND 1987 (Continued)

(in dollars)

Area	1979	1987	Per-cent-age change	Area	1979	1987	Per-cent-age change
Hamilton	4,350	7,172	64.9	Jackson (Continued)			
Jasper	4,407	7,275	65.1	Campbellton	3,334	5,593	67.8
Jennings	4,131	7,054	70.8	Cottondale	4,267	6,926	62.3
White Springs	4,178	6,627	58.6	Graceville	5,039	8,374	66.2
				Grand Ridge	4,850	7,548	55.6
Hardee	5,130	7,832	52.7	Greenwood	5,139	8,476	64.9
Bowling Green	4,110	6,026	46.6	Jacob City	1,873	3,233	72.6
Wauchula	6,313	9,775	54.8	Malone	4,475	6,981	56.0
Zolfo Springs	3,875	6,221	60.5	Marianna	5,009	8,378	67.3
				Sneads	4,969	9,080	82.7
Hendry	5,738	8,939	55.8				
Clewiston	7,645	12,127	58.6	Jefferson	4,570	7,713	68.8
La Belle	5,091	7,755	52.3	Monticello	4,383	6,834	55.9
Hernando	5,881	9,780	66.3	Lafayette	4,934	8,815	78.7
Brooksville	6,184	10,159	64.3	Mayo	4,300	7,904	83.8
Weeki Wachee	5,881	9,780	66.3				
				Lake	6,449	11,837	83.5
Highlands	5,964	10,024	68.1	Astatula	5,492	9,834	79.1
Avon Park	4,630	7,714	66.6	Clermont	6,941	11,880	71.2
Lake Placid	4,869	8,167	67.7	Eustis	7,060	11,916	68.8
Sebring	6,433	10,880	69.1	Fruitland Park	5,656	9,660	70.8
				Groveland	4,538	7,706	69.8
Hillsborough	6,683	11,752	75.8	Howey-in-the-Hills	8,143	15,644	92.1
Plant City	5,405	8,709	61.1	Lady Lake	4,585	8,272	80.4
Tampa	6,385	11,004	72.3	Leesburg	6,344	10,464	64.9
Temple Terrace	8,899	14,891	67.3	Mascotte	3,824	6,745	76.4
				Minneola	5,783	10,953	89.4
Holmes	4,741	8,203	73.0	Montverde	6,771	13,344	97.1
Bonifay	4,594	7,430	61.7	Mount Dora	7,562	13,262	75.4
Esto	3,057	4,819	57.6	Tavares	6,417	11,152	72.3
Noma	2,279	3,652	60.2	Umatilla	5,984	8,860	48.1
Ponce de Leon	4,888	7,523	53.9				
Westville	4,694	7,289	55.3	Lee	7,554	12,948	71.4
				Cape Coral	8,340	12,929	55.0
Indian River	7,976	13,722	72.0	Ft. Myers	6,548	11,419	74.4
Fellsmere	4,900	9,684	97.6	Sanibel	15,604	29,150	86.8
Indian River							
Shores	27,048	39,807	47.2	Leon	6,862	11,923	73.8
Orchid	7,976	13,722	72.0	Tallahassee	6,777	11,631	71.6
Sebastian	5,965	11,952	100.4				
Vero Beach	9,805	18,387	87.5	Levy	5,100	8,579	68.2
				Bronson	4,376	6,858	56.7
Jackson	4,672	7,961	70.4	Cedar Key	4,180	7,419	77.5
Alford	3,670	6,316	72.1	Chiefland	5,710	9,335	63.5
Bascom	6,579	11,087	68.5				

See footnote at end of table.   Continued . . .

Florida Statistical Abstract 1991

Table 5.45. MONEY INCOME: ESTIMATED PER CAPITA AMOUNTS IN THE STATE, COUNTIES
AND MUNICIPALITIES OF FLORIDA, 1979 AND 1987 (Continued)

(in dollars)

Area	1979	1987	Per-cent-age change	Area	1979	1987	Per-cent-age change
Levy (Continued)				Okaloosa	6,422	11,192	74.3
Fanning Springs				Cinco Bayou	5,794	9,915	71.1
(part)	3,803	6,093	60.2	Crestview	4,855	7,614	56.8
Inglis	5,486	9,121	66.3	Destin	8,069	14,429	78.8
Otter Creek	6,271	10,031	60.0	Ft. Walton Beach	7,083	12,199	72.2
Williston	4,824	8,172	69.4	Laurel Hill	3,421	5,658	65.4
Yankeetown	6,494	11,971	84.3	Mary Esther	6,311	10,777	70.8
				Niceville	6,454	11,834	83.4
Liberty	4,730	8,309	75.7	Shalimar	11,136	18,797	68.8
Bristol	5,666	9,871	74.2	Valparaiso	6,894	11,772	70.8
Madison	4,205	6,943	65.1	Okeechobee	5,478	9,224	68.4
Greenville	3,745	5,709	52.4	Okeechobee	5,645	9,433	67.1
Lee	4,418	6,464	46.3				
Madison	4,833	7,335	51.8	Orange	6,985	12,501	79.0
				Apopka	6,541	11,369	73.8
Manatee	7,206	12,357	71.5	Bay Lake	6,985	12,501	79.0
Ana Maria	8,732	15,538	77.9	Belle Isle	9,276	16,238	75.1
Bradenton	6,699	11,464	71.1	Eatonville	4,130	7,706	86.6
Bradenton Beach	7,101	12,965	82.6	Edgewood	9,389	21,785	132.0
Holmes Beach	10,675	18,500	73.3	Lake Buena Vista	11,151	25,921	132.5
Longboat Key				Maitland	11,239	22,243	97.9
(part)	14,445	27,617	91.2	Oakland	5,179	10,757	107.7
Palmetto	5,811	9,695	66.8	Ocoee	5,579	9,940	78.2
				Orlando	6,735	12,042	78.8
Marion	5,813	9,707	67.0	Windermere	12,665	22,069	74.3
Belleview	4,786	8,113	69.5	Winter Garden	5,896	10,023	70.0
Dunnellon	6,398	10,739	67.8	Winter Park	10,083	17,466	73.2
McIntosh	7,339	11,959	63.0				
Ocala	6,175	9,988	61.7	Osceola	6,055	10,770	77.9
Reddick	3,947	6,176	56.5	Kissimmee	6,003	10,865	81.0
				St. Cloud	5,805	10,553	81.8
Martin	8,099	15,256	88.4				
Jupiter Island	20,306	39,042	92.3	Palm Beach	8,899	15,964	79.4
Ocean Breeze Park	6,644	13,078	96.8	Atlantis	23,770	46,122	94.0
Sewall's Point	14,818	28,567	92.8	Belle Glade	5,654	8,876	57.0
Stuart	7,809	14,929	91.2	Boca Raton	12,549	23,679	88.7
				Boynton Beach	7,266	12,854	76.9
Monroe	7,755	14,184	82.9	Briny Breezes	12,208	23,379	91.5
Key Colony Beach	12,597	22,403	77.8	Cloud Lake	6,753	13,213	95.7
Key West	6,688	12,012	79.6	Delray Beach	9,261	15,571	68.1
Layton	7,755	14,184	82.9	Glen Ridge	11,309	22,240	96.7
				Golf Village	61,938	121,396	96.0
Nassau	6,416	11,039	72.1	Golfview	12,182	24,001	97.0
Callahan	5,143	9,210	79.1	Greenacres City	6,744	12,847	90.5
Fernandina Beach	7,013	13,084	86.6	Gulf Stream	49,656	93,005	87.3
Hilliard	5,456	8,442	54.7	Haverhill	7,800	15,331	96.6

See footnote at end of table.

Continued . . .

Florida Statistical Abstract 1991

Table 5.45. MONEY INCOME: ESTIMATED PER CAPITA AMOUNTS IN THE STATE, COUNTIES AND MUNICIPALITIES OF FLORIDA, 1979 AND 1987 (Continued)

(in dollars)

Area	1979	1987	Percentage change	Area	1979	1987	Percentage change
Palm Beach				Pinellas (Continued)			
(Continued)				Largo	7,572	12,728	68.1
Highland Beach	17,839	34,865	95.4	Madeira Beach	8,519	16,438	93.0
Hypoluxo	8,761	16,786	91.6	North Redington			
Juno Beach	14,341	28,340	97.6	Beach	11,720	20,956	78.8
Jupiter	8,345	15,830	89.7	Oldsmar	6,984	12,349	76.8
Jupiter Inlet				Pinellas Park	6,408	11,425	78.3
Colony	14,375	27,999	94.8	Redington Beach	9,859	17,023	72.7
Lake Clarke Shores	10,816	20,068	85.5	Redington Shores	9,677	17,531	81.2
Lake Park	9,374	17,391	85.5	Safety Harbor	7,109	14,137	98.9
Lake Worth	7,186	12,971	80.5	St. Petersburg	6,965	12,170	74.7
Lantana	7,694	14,057	82.7	St. Petersburg			
Manalapan	38,666	76,165	97.0	Beach	10,010	17,293	72.8
Mangonia Park	7,065	13,857	96.1	Seminole	7,125	12,052	69.2
North Palm Beach	11,174	23,135	107.0	South Pasadena	10,812	18,465	70.8
Ocean Ridge	16,474	34,107	107.0	Tarpon Springs	6,526	11,730	79.7
Pahokee	5,479	10,435	90.5	Treasure Island	11,499	21,075	83.3
Palm Beach	25,598	40,512	58.3				
Palm Beach Gardens	10,361	19,783	90.9	Polk	6,445	10,393	61.3
Palm Beach Shores	12,549	23,159	84.5	Auburndale	5,909	9,379	58.7
Palm Springs	8,145	14,195	74.3	Bartow	6,653	9,915	49.0
Riviera Beach	6,804	11,959	75.8	Davenport	5,728	10,063	75.7
Royal Palm Beach	10,377	17,204	65.8	Dundee	4,875	8,134	66.9
South Bay	3,721	6,679	79.5	Eagle Lake	5,759	7,882	36.9
South Palm Beach	16,986	33,047	94.6	Ft. Meade	5,127	6,988	36.3
Tequesta	15,034	26,156	74.0	Frostproof	5,849	9,404	60.8
West Palm Beach	7,528	13,845	83.9	Haines City	5,004	7,898	57.8
				Highland Park	13,183	21,794	65.3
Pasco	6,063	10,797	78.1	Hillcrest Heights	12,554	20,418	62.6
Dade City	6,536	11,778	80.2	Lake Alfred	5,836	9,280	59.0
New Port Richey	5,942	10,540	77.4	Lake Hamilton	6,355	11,508	81.1
Port Richey	6,258	11,048	76.5	Lake Wales	6,102	9,683	58.7
St. Leo	2,550	4,471	75.3	Lakeland	7,142	11,256	57.6
San Antonio	6,522	10,531	61.5	Mulberry	5,043	8,197	62.5
Zephyrhills	5,240	9,284	77.2	Polk City	4,743	8,528	79.8
				Winter Haven	7,255	12,205	68.2
Pinellas	7,610	13,451	76.8				
Belleair	14,204	26,312	85.2	Putnam	5,387	9,109	69.1
Belleair Beach	15,011	31,869	112.3	Crescent City	5,259	8,666	64.8
Belleair Bluffs	12,133	21,182	74.6	Interlachen	4,209	7,092	68.5
Belleair Shore	7,610	13,451	76.8	Palatka	4,659	7,616	63.5
Clearwater	8,202	14,452	76.2	Pomona Park	4,883	8,600	76.1
Dunedin	8,106	13,682	68.8	Welaka	3,888	7,354	89.1
Gulfport	6,509	11,597	78.2				
Indian Rocks Beach	9,516	16,793	76.5	St. Johns	6,665	12,315	84.8
Indian Shores	13,401	24,994	86.5	Hastings	4,520	7,447	64.8
Kenneth City	7,196	12,621	75.4	Marineland (part)	6,665	12,315	84.8

See footnote at end of table. Continued . . .

Table 5.45. MONEY INCOME: ESTIMATED PER CAPITA AMOUNTS IN THE STATE, COUNTIES
AND MUNICIPALITIES OF FLORIDA, 1979 AND 1987 (Continued)

(in dollars)

Area	1979	1987	Per-cent-age change	Area	1979	1987	Per-cent-age change
St. Johns (Continued)				Taylor	5,718	9,358	63.7
St. Augustine	6,022	10,277	70.7	Perry	5,727	9,308	62.5
St. Augustine							
Beach	8,731	14,170	62.3	Union	3,703	6,511	75.8
				Lake Butler	4,838	8,667	79.1
St. Lucie	6,460	10,623	64.4	Raiford	6,472	10,070	55.6
Ft. Pierce	5,547	8,466	52.6	Worthington			
Port St. Lucie	7,794	12,193	56.4	Springs	3,660	5,960	62.8
St. Lucie	9,480	16,531	74.4				
				Volusia	6,588	11,420	73.3
Santa Rosa	6,057	10,501	73.4	Daytona Beach	5,884	10,238	74.0
Gulf Breeze	8,942	15,996	78.9	Daytona Beach			
Jay	7,288	10,800	48.2	Shores	11,448	20,051	75.1
Milton	5,607	9,985	78.1	Deland	5,394	9,229	71.1
				Edgewater	5,831	9,581	64.3
Sarasota	8,449	14,848	75.7	Holly Hill	5,919	9,726	64.3
Longboat Key				Lake Helen	5,043	8,871	75.9
(part)	19,085	32,797	71.8	New Smyrna Beach	6,624	11,419	72.4
North Port	6,546	11,098	69.5	Oak Hill	4,207	6,870	63.3
Sarasota	8,071	14,120	74.9	Orange City	5,471	8,836	61.5
Venice	9,409	15,729	67.2	Ormond Beach	9,394	16,793	78.8
				Pierson	4,549	7,963	75.0
Seminole	7,672	13,594	77.2	Ponce Inlet	8,822	17,759	101.3
Altamonte Springs	8,635	14,976	73.4	Port Orange	6,456	11,211	73.7
Casselberry	7,177	13,200	83.9	South Daytona	6,758	11,702	73.2
Lake Mary	7,782	14,313	83.9				
Longwood	7,185	12,816	78.4	Wakulla	5,111	8,769	71.6
Oviedo	7,631	13,089	71.5	St. Marks	6,107	10,417	70.6
Sanford	5,264	8,568	62.8	Sopchoppy	4,122	6,962	68.9
Winter Springs	7,977	14,274	78.9				
				Walton	5,218	8,252	58.1
Sumter	5,153	8,576	66.4	DeFuniak Springs	4,795	7,174	49.6
Bushnell	6,048	9,478	56.7	Freeport	5,058	7,249	43.3
Center Hill	4,318	7,160	65.8	Paxton	4,253	6,220	46.2
Coleman	4,350	7,042	61.9				
Webster	3,061	4,950	61.7	Washington	4,526	7,825	72.9
Wildwood	4,871	7,995	64.1	Caryville	3,230	5,619	74.0
				Chipley	4,428	7,881	78.0
Suwannee	4,908	8,395	71.0	Ebro	4,267	6,910	61.9
Branford	4,143	6,759	63.1	Vernon	4,129	6,835	65.5
Live Oak	5,050	8,461	67.5	Wausau	4,419	6,993	58.2

Note: See Glossary for definition of money income.

Source: U.S., Department of Commerce, Bureau of the Census, *Current Population
Reports: Local Population Estimates, 1988 Population* and *1987 Per Capita Income
Estimates for Counties and Incorporated Places, South.* Series P-26, No. 88-S-SC.

Florida Statistical Abstract 1991

Table 5.46. POVERTY THRESHOLDS: AVERAGE POVERTY THRESHOLDS FOR A FAMILY OF FOUR
AND THE ANNUAL CONSUMER PRICE INDEX IN THE UNITED STATES, 1978 THROUGH 1989

Year	Average threshold (dollars)	Consumer Price Index (1982-84=100)	Year	Average threshold (dollars)	Consumer Price Index (1982-84=100)
1978	6,662	65.2	1984	10,609	103.9
1979	7,412	72.6	1985	10,989	107.6
1980	8,414	82.4	1986	11,203	109.6
1981	9,287	90.9	1987	11,611	113.6
1982	9,862	96.5	1988	12,092	118.3
1983	10,178	99.6	1989	12,675	124.0

Note: Poverty thresholds are based on a definition developed by the Social
Security Administration in 1964 and revised by a federal interagency committee in
1969 and 1980. Annual adjustments are based on changes in the Consumer Price Index
(CPI). The poverty index is based on money income and does not take into account
noncash benefits, such as food stamps, medicaid, and public housing. Differences in
poverty thresholds based on farm-nonfarm residence have been eliminated. Nonfarm
thresholds now apply to all families. For years prior to 1981, average threshold for
a nonfarm family of four is shown. Beginning in 1987, poverty thresholds are based
on revised processing procedures and are not directly comparable with prior years.
   Source: U.S., Department of Commerce, Bureau of the Census, *Statistical Abstract
of the United States, 1991* and *Survey of Current Business*, May 1990.

Table 5.47. MONEY INCOME: MEDIAN FAMILY INCOME BY SPECIFIED CHARACTERISTICS
IN THE UNITED STATES, 1988 AND 1989

(amounts in dollars)

Specified characteristics	1988	1989	Percentage change in real income
All families	32,191	34,213	1.4
Race of householder			
White	33,915	35,975	1.2
Black	19,329	20,209	-0.3
Spanish origin 1/	21,769	23,446	2.8
Education of householder			
Elementary, total	16,708	17,385	-0.7
High school, 4 years	31,198	32,502	-0.6
College, total	45,429	48,518	1.9
1 to 3 years	37,234	39,740	1.8
4 years	53,214	57,226	2.6
5 or more years	59,197	62,889	1.4
Type of family			
Married-couple families	36,389	38,547	1.1
Wife in paid labor force	42,709	45,266	1.1
Wife not in paid labor force	27,220	28,747	0.8
Male householder, no wife present	26,827	27,847	-1.0
Female householder, no husband present	15,346	16,442	2.2

   1/ Persons of Spanish origin may be of any race.
   Source: U.S., Department of Commerce, Bureau of the Census, *Current Population
Reports: Consumer Income*. Series P-60, No. 172.

Florida Statistical Abstract 1991

Table 5.48. INCOME LEVELS DEFINING POVERTY: AMOUNT OF INCOME BELOW WHICH A PERSON
IS DETERMINED TO BE POOR IN THE UNITED STATES, MARCH 1987 THROUGH 1991

(in dollars)

Family size	1987	1988	1989	1990	1991
1	5,500	5,770	5,980	6,280	6,620
2	7,400	7,730	8,020	8,420	8,880
3	9,300	9,690	10,060	10,560	11,140
4	11,200	11,650	12,100	12,700	13,400
5	13,100	13,610	14,140	14,840	15,660
6	15,000	15,570	16,180	16,980	17,920
7	16,900	17,530	18,220	19,120	20,180
8	18,800	19,490	20,260	21,260	22,440
Amount to add for each additional person	1,900	1,960	2,040	2,140	2,260

Note: These poverty income guidelines are used for administrative purposes; for
instance, for determining whether a person or family is financially eligible for
assistance or services under a particular federal program. The guidelines apply in
all states except Alaska and Hawaii. Data are the same for farm and nonfarm
families.
Source: U.S., National Archives and Records Administration, *Federal Register*,
February 20, 1991. Volume 56, No. 34. Data from U.S., Department of Health and Human
Services.

Table 5.49. POVERTY THRESHOLDS: POVERTY LEVEL INCOMES BY SIZE OF FAMILY IN THE
UNITED STATES, 1985 THROUGH 1988

(in dollars)

Size of family unit	1985	1986	1987	1988
1 person (unrelated individual)	4,974	5,068	5,308	5,534
Under 65 years	5,088	5,186	5,428	5,654
65 years and over	4,690	4,780	5,004	5,212
2 persons	6,366	6,493	6,795	7,077
Householder under 65 years	6,578	6,706	7,019	7,310
Householder 65 years and over	5,916	6,031	6,313	6,575
3 persons	7,799	7,948	8,319	8,667
4 persons	9,997	10,191	10,666	11,108
5 persons	11,832	12,061	12,619	13,141
6 persons	13,369	13,633	14,247	14,834
7 persons	15,152	15,509	16,212	16,763
8 persons	16,840	17,094	17,926	18,628
9 persons or more	20,089	20,465	21,224	22,169

Note: These data were generated by the Congressional Budget Office to reflect
alternative adjustments for inflation, using the CPI-U-X1. Differences in poverty
thresholds for farm families and for families with a female householder, no husband
present, have been eliminated.
Source: U.S., Department of Commerce, Bureau of the Census, *Statistical Abstract
of the United States, 1991*.

Florida Statistical Abstract 1991

Table 5.50. INCOME AND POVERTY STATUS: MEDIAN HOUSEHOLD AND FAMILY INCOME, 1969
AND 1979, AND PERCENTAGE OF 1980 FAMILIES AND PERSONS WITH 1979 INCOMES BELOW
POVERTY LEVEL IN THE STATE AND COUNTIES OF FLORIDA

County	Median income 1/ (dollars)				Percentage of 1980 population with 1979 incomes below poverty level	
	Household 2/		Family 3/			
	1969	1979	1969	1979	Families	Persons
Florida	7,117	14,675	8,267	17,280	9.9	13.5
Alachua	7,058	12,354	8,329	17,072	13.9	23.5
Baker	6,691	14,391	7,714	16,290	12.3	16.6
Bay	6,700	13,271	7,416	15,374	12.8	16.2
Bradford	6,249	11,816	6,905	14,556	17.9	19.8
Brevard	10,413	16,858	11,145	19,388	7.3	9.7
Broward	8,409	16,580	9,539	19,592	6.3	9.1
Calhoun	4,153	10,657	4,866	12,279	19.6	23.7
Charlotte	5,362	13,190	6,255	15,174	6.7	8.9
Citrus	4,806	11,258	5,563	12,948	10.0	13.6
Clay	7,591	18,407	8,430	20,269	8.6	10.0
Collier	8,135	16,620	9,136	19,174	9.5	13.6
Columbia	6,427	12,794	7,354	15,506	15.3	19.7
Dade	7,967	15,571	9,245	18,642	11.9	15.0
De Soto	5,434	11,292	6,320	13,183	16.1	21.1
Dixie	5,062	9,631	5,666	10,920	22.3	25.2
Duval	7,611	14,938	8,671	17,661	12.7	15.8
Escambia	7,303	14,442	8,027	16,586	14.0	17.4
Flagler	4,732	14,562	5,627	16,232	11.8	15.5
Franklin	3,809	9,444	4,338	11,018	23.6	28.3
Gadsden	4,709	11,110	5,598	12,828	26.3	32.6
Gilchrist	5,305	10,778	6,213	11,999	16.1	19.3
Glades	5,306	10,074	6,165	11,427	16.6	21.0
Gulf	6,307	12,089	7,322	15,252	18.3	21.3
Hamilton	4,576	10,565	5,733	12,989	21.8	26.6
Hardee	5,254	12,028	5,792	13,661	19.3	25.8
Hendry	6,419	14,565	7,042	16,344	16.8	21.5
Hernando	5,080	12,366	5,863	13,915	9.7	13.4
Highlands	4,978	11,283	5,863	13,125	12.6	18.8
Hillsborough	7,100	14,868	8,162	17,632	10.7	14.0
Holmes	4,103	9,880	4,754	12,051	21.5	26.9
Indian River	6,415	15,101	7,219	17,607	8.3	12.3
Jackson	4,419	10,636	5,496	12,795	18.5	23.0
Jefferson	4,663	9,786	5,519	11,761	23.7	28.3
Lafayette	4,590	11,090	5,368	12,431	18.1	21.4
Lake	5,479	12,489	6,352	14,392	9.9	14.0
Lee	6,973	14,612	7,878	16,757	7.7	11.0
Leon	7,530	14,369	8,961	18,916	11.8	17.8
Levy	4,872	10,686	5,821	12,464	16.6	20.8
Liberty	5,167	10,541	5,582	13,260	17.9	22.1

See footnotes at end of table.   Continued . . .

Florida Statistical Abstract 1991

Table 5.50.   INCOME AND POVERTY STATUS: MEDIAN HOUSEHOLD AND FAMILY INCOME, 1969
AND 1979, AND PERCENTAGE OF 1980 FAMILIES AND PERSONS WITH 1979 INCOMES BELOW
POVERTY LEVEL IN THE STATE AND COUNTIES OF FLORIDA (Continued)

| County | Median income 1/ (dollars) | | | | Percentage of 1980 population with 1979 incomes below poverty level | |
| | Household 2/ | | Family 3/ | | | |
	1969	1979	1969	1979	Families	Persons
Madison	4,572	10,169	5,743	11,895	26.4	30.2
Manatee	5,439	13,568	6,591	16,191	7.9	11.0
Marion	5,651	11,797	6,595	13,440	14.0	17.9
Martin	6,042	15,749	7,285	18,311	7.3	11.1
Monroe	6,655	13,713	7,334	16,129	10.0	13.4
Nassau	7,369	16,948	8,063	19,473	10.1	12.3
Okaloosa	7,486	15,151	7,876	16,955	8.7	10.9
Okeechobee	5,902	12,074	6,506	14,012	13.2	17.5
Orange	7,838	15,298	8,880	17,705	10.0	13.2
Osceola	5,154	12,984	6,223	15,177	9.3	11.8
Palm Beach	7,771	16,665	9,112	19,817	6.7	10.1
Pasco	4,482	11,645	4,998	13,129	7.7	10.9
Pinellas	6,235	13,404	7,642	16,707	6.5	9.8
Polk	6,566	14,248	7,526	16,512	10.3	14.6
Putnam	5,817	11,438	6,803	13,556	17.0	21.3
St. Johns	5,507	14,213	6,548	16,876	11.0	15.6
St. Lucie	5,529	13,878	6,358	15,884	12.3	17.1
Santa Rosa	7,041	15,085	7,707	16,774	13.9	16.2
Sarasota	6,525	15,069	7,739	17,786	6.1	9.1
Seminole	7,940	18,289	8,900	20,873	7.0	9.2
Sumter	4,883	11,232	5,657	13,318	15.7	20.6
Suwannee	4,852	10,964	5,903	12,775	19.0	23.9
Taylor	5,958	12,285	6,814	15,784	18.0	22.2
Union	5,909	12,321	6,317	14,506	13.4	17.2
Volusia	5,725	12,393	7,036	15,088	9.7	14.0
Wakulla	5,234	12,158	6,128	14,018	15.8	18.1
Walton	4,863	10,687	5,828	12,748	19.3	23.0
Washington	3,867	10,028	4,755	12,140	20.7	25.0

1/ The figure which divides the distribution of all household or family incomes
into two equal groups, one-half below the median and one-half above.

2/ Includes the income received by all household members 15 years old or over,
regardless of family relationship, and by persons living alone or in other nonfamily households.

3/ Includes the total money income received in a calendar year by all family
members 15 years old and over.

Source: U.S., Department of Commerce, Bureau of the Census, 1980 Census of Population and Housing: Summary Tape File 3A (corrected).   1969 data from the 1970
Census of Population and Housing.

Florida Statistical Abstract 1991

LABOR FORCE, EMPLOYMENT, AND EARNINGS

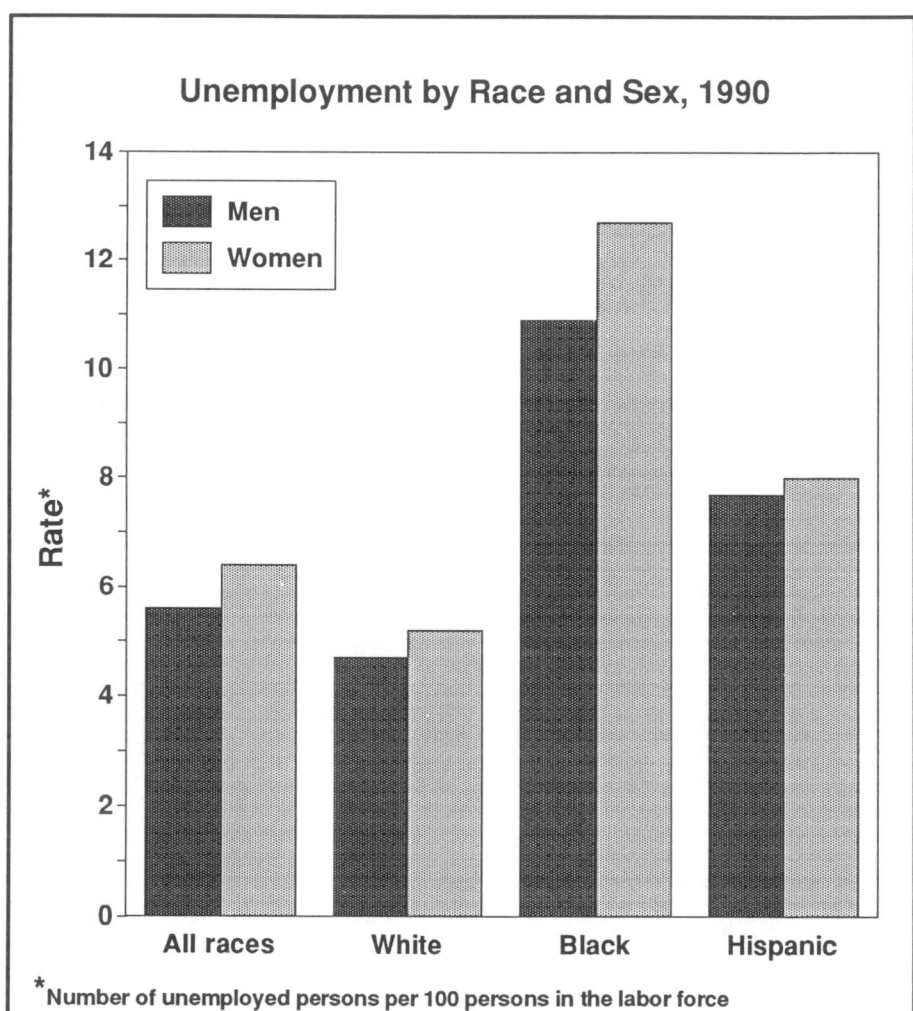

Unemployment by Race and Sex, 1990

Legend:
- Men
- Women

Y-axis: Rate*
(scale 0 to 14)

X-axis categories: All races, White, Black, Hispanic

*Number of unemployed persons per 100 persons in the labor force

Source: Table 6.12

TABLES LISTED BY MAJOR HEADINGS

Table 6.01. NONAGRICULTURAL EMPLOYMENT: EMPLOYMENT BY INDUSTRIAL CLASSIFICATION
IN FLORIDA, 1951 THROUGH 1989

(in thousands)

Year	Total	Min- ing	Con- struc- tion	Manufac- turing	Trans- porta- tion and Public Util- ities 1/	Whole- sale and Retail trade	Finance In- surance and Real Estate	Serv- ices	Govern- ment
1951	759.7	6.5	74.9	114.4	70.1	213.0	34.7	121.6	124.5
1952	808.8	6.7	76.8	121.5	73.3	229.6	37.5	127.3	136.1
1953	848.8	6.9	82.8	129.3	75.8	240.7	40.7	134.5	138.1
1954	882.7	7.1	85.9	135.5	77.6	246.8	45.6	139.0	145.2
1955	965.9	6.4	99.7	147.6	82.0	270.1	51.9	150.8	157.4
1956	1,060.0	7.6	111.7	160.5	89.6	294.1	57.8	166.4	172.3
1957	1,152.7	7.8	122.7	176.1	94.6	313.3	64.6	187.8	185.8
1958	1,185.6	7.7	127.7	180.3	94.4	313.1	70.0	197.2	195.2
1959	1,273.0	7.8	134.6	199.9	97.6	333.4	76.9	215.2	207.6
1960	1,320.6	8.2	124.7	207.5	100.2	349.7	82.1	227.7	220.5
1961	1,333.9	8.3	112.4	211.8	99.8	350.9	84.6	233.8	232.3
1962	1,387.8	8.2	112.7	223.1	99.4	365.0	87.4	244.6	247.4
1963	1,447.4	8.5	120.2	229.3	100.7	375.1	90.8	260.3	262.5
1964	1,526.5	9.2	130.1	237.9	106.0	395.0	93.7	275.9	278.7
1965	1,619.1	9.6	138.8	252.6	109.9	417.7	97.4	291.9	301.2
1966	1,726.8	9.7	137.1	276.1	116.8	443.1	101.7	316.1	326.2
1967	1,816.4	8.9	131.7	293.8	127.1	466.3	106.2	340.1	342.3
1968	1,932.3	8.4	143.6	311.4	135.1	491.5	112.6	367.9	361.8
1969	2,069.9	7.8	169.2	329.2	145.4	521.3	123.0	396.1	377.9
1970	2,152.1	8.3	175.7	322.5	154.5	545.8	131.3	416.2	397.8
1971	2,276.4	8.9	186.8	322.7	161.7	583.5	143.8	449.9	419.1
1972	2,513.1	8.8	230.1	351.3	173.5	643.5	162.4	505.6	437.9
1973	2,778.6	9.2	290.2	380.6	186.7	703.2	182.6	556.2	469.9
1974	2,863.8	9.9	276.1	375.9	189.8	727.6	192.5	581.5	510.5
1975	2,746.4	9.4	182.5	339.4	182.9	713.6	188.3	584.3	546.0
1976	2,784.3	8.8	166.7	354.0	181.4	730.8	191.3	608.5	542.8
1977	2,933.2	9.1	178.9	380.9	185.1	771.0	202.5	640.0	565.7
1978	3,180.6	9.5	209.5	415.5	194.2	836.9	219.3	693.9	601.8
1979	3,381.2	10.1	241.4	443.6	208.5	889.5	235.0	752.6	600.5
1980	3,576.2	11.0	263.9	456.4	220.8	939.8	254.2	811.3	618.8
1981	3,736.9	11.3	283.1	472.2	229.8	987.2	274.3	858.9	620.1
1982	3,761.9	9.6	256.6	456.7	229.9	998.0	276.6	902.0	632.5
1983	3,905.6	9.6	268.8	464.3	231.4	1,037.6	283.2	971.4	639.3
1984	4,209.0	10.2	319.4	502.3	242.5	1,114.1	298.7	1,068.4	652.6
1985	4,410.0	9.0	335.0	515.0	244.0	1,195.0	318.0	1,133.0	673.0
1986	4,599.0	9.0	340.0	517.0	245.0	1,239.0	340.0	1,203.0	697.0
1987	4,848.0	9.0	341.0	530.0	256.0	1,318.0	360.0	1,305.0	734.0
1988	5,067.0	9.0	349.0	541.0	260.0	1,385.0	365.0	1,397.0	774.0
1989	5,276.0	9.0	341.0	541.0	266.0	1,440.0	372.0	1,502.0	805.0

1/ Includes communications.
Note: Totals are revised.
Source: U.S., Department of Labor, Bureau of Labor Statistics, *Employment, Hours, and Earnings, States and Areas, 1939-82* and previous editions, *Supplement to Employment, Hours, and Earnings, States and Areas, Data for 1980-84*, and U.S., Department of Commerce, Bureau of the Census, *Statistical Abstract of the United States, 1991*, and previous editions.

Florida Statistical Abstract 1991

Table 6.10. LABOR FORCE: ESTIMATES BY EMPLOYMENT STATUS IN THE STATE AND COUNTIES OF FLORIDA AND IN THE UNITED STATES, 1988, 1989, AND 1990

County	1988 Labor force	1988 Employ-ment	1988 Unemployment Number	1988 Rate	1989 Labor force	1989 Employ-ment	1989 Unemployment Number	1989 Rate	1990 Labor force	1990 Employ-ment	1990 Unemployment Number	1990 Rate
United States 1/	123,378	116,677	6,701	5.4	125,557	119,030	6,528	5.2	126,424	119,550	6,874	5.4
Florida	6,080,217	5,776,558	303,658	5.0	6,193,075	5,844,658	348,417	5.6	6,365,258	5,986,867	378,392	5.9
Alachua	96,193	93,203	2,990	3.1	95,832	92,821	3,011	3.1	98,808	95,478	3,330	3.4
Baker	7,503	7,076	427	5.7	7,797	7,294	503	6.4	8,091	7,567	524	6.5
Bay	60,114	54,932	5,182	8.6	60,607	54,868	5,739	9.5	60,531	55,401	5,130	8.5
Bradford	9,863	9,554	309	3.1	9,864	9,515	349	3.5	10,261	9,788	473	4.6
Brevard	184,023	175,462	8,561	4.7	187,488	177,696	9,793	5.2	195,550	184,739	10,811	5.5
Broward	635,198	609,010	26,189	4.1	647,224	614,368	32,856	5.1	660,159	623,928	36,231	5.5
Calhoun	3,837	3,490	347	9.0	3,816	3,479	337	8.8	3,924	3,610	314	8.0
Charlotte	32,709	31,328	1,381	4.2	35,561	33,869	1,692	4.8	39,294	37,229	2,065	5.3
Citrus	33,405	31,414	1,991	6.0	34,130	31,920	2,210	6.5	36,783	34,236	2,547	6.9
Clay	45,163	43,140	2,023	4.5	45,136	42,852	2,284	5.1	45,903	43,685	2,218	4.8
Collier	69,815	66,842	2,973	4.3	72,034	68,794	3,240	4.5	78,307	74,082	4,225	5.4
Columbia	19,294	17,859	1,434	7.4	19,549	17,931	1,618	8.3	19,869	18,220	1,649	8.3
Dade	934,558	884,522	50,036	5.4	941,095	880,901	60,194	6.4	952,318	888,469	63,849	6.7
De Soto	7,818	7,455	363	4.6	8,023	7,609	415	5.2	9,160	8,316	844	9.2
Dixie	3,769	3,537	231	6.1	3,829	3,572	257	6.7	3,932	3,652	280	7.1
Duval	346,049	327,444	18,605	5.4	345,362	325,255	20,107	5.8	351,209	331,581	19,628	5.6
Escambia	118,207	111,127	7,080	6.0	117,692	110,293	7,399	6.3	119,439	112,510	6,929	5.8
Flagler	9,589	9,176	413	4.3	10,242	9,723	519	5.1	11,334	10,634	700	6.2
Franklin	5,852	5,529	323	5.5	5,852	5,458	393	6.7	5,459	5,138	321	5.9
Gadsden	19,494	18,407	1,087	5.6	20,170	19,010	1,159	5.7	20,834	19,614	1,220	5.9
Gilchrist	3,263	3,091	172	5.3	3,470	3,273	197	5.7	3,677	3,447	230	6.2
Glades	2,749	2,538	211	7.7	2,988	2,751	237	7.9	3,157	2,876	281	8.9

Continued . . .

See footnotes at end of table.

Table 6.10. LABOR FORCE: ESTIMATES BY EMPLOYMENT STATUS IN THE STATE AND COUNTIES OF FLORIDA AND IN THE UNITED STATES, 1988, 1989, AND 1990 (Continued)

County	1988 Labor force	1988 Employ-ment	1988 Unemployment Number	1988 Unemployment Rate	1989 Labor force	1989 Employ-ment	1989 Unemployment Number	1989 Unemployment Rate	1990 Labor force	1990 Employ-ment	1990 Unemployment Number	1990 Unemployment Rate
Gulf	4,604	4,248	357	7.7	4,511	4,135	377	8.3	4,458	4,122	336	7.5
Hamilton	3,560	3,248	312	8.8	3,734	3,444	290	7.8	3,843	3,523	320	8.3
Hardee	8,643	7,978	665	7.7	8,706	7,944	761	8.7	9,056	8,066	991	10.9
Hendry	10,421	9,226	1,195	11.5	10,937	9,615	1,322	12.1	11,151	9,707	1,444	13.0
Hernando	37,308	35,240	2,068	5.5	37,622	35,221	2,401	6.4	38,674	36,042	2,631	6.8
Highlands	23,667	22,299	1,368	5.8	24,365	22,765	1,600	6.6	26,052	23,997	2,055	7.9
Hillsborough	454,421	433,913	20,507	4.5	456,055	433,672	22,383	4.9	466,231	443,789	22,441	4.8
Holmes	6,152	5,727	424	6.9	6,549	6,096	453	6.9	6,551	6,079	471	7.2
Indian River	37,659	35,110	2,550	6.8	39,915	37,372	2,543	6.4	42,752	38,833	3,919	9.2
Jackson	18,359	17,233	1,126	6.1	18,905	17,753	1,152	6.1	19,411	18,102	1,309	6.7
Jefferson	5,062	4,800	263	5.2	4,896	4,644	251	5.1	5,195	4,930	265	5.1
Lafayette	2,518	2,392	127	5.0	2,736	2,561	175	6.4	2,793	2,639	154	5.5
Lake	54,931	51,899	3,032	5.5	57,683	54,077	3,606	6.3	59,799	55,104	4,695	7.9
Lee	139,577	134,550	5,027	3.6	145,458	139,803	5,655	3.9	152,616	145,877	6,739	4.4
Leon	108,671	105,003	3,668	3.4	112,905	108,448	4,457	3.9	116,364	111,894	4,470	3.8
Levy	9,726	9,134	592	6.1	10,278	9,679	599	5.8	10,698	10,068	630	5.9
Liberty	2,355	2,217	139	5.9	2,659	2,556	103	3.9	3,060	2,949	111	3.6
Madison	7,338	6,862	476	6.5	7,625	7,085	540	7.1	7,835	7,252	583	7.4
Manatee	82,804	79,281	3,523	4.3	86,482	82,499	3,983	4.6	93,021	88,705	4,316	4.6
Marion	78,170	73,739	4,431	5.7	78,497	73,760	4,736	6.0	80,781	75,198	5,583	6.9
Martin	39,706	37,502	2,204	5.6	41,490	38,873	2,617	6.3	42,953	39,817	3,137	7.3
Monroe	42,809	41,694	1,115	2.6	42,007	40,729	1,278	3.0	44,370	42,891	1,479	3.3
Nassau	22,528	21,038	1,490	6.6	22,151	20,897	1,254	5.7	22,623	21,304	1,320	5.8
Okaloosa	63,133	59,551	3,582	5.7	63,401	59,459	3,942	6.2	64,814	60,766	4,047	6.2
Okeechobee	11,513	10,599	914	7.9	12,133	11,064	1,069	8.8	12,678	11,536	1,142	9.0
Orange	370,832	353,752	17,080	4.6	391,094	371,494	19,600	5.0	408,017	385,737	22,279	5.5

See footnotes at end of table.

Continued . . .

Table 6.10. LABOR FORCE: ESTIMATES BY EMPLOYMENT STATUS IN THE STATE AND COUNTIES OF FLORIDA AND IN THE UNITED STATES, 1988, 1989, AND 1990 (Continued)

County	1988 Labor force	1988 Employ-ment	1988 Unemployment Number	1988 Unemployment Rate	1989 Labor force	1989 Employ-ment	1989 Unemployment Number	1989 Unemployment Rate	1990 Labor force	1990 Employ-ment	1990 Unemployment Number	1990 Unemployment Rate
Osceola	48,649	46,546	2,103	4.3	51,561	48,881	2,681	5.2	53,474	50,755	2,719	5.1
Palm Beach	408,843	388,337	20,506	5.0	421,168	395,978	25,190	6.0	430,148	402,062	28,086	6.5
Pasco	96,654	91,264	5,390	5.6	97,493	91,213	6,280	6.4	100,254	93,341	6,912	6.9
Pinellas	401,421	383,857	17,564	4.4	402,374	383,643	18,731	4.7	412,718	392,594	20,124	4.9
Polk	177,915	163,624	14,292	8.0	179,779	164,548	15,231	8.5	182,628	164,891	17,738	9.7
Putnam	24,893	23,125	1,768	7.1	24,815	22,950	1,866	7.5	25,232	23,487	1,745	6.9
St. Johns	39,295	37,290	2,005	5.1	39,297	37,040	2,257	5.7	40,011	37,761	2,250	5.6
St. Lucie	59,794	54,550	5,245	8.8	62,765	56,544	6,221	9.9	66,197	57,917	8,280	12.5
Santa Rosa	29,945	27,952	1,993	6.7	29,869	27,742	2,127	7.1	30,375	28,300	2,075	6.8
Sarasota	120,603	116,479	4,123	3.4	121,840	117,282	4,558	3.7	126,594	121,406	5,188	4.1
Seminole	163,132	155,942	7,190	4.4	172,443	163,763	8,680	5.0	179,038	170,042	8,996	5.0
Sumter	12,140	11,310	830	6.8	12,171	11,310	861	7.1	12,044	11,068	976	8.1
Suwannee	10,824	10,152	672	6.2	11,437	10,585	852	7.4	11,679	10,757	922	7.9
Taylor	9,094	8,441	653	7.2	9,089	8,259	830	9.1	9,203	8,262	941	10.2
Union	4,051	3,901	150	3.7	4,034	3,869	164	4.1	4,176	4,008	168	4.0
Volusia	152,073	145,233	6,840	4.5	155,979	147,556	8,423	5.4	160,040	151,141	8,899	5.6
Wakulla	6,436	6,135	301	4.7	6,458	6,119	339	5.3	6,507	6,190	317	4.9
Walton	12,392	11,512	880	7.1	12,972	12,077	896	6.9	13,932	13,053	879	6.3
Washington	7,135	6,539	596	8.3	6,976	6,406	571	8.2	7,223	6,709	513	7.1

1/ United States numbers are rounded to thousands.
Note: Data are adjusted to 1990 benchmarks and are generated for federal fund allocations. Caution is urged when using these data for short-term economic analysis. Detail may not add to totals because of rounding.

Source: State of Florida, Department of Labor and Employment Security, unpublished data and U.S., Department of Labor, Bureau of Labor Statistics, Employment and Earnings, January 1991.

Florida Statistical Abstract 1991

Table 6.12. EMPLOYMENT: LABOR FORCE STATUS OF THE POPULATION 16 YEARS OLD AND
OVER BY SEX, RACE, HISPANIC ORIGIN, AND MARITAL STATUS IN FLORIDA AND
SPECIFIED METROPOLITAN AREAS, ANNUAL AVERAGES, 1990

Area and population group	Civilian noninstitutional population (1,000)	Civilian labor force Number (1,000)	Percentage of population	Employment Number (1,000)	Percentage of population	Unemployment Number (1,000)	Rate	Error range of rate 1/
Florida								
Total	10,121	6,365	62.9	5,987	59.2	378	5.9	5.6-6.3
Men	4,775	3,414	71.5	3,223	67.5	191	5.6	5.2-6.0
Women	5,346	2,951	55.2	2,764	51.7	188	6.4	5.9-6.8
Both sexes, 16-19 years	655	357	54.5	295	45.0	62	17.5	15.5-19.5
White	8,559	5,324	62.2	5,062	59.1	262	4.9	4.6-5.2
Men	4,064	2,893	71.2	2,757	67.8	137	4.7	4.3-5.2
Women	4,495	2,430	54.1	2,305	51.3	125	5.2	4.7-5.6
Black	1,398	923	66.0	814	58.2	109	11.8	10.6-13.1
Men	633	457	72.2	407	64.3	50	10.9	9.2-12.6
Women	765	466	60.9	406	53.1	59	12.7	10.9-14.6
Hispanic origin	1,256	847	67.5	781	62.2	66	7.8	6.7-8.9
Men	593	470	79.2	434	73.1	36	7.7	6.2-9.1
Women	662	377	57.0	347	52.4	30	8.0	6.4-9.6
Single (never married)	2,177	1,585	72.8	1,432	65.8	153	9.6	8.9-10.4
Married, spouse present	5,792	3,622	62.5	3,472	60.0	149	4.1	3.8-4.5
Other marital status	2,151	1,158	53.8	1,082	50.3	76	6.6	5.8-7.3
Ft. Lauderdale- Hollywood- Pompano Beach PMSA								
Total	1,012	622	61.5	591	58.4	31	5.0	4.0-5.9
Men	460	323	70.2	308	66.9	15	4.6	3.3-5.9
Women	552	300	54.3	283	51.3	16	5.4	4.0-6.8
White	849	499	58.7	478	56.3	21	4.2	3.2-5.1
Men	388	264	67.9	253	65.1	11	4.2	2.8-5.5
Women	461	235	51.0	225	48.9	10	4.1	2.7-5.5
Black	147	111	75.7	102	69.0	10	8.8	5.7-12.0
Men	65	53	82.0	49	76.0	4	7.3	3.1-11.4
Women	83	58	70.8	52	63.5	6	10.3	5.6-14.9
Hispanic origin	62	39	62.9	37	59.4	2	5.5	1.3-9.6
Men	(NA)	(NA)	(NA)	(NA)	(NA)	(NA)	(NA)	(NA)
Women	(NA)	(NA)	(NA)	(NA)	(NA)	(NA)	(NA)	(NA)
Single (never married)	240	183	76.0	171	71.0	12	6.5	4.5-8.5
Married, spouse present	529	322	60.9	309	58.5	13	3.9	2.8-5.1
Other marital status	243	118	48.6	112	45.9	7	5.5	3.3-7.8

See footnotes at end of table. Continued . . .

Florida Statistical Abstract 1991

Table 6.12. EMPLOYMENT: LABOR FORCE STATUS OF THE POPULATION 16 YEARS OLD AND
OVER BY SEX, RACE, HISPANIC ORIGIN, AND MARITAL STATUS IN FLORIDA AND
SPECIFIED METROPOLITAN AREAS, ANNUAL AVERAGES, 1990 (Continued)

Area and population group	Civilian noninstitutional population (1,000)	Civilian labor force		Employment		Unemployment		
		Number (1,000)	Percentage of population	Number (1,000)	Percentage of population	Number (1,000)	Rate	Error range of rate 1/
Miami-Hialeah PMSA								
Total	1,473	960	65.2	888	60.3	72	7.5	6.6-8.4
Men	685	512	74.7	477	69.7	35	6.8	5.6-8.0
Women	788	449	56.9	411	52.1	38	8.4	7.0-9.8
White	1,129	740	65.6	693	61.3	48	6.5	5.5-7.4
Men	532	404	76.0	380	71.4	24	5.9	4.7-7.2
Women	598	337	56.3	313	52.3	24	7.1	5.6-8.6
Black	317	204	64.3	180	56.8	24	11.6	9.0-14.3
Men	140	98	70.0	88	62.7	10	10.5	6.8-14.1
Women	177	106	59.7	92	52.1	13	12.7	8.9-16.5
Hispanic origin	772	519	67.2	476	61.6	43	8.3	6.9-9.7
Men	364	286	78.4	264	72.6	21	7.5	5.7-9.3
Women	408	233	57.2	212	51.9	22	9.2	7.1-11.4
Single (never married)	400	251	62.8	225	56.3	26	10.4	8.3-12.4
Married, spouse present	756	534	70.7	503	66.6	31	5.9	4.8-7.0
Other marital status	317	174	55.0	160	50.3	15	8.5	6.2-10.7
Tampa-St.-Petersburg-Clearwater MSA								
Total	1,675	1,049	62.6	994	59.4	54	5.2	4.4-5.9
Men	776	553	71.3	526	67.9	27	4.8	3.8-5.8
Women	899	496	55.1	468	52.0	28	5.6	4.5-6.7
White	1,510	944	62.5	901	59.7	43	4.6	3.8-5.3
Men	705	503	71.4	481	68.2	23	4.5	3.5-5.5
Women	805	441	54.8	420	52.2	21	4.7	3.6-5.7
Black	140	89	63.0	79	56.1	10	11.0	7.1-14.9
Men	60	41	69.3	38	63.8	3	8.0	3.1-13.0
Women	81	47	58.4	41	50.4	6	13.6	7.7-19.6
Hispanic origin	110	69	62.8	66	60.1	3	4.3	1.5-7.1
Men	51	39	76.6	38	73.7	1	3.8	.3-7.3
Women	59	30	50.8	29	48.3	1	4.9	.4-9.4
Single (never married)	340	255	75.1	235	69.0	21	8.1	6.3-10.0
Married, spouse present	960	604	62.9	584	60.8	20	3.3	2.5-4.1
Other marital status	375	190	50.6	176	46.9	14	7.2	5.1-9.2

(NA) Not available.

1/ If repeated samples were drawn from the same population and an error range
constructed around each sample estimate, in 9 out of 10 cases the true value based
on a complete census of the population would be contained within these error ranges.

Source: U.S., Department of Labor, Bureau of Labor Statistics, *Geographic Profile of Employment and Unemployment, 1990.*

Florida Statistical Abstract 1991

Table 6.18. EMPLOYMENT AND EARNINGS: NUMBER OF JOBS AND PROPRIETORS AND AVERAGE
    EARNINGS PER JOB IN THE STATE AND COUNTIES OF FLORIDA, 1988 AND 1989

County	Wage and salary jobs	Number of proprietors Nonfarm 2/	Farm	Average wage and salary earnings per job (dollars)
		Total employment 1/		
		1988 A/		
Florida	5,502,225	39,618	1,006,997	19,336
Alachua	94,426	1,255	10,630	17,240
Baker	4,651	268	644	14,736
Bay	55,902	103	9,421	16,699
Bradford	5,436	446	863	15,428
Brevard	162,801	595	25,884	21,277
Broward	510,143	450	110,080	20,806
Calhoun	2,615	196	661	13,587
Charlotte	25,161	148	7,175	16,254
Citrus	21,446	332	7,717	15,454
Clay	26,109	270	6,588	15,881
Collier	62,018	224	19,069	17,633
Columbia	14,134	652	2,285	15,857
Dade	915,172	1,514	153,133	21,633
De Soto	7,560	601	1,276	13,580
Dixie	2,430	131	515	15,032
Duval	394,532	504	36,653	20,775
Escambia	123,272	594	13,864	18,693
Flagler	7,239	115	1,405	16,166
Franklin	2,302	0	1,800	12,927
Gadsden	14,049	465	1,515	15,190
Gilchrist	1,740	364	548	13,589
Glades	1,606	176	174	11,159
Gulf	3,692	0	586	19,513
Hamilton	4,417	331	327	21,640
Hardee	6,714	1,091	1,323	12,857
Hendry	9,325	311	1,417	14,296
Hernando	19,627	497	5,080	15,510
Highlands	19,671	604	5,176	13,959
Hillsborough	446,007	3,033	59,250	19,565
Holmes	3,348	656	995	12,854
Indian River	33,424	433	8,664	16,905
Jackson	14,172	1,119	2,191	14,343
Jefferson	3,490	376	510	12,476

See footnotes at end of table.   Continued . . .

Table 6.18.   EMPLOYMENT AND EARNINGS: NUMBER OF JOBS AND PROPRIETORS AND AVERAGE
    EARNINGS PER JOB IN THE STATE AND COUNTIES OF FLORIDA, 1988 AND 1989
    (Continued)

County	Wage and salary jobs	Total employment 1/ Number of proprietors Nonfarm 2/	Farm	Average wage and salary earnings per job (dollars)

County	Wage and salary jobs	Nonfarm 2/	Farm	Average wage and salary earnings per job (dollars)
		1988 A/ (Continued)		
Lafayette	1,177	368	206	12,323
Lake	49,226	1,706	11,991	15,020
Lee	121,141	396	36,669	17,680
Leon	106,943	342	11,660	18,020
Levy	5,409	544	1,905	14,104
Liberty	1,203	96	211	13,739
Madison	4,599	693	840	14,168
Manatee	70,035	749	15,824	16,565
Marion	64,156	1,720	14,228	15,675
Martin	40,217	262	10,005	17,735
Monroe	34,143	0	11,889	16,859
Nassau	12,264	335	2,435	19,450
Okaloosa	68,926	418	10,773	17,643
Okeechobee	7,688	330	1,993	14,222
Orange	422,369	1,337	47,175	20,656
Osceola	34,770	493	6,585	15,297
Palm Beach	383,649	657	82,104	20,979
Pasco	60,609	1,156	17,287	15,668
Pinellas	359,661	218	83,106	18,446
Polk	160,719	2,525	24,900	17,625
Putnam	17,384	605	3,163	16,587
St. Johns	25,948	205	7,439	15,538
St. Lucie	46,455	466	8,997	16,476
Santa Rosa	19,253	545	4,644	16,883
Sarasota	114,693	344	34,068	17,758
Seminole	87,605	568	23,148	18,098
Sumter	6,962	739	1,425	14,729
Suwannee	7,793	1,186	1,594	14,234
Taylor	7,303	201	872	17,473
Union	3,779	238	246	16,242
Volusia	123,026	1,152	29,252	16,065
Wakulla	2,679	108	879	15,167
Walton	7,441	533	1,206	12,730
Washington	4,369	529	859	14,921

See footnotes at end of table.   Continued . . .

Florida Statistical Abstract 1991

Table 6.18. EMPLOYMENT AND EARNINGS: NUMBER OF JOBS AND PROPRIETORS AND AVERAGE
    EARNINGS PER JOB IN THE STATE AND COUNTIES OF FLORIDA, 1988 AND 1989
    (Continued)

County	Total employment 1/ Wage and salary jobs	Number of proprietors Nonfarm 2/	Farm	Average wage and salary earnings per job (dollars)
		1989		
Florida	5,695,692	39,617	1,037,751	19,930
Alachua	96,777	1,255	10,959	18,067
Baker	4,824	268	659	15,180
Bay	57,050	103	9,699	17,110
Bradford	5,919	446	888	15,329
Brevard	170,124	595	26,687	22,117
Broward	528,008	450	113,420	21,056
Calhoun	2,631	196	679	14,506
Charlotte	27,599	148	7,394	16,844
Citrus	22,293	332	7,960	16,631
Clay	27,504	270	6,793	16,338
Collier	67,647	224	19,639	18,539
Columbia	14,697	652	2,350	16,138
Dade	931,476	1,514	157,784	22,128
De Soto	7,871	601	1,317	13,964
Dixie	2,601	131	529	16,389
Duval	401,202	504	37,763	21,417
Escambia	125,749	594	14,284	19,206
Flagler	7,858	115	1,450	16,261
Franklin	2,407	0	1,853	13,465
Gadsden	14,369	465	1,558	15,624
Gilchrist	1,846	364	564	14,401
Glades	1,572	176	177	12,263
Gulf	3,765	0	601	19,440
Hamilton	4,583	331	334	23,224
Hardee	6,909	1,091	1,360	13,591
Hendry	9,794	311	1,461	14,937
Hernando	21,005	497	5,229	16,010
Highlands	20,530	604	5,338	14,482
Hillsborough	457,924	3,032	61,052	20,436
Holmes	3,545	656	1,022	13,141
Indian River	35,897	433	8,936	18,124
Jackson	14,338	1,119	2,256	14,933
Jefferson	3,338	376	522	12,629
Lafayette	1,259	368	212	12,728
Lake	51,237	1,706	12,355	15,722

See footnotes at end of table.   Continued . . .

Table 6.18. EMPLOYMENT AND EARNINGS: NUMBER OF JOBS AND PROPRIETORS AND AVERAGE
    EARNINGS PER JOB IN THE STATE AND COUNTIES OF FLORIDA, 1988 AND 1989
    (Continued)

| County | Total employment 1/ | | | Average wage and salary earnings per job (dollars) |
| | Wage and salary jobs | Number of proprietors | | |
		Nonfarm 2/	Farm	
	1989 (Continued)			
Lee	129,728	396	37,786	18,204
Leon	113,257	342	12,037	18,590
Levy	5,854	544	1,963	14,371
Liberty	1,390	96	216	15,383
Madison	4,737	693	863	14,623
Manatee	74,266	749	16,318	17,127
Marion	65,899	1,720	14,665	16,507
Martin	42,363	262	10,319	18,743
Monroe	34,892	0	12,262	17,755
Nassau	12,478	335	2,505	20,667
Okaloosa	70,827	418	11,109	18,238
Okeechobee	7,895	330	2,050	15,039
Orange	452,717	1,337	48,590	21,130
Osceola	37,654	493	6,791	16,068
Palm Beach	393,223	657	84,631	21,758
Pasco	63,504	1,156	17,823	16,154
Pinellas	368,231	218	85,657	19,153
Polk	167,717	2,525	25,652	18,209
Putnam	17,388	605	3,260	17,048
St. Johns	27,203	205	7,667	16,292
St. Lucie	49,309	466	9,277	17,017
Santa Rosa	19,891	545	4,789	17,500
Sarasota	118,389	344	35,149	18,430
Seminole	91,811	568	23,854	18,767
Sumter	6,964	739	1,467	15,380
Suwannee	7,967	1,186	1,640	14,643
Taylor	7,269	201	896	18,508
Union	3,702	238	254	16,846
Volusia	128,069	1,152	30,152	16,625
Wakulla	2,737	108	904	16,439
Walton	7,868	533	1,240	13,620
Washington	4,345	529	881	15,587

A/ Revised.
1/ Full- and part-time jobs.
2/ Includes only persons who are primarily self-employed.

    Source: U.S., Department of Commerce, Bureau of Economic Analysis, unpublished
data.

Florida Statistical Abstract 1991

Table 6.21.   EMPLOYMENT: AVERAGE MONTHLY EMPLOYMENT COVERED BY UNEMPLOYMENT
COMPENSATION LAW BY INDUSTRY IN FLORIDA, 1989 AND 1990

SIC code	Industry	1989	1990
01-99	All industries	5,281,342	5,400,969
01-09	Agriculture, forestry, and fisheries	148,488	145,229
01	Agricultural production--crops	65,678	63,676
02	Agricultural production--livestock and animal specialties	7,515	7,456
07	Agricultural services	71,872	70,719
08	Forestry	2,118	2,103
09	Fishing, hunting, and trapping	1,013	979
10-14	Mining	9,143	8,886
10	Metal mining	(D)	(D)
12	Coal mining	(D)	(D)
13	Oil and gas extraction	477	506
14	Mining and quarrying of nonmetallic minerals, except fuels	8,261	7,966
15-17	Construction	346,423	329,399
15	Building construction--general contractors and operative builders	82,569	75,664
16	Heavy construction other than building construction-- contractors	55,957	52,608
17	Construction--special trade contractors	207,316	200,553
20-39	Manufacturing	536,234	519,385
20	Food and kindred products	48,442	46,946
21	Tobacco products	1,376	1,057
22	Textile mill products	5,249	3,929
23	Apparel and other finished products made from fabrics and similar materials	32,596	32,971
24	Lumber and wood products, except furniture	24,789	22,254
25	Furniture and fixtures	14,420	13,513
26	Paper and allied products	14,579	14,069
27	Printing, publishing, and allied industries	65,867	65,792
28	Chemicals and allied products	23,317	22,966
29	Petroleum refining and related industries	1,514	1,609
30	Rubber and miscellaneous plastics products	20,782	21,353
31	Leather and leather products	2,510	2,472
32	Stone, clay, glass, and concrete products	25,857	22,889
33	Primary metal industries	5,255	5,525
34	Fabricated metal products, except machinery and transportation equipment	33,984	32,467
35	Industrial and commercial machinery and computer equipment	42,254	42,062
36	Electronic and other electrical equipment and components, except computer equipment	61,200	59,002
37	Transportation equipment	67,368	62,799
38	Measuring, analyzing, and controlling instruments; photographic, medical, and optical goods; watches and clocks	34,390	35,421
39	Miscellaneous manufacturing industries	9,151	8,929

See footnotes at end of table.   Continued . . .

Florida Statistical Abstract 1991

Table 6.21.   EMPLOYMENT: AVERAGE MONTHLY EMPLOYMENT COVERED BY UNEMPLOYMENT
COMPENSATION LAW BY INDUSTRY IN FLORIDA, 1989 AND 1990 (Continued)

SIC code	Industry	1989	1990
40-49	Transportation, communications, and public utilities	308,094	317,511
40	Railroad transportation	(D)	(D)
41	Local and suburban transit and interurban highway passenger transportation	11,854	12,254
42	Motor freight transportation and warehousing	61,428	58,811
43	U.S. postal service	42,111	41,745
44	Water transportation	15,761	17,423
45	Transportation by air	43,863	52,698
46	Pipelines, except natural gas	(D)	(D)
47	Transportation services	21,274	21,593
48	Communications	66,509	67,090
49	Electric, gas, and sanitary services	44,730	45,311
50-51	Wholesale trade	293,406	293,090
50	Wholesale trade--durable goods	171,391	169,995
51	Wholesale trade--nondurable goods	121,172	122,250
52-59	Retail trade	1,149,783	1,161,920
52	Building materials, hardware, garden supply, and mobile home dealers	46,947	46,922
53	General merchandise stores	141,624	138,876
54	Food stores	200,832	206,117
55	Automotive dealers and gasoline service stations	119,859	116,400
56	Apparel and accessory stores	63,831	64,110
57	Home furniture, furnishings, and equipment stores	55,922	55,086
58	Eating and drinking places	383,780	393,584
59	Miscellaneous retail	135,677	139,517
60-67	Finance, insurance, and real estate	369,016	368,784
60	Depository institutions	119,531	113,725
61	Nondeposit credit institutions	24,139	26,013
62	Security and commodity brokers, dealers, exchanges, and services	18,378	18,563
63	Insurance carriers	56,975	59,451
64	Insurance agents, brokers, and service	37,708	39,293
65	Real estate	101,698	99,747
67	Holding and other investment offices	10,094	11,503
70-89	Services	1,773,507	1,882,489
70	Hotels, rooming houses, camps, and other lodging places	136,740	139,644
72	Personal services	60,197	62,249
73	Business services	275,114	301,048
75	Automotive repair services, and parking	53,720	55,557
76	Miscellaneous repair services	23,733	24,316
78	Motion pictures	13,842	14,448
79	Amusement and recreation services	105,496	112,130

See footnotes at end of table.   Continued . . .

Florida Statistical Abstract 1991

Table 6.21. EMPLOYMENT: AVERAGE MONTHLY EMPLOYMENT COVERED BY UNEMPLOYMENT
   COMPENSATION LAW BY INDUSTRY IN FLORIDA, 1989 AND 1990 (Continued)

SIC code	Industry	1989	1990
70-89	Services (Continued)		
80	Health services	436,786	466,996
81	Legal services	52,818	54,477
82	Educational services	349,480	370,515
83	Social services	81,940	88,220
84	Museums, art galleries, botanical and zoological gardens	2,283	2,362
86	Membership organizations	43,789	47,462
87	Engineering, accounting, research, management and related services	119,456	124,278
88	Private households	13,661	14,162
89	Services, NEC	2,135	2,255
91-97	Government	346,671	371,509
91	Executive, legislative, and general government, except finance	167,035	178,873
92	Justice, public order, and safety	63,168	68,477
93	Public finance, taxation, and monetary policy	13,799	14,364
94	Administration of Human Resource programs	39,825	42,096
95	Administration of Environmental Quality and Housing programs	9,199	9,700
96	Adminstration of Economic programs	21,982	26,584
97	National Security and International Affairs	31,236	30,961
99	Nonclassifiable establishments	276	2,453

NEC Not elsewhere classified.
(D) Data withheld to avoid disclosure of information about individual firms.
Note: Totals on county employment tables may not match totals in this table due
to rounding.

Source: State of Florida, Department of Labor and Employment Security, Bureau of
Labor Market Information, "Employment, Wages, and Contributions Report" (ES-202),
unpublished data.

Florida Statistical Abstract 1991

Table 6.22. COVERED EMPLOYMENT AND PAYROLL: AVERAGE MONTHLY REPORTING UNITS
EMPLOYMENT, AND PAYROLL COVERED BY UNEMPLOYMENT COMPENSATION LAW FOR ALL
INDUSTRIES IN THE STATE AND COUNTIES OF FLORIDA, 1990

County	Number of re- porting units	Number of employees	Payroll ($1,000)	County	Number of re- porting units	Number of employees	Payroll ($1,000)
			All industries	(SIC codes 01-99)			
Florida	332,730	5,400,969	9,465,417	Lafayette	87	1,083	1,371
				Lake	3,292	44,181	64,229
Alachua	4,230	94,124	149,024	Lee	8,974	125,723	201,395
Baker	250	5,041	6,635	Leon	5,173	110,845	184,161
Bay	3,293	50,949	73,515	Levy	493	5,391	6,849
Bradford	357	5,574	7,624	Liberty	99	1,402	1,948
Brevard	8,354	161,933	312,351	Madison	317	4,587	6,179
Broward	35,908	503,094	940,414	Manatee	3,936	75,007	112,777
Calhoun	230	2,579	3,500	Marion	4,276	62,789	91,466
Charlotte	2,261	27,432	40,601	Martin	3,310	38,706	65,966
Citrus	1,696	21,586	32,471	Monroe	2,787	30,427	44,605
Clay	1,978	26,105	37,372	Nassau	902	12,087	21,300
Collier	5,590	72,720	110,749	Okaloosa	3,326	53,463	78,268
Columbia	944	13,770	19,602	Okeechobee	664	7,775	10,711
Dade	57,711	872,944	1,684,887	Orange	18,465	430,604	786,487
De Soto	481	7,977	9,810	Osceola	2,027	36,551	50,409
Dixie	202	2,337	3,447	Palm Beach	25,749	363,277	714,170
Duval	15,981	345,823	641,101	Pasco	4,498	61,804	87,262
Escambia	5,558	107,613	178,855	Pinellas	20,837	349,767	585,508
Flagler	587	7,541	10,443	Polk	8,195	156,970	254,168
Franklin	263	2,097	2,574	Putnam	1,040	16,101	25,125
Gadsden	631	14,091	18,971	St. Johns	1,935	26,615	37,972
Gilchrist	160	1,783	2,448	St. Lucie	3,127	45,247	70,846
Glades	92	967	1,368	Santa Rosa	1,303	17,610	24,886
Gulf	248	3,524	6,109	Sarasota	9,156	115,633	185,481
Hamilton	169	4,538	9,122	Seminole	6,536	90,660	150,901
Hardee	533	6,837	8,026	Sumter	472	6,276	8,110
Hendry	570	9,976	14,456	Suwannee	541	7,400	9,670
Hernando	1,634	20,298	28,919	Taylor	436	6,564	11,096
Highlands	1,617	20,399	26,384	Union	141	3,535	5,362
Hillsborough	20,531	440,383	791,436	Volusia	8,328	122,243	177,997
Holmes	240	3,129	3,670	Wakulla	224	2,565	3,684
Indian River	2,947	34,233	56,001	Walton	502	7,771	9,253
Jackson	719	13,355	18,124	Washington	298	4,222	5,844
Jefferson	253	2,875	3,492	Statewide 1/	5,066	48,461	116,460

1/ Reporting units without a fixed location within the state or of unknown county
location.

Source: State of Florida, Department of Labor and Employment Security, Bureau of
Labor Market Information, "Employment, Wages, and Contributions Report" (ES-202),
unpublished data.

Florida Statistical Abstract 1991

Table 6.23. EMPLOYMENT: AVERAGE MONTHLY EMPLOYMENT COVERED BY UNEMPLOYMENT COMPENSATION LAW BY MAJOR INDUSTRY GROUP IN THE STATE AND COUNTIES OF FLORIDA, 1989 AND 1990

1989

County	All industries (01-99)	Agriculture forestry and fisheries (01-09)	Mining (10-14)	Construction (15-17)	Manufacturing (20-39)	Transportation and public utilities (40-49)	Wholesale trade (50-51)	Retail trade (52-59)	Finance insurance and real estate (60-67)	Services (70-89)	Government (91-97)	Other (99)
Florida	5,281,342	148,488	9,143	346,423	536,234	308,094	293,406	1,149,783	369,016	1,773,507	346,671	270
Alachua	90,963	963	(D)	4,246	4,982	2,988	2,289	17,709	4,238	48,898	4,586	(D)
Baker	4,713	429	0	93	301	203	34	721	96	2,284	548	0
Bay	48,549	194	0	2,802	3,465	2,541	1,689	13,965	2,607	15,731	5,551	0
Bradford	5,522	95	(D)	194	679	132	48	1,232	137	1,314	1,660	(D)
Brevard	157,475	1,749	(D)	9,533	29,738	5,158	3,733	33,977	5,821	55,223	12,477	(D)
Broward	492,634	4,761	259	35,159	45,085	26,870	28,849	118,967	39,851	165,039	27,751	39
Calhoun	2,391	129	0	104	303	(D)	66	439	52	577	449	(D)
Charlotte	25,573	460	(D)	2,966	816	1,154	358	7,285	1,846	8,867	1,789	(D)
Citrus	20,858	221	51	1,827	918	2,150	322	5,653	1,182	7,291	1,237	0
Clay	25,658	561	(D)	2,167	1,768	1,170	770	8,569	939	7,902	1,347	(D)
Collier	71,220	13,397	(D)	7,685	2,415	2,484	1,586	14,779	4,994	20,829	2,925	(D)
Columbia	13,632	158	0	1,243	1,697	476	711	3,418	478	4,462	986	0
Dade	863,265	13,020	912	39,919	91,309	74,880	68,669	165,138	70,727	287,984	50,547	155
De Soto	7,481	1,470	(D)	296	380	162	182	1,168	173	2,833	788	(D)
Dixie	2,368	34	(D)	93	567	51	15	502	40	466	574	(D)
Duval	339,554	2,385	(D)	22,601	31,627	29,259	24,807	65,942	37,297	102,343	23,089	(D)
Escambia	106,861	463	118	6,862	9,378	6,658	4,657	24,551	4,791	36,389	12,990	1
Flagler	7,175	177	(D)	651	1,368	232	64	1,436	584	2,240	414	(D)
Franklin	2,276	95	0	47	176	108	178	460	103	809	296	0
Gadsden	13,854	1,330	(D)	499	1,782	312	514	1,749	277	5,951	1,206	(D)
Gilchrist	1,647	137	0	44	107	63	46	204	47	478	517	0

See footnotes at end of table.

Continued . . .

Table 6.23. EMPLOYMENT: AVERAGE MONTHLY EMPLOYMENT COVERED BY UNEMPLOYMENT COMPENSATION LAW BY MAJOR INDUSTRY GROUP IN THE STATE AND COUNTIES OF FLORIDA, 1989 AND 1990 (Continued)

1989 (Continued)

County	All industries (01-99)	Agriculture forestry and fisheries (01-09)	Mining (10-14)	Construction (15-17)	Manufacturing (20-39)	Transportation communication and public utilities (40-49)	Wholesale trade (50-51)	Retail trade (52-59)	Finance insurance and real estate (60-67)	Services (70-89)	Government (91-97)	Other (99)
Glades	942	209	(D)	17	(D)	(D)	(D)	114	(D)	(D)	185	0
Gulf	3,539	153	0	95	1,166	426	21	475	115	728	357	0
Hamilton	4,380	(D)	0	84	319	96	22	385	36	803	593	0
Hardee	6,858	2,354	(D)	237	868	189	324	1,042	210	1,665	448	(D)
Hendry	9,427	3,526	56	427	976	233	127	1,226	276	1,749	934	0
Hernando	19,164	570	(D)	1,635	1,236	962	545	4,893	1,033	6,292	1,736	(D)
Highlands	19,405	2,999	(D)	1,159		827	477	4,987	903	5,439	1,364	(D)
Hillsborough	427,014	11,671	(D)	25,702	40,746	29,317	34,238	80,707	33,909	149,923	20,689	(D)
Holmes	3,235	(D)	(D)	106	843	64	60	525	75	989	518	(D)
Indian River	34,159	3,771	(D)	3,451	2,991	847	606	8,183	1,909	10,184	2,205	(D)
Jackson	12,999	317	0	540	2,011	454	750	2,386	502	3,800	2,206	(D)
Jefferson	2,682	381	0	144	332	146	82	452	111	762	269	(D)
Lafayette	1,147	224	0	14	(D)	(D)	24	65	(D)	(D)	323	0
Lake	44,522	3,100	(D)	3,027	5,328	2,545	1,512	10,602	2,886	12,394	2,811	(D)
Lee	122,028	3,753	(D)	13,213	6,091	6,437	4,424	32,093	8,883	40,475	6,532	(D)
Leon	106,317	681	(D)	5,398	3,140	3,333	3,053	20,697	4,825	38,741	26,431	(D)
Levy	5,390	300	(D)	406	422	217	184	1,394	247	1,506	543	(D)
Liberty	1,262	(D)	0	86	225	66	(D)	124	21	413	312	0
Madison	4,382	269	0	46	1,149	176	123	754	73	1,264	524	0
Manatee	71,362	5,649	(D)	3,134	10,633	2,120	1,907	15,995	3,736	23,888	4,226	(D)
Marion	61,343	2,657	(D)	4,029	10,176	2,077	4,045	14,091	2,948	17,077	4,115	(D)
Martin	38,127	1,831	(D)	4,293	3,582	1,695	816	9,944	2,753	11,251	1,954	(D)
Monroe	29,504	354	(D)	1,853	590	2,250	584	9,220	1,414	10,524	2,660	(D)

See footnotes at end of table.

Continued . . .

Table 6.23. EMPLOYMENT: AVERAGE MONTHLY EMPLOYMENT COVERED BY UNEMPLOYMENT COMPENSATION LAW BY MAJOR INDUSTRY GROUP IN THE STATE AND COUNTIES OF FLORIDA, 1989 AND 1990 (Continued)

1989 (Continued)

County	All industries (01-99)	Agriculture forestry and fisheries (01-09)	Mining (10-14)	Construction (15-17)	Manufacturing (20-39)	Transportation communication and public utilities (40-49)	Wholesale trade (50-51)	Retail trade (52-59)	Finance insurance and real estate (60-67)	Services (70-89)	Government (91-97)	Other (99)
Nassau	11,646	548	0	736	1,726	470	291	2,806	390	3,333	1,342	0
Okaloosa	52,272	305	(D)	3,037	5,153	2,029	1,004	14,139	2,918	16,353	7,322	(D)
Okeechobee	7,550	1,398	0	539	377	239	256	1,770	284	2,149	535	0
Orange	413,042	8,669	(D)	26,227	41,462	28,602	25,777	76,595	26,783	160,305	18,494	(D)
Osceola	34,902	560	(D)	2,694	2,189	804	816	11,055	1,455	13,296	2,027	(D)
Palm Beach	360,630	17,721	27	28,485	33,165	16,968	14,906	79,339	28,133	120,749	21,115	16
Pasco	60,564	3,216	(D)	4,915	4,029	3,146	1,568	17,433	3,209	19,481	3,551	(D)
Pinellas	344,623	2,608	(D)	20,974	49,118	14,416	14,555	83,568	26,763	115,030	17,559	(D)
Polk	159,172	10,411	4,074	9,446	23,195	7,473	8,190	34,610	7,922	44,187	9,660	0
Putnam	15,941	735	93	836	3,715	571	314	3,337	521	4,149	1,666	0
St. Johns	25,030	642	(D)	1,220	3,141	561	828	6,572	885	9,465	1,707	(D)
St. Lucie	45,024	5,313	45	3,672	2,355	3,100	1,516	10,442	2,576	12,783	3,217	0
Santa Rosa	16,451	316	180	1,204	2,001	1,040	370	3,797	513	5,760	1,267	0
Sarasota	110,430	1,338	(D)	10,300	8,491	4,509	3,539	30,038	7,988	39,339	4,832	(D)
Seminole	86,004	1,620	(D)	7,421	11,506	3,507	4,451	23,547	4,629	25,408	3,891	(D)
Sumter	6,287	323	(D)	252	454	450	243	1,724	162	1,640	927	(D)
Suwannee	7,534	373	(D)	430	1,444	425	251	1,866	321	1,836	567	(D)
Taylor	6,511	68	46	(D)	2,275	135	187	1,201	187	1,360	356	(D)
Union	3,415	18	(D)	64	685	276	33	207	45	545	1,533	(D)
Volusia	119,752	3,110	(D)	8,671	12,256	4,805	3,632	31,621	5,939	41,951	7,754	(D)
Wakulla	2,559	51	0	95	667	78	80	500	78	748	259	(D)
Walton	7,356	192	(D)	273	1,257	437	84	1,622	248	2,624	602	(D)
Washington	3,959	93	0	565	598	265	144	576	62	1,340	312	0
Statewide 1/	47,831	1,659	(D)	5,550	812	1,882	16,853	3,200	3,834	11,458	2,514	(D)

See footnotes at end of table.   Continued . . .

Table 6.23. EMPLOYMENT: AVERAGE MONTHLY EMPLOYMENT COVERED BY UNEMPLOYMENT COMPENSATION LAW BY MAJOR INDUSTRY GROUP IN THE STATE AND COUNTIES OF FLORIDA, 1989 AND 1990 (Continued)

1990

County	All industries (01-99)	Agriculture forestry and fisheries (01-09)	Mining (10-14)	Construction (15-17)	Manufacturing (20-39)	Transportation communication and public utilities (40-49)	Wholesale trade (50-51)	Retail trade (52-59)	Finance insurance and real estate (60-67)	Services (70-89)	Government (91-97)	Other (99)
Florida	5,400,969	145,229	8,886	329,399	519,385	317,511	293,090	1,161,920	368,784	1,882,489	371,509	2,439
Alachua	94,124	970	44	4,127	4,781	2,316	2,280	17,762	4,352	51,838	5,620	28
Baker	5,041	(D)	(D)	122	287	184	38	731	99	2,458	613	(D)
Bay	50,949	(D)	219	3,023	3,595	2,524	1,796	14,645	2,641	16,902	5,624	(D)
Bradford	5,574	62	(D)	169	681	143	84	1,229	147	1,339	1,688	(D)
Brevard	161,933	1,695	50	8,737	29,826	5,418	4,567	34,343	5,783	58,313	13,163	30
Broward	503,094	4,750	(D)	33,941	43,256	27,214	29,680	118,777	39,941	175,420	29,667	(D)
Calhoun	2,579	106	0	164	327	(D)	(D)	442	54	637	465	(D)
Charlotte	27,432	516	(D)	2,638	916	1,115	372	8,146	1,819	9,675	2,196	(D)
Citrus	21,586	216	(D)	1,941	844	2,286	358	5,786	1,230	7,518	1,349	(D)
Clay	26,105	594	(D)	2,059	1,476	1,147	764	8,966	894	8,258	1,460	(D)
Collier	72,720	11,977	101	7,709	2,339	2,279	1,539	15,412	5,062	23,076	3,197	24
Columbia	13,770	140	(D)	1,187	1,554	532	764	3,567	414	4,522	1,083	(D)
Dade	872,944	12,544	858	37,748	87,733	78,799	69,582	164,265	69,469	296,489	55,013	438
De Soto	7,977	1,554	(D)	291	(D)	178	179	1,227	187	3,131	863	(D)
Dixie	2,337	44	(D)	73	528	52	10	483	40	471	607	(D)
Duval	345,823	2,366	(D)	21,774	30,171	30,050	23,792	66,195	40,002	106,725	24,516	(D)
Escambia	107,613	478	123	6,556	9,624	6,630	4,400	24,224	4,809	37,366	13,387	12
Flagler	7,541	225	(D)	466	1,348	254	69	1,534	702	2,464	470	(D)
Franklin	2,097	(D)	0	57	131	122	122	415	100	743	352	(D)
Gadsden	14,091	1,624	(D)	487	1,568	291	511	1,747	268	5,996	1,350	(D)
Gilchrist	1,783	212	(D)	36	100	67	70	197	47	497	553	(D)
Glades	967	233	(D)	14	26	(D)	(D)	122	(D)	231	178	(D)

See footnotes at end of table.

Continued . . .

Table 6.23. EMPLOYMENT: AVERAGE MONTHLY EMPLOYMENT COVERED BY UNEMPLOYMENT COMPENSATION LAW BY MAJOR INDUSTRY GROUP IN THE STATE AND COUNTIES OF FLORIDA, 1989 AND 1990 (Continued)

1990 (Continued)

County	All industries (01-99)	Agriculture forestry and fisheries (01-09)	Mining (10-14)	Construction (15-17)	Manufacturing (20-39)	Transportation communication and public utilities (40-49)	Wholesale trade (50-51)	Retail trade (52-59)	Finance insurance and real estate (60-67)	Services (70-89)	Government (91-97)	Other (99)
Gulf	3,524	175	(D)	106	1,151	407	19	456	101	710	396	(D)
Hamilton	4,538	(D)	0	73	(D)	95	28	399	36	846	668	0
Hardee	6,837	2,354	(D)	179	320	185	313	1,032	202	1,711	461	(D)
Hendry	9,976	3,999	(D)	399	902	244	130	1,222	274	1,800	958	(D)
Hernando	20,298	470	(D)	1,495	1,139	1,057	437	5,130	1,111	7,077	1,904	(D)
Highlands	20,399	3,066	(D)	1,130	1,250	860	545	5,059	994	5,995	1,478	(D)
Hillsborough	440,383	11,418	50	23,339	40,073	30,343	33,818	81,184	35,414	162,860	21,800	78
Holmes	3,129	(D)	(D)	99	764	66	47	511	63	989	531	0
Indian River	34,233	3,548	(D)	3,134	2,444	859	584	8,068	2,073	11,094	2,411	(D)
Jackson	13,355	300	(D)	518	1,999	457	777	2,537	501	4,003	2,227	(D)
Jefferson	2,875	360	0	134	333	166	53	463	110	838	415	0
Lafayette	1,083	194	0	(D)	(D)	(D)	27	76	(D)	203	336	(D)
Lake	44,181	2,655	315	3,210	4,712	2,330	1,351	10,245	2,851	13,515	2,976	15
Lee	125,723	3,793	(D)	12,717	5,824	6,982	4,324	32,685	9,175	42,800	7,290	(D)
Leon	110,845	683	(D)	5,329	3,114	3,428	3,049	21,222	4,803	41,331	27,860	(D)
Levy	5,391	386	(D)	461	381	222	151	1,370	264	1,413	585	(D)
Liberty	1,402	(D)	0	82	255	73	(D)	137	(D)	414	405	(D)
Madison	4,587	283	0	50	1,130	170	122	795	74	1,316	642	0
Manatee	75,007	5,623	(D)	2,840	9,908	2,439	1,923	15,973	3,457	28,163	4,594	(D)
Marion	62,789	2,574	127	4,030	10,026	2,108	3,953	14,489	2,936	18,126	4,407	8
Martin	38,706	1,777	(D)	4,064	3,487	1,886	848	10,241	2,223	11,884	2,284	(D)
Monroe	30,427	339	(D)	1,803	594	2,354	580	9,199	1,419	11,437	2,655	(D)
Nassau	12,087	570	(D)	795	1,760	502	316	2,852	380	3,489	1,415	(D)
Okaloosa	53,463	252	(D)	3,095	4,873	2,088	989	14,726	2,684	17,109	7,635	(D)
Okeechobee	7,775	1,643	0	495	274	241	282	1,747	275	2,252	561	0

See footnotes at end of table.

Continued . . .

Table 6.23. EMPLOYMENT: AVERAGE MONTHLY EMPLOYMENT COVERED BY UNEMPLOYMENT COMPENSATION LAW BY MAJOR INDUSTRY GROUP IN THE STATE AND COUNTIES OF FLORIDA, 1989 AND 1990 (Continued)

County	All industries (01-99)	Agriculture forestry and fisheries (01-09)	Mining (10-14)	Construction (15-17)	Manufacturing (20-39)	Transportation communication and public utilities (40-49)	Wholesale trade (50-51)	Retail trade (52-59)	Finance insurance and real estate (60-67)	Services (70-89)	Government (91-97)	Other (99)
					1990 (Continued)							
Orange	430,604	8,371	115	24,922	39,976	29,993	25,966	80,440	26,643	174,173	19,883	116
Osceola	36,551	595	0	2,516	2,046	900	795	11,703	1,579	14,124	2,274	15
Palm Beach	363,277	18,177	22	25,252	32,390	17,839	14,188	80,126	27,197	125,677	22,223	182
Pasco	61,804	3,321	16	4,422	3,908	2,881	1,462	17,522	3,093	21,275	3,871	28
Pinellas	349,767	2,647	19	19,757	46,765	14,534	14,709	84,297	25,417	122,983	18,569	64
Polk	156,970	8,726	4,094	8,825	22,130	8,058	7,936	34,525	7,926	44,499	10,196	51
Putnam	16,101	664	(D)	691	3,691	599	282	3,330	499	4,480	1,774	(D)
St. Johns	26,615	711	(D)	1,236	3,112	598	846	6,768	996	10,510	1,821	(D)
St. Lucie	45,247	5,193	(D)	3,586	2,317	3,044	1,341	10,210	2,563	13,541	3,414	(D)
Santa Rosa	17,610	330	(D)	1,190	2,327	1,033	396	3,885	562	6,317	1,361	(D)
Sarasota	115,633	1,430	(D)	9,451	8,933	4,452	3,684	30,421	8,144	43,346	5,665	(D)
Seminole	90,660	1,554	(D)	8,088	11,463	3,381	4,593	23,604	4,589	29,160	4,153	(D)
Sumter	6,276	339	(D)	258	434	411	187	1,720	197	1,686	940	(D)
Suwannee	7,400	426	(D)	440	1,155	427	261	1,891	294	1,898	588	(D)
Taylor	6,564	78	50	(D)	2,227	139	144	1,244	195	1,413	394	(D)
Union	3,535	23	5	69	639	300	32	203	56	552	1,652	0
Volusia	122,243	3,192	(D)	8,356	11,876	4,937	3,643	32,700	5,729	43,345	8,338	(D)
Wakulla	2,565	54	0	93	692	93	31	481	82	759	277	0
Walton	7,771	189	(D)	334	1,247	467	147	1,661	266	2,646	793	(D)
Washington	4,222	92	0	572	(D)	256	135	627	58	1,407	325	(D)
Statewide 1/	48,461	1,339	(D)	5,756	779	1,598	16,585	2,529	3,165	13,254	2,690	(D)

(D) Data withheld to avoid disclosure of information about individual firms.
1/ Reporting units without a fixed location within the state or of unknown county location.
Source: State of Florida, Department of Labor and Employment Security, Bureau of Labor Market Information, "Employment, Wages, and Contributions Report" (ES-202), unpublished data.

Table 6.40. EMPLOYMENT: NAME AND LOCATION OF CORPORATE HEADQUARTERS OF THE
50 LARGEST EMPLOYERS IN FLORIDA, 1991

Firm and headquarters location	Number of employees	Firm and headquarters location	Number of employees
Barnett Banks, Inc.--Jacksonville, FL	A/	McDonald's Corporation--Oak Brook, IL	C/
Florida Power and Light--Miami, FL	A/	United Technologies Corp.--Hartford, CT	C/
K Mart Corp.--Troy, MI	A/	Walgreen Co.--Deerfield, IL	C/
Publix Super Markets, Inc.--Lakeland, FL	A/		
Sears, Roebuck and Co., Inc.--Chicago, IL	A/	American Express Co.--New York, NY	D/
Southern Bell Telephone and Telegraph Co.--Atlanta, GA	A/	Florida Power Corp.--St. Petersburg, FL	D/
Wal-Mart Stores, Inc.--Bentonville, AR	A/	HCA Health Services of Florida, Inc.--Nashville, TN	D/
Walt Disney World Co.--Lake Buena Vista, FL	A/	Home Depot, Inc.--Atlanta, GA	D/
		Humana, Inc.--Louisville, KY	D/
Winn Dixie Stores, Inc.--Jacksonville, FL	A/	Lockheed Space Operations Co.--Titusville, FL	D/
		Morrison, Inc.--Mobile, AL	D/
American Telephone and Telegraph--Morristown, NJ	B/	Pan American World Airways, Inc.--New York, NY	D/
General Mills Restaurants, Inc.--Orlando, FL	B/	Prudential Services of America--Newark, NJ	D/
Harris Corporation--Melbourne, FL	B/	Scotty's, Inc.--Winter Haven, FL	D/
International Business Machines, Inc.--Armonk, NY	B/	Southeast Banking Corp.--Miami, FL	D/
J. C. Penney Co.--Dallas, TX	B/	Southland Corporation--Dallas, TX	D/
Jack Eckerd Corp.--Clearwater, FL	B/	Steak and Ale of Florida--Dallas, TX	D/
Martin-Marietta Corp.--Bethesda, MD	B/	United Telephone Company of Florida--Altamonte Springs, FL	D/
Staff Leasing, Inc.--Bradenton, FL	B/		
United Parcel Service of America, Inc.--Greenwich, CT	B/	Action Staffing, Inc.--Tampa, FL	E/
		Blue Cross/Blue Shield of Florida, Inc.--Jacksonville, FL	D/
Albertson's, Inc.--Boise, ID	C/	Circle K Corp.--Phoenix, AZ	D/
Beverly Enterprises--Fort Smith, AR	C/	Continental Companies--Miami, FL	D/
Burdine's Inc.--Cincinnati, OH	C/	Denny's, Inc.--Irvine, CA	D/
First Union National Bank of Florida, Inc.--Jacksonville, FL	C/	Domino's Pizza, Inc.--Ann Arbor, MI	E/
GTE Florida, Inc.--Tampa, FL	C/	General Electric Co.--Fairfield, CT	E/
Kash n' Karry Food Stores, Inc.--Tampa, FL	C/	Motorola, Inc.--Schaumberg, IL	E/
Maas Brothers, Inc.--Tampa, FL	C/		

A/ 15,001 and over
B/ 10,001-15,000
C/   7,001-10,000
D/   5,001-7,000
E/   4,000-5,000
Note: Employers are listed alphabetically within employment size ranges.
Source: State of Florida, Department of Commerce, Bureau of Economic Analysis,
unpublished data.

Florida Statistical Abstract 1991

Table 6.57. AVERAGE ANNUAL PAY: PAY OF EMPLOYEES COVERED BY STATE AND FEDERAL
    UNEMPLOYMENT INSURANCE PROGRAMS IN THE UNITED STATES AND THE STATE AND
    METROPOLITAN AREAS OF FLORIDA, 1988 AND 1989

Industry or metropolitan area	1988 (dollars)	1989 (dollars)	Percentage change 1988-89	Ranking of MSAs in the U.S. By 1989 level	Ranking of MSAs in the U.S. By percentage change 1988-89
United States	21,872	22,567	3.2	(X)	(X)
Florida	19,520	20,072	2.8	(X)	(X)
Private industry 1/	19,085	19,572	2.6	(X)	(X)
Agriculture, forestry, and fishing	11,887	12,309	3.6	(X)	(X)
Mining	27,729	28,236	1.8	(X)	(X)
Construction	20,323	21,001	3.3	(X)	(X)
Manufacturing	23,465	24,290	3.5	(X)	(X)
Transportation, communications, and public utilities	26,492	26,426	-0.2	(X)	(X)
Wholesale trade	26,310	27,035	2.8	(X)	(X)
Retail trade	12,122	12,375	2.1	(X)	(X)
Finance, insurance, and real estate	23,977	24,433	1.9	(X)	(X)
Services	19,207	19,907	3.6	(X)	(X)
Government	22,008	22,902	4.1	(X)	(X)
Bradenton	16,740	17,256	3.1	296	149
Daytona Beach	16,231	16,740	3.1	309	149
Ft. Lauderdale-Hollywood-Pompano Beach	20,983	21,198	1.0	119	299
Ft. Myers-Cape Coral	17,753	18,219	2.6	261	200
Ft. Pierce	17,787	18,496	4.0	246	77
Ft. Walton Beach	16,140	16,625	3.0	310	157
Gainesville	17,355	18,122	4.4	266	49
Jacksonville	19,987	20,571	2.9	149	168
Lakeland-Winter Haven	17,861	18,417	3.1	251	149
Melbourne-Titusville-Palm Bay	21,441	22,266	3.8	78	89
Miami-Hialeah	21,871	22,330	2.1	74	250
Naples	16,084	17,135	6.5	298	3
Ocala	16,033	16,803	4.8	307	31
Orlando	19,930	20,373	2.2	155	235
Panama City	16,102	16,473	2.3	311	226
Pensacola	18,059	18,468	2.3	248	226
Sarasota	17,839	18,578	4.1	238	68
Tallahassee	17,951	18,465	2.9	249	168
Tampa-St. Petersburg-Clearwater	18,714	19,456	4.0	203	77
West Palm Beach-Boca Raton-Delray Beach	21,741	22,366	2.9	71	168

(X) Not applicable.   1/ Includes industries not listed separately.
    Note: 1988 data are revised; 1989 data are preliminary. Data are for Metro-
politan Statistical Areas (MSAs) and Primary Metropolitan Statistical Areas (PMSAs)
defined as of June 30, 1989. See Glossary for definitions and map at the front of
the book for area boundaries.
    Source: U.S., Department of Labor, Bureau of Labor Statistics, *Employment and
Wages: Annual Averages, 1989* and *News: Annual Pay Levels for Metropolitan Areas,
1989*, release of September 21, 1990.

Florida Statistical Abstract 1991

SOCIAL INSURANCE AND WELFARE

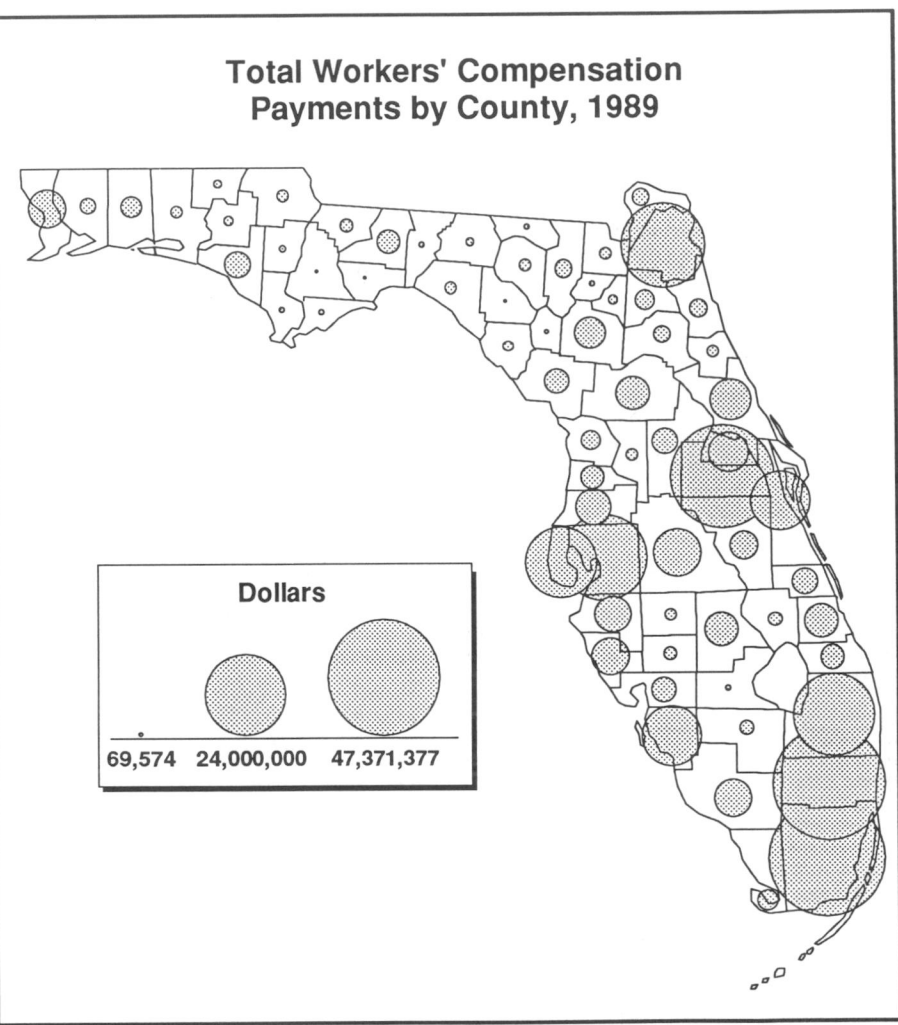

Total Workers' Compensation Payments by County, 1989

Dollars

69,574   24,000,000   47,371,377

Source: Table 7.60

TABLES LISTED BY MAJOR HEADINGS

Table 7.03. MEDICARE: ENROLLMENT IN HOSPITAL AND/OR MEDICAL INSURANCE
BY METROPOLITAN/NONMETROPOLITAN RESIDENCE IN FLORIDA, 1989 AND 1990

Item	Total enrollment		Persons aged 65 and over		Disability benefi- ciaries 1/	
	1989	1990	1989	1990	1989	1990
Florida, total	2,273,962	2,339,153	2,114,028	2,174,124	159,934	165,029
Metropolitan counties 2/	2,026,094	2,082,220	1,886,291	1,937,886	139,803	144,334
With central city	1,804,065	1,853,790	1,681,351	1,727,315	122,714	126,475
Without central city	222,029	228,430	204,940	210,571	17,089	17,859
Nonmetropolitan counties	244,189	254,450	224,249	233,922	19,940	20,528

1/ Persons under age 65 entitled to cash disability benefits for at least 24
consecutive months and also those eligible solely on the basis of end-stage renal
disease.

2/ Counties included in Metropolitan Statistical Areas (MSAs).

Table 7.04. MEDICARE: ENROLLMENT, JULY 1, AND BENEFIT PAYMENTS, FOR CALENDAR YEAR
OF PERSONS AGED 65 AND OVER IN FLORIDA, 1976 THROUGH 1989

Year	Hospital and/or medical insurance		Hospital insurance		Supplementary medical insurance	
	Enroll- ment (1,000)	Benefit payments ($1,000)	Enroll- ment (1,000)	Benefit payments ($1,000)	Enroll- ment (1,000)	Benefit payments ($1,000)
1976	1,313	975,846	1,282	650,381	1,288	325,465
1977	1,374	1,159,707	1,346	765,109	1,347	394,598
1978	1,447	1,329,317	1,418	852,428	1,420	476,889
1979	1,520	1,582,519	1,491	1,008,708	1,492	573,810
1980	1,579	1,927,887	1,549	1,209,668	1,551	718,219
1981	1,626	2,338,909	1,595	1,480,300	1,598	858,609
1982	1,680	2,934,263	1,648	1,898,732	1,651	1,035,531
1983	1,736	3,411,057	1,704	2,178,642	1,709	1,232,415
1984	1,791	4,296,524	1,757	2,775,313	1,765	1,521,211
1985	1,856	5,040,418	1,820	3,267,584	1,829	1,772,834
1986	1,921	5,394,033	1,881	3,347,974	1,893	2,046,059
1987	2,135	5,720,000	2,092	3,275,000	2,095	2,445,000
1988	2,114	5,517,000	2,070	2,869,000	2,072	2,648,000
1989	2,174	6,470,000	2,165	3,340,000	2,129	3,130,000

Note: Geographic classification is based on the address to which the enrollee's
cash benefit check is being mailed or the mailing address recorded in the health
insurance master file. Data from 1985 are estimated.

Source for Tables 7.03 and 7.04: U.S., Department of Health and Human Services,
Health Care Financing Administration, unpublished data.

Florida Statistical Abstract 1991

Table 7.12. SOCIAL SECURITY: NUMBER OF BENEFICIARIES AND AMOUNT OF BENEFITS
IN CURRENT-PAYMENT STATUS BY TYPE OF BENEFICIARY IN THE STATE AND
COUNTIES OF FLORIDA, DECEMBER 31, 1989

Residence of beneficiary	Total	Retired workers 1/	Disabled workers	Husbands or wives	Children	Widows, widowers, parents
			Number of beneficiaries			
Florida	2,576,028	1,757,439	154,441	215,648	147,771	300,729
Alachua	23,475	13,815	1,990	1,825	2,840	3,005
Baker	2,255	1,085	365	175	340	290
Bay	19,495	11,395	1,565	1,870	1,790	2,875
Bradford	3,280	1,830	330	290	365	465
Brevard	73,205	49,380	4,740	6,760	3,995	8,330
Broward	268,660	191,540	12,280	20,540	10,810	33,490
Calhoun	2,005	1,075	180	210	215	325
Charlotte	33,470	25,195	1,425	3,060	945	2,845
Citrus	31,470	22,925	1,705	2,745	1,290	2,805
Clay	11,115	6,740	895	935	1,150	1,395
Collier	34,035	23,695	1,340	4,110	1,335	3,555
Columbia	7,355	4,095	760	655	815	1,030
Dade	269,010	178,950	17,950	20,850	19,375	31,885
De Soto	5,070	3,260	450	405	440	515
Dixie	2,095	1,170	260	185	225	255
Duval	90,950	54,945	7,500	6,635	8,585	13,285
Escambia	38,770	22,165	3,250	3,910	3,510	5,935
Flagler	7,250	5,380	405	595	320	550
Franklin	1,815	1,110	175	130	140	260
Gadsden	7,665	4,035	930	460	1,340	900
Gilchrist	1,630	970	145	140	155	220
Glades	865	560	65	70	80	90
Gulf	2,235	1,155	190	255	240	395
Hamilton	1,860	945	210	160	260	285
Hardee	3,560	2,060	315	295	455	435
Hendry	3,235	1,885	280	265	400	405
Hernando	34,550	25,280	2,105	2,985	1,550	2,630
Highlands	22,970	16,800	1,115	2,075	920	2,060
Hillsborough	125,440	78,280	10,575	9,800	10,615	16,170
Holmes	3,320	1,785	305	350	315	565
Indian River	28,615	20,840	1,175	2,825	950	2,825
Jackson	8,595	4,630	725	740	1,080	1,420
Jefferson	2,075	1,180	170	155	255	315
Lafayette	705	385	60	60	90	110
Lake	45,975	33,035	2,440	4,105	1,790	4,605
Lee	88,510	63,785	4,250	7,990	3,885	8,600
Leon	19,920	12,220	1,450	1,545	1,960	2,745
Levy	5,440	3,315	475	495	470	685
Liberty	900	435	115	75	135	140
Madison	3,150	1,790	265	270	310	515
Manatee	55,405	39,700	2,515	4,780	2,005	6,405
Marion	52,605	36,165	3,765	4,465	3,310	4,900
Martin	29,120	21,435	1,015	2,955	830	2,885
Monroe	10,050	6,870	625	910	495	1,150
Nassau	5,445	2,990	535	490	595	835
Okaloosa	17,745	10,520	1,415	1,835	1,550	2,425
Okeechobee	6,750	4,315	570	560	535	770

See footnotes at end of table.   Continued . . .

Table 7.12. SOCIAL SECURITY: NUMBER OF BENEFICIARIES AND AMOUNT OF BENEFITS
IN CURRENT-PAYMENT STATUS BY TYPE OF BENEFICIARY IN THE STATE AND
COUNTIES OF FLORIDA, DECEMBER 31, 1989 (Continued)

Residence of beneficiary	Total	Retired workers 1/	Disabled workers	Husbands or wives	Children	Widows, widowers, parents
		Number of beneficiaries (Continued)				
Orange	93,825	59,100	7,620	7,470	8,000	11,635
Osceola	16,835	10,865	1,315	1,320	1,430	1,905
Palm Beach	210,345	153,395	7,725	18,205	7,240	23,780
Pasco	95,975	70,630	5,100	7,935	3,425	8,885
Pinellas	233,640	166,900	11,255	17,725	8,390	29,370
Polk	83,065	55,195	5,860	6,745	5,770	9,495
Putnam	13,685	8,255	1,345	1,155	1,250	1,680
St. Johns	15,325	10,010	1,045	1,445	1,065	1,760
St. Lucie	32,380	22,720	2,155	2,520	1,960	3,025
Santa Rosa	9,885	5,420	970	1,115	1,050	1,330
Sarasota	100,300	73,490	3,490	9,870	2,540	10,910
Seminole	31,565	19,915	2,355	2,570	2,860	3,865
Sumter	7,875	5,325	565	680	500	805
Suwannee	5,965	3,470	565	515	560	855
Taylor	3,355	1,850	300	305	375	525
Union	1,085	560	105	85	160	175
Volusia	95,890	66,430	6,175	7,820	4,955	10,510
Wakulla	2,030	1,160	180	170	250	270
Walton	4,530	2,615	410	445	400	660
Washington	3,820	2,110	395	385	345	585
Unknown	1,555	925	145	145	180	160
		Amount of monthly cash benefits ($1,000)				
Florida	1,347,268	994,802	87,228	61,961	44,224	159,053
Alachua	11,400	7,486	1,079	515	845	1,475
Baker	1,000	547	188	41	97	127
Bay	9,159	5,875	877	486	557	1,364
Bradford	1,454	902	177	69	102	204
Brevard	37,701	27,364	2,807	1,865	1,271	4,394
Broward	152,031	115,893	7,173	6,282	3,488	19,195
Calhoun	833	506	94	45	56	132
Charlotte	18,088	14,430	916	889	304	1,549
Citrus	16,508	12,793	1,068	761	403	1,483
Clay	5,404	3,570	523	247	380	684
Collier	19,316	14,633	804	1,363	407	2,109
Columbia	3,256	2,020	413	159	221	443
Dade	134,820	97,841	9,028	5,809	5,556	16,586
De Soto	2,467	1,744	239	106	23	255
Dixie	945	584	145	45	59	112
Duval	44,691	29,652	4,050	1,875	2,582	6,532
Escambia	17,679	11,150	1,789	986	1,024	2,730
Flagler	3,941	3,116	258	172	94	301
Franklin	808	528	92	33	40	115
Gadsden	3,059	1,860	427	103	292	377
Gilchrist	743	477	86	34	50	96
Glades	432	302	40	20	24	46
Gulf	1,066	622	107	73	74	190
Hamilton	766	440	108	34	68	116

See footnotes at end of table.   Continued . . .

Florida Statistical Abstract 1991

Table 7.12. SOCIAL SECURITY: NUMBER OF BENEFICIARIES AND AMOUNT OF BENEFITS
IN CURRENT-PAYMENT STATUS BY TYPE OF BENEFICIARY IN THE STATE AND
COUNTIES OF FLORIDA, DECEMBER 31, 1989 (Continued)

Residence of beneficiary	Total	Retired workers 1/	Disabled workers	Husbands or wives	Children	Widows, widowers, parents
		Amount of monthly cash benefits ($1,000) (Continued)				
Hardee	1,597	1,049	155	73	123	197
Hendry	1,568	1,039	151	73	111	194
Hernando	18,262	14,209	1,363	829	449	1,412
Highlands	11,838	9,271	647	575	254	1,091
Hillsborough	62,769	42,954	5,827	2,735	3,137	8,116
Holmes	1,316	793	158	72	79	214
Indian River	15,687	12,227	699	874	307	1,580
Jackson	3,553	2,156	371	166	278	582
Jefferson	859	553	83	34	64	125
Lafayette	305	191	32	14	23	45
Lake	23,782	18,304	1,398	1,152	515	2,413
Lee	47,744	36,845	2,582	2,349	1,237	4,731
Leon	9,985	6,800	778	453	588	1,366
Levy	2,554	1,694	275	123	142	320
Liberty	380	213	59	17	36	55
Madison	1,297	823	139	58	75	202
Manatee	29,416	22,484	1,447	1,389	611	3,485
Marion	26,703	19,882	2,204	1,210	930	2,477
Martin	16,169	12,740	607	916	272	1,634
Monroe	5,094	3,741	360	255	159	579
Nassau	2,709	1,652	314	138	198	407
Okaloosa	8,131	5,268	780	460	489	1,134
Okeechobee	3,367	2,360	326	149	152	380
Orange	47,297	32,736	4,166	2,085	2,344	5,966
Osceola	8,493	5,985	769	349	421	969
Palm Beach	122,193	95,464	4,545	5,936	2,293	13,955
Pasco	50,466	39,350	3,136	2,186	1,028	4,766
Pinellas	123,463	93,543	6,435	5,072	2,634	15,779
Polk	42,126	30,449	3,243	1,901	1,665	4,868
Putnam	6,509	4,336	762	292	322	797
St. Johns	7,851	5,607	590	428	319	907
St. Lucie	17,080	12,945	1,243	717	556	1,619
Santa Rosa	4,561	2,785	568	279	327	602
Sarasota	55,400	43,171	2,125	3,039	860	6,205
Seminole	16,058	11,061	1,348	715	904	2,030
Sumter	3,779	2,791	311	177	123	377
Suwannee	2,632	1,685	315	122	144	366
Taylor	1,540	958	168	76	101	237
Union	459	268	56	20	42	73
Volusia	49,488	36,757	3,594	2,170	1,482	5,485
Wakulla	899	580	95	40	69	115
Walton	1,950	1,241	226	98	106	279
Washington	1,620	999	208	85	91	237
Unknown	765	515	79	42	44	85

1/ Includes "special age 72" beneficiaries.
Note: Data are estimates based on a 10 percent sample. Detail may not add to
totals because of rounding.
Source: U.S., Department of Health and Human Services, Social Security Administration, *OASDI Beneficiaries by State and County, December 1989.*

Florida Statistical Abstract 1991

Table 7.14. SOCIAL SECURITY: AVERAGE MONTHLY BENEFITS OF BENEFICIARIES AGED 65 AND
   OLDER IN THE STATE AND COUNTIES OF FLORIDA, DECEMBER 31, 1989

(in dollars)

County	All bene-ficiaries	Retired workers	County	All bene-ficiaries	Retired workers
Florida	523.00	566.05	Lafayette	432.62	496.10
			Lake	517.28	554.08
Alachua	485.62	541.87	Lee	539.42	577.64
Baker	443.46	504.15	Leon	501.26	556.46
Bay	469.81	515.58	Levy	469.49	511.01
Bradford	443.29	492.90	Liberty	422.22	489.66
Brevard	515.01	554.15	Madison	411.75	459.78
Broward	565.89	605.06	Manatee	530.93	566.35
Calhoun	415.46	470.70	Marion	507.61	549.76
Charlotte	540.42	572.73	Martin	555.25	594.36
Citrus	524.56	558.04	Monroe	506.87	544.54
Clay	486.19	529.67	Nassau	497.52	552.51
Collier	567.53	617.56	Okaloosa	458.21	500.76
Columbia	442.69	493.28	Okeechobee	498.81	546.93
Dade	501.17	546.75	Orange	504.10	553.91
De Soto	486.59	534.97	Osceola	504.48	550.85
Dixie	451.07	499.15	Palm Beach	580.92	622.34
Duval	491.38	539.67	Pasco	525.82	557.13
Escambia	456.00	503.05	Pinellas	528.43	560.47
Flagler	543.59	579.18	Polk	507.15	551.66
Franklin	445.18	475.68	Putnam	475.63	525.26
Gadsden	399.09	460.97	St. Johns	512.30	560.14
Gilchrist	455.83	491.75	St. Lucie	527.49	569.76
Glades	499.42	539.29	Santa Rosa	461.41	513.84
Gulf	476.96	538.53	Sarasota	552.34	587.44
Hamilton	411.83	465.61	Seminole	508.73	555.41
Hardee	448.60	509.22	Sumter	479.87	524.13
Hendry	484.70	551.19	Suwannee	441.24	485.59
Hernando	528.57	562.06	Taylor	459.02	517.84
Highlands	515.37	551.85	Union	423.04	478.57
Hillsborough	500.39	548.72	Volusia	516.09	553.32
Holmes	396.39	444.26	Wakulla	442.86	500.00
Indian River	548.21	586.71	Walton	430.46	474.57
Jackson	413.38	465.66	Washington	424.08	473.46
Jefferson	413.98	468.64			

Note: Data are estimates based on a 10 percent sample.

Source: U.S., Department of Health and Human Services, Social Security Administration, *OASDI Beneficiaries by State and County, December 1989.*

Florida Statistical Abstract 1991

Table 7.15.   PUBLIC ASSISTANCE: DIRECT AND MEDICAL ASSISTANCE PAYMENTS BY PROGRAM
   IN FLORIDA, FISCAL YEARS 1985-86 THROUGH 1988-89

(amounts rounded to thousands of dollars)

Type of assistance	1985-86	1986-87	1987-88	1988-89
Direct assistance, total	478,733	775,806	784,914	729,477
Basic Supplemental Security Income (SSI)	214,460	487,897	512,484	455,327
Old-Age Assistance (OAA)	71,540	183,068	177,734	151,021
Aid to the Blind (AB)	8,403	6,016	8,897	7,720
Aid to the Disabled (AD)	134,517	296,262	325,853	296,585
SSI State Supplementation 1/	9,240	10,769	11,207	12,485
Aid to Families with Dependent Children (AFDC)	253,496	277,140	253,966	255,122
Medical assistance, total 2/	1,030,344	1,177,980	1,493,272	(NA)
Aid to the Blind	5,765	6,016	7,486	(NA)
Aid to the Disabled	394,885	439,671	527,110	(NA)
Aid to Families with Dependent Children	167,628	209,115	335,742	(NA)
Old-Age Assistance	454,166	508,283	601,460	(NA)

(NA) Not available.
   1/ Payments to persons eligible for state benefits prior to 1974 or eligible
under current state guidelines, but not eligible under federal requirements.
   2/ Data are for federal fiscal year, October 1 through September 30.

Table 7.16.   MEDICAL ASSISTANCE: NUMBER OF RECIPIENTS BY AGE OF RECIPIENT
   IN FLORIDA, FISCAL YEAR 1988-89

Type of service	Total	Aged 5 and under	Aged 6 to 20	Aged 21 to 64	Aged 65 to 84	Aged 85 and over
Unduplicated total	875,585	222,690	215,126	268,448	127,525	41,796
Inpatient hospital	182,657	31,357	34,595	83,807	24,910	7,988
Mental--aged	26,925	855	5,549	18,017	2,139	365
Mentally retarded	3,401	12	404	2,924	55	6
Intermediate care facilities	44,047	82	24	3,354	20,469	20,118
Skilled nursing facilities	20,298	29	18	2,374	10,203	7,674
Physician	560,122	154,589	126,987	177,820	75,873	24,853
Dental	111,854	22,713	61,215	14,933	9,619	3,374
Other practitioners	82,208	3,003	20,089	33,066	19,951	6,099
Outpatient hospital	361,592	95,354	87,381	135,195	35,420	8,242
Clinic	2,183	196	288	691	824	184
Home health	13,583	409	508	6,330	4,382	1,954
Family planning	30,149	70	10,833	19,218	23	5
Lab and X-ray	344,137	85,585	86,855	143,599	20,751	7,347
Prescribed drugs	578,013	129,185	111,551	184,877	115,543	36,857
Early and periodic screening	122,822	86,957	34,246	1,594	20	5
Other care	168,084	20,013	26,522	58,818	45,774	16,957
Rural health clinic	14,256	4,470	3,660	5,127	846	153

Note: Data are for fiscal year ending September 30.

   Source for Tables 7.15 and 7.16:   State of Florida, Department of Health and
Rehabilitative Services, Office of Revenue Management, *Annual Statistical Report,
Fiscal Year 1988-89* prepublication release, and previous editions.

Table 7.18. PUBLIC ASSISTANCE: AMOUNT OF ASSISTANCE AND AVERAGE MONTHLY CASES BY TYPE OF ASSISTANCE IN THE STATE DEPARTMENT OF HEALTH AND REHABILITATIVE SERVICES DISTRICTS, AND COUNTIES OF FLORIDA, FISCAL YEAR 1989-90

| District and county | Total direct assistance | | Aid to Families with Dependent Children | | Supplemental Security Income | | | | | |
| | | | | | Old Age Assistance | | Aid to the Blind | | Aid to the Disabled | |
	Amount (dollars)	Percentage change from 1988-89	Amount (dollars)	Average monthly cases	Amount (dollars)	Average monthly cases	Amount (dollars)	Average monthly cases	Amount (dollars)	Average monthly cases
Florida	908,435,698	27.9	355,455,794	118,798	172,995,762	79,930	9,860,452	3,160	370,123,690	126,045
District 1	41,751,331	30.4	19,523,162	6,662	4,272,185	2,498	528,196	169	17,427,788	5,797
Escambia	27,721,207	31.7	13,612,699	4,576	2,649,998	1,525	314,932	102	11,143,578	3,609
Okaloosa	6,652,428	26.8	2,639,312	935	775,029	443	104,049	33	3,134,038	1,114
Santa Rosa	4,839,616	31.0	2,380,149	833	454,689	277	70,507	22	1,934,271	659
Walton	2,538,080	24.8	891,002	318	392,469	253	38,708	12	1,215,901	415
District 2	53,544,764	32.9	20,667,221	7,195	7,919,568	4,893	773,211	256	24,184,764	8,411
Bay	8,523,935	29.9	3,386,248	1,191	1,068,403	700	97,357	38	3,971,927	1,397
Calhoun	1,933,186	37.0	815,620	273	291,600	181	35,537	10	790,429	276
Franklin	1,235,266	29.6	545,632	191	205,380	148	12,880	5	471,374	173
Gadsden	7,835,489	31.7	3,480,813	1,169	926,533	710	105,448	35	3,322,695	1,185
Gulf	1,352,510	29.6	573,667	205	191,022	124	5,737	4	582,084	206
Holmes	2,348,096	31.1	641,545	229	564,024	339	36,648	11	1,105,879	390
Jackson	6,046,066	27.9	1,536,073	554	1,391,016	773	59,735	20	3,059,242	1,124
Jefferson	2,177,208	30.5	877,664	304	419,266	226	18,705	6	861,573	273
Leon	11,654,856	40.7	5,165,270	1,799	1,323,561	753	219,080	70	4,946,945	1,670
Liberty	715,553	29.6	249,105	90	127,499	66	25,421	9	313,528	135
Madison	3,590,447	28.8	1,111,976	378	581,685	342	71,663	20	1,825,123	564
Taylor	2,145,336	37.9	902,366	324	268,219	174	7,731	5	967,020	336
Wakulla	1,337,478	36.2	586,871	206	143,493	95	13,578	4	593,536	187
Washington	2,649,338	31.1	794,371	282	417,867	262	63,691	19	1,373,409	495
District 3	76,677,522	35.4	35,835,699	12,055	7,485,757	4,762	986,827	317	32,369,239	11,190
Alachua	16,291,592	33.0	8,380,217	2,750	1,237,377	749	201,078	72	6,472,920	2,305
Bradford	2,366,974	35.0	1,117,102	372	258,575	148	28,739	10	962,558	328
Citrus	3,894,490	38.7	1,936,170	697	304,613	221	39,542	14	1,614,165	589
Columbia	5,226,613	42.5	1,845,467	647	733,324	404	69,290	12	2,578,532	869

Continued . . .

Health and Rehabilitative Services Districts

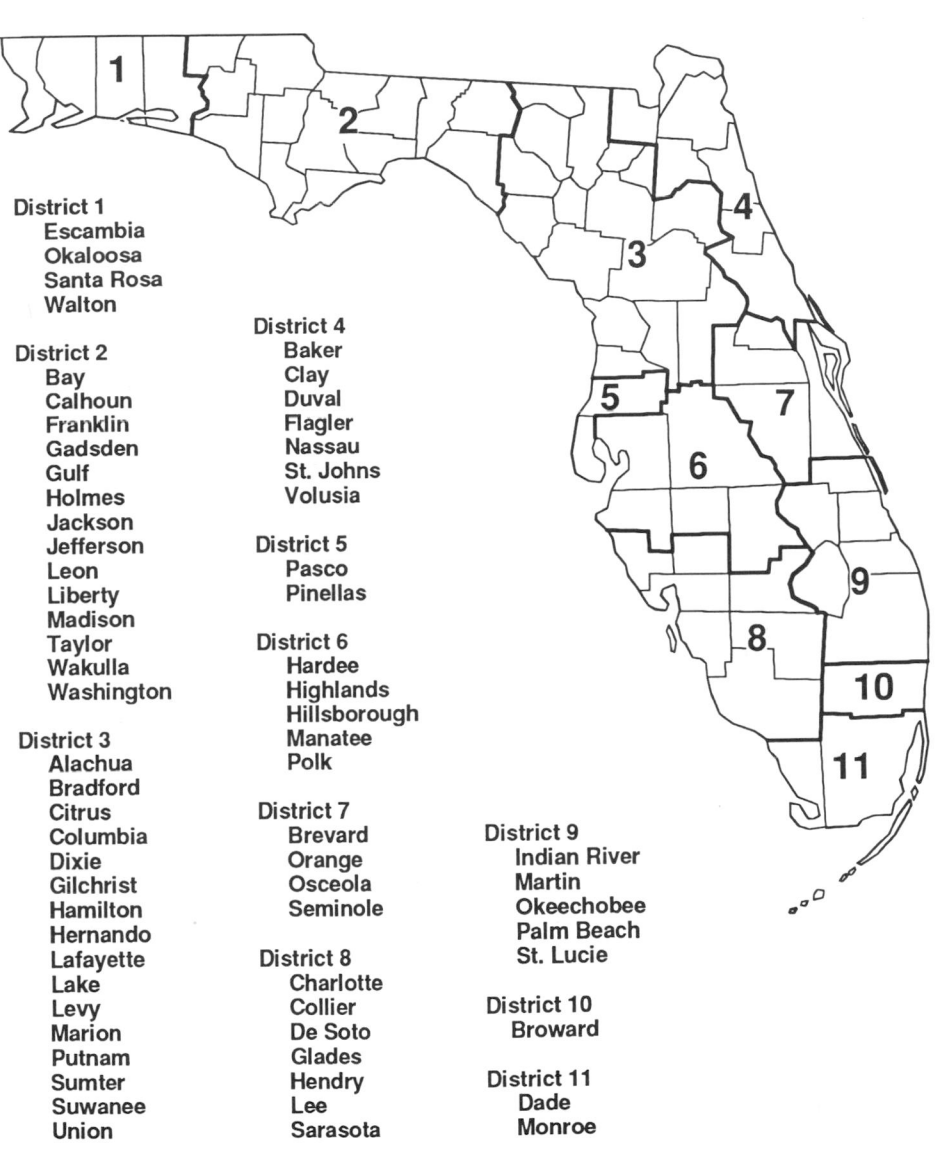

District 1
  Escambia
  Okaloosa
  Santa Rosa
  Walton

District 2
  Bay
  Calhoun
  Franklin
  Gadsden
  Gulf
  Holmes
  Jackson
  Jefferson
  Leon
  Liberty
  Madison
  Taylor
  Wakulla
  Washington

District 3
  Alachua
  Bradford
  Citrus
  Columbia
  Dixie
  Gilchrist
  Hamilton
  Hernando
  Lafayette
  Lake
  Levy
  Marion
  Putnam
  Sumter
  Suwanee
  Union

District 4
  Baker
  Clay
  Duval
  Flagler
  Nassau
  St. Johns
  Volusia

District 5
  Pasco
  Pinellas

District 6
  Hardee
  Highlands
  Hillsborough
  Manatee
  Polk

District 7
  Brevard
  Orange
  Osceola
  Seminole

District 8
  Charlotte
  Collier
  De Soto
  Glades
  Hendry
  Lee
  Sarasota

District 9
  Indian River
  Martin
  Okeechobee
  Palm Beach
  St. Lucie

District 10
  Broward

District 11
  Dade
  Monroe

Table 7.18. PUBLIC ASSISTANCE: AMOUNT OF ASSISTANCE AND AVERAGE MONTHLY CASES BY TYPE OF ASSISTANCE IN THE STATE DEPARTMENT OF HEALTH AND REHABILITATIVE SERVICES DISTRICTS, AND COUNTIES OF FLORIDA, FISCAL YEAR 1989-90 (Continued)

| District and county | Total direct assistance | | Aid to Families with Dependent Children | | Old Age Assistance | | Supplemental Security Income | | | |
| | | | | | | | Aid to the Blind | | Aid to the Disabled | |
	Amount (dollars)	Percentage change from 1988-89	Amount (dollars)	Average monthly cases	Amount (dollars)	Average monthly cases	Amount (dollars)	Average monthly cases	Amount (dollars)	Average monthly cases
District 3 (Cont.)										
Dixie	1,374,676	39.2	631,263	216	124,560	73	29,517	8	589,336	188
Gilchrist	695,276	48.0	315,999	110	91,698	64	4,615	2	282,964	101
Hamilton	1,957,961	28.1	879,577	256	320,688	190	26,427	9	731,269	257
Hernando	4,691,478	41.4	2,343,614	799	300,905	222	58,738	17	1,988,221	680
Lafayette	407,218	29.7	202,853	71	52,441	38	6,133	3	145,791	58
Lake	7,685,706	34.9	3,372,337	1,166	796,175	561	64,904	23	3,452,290	1,235
Levy	2,657,614	30.4	1,193,138	408	314,342	190	25,285	10	1,124,849	379
Marion	13,973,534	37.6	6,247,127	2,123	1,275,718	793	205,288	65	6,245,401	2,094
Putnam	8,246,969	34.0	4,289,351	1,391	680,938	472	115,688	39	3,160,992	1,062
Sumter	3,121,529	29.5	1,389,460	466	316,317	220	51,819	15	1,363,933	463
Suwannee	3,179,783	33.7	1,312,028	459	528,097	337	50,998	15	1,288,660	449
Union	906,109	25.2	379,996	124	149,989	80	8,766	3	367,358	133
District 4	88,871,015	34.5	39,745,092	13,482	8,770,259	5,267	1,213,815	392	39,141,849	12,887
Baker	1,312,169	34.0	637,968	226	126,851	100	20,471	7	526,879	166
Clay	2,812,919	42.2	1,224,361	458	305,524	172	49,395	17	1,233,639	418
Duval	58,115,163	35.3	27,250,955	9,039	5,670,347	3,281	726,268	221	24,467,593	7,811
Flagler	856,578	40.6	420,722	142	84,408	51	3,205	2	348,243	127
Nassau	2,462,919	33.2	979,122	376	276,126	182	15,971	6	1,191,700	410
St. Johns	4,558,990	26.0	1,748,888	626	483,588	324	86,070	36	2,240,444	779
Volusia	18,752,277	33.2	7,483,076	2,615	1,823,415	1,157	312,435	103	9,133,351	3,176
District 5	49,468,797	34.4	23,686,868	8,173	4,432,588	2,775	525,074	196	20,824,267	7,318
Pasco	11,540,180	32.7	5,364,919	1,892	886,349	604	84,893	33	5,204,019	1,819
Pinellas	37,928,617	34.9	18,321,949	6,281	3,546,239	2,171	440,181	163	15,620,248	5,499
District 6	106,362,142	35.3	43,689,172	14,689	12,149,757	6,622	1,193,428	397	49,329,785	16,304
Hardee	2,441,494	31.2	974,312	323	243,330	164	18,724	7	1,205,128	414
Highlands	4,255,498	33.9	1,947,213	676	414,068	267	60,912	20	1,833,305	636
Hillsborough	65,667,050	34.8	27,422,230	9,152	8,180,903	4,259	688,197	234	29,375,720	9,527

Continued . . .

Table 7.18. PUBLIC ASSISTANCE: AMOUNT OF ASSISTANCE AND AVERAGE MONTHLY CASES BY TYPE OF ASSISTANCE IN THE STATE DEPARTMENT OF HEALTH AND REHABILITATIVE SERVICES DISTRICTS, AND COUNTIES OF FLORIDA, FISCAL YEAR 1989-90 (Continued)

District and county	Total direct assistance Amount (dollars)	Per-centage change from 1988-89	Aid to Families with Dependent Children Amount (dollars)	Average monthly cases	Old Age Assistance Amount (dollars)	Average monthly cases	Aid to the Blind Amount (dollars)	Average monthly cases	Aid to the Disabled Amount (dollars)	Average monthly cases
District 6 (Cont.)										
Manatee	8,194,683	37.1	3,625,204	1,251	708,825	466	116,461	34	3,744,193	1,292
Polk	25,803,417	36.4	9,720,213	3,287	2,602,631	1,466	309,134	102	13,171,439	4,435
District 7	71,899,159	39.4	33,895,614	11,429	7,649,798	3,983	780,048	253	29,573,699	9,969
Brevard	17,638,260	40.4	8,931,873	3,009	1,424,475	804	161,614	50	7,120,298	2,360
Orange	40,491,088	38.3	18,611,034	6,212	4,532,500	2,273	479,216	158	16,868,338	5,674
Osceola	3,840,986	57.5	1,863,952	639	408,683	212	38,202	11	1,530,149	513
Seminole	9,928,825	35.8	4,488,755	1,569	1,284,140	694	101,016	34	4,054,914	1,422
District 8	31,396,782	34.3	14,372,036	4,895	3,238,763	1,889	396,093	141	13,389,890	4,913
Charlotte	2,327,889	44.8	891,975	323	335,665	173	39,311	15	1,060,938	373
Collier	4,209,404	19.6	1,993,418	682	594,389	285	70,026	23	1,551,571	656
De Soto	2,034,416	31.4	1,071,729	364	186,785	140	9,610	5	766,292	265
Glades	353,531	30.7	168,936	56	51,159	33	8,322	3	125,114	37
Hendry	2,655,950	36.4	1,642,615	540	204,448	108	19,576	7	789,311	263
Lee	12,792,001	37.7	5,883,409	1,973	1,100,232	662	139,669	49	5,668,691	2,073
Sarasota	7,023,591	35.2	2,719,954	957	766,085	488	109,579	39	3,427,973	1,246
District 9	50,750,276	35.3	23,409,726	7,822	6,660,395	3,271	650,782	205	20,029,373	6,709
Indian River	3,119,480	31.8	1,350,871	471	277,373	193	45,402	14	1,445,834	518
Martin	3,480,168	52.3	1,455,795	492	430,272	268	64,938	23	1,529,163	536
Okeechobee	2,104,559	40.5	822,546	290	194,983	129	32,533	10	1,054,497	355
Palm Beach	32,797,969	35.3	14,659,966	4,905	5,165,381	2,332	438,454	136	12,534,168	4,121
St. Lucie	9,248,100	30.1	5,120,548	1,664	592,386	349	69,455	22	3,465,711	1,179
District 10	51,132,662	40.0	20,630,599	6,922	8,037,767	3,637	505,988	163	21,958,308	7,108
Broward	51,132,662	40.0	20,630,599	6,922	8,037,767	3,637	505,988	163	21,958,308	7,108
District 11	286,581,248	14.2	80,000,605	25,474	102,378,925	40,333	2,306,990	671	101,894,728	35,439
Dade	283,584,316	14.0	79,140,893	25,173	101,679,880	40,035	2,270,010	659	100,493,533	34,997
Monroe	2,996,932	32.3	859,712	301	699,045	298	36,980	12	1,401,195	442

Source: State of Florida, Annual Report of the Comptroller, Fiscal Year 1989-90. Data from Department of Health and Rehabilitative Services.

Table 7.22. PUBLIC ASSISTANCE: VALUE OF FOOD STAMPS AND HOME ENERGY ASSISTANCE
   PAYMENTS AND NUMBER OF HOUSEHOLDS RECEIVING PAYMENTS IN THE STATE
   DEPARTMENT OF HEALTH AND REHABILITATIVE SERVICES DISTRICTS, AND
   COUNTIES OF FLORIDA, FISCAL YEARS ENDING JUNE 30, 1988 AND 1989

(amounts in dollars)

District and county	Value of food stamps issued		Low-income home energy assistance program			
			Payment amount		Number of households	
	1988	1989	1988	1989	1988	1989
Florida	359,216,779	438,487,986	15,889,638	14,394,841	174,490	179,342
District 1	21,191,795	25,748,219	1,281,639	1,144,045	12,355	12,626
Escambia	14,114,929	16,993,468	802,837	714,815	7,740	7,844
Okaloosa	3,098,005	4,094,785	205,888	183,747	1,994	2,047
Santa Rosa	2,664,492	3,166,893	157,314	145,696	1,498	1,592
Walton	1,314,369	1,493,073	115,600	99,787	1,123	1,143
District 2	23,845,103	28,564,170	1,978,798	1,675,350	18,993	18,597
Bay	4,878,672	6,291,959	396,360	359,484	3,744	3,902
Calhoun	825,120	1,010,093	70,242	56,706	666	605
Franklin	614,584	774,771	56,224	55,089	532	582
Gadsden	3,673,326	4,281,815	286,718	247,286	2,827	2,847
Gulf	772,232	833,700	67,380	55,640	624	617
Holmes	1,280,043	1,501,408	111,636	92,302	1,073	1,041
Jackson	1,990,435	2,246,362	199,333	165,391	1,944	1,836
Jefferson	876,384	1,021,234	63,439	51,427	613	578
Leon	4,693,859	5,567,072	376,372	298,801	3,616	3,330
Liberty	235,900	279,181	22,486	18,606	225	204
Madison	1,204,331	1,371,081	98,717	80,023	952	910
Taylor	880,218	1,129,312	60,441	55,315	571	620
Wakulla	701,610	901,389	55,091	45,632	495	488
Washington	1,218,389	1,354,793	114,359	93,648	1,111	1,037
District 3	35,654,422	44,336,851	1,936,839	1,702,687	19,844	19,796
Alachua	6,621,163	8,048,112	399,745	346,441	3,737	3,623
Bradford	988,173	1,123,960	66,711	59,109	655	638
Citrus	2,249,080	3,077,275	74,084	65,275	859	918
Columbia	1,999,264	2,469,159	136,353	131,827	1,322	1,417
Dixie	755,601	874,659	43,676	41,346	398	423
Gilchrist	319,783	382,074	15,697	16,657	149	180
Hamilton	852,862	976,919	64,836	52,851	618	592
Hernando	2,423,991	3,340,638	84,831	66,603	1,018	920
Lafayette	242,964	279,097	19,155	18,014	184	198
Lake	3,758,177	4,771,261	165,601	145,733	1,896	1,888
Levy	1,328,300	1,605,424	83,118	70,654	819	807
Marion	6,970,115	8,707,407	308,001	274,742	3,525	3,585
Putnam	3,813,055	4,761,761	260,270	228,429	2,449	2,419
Sumter	1,775,768	2,146,335	82,531	72,259	937	947
Suwannee	1,201,058	1,400,499	104,299	89,117	1,010	975
Union	355,068	372,271	27,931	23,630	268	266
District 4	37,064,370	44,321,320	2,431,470	2,206,445	23,656	24,137
Baker	779,515	847,875	41,216	29,075	411	326
Clay	1,340,845	1,728,888	68,452	60,760	681	672
Duval	23,911,676	28,998,638	1,693,679	1,576,048	15,679	16,214

See footnotes at end of table.   Continued . . .

Table 7.22. PUBLIC ASSISTANCE: VALUE OF FOOD STAMPS AND HOME ENERGY ASSISTANCE
PAYMENTS AND NUMBER OF HOUSEHOLDS RECEIVING PAYMENTS IN THE STATE
DEPARTMENT OF HEALTH AND REHABILITATIVE SERVICES DISTRICTS, AND
COUNTIES OF FLORIDA, FISCAL YEARS ENDING JUNE 30, 1988 AND 1989
(Continued)

(amounts in dollars)

| District and county | Value of food stamps issued | | Low-income home energy assistance program | | | |
| | | | Payment amount | | Number of households | |
	1988	1989	1988	1989	1988	1989
District 4 (Cont.)						
Flagler	466,603	644,044	32,820	28,247	323	328
Nassau	1,278,281	1,392,296	75,826	59,453	735	673
St. Johns	1,573,153	1,951,687	135,962	122,210	1,303	1,349
Volusia	7,714,297	8,757,892	383,515	330,652	4,524	4,575
District 5	21,451,140	27,766,064	744,543	667,762	8,474	8,698
Pasco	5,857,757	7,562,698	211,621	168,484	2,391	2,214
Pinellas	15,593,383	20,203,366	532,922	499,278	6,083	6,484
District 6	48,605,605	59,040,257	1,646,809	1,444,693	19,154	19,372
Hardee	1,615,268	1,719,816	41,640	28,317	463	365
Highlands	1,761,046	2,354,108	67,306	54,269	781	740
Hillsborough	26,588,060	33,038,575	966,543	882,351	11,237	11,635
Manatee	4,503,544	5,661,247	110,622	100,552	1,303	1,393
Polk	14,137,687	16,266,511	460,698	379,204	5,370	5,239
District 7	27,186,393	34,870,989	955,005	865,708	11,190	11,377
Brevard	8,108,585	10,070,067	225,863	213,788	2,561	2,721
Orange	13,980,742	17,609,332	544,162	480,575	6,421	6,387
Osceola	1,711,111	2,626,726	49,734	42,159	587	551
Seminole	3,385,955	4,564,864	135,246	129,186	1,621	1,718
District 8	15,715,238	18,637,059	426,267	402,794	5,143	5,695
Charlotte	1,058,218	1,331,386	32,858	31,555	420	466
Collier	3,246,220	3,697,629	58,451	63,537	689	863
De Soto	1,195,494	1,338,190	40,549	30,015	474	428
Glades 1/	1,535,757	1,911,585	7,217	7,683	89	101
Hendry 1/	(NA)	(NA)	29,475	33,988	366	488
Lee	5,731,315	6,770,000	169,881	152,595	2,100	2,207
Sarasota	2,948,234	3,588,269	87,836	83,421	1,005	1,142
District 9	23,281,560	27,430,400	656,847	604,349	8,029	8,248
Indian River	1,391,739	1,262,021	41,872	32,794	518	465
Martin	1,208,981	1,382,253	36,924	32,977	473	450
Okeechobee	1,136,933	1,238,097	37,579	30,294	450	426
Palm Beach	14,234,701	17,139,252	381,018	370,068	4,788	5,111
St. Lucie	5,309,206	6,408,777	159,454	138,216	1,800	1,796
District 10	14,498,607	19,177,227	520,556	493,134	6,375	6,665
Broward	14,498,607	19,177,227	520,556	493,134	6,375	6,665
District 11	90,722,546	108,595,430	3,310,865	3,187,874	41,277	44,131
Dade	89,449,328	107,237,758	3,294,774	3,173,432	41,075	43,928
Monroe	1,273,218	1,357,672	16,091	14,442	202	203

(NA) Not available.
1/ Hendry County data are consolidated with Glades County.

Source: State of Florida, Department of Health and Rehabilative Services, Office
of Revenue Management, Statistical Reporting Section, *Annual Statistical Report,
Fiscal Year 1988-89* prepublication release, and previous edition.

Florida Statistical Abstract 1991

Table 7.56. AVERAGE WEEKLY WAGES: AMOUNT RECEIVED BY PERSONS COVERED
BY UNEMPLOYMENT COMPENSATION LAW IN FLORIDA, 1952 THROUGH 1990

(in dollars)

Year	Average weekly wages 1/	Year	Average weekly wages 1/	Year	Average weekly wages 1/
1952	56.89	1965	96.34	1978	195.01
1953	60.47	1966	100.25	1979	210.73
1954	62.61	1967	104.80	1980	227.97
1955	65.13	1968	111.71	1981	252.92
1956	67.42	1969	122.57	1982	271.25
1957	71.22	1970	129.33	1983	288.34
1958	74.43	1971	131.97	1984	306.55
1959	78.28	1972	138.02	1985	314.88
1960	80.89	1973	143.30	1986	329.60
1961	82.64	1974	155.82	1987	344.32
1962	85.50	1975	167.02	1988	362.41
1963	88.23	1976	175.27	1989	382.00
1964	92.54	1977	185.69	1990	392.18

1/ Data prior to 1972 do not include state, local, or federal government figures.
Beginning in 1972 state data were included, and beginning in 1974 local data were
included. Data are for fiscal years from 1971 to date; data are for calendar years
prior to 1971.
Note: In 1956, 1972, and 1978 changes were made extending coverage of workers.

Table 7.57. UNEMPLOYMENT INSURANCE TRANSACTIONS: CONTRIBUTIONS AND DISBURSEMENTS
FOR UNEMPLOYMENT INSURANCE IN FLORIDA, 1952 THROUGH 1990

(rounded to thousands of dollars)

Year	Contributions deposits 1/	Total disbursements 2/	Year	Contributions deposits 1/	Total disbursements 2/	Year	Contributions deposits 1/	Total disbursements 2/
1952	11,448	7,540	1965	45,160	20,273	1978	424,988	136,723
1953	11,266	7,832	1966	40,720	17,410	1979	389,370	135,457
1954	11,225	11,926	1967	37,029	20,639	1980	321,578	197,981
1955	10,433	11,110	1968	34,094	22,343	1981	305,028	206,012
1956	16,247	11,611	1969	42,145	20,875	1982	326,706	379,067
1957	19,005	13,941	1970	48,594	37,306	1983	451,459	406,075
1958	20,118	28,559	1971	57,425	49,704	1984	526,691	279,457
1959	36,721	22,484	1972	71,799	45,441	1985	514,281	277,463
1960	34,766	31,925	1973	85,861	44,962	1986	478,859	315,337
1961	41,970	43,830	1974	99,304	117,453	1987	469,296	285,736
1962	52,392	33,201	1975	263,243	496,688	1988	468,348	304,930
1963	45,079	29,652	1976	342,166	407,060	1989	480,211	355,749
1964	45,956	24,492	1977	360,650	271,917	1990	461,103	488,961

1/ Includes interest, reimbursable interstate and state and local government
benefits.
2/ Includes payable interstate benefits.
Source for Tables 7.56 and 7.57: State of Florida, Department of Labor and Employment Security, Division of Employment Security, Historical Series of Unemployment Insurance Statistical Data, 1937-1979, and unpublished data.

Florida Statistical Abstract 1991

Table 7.58. UNEMPLOYMENT INSURANCE: SPECIFIED DATA FOR FLORIDA, 1986, 1987
    AND 1988

Item	1986	1987	1988
Covered employment			
Average monthly number of workers (1,000)	4,514	4,746	4,968
Total payroll ($1,000,000)	78,493	87,753	96,088
Insured unemployment as percentage			
of covered employment	1.4	1.1	1.0
Number of first payments (1,000)	182	159	163
Average weekly benefit for total unemployment			
Amount (dollars)	124.28	128.39	139.50
Percentage of average weekly wages	37.0	36.1	37.5
Weeks compensated for all unemployment (1,000)	2,433	2,128	2,092
Average actual duration (weeks)	13.3	13.3	12.8
Claimants exhausting benefits			
Number (1,000)	70	62	58
Percentage of first payments	35.8	36.1	36.5
Contributions collected ($1,000,000)	312.7	297.7	291.1
Benefits paid ($1,000,000)	290.6	260.3	277.1
Funds available for benefits at end			
of year ($1,000,000)	1,553.7	1,745.4	1,910.1
Average employer contribution rate 1/	1.0	1.0	0.9

   1/ As a percentage of taxable payroll. The standard contribution rate for most
states is 2.7 percent.
   Source: U.S., Department of Health and Human Services, Social Security Administration, *Social Security Bulletin: Annual Statistical Supplement, 1990*, and
previous editions.

Table 7.59. WORKERS' COMPENSATION: ESTIMATES OF PAYMENTS BY TYPE OF INSURANCE
    IN FLORIDA, 1986 THROUGH 1988

                            (in thousands of dollars)

Item	1986	1987	1988 A/
Total	978,996	1,178,113	1,421,550
Insurance losses paid by private insurance			
carriers 1/	638,996	738,113	888,550
State and federal fund disbursements 2/	0	0	0
Self-insurance payments 3/	340,000	440,000	533,000
Percentage change in total payments from			
previous year	20.2	20.3	20.7

   A/ Preliminary.
   1/ Net cash and medical benefits paid during the calendar year by private insurance carriers under standard workers' compensation policies. Data primarily from
A.M. Best Company.
   2/ Net cash and medical benefits paid by state funds compiled from state reports
(published and unpublished).
   3/ Cash and medical benefits paid by self-insurers, plus the value of medical
benefits paid by employers carrying workers' compensation policies that do not include standard medical coverage. Estimated from available state data.
   Source: U.S., Department of Health and Human Services, Social Security Administration, *Social Security Bulletin*, January 1989 and March 1991.

Florida Statistical Abstract 1991

Table 7.60. WORKERS' COMPENSATION: NUMBER OF INJURIES AND DAYS OF DISABILITY AND
MEDICAL AND COMPENSATION PAYMENTS IN THE STATE AND COUNTIES OF FLORIDA, 1989

County	Work injuries	Days of disability	Payments (dollars)		
			Total	Medical	Compensation
Florida	91,142	23,701,932	389,530,446	208,657,440	180,873,006
Alachua	1,007	244,321	3,698,987	2,135,021	1,563,966
Baker	172	42,641	463,808	270,728	193,080
Bay	778	264,523	2,881,397	1,661,251	1,220,146
Bradford	82	21,395	271,606	181,065	90,541
Brevard	2,685	673,341	12,819,886	4,535,429	8,284,457
Broward	7,390	2,087,464	44,528,268	19,098,267	25,430,001
Calhoun	29	19,714	198,126	107,558	90,568
Charlotte	522	187,790	2,140,668	1,218,314	922,354
Citrus	363	113,324	1,187,176	572,710	614,466
Clay	403	84,065	1,294,967	726,027	568,940
Collier	1,244	325,506	5,155,729	3,216,450	1,939,279
Columbia	241	73,695	969,237	576,229	393,008
Dade	11,172	2,731,971	47,371,377	29,091,823	18,279,554
De Soto	240	55,891	685,944	470,265	215,679
Dixie	61	10,687	291,916	161,735	130,181
Duval	5,299	1,357,046	25,368,223	16,832,651	8,535,572
Escambia	1,380	445,626	5,099,622	3,109,419	1,990,203
Flagler	123	48,458	443,266	221,882	221,384
Franklin	47	7,757	132,846	90,298	42,548
Gadsden	282	52,906	622,239	342,575	279,664
Gilchrist	30	7,112	81,769	60,445	21,324
Glades	37	13,395	130,770	99,665	31,105
Gulf	33	13,730	131,357	49,876	81,481
Hamilton	47	19,922	118,553	68,139	50,414
Hardee	169	26,265	543,040	301,141	241,899
Hendry	377	58,692	818,979	500,481	318,498
Hernando	404	135,380	1,781,768	1,037,920	743,848
Highlands	351	111,467	4,498,786	785,110	3,713,676
Hillsborough	6,971	1,866,428	26,505,292	16,024,577	10,480,715
Holmes	70	27,466	202,677	120,458	82,219
Indian River	646	145,514	2,789,236	1,752,524	1,036,712
Jackson	190	36,279	450,631	271,901	178,730
Jefferson	37	19,121	112,350	72,271	40,079
Lafayette	19	1,269	91,781	48,684	43,097
Lake	834	222,296	2,755,779	1,651,777	1,104,002
Lee	2,253	573,098	12,929,315	6,324,830	6,604,485

See footnote at end of table.   Continued . . .

Table 7.60.   WORKERS' COMPENSATION: NUMBER OF INJURIES AND DAYS OF DISABILITY AND
   MEDICAL AND COMPENSATION PAYMENTS IN THE STATE AND COUNTIES OF FLORIDA, 1989
   (Continued)

County	Work injuries	Days of disability	Payments (dollars) Total	Medical	Compensation
Leon	811	136,560	2,234,754	1,216,171	1,018,583
Levy	117	42,122	2,120,657	202,334	1,918,323
Liberty	22	13,268	91,815	39,377	52,438
Madison	92	15,286	248,378	156,689	91,689
Manatee	1,285	266,291	4,707,287	2,102,163	2,605,124
Marion	1,218	467,483	4,132,886	2,287,553	1,845,333
Martin	734	188,136	2,210,792	1,141,134	1,069,658
Monroe	448	121,124	1,589,633	941,106	648,527
Nassau	252	77,877	994,682	581,183	413,499
Okaloosa	595	102,808	1,631,018	1,007,420	623,598
Okeechobee	188	51,874	717,853	383,284	334,569
Orange	8,329	1,793,047	38,658,637	15,658,237	23,000,400
Osceola	834	231,247	2,901,235	1,769,344	1,131,891
Palm Beach	6,570	1,509,088	24,980,891	12,894,617	12,086,274
Pasco	1,146	292,318	4,918,858	3,253,748	1,665,110
Pinellas	5,096	1,369,274	18,055,485	10,380,092	7,675,393
Polk	2,675	780,769	8,199,252	4,444,706	3,754,546
Putnam	297	91,400	1,008,922	576,558	432,364
St. Johns	352	90,326	1,439,770	775,621	664,149
St. Lucie	1,059	332,452	4,240,393	2,311,941	1,928,452
Santa Rosa	268	125,189	764,117	418,100	346,017
Sarasota	1,842	348,013	5,356,790	3,085,299	2,271,491
Seminole	1,482	338,410	5,790,800	3,745,112	2,045,688
Sumter	115	17,955	384,291	238,115	146,176
Suwannee	122	36,934	446,179	252,368	193,811
Taylor	112	34,903	410,711	231,310	179,401
Union	53	14,207	169,119	88,143	80,976
Volusia	2,049	401,596	6,277,515	3,455,402	2,822,113
Wakulla	42	1,503	69,574	35,842	33,732
Walton	129	35,787	554,271	408,685	145,586
Washington	51	20,704	281,961	151,942	130,019
Out of state	2,271	672,587	9,943,295	5,030,941	4,912,354
Unknown	4,498	1,555,839	24,431,254	15,603,407	8,827,847

Note: Injuries are reported on a place-of-occurrence basis.

Source: State of Florida, Department of Labor and Employment Security, Division
of Workers' Compensation, Workers' Compensation Research and Evaluation Center, *1989
Report on Occupational Injuries.*

Florida Statistical Abstract 1991

Table 7.61. WORKERS' COMPENSATION: NUMBER OF WORK INJURIES BY ACCIDENT TYPE AND COST BY INDUSTRY IN FLORIDA, 1989

Industry 1/	Total	Struck or caught by	Fall	Over-exertion/reaction	Temperature extreme	Radiation/caustics	Electric current	Aircraft/motor vehicle	Other 2/	Medical and compensation cost ($1,000)
					Contact with					
Total	91,142	26,078	21,066	34,047	1,408	1,383	169	3,969	3,022	389,530
Agriculture, forestry, and fisheries	3,403	1,235	796	865	32	132	6	194	143	20,497
Mining	127	45	29	37	5	1	0	7	3	665
Contract construction	15,750	4,903	4,196	5,134	266	213	66	451	521	83,860
Building construction, general contractors	2,201	673	573	758	20	48	9	47	73	11,313
Construction, special trade contractors	11,234	3,472	3,153	3,602	212	109	40	274	372	61,278
Manufacturing	10,507	4,016	1,758	3,737	144	175	17	322	338	39,748
Food and kindred products	2,747	1,225	417	841	42	46	4	110	62	6,241
Transportation, communication, and public utilities	6,164	1,488	1,240	2,547	57	75	13	492	252	22,833
Motor freight transportation	3,029	691	660	1,233	26	29	7	256	127	11,785
Wholesale and retail trade	22,309	6,340	5,343	8,443	551	202	17	708	705	91,760
Wholesale trade	4,355	1,296	829	1,726	39	52	3	250	160	17,563
Retail food	4,708	1,525	960	1,950	41	22	1	71	138	16,550
Retail eating and drinking places	5,154	1,295	1,883	1,298	390	74	6	50	158	21,178
Finance, insurance, and real estate	4,058	962	985	1,756	32	67	3	138	115	15,368
Real estate	3,320	824	777	1,459	27	60	3	83	87	12,963
Services	15,750	3,780	3,715	6,494	195	302	26	679	559	66,017
Miscellaneous business services	3,329	947	800	1,140	31	53	6	219	133	12,311
Medical and other health services	4,862	841	978	2,598	34	115	5	115	176	25,443
Government	10,204	2,466	2,284	4,061	75	192	12	835	279	(NA)
Establishments, NEC	2,870	843	720	973	51	24	9	143	107	(NA)

NEC Not elsewhere classified.
(NA) Not available.
1/ Major industry group totals include data for industries not shown separately.
2/ Includes data on injuries reported with no accident type given.
Source: State of Florida, Department of Labor and Employment Security, Division of Workers' Compensation, Workers' Compensation Research and Evaluation Center, 1989 Report on Occupational Injuries.

GEOGRAPHY AND ENVIRONMENT

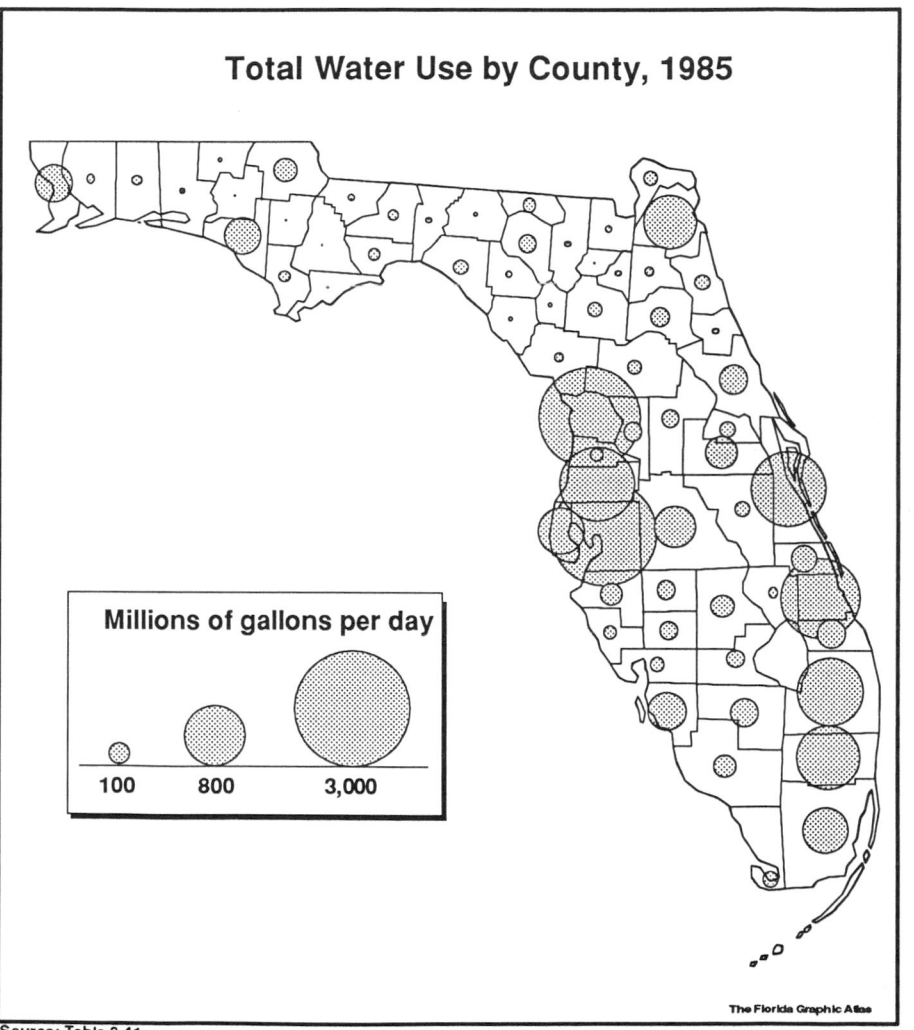

Total Water Use by County, 1985

Millions of gallons per day

100   800   3,000

The Florida Graphic Atlas

Source: Table 8.41

Table 8.01. GEOGRAPHY: LAND AND WATER AREAS, COASTLINE, AND ELEVATIONS OF FLORIDA
OTHER SUNBELT STATES, OTHER POPULOUS STATES, AND THE UNITED STATES, 1980

| State | Area (square miles) | | | Coastline (statute miles) | | Elevation (feet) | | |
	Total	Land 1/	Wa-ter 2/	General coast-line 3/	Tidal shore-line 4/	High-est	Low-est	Ap-prox-imate mean
			Sunbelt states					
Florida	58,664	54,153	4,511	1,350	8,426	345	A/	100
Alabama	51,705	50,767	938	53	607	2,407	A/	500
Arizona	114,000	113,508	492	0	0	12,633	70	4,100
Arkansas	53,187	52,078	1,109	0	0	2,753	55	650
California	158,706	156,299	2,407	840	3,427	14,494	-282	2,900
Georgia	58,910	58,056	854	100	2,344	4,784	A/	600
Louisiana	47,752	44,521	3,230	397	7,721	535	-5	100
Mississippi	47,689	47,233	457	44	359	806	A/	300
New Mexico	121,593	121,335	258	0	0	13,161	2,817	5,700
North Carolina	52,669	48,843	3,826	301	3,375	6,684	A/	700
Oklahoma	69,956	68,655	1,301	0	0	4,973	287	1,300
South Carolina	31,113	30,203	909	187	2,876	3,560	A/	350
Tennessee	42,144	41,155	989	0	0	6,643	182	900
Texas	266,807	262,017	4,790	367	3,359	8,749	A/	1,700
Virginia	40,767	39,704	1,063	112	3,315	5,729	A/	950
			Other populous states					
Illinois	56,345	55,645	700	0	0	1,235	279	600
Indiana	36,185	35,932	253	0	0	1,257	320	700
Massachusetts	8,284	7,824	460	192	1,519	3,491	A/	500
Michigan	58,527	56,954	1,573	0	0	1,980	572	900
New Jersey	7,787	7,468	319	130	1,792	1,803	A/	250
New York	49,108	47,377	1,731	127	1,850	5,344	A/	1,000
Ohio	41,330	41,004	325	0	0	1,550	433	850
Pennsylvania	45,308	44,888	420	0	89	3,213	A/	1,100
United States	3,618,770	3,539,289	79,481	12,383	88,633	20,320	-282	2,500

A/ Sea level.
1/ Dry land and land temporarily or partially covered by water, as marshland,
swamps, etc.; streams and canals under one-eighth statute mile wide; and lakes,
reservoirs, and ponds under 40 acres of area.
2/ Permanent inland water surface, other than included in footnote 1/. Excludes
areas of oceans, bays, sounds, etc. not defined as inland waters.
3/ Figures are lengths of general outline of seacoast. Unit of measure is 30
minutes of latitude on charts at approximate scale of 1:1,200,000.
4/ Figures are lengths of shoreline of outer coast, offshore islands, sounds,
bays, rivers, and creeks to the head of tidewate., and were obtained in 1939-40.

Source: U.S., Department of Commerce, Bureau of the Census, *Statistical Abstract
of the United States, 1990.*

Florida Statistical Abstract 1991

Table 8.03.   LAND AREA: AREA OF THE STATE AND COUNTIES OF FLORIDA, APRIL 1, 1980

County	Square miles	Square kilometers	County	Square miles	Square kilometers
Florida	54,153	140,256	Lafayette	545	1,412
			Lake	954	2,472
Alachua	902	2,335	Lee	803	2,080
Baker	585	1,516	Leon	676	1,751
Bay	758	1,962	Levy	1,100	2,848
Bradford	293	758	Liberty	837	2,168
Brevard	995	2,578	Madison	710	1,840
Broward	1,211	3,137	Manatee	747	1,935
Calhoun	568	1,471	Marion	1,610	4,169
Charlotte	690	1,787	Martin	555	1,437
Citrus	629	1,628	Monroe	1,034	2,678
Clay	592	1,534	Nassau	649	1,681
Collier	1,994	5,165	Okaloosa	936	2,424
Columbia	797	2,063	Okeechobee	771	1,996
Dade	1,955	5,064	Orange	910	2,358
De Soto	636	1,647	Osceola	1,350	3,496
Dixie	701	1,816	Palm Beach	1,993	5,162
Duval	776	2,011	Pasco	738	1,911
Escambia	661	1,711	Pinellas	280	726
Flagler	491	1,271	Polk	1,823	4,722
Franklin	545	1,411	Putnam	733	1,898
Gadsden	518	1,341	St. Johns	617	1,599
Gilchrist	354	916	St. Lucie	581	1,505
Glades	763	1,976	Santa Rosa	1,024	2,651
Gulf	559	1,447	Sarasota	573	1,484
Hamilton	517	1,340	Seminole	298	772
Hardee	637	1,651	Sumter	561	1,454
Hendry	1,163	3,011	Suwannee	690	1,786
Hernando	477	1,236	Taylor	1,058	2,739
Highlands	1,029	2,664	Union	246	637
Hillsborough	1,053	2,727	Volusia	1,113	2,882
Holmes	488	1,263	Wakulla	601	1,557
Indian River	497	1,287	Walton	1,066	2,760
Jackson	942	2,439	Washington	590	1,527
Jefferson	609	1,578			

Note: Differences between 1980 area figures and those reported in previous censuses are attributable to changes in base map scale and detail, methodology for measurement, and occasionally to county boundary change or relocation.   County detail does not add to state total because of rounding.

Source: U.S., Department of Commerce, Bureau of the Census, *1980 Census of Population: Number of Inhabitants, Florida.*   PC80-1-A11.

Florida Statistical Abstract 1991

Table 8.10. LAND USE: VALUE AND PROPORTION OF LAND BY USE IN THE STATE AND COUNTIES OF FLORIDA, 1989

County	Residential Value (million dollars)	Residential Percentage of total value	Commercial Value (million dollars)	Commercial Percentage of total value	Industrial Value (million dollars)	Industrial Percentage of total value	Agricultural Value (million dollars)	Agricultural Percentage of total value	Institutional Value (million dollars)	Institutional Percentage of total value	Miscellaneous 1/ Value (million dollars)	Miscellaneous 1/ Percentage of total value
Florida	322,074.25	64.5	79,956.21	16.0	19,275.37	3.9	10,324.19	2.1	12,981.70	2.6	55,089.75	11.0
Alachua	2,580.27	54.7	611.75	13.0	101.23	2.1	128.01	2.7	111.10	2.4	1,183.59	25.1
Baker	114.90	35.0	20.24	6.2	4.99	1.5	60.31	18.3	7.77	2.4	120.50	36.7
Bay	2,817.01	62.3	627.20	13.9	79.62	1.8	66.29	1.5	74.41	1.6	855.87	18.9
Bradford	203.85	55.9	36.98	10.1	6.73	1.8	55.61	15.3	13.53	3.7	47.65	13.1
Brevard	9,689.48	59.2	1,864.28	11.4	569.97	3.5	109.29	0.7	355.74	2.2	3,766.11	23.0
Broward	35,321.47	71.3	7,602.74	15.4	2,294.62	4.6	185.32	0.4	817.16	1.7	3,300.28	6.7
Calhoun	68.16	40.1	10.72	6.3	3.63	2.1	63.27	37.2	5.24	3.1	18.88	11.1
Charlotte	3,768.16	77.2	674.82	13.8	42.06	0.9	116.50	2.4	89.62	1.8	189.75	3.9
Citrus	2,209.31	70.5	292.23	9.3	27.74	0.9	37.10	1.2	54.03	1.7	512.37	16.4
Clay	1,891.48	73.9	343.10	13.4	39.62	1.5	50.68	2.0	75.62	3.0	159.89	6.2
Collier	8,617.78	73.0	1,360.19	11.5	239.60	2.0	232.40	2.0	201.41	1.7	1,146.34	9.7
Columbia	381.09	47.8	123.01	15.4	20.93	2.6	100.03	12.5	20.41	2.6	152.15	19.1
Dade	49,488.12	61.7	14,648.06	18.3	4,413.08	5.5	850.38	1.1	1,993.55	2.5	8,857.42	11.0
De Soto	252.51	40.8	54.31	8.8	8.50	1.4	192.06	31.0	16.20	2.6	95.72	15.5
Dixie	100.14	52.0	8.57	4.5	2.67	1.4	55.67	28.9	2.28	1.2	23.10	12.0
Duval	11,555.35	52.9	4,155.16	19.0	1,315.26	6.0	77.94	0.4	1,189.74	5.4	3,560.46	16.3
Escambia	3,496.41	51.5	736.40	10.8	205.59	3.0	73.04	1.1	211.67	3.1	2,070.61	30.5
Flagler	1,436.63	77.2	119.27	6.4	21.42	1.2	47.55	2.6	28.27	1.5	208.15	11.2
Franklin	256.74	30.1	28.60	3.4	4.36	0.5	20.81	2.4	5.64	0.7	536.36	62.9
Gadsden	268.47	48.2	38.45	6.9	34.67	6.2	81.80	14.7	19.32	3.5	114.40	20.5
Gilchrist	91.50	53.5	5.19	3.0	0.42	0.2	50.99	29.8	3.48	2.0	19.47	11.4
Glades	164.20	37.4	21.92	5.0	2.49	0.6	112.62	25.7	3.77	0.9	133.84	30.5
Gulf	235.14	57.2	21.50	5.2	16.57	4.0	25.94	6.3	6.68	1.6	104.94	25.5

See footnote at end of table.

Continued . . .

Table 8.10.   LAND USE: VALUE AND PROPORTION OF LAND BY USE IN THE STATE AND COUNTIES OF FLORIDA, 1989 (Continued)

County	Residential Value (million dollars)	Residential Percentage of total value	Commercial Value (million dollars)	Commercial Percentage of total value	Industrial Value (million dollars)	Industrial Percentage of total value	Agricultural Value (million dollars)	Agricultural Percentage of total value	Institutional Value (million dollars)	Institutional Percentage of total value	Miscellaneous 1/ Value (million dollars)	Miscellaneous 1/ Percentage of total value
Hamilton	71.94	34.0	14.68	6.9	48.69	23.0	45.72	21.6	3.78	1.8	26.68	12.6
Hardee	159.43	30.6	34.85	6.7	38.39	7.4	237.39	45.5	14.68	2.8	36.43	7.0
Hendry	375.69	37.4	86.14	8.6	26.46	2.6	312.42	31.1	20.36	2.0	182.80	18.2
Hernando	2,233.90	71.3	294.42	9.4	20.32	0.6	59.51	1.9	60.56	1.9	464.53	14.8
Highlands	1,335.44	60.6	269.16	12.2	40.16	1.8	221.36	10.0	90.88	4.1	246.44	11.2
Hillsborough	15,631.45	59.8	4,666.10	17.9	1,348.35	5.2	435.52	1.7	884.32	3.4	3,155.12	12.1
Holmes	93.19	37.4	16.82	6.8	1.64	0.7	78.28	31.4	13.91	5.6	45.26	18.2
Indian River	3,421.51	73.1	520.95	11.1	108.26	2.3	272.90	5.8	107.58	2.3	250.74	5.4
Jackson	313.24	42.5	65.43	8.9	21.82	3.0	136.69	18.5	28.37	3.8	172.33	23.4
Jefferson	52.68	27.6	17.84	9.4	1.73	0.9	87.94	46.1	7.83	4.1	22.74	11.9
Lafayette	27.55	29.2	2.40	2.5	0.89	0.9	51.64	54.8	2.53	2.7	9.30	9.9
Lake	2,691.47	67.1	452.89	11.3	102.72	2.6	301.29	7.5	97.82	2.4	366.53	9.1
Lee	12,329.69	75.2	2,232.07	13.6	391.17	2.4	99.99	0.6	332.68	2.0	1,011.33	6.2
Leon	3,191.50	46.5	1,091.55	15.9	41.65	0.6	84.63	1.2	218.42	3.2	2,235.76	32.6
Levy	309.39	54.7	40.61	7.2	4.06	0.7	107.54	19.0	9.69	1.7	94.32	16.7
Liberty	34.26	27.4	2.64	2.1	0.84	0.7	24.76	19.8	3.40	2.7	58.92	47.2
Madison	96.08	39.2	17.48	7.1	8.81	3.6	89.60	36.5	9.55	3.9	23.83	9.7
Manatee	5,044.99	64.4	1,145.53	14.6	357.80	4.6	218.68	2.8	304.82	3.9	757.54	9.7
Marion	3,102.32	57.6	668.73	12.4	228.49	4.2	323.98	6.0	126.27	2.3	939.13	17.4
Martin	4,707.63	72.3	698.95	10.7	145.12	2.2	383.19	5.9	115.46	1.8	458.62	7.0
Monroe	4,242.80	65.5	1,156.77	17.9	60.15	0.9	0.19	0.0	104.14	1.6	914.24	14.1
Nassau	1,031.72	68.4	154.34	10.2	65.59	4.3	86.79	5.8	29.24	1.9	141.05	9.3
Okaloosa	2,989.18	72.1	467.21	11.3	38.20	0.9	38.69	0.9	74.08	1.8	539.98	13.0
Okeechobee	446.82	55.3	97.86	12.1	10.18	1.3	134.49	16.6	20.57	2.5	98.69	12.2

See footnote at end of table.

Continued . . .

Table 8.10. LAND USE: VALUE AND PROPORTION OF LAND BY USE IN THE STATE AND COUNTIES OF FLORIDA, 1989 (Continued)

County	Residential Value (million dollars)	Residential Per-cent-age of total value	Commercial Value (million dollars)	Commercial Per-cent-age of total value	Industrial Value (million dollars)	Industrial Per-cent-age of total value	Agricultural Value (million dollars)	Agricultural Per-cent-age of total value	Institutional Value (million dollars)	Institutional Per-cent-age of total value	Miscellaneous 1/ Value (million dollars)	Miscellaneous 1/ Per-cent-age of total value
Orange	14,282.48	51.3	7,331.58	26.3	1,624.03	5.8	882.55	3.2	987.21	3.5	2,723.16	9.8
Osceola	2,009.97	53.1	1,209.93	32.0	88.55	2.3	136.59	3.6	92.05	2.4	248.81	6.6
Palm Beach	36,173.48	70.7	8,226.49	16.1	1,741.60	3.4	622.82	1.2	962.93	1.9	3,404.81	6.7
Pasco	5,721.83	72.3	1,250.46	15.8	108.52	1.4	165.96	2.1	194.90	2.5	476.73	6.0
Pinellas	22,196.55	67.1	5,672.30	17.1	1,274.15	3.9	28.11	0.1	1,080.80	3.3	2,826.25	8.5
Polk	5,581.29	53.9	1,636.44	15.8	498.59	4.8	654.45	6.3	342.58	3.3	1,644.33	15.9
Putnam	957.62	63.4	123.68	8.2	64.18	4.2	48.53	3.2	50.87	3.4	266.06	17.6
St. Johns	2,738.91	74.4	466.24	12.7	46.08	1.3	58.52	1.6	123.60	3.4	248.49	6.7
St. Lucie	3,553.43	63.0	614.13	10.9	130.54	2.3	289.47	5.1	118.79	2.1	933.98	16.6
Santa Rosa	1,576.52	69.6	198.25	8.7	26.09	1.2	94.65	4.2	58.17	2.6	312.32	13.8
Sarasota	10,673.93	74.4	2,057.43	14.3	325.51	2.3	70.93	0.5	341.57	2.4	869.53	6.1
Seminole	6,817.28	75.4	1,333.85	14.8	365.07	4.0	40.51	0.4	162.78	1.8	319.41	3.5
Sumter	273.14	57.2	55.47	11.6	14.56	3.0	71.19	14.9	3.98	0.8	59.21	12.4
Suwannee	214.67	49.6	32.17	7.4	9.37	2.2	100.19	23.2	26.76	6.2	49.44	11.4
Taylor	193.18	44.6	40.80	9.4	50.95	11.8	83.00	19.2	13.51	3.1	51.69	11.9
Union	33.36	23.5	3.91	2.8	2.70	1.9	34.64	24.4	3.20	2.3	64.11	45.2
Volusia	8,777.22	70.9	1,975.12	16.0	315.01	2.5	137.35	1.1	398.09	3.2	777.64	6.3
Wakulla	171.50	41.7	12.14	3.0	7.24	1.8	29.12	7.1	5.88	1.4	185.00	45.0
Walton	1,040.34	74.9	79.90	5.7	9.81	0.7	80.74	5.8	18.83	1.4	160.01	11.5
Washington	145.51	51.8	15.81	5.6	5.56	2.0	68.06	24.2	7.62	2.7	38.61	13.7

1/ Includes lease hold interests, utilities, mining, petroleum and gas lands, subsurface rights, right-of-ways, submerged lands, sewage disposal, borrow pits, wastelands, outdoor recreational/park lands, and governmental lands.

Source: State of Florida, Department of Revenue, unpublished data. Compiled by Armasi, Inc.

Table 8.15. SOLID WASTE: SOLID WASTE TONNAGE BY DISPOSAL PROCESS AND PER CAPITA
   IN THE STATE AND COUNTIES OF FLORIDA, JULY 1, 1989 THROUGH JUNE 30, 1990

(in tons)

County	Total	Recycled	Landfilled	Combusted	Tons per capita per year 1/
Florida	19,358,212	2,827,405	13,402,527	3,128,280	1.47
Alachua	211,139	35,429	172,711	3,000	1.11
Baker	12,791	1,100	11,691	0	0.64
Bay	182,185	15,702	30,321	136,162	1.30
Bradford	16,026	1,050	14,976	0	0.64
Brevard	547,633	72,686	474,947	0	1.31
Broward	1,886,011	214,806	1,503,305	167,900	1.48
Calhoun	4,730	109	2,310	2,310	0.41
Charlotte	144,193	20,906	123,287	0	1.39
Citrus	78,435	10,456	67,979	0	0.82
Clay	85,821	19,569	66,252	0	0.80
Collier	420,374	25,760	394,614	0	2.78
Columbia	48,928	9,928	39,000	0	1.10
Dade	3,173,675	403,945	2,031,525	738,205	1.66
De Soto	18,560	602	17,958	0	0.75
Dixie	5,847	75	5,772	0	0.53
Duval	1,101,264	227,472	873,792	0	1.57
Escambia	345,981	78,578	267,403	0	1.19
Flagler	30,000	553	29,447	0	1.18
Franklin	8,172	290	6,118	1,764	0.93
Gadsden	34,053	5,104	26,635	2,314	0.74
Gilchrist	2,466	74	2,392	0	0.31
Glades	4,500	775	3,725	0	0.56
Gulf	11,346	41	1,800	9,505	0.89
Hamilton	6,802	628	6,174	0	0.65
Hardee	21,395	838	20,557	0	0.93
Hendry	30,061	438	29,623	0	1.12
Hernando	82,215	1,980	80,235	0	0.86
Highlands	67,415	5,815	61,600	0	0.94
Hillsborough	1,192,591	291,118	179,888	721,585	1.38
Holmes	7,543	366	7,177	0	0.41
Indian River	150,123	7,005	132,408	10,710	1.58
Jackson	25,755	41	25,714	0	0.56
Jefferson	11,134	802	10,332	0	0.88
Lafayette	2,532	20	2,512	0	0.46

See footnote at end of table.   Continued . . .

Table 8.15. SOLID WASTE: SOLID WASTE TONNAGE BY DISPOSAL PROCESS AND PER CAPITA
IN THE STATE AND COUNTIES OF FLORIDA, JULY 1, 1989 THROUGH JUNE 30, 1990
(Continued)

(in tons)

County	Total	Recycled	Landfilled	Combusted	Tons per capita per year 1/
Lake	149,067	9,297	139,770	0	0.99
Lee	492,902	74,052	418,850	0	1.46
Leon	208,856	24,177	184,679	0	1.06
Levy	14,114	1,372	12,742	0	0.54
Liberty	2,063	67	1,996	0	0.43
Madison	11,786	18	11,768	0	0.71
Manatee	323,638	34,056	289,582	0	1.64
Marion	246,381	62,956	183,425	0	1.24
Martin	216,452	38,005	178,447	0	2.16
Monroe	102,161	17,594	9,066	75,501	1.27
Nassau	41,751	2,102	39,648	0	0.84
Okaloosa	165,079	9,224	155,855	0	1.02
Okeechobee	25,510	1,185	24,325	0	0.82
Orange	1,385,132	165,234	1,219,898	0	2.05
Osceola	145,793	1,546	144,247	0	1.42
Palm Beach	1,259,488	151,903	721,271	386,314	1.40
Pasco	275,404	35,782	239,622	0	0.98
Pinellas	1,305,658	289,656	143,543	872,458	1.50
Polk	509,590	80,563	429,027	0	1.21
Putnam	65,352	2,717	62,635	0	1.02
St. Johns	102,765	5,825	96,940	0	1.17
St. Lucie	252,123	37,216	214,907	0	1.69
Santa Rosa	60,153	4,350	55,252	551	0.85
Sarasota	593,842	137,842	456,000	0	2.19
Seminole	397,893	5,634	392,259	0	1.36
Sumter	17,089	2,906	14,183	0	0.53
Suwannee	23,494	5,995	17,498	0	0.83
Taylor	21,283	1,606	19,677	0	1.06
Union	12,299	371	11,928	0	1.15
Volusia	915,335	165,335	750,000	0	2.46
Wakulla	12,726	833	11,893	0	0.85
Walton	25,688	3,762	21,926	0	0.86
Washington	5,649	163	5,486	0	0.33

1/ Based on U.S. Bureau of the Census 1990 population counts.

Source: State of Florida, Department of Environmental Regulation, *Solid Waste
Management in Florida, 1990 Annual Report.*

Florida Statistical Abstract 1991

Table 8.35.   WATER USE: WATER WITHDRAWALS AND CONSUMPTION PER DAY IN FLORIDA
   OTHER SUNBELT STATES, AND THE UNITED STATES, 1985

(in millions of gallons per day, except where indicated)

| State | Total | Per capita fresh-water consump-tion (gpd) | Source | | Withdrawals | | | |
| | | | | | Use | | | |
			Ground	Surface	Irri-gation	Public supply	Indus-trial	Thermo-electric
Florida	17,000	554	4,050	13,000	2,910	1,939	679	11,351
Alabama	8,600	2,140	347	8,250	69	654	851	6,920
Arizona	6,430	1,960	3,100	3,330	5,520	645	133	58
Arkansas	5,910	2,500	3,810	2,100	3,870	317	175	1,090
California	49,700	1,420	15,100	34,600	30,600	5,450	1,159	12,180
Georgia	5,450	899	1,000	4,440	453	935	656	3,326
Louisiana	10,400	2,210	1,440	8,980	1,480	675	2,100	5,964
Mississippi	2,510	885	1,580	933	886	328	236	670
New Mexico	3,280	2,320	1,510	1,780	2,820	264	83	59
North Carolina	8,760	1,260	435	8,320	132	764	539	7,266
Oklahoma	1,270	386	568	707	445	547	113	134
South Carolina	6,820	2,040	214	6,610	34	421	1,130	5,186
Tennessee	8,450	1,770	444	8,010	9	697	1,613	6,060
Texas	25,300	1,230	7,410	17,900	8,120	3,095	2,763	11,010
Virginia	7,250	853	341	6,910	52	691	673	5,760
United States	399,000	1,400	74,000	325,000	137,000	39,900	29,300	187,000

gpd gallons per day.
Source: U.S., Department of Commerce, Bureau of the Census, *Statistical Abstract
of the United States, 1991.*

Table 8.40.   WATER USE: FRESHWATER WITHDRAWALS BY CATEGORY OF USE IN FLORIDA, 1970
   1975, 1980, AND 1985

(in millions of gallons per day)

Disposition	1970	1975	1980	1985
Total	6,011.12	6,863.57	7,298.22	6,258.68
Public supply 1/	883.50	1,145.81	1,361.28	1,659.83
Domestic, self-supplied	165.00	202.98	250.88	259.29
Commercial/industrial, self-supplied	926.80	939.61	781.33	708.81
Agricultural irrigation	2,348.92	2,879.63	3,056.90	2,979.30
Power generation, self-supplied 2/	1,686.90	1,695.54	1,847.83	651.45

1/ Public supply refers to municipal or other water utility which serves the
public.
2/ Over ninety percent of power generation withdrawals are saline water.
Source: U.S., Department of the Interior, Geological Survey, *Source, Use, Dispo-
sition of Water in Florida, 1980,* and previous reports, and in cooperation with St.
Johns River Water Management District, *Water Withdrawals and Use by Category in
Florida, 1985.*

Table 8.41. WATER USE: WATER WITHDRAWALS BY SOURCE IN THE STATE AND COUNTIES
OF FLORIDA, 1985

(in millions of gallons per day)

County	Total	Ground Total	Ground Fresh	Ground Saline	Surface Total	Surface Fresh	Surface Saline
Florida	17,056.93	4,106.78	4,030.39	76.39	12,950.15	2,228.29	10,721.86
Alachua	51.46	51.42	51.42	0.00	0.04	0.04	0.00
Baker	8.26	6.07	6.07	0.00	2.19	2.19	0.00
Bay	306.52	12.04	12.04	0.00	294.48	29.88	264.60
Bradford	9.25	9.25	9.25	0.00	0.00	0.00	0.00
Brevard	1,313.37	115.70	115.68	0.02	1,197.67	39.79	1,157.88
Broward	929.42	230.18	230.18	0.00	699.24	5.10	694.14
Calhoun	1.68	1.65	1.65	0.00	0.03	0.03	0.00
Charlotte	54.16	47.67	46.69	0.98	6.49	6.49	0.00
Citrus	2,302.90	25.20	25.20	0.00	2,277.70	0.70	2,277.00
Clay	26.57	21.26	21.26	0.00	5.31	5.31	0.00
Collier	123.69	118.22	118.22	0.00	5.47	5.47	0.00
Columbia	9.86	9.81	9.81	0.00	0.05	0.05	0.00
Dade	491.54	486.05	486.05	0.00	5.49	4.50	0.99
De Soto	83.78	74.93	74.93	0.00	8.85	8.85	0.00
Dixie	4.21	4.06	4.06	0.00	0.15	0.15	0.00
Duval	640.09	159.30	159.30	0.00	480.79	1.37	479.42
Escambia	343.06	84.29	84.29	0.00	258.77	258.77	0.00
Flagler	9.87	8.94	8.94	0.00	0.93	0.93	0.00
Franklin	2.98	2.98	2.98	0.00	0.00	0.00	0.00
Gadsden	16.12	8.45	8.45	0.00	7.67	7.67	0.00
Gilchrist	5.41	5.41	5.41	0.00	0.00	0.00	0.00
Glades	82.08	15.96	15.96	0.00	66.12	66.12	0.00
Gulf	37.88	4.03	4.03	0.00	33.85	33.85	0.00
Hamilton	43.38	43.38	43.38	0.00	0.00	0.00	0.00
Hardee	94.18	94.18	94.18	0.00	0.00	0.00	0.00
Hendry	192.00	33.94	33.94	0.00	158.06	158.06	0.00
Hernando	40.86	40.86	40.86	0.00	0.00	0.00	0.00
Highlands	123.67	100.40	100.40	0.00	23.27	23.27	0.00
Hillsborough	2,645.07	249.30	249.30	0.00	2,395.77	67.91	2,327.86
Holmes	5.47	5.04	5.04	0.00	0.43	0.43	0.00
Indian River	170.61	44.99	44.02	0.97	125.62	107.18	18.44
Jackson	129.33	18.44	18.44	0.00	110.89	110.89	0.00
Jefferson	9.56	8.20	8.20	0.00	1.36	1.36	0.00

Continued . . .

Table 8.41. WATER USE: WATER WITHDRAWALS BY SOURCE IN THE STATE AND COUNTIES
  OF FLORIDA, 1985 (Continued)

(in millions of gallons per day)

County	Total	Ground			Surface		
		Total	Fresh	Saline	Total	Fresh	Saline
Lafayette	7.57	7.31	7.31	0.00	0.26	0.26	0.00
Lake	73.18	64.88	64.88	0.00	8.30	8.30	0.00
Lee	328.56	68.29	60.17	8.12	260.27	11.35	248.92
Leon	36.61	34.44	34.44	0.00	2.17	2.17	0.00
Levy	18.59	14.14	14.14	0.00	4.45	4.45	0.00
Liberty	1.09	1.09	1.09	0.00	0.00	0.00	0.00
Madison	6.00	6.00	6.00	0.00	0.00	0.00	0.00
Manatee	127.49	93.18	93.18	0.00	34.31	34.31	0.00
Marion	53.03	49.14	49.14	0.00	3.89	3.89	0.00
Martin	189.22	46.29	45.99	0.30	142.93	142.93	0.00
Monroe	60.71	60.71	1.60	59.11	0.00	0.00	0.00
Nassau	48.65	46.14	46.14	0.00	2.51	0.93	1.58
Okaloosa	27.67	27.67	27.67	0.00	0.00	0.00	0.00
Okeechobee	29.71	24.44	24.44	0.00	5.27	5.27	0.00
Orange	245.74	191.82	191.82	0.00	53.92	53.92	0.00
Osceola	59.27	53.69	53.69	0.00	5.58	5.58	0.00
Palm Beach	1,033.46	153.93	153.93	0.00	879.53	554.28	325.25
Pasco	1,258.29	126.02	126.02	0.00	1,132.27	0.87	1,131.40
Pinellas	519.82	23.47	23.47	0.00	496.35	0.55	495.80
Polk	398.80	320.36	320.36	0.00	78.44	78.44	0.00
Putnam	90.34	70.27	70.27	0.00	20.07	20.07	0.00
St. Johns	51.29	50.22	50.22	0.00	1.07	1.07	0.00
St. Lucie	1,486.18	68.28	68.28	0.00	1,417.90	163.62	1,254.28
Santa Rosa	16.83	16.68	16.68	0.00	0.15	0.15	0.00
Sarasota	40.83	40.36	33.48	6.88	0.47	0.47	0.00
Seminole	68.72	66.66	66.66	0.00	2.06	2.06	0.00
Sumter	78.62	78.27	78.27	0.00	0.35	0.35	0.00
Suwannee	87.90	21.30	21.30	0.00	66.60	66.60	0.00
Taylor	50.16	48.53	48.53	0.00	1.63	1.63	0.00
Union	2.11	2.11	2.11	0.00	0.00	0.00	0.00
Volusia	212.08	79.08	79.07	0.01	133.00	117.75	15.25
Wakulla	30.34	1.29	1.29	0.00	29.05	0.00	29.05
Walton	6.57	6.05	6.05	0.00	0.52	0.52	0.00
Washington	3.21	3.07	3.07	0.00	0.14	0.14	0.00

    Source: U.S., Department of the Interior, Geological Survey in cooperation with
St. Johns River Water Management District, *Water Withdrawal and Use by Category in
Florida, 1985.*

Table 8.42. WATER USE: PUBLIC SUPPLY WATER WITHDRAWALS AND WATER USE BY TYPE
OF USE IN THE STATE AND COUNTIES OF FLORIDA, 1985

(in millions of gallons per day)

County	Total with- drawal	Total	Resi- dential/ domestic	Insti- tutional/ commercial	Indus- trial	Utility 1/	Other 2/
Florida	1,677.11	1,677.11	1,196.18	250.84	142.20	56.68	31.21
Alachua	21.25	21.25	14.79	3.09	2.98	0.07	0.32
Baker	0.60	0.60	0.52	0.02	0.00	0.02	0.04
Bay	31.92	31.92	16.59	12.44	0.64	1.93	0.32
Bradford	1.34	1.34	0.79	0.26	0.27	0.01	0.01
Brevard	23.30	45.40	36.66	3.18	1.24	4.32	0.00
Broward	187.95	187.95	124.05	37.59	24.43	1.88	0.00
Calhoun	0.39	0.39	0.27	0.12	0.00	0.00	0.00
Charlotte	4.29	10.64	8.93	1.06	0.11	0.54	0.00
Citrus	6.55	6.55	5.77	0.52	0.13	0.13	0.00
Clay	8.40	8.40	7.48	0.20	0.08	0.62	0.02
Collier	25.38	25.38	20.55	3.55	0.25	1.03	0.00
Columbia	1.99	1.99	0.80	0.87	0.30	0.02	0.00
Dade	339.77	328.43	216.76	65.68	42.70	3.29	0.00
De Soto	7.26	0.68	0.60	0.06	0.01	0.01	0.00
Dixie	0.64	0.64	0.57	0.04	0.02	0.01	0.00
Duval	84.86	84.86	53.12	10.61	9.50	5.35	6.28
Escambia	37.62	37.62	19.81	1.97	7.72	2.02	6.10
Flagler	2.22	2.22	1.95	0.08	0.02	0.17	0.00
Franklin	1.20	1.20	0.84	0.24	0.06	0.06	0.00
Gadsden	2.73	2.73	1.87	0.46	0.25	0.15	0.00
Gilchrist	0.34	0.34	0.30	0.03	0.00	0.01	0.00
Glades	0.25	0.25	0.21	0.02	0.01	0.01	0.00
Gulf	0.98	0.98	0.88	0.08	0.01	0.01	0.00
Hamilton	0.73	0.73	0.51	0.07	0.11	0.04	0.00
Hardee	1.32	1.32	1.12	0.13	0.05	0.02	0.00
Hendry	2.89	2.89	2.31	0.14	0.30	0.14	0.00
Hernando	7.88	7.88	6.42	0.90	0.40	0.12	0.04
Highlands	7.88	7.88	5.90	0.39	1.50	0.09	0.00
Hillsborough	165.40	114.09	84.08	10.03	16.99	1.72	1.27
Holmes	0.82	0.82	0.66	0.14	0.00	0.02	0.00
Indian River	8.84	8.84	6.83	0.42	0.36	0.84	0.39
Jackson	2.44	2.44	1.22	0.36	0.79	0.07	0.00
Jefferson	0.60	0.60	0.43	0.15	0.00	0.02	0.00
Lafayette	0.15	0.15	0.12	0.01	0.01	0.01	0.00
Lake	15.34	15.34	12.11	1.03	0.80	1.07	0.33

See footnotes at end of table.   Continued . . .

Florida Statistical Abstract 1991

Table 8.42. WATER USE: PUBLIC SUPPLY WATER WITHDRAWALS AND WATER USE BY TYPE
OF USE IN THE STATE AND COUNTIES OF FLORIDA, 1985 (Continued)

(in millions of gallons per day)

County	Total with- drawal	Total	Water use Resi- dential/ domestic	Insti- tutional/ commercial	Indus- trial	Utility 1/	Other 2/
Lee	31.73	31.73	27.92	2.54	0.32	0.95	0.00
Leon	22.06	22.06	12.57	6.83	0.22	2.06	0.38
Levy	1.19	1.19	0.83	0.11	0.11	0.14	0.00
Liberty	0.25	0.25	0.20	0.03	0.00	0.02	0.00
Madison	1.18	1.18	0.60	0.30	0.24	0.04	0.00
Manatee	30.89	21.49	18.22	1.35	0.88	0.54	0.50
Marion	11.89	11.89	9.45	0.68	0.65	1.11	0.00
Martin	9.33	9.33	7.50	0.58	0.39	0.86	0.00
Monroe	0.00	11.34	3.98	4.71	0.00	2.65	0.00
Nassau	3.04	3.04	1.52	0.26	0.86	0.40	0.00
Okaloosa	17.36	17.36	11.45	3.47	0.00	0.20	2.24
Okeechobee	1.93	1.93	1.31	0.19	0.06	0.37	0.00
Orange	122.60	100.50	60.60	18.29	8.84	8.22	4.55
Osceola	5.69	5.69	4.83	0.40	0.12	0.14	0.20
Palm Beach	146.55	146.55	128.52	8.80	7.33	1.17	0.73
Pasco	75.44	21.11	19.01	1.70	0.00	0.40	0.00
Pinellas	9.45	115.08	84.12	25.66	0.46	3.61	1.23
Polk	54.90	54.90	41.39	7.91	3.62	1.64	0.34
Putnam	2.97	2.97	2.24	0.15	0.13	0.44	0.01
St. Johns	7.01	7.01	5.79	0.14	0.06	0.51	0.51
St. Lucie	10.83	10.83	8.66	0.66	0.97	0.40	0.14
Santa Rosa	7.60	7.60	4.60	2.32	0.08	0.53	0.07
Sarasota	17.09	26.73	22.70	2.93	0.73	0.30	0.07
Seminole	34.86	34.86	27.57	1.81	1.39	1.30	2.79
Sumter	1.31	1.31	1.07	0.12	0.09	0.03	0.00
Suwannee	1.33	1.33	0.94	0.16	0.16	0.07	0.00
Taylor	1.58	1.58	1.11	0.16	0.24	0.07	0.00
Union	0.52	0.52	0.42	0.06	0.03	0.01	0.00
Volusia	36.40	36.40	27.30	2.26	2.18	2.48	2.18
Wakulla	0.59	0.59	0.55	0.02	0.00	0.02	0.00
Walton	2.99	2.99	2.48	0.20	0.00	0.16	0.15
Washington	1.03	1.03	0.91	0.10	0.00	0.02	0.00

1/ Water used in fire fighting, system flushing, and leakage.
2/ Includes power generation, heating and cooling systems, and urban irrigation.
Note: Public supply refers to municipal or other private water utilities which
serves the public. See Table 9.50 for agricultural irrigated water use.

Source: U.S., Department of the Interior, Geological Survey in cooperation with
St. Johns River Water Management District, *Water Withdrawals and Use by Category in
Florida, 1985.*

Table 8.43.   WATER USE: WATER DISCHARGED FROM WASTEWATER TREATMENT FACILITIES
BY TYPE OF FACILITY IN THE STATE AND COUNTIES OF FLORIDA, 1985

(in millions of gallons per day)

County	Total	Muni-cipal	Commer-cial/in-dustrial	County	Total	Muni-cipal	Commer-cial/in-dustrial
Florida	1,392.51	1,121.57	270.94	Lafayette	0.09	0.09	0.00
				Lake	4.83	4.83	0.00
Alachua	15.01	11.80	3.21	Lee	21.91	21.91	0.00
Baker	0.60	0.48	0.12	Leon	14.79	14.79	0.00
Bay	29.79	29.79	0.00	Levy	0.40	0.40	0.00
Bradford	6.25	0.97	5.28	Liberty	0.11	0.11	0.00
Brevard	26.51	26.18	0.33	Madison	0.72	0.72	0.00
Broward	146.64	146.62	0.02	Manatee	17.08	17.08	0.00
Calhoun	0.37	0.37	0.00	Marion	5.71	5.63	0.08
Charlotte	4.39	4.39	0.00	Martin	3.87	3.76	0.11
Citrus	4.39	4.39	0.00	Monroe	7.75	7.75	0.00
Clay	4.61	4.61	0.00	Nassau	37.07	1.85	35.22
Collier	11.03	11.03	0.00	Okaloosa	11.08	10.62	0.46
Columbia	1.10	1.10	0.00	Okeechobee	0.41	0.32	0.09
Dade	250.16	249.67	0.49	Orange	30.67	29.08	1.59
De Soto	0.80	0.72	0.08	Osceola	11.44	7.53	3.91
Dixie	0.46	0.46	0.00	Palm Beach	104.26	94.95	9.31
Duval	98.91	68.66	30.25	Pasco	11.34	11.34	0.00
Escambia	64.96	17.38	47.58	Pinellas	101.46	101.46	0.00
Flagler	1.53	1.53	0.00	Polk	50.22	18.59	31.63
Franklin	1.01	1.01	0.00	Putnam	20.71	1.74	18.97
Gadsden	2.30	1.69	0.61	St. Johns	4.70	4.70	0.00
Gilchrist	0.21	0.21	0.00	St. Lucie	6.72	6.12	0.60
Glades	0.07	0.07	0.00	Santa Rosa	6.87	1.73	5.14
Gulf	33.22	0.68	32.54	Sarasota	17.06	17.06	0.00
Hamilton	0.40	0.40	0.00	Seminole	43.45	39.25	4.20
Hardee	0.89	0.89	0.00	Sumter	0.92	0.68	0.24
Hendry	1.23	1.03	0.20	Suwannee	0.50	0.50	0.00
Hernando	3.66	3.66	0.00	Taylor	25.88	0.88	25.00
Highlands	3.04	2.71	0.33	Union	0.30	0.30	0.00
Hillsborough	80.28	67.56	12.72	Volusia	28.45	28.45	0.00
Holmes	0.41	0.41	0.00	Wakulla	0.01	0.01	0.00
Indian River	3.30	3.30	0.00	Walton	1.55	1.01	0.54
Jackson	1.82	1.73	0.09	Washington	0.52	0.52	0.00
Jefferson	0.31	0.31	0.00				

Note: Discharge is to both surface and ground.
Source: U.S., Department of the Interior, Geological Survey in cooperation with
St. Johns River Water Management District, *Water Withdrawals and Use by Category in
Florida, 1985.*

Florida Statistical Abstract 1991

Table 8.44. WATER RATES: RESIDENTIAL WATER RATES FOR SPECIFIED UTILITIES
   IN FLORIDA, 1988-89

Utility	County	Ownership	Popula-tion served 1/	Cost per 1,000 gallons (dollars)	Monthly cost per 10,000 gallons 2/ (dollars)
Cape Coral	Lee	Public	45,772	1.95	19.60
Clearwater	Pinellas	Public	102,000	1.79	17.90
Cocoa	Brevard	Public	123,673	1.00	13.00
Daytona Beach	Volusia	Public	80,436	1.39	16.90
Deerfield Beach	Broward	Public	44,313	1.01	15.90
Escambia County Utilities	Escambia	Public	178,567	0.96	15.90
Florida Keys Aqueduct Authority 3/	Monroe	Public	73,500	5.56	55.60
Florida Public Utility Company	Nassau	Private	11,928	0.68	13.48
Ft. Myers	Lee	Public	42,044	1.25	14.30
Ft. Pierce	St. Lucie	Public	45,947	1.58	15.80
Ft. Walton Beach	Okaloosa	Public	23,030	0.82	8.20
Gainesville Regional Utility	Alachua	Public	116,650	0.82	11.10
Jacksonville	Duval	Public	355,080	0.51	9.50
Kingsley Service Company	Clay	Private	42,644	0.49	13.95
Miami/Dade Water Authority	Dade	Public	1,536,813	0.92	9.20
Naples	Collier	Public	39,506	0.90	9.00
New Port Richey	Pasco	Public	13,700	1.30	13.00
Ocala	Marion	Public	44,267	0.70	13.20
Orlando Utilities Company	Orange	Public	355,950	0.53	7.60
Palm Coast Utility Corporation	Flagler	Private	11,500	2.64	34.10
Placid Lakes Utility Inc.	Highlands	Private	2,195	0.85	15.35
St. Augustine	St. Johns	Public	15,757	3.30	32.96
St. Petersburg	Pinellas	Public	315,000	0.98	14.20
Sanlando Utility Corporation	Seminole	Private	32,849	0.35	7.43
Sarasota	Sarasota	Public	51,250	1.68	16.80
Seacoast Utility Corporation	Palm Beach	Private	68,538	1.59	22.20
Tallahassee	Leon	Public	123,060	0.84	12.00
Tampa	Hillsborough	Public	434,000	1.03	11.80
West Palm Beach Utilities	Palm Beach	Public	87,466	0.66	20.30
Winter Haven	Polk	Public	34,900	0.74	4/ 22.92

4/ Base charge ($15.52) includes water, sewer, and garbage service fees.
1/ Population served is for 1987.
2/ Includes base and service charges and excludes surcharges and taxes.
3/ Service area includes the city of Key West.

Source: U.S., Department of the Interior, Geological Survey, *Factors that Affect Public Supply Water Use and Projected Public Supply Water Use in Florida for 2000, 2010, and 2020*, unpublished report.

Florida Statistical Abstract 1991

Table 8.70. CLIMATE: TEMPERATURE CHARACTERISTICS AND TOTAL PRECIPITATION AT NATIONAL WEATHER STATION OFFICES IN FLORIDA BY MONTH, 1990

(temperature in degrees Fahrenheit)

Station and characteristics	January	February	March	April	May	June	July	August	September	October	November	December
Apalachicola												
Temperature												
Average maximum	67.3	69.6	72.3	76.8	84.1	90.1	90.5	91.8	88.2	81.2	74.0	69.6
Average minimum	48.1	53.5	53.7	57.7	65.4	72.2	74.3	74.7	69.9	62.3	51.5	51.0
Heating degree days	228	109	87	39	0	0	0	0	0	32	102	190
Cooling degree days	11	21	33	113	309	492	547	571	431	250	42	57
Days with maximum 90 degrees or more	0	0	0	0	2	18	18	26	14	0	0	0
Days with minimum 32 degress or less	0	0	0	0	0	0	0	0	0	0	0	1
Precipitation (inches)	2.4	3.9	4.2	2.2	0.5	2.8	9.3	2.3	5.2	2.0	1.6	1.6
Pensacola												
Temperature												
Average maximum	65.0	68.5	73.2	76.3	83.4	90.9	92.0	94.5	90.1	80.5	73.8	67.3
Average minimum	45.3	50.9	52.6	56.0	65.0	72.5	74.1	73.5	69.6	58.7	50.2	48.1
Heating degree days	302	157	96	54	0	0	0	0	0	43	112	251
Cooling degree days	5	17	39	94	293	510	568	596	453	195	30	31
Days with maximum 90 degrees or more	0	0	0	0	0	19	22	31	20	1	0	0
Days with minimum 32 degress or less	2	0	0	0	0	0	0	0	0	0	0	2
Precipitation (inches)	4.7	5.0	9.2	4.9	4.6	5.5	2.1	2.5	1.5	8.5	1.1	2.0
Tallahassee												
Temperature												
Average maximum	70.6	72.7	78.0	80.8	87.9	93.8	93.6	95.2	92.0	83.8	76.8	71.1
Average minimum	40.9	49.5	48.7	51.4	61.6	68.9	71.1	71.1	66.1	58.2	45.1	46.2
Heating degree days	281	128	97	68	0	0	0	0	0	58	142	228
Cooling degree days	0	26	53	108	308	499	544	572	430	251	30	38
Days with maximum 90 degrees or more	0	0	0	0	0	13	26	30	23	10	0	0
Days with minimum 32 degress or less	7	0	1	0	0	0	0	0	0	0	0	6
Precipitation (inches)	3.1	7.3	3.4	3.4	1.9	4.0	3.4	6.8	4.9	2.5	0.6	4.5

See footnotes at end of table.

Continued . . .

Table 8.70. CLIMATE: TEMPERATURE CHARACTERISTICS AND TOTAL PRECIPITATION AT NATIONAL WEATHER STATION OFFICES IN FLORIDA BY MONTH, 1990 (Continued)

(temperature in degrees Fahrenheit)

Station and characteristics	January	February	March	April	May	June	July	August	September	October	November	December
Jacksonville												
Temperature												
Average maximum	71.2	73.9	77.7	79.2	87.5	92.3	93.4	93.6	91.0	83.5	76.7	72.8
Average minimum	45.4	52.2	52.5	54.3	63.1	69.4	73.5	71.9	67.9	61.8	50.1	48.7
Heating degree days	221	117	70	49	1	0	0	0	0	29	96	191
Cooling degree days	21	66	81	109	327	484	581	557	443	276	56	67
Days with maximum 90 degrees or more	0	0	0	1	13	23	24	29	19	2	0	0
Days with minimum 32 degress or less	3	0	0	0	0	0	0	0	0	0	0	3
Precipitation (inches)	1.8	4.1	1.6	1.3	0.2	1.6	6.5	3.8	2.6	4.5	1.2	1.9
Daytona Beach												
Temperature												
Average maximum	74.0	76.5	77.4	79.6	86.3	90.4	90.6	91.4	88.9	84.0	77.8	77.0
Average minimum	51.4	58.4	55.3	59.6	68.2	70.9	73.1	72.3	72.0	67.9	56.9	53.2
Heating degree days	120	47	37	14	0	0	0	0	0	9	35	96
Cooling degree days	55	124	85	161	385	478	531	528	470	355	114	107
Days with maximum 90 degrees or more	0	0	0	0	10	16	18	21	12	1	0	0
Days with minimum 32 degress or less	0	0	0	0	0	0	0	0	0	0	0	0
Precipitation (inches)	1.4	5.6	1.9	1.5	1.5	2.7	5.9	7.0	1.6	5.9	0.8	0.3
Orlando												
Temperature												
Average maximum	76.9	79.3	80.6	81.9	89.9	91.6	92.0	93.1	91.6	85.9	79.2	77.5
Average minimum	54.6	58.9	58.0	61.1	68.8	72.2	73.6	73.9	72.4	68.3	59.3	55.1
Heating degree days	71	34	11	5	0	0	0	0	0	6	14	69
Cooling degree days	102	156	156	206	453	514	559	581	518	388	149	116
Days with maximum 90 degrees or more	0	0	0	3	15	22	26	28	23	6	0	0
Days with minimum 32 degress or less	0	0	0	0	0	0	0	0	0	0	0	0
Precipitation (inches)	0.2	4.1	1.9	1.7	0.6	6.2	6.7	3.8	2.5	2.1	1.1	0.8

See footnotes at end of table.

Continued . . .

Florida Statistical Abstract 1991

Table 8.70. CLIMATE: TEMPERATURE CHARACTERISTICS AND TOTAL PRECIPITATION AT NATIONAL WEATHER STATION OFFICES IN FLORIDA BY MONTH, 1990 (Continued)

(temperature in degrees Fahrenheit)

Station and characteristics	January	February	March	April	May	June	July	August	September	October	November	December
Lakeland												
Temperature												
Average maximum	78.9	81.4	82.3	84.9	91.6	93.9	94.0	94.4	93.1	87.6	80.2	77.2
Average minimum	55.4	58.7	57.5	60.7	69.4	72.1	73.2	73.1	72.3	67.5	59.4	54.9
Heating degree days	51	25	4	2	0	0	0	0	0	6	15	71
Cooling degree days	125	173	164	243	489	547	586	590	539	403	167	115
Days with maximum 90 degrees or more	0	0	0	4	24	26	27	28	28	14	0	0
Days with minimum 32 degress or less	0	0	0	0	0	0	0	0	0	0	0	0
Precipitation (inches)	0.4	4.3	1.2	1.2	4.4	7.2	7.7	6.4	3.3	2.2	0.9	0.4
Tampa												
Temperature												
Average maximum	76.6	78.8	80.8	82.7	90.0	91.7	91.3	92.7	92.4	87.2	81.5	78.1
Average minimum	55.5	59.5	58.5	61.4	71.0	73.7	73.7	75.0	73.1	68.0	58.9	55.6
Heating degree days	70	32	13	5	0	0	0	0	0	7	11	70
Cooling degree days	107	154	164	225	487	537	549	592	541	406	176	139
Days with maximum 90 degrees or more	0	0	0	0	19	27	25	27	25	14	0	0
Days with minimum 32 degress or less	0	0	0	0	0	0	0	0	0	0	0	0
Precipitation (inches)	0.5	4.6	1.7	1.5	1.8	5.2	10.0	3.3	2.4	2.6	0.7	0.2
Ft. Myers												
Temperature												
Average maximum	80.8	82.0	83.5	86.2	90.1	93.2	93.3	93.6	92.9	88.5	83.3	(NA)
Average minimum	58.4	60.7	60.1	62.5	70.7	72.9	73.9	74.5	73.9	70.3	62.0	(NA)
Heating degree days	31	7	1	1	0	0	0	0	0	2	2	(NA)
Cooling degree days	183	192	219	289	484	549	583	595	560	455	237	(NA)
Days with maximum 90 degrees or more	0	0	1	3	18	28	30	27	27	20	2	(NA)
Days with minimum 32 degress or less	0	0	0	0	0	0	0	0	0	0	0	(NA)
Precipitation (inches)	0.5	3.4	0.9	0.4	3.7	9.0	6.5	15.0	7.4	2.3	0.0	(NA)

See footnotes at end of table.

Continued . . .

Florida Statistical Abstract 1991

Table 8.70. CLIMATE: TEMPERATURE CHARACTERISTICS AND TOTAL PRECIPITATION AT NATIONAL WEATHER STATION OFFICES IN FLORIDA BY MONTH, 1990 (Continued)

(temperature in degrees Fahrenheit)

Station and characteristics	January	February	March	April	May	June	July	August	September	October	November	December
Miami												
Temperature												
Average maximum	81.1	80.8	80.6	82.6	86.8	90.3	91.2	91.5	89.9	84.1	81.7	80.1
Average minimum	66.0	67.1	66.7	67.8	73.7	75.6	75.7	75.8	76.3	75.4	67.0	65.6
Heating degree days	7	4	0	0	0	0	0	0	0	0	0	4
Cooling degree days	279	262	276	314	479	547	578	587	552	467	287	254
Days with maximum 90 degrees or more	0	0	0	1	5	18	20	25	17	1	0	0
Days with minimum 32 degress or less	0	0	0	0	0	0	0	0	0	0	0	0
Precipitation (inches)	0.2	1.2	2.3	7.0	7.8	6.8	4.3	11.1	3.5	2.3	1.7	1.0
West Palm Beach												
Temperature												
Average maximum	79.8	81.3	80.5	81.7	87.0	90.1	91.2	92.4	90.2	86.8	81.4	79.1
Average minimum	64.7	66.3	65.9	66.1	72.4	74.2	75.4	75.0	75.2	73.3	65.5	63.4
Heating degree days	14	7	2	1	0	0	0	0	0	2	0	11
Cooling degree days	247	259	262	276	460	520	574	591	542	474	263	211
Days with maximum 90 degrees or more	0	0	0	0	7	15	24	29	21	5	0	0
Days with minimum 32 degress or less	0	0	0	0	0	0	0	0	0	0	0	0
Precipitation (inches)	1.2	1.4	1.9	2.8	6.7	6.7	10.2	6.6	11.7	3.5	1.2	1.9
Key West												
Temperature												
Average maximum	78.7	80.1	79.8	82.3	86.4	89.6	90.8	92.0	89.5	85.9	80.4	78.8
Average minimum	67.7	70.8	70.1	70.9	77.0	79.1	78.6	79.1	78.1	75.8	70.8	70.3
Heating degree days	2	0	0	0	0	0	0	0	0	0	0	0
Cooling degree days	263	299	315	356	522	588	620	644	575	499	326	309
Days with maximum 90 degrees or more	0	0	0	0	2	17	23	31	16	1	0	0
Days with minimum 32 degress or less	0	0	0	0	0	0	0	0	0	0	0	0
Precipitation (inches)	T	1.1	0.8	1.4	5.5	0.9	4.1	8.0	5.3	5.1	2.9	1.3

T denotes trace. (NA) Not available.
Note: Degree day totals are the sums of the negative (heating) or positive (cooling) departures of average daily temperatures from 65 degrees Fahrenheit.
Source: U.S., Department of Commerce, National Oceanic and Atmospheric Administration, Environmental Data Service, *Climatological Data: Florida,* 1990 monthly reports.

Table 8.74. CLIMATE: CHARACTERISTICS FOR JACKSONVILLE, MIAMI, LOS ANGELES, ATLANTA CHICAGO, AND NEW YORK, SPECIFIED DATES THROUGH 1989

Characteristic	Jackson-ville Florida	Miami Florida	Los Angeles Cali-fornia	Atlanta Georgia	Chicago Illinois	New York New York 1/
Heating degree days 2/ 3/						
January	396	76	286	716	1,352	1,029
February	302	62	233	563	1,092	885
November	164	5	139	394	756	534
December	332	42	255	636	1,156	893
Annual	1,402	199	1,595	3,021	6,455	4,868
Normal temperature 3/						
January average	53.2	67.1	56.0	41.9	21.4	31.8
July average	81.3	82.4	69.0	78.6	73.0	76.7
Annual average	68.0	75.6	62.6	61.2	49.2	54.5
January normal high	64.6	75.0	64.6	51.2	29.2	38.0
July normal high	90.7	88.7	75.3	87.9	83.3	85.3
Annual average high	78.7	82.6	70.1	71.3	58.7	62.2
January normal low	41.7	59.2	47.3	32.6	13.6	25.6
July normal low	71.8	76.2	62.6	69.2	62.7	68.2
Annual average low	57.2	68.7	55.0	51.1	39.7	46.9
Extreme temperatures 4/						
Highest temperature of record	105	98	110	105	104	106
Lowest temperature of record	7	30	23	−8	−27	−15
Length of record (years)	48	47	54	41	31	121
Normal annual precipitation						
Annual 3/ (inches)	52.76	57.55	12.08	48.61	33.34	44.12
Average number of days precipitation 0.01 or more 4/	115	129	35	115	126	121
Length of record 4/ (years)	48	47	54	55	31	120
Average total snow and ice pellets (inches)	T	0.0	T	2.0	39.3	28.5
Length of record 4/ (years)	48	47	54	55	31	121
Average annual percentage of possible sunshine	62	73	A/ 73	61	55	58
Length of record 4/ (years)	38	13	A/ 32	54	9	103
Average annual wind speed (MPH)	8.0	9.3	7.5	9.1	10.3	9.4
Length of record 4/ (years)	40	40	41	51	31	58
Minimum temperature 32° or less						
Length of record 4/	48	25	30	29	31	76
Mean number of days	15	B/	B/	55	133	80
Average relative humidity						
Length of record 4/	53	25	30	29	31	61
Annual (percentage), morning	88	84	79	82	80	72
Afternoon	56	61	64	56	60	56

T denotes trace.   MPH denotes miles per hour.
A/ Record through 1978.   B/ Less than one-half day.
1/ City office data.   2/ For any one day, when the mean temperature is less than 65 degrees F., there exist as many degree days as there are degree differences between the average temperature for the day and 65 degrees F.   3/ Based on 1951-80 period of record.   4/ Record through 1989.
Note: All temperatures are in degrees Fahrenheit.
Source: U.S., Department of Commerce, Bureau of the Census, *Statistical Abstract of the United States, 1991.* Data from U.S. National Oceanic and Atmospheric Administration.

Florida Statistical Abstract 1991

Table 8.76. HURRICANES: AREA OF LANDFALL, NAME, YEAR, FORCE CATEGORY, AND RANK OF
    THE TWENTY-ONE DEADLIEST HURRICANES IN THE UNITED STATES, 1900 THROUGH 1989

Area of landfall/name	Year	Force Category 1/	Deaths Number	Rank
Galveston, Texas/(NA)	1900	4	6,000	1
Lake Okeechobee, Florida/(NA)	1928	4	1,836	2
Florida Keys; S. Texas/(NA)	1919	4	600	3
New England/(NA)	1938	3	600	4
Florida Keys/(NA)	1935	5	408	5
S.W. Louisiana; N. Texas/Audrey	1957	4	390	6
N.E. United States/(NA)	1944	3	390	7
Grand Isle, Louisiana/(NA)	1909	4	350	8
New Orleans, Louisiana/(NA)	1915	4	275	9
Galveston, Texas/(NA)	1915	4	275	10
Mississippi; Louisiana/Camille	1969	5	256	11
Miami, Florida/(NA)	1926	4	243	12
N.E. United States/Diane	1955	1	184	13
S.E. Florida/(NA)	1906	2	164	14
Mississippi; Alabama; Pensacola, Florida/(NA)	1906	3	134	15
N.E. United States/Agnes	1972	1	122	16
South Carolina; North Carolina/Hazel	1954	4	95	17
S.E. Florida; S.E. Louisiana/Betsy	1965	3	75	18
N.E. United States/Carol	1954	3	60	19
S.E. Florida; Louisiana; Mississippi/(NA)	1947	4	51	20
Florida; E. United States/Donna	1960	4	50	21

(NA) Not available.
    1/ Assigned based on the Saffir/Simpson scale. Ratings are 1-5 and a "5" indi-
cates central pressure less than 920 millibars or winds greater than 155 mph or
storm surge higher than 18 feet and damage classified as catastrophic.

Table 8.77. HURRICANES: AREA OF LANDFALL, NAME, YEAR, FORCE CATEGORY, AND RANK OF
    THE TEN COSTLIEST HURRICANES IN THE UNITED STATES, 1900 THROUGH 1989

Area of landfall/name	Year	Force Category 1/	Value of damage 2/ Amount ($1,000)	Rank
South Carolina/Hugo	1989	4	7,000,000	1
Florida; Louisiana/Betsy	1965	3	6,321,225	2
N.E. United States/Agnes	1972	1	6,279,000	3
Mississippi; Alabama/Camille	1969	5	5,128,727	4
N.E. United States/Diane	1955	1	4,108,598	5
New England/(NA)	1938	3	3,515,940	6
Alabama; Mississippi/Frederic	1979	3	3,427,000	7
N. Texas/Alicia	1983	3	2,340,000	8
N.E. United States/Carol	1954	3	2,318,830	9
Texas/Carla	1961	4	1,884,960	10

(NA) Not available.
    1/ Assigned based on the Saffir/Simpson scale. Ratings are 1-5 and a "5" indi-
cates central pressure less than 920 millibars or winds greater than 155 mph or
storm surge higher than 18 feet and damage classified as catastrophic.
    2/ Adjusted to 1989 dollars on basis of U.S. Department of Commerce composite
construction cost indexes.
    Source for Tables 8.76 and 8.77: U.S., Department of Commerce, National Oceanic
and Atmospheric Administration, *The Deadliest, Costliest, and Most Intense United
States Hurricanes of this Century*. NOAA Technical Memorandum NWS NHC 31.

Florida Statistical Abstract 1991

Table 8.80. AIR POLLUTION: PARTICULATE MATTER (PM) CONCENTRATIONS IN SPECIFIED CITIES OF FLORIDA, 1990

Area	Site Address	PM10 concentration (UG/M^3) 2nd highest 24-hour value 1/	Annual geometric mean 2/
Broward County			
Ft. Lauderdale	2101 NW 6th Street	45	24
Ft. Lauderdale	2101 NW 6th Street	41	21
Ft. Lauderdale	500 SW 14th Court, #12	29	16
Dade County			
Miami	6400 NW 27th Avenue	46	25
Miami	NW 36th Street & 72nd Avenue, #3	49	29
Miami	Fire Station NW 12th Avenue & 20th Street, #40	49	30
Miami	Fire Station NW 12th Avenue & 20th Street	48	31
Duval County			
Jacksonville	1070 E Adams Street	56	35
Jacksonville	Sewage Treatment Plant, 2221 Buckman Street	61	33
Jacksonville	Roselle & Copeland adjacent to I-10	60	34
Hendry County			
Clewiston 3/	115 S Lopez Street	35	22
Clewiston 3/	Delta Ranch on SR 832	112	25
Hillsborough County			
Gibsonton	ICWU Building, Highway 41 North	68	37
Tampa	5012 Causeway Boulevard, (Gannon)	39	28
Tampa	HCHD #1, 1105 E Kennedy	41	29
Tampa	Coast Guard Station, Davis Island	46	30
Tampa	Davis Island Coast Guard Station	46	29
Tampa	Seminole Heights School, 6201 Central Avenue	50	31
Orange County			
Orlando	2401 W 33rd Street (Sheriff's Department)	55	32
Orlando	SW Corner of Central Boulevard & Paramore	46	26
Orlando	595 N Primrose	32	23
Palm Beach County			
Belle Glade 3/	SR 717 Belle Glade Municipal Golf	33	20
Belle Glade 3/	273 SE Avenue E (Glades Mercantile)	43	25
Belle Glade 3/	273 SE Avenue E (Glades Mercantile)	44	25
Belle Glade	425 West Canal Street North	38	23
Boca Raton	Marymount College, S Military Trail	20	16
Delray Beach	345 S Congress	35	20
Pahokee 3/	Pahokee Water Treatment Plant	39	22
Pahokee	200 S Barfield Highway (Memorial Hospital)	38	22
County	Twenty Mile Bend	33	17

See footnotes at end of table. Continued . . .

Florida Statistical Abstract 1991

Table 8.80.   AIR POLLUTION: PARTICULATE MATTER (PM) CONCENTRATIONS IN SPECIFIED
    CITIES OF FLORIDA, 1990 (Continued)

Area	Site Address	PM10 concentration (UG/M^3) 2nd highest 24-hour value 1/	PM10 concentration (UG/M^3) Annual geometric mean 2/
Palm Beach County			
(Continued)			
South Bay 3/	Sunshine Sod Company	78	25
Belle Glade 3/	P O Box 484	95	25
Belle Glade 3/	SR 80	47	21
Pahokee 3/	East Shore Drainage District	39	21
Canal Point 3/	US 441 (USDA Research)	39	23
Canal Point 3/	US 98, 1.8 miles south of Hatton	96	26
Palm Beach Gardens	3188 PGA Boulevard (By Courthouse)	30	17
West Palm Beach	Health Department, 901 Evernia Street	26	19
West Palm Beach	3730 Belvedere Road	25	20
Pinellas County			
Largo	1301 Ulmerton Road (Fleet Maintenance)	50	27
Largo	1301 Ulmerton Road (Fleet Maintenance)	48	28
Tarpon Springs	Brooker Creek Park	32	20
Sarasota County			
Sarasota	1642 12th Street (Reverse Osmosis Plant)	50	27
Sarasota	1642 12th Street (Reverse Osmosis Plant)	47	27
Sarasota	Bee Ridge Park on Lockwood Ridge Road	35	21
Venice	448 East Venice Avenue	60	36
Venice	447 East Venice Avenue (Reverse Osmosis)	51	36

UG/M^3 Micrograms per cubic meter.
1/ Florida standard is 150 UG/M^3, not to be exceeded more than once per year.
2/ Florida standard is 50 UG/M^3.
3/ Industy.
Note: Particulate describes airborne solid or liquid particles of about 0.1 to
50 microns in diameter (1 micron = 0.0001 centimeter).   PM consists of sulfate,
nitrate, and acidic particles formed by oxidation of the pollutant gases sulfur
dioxide and nitrogen dioxide; of soot and organic particles released in forest fires
and other low-temperature combustion processes; of lead-containing particles emitted
from motor vehicles; of products of industrial processes and high temperature fuel
combustion; of local soil; and of airborne sea salt.   PM10 is a subset of
particulate matter and refers to airborne particles that are 10 microns or less in
size.
    Source: State of Florida, Department of Environmental Regulation, Division of
Air Resources Management, *Comparison of Air Quality Data with the National Ambient
Air Quality Standards, 1990.*

Florida Statistical Abstract 1991

AGRICULTURE

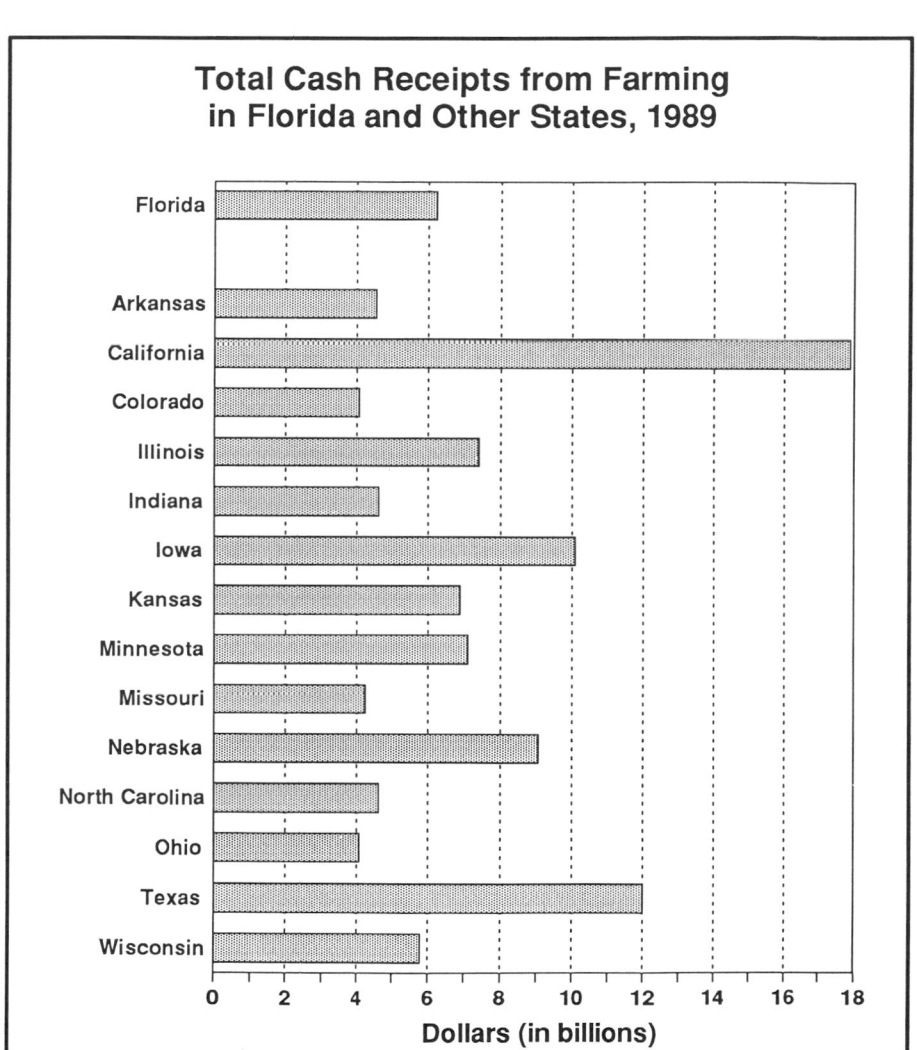

**Total Cash Receipts from Farming
in Florida and Other States, 1989**

Dollars (in billions)

Source: Table 9.42

TABLES LISTED BY MAJOR HEADINGS

TABLES LISTED BY MAJOR HEADINGS

SECTION 9.00
AGRICULTURE (CONTINUED)

TABLES LISTED BY MAJOR HEADINGS

Table 9.04. VETERINARIANS: LICENSED DOCTORS OF VETERINARY MEDICINE IN THE STATE
    AND COUNTIES OF FLORIDA, AUGUST 3, 1991

Location of licensee	Doctors of veterinary medicine	Location of licensee	Doctors of veterinary medicine
Total 1/	5,612	Jefferson	6
NonFlorida	2,797	Lafayette	1
Unknown	0	Lake	34
Alachua	178	Lee	82
Baker	1	Leon	49
Bay	25	Levy	11
Bradford	5	Liberty	0
Brevard	68	Madison	3
Broward	257	Manatee	29
Calhoun	2	Marion	109
Charlotte	17	Martin	25
Citrus	16	Monroe	35
Clay	28	Nassau	6
Collier	32	Okaloosa	31
Columbia	5	Okeechobee	8
Dade	330	Orange	130
De Soto	7	Osceola	18
Dixie	4	Palm Beach	222
Duval	138	Pasco	38
Escambia	51	Pinellas	172
Flagler	6	Polk	65
Franklin	1	Putnam	8
Gadsden	6	St. Johns	23
Gilchrist	2	St. Lucie	26
Glades	0	Santa Rosa	11
Gulf	2	Sarasota	86
Hamilton	2	Seminole	56
Hardee	5	Sumter	9
Hendry	6	Suwannee	11
Hernando	14	Taylor	4
Highlands	12	Union	0
Hillsborough	172	Volusia	70
Holmes	1	Wakulla	2
Indian River	21	Walton	5
Jackson	8	Washington	8

1/ Total includes all licensed persons regardless of current status.

   Source: State of Florida, Department of Professional Regulation, unpublished
data.

Florida Statistical Abstract 1991

Table 9.10. AGRICULTURAL EMPLOYMENT: ESTIMATES OF AVERAGE MONTHLY EMPLOYMENT
OF PROPRIETORS AND WAGE AND SALARY WORKERS IN THE STATE AND COUNTIES
OF FLORIDA, 1988 AND 1989

| | 1988 A/ | | | 1989 | | |
| | | Farm wage and salary employees | | | Farm wage and salary employees | |
County	Farm proprie- tors	Number	As a per- centage of all wage and salary employees	Farm proprie- tors	Number	As a per- centage of all wage and salary employees
Florida	39,618	66,443	1.2	39,617	56,533	1.0
Alachua	1,255	442	0.5	1,255	377	0.4
Baker	268	270	5.8	268	229	4.7
Bay	103	34	0.1	103	29	0.1
Bradford	446	74	1.4	446	63	1.1
Brevard	595	325	0.2	595	278	0.2
Broward	450	1,166	0.2	450	994	0.2
Calhoun	196	95	3.6	196	81	3.1
Charlotte	148	301	1.2	148	256	0.9
Citrus	332	76	0.4	332	65	0.3
Clay	270	256	1.0	270	218	0.8
Collier	224	1,368	2.2	224	1,162	1.7
Columbia	652	138	1.0	652	118	0.8
Dade	1,514	5,075	0.6	1,514	4,320	0.5
De Soto	601	506	6.7	601	431	5.5
Dixie	131	34	1.4	131	29	1.1
Duval	504	505	0.1	504	430	0.1
Escambia	594	152	0.1	594	129	0.1
Flagler	115	150	2.1	115	127	1.6
Franklin	0	0	0.0	0	0	0.0
Gadsden	465	648	4.6	465	551	3.8
Gilchrist	364	224	12.9	364	190	10.3
Glades	176	492	30.6	176	418	26.6
Gulf	0	0	0.0	0	0	0.0
Hamilton	331	70	1.6	331	60	1.3
Hardee	1,091	926	13.8	1,091	790	11.4
Hendry	311	1,182	12.7	311	1,006	10.3
Hernando	497	296	1.5	497	253	1.2
Highlands	604	1,439	7.3	604	1,226	6.0
Hillsborough	3,033	5,057	1.1	3,032	4,302	0.9
Holmes	656	185	5.5	656	157	4.4
Indian River	433	754	2.3	433	643	1.8
Jackson	1,119	381	2.7	1,119	324	2.3
Jefferson	376	397	11.4	376	338	10.1
Lafayette	368	188	16.0	368	160	12.7
Lake	1,706	2,623	5.3	1,706	2,237	4.4

See footnote at end of table.   Continued . . .

Florida Statistical Abstract 1991

Table 9.10. AGRICULTURAL EMPLOYMENT: ESTIMATES OF AVERAGE MONTHLY EMPLOYMENT
OF PROPRIETORS AND WAGE AND SALARY WORKERS IN THE STATE AND COUNTIES
OF FLORIDA, 1988 AND 1989 (Continued)

| | | 1988 A/ | | | 1989 | |
| | | Farm wage and salary employees | | | Farm wage and salary employees | |
County	Farm proprie- tors	Number	As a per- centage of all wage and salary employees	Farm proprie- tors	Number	As a per- centage of all wage and salary employees
Lee	396	1,861	1.5	396	1,581	1.2
Leon	342	142	0.1	342	122	0.1
Levy	544	179	3.3	544	152	2.6
Liberty	96	10	0.8	96	8	0.6
Madison	693	334	7.3	693	284	6.0
Manatee	749	2,381	3.4	749	2,024	2.7
Marion	1,720	1,693	2.6	1,720	1,442	2.2
Martin	262	1,368	3.4	262	1,164	2.7
Monroe	0	0	0.0	0	0	0.0
Nassau	335	192	1.6	335	163	1.3
Okaloosa	418	58	0.1	418	49	0.1
Okeechobee	330	1,120	14.6	330	953	12.1
Orange	1,337	4,906	1.2	1,337	4,174	0.9
Osceola	493	821	2.4	493	699	1.9
Palm Beach	657	15,664	4.1	657	13,303	3.4
Pasco	1,156	679	1.1	1,156	580	0.9
Pinellas	218	268	0.1	218	230	0.1
Polk	2,525	2,754	1.7	2,525	2,348	1.4
Putnam	605	435	2.5	605	371	2.1
St. Johns	205	480	1.8	205	409	1.5
St. Lucie	466	1,389	3.0	466	1,183	2.4
Santa Rosa	545	239	1.2	545	203	1.0
Sarasota	344	240	0.2	344	205	0.2
Seminole	568	712	0.8	568	606	0.7
Sumter	739	236	3.4	739	202	2.9
Suwannee	1,186	305	3.9	1,186	260	3.3
Taylor	201	32	0.4	201	27	0.4
Union	238	76	2.0	238	64	1.7
Volusia	1,152	1,774	1.4	1,152	1,509	1.2
Wakulla	108	17	0.6	108	15	0.5
Walton	533	106	1.4	533	90	1.1
Washington	529	143	3.3	529	122	2.8

A/ Revised.

Source: U.S., Department of Commerce, Bureau of Economic Analysis, unpublished
data.

Florida Statistical Abstract 1991

Table 9.11. AGRICULTURAL EMPLOYMENT: ESTIMATES OF SEASONAL EMPLOYMENT BY PLACE
OF WORKER'S ORIGIN AND BY CROP IN FLORIDA, 1990

	Seasonal hired workers by place of origin			Seasonal hired workers by crop activity			
	For-		Domestic			Flower/		Vege-
			Intra-	Inter-	Cit-	nur-	Sugar-	table
Date	eign	Local	state	state	rus 1/	sery 2/	cane	3/
January 15	8,919	46,979	8,059	12,511	43,929	9,230	9,680	1,897
January 31	9,159	40,090	8,324	8,346	33,066	8,096	9,865	2,046
February 15	9,066	38,797	9,078	10,869	30,782	7,961	9,772	1,999
February 28	7,743	36,700	9,496	9,753	25,790	7,839	8,360	3,457
March 15	4/	33,897	8,398	10,060	21,614	7,819	620	3,397
March 31	4/	30,820	8,193	7,514	17,490	7,201	620	3,312
April 15	4/	29,009	7,568	4,003	15,882	6,799	550	2,708
May 15	4/	27,953	6,649	5,570	10,656	8,501	560	4,414
June 15	4/	22,462	4,469	3,593	6,237	10,462	690	2,491
July 15	4/	22,019	4,456	4,089	7,493	11,293	450	1,863
August 15	4/	17,381	4,980	2,985	5,460	11,488	750	943
September 15	4/	21,570	4,999	4,530	9,742	9,825	920	1,780
October 15	4/	25,269	8,596	6,315	13,095	5,105	1,098	1,599
November 15	10,805	31,483	11,414	10,088	22,451	11,550	12,965	3,971
November 30	8,722	36,137	15,302	12,229	30,980	11,348	10,853	3,933
December 15	8,600	1,287	41,396	23,403	32,050	11,343	10,948	3,551
December 31	8,457	1,230	41,351	19,361	33,941	10,678	10,798	4,022

| | Seasonal hired workers by crop activity (Continued) | | | | | | |
| | | | | | Lemon | | Beans |
Date	Tomato	Celery	Pepper	Sod	and lime	Squash	4/
January 15	2,445	1,590	1,525	465	100	125	25
January 31	2,555	1,655	1,325	550	160	99	4/
February 15	2,830	1,665	1,425	560	150	560	280
February 28	3,630	1,600	1,725	560	150	635	280
March 15	4,340	1,785	1,765	600	225	755	439
March 31	5,525	1,956	1,805	550	225	805	625
April 15	3,225	1,900	2,220	550	250	820	550
May 15	5,965	1,650	2,015	500	400	146	80
June 15	3,145	250	664	360	550	4/	4/
July 15	3,075	375	545	465	1,325	4/	4/
August 15	2,550	95	525	520	1,180	4/	4/
September 15	3,710	150	1,225	545	745	350	4/
October 15	5,125	305	1,625	570	625	690	4/
November 15	6,950	1,350	1,975	515	525	887	516
November 30	5,365	1,350	2,100	515	525	762	523
December 15	4,575	1,525	2,325	465	525	717	480
December 31	2,950	1,350	2,125	515	25	4/	4/

See footnotes at end of table.   Continued . . .

Florida Statistical Abstract 1991

Table 9.11. AGRICULTURAL EMPLOYMENT: ESTIMATES OF SEASONAL EMPLOYMENT BY PLACE
OF WORKER'S ORIGIN AND BY CROP IN FLORIDA, 1990 (Continued)

			Seasonal hired workers by crop activity (Continued)				
Date	Corn 5/	Straw-berry	Cu-cumber	Water-melon	Tobacco	Peanut	All others 6/
January 15	A/	3,100	100	A/	A/	A/	2,232
January 31	A/	5,060	75	A/	A/	A/	2,267
February 15	A/	6,910	97	100	A/	A/	2,719
February 28	A/	7,350	222	185	100	A/	1,809
March 15	125	6,292	200	100	60	A/	2,219
March 31	465	2,200	450	160	75	A/	2,163
April 15	475	650	495	280	500	A/	2,617
May 15	1,229	295	273	860	200	80	2,348
June 15	1,470	A/	148	1,476	450	100	1,831
July 15	365	A/	A/	820	875	270	1,830
August 15	A/	A/	A/	A/	315	160	1,360
September 15	A/	400	310	A/	A/	A/	1,397
October 15	6,466	1,600	510	A/	A/	A/	1,767
November 15	169	550	1,114	A/	A/	A/	924
November 30	190	1,250	1,117	A/	A/	A/	1,579
December 15	200	3,055	788	A/	A/	A/	2,139
December 31	150	2,050	A/	A/	A/	A/	1,775

A/ No workers or small numbers included in all others. 1/ Excludes lemons and
limes.   2/ Foliage, nursery tropical foliage, flower, greenhouse seedling, fern,
gladiola and ornamental bulbs, and nursery workers. 3/ Leafy, mixed, and tropical.
4/ Pole, bush, string, and soybean. 5/ Includes sweet corn. 6/ Includes labor
for field preparation and crops not elsewhere classified.
    Note: Semi-monthly reports are available during months when foreign sugarcane
workers are in Florida. Some duplication of data may be present.
    Source: State of Florida, Department of Labor and Employment Security, Bureau of
Labor Market Information.

Table 9.13. FERTILIZER: MIXTURES AND MATERIALS CONSUMED IN FLORIDA, JULY 1, 1989
THROUGH JUNE 30, 1990

Fertilizer		Container (tons)			Use (tons)	
	Total	Bag	Bulk	Liquid	Farm	Nonfarm
Total	2,178,953	405,227	1,364,981	408,745	1,843,935	335,018
Mixtures	1,723,286	324,450	1,073,848	324,988	1,475,502	247,784
Materials	455,667	80,777	291,133	83,758	368,432	87,234
Nitrogen	175,051	21,993	83,876	69,182	143,777	31,274
Phosphate	31,341	1,780	25,309	4,251	27,113	4,227
Potash	35,703	2,799	31,469	1,436	31,346	4,357
Other 1/	213,572	54,205	150,479	8,889	166,196	47,376

1/ Includes secondary and micronutrient materials, natural organics and gypsum
for direct application. Does not include agriculture liming materials.
    Note: Detail may not add to total because of rounding.
    Source: State of Florida, Department of Agriculture and Consumer Services, *Sum-
mary Report of Fertilizer Materials and Fertilizer Mixtures Consumed in Florida,
Fiscal Year July 1, 1989–June 30, 1990.*

Florida Statistical Abstract 1991

Table 9.15. AGRICULTURAL PRODUCTION: AVERAGE MONTHLY REPORTING UNITS, EMPLOYMENT
AND PAYROLL COVERED BY UNEMPLOYMENT COMPENSATION LAW IN THE STATE AND COUNTIES
OF FLORIDA, 1990

County	Number of re-porting units	Number of employees	Payroll ($1,000)	County	Number of re-porting units	Number of employees	Payroll ($1,000)
			Agricultural production--crops (SIC code 01)				
Florida	2,421	63,738	68,223	Lafayette	(D)	(D)	(D)
				Lake	90	1,172	1,472
Alachua	16	134	98	Lee	38	1,909	1,724
Baker	(D)	(D)	(D)	Leon	6	107	97
Bay	(D)	(D)	(D)	Levy	(D)	(D)	(D)
Bradford	0	0	0	Liberty	(D)	(D)	(D)
Brevard	20	261	257	Madison	(D)	(D)	(D)
Broward	50	727	925	Manatee	75	3,891	3,903
Calhoun	(D)	(D)	(D)	Marion	23	212	216
Charlotte	8	158	314	Martin	35	788	1,016
Citrus	(D)	(D)	(D)	Monroe	(D)	(D)	(D)
Clay	(D)	(D)	(D)	Nassau	(D)	(D)	(D)
Collier	95	7,466	4,397	Okaloosa	(D)	(D)	(D)
Columbia	(D)	(D)	(D)	Okeechobee	15	230	218
Dade	291	5,717	6,517	Orange	188	4,047	5,300
De Soto	34	392	480	Osceola	26	335	387
Dixie	(D)	(D)	(D)	Palm Beach	274	11,028	15,237
Duval	7	200	284	Pasco	49	955	1,120
Escambia	(D)	(D)	(D)	Pinellas	17	292	460
Flagler	8	73	90	Polk	177	2,492	3,234
Franklin	0	0	0	Putnam	28	478	388
Gadsden	25	1,424	1,171	St. Johns	36	348	416
Gilchrist	4	12	13	St. Lucie	43	897	1,251
Glades	(D)	(D)	(D)	Santa Rosa	7	49	44
Gulf	(D)	(D)	(D)	Sarasota	20	424	407
Hamilton	(D)	(D)	(D)	Seminole	26	451	701
Hardee	53	929	779	Sumter	11	179	163
Hendry	42	2,669	3,511	Suwannee	20	277	253
Hernando	(D)	(D)	(D)	Taylor	(D)	(D)	(D)
Highlands	75	1,293	1,602	Union	0	0	0
Hillsborough	249	6,712	4,698	Volusia	120	2,326	2,071
Holmes	(D)	(D)	(D)	Wakulla	0	0	0
Indian River	44	970	1,466	Walton	3	21	23
Jackson	(D)	(D)	(D)	Washington	(D)	(D)	(D)
Jefferson	9	170	136	Statewide 1/	(D)	(D)	(D)

(D) Data withheld to avoid disclosure of information about individual firms.
1/ Reporting units without a fixed location within the state or of unknown county
location.
Note: Three-digit classifications of this two-digit group are listed in Table
9.27.

Source: State of Florida, Department of Labor and Employment Security, Bureau of
Labor Market Information, "Employment, Wages, and Contributions Report" (ES-202),
unpublished data.

Florida Statistical Abstract 1991

Table 9.17.   AGRICULTURAL SERVICES: AVERAGE MONTHLY REPORTING UNITS, EMPLOYMENT
AND PAYROLL COVERED BY UNEMPLOYMENT COMPENSATION LAW IN THE STATE AND
COUNTIES OF FLORIDA, 1990

County	Number of reporting units	Number of employees	Payroll ($1,000)	County	Number of reporting units	Number of employees	Payroll ($1,000)
			Agricultural	services (SIC code 07)			
Florida	7,559	70,833	75,231	Lafayette	(D)	(D)	(D)
				Lake	122	1,359	1,343
Alachua	92	674	654	Lee	226	1,628	1,622
Baker	(D)	(D)	(D)	Leon	79	403	381
Bay	35	127	133	Levy	14	113	122
Bradford	(D)	(D)	(D)	Liberty	(D)	(D)	(D)
Brevard	192	1,156	1,209	Madison	4	15	19
Broward	677	3,873	5,400	Manatee	129	1,536	1,592
Calhoun	(D)	(D)	(D)	Marion	146	1,054	1,164
Charlotte	61	302	362	Martin	97	904	1,116
Citrus	35	188	195	Monroe	33	110	130
Clay	54	296	327	Nassau	23	117	115
Collier	242	4,467	3,113	Okaloosa	47	177	161
Columbia	13	56	55	Okeechobee	(D)	(D)	(D)
Dade	718	6,723	6,754	Orange	434	4,205	5,077
De Soto	46	1,023	936	Osceola	(D)	(D)	(D)
Dixie	(D)	(D)	(D)	Palm Beach	773	6,963	7,724
Duval	307	1,901	2,247	Pasco	140	1,844	1,611
Escambia	75	400	408	Pinellas	424	2,305	2,734
Flagler	21	133	122	Polk	387	5,917	6,471
Franklin	(D)	(D)	(D)	Putnam	23	171	140
Gadsden	(D)	(D)	(D)	St. Johns	46	305	224
Gilchrist	4	20	20	St. Lucie	179	4,252	4,079
Glades	(D)	(D)	(D)	Santa Rosa	27	147	170
Gulf	3	4	2	Sarasota	197	960	1,149
Hamilton	(D)	(D)	(D)	Seminole	166	1,040	1,260
Hardee	85	1,173	836	Sumter	(D)	(D)	(D)
Hendry	46	1,272	1,154	Suwannee	8	48	59
Hernando	51	269	323	Taylor	(D)	(D)	(D)
Highlands	99	1,426	1,484	Union	(D)	(D)	(D)
Hillsborough	452	4,077	4,190	Volusia	178	749	756
Holmes	(D)	(D)	(D)	Wakulla	(D)	(D)	(D)
Indian River	174	2,506	3,016	Walton	9	77	79
Jackson	12	56	53	Washington	7	29	28
Jefferson	9	57	50	Statewide 1/	11	1,276	2,099

(D) Data withheld to avoid disclosure of information about individual firms.
1/ Reporting units without a fixed location within the state or of unknown county
location.
Note: For a list of three-digit code industries included see Table 9.27.

Source: State of Florida, Department of Labor and Employment Security, Bureau of
Labor Market Information, "Employment, Wages, and Contributions Report" (ES-202),
unpublished data.

Florida Statistical Abstract 1991

Table 9.18.　AGRICULTURAL PRODUCTION AND SERVICES:　AVERAGE MONTHLY EMPLOYMENT
COVERED BY UNEMPLOYMENT COMPENSATION LAW IN THE STATE AND COUNTIES
OF FLORIDA, 1990

	Specified agricultural crop production			Specified agricultural services		
County	Vegetables and melons (SIC 016)	Fruits and tree nuts (SIC 017)	Horti-cultural spe-cialties (SIC 018)	Crop services (SIC 072)	Farm labor and management services (SIC 076)	Landscape and horti-cultural services (SIC 078)
Florida	23,045	12,137	23,042	9,176	24,873	26,466
Alachua	(D)	(D)	60	(D)	(D)	316
Baker	(D)	(D)	(D)	0	0	(D)
Bay	0	0	(D)	0	0	39
Bradford	0	0	0	0	0	(D)
Brevard	0	(D)	141	69	265	553
Broward	166	31	528	50	(D)	2,669
Calhoun	0	0	(D)	0	0	(D)
Charlotte	(D)	(D)	(D)	0	(D)	172
Citrus	0	0	(D)	(D)	(D)	87
Clay	0	0	(D)	(D)	0	179
Collier	6,524	268	652	869	2,782	714
Columbia	0	0	(D)	0	(D)	30
Dade	1,728	282	3,440	1,409	1,865	2,281
De Soto	(D)	292	91	123	738	143
Dixie	0	0	(D)	0	0	(D)
Duval	0	0	200	(D)	0	1,377
Escambia	0	0	895	0	0	246
Flagler	52	0	0	0	(D)	67
Franklin	0	0	0	0	0	0
Gadsden	528	0	895	(D)	(D)	(D)
Gilchrist	(D)	0	0	(D)	0	(D)
Glades	0	0	(D)	(D)	(D)	(D)
Gulf	0	(D)	0	0	0	(D)
Hamilton	(D)	0	0	(D)	0	0
Hardee	138	575	215	220	928	17
Hendry	820	(D)	108	192	1,060	(D)
Hernando	0	(D)	(D)	(D)	(D)	195
Highlands	(D)	728	512	(D)	1,040	152
Hillsborough	2,453	2,700	1,510	664	761	1,754
Holmes	(D)	0	0	0	0	(D)
Indian River	(D)	912	17	853	1,135	460
Jackson	(D)	0	(D)	(D)	0	20
Jefferson	(D)	(D)	122	0	0	(D)
Lafayette	0	0	0	0	(D)	(D)
Lake	134	237	801	264	748	243
Lee	830	(D)	1,048	190	357	863
Leon	(D)	0	(D)	0	0	199

See footnotes at end of table.　　　　　　　　　　　　　Continued . . .

Florida Statistical Abstract 1991

Table 9.18. AGRICULTURAL PRODUCTION AND SERVICES: AVERAGE MONTHLY EMPLOYMENT
COVERED BY UNEMPLOYMENT COMPENSATION LAW IN THE STATE AND COUNTIES
OF FLORIDA, 1990 (Continued)

	Specified agricultural crop production			Specified agricultural services		
County	Vegetables and melons (SIC 016)	Fruits and tree nuts (SIC 017)	Horticultural specialties (SIC 018)	Crop services (SIC 072)	Farm labor and management services (SIC 076)	Landscape and horticultural services (SIC 078)
Levy	(D)	0	(D)	(D)	0	49
Liberty	0	0	(D)	(D)	0	0
Madison	0	(D)	(D)	0	0	(D)
Manatee	2,523	504	863	619	340	423
Marion	35	(D)	135	(D)	(D)	307
Martin	(D)	361	345	(D)	(D)	496
Monroe	0	0	(D)	0	0	57
Nassau	0	0	0	0	0	94
Okaloosa	0	(D)	(D)	0	0	59
Okeechobee	0	(D)	96	(D)	(D)	22
Orange	732	526	2,781	236	741	2,707
Osceola	0	93	236	0	(D)	113
Palm Beach	4,952	192	2,909	290	2,282	3,656
Pasco	189	596	161	(D)	1,336	313
Pinellas	(D)	(D)	212	(D)	(D)	1,605
Polk	(D)	1,720	684	947	4,331	406
Putnam	(D)	(D)	407	0	118	18
St. Johns	69	0	(D)	(D)	129	75
St. Lucie	142	717	(D)	1,025	2,910	236
Santa Rosa	0	0	(D)	(D)	0	74
Sarasota	(D)	64	169	(D)	(D)	710
Seminole	(D)	(D)	215	(D)	(D)	760
Sumter	47	0	(D)	(D)	(D)	28
Suwannee	(D)	0	74	(D)	0	(D)
Taylor	0	0	(D)	0	0	(D)
Union	0	0	0	0	0	(D)
Volusia	(D)	28	2,274	(D)	(D)	387
Wakulla	0	0	0	0	(D)	(D)
Walton	(D)	0	0	0	0	68
Washington	0	0	(D)	0	0	25
Statewide 1/	(D)	0	0	(D)	0	(D)

(D) Data withheld to avoid disclosure of information about individual firms.
1/ Reporting units without a fixed location within the state or of unknown county
location.
Note: See Table 9.15 for total crop productions (SIC 01) and Table 9.17 for
total agricultural services (SIC 07).

Source: State of Florida, Department of Labor and Employment Security, Bureau of
Labor Market Information, "Employment, Wages, and Contributions Report" (ES-202),
unpublished data.

Table 9.19. FARM INCOME: GOVERNMENT PAYMENTS BY PROGRAM IN FLORIDA, 1985 THROUGH
    1989

(in thousands of dollars)

Program	1985	1986	1987	1988	1989
Total	30,128	26,119	42,532	32,034	38,323
Conservation 1/	3,071	2,966	6,261	7,779	9,578
Feed grain program	812	3,875	8,602	7,951	4,546
Wheat program	1,307	1,744	1,695	1,787	499
Cotton program	2,231	2,801	3,003	2,379	38
Rice program	277	395	295	174	3,166
Miscellaneous programs 2/	22,430	14,338	22,676	11,964	20,496

1/ Includes amount paid under agriculture and conservation programs.
    2/ Includes Rural Clean Water Program, Clean Lakes Program, Animal Waste Manage-
ment Program, Forest Incentive Program, Water Bank Program, Milk Indemnity Program,
Dairy Termination Program, Emergency Feed Program, Extended Warehouse Storage
Program, Extended Farm Storage, Milk Diversion Program, Disaster Program Crops,
Disaster Program Noncrops, Warehouse Storage Deduction Program, Livestock Emergency
Assistance Program, Interest Penalty Payments Program, Disaster Program, and Loan
Deficiency.

Table 9.20. HOME CONSUMPTION: VALUE OF HOME AGRICULTURAL COMMODITY CONSUMPTION
    IN FLORIDA AND THE UNITED STATES, 1987 THROUGH 1989

(in thousands of dollars)

Item	Florida	United States
1987		
Total	7,191	837,312
Livestock and products	4,206	670,743
Crops	2,985	166,569
1988		
Total	7,836	794,178
Livestock and products	4,799	630,262
Crops	3,037	163,916
1989		
Total	5,207	645,972
Livestock and products	2,561	505,736
Crops	2,646	140,236

Note: Data are for value of farm products consumed directly in farm households
where produced. Data for earlier years are revised.

Source for Tables 9.19 and 9.20: U.S., Department of Agriculture, Economic
Research Service, *Economic Indicators of the Farm Sector: State Financial Summary,
1989.*

Florida Statistical Abstract 1991

Table 9.21.   FARM INCOME AND EXPENSES: FARM LABOR AND PROPRIETORS' INCOME
    IN FLORIDA, 1986 THROUGH 1989

(rounded to thousands of dollars)

Item	1986	1987	1988	1989
Cash receipts from marketing	4,818,960	5,359,848	5,884,143	6,261,096
Total livestock and products	1,093,525	1,174,290	1,218,315	1,300,463
Total crops	3,725,435	4,185,558	4,665,828	4,960,633
Other income	320,262	343,077	321,944	321,749
Government payments	26,119	42,532	32,034	38,322
Imputed income and rent received	294,143	300,545	289,910	283,427
Production expenses	3,205,321	3,432,003	3,518,612	3,828,265
Feed purchased	283,345	276,805	342,091	379,507
Livestock purchased	124,896	153,872	152,143	148,898
Seed purchased	51,462	62,023	62,303	76,451
Fertilizer and lime purchased	339,180	350,645	357,500	445,324
Petroleum products purchased	82,019	78,209	77,408	85,425
Hired farm labor excluding contract labor	794,885	863,655	897,659	970,172
All other production expenses 1/	1,529,534	1,646,794	1,629,508	1,722,488
Value of inventory change	1,165	-68,399	7,374	-28,682
Livestock	6,039	-68,440	1,886	-29,173
Crops	-4,874	0	5,488	491
Derivation of farm labor and proprietors' income:				
Total cash receipts and other income	5,139,222	5,702,925	6,206,087	6,582,845
Less: Total production expenses	3,205,321	3,432,003	3,518,612	3,828,265
Realized net income	1,933,901	2,270,922	2,687,475	2,754,580
Plus: Value of inventory change	1,165	-68,399	7,374	-28,682
Total net income including corporate farms	1,935,066	2,202,523	2,694,849	2,725,898
Less: Corporate farms	166,640	544,219	636,258	803,751
Total net farm proprietors' income	1,768,411	1,658,318	2,058,602	1,922,134
Plus: Farm wages and perquisites	446,846	471,987	473,221	478,329
Plus: Farm other labor income	46,395	46,636	47,095	48,613
Total farm labor and proprietors' income	2,261,652	2,176,941	2,578,918	2,449,076

1/ Includes repair and operation of capital items; depreciation, interest, rent
and taxes; and other miscellaneous expenses.
    Note: Data for 1986 through 1988 are revised.   Detail may not add to total
because of rounding.

    Source: U.S., Department of Commerce, Bureau of Economic Analysis, unpublished
data.

Florida Statistical Abstract 1991

Table 9.22. FARM INCOME AND EXPENSES: DERIVATION OF FARM LABOR AND PROPRIETORS' INCOME IN THE STATE AND COUNTIES OF FLORIDA, 1988 AND 1989

(rounded to thousands of dollars)

1988

County	Cash receipts from marketings	Plus other income 1/	Less production expenses	Plus value of inventory change	Total net farm income	Less corporate farm income	Total net farm proprietors' income	Plus farm wages	Plus farm other labor income	Total farm labor and proprietors' income
Florida	5,884,143	321,944	3,518,612	7,374	2,694,849	636,258	2,058,602	473,221	47,095	2,578,918
Alachua	43,170	6,252	33,477	217	16,162	794	15,368	3,173	309	18,850
Baker	22,621	1,590	15,713	A/	8,521	595	7,926	1,764	179	9,869
Bay	1,944	385	1,679	A/	660	184	476	187	A/	682
Bradford	18,210	1,607	13,524	64	6,357	198	6,159	456	A/	6,659
Brevard	33,782	2,504	15,439	50	20,897	2,825	18,072	3,046	286	21,404
Broward	76,746	6,036	46,255	A/	36,572	9,366	27,206	8,082	788	36,076
Calhoun	7,976	1,417	7,494	369	2,268	189	2,079	448	A/	2,572
Charlotte	22,635	2,547	12,642	54	12,594	3,160	9,434	2,216	221	11,871
Citrus	8,032	1,787	6,358	A/	3,498	442	3,056	420	A/	3,518
Clay	28,520	2,729	24,661	102	6,690	1,861	4,829	2,294	226	7,349
Collier	127,055	3,987	71,771	A/	59,309	4,351	54,958	9,166	930	65,054
Columbia	16,752	3,682	14,790	A/	5,610	535	5,075	947	91	6,113
Dade	340,071	9,111	196,648	54	152,588	26,790	125,799	28,701	2,897	157,397
De Soto	60,201	4,865	54,814	124	10,376	741	9,635	5,261	508	15,404
Dixie	2,398	1,188	1,705	A/	1,898	714	1,184	195	A/	1,398
Duval	39,717	2,747	30,507	A/	11,998	1,854	10,144	3,407	336	13,887
Escambia	13,189	3,520	14,122	55	2,642	133	2,509	774	80	3,363
Flagler	17,173	1,547	11,532	A/	7,232	51	7,181	1,030	104	8,315
Franklin	0	0	0	0	0	0	0	0	0	0
Gadsden	50,427	2,812	33,668	A/	19,612	1,100	18,512	6,162	608	25,282
Gilchrist	36,263	2,192	24,328	169	14,296	1,878	12,418	1,522	151	14,091

See footnotes at end of table.

Continued . . .

Table 9.22. FARM INCOME AND EXPENSES: DERIVATION OF FARM LABOR AND PROPRIETORS' INCOME IN THE STATE AND COUNTIES OF FLORIDA, 1988 AND 1989 (Continued)

(rounded to thousands of dollars)

County	Cash receipts from marketings	Plus other income 1/	Less production expenses	Plus value of inventory change	Total net farm income	Less corporate farm income	Total net farm proprietors' income	Plus farm wages	Plus farm other labor income	Total farm labor and proprietors' income
					1988 (Continued)					
Glades	44,631	5,166	29,206	114	20,705	9,035	11,670	3,948	391	16,009
Gulf	0	0	0	0	0	0	0	0	0	0
Hamilton	11,649	2,859	12,318	A/	2,189	A/	2,151	602	59	2,812
Hardee	105,679	9,522	61,280	209	54,130	10,024	44,106	7,667	746	52,519
Hendry	206,240	7,740	102,159	222	112,043	35,560	76,483	9,315	924	86,722
Hernando	38,990	2,767	27,656	95	14,196	2,140	12,056	2,052	198	14,306
Highlands	152,833	8,217	78,140	261	83,171	17,740	65,431	9,826	973	76,230
Hillsborough	355,055	12,355	184,885	250	182,775	35,580	147,196	28,768	2,928	178,892
Holmes	26,700	3,103	22,600	210	7,413	101	7,312	978	102	8,392
Indian River	143,876	7,440	95,457	A/	55,901	7,860	48,041	6,451	621	55,113
Jackson	51,639	8,289	49,539	63	10,452	296	10,156	2,462	251	12,869
Jefferson	29,171	3,791	24,277	-58	8,627	357	8,270	2,834	283	11,387
Lafayette	42,524	1,843	28,274	152	16,245	1,218	15,027	1,071	110	16,208
Lake	376,276	13,360	157,838	139	231,937	59,789	172,149	27,158	2,602	201,909
Lee	69,004	3,624	34,381	A/	38,268	2,406	35,862	12,020	1,229	49,111
Leon	5,545	2,814	6,843	A/	1,486	125	1,361	735	73	2,169
Levy	17,693	3,083	11,180	85	9,681	503	9,178	925	93	10,196
Liberty	555	331	764	A/	131	0	131	85	A/	224
Madison	30,598	4,625	32,148	99	3,174	115	3,059	2,609	260	5,928
Manatee	219,122	7,121	116,900	186	109,529	25,457	84,072	15,132	1,530	100,734
Marion	114,488	11,204	106,279	290	19,703	2,574	17,129	11,982	1,181	30,292
Martin	147,692	7,155	66,937	156	88,066	17,746	70,320	9,869	977	81,166

See footnotes at end of table.

Continued . . .

Table 9.22. FARM INCOME AND EXPENSES: DERIVATION OF FARM LABOR AND PROPRIETORS' INCOME IN THE STATE AND COUNTIES OF FLORIDA, 1988 AND 1989 (Continued)

(rounded to thousands of dollars)

County	Cash receipts from marketings	Plus other income 1/	Less production expenses	Plus value of inventory change	Total net farm income	Less corporate farm income	Total net farm proprietors' income	Plus farm wages	Plus farm other labor income	Total farm labor and proprietors' income
				1988 (Continued)						
Monroe	0	0	0	0	0	0	0	0	0	0
Nassau	24,757	2,343	24,932	55	2,223	273	1,950	1,200	122	3,272
Okaloosa	8,200	2,235	9,598	194	1,031	66	965	433	A/	1,439
Okeechobee	118,512	5,598	102,628	719	22,201	6,116	16,085	9,802	961	26,848
Orange	377,235	10,031	194,317	90	193,039	38,806	154,234	36,691	3,642	194,567
Osceola	66,182	10,102	42,276	321	34,329	12,802	21,527	5,380	538	27,445
Palm Beach	961,818	20,036	608,367	58	373,545	183,023	190,528	111,696	11,296	313,520
Pasco	121,394	9,430	78,999	166	51,991	11,012	40,979	5,901	550	47,430
Pinellas	19,858	1,236	7,353	A/	13,742	1,803	11,939	2,093	197	14,229
Polk	431,708	21,941	209,457	253	244,445	45,813	198,633	22,966	2,204	223,803
Putnam	31,076	4,203	18,966	106	16,419	1,047	15,372	2,710	270	18,352
St. Johns	63,833	1,891	35,805	204	30,123	5,428	24,695	3,422	344	28,461
St. Lucie	179,422	8,295	84,468	90	103,339	33,728	69,611	11,064	1,088	81,763
Santa Rosa	21,519	4,345	22,275	240	3,829	138	3,691	999	106	4,796
Sarasota	22,423	3,842	12,701	77	13,641	2,075	11,566	1,960	186	13,712
Seminole	37,930	1,995	20,139	A/	19,807	2,495	17,312	3,817	388	21,517
Sumter	34,261	3,475	23,896	191	14,031	985	13,046	2,118	207	15,371
Suwannee	54,993	6,781	49,779	107	12,102	248	11,854	2,951	289	15,094
Taylor	2,487	828	2,117	A/	1,228	A/	1,220	212	A/	1,453
Union	10,103	2,995	7,945	50	5,174	59	5,115	267	A/	5,410
Volusia	104,597	5,358	50,167	69	59,857	3,317	56,540	9,861	1,006	67,407
Wakulla	1,787	425	1,422	A/	789	A/	745	81	A/	833
Walton	18,619	2,904	19,787	193	1,929	280	1,649	814	79	2,542
Washington	14,587	2,741	11,001	106	6,433	267	6,166	1,043	103	7,312

See footnotes at end of table.   Continued . . .

Table 9.22. FARM INCOME AND EXPENSES: DERIVATION OF FARM LABOR AND PROPRIETORS' INCOME IN THE STATE AND COUNTIES OF FLORIDA, 1988 AND 1989 (Continued)

(rounded to thousands of dollars)

1989

County	Cash receipts from marketings	Plus other income 1/	Less production expenses	Plus value of inventory change	Total net farm income	Less corporate farm income	Total net farm proprietors' income	Plus farm wages	Plus farm other labor income	Total farm labor and proprietors' income
Florida	6,261,096	321,749	3,828,265	-28,682	2,725,898	803,751	1,922,134	478,329	48,613	2,449,076
Alachua	47,940	7,417	36,607	-408	18,342	1,088	17,254	3,150	319	20,723
Baker	24,728	1,644	17,070	-121	9,181	773	8,408	1,796	185	10,389
Bay	1,969	358	1,814	A/	509	171	338	176	A/	533
Bradford	21,522	2,090	14,870	-144	8,598	324	8,274	441	A/	8,760
Brevard	32,956	2,426	17,100	-315	17,967	2,932	15,035	2,948	295	18,278
Broward	79,879	5,913	49,662	-335	35,795	11,065	24,730	7,944	813	33,487
Calhoun	8,368	1,355	8,325	-319	1,079	108	971	437	A/	1,454
Charlotte	22,862	2,582	13,841	-353	11,250	3,408	7,842	2,250	228	10,320
Citrus	8,566	1,739	6,930	-99	3,276	500	2,776	389	A/	3,209
Clay	30,481	2,713	26,297	-208	6,689	2,246	4,443	2,346	234	7,023
Collier	151,911	3,911	79,306	-372	76,144	6,743	69,401	9,426	959	79,786
Columbia	18,333	4,112	16,241	-147	6,057	697	5,360	917	94	6,371
Dade	377,787	8,861	213,640	-85	172,923	36,649	136,273	28,567	2,983	167,823
De Soto	60,481	4,759	57,909	-892	6,439	554	5,885	5,331	526	11,742
Dixie	2,666	1,325	1,851	-110	2,030	922	1,108	185	A/	1,312
Duval	42,414	2,684	33,011	-371	11,716	2,186	9,530	3,383	347	13,260
Escambia	13,466	3,089	15,595	-743	217	A/	204	782	83	1,069
Flagler	20,462	1,502	12,702	-80	9,182	79	9,103	1,052	107	10,262
Franklin	0	0	0	0	0	0	0	0	0	0
Gadsden	53,859	2,878	36,288	-144	20,305	1,375	18,930	6,375	628	25,933
Gilchrist	37,428	2,367	25,772	-452	13,571	2,153	11,418	1,531	156	13,105
Glades	48,605	5,094	31,641	-846	21,212	11,174	10,038	4,023	404	14,465

See footnotes at end of table.

Continued . . .

Table 9.22. FARM INCOME AND EXPENSES: DERIVATION OF FARM LABOR AND PROPRIETORS' INCOME IN THE STATE AND COUNTIES OF FLORIDA, 1988 AND 1989 (Continued)

(rounded to thousands of dollars)

1989 (Continued)

County	Cash receipts from marketings	Plus other income 1/	Less production expenses	Plus value of inventory change	Total net farm income	Less corporate farm income	Total net farm proprietors' income	Plus farm wages	Plus farm other labor income	Total farm labor and proprietors' income
Gulf	0	0	0	0	0	0	0	0	0	0
Hamilton	12,769	2,562	13,589	-74	1,668	A/	1,633	610	60	2,303
Hardee	104,338	7,717	67,457	-899	43,699	9,768	33,931	7,662	770	42,363
Hendry	214,523	7,640	112,790	-1,648	107,725	41,271	66,454	9,499	955	76,908
Hernando	40,672	2,667	29,623	-369	13,347	2,429	10,918	1,985	205	13,108
Highlands	149,994	8,091	85,417	-1,133	71,535	18,418	53,117	9,809	1,004	63,930
Hillsborough	378,716	13,077	200,891	-1,137	189,765	44,592	145,172	28,953	3,015	177,140
Holmes	30,644	3,562	25,034	-375	8,797	144	8,653	1,008	104	9,765
Indian River	138,254	7,279	98,988	-397	46,148	7,833	38,315	6,376	641	45,332
Jackson	57,451	7,763	54,907	-1,238	9,069	310	8,759	2,524	259	11,542
Jefferson	30,417	4,004	26,333	-205	7,883	394	7,489	2,895	292	10,676
Lafayette	48,475	1,514	30,970	-317	18,702	1,692	17,010	1,082	112	18,204
Lake	375,452	13,170	174,453	-312	213,857	66,547	147,309	27,278	2,694	177,281
Lee	74,943	3,563	37,372	-168	40,966	3,109	37,857	12,417	1,268	51,542
Leon	5,567	2,610	7,458	A/	671	68	603	703	75	1,381
Levy	19,711	3,368	12,333	-289	10,457	656	9,801	896	95	10,792
Liberty	559	296	800	A/	A/	0	A/	89	A/	130
Madison	33,836	4,486	35,397	-342	2,583	113	2,470	2,667	269	5,406
Manatee	245,876	7,099	127,378	-832	124,765	35,004	89,760	15,370	1,577	106,707
Marion	115,143	11,983	113,090	-491	13,545	2,136	11,409	11,942	1,218	24,569
Martin	147,658	6,990	73,425	-589	80,634	19,614	61,020	9,934	1,010	71,964
Monroe	0	0	0	0	0	0	0	0	0	0
Nassau	27,640	2,271	26,970	-209	2,732	405	2,327	1,207	126	3,660
Okaloosa	8,565	2,174	9,953	-198	588	A/	543	423	A/	1,008

See footnotes at end of table.

Continued . . .

Table 9.22. FARM INCOME AND EXPENSES: DERIVATION OF FARM LABOR AND PROPRIETORS' INCOME IN THE STATE AND COUNTIES OF FLORIDA, 1988 AND 1989 (Continued)

(rounded to thousands of dollars)

County	Cash receipts from marketings	Plus other income 1/	Less production expenses	Plus value of inventory change	Total net farm income	Less corporate farm income	Total net farm proprietors' income	Plus farm wages	Plus farm other labor income	Total farm labor and proprietors' income
					1989 (Continued)					
Okeechobee	125,460	5,706	110,576	-1,679	18,911	6,289	12,622	9,980	995	23,597
Orange	390,607	9,802	211,741	-218	188,450	45,730	142,719	37,207	3,762	183,688
Osceola	65,342	9,963	45,931	-1,381	27,993	12,602	15,391	5,406	555	21,352
Palm Beach	1,115,773	19,493	658,353	-466	476,447	281,789	194,651	115,247	11,666	321,564
Pasco	125,949	9,237	86,516	-686	47,984	12,268	35,716	5,637	569	41,922
Pinellas	19,690	1,201	8,036	A/	12,828	2,032	10,796	2,001	204	13,001
Polk	419,652	21,643	230,665	-1,379	209,251	47,340	161,910	22,566	2,277	186,753
Putnam	33,776	3,985	20,833	-116	16,812	1,294	15,518	2,692	279	18,489
St. Johns	75,514	1,914	39,362	159	38,225	8,315	29,910	3,485	355	33,750
St. Lucie	173,501	8,118	93,444	-659	87,516	34,480	53,036	11,160	1,124	65,320
Santa Rosa	23,132	5,148	24,696	-1,759	1,825	79	1,746	1,004	108	2,858
Sarasota	23,662	2,710	13,677	-472	12,223	2,245	9,978	1,906	193	12,077
Seminole	41,146	1,959	21,940	-89	21,076	3,204	17,872	3,793	399	22,064
Sumter	38,248	4,960	25,758	-669	16,781	1,422	15,359	2,105	213	17,677
Suwannee	62,480	7,682	54,708	-397	15,057	372	14,685	3,018	298	18,001
Taylor	2,725	817	2,307	-56	1,179	A/	1,170	207	A/	1,399
Union	11,635	3,650	8,668	-107	6,510	89	6,421	270	A/	6,721
Volusia	106,887	5,207	54,372	-235	57,487	3,846	53,641	9,912	1,036	64,589
Wakulla	1,917	392	1,538	A/	755	51	704	79	A/	790
Walton	20,915	2,837	21,749	-368	1,635	287	1,348	821	82	2,251
Washington	15,199	2,620	12,295	-222	5,302	265	5,037	1,055	106	6,198

A/ Less than $50,000.
1/ Includes government payments, imputed income, and rent received.
Note: Data for 1988 are revised. See also tables in Section 5.00.
Source: U.S., Department of Commerce, Bureau of Economic Analysis, unpublished data.

Table 9.25. FARM INCOME: ESTIMATED CASH RECEIPTS FROM FARM MARKETINGS BY SPECIFIED
  COMMODITY IN THE UNITED STATES AND LEADING STATES IN RANK ORDER, 1989

(in millions of dollars)

Commodity and state	Cash receipts	Commodity and state	Cash receipts	Commodity and state	Cash receipts
All commodities		**All livestock**		**All crops**	
United States	159,173	United States	83,724	United States	75,449
California	17,515	Texas	6,863	California	12,422
Texas	10,760	Nebraska	5,643	Florida	4,982
Iowa	9,119	Iowa	5,209	Illinois	4,458
Nebraska	8,521	California	5,093	Iowa	3,911
Illinois	6,710	Wisconsin	4,337	Texas	3,897
Minnesota	6,526	Kansas	4,245	Nebraska	2,878
Kansas	6,324	Minnesota	3,716	Minnesota	2,809
Florida	6,203	Arkansas	2,661	Indiana	2,502
Wisconsin	5,278	Colorado	2,649	Washington	2,438
North Carolina	4,551	Pennsylvania	2,595	Ohio	2,114
Greenhouse and nursery (7)		**Eggs (10)**		**Potatoes (13)**	
United States	7,295	United States	3,854	United States	2,288
California	1,586	California	402	Idaho	587
Florida	956	Georgia	286	Washington	299
Texas	477	Indiana	281	California	166
Pennsylvania	288	Pennsylvania	257	Wisconsin	154
Oregon	279	Arkansas	237	Maine	152
New York	262	Texas	223	Colorado	135
Michigan	254	North Carolina	222	Florida	128
New Jersey	233	Ohio	183	North Dakota	93
Oklahoma	224	Alabama	153	Oregon	90
North Carolina	214	Florida	122	Minnesota	88
Tomatoes (15)		**Oranges (16)**		**Peanuts (20)**	
United States	1,824	United States	1,814	United States	1,119
California	809	Florida	1,316	Georgia	494
Florida	741	California	472	Alabama	157
Ohio	45	Arizona	16	Texas	136
Virginia	41	Texas	10	North Carolina	111
South Carolina	25	**Sugarcane (23)**		Virginia	74
Pennsylvania	20	United States	884	Oklahoma	63
New York	19	Florida	433	Florida	59
Indiana	18	Hawaii	215	New Mexico	13
New Jersey	16	Louisiana	209	South Carolina	12
Michigan	16	Texas	27	Arizona	1

Note: Commodities listed here are among 25 leading commodities ranked by value
of farm marketings. The number after the commodity name indicates rank order in
cash receipts in the United States. Receipts include commodity credit corporation
loans. Greenhouse and nursery excludes mushrooms.

Source: U.S., Department of Agriculture, Economic Research Service, *Economic
Indicators of the Farm Sector: State Financial Summary, 1989.*

Florida Statistical Abstract 1991

Table 9.26. FARM INCOME: CASH RECEIPTS BY COMMODITY AND COMMODITY GROUP IN FLORIDA 1987 THROUGH 1989

Commodity	1987 A/ Cash receipts ($1,000)	1987 A/ Percentage of total	1988 A/ Cash receipts ($1,000)	1988 A/ Percentage of total	1989 B/ Cash receipts ($1,000)	1989 B/ Percentage of total
Cash receipts 1/	5,308,133	100.0	5,819,668	100.0	6,202,954	100.0
Crops	4,207,279	79.3	4,687,549	80.5	4,982,354	80.3
Citrus	1,312,791	24.7	1,819,366	31.3	1,730,289	27.9
Grapefruit	320,615	6.0	384,523	6.6	308,751	5.0
K-early citrus fruit	2,535	0.0	2,508	0.0	1,599	0.0
Lemons	4,632	0.1	4,500	0.1	4,240	0.1
Limes	23,580	0.4	20,778	0.4	18,964	0.3
Oranges	882,129	16.6	1,294,173	22.2	1,291,071	20.8
Tangelos	28,115	0.5	35,203	0.6	29,870	0.5
Tangerines	31,099	0.6	51,632	0.9	50,512	0.8
Temples	20,086	0.4	26,049	0.4	25,282	0.4
Other fruits and nuts	105,522	2.0	113,360	1.9	120,354	1.9
Avocados	9,341	0.2	12,677	0.2	13,386	0.2
Mangos	6,600	0.1	5,250	0.1	5,200	0.1
Pecans	3,744	0.1	3,036	0.1	2,270	0.0
Strawberries	67,062	1.3	73,875	1.3	92,188	1.5
Other	18,775	0.4	18,522	0.3	7,310	0.1
Vegetables and melons	1,286,872	24.2	1,185,863	20.4	1,545,012	24.9
Cabbage	26,202	0.5	29,559	0.5	30,433	0.5
Carrots	11,502	0.2	13,486	0.2	15,040	0.2
Celery	43,344	0.8	49,848	0.9	52,456	0.8
Cucumbers	56,368	1.1	65,578	1.1	67,060	1.1
Eggplant	9,634	0.2	10,253	0.2	11,413	0.2
Escarole	12,123	0.2	12,619	0.2	9,607	0.2
Green peppers	137,033	2.6	93,044	1.6	110,181	1.8
Lettuce	37,284	0.7	40,600	0.7	36,155	0.6
Potatoes	106,910	2.0	44,916	0.8	127,658	2.1
Radishes	17,605	0.3	18,685	0.3	19,987	0.3
Snap beans	49,610	0.9	54,300	0.9	54,567	0.9
Squash	37,023	0.7	40,144	0.7	35,958	0.6
Sweet corn	65,520	1.2	72,629	1.2	88,201	1.4
Tomatoes	490,341	9.2	476,036	8.2	740,964	11.9
Watermelons	69,774	1.3	62,556	1.1	45,050	0.7
Other	116,599	2.2	101,610	1.7	100,282	1.6
Field crops	532,891	10.0	584,730	10.0	599,749	9.7
Corn	12,894	0.2	9,628	0.2	11,376	0.2
Cotton	11,895	0.2	9,956	0.2	10,692	0.2
Hay	5,356	0.1	4,372	0.1	4,299	0.1
Peanuts	58,266	1.1	61,493	1.1	59,488	1.0
Soybeans	13,362	0.3	21,224	0.4	18,597	0.3
Sugarcane	382,890	7.2	419,697	7.2	432,955	7.0
Tobacco	22,800	0.4	27,673	0.5	30,327	0.5
Wheat	3,833	0.1	7,263	0.1	6,494	0.1
Other	21,595	0.4	23,424	0.4	25,521	0.4
Foliage and floriculture	521,039	9.8	504,794	8.7	500,547	8.1
Other crops and products	448,164	8.4	479,436	8.2	486,403	7.8
Livestock and products	1,100,854	20.7	1,132,119	19.5	1,220,600	19.7
Milk	343,200	6.5	355,680	6.1	387,960	6.3
Cattle and calves	387,883	7.3	372,431	6.4	376,744	6.1

See footnotes at end of table. Continued . . .

Florida Statistical Abstract 1991

Table 9.26. FARM INCOME: CASH RECEIPTS BY COMMODITY AND COMMODITY GROUP IN FLORIDA 1987 THROUGH 1989 (Continued)

Commodity	1987 A/ Cash receipts ($1,000)	1987 A/ Per-cent-age of total	1988 A/ Cash receipts ($1,000)	1988 A/ Per-cent-age of total	1989 B/ Cash receipts ($1,000)	1989 B/ Per-cent-age of total
Livestock and products (Cont.)						
Poultry and eggs	223,811	4.2	254,036	4.4	307,443	5.0
Broilers	127,099	2.4	156,585	2.7	181,636	2.9
Eggs	94,160	1.8	94,461	1.6	121,869	2.0
Other	2,552	0.0	2,990	0.1	3,938	0.1
Catfish	1,575	0.0	1,439	0.0	1,901	0.0
Hogs	23,550	0.4	19,024	0.3	19,010	0.3
Honey	9,290	0.2	12,852	0.2	6,794	0.1
Other	111,545	2.1	116,657	2.0	120,748	2.0

A/ Revised. B/ Preliminary.

1/ Farm marketings. Includes additional receipts not published.

Source: State of Florida, Department of Agriculture, Florida Agricultural Statistics Service, *Florida Agriculture: Cash Receipts from Farming*, release of September 7, 1990.

Table 9.27. AGRICULTURAL PRODUCTION AND SERVICES: AVERAGE MONTHLY REPORTING UNITS EMPLOYMENT, AND PAYROLL COVERED BY UNEMPLOYMENT COMPENSATION LAW BY INDUSTRY IN FLORIDA, 1990

SIC code	Industry	Number of reporting units	Number of employees	Payroll ($1,000)
01	Agricultural production--crops	2,437	63,676	68,223
011	Cash grains	16	214	244
013	Field crops, except cash grains	164	4,843	9,370
016	Vegetables and melons	428	23,045	17,266
017	Fruits and tree nuts	694	12,128	14,013
018	Horticultural specialities	1,121	23,036	26,799
019	General farms, primarily crop	12	409	531
02	Agricultural production--livestock	586	7,456	9,787
021	Livestock, except dairy, and poultry	200	1,526	2,204
024	Dairy farms	178	3,253	4,377
025	Poultry and eggs	34	1,101	1,304
027	Animal specialties	171	1,546	1,870
029	General farms, primarily animal	3	29	33
07	Agricultural services	7,579	70,719	75,233
071	Soil preparation services	30	202	361
072	Crop services	330	9,164	10,337
074	Veterinary services	1,193	8,083	10,761
075	Animal services, except veterinary	540	1,952	1,983
076	Farm labor and management services	883	24,856	19,795
078	Landscape and horticultural services	4,601	26,460	31,996

Note: Totals on county employment tables may not match totals in this table due to rounding.

Source: State of Florida, Department of Labor and Employment Security, Bureau of Labor Market Information, "Employment, Wages, and Contributions Report" (ES-202), unpublished data.

Florida Statistical Abstract 1991

Table 9.29. FARMS: NUMBER, ACREAGE, AND AGRICULTURAL STABILIZATION AND
CONSERVATION SERVICE (ASCS) PROGRAM PAYMENTS IN THE STATE AND
COUNTIES OF FLORIDA, 1990

			Acreage				ASCS
				Farmland			program
					Pasture-		pay-
	Num-				land and		ments 6/
	ber of			Crop-	range-	Forest-	
County	farms 1/	Total 2/	Total 3/	land 4/	land 5/	land	($1,000)
Florida	62,662	34,660,480	24,300,104	6,875,105	4,551,334	12,869,518	6,395,011
Alachua	2,134	577,280	519,000	227,000	100,000	192,000	157,186
Baker	461	374,400	301,528	13,115	1,506	286,907	28,893
Bay	166	485,120	410,490	9,154	7,200	394,136	30,085
Bradford	500	187,520	173,000	20,000	15,000	138,000	17,753
Brevard	385	636,800	478,050	114,050	284,000	80,000	12,707
Broward	1,154	775,040	28,670	25,370	2,000	1,300	4,100
Calhoun	924	363,520	343,710	48,810	4,900	290,000	116,768
Charlotte	404	441,600	268,170	93,420	104,500	70,250	100,098
Citrus	335	402,560	178,310	31,067	3,163	144,080	27,861
Clay	200	378,880	368,000	40,000	150,000	178,000	7,350
Collier	124	1,276,160	576,400	145,000	170,000	261,400	0
Columbia	1,700	510,080	534,065	104,542	65,000	364,523	114,179
Dade	3,398	1,251,200	85,306	78,706	5,300	1,300	134,023
De Soto	878	407,040	354,000	259,000	55,000	40,000	47,550
Dixie	327	448,640	278,725	10,531	88,244	180,000	30,284
Duval	300	496,640	301,900	18,900	5,000	278,000	23,117
Escambia	1,117	423,040	308,207	62,091	0	246,116	76,781
Flagler	215	314,240	310,100	26,600	24,500	250,000	51,923
Franklin	25	348,800	310,000	700	4,300	305,000	1,198
Gadsden	1,283	331,520	261,800	56,800	5,000	200,000	135,611
Gilchrist	1,250	226,560	216,560	61,265	17,150	138,145	138,474
Glades	300	488,320	443,500	210,000	105,000	128,500	36,945
Gulf	76	357,760	363,000	30,000	5,000	328,000	9,202
Hamilton	797	330,880	333,219	73,219	4,000	256,000	152,470
Hardee	1,500	407,680	326,302	172,712	101,590	52,000	337,206
Hendry	380	744,320	734,000	370,000	189,000	175,000	58,896
Hernando	431	305,280	216,299	23,000	23,000	170,299	25,638
Highlands	691	658,560	600,549	225,051	269,243	106,255	141,030
Hillsborough	4,446	673,920	530,000	150,000	250,000	130,000	240,409
Holmes	1,466	312,320	343,300	85,000	42,000	216,300	249,448
Indian River	660	318,080	210,161	118,889	41,657	49,613	82,313
Jackson	3,350	602,880	576,000	251,000	15,000	310,000	420,911
Jefferson	983	389,760	346,072	69,182	18,000	258,890	176,484
Lafayette	858	348,800	337,868	50,315	18,000	269,553	99,254
Lake	1,486	610,560	515,245	187,537	54,708	273,000	133,809
Lee	451	513,920	244,484	65,311	71,173	108,000	41,505
Leon	670	432,640	304,350	81,350	34,000	189,000	63,927
Levy	1,200	704,000	646,185	126,185	65,000	455,000	140,614
Liberty	377	535,680	268,375	9,000	2,375	257,000	9,322
Madison	1,690	454,400	417,961	107,584	33,000	277,377	187,233

See footnotes at end of table.   Continued . . .

Florida Statistical Abstract 1991

Table 9.29. FARMS: NUMBER, ACREAGE, AND AGRICULTURAL STABILIZATION AND
CONSERVATION SERVICE (ASCS) PROGRAM PAYMENTS IN THE STATE AND
COUNTIES OF FLORIDA, 1990 (Continued)

			Acreage			ASCS
				Farmland		program
					Pasture-	pay-
	Num-			Crop-	land and	Forest-	ments 6/
	ber of				range-		
County	farms 1/	Total 2/	Total 3/	land 4/	land 5/	land	($1,000)
Manatee	766	478,080	329,388	94,959	159,268	75,161	73,298
Marion	1,350	1,030,400	575,000	145,000	155,000	275,000	103,467
Martin	316	355,200	278,000	105,000	153,000	20,000	17,167
Monroe	0	661,760	0	0	0	0	0
Nassau	475	415,360	351,800	13,000	800	338,000	67,367
Okaloosa	1,035	599,040	208,069	79,569	30,000	98,500	107,579
Okeechobee	350	493,440	465,500	242,000	158,500	65,000	305,620
Orange	1,211	582,400	323,984	78,984	45,000	200,000	46,236
Osceola	557	864,000	802,100	297,500	311,000	193,600	38,599
Palm Beach	715	1,275,520	569,135	523,635	45,000	500	15,933
Pasco	1,011	472,320	324,755	97,950	76,350	150,455	61,357
Pinellas	380	179,200	47,000	14,000	18,000	15,000	3,500
Polk	3,518	1,166,720	851,600	255,600	300,000	296,000	202,430
Putnam	687	469,120	330,670	45,670	35,000	250,000	145,062
St. Johns	425	394,880	340,000	40,000	30,000	270,000	154,107
St. Lucie	800	371,840	294,158	225,158	30,000	39,000	150,642
Santa Rosa	1,261	655,360	550,080	74,618	250	475,212	174,037
Sarasota	154	366,720	166,766	13,492	111,157	42,117	9,326
Seminole	390	190,720	116,200	20,200	32,000	64,000	26,732
Sumter	796	359,040	595,000	190,000	60,000	345,000	66,574
Suwannee	2,510	441,600	441,600	211,188	5,000	225,412	210,991
Taylor	230	677,120	296,800	36,800	200,000	60,000	41,499
Union	620	157,440	149,932	35,987	4,500	109,445	70,806
Volusia	920	712,320	529,360	27,360	126,000	376,000	42,505
Wakulla	281	384,640	160,472	12,300	8,000	140,172	74,416
Walton	1,533	682,240	505,222	93,222	4,000	408,000	198,411
Washington	1,279	377,600	334,652	50,457	0	289,000	124,795

1/ The Agricultural Stabilization and Conservation Service defines a farm as a
place producing agricultural commodities for commercial sale. The number of farms
of record is estimated in cooperation with county agents.
2/ Data from 1980 Census.
3/ Does not include public lands, urban areas, large bodies of water, highways,
etc.
4/ Includes established and improved pasture.
5/ Native grasses. Excludes established and improved pasture.
6/ Includes program payments and loans.

Source: U.S., Department of Agriculture, Agricultural Stabilization and Conservation Service, unpublished data.

Florida Statistical Abstract 1991

Table 9.32. AGRICULTURAL LOANS: AMOUNT OUTSTANDING OF REAL ESTATE AND PERSONAL
     AND COLLATERAL LOANS OF ALL OPERATING BANKS IN FLORIDA AND THE UNITED STATES
     DECEMBER 31, 1987, 1988, AND 1989

(in thousands of dollars)

Item	1987	1988	1989 A/
Florida	803,314	903,720	936,882
Farm real estate loans	489,799	578,720	681,157
Non-real estate farm loans	313,515	325,010	255,725
United States	43,496,001	45,215,355	47,428,575
Farm real estate loans	14,455,162	15,416,700	16,646,179
Non-real estate farm loans	29,040,839	29,798,655	30,782,396

A/ Preliminary.
  Note: Includes operator households. Includes loans of national and commercial
mutual savings, stock savings, and private banks. Loans are classified according to
location of bank and, therefore, are not strictly comparable with data for other
lenders which are classified according to location of borrower.

Table 9.33. AGRICULTURAL LOANS: FARM REAL ESTATE DEBT OUTSTANDING BY LENDER
     IN FLORIDA AND THE UNITED STATES, DECEMBER 31, 1988 AND 1989

(in thousands of dollars)

Lender group	Florida		United States	
	1988	1989	1988	1989
Total	2,650,370	2,740,778	82,952,535	80,476,478
Federal land banks 1/	913,021	822,599	30,326,708	28,501,000
Life insurance companies 2/	674,900	787,000	9,581,700	9,597,900
Farmers Home Administration 3/	129,564	115,593	9,606,807	8,719,822
All banks	578,720	681,157	15,416,700	16,646,179
Individuals and others 4/	354,165	334,429	18,020,620	17,011,577

  1/ Includes mortgages in process of foreclosure.
  2/ Includes U.S. legal reserve companies only. Includes regular mortgages and
purchase-money mortgages.
  3/ Includes farm ownership loans, soil and water loans to individuals, rural and
labor housing loans on farms and association loans for grazing, and for Indian tribe
land acquisition.
  4/ Estimated by Economic Research System, U.S. Department of Agriculture.
  Note: Some 1988 data are revised. 1989 data are preliminary.

  Source for Tables 9.32 and 9.33: U.S., Department of Agriculture, *Agricultural
Statistics, 1990*.

Florida Statistical Abstract 1991

Table 9.34.   FARMS: SPECIFIED CHARACTERISTICS OF FARMS IN FLORIDA, 1982 AND 1987

Item	All farms			Farms with sales of $10,000 or more		
	1982	1987	Per-cent-age change	1982	1987	Per-cent-age change
Number of farms	36,352	36,556	0.6	14,754	14,667	-0.6
By size						
1 to 9 acres	6,790	7,300	7.5	1,628	1,968	20.9
10 to 49 acres	12,981	13,346	2.8	3,556	3,919	10.2
50 to 179 acres	8,711	8,379	-3.8	3,662	3,274	-10.6
180 to 499 acres	4,409	4,255	-3.5	2,944	2,706	-8.1
500 to 999 acres	1,660	1,598	-3.7	1,354	1,279	-5.5
1,000 to 1,999 acres	828	789	-4.7	729	708	-2.9
2,000 acres or more	973	889	-8.6	881	813	-7.7
With irrigated land	10,550	11,981	13.6	6,952	7,788	12.0
By SIC code						
Cash grains (011)	1,706	635	-62.8	888	236	-73.4
Field crops, except cash grains (013)	1,852	2,218	19.8	1,073	1,203	12.1
Vegetables and melons (016)	1,692	1,511	-10.7	1,091	1,057	-3.1
Fruits and tree nuts (017)	9,283	8,388	-9.6	4,272	4,007	-6.2
Horticultural spe-cialities (018)	3,560	4,096	15.1	2,244	2,849	27.0
General farms, pri-marily crop (019)	548	434	-20.8	380	219	-42.4
Livestock, except dairy, poultry and animal spe-cialities (021)	13,937	14,738	5.7	2,932	3,296	12.4
Dairy farms (024)	404	358	-11.4	394	358	-9.1
Poultry and eggs (025)	964	746	-22.6	811	629	-22.4
Animal specialities (027)	2,159	3,170	46.8	650	798	22.8
General farms, pri-marily livestock (029)	247	234	-5.3	19	15	-21.1
Selected farm product expenses ($1,000)						
Feed for livestock and poultry	349,630	336,690	-3.7	333,838	322,471	-3.4
Commercial fertilizer	217,332	209,617	-3.5	203,755	198,090	-2.8
Agricultural chemicals	165,343	227,063	37.3	160,214	218,474	36.4
Petroleum products	135,063	104,591	-22.6	161,508	96,529	40.2
Hired farm labor	480,444	721,540	50.2	473,066	716,905	51.5

See footnotes at end of table.   Continued . . .

Table 9.34. FARMS: SPECIFIED CHARACTERISTICS OF FARMS IN FLORIDA, 1982 AND 1987
  (Continued)

Item	All farms			Farms with sales of $10,000 or more		
	1982	1987	Per- cent- age change	1982	1987	Per- cent- age change
Livestock/poultry in- ventory ($1,000)						
Cattle and calves						
Farms	17,822	17,321	-2.8	5,891	5,403	-8.3
Number	2,178,552	1,879,124	-13.7	1,853,035	1,609,538	-13.1
Milk cows						
Farms	1,385	1,073	-22.5	594	503	-15.3
Number	194,550	176,993	-9.0	192,598	175,647	-8.8
Chickens 1/						
Farms	2,891	2,275	-21.3	751	(NA)	(NA)
Number	15,374,588	12,964,760	-15.7	15,267,799	(NA)	(NA)
Crops harvested 2/						
Corn						
Farms	2,987	2,088	-30.1	1,598	1,079	-32.5
Acres	190,254	95,874	-49.6	167,295	82,973	-50.4
Soybeans						
Farms	2,091	708	-66.1	1,590	575	-63.8
Acres	334,401	89,938	-73.1	318,386	86,038	-73.0
Sugarcane						
Farms	123	138	12.2	118	(NA)	(NA)
Acres	343,680	403,014	17.3	343,639	(NA)	(NA)
Hay						
Farms	5,560	5,643	1.5	2,711	2,589	-4.5
Acres	281,747	280,639	-0.4	228,652	219,396	-4.0
Vegetables						
Farms	2,455	2,053	-16.4	1,646	1,456	-11.5
Acres	283,780	311,659	9.8	279,290	308,960	10.6
Orchards						
Farms	11,214	9,965	-11.1	5,078	4,669	-8.1
Acres	938,527	762,068	-18.8	865,428	693,903	-19.8

SIC Standard Industrial Classification. See Glossary.
  (NA) Not available.
  1/ Three months old or older.
  2/ Corn for grain or seed; soybeans for beans; sugarcane for sugar; hay includes
alfalfa, and other tame, small grain, wild, grass silage, green chop, etc.;
vegetables harvested for sale; vegetable acreage is counted only once even when it
is replanted.

Source: U.S., Department of Commerce, Bureau of the Census, *1987 Census of Agriculture: State and County Data, Florida.* AC87-A-9.

Florida Statistical Abstract 1991

Table 9.35. FARMS: NUMBER, LAND IN FARMS, AND VALUE OF LAND AND BUILDINGS IN THE
  STATE AND COUNTIES OF FLORIDA, 1982 AND 1987

County	Number of farms 1982	Number of farms 1987	Land in farms (acres) Total 1982	Land in farms (acres) Total 1987	Average size of farm 1982	Average size of farm 1987	Average value of land and buildings per farm (dollars) 1982	Average value of land and buildings per farm (dollars) 1987
Florida	36,352	36,556	12,814,216	11,194,090	353	306	552,586	543,830
Alachua	1,106	1,161	219,337	192,255	198	166	311,595	284,184
Baker	232	220	32,156	27,937	139	127	349,155	177,109
Bay	93	85	18,676	11,448	201	135	245,043	161,306
Bradford	399	349	40,709	41,178	102	118	130,802	190,212
Brevard	540	495	193,971	165,082	359	333	345,181	423,756
Broward	479	448	74,983	35,909	157	80	996,829	395,098
Calhoun	169	159	55,986	48,166	331	303	284,840	298,088
Charlotte	139	197	217,117	214,364	1,562	1,088	1,353,237	1,143,893
Citrus	293	331	93,183	74,264	318	224	447,874	280,141
Clay	244	244	106,280	83,994	436	344	500,061	580,689
Collier	196	224	279,754	332,177	1,427	1,483	1,642,735	1,755,839
Columbia	573	535	116,586	98,620	203	184	245,264	209,752
Dade	1,483	1,623	87,420	83,061	59	51	461,567	342,513
De Soto	541	654	347,957	351,402	643	537	692,669	721,087
Dixie	118	114	255,854	56,416	2,168	495	726,949	388,298
Duval	470	434	71,472	41,766	152	96	225,623	248,028
Escambia	522	502	78,533	65,426	150	130	201,839	194,191
Flagler	103	104	102,850	83,332	999	801	715,699	712,875
Franklin	5	6	(D)	(D)	(D)	(D)	84,800	(D)
Gadsden	404	348	77,791	62,114	193	178	270,648	243,289
Gilchrist	329	336	96,163	87,500	292	260	336,818	414,080
Glades	170	194	489,319	222,232	2,878	1,146	2,320,729	1,054,114
Gulf	39	35	50,027	33,644	1,283	961	955,333	564,314
Hamilton	278	256	79,837	73,603	287	288	231,428	244,828
Hardee	954	1,130	318,990	303,892	334	269	623,831	493,415
Hendry	298	396	538,360	545,111	1,807	1,377	2,074,993	2,215,972
Hernando	463	431	94,090	66,167	203	154	458,927	296,826
Highlands	564	735	382,875	413,381	679	562	995,011	871,313
Hillsborough	2,748	2,754	329,293	287,951	120	105	317,184	325,425
Holmes	579	572	106,128	86,701	183	152	165,485	118,550
Indian River	422	539	209,222	195,671	496	363	1,326,472	1,189,302
Jackson	960	910	269,239	269,663	280	296	259,942	256,502
Jefferson	314	296	137,431	130,376	438	440	427,564	433,835
Lafayette	308	273	69,387	94,847	225	347	188,211	255,901
Lake	1,637	1,285	310,072	232,657	189	181	584,946	447,166

See footnotes at end of table.   Continued . . .

Florida Statistical Abstract 1991

Table 9.35. FARMS: NUMBER, LAND IN FARMS, AND VALUE OF LAND AND BUILDINGS IN THE STATE AND COUNTIES OF FLORIDA, 1982 AND 1987 (Continued)

County	Number of farms		Land in farms (acres) Total		Average size of farm		Average value of land and buildings per farm (dollars)	
	1982	1987	1982	1987	1982	1987	1982	1987
Lee	349	415	118,552	132,665	340	320	805,711	633,500
Leon	310	302	115,261	101,885	372	337	377,210	452,103
Levy	476	540	193,458	179,608	406	333	313,626	383,861
Liberty	81	80	16,628	17,507	205	219	143,370	121,675
Madison	595	482	175,519	132,173	295	274	238,966	208,608
Manatee	707	766	353,958	329,388	501	430	797,386	759,265
Marion	1,557	1,707	332,694	311,074	214	182	474,531	475,794
Martin	280	316	266,175	231,522	951	733	2,100,586	1,882,291
Monroe	11	16	(D)	27	(D)	2	73,000	(D)
Nassau	304	317	54,131	48,999	178	155	264,655	245,448
Okaloosa	371	322	70,612	62,662	190	195	205,722	274,201
Okeechobee	326	400	381,895	384,169	1,171	960	1,337,160	1,003,723
Orange	1,320	1,125	243,719	161,900	185	144	518,555	489,619
Osceola	464	503	928,502	787,046	2,001	1,565	1,641,991	1,639,801
Palm Beach	800	975	667,817	659,438	835	676	2,022,293	2,202,349
Pasco	1,072	1,011	274,111	218,953	256	217	594,840	478,293
Pinellas	222	166	13,415	8,549	60	52	451,968	220,491
Polk	2,357	2,638	680,156	602,461	289	228	635,272	569,292
Putnam	549	421	144,829	106,993	264	254	288,945	347,653
St. Johns	186	172	72,712	49,414	391	287	580,220	486,269
St. Lucie	433	522	302,810	297,433	699	570	1,418,691	1,597,356
Santa Rosa	479	435	92,066	81,667	192	188	262,600	223,359
Sarasota	317	352	206,976	166,766	653	474	676,022	624,344
Seminole	503	390	66,380	59,933	132	154	281,676	360,221
Sumter	658	705	295,867	253,897	450	360	378,474	347,387
Suwannee	1,030	985	200,607	182,409	195	185	200,642	221,691
Taylor	180	158	101,396	77,346	563	490	267,633	255,975
Union	216	205	63,173	67,317	292	328	318,366	386,156
Volusia	1,037	920	221,212	192,768	213	210	296,793	346,207
Wakulla	96	87	12,874	(D)	134	(D)	169,750	(D)
Walton	470	430	115,353	104,239	245	242	203,304	154,098
Washington	424	318	79,647	61,647	188	194	163,450	124,191

(D) Data withheld to avoid disclosure of information about individual farms.
    Note: Because data for selected items are collected from a sample of operators, the results are subject to sampling variability. Because of changes in reporting procedures, 1982 data have been adjusted to be comparable with 1987 data.

    Source: U.S., Department of Commerce, Bureau of the Census, *1987 Census of Agriculture: State and County Data, Florida.* AC87-A-9.

Florida Statistical Abstract 1991

Table 9.36.   FARMS: LAND IN FARMS BY USE IN THE STATE AND COUNTIES OF FLORIDA
     1987

(in acres)

County	Total land in farms	Cropland Total	Harvested	Wood- land 1/	Pasture- land 2/	Other 3/	Irri- gated land
Florida	11,194,090	3,790,599	2,240,831	2,213,679	4,495,653	694,159	1,622,750
Alachua	192,255	83,340	33,057	42,514	53,841	12,560	9,068
Baker	27,937	9,897	1,942	12,409	2,971	2,660	447
Bay	11,448	3,580	843	6,400	1,006	462	(D)
Bradford	41,178	16,946	5,610	7,586	12,974	3,672	268
Brevard	165,082	27,625	15,045	38,155	95,795	3,507	17,174
Broward	35,909	(D)	8,653	(D)	22,166	2,085	6,125
Calhoun	48,166	32,266	20,288	12,055	2,350	1,495	805
Charlotte	214,364	23,925	9,804	69,183	116,908	4,348	8,807
Citrus	74,264	18,546	5,679	23,126	24,766	7,826	691
Clay	83,994	7,602	3,138	58,067	13,705	4,620	270
Collier	332,177	59,871	39,749	82,386	171,518	18,402	43,147
Columbia	98,620	50,332	15,028	31,338	11,103	5,847	1,597
Dade	83,061	66,313	61,997	3,014	8,277	5,457	53,185
De Soto	351,402	86,702	47,958	20,898	235,058	8,744	48,078
Dixie	56,416	5,799	1,030	19,413	30,422	782	340
Duval	41,766	12,468	4,239	19,275	6,925	3,098	1,341
Escambia	65,426	44,662	32,943	12,544	4,803	3,417	807
Flagler	83,332	11,443	6,753	49,997	20,915	977	5,913
Franklin	(D)	(D)	0	(D)	0	(D)	0
Gadsden	62,114	28,296	10,684	22,638	5,769	5,411	2,025
Gilchrist	87,500	44,092	16,207	23,933	12,739	6,736	4,496
Glades	222,232	32,420	17,092	63,588	(D)	(D)	49,506
Gulf	33,644	9,796	2,120	1,769	(D)	(D)	(D)
Hamilton	73,603	34,612	14,060	23,513	8,983	6,495	2,878
Hardee	303,892	103,265	55,836	33,168	148,561	18,898	43,878
Hendry	545,111	141,185	95,718	46,060	289,297	68,569	144,808
Hernando	66,167	22,732	7,969	18,246	19,620	5,569	608
Highlands	413,381	102,136	60,983	77,138	218,529	15,578	71,665
Hillsborough	287,951	107,594	61,829	50,296	105,410	24,651	37,839
Holmes	86,701	46,179	19,392	24,110	9,946	6,466	602
Indian River	195,671	88,091	74,372	22,873	71,809	12,898	83,771
Jackson	269,663	162,750	93,419	63,059	26,272	17,582	15,541
Jefferson	130,376	45,665	21,981	58,887	18,879	6,945	6,573
Lafayette	94,847	27,111	7,964	20,283	44,164	3,289	2,319
Lake	232,657	111,692	49,258	34,875	60,129	25,961	29,020
Lee	132,665	32,689	17,918	20,066	73,996	5,914	16,812
Leon	101,885	25,973	9,766	57,335	11,785	6,792	747

See footnotes at end of table.   Continued . . .

Florida Statistical Abstract 1991

Table 9.36. FARMS: LAND IN FARMS BY USE IN THE STATE AND COUNTIES OF FLORIDA
     1987 (Continued)

(in acres)

County	Total land in farms	Cropland Total	Cropland Harvested	Wood-land 1/	Pasture-land 2/	Other 3/	Irri-gated land
Levy	179,608	68,062	18,052	42,969	59,010	9,567	3,844
Liberty	17,507	2,408	447	13,911	714	474	29
Madison	132,173	63,439	27,271	41,493	16,741	10,500	2,366
Manatee	329,388	92,525	53,910	77,595	135,136	24,132	41,204
Marion	311,074	112,235	40,000	62,617	116,533	19,689	5,597
Martin	231,522	84,738	69,176	18,550	106,337	21,897	58,665
Monroe	27	(D)	(D)	0	(D)	(D)	6
Nassau	48,999	12,331	4,347	26,392	6,098	4,178	50
Okaloosa	62,662	28,720	12,729	18,156	12,890	2,896	525
Okeechobee	384,169	65,415	32,761	17,763	282,807	18,184	19,280
Orange	161,900	64,300	40,321	59,993	24,994	12,613	34,447
Osceola	787,046	66,965	32,501	62,363	635,781	21,937	25,868
Palm Beach	659,438	573,037	506,710	4,949	46,642	34,810	422,619
Pasco	218,953	64,204	26,121	42,284	91,550	20,915	9,082
Pinellas	8,549	3,225	(D)	1,780	3,171	373	278
Polk	602,461	200,706	137,879	74,664	290,950	36,141	114,996
Putnam	106,993	26,507	12,218	46,095	29,587	4,804	7,601
St. Johns	49,414	25,190	21,895	8,890	6,356	8,978	21,896
St. Lucie	297,433	111,588	93,830	19,502	143,930	22,413	109,809
Santa Rosa	81,667	59,228	40,817	14,153	4,263	4,023	416
Sarasota	166,766	13,492	5,526	42,117	103,906	7,251	4,583
Seminole	59,933	8,626	5,104	17,465	25,442	8,400	3,596
Sumter	253,897	53,091	14,532	40,789	148,503	11,514	3,543
Suwannee	182,409	101,508	41,824	48,439	19,228	13,234	11,131
Taylor	77,346	7,711	1,395	48,011	19,487	2,137	424
Union	67,317	18,397	5,354	30,579	13,539	4,802	1,141
Volusia	192,768	27,371	11,236	113,435	35,431	16,531	5,114
Wakulla	(D)	(D)	1,127	4,540	1,241	(D)	(D)
Walton	104,239	65,054	20,598	20,436	7,825	10,924	867
Washington	61,647	28,561	11,856	22,574	5,479	5,033	341

(D) Data withheld to avoid disclosure of information about individual farms.
1/ Includes woodland pasture.
2/ Pastureland and rangeland other than cropland and woodland pasture.
3/ Land in house lots, ponds, roads, wasteland, etc.
Note: Because data for selected items are collected from a sample of operators,
the results are subject to sampling variabilty.

Source: U.S., Department of Commerce, Bureau of the Census, *1987 Census of Agri-*
culture: State and County Data, Florida. AC87-A-9.

Table 9.37. FARM INCOME: MARKET VALUE OF AGRICULTURAL PRODUCTS SOLD IN THE STATE AND COUNTIES OF FLORIDA, 1982 AND 1987

(In thousands of dollars, except where indicated)

County	All products Total		Average per farm (dollars)		Crops 1/		Livestock, poultry and their products	
	1982	1987	1982	1987	1982	1987	1982	1987
Florida	3,522,103	4,351,383	96,889	119,033	2,518,959	3,317,823	1,003,144	1,033,560
Alachua	35,197	31,998	31,823	27,561	13,873	14,986	21,323	17,012
Baker	17,358	20,960	74,820	95,274	5,445	10,593	11,914	10,367
Bay	1,281	(D)	13,771	(D)	797	600	484	(D)
Bradford	16,923	15,304	42,412	43,850	1,362	1,634	15,560	13,670
Brevard	18,761	21,518	34,742	43,472	14,579	16,599	4,182	4,919
Broward	45,247	43,343	94,461	96,748	27,991	35,403	17,256	7,940
Calhoun	7,743	8,750	45,817	55,030	6,712	6,775	1,031	1,975
Charlotte	13,224	18,508	95,138	93,950	8,748	13,828	4,476	4,680
Citrus	6,033	6,138	20,589	18,544	2,085	1,660	3,948	4,478
Clay	28,334	28,721	116,122	117,710	848	965	27,486	27,756
Collier	66,417	118,854	338,865	530,599	61,333	112,085	5,084	6,769
Columbia	15,617	16,361	27,254	30,582	6,673	5,599	8,944	10,763
Dade	179,643	250,519	121,135	154,356	173,007	243,596	6,636	6,923
De Soto	36,197	72,586	66,907	110,988	22,256	53,052	13,941	19,535
Dixie	1,933	1,468	16,381	12,875	654	408	1,279	1,060
Duval	31,194	22,264	66,371	51,299	4,668	4,261	26,526	18,003
Escambia	12,895	11,746	24,702	23,398	8,191	6,507	4,704	5,239
Flagler	9,721	10,702	94,375	102,905	8,431	9,608	1,289	1,094
Franklin	(D)	28	(D)	4,667	0	0	(D)	28
Gadsden	30,208	39,228	74,772	112,726	24,989	35,460	5,219	3,768
Gilchrist	27,313	15,092	83,018	44,916	4,192	3,530	23,121	11,562
Glades	30,957	36,578	182,103	188,549	14,153	17,590	16,804	18,988

See footnotes at end of table.

Continued . . .

Table 9.37. FARM INCOME: MARKET VALUE OF AGRICULTURAL PRODUCTS SOLD IN THE STATE AND COUNTIES OF FLORIDA, 1982 AND 1987 (Continued)

(In thousands of dollars, except where indicated)

County	All products Total		Average per farm (dollars)		Crops 1/		Livestock, poultry and their products	
	1982	1987	1982	1987	1982	1987	1982	1987
Gulf	3,754	1,444	96,251	41,250	(D)	(D)	(D)	(D)
Hamilton	13,162	12,036	47,347	47,015	7,796	6,732	5,366	5,304
Hardee	58,722	92,873	61,554	82,188	42,477	67,311	16,245	25,562
Hendry	112,248	161,652	376,672	408,212	89,411	139,571	22,837	22,081
Hernando	28,715	24,612	62,020	57,104	5,866	955	22,850	23,656
Highlands	86,463	138,223	153,303	188,059	59,111	106,463	27,352	31,760
Hillsborough	219,038	222,503	79,708	80,793	122,958	137,517	96,080	84,985
Holmes	24,350	28,346	42,055	49,555	6,403	4,659	17,947	23,686
Indian River	74,609	138,975	176,799	257,838	69,805	133,619	4,805	5,356
Jackson	45,784	48,572	47,692	53,375	30,608	30,801	15,176	17,771
Jefferson	21,712	16,736	69,147	56,540	11,219	7,539	10,493	9,197
Lafayette	38,209	38,932	124,056	142,609	5,463	3,478	32,746	35,454
Lake	196,715	75,903	120,168	59,069	181,209	60,423	15,507	15,480
Lee	35,740	73,411	102,406	176,893	33,865	70,914	1,875	2,496
Leon	5,933	4,460	19,140	14,769	2,260	1,288	3,674	3,172
Levy	13,060	16,305	27,437	30,194	7,072	6,815	5,988	9,489
Liberty	676	710	8,344	8,874	313	44	363	666
Madison	32,628	24,374	54,838	50,569	13,156	5,591	19,472	18,783
Manatee	119,933	148,655	169,637	194,067	96,749	125,858	23,184	22,797
Marion	78,528	93,704	50,435	54,894	26,020	13,267	52,508	80,437
Martin	79,628	129,892	284,385	411,051	66,951	115,046	12,677	14,846
Monroe	(D)	(D)	(D)	(D)	(D)	242	(D)	(D)
Nassau	21,632	22,150	71,158	69,872	846	1,028	20,786	21,122
Okaloosa	8,563	5,457	23,081	16,946	3,790	2,274	4,773	3,183
Okeechobee	90,432	114,947	277,398	287,367	5,404	16,442	85,028	98,504

See footnotes at end of table.   Continued . . .

Table 9.37. FARM INCOME: MARKET VALUE OF AGRICULTURAL PRODUCTS SOLD IN THE STATE AND COUNTIES OF FLORIDA, 1982 AND 1987 (Continued)

(in thousands of dollars, except where indicated)

County	All products Total		Average per farm (dollars)		Crops 1/		Livestock, poultry and their products	
	1982	1987	1982	1987	1982	1987	1982	1987
Orange	197,874	197,418	149,905	175,483	186,286	192,405	11,588	5,013
Osceola	39,770	56,986	85,712	113,292	20,908	35,865	18,862	21,121
Palm Beach	534,779	855,172	668,473	877,100	519,451	846,953	15,328	8,220
Pasco	81,169	59,443	75,717	58,796	36,729	14,228	44,440	45,215
Pinellas	10,456	9,368	47,099	56,433	9,662	(D)	794	(D)
Polk	231,195	260,669	98,089	98,813	190,477	219,034	40,718	41,635
Putnam	20,995	27,121	38,242	64,420	14,407	22,589	6,588	4,532
St. Johns	37,508	39,294	201,653	228,455	34,343	37,896	3,165	1,398
St. Lucie	94,910	165,828	219,192	317,678	80,535	155,311	14,374	10,517
Santa Rosa	16,081	19,653	33,571	45,180	12,330	15,980	3,751	3,673
Sarasota	14,179	15,239	44,729	43,293	7,517	9,912	6,662	5,327
Seminole	20,229	19,009	40,218	48,742	18,128	17,201	2,102	1,808
Sumter	23,108	30,776	35,119	43,654	7,457	8,147	15,651	22,629
Suwannee	54,206	64,064	52,628	65,039	17,903	16,920	36,303	47,143
Taylor	2,261	2,447	12,562	15,487	666	689	1,595	1,758
Union	9,300	8,800	43,056	42,928	2,715	2,001	6,586	6,799
Volusia	59,631	63,794	57,503	69,341	45,996	53,814	13,634	9,980
Wakulla	1,458	1,408	15,187	16,180	502	531	956	877
Walton	20,223	18,487	43,029	42,992	6,514	4,099	13,709	14,387
Washington	10,099	8,161	23,818	25,663	3,804	2,209	6,295	5,952

(D) Data withheld to avoid disclosure of information about individual farms.

1/ Includes nursery and greenhouse products.

Note: Because data for selected items are collected from a sample of operators, the results are subject to sampling variability.

Source: U.S., Department of Commerce, Bureau of the Census, 1987 Census of Agriculture: State and County Data, Florida. AC87-A-9.

Table 9.38. FARM OPERATORS: NUMBER OF OPERATORS BY PRINCIPAL OCCUPATION, AGE, AND
RACE AND NUMBER OF FARMS AND ACRES OPERATED BY FEMALES IN THE STATE AND
COUNTIES OF FLORIDA, 1987

| | | Operators | | | Race | | Female operators | |
| | | Principal occupation | | Average age | Spanish ori- | Black and other | Number of | Land in farms |
County	Total	Farming	Other	(years)	gin 1/	races	farms	(acres)
Florida	36,556	15,821	20,735	53.7	624	974	4,606	608,590
Alachua	1,161	440	721	53.3	4	76	158	15,497
Baker	220	77	143	55.0	(D)	5	9	717
Bay	85	28	57	54.3	(D)	(D)	4	434
Bradford	349	119	230	54.1	5	6	36	3,898
Brevard	495	160	335	54.8	9	11	79	7,830
Broward	448	174	274	50.8	24	10	84	1,777
Calhoun	159	68	91	53.5	(D)	3	14	1,735
Charlotte	197	87	110	54.6	(D)	3	21	11,527
Citrus	331	126	205	54.6	(D)	8	33	4,760
Clay	244	81	163	54.1	3	(D)	22	7,071
Collier	224	137	87	52.2	7	4	15	278
Columbia	535	214	321	53.6	5	28	63	10,081
Dade	1,623	719	904	51.6	223	79	206	3,620
De Soto	654	256	398	56.6	3	(D)	84	9,202
Dixie	114	30	84	56.5	(D)	(D)	8	1,862
Duval	434	158	276	54.9	(D)	4	64	1,815
Escambia	502	198	304	54.4	(D)	18	53	4,926
Flagler	104	55	49	51.0	(D)	(D)	6	694
Franklin	6	0	6	52.0	(D)	(D)	0	0
Gadsden	348	127	221	55.4	4	27	29	4,726
Gilchrist	336	143	193	53.5	(D)	(D)	34	7,189
Glades	194	101	93	54.7	(D)	8	17	6,087
Gulf	35	9	26	49.4	(D)	(D)	0	0
Hamilton	256	116	140	53.7	(D)	21	18	3,213
Hardee	1,130	523	607	55.5	10	5	166	20,337
Hendry	396	202	194	53.7	14	9	24	30,142
Hernando	431	178	253	54.1	15	10	62	4,127
Highlands	735	322	413	52.7	3	20	84	36,582
Hillsborough	2,754	1,163	1,591	54.0	65	57	431	25,375
Holmes	572	267	305	52.4	(D)	5	41	5,668
Indian River	539	283	256	55.1	9	6	61	4,094
Jackson	910	463	447	53.9	(D)	108	47	12,458
Jefferson	296	113	183	52.2	(D)	21	26	11,662
Lafayette	273	146	127	51.4	(D)	(D)	28	3,334

See footnotes at end of table.   Continued . . .

Florida Statistical Abstra

Table 9.38.   FARM OPERATORS: NUMBER OF OPERATORS BY PRINCIPAL OCCUPATION, AGE, AND
RACE AND NUMBER OF FARMS AND ACRES OPERATED BY FEMALES IN THE STATE AND
COUNTIES OF FLORIDA, 1987 (Continued)

		Operators				Race	Female operators	
County	Total	Principal occupation Farming	Other	Average age (years)	Spanish ori- gin 1/	Black and other races	Number of farms	Land in farms (acres)
Lake	1,285	546	739	52.9	8	9	177	13,471
Lee	415	189	226	53.8	3	3	53	4,246
Leon	302	82	220	53.2	(D)	36	38	21,056
Levy	540	223	317	54.8	9	22	57	9,980
Liberty	80	25	55	54.0	(D)	3	5	421
Madison	482	223	259	55.8	(D)	42	41	5,035
Manatee	766	372	394	53.6	5	10	104	14,157
Marion	1,707	780	927	53.6	18	81	284	18,864
Martin	316	139	177	51.0	7	3	37	2,553
Monroe	16	7	9	50.2	(D)	(D)	6	(D)
Nassau	317	93	224	52.8	(D)	5	30	5,088
Okaloosa	322	126	196	54.3	(D)	(D)	24	5,844
Okeechobee	400	163	237	52.3	9	(D)	33	18,698
Orange	1,125	543	582	53.0	8	32	187	24,581
Osceola	503	248	255	53.9	5	9	77	31,357
Palm Beach	975	532	443	49.6	48	28	115	10,399
Pasco	1,011	399	612	54.8	26	8	166	22,146
Pinellas	166	66	100	54.3	(D)	(D)	42	(D)
Polk	2,638	1,065	1,573	55.3	11	24	413	33,532
Putnam	421	161	260	53.4	(D)	12	55	11,205
St. Johns	172	107	65	52.7	6	4	15	4,382
St. Lucie	522	257	265	52.7	6	6	57	11,018
Santa Rosa	435	214	221	52.8	(D)	(D)	29	4,746
Sarasota	352	128	224	52.6	(D)	(D)	45	2,633
Seminole	390	157	233	53.8	(D)	13	52	6,976
Sumter	705	291	414	54.8	8	18	113	24,553
Suwannee	985	479	506	53.9	5	25	91	13,432
Taylor	158	58	100	55.6	(D)	(D)	16	1,773
Union	205	72	133	53.5	(D)	(D)	16	2,563
Volusia	920	435	485	52.3	11	9	140	11,905
Wakulla	87	26	61	52.3	3	(D)	7	(D)
Walton	430	194	236	55.7	(D)	3	37	5,720
Washington	318	138	180	55.8	(D)	3	17	1,906
Other	0	0	0	0.0	25	14	0	0

(D) Data withheld to avoid disclosure of information about individual farms.
1/ Persons of Spanish origin may be of any race.
Note: Because data for selected items are collected from a sample of operators,
the results are subject to sampling variability.
Source: U.S., Department of Commerce, Bureau of the Census, *1987 Census of Agriculture: State and County Data, Florida*.   AC87-A-9.

Table 9.42.   FARM INCOME: CASH RECEIPTS FROM FARMING AND VALUE OF HOME CONSUMPTION
IN FLORIDA, OTHER AGRICULTURAL STATES, AND THE UNITED STATES, 1989

(in thousands of dollars)

State	Total Amount	Rank among states	Cash receipts from farming Total	Marketings	Government payments	Value of home consump- tion 1/
Florida	6,246,484	8	6,241,277	6,202,954	38,323	5,207
California	17,900,631	1	17,886,885	17,514,795	372,090	13,746
Texas	12,043,179	2	12,009,127	10,760,414	1,248,713	34,052
Iowa	10,121,888	3	10,100,408	9,119,202	981,206	21,480
Nebraska	9,075,076	4	9,063,393	8,521,087	542,306	11,683
Illinois	7,469,148	5	7,436,377	6,710,436	725,941	32,771
Minnesota	7,151,175	6	7,125,393	6,525,541	599,852	25,782
Kansas	6,930,628	7	6,912,738	6,324,292	588,446	17,890
Wisconsin	5,820,715	9	5,800,303	5,277,971	522,332	20,412
Indiana	4,671,003	10	4,652,184	4,318,493	333,691	18,819
North Carolina	4,661,861	11	4,644,504	4,550,587	93,917	17,357
Arkansas	4,581,036	12	4,570,717	4,131,042	439,675	10,319
Missouri	4,282,560	13	4,256,825	3,900,434	356,391	25,735
Ohio	4,113,537	14	4,086,121	3,812,118	274,003	27,416
Colorado	4,091,717	15	4,082,056	3,898,614	183,442	9,661
United States	170,706,892	(X)	170,060,001	159,173,299	10,886,702	646,891

(X) Not applicable.
1/ Value of farm products consumed directly in farm households where produced.
Note: Data are preliminary.

Table 9.43.   AGRICULTURAL TAXES: AMOUNT LEVIED ON FARM REAL ESTATE IN FLORIDA AND
THE UNITED STATES, 1987 AND 1988

Item	Florida 1987	1988	United States 1/ 1987	1988
Total taxes levied ($1,000,000)	101.4	107.2	4,233.5	4,304.1
Taxes per acre Amount (dollars)	9.34	10.04	4.82	4.91
Taxes per $100 of full value (dollars)	0.58	0.56	0.80	0.77

1/ Excludes Alaska.

Source for Tables 9.42 and 9.43:   U.S., Department of Agriculture, *Agricultural Statistics, 1990.*

Florida Statistical Abstract 1991

Table 9.45. AGRICULTURAL LAND: TOTAL ACREAGE AND ACREAGE OWNED BY NONRESIDENT
ALIENS IN THE STATE AND COUNTIES OF FLORIDA, DECEMBER 1988

County	Estimated total farmland acreage 1/	Acreage foreign-owned 2/		
		Amount	As a percentage of total farmland	County total as a percentage of state total
Florida	24,434,639	519,236	2.12	100.00
Alachua	465,590	11,716	2.52	2.26
Baker	290,862	1,802	0.62	0.35
Bay	410,490	0	0.00	0.00
Bradford	168,000	0	0.00	0.00
Brevard	336,000	6,167	1.84	1.19
Broward	28,670	1,879	6.55	0.36
Calhoun	352,375	2,397	0.68	0.46
Charlotte	255,851	1,508	0.59	0.29
Citrus	263,075	1,096	0.42	0.21
Clay	278,000	7,088	2.55	1.37
Collier	576,448	14,355	2.49	2.76
Columbia	410,523	4,515	1.10	0.87
Dade	85,306	18,540	21.73	3.57
De Soto	354,000	5,073	1.43	0.98
Dixie	398,000	0	0.00	0.00
Duval	301,244	52	0.02	0.01
Escambia	332,994	249	0.07	0.05
Flagler	300,600	0	0.00	0.00
Franklin	310,000	0	0.00	0.00
Gadsden	243,623	6,471	2.66	1.25
Gilchrist	209,000	9,309	4.45	1.79
Glades	443,500	1,192	0.27	0.23
Gulf	350,000	0	0.00	0.00
Hamilton	319,469	1,378	0.43	0.27
Hardee	326,302	2,949	0.90	0.57
Hendry	734,000	8,586	1.17	1.65
Hernando	193,300	0	0.00	0.00
Highlands	600,549	3,900	0.65	0.75
Hillsborough	575,626	13,492	2.34	2.60
Holmes	305,550	0	0.00	0.00
Indian River	262,000	26,527	10.12	5.11
Jackson	576,000	6,488	1.13	1.25
Jefferson	346,073	2,851	0.82	0.55
Lafayette	345,500	0	0.00	0.00
Lake	515,245	13,491	2.62	2.60
Lee	266,400	7,419	2.78	1.43
Leon	304,350	0	0.00	0.00

See footnotes at end of table.   Continued . . .

Florida Statistical Abstract 1991

Table 9.45.   AGRICULTURAL LAND: TOTAL ACREAGE AND ACREAGE OWNED BY NONRESIDENT
ALIENS IN THE STATE AND COUNTIES OF FLORIDA, DECEMBER 1988 (Continued)

County	Estimated total farmland acreage 1/	Acreage foreign-owned 2/		
		Amount	As a percentage of total farmland	County total as a percentage of state total
Levy	692,042	9,872	1.43	1.90
Liberty	268,375	0	0.00	0.00
Madison	417,961	793	0.19	0.15
Manatee	326,000	8,117	2.49	1.56
Marion	585,000	12,241	2.09	2.36
Martin	332,000	26,345	7.94	5.07
Monroe	2	0	0.00	0.00
Nassau	350,884	315	0.09	0.06
Okaloosa	203,630	21,718	10.67	4.18
Okeechobee	465,500	4,053	0.87	0.78
Orange	323,984	27,252	8.41	5.25
Osceola	730,000	15,316	2.10	2.95
Palm Beach	582,552	140,292	24.08	27.02
Pasco	293,000	3,287	1.12	0.63
Pinellas	62,000	55	0.09	0.01
Polk	861,400	6,962	0.81	1.34
Putnam	465,768	776	0.17	0.15
St. Johns	339,000	1,156	0.34	0.22
St. Lucie	364,179	6,340	1.74	1.22
Santa Rosa	454,563	426	0.09	0.08
Sarasota	206,150	6,400	3.10	1.23
Seminole	116,000	2,313	1.99	0.45
Sumter	338,426	4,247	1.25	0.82
Suwannee	426,000	2,004	0.47	0.39
Taylor	668,222	20	Δ/	Δ/
Union	149,932	0	0.00	0.00
Volusia	549,000	10,665	1.94	2.05
Wakulla	159,472	61	0.04	0.01
Walton	512,600	27,720	5.41	5.34
Washington	356,482	0	0.00	0.00

Δ/ Less than 0.005 percent.

1/ Land currently used for agricultural, forestry, or timber production or, if
idle, land used for such purposes within the last five years.

2/ A foreign investor is defined as any nonresident alien, any corporation
incorporated outside the U.S., or any U.S. corporation with 5 percent or more
foreign interest.   A foreign investor holding more than 5 percent or more interest
in any agricultural lands must disclose such holdings.

Note: Data were compiled by the U.S. Department of Agriculture, Agricultural
Stabilization and Conservation Service from disclosure forms filed under the
Agriculture Foreign Investment Disclosure Act of 1978.   Detail may not add to total
because of rounding.

Source: U.S., Department of Agriculture, Agricultural Stabilization and Conservation Service, unpublished data.

Table 9.50.   AGRICULTURAL IRRIGATION: ACREAGE UNDER IRRIGATION AND WATER USE
BY TYPE OF PRODUCT AND SOURCE IN FLORIDA, 1985

(water use in millions of gallons per day)

Product	Acres irri-gated 1/	Irrigated water use		
		Total 2/	Ground	Surface
Total	1,910,505	2,978.51	1,646.31	1,332.20
Vegetable crops	342,750	496.35	396.43	99.92
Cabbage	10,685	13.75	13.73	0.02
Carrots	20,200	18.42	7.34	11.08
Cucumbers	24,548	46.89	46.86	0.03
Peppers	23,092	39.62	39.51	0.11
Potatoes	27,441	37.97	37.97	0.00
Tomatoes	58,154	135.57	132.58	2.99
Sweet corn	65,360	74.32	26.35	47.97
Watercress	150	7.81	7.81	0.00
Other vegetables	113,120	122.00	84.28	37.72
Fruit crops	693,317	1,142.20	650.72	491.48
Blueberries	848	0.83	0.83	0.00
Citrus	610,720	1,009.59	523.68	485.91
Grapes	361	0.33	0.33	0.00
Peaches	1,203	1.81	1.70	0.11
Pecans	2,970	2.63	2.63	0.00
Strawberries	4,750	16.96	16.15	0.81
Watermelons	47,125	51.44	47.15	4.29
Other fruit	25,340	58.61	58.25	0.36
Field crops	485,597	610.31	72.60	537.71
Field corn	42,629	52.39	34.56	17.83
Peanuts	18,586	11.80	8.90	2.90
Rice	3,300	7.69	0.00	7.69
Sorghum	7,875	6.79	6.16	0.63
Soybeans	9,835	7.36	6.01	1.35
Sugar cane	379,250	505.41	0.00	505.41
Tobacco	6,674	7.03	6.89	0.14
Wheat	10,533	5.03	3.51	1.52
Other field crops	6,915	6.81	6.57	0.24
Ornamentals and grasses	388,841	663.26	468.29	194.97
Ferns	6,682	32.29	27.46	4.83
Flowers and foliage	11,124	58.63	47.07	11.56
Woody ornamentals	17,918	99.56	81.22	18.34
Improved pasture	246,438	222.57	163.62	58.95
Sod	32,642	68.72	29.27	39.45
Turf grass 3/	74,037	181.49	119.65	61.84
Animal product	(X)	66.39	58.27	8.12
Livestock	(X)	45.96	37.84	8.12
Fish farming	(X)	20.43	20.43	0.00

(X) Not applicable.
1/ Includes acreage for double cropping.
2/ Excludes the use of discharged wastewater.
3/ Golf courses.

Source: U.S., Department of the Interior, Geological Survey in cooperation with
St. Johns River Water Management District, *Water Withdrawals and Use by Category in
Florida, 1985.*

Florida Statistical Abstract 1991

Table 9.51. CITRUS: ESTIMATED PRODUCTION AND VALUE OF CITRUS BY TYPE IN FLORIDA
CROP YEARS 1985-86 THROUGH 1989-90

Type of citrus	1985-86	1986-87	1987-88	1988-89	1989-90 A/
Production (1,000 boxes)					
All citrus	176,015	181,530	204,100	213,850	154,185
Oranges	119,200	119,700	138,000	146,600	110,200
Early and midseason	64,200	65,800	78,500	85,300	68,100
Late (Valencia)	55,000	53,900	59,500	61,300	42,100
Grapefruit	46,750	49,800	53,850	54,750	35,700
Seedy	3,150	2,900	2,750	3,350	1,400
White seedless	25,600	26,900	29,200	27,700	18,000
Colored seedless	18,000	20,000	21,900	23,700	16,300
Other citrus	10,065	12,030	12,250	12,500	8,285
Temples	2,950	3,400	3,550	3,750	1,400
Tangelos	2,950	4,000	4,200	3,800	2,950
Tangerines 1/	1,150	1,300	1,300	1,400	1,060
Honey tangerines	800	1,040	1,150	1,500	640
K-early citrus	160	220	240	320	210
Limes	1,725	1,450	1,300	1,250	1,650
Lemons	330	620	510	480	375
Value of production ($1,000)					
All citrus	724,921	941,078	1,443,116	1,429,808	908,560
Oranges	469,959	624,771	1,046,700	1,086,319	635,890
Early and midseason	251,366	300,290	527,169	571,082	345,491
Late (Valencia)	218,593	324,481	519,531	515,237	290,399
Grapefruit	191,068	248,120	299,887	243,874	206,805
Seedy	10,301	12,383	13,723	12,328	5,376
White seedless	91,107	119,693	156,360	119,980	95,000
Colored seedless	89,660	116,044	129,804	111,566	106,429
Other citrus	63,894	68,187	96,529	99,615	65,865
Temples	8,870	12,236	20,196	20,474	7,642
Tangelos	11,980	14,891	23,435	23,994	14,313
Tangerines 1/	14,480	15,610	16,407	17,555	17,718
Honey tangerines	8,035	9,953	15,424	19,097	8,777
K-early citrus	1,354	1,479	2,013	1,835	1,189
Limes	13,692	12,424	16,493	14,112	13,634
Lemons	5,483	1,594	2,561	2,548	2,592

A/ Preliminary.
1/ Sunburst tangerines not included prior to 1989-90.
Note: Florida lemons bloom and harvest during the calendar year; data are for
1984 through 1989. Tangerines do not include honey tangerines. Some data are
revised.

Source: State of Florida, Department of Agriculture and Consumer Services,
Florida Agricultural Statistics Service, *Florida Agricultural Statistics: Citrus
Summary, 1989-90.*

Florida Statistical Abstract 1991

Table 9.52. ORANGES AND GRAPEFRUIT: BEARING ACREAGE, PRODUCTION, AND YIELD PER
ACRE IN FLORIDA, OTHER CITRUS STATES, AND THE UNITED STATES, CROP YEARS
1983-84 THROUGH 1989-90

	Oranges			Grapefruit		
State and year	Bearing acreage (1,000 acres)	Produc- tion (1,000 tons)	Yield per acre (tons)	Bearing acreage (1,000 acres)	Produc- tion (1,000 tons)	Yield per acre (tons)
Florida						
1983-84	474.2	5,252	11.1	119.6	1,738	14.5
1984-85	420.1	4,676	11.1	115.5	1,870	16.2
1985-86	367.6	5,364	14.6	105.1	1,987	18.9
1986-87	375.4	5,387	14.4	106.0	2,116	20.0
1987-88	380.2	6,210	16.3	106.0	2,289	21.6
1988-89	388.7	6,597	17.0	106.9	2,327	21.8
1989-90 A/	431.4	4,959	11.5	107.4	1,517	14.1
Arizona						
1983-84	12.6	65	5.2	6.8	80	11.8
1984-85	10.9	77	7.1	7.1	107	15.1
1985-86	11.0	76	6.9	5.7	90	15.8
1986-87	10.9	101	9.3	5.9	88	14.9
1987-88	10.6	68	6.4	6.0	62	10.3
1988-89	10.4	64	6.2	6.5	62	9.5
1989-90 A/	10.2	59	5.8	6.4	70	10.9
California						
1983-84	177.1	1,819	10.3	21.9	238	10.9
1984-85	175.3	1,966	11.2	21.1	289	13.7
1985-86	174.6	2,022	11.6	20.9	266	12.7
1986-87	172.9	2,172	12.6	20.8	305	14.7
1987-88	172.6	2,212	12.8	20.7	298	14.4
1988-89	177.6	2,209	12.4	19.9	283	14.2
1989-90 A/	174.8	2,740	15.7	19.2	286	14.9
Texas						
1983-84	24.3	107	4.4	43.3	128	3.0
1984-85	11.4	0	0.0	19.1	0	0.0
1985-86	8.3	14	1.7	13.5	9	0.7
1986-87	10.3	37	3.6	15.2	77	5.1
1987-88	11.1	61	5.5	16.0	152	9.5
1988-89	12.0	79	6.6	16.9	192	11.4
1989-90 A/	13.0	51	3.9	18.7	80	4.3
United States						
1983-84	688.2	7,243	10.5	191.6	2,184	11.4
1984-85	617.7	6,719	10.9	162.8	2,266	13.9
1985-86	561.5	7,476	13.3	145.2	2,352	16.2
1986-87	569.5	7,697	13.5	147.9	2,586	17.5
1987-88	574.5	8,551	14.9	148.7	2,801	18.8
1988-89	588.7	8,949	15.2	150.2	2,844	18.9
1989-90 A/	629.4	7,809	12.4	151.7	1,953	12.9

A/ Preliminary.
Note: Some data are revised.

Source: State of Florida, Department of Agriculture and Consumer Services,
Florida Agricultural Statistics Service, *Florida Agricultural Statistics: Citrus
Summary, 1989-90.*

Florida Statistical Abstract 1991

Table 9.53.   ORANGES AND GRAPEFRUIT: SEASON AVERAGE ON-TREE PRICES PER BOX AND
VALUE OF PRODUCTION IN FLORIDA AND THE UNITED STATES, CROP YEARS 1982-83
THROUGH 1989-90

Crop year	Season average price (in dollars per box)			Value of production (in thousands of dollars)		
	Total	Fresh use	Process-ing	Total	Fresh use	Process-ing
Oranges 1/						
Florida						
1982-83	5.15	5.94	5.08	718,420	61,273	657,147
1983-84	5.75	7.75	5.61	670,618	59,245	611,373
1984-85	7.10	11.11	6.83	737,923	73,911	664,012
1985-86	3.94	5.33	3.83	469,959	47,746	422,213
1986-87	5.22	6.18	5.14	624,771	54,828	569,943
1987-88	7.58	7.96	7.56	1,046,700	75,749	970,951
1988-89	7.41	7.61	7.40	1,086,319	64,628	1,021,691
1989-90 A/	5.77	10.31	5.51	635,890	60,962	574,928
United States						
1982-83	4.15	4.65	3.98	934,571	275,767	658,804
1983-84	5.92	8.37	5.07	1,007,760	403,283	604,477
1984-85	7.37	10.17	6.29	1,172,733	493,420	679,313
1985-86	4.27	6.38	3.43	755,660	349,010	406,650
1986-87	5.39	7.97	4.45	980,997	427,974	553,023
1987-88	7.18	8.41	6.78	1,424,847	450,588	974,259
1988-89	7.08	8.21	6.76	1,470,672	426,516	1,044,156
1989-90 A/	5.99	8.42	5.04	1,119,703	481,847	637,856
Grapefruit						
Florida						
1982-83	1.96	3.61	0.52	77,221	66,195	11,026
1983-84	2.72	4.19	1.70	111,081	69,817	41,264
1984-85	3.67	5.62	2.66	161,356	84,208	77,148
1985-86	4.09	5.19	3.29	191,067	101,731	89,336
1986-87	4.98	5.89	4.32	248,120	123,342	124,778
1987-88	5.57	6.85	4.61	299,887	158,213	141,674
1988-89	4.45	6.03	3.24	243,874	144,068	99,806
1989-90 A/	5.79	10.00	3.28	206,805	133,424	73,381
United States						
1982-83	1.79	3.18	0.22	108,472	102,169	6,303
1983-84	2.68	4.14	1.37	144,078	107,956	36,122
1984-85	3.95	6.27	2.38	224,962	149,415	75,547
1985-86	4.29	5.85	2.94	250,245	163,452	86,793
1986-87	4.94	6.27	3.79	313,549	190,367	123,182
1987-88	5.43	6.84	4.16	370,452	226,968	143,484
1988-89	4.45	6.12	2.85	309,323	213,177	96,146
1989-90 A/	6.21	10.43	2.81	306,423	235,498	70,925

A/ Preliminary.
1/ Includes early, midseason, and late type (Valencia) oranges.
Note: Charges for picking, hauling, and packing are deducted from the weighted
average of prices obtained from all segments of the citrus industry to arrive at the
final on-tree price received by producers. Some historical data have been revised.
United States data include Arizona, California, Florida, and Texas.
Source: State of Florida, Department of Agriculture and Consumer Services,
Florida Agricultural Statistics Service, *Florida Agricultural Statistics: Citrus
Summary, 1989-90.*

Florida Statistical Abstract 1991

Table 9.54. CITRUS: ESTIMATED PRODUCTION OF PRINCIPAL TYPES OF CITRUS IN THE STATE
AND COUNTIES OF FLORIDA, CROP YEAR 1989-90

(in 1,000 boxes)

Area and county	Total 1/	All oranges	Oranges Early and mid-season	Valencias	All grape-fruit	Specialty fruit 2/
Florida	152,160	110,200	68,100	42,100	35,700	6,260
District						
Indian River	45,208	17,924	9,791	8,133	26,100	1,184
Northern	2,384	1,888	1,385	503	79	417
Central	41,401	35,747	19,791	15,956	3,459	2,195
Western	30,973	28,297	20,387	7,910	1,214	1,462
Southern	32,194	26,344	16,746	9,598	4,848	1,002
County						
Brevard	2,627	1,955	1,106	849	600	72
Broward	78	61	19	42	14	3
Charlotte	2,050	1,873	1,154	719	133	44
Collier	2,542	2,099	1,432	667	397	46
De Soto	10,081	9,457	5,697	3,760	220	404
Glades	1,483	1,422	1,132	290	59	2
Hardee	10,463	9,948	7,694	2,254	158	357
Hendry	11,913	9,619	6,230	3,389	1,964	330
Highlands	12,638	11,158	4,624	6,534	770	710
Hillsborough	6,057	5,482	4,450	1,032	244	331
Indian River	17,808	5,804	3,362	2,442	11,685	319
Lake	850	573	425	148	45	232
Lee	1,747	1,606	953	653	123	18
Manatee	3,838	3,042	2,309	733	497	299
Martin	9,642	7,414	3,564	3,850	1,990	238
Okeechobee	1,611	1,280	962	318	295	36
Orange	1,026	866	582	284	27	133
Osceola	3,674	3,303	2,400	903	188	183
Palm Beach	4,175	2,558	1,763	795	1,274	343
Pasco	325	298	257	41	6	21
Pinellas	48	24	8	16	14	10
Polk	25,346	21,503	12,957	8,546	2,535	1,308
St. Lucie	21,308	8,248	4,599	3,649	12,336	724
Sarasota	486	344	229	115	81	61
Seminole	153	122	95	27	0	31
Volusia	172	123	81	42	44	5
Other 3/	19	18	16	2	1	0

1/ Does not include lemon and lime production.
2/ Includes tangelos, temples, tangerines, and K-early citrus.
3/ Includes Citrus, Hernando, Marion, Putnam, and Sumter counties.
Note: Citrus districts are based on citrus marketings/production areas. Several counties are in more than one district.

Source: State of Florida, Department of Agriculture and Consumer Services, Florida Agricultural Statistics Service, *Florida Agricultural Statistics: Citrus Summary, 1989-90.*

Florida Statistical Abstract 1991

Table 9.55.   CITRUS: ACREAGE BY TYPE OF FRUIT IN THE STATE AND SPECIFIED COUNTIES OF FLORIDA, JANUARY 1, 1990

County	Total 1/	All oranges 1/	Oranges Early and mid-season	Valencias	All grape-fruit	Specialty fruit 2/
Florida	732,522	564,809	274,696	246,483	125,300	42,413
Brevard	10,519	8,098	4,275	3,534	1,983	438
Broward	589	446	132	314	118	25
Charlotte	11,718	10,405	4,987	5,256	846	467
Citrus	103	82	58	2	14	7
Collier	23,565	20,380	9,677	10,525	2,054	1,131
Dade	6,074	0	0	0	0	6,074
De Soto	52,584	49,662	23,177	21,820	1,299	1,623
Glades	7,523	7,190	4,598	2,324	218	115
Hardee	51,069	48,446	32,035	13,309	912	1,711
Hendry	73,754	62,167	28,493	29,868	7,605	3,982
Hernando	598	596	234	2	0	2
Highlands	57,048	49,728	17,133	29,822	3,745	3,575
Hillsborough	26,007	23,891	16,439	5,782	1,024	1,092
Indian River	66,116	29,801	15,013	13,988	34,260	2,055
Lake	13,960	11,616	5,505	2,047	735	1,609
Lee	9,692	8,339	3,696	4,205	610	743
Manatee	20,331	17,584	10,768	5,537	1,934	813
Marion	277	264	207	17	2	11
Martin	46,283	39,779	14,677	23,201	5,119	1,385
Okeechobee	8,541	7,369	4,824	2,431	907	265
Orange	8,399	7,427	3,957	2,454	226	746
Osceola	16,101	13,522	7,926	4,272	1,559	1,020
Palm Beach	15,545	9,875	5,721	4,102	3,181	2,489
Pasco	6,937	6,570	4,330	506	163	204
Pinellas	218	128	46	80	61	29
Polk	99,718	81,578	35,519	35,935	12,619	5,521
Putnam	20	20	18	0	0	0
St. Lucie	94,878	46,444	19,366	24,010	43,518	4,916
Sarasota	2,127	1,503	739	733	429	195
Seminole	1,024	887	592	161	2	135
Sumter	6	5	5	0	1	0
Volusia	1,198	1,007	549	246	156	35

1/ Includes unidentified variety acreage.
2/ Includes limes and lemons surveyed as of November 1990.

Source: State of Florida, Department of Agriculture and Consumer Services, Florida Agricultural Statistics Service, *Florida Agricultural Statistics: Citrus Summary, 1989-90*.

Florida Statistical Abstract 1991

Table 9.56. ORANGE JUICE SALES: GALLONS SOLD AND CONSUMER RETAIL DOLLARS SPENT
IN UNITED STATES FOOD STORES, 1977 THROUGH 1990

Year	Total Amount	Percentage change from pre-vious year	Chilled orange juice 1/	Canned single strength	Frozen concen-trated orange juice
		Reconstituted gallons (rounded to millions)			
1977	715	1	189	29	497
1978	681	-5	204	30	447
1979	709	4	223	28	457
1980	808	14	278	29	501
1981	808	A/	289	27	492
1982	804	A/	295	25	484
1983	863	7	346	23	494
1984	856	-1	378	20	457
1985	817	-5	373	18	426
1986	884	8	437	17	430
1987 B/	700	(X)	361	9	330
1988	660	-6	354	9	297
1989	692	5	395	9	289
1990	622	-10	359	8	254
		Consumer retail dollars (rounded to millions)			
1977	1,327	20	412	66	849
1978	1,630	23	545	85	1,000
1979	1,842	13	655	90	1,097
1980	2,098	14	825	95	1,178
1981	2,405	15	965	98	1,342
1982	2,498	4	1,020	96	1,382
1983	2,628	5	1,156	91	1,381
1984	2,993	14	1,418	91	1,483
1985	3,102	4	1,512	88	1,502
1986	2,871	-7	1,550	77	1,244
1987 B/	2,101	(X)	1,166	43	892
1988	2,415	15	1,405	47	963
1989	2,574	7	1,601	44	929
1990	2,667	4	1,689	42	935

(X) Not applicable.
A/ Decreased by less than one percent.
B/ Data not comparable to previous years due to changes in data collection meth-
ods.
1/ Includes glass and plastic containers and cartons.
Note: Data for 1976-1986 come from an audit of 1,300 food stores throughout the
United States and relate to the retail market only. Data for 1987-90 come from
scanner supermarkets doing over $4 million in retail sales annually. Sales from
these stores are estimated to represent 73 percent of total retail sales.
Source: State of Florida, Department of Citrus, *Market Research Report: A.C.
Nielsen Retail Food Index, Annual Summary, 1986* and previous editions and *Market
Research Report: Nielsen Scantrack, Annual Summary, 1990* and previous edition.

Florida Statistical Abstract 1991

Table 9.62. FIELD CROPS: ACREAGE HARVESTED, PRODUCTION, YIELD, AND VALUE
OF PRODUCTION IN FLORIDA, CROP YEARS 1988 AND 1989

Crop	Harvested acres (1,000) 1988	1989	Unit	Production Total (1,000) 1988	1989	Yield per acre 1988	1989	Production value ($1,000) 1988	1989
Corn for grain	65	80	Bu.	3,770	5,920	58	74	11,310	13,616
Cotton	29	25	1/	34	29	566	557	8,536	9,048
Cottonseed	(X)	(X)	Tons	12	10	(X)	(X)	1,260	936
Hay, all	270	260	Tons	648	598	2	2	44,064	45,448
Peanuts 2/	90	87	Lbs.	228,600	214,890	2,540	2,470	61,493	55,871
Potatoes, all all seasons	36,100	42,600	Cwt.	8,173	8,304	226	195	46,202	129,043
Soybeans 3/	115	120	Bu.	3,335	2,640	29	22	25,013	14,388
Sugarcane 4/	421	420	Tons	13,304	13,188	32	31	433,710	404,872
Tobacco, flue-cured 14	6	7	Lbs.	17,152	17,755	2,680	2,650	28,266	29,757
Wheat	70	65	Bu.	2,520	1,885	36	29	8,316	6,598

(X) Not applicable.
1/ Production in 480 net weight bales. Yield in pounds.
2/ Harvested for dry nuts.
3/ Harvested for beans.
4/ For sugar and seed.
Note: Data for 1988 are revised. All 1989 estimates are preliminary.

Table 9.63. CORN: ACREAGE HARVESTED FOR GRAIN AND BUSHELS PRODUCED IN THE STATE
CROP-REPORTING DISTRICTS, AND SPECIFIED COUNTIES OF FLORIDA, 1989

District and county	Acres harvested	Production (1,000 bushels)	District and county	Acres harvested	Production (1,000 bushels)
Florida	80,000	5,920	District 3--North	20,500	1,332
			Columbia	5,000	225
District 1--West	42,000	3,555	Hamilton	4,000	340
Escambia	11,000	1,100	Madison	3,000	165
Gadsden	2,000	130	Suwannee	6,000	390
Holmes	2,500	213	Other counties	2,500	212
Jackson	10,000	850	District 5--Central	12,000	675
Jefferson	5,000	425	Alachua	3,500	192
Leon	2,500	225	Gilchrist	1,500	68
Okaloosa	2,500	137	Levy	2,000	140
Walton	2,000	130	Marion	1,500	82
Washington	2,000	170	Other counties	3,500	193
Other counties	2,500	175	District 8--South	5,500	358

Note: See accompanying map for counties in crop-reporting districts. Data are
preliminary.

Source for Tables 9.62 and 9.63: State of Florida, Department of Agriculture and
Consumer Services, Florida Agricultural Statistics Service, *Florida Agricultural
Statistics: Field Crops Summary, 1989.*

Florida Statistical Abstract 1991

Crop Reporting Districts

District 1 - West
Bay
Calhoun
Escambia
Franklin
Gadsden
Gulf
Holmes
Jackson
Jefferson
Leon
Liberty
Okaloosa
Santa Rosa
Wakulla
Walton
Washington

District 3 - North
Baker
Columbia
Dixie
Duval
Hamilton
Lafayette
Madison
Nassau
Suwannee
Taylor

District 5 - Central
Alachua
Bradford
Citrus
Clay
Flagler
Gilchrist
Hernando
Hillsborough
Lake
Levy
Marion
Orange
Osceola
Pasco
Pinellas
Polk
Putnam
St. Johns
Seminole
Sumter
Union
Volusia

District 8 - South
Brevard
Broward
Charlotte
Collier
Dade
De Soto
Glades
Hardee
Hendry
Highlands
Indian River
Lee
Manatee
Martin
Monroe
Okeechobee
Palm Beach
St. Lucie
Sarasota

Table 9.64. PEANUTS: ACREAGE HARVESTED AND PRODUCTION IN THE STATE, CROP-REPORTING DISTRICTS, AND SPECIFIED COUNTIES OF FLORIDA, 1989

District and county	Acres harvested	Production (1,000 lbs.)	District and county	Acres harvested	Production (1,000 lbs.)
Florida	87,000	214,890	District 3--North	7,100	19,909
District 1--West	71,200	170,742	Columbia	1,900	3,857
Calhoun	4,050	10,206	Hamilton	200	362
Gadsden	1,450	3,364	Lafayette	200	664
Holmes	6,100	11,773	Madison	600	1,542
Jackson	39,950	97,079	Suwannee	4,100	13,243
Jefferson	1,000	2,510	Other counties	100	241
Leon	450	1,130			
Okaloosa	950	2,137	District 5--Central	8,700	24,239
Santa Rosa	10,250	29,110	Alachua	1,900	5,301
Wakulla	650	988	Gilchrist	500	1,155
Walton	4,300	7,740	Levy	3,350	9,749
Washington	1,650	3,993	Marion	2,450	6,884
Other counties	400	712	Other counties	500	1,150

Note: See accompanying map for counties in crop-reporting districts. Data are preliminary.

Table 9.65. SOYBEANS: ACREAGE HARVESTED FOR BEANS AND BUSHELS PRODUCED IN THE STATE, CROP-REPORTING DISTRICTS, AND SPECIFIED COUNTIES OF FLORIDA, 1989

District and county	Acres harvested	Production (1,000 bushels)	District and county	Acres harvested	Production (1,000 bushels)
Florida	120,000	2,640	District 3--North	20,200	456
District 1--West	88,600	1,945	Columbia	2,500	65
Calhoun	14,300	272	Hamilton	2,700	70
Escambia	15,700	346	Madison	8,700	174
Gadsden	2,400	55	Suwannee	4,900	118
Holmes	6,500	150	Other counties	1,400	29
Jackson	14,000	322			
Jefferson	2,900	70	District 5--Central	10,200	214
Okaloosa	7,600	167	Alachua	4,000	92
Santa Rosa	11,700	257	Gilchrist	2,400	50
Walton	6,600	152	Other counties	3,800	72
Washington	4,500	104			
Other counties	2,400	50	District 8--South	1,000	25

Note: See accompanying map for counties in crop-reporting districts. Data are preliminary.

Source for Tables 9.64 and 9.65: State of Florida, Department of Agriculture and Consumer Services, Florida Agricultural Statistics Service, *Florida Agricultural Statistics: Field Crops Summary, 1989.*

Florida Statistical Abstract 1991

Table 9.66. SUGARCANE AND COTTON: ACREAGE HARVESTED AND PRODUCTION IN THE STATE
   CROP-REPORTING DISTRICTS, AND SPECIFIED COUNTIES OF FLORIDA, 1989

County	Sugarcane for sugar		District and county	Cotton	
	Acres harvested	Production (tons)		Acres harvested	Production (bales)
Florida	405,000	12,717,000	Florida	25,000	29,000
Glades	19,400	599,000	District 1--West	24,650	28,600
Hendry	58,100	1,714,000	Escambia	3,150	4,700
Martin	13,900	431,000	Jackson	4,000	5,200
Palm Beach	313,600	9,973,000	Santa Rosa	12,300	13,500
			Other counties	5,200	5,200
			District 3--North	350	400

Note: Data are preliminary.

Table 9.67. FLUE-CURED TOBACCO: ACREAGE HARVESTED AND PRODUCTION IN THE STATE
   CROP-REPORTING DISTRICTS, AND SPECIFIED COUNTIES OF FLORIDA, 1989

District and county	Acres harvested	Production (pounds)	District and county	Acres harvested	Production (pounds)
Florida	6,700	17,755,000	District 3 (cont.)		
			Lafayette	470	1,410,000
District 1--West	355	725,000	Madison	745	1,807,000
Gadsden	110	220,000	Suwannee	1,695	4,916,000
Jefferson	145	305,000	Taylor	120	312,000
Other counties 1/	100	200,000	District 5--Central	1,360	3,364,000
District 3--North	4,985	13,666,000	Alachua	805	1,932,000
Baker	130	273,000	Bradford	110	275,000
Columbia	695	1,807,000	Gilchrist	160	448,000
Dixie and Nassau	65	159,000	Union	210	525,000
Hamilton	1,065	2,982,000	Other counties 2/	75	184,000

1/ Includes Holmes, Jackson, and Leon counties.
2/ Includes Levy, Marion, and Sumter counties.
Note: See accompanying map for counties in crop-reporting districts. Data are
preliminary.

Source for Tables 9.66 and 9.67: State of Florida, Department of Agriculture and
Consumer Services, Florida Agricultural Statistics Service, *Florida Agricultural
Statistics: Field Crops Summary, 1989.*

Florida Statistical Abstract 1991

Table 9.68. POTATOES: ACREAGE HARVESTED IN THE STATE AND SPECIFIED COUNTIES
OF FLORIDA, 1984 THROUGH 1989

(in acres)

County or season	1984	1985	1986	1987	1988	1989
Florida	33,600	35,100	32,600	35,700	36,100	42,600
Winter	7,400	7,800	7,200	7,100	7,100	7,600
Spring	26,200	27,300	25,400	28,600	29,000	35,000
Dade	5,400	5,500	5,000	5,000	5,200	5,100
Flagler	2,800	3,000	2,000	1,700	2,200	3,000
Putnam	4,200	4,500	4,300	5,600	4,400	4,500
St. Johns	18,000	18,500	18,200	19,200	19,900	20,500
Other counties	3,200	3,600	3,100	4,200	4,400	9,500

Note: 1989 data are preliminary.
Source: State of Florida, Department of Agriculture and Consumer Services,
Florida Agricultural Statistics Service, *Florida Agricultural Statistics: Field
Crops Summary, 1989.*

Table 9.69. VEGETABLES, MELONS, POTATOES, AND STRAWBERRIES: ACREAGE HARVESTED
PRODUCTION, AND VALUE IN FLORIDA, CROP YEAR 1989-90

Crop	Acreage planted	Acreage harvested	Production (1,000 CWT)	Total value ($1,000)
All crops, total	418,055	368,080	65,350	1,325,586
Vegetables, total	273,050	237,350	41,591	952,728
Snap beans 1/	26,500	21,300	1,184	41,869
Cabbage	14,300	12,900	2,774	38,575
Carrots 1/	9,900	7,200	1,080	17,604
Celery	8,900	7,900	2,939	34,237
Sweet corn	58,200	52,000	5,484	83,817
Cucumbers 1/	17,100	16,100	3,783	67,254
Eggplant	2,050	1,950	524	13,537
Escarole	4,000	3,500	423	7,945
Lettuce	10,600	8,000	1,536	31,115
Green peppers	23,100	20,200	3,706	111,246
Radishes	29,000	23,000	1,208	28,497
Squash	13,600	11,700	1,671	36,598
Tomatoes 1/	55,800	51,600	15,279	440,434
Other vegetables 2/	41,105	35,730	3,860	93,477
Watermelons	53,000	45,000	9,000	64,350
Potatoes	45,500	44,700	Δ/ 9,733	Δ/ 139,707
Strawberries	5,400	5,300	1,166	75,324

CWT hundred weight.
Δ/ Production sold.
1/ Fresh and processing.
2/ Fresh and processing vegetables and cantaloupes.
Source: State of Florida, Department of Agriculture and Consumer Services,
Florida Agricultural Statistics Service, *Florida Agricultural Statistics: Vegetable
Summary, 1989-90.*

Florida Statistical Abstract 1991

Table 9.72. LIVESTOCK: CASH RECEIPTS FROM MARKETINGS IN FLORIDA, 1983 THROUGH 1990

(in thousands of dollars, except where indicated)

| Year | Total livestock and products | | Cattle and calves | Hogs | Milk | Poultry and eggs |
	Amount	Percentage of total farm cash receipts				
1983	1,078,395	23	359,015	36,466	346,335	233,537
1984	1,098,633	23	373,133	27,088	304,398	284,588
1985	1,023,070	22	334,247	17,950	333,465	230,047
1986	1,017,626	22	272,920	23,376	346,680	265,630
1987	1,101,730	21	387,883	23,550	343,200	223,246
1988	1,155,908	20	391,171	19,024	355,680	253,446
1989	1,182,052	22	356,668	19,010	387,960	308,032
1990	1,288,877	23	390,561	20,041	421,341	288,108

Note: Data are for calendar year, except for hogs, poultry, and eggs which report for a marketing year of December through November. Beginning in 1985, value of eggs is for total production including consumption on farms where produced. Data do not include government payments. Some data are revised.

Table 9.73. LIVESTOCK INVENTORY: NUMBER ON FARMS IN FLORIDA, LEADING STATE, AND THE UNITED STATES, 1990 OR 1991

(numbers in thousands)

| Type of livestock | Florida | | Leading state | | United States |
	Rank among states	Number	Name	Number	
Cattle and calves 1/	16	1,975	Texas	13,200	98,162
Beef cows 2/	10	1,065	Texas	5,360	33,620
Hogs and pigs 3/	29	130	Iowa	13,800	54,362

1/ January 1, 1990.   2/ January 1, 1991.   3/ December 1990.

Table 9.74. LIVESTOCK: HONEY AND BEESWAX PRODUCTION IN FLORIDA, SPECIFIED YEARS 1980 THROUGH 1990

| Year | Honey | | | | Beeswax | | |
	Number of colonies (1,000)	Production (1,000 pounds)	Price per pound (dollars)	Value ($1,000)	Production (1,000 pounds)	Price per pound (dollars)	Value ($1,000)
1980	350	20,300	0.520	10,556	345	1.82	628
1981	360	24,120	0.537	12,952	362	1.97	713
1988	240	25,200	0.510	12,852	(NA)	(NA)	(NA)
1989	250	15,000	0.480	7,200	(NA)	(NA)	(NA)
1990	220	20,900	0.470	9,823	(NA)	(NA)	(NA)

(NA) Not available.
Note: Some data are revised.
Source for Tables 9.72, 9.73, and 9.74: State of Florida, Department of Agriculture, Florida Agricultural Statistics Service, *Florida Agricultural Statistics: Livestock Summary, 1990.*

Florida Statistical Abstract 1991

Table 9.85.   COMMERCIAL DAIRIES: ANNUAL MILK PRODUCTION IN THE STATE AND COUNTIES
OF FLORIDA, 1989 AND 1990

(in thousands of pounds)

County	1989	1990
Florida	2,447,000	2,528,000
Alachua	73,500	68,700
Broward	33,000	31,800
Clay	122,000	113,500
Duval	61,600	64,100
Escambia	32,500	36,000
Gilchrist	106,000	126,000
Hardee	72,700	108,000
Hernando	48,100	48,100
Highlands	128,000	130,000
Hillsborough	105,000	101,500
Holmes	22,700	26,400
Jackson	40,700	45,600
Jefferson	44,500	44,000
Lafayette	142,000	158,500
Lake	35,200	37,000
Manatee	88,400	87,300
Marion	44,500	46,900
Martin	47,800	41,000
Nassau	82,000	76,600
Okeechobee	624,000	581,500
Pasco	80,900	85,200
Polk	43,500	48,400
Suwannee	63,500	75,900
Washington	17,800	18,000
Other counties 1/	280,100	328,000
Noncommercial 2/	7,000	5,000

1/ Other counties combined to avoid disclosing individual operations include:
Baker, Bradford, Brevard, Calhoun, Charlotte, De Soto, Dixie, Glades, Hamilton,
Indian River, Leon, Levy, Orange, Osceola, Palm Beach, Putnam, St. Lucie, Santa
Rosa, Sarasota, Sumter, and Volusia.
2/ Noncommercial production used on farms where produced.

Source: State of Florida, Department of Agriculture and Consumer Services,
Florida Agricultural Statistics Service, *Florida Agricultural Statistics: Dairy
Summary, 1990.*

Florida Statistical Abstract 1991

Table 9.86. DAIRY PRODUCTION: NUMBER OF MILK COWS AND ANNUAL MILK PRODUCTION
IN FLORIDA, OTHER LEADING PRODUCTION STATES, AND THE UNITED STATES, 1990

State	Milk cows 1/ (1,000)	Total milk (1,000,000 pounds)	Production 2/ Rank among states	Per milk cow (pounds)
Florida	180	2,528	14	14,044
Wisconsin	1,753	24,400	1	13,919
California	1,135	20,953	2	18,461
New York	768	11,102	3	14,456
Minnesota	710	10,006	4	14,093
Pennsylvania	683	9,933	5	14,543
Texas	386	5,539	6	14,350
Michigan	344	5,233	7	15,212
Ohio	342	4,495	8	13,143
Washington	237	4,398	9	18,557
Iowa	305	4,330	10	14,197
Missouri	230	3,040	11	13,217
Idaho	179	2,949	12	16,475
Illinois	195	2,820	13	14,462
United States	10,127	148,284	(X)	14,642

(X) Not applicable.
1/ Average number on farms during year, excluding heifers not yet fresh.
2/ Excludes milk sucked by calves.

Source: State of Florida, Department of Agriculture and Consumer Services,
Florida Agricultural Statistics Service, *Florida Agricultural Statistics: Dairy
Summary, 1990.*

Table 9.87. CHICKENS AND EGGS: CASH RECEIPTS IN FLORIDA, MARKETING YEARS 1984
THROUGH 1990

(in thousands of dollars)

Year	Total	Broilers	Eggs 1/	Other chickens
1984	284,588	126,149	155,306	3,133
1985	230,047	118,796	107,680	3,571
1986	265,630	147,687	114,698	3,245
1987	223,246	127,099	94,160	1,987
1988	253,446	156,585	94,461	2,400
1989	308,032	181,636	123,078	3,318
1990	288,108	152,012	133,610	2,486

1/ Beginning in 1985, value of eggs is for total production including consumption
on farms where produced.
Note: Data are for marketing years beginning December 1 and ending November 30.

Source: State of Florida, Department of Agriculture and Consumer Services,
Florida Agricultural Statistics Service, *Florida Agricultural Statistics: Poultry
Summary, 1990.*

Florida Statistical Abstract 1991

FORESTRY, FISHERIES AND MINERALS

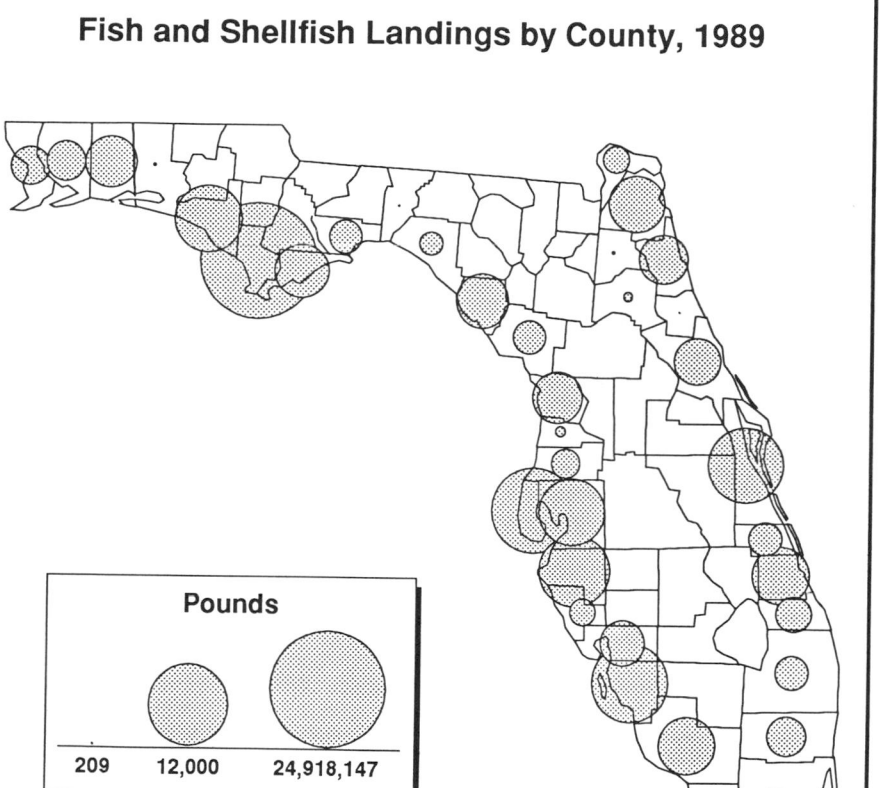

Fish and Shellfish Landings by County, 1989

Pounds

209   12,000   24,918,147

The Florida Graphic Atlas

Source: Table 10.40

SECTION 10.00
FORESTRY, FISHERIES, AND MINERALS

TABLES LISTED BY MAJOR HEADINGS

292

Table 10.07.   FOREST PRODUCTS: HARVEST BY PRODUCT AND BY SPECIES GROUP IN THE STATE
AND COUNTIES OF FLORIDA, 1989

(rounded to thousands of cubic feet)

| County | All products | | Pulpwood | | Saw/veneer logs | | Other products-- |
	Softwood	Hardwood	Softwood	Hardwood	Softwood	Hardwood	softwood
Florida	450,095	32,603	270,713	25,600	157,846	5,416	21,536
Alachua	14,039	622	9,072	503	4,778	63	189
Baker	15,164	77	9,433	15	5,376	62	355
Bay	16,093	1,067	12,566	1,037	3,527	30	0
Bradford	18,738	355	11,685	337	6,809	18	244
Brevard	5,879	0	0	0	67	0	5,812
Broward	0	52	0	52	0	0	0
Calhoun	12,013	929	8,091	290	3,633	639	289
Charlotte	328	0	328	0	0	0	0
Citrus	1,001	38	642	0	356	38	3
Clay	15,669	290	8,264	290	7,405	0	0
Collier	69	0	0	0	69	0	0
Columbia	21,901	428	13,114	373	8,383	55	404
Dade	0	0	0	0	0	0	0
De Soto	2,700	0	2,504	0	17	0	179
Dixie	11,433	2,311	6,674	1,968	4,595	343	164
Duval	10,953	337	5,383	335	5,194	2	376
Escambia	7,048	1,399	5,291	1,399	1,757	0	0
Flagler	10,459	261	5,620	261	4,564	0	275
Franklin	2,638	0	1,521	0	1,117	0	0
Gadsden	7,341	2,237	5,221	1,342	1,967	895	153
Gilchrist	10,412	146	6,176	0	4,030	90	206
Glades	920	0	82	0	0	0	838
Gulf	5,157	11	4,595	4	562	7	0
Hamilton	5,560	411	4,570	86	856	69	134
Hardee	900	0	900	0	0	0	0
Hendry	4,513	0	4,191	0	0	0	322
Hernando	730	59	3	0	522	59	205
Highlands	738	0	33	0	167	0	538
Hillsborough	910	283	0	0	619	283	291
Holmes	9,004	1,035	4,730	1,034	4,188	1	86
Indian River	0	0	0	0	0	0	0
Jackson	9,819	940	4,244	940	5,444	0	131
Jefferson	6,125	1,013	4,557	389	1,469	360	99

Continued . . .

Table 10.07. FOREST PRODUCTS: HARVEST BY PRODUCT AND BY SPECIES GROUP IN THE STATE
AND COUNTIES OF FLORIDA, 1989 (Continued)

(rounded to thousands of cubic feet)

County	All products Softwood	All products Hardwood	Pulpwood Softwood	Pulpwood Hardwood	Saw/veneer logs Softwood	Saw/veneer logs Hardwood	Other products-- softwood
Lafayette	8,801	173	6,061	45	2,690	128	50
Lake	1,827	77	623	0	1,001	77	203
Lee	6	851	6	180	0	0	0
Leon	5,428	226	2,852	98	2,210	128	366
Levy	16,564	2,326	10,553	2,085	5,152	213	859
Liberty	8,498	754	4,510	565	3,434	189	554
Madison	9,054	2,611	5,860	1,914	3,063	441	131
Manatee	15	6	0	0	15	6	0
Marion	14,286	638	7,994	196	6,097	442	195
Martin	0	0	0	0	0	0	0
Monroe	0	0	0	0	0	0	0
Nassau	18,672	1,286	12,164	1,237	5,958	49	550
Okaloosa	7,132	297	2,175	275	4,828	22	129
Okeechobee	111	0	0	0	43	0	68
Orange	765	1,968	540	1,968	140	0	85
Osceola	2,098	46	0	0	1,307	46	791
Palm Beach	0	0	0	0	0	0	0
Pasco	3,053	172	1,635	11	1,355	161	63
Pinellas	29	0	0	0	29	0	0
Polk	5,332	27	183	27	2,109	0	3,040
Putnam	8,980	256	3,618	196	4,960	60	402
St. Johns	8,901	901	5,316	888	2,985	13	600
St. Lucie	152	0	48	0	44	0	60
Santa Rosa	13,383	1,788	9,016	1,788	4,022	0	345
Sarasota	3	0	0	0	3	0	0
Seminole	681	1,476	540	1,476	81	0	60
Sumter	2,122	220	540	196	1,541	24	41
Suwannee	10,265	14	5,229	14	4,869	0	167
Taylor	34,777	663	26,987	338	7,517	325	273
Union	6,099	156	3,383	156	2,617	0	99
Volusia	9,705	274	8,354	198	680	76	671
Wakulla	7,051	0	4,226	0	2,491	0	334
Walton	8,963	339	5,313	338	3,564	1	86
Washington	9,088	757	3,497	756	5,570	1	21

Source: State of Florida, Department of Agriculture and Consumer Services,
Division of Forestry, unpublished data.

Florida Statistical Abstract 1991

Table 10.25. NATIONAL FOREST LAND: GROSS AND NET AREA OF NATIONAL FOREST AND OTHER
LAND ADMINISTERED BY THE FOREST SERVICE IN FLORIDA AND THE UNITED STATES AS OF
SEPTEMBER 30, 1990

(in acres)

Unit name and area	Gross area within unit boundaries	National forest system lands	Other lands within unit boundaries
Total	1,246,201	1,127,133	119,068
National forests			
Apalachicola National Forest	631,260	563,668	67,592
National wilderness areas	32,402	(X)	(X)
Bradwell Bay 1/	24,602	(X)	(X)
Mud Swamp/New River 1/	7,800	(X)	(X)
Choctawhatchee National Forest	684	684	0
Ocala National Forest	430,446	383,049	47,397
National wilderness areas	26,580	(X)	(X)
Alexander Springs 1/	7,700	(X)	(X)
Billies Bay 1/	3,120	(X)	(X)
Juniper Prairie 1/	13,260	(X)	(X)
Little Lake George 1/	2,500	(X)	(X)
National game refuge, Ocala	79,735	(X)	(X)
Osceola National Forest	183,811	179,732	4,079
National wilderness area, Big Gum Swamp 1/	13,600	(X)	(X)
United States	231,098,504	191,395,342	39,703,162

(X) Not applicable.
1/ Acreage estimated pending final map compilation.

Table 10.26. NATIONAL FOREST LAND: NET AREA OF THE NATIONAL FOREST LAND
ADMINISTERED BY THE FOREST SERVICE BY COUNTY IN FLORIDA AND IN THE
UNITED STATES AS OF SEPTEMBER 30, 1990

Area	National forest area	National forest system lands (acres)
Total	(X)	1,127,133
Okaloosa	Choctawhatchee National Forest	523
Walton	Choctawhatchee National Forest	161
Baker	Osceola National Forest	101,403
Columbia	Osceola National Forest	78,329
Franklin	Apalachicola National Forest	21,816
Leon	Apalachicola National Forest	104,470
Liberty	Apalachicola National Forest	265,817
Wakulla	Apalachicola National Forest	171,565
Lake	Ocala National Forest	84,072
Marion	Ocala National Forest	275,362
Putnam	Ocala National Forest	23,615
United States	(X)	187,083,200

(X) Not applicable.
Source for Tables 10.25 and 10.26: U.S., Department of Agriculture, Forest
Service, *Land Areas of the National Forest System as of September 30, 1990.*

Florida Statistical Abstract 1991

Table 10.34. TREE FARMS: NUMBER AND ACREAGE IN FLORIDA, OTHER SELECTED STATES, AND
THE UNITED STATES, JANUARY 1, 1990 AND 1991

State	Number of tree farms		Total acreage	
	1990	1991	1990	1991
Florida	3,652	3,902	7,305,693	6,976,544
Alabama	2,615	2,765	7,447,993	7,531,973
Arkansas	4,400	4,542	5,413,059	5,373,625
California	713	755	3,617,259	3,700,243
Georgia	4,424	4,594	7,926,846	7,789,249
Louisiana	2,999	3,041	4,815,794	4,418,941
Maine	1,871	1,918	8,742,535	7,913,341
Michigan	2,036	2,184	2,434,569	2,765,455
Mississippi	5,367	5,609	4,132,666	4,195,189
North Carolina	3,175	3,139	2,654,987	2,579,683
Oregon	1,068	1,125	6,720,630	6,804,524
South Carolina	1,646	1,728	3,434,366	3,493,520
Tennessee	1,514	1,597	2,149,853	2,161,173
Texas	3,479	3,726	4,527,063	4,565,745
Virginia	2,459	2,723	2,114,985	2,191,487
Washington	984	1,124	6,261,455	6,717,726
United States	67,175	71,495	95,309,259	95,097,329

Note: Data are reported for states with acreage of 2.0 million or more.
Source: American Forest Council, unpublished data.

Table 10.35. FISHERIES: NUMBER OF PROCESSING AND WHOLESALING PLANTS AND AVERAGE
ANNUAL EMPLOYMENT IN FLORIDA, GEOGRAPHIC AREAS, OTHER MAJOR PRODUCTION STATES
AND THE UNITED STATES, 1989

Area	Number of plants			Average annual employment		
	Total	Pro-cessing	Whole-sale	Total	Pro-cessing	Whole-sale
Area						
South Atlantic and Gulf	1,690	657	1,033	21,930	17,393	4,537
New England	934	252	682	8,927	6,182	2,745
Mid-Atlantic	562	191	371	10,332	7,472	2,860
Pacific	1,146	556	590	19,069	16,337	2,732
Inland States	60	39	21	609	540	69
State						
Florida	435	209	226	6,857	5,531	1,326
Maine	383	98	285	2,792	1,978	814
Massachusetts	368	109	259	4,713	3,340	1,373
North Carolina	260	97	163	2,170	1,664	506
Washington	308	145	163	4,149	3,682	467
California	517	129	388	6,634	4,681	1,953
Alaska 1/	267	247	20	7,023	6,978	45
United States 2/	4,459	1,718	2,741	73,179	59,937	13,242

1/ Some data have been estimated.
2/ Includes partial survey of Guam, Hawaii, North Marianas, American Samoa and
Puerto Rico.
Source: U.S., Department of Commerce, National Oceanic and Atmospheric Administration, National Marine Fisheries Service, *Fisheries of the United States, 1990*.

Florida Statistical Abstract 1991

Table 10.40. FISH AND SHELLFISH: QUANTITY OF LANDINGS BY TYPE OF SPECIES AND TRIPS IN THE STATE AND SPECIFIED COUNTIES OF FLORIDA, 1989

Area and county	Landings 1/ (pounds)			Trips 3/
	Total	Fish	Shellfish 2/	
Florida	199,529,670	138,408,918	61,120,752	407,439
East coast	46,116,073	27,985,797	18,130,276	118,230
West coast	146,472,218	104,115,181	42,357,037	285,291
Inland/out of state 4/	6,941,379	6,307,940	633,439	3,918
Bay	8,939,542	8,251,482	688,060	9,200
Brevard	11,169,071	3,504,147	7,664,924	43,301
Broward	2,981,926	2,859,880	122,046	3,258
Charlotte	3,960,115	3,367,517	592,598	10,754
Citrus	5,073,013	2,538,324	2,534,689	16,666
Clay	26,285	16,941	9,344	97
Collier	6,384,921	4,872,913	1,512,008	12,419
Dade	1,560,006	679,973	880,033	8,930
Dixie	5,368,415	3,269,257	2,099,158	18,804
Duval	6,459,901	3,695,713	2,764,188	11,838
Escambia	2,893,772	2,186,221	707,551	6,622
Flagler	209	209	0	7
Franklin	5,462,794	1,256,289	4,206,505	28,953
Gulf	24,918,147	21,857,447	3,060,700	2,735
Hernando	235,294	20,544	214,750	1,747
Hillsborough	9,020,545	6,873,630	2,146,915	5,436
Indian River	2,104,263	2,066,428	37,835	5,910
Jefferson	1,618	1,618	0	8
Lee	11,484,311	7,339,576	4,144,735	32,296
Levy	2,350,378	612,998	1,737,380	8,194
Manatee	9,736,042	9,624,739	111,303	8,697
Martin	2,555,599	2,547,274	8,325	3,902
Monroe	22,019,233	8,993,204	13,026,029	78,690
Nassau	1,334,564	278,666	1,055,898	1,586
Okaloosa	5,059,096	4,660,807	398,289	3,226
Palm Beach	2,171,242	2,111,523	59,719	7,730
Pasco	1,774,118	960,049	814,069	5,166
Pinellas	13,967,564	11,273,242	2,694,322	18,812
Putnam	185,014	27,005	158,009	1,176
St. Johns	4,946,192	472,392	4,473,800	7,842
St. Lucie	6,346,542	6,144,587	201,955	8,558
Santa Rosa	2,948,414	2,787,353	161,061	3,851
Sarasota	1,542,762	1,469,316	73,446	2,303
Taylor	983,364	759,229	224,135	4,255
Volusia	4,275,259	3,581,059	694,200	14,095
Wakulla	2,322,109	1,121,671	1,200,438	6,150
Walton	26,651	17,755	35,547	307

1/ Based on whole weight of species with some exceptions, e.g., stone crabs, sponges. Recorded in county of first sale to dealer.
2/ Includes clams, conch, crabs, lobster, octopus, oysters, scallops, shrimp, sponges, and squid.
3/ Only successful trips of fishermen.
4/ Landings from seafood dealers residing in inland counties or out-of-state who bought Florida produced seafood.
Note: Data are preliminary.
Source: State of Florida, Department of Natural Resources, Marine Fisheries Information System, unpublished data.

Florida Statistical Abstract 1991

Table 10.71. FORESTRY AND FISHING INDUSTRIES: AVERAGE MONTHLY REPORTING UNITS
   EMPLOYMENT, AND PAYROLL COVERED BY UNEMPLOYMENT COMPENSATION LAW BY
   INDUSTRY IN FLORIDA, 1990

SIC code	Industry	Number of reporting units	Number of employees	Payroll ($1,000)
08	Forestry	178	2,103	3,482
081	Timber tracts	48	353	591
083	Forest products	12	80	96
085	Forestry services	118	1,669	2,794
09	Fishing, hunting, and trapping	271	979	1,366
091	Commercial fishing	256	879	1,233
092	Fish hatcheries and preserves	7	62	95
097	Hunting and trapping, and game propagation	7	37	38

Note: Totals on county employment tables may not match totals in this table due
to rounding.

Table 10.72. MINING: AVERAGE MONTHLY REPORTING UNITS, EMPLOYMENT, AND PAYROLL
   COVERED BY UNEMPLOYMENT COMPENSATION LAW BY INDUSTRY IN FLORIDA, 1990

SIC code	Industry	Number of reporting units	Number of employees	Payroll ($1,000)
	Mining	222	8,886	21,239
10	Metal mining	(D)	(D)	(D)
12	Coal mining	(D)	(D)	(D)
13	Oil and gas extraction	61	506	1,714
131	Crude petroleum and natural gas	(D)	(D)	(D)
132	Natural gas liquids	(D)	(D)	(D)
138	Oil and gas fields services	41	226	601
14	Mining and quarrying of nonmetallic minerals, except fuels	163	7,966	18,398
141	Dimension stone	(D)	(D)	(D)
142	Crushed and broken stone, including riprap	52	2,439	5,365
144	Sand and gravel	49	798	1,506
145	Clay, cermanic, and refactory minerals	5	306	670
147	Chemical and fertilizer mineral mining	12	3,962	10,008
148	Nonmetallic minerals services, except fuels	(D)	(D)	(D)
149	Miscellaneous nonmetallic minerals, except fuels	39	396	727

(D) Data withheld to avoid disclosure of information about individual firms.
   Note: Totals on county employment tables may not match totals in this table due
to rounding.

   Source for Tables 10.71 and 10.72: State of Florida, Department of Labor and
Employment Security, Bureau of Labor Market Information, "Employment, Wages, and
Contributions Report" (ES-202), unpublished data.

Florida Statistical Abstract 1991

Table 10.84. PHOSPHATE ROCK PRODUCTION: SALES OR USE BY PRODUCERS BY TYPE OF USE AND BY REGION IN THE UNITED STATES, CROP YEARS 1988-89 AND 1989-90

(in thousand metric tons)

	Year ending June 30, 1989 Domestic 1/				Year ending June 30, 1990 Domestic 1/			
Region	Total	Agri-cultural	Indu-strial	Ex-port 2/	Total	Agri-cultural	Indu-strial	Ex-port 2/
Florida and North Carolina								
Rock	35,618	35,590	28	8,339	36,269	36,189	80	6,838
P205 content	10,799	10,791	8	2,690	10,927	10,904	23	2,207
Idaho, Montana, Tennessee, and Utah								
Rock	5,715	3,735	1,980	202	5,911	3,732	2,179	134
P205 content	1,629	1,093	536	63	1,682	1,092	590	40

1/ Includes rock converted to products and exported.
2/ Exports reported to Bureau of Mines by companies.

Table 10.85. PHOSPHATE ROCK PRODUCTION: PRODUCTION AND SALES BY REGION IN THE UNITED STATES, CROP YEARS 1988-89 AND 1989-90

	Year ending June 30, 1989		Value 1/		Year ending June 30, 1990		Value 1/	
	Thousand metric tons		Total (million	Aver-age per ton (dol-	Thousand metric tons		Total (million	Aver-age per ton (dol-
Item	Rock	P205 con-tent	dollars)	lars)	Rock	P205 con-tent	dollars)	lars)
Mine production	180,546	28,252	(NA)	(NA)	148,693	19,134	(NA)	(NA)
Florida and North Carolina	170,705	25,787	(NA)	(NA)	139,904	16,975	(NA)	NA)
Idaho, Montana, Tennessee, and Utah	9,841	2,465	(NA)	(NA)	8,790	2,158	(NA)	(NA)
Marketable production	49,693	15,079	1,061	21.34	46,391	14,077	1,041	22.44
Florida and North Carolina	43,254	13,238	926	21.41	40,482	12,388	923	22.80
Idaho, Montana, Tennessee, and Utah	6,439	1,841	135	20.97	5,909	1,689	118	19.97
Sold or used by producers	49,911	15,216	1,066	21.36	49,150	14,857	1,104	22.46
Florida and North Carolina	43,996	13,525	941	21.39	43,107	13,134	985	22.85
Idaho, Montana, Tennessee, and Utah	5,915	1,691	125	21.13	6,043	1,723	119	19.69

(NA) Not available.   1/ Calculated value based on weighted sold or used value.
Note: Detail may not add to totals because of rounding.
Source for Tables 10.84 and 10.85: U.S., Department of the Interior, Bureau of Mines, *Mineral Industry Surveys: Phosphate Rock, 1990 Crop Year*, and previous edition.

Table 10.86. PHOSPHATE: RESERVES IN FLORIDA, OTHER STATES, THE UNITED STATES, AND
    OTHER COUNTRIES, 1989

(in millions of metric tons)

Area	Number of deposits	Reserves 1/	Reserve base 2/
State, total	(NA)	1,230	4,440
Florida	(NA)	750	2,540
Idaho	(NA)	90	160
Montana	(NA)	1	1
North Carolina	(NA)	390	790
Tennessee	(NA)	6	10
Utah	(NA)	0	730
Wyoming	(NA)	0	210
Country, total	195	12,585	34,275
Algeria	1	240	240
Australia	5	90	590
Brazil	11	330	370
Canada	1	50	50
China	6	210	210
Christmas Island	1	10	10
Colombia	1	0	100
Egypt	5	0	760
Finland	1	0	70
Israel	4	0	180
Jordan	3	90	480
Mexico	2	10	110
Morocco	10	4,950	20,490
Nauru	1	5	5
Peru	1	310	310
Senegal	2	0	160
South Africa, Republic of	1	2,530	2,530
Syria	2	190	190
Togo	12	0	60
Tunisia	11	0	270
Turkey	1	30	30
United States	94	1,230	4,440
U.S.S.R.	11	1,330	1,330
Venezuela	1	0	10
Western Sahara	1	950	950
Other	6	30	330

(NA) Not available.

1/ Phosphate rock reserves at a cost less than $40 per ton FOB mine. Costs
include capital, operating expenses, taxes, royalties (if applicable), miscellaneous
costs, and a 15 percent rate of return on investment. Costs and resources are as of
January 1989, FOB mine.

2/ Reserve base at a cost less than $100 per ton FOB mine.

Note: Detail may not add to totals because of rounding.

Source: U.S. Department of the Interior, Bureau of Mines, *Phosphate Rock, 1989.*

CONSTRUCTION

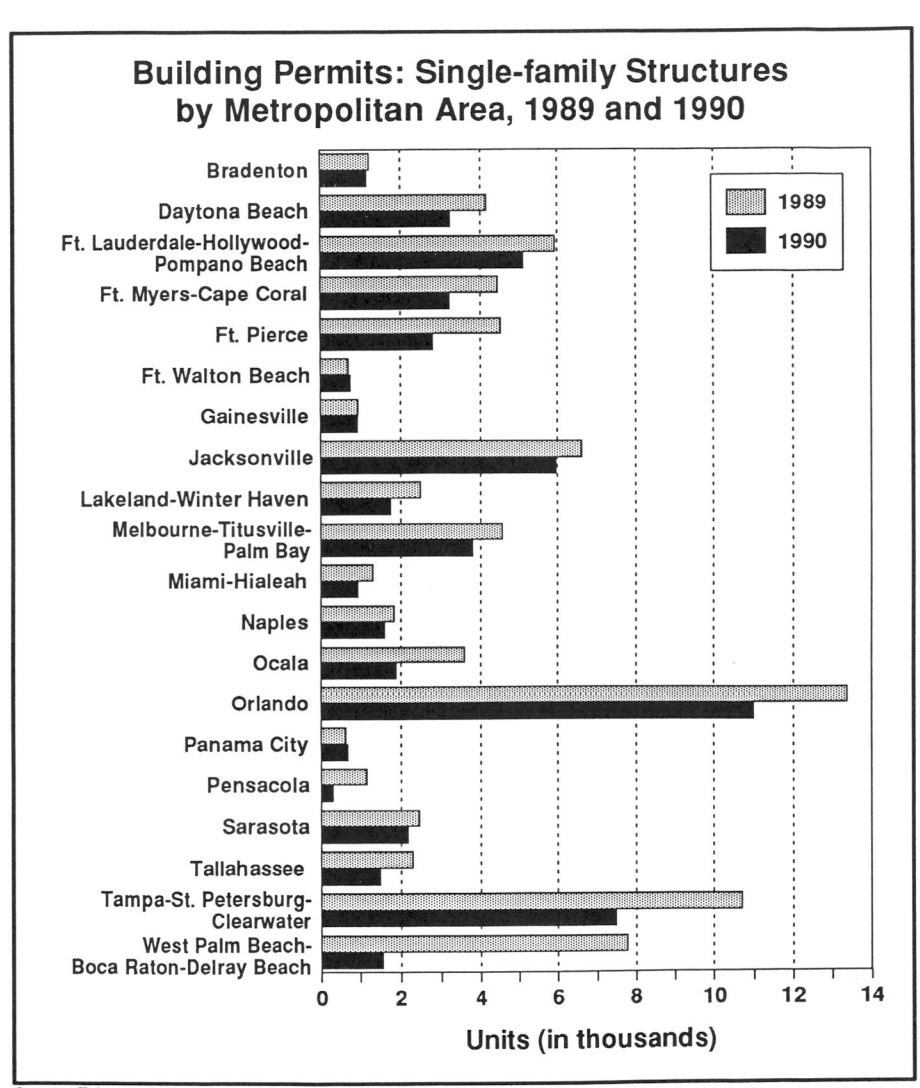

Building Permits: Single-family Structures by Metropolitan Area, 1989 and 1990

Units (in thousands)

1989
1990

Bradenton
Daytona Beach
Ft. Lauderdale-Hollywood-Pompano Beach
Ft. Myers-Cape Coral
Ft. Pierce
Ft. Walton Beach
Gainesville
Jacksonville
Lakeland-Winter Haven
Melbourne-Titusville-Palm Bay
Miami-Hialeah
Naples
Ocala
Orlando
Panama City
Pensacola
Sarasota
Tallahassee
Tampa-St. Petersburg-Clearwater
West Palm Beach-Boca Raton-Delray Beach

Source: Table 11.17

SECTION 11.00
CONSTRUCTION

TABLES LISTED BY MAJOR HEADINGS

Table 11.03. CONSTRUCTION CONTRACTS: VALUE IN FLORIDA AND THE UNITED STATES
1979 THROUGH 1989

(in millions of dollars)

Year	Florida	United States	Year	Florida	United States
1979	12,176	168,446	1986	17,954	248,588
1980	12,847	148,393	1987	19,447	258,090
1981	12,124	153,480	1988 A/	19,587	260,752
1982	10,820	156,240	1989		
1983	14,307	193,602	Total 1/	20,481	261,163
1984	16,926	211,480	Nonresidential	5,939	93,058
1985	17,820	232,277	Residential	11,680	120,436

A/ Revised.   1/ Includes nonbuildings.
Note: Includes new structures/additions/major alterations to existing structures.
Source: U.S., Department of Commerce, Bureau of the Census, *Statistical Abstract
of the United States, 1991.* Data from F.W. Dodge Division.

Table 11.04. BUILDING PERMIT ACTIVITY: NUMBER OF PRIVATE RESIDENTIAL HOUSING UNITS
AUTHORIZED BY BUILDING PERMITS IN FLORIDA, OTHER SUNBELT STATES, OTHER POPULOUS
STATES, AND THE UNITED STATES, 1987 THROUGH 1990

State	1987	1988	1989	1990
Sunbelt states				
Florida	178,764	170,597	164,985	126,929
Alabama 1/	14,523	12,773	12,042	12,258
Arizona	40,181	32,878	23,820	22,773
Arkansas 1/	6,476	6,232	6,339	6,134
California	251,824	253,369	237,694	162,638
Georgia 1/	64,217	63,017	50,457	41,373
Louisiana 1/	8,520	7,270	6,116	5,881
Mississippi 1/	6,632	7,396	6,643	5,397
New Mexico	9,268	6,401	6,658	6,047
North Carolina 1/	54,270	50,322	48,351	40,589
Oklahoma 1/	6,247	5,046	5,622	4,848
South Carolina	23,520	23,102	21,204	18,485
Tennessee 1/	29,919	27,803	24,244	21,548
Texas 1/	50,455	40,479	41,287	46,575
Virginia	66,650	66,487	56,877	40,580
Other populous states				
Illinois	50,447	49,145	42,377	37,563
Indiana	27,273	25,248	26,473	25,329
Massachusetts	40,419	30,482	21,283	15,138
Michigan	46,593	44,907	45,687	39,989
New Jersey	51,462	40,909	30,337	19,390
New York	62,186	54,719	48,735	32,067
Ohio 1/	45,153	45,105	41,228	39,064
Pennsylvania	54,803	53,833	45,483	35,980
United States	1,534,772	1,455,623	1,338,423	1,104,414

1/ Percentage of population in permit-issuing places is less than 90.
Note: Data are from a national sample of 17,000 permit-issuing places, a uni-
verse which accounts for approximately 92 percent of new residential construction.
Some data may be revised. See also Table 24.20.
Source: U.S., Department of Commerce, International Trade Administration, *Con-
struction Review,* March-April 1991.

Florida Statistical Abstract 1991

Table 11.15. BUILDING PERMIT ACTIVITY: NEW HOUSING UNITS AUTHORIZED BY BUILDING
   PERMITS IN THE STATE, COUNTIES, MUNICIPALITIES, AND UNINCORPORATED AREAS OF
   FLORIDA, 1989 AND 1990

	1989			1990		
	Number of	Number of units in--		Number of	Number of units in--	
	monthly	Single-	Multi-	monthly	Single-	Multi-
	reports	family	family	reports	family	family
Area	received	structures	structures	received	structures	structures
Florida	(X)	92,326	48,679	(X)	68,329	34,106
Alachua County	(X)	859	558	(X)	881	256
Alachua	12	35	0	12	58	0
Archer	11	1	24	11	11	0
Gainesville	12	173	6	12	120	8
Hawthorne	12	3	0	12	3	0
High Springs	12	11	0	12	9	0
Micanopy	12	0	0	12	1	0
Newberry	12	4	0	11	6	0
Waldo	12	0	0	11	1	0
Unincorporated	11	632	528	12	672	248
Baker County	(X)	84	0	(X)	98	0
Macclenny	12	17	0	12	27	0
Unincorporated	12	67	0	12	71	0
Bay County	(X)	636	364	(X)	680	44
Callaway	1	0	0	0	(NA)	(NA)
Lynn Haven	12	107	0	12	86	2
Mexico Beach	12	9	0	9	4	4
Panama City	0	(NA)	(NA)	0	(NA)	(NA)
Panama City Beach	12	110	28	12	150	26
Springfield	1	0	0	7	2	0
Unincorporated	12	410	336	12	438	12
Bradford County	(X)	102	0	(X)	71	2
Unincorporated	12	102	0	12	71	2
Brevard County	(X)	4,575	477	(X)	3,813	921
Cape Canaveral	12	40	40	12	2	38
Cocoa	12	110	8	12	73	20
Cocoa Beach	12	8	225	12	2	24
Indialantic	12	13	0	12	9	0
Indian Harbour Beach	12	28	6	12	36	16
Malabar	12	51	0	12	50	0
Melbourne	12	509	36	12	430	379
Melbourne Beach	11	9	0	12	7	0
Melbourne Village	11	1	0	11	0	0
Palm Bay	11	1,220	8	12	1,113	0
Palm Shores	12	24	0	12	45	0
Rockledge	11	248	8	12	210	16
Satellite Beach	12	12	15	12	6	0
Titusville	12	251	82	11	189	75
West Melbourne	12	21	28	12	13	14
Unincorporated	12	2,030	21	12	1,628	339
Broward County	(X)	5,944	6,936	(X)	5,134	5,157
Coconut Creek	12	446	364	12	458	300
Cooper City	12	313	183	12	339	54

See footnotes at end of table.   Continued . . .

Florida Statistical Abstract 1991

Table 11.15. BUILDING PERMIT ACTIVITY: NEW HOUSING UNITS AUTHORIZED BY BUILDING PERMITS IN THE STATE, COUNTIES, MUNICIPALITIES, AND UNINCORPORATED AREAS OF FLORIDA, 1989 AND 1990 (Continued)

	1989			1990		
	Number of	Number of units in--		Number of	Number of units in--	
	monthly	Single-	Multi-	monthly	Single-	Multi-
	reports	family	family	reports	family	family
Area	received	structures	structures	received	structures	structures
Broward County						
(Continued)						
Coral Springs	12	712	1,294	12	434	409
Dania	11	35	334	12	28	19
Davie 1/	12	1,051	242	11	516	148
Deerfield Beach	12	48	46	12	72	294
Ft. Lauderdale	12	73	72	12	37	195
Hacienda Village	0	(NA)	(NA)	0	(NA)	(NA)
Hallandale	12	21	12	12	15	2
Hillsboro Beach	1	0	0	1	0	0
Hollywood	12	115	541	11	42	325
Lauderdale-by-the-sea	12	3	0	12	1	0
Lauderdale Lakes	12	0	0	12	0	0
Lauderhill	0	(NA)	(NA)	6	18	0
Lazy Lake Village	1	0	0	1	0	0
Lighthouse Point	11	21	0	11	12	0
Margate	12	359	138	10	206	12
Miramar	12	289	240	12	191	0
North Lauderdale	12	40	12	12	67	0
Oakland Park	12	32	544	11	23	272
Parkland	11	150	244	12	168	211
Pembroke Park	12	0	0	11	12	0
Pembroke Pines	12	304	1,034	12	396	851
Plantation	7	564	308	12	525	178
Pompano Beach	12	148	135	11	34	700
Sea Ranch Lakes	12	0	0	11	0	0
Sunrise	12	501	654	12	723	688
Tamarac	11	106	497	12	80	473
Wilton Manor	1	0	0	1	0	0
Unincorporated	11	613	42	12	737	26
Calhoun County	(X)	58	0	(X)	51	0
Blountstown	12	7	0	12	5	0
Unincorporated	12	51	0	12	46	0
Charlotte County	(X)	2,628	617	(X)	1,993	724
Punta Gorda	12	185	135	12	170	58
Unincorporated	12	2,443	482	12	1,823	666
Citrus County	(X)	1,449	94	(X)	1,292	66
Crystal River	12	16	0	12	14	0
Inverness	12	145	0	12	144	0
Unincorporated	12	1,288	94	12	1,134	66
Clay County	(X)	1,020	0	(X)	1,006	0
Green Cove Springs	12	34	0	12	48	0
Keystone Heights 2/	(X)	(X)	(X)	2	1	0
Orange Park	12	5	0	12	5	0
Penney Farms	12	2	0	12	3	0
Unincorporated	12	979	0	12	949	0

See footnotes at end of table. Continued . . .

Florida Statistical Abstract 1991

Table 11.15. BUILDING PERMIT ACTIVITY: NEW HOUSING UNITS AUTHORIZED BY BUILDING
PERMITS IN THE STATE, COUNTIES, MUNICIPALITIES, AND UNINCORPORATED AREAS OF
FLORIDA, 1989 AND 1990 (Continued)

		1989			1990	
	Number of	Number of units in--		Number of	Number of units in--	
	monthly	Single-	Multi-	monthly	Single-	Multi-
	reports	family	family	reports	family	family
Area	received	structures	structures	received	structures	structures
Collier County	(X)	1,852	3,588	(X)	1,635	2,753
Everglades	11	0	0	12	2	0
Naples	12	46	63	11	39	57
Unincorporated	10	1,806	3,525	10	1,594	2,696
Columbia County	(X)	223	50	(X)	254	24
Lake City	12	10	0	12	18	24
Unincorporated	12	213	50	12	236	0
Dade County	(X)	1,325	4,897	(X)	935	1,599
Bal Harbour	12	0	0	11	0	0
Bay Harbor Islands	12	0	0	12	0	23
Biscayne Park	12	0	0	12	0	0
Coral Gables	12	119	182	12	83	20
El Portal	0	(NA)	(NA)	11	0	0
Florida City	12	51	68	12	16	0
Golden Beach	11	6	0	12	4	0
Hialeah	11	657	1,862	10	394	291
Hialeah Gardens	12	43	173	12	167	0
Homestead	12	218	200	12	150	62
Indian Creek Village	11	0	0	12	1	0
Islandia	1	0	0	1	0	0
Medley	12	0	0	11	0	0
Miami	12	104	792	11	77	874
Miami Beach	10	8	1,589	11	9	298
Miami Shores	11	3	0	11	2	11
Miami Springs	11	11	0	11	5	0
North Bay	0	(NA)	(NA)	3	0	0
North Miami	12	6	0	11	6	0
North Miami Beach	4	13	0	12	3	0
Opa-Locka	10	4	0	12	2	0
Pennsuco	0	(NA)	(NA)	0	(NA)	(NA)
South Miami	12	16	0	12	11	14
Surfside	12	6	0	12	4	0
Sweetwater	12	60	31	12	1	6
Virginia Gardens	12	0	0	12	0	0
Unincorporated	0	(NA)	(NA)	0	(NA)	(NA)
De Soto County	(X)	117	60	(X)	102	36
Arcadia	12	25	4	9	17	8
Unincorporated	12	92	56	12	85	28
Dixie County	(X)	53	0	(X)	63	0
Horseshoe Beach 2/	(X)	(X)	(X)	1	0	0
Unincorporated	11	53	0	12	63	0
Duval County	(X)	4,268	1,678	(X)	3,743	1,836
Atlantic Beach	12	98	268	12	45	6
Baldwin	12	5	0	12	10	0

See footnotes at end of table.   Continued . . .

Table 11.15.   BUILDING PERMIT ACTIVITY: NEW HOUSING UNITS AUTHORIZED BY BUILDING
PERMITS IN THE STATE, COUNTIES, MUNICIPALITIES, AND UNINCORPORATED AREAS OF
FLORIDA, 1989 AND 1990 (Continued)

	1989			1990		
	Number of	Number of units in--		Number of	Number of units in--	
	monthly	Single-	Multi-	monthly	Single-	Multi-
	reports	family	family	reports	family	family
Area	received	structures	structures	received	structures	structures
Duval County						
(Continued)						
Jacksonville	12	3,897	1,389	11	3,196	1,334
Jacksonville Beach	12	192	0	12	122	194
Neptune Beach	12	76	21	12	16	18
Escambia County	(X)	193	8	(X)	134	42
Pensacola	12	188	8	12	127	42
Unincorporated 3/	12	5	0	12	7	0
Flagler County	(X)	1,070	112	(X)	698	21
Bunnell	5	8	0	0	(NA)	(NA)
Flagler Beach	12	49	13	5	12	0
Marineland	1	0	0	12	0	0
Unincorporated	12	1,013	99	11	686	21
Franklin County	(X)	80	2	(X)	80	0
Apalachicola	12	10	0	12	7	0
Carrabelle	12	3	0	9	0	0
Unincorporated	12	67	2	12	73	0
Gadsden County	(X)	181	0	(X)	151	0
Chattahoochee	12	2	0	12	0	0
Greensboro	12	0	0	12	1	0
Gretna	0	(NA)	(NA)	0	(NA)	(NA)
Quincy	12	17	0	12	19	0
Unincorporated	12	162	0	12	131	0
Gilchrist County	(X)	56	24	(X)	49	0
Trenton	0	(NA)	(NA)	0	(NA)	(NA)
Unincorporated	12	56	24	12	49	0
Glades County	(X)	26	0	(X)	22	0
Unincorporated	12	26	0	11	22	0
Gulf County	(X)	69	11	(X)	80	2
Port St. Joe	12	8	3	12	12	0
Wewahitchka 4/	3	1	0	0	(NA)	(NA)
Unincorporated	12	60	8	12	68	2
Hamilton County	(X)	31	0	(X)	26	0
Jasper	12	2	0	9	4	0
Jennings	0	(NA)	(NA)	0	(NA)	(NA)
White Springs	0	(NA)	(NA)	0	(NA)	(NA)
Unincorporated	11	29	0	12	22	0
Hardee County	(X)	64	55	(X)	57	0
Bowling Green	12	5	0	12	1	0
Wauchula	12	11	53	12	6	0
Zolfo Springs	12	4	2	12	3	0
Unincorporated	12	44	0	12	47	0
Hendry County	(X)	56	0	(X)	76	2
Clewiston	0	(NA)	(NA)	3	0	0
LaBelle 5/	(X)	(X)	(X)	9	9	2
Unincorporated	9	56	0	12	67	0

See footnotes at end of table.   Continued . . .

Table 11.15. BUILDING PERMIT ACTIVITY: NEW HOUSING UNITS AUTHORIZED BY BUILDING
PERMITS IN THE STATE, COUNTIES, MUNICIPALITIES, AND UNINCORPORATED AREAS OF
FLORIDA, 1989 AND 1990 (Continued)

	1989			1990		
	Number of	Number of units in--		Number of	Number of units in--	
	monthly	Single-	Multi-	monthly	Single-	Multi-
	reports	family	family	reports	family	family
Area	received	structures	structures	received	structures	structures
Hernando County	(X)	2,114	51	(X)	1,617	133
Brooksville	12	5	0	11	12	45
Unincorporated	12	2,109	51	12	1,605	88
Highlands County	(X)	867	510	(X)	686	161
Avon Park	12	29	2	12	16	2
Lake Placid	12	9	8	12	10	8
Sebring	11	15	0	12	25	18
Unincorporated	12	814	500	12	635	133
Hillsborough County	(X)	4,100	2,162	(X)	2,454	2,837
Plant City	12	257	12	12	220	216
Tampa	12	675	446	11	386	668
Temple Terrace	12	20	8	12	20	260
Unincorporated	12	3,148	1,696	11	1,828	1,693
Holmes County	(X)	63	8	(X)	65	0
Unincorporated	12	63	8	12	65	0
Indian River County	(X)	1,263	419	(X)	1,027	226
Fellsmere	11	9	0	12	14	0
Indian River Shores	12	54	0	12	36	0
Orchid 2/	(X)	(X)	(X)	1	0	0
Sebastian	12	406	8	12	372	8
Vero Beach	12	82	6	11	45	8
Unincorporated	12	712	405	12	560	210
Jackson County	(X)	157	0	(X)	125	26
Graceville	0	(NA)	(NA)	0	(NA)	(NA)
Unincorporated	12	157	0	12	125	26
Jefferson County	(X)	37	0	(X)	47	0
Unincorporated	12	37	0	12	47	0
Lafayette County	(X)	19	0	(X)	15	0
Mayo	12	3	0	12	1	0
Unincorporated	11	16	0	4	14	0
Lake County	(X)	1,531	487	(X)	2,057	148
Eustis	12	70	47	12	48	2
Fruitland Park	12	6	0	12	9	0
Groveland	0	(NA)	(NA)	0	(NA)	(NA)
Lady Lake	12	95	10	12	512	0
Leesburg	12	63	73	12	29	33
Mascotte	12	7	0	12	3	0
Monteverde	0	(NA)	(NA)	0	(NA)	(NA)
Mount Dora	12	56	170	12	35	8
Tavares	11	25	10	12	25	12
Umatilla	12	3	46	12	9	0
Unincorporated	12	1,206	131	12	1,387	93
Lee County	(X)	4,449	3,269	(X)	3,207	1,101
Cape Coral	12	1,891	169	12	1,143	120
Ft. Myers	12	82	967	12	42	125
Sanibel	12	71	6	12	48	18
Unincorporated	12	2,405	2,127	11	1,974	838

　　See footnotes at end of table.　　　　　　　　　　　　　　　Continued . . .

Florida Statistical Abstract 1991

Table 11.15.   BUILDING PERMIT ACTIVITY: NEW HOUSING UNITS AUTHORIZED BY BUILDING
PERMITS IN THE STATE, COUNTIES, MUNICIPALITIES, AND UNINCORPORATED AREAS OF
FLORIDA, 1989 AND 1990 (Continued)

	1989			1990		
	Number of	Number of units in--		Number of	Number of units in--	
	monthly	Single-	Multi-	monthly	Single-	Multi-
	reports	family	family	reports	family	family
Area	received	structures	structures	received	structures	structures
Leon County	(X)	2,103	1,170	(X)	1,345	978
Tallahassee	12	1,012	964	12	801	919
Unincorporated	12	1,091	206	7	544	59
Levy County	(X)	22	6	(X)	16	6
Cedar Key 2/	(X)	(X)	(X)	2	2	0
Chiefland	12	12	6	12	3	6
Inglis	0	(NA)	(NA)	0	(NA)	(NA)
Williston	12	8	0	12	6	0
Yankeetown	12	2	0	9	5	0
Unincorporated	0	(NA)	(NA)	0	(NA)	(NA)
Liberty County	(X)	0	0	(X)	5	0
Unincorporated	0	(NA)	(NA)	5	5	0
Madison County	(X)	29	9	(X)	46	0
Unincorporated	12	29	9	12	46	0
Manatee County	(X)	1,254	1,273	(X)	1,185	1,118
Anna Maria	12	11	0	12	21	0
Bradenton	12	142	701	12	219	205
Bradenton Beach	12	1	2	12	2	0
Holmes Beach	12	22	22	11	19	6
Longboat Key	12	40	235	12	54	138
Palmetto	12	23	0	12	21	94
Unincorporated	12	1,015	313	11	849	675
Marion County	(X)	3,600	136	(X)	1,908	99
Belleview	12	6	4	12	2	0
Dunnellon	11	11	0	12	2	24
McIntosh	7	3	0	12	1	0
Ocala	12	226	16	12	120	12
Reddick	0	(NA)	(NA)	0	(NA)	(NA)
Unincorporated	12	3,354	116	11	1,783	63
Martin County	(X)	1,502	659	(X)	841	326
Jupiter Island	12	14	0	12	5	0
Ocean Breeze Park	1	0	0	1	0	0
Sewalls Point	12	27	0	12	19	0
Stuart	12	8	78	12	4	88
Unincorporated	12	1,453	581	12	813	238
Monroe County	(X)	38	116	(X)	17	106
Key Colony Beach	12	12	4	11	5	4
Key West	11	25	112	12	11	102
Layton	12	1	0	12	1	0
Unincorporated	0	(NA)	(NA)	0	(NA)	(NA)
Nassau County	(X)	410	109	(X)	349	62
Callahan	12	4	0	12	0	0
Fernandina Beach	12	110	36	12	74	58
Hilliard	12	2	6	12	0	0
Unincorporated	12	294	67	12	275	4

See footnotes at end of table.   Continued . . .

Florida Statistical Abstract 1991

Table 11.15. BUILDING PERMIT ACTIVITY: NEW HOUSING UNITS AUTHORIZED BY BUILDING
    PERMITS IN THE STATE, COUNTIES, MUNICIPALITIES, AND UNINCORPORATED AREAS OF
    FLORIDA, 1989 AND 1990 (Continued)

	1989			1990		
	Number of	Number of units in--		Number of	Number of units in--	
	monthly	Single-	Multi-	monthly	Single-	Multi-
	reports	family	family	reports	family	family
Area	received	structures	structures	received	structures	structures
Okaloosa County	(X)	716	77	(X)	768	94
Crestview	0	(NA)	(NA)	0	(NA)	(NA)
Destin	12	99	3	12	86	0
Ft. Walton Beach	12	11	32	12	15	0
Mary Esther	12	3	0	12	6	0
Niceville	12	81	0	12	63	0
Valparaiso	12	8	4	12	8	0
Unincorporated	8	514	38	10	590	94
Okeechobee County	(X)	161	27	(X)	111	0
Okeechobee	0	(NA)	(NA)	0	(NA)	(NA)
Unincorporated	12	161	27	12	111	0
Orange County	(X)	7,267	5,061	(X)	5,693	3,504
Apopka	12	463	0	12	335	6
Bay Lake	12	0	0	12	0	0
Belle Isle	0	(NA)	(NA)	0	(NA)	(NA)
Eatonville	12	2	2	10	0	2
Edgewood	11	21	0	12	2	0
Lake Buena Vista	12	0	132	11	0	60
Maitland	12	8	0	12	12	0
Oakland	12	4	0	12	9	0
Ocoee	12	239	6	12	381	259
Orlando	12	367	2,700	12	370	877
Winter Garden	12	123	0	12	109	200
Winter Park	12	64	23	11	65	7
Unincorporated	12	5,976	2,198	11	4,410	2,093
Osceola County	(X)	2,130	1,712	(X)	2,505	1,362
Kissimmee	12	468	895	12	193	296
St. Cloud	12	325	14	12	149	226
Unincorporated	11	1,337	803	12	2,163	840
Palm Beach County	(X)	7,782	5,903	(X)	1,566	1,439
Atlantis	12	7	0	12	15	0
Belle Glade	12	29	0	12	7	4
Boca Raton	12	661	430	12	285	576
Boynton Beach	12	436	349	12	103	196
Briny Breezes	0	(NA)	(NA)	3	0	0
Cloud Lake	1	0	0	1	0	0
Delray Beach	12	163	192	12	184	377
Glen Ridge	1	0	0	12	0	0
Golf Village	12	0	0	12	3	0
Golfview	12	0	0	10	0	0
Greenacres City	12	107	584	11	76	32
Haverhill	12	34	0	11	1	0
Highland Beach	12	6	87	11	3	0

    See footnotes at end of table.   Continued . . .

Florida Statistical Abstract 1991

Table 11.15. BUILDING PERMIT ACTIVITY: NEW HOUSING UNITS AUTHORIZED BY BUILDING
PERMITS IN THE STATE, COUNTIES, MUNICIPALITIES, AND UNINCORPORATED AREAS OF
FLORIDA, 1989 AND 1990 (Continued)

	1989			1990		
	Number of	Number of units in--		Number of	Number of units in--	
	monthly	Single-	Multi-	monthly	Single-	Multi-
	reports	family	family	reports	family	family
Area	received	structures	structures	received	structures	structures
Palm Beach County						
(Continued)						
Hypoluxo	12	0	593	12	1	3
Jupiter	12	306	565	12	133	62
Jupiter Inlet Colony	12	2	0	12	1	0
Lake Clarke Shores	12	8	132	12	3	0
Lake Park	12	0	7	12	1	0
Lake Worth	12	18	4	12	6	0
Lantana	12	28	4	12	20	10
Manalapan	12	4	0	12	4	0
Mangonia Park	12	1	0	12	0	0
North Palm Beach	12	5	0	11	2	0
Ocean Ridge	12	10	0	12	9	0
Pahokee 2/	(X)	(X)	(X)	3	0	0
Palm Beach	11	8	0	12	15	0
Palm Beach Shores	12	2	44	12	0	0
Palm Springs	12	5	0	12	0	0
Riviera Beach	11	18	131	12	27	0
Royal Palm Beach						
Village	12	404	0	11	152	0
South Bay 2/	(X)	(X)	(X)	3	0	0
South Palm Beach	12	0	0	12	0	24
Tequesta Village	6	17	0	11	13	0
West Palm Beach	12	150	712	11	80	0
Unincorporated	8	4,893	1,973	0	(NA)	(NA)
Pasco County	(X)	2,080	326	(X)	1,460	81
Dade City	10	7	46	12	6	0
New Port Richey	12	25	84	11	38	18
Port Richey	12	2	0	11	1	0
San Antonio	12	6	0	11	0	0
Zephyrhills	12	37	10	12	34	9
Unincorporated	12	2,003	186	12	1,381	54
Pinellas County	(X)	2,423	1,737	(X)	1,960	1,935
Belleair	12	12	0	12	8	0
Belleair Beach	7	4	0	2	4	0
Clearwater	12	137	301	12	95	925
Dunedin	12	133	363	12	80	160
Gulfport	12	45	14	12	28	0
Indian Rocks Beach	9	3	32	12	13	40
Indian Shores	11	0	2	11	0	0
Kenneth City	12	0	0	12	0	0
Largo	12	54	201	12	39	15
North Redington Beach	12	2	0	12	3	0

See footnotes at end of table.   Continued . . .

Florida Statistical Abstract 1991

Table 11.15. BUILDING PERMIT ACTIVITY: NEW HOUSING UNITS AUTHORIZED BY BUILDING
    PERMITS IN THE STATE, COUNTIES, MUNICIPALITIES, AND UNINCORPORATED AREAS OF
    FLORIDA, 1989 AND 1990 (Continued)

		1989			1990	
	Number of	Number of units in--		Number of	Number of units in--	
	monthly	Single-	Multi-	monthly	Single-	Multi-
	reports	family	family	reports	family	family
Area	received	structures	structures	received	structures	structures
Pinellas County						
(Continued)						
Oldsmar	12	16	38	12	11	10
Pinellas Park	12	43	0	12	128	0
Redington Beach	11	1	0	12	5	0
Redington Shores	12	28	25	12	5	0
Safety Harbor	12	110	8	12	91	0
St. Petersburg	12	269	103	12	143	42
St. Petersburg Beach	9	6	131	12	14	48
Seminole	12	6	0	12	2	0
South Pasadena	12	2	50	12	1	84
Tarpon Springs	0	(NA)	(NA)	0	(NA)	(NA)
Treasure Island	12	41	4	12	39	6
Unincorporated	12	1,511	465	12	1,251	605
Polk County	(X)	2,486	795	(X)	1,775	319
Auburndale	12	47	10	12	36	0
Bartow	12	35	10	12	29	0
Davenport	9	9	0	6	3	0
Dundee	12	14	0	8	4	0
Eagle Lake	12	5	0	12	2	0
Ft. Meade	12	7	0	12	11	0
Frostproof	12	6	0	12	5	0
Haines City	11	21	100	12	21	0
Highland Park	0	(NA)	(NA)	0	(NA)	(NA)
Lake Alfred	12	8	0	12	7	0
Lake Hamilton	12	5	5	12	1	0
Lake Wales	12	27	0	12	26	0
Lakeland	12	257	287	12	222	53
Mulberry	11	0	0	12	4	0
Polk City	11	14	36	12	20	0
Winter Haven	12	61	21	11	38	90
Unincorporated	12	1,970	326	10	1,346	176
Putnam County	(X)	264	6	(X)	229	
Palatka	12	24	6	12	23	0
Welaka	12	3	0	1	0	0
Unincorporated	12	237	0	12	206	0
St. Johns County	(X)	931	111	(X)	868	299
St. Augustine	12	15	0	11	8	3
St. Augustine Beach	12	29	4	12	26	4
Unincorporated	12	887	107	12	834	292
St. Lucie County	(X)	3,038	302	(X)	1,951	313
Ft. Pierce	12	30	144	12	26	72
Port St. Lucie	12	2,511	52	11	1,488	150
St. Lucie Village	10	8	0	12	4	0
Unincorporated	11	489	106	12	433	91

    See footnotes at end of table.   Continued . . .

Florida Statistical Abstract 1991

Table 11.15. BUILDING PERMIT ACTIVITY: NEW HOUSING UNITS AUTHORIZED BY BUILDING
    PERMITS IN THE STATE, COUNTIES, MUNICIPALITIES, AND UNINCORPORATED AREAS OF
    FLORIDA, 1989 AND 1990 (Continued)

	1989			1990		
	Number of	Number of units in--		Number of	Number of units in--	
	monthly	Single-	Multi-	monthly	Single-	Multi-
	reports	family	family	reports	family	family
Area	received	structures	structures	received	structures	structures
Santa Rosa County	(X)	978	48	(X)	160	2
Gulf Breeze	0	(NA)	(NA)	0	(NA)	(NA)
Unincorporated	11	978	48	2	160	2
Sarasota County	(X)	2,469	1,035	(X)	2,179	789
North Port Charlotte	12	278	0	12	304	0
Sarasota	12	55	0	12	55	312
Venice	12	129	54	12	318	9
Unincorporated	11	2,007	981	11	1,502	468
Seminole County	(X)	3,983	799	(X)	2,807	2,479
Altamonte Springs	12	46	372	12	106	163
Casselberry	12	80	0	12	56	892
Lake Mary	12	222	0	12	138	0
Longwood	12	60	8	12	19	0
Oviedo	12	706	186	12	634	8
Sanford	11	155	137	11	115	706
Winter Springs	12	418	0	12	270	12
Unincorporated	12	2,296	96	12	1,469	698
Sumter County	(X)	169	8	(X)	145	5
Bushnell	12	23	0	12	7	0
Center Hill	12	0	0	12	2	0
Coleman	0	(NA)	(NA)	0	(NA)	(NA)
Unincorporated	12	146	8	12	136	5
Suwannee County	(X)	112	24	(X)	133	0
Branford	12	1	0	12	1	0
Live Oak	12	5	24	12	6	0
Unincorporated	12	106	0	12	126	0
Taylor County	(X)	95	9	(X)	81	66
Perry	12	39	4	12	40	66
Unincorporated	12	56	5	12	41	0
Union County	(X)	29	0	(X)	26	0
Unincorporated	12	29	0	12	26	0
Volusia County	(X)	4,180	775	(X)	3,226	595
Daytona Beach	12	160	351	12	144	66
Daytona Beach Shores	12	19	15	12	8	209
Deland	12	60	10	11	64	0
Edgewater	12	332	0	12	230	0
Holly Hill	12	21	0	12	18	0
Lake Helen	12	11	0	12	10	0
New Smyrna Beach	12	148	79	12	115	127
Oak Hill	12	13	0	12	14	0
Orange City	12	24	0	12	55	0
Ormond Beach	12	210	0	10	93	2
Pierson	12	6	0	11	8	2
Ponce Inlet	12	58	0	12	50	0

See footnotes at end of table.   Continued . . .

Florida Statistical Abstract 1991

Table 11.15. BUILDING PERMIT ACTIVITY: NEW HOUSING UNITS AUTHORIZED BY BUILDING
   PERMITS IN THE STATE, COUNTIES, MUNICIPALITIES, AND UNINCORPORATED AREAS OF
   FLORIDA, 1989 AND 1990 (Continued)

Area	Number of monthly reports received	Number of units in-- Single-family structures	Multi-family structures	Number of monthly reports received	Number of units in-- Single-family structures	Multi-family structures
1989				1990		
Volusia County (Continued)						
Port Orange	12	471	143	12	418	53
South Daytona	12	42	8	12	36	8
Unincorporated	12	2,605	169	12	1,963	128
Wakulla County	(X)	86	0	(X)	112	0
Unincorporated	12	86	0	12	112	0
Walton County	(X)	288	9	(X)	328	12
DeFuniak Springs	12	13	0	12	15	0
Unincorporated	12	275	9	12	313	12
Washington County	(X)	82	0	(X)	110	0
Unincorporated	12	82	0	11	110	0

(X) Not applicable.
(NA) Not available.
1/ Includes Hacienda Village as of January 1985.
2/ Previously included in unincorporated. Reporting separately as of October 1990.
3/ Escambia County unincorporated is Pensacola Beach.
4/ Included in unincorporated as of April 1989.
5/ Previously included in unincorporated. Reporting separately as of March 1990.

Note: Data include activity reported by April 1990 and 1991. Only areas which issue permits are listed. County totals are aggregates of reports received. Data for 1989 are revised.

Source: University of Florida, Bureau of Economic and Business Research, *Building Permit Activity in Florida, 1990 Annual Report*, and previous edition.

Florida Statistical Abstract 1991

Table 11.16. BUILDING PERMIT ACTIVITY: VALUE REPORTED ON BUILDING PERMITS ISSUED
    IN THE STATE AND COUNTIES OF FLORIDA, 1990

(rounded to thousands of dollars)

County	Total value	Private Residential 1/	Private Non-residential 2/	Private Additions and alterations	Public
Florida	12,515,982	7,296,378	2,729,242	2,235,557	254,806
Alachua	101,170	57,763	23,687	17,330	2,390
Baker	5,952	3,946	849	1,132	25
Bay	96,425	53,273	25,245	17,907	0
Bradford	6,925	4,150	1,286	1,489	0
Brevard	507,461	362,431	93,252	50,911	867
Broward	1,267,067	781,064	281,005	177,278	27,717
Calhoun	3,309	2,504	100	356	350
Charlotte	258,311	177,764	62,372	18,156	19
Citrus	182,030	46,927	122,148	12,654	300
Clay	90,015	76,160	4,767	5,088	4,000
Collier	378,845	277,749	65,249	35,846	0
Columbia	15,037	10,392	2,577	2,069	0
Dade	520,048	264,572	80,197	155,216	20,064
De Soto	11,723	6,114	2,904	2,705	0
Dixie	8,013	3,350	2,610	2,053	0
Duval	641,170	303,837	184,708	145,255	7,369
Escambia	33,957	12,647	11,742	9,569	0
Flagler	62,526	48,530	10,875	3,121	0
Franklin	10,897	7,365	1,991	1,341	200
Gadsden	15,342	10,351	1,462	3,530	0
Gilchrist	3,214	2,166	733	315	0
Glades	3,229	1,236	967	1,026	0
Gulf	6,285	5,104	621	545	15
Hamilton	2,234	1,238	745	251	0
Hardee	8,983	3,960	3,472	1,550	0
Hendry	14,575	5,620	6,509	2,446	0
Hernando	145,280	88,842	43,023	12,953	462
Highlands	59,577	38,107	10,915	10,556	0
Hillsborough	606,274	309,130	155,909	134,291	6,944
Holmes	3,690	2,252	632	806	0
Indian River	189,320	131,857	31,849	24,615	998
Jackson	11,882	8,133	1,465	2,284	0
Jefferson	5,104	3,458	665	980	0
Lafayette	1,111	791	224	96	0
Lake	225,226	137,284	31,850	20,730	35,363
Lee	527,592	321,756	131,525	58,344	15,968
Leon	191,216	115,530	50,305	23,594	1,787

See footnotes at end of table.   Continued . . .

Florida Statistical Abstract 1991

Table 11.16. BUILDING PERMIT ACTIVITY: VALUE REPORTED ON BUILDING PERMITS ISSUED
    IN THE STATE AND COUNTIES OF FLORIDA, 1990 (Continued)

(rounded to thousands of dollars)

County	Total value	Residential 1/	Private Non-residential 2/	Additions and alterations	Public
Levy	2,357	1,381	360	616	0
Liberty	194	162	0	32	0
Madison	4,450	2,320	545	1,585	0
Manatee	194,562	109,604	58,968	25,394	595
Marion	135,304	76,250	33,730	12,474	12,852
Martin	218,920	145,531	31,976	40,348	1,065
Monroe	15,636	9,376	5,972	286	0
Nassau	38,498	30,783	4,468	3,247	0
Okaloosa	67,633	47,368	11,700	7,300	1,265
Okeechobee	8,926	6,473	1,496	957	0
Orange	1,309,345	715,057	318,756	234,979	40,551
Osceola	292,181	246,648	29,806	14,227	1,500
Palm Beach	995,851	304,423	240,808	445,120	5,500
Pasco	168,842	94,105	58,572	14,435	1,729
Pinellas	678,355	349,607	139,585	175,747	13,413
Polk	314,891	215,097	60,373	34,048	5,374
Putnam	29,598	13,506	8,371	7,721	0
St. Johns	142,033	109,974	20,581	11,462	16
St. Lucie	194,362	137,076	38,590	10,995	7,700
Santa Rosa	10,116	7,813	2,303	0	0
Sarasota	399,466	239,726	70,332	61,344	28,066
Seminole	535,890	359,199	71,341	105,351	0
Sumter	11,668	6,609	3,062	1,948	48
Suwannee	20,147	8,504	9,332	2,212	101
Taylor	13,026	4,811	1,587	2,275	4,354
Union	1,729	1,329	247	154	0
Volusia	419,073	305,394	48,981	59,002	5,699
Wakulla	10,058	7,145	1,338	1,575	0
Walton	28,943	22,208	5,122	1,472	140
Washington	32,913	31,546	505	863	0

1/ Includes single family, multi-family, and mobile homes; motels, hotels,
rooming houses, and other nonhousekeeping residential buildings.
    2/ Includes offices, stores, schools, industrial, and institutional buildings and
other nonresidential structures.
    Note: Data include activity reported by April 1991. Figures are aggregates of
value on monthly reports received from permit-issuing places. See Table 11.15 for a
record of the number of reports received and for changes in permit-issuing status.
A value of (0) thousand dollars indicates the value was between 0 and 500 dollars.
    Source: University of Florida, Bureau of Economic and Business Research, *Build-
ing Permit Activity in Florida, 1990 Annual Report.*

Florida Statistical Abstract 1991

Table 11.17. BUILDING PERMIT ACTIVITY: TOTAL VALUE AND NUMBER OF SINGLE-FAMILY AND MULTIFAMILY UNITS AUTHORIZED BY BUILDING PERMITS IN THE STATE AND METROPOLITAN STATISTICAL AREAS (MSAS) OF FLORIDA, 1989 AND 1990

	1989			1990		
		Units in--			Units in--	
	Total value ($1,000)	Single-family structures	Multi-family structures	Total value ($1,000)	Single family structures	Multi-family structures
MSA 1/						
Florida	15,997,827	92,326	48,679	12,515,982	68,329	34,106
Bradenton	294,268	1,254	1,273	194,562	1,185	1,118
Daytona Beach	512,928	4,180	775	419,073	3,226	595
Ft. Lauderdale-Hollywood- Pompano Beach	1,570,350	5,944	6,936	1,267,067	5,134	5,157
Ft. Myers-Cape Coral	653,918	4,449	3,269	527,592	3,207	1,101
Ft. Pierce	550,657	4,540	961	413,282	2,792	639
Martin County	344,496	1,502	659	218,920	841	326
St. Lucie County	206,161	3,038	302	194,362	1,951	313
Ft. Walton Beach	63,087	716	77	67,633	768	94
Gainesville	113,681	961	558	108,095	952	258
Alachua County	104,306	859	558	101,170	881	256
Bradford County	9,375	102	0	6,925	71	2
Jacksonville	1,081,658	6,629	1,898	911,716	5,966	2,197
Clay County	86,067	1,020	0	90,015	1,006	0
Duval County	752,884	4,268	1,678	641,170	3,743	1,836
Nassau County	86,980	410	109	38,498	349	62
St. Johns County	155,727	931	111	142,033	868	299
Lakeland-Winter Haven	329,802	2,486	795	314,891	1,775	319
Melbourne-Titusville- Palm Bay	570,035	4,575	477	507,461	3,813	921
Miami-Hialeah	700,075	1,325	4,897	520,048	935	1,599
Naples	519,096	1,852	3,588	378,845	1,635	2,753
Ocala	249,502	3,600	136	135,304	1,908	99
Orlando	2,398,254	13,380	7,572	2,137,416	11,005	7,345
Orange County	1,606,234	7,267	5,061	1,309,345	5,693	3,504
Osceola County	277,359	2,130	1,712	292,181	2,505	1,362
Seminole County	514,661	3,983	799	535,890	2,807	2,479
Panama City	124,439	636	364	96,425	680	44
Pensacola	116,141	1,171	56	44,073	294	44
Escambia County	53,384	193	8	33,957	134	42
Santa Rosa County	62,757	978	48	10,116	160	2
Sarasota	459,190	2,469	1,035	399,466	2,179	789
Tallahassee	294,752	2,284	1,170	206,558	1,496	978
Gadsden County	21,824	181	0	15,342	151	0
Leon County	272,928	2,103	1,170	191,216	1,345	978
Tampa-St. Petersburg- Clearwater	2,400,844	10,717	4,276	1,598,751	7,491	4,986
Hernando County	159,384	2,114	51	145,280	1,617	133
Hillsborough County	1,206,033	4,100	2,162	606,274	2,454	2,837
Pasco County	186,062	2,080	326	168,842	1,460	81
Pinellas County	849,365	2,423	1,737	678,355	1,960	1,935
West Palm Beach-Boca Raton-Delray Beach	1,765,002	7,782	5,903	995,851	1,566	1,439

1/ As defined June 30, 1990.
Note: Data for 1989 are revised.
Source: University of Florida, Bureau of Economic and Business Research, *Building Permit Activity in Florida, 1990 Annual Report* and previous edition.

Florida Statistical Abstract 1991

Table 11.25.　MANUFACTURED HOUSING:　SHIPMENTS OF MOBILE HOMES TO FLORIDA, SELECTED
STATES, AND THE UNITED STATES, 1986 THROUGH 1990

State 1/	1986	1987	1988	1989	1990 A/
Florida	24,877	25,865	23,339	22,606	17,297
Alabama	10,508	11,249	11,217	9,227	8,297
Arizona	5,728	5,871	4,717	3,276	3,047
Arkansas	4,394	4,363	3,748	2,803	2,557
California	10,520	9,651	10,517	10,763	9,706
Georgia	16,774	14,797	14,612	11,417	10,160
Illinois	3,355	3,571	3,170	3,071	2,856
Indiana	6,101	6,425	6,759	6,498	6,274
Kentucky	4,844	5,346	5,435	5,648	6,207
Michigan	9,461	9,915	10,334	9,861	9,356
Mississippi	5,383	5,070	4,307	3,510	3,704
Missouri	5,029	4,621	4,348	3,829	3,994
Nevada	1,513	2,006	2,361	2,324	2,386
New York	7,374	7,930	7,937	6,988	5,998
North Carolina	24,232	22,699	19,117	16,653	16,897
Ohio	6,604	6,749	6,883	6,454	6,048
Oregon	2,297	2,910	3,852	4,387	4,905
Pennsylvania	7,423	7,076	7,396	7,094	6,639
South Carolina	13,066	11,811	10,978	10,596	11,090
Tennessee	7,858	9,342	8,859	8,031	6,941
Texas	14,309	8,507	4,239	3,451	4,374
Virginia	6,022	5,861	5,580	4,984	5,452
Washington	4,550	3,873	4,184	4,397	5,645
West Virginia	3,352	3,085	2,651	2,493	2,778
Wisconsin	1,839	2,198	2,449	2,583	2,766
United States	244,347	232,823	218,264	198,083	188,251

A/ Preliminary.
1/ States with 1990 shipments of 2,000 or more are listed.
　　Note:　Shipments figures are based on reports submitted by manufacturers on the
number of mobile homes actually shipped during the survey month.　Shipments to
dealers may not be placed for residential uses in the month as they are shipped.
The number of mobile "homes" used for nonresidential purposes is not known.　These
shipments statistics are produced by the National Conference of States on Building
Codes and Standards, Inc.　See Glossary for definition of mobile home.

　　Source:　U.S., Department of Commerce, Bureau of the Census, *Housing Units
Authorized by Building Permits and Public Contracts:　February 1991*, and previous
editions.

Florida Statistical Abstract 1991

Table 11.40. CONSTRUCTION COST: INDEX OF CONSTRUCTION COSTS IN THE UNITED STATES
ANNUAL AVERAGES, 1988 THROUGH 1990, AND QUARTERLY, 1990

(1987 = 100)

Name of index	Annual averages		
	1988	1989	1990
Bureau of the Census			
Composite, fixed-weighted	103.8	107.2	109.7
Implicit price deflator	104.2	108.0	110.2
Engineering News Record			
Buildings	102.2	103.9	106.5
Construction	102.6	104.5	107.3
Bureau of the Census, houses			
under construction			
Fixed-weighted	103.6	106.7	109.1
Price deflator	104.1	107.9	109.9
Federal Highway Administration			
Composite	106.6	107.7	108.5
Bureau of Reclamation	103.0	107.0	111.0
Turner Construction Company	104.0	107.0	111.0
Handy-Whitman Public Utility			
Buildings	104.0	107.0	108.0
Electric	107.0	111.0	115.0
Gas	106.0	111.0	114.0
Water	103.0	106.0	108.0
C. A. Turner Telephone Plant	101.0	110.0	113.0

	Quarterly, 1990			
	February	May	August	November
Federal Highway Administration				
Composite	111.2	106.0	109.2	108.5
Bureau of Reclamation	110.0	110.0	111.0	113.0
Turner Construction Company	110.0	111.0	112.0	113.0

Note: Data are revised.

Source: U.S., Department of Commerce, Bureau of the Census, *Current Construction Reports: Value of New Construction Put in Place*, March 1991.

Florida Statistical Abstract 1991

Table 11.42. PRODUCER PRICES: INDEX OF PRODUCER PRICES OF MATERIALS USED
IN CONSTRUCTION BY SPECIFIED GROUP AND COMMODITY IN THE UNITED STATES
ANNUAL AVERAGES, 1987 THROUGH 1990

(1982 = 100, except where indicated)

Group and commodity	1987	1988	1989	1990	Percentage change annual 1989 to 1990
All construction materials	109.5	115.7	119.5	119.6	0.1
Softwood lumber	116.1	120.0	127.1	123.8	-2.6
Hardwood lumber	126.8	131.0	128.2	131.0	2.2
General millwork	119.2	123.3	129.2	132.0	2.2
Prefabricated structural members	113.3	116.8	119.3	122.3	2.5
Softwood plywood	109.8	109.1	124.2	119.6	-3.7
Hardwood plywood	92.9	94.2	99.8	102.7	2.9
Particleboard, platen-type 1/	121.1	125.4	128.6	117.3	-8.8
Hardboard	101.9	103.5	101.5	99.2	-2.3
Prefabricated wood buildings and components 2/	105.5	108.2	110.7	113.1	2.2
Mobile homes	104.0	109.3	114.0	117.5	3.1
Prepared paint	108.0	112.2	119.5	124.7	4.4
Builders hardware	117.0	122.5	127.8	133.0	4.1
Bright nails	101.0	104.7	110.4	(NA)	(NA)
Welded wire for concrete reinforcement	98.0	109.2	108.6	109.7	1.0
Concrete reinforcing bars 3/	100.8	113.4	115.5	109.9	-4.8
Aluminum siding 1/	104.0	116.8	(NA)	(NA)	(NA)
Roofing steel	98.0	99.0	105.9	109.2	3.1
Building wire and cable 1/	113.0	154.2	170.1	159.2	-6.4
Metal door sash and trim	112.0	122.4	130.0	131.4	1.1
Metal moulding, trim, and storefronts 4/	99.0	115.8	135.1	137.2	1.6
Steel fencing and fence gates 3/	105.0	109.5	115.4	116.3	0.8
Cast iron pressure and soil pipe and fittings	127.0	132.9	137.6	136.9	-0.5
Plumbing fixtures and brass fittings, group index	120.0	128.7	137.7	144.3	4.8
Vitreous china fixtures	117.0	120.4	123.3	125.6	1.9
Brass fittings	123.0	134.8	146.8	155.8	6.1
Metal fixtures 5/	102.0	106.1	111.6	114.9	3.0
Heating equipment, group index 6/	116.0	119.2	125.1	131.6	5.2
Steam and hot water	121.0	124.9	128.6	132.6	3.1
Warm air furnaces and attachments	112.0	115.1	120.3	129.5	7.6
Water heaters, domestic	111.0	115.5	120.0	124.2	3.5
Domestic heating stoves	117.0	111.4	112.9	113.7	0.7
Unitary air conditioners including heat pumps	107.0	110.1	113.5	117.1	3.2
Steel for buildings	108.0	114.9	119.0	118.9	-0.1
Steel for bridges	(NA)	105.9	115.7	115.8	0.1
Architectural and ornamental metalwork 7/	106.0	113.7	117.5	118.8	1.1

See footnotes at end of table.

Continued . . .

Table 11.42. PRODUCER PRICES: INDEX OF PRODUCER PRICES OF MATERIALS USED
   IN CONSTRUCTION BY SPECIFIED GROUP AND COMMODITY IN THE UNITED STATES
   ANNUAL AVERAGES, 1987 THROUGH 1990 (Continued)

(1982 = 100, except where indicated)

Group and commodity	1987	1988	1989	1990	Percentage change annual 1989 to 1990
Prefab metal buildings 8/	100.0	105.6	110.3	111.5	1.1
Concrete ingredients, group index 6/	110.4	112.0	113.2	115.3	1.9
Sand, gravel, and crushed stone	118.1	120.6	122.8	125.5	2.2
Portland cement	102.7	102.8	102.1	103.7	1.6
Concrete products, group index 6/	109.4	110.0	111.2	113.5	2.1
Building block	120.2	122.1	124.4	126.9	2.0
Concrete pipe	113.0	110.1	107.8	107.7	-0.1
Ready mixed concrete	107.3	107.9	109.3	111.9	2.4
Precast concrete	114.9	118.1	119.7	122.9	2.7
Prestressed concrete	98.2	97.5	98.9	100.1	1.2
Structural clay products, group index 6/	121.4	124.9	127.0	129.9	2.3
Brick and structural clay tile 2/	108.2	110.9	112.2	115.1	2.6
Ceramic floor and wall tile	123.1	127.2	130.2	132.5	1.8
Gypsum products, group index 6/	125.2	112.9	110.0	105.2	-4.4
Wallboard 1/2 inch	120.5	105.3	101.2	94.7	-6.4
Type X wallboard	126.6	110.5	106.7	101.9	-4.5
Cut stone and stone products 2/	110.0	115.1	118.7	121.1	2.0
Hardsurfaced floor coverings	116.1	122.5	129.9	133.2	2.5
Soft surfaced floor coverings	109.3	112.9	115.5	116.9	1.2
Prepared asphalt roofing	91.9	94.3	95.6	95.7	0.1
Sheet, plate, and float glass	103.4	107.7	105.3	98.6	-6.4
Insulation materials	105.0	105.8	106.7	108.4	1.6
Paving mixtures and blocks	100.8	102.7	101.0	101.3	0.3
Plastic construction products, group index 6/	108.4	121.1	120.1	117.1	-2.5
Plumbing products	112.6	128.8	119.2	108.6	-8.9
Plastic pipe and fittings 1/	107.7	123.4	113.9	104.1	-8.6
Lighting fixtures					
Residential	115.1	120.3	127.5	133.4	4.6
Commercial and industrial	112.6	117.3	122.7	127.6	4.0
Construction machinery and equipment	108.9	111.8	117.2	121.6	3.8

(NA) Not available.
1/ December 1982 = 100.
2/ December 1984 = 100.
3/ June 1982 = 100.
4/ June 1983 = 100.
5/ June 1987 = 100.
6/ Includes items not shown separately.
7/ December 1983 = 100.
8/ December 1987 = 100.

Source: U.S., Department of Commerce, International Trade Administration, *Construction Review*, March-April 1991.

Florida Statistical Abstract 1991

Table 11.71. CONSTRUCTION: AVERAGE MONTHLY REPORTING UNITS, EMPLOYMENT
AND PAYROLL COVERED BY UNEMPLOYMENT COMPENSATION LAW BY INDUSTRY IN
FLORIDA, 1990

SIC code	Industry	Number of re-porting units	Number of employees	Payroll ($1,000)
	Construction	37,878	328,825	618,521
15	Building construction--general contractors and operative builders	10,654	75,664	157,082
152	General building contractors--residential buildings	8,166	40,677	78,668
153	Operative builders	335	4,006	9,302
154	General building contractors--nonresidential buildings	2,152	30,980	69,112
16	Heavy construction other than building construction--contractors	2,337	52,608	105,577
161	Highway and street construction, except elevated highways	399	18,421	35,984
162	Heavy construction, except highway and street construction	1,937	34,186	69,593
1622	Bridge, tunnel, and elevated highway construction	52	2,469	5,412
1623	Water, sewer, pipeline, communications, and power line construction	675	15,452	28,884
1629	Heavy construction, NEC	1,210	16,265	35,297
17	Special trade contractors	24,887	200,553	355,862
171	Plumbing, heating, and air-conditioning	4,876	44,104	78,068
172	Painting and paper hanging	2,137	11,685	18,256
173	Electrical work	3,920	41,317	75,301
174	Masonry, stonework, tile setting, and plastering	3,797	33,175	68,324
175	Carpentry and floor work	2,342	11,192	17,096
176	Roofing, siding, and sheet metal work	1,720	13,490	20,383
177	Concrete work	1,825	15,540	24,345
178	Water well drilling	270	1,282	2,215
179	Miscellaneous special trade contractors	3,997	28,765	51,875
1791	Structural steel erection	335	3,796	7,185
1793	Glass and glazing work	410	2,995	5,336
1794	Excavation work	563	3,625	6,362
1795	Wrecking and demolition work	39	380	633
1796	Installation or erection of building equipment, NEC	189	2,018	5,384
1799	Special trade contractors, NEC	2,460	15,949	26,975

NEC Not elsewhere classified.
Note: Totals on county employment tables may not match totals in this table due
to rounding.

Source: State of Florida, Department of Labor and Employment Security, Bureau of
Labor Market Information, "Employment, Wages, and Contributions Report" (ES-202),
unpublished data.

Florida Statistical Abstract 1991

Table 11.73. CONTRACT CONSTRUCTION: AVERAGE MONTHLY REPORTING UNITS, EMPLOYMENT
AND PAYROLL COVERED BY UNEMPLOYMENT COMPENSATION LAW IN THE STATE AND
COUNTIES OF FLORIDA, 1990

County	Number of reporting units	Number of employees	Payroll ($1,000)	County	Number of reporting units	Number of employees	Payroll ($1,000)
			Contract construction (SIC codes 15-17)				
Florida	37,853	329,399	618,521	Lafayette	(D)	(D)	(D)
				Lake	439	3,210	4,958
Alachua	423	4,127	6,358	Lee	1,509	12,717	22,699
Baker	26	122	152	Leon	639	5,329	8,103
Bay	378	3,023	4,347	Levy	49	461	693
Bradford	39	169	224	Liberty	10	82	131
Brevard	1,215	8,737	15,357	Madison	21	50	53
Broward	3,705	33,941	68,405	Manatee	425	2,840	5,128
Calhoun	19	164	228	Marion	568	4,030	5,910
Charlotte	432	2,638	4,335	Martin	475	4,064	7,849
Citrus	290	1,941	2,983	Monroe	360	1,803	3,032
Clay	307	2,059	3,137	Nassau	126	795	1,528
Collier	833	7,709	14,800	Okaloosa	431	3,095	4,304
Columbia	104	1,187	2,047	Okeechobee	82	495	695
Dade	4,066	37,748	74,270	Orange	2,131	24,922	47,015
De Soto	63	291	379	Osceola	287	2,516	4,497
Dixie	11	73	126	Palm Beach	3,054	25,252	51,414
Duval	1,863	21,774	40,411	Pasco	705	4,422	6,500
Escambia	626	6,556	10,960	Pinellas	2,163	19,757	34,706
Flagler	117	466	674	Polk	1,018	8,825	15,164
Franklin	25	57	72	Putnam	136	691	913
Gadsden	71	487	587	St. Johns	234	1,236	1,818
Gilchrist	16	36	27	St. Lucie	522	3,586	6,282
Glades	6	14	18	Santa Rosa	188	1,190	1,628
Gulf	21	106	157	Sarasota	1,308	9,451	16,914
Hamilton	14	73	115	Seminole	936	8,088	15,135
Hardee	41	179	223	Sumter	54	258	325
Hendry	65	399	648	Suwannee	69	440	619
Hernando	322	1,495	2,107	Taylor	(D)	(D)	(D)
Highlands	252	1,130	1,554	Union	9	69	109
Hillsborough	2,224	23,339	60,781	Volusia	1,153	8,356	13,491
Holmes	22	99	100	Wakulla	31	93	102
Indian River	441	3,134	5,310	Walton	62	334	371
Jackson	60	518	596	Washington	31	572	1,083
Jefferson	17	134	199	Statewide 1/	472	5,756	12,259

(D) Data withheld to avoid disclosure of information about individual firms.
1/ Reporting units without a fixed location within the state or of unknown county
location.
Note: Contract construction includes general contractors and operative builders
(SIC code 15), heavy construction contractors (SIC code 16), and special trade
contractors (SIC code 17).
Source: State of Florida, Department of Labor and Employment Security, Bureau of
Labor Market Information, "Employment, Wages, and Contributions Report" (ES-202),
unpublished data.

Florida Statistical Abstract 1991

MANUFACTURING

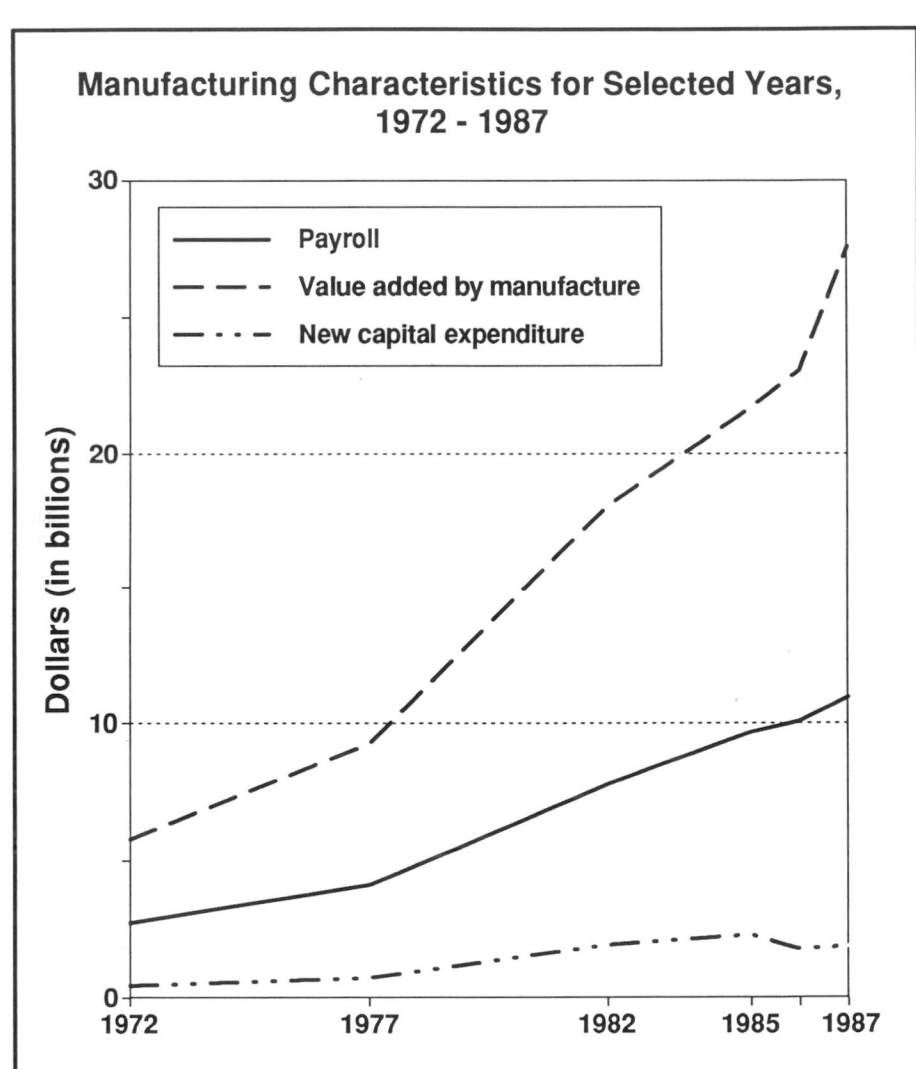

Manufacturing Characteristics for Selected Years, 1972 - 1987

Source: Table 12.01

SECTION 12.00
MANUFACTURING

TABLES LISTED BY MAJOR HEADINGS

TABLES LISTED BY MAJOR HEADINGS

Table 12.01. MANUFACTURING: CHARACTERISTICS IN THE STATE AND SELECTED STANDARD
METROPOLITAN STATISTICAL AREAS (SMSAS) AND STANDARD CONSOLIDATED STATISTICAL
AREAS (SCSAS) OF FLORIDA, SPECIFIED YEARS 1972 THROUGH 1987

Year and source 1/	Number of establishments 2/ Total	Number of establishments 2/ With 20 employees or more	All employees Number (1,000)	All employees Payroll (million dollars)	All employees Percentage of U.S. total	Value added by manufacture 3/ (million dollars)	New capital expenditure (million dollars)
Florida							
1972--census	10,275	2,893	342.9	2,750.3	1.80	5,786.8	463.0
1977--census	12,399	2,915	358.0	4,133.1	1.83	9,255.1	737.3
1982--census	13,723	3,599	454.4	7,773.2	2.37	18,111.8	1,960.6
1985--ASM	(NA)	(NA)	475.7	9,682.0	2.53	21,725.5	2,311.4
1986--ASM	(NA)	(NA)	479.7	10,080.4	2.61	23,080.5	1,780.6
1987--census	15,603	4,046	499.3	10,954.0	2.64	27,574.2	1,910.7
Miami-Ft. Lauderdale SCSA 4/							
1972--census	3,998	1,185	110.9	804.4	0.58	1,606.9	111.9
1977--census	4,890	1,162	114.9	1,163.1	0.59	2,625.7	166.4
1982--census	5,023	1,321	138.6	2,091.5	0.72	4,422.7	346.7
1987--census 5/	5,185	1,338	132.6	2,504.3	0.70	5,700.2	254.0
Ft. Lauderdale-Hollywood SMSA							
1972--census	1,108	248	25.0	195.8	0.13	387.9	31.8
1977--census	1,480	274	29.7	350.3	0.15	828.3	54.1
1982--census	1,629	344	40.3	702.1	0.21	1,579.4	125.6
1987--census 6/	1,790	397	43.3	936.0	0.23	2,138.3	122.0
Miami SMSA							
1972--census	2,890	937	86.0	608.9	0.45	1,219.0	80.0
1977--census	3,410	888	85.1	812.8	0.43	1,797.5	112.3
1982--census	3,394	977	98.4	1,389.5	0.51	2,843.3	221.1
1987--census 7/	3,395	941	89.3	1,568.4	0.47	3,561.9	132.0
Orlando MSA							
1987--census	1,249	358	51.9	1,302.9	0.27	3,197.8	203.4
Tampa-St. Petersburg SMSA							
1977--census	1,753	440	59.7	686.6	0.30	1,558.2	96.0
1982--census	2,078	571	77.2	1,292.3	0.40	2,701.7	266.2
1987--census 8/	2,546	681	84.5	1,834.5	0.05	4,139.8	279.1

(NA) Not available.
1/ Data for the years 1972, 1977, 1982,and 1987 are from the Census of Manufactures. Data for Annual Survey of Manufactures (ASM) years are estimates based on
a representative sample of establishments canvassed annually and may differ from
results of a complete canvas of all establishments. 2/ Includes establishments with
payroll at any time during the year. 3/ Uniform instructions for reporting
inventories were introduced with the 1982 census. Therefore, data for 1982 and
later years are not comparable to prior years. 4/ Consists of Dade and Broward
counties. 5/ Miami-Ft. Lauderdale CMSA. 6/ Ft. Lauderdale-Hollywood-Pompano Beach
PMSA. 7/ Miami-Hialeah PMSA. 8/ Tampa-St. Petersburg-Clearwater MSA.
Note: Data are reported for metropolitan areas with 40,000 manufacturing
employees or more in 1987.   See Glossary for definitions of metropolitan areas and
maps at the front of the book for area boundaries.
Source: U.S., Department of Commerce, Bureau of the Census, *1987 Census of
Manufactures: Florida.* Geographic Area Series MC87-A-10.

Florida Statistical Abstract 1991

Table 12.06. MANUFACTURING: ESTABLISHMENTS, EMPLOYMENT, VALUE ADDED BY MANUFACTURE VALUE OF SHIPMENTS, AND NEW CAPITAL EXPENDITURE IN THE STATE AND COUNTIES OF FLORIDA, 1987

(in millions of dollars, except where indicated)

County	Establish- ments 1/ (number)	All employees 1/ Number (1,000)	Payroll	Value added by manu- facture	Value of ship- ments 2/	New capital expen- diture
Florida	15,603	499.3	10,954.0	27,574.2	56,612.7	1,910.7
Alachua	169	(D)	(D)	(D)	(D)	(D)
Baker	15	0.2	4.2	10.6	43.0	(D)
Bay	114	2.8	64.8	170.3	447.2	(D)
Bradford	29	(D)	(D)	(D)	(D)	(D)
Brevard	387	24.3	665.0	1,412.6	2,500.1	92.1
Broward	1,790	43.3	936.0	2,138.3	3,746.3	122.0
Calhoun	40	0.5	5.6	16.3	34.5	0.8
Charlotte	69	0.6	9.0	21.0	43.1	1.0
Citrus	51	0.9	12.1	35.6	57.2	1.1
Clay	73	1.4	25.1	67.7	178.6	9.8
Collier	136	1.5	29.2	73.8	129.7	5.5
Columbia	47	1.7	28.9	52.2	123.1	4.2
Dade	3,395	89.3	1,568.4	3,561.9	6,734.4	132.0
De Soto	14	(D)	(D)	(D)	(D)	(D)
Dixie	25	0.5	8.0	16.5	43.2	2.6
Duval	743	29.9	693.4	2,395.5	4,874.4	130.2
Escambia	217	(D)	(D)	(D)	(D)	(D)
Flagler	22	0.8	16.4	39.0	95.3	3.8
Franklin	15	0.1	1.1	2.6	8.4	0.1
Gadsden	63	2.0	30.9	73.4	148.4	6.2
Gilchrist	6	1.0	0.6	1.6	3.5	(D)
Glades	7	A/	0.7	0.9	4.2	(D)
Gulf	12	(D)	(D)	(D)	(D)	(D)
Hamilton	12	(D)	(D)	(D)	(D)	(D)
Hardee	17	0.2	3.7	7.1	20.3	0.3
Hendry	15	(D)	(D)	(D)	(D)	(D)
Hernando	59	0.7	12.0	49.5	102.1	2.1
Highlands	55	1.0	17.2	53.3	120.1	3.1
Hillsborough	1,034	36.1	764.5	1,732.5	4,317.3	122.3
Holmes	24	0.7	7.2	11.7	20.5	0.7
Indian River	85	2.4	45.9	165.6	255.0	6.4
Jackson	46	2.0	30.7	69.5	151.8	2.7
Jefferson	24	0.3	4.3	9.7	23.8	0.4
Lafayette	9	0.2	2.3	4.7	10.3	0.6
Lake	155	3.3	54.0	187.1	535.1	21.0
Lee	305	5.6	100.8	239.3	452.0	13.2

See footnotes at end of table.   Continued . . .

Florida Statistical Abstract 1991

Table 12.06. MANUFACTURING: ESTABLISHMENTS, EMPLOYMENT, VALUE ADDED BY MANUFACTURE
   VALUE OF SHIPMENTS, AND NEW CAPITAL EXPENDITURE IN THE STATE AND COUNTIES
   OF FLORIDA, 1987 (Continued)

(in millions of dollars, except where indicated)

County	Establish-ments 1/ (number)	All employees 1/ Number (1,000)	Payroll	Value added by manu-facture	Value of ship-ments 2/	New capital expen-diture
Leon	142	2.6	45.4	106.0	194.6	6.2
Levy	38	0.3	5.1	11.8	25.1	(D)
Liberty	17	0.2	2.7	6.7	18.1	0.4
Madison	35	(D)	(D)	(D)	(D)	(D)
Manatee	215	9.3	198.9	671.0	1,502.8	38.6
Marion	208	6.5	113.4	247.7	545.9	23.5
Martin	132	3.7	78.8	164.7	307.8	7.7
Monroe	87	0.5	9.3	21.3	47.0	2.4
Nassau	59	2.3	63.7	302.3	737.6	27.9
Okaloosa	115	4.7	75.6	180.1	290.8	8.5
Okeechobee	19	0.2	4.2	13.0	71.6	0.7
Orange	836	40.4	1,057.4	2,713.1	4,734.1	173.2
Osceola	69	2.3	47.1	95.2	182.4	9.2
Palm Beach	861	38.5	1,189.6	2,685.6	6,405.7	160.0
Pasco	155	3.6	59.9	189.9	503.4	8.4
Pinellas	1,298	44.0	998.1	2,167.8	3,624.1	146.4
Polk	469	20.7	416.4	1,517.4	4,109.3	83.8
Putnam	61	3.2	77.6	203.0	514.4	(D)
St. Johns	67	1.8	25.6	69.3	145.7	2.2
St. Lucie	99	2.6	46.1	201.9	392.4	4.3
Santa Rosa	45	(D)	(D)	(D)	(D)	(D)
Sarasota	427	8.9	180.2	433.1	692.2	24.9
Seminole	344	9.1	198.4	389.5	738.8	21.0
Sumter	24	0.6	11.0	25.1	88.9	(D)
Suwannee	21	1.1	15.0	19.8	91.4	0.9
Taylor	49	2.7	62.3	216.6	416.1	15.5
Union	9	0.6	8.5	19.1	35.4	0.5
Volusia	359	12.6	264.3	603.7	1,029.7	42.3
Wakulla	12	0.6	15.2	36.4	77.1	(D)
Walton	22	1.2	11.8	18.0	81.6	1.6
Washington	30	0.6	7.0	25.1	47.7	0.8

(D) Data withheld to avoid disclosure of information about individual companies.
A/ Under 50 employees.
1/ Includes establishments with payroll at anytime during the year.
2/ The total value of shipments may include extensive duplication arising from
shipments between establishments in the same industry classification.

Source: U.S., Department of Commerce, Bureau of the Census, *1987 Census of
Manufactures: Florida*. Geographic Area Series MC82-A-10.

Table 12.50. MANUFACTURING INDUSTRY: AVERAGE MONTHLY REPORTING UNITS, EMPLOYMENT
AND PAYROLL COVERED BY UNEMPLOYMENT COMPENSATION LAW BY INDUSTRY IN FLORIDA
1990

SIC code	Industry	Number of reporting units	Number of employees	Payroll ($1,000)
	Manufacturing	14,837	462,037	950,631
20	Food and kindred products	695	46,946	96,758
201	Meat products	90	6,343	9,428
202	Dairy products	35	3,149	6,916
203	Canned, frozen, and preserved fruits, vegetables, and food specialties	111	11,839	25,508
204	Grain mill products	55	780	1,595
205	Bakery products	88	6,922	13,592
206	Sugar and confectionery products	34	2,763	8,228
207	Fats and oils	10	255	485
208	Beverages	66	7,057	18,916
209	Miscellaneous food preparations and kindred products	202	7,834	12,089
21	Tobacco products	33	1,057	2,258
211	Cigarettes	(D)	(D)	(D)
212	Cigars	30	1,047	2,221
213	Chewing and smoking tobacco and snuff	(D)	(D)	(D)
22	Textile mill products	169	3,929	5,866
221	Broadwoven fabric mills, cotton	9	87	106
222	Broadwoven fabric mills, manmade fiber and silk	10	121	153
224	Narrow fabrics and other smallwares mills-- cotton, wool, silk, and manmade fiber	13	312	505
225	Knitting mills	23	1,400	1,765
226	Dyeing and finishing textiles, except wool fabrics and knit goods	70	1,080	1,448
227	Carpets and rugs	5	35	69
228	Yarn and thread mills	4	50	53
229	Miscellaneous textile goods	31	840	1,767
23	Apparel and other finished products made from fabrics and similar materials	1,288	32,971	37,662
231	Men's and boys' suits, coats, and overcoats	8	795	789
232	Men's and boys' furnishings, work clothing, and allied garments	97	5,539	6,180
233	Women's, misses', and juniors' outerwear	550	13,179	14,073
234	Women's, misses', children's, and infants' undergarments	17	1,980	1,892
235	Hats, caps, and millinery	(D)	(D)	(D)
236	Girls', children's, and infants' outerwear	52	2,074	2,224
237	Fur goods	(D)	(D)	(D)
238	Miscellaneous apparel and accessories	33	977	1,268
239	Miscellaneous fabricated textile products	508	7,954	10,726

See footnotes at end of table.   Continued . . .

Florida Statistical Abstract 1991

Table 12.50. MANUFACTURING INDUSTRY: AVERAGE MONTHLY REPORTING UNITS, EMPLOYMENT
AND PAYROLL COVERED BY UNEMPLOYMENT COMPENSATION LAW BY INDUSTRY IN FLORIDA
1990 (Continued)

SIC code	Industry	Number of reporting units	Number of employees	Payroll ($1,000)
24	Lumber and wood products, except furniture	1,191	22,254	35,133
241	Logging	377	2,692	4,417
242	Sawmills and planing mills	89	2,704	4,611
243	Millwork, veneer, plywood, and structural wood members	474	10,012	15,408
244	Wood containers	50	1,172	1,496
245	Wood buildings and mobile homes	36	3,614	6,064
249	Miscellaneous wood products	164	2,058	3,137
25	Furniture and fixtures	559	13,513	20,243
251	Household furniture	288	7,718	10,579
252	Office furniture	37	838	1,299
253	Public building and related furniture	18	473	761
254	Partitions, shelving, lockers, and office and store fixtures	91	2,046	3,526
259	Miscellaneous furniture and fixtures	123	2,437	4,077
26	Paper and allied products	193	14,069	37,389
261	Pulp mills	(D)	(D)	(D)
262	Paper mills	11	2,200	7,440
263	Paperboard mills	(D)	(D)	(D)
265	Paperboard containers and boxes	81	4,205	9,376
267	Converted paper and paperboard products, except containers and boxes	89	4,487	9,974
27	Printing, publishing, and allied industries	3,519	65,792	129,610
271	Newspapers: publishing, or publishing and printing	301	26,827	52,625
272	Periodicals: publishing, or publishing and printing	345	5,976	12,826
273	Books	122	2,617	5,922
274	Miscellaneous publishing	269	4,672	10,233
275	Commercial printing	2,171	20,446	37,511
276	Manifold business forms	23	1,201	2,650
277	Greeting cards	6	78	107
278	Blankbooks, looseleaf binders, and bookbinding and related work	62	1,787	3,003
279	Service industries for the printing trade	217	2,185	4,733
28	Chemicals and allied products	525	22,966	62,564
281	Industrial inorganic chemicals	38	843	2,410
282	Plastics materials and synthetic resins, synthetic rubber, cellulosic and other manmade fibers, except glass	27	2,942	10,231
283	Drugs	48	2,825	7,267
284	Soap, detergents, and cleaning preparations; perfumes, cosmetics, and other toilet preparations	121	2,415	4,780

See footnotes at end of table.   Continued . . .

Florida Statistical Abstract 1991

Table 12.50. MANUFACTURING INDUSTRY: AVERAGE MONTHLY REPORTING UNITS, EMPLOYMENT
AND PAYROLL COVERED BY UNEMPLOYMENT COMPENSATION LAW BY INDUSTRY IN FLORIDA
1990 (Continued)

SIC code	Industry	Number of reporting units	Number of employees	Payroll ($1,000)
28	Chemicals and allied products (Continued)			
285	Paints, varnishes, lacquers, enamels, and allied products	82	1,675	3,650
286	Industrial organic chemicals	27	2,711	8,545
287	Agricultural chemicals	105	8,172	22,193
289	Miscellaneous chemical products	74	1,380	3,489
29	Petroleum refining and related industries	61	1,609	3,677
291	Petroleum refining	(D)	(D)	(D)
295	Asphalt paving and roofing materials	47	1,310	3,165
299	Miscellaneous products of petroleum and coal	(D)	(D)	(D)
30	Rubber and miscellaneous plastics products	754	21,353	36,082
301	Tires and inner tubes	(D)	(D)	(D)
302	Rubber and plastics footwear	(D)	(D)	(D)
305	Gaskets, packing, and sealing devices and rubber and plastics hose and belting	15	912	1,669
306	Fabricated rubber products, NEC	47	1,542	2,612
308	Miscellaneous plastics products	684	16,303	28,625
31	Leather and leather products	64	2,472	2,948
311	Leather tanning and finishing	(D)	(D)	(D)
313	Boot and shoe cut stock and findings	(D)	(D)	(D)
314	Footwear, except rubber	13	429	537
316	Luggage	11	437	484
317	Handbags and other personal leather goods	24	959	1,119
319	Leather goods, NEC	12	460	505
32	Stone, clay, glass, and concrete products	775	22,889	47,332
321	Flat glass	8	35	46
322	Glass and glassware, pressed or blown	13	1,717	4,899
323	Glass products, made of purchased glass	68	1,678	2,514
324	Cement, hydraulic	12	486	1,450
325	Structural clay products	20	880	2,028
326	Pottery and related products	45	234	250
327	Concrete, gypsum, and plaster products	511	16,325	33,004
328	Cut stone and stone products	37	288	531
329	Abrasive, asbestos, and miscellaneous nonmetallic mineral products	59	1,244	2,610
33	Primary metal industries	169	5,525	12,086
331	Steel works, blast furnaces and rolling and finishing mills	30	1,683	4,599
332	Iron and steel foundries	11	729	1,590
333	Primary smelting and refining of nonferrous metals	3	23	82
334	Secondary smelting and refining of nonferrous metals	40	389	756

See footnotes at end of table.   Continued . . .

Table 12.50. MANUFACTURING INDUSTRY: AVERAGE MONTHLY REPORTING UNITS, EMPLOYMENT
AND PAYROLL COVERED BY UNEMPLOYMENT COMPENSATION LAW BY INDUSTRY IN FLORIDA
1990 (Continued)

SIC code	Industry	Number of reporting units	Number of employees	Payroll ($1,000)
33	Primary metal industries (Continued)			
335	Rolling, drawing, and extruding of nonferrous metals	41	2,157	4,079
336	Nonferrous foundries (castings)	29	394	677
339	Miscellaneous primary metal products	12	150	301
34	Fabricated metal products, except machinery and transportation equipment	1,241	32,467	63,439
341	Metal cans and shipping containers	15	1,343	3,690
342	Cutlery, handtools, and general hardware	74	1,437	2,617
343	Heating equipment, except electric and warm air; and plumbing fixtures	22	401	838
344	Fabricated structural metal products	713	19,098	35,187
345	Screw machine products, and bolts, nuts, screws, rivets, and washers	49	892	1,799
346	Metal forgings and stampings	78	2,097	4,012
347	Coating, engraving, and allied services	141	1,593	3,119
348	Ordnance and accessories, except vehicles and guided missiles	24	1,053	2,484
349	Miscellaneous fabricated metal products	123	4,550	9,693
35	Industrial and commercial machinery and computer equipment	1,530	42,062	108,745
351	Engines and turbines	(D)	(D)	(D)
352	Farm and garden machinery and equipment	(D)	(D)	(D)
353	Construction, mining, and materials handling machinery and equipment	106	3,336	7,319
354	Metalworking machinery and equipment	295	4,290	9,060
355	Special industry machinery, except metal-working machinery	110	2,356	5,765
356	General industrial machinery and equipment	156	3,814	8,188
357	Computer and office equipment	65	14,293	48,366
358	Refrigeration and service industry machinery	134	5,345	10,274
359	Miscellaneous industrial and commercial machinery and equipment	586	5,965	11,890
36	Electronic and other electrical equipment and components, except computer equipment	701	59,002	140,308
361	Electric transmission and distribution equipment	36	2,608	4,970
362	Electrical industrial apparatus	56	2,006	3,976
363	Household appliances	18	220	354
364	Electric lighting and wiring equipment	93	2,334	3,579
365	Household audio and video equipment, and audio recordings	49	736	1,316
366	Communications equipment	126	17,863	49,246
367	Electronic components and accessories	233	27,971	65,784

See footnotes at end of table.   Continued . . .

Florida Statistical Abstract 1991

Table 12.50. MANUFACTURING INDUSTRY: AVERAGE MONTHLY REPORTING UNITS, EMPLOYMENT
AND PAYROLL COVERED BY UNEMPLOYMENT COMPENSATION LAW BY INDUSTRY IN FLORIDA
1990 (Continued)

SIC code	Industry	Number of reporting units	Number of employees	Payroll ($1,000)
36	Electronic and other electrical equipment and components, except computer equipment (Continued)			
369	Miscellaneous electrical machinery, equipment, and supplies	89	5,260	11,083
37	Transportation equipment	981	62,799	172,050
371	Motor vehicles and motor vehicle equipment	158	6,811	12,545
372	Aircraft and parts	112	18,471	57,327
373	Ship and boat building and repairing	607	16,520	32,775
374	Railroad equipment	8	410	907
375	Motorcycles, bicycles, and parts	6	47	64
376	Guided missiles and space vehicles and parts	27	19,814	67,438
379	Miscellaneous transportation equipment	61	724	993
38	Measuring, analyzing, and controlling instruments; photographic, medical, and optical goods; watches and clocks	508	35,421	81,574
381	Search, detection, navigation, guidance, aeronautical, and nautical systems, instruments, and equipment	54	13,720	34,874
382	Laboratory apparatus and analytical, optical, measuring, and controlling instruments	166	4,995	10,384
384	Surgical, medical, and dental instruments and supplies	187	10,818	25,118
385	Ophthalmic goods	74	5,574	10,510
386	Photographic equipment and supplies	(D)	(D)	(D)
387	Watches, clocks, clockwork operated devices, and parts	(D)	(D)	(D)
39	Miscellaneous manufacturing industries	704	8,929	14,412
391	Jewelry, silverware, and plated ware	128	1,588	2,777
393	Musical instruments	10	106	173
394	Dolls, toys, games, and sporting and athletic goods	153	1,694	2,440
395	Pens, pencils, and other artists' materials	43	591	1,000
396	Costume jewelry, costume novelties, buttons, and miscellaneous notions, except precious metal	34	725	1,152
399	Miscellaneous manufacturing industries	334	4,223	6,870

NEC Not elsewhere classified.
(D) Data withheld to avoid disclosure of information about individual firms.
Note: Totals on county employment tables may not match totals in this table due
to rounding.

Source: State of Florida, Department of Labor and Employment Security, Bureau of
Labor Market Information, "Employment, Wages, and Contributions Report" (ES-202),
unpublished data.

Florida Statistical Abstract 1991

Table 12.51. MANUFACTURING INDUSTRY: AVERAGE MONTHLY REPORTING UNITS, EMPLOYMENT
AND PAYROLL COVERED BY UNEMPLOYMENT COMPENSATION LAW IN THE STATE AND COUNTIES
OF FLORIDA, 1990

County	Number of reporting units	Number of employees	Payroll ($1,000)	County	Number of reporting units	Number of employees	Payroll ($1,000)
			Manufacturing industry (SIC codes 20-39)				
Florida	15,646	519,385	1,110,138	Lafayette	(D)	(D)	(D)
				Lake	160	4,712	8,395
Alachua	150	4,781	9,380	Lee	332	5,824	10,558
Baker	12	287	462	Leon	151	3,114	6,179
Bay	124	3,595	7,854	Levy	30	381	497
Bradford	22	681	837	Liberty	17	255	392
Brevard	411	29,826	79,882	Madison	33	1,130	1,600
Broward	1,753	43,256	97,492	Manatee	210	9,908	20,417
Calhoun	39	327	427	Marion	221	10,026	16,253
Charlotte	66	916	1,287	Martin	124	3,487	7,547
Citrus	59	844	1,127	Monroe	86	594	885
Clay	79	1,476	2,665	Nassau	57	1,760	5,072
Collier	146	2,339	4,471	Okaloosa	114	4,873	8,136
Columbia	48	1,554	2,253	Okeechobee	24	274	466
Dade	3,274	87,733	154,213	Orange	864	39,976	105,831
De Soto	(D)	(D)	(D)	Osceola	67	2,046	4,874
Dixie	27	528	1,052	Palm Beach	841	32,390	100,754
Duval	734	30,171	67,140	Pasco	154	3,908	6,325
Escambia	233	9,624	23,919	Pinellas	1,279	46,765	100,956
Flagler	34	1,348	2,138	Polk	484	22,130	44,175
Franklin	17	131	150	Putnam	57	3,691	7,964
Gadsden	38	1,568	2,304	St. Johns	77	3,112	5,454
Gilchrist	7	100	128	St. Lucie	115	2,317	4,071
Glades	5	26	44	Santa Rosa	51	2,327	4,305
Gulf	13	1,151	3,156	Sarasota	404	8,933	17,448
Hamilton	(D)	(D)	(D)	Seminole	381	11,463	22,865
Hardee	13	320	448	Sumter	26	434	986
Hendry	19	902	2,273	Suwannee	34	1,155	1,507
Hernando	63	1,139	1,937	Taylor	36	2,227	5,192
Highlands	53	1,250	2,012	Union	18	639	744
Hillsborough	1,011	40,073	77,311	Volusia	349	11,876	22,862
Holmes	32	764	672	Wakulla	14	692	1,401
Indian River	108	2,444	4,638	Walton	18	1,247	1,581
Jackson	35	1,999	2,726	Washington	(D)	(D)	(D)
Jefferson	23	333	357	Statewide 1/	119	779	2,097

(D) Data withheld to avoid disclosure of information about individual firms.
1/ Reporting units without a fixed location within the state or of unknown county
location.
Note: See Table 12.50 for a list of industries.

Source: State of Florida, Department of Labor and Employment Security, Bureau of
Labor Market Information, "Employment, Wages, and Contributions Report" (ES-202),
unpublished data.

Florida Statistical Abstract 1991

Table 12.52. FOOD, TOBACCO, TEXTILE, AND APPAREL PRODUCTS MANUFACTURING: AVERAGE
    MONTHLY REPORTING UNITS, EMPLOYMENT, AND PAYROLL COVERED BY UNEMPLOYMENT
    COMPENSATION LAW IN THE STATE AND COUNTIES OF FLORIDA, 1990

County	Number of re-porting units	Number of employees	Payroll ($1,000)	County	Number of re-porting units	Number of employees	Payroll ($1,000)
				Food and kindred products (SIC code 20)			
Florida	683	47,013	96,757	Lee	15	568	948
Alachua	6	51	66	Marion	16	304	416
Brevard	10	134	178	Monroe	7	49	67
Broward	38	1,560	3,035	Okeechobee	5	62	152
Dade	154	6,099	12,406	Orange	31	3,396	7,721
Duval	38	4,939	11,819	Osceola	7	136	298
Escambia	9	497	856	Palm Beach	28	2,698	7,842
Franklin	7	82	87	Pinellas	29	1,246	2,020
Hendry	6	803	2,112	Polk	46	5,753	11,823
Highlands	3	7	16	Putnam	4	91	115
Hillsborough	72	6,563	12,632	St. Lucie	7	604	1,197
Indian River	6	276	510	Volusia	14	586	914
Jackson	4	69	81	Wakulla	7	188	108
Lake	12	1,623	3,570	Statewide	6	80	135
			Tobacco products (SIC code 21)				
Florida	32	1,057	2,256	Hillsborough	9	429	1,154
Dade	19	102	117				
			Textile mill products (SIC code 22)				
Florida	162	3,938	5,865	Orange	5	24	38
				Palm Beach	3	25	32
Broward	18	363	592	Pinellas	5	31	32
Dade	87	2,728	3,598	Seminole	3	27	25
			Apparel and other textile products (SIC code 23)				
Florida	1,278	33,031	37,663	Martin	12	58	111
Bradford	3	294	258	Monroe	8	55	72
Brevard	17	131	187	Okaloosa	9	901	971
Broward	148	1,546	2,190	Orange	30	306	409
Charlotte	6	31	58	Palm Beach	46	363	520
Collier	4	39	38	Pasco	6	57	44
Dade	681	18,527	20,204	Pinellas	70	1,390	1,991
Duval	26	352	450	Polk	15	447	544
Hillsborough	33	2,132	2,725	Santa Rosa	3	951	1,036
Holmes	3	539	375	Sarasota	25	118	155
Lee	27	276	410	Seminole	19	360	403
Manatee	10	263	359	Volusia	16	173	227
Marion	6	193	249	Statewide	3	2	10

Note: Excluded are counties where data are withheld to avoid disclosure of
information about individual firms. For a list of three-digit code industries
included see Table 12.50. See Table 12.51 for definition of statewide.
    Source: State of Florida, Department of Labor and Employment Security, Bureau of
Labor Market Information, "Employment, Wages, and Contributions Report" (ES-202),
unpublished data.

Florida Statistical Abstract 1991

Table 12.57. LUMBER AND WOOD PRODUCTS, EXCEPT FURNITURE: AVERAGE MONTHLY REPORTING
UNITS, EMPLOYMENT, AND PAYROLL COVERED BY UNEMPLOYMENT COMPENSATION LAW IN THE
STATE AND COUNTIES OF FLORIDA, 1990

County	Number of reporting units	Number of employees	Payroll ($1,000)	County	Number of reporting units	Number of employees	Payroll ($1,000)
		Lumber and wood products, except furniture (SIC code 24)					
Florida	1,173	22,341	35,131	Lafayette	(D)	(D)	(D)
				Lake	28	691	972
Alachua	17	346	502	Lee	25	461	713
Baker	7	41	61	Leon	15	80	104
Bay	22	315	517	Levy	18	188	271
Bradford	7	97	159	Liberty	16	248	388
Brevard	20	417	573	Madison	23	335	529
Broward	51	782	1,411	Manatee	7	183	269
Calhoun	29	195	299	Marion	30	1,264	2,063
Charlotte	(D)	(D)	(D)	Martin	(D)	(D)	(D)
Citrus	3	29	45	Monroe	(D)	(D)	(D)
Clay	17	95	139	Nassau	30	204	352
Collier	7	76	109	Okaloosa	19	334	476
Columbia	21	735	1,090	Okeechobee	(D)	(D)	(D)
Dade	117	2,407	3,573	Orange	40	624	985
De Soto	4	33	55	Osceola	4	48	49
Dixie	21	496	1,024	Palm Beach	41	640	1,118
Duval	43	952	1,816	Pasco	15	212	267
Escambia	31	232	292	Pinellas	42	820	1,319
Flagler	10	174	248	Polk	35	2,332	3,761
Franklin	5	32	45	Putnam	21	638	1,261
Gadsden	(D)	(D)	(D)	St. Johns	7	42	57
Gilchrist	(D)	(D)	(D)	St. Lucie	9	167	269
Glades	(D)	(D)	(D)	Santa Rosa	13	94	117
Gulf	(D)	(D)	(D)	Sarasota	17	527	813
Hamilton	3	39	62	Seminole	17	225	335
Hardee	4	76	108	Sumter	5	41	46
Hendry	(D)	(D)	(D)	Suwannee	12	105	153
Hernando	8	157	235	Taylor	18	410	658
Highlands	(D)	(D)	(D)	Union	13	195	349
Hillsborough	54	1,393	2,012	Volusia	32	508	781
Holmes	20	78	99	Wakulla	0	0	0
Indian River	7	75	90	Walton	3	24	31
Jackson	14	246	351	Washington	13	87	119
Jefferson	12	120	175	Statewide 1/	6	65	157

(D) Data withheld to avoid disclosure of information about individual firms.
1/ Reporting units without a fixed location within the state or of unknown county
location.
Note: For a list of three-digit code industries included see Table 12.50.

Source: State of Florida, Department of Labor and Employment Security, Bureau of
Labor Market Information, "Employment, Wages, and Contributions Report" (ES-202),
unpublished data.

Florida Statistical Abstract 1991

Table 12.63. FURNITURE AND FIXTURES AND PAPER AND ALLIED PRODUCTS: AVERAGE MONTHLY REPORTING UNITS, EMPLOYMENT, AND PAYROLL COVERED BY UNEMPLOYMENT COMPENSATION LAW IN THE STATE AND COUNTIES OF FLORIDA, 1990

County	Number of reporting units	Number of employees	Payroll ($1,000)	County	Number of reporting units	Number of employees	Payroll ($1,000)
			Furniture and fixtures (SIC code 25)				
Florida	552	14,464	20,355	Marion	6	278	374
				Martin	3	41	65
Brevard	7	137	180	Orange	28	710	1,240
Broward	76	1,733	3,021	Palm Beach	37	552	981
Collier	5	75	101	Pasco	6	49	51
Dade	191	4,374	6,279	Pinellas	34	605	799
Duval	33	1,030	1,667	Polk	9	462	600
Escambia	7	523	608	Sarasota	17	207	304
Hillsborough	28	502	772	Seminole	11	260	403
Indian River	4	34	60	Volusia	7	48	62
			Household furniture (SIC code 251)				
Florida	282	7,727	10,577	Marion	6	278	374
				Orange	16	527	938
Broward	36	374	568	Palm Beach	25	257	446
Dade	107	2,637	3,290	Pinellas	16	253	311
Duval	15	323	525	Polk	7	382	520
Escambia	4	446	506	Sarasota	8	115	165
Hillsborough	12	228	344	Seminole	4	44	68
			Paper and allied products (SIC code 26)				
Florida	191	14,081	37,390	Nassau	3	836	2,809
Broward	14	222	396	Orange	11	528	1,189
Dade	44	1,925	3,612	Pinellas	6	133	304
Duval	36	2,372	6,107	Polk	9	680	1,516
Hillsborough	21	772	1,681	Sarasota	5	52	97
Marion	4	115	209	Seminole	4	67	118

Note: Excluded are counties where data are withheld to avoid disclosure of information about individual firms. For a list of three-digit code industries included see Table 12.50. See Table 12.51 for definition of statewide.

Source: State of Florida, Department of Labor and Employment Security, Bureau of Labor Market Information, "Employment, Wages, and Contributions Report" (ES-202), unpublished data.

Florida Statistical Abstract 1991

Table 12.64. CHEMICALS AND ALLIED PRODUCTS AND AGRICULTURAL CHEMICALS: AVERAGE
MONTHLY REPORTING UNITS, EMPLOYMENT, AND PAYROLL COVERED BY UNEMPLOYMENT
COMPENSATION LAW IN THE STATE AND COUNTIES OF FLORIDA, 1990

County	Number of re- porting units	Number of employees	Payroll ($1,000)	County	Number of re- porting units	Number of employees	Payroll ($1,000)
			Chemicals and allied products (SIC code 28)				
Florida	507	23,364	60,983	Orange	33	567	1,542
				Osceola	3	14	18
Brevard	13	260	543	Palm Beach	24	394	1,163
Broward	40	626	1,478	Pinellas	40	953	1,958
Dade	94	3,190	8,071	Polk	40	4,075	10,893
Duval	33	1,652	4,400	Putnam	3	20	98
Hillsborough	52	2,270	5,674	Santa Rosa	4	701	2,365
Lake	10	128	213	Sarasota	6	169	451
Lee	9	348	860	Seminole	16	165	311
Manatee	8	266	668	Volusia	12	447	906
Marion	8	155	284	Statewide	7	151	592
			Agricultural chemicals (SIC code 287)				
Florida	102	8,175	22,191	Manatee	3	232	605
				Orange	9	166	536
Hillsborough	14	1,556	4,218	Polk	21	3,477	9,439
Lake	6	123	201	Seminole	4	108	221

Note: Excluded are counties where data are withheld to avoid disclosure of
information about individual firms. For a list of three-digit code industries in
SIC 28, see Table 12.50. SIC 287 is a part of SIC 28.

Source: State of Florida, Department of Labor and Employment Security, Bureau of
Labor Market Information, "Employment, Wages, and Contributions Report" (ES-202),
unpublished data.

Florida Statistical Abstract 1991

Table 12.67. PRINTING, PUBLISHING, AND ALLIED INDUSTRIES: AVERAGE MONTHLY
REPORTING UNITS, EMPLOYMENT, AND PAYROLL COVERED BY UNEMPLOYMENT
COMPENSATION LAW IN THE STATE AND COUNTIES OF FLORIDA, 1990

County	Number of reporting units	Number of employees	Payroll ($1,000)	County	Number of reporting units	Number of employees	Payroll ($1,000)
			Printing, publishing, and allied industries (SIC code 27)				
Florida	3,501	65,897	129,608	Lafayette	0	0	0
				Lake	28	375	512
Alachua	41	720	1,103	Lee	87	1,341	2,487
Baker	(D)	(D)	(D)	Leon	67	1,516	2,684
Bay	16	366	606	Levy	4	23	28
Bradford	(D)	(D)	(D)	Liberty	(D)	(D)	(D)
Brevard	73	1,163	1,878	Madison	(D)	(D)	(D)
Broward	442	6,370	14,072	Manatee	35	564	1,036
Calhoun	(D)	(D)	(D)	Marion	36	565	927
Charlotte	17	331	371	Martin	28	615	1,087
Citrus	(D)	(D)	(D)	Monroe	21	165	259
Clay	19	189	242	Nassau	7	59	79
Collier	48	757	1,374	Okaloosa	21	321	408
Columbia	7	66	119	Okeechobee	(D)	(D)	(D)
Dade	677	12,388	29,157	Orange	263	6,189	13,462
De Soto	3	34	40	Osceola	13	201	364
Dixie	(D)	(D)	(D)	Palm Beach	220	3,734	8,767
Duval	171	3,796	7,260	Pasco	33	425	565
Escambia	52	996	1,378	Pinellas	280	6,951	13,977
Flagler	3	27	40	Polk	67	1,129	1,927
Franklin	(D)	(D)	(D)	Putnam	4	131	221
Gadsden	(D)	(D)	(D)	St. Johns	17	301	372
Gilchrist	(D)	(D)	(D)	St. Lucie	26	296	420
Glades	(D)	(D)	(D)	Santa Rosa	9	64	92
Gulf	(D)	(D)	(D)	Sarasota	99	1,544	2,660
Hamilton	(D)	(D)	(D)	Seminole	89	712	1,301
Hardee	(D)	(D)	(D)	Sumter	(D)	(D)	(D)
Hendry	(D)	(D)	(D)	Suwannee	5	56	55
Hernando	14	102	113	Taylor	3	26	26
Highlands	10	111	147	Union	0	0	0
Hillsborough	245	8,125	13,001	Volusia	73	1,517	2,593
Holmes	(D)	(D)	(D)	Wakulla	(D)	(D)	(D)
Indian River	30	346	641	Walton	(D)	(D)	(D)
Jackson	4	49	44	Washington	(D)	(D)	(D)
Jefferson	3	40	30	Statewide 1/	35	283	583

(D) Data withheld to avoid disclosure of information about individual firms.
1/ Reporting units without a fixed location within the state or of unknown county
location.
Note: For a list of three-digit code industries included see Table 12.50.

Source: State of Florida, Department of Labor and Employment Security, Bureau of
Labor Market Information, "Employment, Wages, and Contributions Report" (ES-202),
unpublished data.

Florida Statistical Abstract 1991

Table 12.68. COMMERCIAL PRINTING: AVERAGE MONTHLY REPORTING UNITS, EMPLOYMENT, AND
   PAYROLL COVERED BY UNEMPLOYMENT COMPENSATION LAW IN THE STATE AND COUNTIES OF
   FLORIDA, 1990

County	Number of reporting units	Number of employees	Payroll ($1,000)	County	Number of reporting units	Number of employees	Payroll ($1,000)
			Commercial printing (SIC code 275)				
Florida	2,157	20,467	37,506	Levy	(D)	(D)	(D)
				Madison	(D)	(D)	(D)
Alachua	16	170	224	Manatee	20	146	252
Bay	11	188	336	Marion	24	257	405
Brevard	45	299	410	Martin	19	305	564
Broward	284	2,454	4,664	Monroe	11	49	61
Charlotte	11	94	112	Nassau	(D)	(D)	(D)
Citrus	10	37	33	Okaloosa	13	86	91
Clay	13	145	187	Okeechobee	(D)	(D)	(D)
Collier	27	176	320	Orange	156	1,757	3,371
Columbia	5	22	27	Osceola	8	101	185
Dade	437	4,799	9,863	Palm Beach	136	945	1,653
De Soto	(D)	(D)	(D)	Pasco	24	87	115
Duval	113	1,348	2,495	Pinellas	177	2,120	3,901
Escambia	33	460	597	Polk	40	382	580
Flagler	(D)	(D)	(D)	Putnam	(D)	(D)	(D)
Gadsden	(D)	(D)	(D)	St. Johns	7	54	68
Gulf	(D)	(D)	(D)	St. Lucie	20	74	87
Hardee	0	0	0	Santa Rosa	3	29	39
Hendry	(D)	(D)	(D)	Sarasota	63	398	658
Hernando	10	47	59	Seminole	55	367	690
Highlands	(D)	(D)	(D)	Sumter	(D)	(D)	(D)
Hillsborough	161	1,505	2,635	Suwannee	(D)	(D)	(D)
Indian River	14	75	103	Taylor	(D)	(D)	(D)
Jackson	(D)	(D)	(D)	Volusia	44	278	509
Jefferson	(D)	(D)	(D)	Walton	(D)	(D)	(D)
Lake	16	89	108	Washington	(D)	(D)	(D)
Lee	58	351	965				
Leon	31	274	416	Statewide 1/	6	9	33

(D) Data withheld to avoid disclosure of information about individual firms.
   1/ Reporting units without a fixed location within the state or of unknown county
location.

   Source: State of Florida, Department of Labor and Employment Security, Bureau of
Labor Market Information, "Employment, Wages, and Contributions Report" (ES-202),
unpublished data.

Florida Statistical Abstract 1991

Table 12.70. RUBBER AND MISCELLANEOUS PLASTICS PRODUCTS AND LEATHER AND LEATHER
  PRODUCTS: AVERAGE MONTHLY REPORTING UNITS, EMPLOYMENT, AND PAYROLL COVERED
  BY UNEMPLOYMENT COMPENSATION LAW IN THE STATE AND COUNTIES OF FLORIDA, 1990

County	Number of reporting units	Number of employees	Payroll ($1,000)	County	Number of reporting units	Number of employees	Payroll ($1,000)
	Rubber and miscellaneous plastics products (SIC code 30)						
Florida	741	21,397	36,083	Lee	13	212	347
				Leon	4	47	59
Alachua	(D)	(D)	(D)	Manatee	9	281	497
Bay	6	214	437	Marion	14	769	1,373
Brevard	31	320	433	Martin	(D)	(D)	(D)
Broward	92	1,942	3,485	Monroe	(D)	(D)	(D)
Charlotte	(D)	(D)	(D)	Okaloosa	4	43	52
Citrus	(D)	(D)	(D)	Orange	49	1,470	2,707
Clay	3	179	373	Osceola	9	789	2,471
Collier	9	156	254	Palm Beach	33	450	705
Dade	128	5,900	8,859	Pasco	(D)	(D)	(D)
Dixie	(D)	(D)	(D)	Pinellas	71	2,179	3,751
Duval	38	605	913	Polk	38	1,108	1,655
Escambia	5	71	95	Putnam	(D)	(D)	(D)
Franklin	0	0	0	St. Johns	(D)	(D)	(D)
Gadsden	(D)	(D)	(D)	St. Lucie	11	281	450
Hernando	4	101	127	Santa Rosa	(D)	(D)	(D)
Highlands	(D)	(D)	(D)	Sarasota	28	665	1,161
Hillsborough	45	1,085	1,865	Seminole	19	519	846
Holmes	(D)	(D)	(D)	Sumter	(D)	(D)	(D)
Indian River	6	55	93	Volusia	21	674	1,013
Lake	9	291	474	Statewide 1/	(D)	(D)	(D)
	Leather and leather products (SIC code 31)						
Florida	62	2,475	2,947	Highlands	(D)	(D)	(D)
				Hillsborough	(D)	(D)	(D)
Brevard	(D)	(D)	(D)	Lee	(D)	(D)	(D)
Broward	(D)	(D)	(D)	Marion	(D)	(D)	(D)
Citrus	(D)	(D)	(D)	Monroe	3	37	31
Dade	34	1,580	1,917	Palm Beach	3	18	36
Duval	(D)	(D)	(D)	Pinellas	6	422	461
Escambia	(D)	(D)	(D)	Seminole	(D)	(D)	(D)
Hernando	(D)	(D)	(D)	Volusia	(D)	(D)	(D)

(D) Data withheld to avoid disclosure of information about individual firms.
  1/ Reporting units without a fixed location within the state or of unknown county
location.
  Note: For a list of three-digit code industries included see Table 12.50.

  Source: State of Florida, Department of Labor and Employment Security, Bureau of
Labor Market Information, "Employment, Wages, and Contributions Report" (ES-202),
unpublished data.

Florida Statistical Abstract 1991

Table 12.71. STONE, CLAY, GLASS, AND CONCRETE PRODUCTS: AVERAGE MONTHLY REPORTING
UNITS, EMPLOYMENT, AND PAYROLL COVERED BY UNEMPLOYMENT COMPENSATION LAW
IN THE STATE AND COUNTIES OF FLORIDA, 1990

County	Number of reporting units	Number of employees	Payroll ($1,000)	County	Number of reporting units	Number of employees	Payroll ($1,000)
			Stone, clay, glass, and concrete products (SIC code 32)				
Florida	765	22,948	47,337	Leon	12	187	334
				Manatee	19	941	1,835
Alachua	8	134	226	Marion	15	351	574
Bay	4	132	203	Martin	5	105	185
Brevard	15	378	770	Monroe	7	140	220
Broward	88	1,958	4,075	Okaloosa	9	89	137
Charlotte	8	136	263	Okeechobee	4	15	31
Citrus	10	176	253	Orange	41	1,272	2,440
Clay	6	234	494	Osceola	5	136	244
Collier	12	317	665	Palm Beach	46	1,286	2,968
Dade	89	3,238	6,496	Pasco	12	345	541
Duval	37	2,705	6,365	Pinellas	40	781	1,739
Escambia	15	816	1,862	Polk	28	1,147	2,801
Gadsden	5	82	99	St. Johns	3	27	42
Hillsborough	57	2,001	4,422	St. Lucie	10	207	425
Indian River	9	99	211	Sarasota	22	566	1,076
Jackson	4	20	19	Seminole	18	397	655
Lake	17	431	731	Volusia	15	355	599
Lee	26	697	1,361	Walton	3	26	37
			Concrete, gypsum, and plaster products (SIC code 327)				
Florida	504	16,347	33,003	Leon	10	185	332
Alachua	8	133	224	Manatee	14	250	483
Bay	3	113	183	Marion	10	177	362
Brevard	10	342	731	Monroe	6	138	219
Broward	45	1,541	3,297	Okaloosa	6	70	113
Charlotte	8	136	263	Okeechobee	4	15	31
Citrus	7	165	241	Orange	29	1,111	2,204
Clay	4	228	476	Osceola	5	136	244
Collier	9	304	655	Palm Beach	27	1,107	2,608
Dade	49	2,380	4,675	Pasco	10	329	520
Duval	25	1,196	2,522	Pinellas	22	652	1,469
Escambia	11	243	386	Polk	14	413	805
Hillsborough	38	1,547	3,438	St. Lucie	8	206	423
Jackson	3	18	17	Sarasota	17	544	1,045
Lake	11	387	648	Seminole	10	166	322
Lee	19	629	1,280	Volusia	10	289	498

Note: Excluded are counties where data are withheld to avoid disclosure of
information about individual firms. For a list of three-digit code industries see
Table 12.50.
    Source: State of Florida, Department of Labor and Employment Security, Bureau of
Labor Market Information, "Employment, Wages, and Contributions Report" (ES-202),
unpublished data.

Table 12.72. FABRICATED METAL PRODUCTS, EXCEPT MACHINERY AND TRANSPORTATION
EQUIPMENT: AVERAGE MONTHLY REPORTING UNITS, EMPLOYMENT, AND PAYROLL
COVERED BY UNEMPLOYMENT COMPENSATION LAW IN THE STATE AND COUNTIES
OF FLORIDA, 1990

County	Number of reporting units	Number of employees	Payroll ($1,000)	County	Number of reporting units	Number of employees	Payroll ($1,000)

Fabricated metal products, except machinery
and transportation equipment (SIC code 34)

County	Number of reporting units	Number of employees	Payroll ($1,000)	County	Number of reporting units	Number of employees	Payroll ($1,000)
Florida	1,227	32,571	63,434	Lee	21	438	772
				Leon	11	193	397
Alachua	8	436	1,082	Manatee	14	329	573
Bay	12	121	223	Marion	19	956	1,400
Brevard	39	696	1,329	Martin	9	92	316
Broward	136	2,705	6,046	Orange	86	2,266	4,710
Charlotte	4	13	25	Palm Beach	69	861	1,793
Clay	9	183	315	Pasco	9	184	288
Collier	8	81	122	Pinellas	126	3,597	6,463
Dade	223	5,795	9,643	Polk	50	1,238	2,294
Duval	70	3,009	6,274	Putnam	7	151	286
Escambia	24	1,148	2,851	St. Lucie	13	166	285
Hernando	4	38	60	Sarasota	33	1,111	2,306
Hillsborough	105	3,682	7,994	Seminole	37	1,002	1,894
Indian River	7	91	128	Volusia	17	461	879
Lake	11	348	751	Statewide 1/	7	11	65

Fabricated structural metal products (SIC code 344)

County	Number of reporting units	Number of employees	Payroll ($1,000)	County	Number of reporting units	Number of employees	Payroll ($1,000)
Florida	701	19,135	35,187	Marion	10	200	·307
				Martin	5	59	92
Brevard	22	381	717	Orange	49	1,056	2,104
Broward	70	1,685	3,742	Palm Beach	42	633	1,287
Collier	7	30	36	Pasco	5	49	78
Dade	136	3,970	6,282	Pinellas	56	1,979	3,147
Duval	49	1,838	3,384	Polk	35	1,009	1,947
Escambia	13	963	2,563	Putnam	7	151	286
Hillsborough	60	2,148	4,120	St. Lucie	6	92	172
Indian River	5	78	111	Sarasota	16	380	671
Lake	5	259	568	Seminole	19	774	1,330
Lee	16	389	660	Volusia	8	62	90
Leon	5	115	227	Statewide 1/	4	6	34

1/ Reporting units without a fixed location within the state or of unknown county
location.
   Note: Excluded are counties where data are withheld to avoid disclosure of
information about individual firms. For a list of three-digit code industries
included see Table 12.50.
   Source: State of Florida, Department of Labor and Employment Security, Bureau of
Labor Market Information, "Employment, Wages, and Contributions Report" (ES-202),
unpublished data.

Florida Statistical Abstract 1991

Table 12.74. INDUSTRIAL AND COMMERCIAL MACHINERY AND COMPUTER EQUIPMENT: AVERAGE
    MONTHLY REPORTING UNITS, EMPLOYMENT, AND PAYROLL COVERED BY UNEMPLOYMENT
    COMPENSATION LAW IN THE STATE AND COUNTIES OF FLORIDA, 1990

County	Number of reporting units	Number of employees	Payroll ($1,000)	County	Number of reporting units	Number of employees	Payroll ($1,000)
			Industrial and commercial machinery and computer equipment (SIC code 35)				
Florida	1,520	42,183	108,747	Marion	18	430	861
Alachua	11	476	1,153	Martin	7	68	111
Bay	7	159	418	Nassau	3	30	51
Brevard	42	1,916	3,763	Okaloosa	10	219	368
Broward	202	5,667	15,520	Orange	71	3,252	9,991
Charlotte	8	132	230	Osceola	6	79	131
Citrus	5	26	33	Palm Beach	86	6,608	25,361
Clay	9	61	94	Pasco	20	344	664
Collier	16	290	679	Pinellas	196	5,725	14,849
Dade	200	3,307	6,417	Polk	71	1,835	3,427
Duval	76	1,538	3,209	St. Johns	9	91	192
Escambia	23	359	608	St. Lucie	11	191	392
Hernando	9	38	58	Santa Rosa	5	62	116
Hillsborough	102	1,562	2,935	Sarasota	59	814	1,912
Indian River	9	251	468	Seminole	42	3,340	7,936
Lake	13	142	228	Suwannee	3	16	20
Lee	33	448	883	Volusia	45	917	2,080
Manatee	33	659	1,574	Statewide 1/	7	10	45
			Computer and office equipment (SIC code 357)				
Florida	64	14,295	48,367	Broward	16	2,170	7,647
				Dade	7	155	391
Brevard	4	1,485	2,842	Orange	6	383	1,222

1/ Reporting units without a fixed location within the state or of unknown county location.

Note: Excluded are counties where data are withheld to avoid disclosure of information about individual firms. For a list of three-digit code industries included see Table 12.50.

Source: State of Florida, Department of Labor and Employment Security, Bureau of Labor Market information, "Employment, Wages, and Contributions Report" (ES-202), unpublished data.

Florida Statistical Abstract 1991

Table 12.77. ELECTRONIC, AND OTHER ELECTRICAL EQUIPMENT AND COMPONENTS, EXCEPT
    COMPUTER EQUIPMENT: AVERAGE MONTHLY REPORTING UNITS, EMPLOYMENT, AND
    PAYROLL COVERED BY UNEMPLOYMENT COMPENSATION LAW IN THE STATE AND
    COUNTIES OF FLORIDA, 1990

County	Number of reporting units	Number of employees	Payroll ($1,000)	County	Number of reporting units	Number of employees	Payroll ($1,000)
			Electronic and other electrical equipment and components, except computer equipment (SIC code 36)				
Florida	691	59,081	140,304	Leon	8	279	536
				Manatee	14	972	1,860
Brevard	39	11,953	34,518	Marion	6	457	772
Broward	99	10,006	25,438	Martin	4	263	438
Dade	103	2,652	3,958	Orange	50	4,561	10,010
Duval	18	577	1,123	Palm Beach	47	4,435	10,890
Escambia	8	171	219	Pasco	6	86	167
Flagler	5	402	530	Pinellas	90	8,115	19,551
Hernando	5	155	187	Sarasota	20	1,688	4,042
Hillsborough	39	3,947	8,256	Seminole	37	2,829	5,676
Lake	8	192	272	Volusia	19	1,980	5,309
Lee	8	276	450	Statewide 1/	10	11	32
			Communications equipment (SIC code 366)				
Florida	122	17,867	49,247	Hillsborough	11	1,124	2,728
				Leon	4	189	394
Brevard	11	978	2,877	Orange	5	456	915
Broward	18	7,159	19,861	Palm Beach	12	1,917	5,694
Dade	8	78	166	Seminole	6	247	610
			Electronic components and accessories (SIC code 367)				
Florida	229	27,987	65,781	Lee	3	192	282
				Orange	17	2,566	5,762
Brevard	19	10,782	31,245	Palm Beach	21	2,365	4,863
Broward	34	1,868	3,510	Pinellas	39	3,736	8,763
Dade	18	783	1,224	Sarasota	8	266	490
Flagler	3	348	469	Seminole	20	1,757	3,598

1/ Reporting units without a fixed location within the state or of unknown county
location.
    Note: Excluded are counties where data are withheld to avoid disclosure of
information about individual firms. For a list of three-digit code industries
included see Table 12.50.

    Source: State of Florida, Department of Labor and Employment Security, Bureau of
Labor Market Information, "Employment, Wages, and Contributions Report" (ES-202),
unpublished data.

Florida Statistical Abstract 1991

Table 12.83. AIRCRAFT AND BOAT BUILDING: AVERAGE MONTHLY REPORTING UNITS
EMPLOYMENT, AND PAYROLL COVERED BY UNEMPLOYMENT COMPENSATION LAW IN
IN THE STATE AND COUNTIES OF FLORIDA, 1990

County	Number of reporting units	Number of employees	Payroll ($1,000)	County	Number of reporting units	Number of employees	Payroll ($1,000)
			Aircraft and parts (SIC code 372)				
Florida	111	18,476	57,328	Duval	5	588	1,452
				Martin	6	1,453	3,601
Broward	17	843	2,294	Orange	8	401	778
Dade	26	1,833	4,367	Pinellas	6	796	1,900
			Ship and boat building and repairing (SIC code 373)				
Florida	592	16,527	32,774	Lee	23	225	379
				Manatee	20	1,455	3,217
Alachua	9	324	628	Martin	17	211	471
Bay	20	542	924	Monroe	18	66	123
Broward	93	1,525	3,324	Palm Beach	41	766	1,962
Collier	6	45	69	Pinellas	50	1,533	2,528
Dade	101	2,039	4,092	Polk	9	38	44
Duval	22	1,949	4,846	St. Johns	8	228	355
Escambia	15	105	142	Sarasota	15	59	81
Hillsborough	20	1,390	2,851	Seminole	5	121	200
Indian River	6	13	17	Volusia	11	319	574

Note: Excluded are counties where data are withheld to avoid disclosure of
information about individual firms.

Table 12.84. INSTRUMENTS AND RELATED PRODUCTS: AVERAGE MONTHLY REPORTING UNITS
EMPLOYMENT, AND PAYROLL COVERED BY UNEMPLOYMENT COMPENSATION LAW IN THE
STATE AND COUNTIES OF FLORIDA, 1990

County	Number of reporting units	Number of employees	Payroll ($1,000)	County	Number of reporting units	Number of employees	Payroll ($1,000)
			Instruments and related products (SIC code 38)				
Florida	500	35,463	81,574	Martin	7	62	177
Alachua	10	94	136	Okaloosa	9	621	1,361
Bay	5	20	41	Orange	37	1,357	3,677
Brevard	26	3,028	8,162	Palm Beach	31	577	1,414
Broward	44	3,083	6,849	Pasco	4	38	40
Collier	4	83	194	Pinellas	83	9,936	24,726
Dade	77	6,156	15,151	Polk	8	906	1,380
Duval	21	1,852	4,615	St. Lucie	3	100	107
Escambia	5	33	62	Sarasota	14	297	510
Hillsborough	23	1,074	2,900	Seminole	17	587	1,074
Manatee	7	392	629	Volusia	17	2,447	4,081

Note: Excluded are counties where data are withheld to avoid disclosure of
information about individual firms. For a list of three-digit code industries
included see Table 12.50

Source for Tables 12.83 and 12.84: State of Florida, Department of Labor and
Employment Security, Bureau of Labor Market Information, "Employment, Wages, and
Contributions Report" (ES-202), unpublished data.

TRANSPORTATION

Enplaned Passengers by Airport, 1988 and 1989

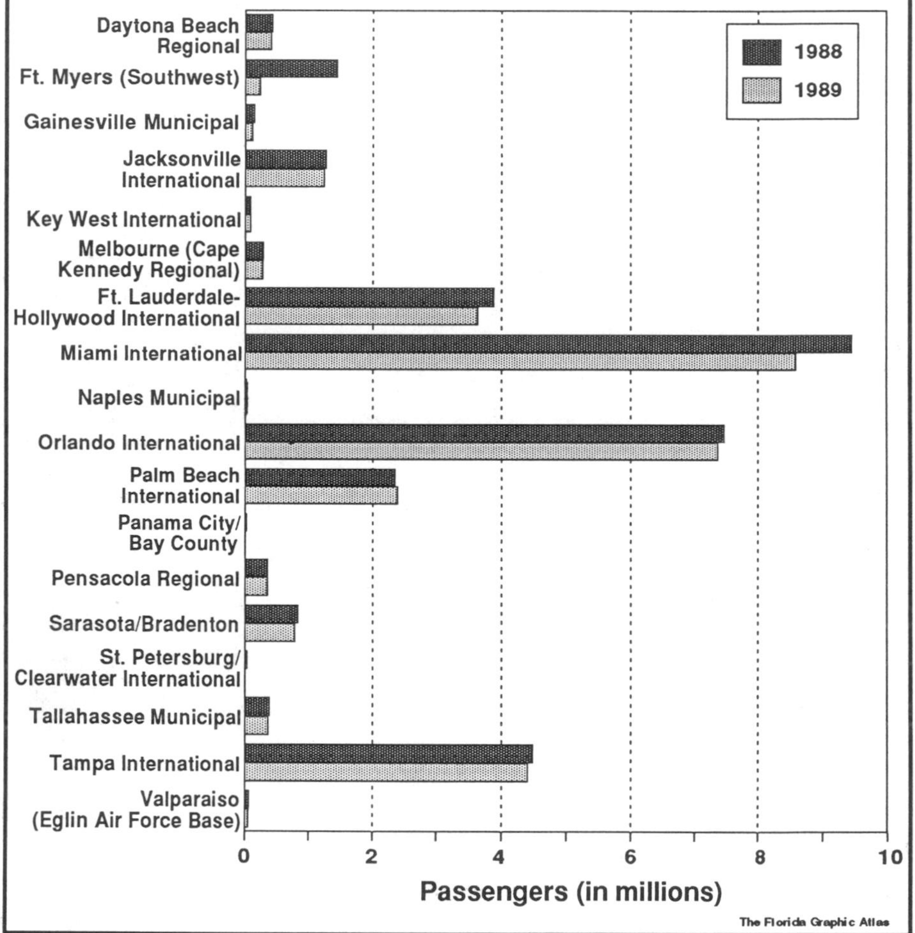

Daytona Beach Regional
Ft. Myers (Southwest)
Gainesville Municipal
Jacksonville International
Key West International
Melbourne (Cape Kennedy Regional)
Ft. Lauderdale-Hollywood International
Miami International
Naples Municipal
Orlando International
Palm Beach International
Panama City/ Bay County
Pensacola Regional
Sarasota/Bradenton
St. Petersburg/ Clearwater International
Tallahassee Municipal
Tampa International
Valparaiso (Eglin Air Force Base)
1988
1989
0
2
4
6
8
10
Passengers (in millions)
The Florida Graphic Atlas

Source: Table 13.92

TABLES LISTED BY MAJOR HEADINGS

Table 13.16. ROADS AND STREETS: EXISTING MILEAGE OF PUBLIC ROADS AND STREETS
BY JURISDICTION IN FLORIDA, DECEMBER 31, 1986 THROUGH 1989

Jurisdiction	1986	1987	1988	1989
Total	99,074	100,423	104,589	107,955
Rural mileage	67,090	68,398	56,658	59,305
Under state control	7,518	7,515	7,669	7,616
Under local control	59,572	60,883	48,989	51,689
County roads	59,307	60,643	48,813	51,513
Other local roads 1/	265	240	176	176
Urban mileage	31,984	32,025	47,931	48,650
Under state control	4,075	4,074	4,162	4,175
Under local control	27,909	27,951	43,769	44,475
County roads	775	1,023	1,201	1,368
Other local roads 1/	7,524	24,053	42,568	43,107

1/ Includes mileage not identified by administrative authority.

Table 13.17. ROADS AND STREETS: EXISTING MILEAGE OF PUBLIC ROADS AND STREETS
BY FUNCTIONAL SYSTEM AND BY PAVEMENT CONDITION IN FLORIDA
DECEMBER 31, 1989

Function	Total existing mileage	Pavement conditions				
		Poor	Fair	Good	Very good	Un- paved
Total	107,955	(NA)	(NA)	(NA)	(NA)	(NA)
Rural	59,305	(NA)	(NA)	(NA)	(NA)	(NA)
Interstate	982	71	0	256	655	0
Other principal arterial	2,601	69	6	1,023	1,503	0
Minor arterial	3,495	51	7	1,331	2,106	0
Major collector	4,674	3,752	110	448	265	99
Minor collector	5,195	4,842	31	0	0	322
Local	42,358	(NA)	(NA)	(NA)	(NA)	(NA)
Urban	48,650	(NA)	(NA)	(NA)	(NA)	(NA)
Interstate	414	7	4	115	288	0
Other freeways and expressways	251	10	0	46	195	0
Other principal arterial	1,941	133	46	767	995	0
Minor arterial	2,416	1,059	23	516	818	0
Collector	4,771	4,629	11	13	54	64
Local	38,857	(NA)	(NA)	(NA)	(NA)	(NA)

(NA) Not available.

Source for Tables 13.16 and 13.17: U.S., Department of Transportation, Federal
Highway Administration, *Highway Statistics, 1989,* and previous editions.

Florida Statistical Abstract 1991

Table 13.20. HIGHWAYS: RECEIPTS AND DISBURSEMENTS FOR HIGHWAYS BY ALL UNITS
OF GOVERNMENT IN FLORIDA, FISCAL YEARS 1985-86 THROUGH 1987-88

(in thousands of dollars)

Item	1985-86	1986-87	1987-88
Total receipts	2,996,197	2,865,714	3,072,617
Bond proceeds, par value 1/	577,348	68,185	100,000
Total current income	2,418,849	2,797,529	2,972,617
Road-user tax revenue 2/	1,558,827	1,720,685	1,817,305
Federal agencies	541,425	557,790	645,261
State agencies	782,402	896,844	822,044
Counties	162,000	182,985	220,000
Municipalities	73,000	83,066	130,000
Road, bridge, and ferry tolls	167,399	226,515	247,913
Appropriations from general fund	185,843	268,230	262,825
Property taxes	145,000	211,681	230,000
Other imposts	127,131	98,002	120,604
Miscellaneous receipts	234,649	272,416	293,970
Total disbursements 3/	2,699,947	2,933,232	3,254,500
Bond redemptions, par value 1/	150,430	120,379	114,227
Total direct expenditure	2,549,517	2,812,853	3,140,273
Capital outlay	1,403,688	1,616,987	1,882,359
State-administered highways	1,016,476	1,190,279	1,390,934
Local rural roads	280,050	288,390	332,077
Local municipal streets	106,010	133,938	158,255
Federal roads and unclassified	1,152	4,380	1,093
Summary: right-of-way only 4/	212,674	177,720	247,193
Maintenance	672,379	708,308	801,042
State-administered highways	155,896	177,599	223,619
Local rural roads	311,950	309,735	342,580
Local municipal streets	201,950	218,252	231,950
Federal roads and unclassified	2,583	2,722	2,893
Administration and miscellaneous	144,694	107,230	84,022
Highway police and safety	219,534	238,386	256,145
Bond interest	109,222	141,942	116,705

1/ Excludes short-term notes and refunding bond issues.

2/ Excludes amounts allocated for collection expenses and nonhighway purposes.
Revenues are segregated according to the collecting agency. Amounts shown for
federal agencies are mostly grants-in-aid payments.

3/ Disbursements are classified by system on which expended, rather than by ex-
pending agencies; capital outlay on county and other local rural roads includes
expenditure from federal, state, and local funds.

4/ Summary of right-of-way costs which are included in local, state, and federal
categories.

Note: This table presents combined summaries of the highway finances of all
government agencies in net amounts; duplications that would otherwise have resulted
from interfund or intergovernmental transfers have been removed. Data may include
estimates.

Source: U.S., Department of Transportation, Federal Highway Administration,
Highway Statistics, 1989, and previous editions.

Table 13.21. HIGHWAY BRIDGES: COUNT OF BRIDGES BY FUNCTIONAL SYSTEM IN FLORIDA
AND THE UNITED STATES, 1988 AND 1989

Functional system	Florida		United States	
	1988	1989	1988	1989
Total	10,229	10,336	576,702	577,296
Rural	5,861	5,877	460,624	467,456
Interstate	709	705	28,869	28,989
Other principal arterial	1,186	1,189	33,021	33,320
Minor arterial	893	892	40,558	40,557
Major collector	625	633	3,746	103,948
Minor collector	641	638	50,002	49,883
Local	1,807	1,820	204,428	210,759
Urban	4,367	4,458	103,164	104,559
Interstate	874	913	23,200	23,483
Other freeways and expressways	348	358	10,306	10,403
Other principal arterial	1,136	1,156	20,789	21,133
Minor arterial	513	521	18,234	18,391
Collector	385	379	11,596	11,703
Local	1,111	1,131	19,039	19,446
Unclassified	1	1	12,914	5,281

Note: Because functional system has been estimated or assigned in some cases,
data may not be precise.

Table 13.22. HIGHWAY SPEED: AVERAGE AND MEDIAN SPEED BY FUNCTIONAL SYSTEM
OF HIGHWAY IN FLORIDA, FISCAL YEAR 1988-89

Functional system of highway	Miles per hour			Percentage exceeding--		
	Average	Median 1/	85th percentile 2/	55 miles per hour	60 miles per hour	65 miles per hour
Statewide	56.9	56.6	63.8	59.4	31.6	11.2
Urban						
Interstate	59.2	58.9	65.8	72.8	43.8	17.1
Other principal and minor arterials	55.4	54.9	62.7	49.3	23.8	7.7
Rural						
Other principal and minor arterials	57.9	57.7	64.4	66.5	35.6	12.4
Major collectors	52.3	51.6	58.7	29.8	9.9	2.7

1/ Median speed is the speed at or below which 50 percent of the vehicles are
traveling.
2/ 85th percentile speed is the speed at or below which 85 percent of the
vehicles are traveling.
Note: Data reflect speeds of all vehicles on sections of roads posted for 55
miles-per-hour speed limits and are based on an annual classification of speed limit
enforcement required annually from each highway agency.

Source for Tables 13.21 and 13.22: U.S., Department of Transportation, Federal
Highway Administration, *Highway Statistics, 1989*, and previous edition.

Florida Statistical Abstract 1991

Table 13.29.   VEHICLE MILES OF TRAVEL: ESTIMATED NUMBER OF MILES BY FUNCTIONAL
SYSTEM OF HIGHWAY IN FLORIDA, 1988 AND 1989

(in millions of miles)

Functional	Total		Rural		Urban	
system of highway	1988	1989	1988	1989	1988	1989
Total	105,319	108,877	29,489	31,385	75,830	77,492
Interstate	17,227	18,224	7,836	8,550	9,391	9,674
Other freeways and expressways	4,383	4,262	0	0	4,383	4,262
Other principal arterial	27,004	28,549	8,586	9,253	18,418	19,296
Minor arterial	19,639	20,430	5,718	6,015	13,921	14,415
Collector	13,557	13,499	4,446	4,475	9,111	9,024
Local	23,509	23,913	2,903	3,092	20,606	20,821

Note: Data are estimated highway travel based on traffic counts taken at
selected highway locations.

Table 13.30.   MOTOR VEHICLES: REGISTRATIONS BY TYPE OF VEHICLE IN FLORIDA, 1973
THROUGH 1989

(rounded to hundreds, except where indicated)

Year	All motor vehicles 1/	Percentage change from previous year	Automobiles	Buses	Trucks	Motorcycles
1973	5,499.2	10.7	4,536.8	8.6	801.8	152.0
1974	5,803.6	5.5	4,704.8	14.7	896.6	187.5
1975	5,560.4	-4.2	4,499.2	17.8	878.4	165.0
1976	6,028.9	8.4	4,835.1	21.6	991.2	180.9
1977	6,444.3	6.9	4,978.9	22.7	1,349.3	93.3
1978	7,068.9	9.7	5,738.0	26.1	1,151.8	152.9
1979	7,519.4	6.4	6,011.0	28.2	1,259.7	220.5
1980	7,833.0	4.2	6,196.6	29.3	1,387.6	219.5
1981	8,194.1	4.6	6,484.6	30.4	1,459.1	220.0
1982	8,561.0	4.5	6,753.6	32.2	1,548.8	226.4
1983	9,041.0	5.6	7,113.9	33.3	1,661.3	232.5
1984	9,635.1	6.6	7,552.4	34.4	1,807.4	240.9
1985	10,096.8	4.8	7,849.1	35.8	1,979.9	232.0
1986	10,591.2	4.9	8,263.3	34.2	2,064.0	229.7
1987	10,903.1	2.9	8,521.6	34.8	2,127.1	219.5
1988	11,183.1	2.6	8,713.2	35.5	2,234.9	199.5
1989	11,410.8	2.0	8,972.7	36.2	2,197.9	203.9

1/ Includes motorcycles.
Note: Excludes vehicles owned by the military service.

Source for Tables 13.29 and 13.30:   U.S., Department of Transportation, Federal
Highway Administration, *Highway Statistics, 1989*, and previous editions.

Table 13.32. MOTOR VEHICLE TAGS: TOTAL TAGS AND PASSENGER CAR TAGS SOLD AND
     REVENUE COLLECTED IN THE STATE AND COUNTIES OF FLORIDA, FISCAL YEAR
     1989-90

County	Total tags		Passenger car tags		
	Number	Per-centage change from 1988-89	Number	Per-centage change from 1988-89	Total revenue ($1,000)
Florida	15,361,833	1.5	8,932,823	1.8	∆/ 351,417
Alachua	188,772	0.7	110,462	-1.8	3,829
Baker	21,935	5.9	9,300	2.1	571
Bay	148,760	7.8	84,064	0.8	3,004
Bradford	29,038	-2.6	13,146	1.0	628
Brevard	475,390	0.2	280,835	0.2	9,622
Broward	1,360,037	0.0	858,145	-0.3	28,946
Calhoun	9,326	-2.1	4,386	0.0	244
Charlotte	140,140	4.7	82,304	5.9	3,052
Citrus	112,528	1.2	60,623	3.1	2,368
Clay	113,546	3.2	64,782	5.6	2,510
Collier	187,863	0.3	114,488	2.8	4,513
Columbia	51,943	3.6	23,641	3.2	1,135
Dade	1,804,221	2.9	1,362,823	1.5	49,352
De Soto	28,964	-1.7	12,041	-0.7	647
Dixie	10,893	3.9	4,325	3.9	282
Duval	788,086	-1.6	452,653	-0.4	17,870
Escambia	263,586	-0.9	173,664	-1.0	6,053
Flagler	37,046	7.6	21,912	12.5	893
Franklin	7,665	2.8	3,979	3.6	183
Gadsden	30,797	7.2	16,070	6.9	722
Gilchrist	12,628	1.5	4,732	3.7	341
Glades	4,835	2.3	1,872	4.6	136
Gulf	11,628	1.1	6,220	1.2	292
Hamilton	8,345	6.7	3,803	2.8	214
Hardee	25,882	-0.4	10,786	0.8	620
Hendry	34,637	-2.1	14,816	-3.9	914
Hernando	105,496	6.1	63,190	8.9	2,362
Highlands	91,417	3.0	45,154	2.9	1,870
Hillsborough	1,040,402	-2.1	572,216	-0.6	23,918
Holmes	14,822	4.6	7,382	1.9	339
Indian River	115,089	2.8	66,952	4.5	2,471
Jackson	43,389	1.4	22,515	1.3	952
Jefferson	10,184	-1.4	4,948	1.1	267
Lafayette	4,828	7.5	1,906	2.6	132
Lake	210,624	2.1	99,944	4.4	4,307
Lee	433,570	4.3	240,556	4.7	9,314
Leon	215,639	-1.9	126,231	-1.8	4,354
Levy	27,975	9.8	12,529	9.1	700

See footnotes at end of table.   Continued . . .

Florida Statistical Abstract 1991

Table 13.32. MOTOR VEHICLE TAGS: TOTAL TAGS AND PASSENGER CAR TAGS SOLD AND
REVENUE COLLECTED IN THE STATE AND COUNTIES OF FLORIDA, FISCAL YEAR
1989-90 (Continued)

County	Total tags Number	Percentage change from 1988-89	Passenger car tags Number	Percentage change from 1988-89	Total revenue ($1,000)
Liberty	5,219	3.1	2,273	2.0	164
Madison	14,594	8.9	7,135	4.5	374
Manatee	279,736	18.2	181,593	24.8	6,868
Marion	249,335	2.8	127,630	4.2	5,256
Martin	140,955	4.1	83,159	4.1	3,017
Monroe	85,329	0.3	44,351	3.6	1,869
Nassau	46,535	5.3	22,456	9.6	1,019
Okaloosa	178,672	-0.1	105,196	0.4	3,357
Okeechobee	38,714	-1.1	16,245	0.7	917
Orange	940,713	2.4	529,232	2.9	22,005
Osceola	157,703	9.6	87,675	8.1	3,285
Palm Beach	829,422	0.9	615,471	3.6	21,998
Pasco	324,349	-2.5	185,360	-1.4	6,609
Pinellas	992,569	-0.4	622,740	0.7	19,929
Polk	509,596	-1.0	251,619	0.5	11,836
Putnam	70,417	-0.7	33,104	0.5	1,465
St. Johns	93,133	7.2	54,493	9.2	2,011
St. Lucie	173,496	-0.5	93,439	2.7	3,677
Santa Rosa	79,049	4.5	43,735	6.2	1,682
Sarasota	358,531	2.6	222,348	5.2	7,413
Seminole	352,270	-3.4	207,408	0.9	6,991
Sumter	35,451	0.8	15,530	3.3	898
Suwannee	34,037	0.9	13,675	2.0	797
Taylor	21,082	6.3	8,907	4.0	498
Union	9,308	16.1	3,494	9.4	477
Volusia	398,915	6.6	244,319	3.6	8,399
Wakulla	13,312	2.7	5,850	6.6	325
Walton	21,922	0.0	11,926	2.1	525
Washington	13,870	0.6	7,369	2.1	338
Office agency 1/	52,278	-27.5	25,696	-40.7	1,231
DHSMV 2/	575,204	10.5	0	0.0	596
Motor carrier service	44,191	2.9	0	0.0	19,463

A/ Does not include $3,795,924.19 in refunds.
1/ Totals include tags and revenue outside computer system.
2/ Sales made by the Department of Highway Safety and Motor Vehicles district
offices.
Note: See Table 2.36 for mobile home and recreational vehicle tag sales.
Source: State of Florida, Department of Highway Safety and Motor Vehicles,
Division of Motor Vehicles, *Tags and Revenue, July 1, 1989 through June 30, 1990*.

Florida Statistical Abstract 1991

Table 13.33.   ACTIVE DRIVERS LICENSES: NUMBER ISSUED BY TYPE AND BY AGE OF DRIVER
IN FLORIDA, JANUARY 1, 1991

Age	Restricted drivers licenses	Operators licenses	Chauffeurs licenses	Age	Restricted drivers licenses	Operators licenses	Chauffeurs licenses
Total	268,530	9,884,875	1,458,997	45	1,449	139,275	30,090
				46	1,434	139,339	30,022
15	36,695	41	0	47	1,236	143,475	30,346
16	29,119	63,102	13	48	1,267	138,319	28,876
17	20,311	97,635	51	49	1,088	121,462	25,821
18	15,915	127,485	813	50	1,061	116,900	24,835
19	14,431	157,041	3,347	51	1,012	111,421	23,377
20	13,266	173,043	6,684	52	1,001	111,022	22,886
21	10,330	174,106	10,344	53	896	106,362	21,527
22	9,091	176,152	14,820	54	882	104,380	20,461
23	8,076	183,871	18,577	55	830	102,945	19,626
24	7,260	198,390	24,139	56	737	101,130	18,899
25	6,816	213,859	28,789	57	746	98,970	17,310
26	6,561	236,877	34,904	58	724	104,842	17,783
27	6,232	243,213	38,906	59	643	103,600	16,354
28	5,924	248,423	42,314	60	736	110,550	16,970
29	5,466	251,560	45,102	61	643	109,419	15,507
30	5,374	250,086	47,404	62	660	115,033	15,406
31	4,951	243,066	47,840	63	593	118,372	15,003
32	4,734	238,041	48,207	64	593	118,712	13,579
33	4,369	236,767	49,443	65	553	121,727	12,784
34	4,065	228,767	49,019	66	538	126,269	11,505
35	3,608	219,698	47,994	67	472	122,870	10,292
36	3,365	214,350	47,722	68	494	121,773	9,534
37	2,983	204,947	45,495	69	461	124,745	8,954
38	2,862	198,703	44,407	70	387	118,788	7,580
39	2,469	189,683	42,937	71	384	107,911	6,870
40	2,409	182,086	40,179	72	326	109,682	5,975
41	2,039	179,902	38,783	73	295	101,482	5,191
42	1,927	178,916	38,361	74	264	95,641	4,395
43	1,856	185,113	38,838	75	240	90,291	3,896
44	1,631	167,113	35,084	Over 75	1,750	666,132	16,827

Note: Data are essentially an inventory of current licenses as of January 1,
1991, according to the records of the Florida Department of Highway Safety and Motor
Vehicles.   Figures do not include licenses that are expired but renewable (less than
one year).

Source: State of Florida, Department of Highway Safety and Motor Vehicles,
Division of Administrative Services, unpublished data.

Florida Statistical Abstract 1991

Table 13.34. ACTIVE DRIVERS LICENSES: NUMBER OF LICENSES BY COUNTY OF DRIVER'S
MAILING ADDRESS AND BY SEX OF LICENSE HOLDER IN THE STATE AND COUNTIES
OF FLORIDA, JANUARY 1, 1991

County of driver's mailing address	Active drivers licenses		County of driver's mailing address	Active drivers licenses	
	Male	Female		Male	Female
Florida	6,201,296	5,411,106	Lake	71,143	65,422
Alachua	82,836	75,472	Lee	163,382	147,192
Baker	6,486	5,857	Leon	79,736	76,209
Bay	63,178	56,255	Levy	11,350	10,229
Bradford	7,764	6,886	Liberty	1,933	1,733
Brevard	196,888	171,510	Madison	6,405	5,559
Broward	629,801	540,181	Manatee	96,405	90,034
Calhoun	3,804	3,519	Marion	93,937	85,997
Charlotte	50,148	47,891	Martin	52,318	46,248
Citrus	41,346	37,719	Monroe	46,601	32,515
Clay	47,368	43,972	Nassau	20,506	18,045
Collier	79,784	67,342	Okaloosa	70,334	62,298
Columbia	17,487	15,991	Okeechobee	15,209	12,142
Dade	893,734	708,591	Orange	332,536	285,658
De Soto	10,164	8,379	Osceola	49,628	42,894
Dixie	4,116	3,547	Palm Beach	444,592	392,824
Duval	301,717	272,036	Pasco	125,237	115,448
Escambia	122,673	110,218	Pinellas	411,472	388,766
Flagler	12,873	11,518	Polk	179,167	160,431
Franklin	3,792	3,287	Putnam	24,871	22,142
Gadsden	14,532	13,006	St. Johns	37,907	35,059
Gilchrist	3,428	3,162	St. Lucie	67,770	59,267
Glades	2,137	1,646	Santa Rosa	37,235	33,404
Gulf	5,103	4,575	Sarasota	139,523	135,226
Hamilton	3,966	3,655	Seminole	126,314	116,707
Hardee	10,409	7,496	Sumter	13,772	12,130
Hendry	12,714	9,365	Suwannee	11,393	10,629
Hernando	47,514	43,883	Taylor	7,519	6,801
Highlands	32,089	28,539	Union	3,123	2,874
Hillsborough	394,128	346,517	Volusia	178,105	157,856
Holmes	6,613	5,915	Wakulla	4,868	4,368
Indian River	48,383	43,925	Walton	10,460	9,202
Jackson	17,038	15,509	Washington	7,245	6,543
Jefferson	4,407	3,775	Unknown county 1/	20,204	4,356
Lafayette	1,509	1,315	Out-of-state 2/	59,167	32,444

1/ Licenses mailed to addresses which do not permit specification of county.
Also includes licenses with incorrect or unknown zip codes.
2/ Licenses mailed to out-of-state addresses.
Note: Data are essentially an inventory of current licenses as of January 1,
1991 according to the records of the Florida Department of Highway Safety and Motor
Vehicles. Figures include restricted, operator, and chauffeur licenses. Figures do
not include licenses that are expired but renewable (less than one year).

Source: State of Florida, Department of Highway Safety and Motor Vehicles,
Division of Administrative Services, unpublished data.

Florida Statistical Abstract 1991

Table 13.36. TRANSPORTATION: AVERAGE MONTHLY REPORTING UNITS, EMPLOYMENT, AND
PAYROLL COVERED BY UNEMPLOYMENT COMPENSATION LAW BY INDUSTRY IN FLORIDA
1990

SIC code	Industry	Number of re-porting units	Number of employees	Payroll ($1,000)
40	Railroad transportation	(D)	(D)	(D)
41	Local and suburban transit and interurban highway passenger transportation	675	12,254	17,049
411	Local and suburban passenger transportation	314	7,605	11,204
412	Taxicabs	111	1,470	1,855
413	Intercity and rural bus transportation	19	604	1,159
414	Bus charter service	74	1,647	2,179
415	School buses	135	762	463
417	Terminal and service facilities for motor vehicle passenger transportation	22	163	189
42	Motor freight transportation and warehousing	4,076	58,811	108,879
421	Trucking and courier services, except air	3,447	54,098	101,819
422	Public warehousing and storage	620	4,628	6,910
423	Terminal and joint terminal maintenance fa-cilities for motor freight transportation	9	84	150
44	Water transportation	892	17,423	35,973
441	Deep sea foreign transportation of freight	28	1,047	3,404
442	Deep sea domestic transportation of freight	16	1,470	4,605
444	Water transportation of freight, NEC	16	834	2,021
448	Water transportation of passengers	130	5,217	10,230
449	Services incidental to water transportation	701	8,853	15,712
45	Transportation by air	825	52,698	123,067
451	Air transportation, scheduled, and air courier services	303	37,783	96,856
452	Air transportation, nonscheduled	150	2,070	4,755
458	Airports, flying fields, and airport terminal services	372	12,844	21,456
47	Transportation services	3,355	21,593	37,698
472	Arrangement of passenger transportation	2,377	13,315	20,715
473	Arrangement of transportation of freight and cargo	888	7,813	16,218
474	Rental of railroad cars	4	44	98
478	Miscellaneous services incidental to transportation	86	421	667

NEC Not elsewhere classified.
(D) Data withheld to avoid disclosure of information about individual firms.
Note: Totals on county employment tables may not match totals in this table due
to rounding.

Source: State of Florida, Department of Labor and Employment Security, Bureau of
Labor Market Information, "Employment, Wages, and Contributions Report" (ES-202),
unpublished data.

Florida Statistical Abstract 1991

Table 13.37. PASSENGER TRANSIT AND MOTOR FREIGHT TRANSPORTATION AND WAREHOUSING
    AVERAGE MONTHLY REPORTING UNITS, EMPLOYMENT, AND PAYROLL COVERED BY
    UNEMPLOYMENT COMPENSATION LAW IN THE STATE AND COUNTIES OF FLORIDA
    1990

County	Number of re- porting units	Number of employees	Payroll ($1,000)	County	Number of re- porting units	Number of employees	Payroll ($1,000)
Local and suburban passenger transit (SIC code 41)							
Florida	664	12,285	17,049	Leon	7	90	129
Alachua	7	35	34	Manatee	3	9	7
Brevard	19	215	241	Monroe	6	209	272
Broward	65	1,295	1,794	Orange	52	2,617	3,539
Charlotte	6	26	24	Osceola	9	97	103
Collier	13	128	146	Palm Beach	38	719	1,011
Dade	102	1,481	2,266	Pasco	11	95	88
Duval	146	1,745	2,245	Pinellas	27	1,445	2,263
Escambia	9	122	179	St. Lucie	9	76	70
Hillsborough	20	631	1,121	Sarasota	14	104	104
Indian River	3	21	20	Volusia	17	314	456
Lee	19	151	160	Statewide 1/	5	51	63
Motor freight transportation and warehousing (SIC code 42)							
Florida	4,052	58,896	108,880	Indian River	29	121	190
				Jackson	8	65	85
Alachua	36	475	801	Lake	46	703	1,084
Baker	9	41	54	Lee	108	851	1,435
Bay	55	520	811	Leon	38	646	1,133
Brevard	89	1,234	1,983	Levy	8	32	36
Broward	341	3,979	6,231	Liberty	7	25	27
Charlotte	21	222	428	Manatee	46	403	586
Citrus	26	148	173	Marion	78	617	1,084
Clay	29	252	345	Martin	22	823	1,727
Collier	63	360	580	Monroe	25	257	494
Columbia	15	143	245	Nassau	18	78	124
Dade	662	8,987	18,564	Okaloosa	32	496	849
De Soto	7	18	21	Okeechobee	8	48	99
Duval	332	10,061	19,582	Orange	286	6,428	14,424
Escambia	109	1,255	1,801	Osceola	15	54	56
Gadsden	9	16	15	Palm Beach	199	2,028	3,831
Gilchrist	4	29	35	Pasco	74	981	1,520
Hamilton	3	63	129	Pinellas	141	1,956	3,212
Hardee	7	16	19	Polk	209	4,335	8,024
Hendry	14	70	112	Putnam	16	85	92
Hernando	24	425	700	St. Johns	14	91	127
Highlands	23	100	132	St. Lucie	48	509	818
Hillsborough	311	5,030	9,078	Santa Rosa	17	70	91

See footnotes at end of table.   Continued . . .

Table 13.37. PASSENGER TRANSIT AND MOTOR FREIGHT TRANSPORTATION AND WAREHOUSING
AVERAGE MONTHLY REPORTING UNITS, EMPLOYMENT, AND PAYROLL COVERED BY
UNEMPLOYMENT COMPENSATION LAW IN THE STATE AND COUNTIES OF FLORIDA
1990 (Continued)

County	Number of reporting units	Number of employees	Payroll ($1,000)	County	Number of reporting units	Number of employees	Payroll ($1,000)

Motor freight transportation and warehousing (SIC code 42) (Continued)

County	Number of reporting units	Number of employees	Payroll ($1,000)	County	Number of reporting units	Number of employees	Payroll ($1,000)
Sarasota	74	723	1,264	Union	17	270	382
Sumter	8	81	116	Volusia	84	644	979
Suwannee	15	87	112	Walton	5	59	91
Taylor	5	29	32	Statewide 1/	64	806	1,305

1/ Reporting units without a fixed location within the state or of unknown county
location.
  Note: Excluded are counties where data are withheld to avoid disclosure of
information about individual firms.   For a list of three-digit code industries
included see Table 13.36.

Table 13.38. WATER AND AIR TRANSPORTATION AND TRANSPORTATION SERVICES: AVERAGE
MONTHLY REPORTING UNITS, EMPLOYMENT, AND PAYROLL COVERED BY UNEMPLOYMENT
COMPENSATION LAW IN THE STATE AND COUNTIES OF FLORIDA, 1990

Water transportation (SIC code 44)

County	Number of reporting units	Number of employees	Payroll ($1,000)	County	Number of reporting units	Number of employees	Payroll ($1,000)
Florida	882	17,456	35,972	Monroe	60	540	700
Bay	33	443	750	Nassau	6	84	155
Brevard	34	718	1,204	Okaloosa	21	84	111
Broward	111	2,089	4,210	Orange	4	50	158
Collier	19	201	343	Palm Beach	50	350	584
Dade	141	6,891	14,840	Pasco	9	40	58
Dixie	5	17	13	Pinellas	52	379	490
Duval	82	2,214	5,849	St. Johns	6	35	68
Escambia	22	472	618	St. Lucie	8	54	83
Hillsborough	58	1,527	3,915	Sarasota	16	140	190
Indian River	5	86	85	Seminole	4	69	106
Lee	35	215	312	Volusia	14	124	142
Manatee	14	136	237	Wakulla	5	36	37
Martin	15	84	133	Statewide 1/	15	40	106

See footnotes at end of table.   Continued . . .

Florida Statistical Abstract 1991

Table 13.38. WATER AND AIR TRANSPORTATION AND TRANSPORTATION SERVICES: AVERAGE
MONTHLY REPORTING UNITS, EMPLOYMENT, AND PAYROLL COVERED BY UNEMPLOYMENT
COMPENSATION LAW IN THE STATE AND COUNTIES OF FLORIDA, 1990 (Continued)

County	Number of reporting units	Number of employees	Payroll ($1,000)	County	Number of reporting units	Number of employees	Payroll ($1,000)
			Transportation by air (SIC code 45)				
Florida	814	52,825	123,068	Leon	11	276	514
				Marion	5	75	104
Alachua	9	177	322	Martin	5	57	84
Bay	7	91	145	Monroe	14	167	263
Brevard	12	285	461	Okaloosa	15	265	672
Broward	100	3,849	10,069	Orange	57	5,967	12,485
Charlotte	4	20	20	Osceola	5	56	101
Collier	8	107	180	Palm Beach	37	1,388	3,085
Dade	268	27,606	68,701	Pinellas	21	388	759
Duval	34	1,794	3,794	Polk	13	139	251
Escambia	23	987	1,872	St. Lucie	6	85	180
Highlands	5	42	47	Santa Rosa	5	495	1,315
Hillsborough	43	6,205	13,657	Sarasota	15	399	787
Indian River	9	61	106	Seminole	9	154	306
Lake	5	18	29	Volusia	20	370	496
Lee	18	1,060	1,975	Statewide 1/	10	47	151
			Transportation services (SIC code 47)				
Florida	3,340	21,632	37,699	Leon	20	150	217
Alachua	12	78	112	Manatee	28	113	143
Bay	16	85	131	Marion	16	49	62
Brevard	60	290	454	Martin	25	83	92
Broward	370	2,347	4,453	Monroe	16	90	340
Charlotte	16	61	62	Okaloosa	15	66	75
Citrus	8	53	58	Orange	197	1,705	2,677
Clay	9	56	122	Osceola	18	78	106
Collier	43	197	262	Palm Beach	216	1,458	2,719
Dade	1,250	8,262	16,245	Pasco	33	112	120
Duval	115	1,648	2,484	Pinellas	192	1,120	1,476
Escambia	25	116	128	Polk	51	369	675
Flagler	6	34	30	St. Johns	12	41	60
Hernando	14	47	54	St. Lucie	22	66	80
Highlands	10	36	41	Santa Rosa	6	20	25
Hillsborough	193	1,140	2,026	Sarasota	67	324	500
Indian River	13	64	79	Seminole	49	191	275
Lake	17	91	120	Volusia	57	271	315
Lee	64	408	463	Statewide 1/	27	48	159

1/ Reporting units without a fixed location within the state or of unknown county
location.
     Note: Excluded are counties where data are withheld to avoid disclosure of
information about individual firms. For a list of three-digit code industries
included see Table 13.36.
     Source for Tables 13.37 and 13.38: State of Florida, Department of Labor and
Employment Security, Bureau of Labor Market Information, "Employment, Wages and
Contributions Report" (ES-202), unpublished data.

Florida Statistical Abstract 1991

Table 13.40. MOTOR VEHICLE REGISTRATIONS: NUMBER OF OUT-OF-STATE VEHICLES
REGISTERED IN FLORIDA BY STATE OF PREVIOUS REGISTRATION, 1986 THROUGH
1990

State in 1990 rank order	1986	1987	1988	1989	1990 Number	1990 Percentage of total
Total	449,520	431,309	401,817	431,403	436,428	100.0
New York	45,032	43,464	42,076	48,099	47,426	10.9
Georgia	31,125	31,612	30,589	33,923	37,216	8.5
New Jersey	25,302	24,938	26,018	30,679	29,739	6.8
Ohio	31,578	28,030	24,494	24,896	23,299	5.3
Michigan	28,570	25,086	21,635	21,996	21,875	5.0
Pennsylvania	22,825	20,596	18,587	19,722	20,532	4.7
Alabama	19,965	19,464	18,308	18,969	20,506	4.7
Virginia	15,437	15,847	15,162	17,168	17,524	4.0
Illinois	22,806	19,797	17,101	17,382	17,380	4.0
North Carolina	15,098	14,344	13,892	15,725	16,872	3.9
Massachusetts	11,643	12,025	13,254	15,749	16,729	3.8
Texas	19,993	22,579	20,227	18,219	16,590	3.8
California	13,021	13,199	13,386	15,449	15,909	3.6
Indiana	15,425	13,804	11,486	11,105	10,996	2.5
Tennessee	11,203	10,909	10,150	10,736	10,958	2.5
Connecticut	9,191	9,463	9,643	11,057	10,833	2.5
Maryland	9,917	9,549	8,867	10,100	10,240	2.3
South Carolina	8,403	8,029	7,557	8,545	9,278	2.1
Kentucky	7,615	7,086	6,269	6,496	6,239	1.4
Louisiana	8,186	9,395	7,920	6,719	6,131	1.4
New Hampshire	3,929	4,029	3,992	4,582	5,281	1.2
Missouri	6,032	5,626	5,340	5,458	5,198	1.2
Wisconsin	6,921	6,216	5,096	5,137	4,937	1.1
Colorado	4,671	4,440	4,530	4,589	4,329	1.0
Mississippi	4,976	4,982	4,618	4,396	4,087	0.9
Maine	2,848	3,151	2,752	3,163	3,454	0.8
West Virginia	4,837	4,180	3,740	3,602	3,433	0.8
Minnesota	4,269	3,765	3,277	3,341	3,233	0.7
Arizona	2,735	2,893	2,679	3,329	3,184	0.7
Rhode Island	2,066	2,199	2,480	2,782	2,997	0.7
Oklahoma	3,523	3,955	3,579	3,351	2,897	0.7
Iowa	3,563	3,201	2,507	2,428	2,329	0.5
Arkansas	2,343	2,484	2,229	2,344	2,224	0.5
Kansas	2,401	2,192	2,050	2,155	2,024	0.5
Washington	1,951	1,782	1,636	1,632	1,805	0.4
Other states	14,531	13,672	12,191	13,131	13,219	3.0
Other areas 1/	4,872	2,846	2,158	2,829	5,240	1.2
Special affidavit	717	480	342	420	285	0.1

1/ Includes Canada, Puerto Rico, other Caribbean islands, and other foreign
countries.

Source: State of Florida, Department of Highway Safety and Motor Vehicles, Division of Motor Vehicles, unpublished data.

Florida Statistical Abstract 1991

Table 13.41. MOTOR VEHICLE REGISTRATIONS: NUMBER OF OUT-OF-STATE VEHICLES
REGISTERED IN FLORIDA BY COUNTY OF REGISTRATION, 1986 THROUGH 1990

| | | | | | 1990 | |
County	1986	1987	1988	1989	Number	Per-centage of total
Florida 1/	449,520	431,309	401,817	431,403	436,428	100.0
Alachua	6,110	5,017	4,559	4,844	4,665	1.1
Baker	295	302	287	304	320	0.1
Bay	6,810	6,844	6,341	6,360	6,664	1.5
Bradford	581	521	504	495	483	0.1
Brevard	15,674	16,726	15,454	16,971	16,256	3.7
Broward	32,707	31,985	30,101	31,051	31,262	7.2
Calhoun	227	221	225	191	192	Δ/
Charlotte	5,718	5,820	5,884	6,335	6,452	1.5
Citrus	4,298	4,134	3,810	4,272	4,232	1.0
Clay	4,598	3,847	3,643	3,850	3,685	0.8
Collier	8,328	8,873	8,140	9,099	8,973	2.1
Columbia	873	882	979	1,310	1,220	0.3
Dade	28,335	28,270	26,873	28,137	30,604	7.0
De Soto	661	697	687	756	769	0.2
Dixie	243	259	227	248	285	0.1
Duval	23,352	23,397	20,617	21,497	22,583	5.2
Escambia	14,318	14,231	12,910	13,774	14,463	3.3
Flagler	1,794	1,935	1,941	2,365	2,100	0.5
Franklin	324	254	237	251	283	0.1
Gadsden	690	638	509	643	732	0.2
Gilchrist	264	236	258	231	240	0.1
Glades	133	165	136	128	129	Δ/
Gulf	457	365	372	375	363	0.1
Hamilton	263	253	194	253	320	0.1
Hardee	659	531	557	632	626	0.1
Hendry	778	775	763	857	847	0.2
Hernando	4,268	4,637	4,436	4,733	4,546	1.0
Highlands	2,801	2,686	2,525	2,736	2,614	0.6
Hillsborough	26,812	27,372	24,950	24,825	25,292	5.8
Holmes	725	657	657	663	759	0.2
Indian River	4,495	3,606	3,453	4,051	3,698	0.8
Jackson	1,699	1,768	1,718	1,770	1,990	0.5
Jefferson	333	314	297	315	327	0.1
Lafayette	58	68	51	55	86	Δ/

See footnotes at end of table.   Continued . . .

Florida Statistical Abstract 1991

Table 13.41. MOTOR VEHICLE REGISTRATIONS: NUMBER OF OUT-OF-STATE VEHICLES
REGISTERED IN FLORIDA BY COUNTY OF REGISTRATION, 1986 THROUGH 1990
(Continued)

					1990	
County	1986	1987	1988	1989	Number	Per-centage of total
Lake	5,575	5,978	5,758	6,240	6,116	1.4
Lee	16,156	15,468	15,540	16,302	16,069	3.7
Leon	5,503	5,933	5,680	6,428	6,687	1.5
Levy	442	500	446	464	592	0.1
Liberty	101	81	89	86	124	A/
Madison	411	387	328	363	414	0.1
Manatee	8,447	7,751	7,247	7,870	8,199	1.9
Marion	7,040	7,664	6,866	7,866	7,960	1.8
Martin	4,659	4,878	4,645	4,784	5,131	1.2
Monroe	4,118	4,280	3,766	3,797	3,720	0.9
Nassau	1,467	1,583	1,553	1,630	1,721	0.4
Okaloosa	11,636	9,522	8,737	8,532	8,770	2.0
Okeechobee	1,239	1,160	1,084	1,151	1,081	0.2
Orange	28,525	23,984	22,586	26,408	26,316	6.0
Osceola	5,678	5,541	5,105	5,873	6,185	1.4
Palm Beach	33,657	29,443	27,216	29,707	28,283	6.5
Pasco	12,086	11,232	9,626	11,445	11,409	2.6
Pinellas	33,626	30,052	26,937	28,243	28,690	6.6
Polk	13,406	12,068	11,803	12,138	12,111	2.8
Putnam	1,709	1,778	1,547	1,593	1,629	0.4
St. Johns	2,818	3,109	2,975	3,347	3,883	0.9
St. Lucie	5,579	5,330	5,196	6,073	5,987	1.4
Santa Rosa	3,241	3,053	3,044	3,112	3,362	0.8
Sarasota	12,725	12,638	11,455	12,062	12,604	2.9
Seminole	12,228	11,758	10,994	12,323	12,175	2.8
Sumter	1,018	963	898	911	1,031	0.2
Suwannee	581	712	627	626	677	0.2
Taylor	427	367	439	427	468	0.1
Union	153	162	136	185	166	A/
Volusia	13,619	13,774	13,416	15,216	15,032	3.4
Wakulla	332	303	327	391	351	0.1
Walton	1,070	1,036	960	930	912	0.2
Washington	567	535	496	503	513	0.1

A/ Less than 0.05 percent.
1/ Includes missing or invalid zip codes.

Source: State of Florida, Department of Highway Safety and Motor Vehicles, Division of Motor Vehicles, unpublished data.

Florida Statistical Abstract 1991

Table 13.45. TRAFFIC STATISTICS: DRIVERS, VEHICLES, MILEAGE, ACCIDENTS, INJURIES
AND DEATHS IN FLORIDA, 1978 THROUGH 1989

Year	Licensed drivers	Registered vehicles	Mileage (millions)	Accidents	Nonfatal injuries	Deaths	Mileage death rate 1/
1978	6,915,219	8,079,308	71,437	326,119	181,019	2,305	3.2
1979	7,341,081	7,724,148	74,651	343,542	190,697	2,635	3.5
1980	7,809,423	7,797,375	75,281	357,720	201,385	2,879	3.8
1981	8,222,403	7,887,881	76,146	368,766	205,437	3,119	4.1
1982	8,598,019	8,622,549	79,497	361,312	195,834	2,710	3.4
1983	8,987,493	9,064,490	81,775	384,614	194,791	2,729	3.3
1984	9,442,763	9,444,964	85,241	237,511	202,889	2,856	3.4
1985	9,630,975	10,827,693	88,057	250,412	216,596	2,870	3.3
1986	9,924,110	11,651,253	87,325	242,381	219,352	2,874	3.3
1987	10,241,063	11,738,273	92,865	240,429	215,886	2,891	3.1
1988	10,648,019	11,997,948	105,030	256,543	230,738	3,152	3.0
1989	11,109,288	12,276,272	(NA)	252,439	230,060	3,033	(NA)

(NA) Not available.
1/ The number of deaths per 100 million vehicle miles traveled.
Note: See Note on Table 13.46.

Table 13.46. REPORTED MOTOR VEHICLE ACCIDENTS: NUMBER OF ACCIDENTS BY CONTRIBUTING
CAUSE IN FLORIDA, 1989

Cause of accident	Total		Urban		Rural	
	Number	Percentage of total	Number	Percentage of total	Number	Percentage of total
Total	391,694	100.0	228,820	100.0	162,874	100.0
Speed too fast	5,899	1.5	2,907	1.3	2,992	1.8
Failed to yield right of way	46,339	11.8	28,377	12.4	17,962	11.0
Disregarded stop sign	3,598	0.9	2,621	1.1	977	0.6
Disregarded other traffic condition	8,682	2.2	6,612	2.9	2,070	1.3
Drove left of center	1,466	0.4	550	0.2	916	0.6
Improper overtaking	6,064	1.5	3,272	1.4	2,792	1.7
Followed too closely	5,249	1.3	3,920	1.7	1,329	0.8
Alcohol, under influence	4,330	1.1	2,372	1.0	1,958	1.2
Careless driving	71,362	18.2	35,077	15.3	36,285	22.3
Mechanical defect	2,425	0.6	1,291	0.6	1,134	0.7
Other	236,280	60.3	141,821	62.0	94,459	58.0

Note: Detail may not add to totals because some accidents may have more than one
contributing cause.   Includes reports and information received by May 21, 1990.
Legally reportable accidents are those involving death, bodily injury, or one or
more of the following circumstances: (1) driver leaves the accident scene where
death, injury, or property damage has occurred; (2) driver is under the influence of
alcohol or drugs; and, (3) a wrecker is required to remove an inoperative vehicle.
Number of noninjury accidents are under-reported effective October 1, 1989 due to
changes in the requirements for written reports.
   Source for Tables 13.45 and 13.46:   State of Florida, Department of Highway
Safety and Motor Vehicles, Division of Florida Highway Patrol, *Florida Traffic Crash
Facts, 1989*.

Table 13.47.   REPORTED MOTOR VEHICLE ACCIDENTS: NUMBER OF ACCIDENTS AND PERSONS
INVOLVED BY TYPE OF ACCIDENT IN FLORIDA, 1989

			Number of accidents			
Type of accident	Total	Fatal	Nonfatal injury	Property damage	Total on roadway	Total off roadway
Total	252,439	2,730	141,720	107,989	204,146	48,293
Motor vehicle in transport	159,587	1,134	98,948	59,505	154,090	5,497
Fixed object	30,834	418	13,567	16,849	14,605	16,229
Other object	729	6	216	507	661	68
Parked motor vehicle	23,183	32	2,499	20,652	9,081	14,102
Pedestrian	8,043	615	7,324	104	6,390	1,653
Bicyclist	6,100	94	5,625	381	5,400	700
Moped	131	4	114	13	127	4
Overturning	6,327	161	4,452	1,714	3,589	2,738
Noncollison	10,708	187	5,758	4,763	4,913	5,795
Motor vehicle on other roadway	236	2	153	81	235	1
Animal	618	1	313	304	578	40
Railway train	133	19	62	52	109	24
Other and not stated	5,810	57	2,689	3,064	4,368	1,442

			Number of persons			
	Total killed	Total injured	Incapac-itating injury	Non-incapac-itating evident injury	Possible injury	No in-jury 1/
Total	3,033	230,060	33,183	77,397	119,480	406,553
Motor vehicle in transport	1,336	175,584	21,533	53,176	100,875	328,755
Fixed object	459	18,251	3,671	8,195	6,385	22,608
Other object	6	269	36	100	133	1,146
Parked motor vehicle	41	3,318	554	1,291	1,473	14,176
Pedestrian	623	7,989	2,364	3,360	2,265	10,113
Bicyclist	94	5,936	1,064	3,088	1,784	7,767
Moped	4	132	29	77	26	195
Overturning	173	6,533	1,516	2,930	2,087	3,733
Noncollison	206	7,724	1,651	3,441	2,632	8,933
Motor vehicle on other roadway	2	324	44	102	178	462
Animal	1	400	66	162	172	613
Railway train	24	91	25	28	38	339
Other and not stated	64	3,509	630	1,447	1,432	7,713

1/ Drivers only.
Note: See Note on Table 13.46.

Source: State of Florida, Department of Highway Safety and Motor Vehicles, Division of Florida Highway Patrol, *Florida Traffic Crash Facts, 1989.*

Table 13.48. REPORTED MOTOR VEHICLE ACCIDENTS: DRIVERS AND MOTOR VEHICLES INVOLVED
IN ACCIDENTS BY AGE, SEX, AND RESIDENCE OF DRIVER AND BY TYPE OF MOTOR VEHICLE
IN FLORIDA, 1989

Item	All accidents	Fatal accidents	Injury accidents
Drivers involved in accidents, total	382,379	1,631	144,513
Age			
15 and under	4,205	36	3,325
16	9,407	21	3,454
17	11,912	35	4,420
18-19	27,226	86	10,410
20-24	58,341	237	22,368
25-34	103,331	403	38,991
35-44	65,142	247	24,031
45-54	37,081	156	13,653
55-64	27,732	126	9,930
65-74	21,397	140	7,686
75 and over	12,087	132	4,603
Not stated	4,518	12	1,642
Sex			
Male	242,265	1,216	82,500
Female	139,303	412	61,942
Not stated	811	3	71
Residence			
Local resident	315,166	1,212	121,249
Resident elsewhere in state	44,446	301	16,339
Nonresident of state	18,530	88	5,787
Foreign	2,966	17	731
Not stated	1,271	13	407
Vehicles involved in accidents, total	487,064	4,487	278,046
Passenger vehicle	357,194	2,905	212,119
Recreational	1,310	8	752
Light truck (pickup)	55,259	645	31,835
Truck (heavy)	10,461	159	5,891
Truck-tractor (all combination)	6,035	240	3,288
Motorcycle	7,054	213	6,206
Off road vehicle	418	6	342
Moped	411	4	372
Bicycle	7,069	99	6,515
Law enforcement vehicle	2,529	20	1,397
Emergency vehicle	388	7	232
Taxi cab	932	6	591
School bus	833	6	479
Bus	1,159	13	708
Special mobile equipment	189	6	118
Farm equipment	139	1	86
Government/military equipment	708	6	370
Other	34,976	143	6,745

Note: See Note on Table 13.46.

Source: State of Florida, Department of Highway Safety and Motor Vehicles, Division of Florida Highway Patrol, *Florida Traffic Crash Facts, 1989*.

Florida Statistical Abstract 1991

Table 13.49. REPORTED MOTOR VEHICLE ACCIDENTS: PERSONS KILLED OR INJURED AND TOTAL
ACCIDENTS IN THE STATE AND COUNTIES OF FLORIDA, 1989

County		Reported accidents					
					Fatal accidents		
						Per-	Persons	Persons
	Total	Rural	Urban	Number	centage	killed	injured
Florida 1/	252,439	108,062	144,377	2,730	1.1	3,033	230,060
Alachua	3,161	1,484	1,677	23	0.7	27	2,837
Baker	140	136	4	4	2.9	5	147
Bay	2,212	1,076	1,136	26	1.2	27	1,912
Bradford	414	215	199	6	1.4	6	345
Brevard	6,155	1,619	4,536	107	1.7	114	6,108
Broward	26,512	4,355	22,157	202	0.8	217	24,188
Calhoun	156	135	21	8	5.1	8	176
Charlotte	1,627	722	905	25	1.5	28	1,589
Citrus	1,041	851	190	20	1.9	22	1,139
Clay	1,167	996	171	22	1.9	25	1,019
Collier	2,951	1,355	1,596	49	1.7	74	2,275
Columbia	725	570	155	21	2.9	23	758
Dade	44,938	22,825	22,113	335	0.7	369	40,232
De Soto	422	292	130	10	2.4	13	460
Dixie	171	171	0	5	2.9	5	204
Duval	14,862	39	14,823	127	0.9	135	11,460
Escambia	5,066	2,660	2,406	62	1.2	66	4,965
Flagler	410	410	0	10	2.4	13	413
Franklin	101	92	9	2	2.0	2	122
Gadsden	835	557	278	18	2.2	23	792
Gilchrist	110	110	0	3	2.7	3	126
Glades	116	116	0	7	6.0	9	110
Gulf	140	118	22	3	2.1	3	156
Hamilton	205	205	0	6	2.9	6	247
Hardee	381	316	65	6	1.6	7	380
Hendry	431	323	108	15	3.5	18	448
Hernando	1,128	986	142	26	2.3	29	1,425
Highlands	881	569	312	19	2.2	22	1,000
Hillsborough	20,592	9,229	11,363	197	1.0	213	17,086
Holmes	198	175	23	8	4.0	8	225
Indian River	1,341	953	388	24	1.8	27	1,368
Jackson	688	507	181	15	2.2	18	683
Jefferson	183	168	15	5	2.7	5	232
Lafayette	42	42	0	0	0.0	0	62
Lake	2,250	1,147	1,103	30	1.3	32	2,059

See footnotes at end of table. Continued . . .

Florida Statistical Abstract 1991

Table 13.49.   REPORTED MOTOR VEHICLE ACCIDENTS: PERSONS KILLED OR INJURED AND TOTAL
ACCIDENTS IN THE STATE AND COUNTIES OF FLORIDA, 1989 (Continued)

| | Reported accidents | | | Fatal accidents | | | |
County	Total	Rural	Urban	Number	Per-centage	Persons killed	Persons injured
Lee	6,508	2,025	4,483	86	1.3	101	5,842
Leon	5,468	1,026	4,442	30	0.5	30	3,669
Levy	315	315	0	10	3.2	10	426
Liberty	62	62	0	2	3.2	2	74
Madison	272	218	54	5	1.8	7	275
Manatee	3,755	2,452	1,303	44	1.2	48	3,498
Marion	3,166	1,944	1,222	54	1.7	64	3,758
Martin	1,917	961	956	29	1.5	30	1,707
Monroe	1,841	860	981	28	1.5	36	1,686
Nassau	779	606	173	13	1.7	17	648
Okaloosa	1,912	1,046	866	16	0.8	18	1,728
Okeechobee	546	418	128	14	2.6	15	630
Orange	16,736	9,428	7,308	140	0.8	156	15,824
Osceola	2,142	1,454	688	58	2.7	69	2,663
Palm Beach	16,723	7,224	9,499	172	1.0	193	14,204
Pasco	3,536	2,724	812	53	1.5	54	4,128
Pinellas	13,398	3,720	9,678	94	0.7	96	12,118
Polk	7,707	3,907	3,800	124	1.6	140	7,633
Putnam	1,004	707	297	18	1.8	18	966
St. Johns	1,476	1,135	341	35	2.4	39	1,542
St. Lucie	2,621	1,314	1,307	45	1.7	56	2,586
Santa Rosa	1,064	816	248	17	1.6	17	1,158
Sarasota	4,521	2,421	2,100	38	0.8	40	4,191
Seminole	3,918	1,642	2,276	38	1.0	40	3,531
Sumter	487	455	32	11	2.3	14	528
Suwannee	406	318	88	4	1.0	5	381
Taylor	394	208	186	7	1.8	7	342
Union	107	107	0	2	1.9	2	92
Volusia	6,961	2,206	4,755	73	1.0	80	6,433
Wakulla	237	237	0	2	0.8	2	224
Walton	484	392	92	12	2.5	13	552
Washington	212	178	34	10	4.7	12	272

1/ Includes data not distributed by county.
Note: See Note on Table 13.46.

Source: State of Florida, Department of Highway Safety and Motor Vehicles, Division of Florida Highway Patrol, *Florida Traffic Crash Facts, 1989.*

Table 13.50.   ALCOHOL-RELATED TRAFFIC ACCIDENTS AND FATALITIES: NUMBER, PERCENTAGE
OF TOTAL, AND ACCIDENTS PER 100,000 POPULATION IN THE STATE AND COUNTIES OF
FLORIDA, 1989

County	Total	Accidents As a percentage of all accidents	Accidents Per 100,000 population	Total	Fatalities As a percentage of all fatalities
Florida 1/	36,312	14.38	287.0	1,492	49.19
Alachua	480	15.19	268.1	12	44.44
Baker	29	20.71	159.8	2	40.00
Bay	482	21.79	383.1	18	66.67
Bradford	79	19.08	343.2	3	50.00
Brevard	1,283	20.84	330.3	67	58.77
Broward	3,210	12.11	260.4	114	52.53
Calhoun	45	28.85	416.6	5	62.50
Charlotte	277	17.03	268.4	11	39.29
Citrus	235	22.57	259.8	16	72.73
Clay	230	19.71	223.3	18	72.00
Collier	532	18.03	370.1	46	62.16
Columbia	139	19.17	331.4	14	60.87
Dade	3,553	7.91	186.1	134	36.31
De Soto	86	20.38	365.5	5	38.46
Dixie	48	28.07	470.0	4	80.00
Duval	1,887	12.70	284.4	71	52.59
Escambia	998	19.70	381.5	30	45.45
Flagler	88	21.46	338.7	9	69.23
Franklin	41	40.59	465.7	2	100.00
Gadsden	207	24.79	503.9	13	56.52
Gilchrist	32	29.09	351.3	1	33.33
Glades	23	19.83	314.4	0	0.00
Gulf	38	27.14	337.0	3	100.00
Hamilton	43	20.98	404.4	3	50.00
Hardee	67	17.59	340.9	2	28.57
Hendry	98	22.74	387.8	8	44.44
Hernando	217	19.24	227.2	12	41.38
Highlands	142	16.12	213.9	9	40.91
Hillsborough	2,674	12.99	325.1	118	55.40
Holmes	53	26.77	341.1	3	37.50
Indian River	262	19.54	301.8	12	44.44
Jackson	110	15.99	266.9	5	27.78
Jefferson	36	19.67	319.2	1	20.00
Lafayette	10	23.81	186.3	0	0.00
Lake	399	17.73	272.4	10	31.25

See footnotes at end of table.   Continued . . .

Florida Statistical Abstract 1991

Table 13.50.   ALCOHOL-RELATED TRAFFIC ACCIDENTS AND FATALITIES: NUMBER, PERCENTAGE
OF TOTAL, AND ACCIDENTS PER 100,000 POPULATION IN THE STATE AND COUNTIES OF
FLORIDA, 1989 (Continued)

| | | Accidents | | | Fatalities |
| | | As a per-
centage
of all | Per
100,000 | | As a per-
centage
of all |
County	Total	accidents	population	Total	fatalities
Lee	1,092	16.78	335.6	53	52.48
Leon	781	14.28	416.6	18	60.00
Levy	109	34.60	431.4	4	40.00
Liberty	17	27.42	359.6	1	50.00
Madison	57	20.96	361.5	5	71.43
Manatee	681	18.14	331.0	21	43.75
Marion	481	15.19	255.8	35	54.69
Martin	405	21.13	420.9	15	50.00
Monroe	483	26.24	629.1	29	80.56
Nassau	160	20.54	367.8	8	47.06
Okaloosa	429	22.44	302.9	10	55.56
Okeechobee	114	20.88	394.0	7	46.67
Orange	2,379	14.21	364.7	79	50.64
Osceola	346	16.15	342.7	31	44.93
Palm Beach	2,334	13.96	277.4	91	47.15
Pasco	620	17.53	226.0	29	53.70
Pinellas	2,054	15.33	243.2	44	45.83
Polk	1,159	15.04	290.5	67	47.86
Putnam	231	23.01	361.4	9	50.00
St. Johns	365	24.73	445.1	28	71.79
St. Lucie	448	17.09	310.9	28	50.00
Santa Rosa	236	22.18	298.4	6	35.24
Sarasota	710	15.70	261.6	16	40.00
Seminole	705	17.99	254.2	22	55.00
Sumter	85	17.45	274.7	1	7.14
Suwannee	64	15.76	242.9	0	0.00
Taylor	107	27.16	623.7	4	57.14
Union	28	26.17	270.6	1	50.00
Volusia	1,268	18.22	352.1	37	46.25
Wakulla	64	27.00	464.1	1	50.00
Walton	119	24.59	438.8	6	46.15
Washington	45	21.23	268.3	5	41.67

1/ Includes data not distributed by county.
Note: See Note on Table 13.46.

Source: State of Florida, Department of Highway Safety and Motor Vehicles,
Division of Florida Highway Patrol, *Florida Traffic Crash Facts, 1989.*

Florida Statistical Abstract 1991

Table 13.60. RAILROADS: MILES OF TRACK AND PERCENTAGE OF STATE SYSTEM
BY RAILROAD COMPANY IN FLORIDA, 1991

Company	Tracks (in miles)	Percent- age of state system	Company	Tracks (in miles)	Percent- age of state system
Total	3,153	100.0	Atlanta and St.		
Burlington Northern	44	1.4	Andrews Bay Line	72	2.3
Florida East Coast	445	14.1	Florida Central	70	2.2
CSXT/AMTRAK	1,742	55.3	Florida Midland	40	1.3
Georgia Southern			Florida Northern	26	0.8
and Florida	157	5.0	Florida West Coast	45	1.4
Southeast Florida			Liveoak Perry and		
Rail Corridor/			South Georgia	52	1.6
AMTRAK Tri-County			Seminole Gulf	118	3.7
Commuter Rail	81	2.7	South Central Florida	102	3.2
Apalachicola Northern	96	3.0	Terminal Companies	63	2.0

Source: State of Florida, Department of Transportation, Office of Planning, unpublished data.

Table 13.70. PORT ACTIVITY: TONNAGE HANDLED IN SPECIFIED PORTS IN FLORIDA, FISCAL
YEAR 1989-90 OR CALENDAR YEAR 1990

Port and type of cargo	Short tons	Port and type of cargo	Short tons
Canaveral (fiscal year		Palm Beach (fiscal year	
1989-90), total	2,879,510	1989-90), total	3,452,100
Exports	817,363	Exports	1,883,929
Imports	2,062,147	Imports	1,568,171
Everglades (calendar year		Panama City (calendar year	
1990), total	17,294,086	1990), total	666,856
Jacksonville 1/ (fiscal year		Exports	453,631
1989-90), total JPA		Imports	106,932
terminals	4,618,386	Domestic	106,293
General cargo exports	158,710	Pensacola (fiscal year	
General cargo imports	567,263	1989-90), total	918,281
Containerized cargo	2,438,861	Exports	730,279
Bulk cargo & petro	926,261	Imports	188,002
Manatee (fiscal year		St. Lucie (calendar year	
1989-90), total	5,279,337	1990), total	154,840
Exports	1,473,942	Exports	20,891
Imports	3,791,384	Imports	133,949
Domestic	14,011	Tampa (fiscal year 1989	
Miami (fiscal year 1989-90),		-90), total	52,000,468
total	3,590,937	Exports	23,529,788
Exports	1,579,809	Imports	28,470,680
Imports	2,011,128		

1/ Tonnage passing through facilities owned by the Jacksonville Port Authority
only; therefore they differ from movements into and out of the Port of Jacksonville.
Source: Data are reported in annual or cumulative monthly reports of each port
authority.

Florida Statistical Abstract 1991

Table 13.90. AIRCRAFT: OPERATIONS AT AIRPORTS WITH FEDERAL AVIATION ADMINISTRATION
(FAA)-OPERATED TRAFFIC CONTROL TOWERS IN FLORIDA, FISCAL YEAR 1989-90

Location and type of operation	Total operations 1/	Air carrier 2/	Air taxi 3/	General aviation 4/	Military
Florida, state total	5,499,444	961,847	495,982	3,873,943	167,672
Itinerant	3,735,459	961,847	495,982	2,186,419	91,211
Local	1,763,985	0	0	1,687,524	76,461
Daytona Beach, total	323,595	15,118	4,676	302,649	1,152
Itinerant	229,236	15,118	4,676	208,609	833
Local	94,359	0	0	94,040	319
Ft. Lauderdale, total	224,120	98,777	54,105	69,704	1,534
Itinerant	218,875	98,777	54,105	64,475	1,518
Local	5,245	0	0	5,229	16
Ft. Lauderdale Executive, total	226,237	1	5,627	220,271	338
Itinerant	185,430	1	5,627	179,464	338
Local	40,807	0	0	40,807	0
Ft. Myers Page Field, total	113,152	0	10,760	101,663	729
Itinerant	70,627	0	10,760	59,387	480
Local	42,525	0	0	42,276	249
Ft. Myers Regional, total	68,731	44,131	11,054	6,411	7,135
Itinerant	63,818	44,131	11,054	5,508	3,125
Local	4,913	0	0	903	4,010
Ft. Pierce, total	195,621	0	2,094	193,421	106
Itinerant	59,893	0	2,094	57,699	100
Local	135,728	0	0	135,722	6
Gainesville, total	105,148	6,956	12,981	81,432	3,779
Itinerant	69,974	6,956	12,981	48,197	1,840
Local	35,174	0	0	33,235	1,939
Hollywood, total	219,344	0	0	218,522	822
Itinerant	74,029	0	0	73,351	678
Local	145,315	0	0	145,171	144
Jacksonville Craig Field, total	198,359	0	7,656	180,937	9,766
Itinerant	107,085	0	7,656	92,479	6,950
Local	91,274	0	0	88,458	2,816
Jacksonville International, total	148,285	54,299	23,571	49,770	20,645
Itinerant	112,809	54,299	23,571	27,524	7,415
Local	35,476	0	0	22,246	13,230
Key West, total	88,147	4,239	23,117	59,450	1,341
Itinerant	64,513	4,239	23,117	36,235	922
Local	23,634	0	0	23,215	419
Melbourne, total	276,910	11,700	7,123	257,698	389
Itinerant	168,433	11,700	7,123	149,373	237
Local	108,477	0	0	108,325	152
Miami International, total	463,066	278,754	99,544	77,542	7,226
Itinerant	463,066	278,754	99,544	77,542	7,226
Local	0	0	0	0	0
Opa-Locka, total	187,655	0	5,904	164,751	17,000
Itinerant	104,841	0	5,904	88,301	10,636
Local	82,814	0	0	76,450	6,364
Orlando Executive, total	181,234	0	12,640	165,681	2,913
Itinerant	140,068	0	12,640	125,391	2,037
Local	41,166	0	0	40,290	876

See footnotes at end of table.   Continued . . .

Florida Statistical Abstract 1991

Table 13.90. AIRCRAFT: OPERATIONS AT AIRPORTS WITH FEDERAL AVIATION ADMINISTRATION
(FAA)-OPERATED TRAFFIC CONTROL TOWERS IN FLORIDA, FISCAL YEAR 1989-90
(Continued)

Location and type of operation	Total operations 1/	Air carrier 2/	Air taxi 3/	General aviation 4/	Military
Orlando International, total	277,799	181,345	61,402	31,427	3,625
Itinerant	277,426	181,345	61,402	31,073	3,606
Local	373	0	0	354	19
Panama City-Bay County, total	161,499	4	14,429	141,505	5,561
Itinerant	73,434	4	14,429	55,696	3,305
Local	88,065	0	0	85,809	2,256
Pensacola, total	146,362	18,610	10,604	72,930	44,218
Itinerant	86,712	18,610	10,604	36,818	20,680
Local	59,650	0	0	36,112	23,538
Pompano Beach Airpark, total	208,108	0	3,463	204,534	111
Itinerant	62,519	0	3,463	58,961	95
Local	145,589	0	0	145,573	16
Sarasota-Bradenton, total	168,191	31,275	13,825	119,715	3,376
Itinerant	133,014	31,275	13,825	84,939	2,975
Local	35,177	0	0	34,776	401
St. Petersburg-Clearwater, total	161,077	2,689	818	133,792	23,778
Itinerant	65,172	2,689	818	54,483	7,182
Local	95,905	0	0	79,309	16,596
St. Petersburg Whitt, total	117,167	0	5,645	110,858	664
Itinerant	53,987	0	5,645	48,156	186
Local	63,180	0	0	62,702	478
Tallahassee, total	159,645	18,429	21,569	112,296	7,351
Itinerant	108,907	18,429	21,569	63,996	4,913
Local	50,738	0	0	48,300	2,438
Tamiami, total	362,050	0	1	361,751	298
Itinerant	135,435	0	1	135,186	248
Local	226,615	0	0	226,565	50
Tampa International, total	227,330	132,465	45,804	47,233	1,828
Itinerant	227,196	132,465	45,804	47,101	1,826
Local	134	0	0	132	2
Vero Beach, total	251,739	29	3,364	248,194	152
Itinerant	161,234	29	3,364	157,708	133
Local	90,505	0	0	90,486	19
West Palm Beach, total	238,873	63,026	34,206	139,806	1,835
Itinerant	217,726	63,026	34,206	118,767	1,727
Local	21,147	0	0	21,039	108

1/ An aircraft arrival at or departure from an airport with FAA traffic control.
2/ Air carrier authorized by the Civil Aeronautics Board to provide scheduled service over specified routes with limited nonscheduled operations.
3/ Performs at least five round trips per week between two or more points and publishes flight schedules or transports mail.
4/ All operations not classified as an air carrier, air taxi, or military.
Note: Itinerant includes all aircraft arrivals and departures other than local. Local includes aircraft operations which operate in the local traffic pattern or within sight of the tower.

Source: U.S., Department of Transportation, Federal Aviation Administration, *FAA Air Traffic Activity, Fiscal Year 1990.*

Florida Statistical Abstract 1991

Table 13.92. AIRPORT ACTIVITY: ENPLANED REVENUE PASSENGERS AND ENPLANED REVENUE
TONS OF CARGO AND MAIL BY AIRPORT IN FLORIDA, 1988 AND 1989

| | Enplaned passengers 1/ | | Enplaned revenue tons 2/ | | | | |
| | | | Total | | 1989 | | |
Airport	1988	1989	1988	1989	Freight	Ex-press	Mail
Florida	33,175,571	21,116,792	320,221	222,584	129,114	2	93,468
Daytona Beach							
Regional	433,958	412,317	567	432	396	Δ/	35
Destin (Ft. Walton							
Beach)	0	0	181	368	368	0	0
Ft. Myers (Page Field)	(X)	0	(X)	220	220	0	0
Ft. Myers (Southwest)	1,460,146	242,542	3,188	528	108	0	420
Ft. Pierce	0	0	0	9	9	0	0
Gainesville Municipal	155,675	120,162	112	60	56	0	4
Jacksonville							
International	1,287,939	1,249,258	11,306	11,175	5,971	0	5,204
Key West International	97,953	89,954	100	84	78	0	6
Melbourne (Cape							
Kennedy Regional)	291,352	288,087	179	166	161	0	5
Ft. Lauderdale-							
Hollywood							
International	3,899,039	3,645,786	36,417	86,211	78,305	Δ/	7,906
Miami International	9,461,760	8,591,936	175,833	232,253	208,916	8	23,329
Naples Municipal	20,357	3,723	Δ/	2	2	0	0
Ocala (Taylor)	(X)	0	(X)	Δ/	Δ/	0	0
Orlando International	7,473,086	7,373,449	47,662	41,086	29,517	6	11,563
Palm Beach							
International	2,360,993	2,403,585	4,310	6,464	2,618	1	3,845
Panama City/Bay County	34,721	686	262	8	4	0	4
Pensacola Regional	362,765	361,181	2,517	1,569	441	0	1,128
Perry-Foley	(X)	0	(X)	1	1	0	0
Sarasota/Bradenton	842,674	794,430	549	570	559	Δ/	11
St. Petersburg/							
Clearwater							
International	43,294	20,351	11	6	4	0	2
Tallahassee Municipal	384,805	371,569	2,429	2,155	1,377	0	778
Tampa International	4,495,349	4,409,261	34,546	36,483	20,562	1	15,920
Valparaiso (Eglin Air							
Force Base)	69,625	67,706	50	39	31	0	8

(X) Not applicable.
Δ/ Less than 0.5 tons.
1/ Includes all revenue passengers boarding aircraft.
2/ Includes originating and transfer tons.
Note: Data are for scheduled and nonscheduled operations.

Source: U.S., Department of Transportation, Federal Aviation Administration,
Airport Activity Statistics of Certified Route Air Carriers, Calendar Year 1989, and
previous edition.

Florida Statistical Abstract 1991

COMMUNICATIONS

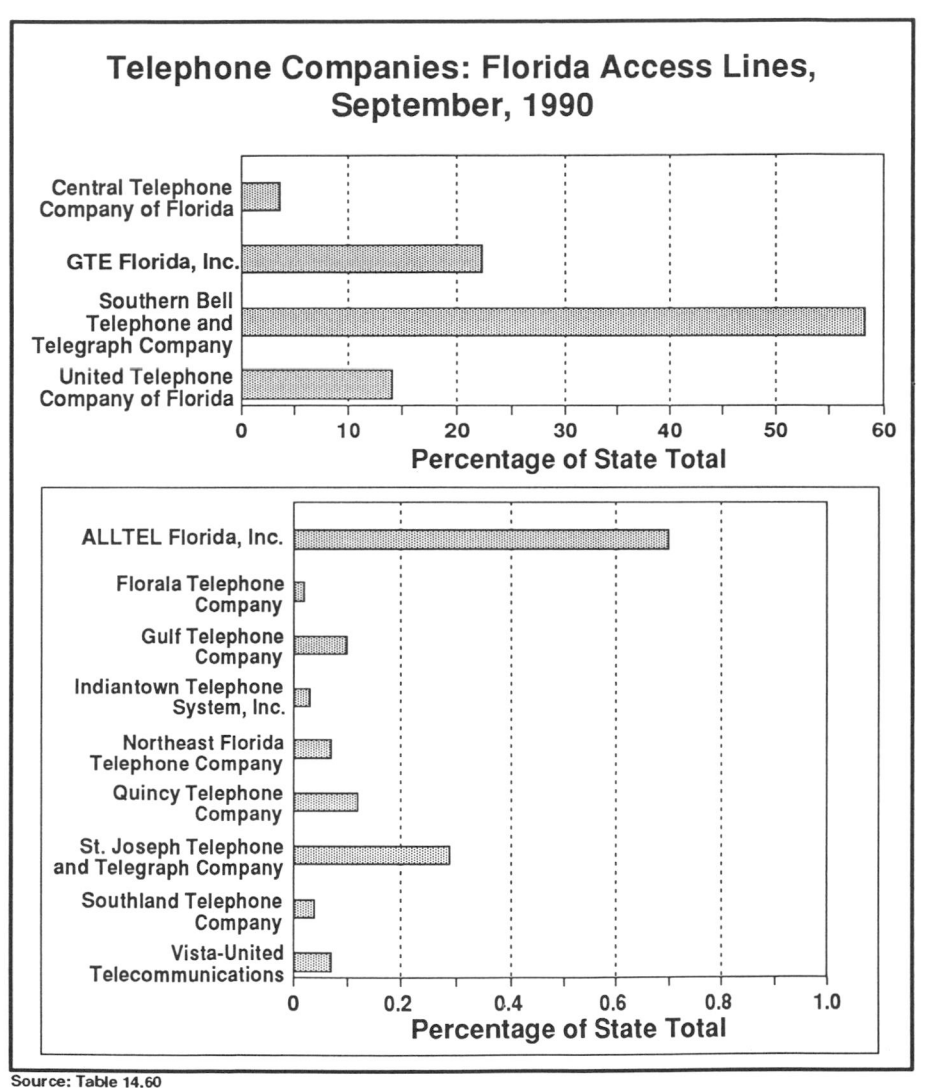

Telephone Companies: Florida Access Lines, September, 1990

Source: Table 14.60

SECTION 14.00
COMMUNICATIONS

TABLES LISTED BY MAJOR HEADINGS

Table 14.05. DAILY AND WEEKLY NEWSPAPERS: LOCATION, NAME, AND CIRCULATION
     IN FLORIDA, 1990

Area	Name	County	Circulation	
	Daily newspapers 1/			
Boca Raton	News	Palm Beach	22,319	VAC
Bradenton	Herald	Manatee	42,154	ABC
Brooksville	Daily Sun Journal	Hernando	1,500	PO
Cape Coral	Daily Breeze	Lee	5,087	PO
Charlotte Harbor	Charlotte Sun Herald	Charlotte	19,412	PO
Daytona Beach	News-Journal	Volusia	93,888	ABC
Deland	Sun News	Volusia	7,596	CAC
Ft. Lauderdale	News	Broward	11,599	ABC
Ft. Lauderdale	Sun-Sentinel	Broward	235,556	ABC
Ft. Myers	News-Press	Lee	88,129	ABC
Ft. Pierce-Port St. Lucie	Tribune	St. Lucie	25,031	ABC
Ft. Walton Beach	Northwest Florida Daily News	Okaloosa	34,298	ABC
Gainesville	Sun	Alachua	55,604	ABC
Inverness	Citrus County Chronicle	Citrus	17,174	ABC
Jacksonville	Florida Times-Union	Duval	179,047	ABC
Key West	Citizen	Monroe	7,923	ABC
Lake City	Reporter	Columbia	9,162	ABC
Lake Wales	Highlander	Polk	3,866	PO
Lakeland	Ledger	Polk	79,684	ABC
Leesburg	Daily Commercial	Lake	27,674	ABC
Marianna	Jackson County Floridan	Jackson	5,540	PO
Melbourne	Florida Today	Brevard	80,999	ABC
Miami	Diario Las Americas	Dade	66,770	PO
Miami	Herald	Dade	428,931	ABC
Naples	Daily News	Collier	36,733	ABC
New Smyrna Beach	Observer	Volusia	5,387	PO
Ocala	Star-Banner	Marion	45,543	ABC
Orange Park	Clay Today	Clay	4,539	PO
Orlando	Sentinel	Orange	279,393	ABC
Palatka	Daily News	Putnam	13,820	ABC
Palm Beach	Daily News	Palm Beach	7,102	PO
Panama City	News-Herald	Bay	36,716	ABC
Pensacola	News Journal	Escambia	59,200	ABC
St. Augustine	Record	St. Johns	14,536	ABC
St. Petersburg	Times	Pinellas	353,130	ABC
Sanford	Herald	Seminole	8,364	PO
Sarasota	Herald-Tribune	Sarasota	122,403	ABC
Stuart	News	Martin	29,348	ABC
Tallahassee	Democrat	Leon	60,834	ABC
Tampa	Tribune	Hillsborough	289,999	ABC
Vero Beach	Press-Journal	Indian River	29,115	ABC
West Palm Beach	Palm Beach Post	Palm Beach	178,683	ABC
Winter Haven	News Chief	Polk	11,218	ABC

See footnotes at end of table.   Continued . . .

Florida Statistical Abstract 1991

Table 14.05. DAILY AND WEEKLY NEWSPAPERS: LOCATION, NAME, AND CIRCULATION
    IN FLORIDA, 1990 (Continued)

Area	Name	County	Circulation	
	Weekly newspapers			
Apopka/Altamonte Springs	Planter	Orange	21,500	2/
Apopka/Orange	Apopka Chief	Orange	2,231	3/
Arcadia	Arcadian	De Soto	8,141	3/
Arcadia/De Soto	De Soto County Times	De Soto	9,547	4/
Auburndale/Lake Alfred	Auburndale Star	Polk	3,250	PO
Avon Park	News-Sun	Highlands	4,524	5/
Bartow	Polk County Democrat	Polk	4,725	3/
Belleview	Voice of South Marion	Marion	1,700	4/
Beverly Hills	Visitor	Citrus	5,500	Free
Boca Raton	Central Boca Times	Palm Beach	7,805	6/
Boca Raton	Monday Paper	Palm Beach	36,395	6/
Boca Raton	Thursday Times	Palm Beach	18,307	6/
Boca Raton	West Boca Times	Palm Beach	19,344	6/
Boca Raton/Pompano Beach	Hi-Riser	Broward	11,049	6/
Bonita Springs	Bonita Banner	Lee	26,600	4/
Boynton Beach	Times	Palm Beach	21,035	6/
Brandon	News	Hillsborough	2,165	3/
Branford	News	Suwannee	1,720	4/
Broward/Palm Beach	Gulfstream Newspapers	Broward	246,654	Free
Bunnell/Palm Coast	Flagler/Palm Coast News-Tribune	Flagler	7,744	3/
Callahan/Hilliard/Yullee	Nassau County Record	Nassau	4,334	3/
Carrabelle	Times	Franklin	926	3/
Cedar Key/Levy	Cedar Key Beacon	Levy	1,500	SNI
Chattahoochee	Twin City News	Gadsden	1,664	3/
Chiefland/Levy	Chiefland Citizen	Levy	16,500	4/
Chipley/Bonita	Washington County News	Washington	2,500	4/
Citrus/Hernando/Pasco	Suncoast News	Pasco	439,700	4/
Clermont/Groveland	South Lake Press	Lake	3,633	3/
Clewiston	News	Hendry	3,207	4/
Cocoa	Tribune	Brevard	49,258	Free
Coral Springs/Broward	Coral Springs Forum	Broward	25,000	2/
Crawfordville/Wakulla	Wakulla News	Wakulla	3,085	3/
Crescent City	Putnam County Courier-Journal	Putnam	1,871	4/
Crestview	North Okaloosa Bulletin	Okaloosa	13,168	7/
Crestview	Okaloosa News-Journal and Bayou Times	Okaloosa	2,958	3/
Cross City	Dixie County Advocate	Dixie	1,894	4/
Dade City	Pasco News	Pasco	5,000	SNI
Deerfield Beach	Thursday Times	Broward	17,500	2/
Deerfield Beach/Lighthouse Point	Observer	Broward	30,000	Free
Delray Beach	Times	Palm Beach	14,193	6/
Destin/Okaloosa	Destin Log	Okaloosa	8,350	4/
East Pasco	Pasco News	Pasco	5,600	SNI
Englewood	Herald-Gulfside	Orange	5,348	3/
Eustis	News	Lake	6,000	SNI
Fernandina Beach	News-Leader	Nassau	8,837	5/

    See footnotes at end of table.   Continued . . .

Table 14.05. DAILY AND WEEKLY NEWSPAPERS: LOCATION, NAME, AND CIRCULATION
    IN FLORIDA, 1990 (Continued)

Area	Name	County	Circulation	

Weekly newspapers (Continued)

Area	Name	County	Circulation	
Florida Keys	Keynoter	Monroe	11,355	8/
Ft. Lauderdale	East Broward Tribune	Broward	32,582	8/
Ft. Lauderdale	Hi-Riser	Broward	16,000	6/
Ft. Lauderdale/Oakland	Eastsider	Broward	17,080	6/
Ft. Meade	Polk County Democrat and Ft. Meade Leader	Polk	1,218	3/
Ft. Myers Beach	Bulletin	Lee	17,500	4/
Franklin County	Apalchicola Times	Franklin	2,757	3/
Frostproof	News	Polk	1,688	3/
Gainesville	Record	Alachua	5,000	SNI
Graceville	News	Jackson	1,378	3/
Greater Orlando	Weekly	Orange	175,000	2/
Greater Seminole	Seminole Beacon	Pinellas	37,200	Free
Green Cove Springs	Clay County Crescent	Clay	3,115	3/
Greenacres/Palm Springs	Thursday Paper	Palm Beach	18,000	2/
Gulf Breeze/Pensacola	Sentinel	Santa Rosa	3,736	3/
Haines City	Herald	Polk	3,090	3/
Hallandale	Digest	Broward	41,000	6/
Hardee County	Herald-Advocate	Hardee	5,440	3/
Havana/Eastern Gadsden	Havana Herald	Gadsden	2,225	3/
High Springs/Alachua	High Springs Herald	Alachua	2,414	3/
Immokalee/LaBelle	Immokalee Bulletin	Collier	3,029	4/
Jacksonville	Advocate	Duval	18,448	9/
Jacksonville Beach	Beaches Leader	Duval	11,171	3/
Jensen Beach	Mirror	Martin	45,000	10/
Jupiter/Tequesta	Courier-Journal	Palm Beach	5,822	3/
Jupiter/Tequesta	Thursday Paper	Broward	12,000	2/
Key Biscayne	Islander News	Dade	3,146	4/
Keystone Heights	Lake Region Monitor	Clay	2,100	SNI
LaBelle	Caloosa Belle	Hendry	6,500	Free
LaBelle	Leader/Immokalee Bulletin	Hendry	8,225	4/
Lake Panasoffkee/Sumter	Sumter Journal	Sumter	2,000	SNI
Lake Placid	Journal	Highlands	4,890	PO
Lake Wales	News	Polk	3,388	3/
Lake Worth	Herald and Coastal Observer	Palm Beach	27,370	8/
Lehigh Acres	Lehigh News	Lee	15,128	3/
Lighthouse Point/Hillsboro Beach	Thursday Times	Broward	14,500	6/
Live Oak	Suwannee Democrat	Suwannee	4,462	3/
Longboat Key	Longboat Observer	Manatee	18,200	4/
Macclenny	Baker County Press	Baker	5,585	3/
Madison County	Carrier	Madison	3,900	SNI
Madison County	Enterprise-Recorder	Madison	2,007	3/
Marco Island/Naples	Marco Island Eagle	Collier	11,693	5/
Margate	Quad City News	Broward	40,000	11/
Margate/Coconut Creek	Forum	Broward	20,000	6/
Marianna/Jackson County	Monitor	Jackson	5,445	3/

See footnotes at end of table.   Continued . . .

Florida Statistical Abstract 1991

Table 14.05. DAILY AND WEEKLY NEWSPAPERS: LOCATION, NAME, AND CIRCULATION
   IN FLORIDA, 1990 (Continued)

Area	Name	County	Circulation	
			Weekly newspapers (Continued)	
Mayo	Free Press	Lafayette	1,550	3/
Miami	Community Newspapers	Dade	137,000	Free
Miami	Today	Dade	33,625	3/
Milton/Santa Rosa	Santa Rosa Free Press	Santa Rosa	12,000	3/
Milton/Santa Rosa	Santa Rosa Press Gazette	Santa Rosa	6,760	3/
Monticello	News	Jefferson	2,368	3/
Moore Haven	Glades County Democrat	Glades	1,327	4/
Mount Dora	Topic	Lake	3,307	4/
Mulberry/Bradley/Lakeland	Mulberry Press/The Press	Polk	7,500	4/
New Port Richey	West Pasco Press	Pasco	1,335	4/
Niceville	Bayou Times	Okaloosa	3,297	4/
Northeast Florida	Advocate	Duval	28,464	11/
Oakland Park/Wilton Manors	Tribune	Broward	10,000	2/
Okeechobee County	Okeechobee News	Okeechobee	5,161	5/
Orange City	Four Towns Enterprise	Volusia	38,000	SNI
Osceola County/St. Cloud	Osceola News-Gazette	Osceola	28,001	3/
Palm Beach County	Jewish Journal	Palm Beach	22,570	6/
Palm Beach/North Palm Beach/				
Juno Beach	Thursday Paper	Broward	18,000	2/
Panama City	Bay-Beach News	Bay	(NA)	SNI
Pensacola	Escambia Sun Press	Escambia	3,500	SNI
Perry	News-Herald	Taylor	3,027	3/
Perry	Taco Times	Taylor	4,680	3/
Pinellas/Pasco	Pinellas County Review	Pinellas and Pasco	3,148	3/
Plant City	Courier	Hillsborough	4,456	PO
Pompano Beach	Pompano Ledger	Broward	48,072	4/
Pompano Beach	Tribune	Broward	13,000	2/
Pompano Beach/Sea Ranch				
Lakes	Observer	Broward	26,000	Free
Port St. Joe	Star	Gulf	2,531	4/
Port St. Lucie	Mirror	Martin	22,000	10/
Port Salerno/Hobo Sound/				
Palm City/Stuart	Mirror	Martin	33,000	10/
Quincy	Gadsden County Times	Gadsden	5,238	3/
Sanibel/Captiva	Island Reporter	Lee	9,124	3/
Sanibel/Captiva	Islander	Lee	7,058	3/
Santa Rosa County	Press-Gazette	Santa Rosa	6,760	4/
Sebring	News-Sun	Highlands	11,500	SNI
Starke	Bradford County Telegraph	Bradford	5,400	SNI
Sumter County	Times	Sumter	3,244	PO
Sun City Center/Hillsborough	Sun	Hillsborough	10,000	Free
Tallahassee	Leon County News	Leon	91	3/
Tampa	Free Press	Hillsborough	1,150	SNI
Tampa/Hillsborough	Reporter	Hillsborough	10,000	Free
Tampa/St. Petersburg	Creative Loafing News-papers	Hillsborough	40,000	6/
Tarpon Springs	Herald	Pinellas	15,200	Free

See footnotes at end of table.   Continued . . .

Table 14.05. DAILY AND WEEKLY NEWSPAPERS: LOCATION, NAME, AND CIRCULATION
   IN FLORIDA, 1990 (Continued)

Area	Name	County	Circulation	
		Weekly newspapers (Continued)		
Tarpon Springs	Holiday Herald	Pinellas	10,500	Free
Titusville	Star-Advocate	Brevard	9,179	Free
Trenton	Gilchrist County Journal	Gilchrist	3,430	SNI
Upper Florida Keys	Reporter	Monroe	7,900	PO
Venice/North Port/Englewood	Venice Gondolier	Sarasota	28,694	5/
Wakulla County	Wakulla News	Wakulla	4,110	3/
Wauchula/Hardee	Herald-Advocate	Hardee	5,357	3/
West Orange County	West Orange Times	Orange	7,205	3/
Wewahitchka	Gulf County Breeze	Gulf	1,400	3/
Williston	Sun-Suwannee Valley News	Levy	1,500	SNI
Winter Park	Sun Herald	Orange	3,543	4/
Zephryhills	News	Pasco	10,035	3/
		College and university newspapers		
Barry College	Barry Buccaneer	Dade	3,000	SNI
Bethune-Cookman College	Voice of the Wildcats	Volusia	2,000	SNI
Brevard Community College	Capsule	Brevard	6,500	SNI
Broward Community College	Observer	Broward	8,000	SNI
Daytona Beach Community College	Bagpiper	Volusia	5,000	SNI
Eckerd College	Triton Tribune	Pinellas	2,200	SNI
Embry Riddle Aero University	Avion	Volusia	8,000	SNI
Florida A & M University	Famuan	Leon	4,000	SNI
Florida Atlantic University	Independent Atlantic Sun	Palm Beach	55,000	SNI
Florida Institute of Technology	Crimson	Brevard	4,500	SNI
Florida International University	Beacon	Dade	8,000	SNI
Florida Southern College	Southern	Polk	2,500	SNI
Florida State University	Flambeau	Leon	22,000	SNI
Hillsborough Community College	Hawkeye	Hillsborough	5,000	SNI
Jacksonville University	Navigator	Duval	3,000	SNI
John B. Stetson University	Stetson Reporter	Volusia	2,000	SNI
Manatee Community College	Lance	Manatee	6,000	SNI
Miami-Dade Community College	Falcon Times	Dade	3,000	SNI
Palm Beach Community College	Beachcomber	Palm Beach	5,000	SNI
Pensacola Junior College	Corsair	Escambia	5,000	SNI
Rollins College	Sandspur	Orange	2,500	SNI
St. Petersburg Junior College	Wooden Horse	Pinellas	6,000	SNI
University of Central Florida	Future	Orange	9,000	SNI
University of Florida	Independent Florida Alligator	Alachua	31,000	SNI
University of Miami	Hurricane	Dade	10,000	SNI
University of Miami Law	Res Ipsa Loquitur	Dade	2,000	SNI

      See footnotes at end of table.   Continued . . .

Florida Statistical Abstract 1991

Table 14.05. DAILY AND WEEKLY NEWSPAPERS: LOCATION, NAME, AND CIRCULATION
  IN FLORIDA, 1990 (Continued)

Area	Name	County	Circulation	

College and university newspapers (Continued)

Area	Name	County	Circulation	
University of North Florida	Spinnaker	Duval	3,000	SNI
University of South Florida	Oracle	Hillsborough	15,000	SNI
University of Tampa	Minaret	Hillsborough	2,000	SNI
University of West Florida	Voyager	Escambia	3,000	SNI
Valencia Community College	Paper	Orange	6,000	SNI

Black newspapers

Coconut Creek	Broward Times	Broward	25,000	SNI
Daytona Beach	Daytona Times	Volusia	13,893	CPVS
Ft. Lauderdale	Westside Gazette	Broward	23,033	CPVS
Ft. Myers	Community Voice	Lee	5,000	TMC
Ft. Pierce	Chronicle	St. Lucie	5,000	SWP/F
Jacksonville	Advocate-Free Press	Duval	16,500	SWP/F
Jacksonville	Chronicle	Duval	5,000	SWP
Jacksonville	North Florida Star News	Duval	24,488	CPVS
Miami	Times	Dade	22,539	ABC
Orlando	Times	Orange	5,710	CPVS
Pensacola	New American Press	Escambia	30,963	CPVS
Pensacola	Voice	Escambia	28,498	CPVS
St. Petersburg	Weekly Challenger	Pinellas	30,000	SWP/F
Sarasota	Weekly Bulletin	Sarasota	18,594	CPVS
Tallahassee	Capitol Outlook	Leon	5,000	CPVS
Tampa	Sentinel-Bulletin	Hillsborough	20,348	CPVS
West Palm Beach	Photo News and Image	Palm Beach	2,090	SWP

Spanish-language newspaper

Hialeah	La Voz De La Calle	Dade	20,000	Free
Hialeah	Sol De Hialeah	Dade	24,000	Free
Miami	Diario Las Americas	Dade	65,856	SNI
Miami	El Nuevo Herald	Dade	102,856	SNI
Miami	El Nuevo Patria	Dade	29,000	4/
Miami Shores	La Voz Catolica	Dade	34,000	SNI
Tampa	El Sol De Florida	Hillsborough	5,000	SNI
Tampa	La Gaceta	Hillsborough	18,200	SNI

VAC Verified Audit Circulation. ABC Circulation from the Audit Bureau of
Circulation; data are usually annual averages. PO Post Office sworn circulation;
data are usually as of a certain date. CAC Certified Audit of Circulations. SNI
Source not indicated. CPVS Community Papers Verification Service. TMC Controlled
circulation. SWP/F Publisher's statement; paid and free distribution. SWP Publisher's statement; paid distribution.
    (NA) Not available.
    1/ Week-day circulation data. Papers with weekend editions may report a higher
circulation for those editions. 2/ Free distribution; PO. 3/ Paid and free distribution; PO. 4/ Paid and free distribution; SNI. 5/ Paid and free distribution;
ABC. 6/ Free distribution; VAC. 7/ Paid and free distribution; CPVS. 8/ Paid
and free distribution; VAC. 9/ Paid distribution; CPVS. 10/ Free distribution;
CAC. 11/ Free distribution; CPVS.
    Source: Editor and Publisher Company, Inc., *Editor and Publisher International
Yearbook, 1991*. (Copyright.)

Florida Statistical Abstract 1991

Table 14.33. POSTAL RECEIPTS: ZIP CODES AND NET REVENUE IN THE STATE AND FIRST
CLASS POST OFFICES OF FLORIDA, FISCAL YEAR 1989-90

First class post office	Zip code	Net revenue (dollars)	Per- cent- age change from prior year	First class post office	Zip code	Net revenue (dollars)	Per- cent- age change from prior year
Florida	(X)	1,694,277,591	4.2	Crestview	32536	1,258,968	9.7
				Cross City	32628	243,012	0.8
Alachua	32615	403,462	-0.6	Crystal River	32629	1,400,692	7.6
Altamonte Springs	32701	7,060,691	6.3	Dade City	33525	1,961,933	4.1
Alva	33920	323,905	-12.4	Dania	33004	1,756,924	-8.0
Anna Maria	33501	240,995	22.8	Davenport	33837	341,872	6.2
Apalachicola	32320	248,486	2.9	Daytona Beach	32114	18,243,210	9.9
Apopka	32703	9,617,513	51.5	Debary	32713	585,947	8.7
Arcadia	33821	993,319	2.0	Deerfield Beach	33441	9,704,516	57.3
Auburndale	33823	1,144,812	0.3	DeFuniak Springs	32433	732,404	3.5
Avon Park	33825	1,033,660	6.9	Deland	32720	3,691,400	0.9
Bartow	33830	2,319,556	3.2	Deleon Springs	32130	468,731	12.6
Bay Pines	33504	251,034	-5.7	Delray Beach	33444	7,004,116	6.7
Belle Glade	33430	813,939	0.0	Destin	32541	1,401,346	2.0
Belleview	32620	796,312	17.3	Dundee	33838	264,718	-9.7
Blountstown	32424	365,085	9.3	Dunedin	34698	3,501,235	-5.7
Boca Raton	33431	23,291,100	9.1	Dunnellon	32630	823,814	8.6
Bonifay	32425	471,103	7.8	Eagle Lake	33839	277,155	-1.0
Bonita Springs	33923	1,545,528	7.5	Eaton Park	33840	848,451	6.0
Boynton Beach	33435	5,318,894	1.2	Edgewater	32032	718,079	8.7
Bradenton	34205	11,115,123	0.5	Eglin Air Force			
Bradenton Beach	34217	541,074	5.6	Base	32542	891,253	19.5
Brandon	33511	4,088,432	5.3	Elfers	34259	1,180,298	-1.7
Brooksville	34601	6,013,777	13.2	Ellenton	34222	578,902	6.2
Bunnell	32110	364,241	9.8	Englewood	34223	2,020,227	6.7
Bushnell	33513	472,247	0.0	Estero	33928	1,049,908	12.8
Callahan	32011	387,724	4.0	Eustis	32726	1,245,462	0.1
Cantonment	32533	478,042	-0.9	Fernandina Beach	32034	1,495,668	4.3
Cape Canaveral	32920	1,128,454	11.0	Flagler Beach	32136	12,737,629	15.0
Captiva	33924	246,691	4.1	Floral City	32636	243,197	4.8
Casselberry	32707	4,765,898	25.9	Ft. Lauderdale	33310	126,336,860	1.3
Chattahoochee	32324	277,915	6.1	Ft. Meade	33841	246,158	1.3
Chiefland	32626	601,567	16.4	Ft. Myers	33906	29,116,785	-1.1
Chipley	32428	572,684	2.2	Ft. Myers Beach	33931	1,289,895	11.0
Clearwater	34625	32,199,058	13.7	Ft. Pierce	34950	9,509,440	9.2
Clermont	32711	883,790	5.3	Ft. Walton Beach	32548	3,648,418	6.0
Clewiston	33440	701,627	5.7	Frostproof	33843	348,872	0.1
Cocoa	32922	3,679,448	0.0	Fruitland Park	34731	372,587	3.9
Cocoa Beach	32931	1,349,116	4.5	Gainesville	32601	17,930,622	4.7
Crawfordville	32327	303,759	9.0	Gibsonton	33534	233,199	-4.1
Crescent City	32112	357,456	3.5	Goldenrod	32733	941,122	19.3

See footnotes at end of table.   Continued . . .

Florida Statistical Abstract 1991

Table 14.33. POSTAL RECEIPTS: ZIP CODES AND NET REVENUE IN THE STATE AND FIRST
    CLASS POST OFFICES OF FLORIDA, FISCAL YEAR 1989-90 (Continued)

First class post office	Zip code	Net revenue (dollars)	Percentage change from prior year	First class post office	Zip code	Net revenue (dollars)	Percentage change from prior year
Gonzalez	32560	234,011	0.4	Lake Worth	33461	8,348,518	-0.4
Graceville	32440	356,558	-0.7	Land O' Lakes	34639	618,642	5.7
Green Cove				Largo	34640	12,595,624	9.5
Springs	32043	696,507	4.7	Lecanto	32661	811,433	11.0
Gulf Breeze	32561	1,282,861	26.5	Leesburg	34748	3,162,188	3.9
Haines City	33844	1,145,459	8.5	Lehigh Acres	33936	2,530,525	22.0
Hallandale	33009	3,526,593	14.5	Live Oak	32060	1,163,267	10.0
Havana	32333	291,348	7.0	Longboat Key	34228	838,211	6.0
Hawthorne	32640	230,944	10.3	Longwood	32750	5,064,217	-2.5
Hernando	32642	302,460	4.6	Loxahatchee	33470	870,069	-1.6
Hialeah	33010	38,591,697	10.4	Lutz	33549	801,649	1.5
Highland City	33846	290,433	14.9	Lynn Haven	32444	789,114	8.9
High Springs	32643	297,111	9.7	Macclenny	32063	446,283	5.5
Hobe Sound	33455	969,138	11.6	Madison	32340	591,092	5.6
Hollywood	33022	31,185,588	-2.2	Maitland	32751	10,577,586	35.0
Homestead	33030	4,148,635	4.3	Malabar	32950	414,428	18.3
Homosassa				Mango	34262	7,514,839	23.9
Springs	32647	765,878	13.3	Marathon	33050	1,211,921	1.2
Immokalee	33934	632,007	-1.6	Marco	33937	1,709,589	4.1
Indian Rocks				Marianna	32446	1,319,914	0.0
Beach	34635	999,886	-18.3	Mary Esther	32569	1,088,593	-1.7
Indiantown	34956	658,933	10.7	Melbourne	32901	14,134,659	8.1
Inverness	32650	2,194,367	7.1	Merritt Island	32952	2,598,135	7.9
Islamorada	33036	404,902	0.6	Miami	33152	209,513,008	-8.1
Jacksonville	32203	163,497,883	5.8	Middleburg	32068	595,768	8.3
Jasper	32052	300,905	13.0	Milton	32570	1,841,206	3.4
Jensen Beach	34957	1,747,167	11.4	Mims	32754	313,335	-2.6
Jupiter	33458	4,460,086	16.7	Monticello	32344	427,712	3.8
Key Largo	33037	1,009,600	1.6	Mount Dora	32757	1,433,668	5.5
Keystone Heights	32656	744,862	2.2	Mulberry	33860	1,364,633	5.1
Key West	33040	3,292,583	-4.6	Naples	33940	13,462,051	8.2
Kissimmee	32741	6,498,185	8.6	New Port Richey	34652	3,464,596	3.3
La Belle	33935	630,274	2.6	New Smyrna Beach	32169	2,135,810	7.8
Lady Lake	32159	722,410	17.5	Niceville	32578	1,039,799	6.9
Lake Alfred	33850	346,903	10.5	Nokomis	34275	975,966	6.2
Lake Butler	32054	273,955	-4.1	Ocala	32678	13,152,737	5.2
Lake City	32055	2,018,766	4.1	Ocoee	34761	748,244	14.1
Lakeland	33802	14,435,943	0.9	Odessa	33556	351,415	3.8
Lake Mary	32746	3,751,570	107.6	Okeechobee	34972	1,353,131	5.3
Lake Placid	33852	826,527	4.2	Oklawaha	32179	381,947	-5.0
Lake Wales	33853	1,766,781	6.6	Oldsmar	34677	1,261,079	9.9

See footnotes at end of table.   Continued . . .

Florida Statistical Abstract 1991

Table 14.33. POSTAL RECEIPTS: ZIP CODES AND NET REVENUE IN THE STATE AND FIRST
CLASS POST OFFICES OF FLORIDA, FISCAL YEAR 1989-90 (Continued)

First class post office	Zip code	Net revenue (dollars)	Percentage change from prior year	First class post office	Zip code	Net revenue (dollars)	Percentage change from prior year
Oneco	34264	575,940	4.9	Santa Rosa	32459	257,590	19.9
Opa-locka	33054	2,810,465	-2.8	Sarasota	34230	22,208,750	1.7
Orange City	32763	2,544,914	9.1	Sebastian	32958	1,027,215	7.9
Orange Park	32073	3,665,381	2.8	Sebring	33870	2,611,006	4.5
Orlando	32862	124,675,540	2.0	Seffner	33584	646,674	-2.0
Ormond Beach	32174	3,519,789	4.1	Shalimar	32579	856,841	3.4
Osprey	34229	674,592	21.4	Sharpes	32959	387,256	4.7
Oviedo	32765	1,217,220	12.7	Silver Springs	32688	796,599	-1.4
Pahokee	33476	285,716	1.5	Starke	32091	758,613	15.4
Palatka	32177	2,052,323	-3.2	Stuart	34994	6,357,241	7.9
Palm Beach	33480	2,915,828	1.4	Summerland Key	33042	614,975	3.7
Palm City	34990	1,126,182	17.7	Sumterville	34267	269,260	1.1
Palmetto	34221	1,043,916	1.0	Tallahassee	32301	36,867,551	6.2
Palm Harbor	34683	3,964,779	21.4	Tallevast	34270	779,116	-6.9
Panama City	32401	8,490,935	3.5	Tampa	33630	181,393,757	10.2
Pensacola	32501	22,443,136	4.9	Tarpon Springs	34689	3,472,578	20.3
Perry	32347	841,786	6.5	Tavares	32778	1,499,382	12.3
Pinellas Park	34665	4,052,593	1.2	Tavernier	33070	549,349	-7.3
Plant City	33566	2,563,601	2.0	Thonotosassa	33592	284,260	4.7
Pompano Beach	33060	24,484,166	4.4	Titusville	32780	4,138,885	7.1
Ponte Vedra				Trenton	32693	259,558	1.3
Beach	32082	1,258,533	4.8	Umatilla	32784	490,885	-5.3
Port Richey	34668	4,281,472	0.1	Valpariso	32580	524,274	-0.8
Port St. Joe	32456	562,877	10.3	Valrico	33594	763,820	-6.2
Port Salerno	34992	633,383	26.7	Venice	34285	5,854,431	4.5
Punta Gorda	33950	7,037,247	5.9	Vero Beach	32960	7,926,256	4.2
Quincy	32351	2,522,171	7.5	Wabasso	32970	1,010,917	-1.9
Riverview	33569	619,560	10.7	Wauchula	33873	749,339	-3.5
Rockledge	32955	1,853,993	0.0	West Palm Beach	33406	38,348,958	6.1
Roseland	32957	290,291	12.0	Wildwood	34785	398,251	0.4
Ruskin	33570	1,886,253	4.6	Williston	32696	338,300	2.1
Safety Harbor	34672	954,706	4.6	Windermere	34786	532,417	7.9
St. Augustine	32084	4,334,829	4.3	Winter Garden	32787	892,751	-0.2
St. Cloud	32769	1,246,298	5.7	Winter Haven	33880	8,833,507	7.8
St. Petersburg	33730	65,211,872	2.4	Winter Park	32789	9,124,187	8.9
Sanford	32771	3,112,663	-2.5	Zephyrhills	33540	2,123,772	5.9
Sanibel	33957	1,134,872	-0.7				

(X) Not applicable.
Note: Data are for first class post offices. Florida totals include revenue
from all post offices.

Source: U.S., Postal Service Headquarters, unpublished data.

Florida Statistical Abstract 1991

Table 14.35. COMMUNICATIONS: AVERAGE MONTHLY REPORTING UNITS, EMPLOYMENT, AND
   PAYROLL COVERED BY UNEMPLOYMENT COMPENSATION LAW BY INDUSTRY IN FLORIDA
   1990

SIC code	Industry	Number of reporting units	Number of employees	Payroll ($1,000)
	Communications	4,587	174,627	419,603
27	Printing, publishing, and allied industries	3,519	65,792	129,610
271	Newspapers	301	26,827	52,625
272	Periodicals	345	5,976	12,826
273	Books	122	2,617	5,922
274	Miscellaneous publishing	269	4,672	10,233
275	Commercial printing	2,171	20,446	37,511
276	Manifold business forms	23	1,201	2,650
277	Greeting cards	6	78	107
278	Blankbooks, looseleaf binders, and book-binding and related work	62	1,787	3,003
279	Service industries for the printing trade	217	2,185	4,733
43	U.S. Postal Service	67	41,745	112,516
48	Communications	1,001	67,090	177,477
481	Telephone communications	360	47,383	133,005
482	Telegraph and other message communications	31	220	610
483	Radio and television broadcasting stations	396	11,518	28,270
4832	Radio broadcasting stations	308	5,806	11,823
4833	Television broadcasting stations	88	5,712	16,446
484	Cable and other pay television services	193	7,715	15,061
489	Communication services, NEC	20	253	531

NEC Not elsewhere classified.
   Note: Newspaper publishing and other print media (SIC code 27) are considered to
be manufacturing in the Standard Industrial Classification system.   Data are
included here because newspapers do compete with the electronic media in providing
communications.   Totals on county employment tables may not match totals in this
table due to rounding.

   Source: State of Florida, Department of Labor and Employment Security, Bureau of
Labor Market Information, "Employment, Wages, and Contributions Report" (ES-202),
unpublished data.

Florida Statistical Abstract 1991

Table 14.36. NEWSPAPER PRINTING AND PUBLISHING, TELEPHONE COMMUNICATIONS, AND
RADIO AND TELEVISION BROADCASTING STATIONS: AVERAGE MONTHLY REPORTING
UNITS, EMPLOYMENT, AND PAYROLL COVERED BY UNEMPLOYMENT COMPENSATION
LAW IN THE STATE AND COUNTIES OF FLORIDA, 1990

County	Number of re-porting units	Number of employees	Payroll ($1,000)	County	Number of re-porting units	Number of employees	Payroll ($1,000)

Newspaper printing and publishing (SIC code 271)

County	Number of re-porting units	Number of employees	Payroll ($1,000)	County	Number of re-porting units	Number of employees	Payroll ($1,000)
Florida	291	26,827	52,627	Monroe	6	98	150
Broward	20	2,156	5,020	Okaloosa	4	225	310
Charlotte	4	231	254	Palm Beach	19	2,043	5,182
Collier	7	490	813	Pasco	4	271	352
Lake	8	270	388	Polk	9	633	1,066
Lee	7	887	1,350	Sarasota	9	857	1,445
Leon	5	408	713	Volusia	8	931	1,592

Telephone communications (SIC code 481)

County	Number of re-porting units	Number of employees	Payroll ($1,000)	County	Number of re-porting units	Number of employees	Payroll ($1,000)
Florida	349	47,386	133,005	Escambia	7	705	2,046
				Orange	21	6,222	18,040
Broward	24	5,146	15,029	Palm Beach	27	2,852	7,811
Columbia	4	159	419	Seminole	9	963	2,739
Dade	40	7,703	22,415	Volusia	10	698	1,912
Duval	15	4,709	13,884	Statewide 1/	7	105	311

Radio and television broadcasting stations (SIC code 483)

County	Number of re-porting units	Number of employees	Payroll ($1,000)	County	Number of re-porting units	Number of employees	Payroll ($1,000)
Florida	383	11,525	28,270	Leon	15	400	676
				Marion	5	135	198
Alachua	8	234	369	Monroe	6	86	123
Bay	15	283	442	Okaloosa	9	102	123
Brevard	15	270	506	Orange	21	959	2,524
Broward	22	643	1,986	Palm Beach	26	1,057	2,524
Collier	10	106	182	Pasco	4	50	61
Dade	40	2,303	7,440	Pinellas	17	693	1,798
Duval	22	831	1,835	Polk	10	148	263
Escambia	11	299	580	St. Johns	3	46	56
Hillsborough	16	836	2,548	St. Lucie	8	184	352
Lake	4	53	80	Sarasota	8	202	425
Lee	15	577	1,218	Volusia	12	190	376

1/ Reporting units without fixed location within the state or of unknown county
location.
Note: Excluded are counties where data are withheld to avoid disclosure of
information about individual firms.

Source: State of Florida, Department of Labor and Employment Security, Bureau of
Labor Market Information, "Employment, Wages, and Contributions Report" (ES-202),
unpublished data.

Florida Statistical Abstract 1991

Table 14.60. TELEPHONE COMPANIES: SPECIFIED CHARACTERISTICS OF COMPANIES
     IN FLORIDA, SEPTEMBER 1990

Companies and headquarters	Number of exchanges	Florida access lines 1/		
		Total number	Percentage of state total	Annual growth rate (percentage)
Florida	282	7,533,652	100.00	4.00
ALLTEL Florida, Inc.				
Live Oak	27	52,690	0.70	4.70
Central Telephone Company of Florida				
Tallahassee	35	276,086	3.70	5.20
Florala Telephone Company				
Florala, Alabama	2	1,711	0.02	3.00
GTE Florida, Inc.				
Tampa	24	1,681,814	22.32	2.40
Gulf Telephone Company				
Perry	2	7,633	0.10	3.50
Indiantown Telephone System, Inc.				
Indiantown	1	2,441	0.03	4.70
Northeast Florida Telephone Company				
Macclenny	2	5,609	0.07	5.60
Quincy Telephone Company				
Quincy	3	9,121	0.12	4.70
St. Joseph Telephone and Telegraph Company				
Port St. Joe	13	21,958	0.29	4.30
Southern Bell Telephone and Telegraph Company				
Miami	102	4,394,649	58.33	3.40
Southland Telephone Company				
Atmore, Alabama	2	3,064	0.04	4.20
United Telephone Company of Florida				
Altamonte Springs	68	1,071,034	14.22	6.60
Vista-United Telecommunications				
Lake Buena Vista	1	5,842	0.07	8.00

1/ An access line is the line going to a home or building for the main telephone located there.

Note: Telephone companies listed above have headquarters in Florida, except as specified. Detail may not add to totals due to rounding.

Source: State of Florida, Public Service Commission, *1990 Annual Report*.

Florida Statistical Abstract 1991

POWER AND ENERGY

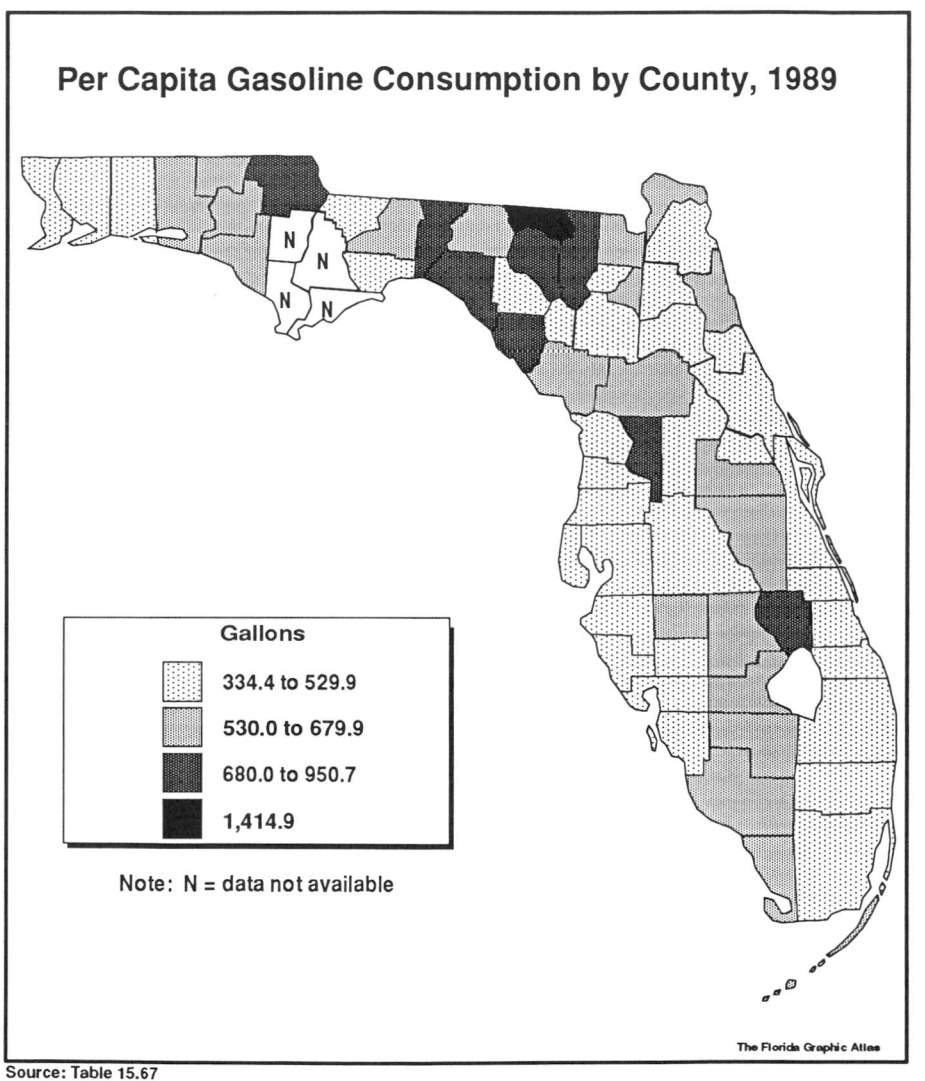

Per Capita Gasoline Consumption by County, 1989

Gallons

- 334.4 to 529.9
- 530.0 to 679.9
- 680.0 to 950.7
- 1,414.9

Note: N = data not available

The Florida Graphic Atlas

Source: Table 15.67

TABLES LISTED BY MAJOR HEADINGS

Table 15.06.   ENERGY CONSUMPTION: ENERGY CONSUMPTION BY TYPE OF FUEL IN FLORIDA
    1979 THROUGH 1989

(in trillions of British thermal units)

Year	Total	Petro-leum 1/	Natural gas	Coal	Nuclear	Renew-ables 2/	Electric inter-state 3/
1979	2,426.9	1,587.5	351.5	202.6	167.4	103.9	13.9
1980	2,485.0	1,601.5	328.2	226.1	182.6	108.6	38.0
1981	2,474.2	1,564.5	356.1	237.5	159.4	110.6	46.2
1982	2,360.1	1,358.7	339.1	240.0	213.9	112.9	95.5
1983	2,425.4	1,357.9	321.0	318.7	161.4	129.1	137.2
1984	2,523.8	1,259.9	318.2	378.5	261.1	140.7	165.5
1985	2,663.3	1,260.6	305.1	472.0	253.7	143.8	228.1
1986	2,713.7	1,435.1	298.9	459.1	238.0	147.0	135.6
1987	2,844.0	1,387.5	313.6	586.3	202.3	158.3	195.9
1988	2,993.7	1,499.6	298.2	611.2	281.4	156.1	147.1
1989	3,073.6	1,512.8	327.9	630.2	224.7	164.0	214.1

1/ Includes asphalt, aviation gasoline, jet fuel, distillates, kerosene, lubri-
cants, motor gasoline, residual fuel, and liquefied petroleum gas.
    2/ Includes hydroelectric, ethanol, woodwaste, and direct solar.
    3/ Combines electric sales and energy losses associated with interstate sales.
Losses estimated to be 7,088 of the 10,400 British thermal units per kilowatt-hour
purchased.
    Note: Data are revised; therefore, numbers will differ from those previously
reported in *Abstract*.

Table 15.07.   ENERGY CONSUMPTION: PER CAPITA ENERGY CONSUMPTION BY TYPE OF FUEL
    IN FLORIDA, 1979 THROUGH 1989

(in millions of British thermal units)

Year	Total	Petro-leum 1/	Natural gas	Coal	Nuclear	Other 2/
1979	254.8	166.7	36.9	21.3	17.6	12.4
1980	252.8	162.9	33.4	23.0	18.6	14.9
1981	242.8	153.5	34.9	23.3	15.6	15.4
1982	226.3	130.3	32.5	23.0	20.5	20.0
1983	227.5	127.4	30.1	29.9	15.1	25.0
1984	229.0	114.3	28.9	34.3	23.7	27.8
1985	234.1	110.8	26.8	41.5	22.3	32.7
1986	230.9	122.1	25.4	39.1	20.3	24.0
1987	234.3	114.3	25.8	48.3	16.7	29.2
1988	239.3	119.9	23.8	48.8	22.5	24.2
1989	238.4	117.4	25.4	48.9	17.4	29.3

1/ Includes asphalt, aviation gasoline, jet fuel, distillates, kerosene, lubri-
cants, motor gasoline, residual fuel, and liquefied petroleum gas.
    2/ Includes renewables and imports/exports of electricity.
    Note: Data are revised; therefore, numbers will differ from those previously
reported in *Abstract*.
    Source for Tables 15.06 and 15.07:   State of Florida, Governor's Energy Office,
Florida Energy Data Report, 1970-1989.

Florida Statistical Abstract 1991

Table 15.08. ENERGY CONSUMPTION: CONSUMPTION OF RENEWABLE ENERGY BY TYPE
      IN FLORIDA, 1984 THROUGH 1989

                    (in trillions of British thermal units)

Type of energy	1984	1985	1986	1987	1988	1989
Total	140.7	143.8	147.0	158.4	157.4	164.0
Direct solar	2.3	3.4	3.7	4.3	4.5	4.7
Indirect solar	136.7	139.6	143.3	153.9	152.9	160.3
Biomass energy, total	134.5	137.1	141.1	151.7	150.8	157.9
Wood	103.1	106.7	113.2	117.7	116.8	115.9
Pulp and paper industry	89.4	92.6	97.7	100.8	100.2	98.9
Residential	13.7	14.1	14.3	14.7	15.2	15.6
Electric utility	0.0	0.0	1.2	2.2	1.4	1.4
Crop residues	13.1	13.3	13.3	13.8	13.8	13.4
Alcohol fuels	4.3	4.9	2.8	1.1	0.6	0.6
Municipal solid waste	14.0	12.2	11.8	19.1	19.6	28.0
Hydroelectric energy	2.2	2.5	2.2	2.2	2.1	2.4

Note: Consumption of renewable energy in Florida from wind systems and animal
waste is negligible (greater than 0 but less than 0.05 trillion British thermal
units) and consumption of geothermal energy is significant, but impossible to
measure. Therefore, these data are not included in this table. Detail may not add to
totals because of rounding. Some data are revised.

Table 15.09. CRUDE OIL AND NATURAL GAS: AMOUNT PRODUCED BY FIELD IN FLORIDA, 1987
      THROUGH 1989

	Crude oil (barrels)			Natural gas (1,000 cubic feet)		
Field	1987	1988	1989	1987	1988	1989
Total	8,269,632	7,746,048	7,296,390	9,181,890	8,452,999	8,911,292
South Florida	2,794,530	2,356,416	1,805,389	210,190	196,192	147,162
Bear Island	351,562	337,823	245,024	29,561	27,815	19,609
Corkscrew	173,537	159,838	108,037	0	0	0
Lake Trafford	10,742	1,790	0	0	0	0
Lehigh Park	170,490	168,605	104,109	16,557	16,493	8,956
Mid-Felda	88,085	79,221	77,195	0	0	0
Raccoon Point	754,428	830,838	682,866	90,770	99,863	81,989
Sunniland	28,077	30,459	5,325	1,861	2,629	482
Sunoco Felda	136,823	82,636	36,591	9,439	4,513	1,308
Townsend Canal	47,817	30,283	46,590	0	0	0
West Felda	1,032,969	634,923	499,652	62,002	44,879	34,818
Northwest Florida	5,475,102	5,389,632	5,491,001	8,971,700	8,256,807	8,764,130
Blackjack Creek	695,496	462,464	519,142	1,106,421	740,047	1,106,557
Bluff Springs	43,434	26,737	15,889	24,404	13,993	5,369
Coldwater Creek	0	5,759	1,766	0	238	203
Jay	4,676,964	4,729,067	4,814,354	7,830,538	7,443,364	7,595,813
McDavid	0	38,417	82,789	0	12,478	35,886
McLellan	27,870	64,107	44,541	10,266	29,549	20,302
Mt. Carmel	31,338	63,081	12,520	71	17,138	0

Source for Tables 15.08 and 15.09: State of Florida, Governor's Energy Office,
Florida Energy Data Report, 1970-1989.

Florida Statistical Abstract 1991

Table 15.14. ELECTRIC UTILITY INDUSTRY: SALES, CUSTOMERS, AND COUNTIES SERVED
   BY PRIVATELY- AND PUBLICLY-OWNED UTILITIES AND BY RURAL ELECTRIC
   COOPERATIVES IN FLORIDA, 1990

Utility	Electricity sales to ultimate customers (MWH)	Number of ultimate customers December 1/	Counties served
Investor-owned systems			
Florida Power	24,878,328	1,135,482	Alachua, Bay, Brevard, Citrus, Columbia, Dixie, Flagler, Franklin, Gadsden, Gilchrist, Gulf, Hamilton, Hardee, Hernando, Highlands, Hillsborough, Jefferson, Lafayette, Lake, Leon, Levy, Liberty, Madison, Marion Orange, Osceola, Pasco, Pinellas, Polk, Seminole, Sumter, Suwannee, Taylor, Volusia, Wakulla
Florida Power and Light	65,222,868	3,158,806	Alachua, Baker, Bradford, Brevard, Broward, Charlotte, Clay, Collier, Columbia, Dade, De Soto, Duval, Flagler, Glades, Hardee, Hendry, Highlands, Indian River, Lee, Manatee, Martin, Monroe, Nassau, Okeechobee, Orange, Osceola, Palm Beach, Putnam, St. Johns, St. Lucie, Sarasota, Seminole, Suwannee, Union, Volusia
Florida Public Utilities	461,570	20,501	Calhoun, Jackson, Liberty, Nassau
Gulf Power	7,775,144	288,282	Bay, Escambia, Holmes, Jackson, Okaloosa, Santa Rosa, Walton, Washington
Tampa Electric	13,435,794	450,603	Hillsborough, Pasco, Pinellas, Polk
Generating municipal systems			
Ft. Pierce	478,675	23,665	St. Lucie
Gainesville	1,217,719	60,324	Alachua
Homestead	250,884	13,832	Dade
Jacksonville	8,104,953	293,949	Duval
Key West	478,492	22,224	Monroe
Kissimmee	658,333	33,966	Osceola
Lake Worth	332,946	24,256	Palm Beach
Lakeland	1,883,476	89,877	Polk
New Smyrna Beach	263,020	18,484	Volusia
Orlando	3,444,566	154,761	Orange
Reedy Creek Utilities	695,555	803	Orange
St. Cloud	229,410	11,736	Osceola
Sebring	160,562	12,224	Highlands
Starke	53,301	2,590	Bradford
Tallahassee	1,822,003	76,525	Leon
Vero Beach	498,528	25,260	Indian River
Wauchula	49,151	2,295	Hardee

See footnotes at end of table.   Continued . . .

Florida Statistical Abstract 1991

Table 15.14. ELECTRIC UTILITY INDUSTRY: SALES, CUSTOMERS, AND COUNTIES SERVED
BY PRIVATELY- AND PUBLICLY-OWNED UTILITIES AND BY RURAL ELECTRIC
COOPERATIVES IN FLORIDA, 1990 (Continued)

Utility	Electricity sales to ultimate customers (MWH)	Number of ultimate customers December 1/	Counties served
Generating rural electric cooperatives			
Florida Keys	456,072	26,844	Monroe
Seminole 2/	0	0	(X)
Nongenerating municipal systems			
Alachua	42,131	1,980	Alachua
Bartow	227,073	9,414	Polk
Blountstown	26,191	1,363	Calhoun
Bushnell	15,645	858	Sumter
Chattahoochee	42,926	1,328	Gadsden
Clewiston	0	0	Hendry
Ft. Meade	35,093	2,747	Polk
Green Cove Springs	75,415	2,364	Clay
Havana	16,841	1,300	Gadsden
Jacksonville Beach	444,612	22,374	Duval
Leesburg	348,572	16,577	Lake
Moore Haven	11,796	10,606	Glades
Mount Dora	61,675	4,631	Lake
Newberry	25,499	810	Alachua
Ocala	871,031	38,766	Marion
Quincy	0	0	Gadsden
Williston	22,021	1,268	Levy
Nongenerating rural electric cooperatives			
Central Florida	216,592	20,728	Alachua, Dixie, Gilchrist, Levy
Choctawhatchee	298,980	21,415	Holmes, Okaloosa, Santa Rosa, Walton
Clay	1,522,979	102,150	Alachua, Baker, Bradford, Clay, Columbia, Duval, Lake, Levy, Marion, Putnam, Union, Volusia
Escambia River	104,183	7,274	Escambia, Santa Rosa
Glades	160,159	11,333	Glades, Hendry, Highlands, Okeechobee
Gulf Coast	141,213	11,902	Bay, Calhoun, Gulf, Jackson, Walton, Washington
Lee County	1,775,400	116,819	Charlotte, Collier, Hendry, Lee
Okefenokee	129,187	8,173	Baker, Duval, Nassau, Okeechobee
Peace River	211,096	18,281	Brevard, De Soto, Hardee, Highlands, Hillsborough, Indian River, Manatee, Osceola, Polk, Sarasota, Sumter
Sumter	812,082	69,583	Citrus, Hernando, Lake, Levy, Marion, Pasco, Sumter

See footnotes at end of table. Continued . . .

Florida Statistical Abstract 1991

Table 15.14. ELECTRIC UTILITY INDUSTRY: SALES, CUSTOMERS, AND COUNTIES SERVED
    BY PRIVATELY- AND PUBLICLY-OWNED UTILITIES AND BY RURAL ELECTRIC
    COOPERATIVES IN FLORIDA, 1990 (Continued)

Utility	Electricity sales to ultimate customers (MWH)	Number of ultimate customers December 1/	Counties served
Nongenerating rural electric cooperatives (Continued)			
Suwannee Valley	185,309	14,346	Columbia, Hamilton, Lafayette, Suwannee
Talquin	546,790	35,981	Gadsden, Leon, Liberty, Wakulla,
Tri-county	134,996	12,270	Dixie, Jefferson, Madison, Taylor
West Florida	228,404	20,149	Calhoun, Holmes, Jackson, Washington
Withlacoochee River	1,718,646	123,835	Citrus, Hernando, Pasco, Polk, Sumter

MWH Megawatt-hours (1,000 kilowatt-hours).
(X) Not applicable.
1/ Year-end monthly average.
2/ Generates only for resale.
Source: State of Florida, Public Service Commission, *Statistics of the Florida Electric Utility Industry, 1990*, prepublication release.

Table 15.15. ELECTRIC, GAS, AND SANITARY SERVICES: AVERAGE MONTHLY REPORTING UNITS
    EMPLOYMENT, AND PAYROLL COVERED BY UNEMPLOYMENT COMPENSATION LAW BY INDUSTRY IN
    FLORIDA, 1990

SIC code	Industry	Number of reporting units	Number of employees	Payroll ($1,000)
49	Electric, gas, and sanitary services	645	45,311	135,710
491	Electric services	109	32,462	107,428
492	Gas production and distribution	45	2,362	5,552
493	Combination electric and gas, and other utility services	27	2,302	5,617
494	Water supply	152	1,577	2,943
495	Sanitary services	308	6,567	14,095
496	Steam and air-conditioning supply	(D)	(D)	(D)
497	Irrigation systems	(D)	(D)	(D)

(D) Data withheld to avoid disclosure of information about individual firms.
Note: State totals on county employment tables may not match totals in this table due to rounding.
Source: State of Florida, Department of Labor and Employment Security, Bureau of Labor Market Information, "Employment, Wages, and Contributions Report" (ES-202), unpublished data.

Florida Statistical Abstract 1991

Table 15.16. ELECTRIC, GAS, AND SANITARY SERVICES: AVERAGE MONTHLY REPORTING UNITS
EMPLOYMENT, AND PAYROLL COVERED BY UNEMPLOYMENT COMPENSATION LAW IN THE STATE
AND COUNTIES OF FLORIDA, 1990

County	Number of re- porting units	Number of employees	Payroll ($1,000)	County	Number of re- porting units	Number of employees	Payroll ($1,000)
Electric, gas, and sanitary services (SIC code 49)							
Florida	631	45,359	135,710	Lee	20	1,251	3,286
				Leon	6	215	396
Bay	8	381	960	Manatee	8	503	1,483
Brevard	11	729	2,334	Marion	20	290	708
Broward	33	2,794	8,911	Monroe	10	630	1,454
Charlotte	6	269	686	Nassau	6	102	268
Collier	15	424	1,005	Okaloosa	11	257	570
Dade	39	7,311	24,658	Orange	36	2,262	6,200
Dixie	4	7	8	Polk	21	567	1,375
Duval	33	2,757	8,046	Putnam	6	295	939
Escambia	15	1,735	4,609	St. Johns	3	106	316
Flagler	4	119	268	St. Lucie	10	1,277	4,874
Franklin	4	37	83	Santa Rosa	13	155	256
Hendry	3	33	75	Sarasota	23	812	2,374
Hernando	5	159	338	Seminole	18	878	2,527
Highlands	9	189	405	Volusia	19	1,303	3,391
Indian River	4	53	157	Walton	10	156	283
Lake	11	226	545	Statewide 1/	13	384	843
Sanitary services (SIC code 495)							
Florida	297	6,584	14,097	Manatee	5	154	281
				Martin	4	11	23
Bay	6	56	113	Monroe	7	103	190
Brevard	6	39	60	Orange	23	279	547
Broward	25	900	2,420	Palm Beach	11	483	1,127
Collier	9	160	345	Pasco	10	103	216
Dade	21	1,088	2,643	Pinellas	13	195	431
Duval	23	498	1,097	Polk	9	171	311
Hillsborough	19	304	537	Sarasota	13	124	220
Lake	6	88	207	Seminole	10	268	522
Lee	9	221	510	Volusia	9	290	467

1/ Reporting units without a fixed location within the state or of unknown county
location.
Note: Excluded are counties where data are withheld to avoid disclosure of
information about individual firms. For a list of three-digit industries included
see Table 15.15.

Source: State of Florida, Department of Labor and Employment Security, Bureau of
Labor Market Information, "Employment, Wages, and Contributions Report" (ES-202),
unpublished data.

Florida Statistical Abstract 1991

Table 15.25. COST OF ELECTRICITY: RESIDENTIAL ELECTRIC RATES CHARGED BY MUNICIPAL
     COOPERATIVE, AND INVESTOR-OWNED UTILITIES IN FLORIDA, DECEMBER 31, 1990

(in dollars)

Utility	Minimum bill or customer charge	500 KWH	750 KWH	1,000 KWH	1,500 KWH
Municipal					
Alachua	8.00	46.43	65.65	84.86	123.29
Bartow	5.50	40.27	57.66	75.04	109.81
Blountstown	3.50	36.08	52.37	68.66	101.24
Bushnell	6.50	42.70	60.80	78.90	115.10
Chattahoochee	3.00	29.02	42.02	55.03	81.05
Clewiston	6.50	42.85	61.03	79.20	115.55
Ft. Meade	8.67	50.87	71.97	93.07	135.27
Ft. Pierce	5.20	41.58	59.76	77.95	114.33
Gainesville	4.85	38.77	55.72	73.71	109.67
Green Cove Springs	6.00	44.39	63.58	82.78	121.16
Havana	6.00	49.37	71.05	92.73	136.10
Homestead	5.50	46.01	66.27	86.52	127.03
Jacksonville	5.50	37.85	54.03	70.20	102.55
Jacksonville Beach	4.50	39.90	57.60	75.30	110.70
Key West	4.76	49.56	71.96	94.36	139.16
Kissimmee	4.88	50.53	73.36	96.18	141.83
Lake Worth	2.65	44.05	64.75	85.45	126.85
Lakeland	3.94	40.02	58.06	76.10	112.18
Leesburg	5.00	39.35	56.53	73.70	108.05
Moore Haven	8.50	47.25	66.63	86.00	124.75
Mount Dora	5.98	40.90	58.87	76.85	112.81
New Smyrna Beach	4.75	47.43	68.76	90.10	132.78
Newberry	5.00	43.17	62.25	81.33	119.50
Ocala	7.00	42.71	60.56	78.41	114.12
Orlando	4.50	40.04	57.80	75.57	111.11
Quincy	2.40	31.65	46.28	60.90	90.15
Reedy Creek Utilities	2.85	32.55	47.40	62.25	91.95
St. Cloud	7.50	49.97	73.40	96.83	143.70
Sebring	9.30	71.25	102.22	133.10	195.14
Starke	6.45	41.20	58.58	75.95	121.70
Tallahassee	3.89	40.44	58.72	76.99	113.54
Vero Beach	7.10	37.90	53.29	68.69	99.49
Wauchula	8.62	43.81	61.40	78.99	114.18
Williston	6.00	47.91	68.87	89.82	131.73

See footnotes at end of table.   Continued . . .

Florida Statistical Abstract 1991

Table 15.25. COST OF ELECTRICITY: RESIDENTIAL ELECTRIC RATES CHARGED BY MUNICIPAL
   COOPERATIVE, AND INVESTOR-OWNED UTILITIES IN FLORIDA, DECEMBER 31, 1990
   (Continued)

(in dollars)

Utility	Minimum bill or customer charge	500 KWH	750 KWH	1,000 KWH	1,500 KWH
Cooperative					
Central Florida	8.50	44.74	62.85	80.97	117.21
Choctawhatchee	11.85	41.45	56.24	71.04	100.64
Clay	7.00	46.55	66.33	86.10	125.65
Escambia River	7.00	39.44	55.66	71.88	104.32
Florida Keys	5.52	43.25	62.12	80.98	118.71
Glades	10.50	52.25	73.13	94.00	135.75
Gulf Coast	7.00	45.25	64.38	83.50	121.75
Lee County	5.00	45.70	66.05	86.40	127.10
Okefenokee	6.09	45.59	65.34	85.09	124.59
Peace River	10.00	51.00	71.50	92.00	133.00
Sumter	8.37	49.96	70.76	91.55	133.14
Suwannee Valley	8.37	51.99	73.80	95.61	139.23
Talquin	7.50	44.20	62.55	80.90	117.60
Tri-county	8.00	53.00	75.50	98.00	143.00
West Florida	6.97	44.07	62.62	81.17	118.27
Withlacoochee River	8.38	44.42	62.43	80.45	116.49
Investor-owned					
Florida Power	5.32	38.39	54.96	71.53	104.68
Florida Power and Light	5.65	39.31	56.13	75.46	114.12
Florida Public Utilities					
Fernandina Beach division	7.00	42.33	60.00	77.66	112.99
Marianna division	6.65	36.99	52.15	67.32	97.66
Gulf Power 1/	8.00	36.47	50.71	64.94	93.41
Tampa Electric	7.00	43.06	61.09	79.12	115.18

KWH Kilowatt-hour.
1/ Summer/winter rates in effect. Winter rates are shown.
Note: Cost excludes local taxes. December 1990 fuel costs are included for
municipal and cooperative utilities. October 1989 through March 1990 fuel costs are
included for investor-owned utilities.

Source: State of Florida, Public Service Commission, *Statistics of the Florida
Electric Utility Industry, 1990*, prepublication release.

Florida Statistical Abstract 1991

Table 15.26. COST OF ELECTRICITY: COMMERCIAL AND INDUSTRIAL ELECTRIC RATES CHARGED BY MUNICIPAL, COOPERATIVE, AND INVESTOR-OWNED UTILITIES IN FLORIDA, DECEMBER 31 1990

(in dollars)

Utility	15,000 KWH	45,000 KWH	150,000 KWH	400,000 KWH	800,000 KWH
Municipal					
Alachua	1,421	3,696	12,267	30,357	60,691
Bartow	1,394	3,575	11,872	29,095	58,171
Blountstown	1,116	3,333	11,095	29,575	59,143
Bushnell	1,349	3,517	11,677	28,922	57,824
Chattahoochee	976	2,821	9,405	23,962	47,924
Clewiston	1,321	3,622	11,990	30,715	61,395
Ft. Meade	1,309	4,014	13,170	32,250	64,410
Ft. Pierce	1,306	3,416	11,316	28,158	56,286
Gainesville	1,207	3,223	10,705	23,749	47,437
Green Cove Springs	1,387	3,585	11,891	25,135	50,146
Havana	1,307	3,909	13,016	34,698	69,390
Homestead	1,429	3,887	13,038	32,743	65,521
Jacksonville	1,121	2,963	9,760	24,600	49,000
Jacksonville Beach	1,551	3,982	13,236	32,436	64,856
Key West	1,767	4,773	15,900	40,095	80,185
Kissimmee	1,627	4,092	13,171	30,281	60,513
Lake Worth	1,437	Δ/ 4,236	Δ/ 14,091	Δ/ 35,074	Δ/ 70,136
Lakeland	1,178	3,133	10,480	24,902	49,428
Leesburg	1,298	3,260	10,827	26,177	52,337
Moore Haven	1,493	3,990	13,248	33,323	66,623
Mount Dora	1,084	3,241	8,636	21,359	42,703
New Smyrna Beach	1,554	4,159	13,786	34,774	69,514
Newberry	1,460	3,600	11,965	28,547	57,079
Ocala	Δ/ 1,110	Δ/ 2,909	Δ/ 9,647	Δ/ 23,283	Δ/ 46,545
Orlando	1,162	2,931	9,736	23,603	47,191
Quincy	1,050	2,753	9,035	22,760	45,460
Reedy Creek Utilities	1,071	2,875	9,548	24,063	48,111
St. Cloud	1,590	4,391	14,580	37,377	74,729
Sebring	2,009	5,358	12,234	30,996	61,956
Starke	1,382	4,127	13,734	36,609	73,209
Tallahassee	1,348	3,385	11,225	27,195	54,365
Vero Beach	1,115	2,881	8,798	21,685	43,311
Wauchula	1,097	3,512	11,556	28,883	57,701
Williston	1,486	3,975	13,210	33,197	66,377

See footnotes at end of table. Continued . . .

Florida Statistical Abstract 1991

Table 15.26. COST OF ELECTRICITY: COMMERCIAL AND INDUSTRIAL ELECTRIC RATES CHARGED
    BY MUNICIPAL, COOPERATIVE, AND INVESTOR-OWNED UTILITIES IN FLORIDA, DECEMBER 31
    1990 (Continued)

(in dollars)

Utility	15,000 KWH	45,000 KWH	150,000 KWH	400,000 KWH	800,000 KWH
Cooperative					
Central Florida	1,380	3,516	11,651	28,038	56,026
Choctawhatchee	993	2,600	9,359	20,956	41,412
Clay	1,252	3,384	11,150	25,810	51,370
Escambia River	1,156	2,975	9,822	24,292	48,544
Florida Keys	1,306	3,827	12,814	33,589	67,203
Glades	1,594	4,440	14,730	34,575	68,975
Gulf Coast	1,092	2,952	9,812	24,812	49,612
Lee County	1,221	3,258	10,825	27,775	55,535
Okefenokee	1,425	3,751	11,968	29,648	58,788
Peace River	1,239	3,174	10,463	25,850	51,650
Sumter	1,133	2,881	9,475	28,978	57,906
Suwannee Valley	1,560	4,159	13,771	34,687	69,334
Talquin	1,394	3,611	11,895	28,160	56,020
Tri-county	1,429	3,562	11,640	27,550	55,000
West Florida	1,109	2,812	9,255	22,750	45,450
Withlacoochee River	1,287	3,349	11,107	27,525	55,025
Investor-owned					
Florida Power	980	2,506	8,439	20,583	41,088
Florida Power and Light	1,145	3,022	9,741	23,823	47,606
Florida Public Utilities Fernandina Beach					
division	1,089	3,058	10,103	26,288	52,538
Marianna division	842	2,312	7,625	19,627	39,219
Gulf Power 1/	903	2,291	8,476	19,393	38,561
Tampa Electric	1,189	2,991	9,889	24,196	48,222

KWH Kilowatt-hour.
A/ Actual demand charge is based on kilovolt-ampere (KVA). An equivalent demand
charge based on kilowatts under the assumption of a 90 percent power factor at peak
demand was used in this comparison.
1/ Summer/winter rates in effect. Winter rates are shown.
Note: Cost excludes local taxes. December 1990 fuel costs are included for
municipal and cooperative utilities. October 1989 through March 1990 fuel costs are
included for investor-owned utilities.

Source: State of Florida, Public Service Commission, *Statistics of the Florida
Electric Utility Industry, 1990*, prepublication release.

Florida Statistical Abstract 1991

Table 15.27. ELECTRIC UTILITY INDUSTRY: CAPACITY, NET GENERATION, FUEL CONSUMPTION
SALES, PER CAPITA CONSUMPTION, AND PRICES IN FLORIDA, 1986 THROUGH 1990

Item	1986	1987	1988	1989	1990
Nameplate capacity, total (MW)	34,412	35,788	36,544	36,523	37,532
Conventional steam	24,503	25,870	26,550	26,431	27,947
Internal combustion and gas turbine	5,086	5,095	5,123	5,241	5,024
Combined cycle	671	671	719	698	596
Hydroelectric	42	42	42	43	43
Steam, nuclear	4,110	4,110	4,110	4,110	3,922
Net generation, total (GWH)	108,465	108,597	124,055	127,142	125,466
By prime mover					
Conventional steam	85,437	86,816	94,842	A/ 104,167	99,570
Internal combustion and					
gas turbine	780	464	459	A/ 1,526	1,154
Combined cycle	(NA)	2,236	2,346	2,807	2,472
Hydroelectric	212	215	210	17	176
Steam, nuclear	22,036	19,049	26,198	21,436	22,095
By fuel type					
Natural gas	14,409	16,238	14,710	17,417	15,919
Coal	42,857	53,390	56,614	63,744	62,110
Residual	28,499	19,548	26,060	25,038	25,905
Distillate	452	338	263	1,113	711
Hydroelectric	212	215	210	17	249
Nuclear	22,036	19,049	26,198	19,814	20,572
By type of ownership					
Investor-owned	89,952	89,075	98,952	98,103	96,490
Municipal	17,862	19,522	25,103	29,039	28,976
Fuel consumed for generation					
Natural gas (billion cubic feet)	133	156	128	158	188
Coal (1,000 short tons)	17,671	22,041	23,376	27,181	26,250
Residual (1,000 barrels)	44,040	29,303	39,325	51,142	38,814
Distillate (1,000 barrels)	959	1,319	1,025	2,864	1,766
U-235 (kilograms)	0	2,970	4,400	3,283	B/ 604
Sales to ultimate consumers, total (GWH)	116,313	122,610	130,222	138,258	143,303
Residential	57,480	60,505	63,996	68,203	71,034
Commercial	36,223	38,638	43,392	45,730	45,770
Industrial	18,982	19,726	18,757	19,908	22,110
Other public utilities	3,628	3,741	4,077	4,417	4,389
Per capita consumption 1/ (KWH)					
Sales per capita, total	9,727	9,945	10,487	11,080	11,432
Residential sales per capita	4,816	4,907	5,154	5,441	5,542
Kilowatt-hours per capita 2/	9,088	8,808	9,991	10,143	10,116

        See footnotes at end of table.   Continued . . .

Florida Statistical Abstract 1991

Table 15.27. ELECTRIC UTILITY INDUSTRY: CAPACITY, NET GENERATION, FUEL CONSUMPTION
SALES, PER CAPITA CONSUMPTION, AND PRICES IN FLORIDA, 1986 THROUGH 1990
(Continued)

Item	1986	1987	1988	1989	1990
Revenues per GWH by class of service ($1,000)	72.3	70.6	70.5	70.5	68.7
Residential	79.8	79.1	78.0	77.4	76.4
Commercial	68.3	64.5	67.1	65.8	65.8
Industrial	57.4	50.3	53.2	55.1	50.0
Other	70.6	103.4	68.1	82.0	67.7

MW Megawatt (1,000 kilowatts). GWH Gigwatt-hours (million kilowatt-hours). KWH
Kilowatt-hours.
(NA) Not available.
A/ Includes combined cycle. B/ Data for Florida Power and Light not available
for publication. 1/ Total sales divided by population. 2/ Net generation divided
by population.
Note: Detail may not add to totals because of rounding.
Source: State of Florida, Public Service Commission, *Statistics of the Florida
Electric Utility Industry, 1990*, prepublication release.

Table 15.41. GAS COMPANIES: TYPICAL GAS BILLS FOR RESIDENTIAL SERVICE OF COMPANIES
IN FLORIDA, DECEMBER 31, 1990

(amounts in dollars)

Company	Minimum bill	20 therms	30 therms	40 therms	50 therms	100 therms
Central Florida Gas Corporation	6.50	21.02	28.29	35.55	42.81	79.12
City Gas Company of Florida	6.00	18.86	25.29	31.73	38.16	70.32
Florida Public Utilities	6.00	18.09	24.13	30.17	36.21	66.43
Indiantown Gas Company	5.00	12.50	16.25	20.00	23.74	42.49
Miller Gas Company	6.00	19.24	25.86	32.48	39.10	72.21
Palm Beach County Utilities	5.00	18.77	25.66	32.55	39.43	73.87
Peoples Gas System, Inc.	7.00	19.45	25.67	31.89	38.11	69.23
Plant City Natural Gas Company	5.00	18.80	25.71	32.61	39.51	74.02
St. Joe Natural Gas Company	3.00	9.65	12.98	16.31	19.64	36.27
South Florida Natural Gas Company	6.00	19.87	26.80	33.73	40.67	75.33
West Florida Natural Gas	6.00	18.04	24.07	30.09	36.11	66.22

1 Therm = 100,000 British thermal units.
Note: Local taxes are excluded.
Source: State of Florida, Public Service Commission, *1990 Annual Report.*

Florida Statistical Abstract 1991

Table 15.42. NATURAL GAS: PRODUCTION, MOVEMENT, AND CONSUMPTION IN FLORIDA AND THE
UNITED STATES, 1988 AND 1989

(quantity in millions of cubic feet)

| | Florida | | United States | |
Item	1988	1989	1988	1989
Marketed production 1/	7,484	7,534	17,808,313	18,044,499
Net interstate movements	290,940	322,766	0	0
Net movements across U.S. borders	0	0	1,219,590	1,274,651
Net storage changes 2/	0	0	-58,734	-321,017
Extraction loss	3,584	3,551	815,844	784,502
Supplemental gas supplies	0	0	101,134	106,745
Unaccounted for 3/	1,407	3,158	344,356	182,217
Consumption, total	293,433	323,591	18,029,588	18,780,192
Delivered to consumers	282,792	310,493	16,319,793	17,079,657
Lease and plant fuel	7,275	8,942	1,095,883	1,070,452
Pipeline fuel	3,366	4,156	613,912	630,083

1/ Gross withdrawals from gas and oil wells less gas used for repressuring, non-
hydrocarbon gases removed, and quantities vented and flared.
2/ Positive numbers indicate an increase in storage, thus a decrease in supply.
3/ Represents an imbalance between available supplies and consumption.
Note: Some data are revised.

Table 15.43. NATURAL GAS: TOTAL AND AVERAGE QUANTITY AND VALUE OF NATURAL GAS
DELIVERED TO CONSUMERS IN FLORIDA, 1989

Item	Total	Resi-dential	Com-mercial	Indus-trial	Electric util-ities
Quantity consumed (MCF)	310,493	13,089	35,105	75,485	186,814
Value ($1,000)	(NA)	(NA)	(NA)	(NA)	(NA)
Consumers (1,000)	(NA)	453	44	A/	(NA)
Average value					
Dollars per thousand					
cubic feet	3.15	8.06	4.85	3.13	2.49
Cents per therm 1/	30.2	77.3	46.5	30.0	23.9
Average consumption					
Quantity (TCF)	(NA)	29	801	164,097	(NA)
Cost per consumer (dollars)	(NA)	233	3,884	(NA)	(NA)

MCF Million cubic feet.
TCF Thousand cubic feet.
(NA) Not available.
A/ Fewer than 500 industrial consumers.
1/ One therm equals 100,000 British Thermal Units.
Note: Beginning in 1987, consumption value is no longer reported.

Source for Tables 15.42 and 15.43: U.S., Department of Energy, Energy Information Administration, *Natural Gas Annual, 1989.*

Table 15.50. NUCLEAR POWER PLANTS: LOCATION AND CAPACITY OF PLANTS IN OPERATION
    IN FLORIDA AND THE UNITED STATES, DECEMBER 31, 1989

Location	Plant	Capacity (net MWe)	Utility	Type of reactor	Date operable
Florida 1/	(X)	3,676	(X)	(X)	(X)
Florida City	Turkey Point 3	666	Florida Power and Light	PWR	Nov-72
Florida City	Turkey Point 4	666	Florida Power and Light	PWR	Jun-73
Ft. Pierce	St. Lucie 1	839	Florida Power and Light	PWR	May-76
Ft. Pierce	St. Lucie 2	839	Florida Power and Light	PWR	Jun-83
Red Level	Crystal River 3	666	Florida Power Corp.	PWR	Jan-77
United States 2/	(X)	97,869	(X)	(X)	(X)

MWe Megawatt electrical.
PWR Pressurized-water reactor.
(X) Not applicable.
1/ 5 plants.
2/ 110 plants.

Source: U.S., Energy Information Administration, *Commercial Nuclear Power 1990:
Prospects for the United States and the World.*

Table 15.51. ENERGY CONSUMPTION: AMOUNT CONSUMED BY SECTOR IN FLORIDA, 1977
    THROUGH 1989

(in trillions of British thermal units)

Year	Total	Residential	Commercial 1/	Industrial 2/	Transportation 3/
1977	2,196.4	520.8	357.2	518.3	800.1
1978	2,316.4	558.5	361.7	543.5	852.8
1979	2,426.9	556.3	375.4	591.9	903.2
1980	2,485.0	581.1	375.0	614.4	914.4
1981	2,474.2	600.8	422.2	545.1	906.0
1982	2,360.1	575.6	424.1	469.2	891.1
1983	2,425.1	599.3	451.7	478.3	895.8
1984	2,523.8	631.0	479.7	503.6	909.5
1985	2,663.3	671.7	537.8	510.1	943.7
1986	2,713.7	690.2	555.7	483.6	984.2
1987	2,844.0	732.5	594.5	497.4	1,019.5
1988	2,993.7	767.9	627.0	511.9	1,086.8
1989	3,073.6	812.7	655.6	489.5	1,115.8

1/ Includes establishments under SIC codes 15-17, 48-49 (except 491 and part of
493), 50-59, 70-89, and 91-93.
2/ Includes establishments under SIC codes 1-14 and 20-39.
3/ Includes establishments under SIC codes 40-47.
Note: Data are revised; therefore, numbers will differ from those previously
reported in *Abstract.*

Source: State of Florida, Governor's Energy Office, *Florida Energy Data Report,
1970-1989.*

Florida Statistical Abstract 1991

Table 15.60. MOTOR FUELS: CONSUMPTION BY USE IN FLORIDA, 1955 THROUGH 1989

(in thousands of gallons)

Year	Total quantity consumed 1/	Nonhighway use 2/	Highway use
1955	1,384,052	174,201	1,194,380
1956	1,549,437	201,969	1,331,698
1957	1,695,294	223,851	1,454,882
1958	1,787,338	243,149	1,525,619
1959	1,933,950	276,033	1,641,576
1960	1,950,650	167,431	1,765,819
1961	1,980,408	160,451	1,800,927
1962	2,071,490	133,801	1,917,987
1963	2,169,084	124,988	2,022,714
1964	2,286,002	112,073	2,160,479
1965	2,409,617	104,646	2,291,031
1966	2,562,586	120,505	2,428,962
1967	2,711,163	135,851	2,561,698
1968	2,959,259	138,496	2,803,754
1969	3,215,457	129,949	3,069,173
1970	3,484,439	153,969	3,312,830
1971	3,771,337	146,210	3,585,727
1972	4,215,995	124,098	4,045,322
1973	4,695,983	126,054	4,494,951
1974	4,510,456	123,058	4,342,185
1975	4,639,217	135,547	4,456,610
1976	4,827,840	136,774	4,650,302
1977	5,023,007	131,635	4,846,201
1978	5,337,604	139,114	5,152,263
1979	5,374,535	142,358	5,171,693
1980	5,293,548	164,430	5,116,312
1981	5,390,545	137,165	5,240,229
1982	5,469,775	139,779	5,317,892
1983	5,723,316	163,810	5,548,590
1984	5,934,391	181,767	5,740,587
1985	6,110,435	254,402	5,843,396
1986	6,394,295	263,337	6,116,961
1987	6,700,629	275,337	6,387,472
1988	6,863,376	281,739	6,530,151
1989	7,034,489	292,036	6,680,708

1/ Includes losses allowed for evaporation and handling.
2/ Gasoline only.
Note: Includes gasoline and all other fuels (except under nonhighway use) under state motor fuel laws.

Source: U.S., Department of Transportation, Federal Highway Administration, *Highway Statistics, 1989*, and previous editions.

Florida Statistical Abstract 1991

Table 15.66. GASOLINE: AVERAGE PRICES IN SELECTED CITIES IN FLORIDA, DECEMBER 1990
AND ANNUALLY IN FLORIDA, 1983 THROUGH 1990

(prices in dollars per gallon)

| | Average pump price | | | | | |
| | Full service unleaded | | | Self-service unleaded | | |
City	Regular	Mid-grade	Premium	Regular	Mid-grade	Premium
Bradenton	1.703	1.785	1.870	1.342	1.450	1.547
Brandon	1.696	1.804	1.850	1.342	1.430	1.529
Cocoa	1.679	1.775	1.880	1.357	1.468	1.559
Daytona Beach	1.632	1.683	1.770	1.358	1.479	1.610
Delray	1.689	1.780	1.830	1.325	1.441	1.504
Ft. Myers	1.679	1.747	1.830	1.353	1.450	1.549
Ft. Pierce	1.602	1.721	1.740	1.360	1.449	1.530
Gainesville	1.637	1.707	1.780	1.366	1.476	1.578
Jacksonville	1.664	1.731	1.800	1.319	1.429	1.520
Lakeland	1.549	1.621	1.700	1.339	1.442	1.528
Lauderhill	1.545	1.643	1.740	1.303	1.428	1.495
Miami	1.525	1.667	1.710	1.292	1.416	1.470
Naples	1.634	1.742	1.750	1.367	1.444	1.525
Ocala	1.531	1.619	1.710	1.355	1.465	1.540
Orlando	1.690	1.780	1.830	1.362	1.452	1.544
Palm Beach	1.645	1.726	1.800	1.315	1.427	1.507
Pensacola	1.676	1.752	1.810	1.312	1.416	1.508
Pompano	1.608	1.689	1.760	1.305	1.423	1.492
Port Charlotte	1.623	1.692	1.770	1.340	1.454	1.542
Port Richey	(NA)	(NA)	(NA)	1.361	1.435	1.535
Sarasota	1.692	1.762	1.810	1.335	1.448	1.542
St. Petersburg	1.585	1.672	1.760	1.327	1.418	1.509
Tallahassee	1.624	1.707	1.800	1.374	1.468	1.574
Tampa	1.654	1.749	1.820	1.341	1.448	1.535
Venice	1.666	1.732	1.780	1.325	1.430	1.525

	Florida average retail prices 1/			
			Constant price	
		Implicit price	(1982 dollars)	
	Nominal	deflator 2/		Percentage
Year	price	(1982 = 100)	Amount	change
1983	95.5	104.1	91.7	(X)
1984	92.9	108.1	85.9	-6.3
1985	94.3	111.6	84.5	-1.6
1986	65.1	114.3	57.0	-32.5
1987	70.1	119.8	58.5	2.6
1988	70.7	124.5	56.8	-2.9
1989	78.5	130.0	60.4	6.3
1990	89.4	136.1	65.7	8.8

(NA) Not available.
(X) Not applicable.
1/ Data from U.S., Department of Energy, Energy Information Administration, *Petroleum Marketing Monthly*, and unpublished data; U.S., Department of Commerce, Bureau of Economic Analysis, *Survey of Current Business*. Prices are in cents per gallon and exclude taxes.
2/ For personal consumption expenditures.
Note: City data are from AAA Clubs of Florida Survey. Some data are revised.
Source: State of Florida, Governor's Energy Office, *1989 Florida Motor Gasoline and Diesel Fuel Report*, and prepublication release.

Florida Statistical Abstract 1991

Table 15.67. GASOLINE: TOTAL AND PER CAPITA GALLONS CONSUMED IN THE STATE AND
COUNTIES OF FLORIDA, 1988 AND 1989

	Total consumption (1,000 gallons)			Per capita consumption (gallons)		
			Per-			Per-
			centage			centage
			change			change
County	1988	1989	1988-89	1988	1989	1988-89
Florida	6,045,971	6,140,500	1.6	490.4	485.4	-1.0
Alachua	92,289	91,349	-1.0	524.2	510.2	-2.7
Baker	9,727	10,179	4.6	546.7	561.0	2.6
Bay	67,101	68,215	1.7	539.4	542.2	0.5
Bradford	11,979	14,054	17.3	520.0	610.6	17.4
Brevard	187,809	195,565	4.1	499.0	503.5	0.9
Broward	545,116	565,959	3.8	451.7	459.2	1.7
Calhoun	(NA)	(NA)	(NA)	(NA)	(NA)	(NA)
Charlotte	46,655	49,062	5.2	481.1	475.4	-1.2
Citrus	39,432	40,601	3.0	459.1	448.9	-2.2
Clay	47,602	48,869	2.7	483.1	474.4	-1.8
Collier	76,138	79,630	4.6	562.7	554.0	-1.6
Columbia	33,012	35,809	8.5	803.6	853.7	6.2
Dade	770,835	800,995	3.9	410.2	419.6	2.3
De Soto	11,340	11,257	-0.7	495.4	478.5	-3.4
Dixie	5,957	7,272	22.1	605.2	712.1	17.7
Duval	329,507	333,306	1.2	502.0	502.4	0.1
Escambia	127,402	126,678	-0.6	489.2	484.2	-1.0
Flagler	12,717	13,690	7.7	550.5	526.8	-4.3
Franklin	(NA)	(NA)	(NA)	(NA)	(NA)	(NA)
Gadsden	17,898	18,589	3.9	432.0	452.5	4.7
Gilchrist	3,036	3,046	0.3	356.0	334.4	-6.1
Glades	4,281	4,334	1.2	597.7	592.5	-0.9
Gulf	(NA)	(NA)	(NA)	(NA)	(NA)	(NA)
Hamilton	14,980	15,043	0.4	1,488.0	1,414.9	-4.9
Hardee	10,701	10,700	0.0	538.7	544.4	1.1
Hendry	14,808	14,393	-2.8	597.2	569.5	-4.6
Hernando	41,685	42,298	1.5	460.4	442.8	-3.8
Highlands	34,786	35,359	1.6	541.1	532.5	-1.6
Hillsborough	390,295	396,064	1.5	482.2	481.5	-0.1
Holmes	8,811	8,573	-2.7	579.1	551.7	-4.7
Indian River	43,165	45,574	5.6	516.0	525.0	1.7
Jackson	29,230	29,007	-0.8	709.7	703.8	-0.8
Jefferson	9,156	8,950	-2.2	814.2	793.7	-2.5

See footnotes at end of table.   Continued . . .

Table 15.67.   GASOLINE: TOTAL AND PER CAPITA GALLONS CONSUMED IN THE STATE AND
    COUNTIES OF FLORIDA, 1988 AND 1989 (Continued)

	Total consumption (1,000 gallons)			Per capita consumption (gallons)		
County	1988	1989	Percentage change 1988-89	1988	1989	Percentage change 1988-89
Lafayette	2,373	2,289	-3.5	452.9	426.4	-5.8
Lake	70,856	73,316	3.5	502.7	500.5	-0.4
Lee	159,430	169,421	6.3	510.5	520.7	2.0
Leon	96,957	100,737	3.9	542.0	537.4	-0.9
Levy	17,682	16,557	-6.4	721.1	655.3	-9.1
Liberty	(NA)	(NA)	(NA)	(NA)	(NA)	(NA)
Madison	10,166	9,946	-2.2	660.4	630.9	-4.5
Manatee	87,671	90,108	2.8	439.1	438.0	-0.2
Marion	112,296	114,811	2.2	620.9	610.5	-1.7
Martin	46,232	49,900	7.9	502.8	518.6	3.2
Monroe	42,592	44,818	5.2	564.4	583.7	3.4
Nassau	31,016	27,734	-10.6	736.6	637.6	-13.4
Okaloosa	72,213	71,466	-1.0	516.5	504.6	-2.3
Okeechobee	20,393	21,280	4.3	726.9	735.4	1.2
Orange	352,616	372,807	5.7	566.6	571.4	0.8
Osceola	62,642	66,329	5.9	658.0	656.9	-0.2
Palm Beach	384,695	398,553	3.6	470.6	473.6	0.7
Pasco	107,691	110,658	2.8	403.4	403.3	0.0
Pinellas	335,201	342,081	2.1	401.9	405.0	0.8
Polk	197,050	205,226	4.1	503.2	514.3	2.2
Putnam	30,080	29,655	-1.4	483.0	463.9	-3.9
St. Johns	49,208	50,078	1.8	628.2	610.6	-2.8
St. Lucie	70,309	73,415	4.4	516.0	509.5	-1.3
Santa Rosa	38,372	38,420	0.1	507.4	485.8	-4.3
Sarasota	119,674	122,382	2.3	452.8	450.9	-0.4
Seminole	115,256	118,158	2.5	435.5	426.1	-2.2
Sumter	30,122	29,417	-2.3	1009.1	950.7	-5.8
Suwannee	17,347	18,393	6.0	674.8	698.1	3.4
Taylor	13,800	14,059	1.9	803.1	819.4	2.0
Union	4,256	4,277	0.5	422.5	413.4	-2.2
Volusia	169,567	175,288	3.4	487.8	486.7	-0.2
Wakulla	5,968	6,552	9.8	441.4	475.2	7.7
Walton	18,485	18,135	-1.9	694.6	668.7	-3.7
Washington	8,227	9,707	18.0	498.4	578.8	16.1

(NA) Not available.
Note: Includes gasohol.

    Source: State of Florida, Governor's Energy Office, *1989 Florida Motor Gasoline
and Diesel Fuel Report*.

Florida Statistical Abstract 1991

WHOLESALE AND RETAIL TRADE

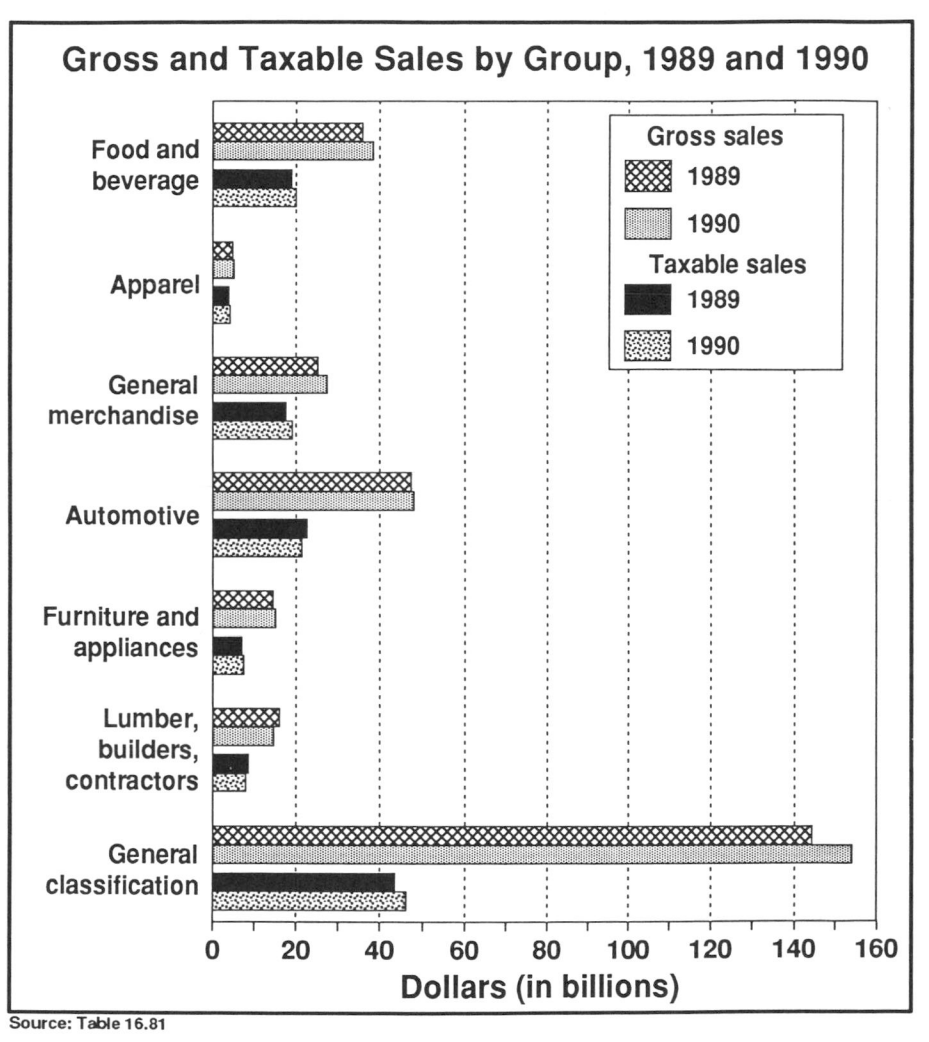

Gross and Taxable Sales by Group, 1989 and 1990

Gross sales
1989
1990

Taxable sales
1989
1990

Food and beverage

Apparel

General merchandise

Automotive

Furniture and appliances

Lumber, builders, contractors

General classification

Dollars (in billions)

Source: Table 16.81

Table 16.01. WHOLESALE TRADE: ESTABLISHMENTS, SALES, AND SALES PER ESTABLISHMENT
IN FLORIDA, CENSUS YEARS 1948 THROUGH 1987

Census year	Establishments		Sales		Sales per establishment	
	Number	Per-centage change	Amount ($1,000)	Per-centage change	Amount (dollars)	Per-centage change
1948	3,718	38.6	1,991,000	281.4	535,503	175.1
1954	5,254	41.3	3,373,000	69.4	641,987	19.9
1958	7,232	37.6	5,511,899	63.4	762,154	18.7
1963	8,896	23.0	7,486,810	35.8	841,593	10.4
1967	9,650	8.5	10,302,824	37.6	1,067,650	26.9
1972	13,450	39.4	19,983,912	94.0	1,485,793	39.2
1977	15,409	14.6	34,380,491	72.0	2,231,195	50.2
1982	19,537	26.8	65,614,610	90.8	3,358,479	50.5
1987	25,636	31.2	97,360,044	48.4	3,797,786	13.1

Table 16.02. WHOLESALE TRADE: NUMBER OF ESTABLISHMENTS AND SALES BY KIND OF
BUSINESS IN FLORIDA, 1987

SIC code	Kind of business	Number of es-tablish-ments	Sales ($1,000)	Sales per estab-lishment (dollars)
	Total	25,636	97,360,044	3,797,786
50	Durable goods	17,092	53,146,057	3,109,411
501	Motor vehicles and automotive parts and supplies	2,575	18,432,893	7,158,405
502	Furniture and home furnishings	1,007	2,122,392	2,107,639
503	Lumber and other construction materials	1,321	4,053,909	3,068,818
504	Sporting, recreational, photographic, and hobby goods, toys, and supplies	2,682	6,856,380	2,556,443
505	Metals and minerals, except petroleum	459	1,933,246	4,211,865
506	Electrical goods	2,035	7,169,533	3,523,112
507	Hardware and plumbing and heating equipment and supplies	1,414	2,603,328	1,841,109
508	Machinery, equipment, and supplies	3,445	6,759,770	1,962,197
509	Miscellaneous durable goods	2,154	3,214,606	1,492,389
51	Nondurable goods	8,544	44,213,987	5,174,858
511	Paper and paper products	886	2,676,697	3,021,103
512	Drugs, drug proprietaries, and druggists' sundries	352	2,112,746	6,002,119
513	Apparel, piece goods, and notions	903	1,336,629	1,480,209
514	Groceries and related products	2,639	20,324,071	7,701,429
515	Farm-product raw materials	107	1,161,188	10,852,224
516	Chemicals and allied products	596	1,762,250	2,956,795
517	Petroleum and petroleum products	468	6,855,296	14,648,068
518	Beer, wine, and distilled alcoholic beverages	211	3,609,591	17,107,066
519	Miscellaneous nondurable goods	2,382	4,375,519	1,836,910

Source for tables 16.01 and 16.02: U.S., Department of Commerce, Bureau of the
Census, *1987 Census of Wholesale Trade: Florida*, and previous editions.

Florida Statistical Abstract 1991

Table 16.06. WHOLESALE AND RETAIL TRADE: SALES IN THE STATE AND COUNTIES
OF FLORIDA, 1987

(in thousands of dollars)

County	Wholesale trade sales	Retail trade sales	County	Wholesale trade sales	Retail trade sales
Florida	97,360,044	87,925,609	Lafayette	2,599	6,138
Alachua	435,481	1,248,707	Lake	515,653	865,023
Baker	(D)	39,651	Lee	954,115	2,522,486
Bay	379,895	924,160	Leon	639,052	1,305,748
Bradford	26,043	98,197	Levy	24,453	103,397
Brevard	1,158,837	2,446,743	Liberty	(D)	8,779
Broward	11,773,113	10,140,827	Madison	48,183	52,769
Calhoun	(D)	35,099	Manatee	1,058,225	1,320,842
Charlotte	(D)	481,422	Marion	1,075,915	1,165,306
Citrus	40,220	424,805	Martin	167,841	775,939
Clay	269,578	616,418	Monroe	139,777	625,320
Collier	346,574	1,133,071	Nassau	53,027	216,498
Columbia	148,497	286,496	Okaloosa	328,338	933,349
Dade	21,772,308	13,047,272	Okeechobee	138,940	153,761
De Soto	(D)	101,256	Orange	9,251,936	5,586,710
Dixie	7,609	33,681	Osceola	504,132	692,951
Duval	14,935,780	4,862,850	Palm Beach	4,101,587	6,622,066
Escambia	1,141,295	1,753,238	Pasco	231,639	1,486,052
Flagler	(D)	99,889	Pinellas	3,078,500	6,625,292
Franklin	(D)	30,636	Polk	2,462,557	2,357,198
Gadsden	349,141	145,559	Putnam	78,059	275,138
Gilchrist	12,828	18,782	St. Johns	167,023	471,058
Glades	(D)	9,147	St. Lucie	491,991	880,138
Gulf	11,791	34,031	Santa Rosa	51,976	278,029
Hamilton	(D)	45,359	Sarasota	788,606	2,360,075
Hardee	85,722	91,594	Seminole	1,677,080	1,815,686
Hendry	40,051	116,204	Sumter	31,789	129,245
Hernando	76,788	398,696	Suwannee	61,046	106,616
Highlands	149,940	394,064	Taylor	39,571	100,193
Hillsborough	14,607,260	5,600,611	Union	(D)	16,071
Holmes	9,675	39,350	Volusia	662,333	2,372,471
Indian River	214,582	589,996	Wakulla	(D)	32,397
Jackson	193,516	206,280	Walton	45,432	90,860
Jefferson	10,680	36,966	Washington	26,706	40,951

(D) Data withheld to avoid disclosure of information about individual companies.

Source: U.S., Department of Commerce, Bureau of the Census, *1987 Census of Wholesale Trade: Florida*, and *1987 Census of Retail Trade: Florida.*

Table 16.11. RETAIL TRADE: ESTABLISHMENTS, SALES, AND SALES PER ESTABLISHMENT
IN FLORIDA, CENSUS YEARS 1939 THROUGH 1987

Census year	Establishments		Retail sales		Sales per establishment	
	Number	Percentage change	Amount ($1,000)	Percentage change	Amount (dollars)	Percentage change
1939	28,614	(NA)	614,464	(NA)	21,474	(NA)
1948	32,513	13.6	2,326,682	278.7	71,562	233.2
1954	41,303	27.0	4,014,417	72.5	97,194	35.8
1958	49,547	20.0	5,839,600	45.5	117,860	21.3
1963	53,293	7.6	7,609,717	30.3	142,790	21.2
1967	58,727	10.2	10,280,334	35.1	175,053	22.6
1972	70,898	20.7	19,430,163	89.0	274,058	56.6
1977	83,013	17.1	31,300,103	61.1	377,051	37.6
1982	88,733	6.9	55,468,945	77.2	625,122	65.8
1987	130,508	47.1	90,295,017	62.8	1,049,131	67.8

(NA) Not available.

Source: U.S., Department of Commerce, Bureau of the Census, *1987 Census of
Retail Trade: Florida* and previous editions, and *1987 Retail Trade: Nonemployer
Statistics Series, South*.

Table 16.12. RETAIL TRADE: ESTABLISHMENTS, SALES, AND INCORPORATION STATUS BY KIND
OF BUSINESS IN FLORIDA, 1987

SIC code	Kind of business	Number of establishments	Sales ($1,000)	Number of unincorporated businesses	
				Individual proprietorships	Partnerships
	Total	83,808	87,925,609	13,814	2,964
52	Building materials and garden supplies stores	4,256	4,699,161	656	133
53	General merchandise stores	1,756	9,911,080	105	15
54	Food stores	10,502	17,001,675	1,554	354
55	Automotive dealers and gasoline service stations	11,818	27,976,297	2,392	335
56	Apparel and accessory stores	9,228	4,002,607	861	227
57	Furniture and home furnishings stores	7,287	4,676,518	1,165	177
58	Eating and drinking places	19,673	9,087,870	3,584	1,073
59	Drug, proprietary and miscellaneous retail	19,288	10,570,401	3,497	650

Source : U.S., Department of Commerce, Bureau of the Census, *1987 Census of
Retail Trade: Florida*, and previous editions.

Florida Statistical Abstract 1991

Table 16.43. WHOLESALE AND RETAIL TRADE: AVERAGE MONTHLY REPORTING UNITS
    EMPLOYMENT, AND PAYROLL COVERED BY UNEMPLOYMENT COMPENSATION LAW
    BY INDUSTRY IN FLORIDA, 1990

SIC code	Industry	Number of reporting units	Number of employees	Payroll ($1,000)
	Wholesale trade	29,972	292,245	691,972
50	Wholesale trade--durable goods	19,116	169,995	420,290
501	Motor vehicles and motor vehicle parts and supplies	2,129	23,182	45,551
502	Furniture and homefurnishings	1,113	7,007	16,292
503	Lumber and other construction materials	1,392	12,790	27,398
504	Professional and commercial equipment and supplies	3,597	37,007	111,638
505	Metals and minerals, except petroleum	432	3,683	9,521
506	Electrical goods	2,679	27,123	72,693
507	Hardware, plumbing and heating equipment and supplies	1,564	13,642	30,905
508	Machinery, equipment, and supplies	4,069	32,794	80,215
509	Miscellaneous durable goods	2,139	12,763	26,079
51	Wholesale trade--nondurable goods	10,856	122,250	271,682
511	Paper and paper products	1,163	14,150	28,704
512	Drugs, drug proprietaries, and druggists' sundries	828	10,145	29,572
513	Apparel, piece goods, and notions	1,151	7,606	15,428
514	Groceries and related products	3,063	45,866	96,998
515	Farm-product raw materials	96	1,248	1,834
516	Chemicals and allied products	825	5,530	15,409
517	Petroleum and petroleum products	510	7,466	18,258
518	Beer, wine, and distilled alcoholic beverages	249	9,291	23,896
519	Miscellaneous nondurable goods	2,968	20,946	41,585
	Retail trade	66,185	1,160,612	1,236,186
52	Building materials, hardware, garden supply, and mobile home dealers	3,775	46,922	62,871
521	Lumber and other building materials dealers	1,099	29,087	39,769
523	Paint, glass, and wallpaper stores	636	3,772	6,025
525	Hardware stores	835	6,258	7,415
526	Retail nurseries, lawn and garden supply stores	839	5,464	6,371
527	Mobile home dealers	364	2,339	3,292
53	General merchandise stores	931	138,876	144,285
531	Department stores	364	124,271	130,638
533	Variety stores	241	5,672	5,571
539	Miscellaneous general merchandise stores	324	8,932	8,076
54	Food stores	5,325	206,117	209,626
541	Grocery stores	3,102	190,034	194,719
542	Meat and fish markets and freezer provisioners	602	3,481	3,819
543	Fruit and vegetable markets	271	1,847	1,980
544	Candy, nut, and confectionery stores	158	1,103	748
545	Dairy products stores	44	1,070	928
546	Retail bakeries	778	6,213	5,086
549	Miscellaneous food stores	367	2,367	2,347

See footnotes at end of table.   Continued . . .

Florida Statistical Abstract 1991

Table 16.43. WHOLESALE AND RETAIL TRADE: AVERAGE MONTHLY REPORTING UNITS
EMPLOYMENT, AND PAYROLL COVERED BY UNEMPLOYMENT COMPENSATION LAW
BY INDUSTRY IN FLORIDA, 1990 (Continued)

SIC code	Industry	Number of re- porting units	Number of employees	Payroll ($1,000)
	Retail trade (Continued)			
55	Automotive dealers and gasoline service stations	8,926	116,400	210,932
551	Motor vehicle dealers (new and used)	1,131	53,489	125,070
552	Motor vehicle dealers (used only)	1,313	5,301	8,985
553	Auto and home supply stores	2,004	19,024	30,009
554	Gasoline service stations	3,325	30,306	31,627
555	Boat dealers	708	4,652	7,927
556	Recreational vehicle dealers	170	1,797	3,516
557	Motorcycle dealers	198	1,183	1,917
559	Automotive dealers, NEC	75	645	1,881
56	Apparel and accessory stores	6,508	64,110	59,496
561	Men's and boys' clothing and accessory stores	549	3,855	5,046
562	Women's clothing stores	2,430	24,265	20,232
563	Women's accessory and specialty stores	335	2,311	2,117
564	Children's and infants' wear stores	249	1,179	927
565	Family clothing stores	653	14,393	13,581
566	Shoe stores	1,293	12,335	11,677
569	Miscellaneous apparel and accessory stores	997	5,770	5,915
57	Home furniture, furnishings, and equipment stores	7,392	55,086	85,598
571	Home furniture and furnishings store	5,049	35,465	53,492
572	Household appliance stores	592	3,856	6,359
573	Radio, television, and computer stores	1,750	15,764	25,747
58	Eating and drinking places	17,245	393,584	292,930
59	Miscellaneous retail	16,083	139,517	170,448
591	Drug stores and proprietary stores	1,360	40,233	51,004
592	Liquor stores	712	4,922	4,697
593	Used merchandise stores	946	3,447	3,762
594	Miscellaneous shopping goods stores	6,697	47,834	51,420
5941	Sporting goods and bicycle shops	1,527	9,402	11,024
5942	Book stores	484	3,982	3,470
5943	Stationery stores	250	2,327	3,428
5944	Jewelry stores	1,522	8,367	12,856
5945	Hobby, toy, and game shops	450	5,892	4,732
5946	Camera and photographic supply stores	151	1,299	1,876
5947	Gift, novelty, and souvenir shops	1,926	12,451	10,431
5948	Luggage and leather goods stores	102	885	1,078
5949	Sewing, needlework, and piece goods stores	283	3,226	2,525
596	Nonstore retailers	723	11,634	17,692
598	Fuel dealers	370	3,627	6,315
599	Retail stores, NEC	5,273	27,819	35,558

NEC Not elsewhere classified.
Note: Totals on county employment tables may not match totals in this table due
to rounding.
Source: State of Florida, Department of Labor and Employment Security, Bureau of
Labor Market Information, "Employment, Wages, and Contributions Report" (ES-202),
unpublished data.

Florida Statistical Abstract 1991

Table 16.44. WHOLESALE TRADE: AVERAGE MONTHLY REPORTING UNITS, EMPLOYMENT, AND
PAYROLL COVERED BY UNEMPLOYMENT COMPENSATION LAW IN THE STATE AND COUNTIES
OF FLORIDA, 1990

County	Number of reporting units	Number of employees	Payroll ($1,000)	County	Number of reporting units	Number of employees	Payroll ($1,000)
			Wholesale trade (SIC codes 50-51)				
Florida	29,947	293,090	691,975	Lafayette	5	27	53
				Lake	195	1,351	2,529
Alachua	227	2,280	4,255	Lee	489	4,324	8,439
Baker	7	38	53	Leon	297	3,049	6,739
Bay	196	1,796	2,899	Levy	31	151	227
Bradford	17	84	109	Liberty	(D)	(D)	(D)
Brevard	476	4,567	9,938	Madison	17	122	155
Broward	3,396	29,680	72,935	Manatee	216	1,923	3,866
Calhoun	(D)	(D)	(D)	Marion	297	3,953	7,428
Charlotte	84	372	792	Martin	144	848	1,936
Citrus	55	358	472	Monroe	102	580	1,075
Clay	127	764	1,595	Nassau	48	316	665
Collier	240	1,539	3,684	Okaloosa	154	989	1,744
Columbia	81	764	1,215	Okeechobee	30	282	493
Dade	7,624	69,582	163,284	Orange	1,932	25,966	59,287
De Soto	22	179	225	Osceola	86	795	1,612
Dixie	5	10	11	Palm Beach	1,606	14,188	38,717
Duval	1,520	23,792	59,325	Pasco	230	1,462	2,845
Escambia	420	4,400	8,468	Pinellas	1,640	14,709	32,129
Flagler	29	69	116	Polk	634	7,936	15,284
Franklin	20	122	151	Putnam	42	282	442
Gadsden	21	511	876	St. Johns	111	846	1,743
Gilchrist	12	70	89	St. Lucie	156	1,341	2,651
Glades	(D)	(D)	(D)	Santa Rosa	85	396	701
Gulf	7	19	27	Sarasota	517	3,684	7,684
Hamilton	7	28	32	Seminole	731	4,593	10,403
Hardee	26	313	365	Sumter	21	187	250
Hendry	20	130	309	Suwannee	35	261	430
Hernando	72	437	711	Taylor	21	144	264
Highlands	71	545	810	Union	7	32	34
Hillsborough	2,290	33,818	83,772	Volusia	427	3,643	6,551
Holmes	12	47	58	Wakulla	14	31	64
Indian River	123	584	3,321	Walton	24	147	180
Jackson	50	777	1,050	Washington	15	135	154
Jefferson	14	53	66	Statewide 1/	2,307	16,585	54,071

(D) Data withheld to avoid disclosure of information about individual firms.
  1/ Reporting units without a fixed location within the state or of unknown county
location.
  Note: For a list of three-digit code industries included see Table 16.43.

  Source: State of Florida, Department of Labor and Employment Security, Bureau of
Labor Market Information, "Employment, Wages, and Contributions Report" (ES-202),
unpublished data.

Florida Statistical Abstract 1991

Table 16.45. RETAIL TRADE: AVERAGE MONTHLY REPORTING UNITS, EMPLOYMENT
AND PAYROLL COVERED BY UNEMPLOYMENT COMPENSATION LAW IN THE STATE
AND COUNTIES OF FLORIDA, 1990

County	Number of reporting units	Number of employees	Payroll ($1,000)	County	Number of reporting units	Number of employees	Payroll ($1,000)
			Retail trade (SIC codes 52-59)				
Florida	66,164	1,161,920	1,236,189	Lafayette	16	76	63
				Lake	755	10,245	10,020
Alachua	912	17,762	15,230	Lee	1,950	32,685	34,932
Baker	79	731	592	Leon	883	21,222	17,839
Bay	861	14,645	12,363	Levy	140	1,370	1,141
Bradford	105	1,229	1,046	Liberty	11	137	109
Brevard	1,852	34,343	32,994	Madison	81	795	737
Broward	6,888	118,777	136,296	Manatee	858	15,973	15,956
Calhoun	55	442	398	Marion	977	14,489	13,861
Charlotte	544	8,146	8,089	Martin	732	10,241	10,933
Citrus	418	5,786	5,121	Monroe	773	9,199	9,824
Clay	456	8,966	8,197	Nassau	224	2,852	2,460
Collier	1,185	15,412	17,512	Okaloosa	867	14,726	12,395
Columbia	246	3,567	3,142	Okeechobee	163	1,747	1,567
Dade	11,021	164,265	198,532	Orange	3,126	80,440	88,634
De Soto	93	1,227	1,020	Osceola	530	11,703	10,906
Dixie	53	483	397	Palm Beach	4,856	80,126	93,268
Duval	2,834	66,195	72,669	Pasco	1,004	17,522	16,352
Escambia	1,274	24,224	22,189	Pinellas	4,095	84,297	87,469
Flagler	119	1,534	1,374	Polk	1,646	34,525	38,614
Franklin	70	415	349	Putnam	265	3,330	3,159
Gadsden	161	1,747	1,581	St. Johns	519	6,768	6,051
Gilchrist	35	197	168	St. Lucie	673	10,210	10,341
Glades	17	122	96	Santa Rosa	291	3,885	3,023
Gulf	73	456	347	Sarasota	1,884	30,421	32,214
Hamilton	48	399	311	Seminole	1,185	23,604	23,692
Hardee	94	1,032	969	Sumter	127	1,720	1,364
Hendry	128	1,222	1,173	Suwannee	132	1,891	1,819
Hernando	389	5,130	4,561	Taylor	138	1,244	1,071
Highlands	355	5,059	4,677	Union	23	203	161
Hillsborough	3,564	81,184	85,784	Volusia	1,936	32,700	30,371
Holmes	59	511	404	Wakulla	48	481	339
Indian River	625	8,068	8,319	Walton	163	1,661	1,255
Jackson	204	2,537	2,266	Washington	66	627	460
Jefferson	52	463	387	Statewide 1/	158	2,529	5,236

1/ Reporting units without a fixed location within the state or of unknown county
location.
Note: For a list of three-digit code industries included see Table 16.43.

Source: State of Florida, Department of Labor and Employment Security, Bureau of
Labor Market Information, "Employment, Wages, and Contributions Report" (ES-202),
unpublished data.

Table 16.81. GROSS AND TAXABLE SALES: SALES REPORTED TO THE DEPARTMENT OF REVENUE BY KIND OF BUSINESS IN FLORIDA, 1989 AND 1990

Code	Description	Gross sales ($1,000) 1989	Gross sales ($1,000) 1990	Taxable sales ($1,000) 1989	Taxable sales ($1,000) 1990
	Total	289,076,440	303,465,606	122,788,168	127,283,855
	Food and beverage group	36,092,389	38,539,862	18,964,793	20,133,108
01	Grocery stores	20,727,183	22,109,463	6,771,680	7,003,534
02	Meat markets, poultry	343,026	345,718	8,473	9,272
03	Seafood dealers	184,225	159,987	19,334	15,049
04	Vegetable and fruit markets	260,149	172,618	34,142	31,639
05	Bakeries	338,586	307,172	75,275	70,728
06	Delicatessens	256,855	347,394	106,813	131,975
07	Candy and confectionery	928,647	964,060	334,397	353,651
08	Restaurants and lunchrooms	11,350,528	12,366,971	10,045,590	10,898,837
09	Taverns, nightclubs, liquor stores	1,703,191	1,766,481	1,569,088	1,618,422
	Apparel group	4,913,691	5,296,288	4,001,770	4,381,429
10	Clothing stores, alterations	3,922,640	4,407,955	3,355,124	3,758,195
11	Shoe stores	960,058	879,566	640,619	617,388
12	Hat shops	30,993	8,767	6,027	5,846
	General merchandise group	25,367,853	27,475,135	17,530,279	19,143,649
13	Department stores	7,401,693	8,096,377	6,891,357	7,464,572
14	Variety stores	3,435,826	4,023,417	2,819,963	3,431,104
15	Drug stores	4,598,213	5,036,077	1,849,360	2,052,296
16	Jewelry, leather, sporting goods	2,551,617	2,664,596	1,656,593	1,790,150
17	Feed, seed, and fertilizer stores	612,445	529,813	104,588	99,890
18	Hardware, paints, machinery	2,869,003	2,771,388	1,577,534	1,517,901
19	Farm implements and supplies	500,648	486,981	250,347	222,215
20	General merchandise stores	2,696,838	3,098,483	1,926,190	2,076,031
21	Second-hand stores	302,986	343,956	184,443	207,318
22	Dry good stores	398,585	424,047	269,904	282,169

Continued . . .

See footnotes at end of table.

Table 16.81. GROSS AND TAXABLE SALES: SALES REPORTED TO THE DEPARTMENT OF REVENUE BY KIND OF BUSINESS IN FLORIDA 1989 AND 1990 (Continued)

Code	Kind of business Description	Gross sales ($1,000) 1989	1990	Taxable sales ($1,000) 1989	1990
	Automotive group	47,571,764	48,149,872	22,694,076	21,512,772
23	Motor vehicle dealers	30,769,608	30,553,711	17,054,470	15,847,136
24	Auto accessories, tires, parts	3,700,982	3,650,800	1,747,682	1,819,377
25	Filling and service stations	6,055,702	6,909,293	905,378	932,891
26	Garages, auto paint and body shops	2,501,356	2,584,963	1,511,345	1,567,097
27	Aircraft dealers	2,207,696	2,363,357	277,613	260,989
28	Motorboat and yacht dealers	2,336,421	2,087,749	1,197,589	1,085,282
	Furniture and appliances group	14,608,724	15,107,911	7,199,581	7,675,106
29	Furniture stores, new and used	3,552,587	3,674,320	2,668,340	2,676,548
30	Household appliances, dinnerware, etc.	1,950,531	1,967,709	979,268	1,038,514
31	Store and office equipment	3,853,157	3,580,019	1,493,779	1,634,434
32	Music stores, radios, televisions	5,252,449	5,885,863	2,058,194	2,325,610
	Lumber, builders, contractors group	16,040,536	14,744,603	8,662,702	8,023,610
33	Building contractors	1,939,892	1,754,696	257,743	210,225
34	Heating and air conditioning	1,456,465	1,328,064	505,750	478,729
35	Electrical and plumbing	3,003,549	2,542,808	1,562,731	1,186,545
36	Decorating, painting, papering	907,433	904,164	560,417	569,264
37	Roofing and sheet metal	404,234	356,163	179,898	177,040
38	Lumber and building materials	8,328,964	7,858,709	5,596,163	5,401,806
	General classification group	144,481,040	154,151,207	43,734,678	46,413,670
39	Hotels, apartment houses, etc. 1/	6,430,018	7,810,361	5,835,670	6,250,370
40	Auctioneers and commission dealers	1,403,753	1,396,484	335,273	330,823
41	Barber and beauty shops	834,333	862,669	304,864	309,255
42	Book stores	535,480	579,738	356,456	388,729
43	Cigar stands and tobacco shops	64,980	48,452	22,627	23,138
44	Florists	507,509	459,017	260,441	280,403
45	Fuel and L.P. gas dealers	5,905,041	5,965,106	354,983	349,326

See footnotes at end of table.

Continued . . .

Table 16.81. GROSS AND TAXABLE SALES: SALES REPORTED TO THE DEPARTMENT OF REVENUE BY KIND OF BUSINESS IN FLORIDA 1989 AND 1990 (Continued)

Code	Kind of business — Description	Gross sales ($1,000) 1989	Gross sales ($1,000) 1990	Taxable sales ($1,000) 1989	Taxable sales ($1,000) 1990
	General classification group (Cont.)				
46	Funeral directors and monuments	169,304	179,529	62,277	60,579
47	Scrap metal, junk yards	392,721	357,418	35,338	29,175
48	Itinerant vendors	307,722	297,448	101,293	98,463
49	Laundry and cleaning services	437,912	447,208	174,318	178,589
50	Machine shops and foundries	612,083	606,008	188,149	182,523
51	Horse, cattle, pet dealers	1,417,103	1,993,177	638,911	800,777
52	Photographers, photo and art supplies	1,124,046	1,233,174	637,803	667,715
53	Shoe repair shops	21,062	21,940	17,110	17,937
54	Storage and warehousing	232,892	294,937	118,489	139,482
55	Gift, card, novelty shops	1,908,621	2,078,376	1,330,276	1,431,090
56	Newsstands	135,131	125,967	46,271	48,135
57	Social clubs and associations	467,896	497,553	355,739	368,111
58	Industrial machinery equipment	5,113,579	5,288,032	1,604,794	1,588,649
59	Admissions	2,153,833	2,444,683	2,062,886	2,328,195
60	Holiday season vendors	26,050	29,308	22,234	20,455
61	Rental of tangible property	3,683,427	3,860,625	2,127,751	2,307,023
62	Fabrication, sales of cabinets, etc.	1,914,578	1,811,470	781,641	716,778
63	Manufacturing and mining	25,211,996	26,386,702	2,904,054	2,968,687
64	Bottlers, softdrinks, etc.	1,094,365	1,051,030	68,601	70,283
65	Pawn shops	70,556	67,713	42,399	45,752
66	Communications	7,355,020	7,864,369	4,436,478	4,698,034
67	Transportation	325,700	269,270	73,014	77,891
68	Graphic arts and printing	2,826,654	3,046,839	1,062,944	1,126,638
69	Insurance, banking, etc.	671,159	661,930	200,521	181,608
70	Sanitary and industrial supplies	1,741,270	1,869,931	359,480	397,340
71	Packaging materials and paper boxes	1,204,779	1,155,360	141,468	137,783
72	Repair of tangible personal property	2,592,032	2,662,734	721,311	773,288
73	Advertising	1,332,872	1,281,850	231,408	229,726

Continued . . .

See footnotes at end of table.

Table 16.81. GROSS AND TAXABLE SALES: SALES REPORTED TO THE DEPARTMENT OF REVENUE BY KIND OF BUSINESS IN FLORIDA 1989 AND 1990 (Continued)

Kind of business		Gross sales ($1,000)		Taxable sales ($1,000)	
Code	Description	1989	1990	1989	1990
	General classification group (Cont.)				
74	Top soil, clay, sand, fill dirt	891,664	809,925	267,627	249,519
75	Trade stamp redemption centers	16,774	4,787	13,906	2,057
76	Nurseries and landscaping	1,100,281	1,164,965	375,252	391,143
77	Vending machines	285,985	297,524	193,952	207,684
78	Importing and exporting	5,387,081	6,315,139	117,851	127,701
79	Medical, dental, surgical, optical	1,891,123	2,173,247	283,062	298,744
80	Wholesale dealers	30,043,219	32,810,472	2,846,675	3,217,052
81	Schools and colleges	99,894	85,189	39,404	39,350
82	Office space and commercial rentals	8,592,704	9,417,684	6,946,198	7,506,527
83	Parking lots, boat docking, storage	338,561	328,848	248,791	241,071
84	Utilities, electricity or gas	9,753,827	10,187,539	2,980,053	3,080,005
86	Dual uses of special fuels	65,419	86,094	6,300	9,920
88	Public works, governmental contractor	64,936	76,267	5,829	9,765
90	Flea markets	90,740	104,219	67,469	75,705
91	Fairs, concessions, carnivals	8,808	8,802	5,161	5,201
92	Other professional services	2,407,881	1,701,654	111,739	38,224
93	Other personal services	643,510	474,168	142,861	121,517
94	Other industrial services	292,038	317,470	52,964	56,648
98	Commercial fisherman	21,978	10,937	1,205	1,471
99	Miscellaneous	2,259,141	2,769,871	1,011,107	1,111,616

1/ Includes sales reported under categories 85 and 89 which are for hotels, rooming houses and apartments.

Note: Data are sales reported to the Florida Department of Revenue for the 5 percent regular sales tax, 5 percent use tax, and 3 percent vehicle and farm equipment sales tax for January 1989. In February 1988 the regular sales and use tax increased to 6 percent; this increase is reflected in the collections from March 1988 through December 1990. Sales occurred, for the most part, from December 1, 1988 through November 30, 1990. Data are not comparable with retail sales reported by the U.S. Bureau of the Census. Data are unaudited.

Source: State of Florida, Department of Revenue, unpublished data.

Table 16.82.   GROSS AND TAXABLE SALES: SALES REPORTED TO THE DEPARTMENT OF REVENUE
IN THE STATE AND COUNTIES OF FLORIDA, 1988, 1989, AND 1990

(rounded to thousands of dollars)

County	Gross sales			Taxable sales		
	1988	1989	1990	1988	1989	1990
Florida	277,485,847	289,076,440	303,465,606	119,103,872	122,788,168	127,283,855
Alachua	2,360,416	2,419,988	2,604,768	1,302,494	1,320,264	1,382,979
Baker	116,430	128,899	137,108	48,877	52,088	60,332
Bay	1,926,886	1,951,744	2,849,439	1,098,600	1,097,110	1,202,933
Bradford	209,787	235,414	257,953	94,924	103,757	102,899
Brevard	5,822,442	6,620,135	7,049,158	2,762,320	2,909,587	3,019,848
Broward	27,796,128	27,935,888	29,318,868	12,206,926	12,544,887	12,872,142
Calhoun	77,574	78,283	89,606	36,541	36,464	40,704
Charlotte	1,092,521	1,248,957	1,331,389	662,080	764,313	846,978
Citrus	775,083	814,467	879,481	463,928	494,320	533,936
Clay	1,210,009	1,245,515	1,331,990	637,401	669,386	711,884
Collier	2,784,481	3,043,700	3,213,882	1,691,847	1,861,079	1,969,000
Columbia	620,240	679,866	674,095	294,713	300,404	310,462
Dade	44,337,829	46,858,387	48,389,729	17,657,647	17,512,645	17,566,759
De Soto	204,254	225,486	242,566	102,464	108,746	117,441
Dixie	93,425	95,467	100,726	33,868	31,780	34,013
Duval	16,853,775	17,252,466	17,469,686	6,469,119	6,330,206	6,513,910
Escambia	4,217,348	4,412,438	4,575,855	1,954,371	1,925,945	2,020,768
Flagler	293,084	259,541	319,737	133,380	144,217	148,698
Franklin	64,269	59,644	67,043	34,475	34,031	39,512
Gadsden	629,801	572,345	536,826	134,993	139,692	143,644
Gilchrist	43,814	43,574	48,385	21,662	20,183	24,163
Glades	41,783	43,764	45,240	18,934	21,873	20,979
Gulf	83,704	135,878	154,462	38,312	35,100	41,914
Hamilton	101,769	86,879	93,052	32,762	31,117	42,820
Hardee	213,071	257,313	222,482	100,087	100,821	97,703
Hendry	512,852	605,505	608,609	141,860	150,720	150,303
Hernando	856,223	965,332	969,038	428,712	480,495	485,658
Highlands	733,187	763,857	792,098	399,527	429,021	443,696
Hillsborough	20,737,746	21,405,870	21,908,717	8,503,873	8,556,432	8,925,381
Holmes	85,721	88,332	87,045	41,752	44,010	44,622
Indian River	1,379,883	1,451,040	1,465,043	704,760	739,511	735,080
Jackson	428,964	459,293	501,842	208,695	212,467	223,257
Jefferson	63,319	64,210	75,031	27,456	26,598	32,210
Lafayette	30,631	33,485	39,465	10,733	9,608	14,094
Lake	1,919,581	1,986,492	2,054,467	965,564	1,005,880	1,036,810
Lee	5,556,319	5,809,780	6,126,005	3,375,709	3,582,772	3,724,535
Leon	3,049,640	3,168,863	3,225,423	1,641,494	1,657,492	1,751,791
Levy	175,250	195,361	211,149	95,257	102,960	115,519

See footnotes at end of table.   Continued . . .

Table 16.82.   GROSS AND TAXABLE SALES: SALES REPORTED TO THE DEPARTMENT OF REVENUE
    IN THE STATE AND COUNTIES OF FLORIDA, 1988, 1989, AND 1990 (Continued)

(rounded to thousands of dollars)

County	Gross sales			Taxable sales		
	1988	1989	1990	1988	1989	1990
Liberty	29,847	30,000	36,940	10,323	9,475	13,186
Madison	165,917	141,057	153,895	45,945	48,126	52,620
Manatee	3,311,235	3,456,761	3,535,664	1,544,912	1,614,723	1,617,601
Marion	3,023,424	3,367,122	3,509,639	1,362,431	1,560,609	1,534,505
Martin	1,737,434	1,867,427	1,893,569	1,000,153	1,079,121	1,097,606
Monroe	1,417,138	1,520,768	1,636,211	965,130	1,037,337	1,093,452
Nassau	740,758	825,158	755,162	222,954	238,386	250,686
Okaloosa	1,748,747	1,798,352	1,916,682	1,005,099	1,036,357	1,097,199
Okeechobee	334,628	380,702	386,758	170,295	189,911	186,420
Orange	20,684,652	22,199,060	23,516,920	9,712,624	10,638,687	11,507,207
Osceola	1,837,824	2,044,507	2,703,442	1,010,098	1,079,961	1,232,694
Palm Beach	16,233,111	16,287,026	16,906,729	8,988,680	9,190,978	9,260,347
Pasco	2,635,256	2,686,783	2,784,280	1,449,088	1,508,777	1,549,898
Pinellas	14,460,238	14,967,283	15,662,251	7,065,867	7,197,390	7,427,990
Polk	7,336,563	7,600,488	8,182,834	3,144,637	3,306,562	3,273,096
Putnam	638,827	671,898	715,050	278,689	282,330	289,272
St. Johns	989,347	1,044,546	1,124,345	567,108	608,783	640,666
St. Lucie	1,907,867	2,030,310	2,012,766	1,038,405	1,086,388	1,073,938
Santa Rosa	651,599	687,583	744,311	277,591	266,474	289,050
Sarasota	4,811,787	4,887,326	5,155,424	2,728,196	2,802,280	2,855,214
Seminole	4,336,594	4,544,836	4,931,004	2,293,416	2,380,572	2,484,382
Sumter	245,330	243,317	278,362	114,246	120,671	119,461
Suwannee	295,011	292,487	368,979	132,843	151,739	140,554
Taylor	274,995	278,324	247,408	106,177	106,511	108,127
Union	68,584	70,786	120,102	24,177	22,651	26,148
Volusia	5,057,919	5,339,093	5,472,674	2,791,914	2,904,493	3,007,878
Wakulla	94,638	109,386	128,977	35,866	33,999	39,636
Walton	251,040	284,718	324,411	144,698	175,085	194,919
Washington	97,737	98,257	107,533	38,865	37,321	42,041
Out of state	34,042,195	35,259,052	37,478,817	6,065,411	6,322,317	6,899,540
In/out state 1/	526,368	358,572	607,011	189,917	162,175	329,148

1/ Reports that have not yet been allocated to counties.
    Note: Data are sales reported to the Florida Department of Revenue for the 5
percent regular sales tax, 5 percent use tax, and 3 percent vehicle and farm equipment sales tax for January 1988.   In February 1988 the regular sales and use tax
increased to 6 percent; this increase is reflected in the collections from March
1988 through December 1990. Sales occurred, for the most part, December 1, 1987
through November 30, 1990.   Kind of business data for counties are available from
the Bureau of Economic and Business Research, University of Florida.   Data are not
comparable with retail sales reported by the U.S. Bureau of the Census.   Data are
unaudited.

    Source: State of Florida, Department of Revenue, unpublished data.

Florida Statistical Abstract 1991

FINANCE, INSURANCE AND REAL ESTATE

FDIC - Insured Commercial Banks, December 31, 1988 and 1989

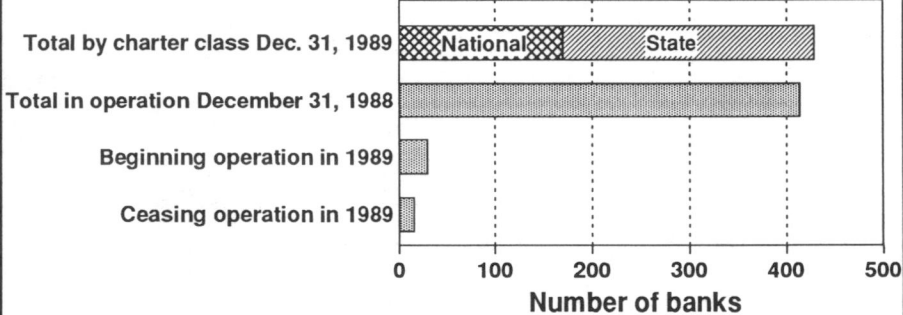

Number of banks

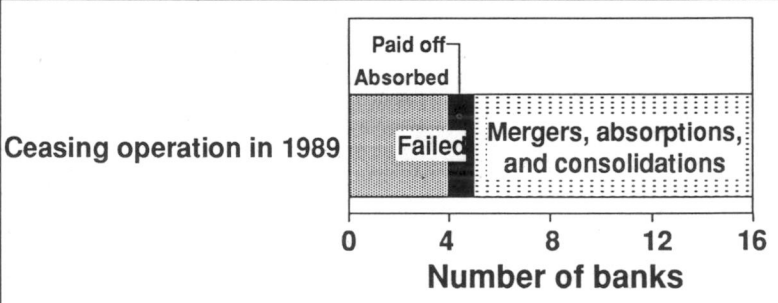

Number of banks

Source: Table 17.07

TABLES LISTED BY MAJOR HEADINGS

TABLES LISTED BY MAJOR HEADINGS

Table 17.07. BANKING OFFICES: NUMBER OF FDIC-INSURED COMMERCIAL BANKS AND TRUST
   COMPANIES BY CHARTER CLASS AND OFFICE TYPE IN FLORIDA, DECEMBER 31, 1988 AND
   1989

		Banks			
Charter class	All offices	Total	Unit banks	Banks oper- ating branches	Branches
Total by charter class	3,310	429	160	269	2,881
National	2,270	171	65	106	2,099
State	1,040	258	95	163	782
Member of Federal Reserve System	195	67	31	36	128
Nonmember of Federal Reserve System	845	191	64	127	654
Total in operation					
December 31, 1988	3,098	415	(NA)	(NA)	2,683
December 31, 1989	3,310	429	(NA)	(NA)	2,881
Net change during 1989	212	14	(NA)	(NA)	198
Beginning operation in 1989	292	30	(NA)	(NA)	262
Ceasing operation in 1989	80	16	(NA)	(NA)	64
Failed banks	50	5	(NA)	(NA)	45
Absorbed	4	4	(NA)	(NA)	(X)
Paid off	1	1	(NA)	(NA)	(X)
Mergers, absorptions, and consolidations	11	11	(NA)	(NA)	(X)
Other	19	0	(NA)	(NA)	19

(NA) Not available.
(X) Not applicable.

Table 17.08. BANKING ACTIVITY: NUMBER OF FDIC-INSURED COMMERCIAL BANKS AND TRUST
   COMPANIES AND AMOUNT OF ASSETS AND DEPOSITS BY ASSET SIZE IN FLORIDA
   DECEMBER 31, 1989

(amounts in millions of dollars)

Size of assets	Number of banks	Assets	Deposits
All banks	429	133,083	111,410
Less than $25 million	104	1,542	1,248
$25 to $50 million	106	3,761	3,355
$50 to $100 million	81	5,551	4,887
$100 to $300 million	82	13,821	12,271
$300 to $500 million	18	7,191	6,330
$500 million to $1 billion	19	13,633	12,050
$1 to $3 billion	11	20,535	16,906
$3 to $10 billion	6	39,205	32,010
$10 billion or more	2	27,843	22,353

   Note: Asset size of bank determined from domestic and foreign consolidated
assets.

   Source for Tables 17.07 and 17.08: Federal Deposit Insurance Corporation,
Statistics on Banking, 1989.

Florida Statistical Abstract 1991

Table 17.09. BANKING ACTIVITY: NUMBER OF FDIC-INSURED COMMERCIAL BANKS AND BANKING
OFFICES AND AMOUNT OF DEPOSITS IN THE STATE AND COUNTIES OF FLORIDA
JUNE 30, 1989

County	Number of banks 1/	Number of banking offices 2/	Amount of deposits ($1,000)		
			Total	IPC	Other 3/
Florida	429	3,175	102,212,898	96,473,040	5,739,866
Alachua	12	45	902,348	874,954	27,394
Baker	2	3	64,247	52,599	11,648
Bay	5	23	505,013	458,870	46,143
Bradford	3	5	85,879	78,808	7,073
Brevard	13	103	2,205,890	2,153,346	52,544
Broward	32	256	8,055,103	7,832,702	222,401
Calhoun	2	2	40,352	38,294	2,058
Charlotte	10	27	863,460	853,216	10,244
Citrus	7	28	715,127	683,707	31,420
Clay	8	22	378,495	345,036	33,459
Collier	17	48	1,708,232	1,660,270	47,962
Columbia	4	8	203,900	191,520	12,380
Dade	74	397	21,745,996	20,358,036	1,387,960
De Soto	3	5	151,606	142,954	8,652
Dixie	1	2	26,075	25,941	134
Duval	16	123	5,574,795	4,999,655	575,139
Escambia	17	68	1,722,979	1,555,326	167,653
Flagler	3	5	166,505	163,427	3,078
Franklin	2	7	40,582	37,322	3,260
Gadsden	5	11	180,287	169,451	10,836
Gilchrist	2	3	41,257	35,315	5,942
Glades	1	1	14,594	11,706	2,888
Gulf	2	4	44,414	39,691	4,723
Hamilton	1	1	29,688	23,893	5,795
Hardee	2	4	165,571	149,089	16,482
Hendry	3	10	151,459	133,253	18,206
Hernando	4	24	759,116	729,098	30,018
Highlands	6	17	625,442	613,204	12,238
Hillsborough	33	198	6,151,662	5,498,520	653,142
Holmes	2	3	61,405	58,634	2,771
Indian River	8	29	1,054,442	1,015,470	38,972
Jackson	5	13	219,398	204,901	14,497
Jefferson	2	2	57,780	55,935	1,845
Lafayette	1	1	22,402	19,483	2,919
Lake	10	41	1,301,474	1,277,915	23,559
Lee	19	97	3,072,584	2,843,802	228,782
Leon	14	46	1,218,772	1,080,394	138,378

See footnotes at end of table.   Continued . . .

Florida Statistical Abstract 1991

Table 17.09.   BANKING ACTIVITY: NUMBER OF FDIC-INSURED COMMERCIAL BANKS AND BANKING
OFFICES AND AMOUNT OF DEPOSITS IN THE STATE AND COUNTIES OF FLORIDA
JUNE 30, 1989 (Continued)

County	Number of banks 1/	Number of banking offices 2/	Amount of deposits ($1,000) Total	IPC	Other 3/
Levy	4	13	141,476	127,695	13,781
Liberty	1	1	16,570	14,572	1,998
Madison	2	4	72,458	66,337	6,121
Manatee	12	55	1,705,274	1,675,978	29,296
Marion	12	45	1,209,954	1,147,589	62,365
Martin	9	41	1,129,159	1,100,418	28,741
Monroe	8	33	754,371	689,255	65,116
Nassau	4	10	167,822	156,908	10,914
Okaloosa	12	40	891,564	785,975	105,589
Okeechobee	3	6	179,284	166,006	13,278
Orange	23	148	4,942,590	4,472,631	469,959
Osceola	9	20	559,684	530,254	29,430
Palm Beach	50	265	7,595,023	7,246,166	348,857
Pasco	14	85	2,079,464	2,039,385	40,079
Pinellas	28	261	7,960,045	7,705,762	254,283
Polk	15	118	2,745,646	2,668,212	77,433
Putnam	5	11	234,853	225,496	9,357
St. Johns	6	20	505,937	498,267	7,670
St. Lucie	8	26	651,218	608,161	43,057
Santa Rosa	7	18	375,592	340,844	34,748
Sarasota	19	107	3,695,614	3,619,312	76,302
Seminole	17	54	1,252,997	1,216,543	36,454
Sumter	2	5	111,964	104,779	7,185
Suwannee	4	5	150,295	142,264	8,031
Taylor	2	4	65,569	58,722	6,847
Union	1	1	27,435	25,011	2,424
Volusia	13	88	2,492,903	2,418,287	74,624
Wakulla	2	3	49,290	42,769	6,521
Walton	3	4	78,458	74,212	4,246
Washington	2	2	42,058	39,493	2,565

IPC Individuals, partnerships, and corporations.
1/ Number of banks in each county includes each bank operating at least one
office within the county, regardless of the location of its main office; therefore,
a bank operating a branch in a second county would be counted as a bank in each
county, but only once in the state total.
2/ Includes each location at which deposit business is transacted.
3/ Transaction, demand, and nontransaction deposits not included under IPC.
Source: Federal Deposit Insurance Corporation, *Data Book: Operating Banks and
Branches, June 30, 1989.*

Table 17.23. STATE CHARTERED BANKS AND TRUST COMPANIES: ASSETS, LIABILITIES
    INCOME, AND EXPENSES BY ASSET SIZE IN FLORIDA, DECEMBER 31, 1990

(in thousands of dollars)

Item	All banks	0-50 million	50-500 million	Over 500 million
Assets	37,247,099	3,672,125	15,176,551	18,398,423
Liabilities	34,659,179	3,298,149	3,372,207	17,337,407
Equity capital	2,587,920	373,976	10,938,859	1,061,016
Operating income	3,668,647	358,053	1,232,630	1,797,000
Operating expenses	3,438,808	355,486	1,491,228	1,681,727
Gains/losses on securities	420	199	1,057,043	-545
Net operating income	230,259	2,766	112,765	114,728
Net income 1/	175,518	-2,391	81,277	96,632

1/ After taxes and extraordinary items.
Note: Nondeposit trust companies and industrial savings banks are excluded.

Source: State of Florida, Office of the Comptroller, *Annual Report of the
Division of Banking, 1990.*

Table 17.24. FAILED BANKS: DEPOSITORS, DEPOSITS, AND DISBURSEMENTS IN FAILED BANKS
    REQUIRING DISBURSEMENTS BY THE FEDERAL DEPOSIT INSURANCE CORPORATION (FDIC)
    IN FLORIDA AND THE UNITED STATES, CUMULATIVE 1934 THROUGH 1989

Item	Florida	United States
Number of banks 1/	23	1,471
Payoff cases	5	401
Assumption cases	18	1,070
Number of depositors 2/	265,138	12,075,654
Payoff cases	10,302	964,262
Assumption cases	254,836	11,111,392
Deposits ($1,000)	2,717,841	90,799,033
Payoff cases	109,420	3,343,771
Assumption cases	2,608,421	87,455,262
Disbursements by FDIC ($1,000)	691,232	25,997,034
Principal disbursements		
Payoff cases	101,515	2,751,428
Assumption cases	589,717	23,245,606

1/ Does not include 23 banks throughout the United States with deposit transfers
to operating banks in 1989.
2/ In assumption cases, number of depositors refers to number of deposit
accounts.

Source: Federal Deposit Insurance Corporation, *1989 Annual Report,* and previous
editions.

Table 17.30. CREDIT UNIONS: FINANCIAL CONDITION OF STATE-CHARTERED CREDIT UNIONS
   IN FLORIDA, DECEMBER 31, 1990

(in thousands of dollars, except where indicated)

Item	Amount	Item	Amount
Number of institutions 1/	145	Gross income, total	276,488
Net loans	1,595,293	Operating expense, total	115,152
Assets, total	2,592,547	Cost of funds	141,952
Shares and deposits, total	2,412,677	Net income	19,384
Liabilities and equity,		Ratio of expense to $100	
total	2,592,547	gross income (dollars)	41.6

1/ Does not include credit unions in liquidation.

Table 17.31. INTERNATIONAL BANKS: NUMBER AND ASSETS OF AGENCIES BY NATION
   OF ORIGIN IN FLORIDA, DECEMBER 31, 1989 AND 1990

Nation of origin	December 1989		December 1990	
	Number	Assets ($1,000)	Number	Assets ($1,000)
Total	40	10,108,763	46	10,791,237
Argentina	1	110,681	1	111,840
Brazil	4	704,118	4	727,320
Cayman Islands	2	485,291	2	89,868
Canada	1	641,243	1	710,889
Columbia	1	157,151	1	168,330
Ecuador	1	97,081	1	96,264
England	3	1,424,928	4	1,956,225
France	3	918,240	3	883,474
Germany	2	1,874,545	2	1,816,355
Israel	3	680,183	3	721,744
Italy	1	244,429	1	275,809
Japan	1	297,988	3	411,198
Korea	(X)	(X)	1	15,651
Netherlands	1	303,517	1	360,054
Panama	1	207,217	1	226,617
Puerto Rico	1	228	1	167
Peru	1	99,387	1	152,868
Republic of Portugal	1	47,171	1	79,751
Spain	6	761,322	7	929,433
Switzerland	2	603,479	2	586,390
United States	1	28,249	1	15,330
Venezuela	3	422,315	4	455,660

(X) Not applicable.

Source for Tables 17.30 and 17.31: State of Florida, Office of the Comptroller,
Annual Report of the Division of Banking, 1990, and previous edition.

Table 17.33. MORTGAGE ACTIVITY: NUMBER AND VALUE OF NEW AND EXISTING RESIDENTIAL
PURCHASE LOANS IN SPECIFIED COUNTIES OF FLORIDA, 1990

	Value		Number of loans	
County	Total 1/	New 2/	Total 1/	New 2/
Alachua	85,957,583	24,737,972	1,038	277
Brevard	393,393,745	148,393,283	4,734	1,862
Broward	1,600,638,677	500,540,821	16,386	4,763
Charlotte	106,801,696	21,187,202	1,230	270
Citrus	27,303,598	4,972,033	343	71
Clay	98,681,160	41,782,805	1,161	511
Collier	400,197,361	155,708,819	3,544	1,473
Dade	1,752,552,371	493,911,665	17,743	5,313
De Soto	5,435,953	208,700	59	2
Duval	537,071,875	228,718,196	6,271	2,701
Escambia	91,097,491	23,418,043	1,114	297
Flagler	34,709,831	16,139,950	431	196
Hernando	39,992,715	12,986,881	513	167
Highlands	17,683,997	1,633,510	188	18
Hillsborough	632,247,078	199,434,885	6,584	2,045
Indian River	97,246,405	20,372,287	855	202
Lake	79,450,476	20,701,920	1,021	292
Lee	467,887,941	106,212,591	4,924	1,254
Leon	163,189,882	44,727,127	1,929	565
Manatee	181,923,493	53,437,261	2,093	600
Marion	54,950,986	12,284,521	699	194
Martin	139,308,350	40,141,990	1,290	396
Monroe	127,476,354	25,826,214	984	201
Nassau	31,944,725	9,770,436	324	97
Okaloosa	98,014,378	31,779,541	1,173	391
Orange	809,744,601	324,679,083	8,991	3,598
Osceola	139,636,500	79,212,088	1,900	1,079
Palm Beach	1,405,210,176	478,793,084	12,705	4,193
Pasco	104,031,221	32,374,377	1,307	397
Pinellas	692,837,554	109,238,518	7,525	1,077
Polk	148,462,707	29,618,037	1,863	408
Putnam	8,838,552	1,027,746	102	16
St. Johns	102,792,208	27,748,392	987	241
St. Lucie	149,008,227	75,195,390	1,879	930
Santa Rosa	43,949,956	14,148,771	572	189
Sarasota	404,253,892	83,323,210	3,770	716
Seminole	482,563,664	213,831,062	5,014	2,205
Sumter	2,283,218	0	22	0
Volusia	254,368,718	84,203,413	3,287	1,163
Walton	24,128,906	7,565,650	228	70

1/ Includes loans for both new and existing homes.
2/ Includes loans for only newly-constructed homes.

Source: TRW REDI Property Data, unpublished data. (Copyright.)

Florida Statistical Abstract 1991

Table 17.34. MORTGAGE ACTIVITY: CHARACTERISTICS OF CONVENTIONAL FIRST MORTGAGE
LOANS CLOSED ON SINGLE-FAMILY HOMES IN THE STATE AND SPECIFIED METROPOLITAN
STATISTICAL AREAS (MSAS) IN FLORIDA, ANNUAL AVERAGES 1987 THROUGH 1990

MSA	1987	1988	1989	1990
Mortgage loan amount ($1,000)				
Florida				
All purposes	74.3	75.5	78.0	87.0
Purchase of new homes	77.0	81.0	87.9	91.6
Purchase of existing homes	73.0	73.8	74.7	84.4
Bradenton	66.1	67.4	70.9	71.6
Daytona Beach	59.2	61.7	58.0	69.6
Ft. Lauderdale-Hollywood-Pompano Beach	75.9	78.7	84.2	93.9
Ft. Myers-Cape Coral	77.9	70.1	73.9	92.3
Ft. Pierce	59.1	65.9	73.0	72.4
Ft. Walton	81.1	123.9	69.2	91.8
Gainesville	67.9	72.4	81.1	83.3
Jacksonville	79.1	81.9	76.6	87.9
Lakeland-Winter Haven	73.2	62.1	78.4	92.4
Melbourne-Titusville-Palm Bay	65.2	67.3	71.8	82.1
Miami-Hialeah	77.4	77.4	84.0	100.7
Ocala	50.5	61.3	48.8	48.1
Orlando	80.7	81.0	82.6	84.3
Panama City	71.0	68.2	40.0	66.2
Pensacola	92.6	85.3	42.7	56.9
Sarasota	76.6	87.4	80.9	77.8
Tallahassee	69.4	74.7	70.3	89.1
Tampa-St. Petersburg-Clearwater	75.0	73.8	74.9	82.2
West Palm Beach-Boca Raton-Delray Beach	81.7	86.1	91.6	101.7
Effective interest rate (percentage)				
Florida				
All purposes	9.0	9.0	10.0	10.0
Purchase of new homes	8.9	8.8	9.8	9.9
Purchase of existing homes	9.0	9.0	10.0	10.0
Bradenton	8.7	8.7	10.1	9.9
Daytona Beach	8.9	9.1	10.1	10.0
Ft. Lauderdale-Hollywood-Pompano Beach	8.9	8.7	9.9	10.1
Ft. Myers-Cape Coral	9.0	8.5	9.9	9.8
Ft. Pierce	8.8	9.0	10.1	10.0
Ft. Walton	8.6	8.7	9.0	9.7
Gainesville	8.7	8.6	9.6	10.0
Jacksonville	9.2	9.2	9.8	10.1
Lakeland-Winter Haven	9.0	8.7	9.8	9.9
Melbourne-Titusville-Palm Bay	8.9	9.5	10.0	9.8
Miami-Hialeah	9.1	8.9	10.1	10.1
Ocala	8.8	9.2	10.3	10.3

See footnotes at end of table.   Continued . . .

Florida Statistical Abstract 1991

Table 17.34. MORTGAGE ACTIVITY: CHARACTERISTICS OF CONVENTIONAL FIRST MORTGAGE
    LOANS CLOSED ON SINGLE-FAMILY HOMES IN THE STATE AND SPECIFIED METROPOLITAN
    STATISTICAL AREAS (MSAS) IN FLORIDA, ANNUAL AVERAGES 1987 THROUGH 1990
    (Continued)

MSA	1987	1988	1989	1990
Effective interest rate (percentage) (Continued)				
Orlando	9.3	9.2	10.1	10.0
Panama City	9.2	9.0	9.3	8.9
Pensacola	8.9	8.9	10.3	10.4
Sarasota	8.4	8.7	9.7	9.4
Tallahassee	9.1	8.9	10.1	9.9
Tampa-St. Petersburg-Clearwater	9.0	8.9	9.9	10.0
West Palm Beach-Boca Raton-Delray Beach	9.1	9.0	10.0	9.9
Purchase price of home ($1,000)				
Florida				
All purposes	100.4	101.2	106.4	119.9
Purchase of new homes	105.7	110.2	119.5	123.9
Purchase of existing homes	98.2	98.3	101.6	116.6
Bradenton	90.6	86.6	93.3	101.2
Daytona Beach	82.9	83.7	81.3	93.6
Ft. Lauderdale-Hollywood-Pompano Beach	103.9	104.2	115.0	129.4
Ft. Myers-Cape Coral	107.0	96.7	102.2	131.0
Ft. Pierce	83.4	90.4	103.1	101.7
Ft. Walton	100.8	163.2	91.0	118.9
Gainesville	82.6	90.4	107.4	115.7
Jacksonville	101.2	107.5	98.3	111.7
Lakeland-Winter Haven	96.3	78.1	104.2	148.0
Melbourne-Titusville-Palm Bay	91.7	88.9	98.9	116.8
Miami-Hialeah	104.0	104.8	116.0	136.6
Ocala	66.2	79.0	65.4	63.5
Orlando	108.0	107.3	108.7	114.0
Panama City	89.9	94.1	41.0	89.5
Pensacola	114.2	110.2	58.3	69.1
Sarasota	102.8	119.1	113.5	115.4
Tallahassee	91.3	97.0	85.4	115.8
Tampa-St. Petersburg-Clearwater	100.3	97.1	100.6	110.0
West Palm Beach-Boca Raton-Delray Beach	111.9	119.6	127.7	144.6

Note: Data are annual weighted averages of loans for single-family mortgages
made by savings and loans associations, mortgage bankers, commercial banks, and
mutual savings banks. Data are collected by a survey conducted during the first
five working days of each month and are subject to sampling variability. Metropolitan areas are defined as MSAs or PMSAs depending on a given year. See the
Glossary for definitions and see the maps at the front of the book for area
boundaries. Some data are revised.

Source: U.S., Federal Home Loan Bank Board, unpublished data.

Florida Statistical Abstract 1991

Table 17.36.   SAVINGS AND LOAN ASSOCIATIONS: NUMBER OF ASSOCIATIONS AND OFFICES
AMOUNT OF SAVINGS, AND NUMBER OF OFFICES BY SIZE OF SAVINGS IN THE STATE AND
COUNTIES OF FLORIDA, JUNE 30, 1990

County	Number of associations	Number of association offices	Savings ($1,000)	Number of offices with savings of (millions of dollars)--				
				0-9.9	10-24.9	25-49.9	50-99.9	100 and over
Florida, total	147	1,695	68,064,372	149	540	561	330	99
No branches	27	27	1,076,193	2	5	11	7	1
1 branch	22	44	1,563,137	6	17	12	7	2
2 branches	10	29	1,062,414	6	8	7	6	2
3-5 branches	29	139	4,100,352	22	52	37	20	2
6-9 branches	12	95	3,296,650	20	26	21	16	3
10 or more branches	47	1,361	56,965,626	93	432	473	274	89
Alachua	4	10	272,544	1	4	4	1	0
Baker	1	1	11,195	0	1	0	0	0
Bay	4	16	398,561	5	7	2	1	1
Bradford	1	1	26,265	0	0	1	0	0
Brevard	8	43	1,129,238	5	21	16	1	0
Broward	41	251	14,561,924	15	54	70	70	40
Calhoun	1	1	10,681	0	1	0	0	0
Charlotte	15	28	869,135	8	7	8	5	0
Citrus	7	15	543,994	4	3	4	3	1
Clay	3	5	78,831	2	2	1	0	0
Collier	12	29	1,013,775	3	12	8	5	1
Columbia	3	4	87,268	1	2	1	0	0
Dade	37	213	12,843,348	4	34	59	75	29
De Soto	2	2	55,537	0	1	1	0	0
Dixie	1	1	6,855	1	0	0	0	0
Duval	9	34	885,826	3	17	10	4	0
Escambia	2	9	240,546	0	6	1	2	0
Flagler	4	5	174,190	0	2	2	1	0
Franklin	1	1	8,978	1	0	0	0	0
Gadsden	0	0	0	0	0	0	0	0
Gilchrist	1	1	6,315	1	0	0	0	0
Glades	0	0	0	0	0	0	0	0
Gulf	1	2	25,515	1	1	0	0	0
Hamilton	1	2	8,973	2	0	0	0	0
Hardee	1	1	39,311	0	0	1	0	0
Hendry	1	2	53,289	0	1	1	0	0
Hernando	12	19	595,650	3	7	6	3	0
Highlands	5	15	363,277	3	7	3	2	0
Hillsborough	20	45	1,232,329	10	15	14	4	1
Holmes	1	1	13,543	0	1	0	0	0
Indian River	9	20	693,446	1	6	9	3	1
Jackson	1	1	47,341	0	0	1	0	0
Jefferson	1	1	10,827	0	1	0	0	0

See footnote at end of table.   Continued . . .

Florida Statistical Abstract 1991

Table 17.36. SAVINGS AND LOAN ASSOCIATIONS: NUMBER OF ASSOCIATIONS AND OFFICES AMOUNT OF SAVINGS, AND NUMBER OF OFFICES BY SIZE OF SAVINGS IN THE STATE AND COUNTIES OF FLORIDA, JUNE 30, 1990 (Continued)

County	Number of associations	Number of association offices	Savings ($1,000)	Number of offices with savings of (millions of dollars)--				
				0- 9.9	10- 24.9	25- 49.9	50- 99.9	100 and over
Lafayette	1	1	4,073	1	0	0	0	0
Lake	8	17	575,109	0	7	8	2	0
Lee	17	62	1,791,820	8	23	27	3	1
Leon	4	14	465,320	1	5	5	3	0
Levy	1	3	33,242	1	2	0	0	0
Liberty	0	0	0	0	0	0	0	0
Madison	1	1	31,753	0	0	1	0	0
Manatee	17	38	1,261,492	2	13	14	9	0
Marion	5	20	769,276	1	4	11	3	1
Martin	13	32	624,104	8	16	7	1	0
Monroe	1	1	10,696	0	1	0	0	0
Nassau	2	3	54,214	1	1	1	0	0
Okaloosa	4	9	163,994	3	4	2	0	0
Okeechobee	3	3	76,437	0	2	1	0	0
Orange	14	43	1,464,034	3	16	16	5	2
Osceola	4	8	281,389	0	4	2	2	0
Palm Beach	44	227	8,606,056	14	74	84	46	9
Pasco	21	46	1,515,885	5	12	23	5	1
Pinellas	27	147	6,339,901	8	44	49	39	7
Polk	8	34	931,129	5	14	12	2	1
Putnam	2	5	155,962	1	1	2	1	0
St. Johns	4	7	161,275	0	4	3	0	0
St. Lucie	8	19	725,867	0	8	4	7	0
Santa Rosa	2	2	19,784	1	1	0	0	0
Sarasota	22	74	2,171,254	6	31	24	13	0
Seminole	13	26	757,031	0	13	9	4	0
Sumter	2	2	52,232	0	1	1	0	0
Suwannee	3	4	73,434	1	2	1	0	0
Taylor	1	1	43,208	0	0	1	0	0
Union	0	0	0	0	0	0	0	0
Volusia	11	62	2,499,747	3	23	28	5	3
Wakulla	0	0	0	0	0	0	0	0
Walton	1	4	70,267	2	1	1	0	0
Washington	1	1	25,880	0	0	1	0	0

Note: Data are for all SAIF-insured (Savings Associations Insurance Fund) savings and loan associations and are the result of a survey. Some data have been estimated. Figures indicate the activity of an association within specific counties whether the county offices are home or branch offices, although some institutions with centralized accounting do not have precise data on savings by office.

Source: U.S., Department of Treasury, Office of Thrift Supervision, *SAIF-Insured Savings Associations: Summary of Savings Accounts by Geographic Area*, June 30, 1990.

Table 17.38.   SAVINGS AND LOAN ASSOCIATIONS: MORTGAGE LOAN ACTIVITY AND
    COMMITMENTS OF FSLIC-INSURED THRIFTS IN FLORIDA AND THE UNITED
    STATES, 1988 AND 1989

(in millions of dollars)

Item	Florida 1988	Florida 1989	United States 1/ 1988	United States 1/ 1989
Net deposit gain	3,820	-483	44,026	-16,158
Net new deposits received	340	-4,108	8,381	73,558
Loans closed, total	12,183	9,923	240,297	189,458
Construction loans, total	3,721	2,897	37,244	29,658
1-4 dwelling units	2,821	2,424	24,049	21,368
5 or more dwelling units	225	110	5,506	3,811
Nonresidential	675	363	7,689	4,477
Permanent loans, total	8,462	7,026	203,052	159,798
1-4 dwelling units	6,558	5,870	159,066	133,348
5 or more dwelling units	242	156	17,337	11,324
Nonresidential	976	457	17,377	9,544
Land	686	544	9,272	5,585
Memo: refinancing loans	1,329	1,223	42,428	30,998
Cash loan repayments	8,151	7,657	127,134	117,847
Net secondary market purchases	325	-4,791	-51,132	-64,680
Gross purchases	4,223	2,544	55,012	41,172
Gross sales	3,898	7,335	106,144	105,853
Commitments to originate mortgage loans 2/				
Made during period	11,550	9,724	232,899	185,629
Outstanding, end of period	1,468	1,034	24,930	19,256
Mortgage loans foreclosed				
During period	907	934	18,859	18,189
Ratio	2.09	2.07	2.70	2.92
Delinquent mortgage loans				
End of Period	2,028	2,121	33,263	36,069
Ratio	4.43	4.95	4.58	4.92

1/ Includes data from the District of Columbia, Puerto Rico, Guam, and the Virgin
Islands.
2/ Commitments to builders, owners, or purchasers of real estate to close mortgage loans in the name of the reporting institution.
Note: Some data are revised.

Source: U.S., Department of Treasury, Office of Thrift Supervision, *Savings and
Home Financing Source Book, 1989.*

Florida Statistical Abstract 1991

Table 17.39. FINANCE, INSURANCE, AND REAL ESTATE: AVERAGE MONTHLY REPORTING UNITS
EMPLOYMENT, AND PAYROLL COVERED BY UNEMPLOYMENT COMPENSATION LAW BY INDUSTRY
IN FLORIDA, 1990

SIC code	Industry	Number of reporting units	Number of employees	Payroll ($1,000)
	Finance, insurance, and real estate	30,126	368,295	781,672
60	Depository institutions	1,657	113,725	213,047
601	Central reserve depository institutions	3	733	1,482
602	Commercial banks	668	72,891	136,212
603	Savings institutions	428	29,824	55,135
606	Credit unions	334	6,504	9,960
608	Foreign banking and branches and agencies of foreign banks	65	2,189	6,436
609	Functions related to depository banking	157	1,581	3,821
61	Nondepository credit institutions	1,984	26,013	58,439
611	Federal and federally-sponsored credit agencies	60	436	763
614	Personal credit institutions	555	7,314	15,866
615	Business credit institutions	150	7,893	16,611
616	Mortgage bankers and brokers	1,218	10,369	25,198
62	Security and commodity brokers, dealers, exchanges, and sevices	1,438	18,563	76,350
621	Security brokers, dealers, flotation companies	773	14,034	60,819
622	Commodity contracts brokers and dealers	(D)	(D)	(D)
623	Security and commodity exchanges	(D)	(D)	(D)
628	Services allied with the exchange of securities or commodities	599	4,185	13,851
63	Insurance carriers	1,812	59,451	144,585
631	Life insurance	569	20,373	47,760
632	Accident and health insurance and medical service plans	134	8,636	20,045
633	Fire, marine, and casualty insurance	452	22,640	60,066
635	Surety insurance	79	743	2,233
636	Title insurance	513	5,981	11,173
637	Pension, health, and welfare funds	51	477	1,327
639	Insurance carriers, NEC	11	600	1,981
64	Insurance agents, brokers, and service	6,506	39,293	88,467
65	Real estate	15,730	99,747	164,366
651	Real estate operators (except developers) and lessors	6,044	39,243	52,130
653	Real estate agents and managers	7,799	39,511	69,140
654	Title abstract offices	190	1,149	1,877
655	Land subdividers and developers	1,696	19,843	41,219
67	Holding and other investment offices	999	11,503	36,418
671	Holding offices	410	8,974	29,006
672	Investment offices	37	131	476
673	Trusts	116	731	1,924
679	Miscellaneous investing	436	1,665	5,011

NEC Not elsewhere classified.
(D) Data withheld to avoid disclosure of information about individual firms.
Note: Totals on county employment tables may not match totals in this table due
to rounding.
Source: State of Florida, Department of Labor and Employment Security, Bureau of
Labor Market Information, "Employment, Wages, and Contributions Report" (ES-202),
unpublished data.

Florida Statistical Abstract 1991

Table 17.40. DEPOSITORY INSTITUTIONS: AVERAGE MONTHLY REPORTING UNITS, EMPLOYMENT
AND PAYROLL COVERED BY UNEMPLOYMENT COMPENSATION LAW IN THE STATE AND COUNTIES
OF FLORIDA, 1990

County	Number of reporting units	Number of employees	Payroll ($1,000)	County	Number of reporting units	Number of employees	Payroll ($1,000)
			Depository institutions (SIC code 60)				
Florida	1,639	113,818	213,045	Lafayette	(D)	(D)	(D)
				Lake	21	1,020	1,688
Alachua	25	1,022	1,617	Lee	42	3,108	5,386
Baker	3	77	117	Leon	38	1,386	2,419
Bay	14	1,021	1,628	Levy	(D)	(D)	(D)
Bradford	5	99	173	Liberty	(D)	(D)	(D)
Brevard	30	1,993	2,958	Madison	(D)	(D)	(D)
Broward	102	12,256	23,886	Manatee	25	1,294	2,162
Calhoun	3	30	38	Marion	21	1,297	2,170
Charlotte	19	705	1,189	Martin	23	941	1,846
Citrus	12	510	818	Monroe	11	677	1,201
Clay	9	197	304	Nassau	10	180	314
Collier	30	1,868	3,641	Okaloosa	20	1,030	1,656
Columbia	8	212	320	Okeechobee	4	150	251
Dade	285	24,427	53,100	Orange	81	7,566	13,676
De Soto	4	102	147	Osceola	12	557	896
Dixie	(D)	(D)	(D)	Palm Beach	112	8,241	17,125
Duval	81	6,152	10,930	Pasco	33	1,597	2,547
Escambia	43	1,823	2,958	Pinellas	83	8,165	13,810
Flagler	5	97	153	Polk	40	2,433	3,791
Franklin	(D)	(D)	(D)	Putnam	10	261	410
Gadsden	8	151	252	St. Johns	8	369	635
Gilchrist	(D)	(D)	(D)	St. Lucie	19	991	1,680
Glades	0	0	0	Santa Rosa	9	251	333
Gulf	4	73	111	Sarasota	48	3,166	5,553
Hamilton	(D)	(D)	(D)	Seminole	29	977	1,618
Hardee	(D)	(D)	(D)	Sumter	(D)	(D)	(D)
Hendry	5	190	320	Suwannee	7	157	270
Hernando	12	623	1,022	Taylor	4	142	228
Highlands	10	436	734	Union	(D)	(D)	(D)
Hillsborough	105	9,656	17,852	Volusia	31	2,309	3,976
Holmes	(D)	(D)	(D)	Wakulla	(D)	(D)	(D)
Indian River	19	735	1,396	Walton	4	81	98
Jackson	9	254	434	Washington	(D)	(D)	(D)
Jefferson	4	53	86	Statewide 1/	9	21	81

(D) Data withheld to avoid disclosure of information about individual firms.
1/ Reporting units without a fixed location within the state or of unknown county
location.
Note: For a list of three-digit code industries included see Table 17.39.

Source: State of Florida, Department of Labor and Employment Security, Bureau of
Labor Market Information, "Employment, Wages, and Contributions Report" (ES-202),
unpublished data.

Florida Statistical Abstract 1991

Table 17.41. NONDEPOSITORY CREDIT INSTITUTIONS: AVERAGE MONTHLY REPORTING UNITS
EMPLOYMENT, AND PAYROLL COVERED BY UNEMPLOYMENT COMPENSATION LAW IN THE
STATE AND COUNTIES OF FLORIDA, 1990

County	Number of re- porting units	Number of employees	Payroll ($1,000)	County	Number of re- porting units	Number of employees	Payroll ($1,000)
			Nondepository credit institutions (SIC code 61)				
Florida	1,966	26,047	58,437	Lafayette	0	0	0
				Lake	10	44	75
Alachua	30	216	371	Lee	51	259	530
Baker	0	0	0	Leon	31	383	784
Bay	17	114	217	Levy	(D)	(D)	(D)
Bradford	(D)	(D)	(D)	Liberty	0	0	0
Brevard	42	189	404	Madison	(D)	(D)	(D)
Broward	(D)	(D)	(D)	Manatee	17	117	187
Calhoun	(D)	(D)	(D)	Marion	23	105	175
Charlotte	9	39	72	Martin	9	45	79
Citrus	(D)	(D)	(D)	Monroe	9	54	112
Clay	12	34	72	Nassau	(D)	(D)	(D)
Collier	22	61	189	Okaloosa	15	89	192
Columbia	7	25	37	Okeechobee	(D)	(D)	(D)
Dade	381	4,791	11,188	Orange	127	1,321	3,328
De Soto	(D)	(D)	(D)	Osceola	6	24	43
Dixie	0	0	0	Palm Beach	149	1,287	3,580
Duval	111	3,923	8,479	Pasco	14	40	70
Escambia	44	396	711	Pinellas	106	841	2,212
Flagler	(D)	(D)	(D)	Polk	33	245	420
Franklin	0	0	0	Putnam	5	24	34
Gadsden	6	15	18	St. Johns	6	37	82
Gilchrist	(D)	(D)	(D)	St. Lucie	20	65	95
Glades	(D)	(D)	(D)	Santa Rosa	9	40	65
Gulf	(D)	(D)	(D)	Sarasota	49	223	495
Hamilton	(D)	(D)	(D)	Seminole	65	356	799
Hardee	(D)	(D)	(D)	Sumter	(D)	(D)	(D)
Hendry	(D)	(D)	(D)	Suwannee	3	19	25
Hernando	(D)	(D)	(D)	Taylor	0	0	0
Highlands	6	18	25	Union	0	0	0
Hillsborough	170	2,656	5,738	Volusia	41	165	299
Holmes	(D)	(D)	(D)	Wakulla	0	0	0
Indian River	9	24	42	Walton	3	17	23
Jackson	7	76	95	Washington	(D)	(D)	(D)
Jefferson	(D)	(D)	(D)	Statewide 1/	43	259	880

(D) Data withheld to avoid disclosure of information about individual firms.
1/ Reporting units without a fixed location within the state or of unknown county
location.
Note: For a list of three-digit code industries included see Table 17.39.

Source: State of Florida, Department of Labor and Employment Security, Bureau of
Labor Market Information, "Employment, Wages, and Contributions Report" (ES-202),
unpublished data.

Florida Statistical Abstract 1991

Table 17.43. INSURANCE CARRIERS: AVERAGE MONTHLY REPORTING UNITS, EMPLOYMENT, AND PAYROLL COVERED BY UNEMPLOYMENT COMPENSATION LAW IN THE STATE AND COUNTIES OF FLORIDA, 1990

County	Number of reporting units	Number of employees	Payroll ($1,000)	County	Number of reporting units	Number of employees	Payroll ($1,000)
			Insurance carriers (SIC code 63)				
Florida	1,796	59,507	144,586	Lafayette	0	0	0
				Lake	15	113	278
Alachua	30	1,256	2,652	Lee	48	631	1,621
Baker	(D)	(D)	(D)	Leon	43	530	1,138
Bay	23	279	614	Levy	(D)	(D)	(D)
Bradford	(D)	(D)	(D)	Liberty	(D)	(D)	(D)
Brevard	39	492	1,338	Madison	(D)	(D)	(D)
Broward	152	3,987	10,907	Manatee	15	140	451
Calhoun	(D)	(D)	(D)	Marion	21	222	609
Charlotte	14	129	328	Martin	15	90	251
Citrus	8	86	159	Monroe	8	43	71
Clay	12	74	217	Nassau	(D)	(D)	(D)
Collier	23	193	507	Okaloosa	22	219	524
Columbia	7	34	87	Okeechobee	(D)	(D)	(D)
Dade	216	8,268	21,677	Orange	141	6,595	15,715
De Soto	(D)	(D)	(D)	Osceola	9	71	166
Dixie	(D)	(D)	(D)	Palm Beach	119	2,289	6,571
Duval	125	15,526	34,896	Pasco	23	237	639
Escambia	43	559	1,330	Pinellas	110	3,594	8,131
Flagler	(D)	(D)	(D)	Polk	45	1,871	4,381
Franklin	(D)	(D)	(D)	Putnam	(D)	(D)	(D)
Gadsden	(D)	(D)	(D)	St. Johns	11	47	90
Gilchrist	0	0	0	St. Lucie	24	230	545
Glades	0	0	0	Santa Rosa	7	27	82
Gulf	(D)	(D)	(D)	Sarasota	42	534	1,428
Hamilton	(D)	(D)	(D)	Seminole	37	714	1,880
Hardee	(D)	(D)	(D)	Sumter	(D)	(D)	(D)
Hendry	(D)	(D)	(D)	Suwannee	3	40	69
Hernando	11	89	204	Taylor	(D)	(D)	(D)
Highlands	(D)	(D)	(D)	Union	(D)	(D)	(D)
Hillsborough	170	8,899	21,483	Volusia	49	598	1,520
Holmes	(D)	(D)	(D)	Wakulla	(D)	(D)	(D)
Indian River	14	70	221	Walton	4	12	26
Jackson	8	75	176	Washington	(D)	(D)	(D)
Jefferson	(D)	(D)	(D)	Statewide 1/	33	365	1,144

(D) Data withheld to avoid disclosure of information about individual firms.
1/ Reporting units without a fixed location within the state or of unknown county location.
Note: For a list of three-digit code industries included see Table 17.39.

Source: State of Florida, Department of Labor and Employment Security, Bureau of Labor Market Information, "Employment, Wages, and Contributions Report" (ES-202), unpublished data.

Florida Statistical Abstract 1991

Table 17.44. INSURANCE AGENTS, BROKERS, AND SERVICE: AVERAGE MONTHLY REPORTING
   UNITS, EMPLOYMENT, AND PAYROLL COVERED BY UNEMPLOYMENT COMPENSATION LAW
   IN THE STATE AND COUNTIES OF FLORIDA, 1990

County	Number of reporting units	Number of employees	Payroll ($1,000)	County	Number of reporting units	Number of employees	Payroll ($1,000)
		Insurance agents, brokers, and service (SIC code 64)					
Florida	6,488	39,296	88,464	Lafayette	0	0	0
				Lake	55	215	376
Alachua	74	313	564	Lee	164	742	1,498
Baker	(D)	(D)	(D)	Leon	126	952	2,074
Bay	53	211	354	Levy	9	35	46
Bradford	6	23	36	Liberty	(D)	(D)	(D)
Brevard	134	669	1,321	Madison	(D)	(D)	(D)
Broward	742	4,087	9,598	Manatee	61	341	695
Calhoun	5	11	18	Marion	82	345	612
Charlotte	32	156	273	Martin	54	226	477
Citrus	28	128	210	Monroe	24	162	358
Clay	31	87	181	Nassau	14	47	69
Collier	73	388	909	Okaloosa	52	214	357
Columbia	11	51	64	Okeechobee	12	53	81
Dade	1,106	7,292	17,194	Orange	428	2,978	7,555
De Soto	8	27	34	Osceola	28	160	306
Dixie	(D)	(D)	(D)	Palm Beach	498	2,766	7,135
Duval	403	2,488	5,920	Pasco	92	352	479
Escambia	110	484	870	Pinellas	466	2,934	6,777
Flagler	6	37	53	Polk	175	979	1,884
Franklin	(D)	(D)	(D)	Putnam	18	93	156
Gadsden	9	40	74	St. Johns	20	87	156
Gilchrist	(D)	(D)	(D)	St. Lucie	49	163	275
Glades	0	0	0	Santa Rosa	25	54	106
Gulf	4	11	19	Sarasota	181	1,279	2,807
Hamilton	(D)	(D)	(D)	Seminole	157	1,027	2,593
Hardee	8	12	17	Sumter	8	26	37
Hendry	11	26	45	Suwannee	11	47	72
Hernando	31	151	233	Taylor	7	13	14
Highlands	19	94	175	Union	(D)	(D)	(D)
Hillsborough	473	4,693	9,718	Volusia	124	698	1,521
Holmes	(D)	(D)	(D)	Wakulla	(D)	(D)	(D)
Indian River	42	213	459	Walton	(D)	(D)	(D)
Jackson	9	41	63	Washington	4	15	18
Jefferson	7	20	27	Statewide 1/	80	455	1,384

(D) Data withheld to avoid disclosure of information about individual firms.
   1/ Reporting units without a fixed location within the state or of unknown county
location.
   Note: For a list of three-digit code industries included see Table 17.39.

   Source: State of Florida, Department of Labor and Employment Security, Bureau of
Labor Market Information, "Employment, Wages, and Contributions Report" (ES-202),
unpublished data.

Florida Statistical Abstract 1991

Table 17.45. REAL ESTATE: AVERAGE MONTHLY REPORTING UNITS, EMPLOYMENT, AND PAYROLL
    COVERED BY UNEMPLOYMENT COMPENSATION LAW IN THE STATE AND COUNTIES OF FLORIDA
    1990

County	Number of reporting units	Number of employees	Payroll ($1,000)	County	Number of reporting units	Number of employees	Payroll ($1,000)
			Real estate	(SIC code 65)			
Florida	15,708	99,855	164,365	Lafayette	0	0	0
				Lake	157	1,344	1,553
Alachua	218	1,405	1,762	Lee	555	4,090	6,524
Baker	4	9	6	Leon	219	1,226	1,528
Bay	145	971	1,003	Levy	14	42	40
Bradford	9	14	15	Liberty	0	0	0
Brevard	432	2,190	2,882	Madison	(D)	(D)	(D)
Broward	1,667	9,224	17,352	Manatee	221	1,389	1,767
Calhoun	(D)	(D)	(D)	Marion	163	873	1,129
Charlotte	137	731	1,112	Martin	195	786	1,666
Citrus	91	475	615	Monroe	138	426	632
Clay	78	478	649	Nassau	30	122	157
Collier	418	2,230	4,846	Okaloosa	172	1,086	1,212
Columbia	26	85	96	Okeechobee	27	54	67
Dade	2,866	19,275	33,706	Orange	839	6,654	12,712
De Soto	11	47	56	Osceola	118	762	1,099
Dixie	(D)	(D)	(D)	Palm Beach	1,393	9,437	18,170
Duval	669	4,954	8,393	Pasco	190	770	983
Escambia	211	1,366	1,307	Pinellas	1,063	6,726	9,253
Flagler	37	540	1,226	Polk	334	2,190	2,979
Franklin	5	17	18	Putnam	33	95	86
Gadsden	12	35	29	St. Johns	85	407	744
Gilchrist	(D)	(D)	(D)	St. Lucie	133	1,037	1,488
Glades	(D)	(D)	(D)	Santa Rosa	56	183	185
Gulf	6	12	9	Sarasota	468	2,124	3,284
Hamilton	(D)	(D)	(D)	Seminole	256	1,385	2,444
Hardee	12	43	64	Sumter	15	121	91
Hendry	18	44	43	Suwannee	9	29	17
Hernando	60	188	221	Taylor	9	29	30
Highlands	66	307	358	Union	(D)	(D)	(D)
Hillsborough	888	7,637	12,842	Volusia	386	1,687	2,374
Holmes	(D)	(D)	(D)	Wakulla	7	15	11
Indian River	152	807	1,423	Walton	24	144	189
Jackson	19	52	55	Washington	7	15	20
Jefferson	(D)	(D)	(D)	Statewide 1/	115	1,404	1,782

(D) Data withheld to avoid disclosure of information about individual firms.
    1/ Reporting units without a fixed location within the state or of unknown county
location.
    Note: For a list of three-digit code industries included see Table 17.39.

    Source: State of Florida, Department of Labor and Employment Security, Bureau of
Labor Market Information, "Employment, Wages, and Contributions Report" (ES-202),
unpublished data.

Florida Statistical Abstract 1991

Table 17.48.   REAL ESTATE: NUMBER OF LICENSED BROKERS AND SALESPERSONS IN THE STATE
AND COUNTIES OF FLORIDA, AUGUST 3, 1991

Location of licensee	Brokers	Broker-sales-persons	Sales-persons	Location of licensee	Brokers	Broker-sales-persons	Sales-persons
Total 1/	35,896	23,910	148,715	Jefferson	14	6	49
NonFlorida	413	352	1,985	Lafayette	5	1	6
Unknown	885	326	1,970	Lake	372	259	1,327
Alachua	455	217	985	Lee	1,258	947	5,974
Baker	9	7	41	Leon	531	282	1,438
Bay	262	161	1,031	Levy	61	36	178
Bradford	23	12	58	Liberty	3	2	2
Brevard	861	734	4,011	Madison	20	4	39
Broward	3,258	2,591	17,547	Manatee	449	361	1,906
Calhoun	5	0	28	Marion	501	274	1,670
Charlotte	289	245	1,449	Martin	465	336	1,613
Citrus	229	180	896	Monroe	307	258	1,155
Clay	183	190	992	Nassau	90	48	232
Collier	798	669	3,906	Okaloosa	432	215	1,300
Columbia	72	40	188	Okeechobee	49	24	198
Dade	4,832	2,873	20,069	Orange	2,125	1,292	9,252
De Soto	44	31	157	Osceola	236	126	1,306
Dixie	20	10	50	Palm Beach	3,241	2,351	14,547
Duval	1,208	900	4,930	Pasco	436	367	2,242
Escambia	348	234	1,276	Pinellas	2,719	1,792	10,659
Flagler	83	62	510	Polk	819	386	2,252
Franklin	24	13	93	Putnam	68	56	237
Gadsden	43	10	75	St. Johns	296	238	1,153
Gilchrist	16	9	47	St. Lucie	408	248	1,647
Glades	7	2	25	Santa Rosa	161	102	597
Gulf	16	5	69	Sarasota	1,297	847	4,598
Hamilton	10	5	12	Seminole	1,077	653	4,474
Hardee	32	14	107	Sumter	42	29	142
Hendry	48	32	192	Suwannee	44	27	121
Hernando	226	142	1,211	Taylor	24	6	28
Highlands	205	75	516	Union	8	1	10
Hillsborough	1,941	1,271	8,143	Volusia	970	625	4,117
Holmes	15	6	43	Wakulla	30	15	95
Indian River	356	233	1,176	Walton	65	27	184
Jackson	37	13	113	Washington	20	5	66

1/ Total includes all licensed persons regardless of current status.

Source: State of Florida, Department of Professional Regulation, unpublished
data.

Florida Statistical Abstract 1991

Table 17.51. INSURANCE INVESTMENTS: TYPE AND VALUE OF INVESTMENTS BY TYPE OF
   INSURER IN FLORIDA, 1990

(in thousands of dollars)

Type of investment	All insurers	Property and casualty	Life	Other 1/
Total investment	34,256,299	11,121,627	22,588,782	545,890
Market value	16,088,586	9,656,556	6,215,894	216,135
Real estate	2,482,545	286,434	2,175,199	20,911
Public sector bonds	10,423,364	8,228,763	2,053,183	141,418
Private sector bonds	2,243,843	576,820	1,623,392	43,631
Preferred stocks	323,227	175,573	147,496	158
Common stocks	615,607	388,966	216,624	10,017
Book value	18,167,715	1,465,071	16,372,889	329,754
Mortgages	15,198,106	437,745	14,492,025	268,335
Other investments	1,051,724	27,489	1,022,252	1,983
Collateral loans	418,065	21,288	393,764	3,012
Short-term investments	466,758	339,506	98,426	28,827
Deposits	397,949	240,252	144,988	12,709
Subsidiaries	635,113	398,791	221,434	14,888

1/ Includes title and fraternal insurers.
   Source: State of Florida, Department of Insurance, *1990 Florida Department of
Insurance Annual Report.*

Table 17.53. BEACH, WINDSTORM, AND FLOOD INSURANCE: POLICIES AND INSURANCE IN
   FORCE IN FLORIDA AND THE UNITED STATES, DECEMBER 31, 1989

Item	Florida	United States
Beach and windstorm plans, 1989		
Applications		
New	11,726	94,665
Renewal	53,040	89,823
Binders or policies issued		
New	7,915	60,832
Renewal	53,040	81,019
Insurance in force, December 31,		
1989 ($1,000)	6,360,121	13,807,973
Flood insurance, December 31,		
1989 Δ/		
Policies in force, total	837,305	2,201,227
National Flood Insurance, direct	42,861	390,447
Write Your Own program	794,444	1,835,089
Insurance in force, total ($1,000)	73,966,493	183,229,984
National Flood Insurance, direct	3,878,264	30,163,528
Write Your Own program	70,088,229	154,711,750

Δ/ Flood insurance available under a program developed jointly by the insurance
business and the Federal Insurance Administration (FIA) and administered by the FIA.
United States includes Guam, Puerto Rico, and the Virgin Islands. In October 1983
the National Flood Insurance program was opened to private insurers under the Write
Your Own program which provided a procedure for government reimbursement of certain
losses.
   Source: Insurance Information Institute, *The Fact Book: 1991 Property/Casualty
Insurance Facts.*

Florida Statistical Abstract 1991

Table 17.60. LIFE INSURANCE: NUMBER OF COMPANIES, POLICIES IN FORCE, PURCHASES
    AND AMOUNT OF LIFE INSURANCE, BENEFIT PAYMENTS, PREMIUM RECEIPTS, AND
    MORTGAGES OWNED BY U.S. LIFE INSURANCE COMPANIES IN FLORIDA AND THE
    UNITED STATES, 1989

Item	Florida	United States
Number of U.S. life insurance companies	47	2,305
Purchases of ordinary life insurance ($1,000,000)	54,637	1,020,719
Insurance in force		
Total		
Number (1,000)	17,885	393,951
Amount ($1,000,000)	379,604	8,694,015
Ordinary		
Number (1,000)	6,750	143,565
Amount ($1,000,000)	237,203	4,939,964
Group		
Number (1,000)	5,075	141,556
Amount ($1,000,000)	126,820	3,469,498
Industrial		
Number (1,000)	2,095	36,614
Amount ($1,000,000)	1,456	24,446
Credit		
Number (1,000)	3,965	72,216
Amount ($1,000,000)	14,125	260,107
Average amount in force 1/ (dollars)	74,900	93,600
Insurance and annuity benefit payments ($1,000)	4,098,300	80,200,500
Death payments	1,238,600	23,261,500
Matured endowments	39,300	726,900
Annuity payments	1,399,100	26,300,200
Disability payments	29,100	554,100
Surrender values	783,600	14,858,600
Policy and contract dividends	608,600	14,499,200
Payments to beneficiaries		
Total		
Number	174,700	2,991,100
Amount ($1,000)	1,238,600	23,261,500
Ordinary		
Number	84,600	1,370,000
Amount ($1,000)	739,000	11,903,700
Group		
Number	45,900	988,900
Amount ($1,000)	470,600	10,883,400
Industrial		
Number	44,200	632,200
Amount ($1,000)	29,000	474,400
Premium receipts of companies ($1,000,000)		
Life	3,012	63,694
Health	3,229	53,293
Mortgages owned by companies ($1,000), total	15,639,900	250,161,900
Farm	787,000	9,597,900
Nonfarm	14,852,900	240,564,000

1/ Average amounts per household. See Glossary for a definition of "household".

Source: American Council of Life Insurance, *1990 Life Insurance Fact Book*.

Table 17.61. LIFE INSURANCE: DIRECT WRITINGS, DIRECT LOSSES, AND LIFE INSURANCE
   IN FORCE IN FLORIDA, 1983 THROUGH 1989

(amounts rounded to thousands of dollars)

Year	Life insurance in force at end of year	Direct writings	Direct losses paid	Losses as a percentage of writings
	All life insurance companies			
1983	191,500,672	2,713,162	813,919	30.0
1984	219,322,109	3,079,336	878,972	28.5
1985	243,113,536	3,501,696	986,017	28.2
1986	264,185,305	3,897,257	1,059,811	27.2
1987	322,472,329	5,246,052	2,805,237	53.5
1988	312,711,163	5,633,515	1,290,565	22.9
1989	344,548,493	5,675,962	1,328,876	23.4
	Florida life insurance companies only			
1983	18,016,444	327,001	84,468	25.8
1984	21,229,983	362,099	91,905	25.4
1985	22,058,452	348,872	97,178	27.8
1986	21,223,054	340,139	85,963	25.3
1987	18,051,822	349,383	86,154	24.7
1988	19,746,098	379,699	96,467	25.4
1989	18,548,502	386,459	97,020	25.1

Note: Includes ordinary, group, industrial, and credit insurance and annuities.

Table 17.62. FRATERNAL INSURANCE SOCIETIES: DIRECT PREMIUMS WRITTEN, BENEFITS
   PAID, AND INSURANCE IN FORCE IN FLORIDA, 1987 THROUGH 1989

(rounded to thousands of dollars)

Year	Life insurance in force at end of year	Direct premiums written		Direct losses paid	
		Life	Accident and health	Life	Accident and health
1987	3,201,595	733,336	3,887	13,166	3,314
1988	3,552,068	659,886	4,105	14,940	3,693
1989	3,907,921	634,901	4,980	18,414	4,744

Source for Tables 17.61 and 17.62: State of Florida, Department of Insurance,
1990 Florida Department of Insurance Annual Report, and previous edition.

Florida Statistical Abstract 1991

Table 17.72. PROPERTY AND CASUALTY INSURANCE: PREMIUMS WRITTEN AND LOSSES PAID BY
    PROPERTY AND CASUALTY, TITLE, AND LIFE INSURANCE COMPANIES IN FLORIDA, 1989

(rounded to thousands of dollars)

| | All companies | | Florida companies | |
Line of business	Direct premiums written	Direct losses paid	Direct premiums written	Direct losses paid
Total	15,723,692	9,653,050	2,888,457	1,726,908
Fire	147,289	66,577	24,817	10,483
Allied lines	177,401	24,304	14,292	2,104
Farmowners' multiple peril	6,924	3,212	1,599	804
Homeowners' multiple peril	935,374	484,116	87,474	38,277
Commercial multiple peril	948,859	357,063	65,536	22,092
Ocean marine	68,394	43,808	3,611	1,391
Inland marine	310,062	129,891	90,108	37,965
Financial guaranty	42,315	3,746	-110	263
Medical malpractice	181,506	103,561	62,420	29,692
Earthquake	1,635	475	1	0
Accident and health, total	4,644,585	3,560,006	1,455,971	1,166,077
Group	3,155,505	2,685,601	1,051,468	904,820
Credit	114,464	37,550	50,404	14,394
Collectively renewable	290,437	196,251	211,223	150,125
Noncancellable	216,463	110,048	2,079	740
Guaranteed renewable	492,539	271,662	32,869	13,772
Nonrenewable for stated reasons only	133,128	84,554	4,527	2,407
Other accident only	8,938	5,548	211	11
All other	233,111	168,792	103,190	79,808
Workers' compensation	1,491,862	1,012,968	93,172	27,646
Other liability	723,794	391,237	67,789	15,598
Private passenger automobile no-fault, PIP	587,116	416,388	122,459	69,390
Other private passenger automobile liability	2,379,280	1,411,939	317,202	138,967
Commercial automobile no-fault, PIP	21,427	12,371	3,511	2,321
Other commercial automobile liability	666,992	405,887	98,360	37,655
Private passenger automobile physical damage	1,400,916	875,341	190,836	91,212
Commercial automobile physical damage	222,318	110,556	30,559	16,183
Aircraft (all perils)	38,908	23,386	500	342
Fidelity	39,064	11,053	2,767	358
Surety	135,851	33,830	31,012	2,180
Glass	1,508	315	51	16
Burglary and theft	5,123	887	395	301
Boiler and machinery	20,229	6,994	51	0
Credit	42,450	40,861	398	284
Title	239,709	28,680	77,960	4,338
All other lines	242,801	93,598	45,716	10,969

PIP Personal injury protection.

Source: State of Florida, Department of Insurance, *1990 Florida Department of Insurance Annual Report*.

Florida Statistical Abstract 1991

PERSONAL AND BUSINESS SERVICES

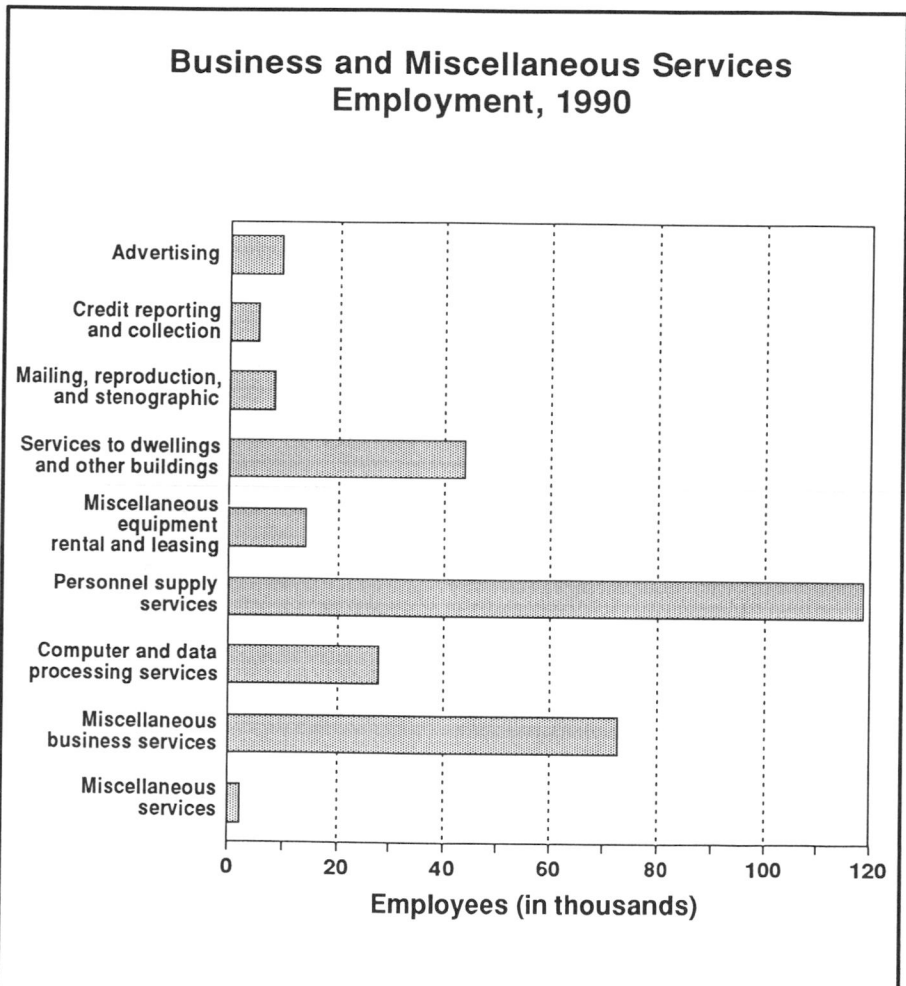

Business and Miscellaneous Services Employment, 1990

Source: Table 18.22

TABLES LISTED BY MAJOR HEADINGS

Table 18.01. AUTOMOTIVE, BUSINESS, AND PROFESSIONAL SERVICES: ESTABLISHMENTS AND RECEIPTS BASED ON 1972 STANDARD INDUSTRIAL CLASSIFICATION CODES FOR FIRMS IN FLORIDA, 1982 AND 1987

SIC Code			Number of establishments		Receipts per establishment		
1972	1987	Kind of business	1982	1987	1982 ($1,000)	1987 ($1,000)	Percentage change
72	72, 7352, 7991 pt.	Personal services	9,509	11,333	1,095,441	1,812,275	65.4
73	73 ex. 7352; 784; 8731, 2, 4; 874	Business services	12,936	21,109	4,539,419	10,252,979	125.9
75	75	Automotive repair, services and parking	6,246	7,930	1,735,526	3,230,507	86.1
76	76	Miscellaneous repair services	3,545	4,398	755,583	1,248,086	65.2
81	81	Legal services	7,377	8,965	1,835,255	3,697,540	101.5
891	871	Engineering, architectural, and surveying services	2,681	3,877	1,114,793	2,251,146	101.9
893	872	Accounting, auditing and bookkeeping services	3,159	4,377	609,573	1,175,297	92.8

Note: Data are for firms subject to federal income tax.

Table 18.02. AUTOMOTIVE, BUSINESS, AND PROFESSIONAL SERVICES: ESTABLISHMENTS, RECEIPTS, AND PAYROLL IN FLORIDA, 1987

SIC Code	Kind of business	Establishments		Receipts ($1,000)	Annual payroll ($1,000)
		Number	Percentage unincorporated 1/		
72	Personal services	10,680	42.4	1,596,527	580,008
73	Business services	16,132	19.2	7,636,598	3,027,387
75	Automotive repair, services, and parking	7,930	32.1	3,230,507	651,537
76	Miscellaneous repair services	4,398	31.4	1,248,086	381,311
81	Legal services	8,965	44.6	3,697,540	1,821,955
87 ex. 8733	Engineering, accounting, research, management, and related services (except noncommercial research organizations)	12,563	24.0	6,004,978	2,646,678

1/ Includes individual proprietorships and partnerships.
Note: Data are for firms subject to federal income tax.

Source for Tables 18.01 and 18.02: U.S., Department of Commerce, Bureau of the Census, *1987 Census of Service Industries: Florida.* SC87-A-10.

Table 18.20. PERSONAL AND HOUSEHOLD SERVICES: AVERAGE MONTHLY REPORTING UNITS
    EMPLOYMENT, AND PAYROLL COVERED BY UNEMPLOYMENT COMPENSATION LAW BY
    INDUSTRY IN FLORIDA, 1990

SIC code	Industry	Number of reporting units	Number of employees	Payroll ($1,000)
72	Personal services	10,156	62,249	62,601
721	Laundry, cleaning, and garment services	3,082	22,585	23,564
722	Photographic studios, portrait	469	2,616	2,864
723	Beauty shops	5,015	25,198	22,798
724	Barber shops	130	488	544
725	Shoe repair shops and shoeshine parlors	170	313	311
726	Funeral service and crematories	434	4,039	6,302
729	Miscellaneous personal services	853	7,007	6,217
88	Private households 1/	10,256	14,162	13,812

1/ Private households which employ workers in domestic services such as cooks,
maids, sitters, butlers, personal secretaries, gardeners and care-takers, and
managers of personal affairs.
    Note: Totals on county employment tables may not match totals in this table due
to rounding.

Table 18.21. AUTOMOTIVE AND MISCELLANEOUS REPAIR SERVICES: AVERAGE MONTHLY
    REPORTING UNITS, EMPLOYMENT, AND PAYROLL COVERED BY UNEMPLOYMENT
    COMPENSATION LAW BY INDUSTRY IN FLORIDA, 1990

SIC code	Industry	Number of reporting units	Number of employees	Payroll ($1,000)
75	Auto repair, services, and parking	8,253	55,557	82,081
751	Automotive rental, no driver	595	17,763	28,939
752	Automobile parking	62	1,952	1,636
753	Automotive repair shops	6,368	26,688	41,673
754	Automotive services, except repair	1,227	9,154	9,833
76	Miscellaneous repair services	4,461	24,316	43,252
762	Electrical repair shops	1,532	8,625	15,359
7622	Radio and television repair shops	426	1,868	3,017
7623	Refrigeration service and repair	447	2,911	5,178
7629	Electrical repair shops, NEC	659	3,844	7,164
763	Watch, clock, and jewelry repair	118	295	350
764	Reupholstery and furniture repair	497	1,533	1,755
769	Miscellaneous repair shops and related services	2,312	13,862	25,788
7692	Welding repair	336	1,666	2,769
7694	Armature rewinding shops	143	1,130	2,308
7699	Repair shops and related services, NEC	1,832	11,066	20,711

    NEC Not elsewhere classified.
    Note: Totals on county employment tables may not match totals in this table due
to rounding.
    Source for Tables 18.20 and 18.21: State of Florida, Department of Labor and
Employment Security, Bureau of Labor Market Information, "Employment, Wages, and
Contributions Report" (ES-202), unpublished data.

Florida Statistical Abstract 1991

Table 18.22. BUSINESS AND MISCELLANEOUS SERVICES: AVERAGE MONTHLY REPORTING UNITS
EMPLOYMENT, AND PAYROLL COVERED BY UNEMPLOYMENT COMPENSATION LAW BY INDUSTRY
IN FLORIDA, 1990

SIC code	Industry	Number of reporting units	Number of employees	Payroll ($1,000)
73	Business services	20,117	301,048	403,997
731	Advertising	1,389	9,517	21,434
7311	Advertising agencies	1,107	6,712	15,142
7312	Outdoor advertising services	81	1,063	2,403
7313	Radio, TV, and publisher representatives	89	752	2,224
7319	Advertising, NEC	112	989	1,665
732	Credit reporting and collection	438	5,428	9,578
7322	Adjustment and collection services	323	3,469	6,367
7323	Credit reporting services	114	1,958	3,212
733	Mailing, reproduction, and stenographic	1,529	8,334	13,877
7331	Direct mail advertising services	204	2,483	3,873
7334	Photocopying and duplicating services	225	1,870	2,496
7335	Commercial photography	179	786	1,691
7336	Commercial art and graphic design	341	1,028	2,215
7338	Secretarial and court reporting services	579	2,166	3,602
734	Services to dwellings and other buildings	3,768	43,901	40,623
7342	Disinfecting and pest control services	1,142	10,410	16,476
7349	Building maintenance services, NEC	2,626	33,490	24,147
735	Miscellaneous equipment rental and leasing	1,733	14,160	25,960
7352	Medical equipment rental and leasing	245	2,211	4,333
7353	Heavy construction equipment rental	436	3,904	8,091
7359	Equipment rental and leasing, NEC	1,051	8,044	13,536
736	Personnel supply services	1,735	118,909	119,359
7361	Employment agencies	671	8,645	11,661
7363	Help supply services	1,064	110,264	107,698
737	Computer and data processing services	2,410	27,952	81,165
7371	Computer programming services	664	4,416	13,855
7372	Prepackaged software	234	3,351	11,580
7373	Computer integrated systems design	198	3,802	12,169
7374	Data processing and preparation	302	10,694	27,378
7375	Information retrieval services	54	1,323	3,196
7376	Computer facilities management services	31	335	981
7377	Computer rental and leasing	59	462	1,560
7378	Computer maintenance and repair	207	1,311	3,648
7379	Computer related services, NEC	659	2,254	6,799
738	Miscellaneous business services	7,112	72,844	92,000
7381	Detective and armored car services	885	29,508	27,614
7382	Security systems services	161	3,138	4,876
7383	News syndicates	34	436	1,828
7384	Photofinishing laboratories	394	2,915	4,098
7389	Business services, NEC	5,636	36,846	53,583
89	Miscellaneous services	394	2,255	6,664

NEC Not elsewhere classified.
Note: Totals on county employment tables may not match totals in this table due
to rounding.
Source: State of Florida, Department of Labor and Employment Security, Bureau of
Labor Market Information, "Employment, Wages, and Contributions Report" (ES-202),
unpublished data.

Florida Statistical Abstract 1991

Table 18.25. ENGINEERING AND MANAGEMENT SERVICES: AVERAGE MONTHLY REPORTING UNITS
  EMPLOYMENT, AND PAYROLL COVERED BY UNEMPLOYMENT COMPENSATION LAW BY INDUSTRY
  IN FLORIDA, 1990

SIC code	Industry	Number of reporting units	Number of employees	Payroll ($1,000)
87	Engineering, accounting, research, management, and related services	14,539	124,278	318,992
871	Engineering, architectural, and surveying services	4,093	43,535	118,712
8711	Engineering services	2,324	31,601	89,760
8712	Architectural services	1,170	6,417	18,131
8713	Surveying services	599	5,517	10,822
872	Accounting, auditing, and bookkeeping services	5,009	30,946	64,148
873	Research, development, and testing services	910	12,173	25,899
8731	Commercial physical and biological research	300	2,973	9,142
8732	Commercial economic, sociological, and educational research	220	4,770	6,694
8733	Noncommercial research organizations	109	1,004	2,434
8734	Testing laboratories	281	3,425	7,629
874	Management and public relations services	4,525	37,622	110,233
8741	Management services	1,778	12,659	33,150
8742	Management consulting services	1,835	6,537	23,482
8743	Public relations services	273	1,105	2,710
8744	Facilities support management services	37	14,339	41,745
8748	Business consulting services, NEC	601	2,981	9,146

NEC Not elsewhere classified.
Note: Totals on county employment tables may not match totals in this table due
to rounding.

Source: State of Florida, Department of Labor and Employment Security, Bureau of
Labor Market Information, "Employment, Wages, and Contributions Report" (ES-202),
unpublished data.

Table 18.30. PERSONAL SERVICES: AVERAGE MONTHLY REPORTING UNITS, EMPLOYMENT, AND
PAYROLL COVERED BY UNEMPLOYMENT COMPENSATION LAW IN THE STATE AND COUNTIES
OF FLORIDA, 1990

County	Number of reporting units	Number of employees	Payroll ($1,000)	County	Number of reporting units	Number of employees	Payroll ($1,000)
			Personal services (SIC code 72)				
Florida	10,131	62,368	62,599	Lafayette	0	0	0
				Lake	112	526	479
Alachua	117	732	657	Lee	235	1,611	1,674
Baker	7	14	8	Leon	139	1,213	1,317
Bay	94	601	491	Levy	6	24	21
Bradford	9	46	30	Liberty	(D)	(D)	(D)
Brevard	273	1,692	1,588	Madison	4	29	32
Broward	1,190	7,484	7,811	Manatee	136	629	635
Calhoun	(D)	(D)	(D)	Marion	125	717	657
Charlotte	72	318	297	Martin	91	467	487
Citrus	49	188	204	Monroe	61	186	187
Clay	79	433	370	Nassau	29	92	83
Collier	149	731	833	Okaloosa	116	525	388
Columbia	19	88	68	Okeechobee	15	68	52
Dade	1,767	10,772	10,838	Orange	527	3,567	3,742
De Soto	14	54	47	Osceola	69	348	284
Dixie	(D)	(D)	(D)	Palm Beach	837	5,043	5,497
Duval	547	3,920	3,911	Pasco	167	842	765
Escambia	173	1,170	1,104	Pinellas	723	4,720	4,658
Flagler	21	89	86	Polk	238	1,343	1,279
Franklin	6	9	8	Putnam	34	158	147
Gadsden	16	64	46	St. Johns	43	268	258
Gilchrist	(D)	(D)	(D)	St. Lucie	85	529	506
Glades	(D)	(D)	(D)	Santa Rosa	34	130	103
Gulf	7	10	6	Sarasota	301	1,791	1,877
Hamilton	(D)	(D)	(D)	Seminole	236	1,475	1,410
Hardee	8	33	32	Sumter	10	34	23
Hendry	11	36	26	Suwannee	8	39	34
Hernando	64	299	256	Taylor	10	42	33
Highlands	41	212	152	Union	(D)	(D)	(D)
Hillsborough	553	4,631	4,632	Volusia	281	1,422	1,289
Holmes	5	13	10	Wakulla	(D)	(D)	(D)
Indian River	92	389	385	Walton	(D)	(D)	(D)
Jackson	13	64	57	Washington	6	20	16
Jefferson	4	17	10	Statewide 1/	25	304	620

(D) Data withheld to avoid disclosure of information about individual firms.
1/ Reporting units without a fixed location within the state or of unknown county
location.
Note: For a list of three-digit code industries included see Table 18.20.

Source: State of Florida, Department of Labor and Employment Security, Bureau of
Labor Market Information, "Employment, Wages, and Contributions Report" (ES-202),
unpublished data.

Florida Statistical Abstract 1991

Table 18.35. BUSINESS SERVICES: AVERAGE MONTHLY REPORTING UNITS, EMPLOYMENT AND PAYROLL COVERED BY UNEMPLOYMENT COMPENSATION LAW IN THE STATE AND COUNTIES OF FLORIDA, 1990

County	Number of reporting units	Number of employees	Payroll ($1,000)	County	Number of reporting units	Number of employees	Payroll ($1,000)
			Business services	(SIC code 73)			
Florida	20,095	301,463	403,993	Lafayette	(D)	(D)	(D)
				Lake	114	1,305	1,239
Alachua	210	2,757	3,061	Lee	516	5,000	5,852
Baker	4	8	9	Leon	331	4,064	5,427
Bay	170	1,902	1,884	Levy	(D)	(D)	(D)
Bradford	7	42	44	Liberty	(D)	(D)	(D)
Brevard	498	6,554	10,697	Madison	6	50	102
Broward	2,700	31,904	43,640	Manatee	183	10,299	11,234
Calhoun	4	5	6	Marion	188	1,890	1,991
Charlotte	86	922	904	Martin	162	1,165	1,695
Citrus	66	798	1,023	Monroe	114	448	524
Clay	101	500	729	Nassau	29	172	236
Collier	302	2,713	3,611	Okaloosa	197	2,149	2,769
Columbia	26	121	166	Okeechobee	(D)	(D)	(D)
Dade	3,534	50,918	74,147	Orange	1,414	27,141	42,121
De Soto	6	45	49	Osceola	83	603	532
Dixie	4	28	24	Palm Beach	1,655	17,395	23,673
Duval	1,027	24,860	31,660	Pasco	171	1,621	1,676
Escambia	317	5,463	5,938	Pinellas	1,374	18,982	26,334
Flagler	(D)	(D)	(D)	Polk	341	4,385	5,301
Franklin	(D)	(D)	(D)	Putnam	35	333	422
Gadsden	8	79	87	St. Johns	92	525	710
Gilchrist	3	9	8	St. Lucie	128	1,595	1,712
Glades	0	0	0	Santa Rosa	65	758	692
Gulf	(D)	(D)	(D)	Sarasota	550	7,593	8,459
Hamilton	(D)	(D)	(D)	Seminole	511	3,946	6,035
Hardee	(D)	(D)	(D)	Sumter	8	17	15
Hendry	12	43	60	Suwannee	16	86	68
Hernando	80	594	599	Taylor	13	35	25
Highlands	55	245	281	Union	(D)	(D)	(D)
Hillsborough	1,489	46,710	59,855	Volusia	420	4,608	5,057
Holmes	7	17	31	Wakulla	5	5	9
Indian River	139	1,295	1,488	Walton	15	165	156
Jackson	12	57	61	Washington	(D)	(D)	(D)
Jefferson	(D)	(D)	(D)	Statewide 1/	418	5,382	8,693

(D) Data withheld to avoid disclosure of information about individual firms.

1/ Reporting units without a fixed location within the state or of unknown county location.

Note: For a list of three-digit code industries included see Table 18.22.

Source: State of Florida, Department of Labor and Employment Security, Bureau of Labor Market Information, "Employment, Wages, and Contributions Report" (ES-202), unpublished data.

Florida Statistical Abstract 1991

Table 18.40. AUTOMOTIVE REPAIR, SERVICES, AND PARKING: AVERAGE MONTHLY REPORTING
  UNITS, EMPLOYMENT, AND PAYROLL COVERED BY UNEMPLOYMENT COMPENSATION LAW IN THE
  STATE AND COUNTIES OF FLORIDA, 1990

County	Number of re-porting units	Number of employees	Payroll ($1,000)	County	Number of re-porting units	Number of employees	Payroll ($1,000)
			Automotive repair, services, and parking (SIC code 75)				
Florida	8,229	55,729	82,082	Lafayette	(D)	(D)	(D)
				Lake	86	318	359
Alachua	113	678	873	Lee	239	1,693	2,619
Baker	4	12	11	Leon	139	1,196	1,555
Bay	80	370	386	Levy	11	28	29
Bradford	5	9	15	Liberty	(D)	(D)	(D)
Brevard	247	1,249	1,577	Madison	(D)	(D)	(D)
Broward	963	7,018	11,674	Manatee	80	483	694
Calhoun	(D)	(D)	(D)	Marion	122	541	654
Charlotte	57	210	307	Martin	71	301	484
Citrus	46	142	147	Monroe	45	154	215
Clay	61	367	400	Nassau	1/	42	64
Collier	118	523	799	Okaloosa	100	504	576
Columbia	29	87	111	Okeechobee	18	58	75
Dade	1,373	10,082	16,611	Orange	481	5,953	8,583
De Soto	10	34	41	Osceola	54	228	392
Dixie	(D)	(D)	(D)	Palm Beach	562	3,628	5,317
Duval	426	3,921	5,897	Pasco	148	569	715
Escambia	175	1,172	1,394	Pinellas	552	3,599	5,029
Flagler	6	12	19	Polk	220	1,096	1,596
Franklin	(D)	(D)	(D)	Putnam	19	61	76
Gadsden	12	63	76	St. Johns	44	156	203
Gilchrist	(D)	(D)	(D)	St. Lucie	92	395	557
Glades	(D)	(D)	(D)	Santa Rosa	39	130	195
Gulf	(D)	(D)	(D)	Sarasota	189	1,163	1,379
Hamilton	(D)	(D)	(D)	Seminole	149	821	1,064
Hardee	9	23	30	Sumter	15	97	109
Hendry	10	28	27	Suwannee	10	19	21
Hernando	36	138	147	Taylor	10	37	44
Highlands	39	94	102	Union	(D)	(D)	(D)
Hillsborough	546	4,760	6,938	Volusia	219	1,033	1,199
Holmes	4	22	22	Wakulla	7	21	30
Indian River	55	204	324	Walton	10	47	55
Jackson	17	46	116	Washington	(D)	(D)	(D)
Jefferson	(D)	(D)	(D)	Statewide 1/	13	29	60

(D) Data withheld to avoid disclosure of information about individual firms.
  1/ Reporting units without a fixed location within the state or of unknown county
location.
  Note: For a list of three-digit code industries included see Table 18.21.

  Source: State of Florida, Department of Labor and Employment Security, Bureau of
Labor Market Information, "Employment, Wages, and Contributions Report" (ES-202),
unpublished data.

Florida Statistical Abstract 1991

Table 18.51. ENGINEERING AND MANAGEMENT SERVICES: AVERAGE MONTHLY REPORTING UNITS
EMPLOYMENT, AND PAYROLL COVERED BY UNEMPLOYMENT COMPENSATION LAW IN THE STATE
AND COUNTIES OF FLORIDA, 1990

County	Number of reporting units	Number of employees	Payroll ($1,000)	County	Number of reporting units	Number of employees	Payroll ($1,000)
Engineering and management services (SIC code 87)								
Florida	14,514	124,473	318,992	Lafayette	(D)	(D)	(D)
				Lake	80	621	1,394
Alachua	241	2,626	6,514	Lee	368	2,600	5,920
Baker	(D)	(D)	(D)	Leon	288	2,142	4,964
Bay	108	1,069	2,405	Levy	14	44	56
Bradford	5	37	70	Liberty	(D)	(D)	(D)
Brevard	406	17,445	50,741	Madison	7	53	113
Broward	1,686	10,468	27,762	Manatee	158	1,436	2,347
Calhoun	(D)	(D)	(D)	Marion	113	614	1,282
Charlotte	64	412	891	Martin	146	878	2,041
Citrus	80	329	898	Monroe	101	366	863
Clay	71	413	745	Nassau	29	103	294
Collier	223	1,316	3,721	Okaloosa	125	2,329	6,262
Columbia	20	88	148	Okeechobee	11	46	78
Dade	2,528	15,767	44,039	Orange	1,028	10,491	29,129
De Soto	5	22	32	Osceola	58	303	594
Dixie	(D)	(D)	(D)	Palm Beach	1,304	7,816	25,853
Duval	689	6,493	16,642	Pasco	130	523	1,005
Escambia	223	1,753	3,659	Pinellas	961	7,637	15,975
Flagler	14	132	288	Polk	284	2,297	5,749
Franklin	4	5	5	Putnam	31	124	210
Gadsden	12	68	121	St. Johns	73	214	490
Gilchrist	(D)	(D)	(D)	St. Lucie	92	660	1,730
Glades	(D)	(D)	(D)	Santa Rosa	41	316	608
Gulf	3	17	18	Sarasota	414	3,168	6,105
Hamilton	(D)	(D)	(D)	Seminole	322	1,838	3,913
Hardee	(D)	(D)	(D)	Sumter	10	28	35
Hendry	10	98	197	Suwannee	9	38	71
Hernando	46	248	556	Taylor	4	16	23
Highlands	36	181	289	Union	(D)	(D)	(D)
Hillsborough	1,040	11,018	29,181	Volusia	299	1,539	3,210
Holmes	7	31	70	Wakulla	(D)	(D)	(D)
Indian River	112	612	1,629	Walton	7	19	45
Jackson	16	69	119	Washington	11	48	60
Jefferson	(D)	(D)	(D)	Statewide 1/	314	5,315	7,596

(D) Data withheld to avoid disclosure of information about individual firms.
1/ Reporting units without a fixed location within the state or of unknown county
location.

Source: State of Florida, Department of Labor and Employment Security, Bureau of
Labor Market Information, "Employment, Wages, and Contributions Report" (ES-202),
unpublished data.

Florida Statistical Abstract 1991

Table 18.56. PROFESSIONAL SERVICES: LICENSED ACCOUNTANTS, ARCHITECTS
AND PROFESSIONAL ENGINEERS IN THE STATE AND COUNTIES OF FLORIDA
AUGUST 3, 1991

Location of licensee	Accountants	Architects	Professional engineers	Location of licensee	Accountants	Architects	Professional engineers
Total 1/	23,851	10,622	27,757	Jefferson	7	3	7
NonFlorida	4,788	5,952	13,376	Lafayette	1	0	1
Unknown	0	0	0	Lake	99	29	82
Alachua	315	109	483	Lee	343	114	338
Baker	3	1	10	Leon	686	148	599
Bay	92	18	119	Levy	6	3	13
Bradford	6	1	5	Liberty	4	0	2
Brevard	331	69	642	Madison	4	0	3
Broward	2,408	396	1,033	Manatee	169	42	122
Calhoun	6	0	2	Marion	122	26	96
Charlotte	43	14	53	Martin	103	49	191
Citrus	32	9	67	Monroe	65	29	47
Clay	114	20	97	Nassau	14	8	34
Collier	205	77	169	Okaloosa	97	21	92
Columbia	38	0	64	Okeechobee	11	0	6
Dade	3,745	1,134	1,720	Orange	1,401	383	1,206
De Soto	5	0	6	Osceola	38	9	58
Dixie	1	0	0	Palm Beach	1,674	432	1,397
Duval	1,288	286	930	Pasco	107	10	88
Escambia	246	77	236	Pinellas	1,342	282	987
Flagler	15	2	18	Polk	332	50	437
Franklin	2	3	2	Putnam	13	4	21
Gadsden	30	6	12	St. Johns	123	30	83
Gilchrist	0	0	2	St. Lucie	92	18	82
Glades	0	0	1	Santa Rosa	52	12	75
Gulf	4	1	3	Sarasota	395	154	270
Hamilton	1	0	1	Seminole	466	119	455
Hardee	8	1	7	Sumter	1	1	4
Hendry	21	3	14	Suwannee	15	2	10
Hernando	34	6	54	Taylor	7	0	9
Highlands	29	4	25	Union	1	0	2
Hillsborough	1,804	354	1,316	Volusia	297	60	303
Holmes	3	1	4	Wakulla	10	0	12
Indian River	113	32	97	Walton	6	3	12
Jackson	16	5	12	Washington	2	0	33

1/ Total includes all licensed persons regardless of current status.

Source: State of Florida, Department of Professional Regulation, unpublished data.

Florida Statistical Abstract 1991

TOURISM AND RECREATION

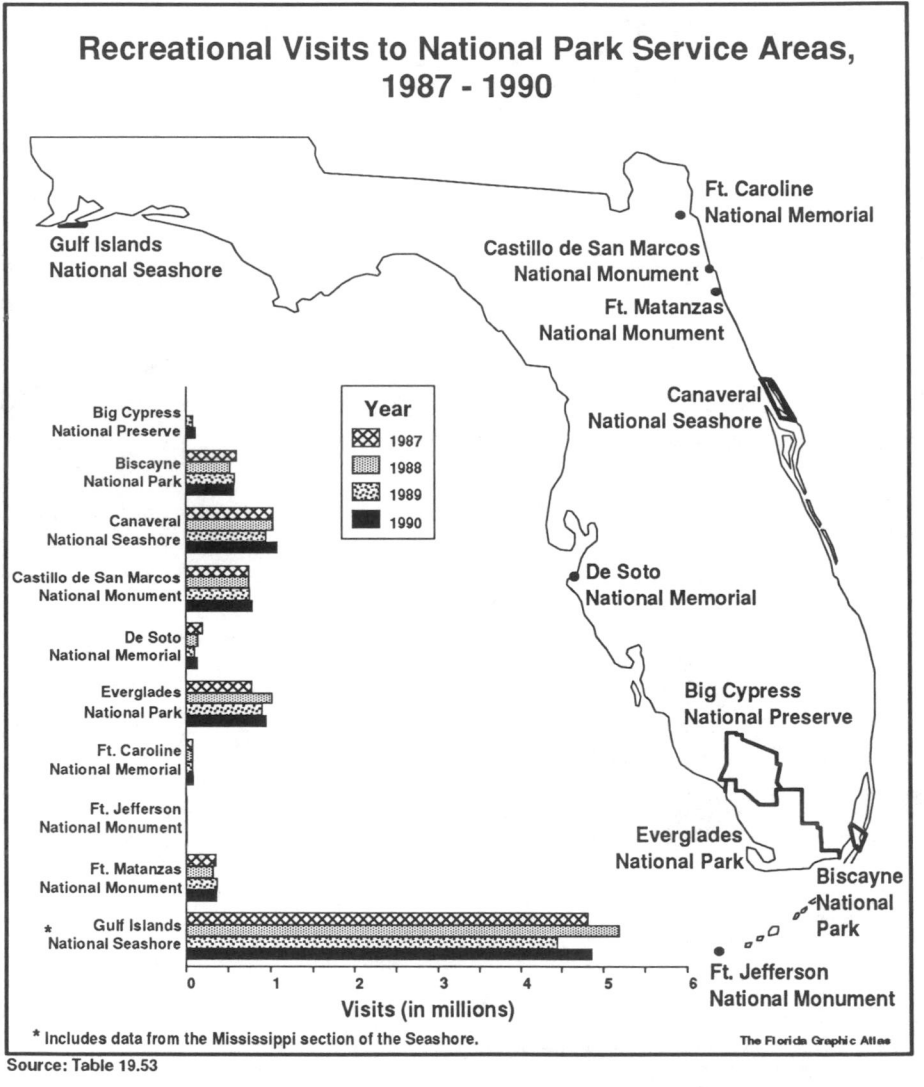

Recreational Visits to National Park Service Areas, 1987 - 1990

Ft. Caroline
National Memorial

Gulf Islands
National Seashore

Castillo de San Marcos
National Monument

Ft. Matanzas
National Monument

Canaveral
National Seashore

Year
- ⊠ 1987
- ▨ 1988
- ▨ 1989
- ■ 1990

De Soto
National Memorial

Big Cypress
National Preserve

Everglades
National Park

Biscayne
National
Park

Ft. Jefferson
National Monument

Chart categories:
- Big Cypress National Preserve
- Biscayne National Park
- Canaveral National Seashore
- Castillo de San Marcos National Monument
- De Soto National Memorial
- Everglades National Park
- Ft. Caroline National Memorial
- Ft. Jefferson National Monument
- Ft. Matanzas National Monument
- * Gulf Islands National Seashore

Visits (in millions)

0 1 2 3 4 5 6

* Includes data from the Mississippi section of the Seashore.

The Florida Graphic Atlas

Source: Table 19.53

Table 19.24. TOURISTS: PERCENTAGE DISTRIBUTION OF VISITORS BY AIR AND AUTOMOBILE
TO FLORIDA BY ORIGIN AND DESTINATION, 1990

State of origin	Travelers by air Percentage	Rank	Travelers by automobile Percentage	Rank	County of destination	Travelers by air Percentage	Rank	Travelers by automobile Percentage	Rank
New York	15.4	1	5.1	3	Orange	14.7	1	11.8	1
New Jersey	7.4	2	(NA)	(NA)	Broward	13.4	2	4.0	8
Pennsylvania	6.2	3	(NA)	(NA)	Dade	12.3	3	(NA)	(NA)
Massachusetts	5.6	4	(NA)	(NA)	Palm Beach	12.2	4	(NA)	(NA)
Ohio	5.6	5	6.4	2	Pinellas	5.4	5	4.5	5
Illinois	5.5	6	3.7	10	Volusia	4.5	6	10.1	3
California	5.1	7	(NA)	(NA)	Hillsborough	4.4	7	3.1	10
Michigan	4.1	8	4.4	7	Lee	3.1	8	(NA)	(NA)
Texas	3.9	9	4.7	4	Sarasota	2.8	9	(NA)	(NA)
Connecticut	3.7	10	(NA)	(NA)	Brevard	2.6	10	3.1	9
Georgia	(NA)	(NA)	15.0	1	Bay	(NA)	(NA)	11.3	2
Tennessee	(NA)	(NA)	4.6	5	Duval	(NA)	(NA)	4.5	6
Alabama	(NA)	(NA)	4.4	6	Escambia	(NA)	(NA)	4.7	4
Ontario	(NA)	(NA)	4.3	8	Okaloosa	(NA)	(NA)	4.3	7
North Carolina	(NA)	(NA)	4.0	9					

(NA) Not available.
Note: Data based on approximately 9,000 person-to-person interviews conducted
annually with visitors to Florida as they are leaving the state. Individuals must
not be residents of Florida and must have been in the state longer than 24 hours.
Source: State of Florida, Department of Commerce, Division of Tourism Research,
unpublished data.

Table 19.25. TRAFFIC COUNTS: AVERAGE DAILY TRAFFIC ENTERING AND LEAVING FLORIDA
AND PASSING OTHER SPECIFIC POINTS, 1990

Location and direction		Average daily traffic	Percentage change from-- 1985	1989
I-275 at Floribraska Ave.	N	61,183	8.0	1.8
(I-275 Tampa)	S	60,430	2.8	501.9
U.S. 1 at Ga. state line	N	4,305	24.2	4.3
(U.S. 1 Ga.)	S	4,214	22.7	2.9
I-75 at Ga. state line	N	13,728	26.3	7.0
(I-75 Ga.)	S	13,677	23.8	4.7
I-95 at Ga. state line	N	19,100	44.5	5.2
(I-95 Ga.)	S	18,836	43.3	5.5
U.S. 231 at Ala. state line	N	5,346	43.8	1.5
(U.S. 231 Ala.)	S	6,062	54.3	11.7
U.S. 27 at Ga. state line	N	2,978	35.9	(NA)
(U.S. 27 Ga.)	S	3,024	37.7	(NA)
I-4 at S.R. 482, Orlando	E	(NA)	(NA)	(NA)
(I-4 Orlando)	W	(NA)	(NA)	(NA)
I-75 at Florida Turnpike	N	14,079	40.4	7.0
(Turnpike Wildwood)	S	13,803	38.1	5.2

(NA) Not available.
Note: Locations are approximate. Abbreviations in parentheses are used in Table
19.26.
Source: State of Florida, Department of Transportation, Division of Transportation Planning, Form TP-228, Annual 1990.

Florida Statistical Abstract 1991

Table 19.26.   TRAFFIC COUNTS: AVERAGE DAILY TRAFFIC ENTERING AND LEAVING FLORIDA
AND PASSING OTHER SPECIFIC POINTS, MONTHS OF 1990

Location and direction		January	February	March	April	May	June
I-95 Georgia	N	15,938	18,085	23,088	24,901	19,770	20,470
	S	17,593	18,738	19,394	19,678	16,619	19,008
U.S. 1 Georgia	N	3,676	3,853	4,417	4,598	4,552	4,459
	S	3,712	3,807	4,163	4,338	4,349	4,394
I-75 Georgia	N	11,506	12,060	18,319	17,001	13,247	15,401
	S	12,118	12,852	15,677	12,893	11,271	14,833
U.S. 27 Georgia	N	2,733	2,756	2,990	3,124	2,972	3,186
	S	2,748	2,747	2,931	3,110	2,917	3,571
U.S. 231 Alabama	N	3,891	4,147	5,748	6,334	5,071	6,360
	S	4,335	4,408	5,577	5,825	5,640	6,671
I-275 Tampa	N	62,117	63,070	65,785	(NA)	63,679	62,507
	S	56,109	59,877	(NA)	58,799	(NA)	56,935
I-4 Orlando	E	(NA)	(NA)	(NA)	(NA)	(NA)	(NA)
	W	(NA)	(NA)	(NA)	(NA)	(NA)	(NA)
Turnpike Wildwood	N	12,409	13,664	17,382	18,229	14,811	(NA)
	S	13,333	14,000	15,325	14,264	12,315	(NA)

		July	August	September	October	November	December
I-95 Georgia	N	(NA)	20,067	15,134	15,274	16,856	19,355
	S	(NA)	20,413	16,654	18,207	18,980	21,045
U.S. 1 Georgia	N	4,558	4,547	4,373	4,195	4,243	4,199
	S	4,495	4,477	4,331	(NA)	4,193	4,189
I-75 Georgia	N	14,914	14,702	11,655	10,906	12,175	12,851
	S	14,827	14,615	12,148	13,026	14,006	15,866
U.S. 27 Georgia	N	3,093	3,055	3,015	2,884	2,944	2,993
	S	3,159	3,085	3,047	2,919	3,035	3,020
U.S. 231 Alabama	N	6,902	6,234	5,982	4,493	4,768	4,225
	S	7,045	7,010	8,289	(NA)	5,915	4,938
I-275 Tampa	N	58,768	61,070	58,448	58,228	58,007	57,786
	S	(NA)	(NA)	64,302	65,028	63,565	62,102
I-4 Orlando	E	(NA)	(NA)	(NA)	(NA)	(NA)	(NA)
	W	(NA)	(NA)	(NA)	(NA)	(NA)	(NA)
Turnpike Wildwood	N	14,331	14,146	11,534	11,836	12,917	13,217
	S	13,813	14,035	12,234	13,717	14,418	15,121

(NA) Not available.
Note: Data are not available for several locations for some months due to
equipment failure or road construction at the count site.   See Table 19.25 for
fuller description of locations.

Source: State of Florida, Department of Transportation, Division of Transportation Planning, Form TP-228, Quarterly reports 1990.

Table 19.45. BOATS: NUMBER REGISTERED BY TYPE IN THE STATE AND COUNTIES OF FLORIDA
FISCAL YEAR 1989-90

County	Pleasure boats	Commer- cial boats	County	Pleasure boats	Commer- cial boats
Florida	687,132	30,922	Lafayette	390	11
			Lake	15,215	306
Alachua	9,105	319	Lee	29,712	1,738
Baker	1,343	2	Leon	11,668	231
Bay	12,769	1,272	Levy	1,916	358
Bradford	1,861	21	Liberty	734	34
Brevard	25,153	1,346	Madison	788	8
Broward	41,296	1,467	Manatee	12,851	613
Calhoun	999	12	Marion	13,396	359
Charlotte	13,213	639	Martin	11,426	467
Citrus	11,771	1,013	Monroe	15,595	3,458
Clay	7,138	208	Nassau	2,920	214
Collier	13,712	1,069	Okaloosa	11,765	571
Columbia	3,412	22	Okeechobee	4,231	253
Dade	49,360	1,323	Orange	29,205	325
De Soto	1,390	251	Osceola	5,297	319
Dixie	1,407	553	Palm Beach	30,878	743
Duval	29,457	925	Pasco	12,793	404
Escambia	15,790	401	Pinellas	44,624	1,673
Flagler	2,478	78	Polk	24,342	425
Franklin	1,185	1,070	Putnam	6,765	402
Gadsden	1,873	55	St. Johns	5,080	302
Gilchrist	1,068	114	St. Lucie	8,534	393
Glades	822	127	Santa Rosa	6,727	263
Gulf	1,883	307	Sarasota	16,756	471
Hamilton	610	2	Seminole	14,218	292
Hardee	1,396	19	Sumter	2,879	117
Hendry	2,343	175	Suwannee	2,009	24
Hernando	5,172	175	Taylor	2,099	265
Highlands	7,352	120	Union	496	6
Hillsborough	39,521	706	Volusia	18,252	879
Holmes	1,315	8	Wakulla	2,157	531
Indian River	7,616	411	Walton	2,365	131
Jackson	3,318	68	Washington	1,324	34
Jefferson	597	24			

Source: State of Florida, Department of Natural Resources, *Vessels Registered in
Florida, Fiscal Year 1989-90.*

Florida Statistical Abstract 1991

Table 19.52. STATE PARKS AND AREAS: ATTENDANCE AT PARKS IN FLORIDA, FISCAL YEARS
1987-88 THROUGH 1990-91

Property designation	County	1987-88	1988-89	1989-90	1990-91
Total	(X)	14,364,898	15,164,968	14,156,980	12,882,651
Addison Blockhouse	Volusia	226	274	963	890
Alfred B. Maclay					
Gardens	Leon	88,077	104,319	120,892	99,915
Amelia Island	Nassau	15,061	17,786	27,763	42,011
Anastasia	St. Johns	368,608	388,988	405,044	373,312
Anclote Key	Pasco, Pinellas	29,441	37,214	40,155	31,515
Bahia Honda	Monroe	311,014	331,014	339,134	331,943
Barnacle, The	Dade	9,455	13,740	14,577	16,522
Big Lagoon	Escambia	75,209	91,773	81,417	68,901
Big Talbot Island	Duval	7,337	10,786	18,803	33,415
Blackwater River	Santa Rosa	57,482	37,540	42,599	45,599
Blue Spring	Volusia	352,464	301,068	324,509	333,461
Bulow Creek	Flagler,				
	Volusia	27,946	28,244	31,470	34,437
Bulow Plantation					
Ruins	Flagler	36,077	26,785	24,580	26,465
Caladesi Island	Pinellas	121,461	148,645	159,787	133,123
Cape Florida	Dade	705,931	746,707	634,110	561,483
Cayo Costa	Lee	88,335	82,985	48,484	88,106
Cedar Key Museum	Levy	31,834	30,538	28,552	26,700
Chekika	Dade	34,222	35,973	32,675	26,059
Collier-Seminole	Collier	62,059	43,475	59,219	57,687
Constitution					
Convention	Gulf	3,414	3,607	2,631	2,503
Crystal River	Citrus	19,573	21,477	22,737	20,799
Dade Battlefield	Sumter	42,793	38,469	38,163	36,224
De Leon Springs	Volusia	171,143	179,537	190,471	191,662
Dead Lakes	Gulf	11,025	10,669	11,161	19,686
Delnor-Wiggins Pass	Collier	379,907	420,488	427,823	315,959
Devil's Millhopper	Alachua	77,176	73,398	65,594	66,873
Don Pedro Island 1/	Charlotte	0	0	3,645	7,707
Eden Gardens	Walton	56,466	63,040	60,306	62,581
Egmont Key	Hillsborough	0	0	41,879	44,163
Fakahatchee Strand	Collier	0	0	28,890	28,480
Falling Waters	Washington	50,154	51,705	34,037	31,949
Faver-Dykes	St. Johns	33,019	19,048	15,598	19,054
Flagler Beach	Flagler	80,645	69,585	75,413	55,423
Florida Caverns	Jackson	123,456	124,800	125,126	127,100
Forest Capital	Taylor	28,720	29,565	29,080	30,062
Ft. Clinch	Nassau	179,502	171,353	174,327	167,533
Ft. Cooper	Citrus	20,847	30,227	37,447	31,793
Ft. Gadsden	Franklin	5,404	5,504	5,151	4,844
Ft. Pierce Inlet	St. Lucie	219,784	222,345	215,255	199,652
Ft. Zackary Taylor	Monroe	119,800	119,070	153,306	190,177
Gamble Plantation	Manatee	37,870	36,026	37,373	41,967
Gasparilla Island	Lee	236,712	216,393	210,456	268,407
Gold Head Branch	Clay	99,053	104,469	99,893	89,758
Grayton Beach	Walton	34,276	33,948	34,804	40,299
Green Mound	Volusia	1,131	1,567	1,350	1,071
Guana River	St. Johns	198,377	225,371	236,882	230,694

See footnotes at end of table.   Continued . . .

Florida Statistical Abstract 1991

Table 19.52.   STATE PARKS AND AREAS: ATTENDANCE AT PARKS IN FLORIDA, FISCAL YEARS
1987-88 THROUGH 1990-91 (Continued)

Property designation	County	1987-88	1988-89	1989-90	1990-91
Henderson Beach	Okaloosa	93,769	83,106	90,464	45,489
Highlands Hammock	Highlands,				
	Hardee	215,990	171,006	152,349	178,695
Hillsborough River	Hillsborough	188,889	167,925	179,482	167,003
Homosassa Springs	Citrus	0	113,302	190,727	206,195
Honeymoon Island	Pinellas	637,936	719,254	809,260	630,812
Hontoon Island	Volusia, Lake	56,800	Δ/ 27,896	Δ/ 21,321	43,292
Hugh Taylor Birch	Broward	204,239	188,212	179,250	222,339
Ichetucknee Springs	Columbia,				
	Suwannee	202,362	180,976	139,057	130,384
Indian Key	Monroe	5,613	7,637	6,541	6,171
Jack Island	St. Lucie	23,084	26,689	23,949	9,475
John Gorrie Museum	Franklin	3,317	4,255	4,347	6,119
John Pennekamp					
Coral Reef	Monroe	495,964	1,356,473	1,335,498	944,663
Jonathan Dickinson	Martin	136,872	141,680	136,784	137,706
Key Largo 1/	Monroe	0	0	0	140
Kingsley Plantation	Duval	15,214	18,888	20,394	23,408
Koreshan	Lee	45,045	38,521	46,347	43,668
Lake Griffin	Lake	24,065	16,429	19,637	18,368
Lake Jackson Mounds	Leon	16,692	15,662	16,464	13,281
Lake Kissimmee	Polk	47,654	47,073	44,960	43,500
Lake Louisa	Lake	17,609	22,133	30,302	30,680
Lake Manatee	Manatee	101,836	62,985	44,329	43,163
Lake Rousseau	Citrus, Levy,				
	Marion	301,265	361,433	235,617	185,759
Lake Talquin	Gadsden, Leon,				
	Liberty	667,491	697,964	478,451	268,700
Lignumvitae Key 1/	Monroe	5,034	5,796	4,937	2,422
Little Manatee River	Hillsborough	23,064	17,527	18,200	18,905
Little Talbot Island	Duval	110,792	117,490	129,797	133,387
Lloyd Beach	Broward	590,818	614,586	613,913	590,483
Long Key	Monroe	106,025	89,717	91,749	95,501
Lovers Key	Lee	8,676	27,161	92,208	74,464
Lower Wekiva River	Lake, Seminole	342	840	982	1,856
MacArthur Beach	Palm Beach	119,750	128,360	91,720	65,869
Madira Bickel Mound	Manatee	2,777	2,378	3,195	3,045
Manatee Springs	Levy	100,037	91,589	114,635	114,730
Marjorie Kinnan					
Rawlings	Alachua	30,225	31,114	30,769	27,168
Myakka River	Manatee,				
	Sarasota	260,643	253,354	274,678	252,370
Natural Bridge					
Battlefield	Leon	6,121	7,796	11,275	16,890
New Smyrna Sugar					
Mill Ruins 1/	Volusia	24,606	30,286	19,897	9,430
North Peninsula	Volusia	0	0	0	10,433
North Shore	Dade	100,056	237,620	152,293	111,301
O'Leno	Alachua,				
	Columbia	62,874	61,846	58,671	54,581
Ochlocknee River	Wakulla	31,461	29,477	24,470	26,669
Oleta River	Dade	164,549	253,242	220,707	198,484

See footnotes at end of table.   Continued . . .

Florida Statistical Abstract 1991

Table 19.52.   STATE PARKS AND AREAS: ATTENDANCE AT PARKS IN FLORIDA, FISCAL YEARS
    1987-88 THROUGH 1990-91 (Continued)

Property designation	County	1987-88	1988-89	1989-90	1990-91
Olustee Battlefield	Baker	19,681	19,019	26,666	30,706
Oscar Scherer	Sarasota	97,467	104,060	119,732	106,313
Paynes Creek	Hardee	46,815	43,122	46,213	48,610
Paynes Prairie	Alachua	74,806	95,851	89,772	83,379
Peacock Springs	Suwannee	0	8,515	14,785	14,029
Perdido Key	Escambia	103,309	57,904	25,508	25,050
Ponce de Leon Springs	Holmes, Walton	38,351	38,212	63,260	53,057
Ravine Gardens	Putnam	191,517	197,019	208,336	181,771
Rock Springs Run	Orange	1,689	2,910	2,355	2,640
Rocky Bayou	Okaloosa	39,368	35,509	34,787	30,965
St. Andrews	Bay	492,307	430,886	405,911	427,847
St. George Island	Franklin	143,161	147,100	159,023	171,486
St. Joseph Peninsula	Gulf	99,367	94,117	83,876	78,856
St. Lucie Inlet	Martin	12,144	15,983	9,942	12,486
St. Marks/Tallahassee Trail	Leon	1,936	35,339	47,400	64,650
San Felasco Hammock	Alachua	14,161	14,518	21,536	23,677
San Marcos de Apalache	Wakulla	10,378	10,106	12,130	14,045
Sebastian Inlet	Brevard, Indian River	1,553,065	1,322,457	617,273	627,595
Shell Island	Bay	151,832	124,769	116,190	141,398
Stephen Foster	Hamilton	59,333	67,526	64,933	51,765
Suwannee River	Hamilton, Madison, Suwannee	39,149	55,150	39,067	32,003
Tenoroc	Polk	16,739	17,749	17,327	16,510
Three Rivers	Jackson	21,312	19,601	19,240	20,072
Tomoka	Volusia	63,020	66,155	68,047	75,373
Torreya	Liberty	18,276	19,295	19,219	17,548
Tosohatchee	Orange	13,936	11,126	11,967	12,970
Waccasassa Bay	Levy	34,729	34,594	36,250	32,307
Wakulla Springs	Wakulla	143,091	163,183	153,425	152,855
Washington Oaks	Flagler	79,917	75,052	74,046	73,799
Weedon Island	Pinellas	106,492	134,969	106,714	97,464
Wekiwa Springs	Orange, Seminole	265,343	258,791	280,404	236,839
Windley Key 1/	Monroe	0	0	0	287
Withlacoochee Trail	Citrus, Pasco, Hernando	0	0	0	158
Ybor City	Hillsborough	24,278	18,650	30,937	22,967
Yulee Sugar Mill Ruins	Citrus	36,750	36,195	36,140	36,212

Δ/ Attendance numbers are lower due to park closing for repairs.
1/ Data are incomplete for 1990-91.
Note: Data include areas reporting actual visitor counts from full-time entrance
stations and areas reporting estimates of attendance from sample counts. Some parks
may have been closed for repairs. Some data are revised. 1990-91 data are
preliminary.
    Source: State of Florida, Department of Natural Resources, Division of Recre-
ation and Parks, unpublished data.

Florida Statistical Abstract 1991

Table 19.53. NATIONAL PARK SYSTEMS: RECREATIONAL VISITS TO NATIONAL PARK SERVICE
    AREAS IN FLORIDA, 1987 THROUGH 1990

Park, monument, or memorial	County	1987 (1,000)	1988 (1,000)	1989 (1,000)	1990 (1,000)
Florida	(X)	8,685.4	9,133.0	8,288.4	7,822.5
Big Cypress Preserve	Broward				
	Hendry	(X)	(X)	81.2	127.8
Biscayne Park	Dade	608.0	531.0	590.0	573.4
Canaveral Seashore	Brevard				
	Volusia	1,037.0	1,038.0	949.2	1,079.0
Castillo de San Marcos					
Monument	St. Johns	755.1	757.1	766.6	789.0
De Soto Memorial	Dade	209.8	152.3	116.7	147.7
Everglades Park	Dade	787.5	1,026.2	913.4	957.9
Ft. Caroline Memorial	Duval	84.5	83.0	91.7	100.9
Ft. Jefferson Monument	Monroe	16.3	16.9	19.4	19.4
Ft. Matanzas Monument	St. Johns	360.3	330.6	383.0	372.1
Gulf Islands Seashore 1/	Escambia				
	Okaloosa				
	Santa Rosa	4,826.9	5,197.9	4,458.4	4,873.7

(X) Not applicable.
1/ Part located in Mississippi; not included in total.
Source: U.S., Department of the Interior, National Park Service, *National Park
Statistical Abstract, 1990*, and previous editions.

Table 19.54. TOURIST DEVELOPMENT TAXES: AMOUNT OF LOCAL OPTION TAX COLLECTIONS AND
    PERCENTAGE CHANGE IN THE STATE AND COUNTIES OF FLORIDA, FISCAL YEARS 1988-89
    AND 1989-90

County	1988-89 ($1,000)	1989-90 Amount ($1,000)	1989-90 Percentage change	County	1988-89 ($1,000)	1989-90 Amount ($1,000)	1989-90 Percentage change
Florida	80,291	104,279	29.9	Leon	674	730	8.3
Alachua	487	514	5.5	Manatee	970	320	-67.0
Bay	1,609	1,788	11.2	Monroe	5,137	5,683	10.6
Brevard	1,558	2,180	39.9	Nassau	123	-5	-104.1
Broward	9,910	10,376	39.9	Okaloosa	0	492	(X)
Charlotte	438	502	4.7	Orange	24,173	37,002	53.1
Citrus	181	188	14.7	Osceola	5,611	8,338	48.6
Columbia	214	218	4.1	Palm Beach	5,659	7,286	28.8
Dade	418	-12	2.0	Pinellas	6,921	8,534	23.3
Duval	1,674	3,693	-102.9	Polk	1,257	1,144	-9.0
Escambia	1,347	19	120.6	St. Johns	210	0	-100.0
Flagler	140	142	-98.6	St. Lucie	705	724	2.7
Hillsborough	4,037	5,541	1.8	Sarasota	1,430	2,235	56.2
Indian River	356	376	37.3	Seminole	848	674	-20.5
Lake	271	328	5.6	Volusia	3,176	4,512	42.1
Lee	224	1	21.0	Walton	533	755	41.6

(X) Not applicable.
Note: The tourist development tax may be levied by counties if approved by local
referendum, and may be one or two percent of each dollar of taxable lease or rental
(hotels and motels, rooming houses and apartments). Data are for sales occurring
June 1988 through May 1990.
Source: State of Florida, Department of Revenue, unpublished data.

Florida Statistical Abstract 1991

Table 19.60.   TOURIST FACILITIES: HOTELS AND MOTELS BY NUMBER OF UNITS AND FOOD SERVICE ESTABLISHMENTS BY SEATING CAPACITY IN THE STATE AND COUNTIES OF FLORIDA, FISCAL YEAR 1990-91

| | Licensed hotels | | Licensed motels | | Food service establishments | |
County	Number	Units	Number	Units	Number of licenses	Seating capacity
Florida	780	126,853	4,013	209,155	44,609	2,782,928
Alachua	2	384	44	2,959	483	31,979
Baker	0	0	3	107	38	1,018
Bay	2	354	217	8,901	593	39,649
Bradford	1	29	14	381	50	2,128
Brevard	11	1,593	105	6,710	1,334	86,534
Broward	95	14,283	440	14,388	4,180	283,912
Calhoun	0	0	3	27	22	1,281
Charlotte	0	0	38	1,273	356	21,243
Citrus	2	99	24	849	333	18,652
Clay	0	0	9	859	250	13,978
Collier	15	3,251	56	2,298	728	49,685
Columbia	0	0	30	1,811	127	6,570
Dade	305	37,477	248	14,529	7,232	347,960
De Soto	0	0	5	131	60	2,083
Dixie	0	0	8	125	28	1,268
Duval	25	4,441	101	7,744	1,963	124,453
Escambia	1	212	66	4,347	652	41,930
Flagler	1	154	13	323	118	7,637
Franklin	1	31	16	366	62	2,570
Gadsden	0	0	6	94	72	2,682
Gilchrist	0	0	1	28	20	866
Glades	0	0	10	218	28	1,361
Gulf	1	14	5	63	31	1,142
Hamilton	0	0	10	382	33	1,100
Hardee	0	0	3	45	63	1,836
Hendry	1	51	15	290	80	3,534
Hernando	0	0	11	451	306	17,667
Highlands	4	325	20	651	207	12,412
Hillsborough	29	7,080	130	7,753	2,709	160,346
Holmes	0	0	6	216	26	1,115
Indian River	0	0	32	1,400	310	19,048
Jackson	0	0	10	471	127	3,691
Jefferson	1	5	6	127	36	1,663
Lafayette	0	0	1	6	10	391
Lake	2	142	52	2,063	497	27,352

See footnote at end of table.   Continued . . .

Florida Statistical Abstract 1991

Table 19.60. TOURIST FACILITIES: HOTELS AND MOTELS BY NUMBER OF UNITS AND FOOD
SERVICE ESTABLISHMENTS BY SEATING CAPACITY IN THE STATE AND COUNTIES
OF FLORIDA, FISCAL YEAR 1990-91 (Continued)

County	Licensed hotels		Licensed motels		Food service establishments	
	Number	Units	Number	Units	Number of licenses	Seating capacity
Lee	18	2,460	152	5,713	1,185	75,303
Leon	8	1,176	45	3,363	551	43,580
Levy	0	0	19	299	99	4,028
Liberty	0	0	1	10	12	434
Madison	0	0	3	116	33	1,334
Manatee	2	299	71	2,707	707	42,184
Marion	4	786	72	2,888	635	30,065
Martin	3	286	24	924	382	25,612
Monroe	16	1,459	159	5,747	636	36,778
Nassau	3	613	28	567	141	8,143
Okaloosa	0	0	57	4,301	490	32,926
Okeechobee	0	0	10	263	111	5,519
Orange	63	26,150	141	26,708	3,058	264,626
Osceola	14	3,768	112	16,332	523	44,277
Palm Beach	56	9,019	174	6,518	3,139	222,240
Pasco	0	0	42	1,822	750	40,615
Pinellas	42	4,721	415	14,243	2,848	199,490
Polk	10	732	106	5,660	1,186	69,100
Putnam	0	0	20	420	167	6,030
St. Johns	5	769	70	2,999	375	22,098
St. Lucie	5	915	33	1,179	485	24,566
Santa Rosa	0	0	12	697	162	6,669
Sarasota	4	560	85	3,261	901	60,999
Seminole	4	570	26	2,491	824	56,369
Sumter	0	0	9	628	128	3,896
Suwannee	1	26	7	227	66	2,430
Taylor	0	0	25	514	50	2,888
Union	0	0	0	0	12	260
Volusia	21	2,192	316	15,600	1,548	98,922
Wakulla	1	27	7	122	38	2,092
Walton	1	400	10	327	158	7,326
Washington	0	0	4	123	45	1,393

Note: Apartment buildings, rooming houses, rental condominiums, transient apartments, and total public lodgings are shown in Table 2.30.

Source: State of Florida, Department of Business Regulation, Division of Hotels
and Restaurants, *Master File Statistics: Public Lodging and Food Service Establishments*, Fiscal Year July 1990 through June 1991.

Florida Statistical Abstract 1991

Table 19.70. TOURIST-RELATED BUSINESSES: GROSS AND TAXABLE SALES AND SALES AND USE
TAX COLLECTIONS BY KIND OF BUSINESS IN FLORIDA, 1988 THROUGH 1990

(rounded to dollars)

Kind of business	Gross sales	Taxable sales	Sales and use tax collections
1988			
Restaurants and lunchrooms	10,518,075,111	9,259,032,413	571,601,588
Taverns and nightclubs	1,713,742,048	1,543,573,821	93,257,060
Hotels, apartment houses, etc.	6,192,143,823	5,541,234,034	340,270,178
Gift, card, and novelty shops	1,806,873,192	1,210,234,407	70,517,574
Newsstands	162,120,837	63,837,363	4,045,867
Admissions	1,956,917,983	1,795,090,701	127,500,374
Holiday season vendors	7,256,060	5,405,771	275,757
Transportation	580,266,098	152,400,771	18,980,142
Filling and service stations	5,835,960,815	913,869,275	54,047,355
1989			
Restaurants and lunchrooms	11,350,527,833	10,045,590,443	637,143,574
Taverns and nightclubs	1,703,190,924	1,569,088,316	99,238,741
Hotels, apartment houses, etc.	6,430,018,076	5,835,669,746	365,852,252
Gift, card, and novelty shops	1,908,620,962	1,330,276,042	83,292,344
Newsstands	135,131,454	46,270,646	3,098,322
Admissions	2,153,833,381	2,062,886,421	141,738,193
Holiday season vendors	26,049,519	22,234,411	1,378,111
Transportation	325,700,288	73,013,630	16,108,917
Filling and service stations	6,055,701,660	905,378,289	55,311,720
1990			
Restaurants and lunchrooms	12,366,970,723	10,898,836,551	686,968,020
Taverns and nightclubs	1,766,480,668	1,618,422,164	104,068,532
Hotels, apartment houses, etc.	7,810,360,922	6,250,370,256	400,784,888
Gift, card, and novelty shops	2,078,375,885	1,431,089,566	89,623,965
Newsstands	125,966,725	48,134,736	3,124,682
Admissions	2,444,682,802	2,328,195,273	158,563,631
Holiday season vendors	29,307,607	20,454,853	1,232,598
Transportation	269,270,394	77,891,057	16,843,405
Filling and service stations	6,909,292,777	932,890,789	58,017,516

Note: Data are sales reported to the Florida Department of Revenue for the 5
percent regular sales tax, 5 percent use tax, and 3 percent vehicle and farm equipment sales tax for January 1988. In February 1988 the regular sales and use tax
increased to 6 percent; this increase is reflected in the collections from March
1988 through December 1990. Sales occurred, for the most part, from December 1,
1987 through November 30, 1990. Kind of business data for counties are available
from the Bureau of Economic and Business Research, University of Florida. Data
includes all sales in the category, not just those to tourists, and are unaudited.
See Table 16.81 for taxable sales for all businesses; see Table 23.43 for tax
collections.

Source: State of Florida, Department of Revenue, unpublished data.

Florida Statistical Abstract 1991

Table 19.73. EATING AND DRINKING PLACES: AVERAGE MONTHLY REPORTING UNITS
EMPLOYMENT, AND PAYROLL COVERED BY UNEMPLOYMENT COMPENSATION LAW IN
THE STATE AND COUNTIES OF FLORIDA, 1990

County	Number of re-porting units	Number of employees	Payroll ($1,000)	County	Number of re-porting units	Number of employees	Payroll ($1,000)
			Eating and drinking places (SIC code 581)				
Florida	17,218	393,610	292,932	Lafayette	(D)	(D)	(D)
				Lake	187	2,856	1,859
Alachua	246	6,844	4,001	Lee	495	11,142	8,286
Baker	13	209	113	Leon	210	8,487	4,860
Bay	243	5,486	3,586	Levy	40	387	216
Bradford	21	415	220	Liberty	(D)	(D)	(D)
Brevard	538	12,429	8,624	Madison	14	126	57
Broward	1,970	40,986	33,431	Manatee	220	5,016	3,542
Calhoun	6	84	44	Marion	209	4,253	2,618
Charlotte	142	2,346	1,485	Martin	179	3,430	2,387
Citrus	107	1,846	1,075	Monroe	271	4,212	3,839
Clay	120	2,657	1,533	Nassau	55	1,075	742
Collier	287	4,942	4,293	Okaloosa	246	6,350	3,970
Columbia	48	1,104	629	Okeechobee	37	364	199
Dade	2,575	49,448	44,375	Orange	831	33,993	28,956
De Soto	18	361	156	Osceola	161	5,933	4,507
Dixie	15	155	80	—Palm Beach	1,283	26,695	22,222
Duval	739	21,056	14,269	Pasco	287	5,426	3,050
Escambia	313	8,208	5,125	Pinellas	1,224	28,808	20,260
Flagler	41	540	324	Polk	363	9,412	5,733
Franklin	20	110	65	Putnam	71	825	470
Gadsden	22	409	220	St. Johns	152	2,579	1,730
Gilchrist	8	33	17	St. Lucie	168	3,111	2,104
Glades	(D)	(D)	(D)	Santa Rosa	65	1,077	543
Gulf	17	121	64	Sarasota	486	10,752	8,054
Hamilton	(D)	(D)	(D)	Seminole	302	7,628	5,136
Hardee	17	171	88	Sumter	33	704	419
Hendry	28	299	187	Suwannee	22	500	285
Hernando	108	1,503	842	Taylor	31	412	227
Highlands	86	1,543	912	Union	(D)	(D)	(D)
Hillsborough	966	26,834	18,498	Volusia	561	12,667	8,456
Holmes	9	149	83	Wakulla	15	246	139
Indian River	137	2,598	1,762	Walton	41	606	352
Jackson	32	506	263	Washington	12	251	155
Jefferson	6	86	41	Statewide 1/	34	637	1,061

(D) Data withheld to avoid disclosure of information about individual firms.
1/ Reporting units without a fixed location within the state or of unknown county
location.

Source: State of Florida, Department of Labor and Employment Security, Bureau of
Labor Market Information, "Employment, Wages, and Contributions Report" (ES-202),
unpublished data.

Table 19.75. TOURIST-RELATED INDUSTRIES: AVERAGE MONTHLY REPORTING UNITS
EMPLOYMENT, AND PAYROLL COVERED BY UNEMPLOYMENT COMPENSATION LAW
BY INDUSTRY IN FLORIDA, 1990

SIC code	Industry	Number of re-porting units	Number of employees	Payroll ($1,000)
413	Intercity and rural bus transportation	19	604	1,159
414	Bus charter service	74	1,647	2,179
4489	Water transportation of passengers, NEC 1/	99	1,762	3,091
451	Air transportation, scheduled	303	37,783	96,856
458	Airports, flying fields, services	372	12,844	21,456
472	Arrangement of passenger transportation	2,377	13,315	20,715
4724	Travel agencies	1,926	9,787	15,025
4725	Tour operators	204	2,034	3,498
4729	Arrangement of passenger transportation, NEC	246	1,493	2,192
5947	Gift, novelty, and souvenir shops	1,926	12,451	10,431
70	Hotels and other lodging places	— 3,636	139,644	146,975
701	Hotels and motels	3,057	134,217	141,284
702	Rooming and boarding houses	96	1,150	894
703	Camps and recreational vehicle parks	422	3,124	3,275
704	Membership-basis organization hotels	60	1,152	1,522
7514	Passenger car rental	345	13,186	18,629
7515	Passenger car leasing	65	316	849
7519	Utility trailer and recreational vehicle leasing	56	972	1,461
78	Motion pictures	1,634	14,448	15,424
781	Motion picture production and allied services	383	2,142	4,917
782	Motion picture distribution and allied services	66	506	1,538
783	Motion picture theaters	244	5,594	3,669
784	Video tape rental	941	6,205	5,299
79	Amusement and recreation services	4,279	112,130	145,364
791	Dance studios, schools, and halls	294	1,385	1,296
792	Producers, orchestras, entertainers	457	6,359	7,963
793	Bowling centers	171	4,343	3,339
794	Commercial sports	525	10,588	19,265
7941	Professional sports clubs and promoters	141	4,111	11,395
7948	Racing, including track operations	383	6,476	7,870
799	Miscellaneous amusement and recreation services	2,830	89,454	113,501
7991	Physical fitness facilities	408	5,467	4,207
7992	Public golf courses	(D)	(D)	(D)
7993	Coin-operated amusement devices	149	992	1,195
7996	Amusement parks	(D)	(D)	(D)
7997	Membership sports and recreation clubs	642	28,887	34,824
7999	Amusement and recreation services, NEC 2/	1,472	15,156	16,137

NEC Not elsewhere classified.
(D) Data withheld to avoid disclosure of information about individual firms.
1/ Includes airboats, excursion boats, sightseeing boats, and water taxis.
2/ Includes miniature golf; golf driving ranges; commercial museums; rental of
bicycles, motorcycles, pleasure boats; carnivals; animal shows; fairs; etc.
Note: Totals on county employment tables may not match totals in this table due
to rounding.

Source: State of Florida, Department of Labor and Employment Security, Bureau of
Labor Market Information, "Employment, Wages, and Contributions Report" (ES-202)
unpublished data.

Florida Statistical Abstract 1991

Table 19.76. HOTELS, ROOMING HOUSES, CAMPS, AND LODGING PLACES: AVERAGE MONTHLY
   REPORTING UNITS, EMPLOYMENT, AND PAYROLL COVERED BY UNEMPLOYMENT COMPENSATION
   LAW IN THE STATE AND COUNTIES OF FLORIDA, 1990

County	Number of reporting units	Number of employees	Payroll ($1,000)	County	Number of reporting units	Number of employees	Payroll ($1,000)
Hotels, rooming houses, camps, and lodging places (SIC code 70)								

County	Number of reporting units	Number of employees	Payroll ($1,000)	County	Number of reporting units	Number of employees	Payroll ($1,000)
Florida	3,614	139,702	146,975	Lafayette	(D)	(D)	(D)
				Lake	41	999	948
Alachua	71	992	698	Lee	114	3,987	4,683
Baker	(D)	(D)	(D)	Leon	63	1,468	1,051
Bay	118	2,193	1,802	Levy	(D)	(D)	(D)
Bradford	(D)	(D)	(D)	Liberty	0	0	0
Brevard	88	2,724	2,211	Madison	(D)	(D)	(D)
Broward	307	11,096	11,958	Manatee	50	815	768
Calhoun	0	0	0	Marion	60	1,180	908
Charlotte	22	421	349	Martin	20	439	494
Citrus	30	583	447	Monroe	151	4,909	5,859
Clay	8	590	511	Nassau	(D)	(D)	(D)
Collier	53	3,893	4,656	Okaloosa	49	1,236	972
Columbia	26	354	221	Okeechobee	9	107	91
Dade	457	20,985	23,277	Orange	185	24,883	29,114
De Soto	8	42	37	Osceola	113	5,748	5,987
Dixie	4	7	3	Palm Beach	168	9,254	11,930
Duval	116	4,018	3,507	Pasco	44	616	500
Escambia	48	1,198	806	Pinellas	292	8,399	8,093
Flagler	9	287	300	Polk	96	2,372	2,197
Franklin	14	86	67	Putnam	13	139	93
Gadsden	(D)	(D)	(D)	St. Johns	60	2,067	2,151
Gilchrist	(D)	(D)	(D)	St. Lucie	31	926	673
Glades	(D)	(D)	(D)	Santa Rosa	12	166	123
Gulf	(D)	(D)	(D)	Sarasota	86	2,135	2,245
Hamilton	3	76	46	Seminole	26	1,377	1,220
Hardee	5	23	17	Sumter	16	179	108
Hendry	11	104	103	Suwannee	7	33	20
Hernando	(D)	(D)	(D)	Taylor	12	139	77
Highlands	19	188	161	Union	0	0	0
Hillsborough	123	7,342	6,938	Volusia	222	5,550	4,552
Holmes	(D)	(D)	(D)	Wakulla	4	19	14
Indian River	26	711	600	Walton	8	863	1,117
Jackson	9	105	71	Washington	(D)	(D)	(D)
Jefferson	(D)	(D)	(D)	Statewide 1/	13	222	648

(D) Data withheld to avoid disclosure of information about individual firms.
  1/ Reporting units without a fixed location within the state or of unknown county
location.
  Note: For a list of three-digit code industries included see Table 19.75.

  Source: State of Florida, Department of Labor and Employment Security, Bureau of
Labor Market Information, "Employment, Wages, and Contributions Report" (ES-202),
unpublished data.

Florida Statistical Abstract 1991

Table 19.78. AMUSEMENT AND RECREATION SERVICES: AVERAGE MONTHLY REPORTING UNITS
    EMPLOYMENT, AND PAYROLL COVERED BY UNEMPLOYMENT COMPENSATION LAW IN THE STATE
    AND COUNTIES OF FLORIDA, 1990

County	Number of re-porting units	Number of employees	Payroll ($1,000)	County	Number of re-porting units	Number of employees	Payroll ($1,000)
			Amusement and recreation services (SIC code 79)				
Florida	4,259	112,299	145,365	Lafayette	0	0	0
				Lake	38	438	447
Alachua	45	982	1,080	Lee	114	1,885	1,921
Baker	(D)	(D)	(D)	Leon	46	1,005	1,199
Bay	92	1,124	984	Levy	10	63	50
Bradford	(D)	(D)	(D)	Liberty	(D)	(D)	(D)
Brevard	89	1,232	1,078	Madison	7	28	21
Broward	521	8,999	9,739	Manatee	50	1,016	1,129
Calhoun	(D)	(D)	(D)	Marion	72	952	952
Charlotte	29	358	341	Martin	60	1,104	1,413
Citrus	28	235	219	Monroe	97	908	1,109
Clay	28	459	461	Nassau	13	77	66
Collier	93	2,208	2,879	Okaloosa	81	518	405
Columbia	14	114	87	Okeechobee	5	22	19
Dade	537	11,264	16,977	Orange	(D)	(D)	(D)
De Soto	7	98	91	Osceola	34	500	456
Dixie	(D)	(D)	(D)	Palm Beach	350	8,652	11,320
Duval	163	3,004	2,866	Pasco	65	665	641
Escambia	64	1,410	1,181	Pinellas	269	4,323	4,479
Flagler	7	193	193	Polk	88	2,361	2,719
Franklin	(D)	(D)	(D)	Putnam	10	50	48
Gadsden	(D)	(D)	(D)	St. Johns	29	769	1,020
Gilchrist	(D)	(D)	(D)	St. Lucie	28	585	587
Glades	(D)	(D)	(D)	Santa Rosa	26	293	281
Gulf	(D)	(D)	(D)	Sarasota	143	2,823	3,398
Hamilton	(D)	(D)	(D)	Seminole	92	1,545	1,771
Hardee	3	7	8	Sumter	6	40	32
Hendry	(D)	(D)	(D)	Suwannee	5	19	24
Hernando	21	444	343	Taylor	3	15	13
Highlands	18	329	261	Union	0	0	0
Hillsborough	243	7,937	8,504	Volusia	139	2,199	2,585
Holmes	(D)	(D)	(D)	Wakulla	(D)	(D)	(D)
Indian River	36	1,128	1,380	Walton	8	165	176
Jackson	11	60	47	Washington	(D)	(D)	(D)
Jefferson	(D)	(D)	(D)	Statewide 1/	49	524	1,104

(D) Data withheld to avoid disclosure of information about individual firms.
    1/ Reporting units without a fixed location within the state or of unknown county
location.
    Note: For a list of three-digit code industries included see Table 19.75.

    Source: State of Florida, Department of Labor and Employment Security, Bureau of
Labor Market Information, "Employment, Wages, and Contributions Report" (ES-202),
unpublished data.

HEALTH, EDUCATION AND CULTURAL SERVICES

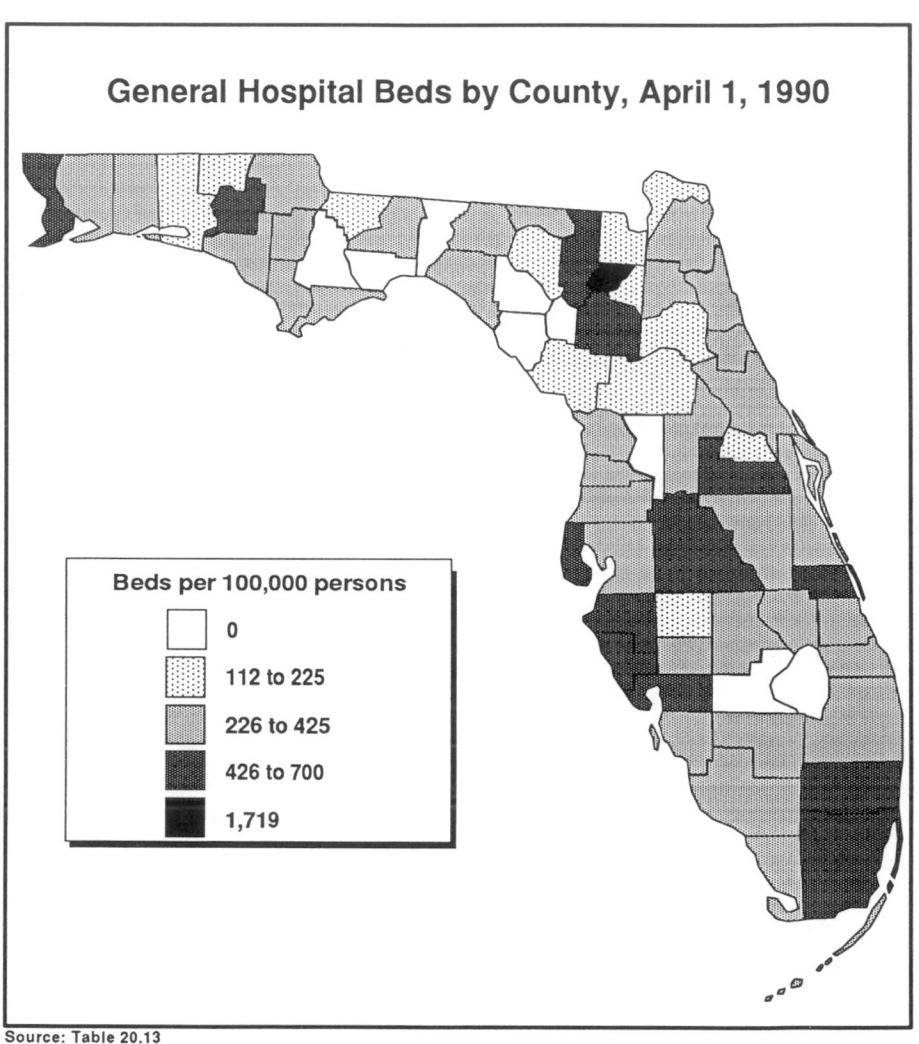

General Hospital Beds by County, April 1, 1990

Beds per 100,000 persons

0
112 to 225
226 to 425
426 to 700
1,719

Source: Table 20.13

TABLES LISTED BY MAJOR HEADINGS

Table 20.01. HEALTH, EDUCATIONAL, AND SOCIAL SERVICES: ESTABLISHMENTS AND RECEIPTS
BASED ON 1972 STANDARD INDUSTRIAL CLASSIFICATION CODES FOR FIRMS IN FLORIDA
1982 AND 1987

SIC Code 1972	SIC Code 1987	Kind of business	Number of establishments 1982	Number of establishments 1987	Receipts per establishment 1982 ($1,000)	Receipts per establishment 1987 ($1,000)	Percentage Change
80 ex.	80 ex.	Health services, except hospitals	18,643	23,906	4,978,365	10,064,191	102.2
806	806						
801	801 pt.	Offices of doctors of medicine	10,098	12,170	2,985,861	5,580,887	86.9
802	802 pt.	Offices of dentists	3,975	4,655	737,010	1,205,092	63.5
803	803	Offices and clinics of doctors of osteopathy	546	610	101,269	189,828	87.4
8041	8041	Offices and clinics of other health practitioners	1,519	2,058	186,794	374,197	100.3
8042	8042						
805	805	Nursing and personal care facilities	364	543	431,568	932,501	116.1
807	807	Medical and dental laboratories	753	971	184,189	392,044	112.8
8049;	801 pt.;	Other health services, NEC	1,388	2,899	351,674	1,389,642	295.2
808,9	802 pt.;						
	8043,9;						
	808,9						
823,4,	823,4,9	Selected educational services	401	623	120,797	324,286	168.5
9							
823	823	Libraries	6	7	320	905	182.8
824	824	Vocational schools	133	219	63,748	207,430	225.4
829	829	Schools and educational services, NEC	262	397	56,729	115,951	104.4
83	83	Social services	1,824	2,832	168,332	458,635	172.5
835	835	Child day care services	1,378	1,910	100,042	232,856	132.8
832,	832,3,6,	Other social services	446	922	68,290	225,779	230.6
3,6,9	9						

NEC Not elsewhere classified.

Table 20.02. HEALTH, EDUCATIONAL, AND SOCIAL SERVICES: ESTABLISHMENTS AND RECEIPTS
FOR FIRMS SUBJECT TO AND EXEMPT FROM FEDERAL INCOME TAX IN FLORIDA, 1987

SIC Code	Kind of business	Subject to federal income tax Number	Subject to federal income tax Receipts	Exempt from federal income tax Number	Exempt from federal income tax Receipts
801 pt.; 802 pt.	Clinics of doctors of medicine and dentists	382	428,965	61	72,010
805	Nursing and personal care facilities	543	932,501	125	251,547
806	Hospitals	142	2,836,850	165	6,693,624
823	Libraries	7	905	9	1,421
824	Vocational schools	219	207,430	31	7,910
835	Child day care services	1,910	232,856	544	101,816

Source for tables 20.01 and 20.02: U.S., Department of Commerce, Bureau of the
Census, *1987 Census of Service Industries: Florida.* SC87-A-10.

Table 20.05. HEALTH, EDUCATIONAL, SOCIAL, AND CULTURAL SERVICES: AVERAGE MONTHLY
    REPORTING UNITS, EMPLOYMENT, AND PAYROLL COVERED BY UNEMPLOYMENT COMPENSATION
    LAW BY INDUSTRY IN FLORIDA, 1990

SIC code	Industry	Number of reporting units	Number of employees	Payroll ($1,000)
80	Health services	25,590	466,996	1,058,333
801	Offices and clinics of doctors of medicine	12,912	82,538	369,796
802	Offices and clinics of dentists	4,781	26,145	55,473
803	Offices and clinics of doctors of osteopathy	591	2,861	8,689
804	Offices of other health practitioners	4,154	18,066	36,494
8041	Offices and clinics of chiropractors	1,580	5,393	10,871
8042	Offices and clinics of optometrists	680	2,528	4,728
8043	Offices and clinics of podiatrists	444	1,763	3,921
8049	Offices and clinics of health practitioners, NEC	1,448	8,381	16,974
805	Nursing and personal care facilities	563	61,726	66,740
8051	Skilled nursing care facilities	502	57,008	61,909
8052	Intermediate care facilities	17	1,812	1,982
8059	Nursing and personal care facilities, NEC	44	2,904	2,849
806	Hospitals	343	229,401	446,465
8062	General medical and surgical hospitals	251	204,208	404,591
8063	Psychiatric hospitals	59	16,340	24,263
8069	Specialty hospitals, except psychiatric	32	8,853	17,610
807	Medical and dental laboratories	1,179	10,774	21,838
8071	Medical laboratories	627	8,328	17,987
8072	Dental laboratories	551	2,446	3,851
808	Home health care services	419	18,441	24,277
809	Miscellaneous health and allied services, NEC	644	17,041	28,561
82	Educational services	1,680	370,515	690,412
821	Elementary and secondary schools	570	257,565	500,491
822	Colleges and universities	256	103,042	175,850
8221	Colleges, universities, and professional schools	209	74,016	133,013
8222	Junior colleges and technical institutes	47	29,026	42,837
823	Libraries	23	836	1,161
824	Vocational schools	229	3,884	5,715
8243	Data processing schools	22	151	290
8244	Business and secretarial schools	22	662	861
8249	Vocational schools, NEC	185	3,070	4,564
829	School and education services, NEC	600	5,186	7,195
83	Social services	4,592	88,220	90,185
832	Individual and family social services	808	14,462	17,140
833	Job training and related services	229	9,072	9,469
835	Child day care services	2,138	24,808	18,449
836	Residential care	1,045	32,833	35,886
839	Social services, NEC	370	7,043	9,242
84	Museums, art galleries, botanical and zoological gardens	103	2,362	2,910
841	Museums and art galleries	76	1,277	1,538
842	Arboreta, botanical and zoological gardens	27	1,085	1,372

NEC Not elsewhere classified.
Note: Totals on county employment tables may not match totals in this table due
to rounding.
Source: State of Florida, Department of Labor and Employment Security, Bureau of
Labor Market Information, "Employment, Wages, and Contributions Report" (ES-202),
unpublished data.

Table 20.06. OFFICES AND CLINICS OF DOCTORS OF MEDICINE: AVERAGE MONTHLY
REPORTING UNITS, EMPLOYMENT, AND PAYROLL COVERED BY UNEMPLOYMENT
COMPENSATION LAW IN THE STATE AND COUNTIES OF FLORIDA, 1990

County	Number of reporting units	Number of employees	Payroll ($1,000)	County	Number of reporting units	Number of employees	Payroll ($1,000)
			Offices and clinics of doctors of medicine (SIC code 801)				
Florida	12,890	82,546	369,798	Lafayette	(D)	(D)	(D)
				Lake	114	652	2,404
Alachua	237	1,432	5,792	Lee	263	2,426	13,800
Baker	4	18	38	Leon	187	1,557	5,756
Bay	107	742	3,555	Levy	9	36	31
Bradford	(D)	(D)	(D)	Liberty	(D)	(D)	(D)
Brevard	328	2,454	11,284	Madison	4	60	133
Broward	1,546	9,822	49,302	Manatee	155	1,142	4,781
Calhoun	(D)	(D)	(D)	Marion	161	1,044	4,416
Charlotte	120	687	3,514	Martin	103	634	2,953
Citrus	69	376	1,537	Monroe	62	223	799
Clay	75	505	1,645	Nassau	16	92	179
Collier	141	604	3,654	Okaloosa	99	753	2,433
Columbia	29	111	414	Okeechobee	20	91	343
Dade	2,753	13,456	61,510	Orange	628	5,160	23,806
De Soto	17	62	200	Osceola	76	430	1,878
Dixie	(D)	(D)	(D)	Palm Beach	994	5,908	29,814
Duval	663	5,082	23,324	Pasco	263	1,770	6,994
Escambia	191	2,247	9,513	Pinellas	865	5,576	24,589
Flagler	11	46	76	Polk	219	2,806	9,015
Franklin	(D)	(D)	(D)	Putnam	38	308	643
Gadsden	11	82	149	St. Johns	61	276	1,149
Gilchrist	(D)	(D)	(D)	St. Lucie	105	521	2,314
Glades	0	0	0	Santa Rosa	38	302	732
Gulf	6	37	96	Sarasota	361	2,250	11,648
Hamilton	(D)	(D)	(D)	Seminole	179	1,265	4,845
Hardee	8	38	87	Sumter	(D)	(D)	(D)
Hendry	10	41	66	Suwannee	8	34	48
Hernando	76	361	1,883	Taylor	14	74	133
Highlands	59	281	905	Union	(D)	(D)	(D)
Hillsborough	925	5,475	23,508	Volusia	275	1,770	7,659
Holmes	5	24	85	Wakulla	(D)	(D)	(D)
Indian River	110	1,017	3,450	Walton	6	25	32
Jackson	21	106	349	Washington	9	35	78
Jefferson	(D)	(D)	(D)	Statewide 1/	9	32	113

(D) Data withheld to avoid disclosure of information about individual firms.
1/ Reporting units without a fixed location within the state or of unknown county
location.

Source: State of Florida, Department of Labor and Employment Security, Bureau of
Labor Market Information, "Employment, Wages, and Contributions Report" (ES-202),
unpublished data.

Florida Statistical Abstract 1991

Table 20.07. OFFICES AND CLINICS OF DENTISTS: AVERAGE MONTHLY REPORTING UNITS EMPLOYMENT, AND PAYROLL COVERED BY UNEMPLOYMENT COMPENSATION LAW IN THE STATE AND COUNTIES OF FLORIDA, 1990

County	Number of reporting units	Number of employees	Payroll ($1,000)	County	Number of reporting units	Number of employees	Payroll ($1,000)
			Offices and clinics of dentisits (SIC code 802)				
Florida	4,765	26,146	55,474	Lafayette	0	0	0
				Lake	44	275	502
Alachua	70	425	840	Lee	109	648	1,473
Baker	(D)	(D)	(D)	Leon	61	423	1,036
Bay	40	256	508	Levy	5	24	26
Bradford	6	28	61	Liberty	(D)	(D)	(D)
Brevard	142	918	1,922	Madison	4	15	19
Broward	574	3,038	6,686	Manatee	74	413	1,002
Calhoun	4	14	17	Marion	55	336	614
Charlotte	27	148	311	Martin	45	199	474
Citrus	20	112	229	Monroe	17	95	178
Clay	40	261	420	Nassau	11	60	113
Collier	67	325	772	Okaloosa	54	258	401
Columbia	8	44	85	Okeechobee	(D)	(D)	(D)
Dade	794	3,700	7,901	Orange	273	1,628	3,692
De Soto	(D)	(D)	(D)	Osceola	19	144	287
Dixie	(D)	(D)	(D)	Palm Beach	427	2,165	4,984
Duval	253	1,521	2,834	Pasco	57	373	814
Escambia	96	543	1,060	Pinellas	361	2,111	4,889
Flagler	5	37	96	Polk	104	617	1,238
Franklin	(D)	(D)	(D)	Putnam	9	61	111
Gadsden	7	28	52	St. Johns	21	105	207
Gilchrist	0	0	0	St. Lucie	45	250	463
Glades	0	0	0	Santa Rosa	20	122	175
Gulf	(D)	(D)	(D)	Sarasota	159	756	1,601
Hamilton	(D)	(D)	(D)	Seminole	94	580	1,197
Hardee	(D)	(D)	(D)	Sumter	(D)	(D)	(D)
Hendry	5	30	43	Suwannee	(D)	(D)	(D)
Hernando	19	135	304	Taylor	(D)	(D)	(D)
Highlands	19	84	165	Union	0	0	0
Hillsborough	289	1,717	3,730	Volusia	116	671	1,252
Holmes	(D)	(D)	(D)	Wakulla	(D)	(D)	(D)
Indian River	41	211	360	Walton	4	12	7
Jackson	8	38	45	Washington	(D)	(D)	(D)
Jefferson	5	13	14	Statewide 1/	(D)	(D)	(D)

(D) Data withheld to avoid disclosure of information about individual firms.
1/ Reporting units without a fixed location within the state or of unknown county location.

Source: State of Florida, Department of Labor and Employment Security, Bureau of Labor Market Information, "Employment, Wages, and Contributions Report" (ES-202), unpublished data.

Florida Statistical Abstract 1991

Table 20.11. NURSING AND PERSONAL CARE FACILITIES AND HOSPITALS: AVERAGE MONTHLY
REPORTING UNITS, EMPLOYMENT, AND PAYROLL COVERED BY UNEMPLOYMENT COMPENSATION
LAW IN THE STATE AND COUNTIES OF FLORIDA, 1990

County	Number of re- porting units	Number of employees	Payroll ($1,000)	County	Number of re- porting units	Number of employees	Payroll ($1,000)

Nursing and personal care facilities (SIC code 805)

County	Units	Employees	Payroll	County	Units	Employees	Payroll
Florida	554	61,735	66,744	Lee	8	1,077	1,084
				Leon	7	631	635
Alachua	9	787	727	Manatee	12	1,255	1,228
Bay	6	540	479	Marion	8	638	577
Brevard	16	1,391	1,352	Martin	5	496	524
Broward	29	3,952	4,659	Okaloosa	7	675	546
Charlotte	7	883	858	Orange	23	2,793	3,078
Citrus	6	605	557	Osceola	4	740	780
Collier	4	707	817	Palm Beach	39	5,613	6,580
Dade	63	6,886	9,457	Pasco	17	1,349	1,371
Duval	23	2,748	2,837	Pinellas	71	7,945	8,921
Escambia	7	975	804	Polk	18	2,183	2,106
Gadsden	3	298	277	St. Johns	6	524	544
Highlands	4	440	378	St. Lucie	6	656	727
Hillsborough	26	2,927	2,846	Sarasota	24	2,595	2,742
Indian River	5	315	386	Seminole	10	844	891
Lake	10	985	1,039	Volusia	24	2,504	2,407

Hospitals (SIC code 806)

County	Units	Employees	Payroll	County	Units	Employees	Payroll
Florida	336	229,429	446,468	Lake	5	2,340	3,656
				Lee	7	5,524	10,800
Alachua	6	8,738	17,142	Manatee	5	3,127	5,823
Bay	4	2,159	3,569	Marion	4	2,304	4,099
Brevard	9	6,170	11,199	Okaloosa	6	1,617	2,746
Broward	25	21,053	40,696	Orange	11	12,667	24,913
Charlotte	4	1,994	3,235	Palm Beach	21	13,930	28,160
Columbia	3	1,381	2,724	Pasco	7	3,077	5,613
Dade	45	39,580	88,388	Pinellas	28	17,906	33,979
Duval	16	14,371	28,734	Polk	8	6,061	11,279
Escambia	7	6,038	10,174	St. Johns	3	978	1,539
Hernando	3	1,323	2,040	Santa Rosa	5	807	1,101
Highlands	3	967	1,600	Sarasota	8	4,844	9,353
Hillsborough	25	17,660	35,771	Seminole	6	3,808	7,664
Indian River	4	1,684	3,111	Volusia	8	5,000	9,230

Note: Excluded are counties where data are withheld to avoid disclosure of
information about individual firms.

Source: State of Florida, Department of Labor and Employment Security, Bureau of
Labor Market Information, "Employment, Wages, and Contributions Report" (ES-202),
unpublished data.

Florida Statistical Abstract 1991

Table 20.13. HEALTH CARE FACILITIES: LICENSED HOSPITALS BY TYPE, BEDS, AND BEDS
   PER 100,000 PERSONS IN THE STATE AND COUNTIES OF FLORIDA, APRIL 1, 1990

| | | | | | | General hospital beds 2/ | |
County	Total	General	General excluding obstetrics	Psychiatric	Other 1/	Total	Per 100,000 persons
Florida	308	116	106	57	29	52,001	406
Alachua	6	3	0	1	2	1,279	685
Baker	2	0	1	1	0	25	129
Bay	3	2	0	1	0	438	323
Bradford	1	0	1	0	0	54	218
Brevard	8	4	0	3	1	1,166	289
Broward	29	9	11	6	3	6,031	485
Calhoun	1	1	0	0	0	36	319
Charlotte	3	2	1	0	0	622	627
Citrus	3	1	1	1	0	283	309
Clay	2	1	1	0	0	256	249
Collier	2	1	0	1	0	381	263
Columbia	2	1	1	0	0	203	466
Dade	39	9	19	6	5	9,305	497
De Soto	2	1	0	1	0	82	338
Dixie	0	0	0	0	0	0	0
Duval	14	5	4	3	2	2,635	384
Escambia	4	3	1	0	0	1,349	473
Flagler	1	0	1	0	0	81	339
Franklin	2	0	1	1	0	29	334
Gadsden	2	1	0	1	0	51	112
Gilchrist	0	0	0	0	0	0	0
Glades	0	0	0	0	0	0	0
Gulf	1	0	1	0	0	45	358
Hamilton	1	1	0	0	0	42	405
Hardee	1	1	0	0	0	50	220
Hendry	1	1	0	0	0	66	253
Hernando	3	1	1	1	0	262	289
Highlands	3	1	1	0	1	277	401
Hillsborough	19	8	6	3	2	3,366	400
Holmes	1	0	1	0	0	34	193
Indian River	3	2	0	0	1	410	449
Jackson	3	1	1	0	1	157	351
Jefferson	0	0	0	0	0	0	0
Lafayette	0	0	0	0	0	0	0
Lake	5	1	2	1	1	544	372

See footnotes at end of table. Continued . . .

Florida Statistical Abstract 1991

Table 20.13. HEALTH CARE FACILITIES: LICENSED HOSPITALS BY TYPE, BEDS, AND BEDS
    PER 100,000 PERSONS IN THE STATE AND COUNTIES OF FLORIDA, APRIL 1, 1990
    (Continued)

County	Total	General	Hospitals General ex- cluding obstet- rics	Psychi- atric	Other 1/	General hospital beds 2/ Total	Per 100,000 persons
Lee	5	1	3	1	0	1,230	379
Leon	4	2	0	0	2	758	394
Levy	1	0	1	0	0	40	159
Liberty	0	0	0	0	0	0	0
Madison	1	1	0	0	0	42	255
Manatee	5	2	0	2	1	870	452
Marion	4	2	0	2	0	406	213
Martin	2	1	0	1	0	336	348
Monroe	4	2	2	0	0	224	284
Nassau	1	1	0	0	0	54	113
Okaloosa	5	1	3	1	0	434	276
Okeechobee	1	1	0	0	0	101	337
Orange	12	6	1	4	1	2,903	444
Osceola	4	1	2	1	0	373	382
Palm Beach	21	7	8	3	3	3,256	376
Pasco	6	4	1	1	0	875	321
Pinellas	23	5	13	3	2	4,329	506
Polk	8	5	2	1	0	1,785	434
Putnam	1	1	0	0	0	141	224
St. Johns	3	1	1	1	0	222	263
St. Lucie	3	1	1	1	0	425	297
Santa Rosa	4	1	2	1	0	268	386
Sarasota	6	2	2	1	1	1,294	490
Seminole	3	1	1	1	0	352	125
Sumter	0	0	0	0	0	0	0
Suwannee	1	1	0	0	0	60	217
Taylor	1	1	0	0	0	48	244
Union	2	0	2	0	0	180	1,719
Volusia	8	3	4	1	0	1,305	362
Wakulla	0	0	0	0	0	0	0
Walton	1	0	1	0	0	50	173
Washington	1	1	0	0	0	81	489

1/ Includes special medical, special tuberculosis, eye, children's, and rehabili-
tation hospitals.
    2/ Total beds include beds in general hospitals and general hospitals, excluding
obstetrics. The rates per 100,000 persons are computed using the April 1, 1989
estimates for Florida and Florida counties. These estimates include inmates.

    Source: State of Florida, Department of Health and Rehabilitative Services,
Office of Licensure and Certification, *List of Licensed Hospitals, Revised 1990*.

Florida Statistical Abstract 1991

Table 20.14. VETERANS ADMINISTRATION HOSPITALS: PATIENTS AND BEDS IN HOSPITAL CARE
AND IN NURSING HOME CARE BY HOSPITAL IN FLORIDA, FISCAL YEAR 1988-89

Item	Bay Pines	Gaines- ville	Lake City	Miami	Tampa
Hospital care					
Average operating beds	666	438	333	627	587
Medical	370	183	245	328	300
Surgical	140	165	65	100	144
Psychiatric	157	90	23	199	143
Patients treated	12,710	10,216	6,849	12,364	11,874
Episodes of care 1/					
Medical	7,736	4,412	4,999	6,840	5,625
Surgical	2,797	4,538	1,494	2,728	3,888
Psychiatric	2,175	1,266	356	2,796	2,361
Average daily census	447	341	242	484	387
Patients in hospitals 9/30/89	380	315	198	462	331
Under 35	24	15	6	44	26
35-44	74	65	19	119	49
45-54	39	35	16	57	37
55-64	94	80	45	95	95
65-74	95	83	76	96	90
75-84	39	34	29	39	31
85 and over	15	3	7	12	3
Nursing home care					
Average operating beds	240	109	120	240	111
Bed occupancy rate (percentage)	93	94	98	93	103
Average daily census	224	102	113	224	114
Admissions	455	67	115	290	183
Discharges/deaths	477	90	115	300	188
Patients treated	707	178	235	526	304
Patients remaining on 9/30/89	230	88	120	226	116
Community nursing homes 2/					
Average daily census	151	67	20	85	139
Admissions	580	151	50	197	519
Discharges/deaths	581	180	48	378	494
Patients treated	719	235	66	454	640
Patients remaining on 9/30/89	138	55	18	76	146

1/ Interhospital transfers are excluded from overall totals but are included in
bed section totals. Patients are classified according to the classification of the
type of bed they occupy rather than a diagnostic basis.
2/ A contract program to place in a community nursing home at Veterans Administration expense those veterans who require skilled or intermediate nursing care in
making the transition from a hospital to the community.

Source: U.S., Department of Veterans Affairs, *Annual Report of the Secretary of
Veterans Affairs, 1989.*

Florida Statistical Abstract 1991

Table 20.16. NURSING HOMES: NUMBER OF LICENSED FACILITIES AND ACCOMMODATIONS
IN THE STATE AND COUNTIES OF FLORIDA, 1991

County	Number of facilities	Number of beds	County	Number of facilities	Number of beds
Florida	571	66,183	Lafayette	0	0
Alachua	6	839	Lake	10	1,012
Baker	2	128	Lee	13	1,528
Bay	5	586	Leon	6	588
Bradford	2	240	Levy	1	180
Brevard	14	1,696	Liberty	0	0
Broward	33	3,960	Madison	2	118
Calhoun	1	150	Manatee	12	1,209
Charlotte	6	808	Marion	6	642
Citrus	6	554	Martin	4	526
Clay	7	795	Monroe	3	360
Collier	6	524	Nassau	2	180
Columbia	1	95	Okaloosa	6	600
Dade	52	7,798	Okeechobee	1	155
De Soto	1	81	Orange	24	3,065
Dixie	0	0	Osceola	5	629
Duval	29	3,387	Palm Beach	43	5,141
Escambia	9	1,132	Pasco	14	1,475
Flagler	1	100	Pinellas	79	8,716
Franklin	2	150	Polk	19	2,045
Gadsden	2	180	Putnam	3	217
Gilchrist	1	120	St. Johns	7	500
Glades	0	0	St. Lucie	6	748
Gulf	1	120	Santa Rosa	3	300
Hamilton	1	60	Sarasota	22	2,540
Hardee	1	79	Seminole	8	964
Hendry	2	180	Sumter	1	180
Hernando	4	540	Suwannee	3	287
Highlands	4	434	Taylor	1	120
Hillsborough	29	3,461	Union	0	0
Holmes	1	120	Volusia	24	2,427
Indian River	6	477	Wakulla	1	120
Jackson	2	300	Walton	2	180
Jefferson	2	157	Washington	1	180

Note: Some accommodation data have been estimated.

Source: State of Florida, Department of Health and Rehabilitative Services,
Office of Licensure and Certification, *Annual Report and Directory of Nursing Home
Facilities, January 1, 1991.*

Florida Statistical Abstract 1991

Table 20.25. HOSPITAL COSTS: AVERAGE COST PER DAY, AVERAGE HOSPITAL STAY, AVERAGE
COST PER STAY, 1988, AND SEMI-PRIVATE ROOM CHARGES, JANUARY 1989 AND 1990
IN FLORIDA AND THE UNITED STATES

Item	Florida	United States
Average cost to hospital per adjusted inpatient day, 1988 A/ (dollars)	646.19	586.33
Average length of hospital stay, 1988 (days)	7.0	7.2
Average semi-private charges		
January 1989 (dollars)	239.00	264.00
January 1990 (dollars)	271.00	297.00
Percentage change in room charges: January 1989 to January 1990	13.4	12.5
Average cost to hospital per adjusted admission, 1988 B/ (dollars)	4,506.01	4,206.73

A/ Covers expense of inpatient care only and is derived by dividing expenses by
inpatient days.

B/ Average expense to the hospital in providing care for one inpatient stay.
Expenses derived by subtracting outpatient expenses from total expenses, and
dividing the resulting amount by total admissions.

Table 20.26. MANAGED HEALTH CARE: NUMBER OF PREFERRED PROVIDER ORGANIZATIONS
(PPOS) AND HEALTH MAINTENANCE ORGANIZATIONS (HMOS) AND ENROLLMENT IN
FLORIDA, OTHER SUNBELT STATES, AND THE UNITED STATES, 1989

State	Number of PPOs	HMOs Number of--	HMOs Enroll- ment	HMOs Percentage of population in--
Florida	25	35	1,300,862	10.6
Alabama	7	8	180,624	4.4
Arizona	13	16	597,896	17.1
Arkansas	1	5	55,739	2.3
California	152	51	8,439,810	29.8
Georgia	16	8	285,616	4.5
Louisiana	13	9	237,110	5.4
Mississippi	3	0	0	0.0
New Mexico	2	5	190,507	12.6
North Carolina	9	12	326,679	5.0
Oklahoma	7	6	169,032	5.2
South Carolina	1	6	74,665	2.2
Tennessee	13	8	231,096	4.7
Texas	39	29	1,197,199	7.1
Virginia	7	14	386,318	6.4
United States	685	590	32,492,784	13.2

Source for Tables 20.25 and 20.26: Health Insurance Association of America,
Source Book of Health Insurance Data, 1990.

Florida Statistical Abstract 1991

Table 20.27. EDUCATIONAL SERVICES: AVERAGE MONTHLY REPORTING UNITS, EMPLOYMENT
AND PAYROLL COVERED BY UNEMPLOYMENT COMPENSATION LAW IN THE STATE AND
COUNTIES OF FLORIDA, 1990

County	Number of reporting units	Number of employees	Payroll ($1,000)	County	Number of reporting units	Number of employees	Payroll ($1,000)
			Educational services (SIC code 82)				
Florida	1,664	370,609	690,412	Leon	48	16,291	26,285
Brevard	38	9,341	17,462	Madison	5	657	1,063
Columbia	6	1,453	2,360	Orange	86	22,828	39,037
Dade	298	61,115	130,258	St. Johns	11	2,531	4,514
Duval	90	19,709	33,815	St. Lucie	17	3,439	6,792
Escambia	30	9,697	16,397	Volusia	40	9,337	17,044
Hillsborough	116	28,279	52,292	Statewide 1/	24	173	321
			Vocational Schools (SIC code 824)				
Florida	216	3,891	5,714	Hillsborough	15	264	433
Alachua	5	27	47	Orange	15	199	267
Broward	28	763	1,358	Palm Beach	22	239	351
Dade	58	1,341	1,665	Pinellas	10	78	124
Duval	13	168	261	Volusia	7	65	124

1/ Reporting units without a fixed location within the state or of unknown county
location.
    Note: Excluded are counties where data are withheld to avoid disclosure of
information about individual firms. See Table 20.05 for a list of educational
services included.

    Source: State of Florida, Department of Labor and Employment Security, Bureau of
Labor Market Information, "Employment, Wages, and Contributions Report" (ES-202),
unpublished data.

Florida Statistical Abstract 1991

Table 20.28. SOCIAL SERVICES: AVERAGE MONTHLY EMPLOYMENT COVERED BY UNEMPLOYMENT COMPENSATION LAW BY TYPE OF SOCIAL SERVICE IN THE STATE AND COUNTIES OF FLORIDA, 1990

County	Total (SIC 83)	Individual and family (SIC 832)	Job training and vocational rehabilitation (SIC 833)	Child day care (SIC 835)	Residential care 1/ (SIC 836)	Social services NEC 2/ (SIC 839)
Florida	88,359	14,475	9,075	24,818	32,847	7,043
Alachua	3,718	177	(D)	615	(D)	201
Baker	96	(D)	0	28	(D)	0
Bay	852	127	55	323	329	(D)
Bradford	93	40	(D)	34	(D)	0
Brevard	1,869	227	450	925	244	20
Broward	7,971	1,349	504	2,698	2,362	1,056
Calhoun	51	(D)	(D)	0	12	0
Charlotte	343	63	(D)	79	136	0
Citrus	631	(D)	(D)	112	204	(D)
Clay	371	(D)	(D)	203	40	0
Collier	901	88	(D)	257	415	41
Columbia	218	11	(D)	116	(D)	(D)
Dade	11,476	2,446	1,252	2,542	4,008	1,226
De Soto	91	(D)	(D)	59	0	0
Dixie	(D)	(D)	(D)	0	0	0
Duval	4,862	1,100	369	1,767	1,415	210
Escambia	2,362	223	197	633	1,048	(D)
Flagler	55	(D)	0	(D)	(D)	0
Franklin	(D)	(D)	0	(D)	0	0
Gadsden	384	(D)	(D)	65	(D)	(D)
Gilchrist	(D)	(D)	0	(D)	0	0
Glades	27	(D)	(D)	(D)	0	0
Gulf	57	(D)	0	(D)	(D)	0
Hamilton	(D)	(D)	0	(D)	0	0
Hardee	402	(D)	(D)	39	75	0
Hendry	158	(D)	(D)	76	(D)	0
Hernando	432	(D)	0	78	(D)	0
Highlands	435	(D)	(D)	88	243	(D)
Hillsborough	5,714	944	329	2,272	1,600	568
Holmes	97	(D)	0	(D)	(D)	(D)
Indian River	457	129	(D)	214	50	(D)
Jackson	(D)	(D)	(D)	78	(D)	(D)
Jefferson	38	(D)	0	(D)	(D)	0
Lafayette	(D)	(D)	0	(D)	(D)	0
Lake	525	19	(D)	197	226	(D)
Lee	4,248	452	214	742	2,766	73
Leon	2,215	443	225	643	692	210
Levy	95	(D)	(D)	50	(D)	0
Liberty	55	(D)	0	(D)	(D)	(D)
Madison	100	(D)	(D)	32	(D)	0

See footnotes at end of table.   Continued . . .

Florida Statistical Abstract 1991

Table 20.28. SOCIAL SERVICES: AVERAGE MONTHLY EMPLOYMENT COVERED BY UNEMPLOYMENT
COMPENSATION LAW BY TYPE OF SOCIAL SERVICE IN THE STATE AND COUNTIES OF
FLORIDA, 1990 (Continued)

County	Total (SIC 83)	Individual and family (SIC 832)	Job training and vocational rehabilitation (SIC 833)	Child day care (SIC 835)	Residential care 1/ (SIC 836)	Social services NEC 2/ (SIC 839)
Manatee	986	194	0	282	362	(D)
Marion	990	220	(D)	418	257	(D)
Martin	522	98	(D)	136	155	(D)
Monroe	183	77	(D)	75	(D)	(D)
Nassau	(D)	(D)	(D)	37	0	0
Okaloosa	865	28	0	347	331	(D)
Okeechobee	425	(D)	(D)	67	(D)	0
Orange	5,053	971	544	1,445	1,596	495
Osceola	349	84	(D)	186	60	(D)
Palm Beach	4,971	857	540	1,635	1,178	759
Pasco	1,521	341	217	343	584	33
Pinellas	7,898	1,323	1,580	1,447	3,207	339
Polk	2,546	371	434	752	952	(D)
Putnam	387	(D)	(D)	107	89	(D)
St. Johns	597	(D)	(D)	187	279	(D)
St. Lucie	671	169	(D)	339	85	(D)
Santa Rosa	265	(D)	0	170	(D)	0
Sarasota	1,999	99	273	252	1,256	118
Seminole	1,276	107	77	750	322	18
Sumter	181	(D)	(D)	18	(D)	0
Suwannee	498	(D)	0	(D)	(D)	(D)
Taylor	88	(D)	(D)	57	0	(D)
Union	(D)	(D)	(D)	(D)	0	0
Volusia	2,391	277	(D)	601	1,164	294
Wakulla	38	(D)	0	(D)	(D)	0
Walton	204	(D)	(D)	(D)	(D)	(D)
Washington	111	0	(D)	22	(D)	(D)
Statewide 3/	128	(D)	0	0	(D)	(D)

NEC Not elsewhere classified.
(D) Data withheld to avoid disclosure of information about individual firms.
1/ Residential social and personal care for children, the aged, and other persons
with limits on ability for self-care, but where medical care is not a major concern.
2/ Includes establishments primarily engaged in community improvement and social
change, such as advocacy groups, fundraising organizations (except contract or fee
basis), health and welfare councils, united fund councils, community action
agencies, etc.
3/ Reporting units without a fixed location within the state or of unknown county
location.

Source: State of Florida, Department of Labor and Employment Security, Bureau of
Labor Market Information, "Employment, Wages, and Contributions Reports" (ES-202),
unpublished data.

Table 20.29. MUSEUMS, ART GALLERIES, BOTANICAL AND ZOOLOGICAL GARDENS: AVERAGE
MONTHLY REPORTING UNITS, EMPLOYMENT, AND PAYROLL COVERED BY UNEMPLOYMENT
COMPENSATION LAW IN THE STATE AND COUNTIES OF FLORIDA, 1990

County	Number of reporting units	Number of employees	Payroll ($1,000)	County	Number of reporting units	Number of employees	Payroll ($1,000)
Museums, art galleries, botanical and zoological gardens (SIC code 84)							
Florida	100	2,363	2,910	Monroe	4	51	63
				Orange	8	328	468
Broward	9	205	270	Palm Beach	12	237	322
Dade	8	125	150	Pinellas	7	125	165
Duval	4	181	235	St. Johns	12	322	301
Hillsborough	4	189	186	Sarasota	4	158	221

Note: Excluded are counties where data are withheld to avoid disclosure of
information about individual firms.

Table 20.30. MEMBERSHIP ORGANIZATIONS: AVERAGE MONTHLY REPORTING UNITS, EMPLOYMENT
AND PAYROLL COVERED BY UNEMPLOYMENT COMPENSATION LAW BY INDUSTRY IN FLORIDA
1990

SIC code	Industry	Number of reporting units	Number of employees	Payroll ($1,000)
86	Membership organizations	6,079	47,462	58,844
861	Business associations	652	3,994	8,310
862	Professional membership organizations	153	2,282	4,498
863	Labor unions and similar labor organizations	516	3,215	4,026
864	Civic, social, and fraternal organizations	4,031	29,374	29,402
865	Political organizations	48	193	363
866	Religious organizations	457	4,085	4,521
869	Memberhip organizations, NEC	220	4,316	7,725

NEC Not elsewhere classified.
Note: State totals on county employment tables may not match totals in this
table due to rounding.

Source for Tables 20.29 and 20.30: State of Florida, Department of Labor and Employment Security, Bureau of Labor Market Information, "Employment, Wages, and
Contributions Report" (ES-202), unpublished data.

Table 20.33. PHYSICIANS: LICENSED DOCTORS OF MEDICINE AND OSTEOPATHY IN THE STATE
    AND COUNTIES OF FLORIDA, AUGUST 3, 1991

Location of licensee	Doctors of-- Medicine	Osteopathy	Location of licensee	Doctors of-- Medicine	Osteopathy
Total 1/	51,513	5,035	Jefferson	4	0
NonFlorida	19,486	3,019	Lafayette	5	0
Unknown	0	0	Lake	210	10
Alachua	1,501	6	Lee	619	71
Baker	18	2	Leon	523	16
Bay	220	15	Levy	20	1
Bradford	16	0	Liberty	4	0
Brevard	685	29	Madison	13	1
Broward	3,050	301	Manatee	389	14
Calhoun	7	1	Marion	294	14
Charlotte	213	14	Martin	217	12
Citrus	133	16	Monroe	161	24
Clay	218	26	Nassau	33	3
Collier	318	14	Okaloosa	247	17
Columbia	94	2	Okeechobee	27	2
Dade	7,390	265	Orange	1,699	124
De Soto	48	0	Osceola	125	11
Dixie	4	3	Palm Beach	2,253	179
Duval	1,972	94	Pasco	360	48
Escambia	675	21	Pinellas	1,997	343
Flagler	25	4	Polk	663	8
Franklin	6	2	Putnam	66	8
Gadsden	54	3	St. Johns	155	5
Gilchrist	4	0	St. Lucie	207	7
Glades	2	0	Santa Rosa	97	4
Gulf	10	1	Sarasota	766	31
Hamilton	6	1	Seminole	489	40
Hardee	14	0	Sumter	12	3
Hendry	21	4	Suwannee	15	0
Hernando	117	6	Taylor	13	0
Highlands	131	2	Union	15	0
Hillsborough	2,438	108	Volusia	600	75
Holmes	11	0	Wakulla	4	1
Indian River	245	7	Walton	19	0
Jackson	45	2	Washington	15	0

1/ Total includes all licensed persons regardless of current status.

Source: State of Florida, Department of Professional Regulation, unpublished
data.

Table 20.35.　DENTISTS AND DENTAL HYGENISTS:　NUMBER LICENSED IN THE STATE AND COUNTIES OF FLORIDA, AUGUST 3, 1991

Location of licensee	Dentists	Dental hygenists	Location of licensee	Dentists	Dental hygenists
Total 1/	10,588	8,156	Jefferson	3	3
NonFlorida	2,856	2,109	Lafayette	1	2
Unknown	0	0	Lake	64	46
Alachua	224	173	Lee	175	137
Baker	4	5	Leon	125	152
Bay	53	45	Levy	5	4
Bradford	9	10	Liberty	1	0
Brevard	220	204	Madison	7	3
Broward	873	700	Manatee	99	77
Calhoun	4	6	Marion	80	80
Charlotte	48	26	Martin	74	67
Citrus	30	29	Monroe	36	31
Clay	56	67	Nassau	14	17
Collier	111	61	Okaloosa	73	75
Columbia	16	12	Okeechobee	8	7
Dade	1,423	651	Orange	412	356
De Soto	6	4	Osceola	24	26
Dixie	3	3	Palm Beach	721	576
Duval	391	372	Pasco	77	54
Escambia	139	181	Pinellas	599	497
Flagler	9	5	Polk	149	130
Franklin	1	1	Putnam	17	12
Gadsden	13	14	St. Johns	46	45
Gilchrist	0	2	St. Lucie	73	70
Glades	0	2	Santa Rosa	25	60
Gulf	3	5	Sarasota	231	137
Hamilton	4	1	Seminole	159	174
Hardee	3	1	Sumter	4	2
Hendry	7	6	Suwannee	4	6
Hernando	33	28	Taylor	4	2
Highlands	34	21	Union	2	1
Hillsborough	439	342	Volusia	175	141
Holmes	4	4	Wakulla	2	3
Indian River	56	49	Walton	6	8
Jackson	15	12	Washington	6	4

1/ Total includes all licensed persons regardless of current status.

　　Source:　State of Florida, Department of Professional Regulation, unpublished data.

Florida Statistical Abstract 1991

Table 20.36.   HEALTH PRACTITIONERS: NUMBER LICENSED IN THE STATE AND COUNTIES
OF FLORIDA, AUGUST 3, 1991

Location of licensee	Chiro- practors	Optome- trists	Podia- trists	Therapists Occupa- tional	Phys- ical	Nursing home adminis- trators	Psy- chol- ogists
Total 1/	5,254	2,112	1,837	3,118	8,350	2,298	2,531
NonFlorida	2,099	663	965	437	2,090	417	403
Unknown	0	0	0	0	0	0	0
Alachua	33	13	5	143	213	25	133
Baker	0	1	0	0	0	3	0
Bay	26	12	4	21	46	13	10
Bradford	3	3	0	1	2	1	0
Brevard	104	40	17	91	170	30	78
Broward	474	167	172	304	836	161	267
Calhoun	1	1	0	0	1	2	0
Charlotte	24	11	12	19	45	16	9
Citrus	17	7	3	12	26	15	3
Clay	20	16	3	19	31	16	9
Collier	45	11	8	28	55	19	10
Columbia	6	5	0	7	11	8	2
Dade	326	218	159	374	1,038	157	455
De Soto	2	1	0	1	3	1	2
Dixie	0	0	0	0	0	0	0
Duval	104	66	35	130	278	72	83
Escambia	38	22	7	40	118	28	49
Flagler	5	0	1	4	4	4	3
Franklin	2	0	1	0	0	3	0
Gadsden	1	2	0	8	2	5	5
Gilchrist	1	0	1	0	0	0	0
Glades	0	0	0	0	2	0	0
Gulf	0	1	0	2	3	1	0
Hamilton	1	0	0	0	0	2	0
Hardee	2	3	1	5	5	1	0
Hendry	5	2	0	4	2	3	0
Hernando	20	9	2	10	31	12	2
Highlands	15	5	1	10	16	10	3
Hillsborough	177	87	48	191	385	94	229
Holmes	2	0	0	0	0	1	0
Indian River	22	9	5	27	59	13	11
Jackson	6	6	0	4	6	7	4

See footnote at end of table.   Continued . . .

Table 20.36. HEALTH PRACTITIONERS: NUMBER LICENSED IN THE STATE AND COUNTIES
    OF FLORIDA, AUGUST 3, 1991 (Continued)

Location of licensee	Chiro- practors	Optome- trists	Podia- trists	Therapists Occupa- tional	Phys- ical	Nursing home adminis- trators	Psy- chol- ogists
Jefferson	1	1	0	3	3	1	0
Lafayette	0	0	0	1	0	0	0
Lake	32	19	6	17	41	28	6
Lee	110	48	27	62	143	46	29
Leon	39	29	7	54	124	28	120
Levy	6	3	0	2	3	5	0
Liberty	0	0	0	0	2	1	0
Madison	1	1	0	0	3	2	0
Manatee	51	26	12	58	81	51	20
Marion	40	19	6	24	56	17	11
Martin	43	16	7	16	35	17	19
Monroe	18	11	0	4	28	7	13
Nassau	3	6	1	4	9	4	2
Okaloosa	19	19	4	27	47	11	17
Okeechobee	5	3	1	1	5	5	0
Orange	149	81	37	150	305	78	75
Osceola	20	6	0	13	32	13	2
Palm Beach	325	119	114	241	488	160	169
Pasco	63	17	10	31	65	36	9
Pinellas	300	117	65	184	689	310	103
Polk	81	42	12	40	101	54	16
Putnam	8	2	0	6	12	5	4
St. Johns	17	9	3	10	47	19	12
St. Lucie	32	10	8	11	42	14	3
Santa Rosa	7	3	0	16	38	12	12
Sarasota	132	43	30	133	187	80	47
Seminole	56	32	20	43	136	49	42
Sumter	3	2	0	1	3	4	0
Suwannee	4	2	0	1	5	6	2
Taylor	3	2	0	0	1	2	0
Union	1	0	0	0	1	0	1
Volusia	98	40	17	69	134	87	25
Wakulla	1	0	0	1	2	1	1
Walton	4	2	0	1	1	2	1
Washington	1	1	0	2	3	3	0

1/ Total includes all licensed persons regardless of current status.

    Source: State of Florida, Department of Professional Regulation, unpublished
data.

Florida Statistical Abstract 1991

Table 20.37. NURSES: LICENSED REGISTERED, PRACTICAL, AND ADVANCED NURSES IN THE
  STATE AND COUNTIES OF FLORIDA, AUGUST 3, 1991

Location of licensee	Total registered and practical nurses 1/	Current registered nurses	Current practical nurses	Current advanced nurses 2/
Total	338,831	124,010	42,812	3,891
NonFlorida	80,258	10,344	1,665	429
Unknown	10,856	6,266	1,175	262
Alachua	5,620	2,910	563	172
Baker	178	111	31	3
Bay	2,615	1,014	441	46
Bradford	223	98	54	4
Brevard	6,954	3,318	962	85
Broward	26,000	11,697	4,308	277
Calhoun	141	44	42	3
Charlotte	2,410	1,063	532	25
Citrus	1,387	620	318	16
Clay	2,158	1,140	302	36
Collier	2,777	1,200	589	38
Columbia	826	394	143	10
Dade	30,665	12,813	3,731	409
De Soto	481	149	143	10
Dixie	78	32	21	1
Duval	12,553	5,548	1,532	149
Escambia	6,555	2,194	1,119	52
Flagler	470	249	67	4
Franklin	114	26	39	0
Gadsden	574	210	146	8
Gilchrist	119	51	36	1
Glades	37	13	7	0
Gulf	156	46	47	3
Hamilton	94	38	30	0
Hardee	226	78	61	3
Hendry	258	100	69	4
Hernando	1,735	786	425	13
Highlands	1,271	464	285	9
Hillsborough	16,067	6,995	2,611	264
Holmes	190	68	56	4
Indian River	1,682	806	279	20
Jackson	736	279	190	17

See footnotes at end of table.   Continued . . .

Florida Statistical Abstract 1991

Table 20.37. NURSES: LICENSED REGISTERED, PRACTICAL, AND ADVANCED NURSES IN THE
   STATE AND COUNTIES OF FLORIDA, AUGUST 3, 1991 (Continued)

Location of licensee	Total registered and practical nurses 1/	Current registered nurses	Current practical nurses	Current advanced nurses 2/
Jefferson	145	52	40	6
Lafayette	44	15	16	0
Lake	2,626	978	653	18
Lee	6,859	3,204	1,191	114
Leon	3,692	1,704	561	94
Levy	344	137	83	3
Liberty	42	10	20	0
Madison	194	57	71	4
Manatee	4,395	1,767	842	24
Marion	2,951	1,426	484	46
Martin	1,905	951	255	38
Monroe	1,419	584	99	22
Nassau	546	269	84	12
Okaloosa	2,456	985	330	31
Okeechobee	374	123	98	12
Orange	13,041	5,486	2,112	130
Osceola	1,525	674	327	8
Palm Beach	16,261	7,750	2,257	225
Pasco	4,468	1,861	1,029	50
Pinellas	23,074	9,307	3,506	305
Polk	6,452	2,701	1,316	54
Putnam	725	216	192	6
St. Johns	1,655	744	317	21
St. Lucie	2,518	1,191	473	22
Santa Rosa	1,713	755	312	31
Sarasota	7,567	3,089	1,456	83
Seminole	5,445	2,840	836	73
Sumter	324	109	101	0
Suwannee	474	172	140	4
Taylor	174	50	53	2
Union	110	53	25	1
Volusia	8,153	3,347	1,303	66
Wakulla	135	54	43	2
Walton	277	93	72	5
Washington	284	92	96	2

1/ Includes current, inactive, and lapsed registered and practical nurses.
2/ Advanced registered nurse practitioners (ARNP).

   Source: State of Florida, Department of Professional Regulation, unpublished
data.

Florida Statistical Abstract 1991

Table 20.38.   HEALTH RELATED RETAILERS: LICENSED DISPENSING OPTICIANS AND
    PHARMACISTS IN THE STATE AND COUNTIES OF FLORIDA, AUGUST 3, 1991

Location of licensee	Dispensing opticians	Pharmacists	Location of licensee	Dispensing opticians	Pharmacists
Total 1/	3,376	16,778	Jefferson	0	9
NonFlorida	370	6,079	Lafayette	0	1
Unknown	0	0	Lake	38	96
Alachua	42	327	Lee	77	278
Baker	0	6	Leon	35	230
Bay	18	102	Levy	1	14
Bradford	1	15	Liberty	0	4
Brevard	80	269	Madison	0	15
Broward	372	1,226	Manatee	43	137
Calhoun	1	13	Marion	51	123
Charlotte	15	76	Martin	15	83
Citrus	14	58	Monroe	11	51
Clay	24	58	Nassau	4	23
Collier	27	106	Okaloosa	12	82
Columbia	4	32	Okeechobee	2	16
Dade	584	1,644	Orange	119	496
De Soto	1	11	Osceola	8	41
Dixie	0	4	Palm Beach	237	780
Duval	121	504	Pasco	58	123
Escambia	41	202	Pinellas	260	894
Flagler	1	15	Polk	66	235
Franklin	0	6	Putnam	7	31
Gadsden	2	29	St. Johns	15	69
Gilchrist	1	1	St. Lucie	26	83
Glades	1	0	Santa Rosa	2	67
Gulf	1	6	Sarasota	83	290
Hamilton	0	5	Seminole	54	272
Hardee	0	8	Sumter	1	4
Hendry	0	18	Suwannee	1	11
Hernando	22	61	Taylor	0	9
Highlands	12	47	Union	1	8
Hillsborough	299	834	Volusia	74	309
Holmes	0	12	Wakulla	1	5
Indian River	17	58	Walton	2	16
Jackson	1	31	Washington	0	10

1/ Total includes all licensed persons regardless of current status.

    Source: State of Florida, Department of Professional Regulation, unpublished
data.

Florida Statistical Abstract 1991

Table 20.40. PUBLIC LIBRARIES: OPERATING EXPENDITURE AND NUMBER OF VOLUMES
IN REGIONS AND COUNTIES OF FLORIDA, FISCAL YEAR 1989-90

Area and library	Total operating expenditure (dollars)	Number of volumes 1/	Area and library	Total operating expenditure (dollars)	Number of volumes 1/
Regional and multi-county systems			Flagler		
			Flagler Beach	31,784	16,430
Central Florida			Flagler County		
Regional 2/	1,288,586	129,673	Public	135,014	19,374
Charlotte-Glades	795,413	126,082	Gadsden		
Jacksonville			Gadsden County	233,242	36,038
Public 3/	9,606,009	1,926,308	Hardee		
Northwest Regional 4/	858,651	143,842	Hardee County		
Seminole Tribal	77,583	10,000	Public	75,420	19,570
Suwannee River			Hendry		
Regional 5/	472,527	119,702	Hendry County	154,119	48,142
West Florida			Hernando		
Regional 6/	1,570,287	266,082	Hernando County	817,463	125,000
County			Highlands		
Alachua			Highlands County		
Alachua County Library District	3,368,461	335,743	Public	378,318	72,958
Bradford			Hillsborough		
Bradford County	103,113	26,314	Tampa-Hillsborough	11,681,916	1,176,857
Brevard			Indian River		
Brevard County	5,858,879	703,591	Indian River County	671,957	123,233
Broward			Jackson		
Broward County	20,930,152	1,399,372	Jackson County	172,781	32,353
Lighthouse Point	146,584	22,400	Jefferson		
Oakland Park	341,300	39,000	Jefferson County	147,210	20,000
Pompano Beach	1,133,395	100,000	Lake		
Wilton Manors	157,675	24,347	Lake County	1,048,810	197,353
Calhoun			Leesburg	375,862	131,977
Calhoun County	104,739	17,000	Lee		
Citrus			Ft. Myers Beach	166,593	39,884
Citrus County	1,055,650	116,000	Lee County	4,579,138	341,994
Clay			Sanibel Public	129,950	22,332
Clay County	790,447	110,418	Leon		
Collier			Leon County	1,901,455	220,443
Collier County	1,520,468	184,002	Manatee		
Columbia			Manatee County	2,007,877	212,745
Columbia County	291,436	70,938	Martin		
Dade			Martin County	1,086,981	90,637
Brockway Memorial	242,196	60,874	Monroe		
Hialeah J. F. Kennedy	852,623	177,601	Monroe County	871,092	142,716
Lafe Allen			Okaloosa		
Memorial	362,381	62,000	Ft. Walton Beach	192,491	42,722
Miami-Dade	24,630,593	2,483,184	Mary Esther Public	60,150	8,571
North Miami	558,936	96,006	Niceville	116,066	20,200
Opa-Locka	75,430	16,871	Robert L. F. Sikes	88,062	40,658
Surf-Bal-Bay	95,688	24,000	Valparaiso	48,481	41,000
De Soto			Okeechobee		
De Soto County	69,790	20,255	Okeechobee County	89,645	22,394

See footnotes at end of table.   Continued . . .

Florida Statistical Abstract 1991

Table 20.40. PUBLIC LIBRARIES: OPERATING EXPENDITURE AND NUMBER OF VOLUMES
IN REGIONS AND COUNTIES OF FLORIDA, FISCAL YEAR 1989-90 (Continued)

Area and library	Total operating expenditure (dollars)	Number of volumes 1/	Area and library	Total operating expenditure (dollars)	Number of volumes 1/
Orange			Polk (Continued)		
Maitland	226,060	38,753	Ft. Meade	77,810	21,176
Orange County	10,972,236	1,301,597	Haines City	95,260	22,627
Winter Park	613,436	109,663	Lake Alfred	38,253	22,610
Osceola			Lake Wales	146,313	44,122
Osceola County	1,401,936	102,000	Lakeland	746,830	125,351
Palm Beach			Latt Maxcy	73,660	27,424
Boynton Beach	798,272	105,554	Polk City	3,203	3,500
Lake Park	119,543	33,200	Winter Haven	316,550	49,346
Lake Worth	432,525	73,492	Putnam		
North Palm Beach	292,948	40,908	Putnam County	266,881	53,620
Palm Beach System	8,394,098	479,347	St. Johns		
Palm Springs	266,228	30,946	St. Johns County		
West Palm Beach	768,402	118,763	Public	501,797	71,262
Pasco			St. Lucie		
New Port Richey	227,753	39,000	St. Lucie County	1,825,517	156,675
Pasco County	4,151,343	101,002	Sarasota		
Zephyrhills	62,889	31,676	Sarasota County	2,702,885	379,148
Pinellas			Seminole		
Clearwater	2,515,982	381,271	Altamonte Springs	102,161	21,538
Dunedin	796,612	81,312	Seminole County	3,434,768	238,387
Gulf Beaches	176,471	45,488	Sumter		
Gulfport	195,225	56,206	George Nichols	7,880	25,000
Largo	895,787	135,587	Panasoffkee		
Oldsmar City	118,473	10,000	Community	7,503	14,730
Palm Harbor	411,544	58,010	Taylor		
Pinellas Park	457,123	51,262	Taylor County	108,378	49,100
St. Petersburg	2,084,016	501,062	Volusia		
St. Petersburg			Volusia County	4,444,284	594,213
Beach	122,200	44,574	Wakulla		
Seminole Library	34,779	28,842	Wakulla County		
Tarpon Springs	228,254	38,395	Public	96,549	28,300
Polk			Walton		
Auburndale	89,994	36,000	Walton/DeFuniak	162,058	35,981
Bartow	189,570	38,161			

1/ Includes volumes of books and bound periodicals.
2/ Serves Citrus, Levy, and Marion counties.
3/ Serves Duval and Nassau counties.
4/ Serves Bay, Gulf, Holmes, Liberty, and Washington counties.
5/ Serves Dixie, Gilchrist, Hamilton, Lafayette, Madison, and Suwannee counties.
6/ Serves Escambia and Santa Rosa counties.
Note: Libraries are omitted if they failed to report to the Division of Library
Services or if they failed to meet or are not part of a system which met all of the
following criteria: at least 10 hours of public service per week, a book collection
of at least 2,000 volumes, at least 200 volumes purchased a year, and expenditure of
at least $1,000 per year.

Source: State of Florida, Department of State, Division of Library Services,
1991 Florida Library Directory with Statistics.

Table 20.56. PUBLIC ELEMENTARY AND SECONDARY SCHOOLS: DISTRIBUTION OF
    ADMINISTRATIVE AND INSTRUCTIONAL STAFF IN THE STATE AND COUNTIES OF
    FLORIDA, FALL 1990

		Administrative staff						
County	Total	Total	Offi-cials adminis-trators managers	Consul-tants/super-visors of instruc-tion	Princi-pals	Assist-ant princi-pals	Community education coor-dinators	Deans/curri-culum coordi-nators
Florida	128,101	8,978	2,201	798	2,314	2,771	156	738
Alachua	1,702	139	42	25	39	28	5	0
Baker	277	27	12	0	6	8	1	0
Bay	1,576	100	24	11	31	34	0	0
Bradford	319	33	15	1	8	6	0	3
Brevard	3,792	236	53	2	72	31	0	78
Broward	10,147	665	93	75	180	317	0	0
Calhoun	166	13	8	0	5	0	0	0
Charlotte	875	72	24	5	19	17	4	3
Citrus	906	61	18	6	18	13	0	6
Clay	1,431	116	40	5	24	47	0	0
Collier	1,484	99	28	13	29	26	3	0
Columbia	519	32	13	0	10	6	0	3
Dade	18,998	1,279	268	61	303	477	46	124
De Soto	300	27	12	0	6	6	1	2
Dixie	144	15	8	0	4	3	0	0
Duval	7,256	539	124	29	147	101	47	91
Escambia	3,185	259	71	29	62	26	7	64
Flagler	323	29	20	2	5	2	0	0
Franklin	122	12	6	0	4	2	0	0
Gadsden	596	62	18	5	16	7	0	16
Gilchrist	126	13	8	0	3	2	0	0
Glades	73	8	4	1	2	0	0	1
Gulf	171	18	8	2	6	2	0	0
Hamilton	191	20	7	3	6	2	2	0
Hardee	324	31	18	2	6	5	0	0
Hendry	383	40	15	2	11	12	0	0
Hernando	880	56	21	1	16	15	3	0
Highlands	647	57	18	8	13	18	0	0
Hillsborough	8,814	556	54	123	144	137	14	84
Holmes	246	19	6	3	7	3	0	0
Indian River	805	63	29	3	19	8	1	3
Jackson	606	44	14	2	15	11	0	2
Jefferson	171	20	10	1	4	3	1	1

    See footnote at end of table.   Continued . . .

Table 20.56. PUBLIC ELEMENTARY AND SECONDARY SCHOOLS: DISTRIBUTION OF
    ADMINISTRATIVE AND INSTRUCTIONAL STAFF IN THE STATE AND COUNTIES OF
    FLORIDA, FALL 1990 (Continued)

						Instructional staff			
	Teachers					Visit-			
	Ele-mentary (pre-kinder-garten-6)	Second-ary (7-12)	Excep-tional student edu-cation	Other	Guid-ance coun-selors	ing teach-ers/ social workers	School psycho-logists	Librar-ians/ audio-visual workers	Other 1/
County									
Florida	47,780	41,279	14,818	4,211	4,609	578	769	2,521	2,558
Alachua	618	593	189	8	64	0	11	45	35
Baker	110	86	28	5	9	1	1	5	5
Bay	528	540	222	52	57	6	13	37	21
Bradford	112	121	29	0	11	0	2	8	3
Brevard	1,575	1,073	485	120	123	7	17	83	73
Broward	3,991	2,921	912	644	368	81	79	185	301
Calhoun	61	54	21	4	7	0	0	5	1
Charlotte	294	337	79	8	28	4	5	14	34
Citrus	333	303	107	15	30	3	5	19	30
Clay	565	487	167	2	38	2	8	27	19
Collier	597	490	164	7	60	3	12	29	23
Columbia	224	174	50	1	16	1	3	11	7
Dade	7,321	5,780	1,944	1,077	821	87	141	313	235
De Soto	121	95	28	13	9	1	1	5	0
Dixie	65	40	17	0	4	0	0	3	0
Duval	2,910	2,072	1,070	129	210	37	38	151	100
Escambia	1,156	1,113	380	20	113	17	14	62	51
Flagler	99	104	37	21	11	0	1	5	16
Franklin	53	33	10	4	5	0	0	4	1
Gadsden	220	181	60	18	21	3	5	16	10
Gilchrist	48	50	10	0	3	0	0	2	0
Glades	30	24	6	0	2	0	1	2	0
Gulf	58	64	17	1	6	0	1	4	2
Hamilton	63	63	24	1	8	0	1	5	6
Hardee	114	109	31	20	7	1	1	7	3
Hendry	157	114	35	9	14	0	2	9	3
Hernando	307	356	80	11	37	5	4	17	7
Highlands	224	205	83	13	28	3	2	14	18
Hillsborough	3,529	2,631	1,163	170	338	60	45	178	144
Holmes	98	91	22	0	5	0	1	7	3
Indian River	340	253	86	7	18	1	6	19	12
Jackson	225	217	56	25	22	0	2	12	3
Jefferson	52	60	20	5	5	1	0	4	4

See footnote at end of table.   Continued . . .

Florida Statistical Abstract 1991

Table 20.56. PUBLIC ELEMENTARY AND SECONDARY SCHOOLS: DISTRIBUTION OF
ADMINISTRATIVE AND INSTRUCTIONAL STAFF IN THE STATE AND COUNTIES OF
FLORIDA, FALL 1990 (Continued)

County	Total	Total	Offi-cials adminis-trators managers	Consul-tants/ super-visors of instruc-tion	Princi-pals	Assist-ant princi-pals	Community education coor-dinators	Deans/ curri-culum coordi-nators
Lafayette	84	10	5	2	2	0	0	1
Lake	1,476	99	15	9	38	27	0	10
Lee	2,913	249	85	32	54	51	0	27
Leon	1,987	131	30	3	38	60	0	0
Levy	370	36	14	3	11	7	1	0
Liberty	88	12	8	0	4	0	0	0
Madison	237	26	7	5	7	4	1	2
Manatee	1,797	141	31	26	34	26	1	23
Marion	2,038	142	35	17	38	32	6	14
Martin	884	71	17	9	16	19	1	9
Monroe	577	24	9	0	12	3	0	0
Nassau	531	40	14	0	14	7	1	4
Okaloosa	1,778	119	29	17	38	24	0	11
Okeechobee	377	30	11	1	7	9	0	2
Orange	7,970	496	144	49	116	152	0	35
Osceola	1,193	81	26	1	20	32	2	0
Palm Beach	7,849	509	84	6	117	302	0	0
Pasco	2,326	173	41	24	38	56	1	13
Pinellas	6,885	466	78	52	124	189	5	18
Polk	4,648	346	96	47	84	99	0	20
Putnam	858	75	30	3	16	17	0	9
St. Johns	846	75	19	4	17	19	1	15
St. Lucie	1,365	107	31	7	23	28	0	18
Santa Rosa	1,074	68	20	5	23	20	0	0
Sarasota	1,989	129	43	11	33	34	0	8
Seminole	3,128	220	54	28	43	82	0	13
Sumter	347	26	14	0	10	2	0	0
Suwannee	353	27	11	0	6	8	1	1
Taylor	265	23	12	0	7	3	0	1
Union	138	18	8	3	3	3	0	1
Volusia	3,279	160	32	7	59	62	0	0
Wakulla	222	25	17	0	5	3	0	0
Walton	331	33	10	6	9	7	0	1
Washington	343	31	12	1	8	9	0	1

See footnote at end of table.   Continued . . .

Table 20.56. PUBLIC ELEMENTARY AND SECONDARY SCHOOLS: DISTRIBUTION OF
   ADMINISTRATIVE AND INSTRUCTIONAL STAFF IN THE STATE AND COUNTIES OF
   FLORIDA, FALL 1990 (Continued)

	Instructional staff								
	Teachers					Visit-ing		Librar-ians/	
County	Ele-mentary (pre-kinder-garten-6)	Second-ary (7-12)	Excep-tional student edu-cation	Other	Guid-ance coun-selors	teach-ers/ social workers	School psycho-logists	audio-visual workers	Other 1/
Lafayette	32	30	5	0	3	0	0	2	2
Lake	491	479	183	57	59	5	9	34	60
Lee	987	1,033	354	19	116	22	24	69	40
Leon	763	524	281	91	84	7	9	41	56
Levy	133	124	43	9	10	2	0	9	4
Liberty	28	32	10	3	1	0	0	2	0
Madison	79	93	20	3	9	0	0	4	3
Manatee	717	573	217	21	61	8	9	37	13
Marion	836	667	213	22	72	13	12	39	22
Martin	344	269	103	42	26	0	5	16	8
Monroe	216	181	82	22	17	4	5	6	20
Nassau	182	193	71	3	19	2	3	14	4
Okaloosa	700	665	150	7	62	1	9	40	25
Okeechobee	168	111	34	10	11	0	2	8	3
Orange	2,543	2,823	870	408	281	38	45	153	313
Osceola	447	432	94	31	48	0	7	23	30
Palm Beach	2,871	2,452	1,157	233	248	0	39	117	223
Pasco	912	731	288	40	86	8	14	50	24
Pinellas	2,063	2,627	787	242	230	55	47	135	233
Polk	1,835	1,550	527	79	160	11	33	101	6
Putnam	312	292	78	19	37	3	6	19	17
St. Johns	298	254	74	74	37	1	5	14	14
St. Lucie	563	449	119	11	42	9	4	29	32
Santa Rosa	410	398	99	9	38	2	5	26	19
Sarasota	675	566	382	77	62	13	13	35	37
Seminole	1,139	1,127	352	78	110	17	14	56	15
Sumter	131	127	28	0	13	0	1	9	12
Suwannee	141	119	19	22	15	1	1	6	2
Taylor	99	82	30	4	9	1	1	6	10
Union	54	45	11	0	4	0	1	3	2
Volusia	1,132	1,079	420	106	117	31	21	91	122
Wakulla	73	85	24	2	7	0	0	5	1
Walton	129	113	31	5	8	0	2	8	2
Washington	79	120	30	52	9	0	1	7	14

1/ Nonadministrative/instructional professional staff.
   Source: State of Florida, Department of Education, Division of Public Schools,
MIS Statistical Brief: Staff in Florida Public Schools, Fall 1990 and *Instructional
Staff in Florida Public Schools, Fall 1990.* Series 91-10B and 91-08B.

Florida Statistical Abstract 1991

Table 20.59. PUBLIC ELEMENTARY AND SECONDARY SCHOOLS: NUMBER AND AVERAGE SALARY
   OF SPECIFIED DISTRICT STAFF PERSONNEL IN THE COUNTIES OF FLORIDA, 1989-90

(salaries in dollars)

| County | Superin-tendent salary | Principals | | | | | | Board members | |
| | | High school | | Junior high/ middle school | | Elementary | | | |
		Num-ber	Salary	Num-ber	Salary	Num-ber	Salary	Num-ber	Salary
Alachua	94,600	6	·57,656	6	51,936	21	46,110	5	18,416
Baker	65,344	2	50,353	1	49,930	1	49,930	5	13,521
Bay	63,893	3	55,997	6	51,071	17	49,509	5	17,482
Bradford	54,078	1	49,145	1	44,998	5	42,562	5	13,784
Brevard	85,000	10	56,945	14	51,127	47	49,355	6	20,492
Broward	108,000	25	65,041	28	55,315	106	52,080	7	22,483
Calhoun	62,913	3	46,200	1	43,500	1	45,200	5	13,131
Charlotte	74,402	3	61,346	4	51,361	7	52,340	5	16,598
Citrus	66,951	3	50,595	3	48,697	8	47,472	5	16,346
Clay	65,856	5	50,893	4	49,952	13	47,970	5	16,831
Collier	86,400	5	63,700	4	54,670	15	52,300	5	17,407
Columbia	55,215	1	48,420	1	48,120	7	45,491	5	14,614
Dade	163,922	28	68,503	49	65,122	181	62,254	7	22,483
De Soto	49,622	1	44,278	1	41,596	3	41,248	5	13,904
Dixie	63,013	1	36,000	0	0	2	37,018	5	13,125
Duval	116,800	21	56,376	26	52,031	103	47,786	7	21,474
Escambia	84,706	12	50,888	9	50,624	38	47,735	5	19,507
Flagler	66,297	1	49,168	1	48,618	3	41,574	5	13,650
Franklin	52,610	2	42,035	0	0	2	41,693	5	12,870
Gadsden	68,477	4	49,022	2	46,555	7	46,357	5	14,817
Gilchrist	50,000	2	45,726	0	0	0	0	5	12,691
Glades	49,103	1	38,080	0	0	1	39,580	5	12,645
Gulf	60,743	2	43,116	0	0	3	40,344	5	13,219
Hamilton	51,521	1	47,269	1	44,278	3	41,847	5	13,087
Hardee	53,379	1	44,147	1	37,080	4	35,152	5	13,687
Hendry	62,800	2	50,200	2	49,000	5	48,200	5	13,838
Hernando	59,950	4	51,269	3	50,088	8	48,732	5	16,336
Highlands	73,731	3	56,362	3	50,946	6	50,247	5	15,600
Hillsborough	102,001	14	61,302	24	56,215	96	52,257	7	21,936
Holmes	48,336	4	41,032	1	38,070	2	40,775	5	13,439
Indian River	75,000	1	60,467	4	52,763	12	49,734	5	16,394
Jackson	65,364	6	45,633	1	41,900	6	43,833	5	14,692
Jefferson	49,944	1	42,850	1	41,812	1	34,315	5	13,219
Lafayette	50,703	1	40,168	0	0	1	37,418	5	12,222
Lake	69,138	7	50,082	8	49,514	18	48,267	5	17,626
Lee	83,175	9	58,960	10	49,580	30	47,258	5	19,522
Leon	66,810	4	53,960	6	50,842	22	45,449	5	18,480
Levy	56,698	5	43,411	1	40,095	3	41,262	5	13,793

See footnote at end of table.   Continued . . .

Table 20.59. PUBLIC ELEMENTARY AND SECONDARY SCHOOLS: NUMBER AND AVERAGE SALARY
OF SPECIFIED DISTRICT STAFF PERSONNEL IN THE COUNTIES OF FLORIDA, 1989-90
(Continued)

(salaries in dollars)

County	Superin-tendent salary	Principals High school Num-ber	Principals High school Salary	Junior high/ middle school Num-ber	Junior high/ middle school Salary	Elementary Num-ber	Elementary Salary	Board members Num-ber	Board members Salary
Liberty	48,621	2	44,290	0	0	1	44,490	5	12,134
Madison	50,506	1	40,000	4	38,197	2	37,596	5	13,394
Manatee	91,427	4	57,295	5	51,825	23	50,053	5	18,501
Marion	68,800	7	56,940	7	53,002	20	49,967	5	18,405
Martin	60,869	2	51,116	4	48,276	7	47,140	5	16,579
Monroe	83,003	2	54,116	1	59,218	3	51,656	5	16,000
Nassau	72,374	3	54,248	3	50,766	8	48,828	5	14,782
Okaloosa	75,124	6	57,857	6	56,153	19	53,252	5	17,878
Okeechobee	65,000	1	55,508	1	52,096	5	47,438	5	13,993
Orange	108,098	11	60,256	17	51,627	74	50,436	7	21,306
Osceola	68,905	3	54,549	5	52,038	12	52,072	5	16,639
Palm Beach	104,065	22	64,487	22	59,097	69	53,209	7	21,999
Pasco	84,627	6	57,853	6	49,955	23	45,754	5	19,013
Pinellas	99,999	15	59,067	23	55,479	74	51,973	7	21,983
Polk	87,559	11	56,122	17	53,859	60	46,222	5	20,703
Putnam	68,245	3	52,832	4	50,019	8	47,566	5	15,389
St. Johns	66,677	2	51,625	3	48,949	8	48,238	5	16,123
St. Lucie	84,000	4	55,503	2	55,462	16	50,501	5	17,523
Santa Rosa	59,222	5	50,684	5	48,726	12	46,298	5	15,628
Sarasota	84,057	10	57,095	5	52,939	18	52,469	5	19,275
Seminole	86,263	7	63,348	9	55,414	26	51,999	5	19,363
Sumter	60,937	2	53,675	2	48,988	5	47,525	5	14,051
Suwannee	54,500	3	47,210	1	46,387	2	46,387	5	13,900
Taylor	51,124	2	41,869	1	43,962	3	42,846	5	13,532
Union	67,051	1	48,591	1	43,741	1	41,657	5	13,123
Volusia	92,516	11	56,401	8	54,731	36	49,157	5	20,105
Wakulla	57,054	1	46,472	1	44,902	3	42,076	5	13,305
Walton	53,896	3	46,090	1	45,890	4	44,190	5	14,265
Washington	57,313	2	46,938	2	43,877	2	43,673	5	13,400

Note: The number of months worked varies from district to district. Salaries
have not been adjusted for a full 12-month calendar year.

Source: State of Florida, Department of Education, Division of Public Schools,
MIS Statistical Brief: District Staff Salaries, 1989-90. Series 91-06B.

Florida Statistical Abstract 1991

Table 20.60. PUBLIC ELEMENTARY AND SECONDARY SCHOOLS: NUMBER AND AVERAGE SALARY
OF CLASSROOM TEACHERS BY DEGREE ATTAINMENT IN THE STATE AND COUNTIES
OF FLORIDA, 1990-91

(salaries in dollars)

County	Total Number	Total Average salary	Bachelor's Number	Bachelor's Average salary	Master's Number	Master's Average salary	Specialist Num-ber	Specialist Average salary	Doctorate Num-ber	Doctorate Average salary
Florida	115,924	30,555	69,141	28,069	43,287	33,810	2,498	40,132	998	37,632
Alachua	1,550	27,487	664	24,362	777	29,441	85	31,754	24	35,575
Baker	247	26,439	169	25,004	76	29,480	2	32,168	0	0
Bay	1,356	28,152	932	27,147	400	30,199	18	32,384	6	35,054
Bradford	282	26,402	187	24,764	87	29,350	4	30,614	4	34,627
Brevard	3,520	29,107	2,082	27,024	1,377	32,029	43	34,261	18	34,228
Broward	9,666	34,309	5,517	32,226	3,790	36,768	255	40,682	104	39,589
Calhoun	150	28,994	107	27,597	39	32,392	2	36,900	2	29,588
Charlotte	791	27,057	435	24,328	340	30,248	5	32,021	11	34,103
Citrus	829	27,149	498	25,025	317	30,347	11	30,251	3	30,500
Clay	1,297	26,645	863	25,174	426	29,518	7	32,071	1	34,750
Collier	1,382	33,953	693	30,847	646	36,870	30	39,647	13	41,476
Columbia	485	28,084	316	26,315	156	31,311	10	31,788	3	34,250
Dade	15,866	37,573	8,156	33,526	6,483	41,173	973	46,164	254	42,721
De Soto	270	29,066	184	27,791	82	31,835	1	34,225	3	29,874
Dixie	121	23,987	86	22,500	31	27,381	3	28,202	1	34,063
Duval	6,583	28,976	4,146	26,869	2,331	32,385	65	36,044	41	37,000
Escambia	2,910	28,166	1,593	25,639	1,271	31,145	20	32,528	26	34,057
Flagler	258	26,441	171	25,341	85	28,631	2	27,398	0	0
Franklin	110	25,624	69	23,647	40	28,864	1	32,388	0	0
Gadsden	501	26,435	309	25,180	187	28,450	4	29,362	1	25,565
Gilchrist	117	25,134	72	23,580	41	27,848	3	25,457	1	24,780
Glades	66	26,892	45	24,967	21	31,017	0	0	0	0
Gulf	152	26,025	106	24,817	45	28,789	0	0	1	29,730
Hamilton	164	26,148	128	25,318	33	28,811	3	32,283	0	0
Hardee	266	28,969	200	27,802	66	32,504	0	0	0	0
Hendry	349	26,842	271	25,802	74	30,367	2	33,570	2	30,545
Hernando	816	26,598	484	24,332	316	29,768	9	34,123	7	30,501
Highlands	582	27,545	398	25,998	180	30,888	2	29,609	2	32,352
Hillsborough	8,041	28,966	5,024	26,740	2,895	32,558	69	35,815	53	34,926
Holmes	214	27,621	130	25,730	82	30,483	1	32,793	1	33,595
Indian River	729	28,884	467	27,390	249	31,339	9	35,666	4	35,231
Jackson	562	26,412	296	24,246	251	28,683	13	31,013	2	32,007
Jefferson	151	25,736	104	24,475	44	28,546	3	28,217	0	0

Continued . . .

Table 20.60.   PUBLIC ELEMENTARY AND SECONDARY SCHOOLS: NUMBER AND AVERAGE SALARY
OF CLASSROOM TEACHERS BY DEGREE ATTAINMENT IN THE STATE AND COUNTIES
OF FLORIDA, 1990-91 (Continued)

(salaries in dollars)

County	Total		Bachelor's		Master's		Specialist		Doctorate	
	Number	Average salary	Number	Average salary	Number	Average salary	Number	Average salary	Number	Average salary
Lafayette	76	25,083	57	23,916	19	28,582	0	0	0	0
Lake	1,388	27,944	889	26,034	477	31,329	5	27,900	17	32,841
Lee	2,654	28,450	1,526	26,223	1,068	31,304	35	33,643	25	35,140
Leon	1,683	28,365	885	26,461	750	30,322	28	32,829	20	33,009
Levy	330	26,444	206	25,071	118	28,724	5	29,540	1	24,680
Liberty	77	28,376	54	27,074	22	31,291	1	34,560	0	0
Madison	208	26,627	127	25,395	79	28,463	0	0	2	32,304
Manatee	1,623	29,134	916	26,468	653	32,221	42	36,653	12	38,351
Marion	1,892	25,570	1,273	24,217	577	28,132	28	31,439	14	31,299
Martin	834	29,200	513	27,194	297	32,146	15	35,532	9	35,790
Monroe	528	32,235	318	31,045	205	33,982	3	34,993	2	38,114
Nassau	492	28,858	306	26,913	181	32,071	4	33,454	1	23,940
Okaloosa	1,653	29,147	983	27,537	648	31,373	12	35,255	10	35,917
Okeechobee	341	25,791	233	27,439	101	31,938	7	37,235	0	0
Orange	7,115	27,993	4,408	25,971	2,583	31,444	76	34,510	48	34,235
Osceola	1,104	25,874	744	24,279	337	29,082	13	30,493	10	30,467
Palm Beach	7,069	33,851	4,404	31,569	2,435	37,272	155	41,897	75	40,165
Pasco	2,200	26,326	1,457	24,883	716	29,119	17	28,962	10	32,010
Pinellas	6,580	30,196	3,977	28,467	2,459	32,687	90	35,287	54	35,556
Polk	4,298	27,871	2,974	26,261	1,250	31,412	56	33,581	18	30,264
Putnam	765	27,442	495	25,928	260	30,274	7	28,771	3	28,810
St. Johns	791	28,120	520	26,882	271	30,496	0	0	0	0
St. Lucie	1,235	30,419	757	28,292	449	33,605	22	37,120	7	35,016
Santa Rosa	1,010	28,131	618	26,255	380	31,041	8	33,131	4	31,577
Sarasota	1,874	34,031	902	30,407	892	36,914	62	43,225	18	41,080
Seminole	2,891	28,993	1,715	26,133	1,094	32,882	64	36,882	18	37,053
Sumter	319	28,841	224	27,358	90	32,394	5	31,350	0	0
Suwannee	310	28,956	215	27,553	94	32,102	1	34,850	0	0
Taylor	233	29,193	146	26,739	81	33,057	3	33,960	3	39,559
Union	122	24,750	88	23,933	34	26,864	0	0	0	0
Volusia	3,074	26,828	1,813	24,712	1,164	29,693	71	31,888	26	32,351
Wakulla	199	25,862	130	24,848	67	27,743	2	28,775	0	0
Walton	299	26,229	214	25,179	80	28,701	3	31,675	2	31,555
Washington	274	27,827	152	26,148	118	29,861	3	30,904	1	33,655

Source: State of Florida, Department of Education, Division of Public Schools,
MIS Statistical Brief: Teachers' Salary, Experience, and Degree Level, 1990-91.
Series 91-11B.

Florida Statistical Abstract 1991

Table 20.62. PUBLIC ELEMENTARY AND SECONDARY SCHOOLS: STUDENT-TEACHER RATIOS AND
    SPECIFIED PERSONNEL PERCENTAGES AND RATIOS IN THE STATE AND COUNTIES OF
    FLORIDA, SCHOOL YEAR 1989-90

County	FTE students per FTE teacher Elementary 1/	Secondary	Percentage of full-time staff who are-- Teachers	Administrators	Ratio of teacher aides to teachers 2/	Percentage of personnel resigning 3/
Florida	22.47	18.71	50.46	4.34	1:5.1	5.5
Alachua	24.36	17.97	53.57	5.38	1:6.2	9.3
Baker	23.12	20.43	45.57	5.36	1:3.9	4.7
Bay	24.02	16.45	49.90	3.89	1:4.5	5.7
Bradford	20.68	14.32	50.38	5.73	1:4.5	5.1
Brevard	21.54	21.45	50.85	3.90	1:8.5	6.3
Broward	23.76	21.58	53.39	4.21	1:6.2	6.6
Calhoun	19.00	20.26	57.33	6.03	1:66.5	5.8
Charlotte	20.85	19.86	40.65	3.59	1:5.2	4.8
Citrus	19.39	14.50	47.70	3.98	1:3.9	3.1
Clay	21.43	19.34	54.44	4.86	1:14.9	6.6
Collier	20.67	16.98	48.90	3.30	1:4.1	5.5
Columbia	21.64	18.28	45.85	3.18	1:4.2	5.7
Dade	22.06	21.81	59.41	4.74	1:9.2	1.5
De Soto	19.81	17.38	48.58	5.67	1:4.1	6.8
Dixie	18.15	17.83	46.12	5.81	1:3.6	9.7
Duval	22.56	20.02	51.43	4.59	1:4.2	9.1
Escambia	21.87	16.80	49.21	5.58	1:5.0	5.0
Flagler	23.51	16.27	48.39	5.65	1:6.5	4.6
Franklin	18.36	16.39	49.75	5.53	1:5.8	6.6
Gadsden	20.33	16.97	44.61	5.35	1:2.3	13.0
Gilchrist	21.94	15.27	47.96	6.33	1:3.8	1.8
Glades	18.29	14.50	51.13	6.02	1:4.5	9.4
Gulf	18.97	17.19	47.77	5.15	1:3.9	11.9
Hamilton	19.52	19.69	45.10	7.72	1:3.5	7.0
Hardee	19.87	17.23	40.87	4.99	1:2.4	5.7
Hendry	20.66	19.91	42.28	5.37	1:3.1	6.3
Hernando	25.32	15.37	44.02	4.09	1:4.2	3.6
Highlands	20.71	19.55	46.90	4.67	1:3.6	5.5
Hillsborough	20.85	19.41	48.78	3.99	1:4.6	6.2
Holmes	19.11	16.95	53.80	5.43	1:3.7	4.2
Indian River	19.79	18.79	51.13	4.69	1:8.5	0.3
Jackson	19.51	15.35	51.78	3.98	1:7.3	6.3
Jefferson	23.65	14.21	42.14	6.29	1:3.4	6.2
Lafayette	19.65	15.31	49.63	4.44	1:11.2	5.0
Lake	24.18	17.44	50.44	4.13	1:6.0	3.5
Lee	26.56	16.95	42.44	5.39	1:3.2	6.6
Leon	19.91	19.85	45.89	3.54	1:4.2	7.1

See footnotes at end of table.   Continued . . .

Florida Statistical Abstract 1991

Table 20.62. PUBLIC ELEMENTARY AND SECONDARY SCHOOLS: STUDENT-TEACHER RATIOS AND
SPECIFIED PERSONNEL PERCENTAGES AND RATIOS IN THE STATE AND COUNTIES OF
FLORIDA, SCHOOL YEAR 1989-90 (Continued)

County	FTE students per FTE teacher		Percentage of full-time staff who are--		Ratio of teacher aides to teachers 2/	Percentage of personnel resigning 3/
	Elementary 1/	Secondary	Teachers	Administrators		
Levy	20.63	14.52	47.19	5.94	1:5.0	11.8
Liberty	22.56	17.60	46.81	7.80	1:4.4	0.0
Madison	20.05	14.97	49.26	6.37	1:4.7	2.5
Manatee	21.50	17.40	47.37	5.17	1:5.2	1.7
Marion	20.45	17.84	46.38	3.92	1:3.9	8.1
Martin	20.43	17.72	47.31	4.53	1:5.7	9.4
Monroe	22.82	18.65	42.31	2.50	1:3.7	10.3
Nassau	24.45	20.81	42.97	4.02	1:2.4	5.1
Okaloosa	20.70	16.67	50.07	3.94	1:9.5	5.1
Okeechobee	20.56	21.06	44.78	4.29	1:3.4	7.3
Orange	24.23	15.54	46.19	3.56	1:4.0	6.6
Osceola	26.91	19.59	44.93	3.57	1:4.5	11.4
Palm Beach	25.36	19.67	50.83	3.67	1:3.9	4.1
Pasco	20.93	19.52	48.65	4.15	1:4.7	6.2
Pinellas	24.27	15.39	52.08	4.14	1:5.6	6.4
Polk	20.37	17.61	51.47	4.64	1:6.0	5.9
Putnam	23.56	15.23	44.01	5.61	1:3.7	5.7
St. Johns	22.06	18.80	47.79	4.68	1:3.3	4.9
St. Lucie	21.22	18.62	46.15	4.12	1:3.8	8.0
Santa Rosa	21.67	16.54	55.81	4.65	1:6.6	3.8
Sarasota	23.41	18.21	48.10	3.81	1:5.8	4.4
Seminole	24.22	18.03	52.04	4.35	1:6.3	6.1
Sumter	20.26	17.77	42.53	4.06	1:2.7	5.1
Suwannee	20.99	21.91	47.69	5.28	1:4.5	5.6
Taylor	22.21	16.95	45.14	4.97	1:4.5	5.7
Union	22.92	15.34	47.22	7.41	1:7.3	17.2
Volusia	23.53	19.50	46.70	3.98	1:4.6	3.5
Wakulla	23.71	15.81	51.27	7.37	1:6.5	6.6
Walton	18.29	15.86	56.96	6.24	1:3.3	5.1
Washington	20.59	18.83	45.03	5.85	1:2.8	5.1

FTE Full-time equivalent.
1/ Grades K-6.
2/ Classroom teachers.
3/ Instructional personnel, 1988-89.

Source: State of Florida, Department of Education, Division of Public Schools,
Profiles of Florida School Districts, 1989-90, Student and Staff Data.

Table 20.63. PUBLIC ELEMENTARY AND SECONDARY SCHOOLS: ALL FUNDS REVENUE BY MAJOR
SOURCE IN THE STATE AND COUNTIES OF FLORIDA, SCHOOL YEAR 1988-89

County	Total all revenue receipts ($1,000)	Revenue per FTE (dollars)	Federal sources ($1,000)	State sources ($1,000)	Local sources ($1,000)
Florida	8,516,761	4,533	542,291	4,529,730	3,444,739
Alachua	110,041	4,319	8,654	71,868	29,519
Baker	20,576	5,009	1,210	17,351	2,016
Bay	91,012	4,059	7,027	57,035	26,950
Bradford	17,298	3,972	1,330	14,038	1,930
Brevard	241,839	4,650	14,932	123,805	103,102
Broward	762,466	4,657	37,010	354,979	370,478
Calhoun	9,548	4,324	992	7,223	1,331
Charlotte	55,372	4,665	2,419	21,138	31,815
Citrus	52,813	4,609	3,025	25,258	24,531
Clay	80,404	3,914	4,250	57,757	18,397
Collier	110,014	5,388	7,702	25,735	76,577
Columbia	43,222	5,430	2,675	35,277	5,270
Dade	1,409,330	4,333	100,256	832,783	476,291
De Soto	18,442	7,366	1,598	12,765	4,079
Dixie	8,083	4,471	826	5,901	1,355
Duval	484,414	4,538	32,512	286,566	165,336
Escambia	185,297	4,278	15,974	125,018	44,305
Flagler	19,315	5,027	676	8,118	10,521
Franklin	7,491	4,928	746	4,449	2,296
Gadsden	38,916	4,463	6,132	29,199	3,585
Gilchrist	7,547	4,363	608	6,043	896
Glades	4,930	5,502	560	2,029	2,341
Gulf	10,582	4,464	850	6,804	2,928
Hamilton	11,274	4,754	1,509	7,161	2,605
Hardee	21,242	4,451	3,198	13,682	4,362
Hendry	26,488	4,533	2,318	15,413	8,757
Hernando	54,244	4,649	2,155	28,941	23,148
Highlands	41,930	4,785	3,822	23,040	15,069
Hillsborough	583,706	4,534	46,439	338,426	198,841
Holmes	14,391	4,428	1,232	11,407	1,751
Indian River	52,922	4,778	2,916	18,880	31,127
Jackson	32,683	3,955	2,879	26,194	3,610
Jefferson	10,588	4,782	1,107	8,074	1,407
Lafayette	4,508	4,312	363	3,456	688

See footnote at end of table.   Continued . . .

Table 20.63. PUBLIC ELEMENTARY AND SECONDARY SCHOOLS: ALL FUNDS REVENUE BY MAJOR
    SOURCE IN THE STATE AND COUNTIES OF FLORIDA, SCHOOL YEAR 1988-89 (Continued)

County	Total all revenue receipts ($1,000)	Revenue per FTE (dollars)	Revenue receipts from-- Federal sources ($1,000)	State sources ($1,000)	Local sources ($1,000)
Lake	88,969	4,235	5,749	56,840	26,380
Lee	196,147	4,673	10,279	81,127	104,741
Leon	129,409	4,424	7,933	81,097	40,380
Levy	21,479	4,621	1,695	15,822	3,962
Liberty	5,072	4,620	557	3,897	618
Madison	13,543	4,311	1,560	10,380	1,603
Manatee	121,424	4,633	7,271	55,990	58,163
Marion	120,602	4,285	9,019	73,394	38,189
Martin	64,049	5,232	2,777	15,641	45,631
Monroe	41,810	5,056	3,000	8,408	30,402
Nassau	35,765	4,264	1,800	24,017	9,949
Okaloosa	101,993	3,976	8,438	66,752	26,803
Okeechobee	24,068	4,227	2,093	16,731	5,243
Orange	459,823	4,474	26,111	221,386	212,326
Osceola	71,629	4,375	3,036	37,066	31,527
Palm Beach	555,787	5,334	26,682	161,447	367,658
Pasco	150,769	4,555	9,099	81,884	59,786
Pinellas	449,690	4,528	21,818	215,703	212,169
Polk	265,226	3,999	19,495	168,075	77,657
Putnam	51,584	4,510	4,138	30,716	16,730
St. Johns	55,981	4,321	3,143	29,448	23,391
St. Lucie	89,067	4,528	6,411	39,597	43,059
Santa Rosa	60,770	4,146	3,984	39,779	17,007
Sarasota	153,819	5,117	7,555	52,098	94,166
Seminole	187,773	4,150	8,166	111,679	67,928
Sumter	21,203	4,160	1,832	15,663	3,708
Suwannee	32,541	5,910	1,940	27,252	3,349
Taylor	16,090	4,324	1,292	10,764	4,034
Union	7,732	4,172	513	6,462	756
Volusia	222,106	4,972	10,745	105,117	106,244
Wakulla	18,106	5,959	828	14,933	2,345
Walton	20,762	4,831	1,677	9,645	9,441
Washington	19,046	4,754	1,754	15,107	2,185

FTE Full-time equivalent.

Source: State of Florida, Department of Education, Division of Public Schools,
Profiles of Florida School Districts, 1988-89, Financial Data.

Florida Statistical Abstract 1991

Table 20.65. PUBLIC ELEMENTARY AND SECONDARY SCHOOLS: ALL FUNDS EXPENDITURE BY
MAJOR TYPE IN THE STATE AND COUNTIES OF FLORIDA, SCHOOL YEAR 1988-89

County	Total expenditure all funds ($1,000)	Total current expenditure ($1,000)	Current expenditure per FTE (dollars)	Capital outlay ($1,000)	Debt service ($1,000)
Florida	8,793,842	7,428,657	3,954	1,098,061	267,124
Alachua	106,895	95,721	3,757	6,020	5,154
Baker	28,918	16,288	3,965	12,435	195
Bay	91,580	83,539	3,726	7,693	348
Bradford	17,375	16,926	3,887	118	331
Brevard	228,337	206,346	3,967	19,419	2,572
Broward	788,845	656,394	4,009	116,174	16,277
Calhoun	9,088	8,166	3,698	873	49
Charlotte	67,929	45,974	3,873	17,685	4,270
Citrus	50,016	45,818	3,999	3,272	926
Clay	79,754	73,923	3,598	5,016	816
Collier	107,512	88,450	4,332	16,691	2,371
Columbia	36,732	29,629	3,722	6,662	442
Dade	1,463,531	1,291,090	3,970	158,021	14,420
De Soto	18,727	16,957	4,014	1,414	356
Dixie	8,436	8,058	4,458	251	127
Duval	487,859	410,358	3,844	60,996	16,505
Escambia	190,321	172,970	3,993	11,684	5,668
Flagler	18,807	15,366	3,999	861	2,580
Franklin	8,030	6,968	4,584	504	558
Gadsden	39,052	37,334	4,282	1,526	192
Gilchrist	7,483	7,191	4,158	220	72
Glades	4,638	4,309	4,809	249	79
Gulf	10,170	9,690	4,087	146	334
Hamilton	11,908	11,401	4,808	337	170
Hardee	19,898	18,787	3,937	652	459
Hendry	33,207	23,555	4,031	8,934	718
Hernando	66,068	43,719	3,747	17,792	4,557
Highlands	47,976	37,104	4,234	9,033	1,839
Hillsborough	561,030	492,791	3,828	48,306	19,932
Holmes	14,526	13,039	4,012	1,283	204
Indian River	51,534	44,338	4,003	3,584	3,612
Jackson	34,371	31,330	3,791	2,433	608
Jefferson	10,587	8,935	4,036	1,510	141
Lafayette	4,695	4,421	4,229	109	166

See footnote at end of table.   Continued . . .

Florida Statistical Abstract 1991

Table 20.65. PUBLIC ELEMENTARY AND SECONDARY SCHOOLS: ALL FUNDS EXPENDITURE BY
MAJOR TYPE IN THE STATE AND COUNTIES OF FLORIDA, SCHOOL YEAR 1988-89
(Continued)

County	Total expenditure all funds ($1,000)	Total current expenditure ($1,000)	Current expenditure per FTE (dollars)	Capital outlay ($1,000)	Debt service ($1,000)
Lake	88,468	80,058	3,810	7,579	831
Lee	198,574	171,566	4,088	18,731	8,277
Leon	139,190	113,710	3,887	17,023	8,456
Levy	21,259	19,481	4,191	1,509	269
Liberty	5,011	4,765	4,341	106	141
Madison	13,883	13,236	4,213	271	376
Manatee	119,219	103,182	3,937	13,513	2,523
Marion	131,165	110,935	3,942	15,917	4,313
Martin	62,694	52,947	4,325	8,188	1,559
Monroe	44,051	40,380	4,883	2,980	691
Nassau	35,190	31,782	3,789	2,992	416
Okaloosa	112,784	94,222	3,673	16,089	2,473
Okeechobee	22,842	21,692	3,810	691	459
Orange	459,232	396,098	3,854	40,240	22,894
Osceola	86,263	57,242	3,496	22,717	6,304
Palm Beach	614,561	462,963	4,443	121,772	29,827
Pasco	163,012	126,702	3,828	25,639	10,671
Pinellas	444,019	387,894	3,906	47,330	8,795
Polk	268,233	249,428	3,761	15,618	3,187
Putnam	71,243	46,111	4,032	22,282	2,851
St. Johns	53,242	49,195	3,797	3,617	431
St. Lucie	106,086	77,443	3,937	24,438	4,205
Santa Rosa	60,740	54,912	3,746	5,154	674
Sarasota	162,553	133,273	4,433	26,811	2,469
Seminole	215,415	164,503	3,636	40,169	10,743
Sumter	20,947	20,016	3,927	577	354
Suwannee	24,625	20,727	3,764	3,732	165
Taylor	16,322	14,742	3,962	1,347	233
Union	7,944	7,309	3,944	493	142
Volusia	245,164	177,459	3,973	43,273	24,432
Wakulla	16,233	11,455	3,770	4,247	531
Walton	19,402	18,168	4,228	947	286
Washington	18,439	18,176	4,536	167	96

FTE Full-time equivalent.

Source: State of Florida, Department of Education, Division of Public Schools,
Profiles of Florida School Districts, 1988-89, Financial Data.

Florida Statistical Abstract 1991

Table 20.66. PUBLIC ELEMENTARY AND SECONDARY SCHOOLS: ALL FUNDS EXPENDITURE BY
    FUNCTION IN THE STATE AND COUNTIES OF FLORIDA, SCHOOL YEAR 1988-89

(rounded to thousands of dollars)

County	Total all funds	Instructional support services	Instruction	Non-instructional
Florida	7,623,247	755,686	4,229,215	2,638,346
Alachua	96,091	10,343	50,862	34,885
Baker	16,433	1,487	8,409	6,537
Bay	83,861	7,728	50,593	25,540
Bradford	16,926	1,645	9,547	5,734
Brevard	216,139	18,326	113,781	84,032
Broward	656,394	82,643	361,664	212,088
Calhoun	8,166	799	4,669	2,698
Charlotte	46,230	4,051	25,317	16,861
Citrus	47,192	5,314	25,101	16,777
Clay	73,923	6,277	39,845	27,801
Collier	92,861	7,941	52,440	32,480
Columbia	29,629	2,276	17,133	10,219
Dade	1,291,731	116,282	780,649	394,800
De Soto	16,957	1,437	9,630	5,891
Dixie	8,058	801	4,311	2,947
Duval	411,291	45,546	226,698	139,047
Escambia	184,690	19,774	97,769	67,147
Flagler	15,366	1,255	8,356	5,756
Franklin	6,968	381	4,055	2,531
Gadsden	37,334	4,276	21,030	12,028
Gilchrist	7,191	663	4,191	2,338
Glades	4,582	501	2,589	1,492
Gulf	9,691	854	5,199	3,639
Hamilton	11,401	1,126	5,646	4,629
Hardee	18,790	2,050	10,621	6,119
Hendry	23,555	1,935	12,630	8,990
Hernando	45,553	4,140	23,659	17,754
Highlands	37,105	4,462	19,060	13,584
Hillsborough	518,399	49,603	276,869	191,927
Holmes	13,039	889	7,842	4,308
Indian River	44,338	4,696	24,593	15,049
Jackson	31,432	2,724	18,290	10,418
Jefferson	8,985	876	4,807	3,302
Lafayette	4,421	295	2,200	1,926
Lake	83,514	9,012	44,299	30,203

Continued . . .

Florida Statistical Abstract 1991

Table 20.66. PUBLIC ELEMENTARY AND SECONDARY SCHOOLS: ALL FUNDS EXPENDITURE BY
FUNCTION IN THE STATE AND COUNTIES OF FLORIDA, SCHOOL YEAR 1988-89
(Continued)

(rounded to thousands of dollars)

County	Total all funds	Instructional support services	Instruction	Non-instructional
Lee	183,906	19,798	90,829	73,279
Leon	113,854	12,461	63,705	37,688
Levy	19,526	2,086	10,773	6,667
Liberty	4,765	419	2,603	1,743
Madison	13,236	1,287	7,128	4,821
Manatee	110,534	10,222	56,904	43,408
Marion	111,606	12,824	62,779	36,004
Martin	52,947	5,515	27,830	19,602
Monroe	42,176	3,181	20,618	18,377
Nassau	31,782	2,273	16,904	12,604
Okaloosa	94,222	9,553	53,212	31,457
Okeechobee	21,692	1,979	11,949	7,764
Orange	420,292	44,294	225,900	150,097
Osceola	60,918	7,114	30,429	23,376
Palm Beach	504,642	39,311	275,661	189,670
Pasco	137,327	14,579	68,864	53,883
Pinellas	390,615	37,109	231,695	121,811
Polk	250,416	23,837	142,838	83,740
Putnam	59,072	5,077	24,606	29,389
St. Johns	51,600	4,275	30,024	17,301
St. Lucie	77,443	9,891	43,001	24,551
Santa Rosa	55,225	5,170	30,649	19,406
Sarasota	134,266	13,270	73,041	47,955
Seminole	165,848	19,272	92,017	54,559
Sumter	20,016	1,965	11,231	6,820
Suwannee	20,727	1,319	11,518	7,890
Taylor	14,742	1,474	8,039	5,230
Union	7,361	753	3,646	2,962
Volusia	178,735	19,439	98,840	60,456
Wakulla	11,475	970	5,909	4,597
Walton	18,168	1,266	10,549	6,353
Washington	25,879	1,297	11,172	13,410

Source: State of Florida, Department of Education, Division of Public Schools,
Selected Statistical Profiles of Florida School Districts, 1988-89.

Florida Statistical Abstract 1991

Table 20.67. PUBLIC ELEMENTARY AND SECONDARY SCHOOLS: OPERATING TAX MILLAGE
OPERATING TAX YIELD, ASSESSED VALUE OF NONEXEMPT PROPERTY, AND ASSESSED
VALUATION PER FTE STUDENT IN THE STATE AND COUNTIES OF FLORIDA, SCHOOL
YEAR 1988-89

County	Operating tax millage	Operating tax yield ($1,000)	Assessed value of nonexempt property	
			Amount ($1,000)	Valuation per FTE student (dollars)
Florida	(X)	2,249,040	378,530,274	164,375
Alachua	6.277	17,394	2,916,998	93,818
Baker	6.272	883	148,166	28,648
Bay	6.183	19,399	3,302,566	118,806
Bradford	6.323	1,307	217,607	40,766
Brevard	6.281	61,870	10,368,848	184,188
Broward	6.390	243,398	40,095,220	199,364
Calhoun	5.543	642	121,971	46,096
Charlotte	6.286	22,197	3,717,040	260,644
Citrus	6.292	17,025	2,848,189	200,746
Clay	6.340	11,243	1,866,740	75,684
Collier	6.182	54,342	9,253,063	377,322
Columbia	6.271	3,207	538,401	55,758
Dade	6.193	328,105	55,768,339	141,449
De Soto	6.238	2,610	440,424	85,436
Dixie	6.147	851	145,645	66,323
Duval	6.186	91,829	15,625,962	117,045
Escambia	6.563	27,260	4,372,158	79,972
Flagler	6.223	7,080	1,197,574	260,682
Franklin	5.851	1,524	274,138	150,791
Gadsden	6.185	2,098	357,039	33,971
Gilchrist	6.151	681	116,614	55,930
Glades	6.148	1,705	291,979	265,919
Gulf	6.364	2,388	394,918	138,811
Hamilton	5.832	1,933	348,883	116,488
Hardee	6.336	2,814	467,549	82,987
Hendry	6.173	5,151	878,387	127,229
Hernando	6.266	13,773	2,313,811	164,907
Highlands	6.193	9,624	1,635,817	150,669
Hillsborough	6.347	125,412	20,799,296	129,873
Holmes	5.595	732	137,766	35,691
Indian River	6.199	22,250	3,778,132	279,448
Jackson	5.605	2,206	414,331	41,945
Jefferson	6.147	859	147,118	55,162
Lafayette	6.602	441	70,289	58,234

See footnotes at end of table.   Continued . . .

Florida Statistical Abstract 1991

Table 20.67. PUBLIC ELEMENTARY AND SECONDARY SCHOOLS: OPERATING TAX MILLAGE
OPERATING TAX YIELD, ASSESSED VALUE OF NONEXEMPT PROPERTY, AND ASSESSED
VALUATION PER FTE STUDENT IN THE STATE AND COUNTIES OF FLORIDA, SCHOOL
YEAR 1988-89 (Continued)

County	Operating tax millage	Operating tax yield ($1,000)	Assessed value of nonexempt property Amount ($1,000)	Valuation per FTE student (dollars)
Lake	6.242	17,451	2,942,869	113,092
Lee	6.257	74,560	12,543,396	243,779
Leon	6.150	21,146	3,619,365	98,647
Levy	6.283	2,568	430,159	74,603
Liberty	5.437	420	81,363	62,299
Madison	6.226	1,117	188,803	49,659
Manatee	6.150	38,722	6,627,630	206,758
Marion	6.380	23,914	3,945,494	115,123
Martin	6.154	31,419	5,374,245	355,087
Monroe	6.073	25,778	4,468,118	441,732
Nassau	6.301	6,464	1,079,862	107,470
Okaloosa	6.148	17,745	3,038,151	153,620
Okeechobee	6.146	3,583	613,719	90,720
Orange	6.205	138,435	23,484,387	191,417
Osceola	6.370	18,611	3,075,385	159,727
Palm Beach	6.322	234,024	38,965,603	300,343
Pasco	6.203	34,062	5,780,200	142,503
Pinellas	6.150	149,575	25,601,234	203,443
Polk	6.217	53,566	9,069,559	113,457
Putnam	6.283	10,420	1,745,721	127,008
St. Johns	6.378	16,494	2,722,116	170,676
St. Lucie	6.349	31,408	5,207,224	222,075
Santa Rosa	6.188	10,532	1,791,605	103,173
Sarasota	6.242	66,795	11,264,093	291,536
Seminole	6.309	43,656	7,283,786	134,002
Sumter	6.278	2,320	388,928	64,735
Suwannee	6.036	1,867	325,661	49,538
Taylor	6.283	2,753	461,194	100,434
Union	6.193	399	67,843	30,950
Volusia	6.204	55,665	9,444,683	171,348
Wakulla	6.283	1,190	199,407	55,253
Walton	6.473	6,908	1,123,401	220,318
Washington	6.392	1,239	204,094	44,205

FTE Full-time equivalent.
(X) Not applicable.
Source: State of Florida, Department of Education, Division of Public Schools,
Profiles of Florida School Districts, 1988-89, Financial Data.

Florida Statistical Abstract 1991

Table 20.69. PUBLIC ELEMENTARY AND SECONDARY SCHOOLS: EXPENDITURE FOR PUPIL
    TRANSPORTATION SERVICES IN THE STATE AND COUNTIES OF FLORIDA, SCHOOL
    YEAR 1988-89

(in dollars)

County	1988-89	County	1988-89
Florida	281,414,557	Lafayette	336,593
Alachua	3,917,430	Lake	3,388,899
Baker	1,096,582	Lee	7,557,506
Bay	3,761,188	Leon	4,321,605
Bradford	789,228	Levy	1,163,254
Brevard	9,452,497	Liberty	235,477
Broward	16,267,508	Madison	825,950
Calhoun	415,515	Manatee	4,872,609
Charlotte	2,098,246	Marion	5,689,821
Citrus	2,833,628	Martin	2,504,293
Clay	3,563,361	Monroe	1,929,525
Collier	3,256,988	Nassau	1,931,232
Columbia	1,765,452	Okaloosa	3,749,825
Dade	28,367,695	Okeechobee	1,131,252
De Soto	799,450	Orange	16,260,016
Dixie	425,008	Osceola	2,112,055
Duval	18,649,151	Palm Beach	12,548,226
Escambia	7,017,975	Pasco	7,131,688
Flagler	883,345	Pinellas	11,880,875
Franklin	197,564	Polk	8,875,272
Gadsden	1,969,168	Putnam	2,678,752
Gilchrist	378,264	St. Johns	2,180,702
Glades	176,740	St. Lucie	4,972,234
Gulf	572,058	Santa Rosa	2,880,107
Hamilton	554,872	Sarasota	5,889,500
Hardee	1,080,521	Seminole	8,787,213
Hendry	1,452,549	Sumter	1,106,004
Hernando	2,767,295	Suwannee	1,440,971
Highlands	1,916,132	Taylor	991,538
Hillsborough	22,619,291	Union	372,524
Holmes	684,314	Volusia	4,837,921
Indian River	1,635,213	Wakulla	1,042,819
Jackson	1,649,842	Walton	1,126,850
Jefferson	711,441	Washington	935,938

    Source: State of Florida, Department of Education, Division of Public Schools,
Profiles of Florida School Districts, 1988-89, Financial Data.

Florida Statistical Abstract 1991

Table 20.73. PUBLIC COMMUNITY COLLEGES: REVENUE AND EXPENDITURE BY INSTITUTION
IN FLORIDA, FISCAL YEARS 1987-88 AND 1988-89

(in dollars)

Community college	Total revenue		Total educational and general expenditure	
	1987-88	1988-89	1987-88	1988-89
Total	587,623,775	662,452,595	585,621,397	650,602,834
Brevard	28,351,410	32,395,988	28,634,109	31,134,458
Broward	42,279,951	48,851,902	43,494,597	46,543,718
Central Florida	9,957,149	11,518,076	10,460,295	11,662,971
Chipola	5,307,885	6,384,397	4,986,840	6,011,371
Daytona Beach	25,949,246	29,370,015	26,119,663	29,361,866
Edison	11,890,535	13,655,503	11,689,283	13,072,668
Florida Community College at Jacksonville	50,252,871	54,496,873	50,219,240	52,952,887
Florida Keys	4,541,362	4,881,182	4,425,321	5,106,159
Gulf Coast	9,531,423	10,873,896	9,448,212	10,663,905
Hillsborough	26,732,619	29,241,306	27,249,564	29,346,044
Indian River	17,533,853	20,112,582	18,051,119	20,007,631
Lake City	8,299,083	9,653,164	8,470,713	9,014,224
Lake Sumter	4,768,696	5,528,579	4,528,446	5,385,245
Manatee	13,443,951	15,465,308	13,676,854	15,267,494
Miami-Dade	113,985,495	125,757,709	113,139,161	125,363,257
North Florida	3,686,094	4,138,720	3,405,341	4,174,980
Okaloosa-Walton	8,637,877	10,210,668	8,585,947	9,989,258
Palm Beach	26,179,739	28,970,278	26,061,734	28,395,809
Pasco-Hernando	6,642,255	7,738,638	6,635,573	8,040,145
Pensacola	28,647,108	31,126,630	28,507,485	30,357,831
Polk	10,684,806	12,199,284	10,682,919	11,996,283
St. Johns River	4,563,957	5,689,703	4,514,750	5,611,308
St. Petersburg	35,309,835	39,292,420	34,166,601	37,671,925
Santa Fe	24,933,738	27,125,769	24,877,499	27,372,883
Seminole	18,655,485	21,804,519	18,081,010	22,169,299
South Florida	5,784,360	7,338,715	5,768,280	7,402,546
Tallahassee	12,940,552	15,548,264	12,533,087	15,488,876
Valencia	28,132,440	33,082,507	27,207,754	31,037,793

Source: State of Florida, Department of Education, Division of Community
Colleges, *Report for Florida Community Colleges: The Fact Book, 1989-90.*

Table 20.74.   FEDERAL AID: SPECIFIED FEDERAL HEALTH AND EDUCATION PROGRAM
   EXPENDITURES IN FLORIDA, OTHER SUNBELT STATES, AND THE UNITED STATES
   1989

(in millions of dollars)

State	Total 1/	Compensatory education for the disadvantaged	Medicaid	ETA employment/ training
Florida	4,095	182	1,139	105
Alabama	1,802	82	407	69
Arizona	1,305	49	263	49
Arkansas	1,106	50	263	32
California	11,936	455	3,260	325
Georgia	3,089	110	830	57
Louisiana	2,304	95	891	57
Mississippi	1,366	75	416	37
New Mexico	907	31	185	19
North Carolina	2,498	92	841	77
Oklahoma	1,508	38	464	32
South Carolina	1,455	60	445	41
Tennessee	2,353	80	830	65
Texas	5,974	291	1,421	141
Virginia	2,119	76	462	51
United States	121,079	4,155	34,506	3,020

ETA Employment and Training Administration.
1/ Includes other amounts not shown separately.

Table 20.75.   STATE ARTS AGENCIES: STATE LEGISLATIVE APPROPRIATIONS FOR ARTS
   AGENCIES IN FLORIDA AND THE UNITED STATES, FISCAL YEARS 1983-84 THROUGH
   1989-90

(in thousands of dollars, except as indicated)

Year	Florida	United States 1/
1983-84	5,264	135,797
1984-85	9,045	161,413
1985-86	9,761	195,622
1986-87	12,710	216,082
1987-88 Δ/	17,340	242,842
1988-89	24,179	270,652
1989-90	23,622	284,101
Per capita 2/ (cents)	188.0	113.0

Δ/ Revised.
1/ Includes outlying areas.
2/ Based on enumerated resident population as of July 1, 1988.
   Source for Tables 20.74 and 20.75: U.S., Department of Commerce, Bureau of the
Census, *Statistical Abstract of the United States, 1991*, and previous editions.

Florida Statistical Abstract 1991

GOVERNMENT
AND ELECTIONS

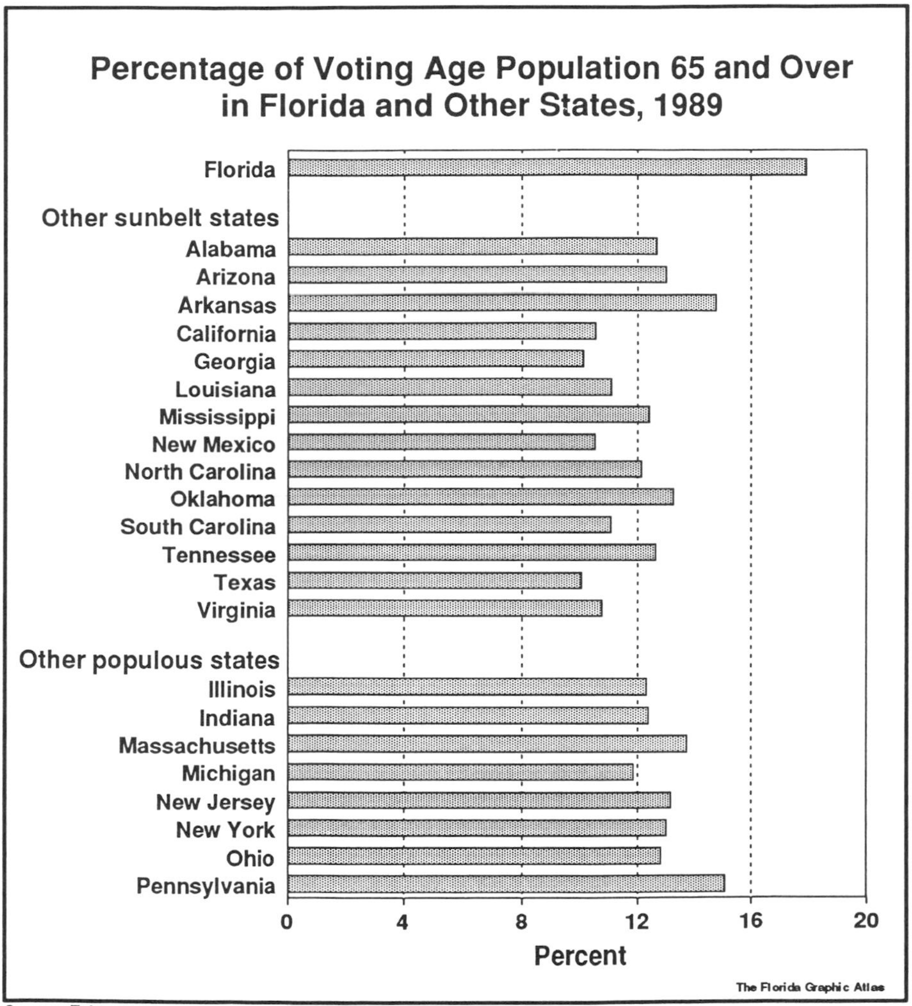

Percentage of Voting Age Population 65 and Over in Florida and Other States, 1989

Florida

Other sunbelt states
Alabama
Arizona
Arkansas
California
Georgia
Louisiana
Mississippi
New Mexico
North Carolina
Oklahoma
South Carolina
Tennessee
Texas
Virginia

Other populous states
Illinois
Indiana
Massachusetts
Michigan
New Jersey
New York
Ohio
Pennsylvania

0   4   8   12   16   20

Percent

The Florida Graphic Atlas

Source: Table 21.24

Table 21.01. GOVERNMENTAL UNITS: NUMBER OF UNITS BY TYPE IN FLORIDA AND THE UNITED
STATES, 1987

Type of unit	Florida	United States
<u>All units</u>	966	83,237
Federal government	0	1
State government	1	50
Local government	965	83,186
County 1/	66	3,042
Municipal	390	19,200
Township	0	16,691
School districts	95	14,721
Special districts	414	29,532
Single-function	398	27,481
Education services	5	1,543
Education 2/	2	713
Libraries	3	830
Social services	43	1,267
Hospitals	29	783
Health	14	484
Transportation	20	1,265
Highways	6	621
Airports	4	369
Other 3/	10	275
Fire protection	48	5,070
Environment and housing	245	12,589
Natural resources 4/	133	6,360
Drainage and flood control	62	2,772
Irrigation	7	854
Soil and water conservation	60	2,469
Other	4	265
Parks and recreation	11	1,004
Housing and community development	98	3,464
Sewerage	3	1,607
Sanitation other than sewerage	0	154
Utilities	19	3,471
Water supply	12	3,060
Other 5/	7	411
Cemeteries	0	1,627
Industrial development and mortgage credit	3	92
Other single-function districts	15	557
Multiple-function	16	2,051
Natural resources and water supply	2	98
Sewerage and water supply	4	1,168
Other	10	785

1/ In 1968, Duval County and the City of Jacksonville consolidated to form one
government, designated the City of Jacksonville. Jacksonville is counted as a
municipal government, rather than as a county government, in census reporting.
2/ Primarily school building authorities.
3/ Includes parking facilities and water transport and terminals.
4/ Functions within the "natural resources" category overlap.
5/ Includes electric power, gas supply, and transit.

Source: U.S., Department of Commerce, Bureau of the Census, *1987 Census of
Governments, Volume I, No. 1: Governmental Organization.*

Florida Statistical Abstract 1991

Table 21.07. LOCAL GOVERNMENTS AND PUBLIC SCHOOL SYSTEMS: NUMBER OF POLITICAL
    UNITS AND ELECTED OFFICIALS BY TYPE OF GOVERNMENT IN THE STATE AND
    COUNTIES OF FLORIDA, 1987

County	Political units Munici- palities	School dis- tricts	Special dis- tricts	Elected officials County	Munici- palities	School dis- tricts	Special dis- tricts
Florida	390	95	414	751	2,255	416	1,017
Alachua	9	2	3	10	48	6	4
Baker	2	1	3	10	10	6	5
Bay	8	2	6	11	40	6	8
Bradford	4	1	1	11	26	6	3
Brevard	15	2	14	8	83	6	30
Broward	28	2	29	13	156	8	64
Calhoun	2	1	0	10	11	6	0
Charlotte	1	1	6	10	5	6	5
Citrus	2	1	2	12	12	6	6
Clay	4	1	3	11	21	6	5
Collier	2	1	11	10	13	6	28
Columbia	2	2	4	13	10	6	5
Dade	26	2	4	10	150	8	3
De Soto	1	1	3	12	7	6	10
Dixie	2	1	1	11	12	6	5
Duval 1/	5	2	2	(X)	62	8	5
Escambia	2	2	4	12	16	6	10
Flagler	4	1	5	9	23	6	14
Franklin	2	1	6	10	10	6	10
Gadsden	5	1	1	11	31	6	5
Gilchrist	3	1	3	17	18	6	11
Glades	1	1	2	11	5	6	8
Gulf	3	1	3	10	14	6	8
Hamilton	3	1	2	10	15	6	1
Hardee	3	1	2	11	20	6	5
Hendry	2	1	15	10	10	6	49
Hernando	2	1	4	10	8	6	5
Highlands	3	2	4	10	19	6	8
Hillsborough	3	2	6	12	24	8	14
Holmes	5	1	1	10	28	6	0
Indian River	5	1	11	30	26	6	45
Jackson	11	2	6	10	62	6	9
Jefferson	1	1	1	10	9	6	5
Lafayette	1	1	1	10	7	6	2

See footnotes at end of table.   Continued . . .

Florida Statistical Abstract 1991

Table 21.07. LOCAL GOVERNMENTS AND PUBLIC SCHOOL SYSTEMS: NUMBER OF POLITICAL
UNITS AND ELECTED OFFICIALS BY TYPE OF GOVERNMENT IN THE STATE AND
COUNTIES OF FLORIDA, 1987 (Continued)

	Political units			Elected officials			
County	Munici-palities	School dis-tricts	Special dis-tricts	County	Munici-palities	School dis-tricts	Special dis-tricts
Lake	14	2	6	11	77	6	5
Lee	3	2	29	10	19	6	112
Leon	1	2	6	12	5	6	10
Levy	7	1	3	11	38	6	10
Liberty	1	1	0	13	7	6	0
Madison	3	2	2	10	17	6	5
Manatee	6	2	19	10	38	6	35
Marion	5	2	5	10	29	6	5
Martin	4	1	5	7	22	6	15
Monroe	3	2	7	11	26	6	10
Nassau	3	1	5	10	19	6	13
Okaloosa	9	2	9	11	57	6	25
Okeechobee	1	1	2	45	6	6	8
Orange	13	2	10	11	73	8	18
Osceola	2	1	1	10	10	6	5
Palm Beach	37	2	37	10	206	8	113
Pasco	6	2	5	10	31	6	7
Pinellas	24	2	13	9	132	8	13
Polk	17	2	11	10	93	6	20
Putnam	5	2	5	11	28	6	5
St. Johns	3	1	7	10	17	6	27
St. Lucie	3	2	5	11	18	6	11
Santa Rosa	3	1	8	12	21	6	22
Sarasota	3	1	15	10	17	6	61
Seminole	7	2	3	10	39	6	5
Sumter	5	1	1	10	30	6	5
Suwannee	2	1	3	9	15	6	5
Taylor	1	1	1	10	5	6	5
Union	3	1	2	10	17	6	5
Volusia	14	2	12	11	72	6	24
Wakulla	2	1	2	10	10	6	5
Walton	3	1	3	10	20	6	8
Washington	5	1	3	11	30	6	5

(X) Not applicable.
1/ County-type area without any county government.
Note: School districts include community college districts.
   Source: U.S., Department of Commerce, Bureau of the Census, *1987 Census of
Governments, Volume I, No. 2: Popularly Elected Officials.*

Florida Statistical Abstract 1991

Table 21.24. VOTING-AGE POPULATION: ESTIMATES BY AGE IN FLORIDA, OTHER
    SUNBELT STATES, OTHER POPULOUS STATES, AND THE UNITED STATES
    JULY 1, 1989

State	Population		Percentage by age			
	Total (1,000)	Aged 18 and over (1,000)	Aged 18 to 24	Aged 25 to 44	Aged 45 to 64	Aged 65 and over
	Sunbelt states					
Florida	12,671	9,799	9.4	28.9	21.1	18.0
Alabama	4,118	3,010	10.9	31.1	18.4	12.7
Arizona	3,556	2,575	10.5	31.2	17.7	13.0
Arkansas	2,406	1,756	10.4	29.1	18.7	14.8
California	29,063	21,350	10.4	34.4	18.1	10.6
Georgia	6,436	4,639	11.3	32.5	18.1	10.1
Louisiana	4,382	3,109	11.1	32.2	16.5	11.1
Mississippi	2,621	1,852	11.4	29.5	17.3	12.4
New Mexico	1,528	1,074	10.5	31.9	17.3	10.5
North Carolina	6,571	4,929	11.3	32.3	19.3	12.1
Oklahoma	3,224	2,371	10.6	31.9	17.7	13.3
South Carolina	3,512	2,558	11.5	32.4	17.8	11.1
Tennessee	4,940	3,685	10.7	32.0	19.2	12.7
Texas	16,991	12,038	10.9	33.2	16.7	10.1
Virginia	6,098	4,615	11.5	34.2	19.3	10.8
	Other populous states					
Illinois	11,658	8,678	10.5	32.4	19.1	12.3
Indiana	5,593	4,133	10.9	31.8	18.7	12.4
Massachusetts	5,913	4,576	11.1	33.2	19.3	13.7
Michigan	9,273	6,829	11.0	32.2	18.5	11.9
New Jersey	7,736	5,903	10.2	31.6	21.3	13.2
New York	17,950	13,600	10.6	31.5	20.7	13.0
Ohio	10,907	8,090	10.5	31.4	19.4	12.8
Pennsylvania	12,040	9,199	10.2	30.8	20.2	15.1
United States	248,239	184,157	10.6	32.4	18.7	12.5

    Source: U.S., Department of Commerce, Bureau of the Census, *Current Population
Reports: Population Estimates and Projections.* Series P-25, No. 1058.

Florida Statistical Abstract 1991

Table 21.25.   VOTING-AGE POPULATION: CENSUS COUNTS, APRIL 1, 1980 AND
1990, OF PERSONS AGED 18 AND OVER IN THE STATE AND COUNTIES OF
FLORIDA

County	1980	1990	County	1980	1990
Florida	7,386,678	10,071,689	Lafayette	2,725	4,198
			Lake	81,114	121,841
Alachua	115,910	142,081	Lee	160,211	269,543
Baker	10,265	12,855	Leon	111,059	149,368
Bay	69,289	94,745	Levy	14,332	19,644
Bradford	14,360	17,109	Liberty	2,989	4,221
Brevard	204,925	311,524	Madison	10,011	12,009
Broward	803,970	998,870	Manatee	117,438	171,091
Calhoun	6,443	8,140	Marion	90,417	151,741
Charlotte	49,205	93,687	Martin	50,804	83,162
Citrus	44,295	77,049	Monroe	50,696	64,469
Clay	44,323	75,452	Nassau	22,027	32,037
Collier	66,102	121,759	Okaloosa	76,763	106,461
Columbia	24,285	30,712	Okeechobee	13,729	21,577
Dade	1,235,784	1,469,084	Orange	345,582	516,005
De Soto	13,864	18,199	Osceola	36,555	80,579
Dixie	5,504	7,997	Palm Beach	453,779	693,965
Duval	407,674	498,625	Pasco	157,739	230,908
Escambia	166,352	196,418	Pinellas	589,818	700,203
Flagler	8,429	23,222	Polk	234,146	307,640
Franklin	5,309	6,814	Putnam	36,226	48,528
Gadsden	27,592	28,941	St. Johns	37,689	65,196
Gilchrist	4,000	7,245	St. Lucie	64,210	115,549
Glades	4,297	5,735	Santa Rosa	38,588	59,434
Gulf	7,370	8,681	Sarasota	166,784	234,065
Hamilton	5,707	7,774	Seminole	127,079	214,622
Hardee	12,875	13,811	Sumter	17,828	24,572
Hendry	12,097	17,695	Suwannee	15,350	19,682
Hernando	35,049	82,467	Taylor	11,456	12,288
Highlands	37,068	55,614	Union	8,018	7,617
Hillsborough	470,929	631,780	Volusia	203,828	297,689
Holmes	10,365	11,857	Wakulla	7,369	10,182
Indian River	46,159	72,722	Walton	15,588	21,166
Jackson	27,571	31,096	Washington	10,202	12,649
Jefferson	7,162	8,028			

Note: Detail may not add to total because of rounding.

Source: University of Florida, Bureau of Economic and Business Research, Population Program, *Population Studies*, August 1991, Volume 24, Bulletin No. 97-98.

Table 21.30.   REGISTERED VOTERS: VOTERS BY PARTY IN THE STATE AND COUNTIES
    OF FLORIDA, OCTOBER 8, 1990

County	Total	Democratic Total	Democratic Black	Republican Total	Republican Black	Other 1/	Number of precincts
Florida	6,031,161	3,149,747	538,802	2,448,488	27,348	432,926	4,536
Alachua	78,625	50,112	8,862	23,499	392	5,014	46
Baker	8,202	7,712	963	463	5	27	8
Bay	55,523	36,517	3,873	16,166	225	2,840	32
Bradford	8,456	7,044	1,173	1,166	16	246	24
Brevard	205,118	92,235	8,851	99,134	629	13,749	126
Broward	635,221	352,911	49,883	231,140	3,255	51,170	537
Calhoun	5,380	5,162	597	201	6	17	13
Charlotte	67,443	26,180	941	37,300	121	3,963	45
Citrus	52,500	28,469	707	20,074	18	3,957	29
Clay	44,273	21,436	1,314	19,932	102	2,905	32
Collier	66,528	18,146	798	43,626	54	4,756	80
Columbia	18,511	15,031	2,697	3,234	59	246	30
Dade	673,838	368,210	122,169	252,219	6,720	53,409	504
De Soto	10,354	8,071	1,080	2,126	31	157	15
Dixie	7,552	6,945	578	537	8	70	12
Duval	304,169	197,247	66,519	90,434	2,160	16,488	223
Escambia	121,389	78,936	17,302	37,747	533	4,706	95
Flagler	15,723	7,496	877	7,021	82	1,206	19
Franklin	5,744	5,302	695	391	3	51	7
Gadsden	18,998	17,718	10,195	1,106	148	174	12
Gilchrist	4,856	4,316	142	469	0	71	10
Glades	4,195	3,392	407	686	9	117	12
Gulf	7,182	6,681	1,177	468	10	33	14
Hamilton	5,562	5,320	1,740	225	16	17	8
Hardee	7,584	6,502	559	993	31	89	11
Hendry	8,584	6,458	1,019	1,865	38	261	17
Hernando	67,012	31,708	1,279	30,270	88	5,034	38
Highlands	35,353	18,853	1,641	15,304	59	1,196	20
Hillsborough	347,626	195,766	34,976	124,738	1,591	27,122	208
Holmes	7,945	7,493	153	417	1	35	16
Indian River	50,974	18,894	2,347	28,545	134	3,535	36
Jackson	18,356	16,306	3,782	1,930	93	120	26
Jefferson	6,234	5,623	2,391	518	29	93	13
Lafayette	3,138	3,008	187	125	2	5	5

See footnotes at end of table.   Continued . . .

Table 21.30.   REGISTERED VOTERS: VOTERS BY PARTY IN THE STATE AND COUNTIES
OF FLORIDA, OCTOBER 8, 1990 (Continued)

County	Total	Democratic Total	Black	Republican Total	Black	Other 1/	Number of pre- cincts
Lake	71,100	30,998	3,284	36,642	161	3,460	69
Lee	161,485	62,417	4,149	86,836	526	12,232	101
Leon	99,577	67,405	19,591	24,973	680	7,199	76
Levy	12,300	10,060	1,061	2,042	23	198	13
Liberty	2,909	2,834	323	74	0	1	8
Madison	7,231	6,500	2,312	660	50	71	11
Manatee	119,725	49,711	5,099	61,466	278	8,548	85
Marion	90,574	48,354	7,035	35,807	350	6,413	75
Martin	55,904	17,273	1,403	34,594	171	4,037	30
Monroe	40,308	21,157	1,445	15,777	94	3,374	25
Nassau	19,319	14,350	1,626	4,263	38	706	13
Okaloosa	64,879	31,604	7,745	30,230	280	3,045	39
Okeechobee	12,776	9,550	781	2,954	75	272	11
Orange	233,559	105,584	23,529	112,227	1,447	15,748	167
Osceola	49,508	23,868	1,355	20,968	138	4,672	40
Palm Beach	461,956	224,034	29,979	190,127	1,772	47,795	316
Pasco	161,541	78,340	1,450	70,826	108	12,375	94
Pinellas	492,578	206,235	24,961	236,835	1,896	49,508	316
Polk	154,766	92,315	13,516	58,291	442	4,160	130
Putnam	31,738	23,377	3,814	7,026	221	1,335	41
St. Johns	41,539	22,625	2,722	16,864	98	1,757	29
St. Lucie	72,075	34,054	6,634	31,555	309	12,983	48
Santa Rosa	47,263	30,429	1,393	15,107	83	8,210	25
Sarasota	177,095	57,275	3,199	106,851	406	2,050	107
Seminole	115,203	43,636	5,481	63,256	381	6,523	95
Sumter	13,588	9,368	1,309	3,793	32	427	17
Suwannee	12,401	10,511	1,526	1,735	27	155	15
Taylor	8,210	7,330	1,105	818	23	62	14
Union	4,048	3,863	561	157	3	28	8
Volusia	184,087	95,584	10,495	76,447	505	12,056	136
Wakulla	8,075	7,043	935	904	12	128	12
Walton	16,117	12,366	950	3,362	32	389	33
Washington	9,579	8,497	1,160	952	19	130	14

1/ Includes registered Conservative, Libertarian, New Alliance, and Populist
voters, and those with no party affiliation specified.
Note: See Table 21.25 for voting-age population.

Source: State of Florida, Department of State, Division of Elections, *Elections
1990: Official Election Returns, November 6, 1990.*

Florida Statistical Abstract 1991

Table 21.32.   ELECTION RESULTS: VOTES CAST FOR PRESIDENT AND VICE PRESIDENT IN THE
GENERAL ELECTION BY PARTY IN THE STATE AND COUNTIES OF FLORIDA, NOVEMBER 8
1988

County	Bush and Quayle (Repub-lican)	Dukakis and Bentson (Demo-crat)	Other par-ties 1/	County	Bush and Quayle (Repub-lican)	Dukakis and Bentson (Demo-crat)	Other par-ties 1/
Florida	2,618,885	1,656,701	26,727	Lafayette	1,450	722	12
				Lake	37,314	16,762	479
Alachua	30,124	29,375	662	Lee	87,247	40,709	908
Baker	3,414	1,353	8	Leon	36,032	33,446	631
Bay	31,712	11,582	450	Levy	5,250	3,433	104
Bradford	4,218	2,386	29	Liberty	1,419	709	47
Brevard	104,721	42,967	1,300	Madison	2,556	1,950	15
Broward	220,196	218,211	2,015	Manatee	51,160	26,618	300
Calhoun	2,420	1,329	33	Marion	41,488	20,679	334
Charlotte	28,879	15,967	292	Martin	31,270	11,486	316
Citrus	21,052	12,177	218	Monroe	15,919	10,151	320
Clay	25,882	7,766	121	Nassau	8,366	4,138	57
Collier	38,910	12,768	291	Okaloosa	40,295	9,726	320
Columbia	7,759	4,072	82	Okeechobee	4,733	3,007	48
Dade	270,672	216,847	2,357	Orange	117,141	53,991	1,510
De Soto	4,237	2,181	40	Osceola	21,350	9,811	214
Dixie	2,027	1,366	0	Palm Beach	181,408	144,143	1,520
Duval	127,875	74,832	1,004	Pasco	63,788	50,369	598
Escambia	64,774	29,934	523	Pinellas	210,971	152,374	1,898
Flagler	6,494	4,241	34	Polk	77,065	38,236	687
Franklin	1,911	1,283	73	Putnam	11,621	8,569	107
Gadsden	5,987	6,368	213	St. Johns	19,164	7,999	156
Gilchrist	1,854	1,137	20	St. Lucie	32,241	17,427	314
Glades	1,546	1,034	12	Santa Rosa	18,948	5,251	143
Gulf	3,040	1,687	142	Sarasota	84,585	42,095	707
Hamilton	2,062	1,314	16	Seminole	60,328	22,627	621
Hardee	3,636	1,688	108	Sumter	5,933	3,900	60
Hendry	3,962	2,036	34	Suwannee	5,859	3,126	130
Hernando	21,179	15,432	231	Taylor	4,054	1,762	55
Highlands	16,713	8,087	127	Union	1,643	691	14
Hillsborough	150,065	98,969	1,549	Volusia	74,116	55,437	1,517
Holmes	4,221	1,639	36	Wakulla	3,157	1,605	42
Indian River	24,619	10,447	252	Walton	7,481	3,231	82
Jackson	8,392	5,002	100	Washington	4,366	2,139	46
Jefferson	2,326	2,055	17	Absentees 2/	2,288	850	26

1/ Libertarian, New Alliance, and write-in candidates.
2/ Absentees counted per: Division of Elections Rule 1C-7.13.   These votes are
included in state totals but not in county detail.
Source: State of Florida, Department of State, Division of Elections, *Tabulation
of Official Votes: Florida General Election, November 8, 1988.*

Florida Statistical Abstract 1991

Table 21.33. ELECTION RESULTS: VOTES CAST FOR UNITED STATES SENATOR, NOVEMBER 4
  1986 AND NOVEMBER 8, 1988, AND FOR GOVERNOR AND LIEUTENANT GOVERNOR
  NOVEMBER 6, 1990, IN THE STATE AND COUNTIES OF FLORIDA

| | United States Senator 1/ | | | | Governor/Lieutenant Governor--1990 C/ | |
| | 1986 A/ | | 1988 B/ | | Lawton Chiles/ Buddy MacKay | Bob Martinez/ Allison Defoor |
County	Bob Graham (D)	Paula Hawkins (R)	Connie Mack (R)	Buddy MacKay (D)	(D)	(R)
Florida	1,877,543	1,552,376	2,051,071	2,016,553	1,995,206	1,535,068
Alachua	29,950	13,332	18,805	42,181	33,616	15,988
Baker	2,195	1,872	2,711	2,495	2,150	1,957
Bay	12,448	17,080	23,733	15,800	14,236	16,966
Bradford	3,497	2,229	2,940	3,766	3,241	2,468
Brevard	59,596	57,330	90,276	64,391	61,741	65,641
Broward	227,862	139,967	171,197	239,438	217,422	113,869
Calhoun	1,663	1,475	1,729	1,814	1,887	1,407
Charlotte	14,465	20,520	23,816	20,296	20,012	21,673
Citrus	15,977	13,811	16,440	20,045	19,282	16,152
Clay	11,008	12,300	22,770	11,733	9,704	16,256
Collier	13,605	22,483	36,417	15,906	18,882	26,505
Columbia	6,100	4,642	5,716	6,887	5,360	4,657
Dade	230,493	181,787	201,148	225,341	232,542	138,417
De Soto	3,117	2,607	3,579	3,514	3,125	2,350
Dixie	2,419	1,370	1,266	2,541	2,486	1,096
Duval	88,523	68,123	107,478	82,345	75,326	83,023
Escambia	27,726	39,110	55,971	33,872	30,468	39,383
Flagler	3,940	3,214	5,945	5,208	5,215	5,390
Franklin	1,328	1,417	1,365	1,502	2,142	758
Gadsden	6,640	3,220	4,102	7,504	6,839	3,495
Gilchrist	1,757	920	1,132	2,133	1,644	1,229
Glades	1,226	1,105	1,258	1,471	1,275	1,025
Gulf	2,087	2,215	2,067	2,163	2,671	1,728
Hamilton	1,403	1,009	1,276	1,889	1,694	992
Hardee	2,632	1,894	2,507	2,579	2,627	2,019
Hendry	2,394	2,445	3,393	3,043	2,354	2,107
Hernando	18,900	15,512	19,036	24,094	24,453	17,434
Highlands	11,170	10,060	14,151	12,525	12,270	11,227
Hillsborough	125,800	75,585	85,757	103,330	129,322	76,891
Holmes	1,966	2,626	3,269	2,343	2,230	2,057
Indian River	12,259	14,424	21,790	13,852	13,838	17,943
Jackson	5,466	5,438	6,624	6,082	6,608	4,681
Jefferson	2,274	1,164	1,634	3,172	2,588	1,271
Lafayette	1,014	695	826	1,297	1,038	767
Lake	20,927	20,577	28,661	23,803	22,624	23,019
Lee	44,212	56,328	76,560	54,911	48,784	60,408
Leon	35,905	17,463	24,855	43,359	45,438	20,085

See footnotes at end of table.   Continued . . .

Florida Statistical Abstract 1991

Table 21.33. ELECTION RESULTS: VOTES CAST FOR UNITED STATES SENATOR, NOVEMBER 4
1986 AND NOVEMBER 8, 1988, AND FOR GOVERNOR AND LIEUTENANT GOVERNOR
NOVEMBER 6, 1990, IN THE STATE AND COUNTIES OF FLORIDA (Continued)

| County | United States Senator 1/ | | | | Governor/Lieutenant Governor--1990 C/ | |
| | 1986 A/ | | 1988 B/ | | Lawton Chiles/ Buddy MacKay | Bob Martinez/ Allison Defoor |
	Bob Graham (D)	Paula Hawkins (R)	Connie Mack (R)	Buddy MacKay (D)	(D)	(R)
Levy	3,874	3,024	3,353	5,177	4,090	3,153
Liberty	861	738	914	1,131	1,088	739
Madison	2,633	1,552	1,994	3,020	2,510	1,832
Manatee	33,716	33,830	43,148	39,876	37,920	31,594
Marion	25,020	23,285	30,494	34,269	26,588	30,522
Martin	14,328	18,972	24,630	15,089	15,344	21,229
Monroe	8,738	10,837	12,634	13,710	11,179	7,034
Nassau	4,929	4,289	7,299	5,708	4,962	6,324
Okaloosa	11,934	22,839	34,263	13,937	17,794	22,049
Okeechobee	2,841	2,848	3,448	3,951	3,495	2,566
Orange	70,787	66,479	100,257	78,021	80,762	65,360
Osceola	11,244	11,008	18,294	13,394	13,601	12,381
Palm Beach	146,760	107,240	131,223	141,831	154,085	106,110
Pasco	56,009	40,343	52,351	64,677	61,172	38,783
Pinellas	179,940	128,046	171,573	190,344	189,108	109,236
Polk	58,092	41,321	59,299	59,722	58,654	45,671
Putnam	9,146	6,897	9,285	12,549	9,736	8,184
St. Johns	9,565	10,430	16,936	10,944	10,267	11,894
St. Lucie	17,176	18,766	23,450	18,825	58,941	53,153
Santa Rosa	6,730	13,865	18,911	9,022	36,027	32,107
Sarasota	43,420	58,093	57,979	53,307	10,399	14,626
Seminole	29,823	29,633	50,679	34,197	20,040	19,487
Sumter	4,744	3,320	3,542	5,310	5,107	3,409
Suwannee	3,261	3,617	4,006	4,790	3,532	3,566
Taylor	2,668	1,809	2,857	2,768	2,598	2,411
Union	1,467	846	1,157	1,252	1,559	777
Volusia	55,349	41,084	61,776	60,231	56,982	49,606
Wakulla	2,294	1,757	2,213	2,834	3,087	2,049
Walton	3,423	5,023	5,837	4,340	4,818	4,303
Washington	2,515	2,748	3,327	2,866	2,627	2,579
Overseas military absentees	312	488	1,742	836	(X)	(X)

(D) Democrat.   (R) Republican.
(X) Not applicable.
A/ Does not include 77 write-in votes.
B/ Does not include 585 write-in votes.
C/ Does not include 597 write-in votes.
1/ Absentee ballots counted per: Division of Election Rule 1C-7.013. These
votes are included in state but not in county detail.
    Source: State of Florida, Department of State, Division of Elections, *Tabulation
of Official Votes: Florida General Election, November 8, 1988*, and previous edition
and *Elections 1990: Official General Election Returns, November 6, 1990*.

Florida Statistical Abstract 1991

Table 21.35. ELECTIONS: WOMEN HOLDING PUBLIC OFFICE BY OFFICE IN FLORIDA
    AND THE UNITED STATES, 1985, 1988, OR 1990

Area	Mayors and city councils 1985	County governing boards 1988	1990 A/ State legisla- ture	1990 A/ Statewide elected office 1/
Florida	311	51	26	1
United States	14,672	1,653	1,273	46

A/ As of July.

1/ Excludes judiciary, appointed cabinet-level positions, elections to executive posts by the legislature, and elected members of university Board of Trustees or Board of Education.

Source: U.S., Department of Commerce, Bureau of the Census, *Statistical Abstract of the United States, 1991.*

Table 21.36. ELECTIONS: BLACK ELECTED OFFICIALS BY OFFICE IN FLORIDA, THE SOUTH
    AND THE UNITED STATES, JANUARY 1989 AND 1990

Office	Florida 1989	Florida 1990	South 1/ 1989	South 1/ 1990	United States 1989	United States 1990
Total	179	177	4,854	4,955	7,191	7,335
U.S. and state legislatures 2/	11	11	232	233	441	440
City and county offices 3/	129	124	3,297	3,362	4,388	4,481
Law enforcement 4/	22	23	419	431	760	769
Education 5/	17	19	906	929	1,602	1,645

1/ Includes Alabama, Arkansas, Delaware, District of Columbia, Florida, Georgia, Kentucky, Louisiana, Maryland, Mississippi, North Carolina, Oklahoma, South Carolina, Tennessee, Texas, Virginia, and West Virginia.

2/ Includes elected state administrators.

3/ County commissioners, councilmen, mayors, vice mayors, aldermen, regional officers, and others.

4/ Judges, magistrates, constables, marshals, sheriffs, justices of the peace, and others.

5/ Members of state education agencies, college boards, school boards, and others.

Source: Joint Center for Political Studies, Washington, DC, *Black Elected Officials: A National Roster,* annual. (Copyright.)

Table 21.37. ELECTION RESULTS: POPULAR VOTES CAST FOR UNITED STATES PRESIDENT
    IN FLORIDA AND THE UNITED STATES, 1976 THROUGH 1988

Year	Florida Total votes cast (1,000)	Florida Per- centage for leading party	United States Total votes cast (1,000)	United States Per- centage for leading party	Year	Florida Total votes cast (1,000)	Florida Per- centage for leading party	United States Total votes cast (1,000)	United States Per- centage for leading party
1976	3,151	D-51.9	81,556	D-50.1	1984	4,180	R-65.3	92,653	R-58.8
1980	3,687	R-55.5	86,515	R-50.7	1988	4,302	R-60.9	91,595	R-53.4

D Democrat.   R Republican.

Note: Total votes cast includes other parties.

Source: Elections Research Center, Washington, DC, *America Votes,* biennial. (Copyright.)

Florida Statistical Abstract 1991

Table 21.42. COMPOSITION OF CONGRESS AND STATE LEGISLATURES: NUMBER OF UNITED
STATES REPRESENTATIVES AND SENATORS AND STATE LEGISLATORS BY PARTY
AFFILIATION, SPECIFIED YEARS 1980 THROUGH 1991

	Florida				United States			
	Demo- crats	Repub- licans	Demo- crats	Repub- licans	Demo- crats	Repub- licans	Demo- crats	Repub- licans
Year 1/	U.S. represent- atives		U.S. senators		U.S. represent- atives		U.S. senators	
1984	13	6	1	1	267	167	45	55
1985	12	7	1	1	252	182	47	53
1986	12	7	1	1	253	182	47	53
1987	12	7	2	0	258	177	55	45
1989	10	9	1	1	259	174	55	45
1991	9	10	1	1	267	167	56	43
Year 1/	State represent- atives		State senators		State represent- atives		State senators	
1980	81	39	27	13	3,289	2,190	1,182	742
1982	84	36	32	8	3,429	2,006	1,210	725
1984	77	43	32	8	3,136	2,316	1,187	753
1986	75	45	25	15	3,294	2,164	1,177	762
1988	73	47	23	17	3,277	2,176	1,192	751

1/ U.S. representative and senator data refer to the beginning of the first
session. State legislative data refer to election years.
Note: Excludes vacancies and persons classified as Independents.
Source: Congressional Quarterly, Inc. Washington, DC, *Congressional Quarterly
Weekly Report*, Vol. 48, No. 45, November 10, 1990. (Copyright.); and The Council of
States Governments, Lexington, Kentucky, 1982-1984, *Book of the States*, biennial;
beginning 1986, *State Executive Officials and the Legislatures*, biennial.
(Copyright.)

Table 21.43. APPORTIONMENT: MEMBERSHIP IN THE UNITED STATES HOUSE
OF REPRESENTATIVES FOR FLORIDA AND THE UNITED STATES, 1840
THROUGH 1990

Census of--	Florida	United States	Census of--	Florida	United States
1840	A/ 1	232	1930	5	435
1850	1	237	1940	6	435
1860	1	243	1950	8	437
1870	2	293	1960	12	435
1880	2	332	1970	15	435
1890	2	357	1980	19	435
1900	3	391	1990	23	435
1910	4	435			

A/ Assigned after apportionment.
Note: Total membership includes representatives assigned to newly admitted
states after the apportionment acts. Population figures used for apportionment
purposes are those determined for states by each decennial census.
Source: U.S., Department of Commerce, Bureau of the Census, *1990 Census Profile:
Population Trends and Congressional Apportionment*, No. 1, March 1991.

Florida Statistical Abstract 1991

COURTS AND LAW
ENFORCEMENT

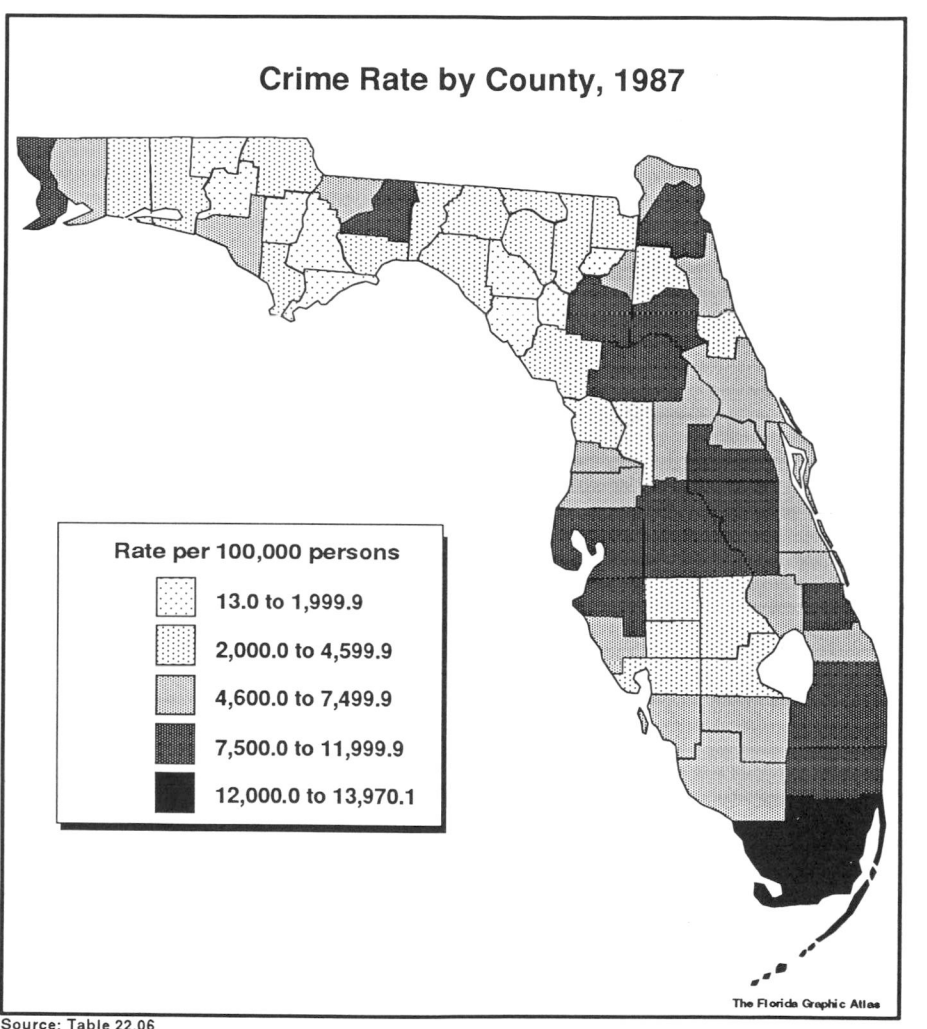

Crime Rate by County, 1987

Rate per 100,000 persons

- 13.0 to 1,999.9
- 2,000.0 to 4,599.9
- 4,600.0 to 7,499.9
- 7,500.0 to 11,999.9
- 12,000.0 to 13,970.1

The Florida Graphic Atlas

Source: Table 22.06

TABLES LISTED BY MAJOR HEADINGS

Table 22.03. CRIMINAL OFFENSES: CRIME INDEX OFFENSES BY TYPE OF OFFENSE IN FLORIDA
1987 THROUGH 1990

Index offenses 1/	Total crime	Mur- der	Forc- ible rape	Rob- bery	Aggra- vated assault	Bur- glary	Larceny	Motor ve- hicle theft
			Violent crime			Nonviolent crime		
Number of index offenses 2/								
1987	1,021,283	1,368	6,017	42,830	72,815	271,047	545,932	81,274
1988	919,886	1,008	3,852	33,010	54,044	201,810	408,763	62,976
1989	1,120,515	1,405	6,299	51,188	81,683	289,254	583,702	102,086
1990	1,122,935	1,387	6,747	54,015	93,042	275,104	585,919	101,358
Percentage change from previous year								
1987	6.3	-0.2	-2.2	0.0	3.1	4.5	7.0	16.4
1988	-9.9	-26.3	-36.0	-22.9	-25.8	-25.5	-25.1	-22.5
1989	21.8	39.4	63.5	55.1	51.1	43.3	42.8	62.1
1990	0.2	-1.3	7.1	5.5	13.9	-4.9	0.4	-0.7
Rate per 100,000 population								
1987	8,479.9	11.4	50.0	355.6	604.6	2,250.5	4,533.0	674.8
1988	7,407.9	8.1	31.0	265.8	435.2	1,625.2	3,291.8	507.2
1989	8,755.9	11.0	49.2	400.0	638.3	2,260.3	4,561.1	797.7
1990	8,539.4	10.7	52.1	417.5	719.1	2,126.3	4,528.7	783.4
Percentage change from previous year								
1987	2.9	-3.4	-5.3	-3.2	-0.2	1.2	3.5	12.7
1988	-12.6	-28.9	-38.0	-25.3	-28.0	-27.8	-27.4	-24.8
1989	18.2	35.8	58.7	50.5	46.7	39.1	38.6	57.3
1990	-2.5	-2.5	6.0	4.4	12.7	-5.9	-0.7	-1.8
Percentage cleared								
1987	22.5	65.0	59.4	25.8	61.9	16.6	19.7	20.7
1988	25.1	57.1	49.3	22.1	55.0	14.2	16.7	15.9
1989	27.9	60.7	55.8	25.0	60.1	15.0	17.8	17.4
1990	21.0	60.3	52.6	23.8	55.8	14.9	18.0	16.6

1/ The crimes selected for use in the index are chosen based on their serious
nature, their frequency of occurrence, and the reliability of reporting from
citizens to law enforcement agencies. The Crime Index is used as a basic measure of
crime.

2/ Actual offenses known to law enforcement officers, not the number of persons
who commited them or number of injuries they caused.

Note: Rates may not add to totals due to rounding. 1988 data represent
approximately 75 percent of the estimated actual reportable crimes in Florida due to
changes in crime reporting standards and procedures. 1989 represents the first full
year of data under this enhanced program. Definitions of some offense categories
changed so caution should be exercised in comparing data after 1987 to numbers
published in previous *Abstracts*.

Source: State of Florida, Department of Law Enforcement, *Crime in Florida: 1990
Annual Report*, previous editions, and unpublished data.

Table 22.04. CRIMINAL OFFENSES: NUMBER OF ARRESTS BY AGE, SEX, RACE, AND OFFENSE
IN FLORIDA, 1990

Offense	Age Under 18	Age 18 and over	Sex Male	Sex Female	Race White	Race Black	Other
Total	88,911	667,839	625,894	130,856	479,193	275,552	2,005
Murder	206	1,175	1,251	130	518	861	2
Forcible rape	348	2,257	2,578	27	1,452	1,148	5
Forcible sodomy	128	342	455	15	299	171	0
Forcible fondling	230	913	1,110	33	816	323	4
Robbery	2,871	10,342	12,305	908	4,086	9,111	16
Aggravated assault	5,445	32,779	32,165	6,059	19,623	18,490	111
Burglary	10,859	23,386	32,045	2,200	20,407	13,735	103
Larceny	24,985	75,513	68,353	32,145	61,502	38,641	355
Motor vehicle theft	5,591	8,675	12,890	1,376	7,046	7,184	36
Manslaughter	13	156	146	23	137	30	2
Kidnap/abduction	46	616	593	69	448	212	2
Arson	198	503	596	105	461	239	1
Simple assault	5,388	28,922	29,410	4,900	21,312	12,915	83
Drug/narcotic sale	1,392	19,377	17,617	3,152	7,828	12,921	20
Drug/narcotic possession	3,798	52,607	47,092	9,313	28,065	28,283	57
Bribery	2	71	66	7	58	15	0
Embezzlement	140	1,505	1,106	539	1,096	546	3
Fraud	434	7,249	5,567	2,116	5,774	1,894	15
Counterfeit/forgery	255	4,545	3,461	1,339	3,164	1,622	14
Extortion/blackmail	55	310	336	29	231	133	1
Intimidation	1,268	11,623	10,846	2,045	7,287	5,573	31
Prostitution/ commercialized sex	126	10,182	5,318	4,990	7,043	3,225	40
Non-forcible sex offense	272	4,392	4,147	517	3,898	752	14
Stolen property: buy/receive/possession	1,098	5,513	5,847	764	3,685	2,906	20
Driving under influence	359	61,860	52,945	9,274	57,720	4,138	361
Destruction/damage/ vandalism	2,665	3,466	5,463	668	4,455	1,646	30
Gambling	52	1,052	1,014	90	343	756	5
Weapon violations	1,648	9,262	10,048	862	5,426	5,460	24
Liquor law violations	2,854	37,937	35,206	5,585	34,155	6,540	96
Miscellaneous	16,185	251,309	225,918	41,576	170,858	96,082	554

Note: A person is counted each time he/she is arrested or summoned; therefore,
arrest counts do not reflect the specific number of persons arrested since one individual may be arrested several times for the same or different crimes. Arrest data
are useful for measuring law enforcement activity and involvement in criminal acts
by the age, sex, and race of perpetrators.

Source: State of Florida, Department of Law Enforcement, *Crime in Florida: 1990
Annual Report*, and unpublished data.

Florida Statistical Abstract 1991

Table 22.05. CRIMINAL OFFENSES: NUMBER OF NARCOTIC DRUG ARRESTS FOR SALE AND
POSSESSION BY AGE, RACE, AND SEX IN FLORIDA, 1990

		Age		Race		Sex	
Classification	Total	Under 18	Over 18	White	Black	Male	Female
		Sale/manufacture					
Total	21,181	1,411	19,770	8,013	13,148	17,981	3,200
Amphetamine	74	6	68	71	3	51	23
Barbiturate	74	2	72	69	5	55	19
Cocaine	15,277	1,072	14,205	4,197	11,068	12,989	2,288
Heroin	88	2	86	17	70	72	16
Hallucinogen	167	31	136	152	15	148	19
Marijuana	3,867	245	3,622	2,362	1,503	3,294	573
Opium/derivative	58	0	58	51	7	35	23
Paraphernalia/ equipment	37	2	35	14	23	33	4
Synthetic	73	2	71	52	21	57	16
Unknown	1,058	27	1,031	704	349	915	143
Other	408	22	386	324	84	332	76
		Possession/use					
Total	59,279	4,022	55,257	29,394	29,827	49,496	9,783
Amphetamine	158	4	154	148	10	110	48
Barbiturate	170	11	159	152	17	125	45
Cocaine	30,215	2,000	28,215	10,375	19,827	24,938	5,277
Heroin	193	0	193	93	100	161	32
Hallucinogen	318	33	285	285	33	282	36
Marijuana	21,273	1,713	19,560	14,970	6,266	18,688	2,585
Opium/derivative	70	1	69	61	8	54	16
Paraphernalia/ equipment	6,005	207	5,798	2,622	3,379	4,471	1,534
Synthetic	120	3	117	97	23	92	28
Unknown	270	16	254	168	102	218	52
Other	487	34	453	423	62	357	130

Source: State of Florida, Department of Law Enforcement, *Crime in Florida: 1990
Annual Report*, and unpublished data.

Florida Statistical Abstract 1991

Table 22.06. CRIMINAL OFFENSES: CRIME INDEX OFFENSES, CRIME RATES, AND PERCENTAGE
OF OFFENSES CLEARED IN THE STATE AND COUNTIES OF FLORIDA, 1990

County	Crime index offenses Total 1/	Vio-lent 2/	Nonvio-lent 3/	Crime rate per 100,000 population 1990	Percentage change 1989-90	Per-centage cleared 4/
Florida	1,122,935	160,554	962,381	8,539.4	-2.5	21.0
Alachua	18,688	2,475	16,213	9,791.9	3.6	21.7
Baker	676	145	531	3,398.0	17.3	42.9
Bay	8,341	818	7,523	6,062.0	0.4	36.4
Bradford	1,394	210	1,184	5,675.2	13.7	27.3
Brevard	29,863	2,989	26,874	7,114.4	8.3	18.5
Broward	110,950	12,761	98,189	8,737.5	0.0	23.4
Calhoun	89	36	53	781.4	-20.0	78.7
Charlotte	2,986	162	2,824	2,809.9	-5.4	20.4
Citrus	3,102	258	2,844	3,281.2	1.9	23.6
Clay	5,143	676	4,467	4,871.2	11.5	35.4
Collier	9,740	1,181	8,559	6,335.0	-8.5	24.7
Columbia	2,490	422	2,068	5,558.4	34.6	35.8
Dade	258,704	44,411	214,293	13,587.2	-2.7	18.1
De Soto	1,043	207	836	4,220.8	19.2	40.5
Dixie	394	93	301	3,464.3	862.3	25.1
Duval	67,703	11,766	55,937	9,641.6	-5.5	23.2
Escambia	20,964	2,926	18,038	7,266.8	-15.5	23.9
Flagler	1,188	176	1,012	4,487.1	18.4	30.2
Franklin	51	28	23	578.8	67.4	96.1
Gadsden	1,966	554	1,412	4,215.7	-13.5	36.5
Gilchrist	49	10	39	606.4	4564.6	6.1
Glades	293	55	238	3,522.9	-22.3	16.0
Gulf	222	50	172	1,731.3	-25.3	32.4
Hamilton	388	78	310	3,623.8	-3.6	38.9
Hardee	1,198	184	1,014	5,187.0	46.2	33.2
Hendry	1,425	263	1,162	5,303.9	7.7	25.9
Hernando	5,388	735	4,653	5,661.3	-6.2	25.4
Highlands	4,046	604	3,442	5,639.8	23.2	20.5
Hillsborough	79,313	14,061	65,252	9,280.2	-11.6	13.4
Holmes	232	79	153	1,265.2	36.2	29.7
Indian River	5,147	561	4,586	5,360.5	2.2	24.7
Jackson	1,102	184	918	2,405.5	-26.0	37.6
Jefferson	588	144	444	4,559.6	53.0	42.2
Lafayette	30	24	6	527.1	67.5	120.0
Lake	7,399	1,089	6,310	4,884.2	-5.9	29.0
Lee	17,462	1,883	15,579	5,159.8	4.9	20.0

See footnotes at end of table.   Continued . . .

Florida Statistical Abstract 1991

Table 22.06. CRIMINAL OFFENSES: CRIME INDEX OFFENSES, CRIME RATES, AND PERCENTAGE
OF OFFENSES CLEARED IN THE STATE AND COUNTIES OF FLORIDA, 1990 (Continued)

County	Crime index offenses			Crime rate per 100,000 population		Per-centage cleared 4/
	Total 1/	Vio-lent 2/	Nonvio-lent 3/	1990	Percentage change 1989-90	
Leon	21,371	3,162	18,209	10,750.3	10.0	31.4
Levy	1,334	254	1,080	5,174.2	18.5	32.8
Liberty	49	14	35	879.7	2.1	87.8
Madison	511	125	386	2,899.1	-15.9	25.6
Manatee	16,404	2,183	14,221	8,148.5	0.9	22.6
Marion	14,871	2,255	12,616	7,491.7	-3.4	38.6
Martin	5,126	415	4,711	5,006.6	-19.6	17.3
Monroe	10,478	1,327	9,151	12,962.7	-0.8	17.3
Nassau	1,813	235	1,578	3,709.7	-27.0	25.5
Okaloosa	5,728	532	5,196	3,529.9	-3.8	25.9
Okeechobee	1,540	243	1,297	5,008.6	6.1	32.9
Orange	65,019	9,287	55,732	9,526.8	2.3	17.3
Osceola	10,157	997	9,160	9,593.2	10.0	20.3
Palm Beach	85,946	10,472	75,474	9,621.1	0.6	18.7
Pasco	12,583	1,030	11,553	4,483.8	-4.8	25.3
Pinellas	68,015	9,599	58,416	7,866.4	-3.6	23.4
Polk	38,342	4,804	33,538	9,097.9	-8.3	20.3
Putnam	5,532	982	4,550	8,671.5	-0.5	29.7
St. Johns	5,602	698	4,904	6,416.7	0.2	26.8
St. Lucie	11,373	1,541	9,832	7,573.2	-10.6	22.8
Santa Rosa	3,240	470	2,770	4,578.4	-20.0	26.7
Sarasota	19,653	1,734	17,919	7,446.0	4.9	17.4
Seminole	17,611	1,942	15,669	5,949.0	-3.2	20.9
Sumter	1,326	263	1,063	4,130.8	-4.1	33.1
Suwannee	1,125	104	1,021	3,921.2	81.0	29.4
Taylor	696	203	493	3,479.7	-15.6	66.5
Union	95	9	86	907.4	2.2	67.4
Volusia	26,640	3,216	23,424	7,154.6	3.1	24.3
Wakulla	291	51	240	1,928.6	-43.0	30.6
Walton	581	86	495	1,933.3	-22.9	26.3
Washington	126	23	103	760.7	-29.9	32.5

1/ Actual offenses known to law enforcement officers, not the number of persons
who committed them or number of injuries they caused.

2/ Includes murder, forcible sex, robbery, and aggravated assault.

3/ Includes breaking and entering (burglary), larceny, and auto theft.

4/ Clearance of an offense occurs when an offender is identified, charged, and
taken custody, or occasionally when some element beyond law enforcement control
precludes formal charges against the offender.

Note: Data are aggregates of offenses reported to municipal, county, and state
law enforcement agencies and campus police departments.

Source: State of Florida, Department of Law Enforcement, *Crime in Florida: 1990
Annual Report*, and unpublished data.

Table 22.07. CRIMINAL OFFENSES: CRIME INDEX OFFENSES AND CRIME RATES IN THE STATE
COUNTIES, AND SPECIFIED AREAS OF FLORIDA, 1990

Area	Number of index offenses 1/	Crime rate per 100,000 population	Area	Number of index offenses 1/	Crime rate per 100,000 population
Florida	1,122,935	8,539.4	Brevard (Continued)		
			Titusville	2,939	6,712.5
Alachua	18,688	9,791.9	West Melbourne	494	5,763.6
Sheriff's office	5,981	6,660.0	State agencies	3	(X)
Alachua	476	8,913.9			
Archer	253	18,400.0	Broward	110,950	8,737.5
Gainesville	9,753	11,334.4	Sheriff's office	12,637	7,900.1
Hawthorne	244	17,354.2	Coconut Creek	916	3,340.4
High Springs	155	5,281.1	Cooper City	679	3,648.2
Micanopy	112	14,545.5	Coral Springs	3,053	3,955.5
Newberry	274	13,204.8	Dania	2,088	14,868.6
University of			Davie	3,250	7,238.0
Florida	1,382	(X)	Deerfield Beach	4,038	7,919.4
Waldo	58	5,282.3	Ft. Lauderdale	25,555	16,947.6
			Hallandale	2,660	6,884.8
Baker	676	3,398.0	Hillsboro Beach	19	1,116.3
Sheriff's office	676	3,398.0	Hollywood	12,833	10,152.5
			Lauderdale Lakes	2,873	10,410.9
Bay	8,341	6,062.0	Lauderdale-by-the-sea	159	6,041.0
Sheriff's office	2,569	4,654.6	Lauderhill	3,788	8,267.3
Callaway	552	4,273.4	Lighthouse Point	378	3,331.6
Cedar Grove	17	1,010.7	Margate	1,907	4,312.0
Florida State			Miramar	2,102	5,199.9
University	1	(X)	North Lauderdale	1,564	5,715.7
Lynn Haven	364	3,529.9	Oakland Park	4,161	16,058.8
Mexico Beach	82	6,623.6	Parkland	104	3,544.6
Panama City	3,265	9,010.1	Pembroke Park	657	10,320.5
Panama City Beach	1,215	20,829.8	Pembroke Pines	2,873	4,463.1
Parker	79	1,632.9	Plantation	6,123	8,607.1
Springfield	195	2,086.9	Pompano Beach	10,194	14,415.6
State agencies	2	(X)	Sea Ranch Lakes	15	2,678.6
			Sunrise	3,433	5,581.4
Bradford	1,394	5,675.2	Tamarac	1,859	4,224.9
Sheriff's office	509	2,708.3	Wilton Manors	1,020	8,321.1
Starke	884	15,323.3	State agencies	12	(X)
State agencies	1	(X)			
			Calhoun	89	781.4
Brevard	29,863	7,114.4	Sheriff's office	22	272.1
Sheriff's office	9,350	5,504.0	Altha	0	0.0
Cocoa	2,591	14,040.3	Blountstown	67	2,390.3
Cocoa Beach	1,333	9,993.3			
Indialantic	180	5,819.6	Charlotte	2,986	2,809.9
Indian Harbour Beach	333	4,177.1	Sheriff's office	2,518	2,667.6
Melbourne	6,990	10,982.5	Punta Gorda	468	3,940.4
Melbourne Beach	139	4,338.3			
Palm Bay	4,096	6,743.2	Citrus	3,102	3,281.2
Rockledge	1,024	6,152.0	Sheriff's office	2,186	2,600.0
Satellite Beach	391	3,750.2	Crystal River	582	14,749.1

See footnotes at end of table.   Continued . . .

Table 22.07. CRIMINAL OFFENSES: CRIME INDEX OFFENSES AND CRIME RATES IN THE STATE COUNTIES, AND SPECIFIED AREAS OF FLORIDA, 1990 (Continued)

Area	Number of index offenses 1/	Crime rate per 100,000 population	Area	Number of index offenses 1/	Crime rate per 100,000 population
Citrus (Continued)			De Soto	1,043	4,220.8
Inverness	334	5,125.8	Sheriff's office	698	3,752.3
			Arcadia	345	5,647.4
Clay	5,143	4,871.2			
Sheriff's office	4,150	4,545.6	Dixie	394	3,464.3
Green Cove Springs	421	9,118.5	Sheriff's office	328	3,621.5
Orange Park	572	5,917.6	Cross City	66	2,849.7
Collier	9,740	6,335.0	Duval	67,703	9,641.6
Sheriff's office	8,071	6,084.5	Atlantic Beach	0	0.0
Naples	1,669	7,910.3	Jacksonville	66,626	10,026.5
			Jacksonville Interna-		
Columbia	2,490	5,558.4	tional Airport	55	(X)
Sheriff's office	825	2,358.4	Jacksonville Beach	440	2,287.1
Lake City	1,665	16,962.1	Neptune Beach	473	7,190.6
			University of North		
Dade	258,704	13,587.2	Florida	108	(X)
Metro-Dade	125,445	12,094.3	State agencies	1	(X)
Bal Harbour	142	4,241.3			
Bay Harbor Islands	113	2,316.5	Escambia	20,964	7,266.8
Biscayne Park	68	2,260.6	Sheriff's office	16,010	7,270.2
Coral Gables	5,525	13,214.2	Century	157	6,111.3
El Portal	190	10,740.5	Pensacola	4,671	7,108.8
Florida City	1,208	18,570.3	University of West		
Florida International			Florida	124	(X)
University	323	(X)	State agencies	2	(X)
Golden Beach	17	2,579.7			
Hialeah	18,233	10,484.3	Flagler	1,188	4,487.1
Hialeah Gardens	545	10,049.8	Sheriff's office	788	3,829.1
Homestead	4,051	16,397.5	Bunnell	216	9,953.9
Medley	375	67,934.8	Flagler Beach	184	4,936.9
Miami	68,246	19,479.5			
Miami Beach	15,376	15,719.8	Franklin	51	578.8
Miami Shores	1,159	12,718.1	Sheriff's office	36	575.3
Miami Springs	1,375	11,450.7	Apalachicola	12	469.9
Miccosukee Police			State agencies	3	(X)
Department	32	(X)			
North Bay Village	201	3,891.6	Gadsden	1,966	4,215.7
North Miami	6,402	14,964.9	Sheriff's office	953	3,122.2
North Miami Beach	3,968	11,216.6	Chattahoochee	68	1,456.4
Opa-Locka	3,146	22,497.1	Havana	119	4,064.2
South Miami	1,397	13,240.5	Quincy	826	9,700.5
Surfside	441	10,601.0			
Sweetwater	244	2,217.6	Gilchrist	49	606.4
Virginia Gardens	190	8,784.1	Sheriff's office	49	606.4
West Miami	259	4,480.2			
State agencies	33	(X)			

See footnotes at end of table.

Continued . . .

Florida Statistical Abstract 1991

Table 22.07. CRIMINAL OFFENSES: CRIME INDEX OFFENSES AND CRIME RATES IN THE STATE
COUNTIES, AND SPECIFIED AREAS OF FLORIDA, 1990 (Continued)

Area	Number of index offenses 1/	Crime rate per 100,000 population	Area	Number of index offenses 1/	Crime rate per 100,000 population
Glades	293	3,522.9	Indian River	5,147	5,360.5
Sheriff's office	293	3,522.9	Sheriff's office	2,969	4,615.9
			Fellsmere	85	4,543.0
Gulf	222	1,731.3	Indian River Shores	18	849.1
Sheriff's office	144	2,146.1	Sebastian	443	4,673.0
Port St. Joe	78	1,854.9	Vero Beach	1,632	8,954.2
Wewahitchka	0	0.0			
			Jackson	1,102	2,405.5
Hamilton	388	3,623.8	Sheriff's office	697	2,041.2
Sheriff's office	337	4,320.5	Graceville	150	5,206.5
Jasper	51	2,415.9	Marianna	238	3,412.7
White Springs	0	0.0	Sneads	17	938.7
Hardee	1,198	5,187.0	Jefferson	588	4,559.6
Sheriff's office	833	5,394.4	Sheriff's office	377	3,814.2
Bowling Green	36	1,359.5	Monticello	211	7,005.3
Wauchula	317	9,420.5			
Zolfo Springs	12	731.3	Lafayette	30	527.1
			Sheriff's office	30	527.1
Hendry	1,425	5,303.9			
Sheriff's office	916	4,358.8	Lake	7,399	4,884.2
Clewiston	252	4,306.2	Sheriff's office	3,240	3,928.4
Seminole Indian			Clermont	438	6,454.5
Reservation	257	(X)	Eustis	563	4,117.9
			Fruitland Park	70	2,524.3
Hernando	5,388	5,661.3	Groveland	166	7,374.5
Sheriff's office	4,262	4,867.2	Howey-in-the-Hills	10	1,517.5
Brooksville	1,126	14,802.2	Lady Lake	83	1,123.1
			Leesburg	1,930	12,879.5
Highlands	4,046	5,639.8	Mascotte	121	6,744.7
Sheriff's office	2,211	4,148.1	Minneola	21	1,728.4
Avon Park	700	8,410.4	Mount Dora	460	6,229.7
Sebring	1,135	11,219.8	Tavares	236	3,171.6
			Umatilla	61	2,290.6
Hillsborough	79,313	9,280.2			
Sheriff's office	35,556	6,753.5	Lee	17,462	5,159.8
Plant City	2,842	12,862.6	Sheriff's office	7,208	3,251.1
Tampa	38,639	13,408.8	Cape Coral	3,854	5,765.7
Tampa International			Ft. Myers	6,261	14,095.0
Airport	654	(X)	Sanibel	139	2,547.7
Temple Terrace	886	4,947.8			
University of South			Leon	21,371	10,750.3
Florida	736	(X)	Sheriff's office	3,206	4,851.8
			Florida A & M		
Holmes	232	1,265.2	University	193	(X)
Sheriff's office	140	900.8	Florida State		
Bonifay	92	3,290.4	University	775	(X)

See footnotes at end of table.   Continued . . .

Florida Statistical Abstract 1991

Table 22.07. CRIMINAL OFFENSES: CRIME INDEX OFFENSES AND CRIME RATES IN THE STATE
   COUNTIES, AND SPECIFIED AREAS OF FLORIDA, 1990 (Continued)

Area	Number of index offenses 1/	Crime rate per 100,000 population	Area	Number of index offenses 1/	Crime rate per 100,000 population
Leon (Continued)			Okaloosa (Continued)		
Tallahassee	17,195	12,956.2	Crestview	616	6,523.4
State agencies	2	(X)	Ft. Walton Beach	1,533	6,485.9
			Niceville	127	1,100.8
Levy	1,334	5,174.2	Okaloosa Air Terminal	0	(X)
Sheriff's office	916	4,320.3	Valparaiso	32	475.3
Chiefland	252	11,775.7	State agencies	1	(X)
Williston	166	6,803.3			
			Okeechobee	1,540	5,008.6
Liberty	49	879.7	Sheriff's office	1,272	4,918.6
Sheriff's office	49	879.7	Okeechobee	268	5,485.1
Madison	511	2,899.1	Orange	65,019	9,526.8
Sheriff's office	399	3,099.5	Sheriff's office	34,226	7,834.3
Greenville	0	0.0	Apopka	1,754	12,918.0
Madison	111	3,098.0	Eatonville	215	8,049.4
			Edgewood	118	10,111.4
Manatee	16,404	8,148.5	Maitland	689	7,370.6
Sheriff's office	9,994	7,280.0	Ocoee	683	5,252.2
Bradenton	4,704	11,376.9	Orlando	23,750	13,829.8
Bradenton Beach	41	2,209.1	University of Central		
Holmes Beach	296	6,498.4	Florida	254	(X)
Longboat Key	138	2,010.5	Windermere	19	1,250.0
Palmetto	1,231	13,081.8	Winter Garden	924	9,943.0
			Winter Park	2,384	10,231.3
Marion	14,871	7,491.7	State agencies	3	(X)
Sheriff's office	6,830	4,623.0			
Belleview	212	7,825.8	Osceola	10,157	9,593.2
Dunnellon	104	5,768.2	Sheriff's office	5,543	8,794.6
Ocala	7,725	16,703.4	Kissimmee	3,846	12,506.1
			St. Cloud	768	6,348.7
Martin	5,126	5,006.6			
Sheriff's office	3,881	4,352.2	Palm Beach	85,946	9,621.1
Jupiter Island	25	5,470.5	Sheriff's office	31,256	7,852.6
Sewalls Point	8	470.0	Atlantis	71	4,183.9
Stuart	1,212	10,966.3	Belle Glade	2,906	16,959.4
			Boca Raton	3,701	5,862.5
Monroe	10,478	12,962.7	Boynton Beach	4,888	9,970.2
Sheriff's office	4,644	8,807.5	Briny Breezes	5	1,326.3
Key West	5,830	20,744.4	Delray Beach	7,180	14,154.5
State agencies	4	(X)	Florida Atlantic		
			University	157	(X)
Nassau	1,813	3,709.7	Greenacres City	1,322	4,904.1
Sheriff's office	1,082	2,739.5	Gulf Stream	29	5,461.4
Fernandina Beach	731	7,796.5	Highland Beach	25	765.2
			Hypoluxo	87	9,456.5
Okaloosa	5,728	3,529.9	Juno Beach	161	6,892.1
Sheriff's office	3,419	3,082.3	Jupiter	1,590	5,335.4

   See footnotes at end of table.   Continued . . .

Florida Statistical Abstract 1991

Table 22.07. CRIMINAL OFFENSES: CRIME INDEX OFFENSES AND CRIME RATES IN THE STATE
COUNTIES, AND SPECIFIED AREAS OF FLORIDA, 1990 (Continued)

Area	Number of index offenses 1/	Crime rate per 100,000 population	Area	Number of index offenses 1/	Crime rate per 100,000 population
Palm Beach (Continued)			Pinellas (Continued)		
Jupiter Inlet Colony	0	0.0	Pinellas County Campus		
Lake Clarke Shores	130	3,529.7	Police	424	(X)
Lake Park	1,144	16,510.3	Pinellas Park	3,291	7,635.9
Lake Worth	4,162	15,122.4	Redington Beach 2/	100	3,344.5
Lantana	852	9,898.9	Redington Shores	72	2,589.0
Manalapan	20	5,194.8	Safety Harbor	771	5,300.8
Mangonia Park	411	32,619.0	St. Petersburg	29,329	11,802.4
North Palm Beach	511	3,997.2	St. Petersburg Beach	1,071	10,434.5
Ocean Ridge	41	2,548.2	Seminole	516	5,692.2
Pahokee	475	7,354.1	South Pasadena	289	4,704.5
Palm Beach	576	5,405.4	Tarpon Springs	1,334	7,312.0
Palm Beach County			Treasure Island	533	7,156.3
School Board	1,105	(X)	University of South		
Palm Beach Gardens	2,133	7,419.9	Florida	46	(X)
Palm Beach Shores	43	3,287.5	State agencies	1	(X)
Palm Springs	645	6,264.6			
Riviera Beach	6,409	21,973.5	Polk	38,342	9,097.9
Royal Palm Beach	644	4,311.7	Sheriff's office	17,140	6,844.6
South Bay	367	9,371.8	Auburndale	738	8,754.4
South Palm Beach	17	1,179.7	Bartow	1,862	11,321.9
Tequesta	105	2,328.2	Davenport	57	2,792.7
West Palm Beach	12,773	17,086.7	Dundee	234	8,941.5
State agencies	5	(X)	Eagle Lake	52	2,631.6
			Ft. Meade	352	5,777.1
Pasco	12,583	4,483.8	Frostproof	147	4,719.1
Sheriff's office	9,632	3,868.7	Haines City	1,199	9,030.7
Dade City	738	13,183.3	Lake Alfred	274	7,615.3
New Port Richey	1,242	8,706.0	Lake Hamilton	194	12,412.0
Port Richey	109	4,203.6	Lake Wales	1,489	16,147.9
St. Leo	0	0.0	Lakeland	9,563	12,914.9
Zephyrhills	862	10,857.8	Mulberry	385	10,860.4
			Winter Haven	4,656	18,583.9
Pinellas	68,015	7,866.4			
Sheriff's office	12,825	5,069.9	Putnam	5,532	8,671.5
Belleair	66	1,641.8	Sheriff's office	3,515	6,883.8
Belleair Beach	47	2,721.5	Cresent City	189	10,505.8
Belleair Bluffs	91	3,592.6	Palatka	1,828	16,718.5
Clearwater	9,597	9,435.9			
Dunedin	1,513	4,252.7	St. Johns	5,602	6,416.7
Gulfport	950	8,035.9	Sheriff's office	3,644	5,066.5
Indian Rocks Beach	345	7,552.5	St. Augustine	1,839	15,455.1
Indian Shores	112	8,223.2	St. Augustine Beach	119	3,417.6
Kenneth City	221	5,152.7			
Largo	3,566	5,199.4	St. Lucie	11,373	7,573.2
Madeira Beach	341	6,353.6	Sheriff's office	3,447	5,956.2
Oldsmar	564	8,022.8	Ft. Pierce	5,387	14,056.5

See footnotes at end of table.   Continued . . .

Table 22.07. CRIMINAL OFFENSES: CRIME INDEX OFFENSES AND CRIME RATES IN THE STATE COUNTIES, AND SPECIFIED AREAS OF FLORIDA, 1990 (Continued)

Area	Number of index offenses 1/	Crime rate per 100,000 population	Area	Number of index offenses 1/	Crime rate per 100,000 population
St. Lucie (Continued)			Taylor	696	3,479.7
Port St. Lucie	2,539	4,703.8	Sheriff's office	91	773.1
			Perry	605	7,350.3
Santa Rosa	3,240	4,578.4			
Sheriff's office	2,494	4,358.5	Union	95	907.4
Gulf Breeze	311	5,008.1	Sheriff's office	95	907.4
Milton	435	5,929.7			
			Volusia	26,640	7,154.6
Sarasota	19,653	7,446.0	Sheriff's office	5,768	3,789.0
Sheriff's office	10,398	5,569.7	Daytona Beach	10,462	15,960.1
North Port	450	4,614.9	Daytona Beach Regional	6	0.0
Sarasota	7,905	15,282.2	Daytona Beach Shores	497	18,698.3
University of South			Deland	2,902	16,427.0
Florida	48	(X)	Edgewater	659	4,635.9
Venice	852	5,401.3	Holly Hill	1,113	9,408.3
			Lake Helen	53	2,109.0
Seminole	17,611	5,949.0	New Smyrna Beach	1,376	8,293.7
Sheriff's office	6,413	4,150.4	Oak Hill	25	2,106.1
Altamonte Springs	4,102	10,713.5	Orange City	322	7,458.9
Casselberry	1,719	9,404.7	Ormond Beach	1,186	3,772.6
Lake Mary	146	2,393.8	Ponce Inlet	20	1,147.4
Longwood	921	6,568.7	Port Orange	1,397	3,729.8
Oviedo	738	6,557.7	South Daytona	491	3,790.0
Sanford	2,990	9,727.1	Volusia County Beach		
Winter Springs	582	2,548.4	Management	361	(X)
			State agencies	2	(X)
Sumter	1,326	4,130.8			
Sheriff's office	929	3,900.4	Wakulla	291	1,928.6
Bushnell	92	5,886.1	Sheriff's office	291	1,928.6
Center Hill	14	1,637.4			
Coleman	32	3,177.8	Walton	581	1,933.3
Webster	72	9,424.1	Sheriff's office	460	1,899.4
Wildwood	187	4,568.8	DeFuniak Springs	121	2,073.7
Suwannee	1,125	3,921.2	Washington	126	760.7
Sheriff's office	926	4,380.3	Sheriff's office	95	721.7
Live Oak	199	2,635.8	Chipley	31	911.8

(X) Not applicable.

1/ Actual offenses known to enforcement officers. Index offenses include murder, forcible sex, robbery, aggravated assault, burglary, larceny, and auto theft.

2/ Includes North Redington Beach.

Note: The data reflected in this table is by geographic jurisdiction and is not intended to depict an individual law enforcement agency's activity. Sheriff's office totals include the activity occurring within those incorporated jurisdictions who do not report directly to Uniform Crime Reporting (UCR) program. County totals reflect all UCR activity occurring within that county. State agencies are listed only for counties with state agency activity.

Source: State of Florida, Department of Law Enforcement, *Crime in Florida: 1990 Annual Report*, and unpublished data.

Table 22.08. CRIME RATES: PROPERTY AND VIOLENT CRIME RATES IN FLORIDA AND THE
UNITED STATES, 1980 THROUGH 1989

(rates per 100,000 population)

Year	Florida			United States		
	All crime	Property crime 1/	Violent crime 2/	All crime	Property crime 1/	Violent crime 2/
1980	8,402.0	7,418.4	983.5	5,899.9	5,319.1	580.8
1981	8,032.5	7,067.4	965.1	5,799.9	5,223.0	576.9
1982	7,465.2	6,568.4	896.8	5,586.1	5,024.0	562.1
1983	6,781.1	5,954.4	826.7	5,175.0	4,637.4	537.7
1984	6,821.2	5,953.3	868.0	5,031.3	4,492.1	539.2
1985	7,574.2	6,633.1	941.1	5,206.7	4,650.5	556.2
1986	8,228.4	7,191.9	1,036.5	5,480.4	4,862.6	617.7
1987	8,503.2	7,478.7	1,024.4	5,550.0	4,940.3	609.7
1988 Δ/	8,937.6	7,819.9	1,117.7	5,664.2	5,027.1	637.2
1989	8,804.5	7,695.1	1,109.4	5,741.0	5,077.9	663.1

Δ/ Data for Florida were unavailable and are estimates.
1/ Includes burglary, larceny-theft, and motor vehicle theft.
2/ Includes murder, forcible rape, robbery, and aggravated assault.
Note: Some data are revised.

Source: U.S., Department of Justice, Federal Bureau of Investigation, *Crime in
the United States, 1989*, and previous editions.

Table 22.09. CAPITAL PUNISHMENT: PRISONERS UNDER SENTENCE OF DEATH IN FLORIDA, THE
SOUTH, AND THE UNITED STATES, DECEMBER 31, 1988 AND 1989

Item	Florida		South 1/		United States
	Number	Percentage of United States	Number	Percentage of United States	United States
Prisoners under sentence of death on 12-31-88 Δ/	287	13.6	1,246	58.9	2,117
Changes during 1989					
Received under death sentence	37	14.7	145	57.8	251
Removed from death row 2/	33	32.4	68	66.7	102
Executed	2	12.5	13	81.3	16
Prisoners under sentence of death on 12-31-89	289	12.8	1,310	58.2	2,250
Women under sentence of death 12-31-89	2	8.0	14	56.0	25

Δ/ Revised.
1/ Includes Alabama, Arkansas, Delaware, Florida, Georgia, Kentucky, Louisiana,
Maryland, Mississippi, North Carolina, Oklahoma, South Carolina, Tennessee, Texas,
and Virginia.
2/ Excludes executions. Includes suicide, murder, and death by natural causes.

Source: U.S., Department of Justice, Bureau of Justice Statistics, *Bureau of
Justice Statistics Bulletin: Capital Punishment, 1989.*

Florida Statistical Abstract 1991

Table 22.10. PRISONERS: NUMBER UNDER JURISDICTION OF STATE AND FEDERAL
CORRECTIONAL AUTHORITIES, DECEMBER 31, 1987 THROUGH 1990

Item	1987	1988	1989 A/	1990 B/
Florida				
Total prisoners	32,445	34,732	39,999	44,387
Percentage change from				
previous year	0.6	7.0	15.2	11.0
Prisoners sentenced to more				
than a year	32,360	34,681	39,966	44,387
Per 100,000 resident population	265	278	311	336
United States				
Total prisoners	584,435	627,588	712,557	771,243
Percentage change from				
previous year	7.2	7.4	13.5	8.2
Prisoners sentenced to more				
than a year	560,459	603,720	680,955	739,763
Per 100,000 resident population	228	246	274	293

A/ Revised.
B/ Preliminary.

Source: U.S., Department of Justice, Bureau of Justice Statistics, *Bureau of Justice Statistics Bulletin: Prisoners in 1990*, and previous editions.

Table 22.11. POPULATION UNDER CRIMINAL SENTENCE: INCARCERATED INMATES AND PERSONS
ON PAROLE AND/OR PROBATION UNDER SUPERVISION OF THE FLORIDA DEPARTMENT OF
CORRECTIONS, JUNE 30, 1986 THROUGH 1990

Item	1986	1987	1988	1989	1990
Under supervision, total	107,160	113,151	109,328	114,071	125,561
Incarcerated inmates	29,712	32,764	33,681	38,059	42,733
White male	13,622	14,063	14,202	15,549	16,595
White female	577	734	800	1,000	1,162
Black male	14,026	16,014	16,852	19,495	22,592
Black female	792	953	1,058	1,344	1,580
Other male	695	1,000	769	671	804
Other female	0	0	0	0	0
Offenders under					
community supervision 1/	74,078	77,310	72,286	72,628	79,033
Population under					
pretrial supervision	3,370	3,131	3,361	3,384	3,795

1/ Parolees and probationers.

Source: State of Florida, Department of Corrections, *Annual Report, 1989-1990*, and previous editions.

Florida Statistical Abstract 1991

Table 22.12. POPULATION UNDER CRIMINAL SENTENCE: INCARCERATED OFFENDERS BY COUNTY
OF COMMITMENT AND BY RACE AND PROBATIONERS AND PAROLEES BY COUNTY OF
SUPERVISION AND BY RACE IN THE STATE AND COUNTIES OF FLORIDA
JUNE 30, 1990

| | Incarcerated offenders | | | | Probationers and parolees | | | |
County	Total	White	Black	Other races	Total	White	Black	Other races
Florida	42,733	17,757	24,172	804	96,540	62,999	32,863	678
Alachua	585	173	409	3	1,661	821	838	2
Baker	46	30	16	0	67	47	20	0
Bay	496	285	211	0	1,647	1,157	478	12
Bradford	99	42	57	0	199	130	69	0
Brevard	786	408	369	9	2,619	1,975	631	13
Broward	5,765	2,217	3,507	41	9,464	5,859	3,510	95
Calhoun	19	6	13	0	101	67	34	0
Charlotte	131	90	40	1	384	339	44	1
Citrus	118	110	8	0	603	547	55	1
Clay	199	122	77	0	496	425	70	1
Collier	337	224	105	8	1,155	980	170	5
Columbia	213	96	115	2	677	382	295	0
Dade	5,635	2,140	3,317	178	9,115	5,014	3,912	189
De Soto	132	38	89	5	232	159	73	0
Dixie	42	23	19	0	133	101	32	0
Duval	3,214	915	2,282	17	4,934	2,693	2,227	14
Escambia	1,072	416	648	8	2,873	1,555	1,315	3
Flagler	48	18	29	1	179	121	57	1
Franklin	36	22	14	0	81	59	22	0
Gadsden	258	28	227	3	827	139	685	3
Gilchrist	8	8	0	0	51	48	3	0
Glades	14	4	9	1	48	33	14	1
Gulf	30	12	18	0	137	84	53	0
Hamilton	83	27	56	0	103	40	63	0
Hardee	83	43	33	7	221	187	30	4
Hendry	63	15	43	5	187	102	80	5
Hernando	186	122	62	2	602	519	82	1
Highlands	186	67	114	5	374	238	134	2
Hillsborough	4,496	1,756	2,500	240	9,553	6,067	3,360	126
Holmes	43	39	3	1	121	109	12	0
Indian River	260	109	150	1	743	521	221	1
Jackson	142	62	78	2	328	181	147	0
Jefferson	66	14	52	0	115	27	87	1
Lafayette	17	13	4	0	23	18	5	0

See footnote at end of table.   Continued . . .

Florida Statistical Abstract 1991

Table 22.12. POPULATION UNDER CRIMINAL SENTENCE: INCARCERATED OFFENDERS BY COUNTY
OF COMMITMENT AND BY RACE AND PROBATIONERS AND PAROLEES BY COUNTY OF
SUPERVISION AND BY RACE IN THE STATE AND COUNTIES OF FLORIDA
JUNE 30, 1990 (Continued)

| County | Incarcerated offenders | | | | Probationers and parolees | | | |
	Total	White	Black	Other races	Total	White	Black	Other races
Lake	388	173	213	2	1,134	821	309	4
Lee	745	345	375	25	1,821	1,357	456	8
Leon	754	174	577	3	2,116	905	1,205	6
Levy	27	14	12	1	191	134	57	0
Liberty	11	7	4	0	39	28	10	1
Madison	63	17	45	1	193	59	134	0
Manatee	546	252	281	13	1,505	1,038	466	1
Marion	573	291	276	6	1,946	1,393	550	3
Martin	284	119	160	5	715	559	152	4
Monroe	414	253	156	5	895	728	162	5
Nassau	84	40	43	1	238	167	70	1
Okaloosa	278	149	126	3	984	802	181	1
Okeechobee	76	34	41	1	213	163	50	0
Orange	2,316	914	1,343	59	6,643	3,938	2,645	60
Osceola	180	93	84	3	629	536	89	4
Palm Beach	1,626	584	1,021	21	3,832	2,586	1,226	20
Pasco	555	439	109	7	1,613	1,527	82	4
Pinellas	3,208	1,484	1,690	34	7,154	5,186	1,960	8
Polk	1,726	839	863	24	3,275	2,263	1,001	11
Putnam	346	147	196	3	483	307	175	1
St. Johns	255	111	143	1	607	432	173	2
St. Lucie	638	170	461	7	1,340	819	518	3
Santa Rosa	117	92	24	1	531	474	55	2
Sarasota	484	237	238	9	1,403	1,134	267	2
Seminole	386	204	179	3	2,299	1,666	620	13
Sumter	118	43	73	2	372	260	110	2
Suwannee	126	62	62	2	210	143	67	0
Taylor	105	32	73	0	301	165	136	0
Union	59	27	32	0	76	49	26	1
Volusia	1,108	560	532	16	3,241	2,224	988	29
Wakulla	52	31	20	1	107	86	20	1
Walton	50	37	13	0	240	199	41	0
Washington	43	27	14	2	138	104	34	0
Interstate	84	62	19	3	3	3	0	0

Note: Detail may not add to totals because of rounding.

Source: State of Florida, Department of Corrections, *Annual Report, 1989-1990*,
and unpublished data.

Florida Statistical Abstract 1991

Table 22.50. LEGAL SERVICES, JUSTICE, PUBLIC ORDER, AND SAFETY: AVERAGE MONTHLY
REPORTING UNITS, EMPLOYMENT, AND PAYROLL COVERED BY UNEMPLOYMENT COMPENSATION
LAW BY INDUSTRY IN FLORIDA, 1990

SIC code	Item	Number of reporting units	Number of employees	Payroll ($1,000)
7381	Detective, guard, and armored car services	885	29,508	27,614
81	Legal services	9,661	54,477	199,944
92	Justice, public order, and safety	805	68,477	143,892
921	Courts	183	8,339	14,782
922	Public order and safety	622	60,138	129,110
9221	Police protection	200	27,312	59,700
9222	Legal counsel and prosecution	223	10,586	28,072
9223	Correctional institutions	109	20,661	37,844
9224	Fire protection	64	1,467	3,256
9229	Public order and safety, NEC	24	112	238

NEC Not elsewhere classified.
Note: Totals on county employment tables may not match totals in this table due
to rounding.

Source: State of Florida, Department of Labor and Employment Security, Bureau of
Labor Market Information, "Employment, Wages, and Contributions Report" (ES-202),
unpublished data.

Table 22.51. LAWYERS: TOTAL LAWYERS AND MEMBERS IN GOOD STANDING OF THE FLORIDA
BAR BY SECTION IN FLORIDA, JUNE 3, 1991

Section	Number of members	Section	Number of members
Members in good standing, total	46,218	Members in sections (continued)	
Florida	36,484		
Out-of-state	9,634	Environmental and and land use	1,898
Foreign	100	Administrative	785
Members in sections, total	20,462	Practice, management,	
Tax	2,021	and technology	756
Real property, probate	7,421	Labor and employment	628
Trial	6,079	International	821
General	1,971	Entertainment,arts,	
Family	2,527	and sports	648
Local government	964	Health	617
Workers' compensation	991	Public interest	198
Criminal	1,892	Elder	153
Governmental	384		

Source: The Florida Bar, release from the Records Department, June 3, 1991.

Florida Statistical Abstract 1991

Table 22.52. LAWYERS: MEMBERS IN GOOD STANDING OF THE FLORIDA BAR BY COUNTY
     JUNE 3, 1991

County	Number of members	County	Number of members
Florida, total	46,218	Lafayette	1
Florida, in state only	36,484	Lake	161
		Lee	592
Alachua	585	Leon	1,991
Baker	3	Levy	17
Bay	163	Liberty	0
Bradford	16	Madison	10
Brevard	578	Manatee	302
Broward	4,178	Marion	273
Calhoun	6	Martin	270
Charlotte	82	Monroe	191
Citrus	65	Nassau	23
Clay	80	Okaloosa	177
Collier	415	Okeechobee	24
Columbia	54	Orange	2,613
Dade	9,403	Osceola	72
De Soto	19	Palm Beach	3,174
Dixie	2	Pasco	206
Duval	1,821	Pinellas	2,048
Escambia	505	Polk	584
Flagler	29	Putnam	57
Franklin	10	St. Johns	108
Gadsden	37	St. Lucie	193
Gilchrist	4	Santa Rosa	46
Glades	1	Sarasota	794
Gulf	7	Seminole	376
Hamilton	8	Sumter	21
Hardee	11	Suwannee	35
Hendry	21	Taylor	14
Hernando	71	Union	4
Highlands	55	Volusia	656
Hillsborough	2,949	Wakulla	12
Holmes	8	Walton	15
Indian River	189	Washington	7
Jackson	24	Out-of-State 1/	9,634
Jefferson	18	Foreign 1/	100

1/ Members of the Bar practicing out of state or in foreign countries.

Source: The Florida Bar, release from the Records Department, June 3, 1991.

Florida Statistical Abstract 1991

Table 22.55. LEGAL SERVICES: AVERAGE MONTHLY REPORTING UNITS, EMPLOYMENT, AND
PAYROLL COVERED BY UNEMPLOYMENT COMPENSATION LAW IN THE STATE AND COUNTIES
OF FLORIDA, 1990

County	Number of reporting units	Number of employees	Payroll ($1,000)	County	Number of reporting units	Number of employees	Payroll ($1,000)
			Legal services	(SIC code 81)			
Florida	9,645	54,484	199,939	Lafayette	0	0	0
				Lake	70	283	708
Alachua	128	640	1,613	Lee	165	1,158	3,332
Baker	(D)	(D)	(D)	Leon	230	1,886	7,121
Bay	53	265	743	Levy	8	17	30
Bradford	7	27	42	Liberty	0	0	0
Brevard	172	818	2,656	Madison	4	17	22
Broward	1,300	6,058	22,273	Manatee	88	457	1,296
Calhoun	(D)	(D)	(D)	Marion	92	432	1,391
Charlotte	27	215	562	Martin	77	427	1,258
Citrus	25	124	323	Monroe	50	216	549
Clay	25	106	243	Nassau	11	34	62
Collier	129	664	2,046	Okaloosa	80	258	571
Columbia	19	66	191	Okeechobee	10	36	58
Dade	2,554	13,669	58,507	Orange	579	4,940	18,572
De Soto	7	11	20	Osceola	25	95	157
Dixie	(D)	(D)	(D)	Palm Beach	794	4,817	19,024
Duval	434	2,892	11,464	Pasco	88	389	1,040
Escambia	135	846	2,599	Pinellas	605	2,974	9,584
Flagler	9	26	46	Polk	179	960	2,948
Franklin	(D)	(D)	(D)	Putnam	25	67	129
Gadsden	11	38	51	St. Johns	24	83	179
Gilchrist	(D)	(D)	(D)	St. Lucie	61	306	1,049
Glades	0	0	0	Santa Rosa	13	68	173
Gulf	5	13	15	Sarasota	227	1,295	4,383
Hamilton	(D)	(D)	(D)	Seminole	111	403	1,035
Hardee	4	16	28	Sumter	9	21	34
Hendry	7	22	41	Suwannee	11	25	38
Hernando	17	75	147	Taylor	6	17	36
Highlands	29	98	208	Union	(D)	(D)	(D)
Hillsborough	590	4,751	17,633	Volusia	210	988	2,764
Holmes	(D)	(D)	(D)	Wakulla	4	8	13
Indian River	50	257	779	Walton	8	14	14
Jackson	11	24	27	Washington	(D)	(D)	(D)
Jefferson	5	12	14	Statewide 1/	4	6	31

(D) Data withheld to avoid disclosure of information about individual firms.
1/ Reporting units without a fixed location within the state or of unknown county
location.
Note: These data include establishments which are engaged in offering legal
advice or services and which are headed by a member of the Bar.

Source: State of Florida, Department of Labor and Employment Security, Bureau of
Labor Market Information, "Employment, Wages, and Contributions Report" (ES-202),
unpublished data.

Florida Statistical Abstract 1991

GOVERNMENT FINANCE
AND EMPLOYMENT

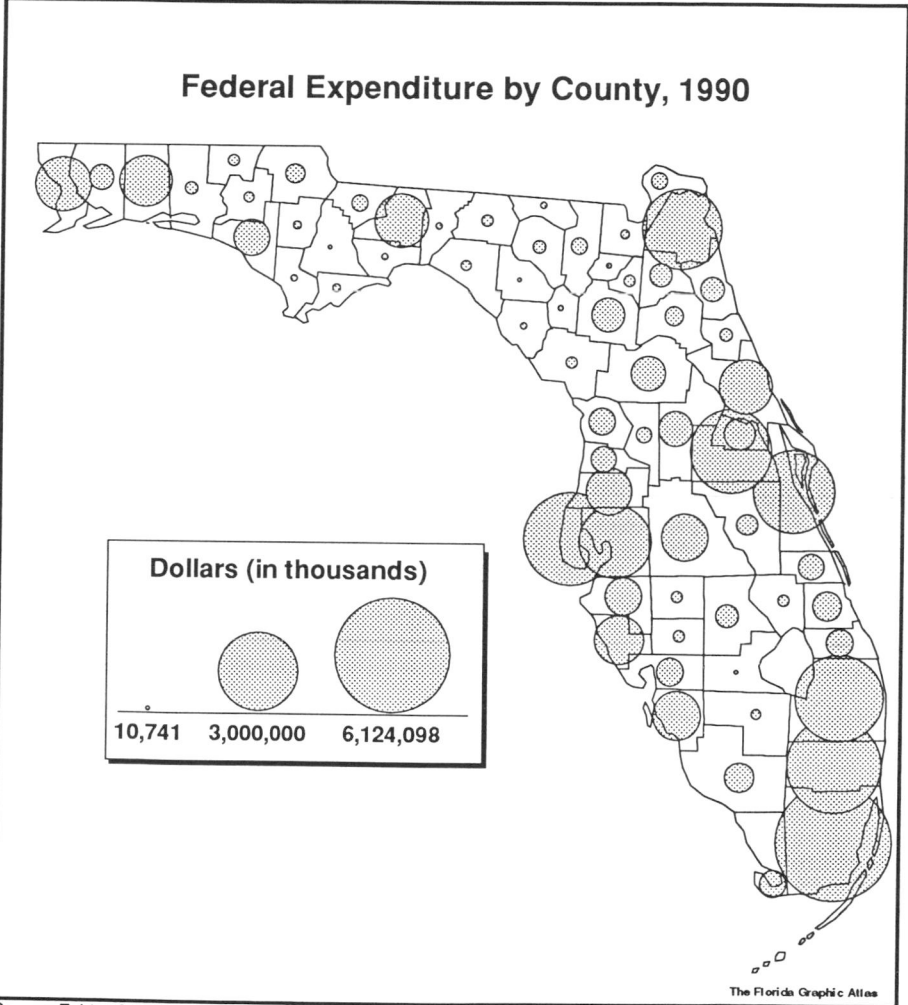

Federal Expenditure by County, 1990

Dollars (in thousands)

10,741   3,000,000   6,124,098

The Florida Graphic Atlas

TABLES LISTED BY MAJOR HEADINGS

561

Table 23.07. FEDERAL GOVERNMENT: EXPENDITURE BY AGENCY AND BY SPECIFIED PROGRAM
  IN FLORIDA AND THE UNITED STATES, FISCAL YEAR 1989-90

(in thousands of dollars)

Item	Florida	United States
Total (19)	51,359,000	1,002,703,000
Grants to state and local governments (50)	4,576,009	134,456,902
Department of Agriculture	434,664	11,852,634
Agricultural Marketing Service	1,445	379,894
Funds for strengthening markets	1,370	378,658
Cooperative projects in marketing	75	1,236
Cooperative State Research Service--agriculture		
experiment stations	8,016	366,376
Extension Service--extension activities	7,501	343,357
Farmers Home Administration	6,800	183,694
Food and Nutrition Service	403,821	10,023,143
Child nutrition programs	238,594	4,811,747
Food stamp program	45,107	2,230,286
Special supplemental food program (WIC)	84,949	2,111,431
Commodity distributions 1/	17,143	403,000
Food donations	11,774	283,952
Temporary emergency food assistance	6,136	164,922
Special milk program	118	17,805
Food Safety and Inspection Service--meat and		
poultry inspection	2,178	36,206
Forest Service	4,726	420,576
Soil Conservation Service	177	99,388
Department of Commerce	6,602	300,851
Economic Development Administration--development	1,240	156,332
assistance programs		
National Oceanic and Atmospheric Administration	4,778	121,970
Corporation for Public Broadcasting--public		
broadcasting fund	8,329	237,831
Department of Defense 2/	2,685	175,978
Department of Education	460,706	11,176,099
Bilingual education and minority language affairs	5,355	151,677
Educational Research and Improvement-libraries	5,351	126,887
Office of Elementary and Secondary Education	260,133	6,378,454
Office of Postsecondary Education	3,472	98,147
Office of Special Education and Rehabilitative Services	132,415	3,117,633
Office of Vocational and Adult Education	53,810	1,287,089
Department of Energy	1,307	208,400
Environmental Protection Agency	133,175	2,885,944
Construction of wastewater treatment works	116,148	2,293,892
Abatement, control, and compliance	7,057	397,393
Hazardous substance response trust fund	9,970	194,659
Equal Employment Opportunity Commission	953	19,219
Federal Emergency Management Agency	11,373	1,256,290
Funds Appropriated to the President--		
Appalachian regional development programs	0	111,578
Department of Health and Human Services	2,188,777	65,487,011
Alcohol, Drug Abuse, and Mental Health Administration	65,329	1,314,218
Family Support Administration	346,060	15,139,727
Family support payments (AFDC)	272,923	12,246,000
Low income home energy assistance	15,382	1,314,000

See footnotes at end of table.   Continued . . .

Table 23.07. FEDERAL GOVERNMENT: EXPENDITURE BY AGENCY AND BY SPECIFIED PROGRAM
IN FLORIDA AND THE UNITED STATES, FISCAL YEAR 1989-90 (Continued)

(in thousands of dollars)

Item	Florida	United States
Grants to state and local governments (Continued)		
Department of Health and Human Services (Continued)		
Family Support Administration (Continued)		
Community service block grant	12,309	351,000
Refugee assistance	17,536	391,000
Assistance for legalized aliens	12,834	544,000
Other	15,076	293,727
Health Care Financing Administration--medical		
assistance (Medicaid)	1,426,640	40,857,263
Health Resources and Services Administration	59,893	1,246,462
Human Development Services	275,523	6,619,566
Social services block grant	146,837	2,745,821
Human development services	104,228	2,815,671
Family social services	24,458	1,058,074
Public Health Service	14,160	283,975
AIDS drug reimbursement	2,560	28,064
Centers for Disease Control	11,600	255,911
Social Security Administration, supplemental		
security income	1,172	25,800
Department of Housing and Urban Development	437,722	12,524,339
Community development	122,621	2,817,769
Emergency shelters and homeless assistance	1,794	49,263
Low rent housing--operating assistance	49,885	1,758,977
Lower income housing assistance	233,164	7,372,331
Institute of Museum Services	183	9,447
Department of Interior	10,419	1,608,226
National Park Service	1,850	58,797
Department of Justice	15,052	330,071
Department of Labor	188,409	5,833,247
Employment and Training Administration	187,615	5,734,997
Job Training Partnership Act	107,563	3,079,386
State unemployment insurance and employment		
service operations	80,052	2,580,110
National Foundation on the Arts and the Humanities--		
National Endowment for the Arts	776	30,142
Tennessee Valley Authority-payments in lieu of taxes	0	232,868
Department of Transportation	674,820	18,982,634
Federal Aviation Administration--airport and		
airway trust fund	95,045	1,220,154
Federal Highway Administration	479,181	13,836,692
Urban Mass Transportation Administration	92,996	3,754,357
Department of the Treasury-Customs Bureau and IRS rebates	0	385,693
Department of Veterans Affairs	14	134,675
Other-payment of District of Columbia and Metro subsidy	0	663,320
Salary and wage expenditure (29)	6,595,657	146,094,692
Department of Defense 2/	3,525,086	69,103,253
Military	2,503,725	39,443,768
Active	2,349,601	33,847,026
Inactive	154,124	5,596,742
Civilian	1,021,361	29,659,485
All other federal	3,070,571	76,991,439

See footnotes at end of table.   Continued . . .

Table 23.07. FEDERAL GOVERNMENT: EXPENDITURE BY AGENCY AND BY SPECIFIED PROGRAM
    IN FLORIDA AND THE UNITED STATES, FISCAL YEAR 1989-90 (Continued)

(in thousands of dollars)

Item	Florida	United States
Direct payments to individuals (1)	32,881,651	497,695,773
Social Security	16,367,115	243,606,965
Retirement insurance payments	12,206,580	168,800,923
Survivors insurance payments	2,837,045	50,192,744
Disability insurance payments	1,323,490	24,613,298
Medicare	7,801,171	112,342,934
Hospital insurance payments	4,384,602	68,254,950
Supplementary medical insurance payments	3,416,569	44,087,984
Federal retirement and disability payments	4,624,653	53,120,905
Military	2,189,189	21,235,041
Civilian 3/	2,435,464	31,885,864
Federal payments for unemployment compensation	410,732	17,360,376
Veterans compensation for service connected disability	767,657	9,242,757
Veterans pensions for nonservice connected disability	127,899	2,555,468
Veterans compensation for service connected death (DIC)	191,876	2,278,937
Pensions to veterans' surviving spouses and children	59,011	1,293,085
Veterans educational assistance (GI Bill)	18,547	342,750
Other veterans benefit programs	20,169	371,683
Supplemental security income payments	601,727	11,747,888
Food stamps	605,058	13,998,950
Social insurance payments for railroad workers	365,210	7,269,712
Housing assistance	201,892	5,898,533
Pell grant program	168,987	4,323,651
Excess earned income tax credits	283,858	4,710,518
National guaranteed student loan interest subsidies	88,744	2,570,100
Federal workers compensation	90,811	1,347,172
Black lung payments	29,886	1,431,956
Procurement contracts (26) A/	6,616,097	188,530,641
Department of Defense	4,657,397	135,259,039
Postal Service	241,981	4,746,664
Other programs (48)	689,115	35,925,238
Grants	179,618	11,057,422
Department of Health and Human Services--		
research programs	92,242	6,767,961
National Science Foundation	31,071	1,808,961
Direct payments--other than for individuals	509,497	24,867,816
Department of Agriculture	60,051	10,703,038
Postal Service	101,313	1,987,338
National flood insurance claim payments	2,863	539,203

A/ Value of annual contract actions; actual outlays for U.S. Postal Service only.
Multiple year obligations of less than 3 years duration may be included.
    1/ Value of commodities distributed to states under Agricultural Marketing
Service and Commodity Credit Corporation programs.
    2/ Includes salaries, wages and compensations such as housing allowances; distri-
bution based on duty station.
    3/ Includes retirement and disability payments to former postal employees.
    Note: The number (after major expenditure categories) indicates Florida's rank
among the states in per capita distribution of federal funds. Expenditures
classified as "other" may not be specified in the table and are contained in the
totals for major expenditure categories.
    Source: U.S., Department of Commerce, Bureau of the Census, *Federal Expenditures
by State for Fiscal Year 1990.*

Florida Statistical Abstract 1991

Table 23.08. FEDERAL GOVERNMENT: EXPENDITURE BY TYPE IN THE STATE AND COUNTIES
   OF FLORIDA AND THE UNITED STATES, 1990

(in thousands of dollars, except were indicated)

County	Direct expenditure Total	Defense Department	Grants	Wages and salaries	Direct payment to individuals Total	Retirement and disability
Florida	51,587,395	10,374,558	4,795,695	6,595,657	33,070,463	23,235,281
Alachua	571,892	51,305	123,558	99,456	306,195	216,116
Baker	33,415	2,407	3,217	1,831	28,078	19,375
Bay	638,335	340,844	26,957	231,485	310,989	247,444
Bradford	54,123	7,413	6,690	5,172	41,092	29,829
Brevard	3,301,742	915,820	55,618	331,121	1,044,667	871,826
Broward	4,055,035	139,879	226,920	255,402	3,453,534	2,217,731
Calhoun	29,881	1,302	5,367	1,183	21,857	15,233
Charlotte	412,083	22,229	7,464	8,993	393,360	306,007
Citrus	345,058	17,039	12,751	7,184	323,723	262,611
Clay	235,491	78,171	8,865	12,829	203,980	172,660
Collier	442,159	34,052	24,115	20,921	373,243	302,874
Columbia	130,762	3,614	12,809	28,329	90,567	67,831
Dade	6,124,098	416,934	1,083,441	803,156	3,958,219	2,163,411
De Soto	63,480	2,770	5,938	2,189	54,943	40,241
Dixie	27,478	1,780	2,953	1,132	23,152	17,814
Duval	3,230,913	1,431,565	216,614	1,315,642	1,437,308	1,029,667
Escambia	1,433,215	753,684	79,417	572,230	674,406	527,176
Flagler	88,099	4,810	5,086	3,364	77,491	64,834
Franklin	29,351	1,917	6,244	1,347	21,586	14,834
Gadsden	141,751	5,296	24,099	32,577	77,581	52,493
Gilchrist	21,512	1,002	1,828	646	18,094	13,237
Glades	13,221	482	1,768	364	10,948	7,624
Gulf	31,350	2,550	3,363	772	26,937	19,942
Hamilton	28,025	940	6,433	912	19,405	13,182
Hardee	47,245	1,532	7,890	2,116	36,279	25,940
Hendry	48,027	3,974	5,558	3,456	36,601	25,027
Hernando	364,426	9,920	9,860	9,952	342,477	283,498
Highlands	268,246	21,803	12,161	14,499	239,214	191,167
Hillsborough	2,596,593	575,305	229,277	518,186	1,598,941	1,171,372
Holmes	51,070	3,976	8,419	2,316	38,166	27,579
Indian River	362,343	30,280	8,617	14,546	320,545	252,291
Jackson	163,588	6,495	19,707	41,525	91,237	63,808
Jefferson	32,097	928	8,863	1,117	20,902	15,366
Lafayette	10,741	596	1,387	478	8,361	6,032
Lake	520,645	34,504	20,862	18,511	468,959	368,680

See footnote at end of table.   Continued . . .

Table 23.08. FEDERAL GOVERNMENT: EXPENDITURE BY TYPE IN THE STATE AND COUNTIES
  OF FLORIDA AND THE UNITED STATES, 1990 (Continued)

(in thousands of dollars, except were indicated)

County	Total	Defense Department	Grants	Wages and salaries	Total	Retirement and disability
					Direct payment to individuals	
Lee	1,130,491	47,983	74,977	61,158	979,157	768,463
Leon	1,336,517	42,149	996,970	62,704	261,581	190,424
Levy	72,178	3,788	7,081	2,924	60,162	46,564
Liberty	12,896	693	2,119	1,050	9,523	7,076
Madison	48,273	1,598	11,921	2,020	32,608	23,103
Manatee	666,473	26,960	26,505	20,007	623,429	464,136
Marion	645,233	57,345	36,592	23,328	551,957	446,935
Martin	364,484	54,251	8,969	11,710	298,553	238,008
Monroe	300,277	115,341	26,461	99,064	145,274	107,661
Nassau	123,762	18,561	6,895	34,169	78,185	62,739
Okaloosa	1,245,770	957,296	26,014	555,044	396,124	346,923
Okeechobee	77,669	2,234	6,337	2,641	67,639	48,402
Orange	3,257,416	1,810,286	142,068	580,479	1,252,148	939,934
Osceola	215,755	21,282	8,655	9,602	187,154	134,796
Palm Beach	3,724,327	895,265	133,082	177,964	2,451,334	1,768,836
Pasco	1,063,907	98,520	41,398	26,790	976,479	734,059
Pinellas	4,016,421	629,517	123,448	243,812	2,973,076	2,119,652
Polk	1,035,736	52,236	81,267	55,798	882,675	687,429
Putnam	176,641	11,330	21,273	6,391	146,767	108,595
St. Johns	282,470	57,191	38,519	20,301	197,636	156,460
St. Lucie	425,650	10,439	33,284	16,941	371,703	296,022
Santa Rosa	283,073	125,511	15,842	88,371	164,332	134,896
Sarasota	1,215,627	81,780	31,177	33,701	1,099,531	837,369
Seminole	500,776	68,141	44,727	22,488	423,646	339,303
Sumter	114,367	4,703	9,392	2,719	100,543	80,611
Suwannee	84,436	4,566	11,966	3,447	65,361	49,529
Taylor	49,315	6,853	6,334	2,144	36,153	25,498
Union	19,346	1,373	4,648	636	12,825	8,638
Volusia	1,353,304	219,088	70,095	50,595	1,060,873	788,609
Wakulla	31,290	1,914	4,654	1,808	23,512	17,486
Walton	86,059	14,942	10,713	8,095	65,194	49,002
Washington	61,903	4,202	12,108	1,938	46,504	32,584
Undistributed	1,618,062	103	436,091	878	835,789	50,786
United States 1/	1,010,376	225,767	147,994	146,095	502,889	334,228

1/ Rounded to millions of dollars.

Source: U.S., Department of Commerce, Bureau of the Census, *Consolidated Federal
Funds Report, Fiscal Year 1990, Volume I: County Areas.*

Table 23.15. DEFENSE CONTRACTS: AWARDS AND PAYROLL IN FLORIDA, OTHER SUNBELT
STATES, OTHER POPULOUS STATES, AND THE UNITED STATES, FISCAL YEARS 1986-87
THROUGH 1988-89

(in millions of dollars)

State	Contract awards 1/			Payroll 2/		
	1986-87	1987-88	1988-89	1986-87	1987-88	1988-89
Sunbelt states						
Florida	5,797	5,328	4,452	3,623	2,990	3,246
Alabama	1,661	1,826	1,392	1,301	1,291	1,378
Arizona	3,211	2,652	2,847	793	806	894
Arkansas	738	422	370	322	649	336
California	24,515	23,458	23,125	9,568	9,842	10,529
Georgia	3,512	1,616	1,864	2,245	2,229	2,762
Louisiana	1,685	1,439	1,693	730	695	925
Mississippi	1,474	2,422	1,235	690	708	692
New Mexico	584	663	625	635	635	640
North Carolina	1,243	1,241	1,104	2,311	2,540	2,673
Oklahoma	608	541	659	1,305	1,365	1,358
South Carolina	571	566	568	1,690	1,757	1,912
Tennessee	986	1,207	1,118	389	409	393
Texas	8,654	9,001	9,263	4,381	4,394	4,908
Virginia	7,807	10,238	5,897	7,216	7,693	7,634
Other populous states						
Illinois	1,924	1,500	1,249	1,340	1,293	1,290
Indiana	2,231	1,518	1,763	565	571	597
Massachusetts	8,685	7,212	8,757	541	652	650
Michigan	1,866	1,270	1,266	550	536	557
New Jersey	3,283	3,359	3,393	1,185	1,216	1,205
New York	9,625	7,706	6,552	993	1,151	1,293
Ohio	4,550	5,060	5,069	1,292	1,136	1,434
Pennsylvania	3,845	3,309	2,828	1,694	1,828	1,699
United States	133,262	125,767	119,917	60,331	61,782	66,180

1/ State data include net value of contracts over $25,000 for military awards for
supplies, services, and construction.
2/ Data are estimates and cover active duty military and direct hire civilian
personnel, including Army Corps of Engineers.
Note: Data refer to awards in year specified and to state in which prime con-
tractor is located. Expenditure may extend over several years and work may be performed by a subcontractor in another state.

Source: U.S., Department of Commerce, Bureau of the Census, *Statistical Abstract
of the United States, 1991.*

Florida Statistical Abstract 1991

Table 23.29. STATE GOVERNMENT: PER CAPITA AMOUNTS OF REVENUE, EXPENDITURE, AND
  INDEBTEDNESS IN FLORIDA AND THE UNITED STATES, FISCAL YEAR 1988-89

(in dollars)

Item	Florida	United States
Revenue, total 1/	1,748.85	2,368.65
General revenue, total	1,522.29	1,947.83
Intergovernmental		
Federal	279.88	437.08
Local	6.29	30.41
Taxes, total 1/	983.00	1,147.02
General sales	602.79	377.23
Motor fuel sales	59.35	72.81
Individual income	0.00	358.16
Charges and miscellaneous, total 1/	253.13	333.33
Higher education charges	33.85	85.47
Hospital charges	7.74	34.43
Interest income	73.15	101.83
Expenditure, total 1/	1,576.62	2,120.37
General expenditure, total 1/	1,494.82	1,895.00
Education, total 1/	578.20	699.35
Higher education	181.65	248.77
Public welfare	218.81	374.54
Hospitals	36.73	86.48
Health	93.93	69.41
Highways	155.46	172.41
Police	16.36	19.16
Correction	59.88	60.64
Interest on general debt	52.72	82.20
Exhibit: salaries and wages	315.98	387.37
Debt at end of fiscal year, total	707.69	1,193.76
Long-term debt		
Full faith credit	148.85	284.80
Nonguaranteed	558.37	899.88
Short-term	0.47	9.09
Long-term debt by function		
Public debt for private purposes	175.93	561.21
Education	287.52	129.40
Utility	0.00	49.22
Cash and security holdings, total	2,314.36	3,557.63
Insurance trust 1/	1,387.99	2,274.24
Other than insurance trust, total 1/	926.37	1,283.39
Offsets to debt	378.68	706.80
Bond funds	80.61	83.57
Other	467.08	493.02

1/ Includes amounts for categories not shown separately.
  Note: Per capita amounts are based on U.S. Census Bureau population figures for
July 1, 1989.

  Source: U.S., Department of Commerce, Bureau of the Census, *State Government
Finances in 1989.*

Florida Statistical Abstract 1991

Table 23.31.   STATE TREASURER OF FLORIDA: RESOURCES AND LIABILITIES, FISCAL YEAR
      1989-90

(in dollars)

	Balance sheet for fiscal year ending June 30, 1990
Item	Resources
Office cash	
Currency and coin	99,109.63
Fraudulent warrants receivable	0.00
Bank deposits	
U.C. benefit investment account	A/ 2,004,163,077.98
Demand accounts	B/ 435,550,888.82
Time deposit accounts	1,588,541,000.00
Total bank deposits	4,028,254,966.80

(The above does not include $8,099,123.23 held in special accounts known as "clear-
ing accounts" and "revolving funds" outside the state treasury.)

Total all securities held by treasury	C/ 3,571,238,535.71
Total state-owned resources in treasurer's custody	7,599,592,612.14

	Liabilities
State funds subject to comptroller's warrant	
General revenue fund	602,462,539.95
Trust fund	6,751,213,605.94
Working capital fund	D/ 0.00
Infra-structure trust fund	245,885,580.23
Total four funds	7,599,561,726.12
Fraudulent warrants reserve	0.00
Adjustments	E/ 30,886.02
Total liabilities	7,599,592,612.14

A/ Represents U.S. benefit funds held and invested by the federal government,
administered by the Treasury.
B/ Includes per reconciled cash balance of $169,208,307.87, a difference of
$266,342,580.95 which represents items in transit.
C/ Total market value of all securities held by Treasury $3,557,217,045.65.
D/ Working capital funds are invested within the Trust Fund Investment Program.
E/ Represents "Purchased Interest".

Source: State of Florida, *Report of the State Treasurer for the Fiscal Year
Ending June 30, 1990.*

Florida Statistical Abstract 1991

Table 23.35. STATE GOVERNMENT: TAX REVENUE BY FUND TYPE IN FLORIDA, FISCAL YEAR
1989-90

(in thousands of dollars)

Tax	Total	General	Fund type Special revenue	Expendable trust
Total	13,116,385	9,795,111	3,034,421	286,853
Sales	8,245,664	8,212,679	32,985	0
Alcoholic beverage	450,566	450,566	0	0
Cigarette	337,114	12,451	324,663	0
Corporate income	805,703	805,703	0	0
Unemployment compensation	286,853	0	0	286,853
Estate	257,820	257,820	0	0
Pari-mutuel wagering	106,599	55,892	50,707	0
Motor fuel	714,715	0	714,715	0
Documentary stamps	429,597	0	429,597	0
Gross receipts utilities	300,106	0	300,106	0
Intangible personal property	418,172	0	418,172	0
Insurance Premium	294,183	0	294,183	0
Hospital public assistance	141,874	0	141,874	0
Severance tax on solid minerals	56,449	0	56,449	0
Workers' compensation special disability	88,094	0	88,094	0
Citrus excise	47,188	0	47,188	0
Aviation fuel	43,419	0	43,419	0
Pollutant	58,634	0	58,634	0
Oil and gas production	9,524	0	9,524	0
Utility regulatory	18,885	0	18,885	0
Other	5,226	0	5,226	0

Source: State of Florida, *Florida Comprehensive Annual Financial Report*, Fiscal
Year Ended June 30, 1990.

Table 23.36. STATE GOVERNMENT: TAX COLLECTIONS IN FLORIDA, SPECIFIED SUNBELT
STATES, AND THE UNITED STATES, 1989

(in millions of dollars)

State	Total 1/	Sales and gross receipts Total 1/	General	Motor fuels	Alcoholic and tobacco products	Corpora- tion net income	Motor ve- hicle and drivers' licenses
Florida	12,456	9,879	7,638	752	789	725	499
Arizona	4,061	2,470	1,842	337	92	200	204
California	41,214	16,205	12,732	1,308	645	5,063	1,165
Georgia	6,347	2,812	2,026	426	204	525	97
North Carolina	7,369	2,916	1,702	610	163	789	271
Texas	13,974	10,962	6,947	1,501	748	(X)	753
Virginia	6,621	2,608	1,290	612	113	347	275
United States	284,042	138,249	93,414	18,029	8,154	23,861	10,145

(X) Not applicable.
1/ Includes amounts for types of taxes not shown separately.
Source: U.S., Department of Commerce, Bureau of the Census, *Government Finances:
State Government Tax Collections, 1989*. GF-89-1

Florida Statistical Abstract 1991

Table 23.40. STATE GOVERNMENT: REVENUE, EXPENDITURE, AND CHANGE IN FUND BALANCE
BY FUND TYPE IN FLORIDA, FISCAL YEAR 1989-90

(in thousands of dollars)

Item	Total 1/	General	Special revenue	Expendable trust
Beginning fund balance, July 1, 1989	6,042,078	645,662	2,783,324	2,088,199
Revenue, total	19,563,015	10,201,618	8,745,872	556,720
Taxes 2/	13,116,385	9,795,111	3,034,421	286,853
Licenses and permits	605,873	39,964	565,909	0
Fees and charges	775,180	146,995	625,253	1,285
Grants and donations	3,993,950	771	3,985,231	2,993
Interest and dividends	552,183	124,207	218,867	184,434
Fines, forfeits and judgements	110,177	480	109,697	0
Insurance contributions	0	0	0	0
Refunds	232,396	94,090	128,082	10,194
Other	176,871	0	78,412	70,961
Expenditure, total	19,462,976	9,076,807	9,317,369	426,535
Current				
Economic opportunities, agri-culture and employment	1,040,227	71,508	544,865	419,987
Public safety	1,298,654	1,128,875	169,595	0
Education	6,759,937	4,630,144	2,123,986	5,561
Health and social concerns	5,678,086	2,485,897	3,186,728	0
Housing and community development	90,000	7,934	81,966	0
Natural resources and enviro-mental management	426,175	134,748	282,621	0
Recreational and cultural opportunities	113,564	36,281	60,475	0
Transportation	430,841	0	430,014	827
Government direction and support services	2,045,579	498,139	1,530,738	0
Capital outlay	1,184,776	73,420	886,940	160
Debt service				
Principle retirement	113,992	8,643	8,530	0
Interest and fiscal charges	281,145	1,218	10,911	0
Excess (deficiency) of revenues over expenditures	100,039	1,124,811	-571,497	130,185
Other financing sources (uses)	-93,781	-1,125,943	431,855	67
Excess (deficiency) of revenues and other financing sources over expenditures and other financing uses	6,258	-1,132	-139,642	130,252
Change in reserve for inventories	2,492	1,591	901	0
Ending Fund Balance, June 30, 1990	6,098,140	646,121	2,691,895	2,218,451

1/ Total presented only to facilitate financial analysis. Includes fund types
and account groups that use differing basis of accounting, restricted and un-
restricted amounts, and interfund transactions which have not been eliminated.

2/ Florida levies neither a personal income tax nor an ad valorem tax on real or
tangible personal property. Taxes are, however, the principal means of financing
state operations. See Table 23.35 for tax revenue by source and type.

Source: State of Florida, *Florida Comprehensive Annual Financial Report*, Fiscal
Year Ended June 30, 1990.

Table 23.41.   STATE GOVERNMENT: EXPENDITURE BY AGENCY IN FLORIDA, FISCAL YEAR
   1989-90

Agency number	Agency name	Amount ($1,000)
	Expenditure, total	47,300,495
11	Legislative branch	121,191
21	Judicial branch	229,784
22	State courts system	150,108
31	Executive Office of the Governor	97,972
36	Department of the Lottery	2,096,014
41	Department of Legal Affairs	59,793
42	Department of Agriculture and Consumer Services	167,365
44	Department of Banking and Finance	4,695,991
45	Department of State	120,889
46	Department of Insurance	5,863,598
47	Department of Commerce	39,259
48	Department of Education	8,904,003
49	Division of Universities	2,503,109
50	Department of Veterans' Affairs	7,239
51	Department of Administration	3,348,542
52	Department of Community Affairs	182,557
53	Department of Business Regulation	452,724
54	Department of Labor and Employment Security	1,182,719
55	Department of Transportation	2,408,203
56	Department of Environmental Regulation	559,747
57	Department of Citrus	68,261
58	Department of Professional Regulation	64,427
60	Department of Health and Rehabilitative Services	5,936,207
61	Public Service Commission	36,964
62	Department of Military Affairs	13,152
70	Department of Corrections	831,874
71	Department of Law Enforcement	95,155
72	Department of General Services	333,012
73	Department of Revenue	5,445,518
74	Department of Natural Resources	514,639
76	Department of Highway Safety and Motor Vehicle	702,316
77	Game and Freshwater Fish Commission	63,011
78	Parole and Probation Commission	5,120
82	Commissioners for the Promotion of Uniformity of Legislation in the United States	33

Source: State of Florida, *Annual Report of the Comptroller, Fiscal Year 1989-90.*

Florida Statistical Abstract 1991

Table 23.43. STATE GOVERNMENT: SALES AND USE TAX COLLECTIONS BY TRADE CLASSIFICATION
IN FLORIDA, FISCAL YEARS 1988-89 AND 1989-90

Group	1988-89 ($1,000)	1989-90 ($1,000)	Percentage change
All classifications, total	7,611,369	8,153,904	7.1
Food and beverage group	1,130,165	1,218,063	7.8
Grocery stores	395,559	422,303	6.8
Meat markets	649	655	1.0
Seafood dealers	1,105	969	-12.3
Vegetables and fruit markets	2,214	2,137	-3.5
Bakeries	5,735	4,889	-14.7
Delicatessens	5,595	7,549	34.9
Candy, confectionery, concession stands	21,146	21,679	2.5
Restaurants, lunchrooms, catering services	601,326	658,625	9.5
Taverns, night clubs, bars, liquor stores	96,836	99,257	2.5
Apparel group	232,507	256,229	10.2
Clothing stores	194,119	218,217	12.4
Shoe stores	38,038	37,660	-1.0
Hat shops	351	352	0.4
General merchandise group	1,021,297	1,127,228	10.4
Department stores	402,056	447,491	11.3
Variety stores	154,318	189,213	22.6
Drug stores	106,910	121,920	14.0
Jewelry, leather, and sporting goods	98,728	104,441	5.8
Feed, seed, fertilizer stores	5,861	6,094	4.0
Hardware, paints, and machinery	93,212	94,625	1.5
Farm implements and supplies	13,313	13,152	-1.2
General merchandise stores	120,590	121,642	0.9
Second-hand stores, antique shops, flea markets	10,781	11,840	9.8
Dry goods stores	15,529	16,810	8.2
Automotive group	1,473,193	1,501,497	1.9
Motor vehicle dealers, trailers, campers	1,141,885	1,153,410	1.0
Auto accessories, tires, and parts	100,170	109,073	8.9
Filling and service stations, car wash	54,390	56,361	3.6
Garage and repair shops	87,552	94,535	8.0
Aircraft dealers	17,306	18,341	6.0
Motorboat and yacht dealers	71,891	69,777	-2.9
Furniture and appliances group	429,938	469,216	9.1
Furniture stores, new and used	158,705	165,452	4.3
Household appliances, dinnerware, etc.	54,916	62,454	13.7
Store and office equipment	97,070	102,991	6.1
Music stores, radios, and televisions	119,247	138,319	16.0
Lumber, builders, and contractors group	542,378	539,670	-0.5
Building contractors	28,274	24,028	-15.0
Heating and air conditioning	32,753	33,982	3.8
Electrical and plumbing	96,681	85,718	-11.3
Decorating, painting, and papering	34,785	35,447	1.9
Roofing and sheet metal	11,318	11,314	0.0
Lumber and building materials	338,568	349,181	3.1
General classification group	2,781,892	3,042,001	9.4
Hotels, apartment houses, etc.	336,997	382,980	13.6
Auctioneers and commission dealers	20,674	21,837	5.6
Barber and beauty shops	18,270	19,030	4.2
Book stores	20,274	22,809	12.5
Cigar stands and tobacco shops	1,356	1,415	4.4
Florists	15,415	16,850	9.3

Continued . . .

Table 23.43. STATE GOVERNMENT: SALES AND USE TAX COLLECTIONS BY TRADE CLASSIFICATION
IN FLORIDA, FISCAL YEARS 1988-89 AND 1989-90 (Continued)

Group	1988-89 ($1,000)	1989-90 ($1,000)	Percentage change
General classification group (Continued)			
Fuel dealers, L.P. gas dealers	20,569	22,044	7.2
Funeral directors monuments	3,529	3,588	1.7
Scrap metal and junk yards	2,207	2,039	-7.6
Itinerant vendors	6,785	5,988	-11.7
Laundry, cleaning services, alterations	10,536	11,214	6.4
Machine shops and foundries	11,452	11,869	3.6
Horse, cattle, and pet dealers	32,168	46,151	43.5
Photographers, photo supplies, art galleries	37,819	39,909	5.5
Shoe repair shops	1,129	1,036	-8.2
Storage and warehousing	6,504	8,192	26.0
Gift, card, and novelty stores, taxidermy	78,503	84,694	7.9
Newsstands	3,288	3,208	-2.4
Social clubs and associations	22,121	22,142	0.1
Industrial machinery equipment	102,828	101,221	-1.6
Admissions	125,344	153,686	22.6
Holiday season vendors, Christmas trees	647	1,403	116.9
Rental of tangible property	125,370	138,009	10.1
Fabrication and sales of cabinets, etc.	52,504	50,693	-3.4
Manufacturing and mining	243,599	257,961	5.9
Bottlers (beer and softdrinks)	5,232	5,604	7.1
Pawn shops	2,532	2,790	10.2
Communications	267,579	289,155	8.1
Transportation	16,049	15,180	-5.4
Graphic arts and printing	67,524	70,340	4.2
Insurance, banking, information services, etc.	15,447	13,805	-10.6
Sanitary and industrial supplies	21,720	26,660	22.7
Packaging materials and paper boxes	11,069	10,928	-1.3
Repair of tangible personal property	43,102	46,955	8.9
Advertising	14,223	14,912	4.8
Topsoil, clay, sand, and fill dirt	21,971	20,991	-4.5
Trade stamp redemption centers	1,111	308	-72.3
Nurseries and landscaping	22,848	24,146	5.7
Vending machines	12,096	13,519	11.8
Importing and exporting	7,122	7,111	-0.2
Medical, dental, surgical, hospital supplies	20,206	20,515	1.5
Wholesale dealers	170,282	192,401	13.0
Schools and educational institutions	2,273	2,422	6.6
Office space and commercial rentals	416,687	456,382	9.5
Parking lots, boat docking, and storage	15,474	15,476	0.0
Utilities, electric or gas	207,605	228,607	10.1
Dual users of special fuels	436	540	23.8
Public works, government contractors	1,841	845	-54.1
Flea market vendors	3,880	4,400	13.4
Carnival concessions	306	270	-11.8
Other professional services	10,816	3,394	-68.6
Other personal services	10,864	8,609	-20.8
Other industrial services	4,112	3,933	-4.3
Commercial fisherman	78	92	18.1
Miscellaneous	87,525	111,743	27.7

Source: State of Florida, Department of Revenue, unpublished data.

Florida Statistical Abstract 1991

Table 23.45. STATE GOVERNMENT: TAX COLLECTIONS BY OR WITHIN COUNTIES BY TYPE
OF TAX COLLECTED IN THE STATE AND COUNTIES OF FLORIDA, FISCAL YEAR 1989-90

(rounded to thousands of dollars)

County	Total 1/	Sales and use taxes	Motor vehicle licenses	Pari-mutuel wagering taxes	Docu-mentary stamp tax
Florida	9,044,336	8,153,937	351,356	109,552	429,491
Alachua	92,403	85,673	3,829	0	2,901
Baker	4,370	3,587	571	0	212
Bay	77,424	71,746	3,004	0	2,674
Bradford	7,617	6,816	628	0	173
Brevard	220,075	198,818	9,622	368	11,267
Broward	906,983	812,457	28,947	18,765	46,814
Calhoun	2,731	2,403	244	0	84
Charlotte	62,191	53,764	3,052	0	5,375
Citrus	37,629	33,019	2,368	0	2,242
Clay	49,269	44,711	2,510	0	2,048
Collier	144,910	124,861	4,513	0	15,536
Columbia	20,888	19,163	1,135	0	590
Dade	1,232,661	1,108,587	49,352	21,204	53,518
De Soto	8,281	7,188	647	0	446
Dixie	2,399	1,999	282	0	118
Duval	444,424	405,784	17,870	3,325	17,445
Escambia	145,664	132,109	6,053	3,299	4,203
Flagler	11,912	9,635	893	0	1,384
Franklin	2,777	2,287	183	0	307
Gadsden	10,437	9,209	722	216	290
Gilchrist	1,856	1,364	341	0	151
Glades	1,815	1,527	136	0	152
Gulf	5,140	4,694	292	0	154
Hamilton	6,543	6,206	214	0	123
Hardee	7,344	6,242	620	0	482
Hendry	10,605	9,428	914	0	263
Hernando	38,886	34,035	2,362	0	2,489
Highlands	31,769	28,092	1,870	0	1,807
Hillsborough	616,239	557,046	23,918	10,359	24,916
Holmes	3,224	2,786	339	0	99
Indian River	54,428	47,148	2,471	0	4,809
Jackson	18,828	13,905	952	3,274	697
Jefferson	4,038	2,038	267	1,567	166
Lafayette	859	669	132	0	58
Lake	73,902	65,577	4,307	0	4,018
Lee	269,256	236,256	9,314	6,093	17,593
Leon	117,632	107,986	4,354	0	5,292

See footnote at end of table.   Continued . . .

Florida Statistical Abstract 1991

Table 23.45. STATE GOVERNMENT: TAX COLLECTIONS BY OR WITHIN COUNTIES BY TYPE
OF TAX COLLECTED IN THE STATE AND COUNTIES OF FLORIDA, FISCAL YEAR 1989-90
(Continued)

(rounded to thousands of dollars)

County	Total 1/	Sales and use taxes	Motor vehicle licenses	Pari-mutuel wagering taxes	Docu-mentary stamp tax
Levy	8,382	7,173	700	0	509
Liberty	974	764	164	0	46
Madison	3,715	3,193	374	0	148
Manatee	124,125	111,374	6,868	0	5,883
Marion	109,063	99,017	5,256	422	4,368
Martin	81,568	71,648	3,017	0	6,903
Monroe	71,293	64,661	1,869	148	4,615
Nassau	20,833	18,691	1,019	0	1,123
Okaloosa	73,572	67,244	3,357	0	2,971
Okeechobee	13,854	12,299	917	0	638
Orange	769,947	718,829	22,005	0	29,113
Osceola	83,516	75,178	3,285	0	5,053
Palm Beach	677,860	597,917	21,998	11,459	46,486
Pasco	111,925	99,491	6,609	0	5,825
Pinellas	524,487	471,859	19,929	7,944	24,755
Polk	247,315	220,413	11,836	0	15,066
Putnam	24,278	22,126	1,465	0	687
St. Johns	51,031	43,540	2,011	2,276	3,204
St. Lucie	80,203	69,502	3,677	776	6,248
Santa Rosa	21,435	18,337	1,682	0	1,416
Sarasota	205,456	181,141	7,413	3,584	13,318
Seminole	181,432	155,994	6,991	7,583	10,864
Sumter	10,471	9,054	898	0	519
Suwannee	9,961	8,657	797	0	507
Taylor	9,562	8,931	498	0	133
Union	2,276	1,721	477	0	78
Volusia	206,778	190,381	8,399	5,438	2,560
Wakulla	2,863	2,342	325	0	196
Walton	12,920	11,438	525	0	957
Washington	4,485	2,549	338	1,453	145
Suspense	0	0	0	0	0
Other	555,150	529,661	21,228	0	4,261
Refunds	-3,796	0	-3,796	0	0

1/ Does not include gasoline taxes; see Table 23.47 for gasoline tax collections.

Source: Columns 2, 5, State of Florida, Department of Revenue, unpublished data;
Column 3, State of Florida, Department of Highway Safety and Motor Vehicles,
Division of Motor Vehicles, *Tags and Revenue, July 1, 1988-June 30, 1990*; Column 4,
State of Florida, Department of Business Regulation, Division of Pari-Mutuel
Wagering, *59th Annual Report*, Fiscal Year Ending June 30, 1990.

Florida Statistical Abstract 1991

Table 23.46. STATE GOVERNMENT: GASOLINE AND GASOHOL TAX COLLECTIONS IN FLORIDA
      FISCAL YEARS 1963-64 THROUGH 1989-90

Fiscal year	Gallons sold	Tax rate (cents)	Tax collected 1/ (dollars)
		Gasoline	
1963-64	2,032,053,873.3	7	142,243,771.13
1964-65	2,158,362,499.2	7	151,085,374.93
1965-66	2,293,644,569.4	7	160,555,119.86
1966-67	2,426,636,427.0	7	169,864,549.90
1967-68	2,597,662,590.4	7	181,836,381.33
1968-69	2,821,029,238.4	7	197,472,046.70
1969-70	3,054,891,901.3	7	213,842,433.12
1970-71	3,341,148,943.8	7	233,880,426.09
1971-72	3,685,131,310.5	7/8	291,484,318.30
1972-73	4,080,699,270.9	8	326,454,941.67
1973-74	4,157,754,572.7	8	332,617,165.82
1974-75	4,243,123,105.1	8	339,449,848.41
1975-76	4,326,195,422.0	8	346,095,633.76
1976-77	4,483,397,014.2	8	358,671,761.14
1977-78	4,721,812,693.4	8	377,745,015.47
1978-79	4,961,448,003.1	8	396,915,840.25
1979-80	4,765,935,970.1	8	381,274,877.61
1980-81	4,681,857,035.4	8	374,548,562.90
1981-82	4,746,090,470.3	8	379,687,237.63
1982-83	4,686,388,610.8	5.7/8/9.7	387,286,074.47
1983-84	4,709,246,332.0	5.7/8/9.7	455,678,899.26
1984-85	4,739,366,278.0	5.7/9.7	458,188,999.77
1985-86	5,003,004,954.0	5.7/9.7	483,953,518.77
1986-87	5,493,474,844.7	5.7/9.7	484,754,881.20
1987-88	5,869,584,946.8	5.7/9.7	569,328,353.84
1988-89	5,995,884,170.5	5.7/9.7	581,596,538.65
1989-90	6,087,306,071.0	5.7/9.7	590,082,229.69
		Gasohol	
1980-81	40,041,320.0	3	1,201,239.60
1981-82	70,917,324.0	3	2,127,519.72
1982-83	174,716,609.0	3	5,241,498.27
1983-84	450,407,246.3	3/5.7	24,795,573.66
1984-85	580,254,644.0	5.7	32,540,874.16
1985-86	502,585,415.4	5.7/7.7	37,559,028.18
1986-87	216,061,242.3	7.7	16,636,263.27
1987-88	90,593,367.2	7.7/9.7	8,494,772.51
1988-89	83,299,691.4	9.7	8,081,088.78
1989-90	72,191,842.3	9.7	7,027,562.96

1/ Includes collection fees.
Source: State of Florida, Department of Revenue, unpublished data.

Florida Statistical Abstract 1991

Table 23.48. STATE GOVERNMENT: DISTRIBUTION OF TAXES AND OTHER FUNDS TO COUNTIES
 BY MAJOR SOURCE IN THE STATE AND COUNTIES OF FLORIDA, FISCAL YEAR 1989-90

(rounded to thousands of dollars)

County	Total 1/	2 cents gas and special fuel tax to State Board of Admin- istration for county road bonds	1/2 cent sales tax	Gasoline and special fuel	Mosquito control state matching	Revenue sharing tax	Insur- ance agents and solici- tors county license trust fund	Bever- age li- censes
Florida	973,849	191,435	450,102	56,412	2,768	235,183	1,912	4,745
Alachua	11,977	2,891	4,635	852	0	3,065	21	67
Baker	1,919	699	246	206	25	293	2	2
Bay	9,529	2,218	3,813	654	63	2,250	17	68
Bradford	1,914	530	394	156	26	357	2	3
Brevard	23,759	5,311	9,968	1,565	107	6,154	44	163
Broward	70,515	14,274	32,832	4,206	51	17,995	201	510
Calhoun	1,568	605	159	178	0	176	3	1
Charlotte	9,112	1,694	4,299	499	72	2,057	10	35
Citrus	6,738	1,397	2,604	412	49	1,795	8	26
Clay	8,050	1,572	3,467	463	0	2,076	7	18
Collier	18,151	3,244	9,702	956	150	3,406	32	79
Columbia	4,510	1,360	1,396	401	34	860	4	9
Dade	127,529	21,560	63,156	6,353	80	35,045	230	658
De Soto	2,338	787	470	232	0	398	3	3
Dixie	1,739	752	148	221	0	168	2	2
Duval	60,667	9,120	33,967	2,688	128	13,987	119	212
Escambia	20,880	3,752	9,432	1,106	28	5,781	37	106
Flagler	2,438	668	658	197	39	419	3	7
Franklin	1,699	731	147	216	17	135	2	5
Gadsden	3,026	932	644	274	23	695	4	7
Gilchrist	1,145	364	106	107	0	118	1	1
Glades	1,860	890	103	262	17	137	1	2
Gulf	1,836	659	286	194	34	212	2	2
Hamilton	2,127	844	383	249	0	199	2	3
Hardee	2,222	779	377	230	4	383	2	1
Hendry	3,224	1,290	586	380	27	436	2	4
Hernando	6,819	1,312	2,811	386	42	1,799	9	15
Highlands	5,827	1,690	1,910	498	0	1,263	7	13
Hillsborough	66,735	10,636	34,798	3,134	68	17,218	154	281
Holmes	1,811	637	232	188	17	287	2	1
Indian River	7,319	1,488	3,086	438	61	1,752	14	32
Jackson	4,081	1,593	850	469	0	711	5	6
Jefferson	1,902	812	169	239	19	212	2	2
Lafayette	1,242	499	68	147	0	79	1	A/
Lake	10,122	2,624	3,711	773	43	2,456	17	52
Lee	28,511	4,420	15,261	1,303	150	6,689	57	151

See footnotes at end of table.   Continued . . .

Florida Statistical Abstract 1991

Table 23.48. STATE GOVERNMENT: DISTRIBUTION OF TAXES AND OTHER FUNDS TO COUNTIES
BY MAJOR SOURCE IN THE STATE AND COUNTIES OF FLORIDA, FISCAL YEAR 1989-90
(Continued)

(rounded to thousands of dollars)

County	Total 1/	2 cents gas and special fuel tax to State Board of Administration for county road bonds	1/2 cent sales tax	Gasoline and special fuel	Mosquito control state matching	Revenue sharing tax	Insurance agents and solicitors county license trust fund	Beverage licenses
Leon	12,309	2,814	5,127	829	41	2,960	35	58
Levy	3,026	1,296	455	382	29	407	3	8
Liberty	1,564	748	64	220	0	83	2	Δ/
Madison	2,404	1,095	249	323	19	269	3	1
Manatee	15,476	2,808	7,406	827	60	3,822	26	81
Marion	16,027	3,787	6,848	1,116	0	3,744	24	62
Martin	10,478	1,610	5,624	474	56	2,212	16	39
Monroe	9,724	2,511	4,049	740	150	1,736	7	85
Nassau	4,179	1,191	1,270	351	33	873	5	9
Okaloosa	10,457	2,393	4,051	705	29	2,748	15	69
Okeechobee	3,475	1,145	948	337	0	591	3	5
Orange	72,230	8,972	44,300	2,644	93	15,364	135	277
Osceola	10,028	2,440	4,414	719	30	1,939	8	31
Palm Beach	62,237	10,480	31,839	3,088	61	15,765	153	404
Pasco	18,215	3,222	7,918	949	63	5,510	34	73
Pinellas	47,799	8,896	21,968	2,622	90	13,253	160	363
Polk	30,552	6,723	13,533	1,981	60	7,639	49	119
Putnam	5,027	1,380	1,587	407	20	1,165	5	16
St. Johns	7,604	1,699	3,162	501	61	1,689	9	37
St. Lucie	9,105	2,104	3,564	620	90	2,224	13	43
Santa Rosa	6,339	1,765	1,353	520	24	1,257	7	4
Sarasota	22,656	3,273	12,056	964	81	5,660	56	120
Seminole	18,132	2,917	8,853	860	0	4,910	45	100
Sumter	3,314	1,392	530	410	0	529	3	4
Suwannee	2,912	1,067	561	314	33	485	4	1
Taylor	2,870	1,169	535	344	22	347	2	4
Union	1,255	385	163	113	21	125	2	1
Volusia	22,420	4,836	9,597	1,425	143	5,746	52	175
Wakulla	1,830	655	228	193	27	276	2	2
Walton	3,534	1,330	780	392	40	535	3	8
Washington	1,829	699	200	206	16	257	2	1

Δ/ Less than $500.
1/ State total includes $29,915,500 pari-mutuel wagering funds. All county totals
include $446,500 pari-mutuel wagering funds. Totals also include the following
distribution from gas and oil production taxes: Florida, $1,376,606; Collier County,
$135,082; Escambia County, $191,207; Hendry County, $53,758; Lee County, $33,562;
and Santa Rosa County, $962,998.
Source: State of Florida, *Annual Report of the Comptroller, Fiscal Year 1989-90.*

Table 23.49. STATE GOVERNMENT: DISTRIBUTION FROM THE GENERAL REVENUE AND
   TRUST FUNDS TO SCHOOL DISTRICTS IN THE STATE AND COUNTIES OF FLORIDA
   FISCAL YEAR 1989-90

(rounded to thousands of dollars)

County	Total disburse- ments	Distribution from--	
		General reve- nue funds	Trust funds
Florida	6,413,704	4,616,449	1,797,255
Alachua	87,690	65,170	22,520
Baker	16,929	12,803	4,126
Bay	69,536	52,521	17,015
Bradford	16,482	12,290	4,192
Brevard	146,943	109,987	36,956
Broward	450,516	331,719	118,798
Calhoun	8,934	6,374	2,560
Charlotte	26,394	18,646	7,748
Citrus	31,746	23,429	8,317
Clay	67,219	52,409	14,811
Collier	34,132	16,992	17,140
Columbia	31,307	21,831	9,476
Dade	1,062,536	793,851	268,685
De Soto	14,937	11,218	3,719
Dixie	7,422	5,346	2,076
Duval	337,933	258,285	79,648
Escambia	157,522	118,382	39,140
Flagler	9,184	6,431	2,753
Franklin	5,294	3,609	1,686
Gadsden	36,632	24,840	11,792
Gilchrist	7,079	5,335	1,745
Glades	3,184	1,592	1,591
Gulf	7,546	5,475	2,070
Hamilton	8,431	5,896	2,536
Hardee	18,254	12,524	5,730
Hendry	19,184	13,623	5,561
Hernando	37,148	26,743	10,405
Highlands	29,273	21,387	7,886
Hillsborough	386,075	291,244	94,831
Holmes	14,184	9,554	4,630
Indian River	23,390	16,038	7,352
Jackson	31,135	23,376	7,759
Jefferson	10,273	6,434	3,839
Lafayette	4,138	3,056	1,082
Lake	67,837	50,446	17,392
Lee	88,453	64,408	24,045
Leon	97,100	73,874	23,226

Continued . . .

Table 23.49. STATE GOVERNMENT: DISTRIBUTION FROM THE GENERAL REVENUE AND
   TRUST FUNDS TO SCHOOL DISTRICTS IN THE STATE AND COUNTIES OF FLORIDA
   FISCAL YEAR 1989-90 (Continued)

(rounded to thousands of dollars)

County	Total disburse- ments	Distribution from--	
		General reve- nue funds	Trust funds
Levy	18,856	13,915	4,940
Liberty	4,574	3,348	1,226
Madison	12,983	9,280	3,704
Manatee	66,457	48,628	17,828
Marion	93,673	69,776	23,897
Martin	17,351	10,760	6,591
Monroe	31,817	20,032	11,786
Nassau	7,180	2,813	4,366
Okaloosa	80,430	61,296	19,133
Okeechobee	26,518	14,608	11,910
Orange	274,647	203,122	71,525
Osceola	49,374	37,805	11,569
Palm Beach	186,471	125,813	60,658
Pasco	99,626	74,520	25,106
Pinellas	248,987	180,452	68,535
Polk	211,248	158,081	53,168
Putnam	38,919	27,851	11,068
St. Johns	49,101	36,521	12,580
St. Lucie	60,468	41,638	18,830
Santa Rosa	129,716	102,211	27,505
Sarasota	35,928	26,898	9,030
Seminole	52,817	38,275	14,542
Sumter	19,189	14,026	5,163
Suwannee	24,318	15,538	8,780
Taylor	13,635	9,903	3,732
Union	8,191	5,679	2,512
Volusia	126,611	93,876	32,735
Wakulla	13,063	9,352	3,711
Walton	10,853	7,876	2,977
Washington	18,609	13,257	5,352
Other	910,120	562,161	347,959

   Source: State of Florida, *Annual Report of the Comptroller, Fiscal Year 1989-90.*
Data from Department of Education.

Florida Statistical Abstract 1991

Table 23.50. STATE GOVERNMENT: LOTTERY SALES AND APPROPRIATIONS FOR EDUCATION IN
THE COUNTIES OF FLORIDA, FISCAL YEARS 1988-89 AND 1989-90

(rounded to thousands of dollars)

County and item	Lottery sales			Appropriations for education 1/		
	Total to date	1988-89	1989-90 A/	Total to date	1988-89	1989-90 A/
Florida	5,832,124	1,991,564	2,280,450	2,541,375	327,665	1,151,855
Alachua	53,787	18,682	21,439	21,134	3,309	8,503
Baker	5,530	1,930	2,349	3,810	594	1,513
Bay	67,218	22,412	27,150	18,538	2,860	7,552
Bradford	7,373	2,724	2,613	3,809	626	1,535
Brevard	178,992	60,890	69,571	43,641	6,513	17,680
Broward	623,378	211,247	239,546	138,939	20,650	53,564
Calhoun	2,912	1,018	1,100	2,102	341	851
Charlotte	40,566	13,275	16,368	10,058	1,454	4,079
Citrus	38,435	13,055	14,647	10,080	1,512	4,065
Clay	34,431	12,215	13,394	16,148	2,518	6,528
Collier	58,555	19,346	22,528	17,384	2,617	7,005
Columbia	18,752	6,523	7,737	6,845	1,082	2,802
Dade	1,048,314	365,112	399,739	274,925	41,094	111,324
De Soto	8,377	2,967	3,224	3,773	609	1,500
Dixie	2,983	1,120	1,031	1,762	303	691
Duval	279,045	96,126	109,316	88,298	14,012	35,409
Escambia	173,906	58,944	72,879	37,183	5,732	14,759
Flagler	11,499	3,898	4,798	3,851	518	1,654
Franklin	3,863	1,373	1,502	1,484	281	581
Gadsden	16,658	5,615	6,969	7,684	1,233	3,097
Gilchrist	1,855	667	736	1,708	301	674
Glades	2,542	788	993	987	194	387
Gulf	4,433	1,564	1,624	2,210	370	891
Hamilton	33,755	12,190	17,272	2,258	383	908
Hardee	5,787	1,985	2,210	4,192	641	1,679
Hendry	11,425	3,929	4,278	5,070	798	2,052
Hernando	40,389	13,667	16,282	10,388	1,464	4,243
Highlands	24,207	8,143	9,696	7,749	1,194	3,099
Hillsborough	339,221	114,807	127,853	105,653	16,703	42,230
Holmes	13,385	4,907	5,857	2,976	485	1,196
Indian River	37,133	12,480	14,218	9,319	1,444	3,743
Jackson	43,675	15,407	20,425	6,948	1,084	2,783
Jefferson	18,085	6,833	8,749	2,176	358	882
Lafayette	988	368	419	1,077	197	414
Lake	61,957	21,322	25,240	17,758	2,673	7,333
Lee	132,352	44,204	50,577	34,823	5,416	14,047

See footnotes at end of table.   Continued . . .

Florida Statistical Abstract 1991

Table 23.50.   STATE GOVERNMENT: LOTTERY SALES AND APPROPRIATIONS FOR EDUCATION IN
THE COUNTIES OF FLORIDA, FISCAL YEARS 1988-89 AND 1989-90 (Continued)

(rounded to thousands of dollars)

County and item	Lottery sales			Appropriations for education 1/		
	Total to date	1988-89	1989-90 A/	Total to date	1988-89	1989-90 A/
Leon	64,268	22,166	26,264	24,580	3,724	9,921
Levy	10,978	3,845	4,192	4,315	690	1,780
Liberty	1,567	542	599	1,234	259	472
Madison	10,373	3,741	4,689	2,991	481	1,201
Manatee	76,814	25,971	30,649	21,177	3,411	8,459
Marion	83,117	28,476	31,940	24,211	3,552	9,877
Martin	40,573	14,189	16,741	10,472	1,667	4,279
Monroe	39,624	13,286	15,081	7,486	1,232	3,011
Nassau	57,153	20,684	26,237	7,219	1,107	2,959
Okaloosa	61,313	20,304	24,152	20,173	3,149	8,193
Okeechobee	13,764	4,784	4,915	4,996	782	2,002
Orange	298,206	98,987	118,097	85,565	12,609	34,807
Osceola	51,346	16,845	20,916	13,982	1,946	5,560
Palm Beach	377,270	128,804	147,325	90,301	13,732	36,915
Pasco	114,414	38,989	43,436	27,803	4,113	11,407
Pinellas	367,827	123,654	139,521	81,341	12,697	32,451
Polk	167,687	58,502	63,802	53,364	8,205	21,460
Putnam	26,513	9,500	10,185	10,104	1,530	4,069
St. Johns	29,925	10,288	11,941	11,068	1,705	4,483
St. Lucie	62,989	21,237	24,776	17,736	2,512	7,200
Santa Rosa	26,280	8,855	10,282	12,076	1,853	4,878
Sarasota	104,717	35,384	40,059	26,561	3,972	10,651
Seminole	94,161	31,359	36,772	36,993	5,601	14,917
Sumter	11,088	3,740	4,750	4,625	718	1,871
Suwannee	7,887	2,776	3,313	4,846	741	1,960
Taylor	6,345	2,214	2,506	3,432	536	1,405
Union	2,705	1,003	1,040	1,804	305	707
Volusia	156,100	52,712	62,452	37,450	5,656	14,978
Wakulla	4,254	1,416	1,768	2,823	440	1,144
Walton	12,488	4,088	5,709	3,950	646	1,666
Washington	4,616	1,491	2,013	3,347	548	1,330
K-12, total	(X)	(X)	(X)	1,713,303	258,597	678,146
Community colleges	(X)	(X)	(X)	218,092	38,092	79,728
Universities	(X)	(X)	(X)	323,725	24,807	141,354
Other programs	(X)	(X)	(X)	62,508	6,169	39,763
Fixed capital outlay	(X)	(X)	(X)	223,746	0	212,864

K-12 Kindergarten through 12th grade.
(X) Not applicable.
A/ Includes appropriation from special session totaling $155,900,030.
1/ Amounts are distributed as of June 30 each year.
Source: State of Florida, Department of the Lottery, *Lottery Facts: Three Years*.

Florida Statistical Abstract 1991

Table 23.51. STATE GOVERNMENT: FUNDS DISTRIBUTED TO SELECTED CITIES BY SOURCE
IN FLORIDA, FISCAL YEAR 1989-90

(rounded to thousands of dollars)

City	Total	1/2¢ sales tax	Municipal financial assistance trust fund	Revenue sharing trust fund	Beverage licenses	Mobile home licenses	Municipal firefighters' pension fund	Municipal police officers' retirement fund
Florida 1/	484,702	233,216	25,603	208,834	5,166	2,840	3,254	5,789
Jacksonville	12,506	318	1,349	7,694	271	371	993	1,510
Miami	26,698	15,117	560	10,741	250	31	0	0
Tampa	24,293	13,862	1,390	8,681	238	122	0	0
St. Petersburg	16,595	8,379	792	7,217	114	93	0	0
Hialeah	12,521	6,831	254	5,338	85	14	0	0
Orlando	19,559	12,928	1,137	5,297	136	61	0	0
Ft. Lauderdale	10,412	5,787	293	4,078	224	30	0	0
Tallahassee	9,185	4,587	305	3,896	77	46	272	0
Hollywood	8,898	4,825	245	3,732	79	17	0	0
Clearwater	6,534	3,429	325	2,605	98	77	0	0
Miami Beach	6,994	4,009	148	2,740	97	0	0	0
Gainesville	5,773	2,611	266	2,809	56	33	0	0
Coral Springs	4,611	2,599	135	1,846	31	0	0	0
Cape Coral	5,212	3,165	439	1,578	30	A/	0	0
Pompano Beach	4,811	2,721	138	1,875	58	19	0	0
Lakeland	5,013	2,570	379	1,980	44	40	0	0
West Palm Beach	5,982	3,507	262	2,113	71	29	0	0
Plantation	4,253	2,401	124	1,689	31	8	0	0
Largo	4,607	2,217	211	1,939	34	207	0	0
Pembroke Pines	3,973	2,139	111	1,680	18	24	0	0
Sunrise	3,926	2,147	110	1,645	24	A/	0	0
Palm Bay	3,212	1,672	173	1,339	19	8	0	0
Daytona Beach	4,761	2,254	272	1,789	97	35	133	181
Boca Raton	4,559	2,830	212	1,456	59	2	0	0
Melbourne	4,128	1,956	198	1,660	52	66	0	197
Pensacola	4,864	2,260	507	2,024	62	11	0	0
Port St. Lucie	2,590	1,368	160	1,030	13	19	0	0
Sarasota	5,401	2,702	392	1,453	62	13	287	493
North Miami	3,365	1,769	65	1,310	20	3	42	157
Lauderhill	3,066	1,702	86	1,262	16	0	0	0
Davie	2,869	1,480	76	1,050	30	33	76	123
Delray Beach	3,569	2,157	162	1,212	37	1	0	0
Deerfield Beach	3,282	1,842	95	1,300	34	12	0	0
Boynton Beach	4,111	2,195	165	1,325	40	21	142	224
Ft. Myers	4,732	2,454	332	1,317	42	5	155	426

A/ Less than $500.
1/ Includes amounts for municipalities not shown separately.
Note: Data are reported for the 35 most populous cities in Florida in 1990.
Cities are listed by population rank.

Source: State of Florida, *Annual Report of the Comptroller, Fiscal Year 1989-90.*

Florida Statistical Abstract 1991

Table 23.53. ALCOHOLIC BEVERAGE LICENSES: NUMBER OF LICENSES ISSUED BY THE STATE DIVISION OF BEVERAGES BY TYPE OF LICENSE IN THE STATE AND COUNTIES OF FLORIDA LICENSE YEAR JULY 1, 1989 THROUGH JUNE 30, 1990

County	Total	1-APS	1-COP	2-APS	2-COP	3-PS	COP	3M	MFG	KLD/IMP BSA	DST	11-C	RT
Florida	38,052	3,040	1,300	13,308	9,728	1,212	7,334	118	26	95	154	1,707	30
Alachua	499	23	35	198	119	7	101	0	2	0	2	12	0
Baker	58	11	4	28	7	2	5	0	0	0	0	1	0
Bay	610	28	41	187	191	7	135	4	0	0	3	14	0
Bradford	72	3	6	35	15	1	9	0	0	0	0	3	0
Brevard	1,196	40	42	425	332	34	237	1	0	2	3	79	1
Broward	3,601	179	60	1,290	1,044	113	781	21	0	4	17	88	4
Calhoun	34	1	8	16	5	4	0	0	0	0	0	0	0
Charlotte	284	4	5	103	67	11	65	0	0	0	0	29	0
Citrus	281	8	12	103	77	6	45	0	0	0	0	30	0
Clay	230	17	10	98	44	11	31	0	0	0	0	18	1
Collier	607	19	15	191	157	21	135	1	0	0	2	66	0
Columbia	158	16	13	71	22	1	25	0	0	0	3	7	0
Dade	5,229	532	85	1,708	1,631	209	867	21	2	38	30	103	3
De Soto	65	1	4	29	13	2	11	0	0	0	0	5	0
Dixie	46	2	2	18	15	1	8	0	0	0	0	0	0
Duval	1,856	143	120	796	399	10	300	3	2	5	10	67	1
Escambia	791	83	37	287	167	14	164	1	1	4	2	30	1
Flagler	123	3	6	37	44	2	23	0	0	0	0	8	0
Franklin	65	3	3	20	15	0	23	0	0	0	0	1	0
Gadsden	162	23	37	53	26	7	14	0	0	0	0	1	1
Gilchrist	29	4	0	14	3	1	7	0	0	0	0	0	0
Glades	40	2	4	13	12	0	9	0	0	0	0	0	0
Gulf	48	8	0	14	12	1	11	0	0	0	0	2	0
Hamilton	59	8	17	28	1	4	1	0	0	0	0	0	0
Hardee	49	23	7	9	10	0	0	0	0	0	0	0	0
Hendry	99	3	3	48	28	0	12	0	0	0	0	5	0
Hernando	236	18	9	79	68	12	31	0	0	0	0	19	0
Highlands	229	32	12	73	47	7	32	0	0	0	1	25	0
Hillsborough	2,044	428	48	553	397	70	424	3	4	21	9	84	3
Holmes	52	11	8	22	5	6	0	0	0	0	0	0	0
Indian River	286	22	5	106	55	8	58	0	0	0	0	32	0
Jackson	161	34	46	55	10	16	0	0	0	0	0	0	0
Jefferson	55	9	6	18	13	3	3	0	0	0	0	2	1
Lafayette	12	3	2	3	4	0	0	0	0	0	0	0	0
Lake	452	31	12	195	102	11	75	0	1	0	1	24	0
Lee	1,107	46	25	373	278	50	221	2	1	0	8	102	1
Leon	451	23	29	187	106	17	69	0	2	0	4	14	0
Levy	130	8	9	47	28	2	28	0	0	0	0	8	0
Liberty	16	10	6	0	0	0	0	0	0	0	0	0	0
Madison	58	30	12	13	3	0	0	0	0	0	0	0	0
Manatee	554	37	21	200	126	18	125	0	0	0	1	26	0

See footnotes at end of table.   Continued . . .

Table 23.53. ALCOHOLIC BEVERAGE LICENSES: NUMBER OF LICENSES ISSUED BY THE STATE DIVISION OF BEVERAGES BY TYPE OF LICENSE IN THE STATE AND COUNTIES OF FLORIDA LICENSE YEAR JULY 1, 1989 THROUGH JUNE 30, 1990 (Continued)

County	Total	1-APS	1-COP	2-APS	2-COP	3-PS	COP	3M	MFG	KLD/IMP BSA	DST	11-C	RT
Marion	592	27	26	264	155	17	76	0	0	1	3	22	1
Martin	405	21	9	134	123	15	60	1	0	0	0	42	0
Monroe	622	53	12	126	189	11	186	9	0	0	3	32	1
Nassau	155	29	5	56	27	1	28	1	0	0	0	8	0
Okaloosa	470	19	21	160	110	11	122	1	0	0	4	22	0
Okeechobee	138	25	4	46	37	3	16	0	0	0	0	7	0
Orange	1,897	92	44	714	509	43	388	23	1	6	6	71	0
Osceola	393	15	15	151	93	15	93	1	0	0	0	10	0
Palm Beach	2,580	159	51	859	615	108	616	7	2	7	11	143	2
Pasco	635	105	18	177	163	27	95	0	0	0	2	48	0
Pinellas	2,407	209	41	733	633	120	555	3	1	5	7	99	1
Polk	1,121	83	38	523	223	21	159	2	5	0	7	60	0
Putnam	195	15	12	82	38	3	35	0	0	0	0	10	0
St. Johns	372	20	18	115	97	5	73	0	0	1	1	41	1
St. Lucie	445	19	11	210	93	20	61	1	0	1	2	26	1
Santa Rosa	164	32	22	79	31	0	0	0	0	0	0	0	0
Sarasota	814	24	17	247	244	28	195	1	1	0	4	52	1
Seminole	699	32	14	257	185	33	135	0	0	0	3	37	3
Sumter	97	5	2	48	19	3	14	0	0	0	0	6	0
Suwannee	82	33	13	25	11	0	0	0	0	0	0	0	0
Taylor	91	8	11	36	13	0	18	0	0	0	0	5	0
Union	22	2	2	12	0	0	5	0	0	0	0	1	0
Volusia	1,238	41	41	417	357	32	280	10	0	0	4	54	2
Wakulla	60	9	10	15	14	2	10	0	0	0	0	0	0
Walton	171	14	9	59	46	5	29	1	1	0	1	6	0
Washington	53	20	8	20	5	0	0	0	0	0	0	0	0

1/ Types of licenses:
1-APS: To sell only beer by the package.
1-COP: To sell only beer to consume on premises and by the package.
2-APS: To sell only beer and wine by the package.
2-COP: To sell only beer and wine to consume on premises and by the package.
3-PS: To sell all alcoholic beverages by the package.
COP: To sell all alcoholic beverages to consume on premises and by the package.
3M: Same as COP, except with more than 3 bars.
MFG: To manufacture wines, wines/cordials, malt beverages, or distilled spirits.
KLD/IMP BSA: To distribute all alcoholic beverages and/or to import and act as broker sales agent.
DST: To distribute only beer and wine or to distribute beverages of not more than 3.2 percent in "dry" counties.
11-C: To sell all alcoholic beverages in a club to members and guests.
RT: To sell all alcoholic beverages at a race track.

Source: State of Florida, Department of Business Regulation, Division of Beverages, *Number of Each Type of License, By County, Issued During License Year Beginning July 1, 1989, Ending June 30, 1990.*

Florida Statistical Abstract 1991

Table 23.54. PARI-MUTUEL WAGERING: PERFORMANCES, ATTENDANCE, AND REVENUE BY TYPE
OF EVENT IN FLORIDA, FISCAL YEARS 1986-87 THROUGH 1989-90

| | | Number of-- | | Pari-mutuel | Revenue |
| | | Perform- | Paid | handle | to state |
Item	Days	ances	attendance	(dollars)	(dollars)
All tracks and frontons					
1986-87	3,821	5,202	16,505,736	1,954,603,904	124,633,435
1987-88	4,963	6,833	16,708,292	2,006,768,479	125,376,775
1988-89	5,170	7,160	15,719,962	1,850,283,419	113,359,942
1989-90	4,992	6,931	15,401,516	1,770,122,929	109,544,230
Thoroughbred tracks					
1986-87	374	374	2,374,923	467,150,509	12,575,762
1987-88	377	377	2,293,336	462,843,392	12,417,864
1988-89	374	374	2,268,652	446,336,224	11,822,798
1989-90	389	389	2,290,363	444,608,090	10,137,443
Harness tracks					
1986-87	120	120	505,697	67,290,552	1,305,100
1987-88	170	170	638,177	85,095,287	1,656,475
1988-89	165	168	619,393	74,142,828	1,287,792
1989-90	150	153	565,216	66,660,012	937,942
Quarter horse tracks					
1986-87	46	46	87,400	8,865,521	63,061
1987-88	20	20	36,273	3,697,152	26,990
1988-89	0	0	0	0	0
1989-90	0	0	0	0	0
Greyhound tracks					
1986-87	1,925	2,719	8,794,823	996,674,064	80,200,163
1987-88	2,522	3,568	8,920,354	1,024,810,413	81,768,779
1988-89	2,757	3,903	9,092,595	1,002,169,566	78,758,074
1989-90	2,709	3,853	8,679,067	933,781,921	76,316,509
Jai alai frontons					
1986-87	1,356	1,943	4,742,893	414,623,258	30,489,349
1987-88	1,874	2,698	4,820,152	430,322,235	29,506,667
1988-89	1,874	2,715	3,739,322	327,634,801	21,491,278
1989-90	1,744	2,536	3,866,870	325,072,906	22,152,336

Note: These data represent the distribution of revenue derived from pari-mutuel
performances and do not represent the total revenue received by the Division of
Pari-Mutuel Wagering. Excluded are such items as licenses, fees, escheated tickets,
charity, scholarship performances, and other miscellaneous items.

Source: State of Florida, Department of Business Regulation, Division of Pari-
Mutuel Wagering, *59th Annual Report*, Fiscal Year Ending June 30, 1990.

Table 23.58. STATE GOVERNMENT RETIREMENT SYSTEMS: MEMBERSHIP, PAYROLL
   CONTRIBUTIONS, ANNUITANTS, AND BENEFITS IN FLORIDA, JUNE 30, 1990

System	Active member-ship	Annual payroll ($1,000)	Accu-mulated contri-butions ($1,000)	Annu-itants	Annual benefits Total paid ($1,000)	Average (dol-lars)
Total	529,872	11,997,274	481,098	107,259	744,844	(X)
Average salary (dollars)	(X)	22,642	(X)	(X)	6,944	6,944
Florida retirement system	525,879	11,837,572	294,128	92,259	657,086	(X)
Regular members	479,500	10,560,313	267,172	87,693	608,387	6,938
Senior management members	578	36,218	1,406	36	974	27,067
Special risk members	43,738	1,137,910	17,589	3,939	35,580	9,033
Administrative support	245	7,941	356	21	350	16,669
Elected state officer class members	1,818	95,190	7,605	570	11,795	20,694
Teachers retirement system	3,802	155,478	184,400	8,336	64,474	7,734
Survivors' benefits	(X)	(X)	(X)	1,165	2,212	1,899
State and county officers and employees retirement system	191	4,224	2,570	5,346	19,039	3,561
Highway patrol pension trust fund	0	0	0	118	1,330	11,274
Judicial retirement system	0	0	0	35	703	20,073

(X) Not applicable.

Table 23.59. STATE GOVERNMENT RETIREMENT SYSTEMS: ANNUITANTS AND BENEFITS BY AGE
   OF RETIREMENT IN FLORIDA, JUNE 30, 1990

Retirement age	Retirees Number	Annualized benefits (dollars)	Joint annuitants Number	Annualized benefits (dollars)
Total	95,751	687,803,266	10,343	54,829,153
Under age 50	2,512	12,233,604	640	3,090,901
50-54	6,714	49,984,010	1,080	5,406,663
55-59	18,751	145,959,990	2,096	11,725,954
60-64	39,385	283,148,511	3,406	18,992,116
65-69	23,712	164,899,478	2,367	11,786,972
70-74	3,898	27,319,911	574	3,103,569
75-79	655	3,701,498	124	502,262
Age 80 and over	124	556,264	56	220,715

Note: Annuitants include all retired persons or survivors of retired persons who
are receiving monthly benefits. Does not include 1,165 persons receiving monthly
benefits from the survivors' benefit trust fund or the 538 annuitants under various
general revenue pensions.

Source for Tables 23.58 and 23.59: State of Florida, Department of Administration, Division of Retirement, *Florida Retirement System: July 1, 1989-June 30, 1990
Annual Report*.

Table 23.60. STATE RETIREMENT SYSTEM: REVENUE, EXPENDITURE, AND BALANCES OF THE
FLORIDA RETIREMENT SYSTEM, FISCAL YEARS 1988-89 AND 1989-90

Item	1988-89	1989-90
Revenue, total	2,857,689,184	3,537,044,173
Contributions	1,576,825,604	1,838,003,745
Investment earnings	1,114,881,773	1,267,846,598
Earnings from other trust funds 1/	454,679	470,165
Gain/loss on sale of investments	175,197,268	430,185,046
Other revenue and prior year adjustments	-9,670,140	538,619
Expenditure, total	755,621,745	803,694,993
Benefit payments	654,617,894	729,870,532
Refunds	2,306,815	2,519,783
Operating expenses	11,636,887	9,747,394
Contractural investment management commissions and fees	18,840,340	23,306,038
Interest expense for repurchase agreements	67,971,827	38,184,871
Transfers to other funds	2,503	0
Other expenses	245,479	66,375
Net addition to fund balance	2,102,067,439	2,733,349,180
Prior year fund balance	14,027,592,570	16,129,660,009
Year end fund balance (June 30)	16,129,660,009	18,863,009,189

1/ Includes social security, savings bonds, and medicare.

Table 23.61. STATE RETIREMENT SYSTEM: RETIREMENT TRUST FUND BALANCES, FISCAL
YEARS 1988-89 AND 1989-90

Trust fund	1988-89	1989-90
Total	16,151,406,537	18,900,872,243
Florida Retirement System	16,129,660,009	18,863,009,189
Health Insurance Subsidy	18,508,422	33,923,672
Institute of Food and Agricultural Sciences (IFAS) Supplemental Retirement Program	2,971,796	3,673,602
Optional Retirement Program	266,310	265,780

Source for Tables 23.60 and 23.61: State of Florida, Department of Administration, Division of Retirement, *Florida Retirement System: July 1, 1989-June 30, 1990 Annual Report*.

Florida Statistical Abstract 1991

Table 23.70. FEDERAL, STATE, AND LOCAL GOVERNMENT: AVERAGE MONTHLY REPORTING UNITS
EMPLOYMENT, AND PAYROLL COVERED BY UNEMPLOYMENT COMPENSATION LAW IN THE STATE
AND COUNTIES OF FLORIDA, 1990

County	Number of reporting units	Number of employees	Payroll ($1,000)	County	Number of reporting units	Number of employees	Payroll ($1,000)
			Federal, state, and local government (SIC codes 91-97)				
Florida	3,848	371,509	755,405	Lafayette	18	336	539
				Lake	63	2,976	4,887
Alachua	97	5,620	12,010	Lee	100	7,290	13,634
Baker	29	613	1,036	Leon	216	27,860	56,371
Bay	76	5,624	10,874	Levy	29	585	817
Bradford	32	1,688	2,856	Liberty	18	405	609
Brevard	89	13,163	28,102	Madison	27	642	1,010
Broward	137	29,667	66,250	Manatee	56	4,594	7,916
Calhoun	25	465	742	Marion	63	4,407	7,236
Charlotte	36	2,196	3,591	Martin	46	2,284	4,236
Citrus	35	1,349	2,111	Monroe	53	2,655	5,815
Clay	39	1,460	2,413	Nassau	28	1,415	3,722
Collier	49	3,197	6,361	Okaloosa	66	7,635	15,406
Columbia	51	1,083	1,770	Okeechobee	26	561	855
Dade	161	55,013	122,559	Orange	136	19,883	41,482
De Soto	28	863	1,320	Osceola	37	2,274	4,033
Dixie	27	607	973	Palm Beach	156	22,223	48,853
Duval	118	24,516	52,933	Pasco	45	3,871	6,364
Escambia	95	13,387	30,868	Pinellas	113	18,569	36,663
Flagler	25	470	774	Polk	97	10,196	18,890
Franklin	26	352	533	Putnam	39	1,774	3,036
Gadsden	49	1,350	2,126	St. Johns	46	1,821	3,089
Gilchrist	24	553	878	St. Lucie	60	3,414	5,992
Glades	17	178	264	Santa Rosa	40	1,361	2,531
Gulf	27	396	534	Sarasota	65	5,665	9,968
Hamilton	26	668	1,087	Seminole	50	4,153	7,708
Hardee	32	461	683	Sumter	32	940	1,457
Hendry	32	958	1,592	Suwannee	36	588	973
Hernando	32	1,904	3,465	Taylor	27	394	589
Highlands	42	1,478	2,369	Union	21	1,652	2,935
Hillsborough	130	21,800	44,971	Volusia	80	8,338	14,265
Holmes	27	531	775	Wakulla	23	277	389
Indian River	43	2,411	4,527	Walton	33	793	1,142
Jackson	55	2,227	3,868	Washington	29	325	454
Jefferson	26	415	592	Statewide 1/	137	2,690	5,732

1/ Reporting units without a fixed location within the state or of unknown county
location.
Note: For a list of two-, three-, and four-digit categories included, see Table
23.71.

Source: State of Florida, Department of Labor and Employment Security, Bureau of
Labor Market Information, "Employment, Wages, and Contributions Report" (ES-202),
unpublished data.

Table 23.71. FEDERAL, STATE, AND LOCAL GOVERNMENT: AVERAGE MONTHLY REPORTING UNITS
EMPLOYMENT, AND PAYROLL COVERED BY UNEMPLOYMENT COMPENSATION LAW BY LEVEL OF
GOVERNMENT AND BY ACTIVITY IN FLORIDA, 1990

SIC code	Activity	Number of reporting units	Number of employees	Payroll ($1,000)
	Federal government (SIC codes 91-97)			
91	Executive, legislative, and general government, except finance	17	1,200	1,422
92	Justice, public order, and safety	82	5,282	16,118
921	Courts	17	1,077	2,844
922	Public order and safety	65	4,205	13,274
9221	Police protection	25	969	3,344
9222	Legal counsel and prosecution	12	2,250	7,266
9223	Correctional institutions	5	969	2,620
9229	Public order and safety, NEC	22	15	45
93	Public finance, taxation, and monetary policy	53	5,283	14,688
94	Administration of human resource programs	85	2,664	6,826
941	Administration of educational programs	1	3	9
943	Administration of public health programs	27	157	456
944	Administration of social, human resource, and income maintenance programs	47	1,935	4,895
945	Administration of veterans' affairs, except health and insurance	9	568	1,466
95	Administration of environmental quality and housing programs	156	1,758	4,120
951	Administration of environmental quality programs	152	1,454	3,326
9511	Air and water resource and solid waste management	4	79	237
9512	Land, mineral, wildlife, and forest conservation	148	1,374	3,089
953	Administration of housing and urban development programs	4	303	795
96	Administration of economic programs	286	12,509	32,638
961	Administration of general economic programs	130	4,746	5,499
962	Regulation and administration of transportation programs	24	3,178	12,512
963	Regulation and administration of communications, electric, gas, and other utilities	3	46	148
964	Regulation of agricultural marketing and commodities	101	1,426	4,039
965	Regulation, licensing, and inspection of miscellaneous commercial sectors	26	426	1,191
966	Space research and technology	1	2,685	9,249
97	National security and international affairs	102	30,654	77,381
971	National security	94	30,460	76,814
972	International affairs	8	193	568

See footnote at end of table.   Continued . . .

Table 23.71. FEDERAL, STATE, AND LOCAL GOVERNMENT: AVERAGE MONTHLY REPORTING UNITS
EMPLOYMENT, AND PAYROLL COVERED BY UNEMPLOYMENT COMPENSATION LAW BY LEVEL OF
GOVERNMENT AND BY ACTIVITY IN FLORIDA, 1990 (Continued)

SIC code	Activity	Number of reporting units	Number of employees	Payroll ($1,000)
	State government (SIC codes 91-97)			
91	Executive, legislative, and general government, except finance	200	6,043	12,126
911	Executive offices	23	319	838
912	Legislative bodies	79	1,521	3,141
919	General government, NEC	97	4,202	8,148
92	Justice, public order, and safety	555	32,004	65,519
921	Courts	108	923	1,778
922	Public order and safety	447	31,081	63,741
9221	Police protection	110	3,126	7,717
9222	Legal counsel and prosecution	211	8,336	20,807
9223	Correctional institutions	103	19,349	34,644
9224	Fire protection	21	174	380
9229	Public order and safety, NEC	1	94	193
93	Public finance, taxation, and monetary policy	159	3,817	7,112
94	Administration of human resource programs	312	39,242	66,654
941	Administration of educational programs	23	2,005	3,963
943	Administration of public health programs	128	32,875	55,369
944	Administration of social, human resource, and income maintenance programs	145	4,223	7,083
945	Administration of veterans' affairs, except health and insurance	14	139	239
95	Administration of environmental quality and housing programs	281	4,022	8,414
951	Administration of environmental quality programs	274	3,833	7,998
9511	Air and water resource and solid waste management	27	1,305	2,929
9512	Land, mineral, wildlife, and forest conservation	247	2,528	5,069
953	Administration of housing and urban development programs	6	188	416
96	Administration of economic programs	644	12,538	21,074
961	Administration of general economic programs	19	362	692
962	Regulation and administration of transportation programs	164	6,100	9,525
963	Regulation and administration of communications, electric, gas, and other utilities	5	386	952
964	Regulation of agricultural marketing and commodities	236	2,429	4,273
965	Regulation, licensing, and inspection of miscellaneous commercial sectors	220	3,259	5,632
97	National security and international affairs	26	307	412

See footnote at end of table.   Continued . . .

Florida Statistical Abstract 1991

Table 23.71. FEDERAL, STATE, AND LOCAL GOVERNMENT: AVERAGE MONTHLY REPORTING UNITS EMPLOYMENT, AND PAYROLL COVERED BY UNEMPLOYMENT COMPENSATION LAW BY LEVEL OF GOVERNMENT AND BY ACTIVITY IN FLORIDA, 1990 (Continued)

SIC code	Activity	Number of reporting units	Number of employees	Payroll ($1,000)
	Local government (SIC codes 91-97)			
91	Executive, legislative, and general government, except finance	474	171,629	337,482
911	Executive offices	25	1,364	603
912	Legislative bodies	68	51,763	93,274
913	Executive and legislative offices combined	377	118,185	243,077
919	General government, NEC	4	316	528
92	Justice, public order, and safety	167	31,190	62,255
921	Courts	58	6,338	10,159
922	Public order and safety	109	24,851	52,095
9221	Police protection	65	23,216	48,639
9223	Correctional institutions	1	342	580
9224	Fire protection	42	1,293	2,876
93	Public finance, taxation, and monetary policy	132	5,262	9,330
94	Administration of human resource programs	4	189	350
943	Administration of public health programs	1	21	28
944	Administration of social, human resource, and income maintenance programs	2	164	317
945	Administration of veterans' affairs, except health and insurance	1	3	6
95	Administration of environmental quality and housing programs	99	3,920	8,640
951	Administration of environmental quality programs	55	3,278	7,428
9511	Air and water resource and solid waste management	45	3,244	7,387
9512	Land, mineral, wildlife, and forest conservation	10	33	42
953	Administration of housing and urban development programs	44	642	1,212
9531	Administration of housing programs	16	130	201
9532	Administration of urban planning and community and rural development	28	512	1,011
96	Administration of economic programs	32	1,536	2,841
961	Administration of general economic programs	8	382	313
962	Regulation and administration of transportation programs	20	953	2,189
963	Regulation and administration of communications, electric, gas, and other utilities	2	187	323
964	Regulation of agricultural marketing and commodities	1	6	7
965	Regulation, licensing, and inspection of miscellaneous commercial sectors	1	6	8

NEC Not elsewhere classified.
Source: State of Florida, Department of Labor and Employment Security, Bureau of Labor Market Information, "Employment, Wages, and Contributions Report" (ES-202), unpublished data.

Florida Statistical Abstract 1991

Table 23.75. STATE AND LOCAL GOVERNMENT: OPTIONAL GAS TAX RATES AND COLLECTIONS
IN THE STATE AND COUNTIES OF FLORIDA, FISCAL YEAR, 1989-90

(amounts in dollars)

County	Tax rate	Total collections	Service charge 1/	County	Tax rate	Total collections	Service charge 1/
Florida	(X)	401,476,996	24,088,620	Lafayette	0.04	104,292	6,258
				Lake	0.06	5,044,270	302,656
Alachua	0.06	5,831,138	349,868	Lee	0.06	10,369,382	622,163
Baker	0.06	710,014	42,601	Leon	0.06	6,565,267	393,916
Bay	0.06	4,018,028	241,082	Levy	0.06	1,140,403	68,424
Bradford	0.06	920,208	55,212	Liberty	0.00	0	0
Brevard	0.06	12,814,449	768,867	Madison	0.03	888,184	53,291
Broward	0.06	35,952,137	2,157,128	Manatee	0.06	5,968,520	358,111
Calhoun	0.00	0	0	Marion	0.06	8,145,997	488,760
Charlotte	0.06	3,353,394	201,204	Martin	0.06	3,208,793	192,528
Citrus	0.06	2,540,290	152,417	Monroe	0.06	2,827,389	169,643
Clay	0.06	3,174,154	190,449	Nassau	0.06	2,256,685	135,401
Collier	0.06	5,149,444	308,967	Okaloosa	0.05	3,753,348	225,201
Columbia	0.06	2,608,742	156,525	Okeechobee	0.06	1,428,927	85,736
Dade	0.06	50,665,128	3,039,908	Orange	0.06	26,111,660	1,566,700
De Soto	0.06	737,255	44,235	Osceola	0.06	4,528,757	271,725
Dixie	0.06	430,285	25,817	Palm Beach	0.06	25,823,602	1,549,416
Duval	0.06	24,477,756	1,468,665	Pasco	0.06	6,998,685	419,921
Escambia	0.06	8,417,598	505,056	Pinellas	0.06	21,121,384	1,267,283
Flagler	0.04	635,707	38,142	Polk	0.06	14,975,780	898,547
Franklin	0.00	0	0	Putnam	0.06	1,910,413	114,625
Gadsden	0.06	1,321,549	79,293	St. Johns	0.06	3,683,539	221,012
Gilchrist	0.06	200,328	12,020	St. Lucie	0.06	5,094,378	305,663
Glades	0.04	198,740	11,924	Santa Rosa	0.06	2,482,439	148,946
Gulf	0.06	251,711	15,103	Sarasota	0.06	7,893,847	473,631
Hamilton	0.03	817,549	49,053	Seminole	0.06	7,517,712	451,063
Hardee	0.06	661,433	39,686	Sumter	0.04	2,153,059	129,184
Hendry	0.02	402,352	24,141	Suwannee	0.06	1,393,585	83,615
Hernando	0.06	2,957,357	177,441	Taylor	0.04	702,394	42,144
Highlands	0.06	2,344,561	140,674	Union	0.05	450,716	27,043
Hillsborough	0.06	26,727,121	1,603,627	Volusia	0.06	10,407,572	624,454
Holmes	0.05	589,953	35,397	Wakulla	0.04	305,035	18,302
Indian River	0.06	3,306,540	198,392	Walton	0.05	1,045,023	62,701
Jackson	0.05	2,129,389	127,763	Washington	0.04	429,219	25,753
Jefferson	0.02	402,430	24,146				

(X) Not applicable.
1/ Six percent charge imposed on collections for state general revenue fund.
Note: Detail may not add to totals because of rounding.

Source: State of Florida, Department of Revenue, unpublished data.

Florida Statistical Abstract 1991

Table 23.76. STATE AND LOCAL GOVERNMENT: EMPLOYMENT BY FUNCTION, PAYROLL, AND
AVERAGE EARNINGS OF STATE AND LOCAL GOVERNMENTS IN FLORIDA AND THE UNITED
STATES, OCTOBER 1989

| | Florida | | United States | |
Item	State and local	State only	State and local	State only
Total employees, all functions	691,244	169,586	14,764,958	4,364,638
Full-time only	577,626	135,807	11,401,170	3,241,356
Full-time equivalent employees, all functions	629,303	149,896	12,722,746	3,708,606
Education, total	287,963	36,441	6,297,210	1,359,759
Higher education	53,767	34,858	1,473,226	1,235,127
Elementary and secondary schools	232,613	0	4,725,782	26,430
Other education	A/	1,583	A/	98,202
Libraries 1/	3,776	B/	92,758	B/
Public welfare	12,987	7,830	441,500	200,874
Hospitals	49,943	17,281	1,052,098	534,544
Health	17,351	12,067	313,251	148,008
Social insurance administration	A/	3,758	A/	101,218
Highways	23,632	9,599	540,469	255,228
Air and water transportation	3,053	0	44,330	7,279
Police protection	40,844	3,389	680,222	88,700
Police officers only	28,404	2,033	517,390	58,613
Fire protection	15,964	B/	248,603	B/
Correction	36,123	24,970	469,215	303,020
Natural resources	10,368	6,749	174,817	142,825
Parks and recreation	14,489	1,041	220,183	35,317
Housing and community development	2,928	B/	102,949	B/
Sewerage 1/	6,919	B/	115,162	B/
Solid waste management 1/	7,125	B/	107,513	B/
Government administration				
Judicial and legal	17,326	8,333	277,198	105,415
Financial and other government administration	29,100	7,899	530,832	181,877
Public utilities				
Water supply 1/	8,694	B/	140,257	B/
Gas supply and electric power 1/	5,533	B/	89,357	B/
Transit 1/	A/	4,687	A/	201,950
Liquor stores	A/	0	A/	10,436
All other and unallocable	26,740	10,129	471,218	205,094
October payroll, total ($1,000)	1,306,805	303,609	28,127,164	8,443,056
Average earnings 2/ (dollars)	2,149	2,083	2,293	2,372

A/ State government only.
B/ Local government only.
1/ United States totals include state government amounts for some states.
2/ Of full-time employees.

Source: U.S., Department of Commerce, Bureau of the Census, *Public Employment in 1989.*

Florida Statistical Abstract 1991

Table 23.77. LOCAL GOVERNMENT: EMPLOYMENT BY FUNCTION, PAYROLL, AND AVERAGE
EARNINGS OF COUNTY GOVERNMENTS IN SPECIFIED COUNTIES OF FLORIDA
OCTOBER 1989

Item	Alachua	Bay	Brevard	Broward	Collier
Population, 1989	179,057	125,815	388,378	1,232,492	143,749
Total employees, all functions	1,372	522	3,023	8,609	1,749
Full-time only	1,166	505	2,820	8,162	1,674
Full-time equivalent	1,256	510	2,923	8,391	1,713
Highways	112	124	243	389	154
Public welfare	80	5	54	182	20
Hospitals	0	0	0	0	0
Health	68	4	142	512	89
Police protection	271	141	387	1,472	443
Police officers only	173	98	205	713	301
Correction	223	0	210	886	204
Parks and recreation	9	17	271	461	69
Financial and other government administration	287	91	361	916	217
All other functions	153	102	904	2,762	337
October payroll, total ($1,000)	2,279	775	5,180	19,602	3,550
Average earnings 1/ (dollars)	1,893	1,521	1,800	2,363	2,091

Item	Dade	Escambia	Hills-borough	Lake	Lee 2/
Population, 1989	1,908,945	261,602	822,621	146,483	325,374
Total employees, all functions	31,104	2,559	12,121	811	2,041
Full-time only	28,839	2,414	10,908	781	1,917
Full-time equivalent	30,200	2,491	11,519	793	1,999
Highways	699	198	686	125	209
Public welfare	1,712	171	624	10	123
Hospitals	7,029	559	3,513	0	0
Health	832	87	532	51	112
Police protection	2,633	380	1,281	161	292
Police officers only	2,571	260	793	96	208
Correction	1,617	364	735	89	137
Parks and recreation	1,592	0	266	5	162
Financial and other government administration	1,733	297	916	138	345
All other functions	10,652	381	1,925	158	569
October payroll, total ($1,000)	80,356	4,176	24,646	1,279	3,378
Average earnings 1/ (dollars)	2,732	1,683	2,154	1,621	1,719

See footnotes at end of table. Continued . . .

Table 23.77. LOCAL GOVERNMENT: EMPLOYMENT BY FUNCTION, PAYROLL, AND AVERAGE
EARNINGS OF COUNTY GOVERNMENTS IN SPECIFIED COUNTIES OF FLORIDA
OCTOBER 1989 (Continued)

Item	Leon	Manatee	Marion	Okaloosa	Orange
Population, 1989	187,467	205,713	188,071	141,624	652,399
Total employees, all functions	1,041	2,224	1,101	797	6,687
Full-time only	973	2,028	1,081	762	6,299
Full-time equivalent	1,011	2,107	1,090	791	6,420
Highways	135	301	146	144	473
Public welfare	20	45	5	5	336
Hospitals	0	0	0	0	0
Health	121	144	17	51	131
Police protection	260	346	313	147	1,072
Police officers only	180	220	144	112	683
Correction	150	209	193	72	987
Parks and recreation	10	175	21	6	233
Financial and other government administration	120	252	170	104	622
All other functions	191	582	189	250	1,997
October payroll, total ($1,000)	1,854	3,862	1,803	1,289	13,771
Average earnings 1/ (dollars)	1,862	1,860	1,659	1,655	2,166

Item	Palm Beach	Pasco	Pinellas	Polk 3/	St. Lucie 2/
Population, 1989	841,490	274,363	844,628	399,022	144,090
Total employees, all functions	7,469	2,140	4,856	3,349	1,120
Full-time only	7,214	2,060	4,789	3,074	1,111
Full-time equivalent	7,353	2,102	4,822	3,182	1,114
Highways	533	185	307	309	105
Public welfare	630	68	74	119	0
Hospitals	0	0	0	505	0
Health	154	23	97	217	0
Police protection	1,274	432	893	533	154
Police officers only	803	281	569	332	109
Correction	644	137	628	309	115
Parks and recreation	393	89	210	36	140
Financial and other government administration	880	295	574	260	238
All other functions	2,046	668	1,412	495	288
October payroll, total ($1,000)	15,204	3,517	10,000	5,455	1,734
Average earnings 1/ (dollars)	2,087	1,686	2,083	1,733	1,558

See footnotes at end of table.   Continued . . .

Table 23.77. LOCAL GOVERNMENT: EMPLOYMENT BY FUNCTION, PAYROLL, AND AVERAGE
    EARNINGS OF COUNTY GOVERNMENTS IN SPECIFIED COUNTIES OF FLORIDA
    OCTOBER 1989 (Continued)

Item	Sarasota	Semi-nole	Volusia
Population, 1989	271,403	277,330	360,171
Total employees, all functions	2,309	1,792	2,455
Full-time only	2,115	1,646	2,355
Full-time equivalent	2,232	1,680	2,248
Highways	210	174	247
Public welfare	10	9	25
Hospitals	0	0	0
Health	95	49	85
Police protection	426	260	373
Police officers only	251	160	242
Correction	132	201	359
Parks and recreation	162	41	177
Financial and other government administration	308	221	340
All other functions	841	490	421
October payroll, total ($1,000)	4,099	3,240	3,973
Average earnings 1/ (dollars)	1,874	1,938	1,660

1/ Of full-time employees.
2/ Data are for October 1986.
3/ Data are for October 1988.
Note: Population estimates from University of Florida, Bureau of Economic and
Business Research, Population Program, *Special Population Reports*, May 1991.

Source: U.S., Department of Commerce, Bureau of the Census, *County Government
Employment in 1989.*

Florida Statistical Abstract 1991

Table 23.78. LOCAL GOVERNMENT: EMPLOYMENT BY FUNCTION, PAYROLL, AND AVERAGE
EARNINGS OF CITY GOVERNMENTS IN SPECIFIED MUNICIPALITIES OF FLORIDA
OCTOBER 1989

Item	Clear-water	Ft. Lauder-dale 1/	Gaines-ville 2/	Hialeah
Population, 1989	101,082	150,631	85,663	172,964
Total employees, all functions	1,672	2,320	1,619	(NA)
Full-time only	1,392	2,059	1,592	(NA)
Full-time equivalent	1,520	2,180	1,607	(NA)
Highways	124	153	136	(NA)
Police protection	353	699	330	(NA)
Police officers only	230	699	222	(NA)
Fire protection	141	286	145	(NA)
Firefighters only	133	286	124	(NA)
Solid waste management	106	27	0	(NA)
Parks and recreation	69	347	64	(NA)
Government administration				
Judicial and legal	8	18	13	(NA)
Financial and other	113	118	62	(NA)
Utilities	111	135	652	(NA)
Water supply only	53	135	104	(NA)
All other and unallocable	495	397	205	(NA)
October payrolls, total ($1,000)	3,674	5,336	3,929	(NA)
Average earnings 3/ (dollars)	2,493	2,458	2,451	(NA)

Item	Holly-wood	Jackson-ville	Miami	Miami Beach
Population, 1989	126,380	647,440	371,444	98,047
Total employees, all functions	1,563	11,607	4,373	1,522
Full-time only	1,355	9,580	3,938	1,472
Full-time equivalent	1,464	10,720	4,254	1,496
Highways	83	583	140	34
Police protection	495	1,626	1,575	453
Police officers only	302	1,088	1,114	279
Fire protection	223	801	760	216
Firefighters only	207	783	673	209
Solid waste management	94	391	530	56
Parks and recreation	143	545	333	283
Government administration				
Judicial and legal	11	335	61	15
Financial and other	108	858	657	224
Utilities	70	1,822	0	37
Water supply only	70	334	0	37
All other and unallocable	237	3,759	198	178
October payrolls, total ($1,000)	4,102	22,402	12,069	4,250
Average earnings 3/ (dollars)	2,901	2,200	2,989	2,861

See footnotes at end of table. Continued . . .

Table 23.78. LOCAL GOVERNMENT: EMPLOYMENT BY FUNCTION, PAYROLL, AND AVERAGE
EARNINGS OF CITY GOVERNMENTS IN SPECIFIED MUNICIPALITIES OF FLORIDA
OCTOBER 1989 (Continued)

Item	Orlando 4/	St. Peters- burg	Talla- hassee	Tampa
Population, 1989	166,181	246,769	130,284	287,917
Total employees, all functions	4,273	3,058	2,625	4,044
Full-time only	4,061	2,688	2,334	3,897
Full-time equivalent	4,140	2,836	2,467	3,972
Highways	157	81	287	313
Police protection	708	673	401	1,046
Police officers only	488	454	259	800
Fire protection	356	331	219	475
Firefighters only	307	303	204	427
Solid waste management	182	213	117	150
Parks and recreation	280	364	162	464
Government administration				
Judicial and legal	28	19	2	29
Financial and other	361	284	339	450
Utilities	1,060	190	543	246
Water supply only	195	190	86	246
All other and unallocable	1,008	681	397	799
October payrolls, total ($1,000)	7,986	6,347	5,228	9,295
Average earnings 3/ (dollars)	1,949	2,289	2,170	2,364

(NA) Not Available
1/ Data are for October 1987.
2/ Data are for October 1988.
3/ Of full-time employees.
4/ Data are for October 1985.
   Note: Population estimates from University of Florida, Bureau of Economic and
Business Research, Population Program, *Florida Estimates of Population, April 1,
1989: State, Counties, and Municipalities*.

   Source: U.S., Department of Commerce, Bureau of the Census, *City Employment in
1989.*

Florida Statistical Abstract 1991

Table 23.81. LOCAL GOVERNMENT: REVENUE AND EXPENDITURE BY SOURCE OR FUNCTION AND
    BY TYPE OF GOVERNMENT IN FLORIDA, FISCAL YEARS ENDING SEPTEMBER 30, 1988 AND
    1989

(rounded to thousands of dollars)

| | Statewide total | | County government | |
Item	1987-88	1988-89	1987-88	1988-89
Revenue, total	24,180,545	27,421,411	10,533,614	12,352,918
Taxes	5,082,916	5,599,515	2,906,239	3,225,356
Licenses and permits	220,367	253,951	91,404	108,755
Intergovernmental revenue	2,340,662	2,600,026	1,270,273	1,351,318
Charges for services	7,135,919	8,072,561	2,140,057	2,385,610
Fines and forfeitures	166,304	181,400	99,652	108,791
Miscellaneous	2,396,599	2,982,455	1,090,329	1,421,982
Other financing sources	6,837,777	7,731,502	2,935,659	3,751,105
Expenditure, total	24,634,621	27,000,124	10,654,071	12,062,013
General government	1,960,937	2,218,633	1,260,828	1,370,482
Public safety	3,180,038	3,601,094	1,716,164	1,963,212
Physical environment	4,552,682	5,177,234	927,457	1,063,935
Transportation	2,055,200	2,375,645	1,300,643	1,516,430
Economic environment	589,844	648,352	226,233	229,385
Human services	2,242,002	2,528,608	900,570	1,006,600
Culture/recreation	1,077,975	1,100,018	449,308	456,219
Debt service	2,343,925	2,441,682	747,945	1,389,398
Other financing uses	6,632,019	6,908,859	3,124,921	3,066,353

| | City government | | Special districts | |
	1987-88	1988-89	1987-88	1988-89
Revenue, total	7,898,459	8,594,244	5,748,472	6,474,249
Taxes	1,778,913	1,931,989	397,764	442,171
Licenses and permits	127,326	140,696	1,636	4,500
Intergovernmental revenue	825,609	910,316	244,780	338,392
Charges for services	2,292,634	2,556,825	2,703,228	3,130,125
Fines and forfeitures	66,594	72,544	58	65
Miscellaneous	836,056	1,081,670	470,213	478,803
Other financing sources	1,971,326	1,900,204	1,930,792	2,080,192
Expenditure, total	7,966,635	8,723,809	6,013,915	6,214,302
General government	651,134	768,716	48,975	79,435
Public safety	1,411,331	1,578,643	52,543	59,239
Physical environment	2,018,886	2,235,290	1,606,339	1,878,009
Transportation	481,704	559,574	272,853	299,642
Economic environment	177,815	185,242	185,796	233,724
Human services	86,098	94,103	1,255,333	1,427,905
Culture/recreation	600,806	626,155	27,861	17,644
Debt service	748,256	503,741	847,723	548,543
Other financing uses	1,790,604	2,172,345	1,716,493	1,670,161

Source: State of Florida, Department of Banking and Finance, *Local Government
Financial Report, Fiscal Year 1988-89,* and previous edition.

Florida Statistical Abstract 1991

Table 23.82. LOCAL GOVERNMENT: REVENUE AND EXPENDITURE PER CAPITA, PERSONAL
    SERVICES EXPENDITURE, AND INDEBTEDNESS OF COUNTY GOVERNMENTS OF FLORIDA
    FISCAL YEAR ENDING SEPTEMBER 30, 1989

(rounded to dollars)

County 1/	Total revenue per capita 2/	Total expenditure per capita 2/	Personal services expenditure 3/	Bonded indebtedness	Other long-term debt
Florida 4/	976.4	953.4	2,445,763,997	7,964,162,117	1,094,367,827
Alachua	605.7	624.6	37,372,064	44,200,000	4,947,884
Baker	522.3	495.2	2,873,967	80,000	1,279,253
Bay	713.2	738.4	15,232,294	84,857,000	13,856,063
Bradford	364.4	352.2	2,932,503	431,000	641,850
Brevard	835.5	715.3	74,824,841	270,880,856	36,021,028
Broward	1,343.6	1,263.2	297,902,000	896,827,000	123,807,000
Calhoun	464.6	482.1	1,516,201	635,000	643,646
Charlotte	875.8	850.0	28,690,076	2,390,000	24,670,698
Citrus	587.1	577.1	19,026,395	477,000	20,623,612
Clay	457.3	452.9	15,824,168	5,695,000	1,425,310
Collier	1,412.3	1,292.5	51,981,258	140,335,111	9,324,630
Columbia	511.9	494.6	5,822,954	5,735,203	920,875
Dade	1,639.2	1,706.7	140,298,000	2,474,337,000	260,334,000
De Soto	430.0	392.1	4,591,584	365,000	1,086,467
Dixie	778.0	803.6	2,237,390	25,000	950,251
Escambia	941.5	1,134.2	63,272,247	90,511,750	16,209,596
Flagler	891.3	781.8	6,054,307	11,255,646	861,045
Franklin	1,099.2	1,248.6	3,487,467	1,765,000	174,230
Gadsden	569.3	545.9	5,093,602	11,392,933	1,497,217
Gilchrist	741.4	527.1	1,693,591	625,000	94,144
Glades	1,010.6	989.0	2,896,610	0	785,997
Gulf	618.7	581.9	2,478,906	2,171,300	478,175
Hamilton	614.5	641.8	2,795,607	1,930,000	334,980
Hardee	1,019.4	968.1	5,163,880	5,995,000	706,696
Hendry	759.5	734.7	6,207,977	8,993,000	478,457
Hernando	684.8	632.0	18,012,038	43,963,129	3,421,413
Highlands	446.0	442.6	13,295,809	1,165,000	2,570,556
Hillsborough	882.8	947.4	241,521,331	767,283,000	104,585,000
Holmes	350.0	389.3	2,072,652	3,481,000	349,429
Indian River	1,298.0	1,111.0	27,940,221	41,756,386	14,612,231
Jackson	421.9	426.1	5,157,290	12,976,000	99,277
Jefferson	548.8	571.3	2,562,421	0	224,841
Lafayette	560.1	528.1	1,123,733	611,000	111,298
Lake	482.5	474.3	21,995,108	38,713,000	7,990,747
Lee	1,172.6	1,277.6	76,098,579	360,253,573	18,477,235
Leon	557.0	531.1	28,038,759	51,313,653	6,068,499

See footnotes at end of table.   Continued . . .

Table 23.82.   LOCAL GOVERNMENT: REVENUE AND EXPENDITURE PER CAPITA, PERSONAL
SERVICES EXPENDITURE, AND INDEBTEDNESS OF COUNTY GOVERNMENTS OF FLORIDA
FISCAL YEAR ENDING SEPTEMBER 30, 1989 (Continued)

(rounded to dollars)

County 1/	Total revenue per capita 2/	Total expendi- ture per capita 2/	Personal services expendi- ture 3/	Bonded indebted- ness	Other long-term debt
Levy	541.6	584.2	5,173,942	2,140,000	522,434
Liberty	610.0	677.6	1,462,225	2,040,000	120,986
Madison	740.3	414.7	2,402,319	4,400,000	112,329
Manatee	1,064.4	1,099.0	60,787,759	213,457,666	31,848,116
Marion	486.5	415.3	28,061,051	30,755,399	6,645,734
Martin	944.7	1,025.5	28,452,693	45,811,218	13,446,205
Monroe	1,399.2	1,157.5	31,588,187	18,022,347	2,338,122
Nassau	1,003.5	695.5	8,010,160	10,420,000	779,526
Okaloosa	455.2	389.3	20,331,224	49,323,663	936,685
Okeechobee	663.5	643.5	7,109,068	7,365,000	1,174,684
Orange	1,171.5	1,098.7	195,097,051	482,757,219	76,878,148
Osceola	1,421.6	1,054.2	22,691,770	44,706,080	752,479
Palm Beach	1,017.1	1,061.3	226,028,946	478,120,261	113,600,174
Pasco	1,759.7	1,512.2	54,190,200	334,593,503	5,255,321
Pinellas	707.3	589.9	159,633,971	313,358,189	42,959,776
Polk	498.4	484.8	84,028,235	62,144,624	9,343,006
Putnam	752.4	602.1	10,453,558	20,097,171	2,933,279
St. Johns	1,066.2	800.4	19,659,719	50,400,000	1,260,740
St. Lucie	867.1	651.2	18,776,816	19,212,500	47,668,827
Santa Rosa	475.1	488.8	11,248,797	13,390,526	5,813,021
Sarasota	926.8	773.1	62,402,772	134,136,051	12,470,583
Seminole	581.2	595.2	50,725,563	125,231,125	5,693,928
Sumter	557.7	542.4	4,624,199	5,540,000	2,331,211
Suwannee	470.0	443.8	4,230,582	535,000	1,704,559
Taylor	480.3	438.2	1,506,109	540,000	490,007
Union	397.5	362.7	1,449,914	425,000	1,352,830
Volusia	548.6	562.3	73,561,899	104,244,335	20,339,711
Wakulla	681.9	651.7	2,898,872	2,502,700	541,645
Walton	902.0	855.6	8,710,399	5,067,000	998,777
Washington	345.6	352.7	2,378,167	0	3,391,354

1/ Duval County data are to be found in Table 23.85 under City of Jacksonville.
2/ Total revenue and expenditure from Tables 23.83 and 23.84 divided by April 1,
1989 population estimates.
3/ Amounts paid for salary and wages and employee benefits. These amounts are
included in the functional distribution on Table 23.84.
4/ Does not include Duval County/Jacksonville.

Source: State of Florida, Department of Banking and Finance, *Local Government
Financial Report, Fiscal Year 1988-89.*

Florida Statistical Abstract 1991

Table 23.83. LOCAL GOVERNMENT: REVENUE BY SOURCE OF COUNTY GOVERNMENTS IN FLORIDA
    FISCAL YEARS ENDING SEPTEMBER 30, 1988 AND 1989

(rounded to thousands of dollars)

County 1/	Total revenue	Revenue from taxes	Revenue from licenses and permits	Inter-govern-mental revenue	Charges for services	Miscel-lane-ous 2/	Other financing sources 3/
			1987-88				
Florida 4/	10,533,614	2,906,239	91,404	1,270,273	2,140,057	1,189,981	2,935,659
Alachua	120,956	40,418	0	12,204	12,076	7,728	48,530
Baker	7,870	1,754	62	2,321	1,634	238	1,862
Bay	83,395	17,974	382	10,475	13,214	3,901	37,449
Bradford	7,262	1,802	57	1,748	1,363	475	1,818
Brevard	264,690	70,732	1,411	33,349	43,788	25,694	89,716
Broward	749,913	242,776	1,634	101,689	160,632	89,393	153,789
Calhoun	2,887	1,086	14	1,328	111	129	218
Charlotte	73,326	20,100	1,580	8,567	11,088	21,915	10,075
Citrus	50,659	21,244	675	8,463	5,791	7,500	6,985
Clay	43,327	15,917	1,011	7,337	4,156	1,233	13,672
Collier	165,995	47,693	4,242	18,279	23,372	24,357	48,052
Columbia	19,254	6,073	103	3,866	1,127	2,561	5,523
Dade	3,005,349	738,295	23,711	327,181	980,996	331,877	603,289
De Soto	8,694	4,168	179	2,033	805	1,371	138
Dixie	5,333	1,541	79	1,537	198	513	1,464
Escambia	148,263	41,626	190	25,989	33,202	18,152	29,105
Flagler	18,493	4,976	426	2,313	1,498	1,844	7,435
Franklin	7,427	2,476	28	1,368	239	824	2,491
Gadsden	16,760	4,759	92	4,119	1,447	1,622	4,721
Gilchrist	4,153	1,239	39	921	379	297	1,279
Glades	6,589	2,478	36	1,434	171	579	1,891
Gulf	6,483	2,708	55	1,481	492	136	1,610
Hamilton	8,191	1,985	22	2,147	878	444	2,714
Hardee	10,777	4,027	71	2,431	932	902	2,413
Hendry	25,030	7,116	77	2,988	1,137	877	12,835
Hernando	75,202	17,207	1,189	5,493	8,312	8,828	34,172
Highlands	28,800	13,653	611	5,765	3,328	4,192	1,251
Hillsborough	923,732	224,174	3,923	86,121	121,970	103,125	384,418
Holmes	9,043	1,596	24	1,954	257	380	4,832
Indian River	103,866	32,069	244	7,974	11,025	11,145	41,409
Jackson	13,351	5,579	97	3,394	1,002	1,107	2,171
Jefferson	4,703	1,308	27	2,326	359	416	266
Lafayette	2,751	755	15	941	83	272	686
Lake	100,636	18,821	879	11,942	6,832	7,805	54,358

See footnotes at end of table.   Continued . . .

Table 23.83. LOCAL GOVERNMENT: REVENUE BY SOURCE OF COUNTY GOVERNMENTS IN FLORIDA
FISCAL YEARS ENDING SEPTEMBER 30, 1988 AND 1989 (Continued)

(rounded to thousands of dollars)

County 1/	Total revenue	Revenue from taxes	Revenue from licenses and permits	Inter-govern-mental revenue	Charges for services	Miscel-lane-ous 2/	Other financing sources 3/
			1987-88 (Continued)				
Lee	390,807	66,550	3,003	31,651	62,251	45,070	182,281
Leon	72,368	25,014	727	13,414	6,074	4,485	22,653
Levy	16,889	4,254	108	2,178	684	1,690	7,975
Liberty	3,357	590	6	1,741	175	261	585
Madison	6,579	1,859	39	1,779	297	640	1,964
Manatee	232,522	51,714	1,927	35,833	56,848	26,528	59,672
Marion	65,622	27,679	1,292	16,447	7,245	9,175	3,785
Martin	76,860	31,090	1,912	10,146	11,892	13,620	8,199
Monroe	83,518	33,484	1,920	12,589	10,828	6,842	17,855
Nassau	19,391	7,308	479	3,956	2,219	658	4,771
Okaloosa	64,763	12,180	558	11,470	12,986	4,098	23,471
Okeechobee	18,571	7,380	143	2,735	1,034	1,285	5,994
Orange	663,499	182,087	6,468	85,181	103,084	65,192	221,487
Osceola	67,724	23,767	1,183	9,031	7,181	4,695	21,867
Palm Beach	801,618	236,018	10,994	76,513	93,837	115,670	268,585
Pasco	181,524	51,328	1,877	22,941	29,478	28,153	47,747
Pinellas	554,230	186,844	3,010	66,642	131,925	52,153	113,656
Polk	189,653	59,562	1,979	37,638	38,734	23,535	28,205
Putnam	39,150	12,254	53	4,728	3,502	3,864	14,748
St. Johns	68,979	22,234	804	7,375	8,688	5,102	24,775
St. Lucie	113,752	35,825	1,668	9,523	8,676	26,392	31,669
Santa Rosa	32,380	7,236	571	5,326	3,781	2,469	12,996
Sarasota	180,144	60,540	2,701	24,423	28,023	28,158	36,298
Seminole	188,406	41,123	2,063	18,173	20,352	13,007	93,688
Sumter	16,732	4,168	199	3,834	1,018	873	6,642
Suwannee	11,302	3,856	66	2,604	665	1,072	3,040
Taylor	7,287	3,225	33	2,433	313	854	429
Union	4,698	890	18	891	241	496	2,162
Volusia	193,104	72,416	2,051	27,166	29,648	19,015	42,808
Wakulla	11,847	2,110	111	5,108	303	929	3,286
Walton	24,539	9,485	200	3,798	3,855	1,802	5,399
Washington	8,644	2,042	58	1,526	325	362	4,331

See footnotes at end of table.   Continued . . .

Table 23.83. LOCAL GOVERNMENT: REVENUE BY SOURCE OF COUNTY GOVERNMENTS IN FLORIDA
FISCAL YEARS ENDING SEPTEMBER 30, 1988 AND 1989 (Continued)

(rounded to thousands of dollars)

County 1/	Total revenue	Revenue from taxes	Revenue from licenses and permits	Inter-govern-mental revenue	Charges for services	Miscel-lane-ous 2/	Other financing sources 3/
				1988-89			
Florida 4/	12,352,918	3,225,356	108,755	1,351,318	2,385,610	1,530,773	3,751,105
Alachua	108,446	42,194	0	13,760	14,570	9,384	28,538
Baker	9,478	1,841	68	2,258	1,296	653	3,362
Bay	89,730	21,913	392	9,905	16,256	7,030	34,235
Bradford	8,388	2,127	61	1,783	466	1,508	2,445
Brevard	324,492	77,460	2,212	40,853	50,180	39,224	114,564
Broward	1,655,976	267,362	4,037	110,639	180,278	156,588	937,072
Calhoun	5,019	1,197	15	1,534	133	176	1,964
Charlotte	90,372	24,754	2,214	9,841	14,013	26,748	12,803
Citrus	53,097	23,505	626	8,671	5,593	11,462	3,239
Clay	47,113	19,482	749	8,364	4,014	1,511	12,992
Collier	203,021	53,985	6,360	25,865	26,321	33,493	56,997
Columbia	21,473	6,879	105	3,984	1,913	2,653	5,940
Dade	3,129,209	820,932	28,527	320,305	1,108,777	385,058	465,610
De Soto	10,116	4,563	198	2,337	1,042	1,371	605
Dixie	7,945	2,117	36	2,733	230	495	2,335
Escambia	246,287	43,306	204	28,057	37,472	18,732	118,517
Flagler	23,160	5,779	586	2,497	2,025	2,320	9,952
Franklin	9,677	2,451	40	1,524	234	1,065	4,363
Gadsden	23,385	5,244	114	4,615	1,727	1,871	9,815
Gilchrist	6,754	1,378	51	2,844	403	604	1,474
Glades	7,393	2,621	49	1,570	235	664	2,255
Gulf	6,976	2,874	16	1,461	580	175	1,870
Hamilton	6,533	2,583	16	2,600	715	468	151
Hardee	20,034	4,481	80	2,752	787	1,342	10,593
Hendry	19,195	7,732	89	3,380	1,433	1,539	5,023
Hernando	65,421	20,936	1,236	7,211	8,948	7,704	19,386
Highlands	29,613	13,297	617	6,936	3,535	4,067	1,160
Hillsborough	726,212	234,532	5,217	97,363	128,947	120,819	139,333
Holmes	5,438	1,857	41	2,101	349	255	835
Indian River	112,678	33,371	285	8,643	13,234	24,202	32,942
Jackson	17,388	6,814	99	4,427	1,317	900	3,832
Jefferson	6,188	1,627	25	3,062	407	538	530
Lafayette	3,007	788	0	1,078	166	214	761
Lake	70,680	21,769	986	12,914	5,807	11,054	18,150
Lee	381,520	78,762	4,748	39,449	68,578	40,462	149,521
Leon	104,423	29,427	782	13,049	6,742	6,426	47,998

See footnotes at end of table.   Continued . . .

Table 23.83. LOCAL GOVERNMENT: REVENUE BY SOURCE OF COUNTY GOVERNMENTS IN FLORIDA
    FISCAL YEARS ENDING SEPTEMBER 30, 1988 AND 1989 (Continued)

(rounded to thousands of dollars)

County 1/	Total revenue	Revenue from taxes	Revenue from licenses and permits	Inter-govern-mental revenue	Charges for services	Miscel-lane-ous 2/	Other financing sources 3/
			1988-89 (Continued)				
Levy	13,684	4,458	105	2,817	1,240	1,586	3,478
Liberty	2,884	613	8	1,363	268	259	374
Madison	11,672	2,437	61	1,681	364	856	6,273
Manatee	218,966	53,950	2,315	27,402	58,566	29,161	47,572
Marion	91,491	32,120	1,431	18,295	7,971	10,271	21,402
Martin	90,893	38,644	1,959	11,349	14,811	19,869	4,261
Monroe	107,434	39,005	2,053	18,691	12,207	8,985	26,493
Nassau	43,650	8,552	402	5,108	3,241	2,164	24,183
Okaloosa	64,469	12,827	651	12,400	15,773	5,150	17,668
Okeechobee	19,199	7,590	167	3,090	1,316	1,381	5,655
Orange	764,264	208,105	6,937	88,546	92,578	118,385	249,713
Osceola	143,544	26,781	1,197	9,563	8,255	9,842	87,905
Palm Beach	855,869	270,651	12,800	87,498	113,296	116,437	255,187
Pasco	482,795	59,654	1,763	23,385	32,786	45,781	319,427
Pinellas	597,383	199,628	3,015	57,357	144,856	71,236	121,292
Polk	198,882	64,904	2,287	47,307	41,378	26,991	16,014
Putnam	48,090	12,872	410	4,783	3,323	5,186	21,517
St. Johns	87,438	23,357	681	6,858	10,195	12,639	33,708
St. Lucie	124,948	39,233	1,093	11,664	9,615	7,814	55,529
Santa Rosa	37,577	10,323	624	6,372	4,139	2,303	13,817
Sarasota	251,528	63,142	3,017	26,441	35,060	50,351	73,518
Seminole	161,172	47,370	1,910	19,857	22,471	27,616	41,948
Sumter	17,258	5,281	189	3,572	1,151	1,337	5,728
Suwannee	12,382	4,249	75	3,005	982	1,140	2,931
Taylor	8,240	3,637	36	2,668	654	1,001	245
Union	4,113	988	35	1,005	356	566	1,164
Volusia	197,594	79,426	2,245	29,164	33,952	25,912	26,895
Wakulla	9,402	2,172	150	3,231	283	1,397	2,170
Walton	24,462	9,596	189	4,427	5,578	2,173	2,500
Washington	5,795	1,851	72	2,056	226	210	1,380

1/ Duval County data are to be found in Table 23.86 under City of Jacksonville.
    2/ Includes fines and forfeitures, interest earnings, rents and royalties, spe-
cial assessments, contributions, etc.
    3/ Includes interfund transfers, contributions from enterprises, debt proceeds,
trust fund receipts, and other nonrevenue receipts.
    4/ Does not include Duval County/Jacksonville.

Source: State of Florida, Department of Banking and Finance, *Local Government
Financial Report, Fiscal Year 1988-89*, and previous edition.

Table 23.84. LOCAL GOVERNMENT: EXPENDITURE BY FUNCTION OF COUNTY GOVERNMENTS
    IN FLORIDA, FISCAL YEARS ENDING SEPTEMBER 30, 1988 AND 1989

(rounded to thousands of dollars)

County 1/	Total	General govern- mental services	Public safety	Physical envi- ronment	Trans- porta- tion	Human services	Miscella- neous 2/
				1987-88			
Florida 3/	10,654,071	1,260,828	1,716,164	927,457	1,300,643	900,570	4,548,408
Alachua	103,600	18,829	24,089	3,119	7,151	4,548	45,864
Baker	7,520	1,308	1,669	444	1,132	388	2,579
Bay	72,520	6,764	10,963	20,734	5,686	2,451	25,922
Bradford	6,619	2,104	1,085	344	712	389	1,983
Brevard	255,625	38,018	34,474	48,955	20,872	8,052	105,255
Broward	768,409	117,235	148,777	57,055	127,755	33,210	284,377
Calhoun	3,046	975	685	122	588	121	555
Charlotte	73,080	14,288	15,006	5,285	13,502	3,917	21,081
Citrus	49,731	7,201	12,177	4,383	7,782	3,160	15,027
Clay	42,669	4,994	10,240	2,606	7,951	1,457	15,422
Collier	157,088	19,190	29,690	17,701	11,199	3,860	75,447
Columbia	20,776	2,498	4,165	1,389	5,227	775	6,722
Dade	3,136,978	188,104	398,779	263,711	494,052	537,906	1,254,426
De Soto	8,169	2,010	2,800	563	1,783	355	657
Dixie	5,273	1,053	1,078	236	835	87	1,983
Escambia	154,900	32,932	29,910	5,779	9,144	20,358	56,777
Flagler	15,738	3,158	3,164	176	3,041	369	5,829
Franklin	6,866	1,254	1,364	383	990	333	2,541
Gadsden	16,939	2,578	3,035	959	2,283	1,675	6,411
Gilchrist	4,078	953	919	97	476	144	1,489
Glades	6,773	1,598	1,412	353	1,050	197	2,163
Gulf	6,507	1,364	1,070	367	986	655	2,065
Hamilton	8,035	1,072	1,873	186	1,126	561	3,216
Hardee	10,771	2,346	2,751	382	2,065	432	2,795
Hendry	19,962	2,701	4,166	618	2,629	586	9,261
Hernando	82,783	13,309	15,698	5,294	8,988	1,384	38,108
Highlands	25,832	7,820	7,693	1,250	4,675	1,761	2,631
Hillsborough	955,033	117,499	139,438	102,274	56,467	65,249	474,105
Holmes	8,598	953	845	161	2,403	244	3,991
Indian River	99,365	8,628	17,442	7,228	7,578	2,136	56,353
Jackson	15,276	2,991	2,645	134	5,327	610	3,568
Jefferson	4,952	874	1,113	302	1,279	119	1,264
Lafayette	2,809	663	366	125	594	31	1,030
Lake	59,045	8,493	15,645	2,110	9,080	3,079	20,639

See footnotes at end of table.   Continued . . .

Table 23.84. LOCAL GOVERNMENT: EXPENDITURE BY FUNCTION OF COUNTY GOVERNMENTS
IN FLORIDA, FISCAL YEARS ENDING SEPTEMBER 30, 1988 AND 1989 (Continued)

(rounded to thousands of dollars)

County 1/	Total	General governmental services	Public safety	Physical environment	Transportation	Human services	Miscellaneous 2/
			1987-88 (Continued)				
Lee	395,398	41,774	26,109	24,227	50,218	7,151	245,918
Leon	81,529	21,226	13,097	3,481	8,931	2,467	32,326
Levy	19,735	2,554	5,120	440	2,202	456	8,963
Liberty	3,212	1,088	578	167	467	39	873
Madison	6,550	1,385	1,364	387	944	254	2,216
Manatee	229,546	37,418	27,270	36,127	21,235	8,867	98,627
Marion	65,099	14,535	23,176	6,013	10,711	6,022	4,641
Martin	86,973	23,826	25,915	7,934	11,341	3,210	14,746
Monroe	78,636	14,636	19,885	8,546	4,321	4,702	26,545
Nassau	19,342	3,755	4,678	915	3,218	813	5,963
Okaloosa	66,418	8,586	9,107	9,149	10,176	2,017	27,382
Okeechobee	18,107	2,887	4,915	423	1,848	745	7,289
Orange	730,719	58,103	115,000	61,493	58,502	20,348	417,273
Osceola	70,728	11,382	15,826	1,831	9,245	2,336	30,107
Palm Beach	790,152	102,742	125,962	36,632	92,133	50,645	382,038
Pasco	184,408	32,122	28,515	20,895	14,722	3,606	84,547
Pinellas	545,678	71,615	102,251	92,324	40,418	20,301	218,769
Polk	187,962	30,922	52,831	13,525	20,118	33,946	36,619
Putnam	35,189	8,598	6,577	1,026	4,025	990	13,973
St. Johns	55,121	8,621	14,870	4,896	6,472	4,140	16,122
St. Lucie	115,106	18,112	17,622	1,706	8,314	3,463	65,890
Santa Rosa	35,451	4,660	5,547	3,333	4,237	1,113	16,560
Sarasota	182,862	29,680	35,249	18,782	26,449	6,423	66,280
Seminole	158,985	23,220	28,931	9,629	14,395	2,454	80,354
Sumter	19,551	2,310	7,338	631	3,157	622	5,491
Suwannee	11,431	2,015	2,026	409	2,374	343	4,263
Taylor	6,948	1,356	2,012	337	2,087	374	782
Union	4,612	899	697	33	1,011	167	1,805
Volusia	193,040	39,240	41,492	6,488	33,843	7,879	64,097
Wakulla	10,397	1,241	1,564	340	690	228	6,334
Walton	21,195	3,260	3,251	406	3,198	3,517	7,563
Washington	8,625	1,299	1,165	106	3,231	330	2,494

See footnotes at end of table.   Continued . . .

Florida Statistical Abstract 1991

Table 23.84. LOCAL GOVERNMENT: EXPENDITURE BY FUNCTION OF COUNTY GOVERNMENTS
IN FLORIDA, FISCAL YEARS ENDING SEPTEMBER 30, 1988 AND 1989 (Continued)

(rounded to thousands of dollars)

County 1/	Total	General govern- mental services	Public safety	Physical envi- ronment	Trans- porta- tion	Human services	Miscella- neous 2/
				1988-89			
Florida 3/	12,062,013	1,370,482	1,963,212	1,063,935	1,516,430	1,006,600	5,141,355
Alachua	111,839	21,274	27,416	3,562	8,759	3,728	47,101
Baker	8,986	1,428	1,858	229	1,776	487	3,208
Bay	92,898	6,869	12,420	26,197	9,362	2,833	35,215
Bradford	8,106	2,311	1,301	485	1,038	455	2,517
Brevard	277,814	38,312	36,292	41,504	27,397	7,306	127,002
Broward	1,556,920	113,655	181,340	83,049	142,142	38,423	998,311
Calhoun	5,207	1,147	806	128	676	81	2,369
Charlotte	87,718	17,249	18,194	5,514	19,526	4,249	22,985
Citrus	52,194	7,974	13,443	3,234	7,310	3,570	16,665
Clay	46,660	5,581	12,906	3,291	7,452	1,980	15,449
Collier	185,803	28,516	36,887	20,211	12,975	5,488	81,725
Columbia	20,746	2,951	5,202	952	3,470	644	7,526
Dade	3,258,051	194,846	466,594	264,739	563,257	604,698	1,163,917
De Soto	9,225	2,113	3,157	363	2,189	394	1,008
Dixie	8,206	1,220	1,217	229	3,338	128	2,074
Escambia	296,698	32,390	32,375	8,027	10,309	24,167	189,431
Flagler	20,315	3,753	4,642	1,884	2,632	543	6,862
Franklin	10,992	1,250	3,639	1,211	1,480	389	3,023
Gadsden	22,425	2,836	7,017	1,031	1,929	1,660	7,951
Gilchrist	4,802	1,124	934	156	550	407	1,632
Glades	7,234	1,708	1,530	283	1,134	269	2,310
Gulf	6,561	1,364	1,145	446	643	773	2,191
Hamilton	6,823	1,362	1,943	251	1,360	591	1,315
Hardee	19,026	2,660	3,319	307	5,776	987	5,977
Hendry	18,567	3,873	4,624	935	2,366	741	6,029
Hernando	60,372	13,512	13,543	3,598	7,188	1,804	20,727
Highlands	29,391	7,372	8,635	4,093	5,584	1,988	1,719
Hillsborough	779,340	114,124	161,984	123,846	58,311	60,954	260,121
Holmes	6,049	1,090	868	186	1,458	291	2,155
Indian River	96,442	10,648	19,620	7,446	7,657	2,561	48,510
Jackson	17,561	3,032	3,684	201	4,396	689	5,560
Jefferson	6,443	1,277	1,572	320	1,228	145	1,899
Lafayette	2,835	682	451	141	449	48	1,065
Lake	69,475	10,616	18,744	3,348	7,594	3,899	25,274

See footnotes at end of table.   Continued . . .

Table 23.84. LOCAL GOVERNMENT: EXPENDITURE BY FUNCTION OF COUNTY GOVERNMENTS
    IN FLORIDA, FISCAL YEARS ENDING SEPTEMBER 30, 1988 AND 1989 (Continued)

(rounded to thousands of dollars)

County 1/	Total	General govern- mental services	Public safety	Physical envi- ronment	Trans- porta- tion	Human services	Miscella- neous 2/
			1988-89 (Continued)				
Lee	415,684	50,538	31,080	26,877	59,762	8,049	239,377
Leon	99,571	21,261	16,865	4,135	6,531	2,464	48,315
Levy	14,760	3,241	3,603	670	2,001	620	4,625
Liberty	3,204	872	562	103	713	134	821
Madison	6,539	1,339	1,452	355	779	312	2,302
Manatee	226,075	31,859	26,622	56,249	19,968	7,964	83,414
Marion	78,109	21,567	24,785	2,374	17,067	6,062	6,255
Martin	98,669	16,000	33,052	9,837	11,574	4,004	24,203
Monroe	88,874	17,500	21,837	8,927	6,915	5,054	28,641
Nassau	30,253	3,958	5,403	1,075	3,435	898	15,484
Okaloosa	55,130	9,422	10,745	10,026	8,547	1,941	34,879
Okeechobee	18,620	2,982	5,227	544	2,152	772	6,943
Orange	716,814	91,188	130,966	72,324	77,087	26,553	318,696
Osceola	106,445	11,540	16,902	1,779	9,069	2,999	64,157
Palm Beach	893,076	117,030	143,998	44,758	142,481	59,837	384,972
Pasco	414,892	28,664	33,311	23,373	20,207	4,675	304,662
Pinellas	498,206	80,029	117,445	101,588	52,386	24,846	121,912
Polk	193,465	34,406	49,288	13,896	21,314	36,150	38,413
Putnam	38,483	8,571	7,414	2,101	4,309	1,218	14,869
St. Johns	65,642	10,741	14,970	5,342	7,552	2,786	24,252
St. Lucie	93,833	23,188	19,376	2,472	11,151	3,926	33,720
Santa Rosa	38,661	5,221	6,330	3,829	5,406	1,245	16,630
Sarasota	209,834	44,362	37,988	34,140	26,053	6,996	60,296
Seminole	165,064	24,840	31,591	13,006	21,226	4,709	69,692
Sumter	16,784	2,398	3,834	485	2,915	568	6,584
Suwannee	11,692	2,264	2,135	844	1,904	398	4,148
Taylor	7,519	852	891	400	2,374	302	2,699
Union	3,752	822	701	110	478	189	1,453
Volusia	202,533	35,768	49,244	9,312	32,385	8,358	67,466
Wakulla	8,987	2,808	1,612	799	993	0	2,775
Walton	23,204	3,778	3,564	709	3,993	5,089	6,071
Washington	5,915	1,358	1,115	102	994	114	2,233

1/ Duval County data to be found in Table 23.87 under City of Jacksonville.
    2/ Includes economic environment, culture/recreation, debt service, and other fi-
nancing uses.
    3/ Does not include Duval County/Jacksonville.
    Note: See Table 23.82 for personal services expenditure, salaries and wages, and
employee benefits included in the functional distribution.
    Source: State of Florida, Department of Banking and Finance, *Local Government
Financial Report, Fiscal Year 1988-89*, and previous edition.

Table 23.85. LOCAL GOVERNMENT: REVENUE AND EXPENDITURE PER CAPITA, PERSONAL
   SERVICES EXPENDITURE, AND INDEBTEDNESS OF CITY GOVERNMENTS SERVING
   A 1989 POPULATION OF 45,000 OR MORE IN FLORIDA, FISCAL YEAR ENDING
   SEPTEMBER 30, 1989

(rounded to dollars)

City	Total revenue per capita 1/	Total expenditure per capita 1/	Personal services expenditure 2/	Bonded indebtedness	Other long-term debt
Jacksonville	1,062.6	1,150.6	261,812,743	500,585,192	106,952,568
Miami	1,446.2	1,386.8	196,062,000	432,788,000	93,206,000
Tampa	1,423.9	1,624.4	113,865,949	535,012,307	13,142,487
St. Petersburg	1,661.9	1,658.3	99,190,316	271,595,817	43,570,338
Hialeah	632.9	646.0	68,129,893	6,970,000	65,447,800
Orlando	1,982.8	2,174.5	92,554,329	402,039,951	120,772,528
Ft. Lauderdale	1,435.9	1,413.5	91,120,746	115,764,843	26,691,870
Tallahassee	2,757.6	2,715.5	65,090,500	174,641,500	36,349,900
Hollywood	829.7	849.3	58,536,477	32,944,091	9,903,896
Clearwater	2,000.9	1,991.3	47,633,038	105,544,370	14,341,813
Miami Beach	1,664.2	1,974.9	66,762,951	157,045,000	19,909,322
Gainesville	3,850.6	3,953.4	48,839,438	365,486,388	79,981,528
West Palm Beach	1,542.6	1,513.3	48,204,173	48,666,702	68,285
Coral Springs	781.3	811.1	22,486,849	46,267,363	26,822,634
Lakeland	3,520.2	3,601.2	47,920,039	292,576,593	60,555,600
Pompano Beach	1,433.9	1,305.8	33,999,295	46,133,094	19,634,429
Largo	576.0	571.2	18,145,494	17,796,973	2,954,498
Plantation	1,282.1	1,386.4	14,718,669	64,730,243	780,594
Daytona Beach	1,234.8	1,177.5	27,841,082	26,580,037	26,906,523
Pensacola	1,803.6	1,789.4	26,719,714	65,326,361	45,089,335
Cape Coral	1,059.0	810.1	20,576,252	63,838,312	1,647,137
Boca Raton	2,163.5	1,919.1	34,756,499	106,917,252	94,619,187
Melbourne	1,328.4	1,294.8	22,068,544	70,045,324	4,596,676
Pembroke Pines	965.5	967.9	20,465,285	25,395,000	1,936,868
Sunrise	1,279.6	1,172.3	22,945,335	104,582,772	5,712,742
Palm Bay	553.8	516.5	11,809,160	16,075,000	2,134,703
Sarasota	2,457.3	2,590.9	28,220,941	85,511,321	8,176,355
Deerfield Beach	778.5	771.8	16,298,428	25,933,945	4,067,139
Delray Beach	1,139.5	1,267.8	21,932,941	51,630,366	3,813,925
Port St. Lucie	676.7	359.9	6,902,941	14,000,000	2,178,581
Boynton Beach	1,318.6	1,466.4	25,620,388	41,275,784	15,133,424
Ocala	2,815.8	2,544.5	21,937,350	103,615,979	8,732,167
Lauderhill	519.3	509.7	8,319,411	16,345,000	1,673,399

1/ Total revenue and expenditure from Tables 23.86 and 23.87 divided by April 1,
1989 population estimates.
   2/ Amounts paid for salary and wages and employee benefits. These amounts are
included in the functional distribution on Table 23.87.
   Source: State of Florida, Department of Banking and Finance, *Local Government
Financial Report, Fiscal Year 1988-89.*

Florida Statistical Abstract 1991

Table 23.86. LOCAL GOVERNMENT: REVENUE BY SOURCE OF CITY GOVERNMENTS SERVING
A 1989 POPULATION OF 45,000 OR MORE IN FLORIDA, FISCAL YEARS ENDING
SEPTEMBER 30, 1988 AND 1989

(rounded to thousands of dollars)

City	Total revenue	Revenue from taxes	Revenue from licenses and permits	Inter-govern-mental revenue	Charges for services	Miscel-lane-ous 1/	Other financ-ing sources 2/
			1987-88				
Jacksonville	818,346	218,890	5,473	156,562	116,123	56,638	264,660
Miami	495,990	170,097	5,384	53,887	41,813	41,670	183,139
Tampa	502,752	90,543	7,602	43,643	103,269	39,088	218,608
St. Petersburg	347,415	69,605	2,833	28,655	74,154	48,346	123,823
Hialeah	102,766	39,403	3,177	22,216	25,252	6,188	6,530
Orlando	283,865	55,570	3,459	34,433	51,898	88,834	49,671
Ft. Lauderdale	181,311	66,065	4,334	19,045	55,817	23,566	12,484
Tallahassee	291,189	17,954	1,367	13,622	170,642	26,116	61,487
Hollywood	93,355	36,960	1,919	13,804	25,175	10,083	5,415
Clearwater	108,980	29,879	1,940	10,767	46,122	10,728	9,544
Miami Beach	136,227	73,235	2,916	12,882	25,099	17,047	5,047
Gainesville	229,248	15,346	1,046	7,891	118,907	25,977	60,081
West Palm Beach	96,421	36,684	1,852	8,492	30,816	10,524	8,052
Coral Springs	40,891	16,596	1,576	4,634	7,595	7,210	3,280
Lakeland	254,785	11,207	1,217	8,716	154,036	22,102	57,508
Pompano Beach	71,530	24,834	1,869	6,564	19,230	8,023	11,008
Largo	37,513	9,374	691	9,082	10,287	6,295	1,784
Plantation	59,936	13,499	2,422	5,612	13,083	12,425	12,894
Daytona Beach	65,910	17,123	1,237	5,966	21,719	13,611	6,254
Pensacola	111,694	13,638	735	9,879	40,022	2,683	44,737
Cape Coral	40,874	11,398	1,937	5,012	12,015	5,841	4,671
Boca Raton	112,386	30,971	1,950	10,162	21,202	15,702	32,398
Melbourne	76,558	13,444	851	4,898	25,188	13,079	19,099
Pembroke Pines	37,256	10,270	2,314	6,952	10,507	6,494	720
Sunrise	60,973	13,266	3,139	3,898	24,258	13,420	2,992
Palm Bay	24,281	12,438	934	3,124	1,722	3,501	2,562
Sarasota	71,352	20,288	1,344	11,046	22,638	5,940	10,097
Deerfield Beach	34,896	11,233	895	3,716	12,771	4,812	1,470
Delray Beach	55,447	17,102	1,381	4,235	14,363	6,757	11,609
Port St. Lucie	14,635	4,805	1,360	2,395	3,592	824	1,660
Boynton Beach	51,100	15,045	1,587	3,706	16,789	10,328	3,645
Ocala	140,062	7,104	607	7,272	69,901	7,151	48,027
Lauderhill	22,544	8,817	1,000	3,295	5,490	2,061	1,880

See footnotes at end of table.

Continued . . .

Table 23.86. LOCAL GOVERNMENT: REVENUE BY SOURCE OF CITY GOVERNMENTS SERVING
A 1989 POPULATION OF 45,000 OR MORE IN FLORIDA, FISCAL YEARS ENDING
SEPTEMBER 30, 1988 AND 1989 (Continued)

(rounded to thousands of dollars)

City	Total revenue	Revenue from taxes	Revenue from licenses and permits	Inter-govern-mental revenue	Charges for services	Miscel-lane-ous 1/	Other financ-ing sources 2/
			1988-89				
Jacksonville	687,970	248,049	5,561	169,277	129,555	64,751	70,778
Miami	537,183	174,155	5,696	61,617	50,448	76,338	168,929
Tampa	409,957	99,264	9,301	53,527	114,206	32,378	101,281
St. Petersburg	410,113	74,174	3,521	23,491	83,261	126,148	99,519
Hialeah	109,467	43,575	3,506	20,583	27,331	10,925	3,548
Orlando	329,509	64,431	3,788	59,097	63,595	56,285	82,313
Ft. Lauderdale	216,289	68,858	4,215	17,333	59,346	29,076	37,460
Tallahassee	359,267	19,097	1,410	13,358	187,929	38,744	98,729
Hollywood	104,854	39,305	2,186	15,855	28,423	9,229	9,856
Clearwater	202,259	31,233	1,978	10,314	51,908	12,948	93,879
Miami Beach	163,167	69,775	4,090	12,793	25,280	25,287	25,943
Gainesville	329,855	15,622	919	8,552	133,404	44,844	126,513
West Palm Beach	114,593	38,469	2,166	10,552	34,074	9,986	19,345
Coral Springs	57,668	19,329	1,591	4,955	7,983	7,227	16,583
Lakeland	256,224	12,566	1,204	9,860	159,655	25,701	47,239
Pompano Beach	102,068	26,472	2,153	7,071	22,437	10,362	33,574
Largo	38,599	10,671	877	8,921	11,014	4,818	2,297
Plantation	84,711	14,643	2,817	12,652	14,730	6,541	33,326
Daytona Beach	80,080	19,456	1,310	6,002	23,535	10,487	19,291
Pensacola	115,924	14,975	809	10,491	36,355	10,410	42,883
Cape Coral	66,550	13,320	2,004	5,896	14,846	8,194	22,289
Boca Raton	133,123	34,637	2,611	14,587	23,216	19,800	38,272
Melbourne	81,403	14,101	947	6,812	25,568	9,968	24,007
Pembroke Pines	58,741	11,978	2,544	5,731	11,912	18,897	7,681
Sunrise	75,741	14,150	3,395	4,853	24,855	13,139	15,349
Palm Bay	31,385	13,515	1,059	3,126	2,348	3,189	8,150
Sarasota	127,243	21,449	1,461	14,182	28,182	17,890	44,079
Deerfield Beach	38,926	12,815	690	4,414	13,961	5,234	1,813
Delray Beach	55,826	18,229	1,250	4,491	14,942	6,821	10,093
Port St. Lucie	32,517	5,867	1,457	2,551	3,879	2,097	16,666
Boynton Beach	62,567	18,750	1,823	4,256	18,195	11,760	7,783
Ocala	129,001	8,295	621	7,721	74,861	8,388	29,115
Lauderhill	23,392	8,953	726	3,426	5,890	2,595	1,802

1/ Includes fines and forfeitures, interest earnings, rents and royalties,
special assessments, contributions, etc.

2/ Includes interfund transfers, contributions from enterprises, debt proceeds,
trust fund receipts, and other nonrevenue receipts.

Source: State of Florida, Department of Banking and Finance, *Local Government
Financial Report, Fiscal Year 1988-89*, and previous edition.

Florida Statistical Abstract 1991

Table 23.87. LOCAL GOVERNMENT: EXPENDITURE BY FUNCTION OF CITY GOVERNMENTS SERVING
   A 1989 POPULATION OF 45,000 OR MORE IN FLORIDA, FISCAL YEARS ENDING SEPTEMBER 30
   1988 AND 1989

(rounded to thousands of dollars)

City	Total	General governmental services	Public safety	Physical environment	Transportation	Human services	Miscellaneous 1/
			1987-88				
Jacksonville	708,765	50,116	158,406	89,544	65,875	38,139	306,683
Miami	554,103	85,798	117,938	37,591	32,298	0	280,478
Tampa	547,126	14,430	66,929	108,062	19,422	795	337,488
St. Petersburg	362,810	18,802	54,916	60,599	15,816	899	211,775
Hialeah	109,248	17,054	36,150	30,521	2,247	157	23,119
Orlando	300,277	18,731	48,068	59,204	17,602	1,073	155,599
Ft. Lauderdale	180,517	16,193	52,738	44,978	11,244	0	55,363
Tallahassee	289,095	7,952	21,217	125,367	26,442	1,640	106,476
Hollywood	99,821	6,314	36,807	23,672	8,324	182,145	24,520
Clearwater	111,706	5,877	21,512	36,966	11,314	407	35,630
Miami Beach	161,973	13,513	47,831	19,501	7,390	609	73,128
Gainesville	214,405	9,502	21,386	116,840	11,103	477	55,097
West Palm Beach	90,708	11,695	21,483	23,372	4,721	0	29,437
Coral Springs	48,481	6,340	12,827	10,066	3,040	0	16,208
Lakeland	255,351	7,978	12,182	131,203	7,470	32	96,485
Pompano Beach	63,739	5,432	23,138	19,550	2,423	0	13,195
Largo	41,821	3,772	12,170	12,698	447	0	12,734
Plantation	63,017	4,945	11,455	14,034	1,039	0	31,543
Daytona Beach	79,875	4,468	16,557	19,497	4,741	235	34,377
Pensacola	116,007	7,198	12,955	28,054	10,516	206	57,076
Cape Coral	43,485	6,135	8,438	11,509	4,930	0	12,475
Boca Raton	126,727	5,426	18,664	24,082	7,972	275	70,307
Melbourne	75,424	4,043	10,849	12,664	7,487	212	40,168
Pembroke Pines	43,841	8,156	12,400	8,975	968	343	12,999
Sunrise	52,719	4,291	12,035	23,365	1,746	0	11,282
Palm Bay	22,585	3,847	7,576	2,202	2,990	80	5,889
Sarasota	83,887	4,753	17,427	17,889	9,998	0	33,819
Deerfield Beach	38,205	6,392	8,658	12,908	1,726	525	7,996
Delray Beach	63,127	4,837	15,025	18,156	1,121	145	23,843
Port St. Lucie	14,176	1,904	3,530	3,045	1,368	148	4,180
Boynton Beach	53,117	7,726	12,711	12,703	1,047	129	18,800
Ocala	142,144	5,594	9,366	56,134	3,343	0	67,706
Lauderhill	20,536	2,259	7,215	4,798	741	569	4,952

See footnotes at end of table.   Continued . . .

Florida Statistical Abstract 1991

Table 23.87. LOCAL GOVERNMENT: EXPENDITURE BY FUNCTION OF CITY GOVERNMENTS SERVING
    A 1989 POPULATION OF 45,000 OR MORE IN FLORIDA, FISCAL YEARS ENDING SEPTEMBER 30
    1988 AND 1989 (Continued)

(rounded to thousands of dollars)

City	Total	General govern- mental services	Public safety	Physical envi- ronment	Trans- porta- tion	Human ser- vices	Miscel- lane- ous 1/
			1988-89				
Jacksonville	744,933	60,468	208,144	116,543	84,438	41,882	233,457
Miami	515,130	107,836	128,197	34,349	24,708	0	220,040
Tampa	467,698	13,150	70,576	103,401	26,860	608	253,104
St. Petersburg	409,224	21,756	56,074	65,129	25,437	929	239,900
Hialeah	111,736	15,354	36,494	30,247	5,319	170	24,153
Orlando	361,367	24,305	53,276	66,531	25,245	1,178	190,834
Ft. Lauderdale	212,920	18,683	56,085	48,046	13,798	0	76,309
Tallahassee	353,793	28,931	27,457	134,258	24,750	1,460	136,937
Hollywood	107,334	8,260	40,264	27,993	6,427	178	24,212
Clearwater	201,281	7,748	23,308	41,594	11,680	605	116,346
Miami Beach	193,636	19,491	45,326	21,164	15,339	669	91,646
Gainesville	338,659	9,672	21,595	130,788	13,261	670	162,673
West Palm Beach	112,412	28,772	24,300	25,743	4,910	0	28,689
Coral Springs	59,873	8,157	11,625	10,231	2,770	0	27,089
Lakeland	262,120	7,773	14,118	134,054	10,264	41	95,871
Pompano Beach	92,949	8,833	24,965	20,741	3,617	0	34,794
Largo	38,277	3,421	10,896	11,800	1,493	0	10,666
Plantation	91,598	4,103	12,014	20,363	514	0	54,604
Daytona Beach	76,366	4,461	18,199	20,449	4,785	155	28,319
Pensacola	115,012	7,131	14,655	27,564	10,354	232	55,075
Cape Coral	50,909	9,031	9,608	12,562	5,009	0	14,699
Boca Raton	118,082	7,664	18,528	25,262	7,258	291	59,079
Melbourne	79,344	4,366	12,102	14,214	7,043	262	41,357
Pembroke Pines	58,887	4,496	13,753	8,942	1,674	328	29,694
Sunrise	69,389	5,074	22,192	25,020	2,342	0	14,762
Palm Bay	29,272	6,051	8,697	3,126	4,115	102	7,182
Sarasota	134,159	5,208	18,794	22,595	6,526	0	81,038
Deerfield Beach	38,591	6,761	9,061	13,828	1,545	742	6,653
Delray Beach	62,115	6,087	16,201	15,517	1,888	177	22,246
Port St. Lucie	17,295	2,358	4,693	4,076	2,024	186	3,959
Boynton Beach	69,582	10,775	14,408	16,050	1,143	725	26,481
Ocala	116,572	3,968	11,299	55,427	5,448	0	40,429
Lauderhill	22,960	2,753	7,756	5,752	575	659	5,465

1/ Includes economic environment, culture/recreation, debt service, and other
financing uses.
    Note: See Table 23.85 for personal services expenditure, salaries and wages, and
employee benefits included in the functional distribution.
    Source: State of Florida, Department of Banking and Finance, *Local Government
Financial Report, Fiscal Year 1988-89*, and previous edition.

Florida Statistical Abstract 1991

Table 23.88. LOCAL GOVERNMENT: REVENUE, EXPENDITURE, AND MILLAGE RATE OF SPECIAL
DISTRICTS WITH REVENUE OVER $6,000,000 IN SPECIFIED COUNTIES OF FLORIDA
FISCAL YEAR ENDING SEPTEMBER 30, 1989

District and county location	Total revenue ($1,000)	Unit-wide millage rate	Total expenditure and uses ($1,000)
Alachua County Health Facility Authority (Alachua)	18,634	0.000	1,938
Baker Hospital Authority (Baker)	6,822	5.000	6,833
Bay Medical Center (Bay)	112,402	0.000	121,506
Canaveral Port Authority (Brevard)	18,774	0.000	9,625
North Brevard Hospital (Brevard)	39,896	0.747	37,123
Broward Housing Authority (Broward)	12,183	0.000	11,876
Coral Springs Improvement (Broward)	34,653	0.000	31,930
Ft. Lauderdale Housing Authority (Broward)	23,104	0.000	19,770
Indian Trace Community Development (Broward)	21,256	0.000	32,610
North Broward Hospital (Broward)	326,476	2.103	345,948
North Springs Improvement (Broward)	18,152	0.000	18,194
Performing Arts Center Authority (Broward	11,384	0.000	10,465
South Broward Hospital (Broward)	198,953	2.120	197,953
Citrus Memorial Hospital (Citrus)	33,098	0.384	34,474
Hialeah Housing Authority (Dade)	9,104	0.000	8,221
Miami Beach Housing Authority (Dade)	19,867	0.000	19,055
First Coast Medical Center (Duval)	17,707	0.150	18,752
Jacksonville Port Authority (Duval)	100,820	0.000	103,632
Jacksonville Electric Authority (Duval)	954,723	0.000	971,826
Escambia Utility Authority (Escambia)	117,421	0.000	119,721
Dunes Community Development (Flagler)	15,060	0.000	7,127
Hardee Memorial Hospital (Hardee)	6,478	0.000	6,502
Hendry Hospital (Hendry)	8,679	1.500	8,894
Sebring Utility Commission (Highlands)	21,083	0.000	29,414
Hillsborough Aviation Authority (Hillsborough)	314,766	0.000	142,286
Hillsborough County Hospital Authority (Hillsborough)	236,283	0.000	243,808
Tampa Port Authority (Hillsborough)	37,742	0.000	38,029
Tampa Housing Authority (Hillsborough)	35,786	0.000	34,421
Hillsborough Transit Authority (Hillsborough)	35,914	0.500	37,737
Indian River Hospital (Indian River)	10,116	1.130	10,526
Jackson County Hospital (Jackson)	11,836	0.000	11,673
South Lake Hospital (Lake)	8,971	2.000	9,640
Ft. Myers Housing Authority (Lee)	8,158	0.000	8,756
Lee Memorial Hospital (Lee)	125,213	0.000	136,596
Lee County Mosquito Control (Lee)	6,638	0.485	6,920
Tallahassee Housing Authority (Leon)	10,080	0.000	9,599
Leon County Research-Development Authority (Leon)	6,609	0.000	7,158
Key West Utility Board (Monroe)	43,654	0.000	53,724
Lower Florida Keys Hospital (Monroe)	19,303	1.639	23,527
Nassau General Hospital (Nassau)	9,239	1.154	8,592
Okaloosa County Gas (Okaloosa)	15,244	0.000	23,247
Greater Orlando Aviation Authority (Orange)	328,567	0.000	354,384
Orange County Housing Finance Authority (Orange)	184,447	0.000	99,785
Orlando Housing Authority (Orange)	24,268	0.000	26,365
Orlando Utilities Commission (Orange)	637,862	0.000	439,504
West Orange Memorial Hospital (Orange)	27,648	0.587	27,256
Kissimmee Utility Authority (Osceola)	60,479	0.000	59,468

Continued . . .

Table 23.88. LOCAL GOVERNMENT: REVENUE, EXPENDITURE, AND MILLAGE RATE OF SPECIAL
DISTRICTS WITH REVENUE OVER $6,000,000 IN SPECIFIED COUNTIES OF FLORIDA
FISCAL YEAR ENDING SEPTEMBER 30, 1989 (Continued)

District and county location	Total revenue ($1,000)	Unit-wide millage rate	Total expen-diture and uses ($1,000)
Acme Improvement (Palm Beach)	16,985	0.000	14,952
Child Service Council (Palm Beach)	6,206	0.153	3,944
Greater Boca Raton Beach Tax (Palm Beach)	8,453	1.071	6,288
Lake Worth Drainage (Palm Beach)	7,084	0.000	6,218
Northern Palm Beach Water Control (Palm Beach)	41,831	0.000	35,544
Palm Beach County Housing Finance Authority (Palm Beach)	100,556	0.000	98,852
Palm Beach Solid Waste Authority (Palm Beach)	146,425	0.000	142,151
Seacoast Utility Authority (Palm Beach)	112,586	0.000	107,848
Southeast Palm Beach Hospital (Palm Beach)	10,478	0.680	13,716
Southwest Palm Beach Hospital (Palm Beach)	15,906	7.418	15,514
Pinellas Suncoast Transit Authority (Pinellas)	36,991	0.514	38,057
Pinellas Housing Authority (Pinellas)	9,908	0.000	9,453
Juvenile Welfare Board (Pinellas)	15,160	0.436	15,246
St. Petersburg Housing Authority (Pinellas)	18,886	0.000	17,885
St. Augustine-Johns Airport (St. Lucie)	6,156	0.200	10,587
Fort Pierce Housing Authority (St. Lucie)	9,171	0.000	10,002
St. Lucie-Ft. Pierce Fire (St. Lucie)	11,688	2.100	10,092
Sarasota Memorial Hospital (Sarasota)	211,026	0.306	219,785
Halifax Hospital (Volusia)	152,733	2.468	157,343
Volusia County Educational Facility Authority (Volusia)	10,723	0.000	656
Southeast Volusia Hospital (Volusia)	19,798	1.898	23,945
West Volusia Hospital Authority (Volusia)	58,277	2.610	60,401
East Central Florida Regional Planning Council (Multicounty)	9,528	0.000	9,489
Tampa Bay Regional Planning Council (Multicounty)	16,110	0.000	15,896
First Florida Government Finance Commission (Multicounty)	48,607	0.000	45,969
First Municipal Loan Council (Multicounty)	19,145	0.000	61,713
Sunshine State Government Finance Commission (Multicounty)	29,152	0.000	26,776
South Florida Water Management (Multicounty)	139,625	0.272	132,700
Florida Municipal Power Agency (Multicounty)	158,340	0.000	170,798
Reedy Creek Improvement (Multicounty)	125,075	9.504	144,143
Northwest Florida Water Management (Multicounty)	9,213	0.050	8,656
St. Johns River Water Management (Multicounty)	46,059	0.281	52,918
Southwest Florida Water Management (Multicounty)	50,464	0.365	43,129
Suwannee River Water Management (Multicounty)	14,083	0.300	18,437
Florida Inland Navigation (Multicounty)	8,129	0.040	5,108
Orange-Seminole-Osceola Transportation Authority (Multicounty)	18,286	0.000	19,685
Sarasota-Manatee Airport Authority (Multicounty)	48,192	0.000	48,786
Englewood Water District (Multicounty)	7,357	1.500	7,598
Loxahatchee Environment Control (Multicounty)	8,087	0.000	8,717
West Coast Regional Water Supply (Multicounty)	21,822	0.000	27,142

Source: State of Florida, Department of Banking and Finance, *Local Government Financial Report, Fiscal Year 1988-89.*

Florida Statistical Abstract 1991

Table 23.89. PROPERTY VALUATIONS: NET ASSESSED VALUES OF REAL, PERSONAL, AND
RAILROAD PROPERTY IN FLORIDA, JANUARY 1, 1955 THROUGH 1990

(amounts rounded to thousands of dollars)

Year	Total Amount	Percentage change from previous year	Real property Amount	Percentage of total	Personal property Amount	Percentage of total	Railroad and private car lines Amount	Percentage of total
1955	6,945,377	12.71	5,923,764	85.29	887,361	12.78	134,252	1.93
1956	7,784,905	12.09	6,744,681	86.64	906,056	11.64	134,168	1.72
1957	9,199,610	18.17	8,039,628	87.39	1,031,410	11.21	128,572	1.40
1958	10,913,540	18.63	9,591,706	87.88	1,183,271	10.84	138,563	1.28
1959	12,167,304	11.49	10,706,612	88.00	1,319,246	10.84	141,447	1.16
1960	14,789,849	21.55	12,945,632	87.53	1,686,093	11.40	158,124	1.07
1961	16,678,864	12.77	14,659,588	87.89	1,855,228	11.12	164,049	0.99
1962	18,354,359	10.05	16,157,399	88.03	2,030,580	11.06	166,381	0.91
1963	19,210,827	4.67	16,890,665	87.92	2,152,967	11.21	167,195	0.87
1964	23,994,036	24.90	21,140,438	88.11	2,674,478	11.14	179,121	0.75
1965	29,760,016	24.03	26,233,082	88.15	3,321,356	11.16	205,578	0.69
1966	36,253,654	21.82	31,943,021	88.11	4,036,480	11.13	274,153	0.76
1967	40,606,927	12.01	35,154,260	86.57	5,162,026	12.71	290,640	0.72
1968	42,060,610	3.58	36,637,166	87.10	5,125,541	12.19	297,903	0.71
1969	45,180,722	7.42	39,697,479	87.86	5,187,897	11.48	295,346	0.66
1970	51,247,667	13.43	45,066,274	87.94	5,915,000	11.54	266,393	0.52
1971	59,967,320	17.01	51,822,900	86.42	7,845,286	13.08	299,134	0.50
1972	67,053,619	11.82	56,610,767	84.43	10,134,332	15.11	308,520	0.46
1973	82,146,275	22.51	69,936,535	85.14	11,870,966	14.45	338,774	0.41
1974	107,894,309	31.34	92,979,953	86.18	14,570,730	13.50	343,627	0.32
1975	120,558,360	11.74	103,460,245	85.82	16,690,698	13.84	407,417	0.34
1976	128,700,512	6.75	109,217,279	84.86	19,072,710	14.82	410,523	0.32
1977	139,650,757	8.51	118,232,881	84.66	20,925,041	14.98	492,835	0.35
1978	151,271,654	8.24	129,382,344	85.53	21,393,945	14.14	495,365	0.33
1979	159,642,320	5.53	135,705,468	84.38	24,422,967	15.30	513,884	0.32
1980	187,750,045	17.61	164,755,192	87.75	22,480,384	11.97	514,470	0.27
1981	237,140,341	26.31	211,148,696	89.04	25,579,874	10.79	411,772	0.17
1982	272,997,005	15.12	244,424,808	89.53	28,194,359	10.53	377,839	0.14
1983	298,583,050	9.37	266,304,607	89.19	31,858,923	10.67	419,519	0.14
1984	323,647,775	8.39	288,392,562	89.11	34,820,448	10.76	434,765	0.13
1985	356,061,973	10.02	317,508,051	89.17	38,100,514	10.70	453,408	0.13
1986	385,126,891	8.16	343,168,089	89.11	41,389,766	10.75	569,036	0.15
1987	417,508,830	8.41	372,504,470	89.22	44,326,033	10.62	678,327	0.16
1988	446,103,804	6.80	398,216,681	89.27	47,192,039	10.58	695,085	0.16
1989	485,766,305	8.90	434,583,860	89.46	50,554,052	10.41	628,394	0.13
1990	524,248,524	7.92	469,498,829	89.56	54,114,754	10.32	634,941	0.12

Note: Net assessed value is total assessed or just value less nontaxable value
of property having a classified use value. Classified use value is the value at
which agricultural land and certain privately owned park and recreation land is
assessed for tax purposes. The "highest and best" use principle is relaxed and
assessment is based on current use only. Some data are revised.

Source: State of Florida, Department of Revenue, *Florida Ad Valorem Valuations
and Tax Data, 1990.*

Florida Statistical Abstract 1991

Table 23.90. PROPERTY VALUATIONS: ASSESSED AND TAXABLE VALUES BY CATEGORY
OF REAL PROPERTY IN FLORIDA, JANUARY 1, 1989 AND 1990

(rounded to thousands of dollars)

Category	Just value 1/ 1989	Just value 1/ 1990 A/	Taxable value 2/ 1989	Taxable value 2/ 1990 A/
Total	512,185,685	553,720,860	363,840,923	396,080,599
Residential				
Vacant	25,657,906	27,378,716	25,396,138	27,049,444
Single-family	189,043,089	206,797,189	134,937,939	151,054,377
Mobile homes	7,652,807	8,211,105	4,037,968	4,410,448
Multifamily				
10 units or more	14,981,521	16,085,001	14,785,966	15,862,355
9 units or less	11,964,701	11,611,085	10,909,171	10,571,059
Condominiums	60,125,563	66,600,700	50,023,571	55,685,968
Cooperatives	2,492,822	2,625,038	1,810,959	1,907,752
Retirement homes	1,450,585	1,654,204	1,194,734	1,375,092
Commercial				
Vacant	8,354,831	8,617,028	8,240,028	8,503,402
Improved	70,291,049	75,643,287	69,483,180	74,735,373
Industrial				
Vacant	2,753,397	2,943,881	2,698,305	2,894,329
Improved	16,295,373	17,549,004	16,206,842	17,460,159
Agricultural	32,029,983	33,440,373	9,026,633	9,098,293
Institutional	12,964,964	14,198,393	3,237,793	3,501,845
Government	42,117,774	46,211,350	457,188	508,134
Leasehold	1,093,119	1,133,639	572,811	605,395
Miscellaneous	4,824,255	5,136,210	3,225,006	3,439,959
Nonagricultural	8,091,946	7,868,296	7,596,691	7,409,269

A/ Totals include centrally assessed values not shown elsewhere.

1/ The value of property for tax purposes as determined by the elected county property appraiser. Value is determined at the highest and best use of property, except for special classes provided for in Florida Statutes.

2/ The value against which millage rates are applied to compute the amount of tax levied. Total taxable value makes up the ad valorem tax base for units of government in Florida.

Source: State of Florida, Department of Revenue, *Florida Ad Valorem Valuations and Tax Data, 1990,* and previous edition.

Florida Statistical Abstract 1991

Table 23.91. PROPERTY VALUATIONS: ASSESSED, EXEMPT, AND TAXABLE VALUES OF REAL
    PROPERTY IN THE STATE AND COUNTIES OF FLORIDA, JANUARY 1, 1989 AND 1990

(rounded to thousands of dollars)

County	Just values 1/		Exempt and immune values		Taxable values 2/	
	1989	1990	1989	1990	1989	1990
Florida	510,639,283	553,716,226	148,067,989	157,252,768	362,173,329	396,038,215
Alachua	5,177,739	5,403,741	2,569,029	2,613,751	2,608,710	2,789,990
Baker	514,665	528,038	384,052	390,579	130,613	137,459
Bay	5,041,885	5,230,709	2,113,653	2,235,706	2,928,232	2,995,003
Bradford	554,618	564,563	346,618	350,212	208,000	214,351
Brevard	16,653,353	19,463,263	6,477,358	8,231,483	10,175,995	11,231,780
Broward	49,813,759	53,845,644	11,395,567	11,805,031	38,418,192	42,040,613
Calhoun	295,137	301,872	190,496	192,093	104,641	109,779
Charlotte	5,007,302	6,092,198	1,136,811	1,286,695	3,870,492	4,805,503
Citrus	3,285,783	3,594,052	1,099,720	1,208,413	2,186,063	2,385,639
Clay	2,871,547	3,091,031	1,051,471	1,090,260	1,820,076	2,000,771
Collier	12,334,711	14,326,125	2,044,924	2,221,429	10,289,787	12,104,696
Columbia	1,070,251	1,115,596	607,835	616,560	462,417	499,036
Dade	70,469,653	75,917,233	18,431,571	18,976,327	52,038,082	56,940,907
De Soto	999,307	1,018,995	581,287	570,669	418,021	448,326
Dixie	420,877	440,159	289,457	300,004	131,420	140,155
Duval	22,228,019	23,280,768	8,165,719	8,485,110	14,062,299	14,795,657
Escambia	7,414,868	8,057,565	4,220,503	4,319,863	3,194,364	3,737,703
Flagler	2,043,831	2,172,335	470,449	501,123	1,573,382	1,671,211
Franklin	1,070,042	1,085,835	807,925	812,226	262,116	273,609
Gadsden	677,023	711,102	410,657	429,215	266,366	281,887
Gilchrist	332,910	341,960	223,834	225,232	109,076	116,727
Glades	818,567	845,479	544,115	558,854	274,452	286,626
Gulf	529,984	546,479	267,945	275,199	262,039	271,280
Hamilton	345,505	350,856	192,039	192,221	153,467	158,635
Hardee	1,114,767	1,161,384	713,997	751,742	400,770	409,641
Hendry	1,865,760	1,967,469	1,132,058	1,185,675	733,701	781,794
Hernando	3,400,040	3,826,068	1,147,164	1,232,835	2,252,876	2,593,233
Highlands	2,376,108	2,537,759	865,139	952,147	1,510,969	1,585,612
Hillsborough	27,451,729	28,718,301	8,912,504	9,147,827	18,539,225	19,570,475
Holmes	388,767	398,121	276,832	278,954	111,935	119,167
Indian River	4,954,817	5,346,943	1,102,180	1,143,628	3,852,637	4,203,315
Jackson	1,002,970	1,031,625	640,138	650,836	362,832	380,788
Jefferson	325,553	352,433	207,751	214,436	117,802	137,997
Lafayette	223,559	226,293	161,509	162,704	62,050	63,589
Lake	4,272,219	4,571,001	1,429,837	1,490,256	2,842,382	3,080,745
Lee	16,948,959	19,459,028	3,502,445	3,879,781	13,446,514	15,579,246
Leon	7,093,389	7,474,448	3,575,593	3,668,163	3,517,796	3,806,285

See footnotes at end of table.   Continued . . .

Table 23.91. PROPERTY VALUATIONS: ASSESSED, EXEMPT, AND TAXABLE VALUES OF REAL
PROPERTY IN THE STATE AND COUNTIES OF FLORIDA, JANUARY 1, 1989 AND 1990
(Continued)

(rounded to thousands of dollars)

County	Just values 1/		Exempt and immune values		Taxable values 2/	
	1989	1990	1989	1990	1989	1990
Levy	654,285	731,994	277,744	285,850	376,541	446,144
Liberty	147,111	154,042	100,723	106,293	46,388	47,749
Madison	402,546	421,959	255,058	266,415	147,488	155,543
Manatee	8,451,225	8,919,191	2,370,473	2,419,633	6,069,816	6,488,840
Marion	6,167,183	6,735,688	2,525,857	2,764,211	3,641,326	3,971,477
Martin	7,092,806	8,344,561	1,652,313	2,132,127	5,329,130	6,100,808
Monroe	6,479,704	7,006,608	1,355,473	1,390,348	5,124,231	5,616,260
Nassau	1,632,414	1,752,367	520,674	555,099	1,111,741	1,197,268
Okaloosa	4,166,140	4,276,828	1,266,952	1,302,890	2,899,188	2,973,938
Okeechobee	1,098,286	1,150,220	510,754	529,758	587,532	620,462
Orange	28,630,827	33,061,370	6,748,477	8,016,495	21,882,350	25,044,876
Osceola	4,298,547	4,970,493	1,223,875	1,423,764	3,074,672	3,546,729
Palm Beach	52,536,336	55,760,549	11,208,219	11,633,264	41,328,116	44,127,285
Pasco	8,554,078	8,901,856	3,039,712	3,133,283	5,514,365	5,768,573
Pinellas	32,909,260	35,163,284	8,845,445	9,202,348	24,063,815	25,960,935
Polk	10,767,815	11,217,863	3,433,156	3,710,029	7,334,659	7,507,834
Putnam	1,684,922	1,786,888	729,941	753,624	954,981	1,033,264
St. Johns	3,754,110	4,133,610	838,557	933,245	2,915,553	3,200,365
St. Lucie	6,344,889	7,098,631	1,627,133	1,697,743	4,448,889	5,104,788
Santa Rosa	2,593,751	2,718,170	980,893	1,015,940	1,612,858	1,702,231
Sarasota	14,495,761	15,593,167	3,127,266	3,254,290	11,368,495	12,338,878
Seminole	9,208,030	10,119,513	2,094,057	2,207,244	7,113,973	7,912,269
Sumter	705,977	738,103	411,985	425,831	293,992	312,272
Suwannee	598,916	624,610	353,332	361,940	245,584	262,671
Taylor	693,986	713,757	398,404	401,164	295,581	312,593
Union	194,976	202,470	144,856	150,403	50,120	52,067
Volusia	12,691,103	13,643,838	3,467,758	3,632,558	9,216,545	10,004,480
Wakulla	464,644	489,266	307,735	318,946	156,908	170,319
Walton	1,448,865	1,499,892	345,991	362,495	1,102,875	1,137,398
Washington	380,617	388,966	214,993	218,299	165,823	170,668

1/ The value of property for tax purposes as determined by the elected county
property appraiser before deduction of exemptions and immunities. Value is determined at the highest and best use of property, except for special classes provided
for in Florida Statutes.

2/ The value against which millage rates are applied to compute the amount of tax
levied. The tax base of a unit of local government also includes the taxable value
of personal property and centrally assessed property.

Source: State of Florida, Department of Revenue, *Florida Ad Valorem Valuations
and Tax Data, 1990.*

Florida Statistical Abstract 1991

Table 23.92. LOCAL GOVERNMENT: ASSESSED AND TAXABLE VALUES, MILLAGE RATES, AND
   TAXES ON MUNICIPAL REAL, PERSONAL, AND RAILROAD PROPERTY IN THE STATE
   COUNTIES, AND MUNICIPALITIES WITH A 1990 POPULATION OVER 15,000 IN
   FLORIDA, 1990

(rounded to thousands of dollars, except where indicated)

County and municipality	Total assessed value	Exemption value Homestead	Other 1/	Taxable value	Oper- ating mil- lage rate	Taxes
Florida TMP 2/	290,521,266	31,582,342	40,143,678	218,795,247	4.8520	1,061,539
Alachua TMP	3,902,535	417,720	1,933,220	1,551,595	5.4960	8,528
Gainesville	3,554,110	341,777	1,862,679	1,349,654	5.5850	7,538
Baker TMP	93,011	20,862	18,000	54,149	3.5550	192
Bay TMP	2,643,514	382,116	387,623	1,873,775	2.0240	3,792
Panama City	1,244,195	169,432	271,511	803,253	3.9706	3,189
Bradford TMP	184,161	30,748	65,214	88,198	2.8890	255
Brevard TMP	10,547,537	1,454,558	1,467,946	7,625,032	2.9760	22,696
Cocoa	519,804	83,367	103,113	333,324	4.2000	1,400
Melbourne	2,980,530	308,895	847,968	1,823,667	3.6765	6,705
Palm Bay	2,147,787	346,069	89,452	1,712,266	1.9914	3,410
Rockledge	570,320	109,622	66,175	394,523	4.4900	1,771
Titusville	1,369,429	237,940	197,118	934,371	3.8830	3,628
Broward TMP	52,951,744	6,882,436	2,913,319	42,755,988	4.3420	185,639
Coconut Creek	1,194,089	195,218	83,196	915,675	2.9000	2,655
Cooper City	728,971	136,559	22,833	569,581	4.2700	2,432
Coral Springs	3,611,817	365,612	154,342	3,091,865	3.7979	11,743
Davie	2,156,480	253,758	231,436	1,671,287	4.3100	7,203
Deerfield Beach	2,570,403	383,371	89,347	2,097,685	4.5122	9,465
Ft. Lauderdale	10,532,105	782,391	931,779	8,817,935	4.5274	39,922
Hallandale	1,559,047	230,928	32,426	1,295,692	5.7956	7,509
Hollywood	5,426,636	769,304	454,002	4,203,330	5.6740	23,850
Lauderdale Lakes	819,115	175,107	39,196	604,812	1.7500	1,058
Lauderhill	1,564,399	261,752	20,621	1,282,026	3.2500	4,167
Margate	1,460,821	315,556	42,962	1,102,303	3.6963	4,074
Miramar	1,213,085	260,390	108,665	844,030	4.6140	3,894
North Lauderdale	640,733	139,441	31,160	470,134	4.1085	1,932
Oakland Park	1,238,206	132,102	71,910	1,034,195	4.9512	5,121
Pembroke Pines	2,462,537	470,249	211,570	1,780,718	3.7968	6,761
Plantation	3,710,949	426,888	156,698	3,127,363	2.4900	7,787
Pompano Beach	4,515,607	421,393	266,823	3,827,391	4.9564	18,970
Sunrise	2,454,534	459,111	117,325	1,878,098	4.7400	8,902
Tamarac	1,792,445	397,278	33,111	1,362,057	4.5818	6,241
Calhoun TMP	55,050	13,704	12,923	28,423	1.3690	39
Charlotte TMP	1,044,339	83,046	80,297	880,996	3.2710	2,882
Citrus TMP	419,700	56,526	43,742	319,433	7.4710	2,387
Clay TMP	536,948	86,370	61,063	389,515	2.9960	1,167
Collier TMP	4,144,056	171,326	289,950	3,682,780	1.0440	3,845
Naples	4,116,017	169,166	285,645	3,661,205	1.0017	3,667
Columbia TMP	311,233	39,999	73,386	197,848	3.6580	724

See footnotes at end of table.   Continued . . .

Florida Statistical Abstract 1991

Table 23.92. LOCAL GOVERNMENT: ASSESSED AND TAXABLE VALUES, MILLAGE RATES, AND
      TAXES ON MUNICIPAL REAL, PERSONAL, AND RAILROAD PROPERTY IN THE STATE
      COUNTIES, AND MUNICIPALITIES WITH A 1990 POPULATION OVER 15,000 IN
      FLORIDA, 1990 (Continued)

(rounded to thousands of dollars, except where indicated)

County and municipality	Total assessed value	Exemption value Homestead	Other 1/	Taxable value	Oper- ating mil- lage rate	Taxes
Dade TMP	38,248,545	3,208,698	4,861,240	29,078,608	7.9550	231,329
Coral Gables	4,518,165	229,118	482,216	3,806,832	4.3120	16,415
Hialeah	4,957,546	697,315	483,516	3,776,715	7.3940	27,925
Homestead	623,974	66,594	101,484	455,897	8.1272	3,705
Miami	15,562,527	989,178	3,613,834	10,959,515	9.5995	105,206
Miami Beach	4,581,146	305,133	603,726	3,672,288	9.9660	36,598
North Miami	1,479,230	228,085	166,263	1,084,881	6.6910	7,259
North Miami Beach	1,286,290	195,478	115,451	975,361	8.1200	7,920
Opa-locka	423,851	37,983	52,971	332,896	9.1000	3,029
De Soto TMP	165,959	29,622	39,229	97,107	7.9220	769
Dixie TMP	34,056	9,545	5,181	19,330	0.9050	17
Duval TMP	7,696,937	760,057	2,187,810	4,749,069	1.1420	5,425
Jacksonville	6,231,655	538,603	2,082,680	3,610,371	0.5088	1,837
Jacksonville Beach	721,495	103,528	59,932	558,034	3.0225	1,687
Escambia TMP	2,216,783	350,064	530,800	1,335,918	3.7070	4,953
Pensacola	2,048,559	342,855	387,897	1,317,807	3.7470	4,938
Flagler TMP	345,820	35,156	37,995	272,670	2.9400	802
Franklin TMP	124,017	30,812	22,903	69,801	4.0620	284
Gadsden TMP	328,451	66,471	131,623	130,357	1.6470	215
Gilchrist TMP	34,671	9,570	5,634	19,466	0.3860	8
Glades TMP	34,950	6,599	9,103	19,248	4.8300	93
Gulf TMP	272,601	34,074	16,422	222,105	5.4010	1,200
Hamilton TMP	61,218	14,024	15,719	31,475	2.1710	68
Hardee TMP	120,772	30,421	18,866	71,485	5.4580	390
Hendry TMP	352,689	41,194	110,106	201,389	3.9200	789
Hernando TMP	292,560	26,600	69,155	196,805	7.7240	1,520
Highlands TMP	560,377	95,680	107,331	357,365	7.5580	2,701
Hillsborough TMP	15,369,196	1,667,808	3,041,728	10,559,659	6.3110	66,638
Plant City	804,737	114,102	113,005	577,631	4.7000	2,715
Tampa	13,796,311	1,455,730	2,892,433	9,348,149	6.5390	61,128
Temple Terrace	768,147	97,977	36,291	633,879	4.4100	2,795
Holmes TMP	85,799	18,361	22,411	45,027	0.1000	5
Indian River TMP	2,363,506	214,151	156,643	1,992,712	2.9670	5,912
Vero Beach	1,245,817	109,256	122,066	1,014,496	2.4500	2,486
Jackson TMP	295,138	62,840	78,883	153,415	1.8970	291
Jefferson TMP	60,724	12,388	12,603	35,733	8.4100	301
Lafayette TMP	13,284	3,219	3,836	6,229	2.0000	12
Lake TMP	2,170,815	398,478	212,720	1,559,617	4.6760	7,292

See footnotes at end of table.   Continued . . .

Table 23.92. LOCAL GOVERNMENT: ASSESSED AND TAXABLE VALUES, MILLAGE RATES, AND
TAXES ON MUNICIPAL REAL, PERSONAL, AND RAILROAD PROPERTY IN THE STATE
COUNTIES, AND MUNICIPALITIES WITH A 1990 POPULATION OVER 15,000 IN
FLORIDA, 1990 (Continued)

(rounded to thousands of dollars, except where indicated)

County and municipality	Total assessed value	Exemption value Homestead	Other 1/	Taxable value	Oper- ating mil- lage rate	Taxes
Lee TMP	7,825,851	710,695	575,372	6,539,784	4.0600	26,550
Cape Coral	3,798,051	517,048	165,275	3,115,728	4.4471	13,856
Ft. Myers	2,243,050	150,323	375,980	1,716,748	5.0000	8,584
Leon TMP	6,361,162	502,192	2,916,059	2,942,911	3.2000	9,417
Tallahassee	6,361,162	502,192	2,916,059	2,942,911	3.2000	9,417
Levy TMP	229,321	41,744	22,149	165,428	4.1290	683
Liberty TMP	18,040	3,864	6,610	7,567	1.0000	8
Madison TMP	86,113	18,019	17,023	51,070	4.8960	250
Manatee TMP	3,085,762	351,728	341,936	2,392,097	2.1740	5,201
Bradenton	1,625,284	236,261	242,541	1,146,482	2.3446	2,688
Marion TMP	1,950,257	226,771	211,797	1,511,689	5.2100	7,876
Ocala	1,788,055	193,508	195,424	1,399,123	5.1700	7,233
Martin TMP	1,647,561	93,352	220,063	1,334,146	2.8110	3,750
Monroe TMP	2,540,520	96,390	759,453	1,684,677	4.6600	7,851
Key West	2,342,726	89,065	755,377	1,498,284	5.0800	7,611
Nassau TMP	794,059	65,736	226,343	501,980	6.7130	3,370
Okaloosa TMP	2,244,316	334,013	152,683	1,757,620	3.2890	5,780
Ft. Walton Beach	638,733	122,303	55,177	461,253	5.4660	2,521
Okeechobee TMP	180,164	24,719	27,350	128,095	4.1500	532
Orange TMP	18,097,976	1,083,713	3,028,845	13,785,419	4.0410	55,709
Orlando	10,135,531	622,575	2,573,072	6,839,884	6.0666	41,495
Winter Park	1,989,188	141,246	307,568	1,540,375	3.6080	5,558
Osceola TMP	1,344,681	181,193	114,369	1,049,119	4.4560	4,674
Kissimmee	969,585	105,824	71,582	792,179	4.5453	3,601
Palm Beach TMP	35,598,155	2,950,990	3,155,118	29,392,047	4.9540	145,601
Belle Glade	273,365	38,722	76,995	157,648	8.7639	1,382
Boca Raton	7,499,081	456,269	682,610	6,360,202	3.5419	22,527
Boynton Beach	2,384,613	356,995	209,656	1,817,963	7.7528	14,094
Delray Beach	2,851,751	334,705	179,898	2,337,148	6.1500	14,373
Greenacres City	680,202	110,423	17,798	551,980	4.1500	2,291
Jupiter	2,244,842	168,123	235,045	1,841,673	1.5484	2,852
Lake Worth	948,162	159,616	137,303	651,244	6.9284	4,512
Palm Beach Gardens	2,524,894	153,383	167,430	2,204,081	3.3330	7,346
Riviera Beach	1,599,429	126,689	157,829	1,314,911	8.9500	11,768
West Palm Beach	4,714,797	330,551	846,039	3,538,207	7.8165	27,656
Pasco TMP	1,260,465	174,537	207,075	878,854	5.5470	4,875
Pinellas TMP	26,613,955	3,832,778	1,650,343	20,030,834	5.5740	111,647
Clearwater	5,356,661	583,855	648,242	4,124,564	5.2037	21,463
Dunedin	1,482,959	249,764	267,495	965,700	5.1440	4,968
Largo	2,120,561	334,102	157,206	1,629,253	3.2200	5,246
Pinellas Park	1,721,467	281,904	128,567	1,310,995	4.2000	5,506

See footnotes at end of table.

Continued . . .

Table 23.92. LOCAL GOVERNMENT: ASSESSED AND TAXABLE VALUES, MILLAGE RATES, AND
TAXES ON MUNICIPAL REAL, PERSONAL, AND RAILROAD PROPERTY IN THE STATE
COUNTIES, AND MUNICIPALITIES WITH A 1990 POPULATION OVER 15,000 IN
FLORIDA, 1990 (Continued)

(rounded to thousands of dollars, except where indicated)

County and municipality	Total assessed value	Exemption value Homestead	Other 1/	Taxable value	Oper- ating mil- lage rate	Taxes
Pinellas (Continued)						
Safety Harbor	655,344	166,194	59,356	479,794	3.7527	1,801
St. Petersburg	9,139,270	1,553,178	1,091,459	6,494,633	8.8000	57,153
Tarpon Springs	848,588	110,765	81,990	655,833	5.2491	3,443
Polk TMP	5,763,490	761,683	1,427,834	3,573,973	3.9440	14,096
Lakeland	3,012,495	328,119	891,217	1,793,159	3.0000	5,379
Winter Haven	954,431	116,085	186,247	652,100	5.4000	3,521
Putnam TMP	473,552	65,390	168,168	239,994	8.0240	1,926
St. Johns TMP	745,220	86,901	140,466	517,852	4.9760	2,577
St. Lucie TMP	3,685,686	500,148	374,023	2,811,514	3.8840	10,920
Ft. Pierce	1,298,650	145,287	278,694	874,670	4.3675	3,820
Port St. Lucie	2,362,724	350,592	95,229	1,916,903	3.6934	7,080
Santa Rosa TMP	544,594	74,956	128,091	341,548	1.8250	623
Sarasota TMP	6,010,120	509,188	810,707	4,690,226	4.2240	19,813
Sarasota	3,418,401	278,870	603,259	2,536,272	5.2700	13,366
Venice	1,095,356	108,718	167,286	819,351	3.8060	3,118
Seminole TMP	5,325,953	722,120	365,991	4,237,842	4.8110	20,388
Altamonte Springs	1,626,679	140,423	109,380	1,376,876	4.9900	6,871
Casselberry	601,970	109,816	18,318	473,836	3.6922	1,749
Sanford	919,141	142,300	152,333	624,508	6.8759	4,294
Winter Springs	726,579	135,589	18,272	572,718	3.6153	2,071
Sumter TMP	127,161	27,698	9,930	89,532	4.0620	364
Suwannee TMP	144,714	31,730	31,341	81,643	4.9980	408
Taylor TMP	185,068	34,939	37,991	112,138	5.1000	572
Union TMP	42,423	7,341	17,486	17,595	2.5230	44
Volusia TMP	9,197,534	1,238,711	862,313	7,096,510	4.5540	32,317
Daytona Beach	2,807,311	278,336	418,385	2,110,590	5.5650	11,745
Deland	651,287	75,256	144,928	431,103	7.0000	3,018
Edgewater	424,565	105,290	10,470	308,805	4.6000	1,421
New Smyrna Beach	1,030,656	125,348	69,090	836,218	5.0500	4,223
Ormond Beach	1,519,362	214,054	79,173	1,226,135	2.6960	3,306
Port Orange	1,070,576	219,490	60,692	790,395	4.3000	3,399
Wakulla TMP	71,888	6,096	43,322	22,471	0.9390	21
Walton TMP	136,482	30,813	26,663	79,006	4.2500	336
Washington TMP	106,329	26,949	21,636	57,744	3.4820	201

TMP Total municipal property.
1/ Includes governmental, institutional, and miscellaneous other exempt proper-
ties.
2/ 1989 data as reported by the source and published in the *1990 Florida
Statistical Abstract* have been corrected. The 1989 data are as follows: total
assessed value, $269,060,477,149; homestead exemption value, $30,747,074,773; other
exemption value, $37,138,663,660; taxable value, $201,174,738,716; operating millage
rate, 4.8251; and taxes, $970,705,452.
Source: State of Florida, Department of Revenue, *Florida Ad Valorem Valuations
and Tax Data, 1990.*

Florida Statistical Abstract 1991

Table 23.93. LOCAL GOVERNMENT: AD VALOREM MILLAGE RATES IN THE COUNTIES
   OF FLORIDA, JANUARY 1, 1990

County	Total county-wide millage	County government Oper-ating millage	Debt service millage	District school board Oper-ating millage	Debt service millage	Other mill-age 1/
Alachua	23.1923	9.2500	0.0300	8.6970	2.5400	2.6753
Baker	23.5403	9.0200	0.0000	8.8770	0.0000	5.6433
Bay	13.5366	5.6320	0.0828	7.7730	0.0000	0.0488
Bradford	16.3990	8.0270	0.0000	8.3720	0.0000	0.0000
Brevard	14.3530	4.2450	0.0000	8.9220	0.0000	1.1860
Broward	17.0435	6.0159	0.8170	8.9900	0.6186	0.6020
Calhoun	15.7568	10.0000	0.0000	5.7080	0.0000	0.0488
Charlotte	13.7679	4.5370	0.0000	8.4132	0.6964	0.1213
Citrus	18.2057	8.2840	0.0000	8.9730	0.0000	0.9487
Clay	17.4692	8.2392	0.0000	8.8720	0.0000	0.3580
Collier	13.1039	3.3502	0.0058	8.2500	0.0000	1.4979
Columbia	19.3823	8.6700	0.0000	8.5010	0.0000	2.2113
Dade	18.9310	8.1180	1.2100	8.6660	0.3350	0.6020
De Soto	16.9630	8.2500	0.0000	8.2490	0.0000	0.4640
Dixie	19.2793	10.0000	0.0000	8.7620	0.0000	0.5173
Duval	21.8247	11.3457	0.1860	8.7300	1.1500	0.4130
Escambia	17.4510	7.9980	0.0000	9.4040	0.0000	0.0490
Flagler	13.9313	4.4800	0.3333	6.7310	1.9740	0.4130
Franklin	16.6998	9.3000	0.0000	7.3510	0.0000	0.0488
Gadsden	16.9318	10.0000	0.0000	6.8830	0.0000	0.0488
Gilchrist	19.3023	10.0000	0.0000	8.7850	0.0000	0.5173
Glades	18.5300	9.6000	0.0000	8.3830	0.0000	0.5470
Gulf	15.2218	8.4470	0.0000	6.7260	0.0000	0.0488
Hamilton	16.1913	8.5000	0.0000	7.1740	0.0000	0.5173
Hardee	18.3060	10.0000	0.0000	7.8420	0.0000	0.4640
Hendry	19.6670	7.9800	0.0000	9.0900	0.5500	2.0470
Hernando	17.2280	7.8580	0.1000	8.8700	0.0000	0.4000
Highlands	16.9200	7.9500	0.0000	8.9700	0.0000	0.0000
Hillsborough	18.7748	8.6622	0.0544	8.8770	0.4931	0.6881
Holmes	16.7888	10.0000	0.0000	6.7400	0.0000	0.0488
Indian River	14.1894	5.1512	0.3594	7.8623	0.4585	0.3580
Jackson	15.7098	8.7000	0.0000	6.9610	0.0000	0.0488
Jefferson	17.3593	9.1323	0.0000	8.2270	0.0000	0.0000
Lafayette	18.2423	10.0000	0.0000	7.7250	0.0000	0.5173
Lake	14.4580	4.9380	0.0000	8.7490	0.0000	0.7710
Lee	14.3925	5.2170	0.0000	8.5580	0.0000	0.6175

   See footnote at end of table.   Continued . . .

Florida Statistical Abstract 1991

Table 23.93. LOCAL GOVERNMENT: AD VALOREM MILLAGE RATES IN THE COUNTIES
OF FLORIDA, JANUARY 1, 1990 (Continued)

County	Total county-wide millage	County government Oper-ating millage	County government Debt service millage	District school board Oper-ating millage	District school board Debt service millage	Other mill-age 1/
Leon	18.9618	8.0900	0.0000	8.8560	1.9670	0.0488
Levy	18.5500	9.5000	0.0000	9.0500	0.0000	0.0000
Liberty	17.2680	10.0000	0.0000	7.2200	0.0000	0.0488
Madison	18.2443	10.0000	0.0000	7.7270	0.0000	0.5173
Manatee	16.8153	6.4732	0.6103	8.7910	0.2137	0.7271
Marion	14.8750	5.6600	0.0000	8.2150	1.0000	0.0000
Martin	15.9250	5.4420	0.6830	8.9190	0.1500	0.7310
Monroe	11.4935	5.1810	0.0000	5.8570	0.0000	0.4555
Nassau	17.0432	7.9552	0.0000	8.7300	0.0000	0.3580
Okaloosa	11.7748	4.0000	0.0000	7.7260	0.0000	0.0488
Okeechobee	19.0740	10.0000	0.8430	8.2310	0.0000	0.0000
Orange	13.5599	5.2889	0.0000	8.2710	0.0000	0.0000
Osceola	16.6433	6.7423	0.0000	8.7960	1.1050	0.0000
Palm Beach	16.2002	4.6000	0.2314	8.6340	0.6590	2.0758
Pasco	19.3050	9.1860	0.3210	8.2590	1.1390	0.4000
Pinellas	15.3964	5.9220	0.0120	8.7660	0.0000	0.6964
Polk	15.4320	7.1000	0.0000	8.3320	0.0000	0.0000
Putnam	16.5430	7.8920	0.0000	8.6510	0.0000	0.0000
St. Johns	16.7580	6.2290	0.4010	8.2350	1.2800	0.6130
St. Lucie	19.4327	7.1572	0.0000	9.3080	0.0000	2.9675
Santa Rosa	14.8668	6.9720	0.0000	7.8460	0.0000	0.0488
Sarasota	13.6497	3.6517	0.2475	8.7750	0.0400	0.9355
Seminole	16.0613	5.4146	0.1197	8.9540	1.2150	0.3580
Sumter	19.3290	10.0000	0.0000	8.9290	0.0000	0.4000
Suwannee	18.3843	9.1360	0.0000	8.7310	0.0000	0.5173
Taylor	15.1513	5.9070	0.0000	8.7270	0.0000	0.5173
Union	19.4903	10.0000	0.0000	8.4730	0.0000	1.0173
Volusia	15.1520	5.1910	0.0000	7.8310	1.7170	0.4130
Wakulla	18.8977	9.7029	0.0000	8.5660	0.5800	0.0488
Walton	15.9888	7.4450	0.0000	8.4950	0.0000	0.0488
Washington	17.0390	10.0000	0.0000	6.9890	0.0000	0.0500

1/ Includes county government special service districts and independent special
service districts.

Source: State of Florida, Department of Revenue, *Florida Ad Valorem Valuations
and Tax Data, 1990.*

Florida Statistical Abstract 1991

Table 23.94. LOCAL GOVERNMENT: AD VALOREM TAXES IN THE STATE AND COUNTIES OF FLORIDA, 1990

(rounded to thousands of dollars)

| | Total taxes levied | | Municipal taxes | County taxes | | | | | | | | Less than county-wide | |
| | | | | | County-wide | | | | | | | | |
	Amount	Per-centage change 1988-1989		Total	County government Operating levy	County government Debt service	District school board Operating levy	District school board Debt service	Special service districts Debt service	Independent service districts Debt service	County government special services districts	Independent special services districts
Florida	9,500,333	10.94	1,158,755	7,911,475	2,877,502	152,482	3,875,889	194,953	38,493	319,464	115,388	314,715
Alachua	93,187	15.25	8,727	84,460	30,267	98	28,458	8,311	0	7,166	0	0
Baker	4,240	6.61	193	4,047	1,585	0	-,560	0	74	828	0	0
Bay	53,495	3.18	3,884	48,318	19,906	293	27,645	0	0	172	1,293	0
Bradford	4,927	16.35	255	4,532	2,218	0	2,314	0	0	0	0	140
Brevard	231,741	13.38	26,437	201,719	53,420	0	112,276	0	16,020	5,197	1,630	1,955
Broward	1,129,093	9.42	203,448	802,714	283,336	38,479	423,410	29,135	0	28,353	6,008	116,924
Calhoun	2,166	4.46	39	2,127	1,346	0	774	0	0	7	0	0
Charlotte	83,881	23.50	2,998	76,860	23,807	0	44,146	3,654	0	636	1,519	2,504
Citrus	63,772	18.54	2,387	58,889	26,796	0	29,024	0	1,077	1,992	1,698	798
Clay	41,537	11.04	1,167	40,370	19,040	0	20,502	0	0	827	0	0
Collier	194,982	17.15	4,080	176,148	42,743	74	105,257	0	13,944	5,167	0	14,755
Columbia	12,866	7.74	724	12,142	5,431	0	5,325	0	122	1,264	0	0
Dade	1,663,300	16.78	276,672	1,386,628	518,036	77,214	553,005	21,377	0	38,416	0	0
De Soto	9,601	13.52	769	8,832	4,295	0	4,295	0	0	242	0	0
Dixie	3,665	9.67	17	3,647	1,637	0	1,434	0	0	85	0	0
Duval	398,278	12.37	6,000	384,728	188,164	3,297	154,725	20,382	0	7,320	0	7,551
Escambia	91,295	11.45	5,180	86,115	38,312	0	47,556	0	0	248	0	0
Flagler	27,460	8.43	849	25,144	8,086	602	12,148	3,563	0	745	940	527
Franklin	5,284	4.18	284	4,930	2,746	0	2,170	0	0	14	0	70
Gadsden	7,313	15.72	215	7,099	3,876	0	2,779	0	424	20	0	0
Gilchrist	2,731	19.77	8	2,664	1,380	0	1,212	0	0	71	59	0

Continued . . .

Table 23.94. LOCAL GOVERNMENT: AD VALOREM TAXES IN THE STATE AND COUNTIES OF FLORIDA, 1990 (Continued)

(rounded to thousands of dollars)

| | Total taxes levied | | Munic-ipal taxes | County taxes | | | | | | | Less than county-wide | |
| | Amount | Per-cent-age change 1988-1989 | | Total | County government | | District school board | | Spec-ial ser-vice dis-tricts | Inde-pendent ser-vice dis-tricts | County govern-ment special ser-vices dis-tricts | Inde-pendent special ser-vices dis-tricts |
					Operat-ing levy	Debt ser-vice	Operat-ing levy	Debt ser-vice				
Glades	6,210	7.44	93	6,006	3,112	0	2,717	0	0	177	0	111
Gulf	8,197	11.38	1,200	6,928	3,827	0	3,029	0	0	22	70	0
Hamilton	6,921	2.38	68	6,852	3,597	0	3,036	0	0	219	0	0
Hardee	9,470	1.98	390	9,080	4,960	0	3,890	0	0	230	0	0
Hendry	20,192	11.19	789	19,258	7,814	0	8,901	539	0	2,004	0	144
Hernando	57,360	20.59	1,520	51,599	23,535	300	26,566	0	0	1,198	3,713	528
Highlands	34,232	9.01	2,710	30,662	14,407	0	16,255	0	0	0	0	859
Hillsborough	593,898	7.33	66,637	502,143	206,736	1,298	211,863	11,769	0	16,423	10,152	14,966
Holmes	2,594	2.14	5	2,590	1,540	0	1,043	0	0	8	0	0
Indian River	86,582	11.46	5,912	68,433	23,349	1,629	35,637	2,078	0	1,623	5,611	6,626
Jackson	8,438	18.15	294	7,651	4,181	0	3,446	0	0	24	389	104
Jefferson	3,412	-6.87	301	3,078	1,619	0	1,459	0	0	0	0	34
Lafayette	1,450	0.46	12	1,438	788	0	609	0	0	41	0	0
Lake	65,951	11.59	7,292	52,386	17,888	0	31,693	0	0	2,793	2,194	4,078
Lee	317,993	15.88	30,201	255,642	87,503	0	143,540	0	0	10,439	1,820	30,330
Leon	91,441	11.76	9,500	80,852	34,495	0	37,761	8,387	0	208	0	1,089
Levy	10,530	19.09	683	9,509	4,870	0	4,639	0	0	4	0	338
Liberty	1,339	9.14	8	1,332	771	0	557	0	0	0	0	0
Madison	4,040	14.48	250	3,790	2,074	0	1,609	0	0	108	0	0
Manatee	135,829	9.75	5,299	130,517	48,863	4,600	66,359	1,613	0	5,489		12
Marion	87,797	18.54	7,925	76,570	25,921	0	37,622	4,580	0	4,976	1,411	1,890
Martin	121,952	14.62	5,363	112,846	37,047	4,650	60,718	1,021	0		3,743	0
Monroe	92,329	9.80	7,851	67,993	30,650	0	34,649	0	0	2,695	8,924	7,561

Continued . . .

Table 23.94. LOCAL GOVERNMENT: AD VALOREM TAXES IN THE STATE AND COUNTIES OF FLORIDA, 1990 (Continued)

(rounded to thousands of dollars)

	Total taxes levied		Municipal taxes	Total	County taxes							
					County-wide						Less than county-wide	
	Amount	Percentage change 1988-1989			County government Operating levy	Debt service	District school board Operating levy	Debt service	Special service districts	Independent service districts	County government special services districts	Independent special services districts
Nassau	28,914	14.46	3,370	25,084	11,309	0	12,411	0	0	509	8	453
Okaloosa	47,663	4.86	5,780	38,752	13,145	0	25,431	0	0	161	0	3,131
Okeechobee	14,415	7.84	591	13,446	7,049	594	5,802	0	0	0	0	378
Orange	560,342	11.32	55,708	485,703	155,088	0	242,408	0	0	0	514	18,417
Osceola	72,961	15.85	4,825	65,987	26,655	0	34,774	4,368	0	0	0	2,149
Palm Beach	991,855	6.65	159,765	776,740	220,553	11,095	413,968	31,597	0	99,527	43,859	11,491
Pasco	140,016	10.21	4,875	127,716	60,772	2,124	54,639	7,535	0	2,646	5,230	2,194
Pinellas	615,636	8.10	114,588	481,806	169,860	349	254,634	0	598	31,250	0	19,242
Polk	177,471	11.35	14,096	156,852	72,165	0	84,687	0	0	0	0	6,523
Putnam	33,471	11.78	1,926	30,231	14,358	0	15,783	0	0	0	661	654
St. Johns	64,449	8.70	2,577	59,374	21,877	1,408	28,922	4,496	0	0	1,531	966
St. Lucie	138,201	20.57	10,920	124,639	45,159	0	58,729	0	0	2,153	1,667	974
Santa Rosa	30,251	4.80	623	29,389	13,746	0	15,546	0	4,963	15,787	0	239
Sarasota	207,816	10.37	23,275	183,965	49,216	3,336	118,266	539	1,233	11,376	576	0
Seminole	175,496	47.14	21,520	153,976	47,204	1,044	78,059	10,592	0	3,121	0	0
Sumter	8,897	9.31	364	8,464	4,379	0	3,910	0	0	175	0	0
Suwannee	7,074	8.72	408	6,666	3,313	0	3,166	0	0	188	0	70
Taylor	8,704	6.74	572	7,758	3,025	0	4,468	0	0	265	374	0
Union	1,501	2.73	44	1,457	748	0	633	0	37	39	0	0
Volusia	253,688	11.61	33,734	176,365	58,308	0	87,962	19,286	0	4,639	9,650	33,939
Wakulla	4,279	5.92	21	4,257	2,186	0	1,930	131	0	11	0	0
Walton	20,244	4.52	336	19,764	9,196	0	10,508	0	0	60	144	0
Washington	4,019	-0.28	201	3,818	2,218	0	1,588	0	0	11	0	0

Source: State of Florida, Department of Revenue, Florida Ad Valorem Valuations and Tax Data, 1990.

ECONOMIC INDICATORS AND PRICES

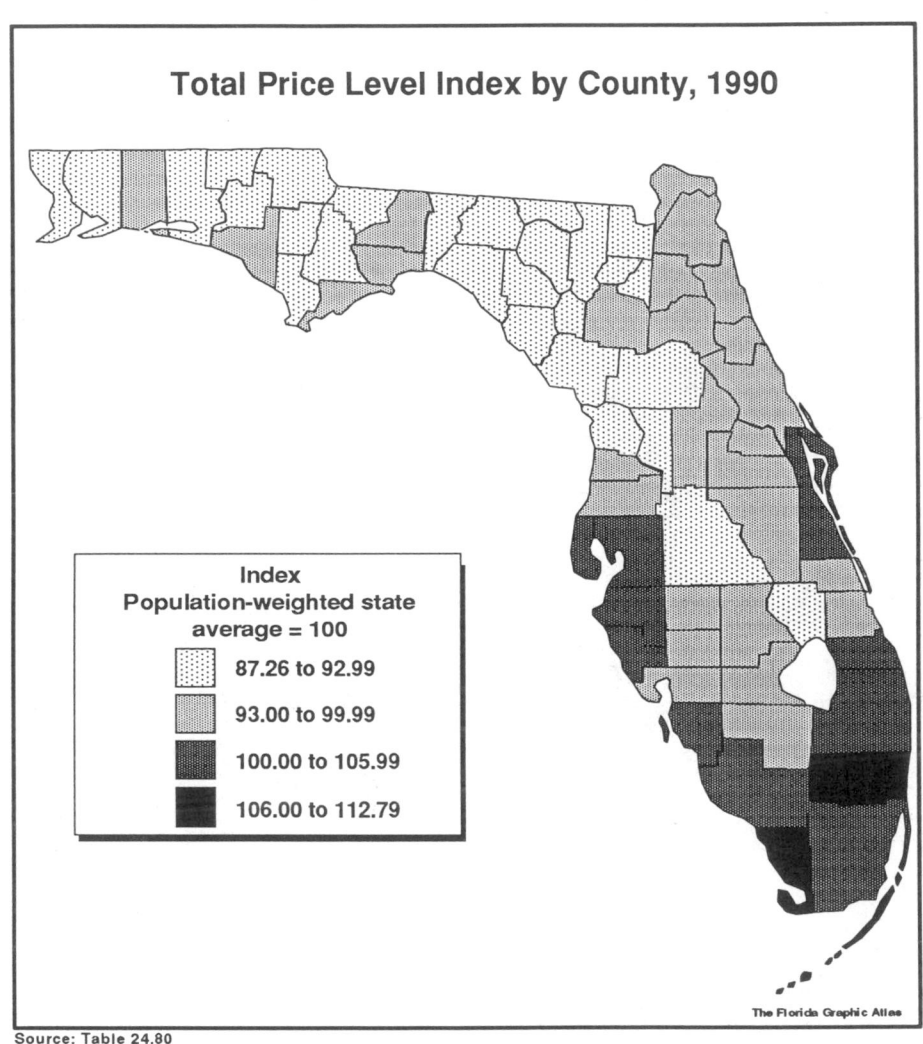

Total Price Level Index by County, 1990

Index
Population-weighted state
average = 100

87.26 to 92.99

93.00 to 99.99

100.00 to 105.99

106.00 to 112.79

The Florida Graphic Atlas

Source: Table 24.80

Table 24.12. ECONOMIC INDICATORS: SPECIFIED INDICATORS OF THE FLORIDA ECONOMY
JANUARY 1979 THROUGH DECEMBER 1990

(not adjusted for seasonal variation)

Month and year	Unem- ploy- ment rate	Nonfarm wage and salary employ- ment 1/ (1,000)	Sales and use tax collec- tions 2/	Month and year	Unem- ploy- ment rate	Nonfarm wage and salary employ- ment 1/ (1,000)	Sales and use tax collec- tions 2/
1979				**1982**			
January	7.5	3,166.0	195.2	January	7.7	3,646.5	277.1
February	5.8	3,193.4	159.6	February	7.1	3,663.4	213.7
March	5.8	3,243.4	163.2	March	8.6	3,689.5	220.9
April	5.3	3,199.6	191.6	April	7.9	3,674.1	262.6
May	5.1	3,193.2	173.7	May	7.3	3,655.6	250.6
June	6.0	3,210.2	166.1	June	7.7	3,643.8	262.1
July	6.6	3,110.2	177.9	July	7.5	3,506.5	283.9
August	6.1	3,148.5	167.4	August	7.8	3,511.6	265.1
September	6.5	3,227.8	171.8	September	8.2	3,594.1	270.8
October	6.3	3,273.6	166.3	October	9.2	3,616.6	278.9
November	5.9	3,318.1	175.6	November	9.5	3,649.7	270.6
December	5.2	3,363.5	182.6	December	9.5	3,700.0	278.7
1980				**1983**			
January	5.7	3,415.5	220.0	January	10.4	3,680.7	371.7
February	5.1	3,450.9	188.9	February	9.5	3,707.1	287.0
March	4.9	3,478.6	195.1	March	8.9	3,745.7	295.4
April	4.8	3,461.4	216.9	April	8.4	3,761.2	356.2
May	5.3	3,450.8	198.5	May	8.7	3,764.4	318.0
June	6.6	3,445.9	189.4	June	8.8	3,776.4	315.5
July	7.6	3,334.2	195.4	July	8.2	3,682.5	328.2
August	6.3	3,360.7	189.4	August	8.2	3,694.8	313.0
September	6.8	3,446.7	190.7	September	8.1	3,816.8	314.7
October	6.8	3,482.6	194.8	October	8.6	3,857.3	322.0
November	5.5	3,521.5	203.3	November	8.1	3,907.3	438.8
December	5.0	3,578.2	199.0	December	7.5	3,964.6	374.7
1981				**1984**			
January	6.4	3,584.6	260.7	January	7.4	3,974.1	385.7
February	6.3	3,605.7	203.3	February	6.1	4,006.6	338.9
March	6.4	3,639.5	212.9	March	5.4	4,064.8	377.8
April	5.4	3,639.6	247.7	April	5.7	4,064.3	402.2
May	6.7	3,631.9	227.4	May	6.1	4,074.8	378.8
June	6.4	3,637.1	219.6	June	6.6	4,086.5	384.5
July	6.5	3,508.0	231.5	July	6.8	3,967.1	370.1
August	6.7	3,514.6	218.0	August	6.2	4,008.2	358.7
September	8.1	3,593.4	220.2	September	6.2	4,098.9	358.3
October	7.9	3,611.5	219.9	October	7.0	4,128.1	362.6
November	7.6	3,630.5	214.1	November	6.2	4,187.1	372.4
December	7.3	3,668.8	216.5	December	6.1	4,237.8	408.7

See footnotes at end of table.   Continued . . .

Table 24.12. ECONOMIC INDICATORS: SPECIFIED INDICATORS OF THE FLORIDA ECONOMY
     JANUARY 1979 THROUGH DECEMBER 1990 (Continued)

(not adjusted for seasonal variation)

Month and year	Unemploy- ment rate	Nonfarm wage and salary employ- ment 1/ (1,000)	Sales and use tax collec- tions 2/	Month and year	Unemploy- ment rate	Nonfarm wage and salary employ- ment 1/ (1,000)	Sales and use tax collec- tions 2/
1985				**1988**			
January	6.5	4,211.0	418.5	January	5.0	4,795.5	622.4
February	5.8	4,239.5	381.1	February	5.0	4,854.9	514.1
March	5.9	4,285.7	400.1	March	4.7	4,905.7	603.5
April	6.1	4,279.4	435.3	April	5.0	4,884.9	676.5
May	4.9	4,285.0	409.4	May	4.7	4,886.6	620.0
June	6.9	4,274.3	404.8	June	4.8	4,897.2	611.6
July	7.0	4,164.5	391.5	July	5.1	4,769.1	616.0
August	5.8	4,198.6	393.8	August	5.0	4,794.3	586.3
September	6.5	4,280.3	391.2	September	5.1	4,920.3	594.2
October	5.3	4,317.3	395.2	October	4.9	4,959.0	584.3
November	5.5	4,369.1	410.0	November	5.2	5,021.6	596.8
December	5.6	4,417.3	443.2	December	5.4	5,084.9	638.9
1986				**1989**			
January	5.6	4,383.7	463.2	January	5.9	5,009.0	722.3
February	5.4	4,417.7	401.8	February	5.2	5,067.1	615.2
March	5.8	4,459.4	433.2	March	4.7	5,124.8	649.2
April	5.4	4,452.0	461.2	April	5.1	5,065.2	715.5
May	5.3	4,456.2	441.1	May	6.1	5,082.0	646.5
June	6.0	4,442.0	440.5	June	6.1	5,090.1	646.1
July	6.9	4,336.0	427.5	July	6.0	4,948.4	639.5
August	5.9	4,382.5	436.0	August	5.4	4,994.9	612.4
September	6.3	4,463.5	431.8	September	5.7	5,109.0	644.4
October	5.8	4,510.7	446.7	October	5.7	5,120.2	619.1
November	5.6	4,569.2	442.4	November	5.6	5,187.2	636.8
December	4.6	4,622.9	478.8	December	5.8	5,247.8	662.6
1987				**1990**			
January	5.8	4,585.1	520.0	January	5.8	5,168.2	745.6
February	5.2	4,629.3	425.9	February	5.8	5,223.8	652.7
March	5.4	4,677.5	460.4	March	5.0	5,281.1	668.8
April	5.2	4,685.4	511.9	April	5.5	5,237.8	742.0
May	5.1	4,695.7	484.5	May	5.4	5,243.8	679.0
June	5.3	4,697.5	469.3	June	6.6	5,234.6	852.9
July	5.9	4,589.2	479.2	July	6.1	5,082.7	671.6
August	5.7	4,599.5	500.4	August	6.8	5,128.0	654.8
September	5.3	4,722.2	524.5	September	6.2	5,192.4	650.1
October	5.0	4,762.2	540.8	October	6.2	5,198.0	623.5
November	5.1	4,813.8	541.9	November	6.3	5,242.4	651.1
December	5.0	4,865.4	596.7	December	5.5	5,265.1	702.8

1/ Data are for employment covered by unemployment compensation.
2/ Data are in millions, rounded to thousands of dollars.
     Source: University of Florida, Bureau of Economic and Business Research, BEBR
Data Base. Data are from State of Florida, Department of Employment Security and
Department of Revenue, unpublished data.

Florida Statistical Abstract 1991

Table 24.20. BUILDING PERMIT ACTIVITY: NUMBER OF PUBLIC AND PRIVATE RESIDENTIAL
  HOUSING UNITS AUTHORIZED BY BUILDING PERMITS IN FLORIDA AND THE UNITED STATES
  1979 THROUGH 1990

Month	1979	1980	1981	1982	1983	1984
Florida						
Annual total 1/	175,705	174,451	146,557	103,813	189,440	204,925
January	12,517	13,374	14,625	8,756	11,140	15,622
February	13,320	13,198	13,961	8,112	13,027	16,967
March	25,373	15,154	16,321	8,558	16,739	19,856
April	12,755	12,102	16,645	9,073	15,166	17,198
May	14,582	11,400	14,499	8,945	17,024	19,643
June	15,112	14,096	13,265	9,324	18,301	18,187
July	12,660	13,833	12,611	7,928	15,924	16,763
August	14,834	14,522	9,823	8,005	18,460	16,483
September	13,692	19,155	9,479	8,772	17,206	13,882
October	15,015	17,829	8,115	10,442	15,137	14,508
November	11,997	14,123	7,067	9,476	15,049	14,019
December	11,488	16,473	7,327	11,022	14,464	15,703
United States						
Annual total	1,562,014	1,207,174	997,697	1,006,768	1,613,254	1,664,663

	1985	1986	1987	1988	1989	1990
Florida						
Annual total 1/	202,615	195,525	178,764	170,597	164,985	126,929
January	14,750	14,708	15,005	11,786	13,582	14,982
February	13,311	18,168	13,279	12,243	13,404	9,318
March	17,981	15,592	17,625	15,721	14,163	12,228
April	19,752	16,562	16,006	13,935	14,593	12,314
May	18,892	16,043	14,580	14,918	17,165	11,836
June	17,388	18,817	16,843	19,255	17,454	12,078
July	17,196	19,131	15,522	13,523	11,756	11,113
August	15,538	14,278	15,895	15,656	13,657	10,667
September	19,278	15,678	15,541	14,614	12,393	8,700
October	16,660	15,809	13,779	13,578	12,754	8,622
November	13,563	12,282	10,794	13,239	11,483	8,592
December	20,150	14,060	13,077	12,911	11,279	6,933
United States						
Annual total	1,733,266	1,769,443	1,534,772	1,455,623	1,338,423	1,104,414

1/ Annual total reflects revisions not distributed to months.
  Note: To arrive at state totals, data for metropolitan areas (MSAs and PMSAs)
were taken from reports submitted by all places within these areas. Estimates of
the data for nonmetropolitan areas in Florida and the United States were based on a
sample of 14,000 permit issuing places prior to 1980; 16,000 places for 1980-1984;
and 17,000 places for 1985-1990. Beginning with January 1986, data exclude public
housing units. See Glossary for metropolitan area definitions and see map at the
front of the book for area boundaries.

  Source: U.S., Department of Commerce, International Trade Administration, *Construction Review*, March-April 1991, and previous editions.

Florida Statistical Abstract 1991

Table 24.30. GROSS AND TAXABLE SALES AND SALES TAXES PAID: SALES REPORTED TO THE
DEPARTMENT OF REVENUE IN FLORIDA, 1960 THROUGH 1990

(sales and taxes rounded to dollars)

Year	Gross sales	Taxable sales	Net sales taxes paid	Number of reports
1960	14,130,478,811	6,272,733,406	172,712,451	(NA)
1961	14,049,302,775	6,276,434,950	172,872,270	(NA)
1962	15,320,661,116	7,090,619,990	187,473,059	(NA)
1963	16,103,205,516	7,470,457,359	207,577,878	1,375,162
1964	18,243,239,834	8,680,873,802	245,010,164	1,795,111
1965	20,159,138,762	9,306,446,815	270,654,499	1,822,855
1966	22,070,877,464	10,052,183,902	292,635,382	1,848,519
1967	23,523,783,328	10,738,028,301	314,139,054	1,868,644
1968	28,188,063,900	13,361,484,763	467,573,056	2,102,650
1969	33,441,677,220	16,246,816,932	616,919,658	2,324,350
1970	36,834,259,466	18,339,123,013	681,920,445	2,394,366
1971	41,255,223,174	20,272,358,516	784,708,762	2,528,429
1972	49,280,284,464	23,884,881,400	947,086,120	2,508,097
1973	59,294,867,904	28,264,125,745	1,136,864,712	2,495,557
1974	65,887,520,411	29,785,250,309	1,216,071,766	2,689,313
1975	66,764,958,864	29,329,230,180	1,197,020,925	2,845,986
1976	73,791,141,256	32,215,852,176	1,323,271,879	2,962,711
1977	82,783,600,922	36,274,024,296	1,500,074,880	2,788,578
1978	98,227,927,655	43,640,280,027	1,816,192,620	2,844,083
1979	114,373,759,327	50,555,056,774	2,074,119,153	3,005,717
1980	136,318,330,861	58,177,097,809	2,383,348,768	3,177,162
1981	156,619,282,052	66,750,301,522	2,691,772,260	3,214,217
1982	161,796,458,854	66,663,022,175	3,143,878,949	3,451,004
1983	168,492,566,327	73,906,494,761	4,035,324,107	3,632,967
1984	195,758,800,411	84,639,051,288	4,498,315,417	3,735,161
1985	210,089,814,330	89,673,013,371	4,874,199,447	3,887,677
1986	223,601,586,263	98,612,192,144	5,304,286,552	4,249,174
1987	259,753,403,821	113,379,458,921	6,053,620,606	5,054,411
1988	277,485,847,435	119,103,871,758	7,299,532,184	5,115,463
1989	289,076,440,275	122,788,168,387	7,834,635,188	5,101,085
1990	303,465,606,024	127,283,855,200	8,242,728,990	5,177,268

(NA) Not available.
Note: These sales were reported to the Department of Revenue for the 5 percent
regular sales tax, the 5 percent use tax, and the 3 percent vehicle and farm equipment sales tax from January to December of each year. The sales occurred, for the
most part, from December of the previous year through November of the posted year.
In February 1988 the regular sales and use tax increased to 6 percent; this increase
is reflected in the collections from March 1988. These data are not comparable with
retail sales figures reported by the Bureau of the Census because of differences in
definitions of retailers and retail sales. At various times, changes in the rate of
the taxes or in the items to be taxed or excluded have been made. Data are
unaudited.

Source: State of Florida, Department of Revenue, unpublished data.

Florida Statistical Abstract 1991

Table 24.72. CONSUMER AND PRODUCER PRICE INDEXES: ANNUAL AVERAGES AND PERCENTAGE
CHANGES FOR ALL URBAN CONSUMERS INDEX AND PRODUCER PRICE INDEX IN THE UNITED
STATES, 1974 THROUGH 1990

			Consumer prices 1/			
	All items		Commodities		Services	
		Percentage		Percentage		Percentage
Year	Index	change	Index	change	Index	change
1974	49.3	11.0	53.5	12.2	43.8	9.2
1975	53.8	9.1	58.2	8.8	48.0	9.6
1976	56.9	5.8	60.7	4.3	52.0	8.3
1977	60.6	6.5	64.2	5.8	56.0	7.7
1978	65.2	7.6	68.8	7.2	60.8	8.6
1979	72.6	11.3	76.6	11.3	67.5	11.0
1980	82.4	13.5	86.0	12.3	77.9	15.4
1981	90.9	10.3	93.2	8.4	88.1	13.1
1982	96.5	6.2	97.0	4.1	96.0	9.0
1983	99.6	3.2	99.8	2.9	99.4	3.5
1984	103.9	4.3	103.2	3.4	104.6	5.2
1985	107.6	3.6	105.4	2.1	109.9	5.1
1986	109.6	1.9	104.4	-0.9	115.4	5.0
1987	113.6	3.6	107.7	3.2	120.2	4.2
1988	118.3	4.1	111.5	3.5	125.7	4.6
1989	124.0	4.8	116.7	4.7	131.9	4.9
1990	130.7	5.4	122.8	5.2	139.2	5.5

			Producer prices 2/			
	All commodities		Farm products, proc-essed foods, and feeds		Industrial commodities	
		Percentage		Percentage		Percentage
Year	Index	change	Index	change	Index	change
1974	53.5	18.9	71.3	11.6	49.2	22.1
1975	58.4	9.2	74.0	3.8	54.9	11.6
1976	61.1	4.6	73.6	-0.5	58.4	6.4
1977	64.9	6.2	75.9	3.1	62.5	7.0
1978	69.9	7.7	83.0	9.4	67.1	7.4
1979	78.7	12.6	92.3	11.2	75.7	12.8
1980	89.8	14.1	98.3	6.5	88.0	16.2
1981	98.0	9.1	101.1	2.8	97.4	10.7
1982	100.0	2.0	100.0	-1.1	100.0	2.7
1983	101.3	1.3	102.0	2.0	101.1	1.1
1984	103.7	2.4	105.5	3.4	103.3	2.2
1985	103.1	-0.6	100.7	-4.5	103.7	0.4
1986	100.2	-2.8	101.2	0.5	99.9	-3.7
1987	102.8	2.6	103.7	2.5	102.6	2.7
1988	106.9	4.0	110.0	6.1	106.3	3.6
1989	112.2	5.0	115.4	4.9	111.6	5.0
1990	116.3	3.7	118.6	2.8	115.8	3.8

1/ 1982-84 = 100.
2/ 1982 = 100. Prior to 1978 this series was designated as wholesale prices.
Note: See Appendix for discussion of consumer and producer price indexes.

Source: U.S., Department of Commerce, Bureau of Economic Analysis, *Survey of
Current Business*, May 1991.

Florida Statistical Abstract 1991

Table 24.73. CONSUMER PRICE INDEXES: INDEXES BY COMMODITY IN THE UNITED STATES
1989 AND 1990

(1982-84 = 100, except where indicated)

Index expenditure category and commodity	Relative impor- tance December 1990	Annual average index 1989	Annual average index 1990	Percentage change 1989 to 1990
Wage earners and clerical workers index (CPI-W), all items	100.0	122.6	129.0	5.2
All urban consumers index (CPI-U), all items	100.0	124.0	130.7	5.4
Food and beverages	17.7	124.9	132.1	5.8
Food	16.2	125.1	132.4	5.8
Food at home	10.1	124.2	132.3	6.5
Cereals and bakery products	1.4	132.4	140.0	5.7
Meats, poultry, fish, and eggs	3.2	121.3	130.0	7.2
Dairy products	1.3	115.6	126.5	9.4
Fruits and vegetables	1.8	138.0	149.0	8.0
Other food at home	2.4	119.1	123.4	3.6
Sugar and sweets	0.3	119.4	124.7	4.4
Fats and oils	0.3	121.2	126.3	4.2
Nonalcoholic beverages	0.8	111.3	113.5	2.0
Other prepared food	1.0	125.5	131.2	4.5
Food away from home	6.1	127.4	133.4	4.7
Alcoholic beverages	1.5	123.5	129.3	4.7
Housing	41.4	123.0	128.5	4.5
Shelter	27.7	132.8	140.0	5.4
Renters' costs 1/	7.9	138.9	146.7	5.6
Rent, residential	5.8	132.8	138.4	4.2
Other renters' costs	2.1	140.7	154.3	9.7
Homeowners' costs 1/	19.5	137.3	144.6	5.3
Owners' equivalent rent 1/	19.2	137.4	144.8	5.4
Household insurance 1/	0.4	132.6	135.3	2.0
Maintenance and repairs	0.2	118.0	122.2	3.6
Maintenance and repair services	0.1	120.6	126.4	4.8
Maintenence and repair commodities	0.1	114.6	116.6	1.7
Fuel and other utilities	7.3	107.8	111.6	3.5
Fuels	4.1	100.9	104.5	3.6
Fuel oil and other household fuel commodities	0.5	81.7	99.3	21.5
Gas (piped) and electricity	3.6	107.5	109.3	1.7
Other utilities and public services	3.2	127.1	131.7	3.6
Household furnishings and operation	6.4	111.2	113.3	1.9
Housefurnishings	3.8	105.5	106.7	1.1
Housekeeping supplies	1.2	120.9	125.2	3.6
Housekeeping services 2/	1.4	117.3	120.1	2.4
Apparel and upkeep	6.1	118.6	124.1	4.6
Apparel commodities	5.5	116.7	122.0	4.5
Men's and boys' apparel	1.5	117.0	120.4	2.9
Women's and girls' apparel	2.5	116.4	122.6	5.3
Infants' and toddlers' apparel	0.2	119.1	125.8	5.6
Footwear	0.8	114.4	117.4	2.6

See footnotes at end of table.   Continued . . .

Table 24.73. CONSUMER PRICE INDEXES: INDEXES BY COMMODITY IN THE UNITED STATES
1989 AND 1990 (Continued)

(1982-84 = 100, except where indicated)

Index expenditure category and commodity	Relative impor- tance December 1990	Annual average index 1989	Annual average index 1990	Percentage change 1989 to 1990
All urban consumers index (CPI-U) (Continued)				
Apparel and upkeep (Continued)				
Apparel commodities (Continued)				
Other apparel commodities	0.5	122.1	131.8	7.9
Apparel services 3/	0.6	129.4	136.7	5.6
Transportation	17.8	114.1	120.5	5.6
Private transportation	16.2	112.9	118.8	5.2
New vehicles	5.0	119.2	121.4	1.8
New cars	4.0	119.2	121.0	1.5
Used Cars	1.1	120.4	117.6	-2.3
Motor fuel	4.1	88.5	101.2	14.4
Gasoline	0.0	88.5	101.0	14.1
Maintenance and repair	1.5	124.9	130.1	4.2
Other private transportation	4.5	135.8	142.5	4.9
Other private transportation commodities 4/	0.7	101.5	102.3	0.8
Other private transportation services 5/	3.8	143.2	151.4	5.7
Public transportation	1.6	129.5	142.6	10.1
Medical care	6.4	149.3	162.8	9.0
Medical care commodities	1.2	150.8	163.4	8.4
Medical care services 6/	5.2	148.9	162.7	9.3
Professional medical services	3.1	146.4	156.1	6.6
Entertainment 7/	4.3	126.5	132.4	4.7
Entertainment commodities	2.0	119.8	124.0	3.5
Entertainment services	2.3	135.4	143.2	5.8
Other goods and services	6.4	147.7	159.0	7.7
Tobacco and smoking products	1.5	164.4	181.5	10.4
Personal care	1.2	125.0	130.4	4.3
Toilet goods and personal care appliances	0.6	123.2	128.2	4.1
Personal care services	0.6	126.8	132.8	4.7
Personal and educational expenses	3.6	158.1	170.2	7.7
School books and supplies	0.2	158.0	171.3	8.4
Personal and educational services	3.4	158.3	170.4	7.6
Commodity and service group, all items	100.0	124.0	130.7	5.4
Commodities	45.3	116.7	122.8	5.2
Food and beverages	17.7	124.9	132.1	5.8
Commodities less food and beverages	27.6	111.6	117.0	4.8
Nondurables less food and beverages	16.9	111.2	119.6	7.6
Apparel commodities	5.5	116.7	122.0	4.5
Nondurables less food, beverages, and apparel	11.4	111.0	121.1	9.1
Durables	10.7	112.2	113.4	1.1

See footnotes at end of table.

Continued . . .

Table 24.73. CONSUMER PRICE INDEXES: INDEXES BY COMMODITY IN THE UNITED STATES
   1989 AND 1990 (Continued)

(1982-84 = 100, except where indicated)

Index expenditure category and commodity	Relative impor- tance December 1990	Annual average index 1989	1990	Percentage change 1989 to 1990
Commodity and service group, all items (Continued)				
Services	54.7	131.9	139.2	5.5
Rent of shelter 1/	27.0	138.0	145.5	5.4
Household services less rent of shelter 1/	8.8	118.7	121.7	2.5
Transportation services	6.9	135.6	144.2	6.3
Medical care services	5.2	148.9	162.7	9.3
Other services	6.8	140.9	150.2	6.6
Special indexes				
All items less food	83.8	123.7	130.3	5.3
All items less shelter	72.3	121.6	128.2	5.4
All items less homeowners' costs 1/	80.5	125.3	132.1	5.4
All items less medical care	93.6	122.4	128.8	5.2
Commodities less food	29.1	112.0	117.4	4.8
Nondurables less food	18.4	111.7	119.9	7.3
Nondurables less food and apparel	12.9	111.3	120.9	8.6
Nondurables	34.6	118.2	126.0	6.6
Services less rent of shelter 1/	27.7	135.1	142.7	5.6
Services less medical care	49.5	130.1	136.8	5.1
Energy	8.2	94.3	102.1	8.3
All items less energy	91.8	128.1	134.7	5.2
All items less food and energy	75.6	129.0	135.5	5.0
Commodities less food and energy	24.5	119.6	123.6	3.3
Energy commodities	4.6	87.9	101.2	15.1
Services less energy	51.1	134.4	142.3	5.9
Purchasing power of the consumer dollar (1982-84=$1.00; data in dollars)	0.0	0.8	0.8	-5.1

1/ Indexes on a December 1982=100 base.
2/ Includes postage, moving and storage, household laundry and dry cleaning services, and appliance and furniture repair.
3/ Apparel laundry and dry cleaning services.
4/ Includes motor oil, coolants, tires, and auto parts.
5/ Includes insurance, finance charges, registration and license fees, and auto rental.
6/ Includes professional services and hospital charges.
7/ Includes newspapers, magazines, books, sporting goods and equipment, toys, hobbies, music and photographic equipment, and pet supplies; also fees and admission to sporting events and other entertainment.
Note: See Appendix for explanation of CPI-W and CPI-U.

Source: U.S., Department of Labor, Bureau of Labor Statistics, *CPI Detailed Report*, January 1991.

Florida Statistical Abstract 1991

Table 24.74. CONSUMER PRICE INDEXES: INDEXES FOR ALL URBAN CONSUMERS BY CATEGORY
AND COMMODITY IN MIAMI-FT. LAUDERDALE AND TAMPA-ST. PETERSBURG-CLEARWATER
FLORIDA, ANNUAL AVERAGE, 1990 AND MIAMI-FT. LAUDERDALE, FLORIDA, JANUARY
1989, 1990, AND 1991

(1982-84 = 100)

| | | Annual average | | |
| | Miami-Ft. Lauderdale | | Tampa-St. Petersburg Clearwater | |
Expenditure category and commodity	1990	Percentage change 1989 to 1990	1990	Percentage change 1989 to 1990
All items	128.0	5.3	111.7	4.2
Food and beverages	134.3	6.9	112.4	5.7
Food	135.9	7.2	113.7	6.3
Food at home	133.6	7.1	114.0	7.2
Cereals and bakery products	132.3	9.2	124.0	6.2
Meats, poultry, fish, and eggs	124.0	5.3	110.8	9.4
Meats, poultry, and fish	124.7	5.4	110.3	9.8
Dairy products	126.5	7.2	119.1	10.1
Fruits and vegetables	175.6	12.3	125.3	8.5
Other foods at home	119.9	3.1	104.1	2.2
Food away from home	141.1	7.6	113.6	5.7
Alcoholic beverages	119.8	3.9	104.6	2.4
Housing	120.4	3.6	108.3	3.3
Shelter	122.6	4.3	112.0	5.6
Renters' costs 1/	125.0	3.0	102.2	4.5
Rent, residential	117.3	2.4	110.1	4.6
Other renters' costs	166.2	5.4	78.4	4.4
Homeowners' costs 1/	125.9	4.1	115.6	5.7
Owners' equilvalent rent 1/	125.2	4.1	115.5	5.8
Fuel and other utilities	109.3	0.2	105.7	3.6
Fuels	107.7	-0.5	100.5	2.9
Fuel oil and other household fuel commodoties	139.5	20.1	119.0	17.6
Gas (piped) and electricity	107.2	-0.8	99.7	2.3
Household furnishings and operation	123.7	4.6	99.9	-3.5
Apparel and upkeep	135.6	3.3	114.7	2.7
Apparel commodities	131.4	2.6	115.1	2.7
Men's and boys' apparel	138.0	3.4	117.9	1.3
Women's and girls' apparel	128.4	1.3	114.3	3.9
Footwear	148.7	4.8	105.3	-1.5
Transportation	121.6	5.9	110.8	3.9
Private transportation	120.5	5.4	111.0	4.1
Public transportation	134.0	12.9	109.0	2.7
Medical care	151.8	8.0	133.2	7.2
Entertainment	121.0	2.7	103.3	1.4
Other goods and services	153.2	9.6	117.0	7.1
Personal care	118.8	3.3	114.1	7.0

See footnotes at end of table.   Continued . . .

Table 24.74. CONSUMER PRICE INDEXES: INDEXES FOR ALL URBAN CONSUMERS BY CATEGORY
AND COMMODITY IN MIAMI-FT. LAUDERDALE AND TAMPA-ST. PETERSBURG-CLEARWATER
FLORIDA, ANNUAL AVERAGE, 1990 AND MIAMI-FT. LAUDERDALE, FLORIDA, JANUARY
1989, 1990, AND 1991 (Continued)

(1982-84 = 100)

Expenditure category and commodity	Miami-Ft. Lauderdale			Percentage change 1990 to 1991
	January			
	1989	1990	1991	
All items	120.0	124.6	131.5	5.5
Food and beverages	122.3	134.1	136.0	1.4
Food	123.5	136.2	136.7	.4
Food at home	119.9	138.1	132.8	-3.8
Cereals and bakery products	118.5	123.8	134.8	8.9
Meats, poultry, fish, and eggs	115.5	119.8	125.7	4.9
Meats, poultry, and fish	116.8	119.3	126.1	5.7
Dairy products	117.0	121.9	131.3	7.7
Fruits and vegetables	138.5	217.4	159.3	-26.7
Other foods at home	114.5	121.3	122.5	1.0
Food away from home	129.3	136.7	143.2	4.8
Alcoholic beverages	112.0	117.0	128.3	9.7
Housing	115.2	116.7	122.3	4.8
Shelter	116.6	118.3	124.2	5.0
Renters' costs 1/	120.9	121.8	126.1	3.5
Rent, residential	112.6	115.5	118.2	2.3
Other renters' costs	165.7	154.7	168.8	9.1
Homeowners' costs 1/	118.9	121.1	127.7	5.5
Owners' equivalent rent 1/	118.4	120.4	127.1	5.6
Fuel and other utilities	109.0	108.6	113.4	4.4
Fuels	107.0	107.3	114.5	6.7
Fuel oil and other household fuel commodoties	116.3	136.4	142.2	4.3
Gas (piped) and electricity	106.8	106.7	114.0	6.8
Household furnishings and operation	116.7	118.7	124.3	4.7
Apparel and upkeep	131.0	130.4	135.6	4.0
Apparel commodities	127.6	126.7	130.7	3.2
Men's and boys' apparel	135.1	133.3	134.3	.8
Women's and girls' apparel	121.0	117.1	124.6	6.4
Footwear	144.9	146.8	153.9	4.8
Transportation	113.9	118.8	129.4	8.9
Private transportation	113.5	118.2	127.9	8.2
Public transportation	116.0	124.8	146.7	17.5
Medical care	137.9	143.3	159.7	11.4
Entertainment	116.0	119.6	127.3	6.4
Other goods and services	137.6	143.7	161.0	12.0
Personal care	114.6	117.6	121.2	3.1

1/ Indexes on a November 1982=100 base for Miami-Ft. Lauderdale.
   Note: The Miami-Ft. Lauderdale and Tampa-St. Petersburg-Clearwater areas are two
of several metropolitan areas for which a consumer price index is issued bimonthly.

Source: U.S., Department of Labor, Bureau of Labor Statistics, *CPI Detailed
Report*, January 1991.

Florida Statistical Abstract 1991

Table 24.75. PRODUCER PRICE INDEXES: INDEXES BY STAGE OF PROCESSING, BY DURABILITY
OF PRODUCT, AND BY COMMODITY IN THE UNITED STATES, ANNUAL AVERAGES, 1989 AND
1990, AND APRIL 1991

(1982 = 100, not seasonally adjusted)

Item	Annual average 1989	Annual average 1990	April 1991
All commodities	112.2	116.3	116.0
By stage of processing			
Crude materials for further processing	103.1	108.9	101.2
Intermediate materials, supplies, etc.	112.0	114.5	114.0
Finished goods 1/	113.6	119.2	120.9
Finished consumer goods	112.1	118.2	119.7
Capital equipment	118.8	122.9	125.7
By durability of product			
Durable goods	119.0	121.2	122.7
Nondurable goods	107.1	112.2	111.0
Manufactures, total	114.3	118.1	118.6
Durable manufactures	118.3	120.7	122.4
Nondurable manufactures	110.2	115.2	114.7
Farm products, processed foods and feeds	115.4	118.6	118.2
Farm products	110.9	112.2	109.4
Foods and feeds, processed	117.8	121.9	122.7
Industrial commodities	111.6	115.8	115.5
Chemical and allied products	123.0	123.6	126.2
Fuels and related products and power	72.9	82.2	78.1
Furniture and household durables	116.9	119.1	121.0
Hides, skins, and leather products	136.3	141.7	141.2
Lumber and wood products	126.7	129.7	128.8
Machinery and equipment	117.4	120.7	123.1
Metals and metal products	124.1	123.0	121.3
Nonmetallic mineral products	112.6	114.7	117.3
Pulp, paper, and allied products	137.8	141.3	143.1
Rubber and plastics products	112.6	113.6	115.8
Textile products and apparel	112.3	114.9	116.0
Transportation equipment 1/	117.7	121.5	124.9
Motor vehicles and equipment	116.2	118.2	121.5

1/ Includes data for items not shown separately.
Note: See Appendix for discussion of producer price indexes.

Source: U.S., Department of Commerce, Bureau of Economic Analysis, *Survey of
Current Business*, May 1991.

Florida Statistical Abstract 1991

Table 24.76. CONSUMER ENERGY PRICES: NATURAL GAS, ELECTRICITY, FUEL OIL, AND
GASOLINE PRICES, U.S. CITY AVERAGE AND MIAMI-FT. LAUDERDALE, JUNE 1990
THROUGH MAY 1991

(amounts in dollars)

Month and year	Piped gas per 40 therms U.S. city average	Miami-Ft. Lauderdale	Electricity per 500 kilowatt-hours U.S. city average	Miami-Ft. Lauderdale	#2 fuel oil per gallon-- U.S. city average	All types gasoline per gallon U.S. city average	Miami-Ft. Lauderdale
1990							
June	25.885	28.874	43.665	44.519	0.908	1.140	1.106
July	25.439	30.933	43.531	44.746	0.880	1.139	1.103
August	25.600	31.123	43.484	44.746	0.998	1.246	1.162
September	25.852	30.644	43.605	44.746	1.165	1.347	1.224
October	25.769	32.785	42.296	44.768	1.330	1.431	1.333
November	25.474	36.411	42.125	44.768	1.305	1.432	1.362
December	25.945	37.251	42.145	44.768	1.273	1.410	1.368
1991							
January	26.438	37.303	43.226	47.143	1.235	1.304	1.287
February	26.070	37.884	43.413	47.143	1.170	1.198	1.182
March	25.781	36.174	43.467	47.143	1.086	1.138	1.113
April	25.459	36.372	42.961	44.813	1.016	1.159	1.119
May	26.307	35.469	43.547	44.813	0.968	1.209	1.163

Source: U.S., Department of Labor, Bureau of Labor Statistics, *CPI Detailed
Report*, monthly releases.

Table 24.77. ELECTRICITY PRICES: COST PER KILOWATT-HOUR OF ELECTRICITY BY CLASS
OF SERVICE OF THE FLORIDA ELECTRIC UTILITY INDUSTRY, 1978 THROUGH 1990

(in cents)

Year	Total	Resi- dential	Com- mercial	Indus- trial	Street and highway lighting	Other public author- ities	Inter- depart- mental
1978	3.90	4.97	4.26	2.91	5.42	3.60	4.40
1979	4.32	4.50	4.72	3.24	5.76	4.20	4.84
1980	5.18	5.32	5.51	4.30	7.91	4.74	5.07
1981	6.61	6.90	6.87	5.41	9.41	5.95	5.67
1982	6.60	7.07	6.45	5.38	9.81	5.97	6.64
1983	6.98	7.69	5.95	6.71	(NA)	7.37	(NA)
1984	7.91	8.81	7.00	6.79	(NA)	9.85	(NA)
1985	7.63	8.42	7.38	6.02	(NA)	7.22	(NA)
1986	7.23	7.98	6.83	5.74	(NA)	7.06	(NA)
1987	7.06	7.91	6.45	5.03	(NA)	10.34	(NA)
1988	7.05	7.80	6.71	5.32	(NA)	6.81	(NA)
1989	7.05	7.74	6.58	5.51	(NA)	8.20	(NA)
1990	6.87	7.64	6.58	5.00	(NA)	6.77	(NA)

(NA) Not available.
Note: Cost by class of service is defined as revenue by class of service/kilo-
watt-hour consumption by class of service.
Source: State of Florida, Public Service Commission, *Statistics of the Florida
Electric Utility Industry, 1990*, prepublication release.

Florida Statistical Abstract 1991

Table 24.78. INDUSTRIAL AND COMMERCIAL FAILURES: NUMBER AND LIABILITIES IN FLORIDA
AND THE UNITED STATES, 1983 THROUGH 1989

	Florida			United States		
		Failures			Failures	
	New busi-		Current li-	New busi-		Current li-
	ness incor-	Num-	abilities 2/	ness incor-	Num-	abilities 2/
Year	porations	ber 1/	($1,000,000)	porations	ber 1/	($1,000,000)
1983	(NA)	1,425	645.0	(NA)	31,334	16,072.9
1984	66,999	2,588	1,045.0	634,991	52,078	29,269.0
1985	71,600	2,794	2,277.1	662,000	57,253	33,376.0
1986	77,600	3,333	(NA)	702,700	61,616	(NA)
1987	79,400	3,201	(NA)	685,600	61,111	(NA)
1988 A/	75,000	3,135	(NA)	685,100	57,098	(NA)
1989 B/	80,000	3,158	(NA)	677,400	50,389	(NA)

(NA) Not available. A/ Revised. B/ Preliminary.
1/ Includes firms discontinuing following assignment, voluntary or involuntary
petition in bankruptcy, attachment, execution, foreclosure, etc.; voluntary withdrawals from business with known loss to creditors; also enterprises involved in
court action, such as receivership and reorganization or arrangement which may or
may not lead to discontinuance; and business making voluntary compromise with creditors out of court. 2/ Liablilities exclude long-term publicly held obligations;
offsetting assets are not taken into account.
    Note: Data exclude railroad failures and real estate and financial companies.
    Source: Dun & Bradstreet Corporation, New York, NY, *New Business Incorporations*,
monthly, and *Business Failure Report*, annual. (Copyright.)

Table 24.79. PRICE LEVEL INDEX: RELATIVE WEIGHTS ASSIGNED TO SELECTED ITEMS PRICED
FOR THE FLORIDA PRICE LEVEL INDEX, 1990

Item	Number of items	Weight	Item	Number of items	Weight
Food group	32	21.728	Housing group	28	38.264
Beer		1.432	Apartment rent,		
Cup of coffee		1.335	monthly		6.281
Hamburger lunch		7.274	Electricity		
Soft drink, served		1.335	500 kilowatt-hours		1.847
Transportation group	15	17.829	1,000 kilowatt-hours		1.847
Auto insurance			Hotel-motel rate		1.316
Liability		1.121	House purchase price		16.322
Physical damage		1.121	Nonlocal phone service		1.058
Auto repair charge		1.283	Residential telephone		
Chevrolet Cavalier		3.859	service		1.073
Ford Mustang		3.859	Health, recreation,		
Gasoline, unleaded			and personal		
self-service		3.513	services group	25	14.658
Apparel group	17	7.522	College tuition		2.111
Woman's shirtwaist			Movie rental		1.473
dress		1.189	Safety deposit box fee		1.043

    Note: Items weighted one percent or more are included. See also note on Table
24.80 and discussion under this section in the Appendix.
    Source: State of Florida, Office of the Governor, Office of Planning and
Budgeting, *Florida Price Level Index, 1990*.

Florida Statistical Abstract 1991

Table 24.80.   PRICE LEVEL INDEX: TOTAL INDEX AND INDEXES OF PRICES OF MAJOR ITEMS
IN THE COUNTIES OF FLORIDA, 1990

(population-weighted state average = 100)

County	Florida Price Level Index Index	Rank among coun- ties	Food	Housing	Apparel	Transpor- tation	Health recrea- tion, and personal services
Alachua	95.97	24	100.24	92.11	102.70	97.02	93.88
Baker	89.01	64	94.53	81.25	95.92	95.11	88.40
Bay	93.82	35	97.87	86.73	89.56	104.03	94.67
Bradford	90.61	58	95.56	83.42	92.85	93.18	96.32
Brevard	100.55	11	109.37	96.39	95.95	100.17	99.32
Broward	107.76	2	107.77	113.29	106.05	100.93	103.04
Calhoun	90.73	56	99.35	81.06	92.83	97.80	91.15
Charlotte	96.62	23	100.31	91.94	94.29	101.95	97.01
Citrus	91.03	54	97.03	86.05	89.51	97.51	86.50
Clay	94.60	32	96.42	93.46	93.73	94.66	94.85
Collier	103.16	4	102.89	101.48	126.22	98.34	101.84
Columbia	91.88	48	95.56	84.04	92.66	100.74	94.33
Dade	105.06	3	95.62	110.09	105.96	105.36	107.13
De Soto	93.41	36	100.97	84.47	99.41	99.39	93.05
Dixie	91.98	47	98.28	83.06	97.10	99.54	92.19
Duval	97.42	20	101.78	93.80	100.30	97.94	97.25
Escambia	92.75	42	92.75	88.20	99.90	97.44	94.82
Flagler	95.44	29	97.03	94.27	102.35	96.27	91.13
Franklin	93.07	38	100.60	85.87	101.74	95.13	91.81
Gadsden	92.91	39	94.99	86.87	94.39	98.52	97.07
Gilchrist	90.97	55	98.12	80.76	99.64	95.91	94.39
Glades	98.07	19	102.60	97.13	92.18	97.15	97.16
Gulf	91.57	49	99.79	83.66	94.65	98.07	88.38
Hamilton	91.40	50	103.30	81.28	102.56	91.27	91.74
Hardee	91.34	51	97.24	82.26	94.73	101.29	90.31
Hendry	96.84	22	102.92	90.28	95.05	100.61	99.70
Hernando	94.23	33	101.48	92.12	75.93	99.70	90.30
Highlands	95.51	28	103.74	90.08	98.69	98.14	90.76
Hillsborough	100.67	10	100.56	101.87	95.03	100.81	100.55
Holmes	90.55	59	99.28	80.32	92.29	98.72	91.04
Indian River	97.37	21	96.93	96.18	97.79	101.17	96.22
Jackson	89.82	61	95.62	79.68	89.90	102.83	89.79
Jefferson	90.64	57	95.65	78.27	107.53	96.80	97.32
Lafayette	89.73	62	93.25	81.51	90.80	96.98	95.23
Lake	95.17	30	98.77	90.99	96.90	96.85	96.85
Lee	100.09	12	99.50	100.19	103.23	96.65	103.43
Leon	98.17	17	100.62	92.88	111.64	100.79	97.27
Levy	89.43	63	91.51	84.30	83.02	95.55	94.73

See footnote at end of table.   Continued . . .

Florida Statistical Abstract 1991

Table 24.80. PRICE LEVEL INDEX: TOTAL INDEX AND INDEXES OF PRICES OF MAJOR ITEMS
    IN THE COUNTIES OF FLORIDA, 1990 (Continued)

(population-weighted state average = 100)

County	Florida Price Level Index Index	Rank among coun- ties	Food	Housing	Apparel	Transpor- tation	Health recrea- tion, and personal services
Liberty	92.14	46	100.95	80.46	104.96	98.32	92.89
Madison	87.26	67	95.20	79.26	95.19	95.62	79.95
Manatee	101.20	9	103.45	102.91	97.67	97.57	99.46
Marion	92.43	44	97.24	85.15	94.59	98.94	93.73
Martin	102.48	6	106.13	103.30	92.87	104.39	96.94
Monroe	112.79	1	106.17	130.36	102.00	99.43	101.28
Nassau	95.69	25	96.70	93.97	95.75	95.27	98.84
Okaloosa	94.16	34	103.03	85.36	99.80	95.48	97.20
Okeechobee	92.90	41	95.33	89.50	76.57	101.82	94.93
Orange	98.58	14	98.63	98.04	96.26	97.51	102.42
Osceola	98.33	15	105.48	96.47	95.98	98.44	92.25
Palm Beach	102.35	7	96.87	105.01	106.85	100.15	105.11
Pasco	94.79	31	99.62	91.95	88.94	99.29	91.43
Pinellas	101.84	8	101.57	103.82	101.98	98.14	101.79
Polk	92.63	43	94.98	89.28	85.92	98.03	94.05
Putnam	93.28	37	98.41	89.10	89.68	98.03	91.40
St. Johns	98.08	18	104.00	97.86	84.53	99.56	93.98
St. Lucie	98.67	13	100.49	96.04	94.62	99.84	102.94
Santa Rosa	91.07	53	92.32	82.79	91.09	100.43	98.46
Sarasota	102.60	5	102.21	103.96	105.70	100.30	101.01
Seminole	98.20	16	100.80	94.87	98.37	100.62	99.28
Sumter	92.36	45	97.61	85.84	92.15	98.85	92.31
Suwannee	87.57	66	94.37	79.88	84.27	95.81	87.36
Taylor	90.25	60	97.20	81.34	95.97	95.66	91.70
Union	91.18	52	99.40	80.62	101.01	94.06	95.73
Volusia	95.52	27	96.63	95.33	95.86	97.64	91.37
Wakulla	95.55	26	109.36	82.92	109.22	98.13	94.42
Walton	92.91	39	105.63	83.41	95.14	95.25	91.84
Washington	87.97	65	96.36	77.83	89.84	98.73	85.54

Note: The Florida Price Level Index is a set of numbers which reflects the price
level in each county relative to population-weighted statewide average (100 for each
category) for a particular point in time, 1990. It measures price level differences
from place to place in contrast to the consumer price index prepared by the U.S.
Bureau of Labor Statistics, which measures price level changes from month to month.
The basis for these comparisons is one of fixed standard of living which represents
the consumption pattern of a typical wage earner or clerical worker. The index
measures in each county the relative cost of living by this standard. See Table
24.79 for relative weights of items priced.

Source: State of Florida, Office of the Governor, Office of Planning and
Budgeting, *Florida Price Level Index, 1990*.

Florida Statistical Abstract 1991

Table 24.85. CONSUMER CONFIDENCE INDEX: TOTAL INDEX AND COMPONENTS OF THE FLORIDA
CONSUMER CONFIDENCE INDEX BY MONTH, JUNE 1987 THROUGH JULY 1991

(1966 = 100)

Year	Month	Index 1/	Current personal 2/	Future personal 3/	U.S. 1 year 4/	U.S. 5 years 5/	House-hold purchases 6/
1987	6	95.23	92.34	106.91	89.84	69.68	117.36
	7	91.81	89.96	100.39	90.99	68.82	108.90
	9	98.83	95.27	108.49	97.28	76.01	117.11
	10	101.48	96.99	112.29	96.55	86.50	115.06
	11	95.27	94.33	110.87	90.49	82.36	98.32
1988	1	94.05	88.59	109.40	90.90	77.02	104.34
	2	91.79	88.37	105.76	91.24	71.27	102.31
	3	90.96	86.04	104.46	87.80	72.77	103.73
	5	101.51	100.92	108.21	98.16	87.08	113.16
	6	105.07	101.15	111.38	105.84	94.90	112.09
	7	97.74	92.52	104.54	94.11	85.28	112.22
	9	95.35	91.91	104.04	96.01	81.52	103.25
	10	96.24	88.73	106.41	95.51	85.22	105.32
	11	96.87	93.28	103.85	93.51	87.88	105.85
1989	1	98.01	90.84	101.28	100.59	83.70	113.63
	2	99.91	98.05	104.53	100.29	91.68	105.00
	3	97.60	94.72	107.18	93.21	89.87	103.03
	5	96.71	92.96	105.18	90.79	92.47	102.13
	6	100.70	94.19	110.61	94.88	96.54	107.29
	7	95.24	90.77	107.00	88.27	84.07	106.09
	9	92.18	89.64	103.50	90.34	74.37	103.03
	10	94.35	92.57	103.53	87.86	79.45	108.37
	11	92.76	89.07	102.58	88.02	80.36	103.78
1990	1	87.64	86.77	96.63	75.88	71.40	107.51
	2	88.90	88.01	95.56	80.69	71.93	108.52
	3	90.50	86.27	97.88	85.65	71.69	110.98
	4	91.40	91.38	99.07	85.97	77.01	103.48
	6	89.40	86.86	105.50	73.23	76.01	105.50
	7	82.20	82.53	94.21	68.27	66.64	99.23
	9	74.50	81.92	93.84	47.36	65.31	84.26
	10	66.80	73.59	85.23	36.63	69.03	69.31
	11	68.30	74.34	90.31	35.60	67.68	73.65
1991	1	73.00	76.46	93.46	40.99	84.85	69.21
	2	77.30	72.25	95.50	57.00	84.12	77.84
	3	89.00	74.14	104.23	88.19	96.39	82.10
	4	85.50	76.95	96.10	82.62	86.53	85.45
	6	85.10	76.28	98.95	83.25	74.24	92.67
	7	82.10	75.43	97.98	82.18	62.33	92.59

1/ Based on a monthly telephone survey of approximately 500 randomly selected
Florida households. Survey is not taken in August and December, in April 1988-89
and in May 1990-91. Compiled from survey responses giving views of personal
financial and general business conditions. 2/ Personal financial conditions at
time of survey as compared to previous year. 3/ Personal financial condition
anticipated a year from time of survey. 4/ U.S. business conditions anticipated a
year from time of survey. 5/ U.S. business conditions anticipated five years from
time of survey. 6/ Perception that the time of survey is a good time to buy major
household items.

Source: University of Florida, Bureau of Economic and Business Research, Survey
Program, *Florida Economic and Consumer Survey*, July 1991.

STATE COMPARISONS

Public Welfare Expenditure in Florida and Other States, 1988-89

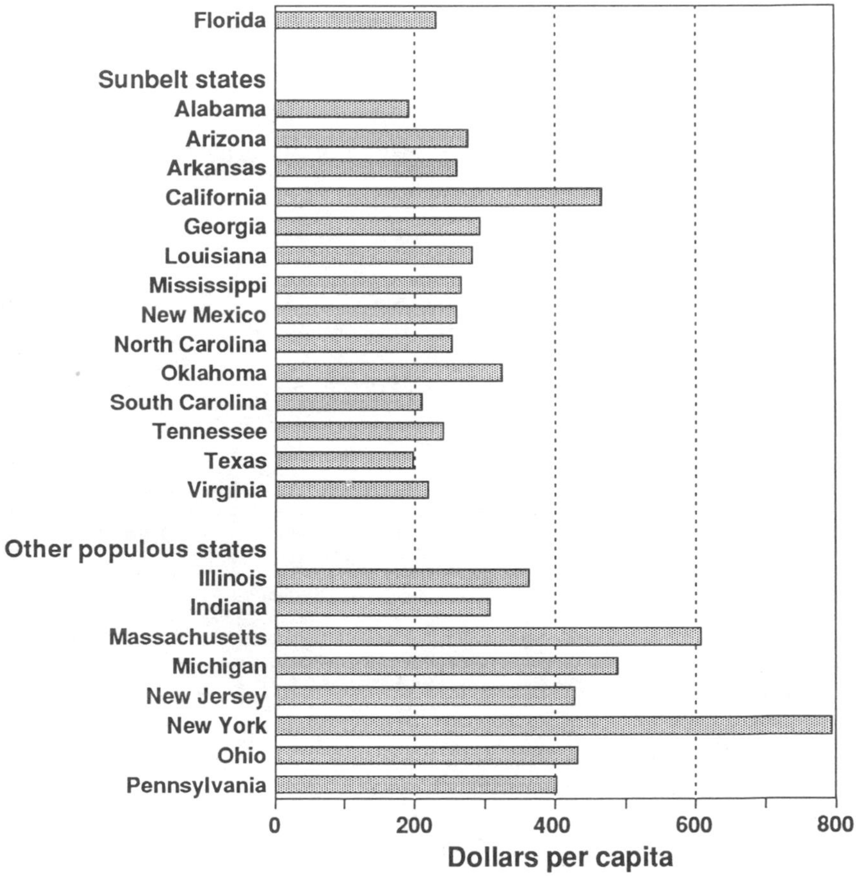

Florida

Sunbelt states
Alabama
Arizona
Arkansas
California
Georgia
Louisiana
Mississippi
New Mexico
North Carolina
Oklahoma
South Carolina
Tennessee
Texas
Virginia

Other populous states
Illinois
Indiana
Massachusetts
Michigan
New Jersey
New York
Ohio
Pennsylvania

0   200   400   600   800

Dollars per capita

The Florida Graphic Atlas

Source: Table 25.01, Government

Table 25.01. SOCIAL STATISTICS AND INDICATORS: DEMOGRAPHIC, ECONOMIC, SOCIAL, AND PHYSICAL CHARACTERISTICS OF FLORIDA, OTHER SUNBELT STATES, OTHER POPULOUS STATES, AND THE UNITED STATES

	Population					
	July 1, 1989 A/		April 1, 1990 A/			
State	Total (1,000)	Percentage of population aged 65 and over	Total (1,000)	Rank among states	Persons per square mile of land area	Percentage change 1980-90
			Sunbelt states			
Florida	12,671	18.0	12,938	4	239.6	32.7
Alabama	4,118	12.7	4,041	22	79.6	3.8
Arizona	3,556	13.1	3,665	24	32.3	34.8
Arkansas	2,406	14.8	2,351	33	45.1	2.8
California	29,063	10.6	29,760	1	190.8	25.7
Georgia	6,436	10.1	6,478	11	111.9	18.6
Louisiana	4,382	11.1	4,220	21	96.9	0.3
Mississippi	2,621	12.4	2,573	31	54.9	2.1
New Mexico	1,528	10.5	1,515	37	12.5	16.3
North Carolina	6,571	12.1	6,629	10	136.1	12.7
Oklahoma	3,224	13.3	3,146	28	45.8	4.0
South Carolina	3,512	11.1	3,487	25	115.8	11.7
Tennessee	4,940	12.6	4,877	17	118.3	6.2
Texas	16,991	10.1	16,987	3	64.9	19.4
Virginia	6,098	10.8	6,187	12	156.3	15.7
			Other populous states			
Illinois	11,658	12.3	11,431	6	205.6	B/
Indiana	5,593	12.4	5,544	14	154.6	1.0
Massachusetts	5,913	13.8	6,016	13	767.6	4.9
Michigan	9,273	11.9	9,295	8	163.6	0.4
New Jersey	7,736	13.2	7,730	9	1042.0	5.0
New York	17,950	13.0	17,990	2	381.0	2.5
Ohio	10,907	12.8	10,847	7	264.9	0.5
Pennsylvania	12,040	15.1	11,882	5	265.1	0.1
United States	248,239	12.5	248,710	(X)	70.3	9.8

(X) Not applicable.
A/ Provisional.
B/ Less than 0.01 percent.

Source: U.S., Department of Commerce, Bureau of the Census, *Statistical Abstract of the United States, 1991.*

Florida Statistical Abstract 1991

Table 25.01. SOCIAL STATISTICS AND INDICATORS: DEMOGRAPHIC, ECONOMIC, SOCIAL, AND
    PHYSICAL CHARACTERISTICS OF FLORIDA, OTHER SUNBELT STATES, OTHER POPULOUS
    STATES, AND THE UNITED STATES (Continued)

	Mobility status between 1975 and 1980 A/	Population (Continued) Percentage of resident population, 1990				
State		White	Black	Other races	Hispanic origin 1/	Living in metro politan areas 2/
		Sunbelt states				
Florida	19.6	83.1	13.6	3.3	12.2	90.8
Alabama	8.9	73.6	25.3	1.1	0.6	67.4
Arizona	23.9	80.8	3.0	16.1	18.8	79.0
Arkansas	12.4	82.7	15.9	1.4	0.8	40.1
California	8.5	69.0	7.4	23.6	25.8	95.7
Georgia	11.5	71.0	27.0	2.0	1.7	65.0
Louisiana	8.4	67.3	30.8	1.9	2.2	69.5
Mississippi	9.2	63.5	35.6	1.0	0.6	30.1
New Mexico	17.4	75.6	2.0	22.4	38.2	48.4
North Carolina	9.8	75.6	22.0	2.5	1.2	56.7
Oklahoma	13.7	82.1	7.4	10.4	2.7	59.4
South Carolina	11.5	69.0	29.8	1.1	0.9	60.6
Tennessee	10.6	83.0	16.0	1.0	0.7	67.7
Texas	11.0	75.2	11.9	12.9	25.5	81.6
Virginia	13.9	77.4	18.8	3.8	2.6	72.5
		Other populous states				
Illinois	6.1	78.3	14.8	6.9	7.9	82.7
Indiana	7.6	90.6	7.8	1.6	1.8	68.5
Massachusetts	7.0	89.8	5.0	5.2	4.8	90.4
Michigan	5.1	83.4	13.9	2.7	2.2	80.1
New Jersey	7.8	79.3	13.4	7.3	9.6	100.0
New York	3.8	74.4	15.9	9.7	12.3	91.1
Ohio	5.7	87.8	10.6	1.6	1.3	79.0
Pennsylvania	5.2	88.5	9.2	2.3	2.0	84.8
United States	9.7	80.3	12.1	7.7	9.0	77.5

A/ Percentage of persons aged 5 and over, April 1, 1980, who lived in a different
state on April 1, 1975.
    1/ Persons of Hispanic origin may be of any race.
    2/ Population in metropolitan statistical areas as defined through June 30, 1990.
See Glossary for definition.

    Source: Column 1, U.S., Department of Commerce, Bureau of the Census, *1980
Census of Population: Supplementary Report*. PC80-S-1-9; Columns 2, 3, 4, 5, U.S.,
Department of Commerce, Bureau of the Census, *News*. Release of June 12, 1991;
Column 6, U.S., Department of Commerce, Bureau of the Census, *Statistical Abstract
of the United States, 1991*.

Florida Statistical Abstract 1991

Table 25.01. SOCIAL STATISTICS AND INDICATORS: DEMOGRAPHIC, ECONOMIC, SOCIAL, AND
PHYSICAL CHARACTERISTICS OF FLORIDA, OTHER SUNBELT STATES, OTHER POPULOUS
STATES, AND THE UNITED STATES (Continued)

	Households		Housing		Year-round housing units, 1980	
State	Per-centage change 1980-1990	Persons per household 1990	New privately-owned units permitted 1989 (1,000)	Percent-age with 5 or more units in structure	Per-centage owner-occupied	Median value of owner-occupied units 1/ (dollars)
			Sunbelt states			
Florida	37.1	2.46	165.0	23.7	68.3	45,100
Alabama	12.3	2.62	12.0	9.1	70.1	33,900
Arizona	43.0	2.62	23.8	16.3	68.3	54,800
Arkansas	9.2	2.57	6.3	7.2	70.5	31,100
California	20.3	2.79	237.7	24.0	55.9	84,500
Georgia	26.4	2.66	50.5	14.0	65.0	36,900
Louisiana	6.2	2.74	6.1	11.1	65.5	43,000
Mississippi	10.2	2.75	6.6	6.0	71.0	31,400
New Mexico	22.9	2.74	6.7	12.2	68.1	45,300
North Carolina	23.2	2.54	48.4	8.5	68.4	36,000
Oklahoma	7.8	2.53	5.5	10.1	70.7	35,600
South Carolina	22.1	2.68	21.2	8.4	70.2	35,100
Tennessee	14.5	2.56	24.2	11.5	68.6	35,600
Texas	23.2	2.73	41.3	18.4	64.3	39,100
Virginia	23.0	2.61	56.9	16.2	65.6	48,000
			Other populous states			
Illinois	3.9	2.65	42.4	22.3	62.6	52,800
Indiana	7.2	2.61	26.5	10.8	71.7	37,200
Massachusetts	10.5	2.58	21.3	20.5	57.5	48,400
Michigan	7.0	2.66	45.7	12.5	72.7	39,000
New Jersey	9.7	2.70	30.3	20.9	62.0	60,200
New York	4.7	2.63	48.7	35.8	48.6	45,600
Ohio	6.6	2.59	41.2	14.1	68.4	44,900
Pennsylvania	6.5	2.57	45.5	12.2	69.9	39,100
United States	14.4	2.63	1,338.4	17.5	64.4	47,200

1/ Includes one-family houses on less than 10 acres without a commercial office
on the property. Excludes condominiums, mobile homes, etc.

Source: U.S., Department of Commerce, Bureau of the Census, *Statistical Abstract
of the United States, 1991*, and previous editions.

Florida Statistical Abstract 1991

Table 25.01. SOCIAL STATISTICS AND INDICATORS: DEMOGRAPHIC, ECONOMIC, SOCIAL, AND
    PHYSICAL CHARACTERISTICS OF FLORIDA, OTHER SUNBELT STATES, OTHER POPULOUS
    STATES, AND THE UNITED STATES (Continued)

			Vital statistics			
		Rate per 1,000 persons 1/			Suicides per 100,000 persons	Per-centage of total births to teenage mothers
State	Live births 1988	Deaths 1988	Marriages 1989 A/	Divorces 1989 A/	1987-88 B/	1988
			Sunbelt states			
Florida	14.9	10.6	10.9	6.3	16.7	13.7
Alabama	14.8	9.5	10.2	6.1	12.1	17.4
Arizona	18.8	7.9	10.1	6.5	19.5	13.8
Arkansas	14.6	10.4	14.4	6.8	12.6	18.9
California	18.8	7.6	8.1	4.3	13.7	11.1
Georgia	16.7	8.1	9.8	4.7	13.4	16.5
Louisiana	16.8	8.5	8.9	(NA)	13.1	16.8
Mississippi	16.1	9.5	9.3	4.9	11.3	20.7
New Mexico	17.9	6.9	8.3	5.0	22.8	15.7
North Carolina	15.0	8.9	7.7	4.9	12.1	16.0
Oklahoma	14.6	9.3	10.3	7.1	12.8	16.0
South Carolina	15.9	8.5	15.5	4.2	9.9	16.8
Tennessee	14.4	9.4	13.2	6.5	13.4	17.2
Texas	18.0	7.3	10.3	5.5	13.4	15.2
Virginia	15.5	7.9	11.3	4.2	12.6	11.2
			Other populous states			
Illinois	15.9	9.1	7.2	4.0	10.8	12.5
Indiana	14.7	9.0	9.9	(NA)	11.6	14.1
Massachusetts	15.0	9.6	9.0	2.6	8.6	8.2
Michigan	15.1	8.7	8.4	4.3	11.8	12.5
New Jersey	15.3	9.5	7.8	3.3	7.0	8.9
New York	15.7	9.8	9.0	3.3	6.7	9.4
Ohio	14.8	9.2	9.0	4.5	11.2	13.5
Pennsylvania	13.8	10.5	7.1	3.2	12.4	10.9
United States	15.9	8.8	9.7	4.7	12.4	12.5

(NA) Not available.
A/ Preliminary.
B/ Place of residence and excludes nonresidents of the United States and members
of the armed forces abroad. Data are for June 30, 1987 to July 1, 1988.
1/ Birth and death rates are by place of residence and exclude nonresidents of
the United States and members of the armed forces abroad. Marriage and divorce
rates are by place of occurrence. Divorces include annulments.

Source: U.S., Department of Commerce, Bureau of the Census, *Statistical Abstract
of the United States, 1991.*

Florida Statistical Abstract 1991

Table 25.01. SOCIAL STATISTICS AND INDICATORS: DEMOGRAPHIC, ECONOMIC, SOCIAL, AND
PHYSICAL CHARACTERISTICS OF FLORIDA, OTHER SUNBELT STATES, OTHER POPULOUS
STATES, AND THE UNITED STATES (Continued)

| | | Community hospitals 1/ | | Health | Public | |
State	Beds per 1,000 population 2/ 1988	Average hospital cost per inpatient day 3/ 1988 (dollars)	Average length of hospital stay 1988 (days)	Active physicians per 100,000 persons 1988 A/	health expenditure per 100,000 persons 1989 B/ (dollars)	Hazardous waste sites 1990 C/
			Sunbelt states			
Florida	4.2	646.19	7.0	203	2,974	51
Alabama	4.6	505.77	6.9	151	3,292	12
Arizona	2.9	759.71	6.0	191	10,559	11
Arkansas	4.5	462.91	6.5	144	2,809	10
California	2.9	804.16	6.3	242	2,800	88
Georgia	4.1	515.96	6.8	167	3,783	13
Louisiana	4.4	604.78	6.3	184	2,648	11
Mississippi	5.4	375.23	6.9	125	4,042	2
New Mexico	2.8	669.71	5.6	173	3,925	10
North Carolina	3.4	487.00	7.3	179	4,417	22
Oklahoma	4.0	546.78	6.7	145	3,158	11
South Carolina	3.3	473.92	7.0	158	5,244	23
Tennessee	4.8	517.45	6.9	167	4,507	14
Texas	3.7	628.21	6.2	169	3,128	28
Virginia	3.5	528.72	7.0	204	3,428	20
			Other populous states			
Illinois	4.3	632.96	7.4	210	2,983	37
Indiana	4.1	571.87	6.6	151	2,519	35
Massachusetts	4.0	671.05	7.8	322	4,784	25
Michigan	3.8	643.92	7.4	180	5,082	78
New Jersey	3.7	509.50	7.4	234	3,498	109
New York	4.2	529.68	9.6	307	5,428	83
Ohio	4.2	612.13	6.9	191	2,749	33
Pennsylvania	4.4	583.14	7.6	227	2,515	95
United States	3.9	586.33	7.2	210	4,299	1,197

A/ Excludes federal physicians and doctors of osteopathy. Rates are per 100,000
civilian population.   B/ Based on total resident population estimated as of July 1,
1989.   C/ Includes proposed and final sites listed on the National Priorities List
for the Superfund program.   1/ All nonfederal short-stay hospitals.   2/ Rates per
1,000 civilian population.   3/ Covers expense of inpatient care only and is derived
by dividing expenses by inpatient days.

Source: Columns 1, U.S., Department of Health and Human Services, Public Health
Service, *Health United States, 1990*; Columns 2, 3, 5, Health Insurance Association
of America, *Source Book of Health Insurance Data, 1990*; Column 4, American Medical
Association, Chicago, IL, *Physician Characteristics and Distribution in the U.S.*
(Copyright.); Column 6, U.S., Department of Commerce, Bureau of the Census,
Statistical Abstract of the United States, 1991.

Florida Statistical Abstract 1991

Table 25.01. SOCIAL STATISTICS AND INDICATORS: DEMOGRAPHIC, ECONOMIC, SOCIAL, AND
   PHYSICAL CHARACTERISTICS OF FLORIDA, OTHER SUNBELT STATES, OTHER POPULOUS
   STATES, AND THE UNITED STATES (Continued)

| | Attainment, 1989 A/ | | Public elementary and secondary schools | | | |
State	Percent-age high school gradu-ates	Per-centage college graduates	Enroll-ment rate fall 1988 B/	Average salary of teachers 1989-90 ($1,000)	Current expendi-ture per pupil in ADA 1989-1990 (dollars)	Number of higher education institutions 1988 C/
			Sunbelt states			
Florida	77.9	19.8	88.4	28.8	5,051	98
Alabama	63.2	11.6	88.5	25.5	3,314	89
Arizona	80.6	22.2	88.1	29.4	3,853	39
Arkansas	67.6	14.8	91.6	22.0	3,272	38
California	78.6	26.4	90.3	36.4	4,598	316
Georgia	71.1	18.2	86.6	27.9	4,456	97
Louisiana	70.9	16.6	85.2	24.3	3,457	37
Mississippi	67.7	15.6	87.6	24.4	3,151	49
New Mexico	74.6	20.6	92.7	25.1	4,180	28
North Carolina	71.3	18.3	91.2	27.8	4,386	130
Oklahoma	75.4	17.1	91.3	23.1	3,484	50
South Carolina	69.8	16.6	89.3	27.2	3,731	66
Tennessee	65.4	15.7	89.3	27.1	3,503	88
Texas	74.3	21.7	93.9	27.5	4,058	184
Virginia	74.3	27.3	94.4	30.9	5,000	81
			Other populous states			
Illinois	77.2	21.1	83.7	32.8	4,853	173
Indiana	78.0	13.8	89.6	30.5	4,126	83
Massachusetts	80.7	28.1	88.3	34.2	6,170	125
Michigan	77.0	17.3	89.1	36.0	5,073	101
New Jersey	79.4	25.7	83.0	35.7	8,439	65
New York	76.7	22.8	83.5	38.9	8,094	340
Ohio	77.6	17.6	86.8	31.2	4,394	161
Pennsylvania	76.8	18.6	80.7	33.3	5,670	223
United States	(NA)	(NA)	88.6	31.2	4,890	3,690

ADA Average daily attendance.
   (NA) Not available.
   A/ Percentage of persons age 25 and over who are high school graduates or college
graduates.
   B/ Public school enrollment, fall 1988, as a percentage of persons 5-17 on
July 1, 1988.
   C/ Includes universities, colleges, professional schools, junior and teachers
colleges, both public and private. Branch campuses count as separate institutions.
   Source: Columns 1, 2, 3, 6, U.S., Department of Commerce, Bureau of the Census,
Statistical Abstract of the United States, 1991, and previous edition; Columns 4, 5,
National Education Association. 1991. *Estimates of School Statistics 1989-90.*
Washington, D.C.: NEA. Reprinted by permission.

Florida Statistical Abstract 1991

Table 25.01. SOCIAL STATISTICS AND INDICATORS: DEMOGRAPHIC, ECONOMIC, SOCIAL, AND
PHYSICAL CHARACTERISTICS OF FLORIDA, OTHER SUNBELT STATES, OTHER POPULOUS
STATES, AND THE UNITED STATES (Continued)

State	Daily newspaper circulation per 100 persons 1989 A/	State legislature appropriations for state arts agencies per capita 1989-90 (dollars)	Number of commercial TV stations 1985	Tidal shoreline 1/ (statute miles)	Average annual days with rainfall .01 inch or more	Normal seasonal heating degree days 65 degrees base 2/
			Sunbelt states			
Florida	25	1.88	41	8,426	116	1,402
Alabama	18	0.47	20	607	123	1,695
Arizona	21	0.70	14	0	36	1,442
Arkansas	23	0.42	10	0	103	3,152
California	23	0.58	63	3,427	36	1,595
Georgia	18	0.52	24	2,344	115	3,021
Louisiana	18	0.20	19	7,721	114	1,490
Mississippi	15	0.19	12	359	109	2,389
New Mexico	21	0.57	12	0	61	4,414
North Carolina	22	0.77	24	3,375	111	3,531
Oklahoma	23	0.98	16	0	82	3,735
South Carolina	19	0.99	14	2,876	109	2,629
Tennessee	20	0.80	24	0	106	3,207
Texas	21	0.16	70	3,359	78	2,407
Virginia	42	0.87	17	3,315	113	3,960
			Other populous states			
Illinois	23	0.92	30	0	127	6,455
Indiana	28	0.42	24	0	125	5,650
Massachusetts	36	2.11	12	1,519	126	5,593
Michigan	27	1.34	27	0	135	6,563
New Jersey	22	2.55	5	1,792	112	5,086
New York	43	3.33	33	1,850	121	4,868
Ohio	25	1.12	33	0	137	5,686
Pennsylvania	26	1.08	29	89	117	4,947
United States	26	1.13	887	88,633	(X)	(X)

(X) Not applicable.

A/ Based on total resident population estimated as of July 1, 1989.

1/ Lengths of shoreline of outer coast, offshore islands, sounds, bays, rivers,
and creeks to the head of tidewater were obtained in 1939-49.

2/ Sums of the negative departures of the average daily temperature from 65
degrees fahrenheit. Period of record is 1951-80.

Note: Climate data are for a major city in each state.

Source: Column 1, Editor and Publisher Co., New York, NY, *Editor & Publisher
International Yearbook*, annual, (Copyright.); Columns 2, 4, 5, 6, U.S., Department
of Commerce, Bureau of the Census, *Statistical Abstract of the United States, 1991*;
Column 3, U.S., Department of Commerce, Bureau of the Census, *State and Metropolitan
Area Data Book, 1986*.

Florida Statistical Abstract 1991

Table 25.01. SOCIAL STATISTICS AND INDICATORS: DEMOGRAPHIC, ECONOMIC, SOCIAL, AND
PHYSICAL CHARACTERISTICS OF FLORIDA, OTHER SUNBELT STATES, OTHER POPULOUS
STATES, AND THE UNITED STATES (Continued)

	Personal finances					
State	Average monthly electric bills January 1 1988 A/ (dollars)	Insured thrift institution assets per capita December 1988 B/ (dollars)	Average amount of life in- surance in force per household 1989 C/ (dollars)	Auto- mobile regis- trations per 1,000 persons 1989 B/	State gaso- line tax December 31, 1989 (cents per gallon)	State lottery ticket sales per capita 1989 D/ (dollars)
			Sunbelt states			
Florida	59.41	7,197	74,900	711	9.7	136
Alabama	49.79	2,632	93,600	744	13.0	(X)
Arizona	60.94	6,985	79,400	560	17.0	67
Arkansas	61.60	2,704	60,300	347	13.5	(X)
California	65.27	13,963	89,700	578	9.0	86
Georgia	49.49	3,189	104,300	591	7.5	(X)
Louisiana	49.07	3,415	87,000	453	16.0	(X)
Mississippi	50.19	2,007	75,700	525	18.0	(X)
New Mexico	60.16	3,598	75,600	506	14.0	(X)
North Carolina	56.69	3,269	89,100	563	15.7	(X)
Oklahoma	50.29	3,409	74,500	522	16.0	(X)
South Carolina	54.30	3,396	90,300	526	16.0	(X)
Tennessee	43.01	2,482	88,500	710	17.0	(X)
Texas	51.75	6,596	98,700	502	15.0	(X)
Virginia	54.55	4,991	105,200	596	17.5	64
			Other populous states			
Illinois	50.89	5,848	102,600	564	13.0	123
Indiana	58.49	2,573	89,000	557	15.0	(X)
Massachusetts	62.74	10,754	104,700	557	11.0	219
Michigan	49.32	4,138	93,700	608	15.0	116
New Jersey	69.75	9,091	121,100	696	10.5	152
New York	73.32	10,073	101,300	494	8.0	94
Ohio	61.09	5,057	90,400	654	14.8	122
Pennsylvania	63.09	5,576	96,500	528	12.0	122
United States	57.39	6,654	93,600	582	(NA)	69

(X) Not applicable.
(NA) Not available.
A/ Average for 750 kilowatt-hours (KWH) of residential service in cities with a
population of 2,500 or more. B/ Based on resident population estimated as of July 1.
C/ See Glossary for definition of "household". D/ Sales reported are less
commissions. Based on resident population estimated as of July 1.
Source: Column 1, U.S., Department of Energy, Energy Information Administration,
Electric Sales, Revenue, and Bills, 1988; Column 2, U.S. League of Savings Insti-
tutions, *1989 Savings Institutions Sourcebook*; Column 3, American Council of Life
Insurance, *1990 Life Insurance Fact Book*; Columns 4, 5, U.S., Department of
Commerce, Bureau of the Census, *Statistical Abstract of the United States, 1991*;
Column 6, U.S., Department of Commerce, Bureau of the Census, *State Government
Finances in 1989*.

Florida Statistical Abstract 1991

Table 25.01. SOCIAL STATISTICS AND INDICATORS: DEMOGRAPHIC, ECONOMIC, SOCIAL, AND
PHYSICAL CHARACTERISTICS OF FLORIDA, OTHER SUNBELT STATES, OTHER POPULOUS
STATES, AND THE UNITED STATES (Continued)

			Income and wealth			
					Personal income	
		Percent-age of	Average	Average	Per	Total personal income
	Median	persons	adjusted	total	capita	percentage
	family	below	gross	income	amount	change
	income	poverty	income	tax	1990 A/	1989 to
	1979	level	1989 A/	1989 A/	(dollars)	1990
State	(dollars)	1979	(dollars)	(dollars)		
			Sunbelt states			
Florida	17,280	13.5	28,420	5,121	18,586	7.2
Alabama	16,347	18.9	24,523	3,946	14,826	6.4
Arizona	19,017	13.2	26,173	4,218	16,297	6.0
Arkansas	14,641	19.0	21,702	3,378	14,218	6.9
California	21,537	11.4	31,805	5,526	20,795	7.4
Georgia	17,414	16.6	27,280	4,405	16,944	6.2
Louisiana	18,088	18.6	23,295	4,007	14,391	7.2
Mississippi	14,591	23.9	20,874	3,358	12,735	5.9
New Mexico	16,928	17.6	22,608	3,633	14,228	6.9
North Carolina	16,792	14.8	25,877	4,037	16,203	7.0
Oklahoma	17,668	13.4	23,926	3,880	15,444	6.5
South Carolina	16,978	16.6	24,158	3,659	15,099	9.9
Tennessee	16,564	16.5	25,082	4,194	15,798	5.9
Texas	19,618	14.7	26,413	4,907	16,759	8.0
Virginia	20,018	11.8	30,808	4,896	19,746	5.5
			Other populous states			
Illinois	22,746	11.0	30,722	5,406	20,303	5.5
Indiana	20,535	9.7	26,414	4,225	16,864	5.6
Massachusetts	21,166	9.6	32,586	5,374	22,642	3.6
Michigan	22,107	10.4	29,365	4,817	18,346	4.9
New Jersey	22,906	9.5	35,808	6,162	24,968	5.1
New York	20,180	13.4	33,672	5,730	21,975	5.8
Ohio	20,909	10.3	26,612	4,182	17,473	5.7
Pennsylvania	19,995	10.5	27,875	4,591	18,672	5.9
United States	19,917	12.4	28,705	4,820	18,685	6.4

A/ Preliminary data from a sample of individual income tax forms.

Source: Columns 1, 2, U.S., Department of Commerce, Bureau of the Census,
Statistical Abstract of the United States, 1991; Columns 3, 4, U.S., Department of
the Treasury, Internal Revenue Service, *Statistics of Income: SOI Bulletin*, Spring
1991; Columns 5, 6, U.S., Department of Commerce, Bureau of Economic Analysis,
Survey of Current Business, April 1991.

Florida Statistical Abstract 1991

Table 25.01. SOCIAL STATISTICS AND INDICATORS: DEMOGRAPHIC, ECONOMIC, SOCIAL, AND
   PHYSICAL CHARACTERISTICS OF FLORIDA, OTHER SUNBELT STATES, OTHER POPULOUS
   STATES, AND THE UNITED STATES (Continued)

| | Social insurance and welfare | | | | | |
State	Average monthly social security benefits 1990 A/ (dollars)	Average weekly state unemploy- ment bene- fits 1989 (dollars)	Public aid recipients as a per- centage of population 1989 B/	Average monthly AFDC pay- ment per family 1989 (dollars)	Average Medicaid benefits per recipient 1988 (dollars)	Number of SSI recipients 1989 (1,000)
			Sunbelt states			
Florida	556.17	145	4.2	253	1,944	210.9
Alabama	486.53	108	6.3	114	1,456	C/ 130.9
Arizona	556.10	117	4.1	271	(NA)	C/ 40.9
Arkansas	479.06	131	6.0	193	1,903	74.5
California	559.01	121	8.8	620	1,422	815.3
Georgia	498.22	136	6.6	261	2,058	156.9
Louisiana	484.24	105	9.2	167	1,794	130.0
Mississippi	454.00	109	11.0	118	1,131	112.5
New Mexico	495.35	125	5.7	225	2,067	C/ 29.6
North Carolina	506.92	146	5.3	238	2,328	C/ 144.7
Oklahoma	517.87	145	5.0	288	2,376	C/ 59.0
South Carolina	502.33	121	5.5	208	1,730	C/ 88.7
Tennessee	499.88	109	6.7	170	1,858	135.7
Texas	517.08	160	4.9	168	1,831	D/ 282.3
Virginia	515.46	141	3.8	260	2,319	C/ 92.0
			Other populous states			
Illinois	584.71	160	6.7	320	1,780	C/ 164.4
Indiana	572.46	105	3.6	263	3,442	C/ 56.8
Massachusetts	563.35	212	6.0	559	3,674	115.2
Michigan	582.52	190	8.3	480	1,636	136.0
New Jersey	609.36	192	5.1	357	3,223	100.0
New York	591.29	166	7.6	530	4,163	390.5
Ohio	558.69	130	7.1	314	2,112	147.1
Pennsylvania	573.28	182	5.8	356	2,072	180.6
United States	544.44	152	6.1	388	2,127	4,592.0

AFDC Aid to Families with Dependent Children.   SSI Supplemental Security Income.
(NA) Not available.   A/ Data are for December 1990 and include retired workers,
disabled workers, survivors, and children.   B/ June recipients of Aid to Families
with Dependent children (AFDC) and federal Supplemental Security Income (SSI) as a
percentage of resident population, July 1.   C/ Data for persons with federal SSI
payments only; state has state-administered supplementation.   D/ Data for persons
with federal SSI payments only; state supplementary payments not made.
   Source: Column 1, U.S., Department of Health and Human Services, Social Security
Administration, *Social Security Bulletin*, June 1991; Columns 2, 3, 4, 6, U.S.,
Department of Commerce, Bureau of the Census, *Statistical Abstract of the United
States, 1991;* Column 5, Health Insurance Association of America, *Source Book of
Health Insurance Data, 1990.*

Florida Statistical Abstract 1991

Table 25.01. SOCIAL STATISTICS AND INDICATORS: DEMOGRAPHIC, ECONOMIC, SOCIAL, AND
   PHYSICAL CHARACTERISTICS OF FLORIDA, OTHER SUNBELT STATES, OTHER POPULOUS
   STATES, AND THE UNITED STATES (Continued)

			Employment			
				Average weekly		
			Average annual	earnings for manu-	Annual average	
	Labor force participation rate, 1989 A/		pay 1989 B/	facturing 1990 C/	unemployment rate, 1989 A/	
State	Male	Female	(dollars)	(dollars)	Male	Female
			Sunbelt states			
Florida	71.3	54.9	20,072	365.49	5.1	6.2
Alabama	73.4	52.0	19,593	384.58	6.1	8.2
Arizona	74.8	56.2	20,808	415.95	5.3	5.1
Arkansas	71.3	56.0	17,418	348.91	6.9	7.6
California	77.9	57.9	24,921	466.09	5.1	5.1
Georgia	77.0	59.8	21,071	373.73	4.7	6.5
Louisiana	72.7	49.1	19,750	498.07	7.8	8.1
Mississippi	71.8	52.7	17,047	329.78	6.6	9.1
New Mexico	73.8	54.4	18,667	368.74	7.4	5.7
North Carolina	77.7	60.4	19,320	350.32	3.2	3.8
Oklahoma	73.0	55.4	19,530	438.04	5.6	5.6
South Carolina	76.6	56.8	18,797	362.78	4.3	5.2
Tennessee	73.2	54.2	19,712	368.63	4.8	5.5
Texas	79.9	58.9	21,740	437.65	6.5	7.1
Virginia	77.9	61.3	21,879	406.83	3.3	4.6
			Other populous states			
Illinois	78.7	58.5	24,211	472.47	6.1	5.8
Indiana	78.1	59.5	20,931	496.84	4.5	5.1
Massachusetts	77.7	61.0	25,233	463.57	4.3	3.6
Michigan	75.6	58.5	24,853	579.35	7.2	7.0
New Jersey	76.4	56.8	26,780	486.86	4.3	3.9
New York	74.6	52.8	27,303	439.96	5.4	4.8
Ohio	75.2	56.8	21,986	535.94	5.7	5.4
Pennsylvania	73.4	52.8	22,312	449.33	4.7	4.2
United States	76.4	57.4	22,567	(NA)	5.2	5.4

(NA) Not available.

A/ Percentage of civilian noninstitutional population of each specified group in
the civilian labor force. Includes persons 16 years old and over.

B/ Data are for workers covered by state and federal unemployment insurance
programs.

C/ Average weekly earnings of production workers on manufacturing payrolls.

Source: Columns 1, 2, 5, 6, U.S., Department of Commerce, Bureau of the Census,
Statistical Abstract of the United States, 1991; Column 3, U.S., Department of
Labor, Bureau of Labor Statistics, *Employment and Wages: Annual Averages, 1990*;
Column 4, U.S., Department of Labor, Bureau of Labor Statistics, *Employment and
Earnings*, May 1991.

Florida Statistical Abstract 1991

Table 25.01. SOCIAL STATISTICS AND INDICATORS: DEMOGRAPHIC, ECONOMIC, SOCIAL, AND
PHYSICAL CHARACTERISTICS OF FLORIDA, OTHER SUNBELT STATES, OTHER POPULOUS
STATES, AND THE UNITED STATES (Continued)

			Employment (Continued)			
			Percentage distribution of nonagricultural employment, 1990 A/			
State	Construc- tion	Manu- facturing	Whole- sale and retail trade	Finance insurance and real estate	Services	Govern- ment
			Sunbelt states			
Florida	6.0	9.7	27.0	6.9	29.6	15.6
Alabama	5.0	23.5	21.7	4.5	19.4	19.9
Arizona	5.6	12.4	24.8	6.3	27.2	17.3
Arkansas	4.1	25.1	22.3	4.1	20.6	17.2
California	5.2	16.5	23.5	6.6	27.0	16.1
Georgia	4.9	18.7	24.9	5.4	21.4	17.8
Louisiana	5.7	11.5	23.3	4.9	23.5	20.6
Mississippi	3.9	26.2	21.2	4.2	17.2	21.8
New Mexico	5.2	7.5	23.8	4.5	25.4	25.9
North Carolina	5.3	27.6	23.0	4.3	19.1	15.8
Oklahoma	3.2	14.0	23.3	5.0	23.0	22.2
South Carolina	6.5	24.7	22.5	4.3	19.1	18.3
Tennessee	4.2	23.8	23.6	4.7	22.2	16.0
Texas	4.7	14.0	24.3	6.1	24.2	18.1
Virginia	6.3	14.7	22.6	5.3	25.4	20.0
			Other populous states			
Illinois	4.1	18.7	23.9	7.1	25.4	14.5
Indiana	4.7	25.2	23.8	4.9	21.0	14.9
Massachusetts	3.3	17.5	23.5	7.2	30.8	13.2
Michigan	3.5	23.8	23.9	4.8	23.8	15.9
New Jersey	4.0	16.4	23.9	6.5	27.0	15.6
New York	3.8	13.8	20.5	9.5	29.2	17.9
Ohio	4.1	22.7	24.0	5.2	24.4	14.8
Pennsylvania	4.4	19.6	22.8	5.8	28.0	13.7
United States	4.7	17.3	23.7	6.2	25.6	16.6

A/ Does not include mining and transportation and public utilities.

Source: U.S., Department of Labor, Bureau of Labor Statistics, *Employment and
Earnings*, May 1991.

Florida Statistical Abstract 1991

Table 25.01. SOCIAL STATISTICS AND INDICATORS: DEMOGRAPHIC, ECONOMIC, SOCIAL, AND
   PHYSICAL CHARACTERISTICS OF FLORIDA, OTHER SUNBELT STATES, OTHER POPULOUS
   STATES, AND THE UNITED STATES (Continued)

State	Jobs won/lost 1978-88 (1,000)	Rank among states in employment 1989	Union member-ship as a percentage of employ-ment 1988	As a per-centage of gross state product 1986	Farm cash receipts 1989 A/ Amount (million dollars)	Rank among states
			Sunbelt states			
Florida	125.3	14	B/ 8.9	10.8	6,203	8
Alabama	10.1	20	B/ 15.3	23.5	2,628	25
Arizona	63.0	30	B/ 3.8	13.5	1,902	31
Arkansas	10.9	26	B/ 12.0	24.6	4,131	12
California	272.7	1	22.6	18.3	17,515	1
Georgia	58.2	11	B/ 11.9	20.9	3,869	15
Louisiana	-39.4	32	B/ 20.4	13.0	1,661	32
Mississippi	3.2	24	B/ 8.1	27.2	2,292	27
New Mexico	6.5	43	10.4	8.0	1,424	34
North Carolina	59.7	8	B/ 4.6	31.4	4,551	10
Oklahoma	-9.6	33	17.1	14.3	3,594	18
South Carolina	-7.6	19	B/ 3.1	26.7	1,225	36
Tennessee	-17.8	15	B/ 13.5	25.0	1,921	30
Texas	-4.0	6	B/ 15.1	16.0	10,760	2
Virginia	17.9	17	B/ 12.2	17.9	2,058	29
			Other populous states			
Illinois	-304.5	5	33.3	20.2	6,710	5
Indiana	-108.5	10	37.6	29.8	4,318	11
Massachusetts	-66.5	12	19.9	21.7	429	43
Michigan	-232.4	7	53.6	31.0	2,941	21
New Jersey	-120.7	9	24.8	19.7	660	40
New York	-272.8	2	48.2	16.5	2,857	23
Ohio	-274.1	3	40.9	29.2	3,812	16
Pennsylvania	-312.0	4	40.7	22.1	3,581	19
United States	-966.0	(X)	24.9	19.7	159,174	(X)

(X) Not applicable.
A/ Includes net commodity credit loans.
B/ State has right-to-work law.

   Source: Column 1, State of Florida, Department of Commerce, Division of Economic
Development, *Florida and the Other Forty-nine, 1989*; Columns 2, 3, 4, U.S.,
Department of Commerce, Bureau of the Census, *Statistical Abstract of the United
States, 1991,* and previous edition; Columns 5, 6, U.S., Department of Agriculture,
Economic Research Service, *Economic Indicators of the Farm Sector: State Financial
Summary, 1989.*

Florida Statistical Abstract 1991

Table 25.01. SOCIAL STATISTICS AND INDICATORS: DEMOGRAPHIC, ECONOMIC, SOCIAL, AND
PHYSICAL CHARACTERISTICS OF FLORIDA, OTHER SUNBELT STATES, OTHER POPULOUS
STATES, AND THE UNITED STATES (Continued)

	Public life and community					
	Percentage of voting-age population casting votes for--			Total crimes	Adults under cor- rectional	Fatal motor
State	Presi- dent 1988	U.S. represent- atives 1988	Hispanic elected officals 1989	per 100,000 persons 1989	supervision per 10,000 persons 1988 A/	vehicle accident rate 1989 B/
	Sunbelt states					
Florida	44.7	C/ 31.9	62	8,804.5	237.5	2.47
Alabama	45.8	39.5	0	4,627.8	157.5	2.25
Arizona	45.0	44.3	268	8,059.7	181.1	2.21
Arkansas	47.0	C/ 34.7	1	4,555.7	155.5	2.83
California	47.4	45.1	580	6,763.4	217.3	1.94
Georgia	38.8	36.6	0	7,073.1	356.6	1.88
Louisiana	51.3	6.6	7	6,241.3	201.2	2.05
Mississippi	51.1	49.9	0	3,515.3	107.7	2.71
New Mexico	47.3	42.4	647	6,573.8	110.1	2.96
North Carolina	43.4	40.9	0	5,253.8	198.1	2.17
Oklahoma	48.7	C/ 32.5	5	5,502.6	154.1	1.73
South Carolina	38.9	39.3	1	5,619.2	195.8	2.73
Tennessee	44.7	38.7	0	4,513.6	155.1	2.14
Texas	44.2	39.4	1,693	7,926.9	368.3	1.83
Virginia	48.2	41.6	0	4,211.4	102.0	1.55
	Other populous states					
Illinois	53.3	50.4	41	5,639.2	158.0	1.90
Indiana	53.3	51.8	9	4,440.0	185.3	1.57
Massachusetts	58.1	52.0	7	5,136.0	239.2	1.38
Michigan	54.0	50.9	10	5,968.3	235.7	1.83
New Jersey	52.1	47.1	53	5,269.4	176.5	1.36
New York	48.1	40.6	71	6,293.2	166.1	1.96
Ohio	55.1	51.7	8	4,733.2	138.8	1.86
Pennsylvania	50.1	45.8	10	3,360.4	186.1	2.04
United States	50.2	44.9	3,783	5,741.0	204.1	1.93

A/ Rate calculated for persons 18 years old and over. Excludes juveniles,
persons incarcerated in mental health institutions in lieu of prison, persons held
by the armed services, persons held on Indian reservations, parolees under county
jurisdiction, parolees whose sentences were for one year or less, and court
probationers (those not placed under the supervisory authority of a probation
agency).   B/ Rate per 100 million vehicle-miles of travel.   C/ State law does not
require tabulation of votes in uncontested elections.
    Source: Columns 1, 2, Elections Research Center, Washington, D.C., *America
Votes*, biennial. (Copyrighted.); Columns 3, 5, U.S., Department of Commerce, Bureau
of the Census, *Statistical Abstract of the United States, 1991*; Column 4, U.S.,
Department of Justice, Federal Bureau of Investigation, *Crime in the United States,
1989*; Column 6, U.S., Department of Transportation, Federal Highway Administration,
Highway Statistics, 1989.

Table 25.01. SOCIAL STATISTICS AND INDICATORS: DEMOGRAPHIC, ECONOMIC, SOCIAL, AND
PHYSICAL CHARACTERISTICS OF FLORIDA, OTHER SUNBELT STATES, OTHER POPULOUS
STATES, AND THE UNITED STATES (Continued)

		Government				
		State and local government direct general expenditure, per capita, 1988-89 (dollars)				
State	Total	Education	Public welfare	Health and hospitals	Highways	Police protection
			Sunbelt states			
Florida	2,833	911	232	271	222	135
Alabama	2,412	935	193	384	212	73
Arizona	3,212	1,150	277	147	383	148
Arkansas	2,047	848	261	193	191	56
California	3,357	1,089	467	299	141	143
Georgia	2,784	973	293	461	200	91
Louisiana	2,705	845	283	318	210	102
Mississippi	2,413	909	267	378	212	61
New Mexico	3,040	1,137	260	248	359	110
North Carolina	2,516	1,043	254	282	197	89
Oklahoma	2,484	946	325	250	237	72
South Carolina	2,462	977	211	373	165	75
Tennessee	2,389	816	241	308	222	80
Texas	2,576	1,051	198	217	248	89
Virginia	2,915	1,112	220	261	316	100
			Other populous states			
Illinois	2,712	928	363	173	240	125
Indiana	2,514	1,055	307	243	189	65
Massachusetts	3,646	994	609	364	187	130
Michigan	3,211	1,223	489	333	193	118
New Jersey	3,618	1,202	428	198	271	144
New York	4,607	1,325	795	474	248	174
Ohio	2,702	995	433	229	186	96
Pennsylvania	2,732	1,002	403	153	226	81
United States 1/	3,059	1,063	383	273	234	112

1/ Average.

Source: U.S., Department of Commerce, Bureau of the Census, *Government Finances in 1988-89.*

Florida Statistical Abstract 1991

Table 25.01. SOCIAL STATISTICS AND INDICATORS: DEMOGRAPHIC, ECONOMIC, SOCIAL, AND
    PHYSICAL CHARACTERISTICS OF FLORIDA, OTHER SUNBELT STATES, OTHER POPULOUS
    STATES, AND THE UNITED STATES (Continued)

		Government (Continued)				
		Federal government expenditure per capita, 1989-90 (dollars)				
State	Total	Grants to state and local governments	Salaries and wages	Direct payments to individuals	Pro-curement	Other
			Sunbelt states			
Florida	3,970	354	510	2,541,049	511	53
Alabama	4,272	520	682	2,126	839	106
Arizona	4,112	442	558	2,014	1,001	97
Arkansas	3,509	532	396	2,249	166	167
California	3,891	468	596	1,729	991	107
Georgia	3,265	484	683	1,673	344	80
Louisiana	3,582	630	442	1,817	565	129
Mississippi	3,912	620	500	2,041	628	122
New Mexico	5,703	633	897	1,882	2,149	142
North Carolina	3,043	444	538	1,741	240	80
Oklahoma	3,753	498	725	2,076	278	176
South Carolina	3,919	542	690	1,777	764	145
Tennessee	3,701	557	456	1,942	678	67
Texas	3,428	406	533	1,699	660	131
Virginia	5,874	361	1,665	2,024	1,643	180
			Other populous states			
Illinois	3,210	462	416	1,985	228	120
Indiana	3,051	437	325	1,808	356	126
Massachusetts	4,949	641	440	2,203	1,464	202
Michigan	3,142	511	262	2,116	183	70
New Jersey	3,664	514	439	2,105	557	48
New York	3,918	876	357	2,090	479	116
Ohio	3,496	497	362	2,008	557	73
Pennsylvania	3,823	515	433	2,425	350	100
United States 1/	3,974	533	579	1,973	747	142

1/ Average.

Source: U.S., Department of Commerce, Bureau of the Census, *Federal Expenditures
by State for Fiscal Year 1990.*

Florida Statistical Abstract 1991

APPENDIX. EXPLANATORY NOTES AND SOURCES

SECTION 1.00. POPULATION

EXPLANATORY NOTES. The Bureau of Economic and Business Research Population Program prepared a revised series of intercensal population estimates for the 1980s which appears in Table 1.20. Extreme caution must be exercised when deriving annual changes from successive estimates. Calculating such changes can lead to inaccurate conclusions regarding population growth, especially for small places. The best base of any estimate of population change is generally the most recent census enumeration.

Counties and municipalities are legal and political entities, but, from a sociological point of view the community of which a person considers himself or herself to be a part may not correspond to such an entity. Terms like "Greater Jacksonville" or "the Miami area" are used to indicate the real community. People do not hesitate to cross city or county limits or even state lines to work, to buy or sell, or to seek cultural, medical, recreational, or social services. For this reason, the U.S. Office of Management and Budget has designated areas known as Metropolitan Statistical Areas (MSAs). An MSA is a geographic area with a large population nucleus together with adjacent communities which have a high degree of economic and social integration with that nucleus. These areas were designated as Standard Metropolitan Statistical Areas (SMSAs) before January 1983. New MSA designations were announced effective June 1983 and other areas have been designated since that date; further, some areas were redesignated as Primary Metroplitan Statistical Ares (PMSAs) and Consolidated Metropolitan Statistical Areas (CMSAs).

Under the new criteria, generally an area qualifies for recognition as a MSA in one of two ways: if there is a city of at least 50,000 population or an urbanized area of at least 50,000 with a total metropolitan population of at least 100,000. A MSA may include a single county or several counties which have close economic and social ties to a central city or urban area. In metropolitan complexes of one million or more population, separate component areas (previously MSAs or SMSAs) are defined if specified criteria are met. Such areas are designated PMSAs and any area containing PMSAs is designated as a CMSA.

In Florida, MSAs are defined in terms of entire counties. Population living in MSAs may be referred to as the metropolitan population. There are twenty designated metropolitan areas in Florida; nineteen were designated effective June 1983 and Naples-Collier County was designated June 1984. Two SMSAs were redefined as PMSAs in 1983--Ft. Lauderdale-Hollywood-Pompano Beach and Miami-Hialeah. Together they comprise the Miami-Ft. Lauderdale CMSA. See Table 1.65 for population figures and the map at the front of this book for the list of counties in each Florida MSA. There is also at the front of the book a map showing the SMSA designations prior to 1983.

Agencies of the state government have grouped counties into different districts. There are eleven planning districts, each containing several counties which have common interests and needs for planning community development. A map on page 33 shows the county assignment for planning districts. Department of Health and Rehabilitative Services districts are mapped on page 201 and crop districts boundaries are shown on page 284.

SOURCES. The census of population taken once every ten years by the U.S. Bureau of the Census provides basic statistics about population. Selected Florida data from the 1990 census are included in this *Abstract*. Some detailed data have been released by the Census Bureau in Summary Tape File 1A. More detailed data from the 1990 census will be released periodically through 1993 in printed, computer tape and CD-Rom format.

At the back of this *Abstract* is an index of census information which appears in previous editions. The Bureau of Economic and Business Research published a collection of county 1980 census data titled *1980 Census Handbook: Florida Counties*. This volume also includes some 1970 data for comparison and information on how to use census data, primary census sources, and census definitions.

In addition to the decennial censuses, the Census Bureau issues a series of *Current Population Reports*, known as P-Series. These contain national, regional, and sometimes state population statistics resulting from periodic surveys, special censuses, and cooperative estimation and projection efforts between the individual states and the Census Bureau.

Between census years, estimates of the population of the state, counties, and municipalities of Florida are made by the Population Program, Bureau of Economic and Business Research (BEBR), University of Florida. These are released annually in *Florida Estimates of Population*.

The *Abstract* contains estimates and projections of population by age, race, and sex. Benchmark data are from the 1990 census. The age, race, and sex estimates and projections are developed by the Bureau of Economic and Business Research. Voting age population estimates are presented in Section 21.00.

Data on veterans come from the U.S. Veterans Administration in Washington, which releases reports on the age, location, and period of service of veterans. Data on immigrants are from the U.S. Immigration and Naturalization Services.

SECTION 2.00. HOUSING

SOURCES. The decennial census of housing is taken simultaneously with the census of population and provides basic information about people in their living arrangements. This *Abstract* contains a summary housing table (2.01) from the 1990 census. (For additional discussion of census data see source notes to Section 1.00 of this Appendix.) The Census Bureau issues subject series that provide statistics compiled on subjects from the decennial or special censuses and surveys. Table 2.08 presents information on housing characteristics from reports of the American Housing Survey (formerly Annual Housing Survey), which are included in the *Current Housing Reports* series.

The Bureau of Economic and Business Research (BEBR), University of Florida makes annual estimates of the number of households and average household size for intercensal years. These estimates are published in the series, *Population Studies*.

Three agencies of the State of Florida provide information relating to housing. The Division of Motor Vehicles of the Department of Highway Safety and Motor Vehicles annually publishes the number of tags sold to owners of mobile homes and recreational vehicles. The Division of Hotels and Restaurants of the State Department of Business Regulation publishes statistics on apartment houses, rooming houses, and licensed lodgings. The Department of Health and Rehabilitative Services maintains on-line the *Directory of Adult Congregate Living Facilities*.

The Florida Association of Homes for the Aging provides a list of homes with locations, number of units and beds in their annual *Directory of Members*.

SECTION 3.00. VITAL STATISTICS AND HEALTH

EXPLANATORY NOTES. Vital statistics usually include data on births, infant deaths, abortions, illegitimate births, marriages, divorces, annulments, and deaths by cause. For births and deaths, "resident" is the term which indicates births or deaths among residents of a specified area regardless of where the event occurred. "Recorded" is the term used to identify births or deaths occurring in a specified area regardless of the usual residence of the person counted. The birth and death figures in this section are resident data. Marriages and dissolutions of marriage are reported by place of occurrence.

SOURCES. The Public Health Statistics Section of the Florida Department of Health and Rehabilitative Services (HRS) is the principal source of vital statistics data for Florida and its counties. Data are released monthly in *Vital News* and later accumulated in an annual report, *Florida Vital Statistics.*

The National Center for Health Statistics in the *Vital Statistics of the United States*, annual, and *Monthly Vital Statistics Report* provides national and state vital statistics data.

Morbidity statistics, except acquired immuno-deficiency syndrome (AIDS) data, are available from the Health Program Office of the HRS. Statistics on AIDS are available from the AIDS Program Office of the HRS.

SECTION 4.00. EDUCATION

SOURCES. The principal sources of information on education in Florida include the annual *Profiles of Florida School Districts*, reports from the Management Information Services (MIS) of the Division of Public Schools, and other publications of the Florida Department of Education.

Enrollment information about the State University System is available in the *Fact Book*, published by the Florida Board of Regents. Data on public community colleges come from reports of the Division of Community Colleges of the Florida Department of Education.

Public and private colleges and universities in Florida are included in the *Directory of Post-Secondary Institutions*, published by the U.S. Department of Education, Center for Educational Statistics.

The census of population taken every ten years also provides information about education, such as school enrollment and educational attainment.

Data on the extent of public education, the level achieved by the pupils, and the availability and enrollments of schools, colleges, and universities are included in Section 4.00. Employment and finances of educational institutions and data on educational services are in Section 20.00. Additional information on the public funding of education is in Section 23.00.

SECTION 5.00. INCOME AND WEALTH

EXPLANATORY NOTES. The earnings components of personal income are allocated on a place-of-work basis. These earnings are converted to a place-of-residence basis by means of a residence adjustment factor. Property income and transfer payments are then added to earnings, resulting in total income on a place-of-residence basis. This conversion is illustrated in Table 5.14. The first basis, earnings by place-of-work, is useful in the analysis of the income structure of a given area in terms of industrial markets and purchasing power. Expressed on a per capita basis, the latter basis, earnings by place-of-residence, is an indicator of living standards and welfare level. (The population estimates on which the per capita amounts are based are those of the U.S. Bureau of the Census and are not the estimates shown in the population section of this publication.) See Section 9.00 for estimates of farm income.

Families and unrelated individuals are classified as being above or below the poverty level by comparing their calendar year income to an income cutoff or "poverty threshold." The income cutoffs vary by family size, number of children, and age of the family householder or unrelated individual. Poverty status is determined for all families (and, by implication, all family members). Poverty status is also determined for persons not in families, except for inmates of institutions, members of the armed forces living in barracks, college students living in dormitories, and unrelated individuals under 15 years old.

The poverty thresholds are revised annually to reflect changes in the Consumer Price Index. The poverty threshold for a family of four with two children under 18 in 1989 was $12,675. Poverty thresholds are computed on a national basis only. No attempt has been made to adjust these thresholds for regional, state, or other local variations in the cost of living. However, the Congressional Budget Office has developed thresholds based on alternative adjustments for inflation using the CPI-X1. These data are presented in Table 5.49.

The *Federal Register* published by the U.S. National Archives and Records Administration contains poverty thresholds which are used in various federal and state employment programs. In 1991, the poverty threshold for a family of four was $13,400.

The Statistics of Income series data published by the U.S. Internal Revenue Service are based on the tax-defined concept, adjusted gross income (AGI), which excludes certain types of income. Caution should be exercised in comparing this data over time as annual changes in tax law will continue to affect the definition of AGI.

State data showing distribution of income by income class is no longer published by the U.S. Internal Revenue Service. Table 5.03 presents percentage of income in the state distributed by household size and income class based on results from the Florida Consumer Survey, Bureau of Economic and Business Research, University of Florida.

SOURCES. The source for statistics on personal income in Florida is the U.S. Department of Commerce, Bureau of Economic Analysis (BEA). The BEA has made comprehensive estimates of personal income, by type and industrial source, covering all metropolitan areas and counties in the nation for selected years from 1929 through 1989. Annual estimates are published in *Survey of Current Business* monthly reports.

In Table 5.50, the "benchmark" income data for 1979 for households and families by county in the state are from the 1980 Census of Population. Estimates of money income are published by the U.S. Bureau of the Census in *Current Population Reports*, Series P-26 and P-60. (See Tables 5.45 and 5.47.)

A source for income data is the U.S. Internal Revenue Service. Data such as income sources, tax deductions and credits are from statistical samplings of individual tax returns and are reported in the series *Statistics of Income* and *Individual Income Tax Returns*. Other publications of the IRS, *Partnership Returns and Corporation Tax Returns*, provide additional measures of income and wealth.

The data on income distribution for the state by income class are from the Florida Consumer Survey of the Bureau of Economic and Business Research, University of Florida. Updated estimates of national poverty thresholds are published annually in the *Statistical Abstract of the United States* and the *Federal Register*.

SECTION 6.00. LABOR FORCE, EMPLOYMENT AND EARNINGS

EXPLANATORY NOTES. Tables of employment and payroll devoted to individual industries and nonprofit organizations are presented in this section and in other sections of *Abstract*. Data are from the State Unemployment Insurance Program and are often termed "covered employment" or "ES-202" data. Any firm or nonprofit establishment whose employees are covered by state and federal unemployment laws must submit monthly reports on the number of persons on its payroll and the amount employees were paid. The data this reporting generates provide useful measures of the impact of various kinds of industries, firms, or other organizations on the economies of the state and counties. The Bureau of Labor Market Information of the Florida Department of Labor and Employment Security compiles these statistics.

Covered employment data include most employed persons in Florida, but certain workers are specifically excluded from coverage. These are some

671

agricultural and domestic employees, self-employed workers, and elected officials. Included among the excluded self-employed are such occupations as insurance or real estate agents whose earnings are from commissions. Certain nonprofit organizations such as churches may elect to participate in the program.

Also missing from the tables are data for the state or counties in which there were so few units that the information for an individual establishment might be made public or estimated by competitors. In these instances and when one firm in a specific category or county has 80 percent of the employment of all the business in that category or county, no data are reported. Often data may be undisclosed at the level of the county or 3-digit SIC industry group but is reported in aggregate at the state level. New disclosure guidelines adopted by the Department of Labor and Employment Security in keeping with federal rules prevent publication of reporting units and employment ranges for undisclosed establishments as published in covered employment tables in previous *Abstracts*.

The derivation and meaning of SIC codes are briefly discussed in the Preface and Glossary which lists the major industrial groups and codes. Table 6.21 presents data for all covered employees by industry and Tables 6.22 and 6.23 present employment data by county. Tables in various sections present state and county data by major industries and industry sub-groupings, such as Tables 12.50 and 12.52, 13.36 and 13.37, etc.

Detailed employment data for governments appear in Section 23.00.

SOURCES. The basis of statistics on the employment status of the population is a monthly Current Population Survey (CPS) conducted by the U.S. Bureau of the Census. The U.S. Bureau of Labor Statistics publishes monthly data from the CPS in *Employment and Earnings* and other related publications listed below. The Bureau of Labor Market Information, Department of Labor and Employment Security of the State of Florida has the responsibility of preparing estimates of employment status following procedures developed in cooperation with the U.S. Bureau of Labor Statistics. The Bureau of Labor Market Information publishes information about Florida in *Florida Employment Trends*, about metropolitan areas in *Labor Market Trends*, and releases special reports on small counties. Different samples are used to prepare these sets of employment and unemployment estimates.

The U.S. Bureau of Labor Statistics compiles statistics and publishes data on nonagricultural employment in Florida and its metropolitan areas. Its publications include *Employment and Earnings: States and Areas*, monthly *Employment and Earnings, Geographic Profile of Employment and Unemployment, Monthly Labor Review*, and the *Handbook of Labor Statistics*. It also publishes a series of bulletins under the title *News*.

The Florida Department of Commerce, Bureau of Economic Analysis publishes a periodic listing of the fifty largest employers in the state.

Statistics on seasonal agricultural employment are available from the Florida Department of Labor and Employment Security, Bureau of Labor Market Information. The U.S. Bureau of Economic Analysis provides data on farm proprietors and wage and salary workers. Farm employment data appear in Section 9.00.

Another source of data on employment by county and industry, *County Business Patterns*, is published each year by the U.S. Bureau of the Census. It provides information on employment by SIC code in the state and counties of Florida.

SECTION 7.00. SOCIAL INSURANCE AND WELFARE

EXPLANATORY NOTES. For purposes of managing state-administered public assistance programs, the state has been divided into eleven Health and Rehabilitative Service districts; a map showing these districts appears on page 201.

SOURCES. The source of statistics on Social Security programs is the U.S. Department of Health and Human Services, Social Security Administration, *Social Security Bulletin* which is published monthly with an annual statistical supplement.   The Department also publishes data on state programs in *OASDI Beneficiaries by State and County* and releases unpublished data.

Data on unemployment insurance are published in the *Social Security Bulletin: Annual Statistical Supplement.* The Division of Unemployment Insurance of the Florida Department of Labor and Employment Security has published a report entitled *Unemployment Insurance, Financial Data Handbook, 1938-82* and can supplement it with unpublished data. Workers' compensation program data are published periodically in the *Social Security Bulletin.* County data on injuries and cost by industry are reported in the Florida Department of Labor and Employment Security, Division of Workers' Compensation, *Report on Occupational Injuries.*

The Health Care Financing Administration in the U.S. Department of Health and Human Services provides unpublished data on Medicare and Medicaid.

Four public assistance programs--for the aged, the blind, the permanently and totally disabled, and dependent children--are administered by the state but are financed in part by the federal government in grants to states under the Social Security Act. The principal source of state and national data on these programs is the U.S. Department of Health and Human Services. The principal source of data on Florida and its counties is the Florida Department of Health and Rehabilitative Services, Office of Revenue Management *Annual Statistical Report.* Information about state assistance is also reported in the Comptroller's *Florida Comprehensive Annual Financial Report.*

SECTION 8.00. GEOGRAPHY AND ENVIRONMENT

SOURCES. Tables in this section which contain information relating to temperature, precipitation, and other climatic phenomena present data supplied by the Environmental Data Service of the National Oceanic and Atmospheric Administration (NOAA), U.S. Department of Commerce. Their publications are issued both annually and monthly under the title, *Climatological Data, Florida.* Hurricane data are published in periodic NOAA technical memoranda.

The 1980 Census of Population report *Number of Inhabitants, Florida* (PC80-1-A11) provides information on the area of the state and counties of Florida.

The Bureau of Air Quality Management, Florida Department of Environmental Regulation provides information on air pollution in the report *Comparison of the Air Quality Data with the National Ambient Air Quality Standards.*

The Florida Department of Revenue annually reviews the ad valorem tax rolls submitted by county property appraisers and Armasi, Inc. compiles data from the tax rolls making the data available with software that displays data geographically by county. Table 8.10 presents land use values by county summarized from the Department of Revenue files by Armasi, Inc.

Data on water use is collected by the five water management districts in the state and the Florida Department of Environmental Regulation. Some water use data is obtained from utilities and information on agricultural irrigation is collected by the Institute of Food and Agricultural Services (IFAS) at the University of Florida. The water use data in Tables 8.40 through 8.43 and 9.50 were compiled from these various sources by the St. Johns River Water Management District under special contract with the United States Geological Survey, Florida District. Utility water rates are reported in the unpublished geological survey report *Factors that Affect Public Supply Water Use in Florida and Projected Public Supply Water Use in Florida for 2000, 2010, and 2020.*

Solid waste data is published by the Florida Department of Environmental Regulation in the annual report, *Solid Waste Management in Florida.*

SECTION 9.00. AGRICULTURE

EXPLANATORY NOTES. A census of agriculture was first taken in 1840 and has been taken every five years. Congress authorized agricultural censuses to be taken in 1978 and 1982 to coincide with the quinquennial economic censuses. After 1982, the agricultural census again reverted to a five-year cycle to be taken in years ending in "2" and "7." Data from the 1987 census dealing with the characteristics of farms and farm operators are presented in this section. An index at the back of this book lists census tables appearing in previous *Abstracts*. As defined since the 1978 census, a farm is "any place from which $1,000 or more of agricultural products were sold or normally would have been sold during the census year." Because data for selected items are collected from a sample of operators, the results are subject to sampling variability. Dollar values have not been adjusted for changes in price levels between census years.

When comparisons are made between Florida and other states, the other states selected either have a similar climate (the southern tier of sunbelt states) or produce similar crops (citrus in Arizona and California, sugarcane in Hawaii and Louisiana, etc.).

SOURCES. Timely and detailed data on farm receipts, income, production, and value of farm marketings are provided in tables based on annual publications of the U.S. Department of Agriculture, *Agricultural Statistics, Economic Indicators of the Farm Sector*, and other publications. Some data on farm income are presented in Section 5.00.

Data primarily covering characteristics of farms and farm operators is from the *1987 Census of Agriculture* reports published by the U.S. Department of Commerce, Bureau of the Census.

Agricultural employment information comes from the Bureau of Economic Analysis, U.S. Department of Commerce and from the Bureau of Labor Market Information, Florida Department of Labor and Employment Security. (See discussion under Section 6.00 of this Appendix.)

Expanded coverage of the Florida Unemployment Compensation Law beginning in 1978 has permitted the Florida Department of Labor and Employment Security to supply more comprehensive data on establishments, employees, and payroll of agricultural establishments, SIC codes 01, 02, and 07, that meet minimum employment and payroll standards.

Information about citrus production, other crop cultivation, and consumption of fertilizers is from the Florida Agricultural Statistics Service, Florida Department of Agriculture and Consumer Services. A complete series of crop estimates for the state dating back to 1919 are available from the Reporting Service upon request. The Florida Department of Citrus provides information on orange juice sales from A. C. Nielsen market research reports. The Florida Department of Professional Regulation has data on veterinarians licensed in the state.

The U.S. Department of Agriculture, Agricultural Stabilization and Conservation Service provides information on government payments and makes estimates of the number of farms. This agency also collects reports on nonresident alien ownership of agricultural land and has provided unpublished state and county estimates.

Information on irrigated water use in agriculture is obtained from the St. Johns River Water Management District and the Institute of Food and Agricultural Services (IFAS) at the University of Florida.

SECTION 10.00 FORESTRY, FISHERIES, AND MINERALS

SOURCES. The American Forest Institute provides data on tree farms. Forestry employment and payroll data come from the Florida Department of Labor and Employment Security, as does similar information for fishing and mining. (See discussion under Section 6.00 of this Appendix.) Acreage devoted to commercial forests by county is estimated by the Forest Service of the U.S. Department of Agriculture. The Division of Forestry of the Florida Department of Agriculture and Consumer Services provides data on the harvest of forest products.

The Florida Department of Natural Resources provides unpublished data on fish landings. The National Marine Fisheries Services, of the U.S. Department of Commerce, publishes data on fishery products, plants, and cooperatives in its annual *Fisheries of the United States*. Table 19.45 in Section 19.00 gives information on the number of commercial boats registered in the state and counties of Florida.

Basic data on the production of minerals are from the *Minerals Yearbook* and specific industry reports of the Bureau of Mines of the U.S. Department of Interior. One industry report, *Phosphate Rock*, provides statistics on phosphate mining in Florida, other states and outside the United States. Every five years the U.S. Bureau of the Census conducts an economic census which includes a census of mineral industries.

The U.S. Department of Agriculture, Forest Service, publishes data on national forests in *Land Areas of the National Forest System.*

SECTION 11.00. CONSTRUCTION

SOURCES. Statistics on building construction activity and characteristics of that industry (SIC codes 15-17) are in this section. The principal sources of building permit data for Florida are the Bureau of Economic and Business Research (BEBR), University of Florida and the U.S. Bureau of the Census. The BEBR publishes monthly and annual summaries on the type and value of building permits for construction issued by local administrative offices throughout Florida in *Building Permit Activity in Florida.* The BEBR prepares projections of housing starts for Florida and its major metropolitan areas and makes them available exclusively to subscribers of *The Florida Outlook*. The Census Bureau publishes building permit and housing starts data in its monthly *Construction Reports* series. *Housing Units Authorized by Building Permits* provides monthly and annual information on shipments of mobile homes in addition to building permit data.

Every five years the U.S. Bureau of the Census conducts an economic census which includes the census of construction industries. Data from the census covers items such as receipts, employment, payroll, and value added. Tables in previous *Abstracts* present data from earlier censuses. Refer to the index of census tables in the back of this edition.

Additional sources of data on construction in the various states are reports available from F.W. Dodge Company, a division of McGraw-Hill, Inc. and the *Construction Review*, published monthly by the International Trade Administration of the U.S. Department of Commerce.

Data on employment and payrolls are supplied by the Florida Department of Labor and Employment Security. (See discussion under Section 6.00 of this Appendix.)

SECTION 12.00. MANUFACTURING

SOURCES. Major industry divisions for manufacturing comprise SIC codes 20-39. Data on the number of units, employees, and payroll for these establishments were obtained from the Bureau of Labor Market Information of the Florida Department of Labor and Employment Security. A number of industries are detailed in tables in this section and many include county breakdowns.

The U.S. Bureau of the Census conducts a complete count of manufactures every five years as part of its comprehensive economic census. The Bureau of the Census also conducts, in intervening years, a sample survey called the *Annual Survey of Manufactures*. The annual survey program includes information on employment related to the export of manufactured goods.

The Bureau of Economic Analysis of the Florida Department of Commerce prepares a report which is periodically updated, *Florida's Largest Manufacturing Firms.*

675

SECTION 13.00. TRANSPORTATION

SOURCES. The U.S. Department of Transportation provides data on roads and highways, tax receipts, and vehicles in *Highway Statistics*, a publication of the Federal Highway Administration. The same agency publishes annually a report entitled *Fatal and Injury Accident Rates on Federal-Aid and Other Highway Systems*. Information about licenses and drivers of motor vehicles comes from the Florida Department of Highway Safety and Motor Vehicles which also publishes *Traffic Crash Facts*.

Every five years the Bureau of the Census conducts an economic census which includes a census of transportation. The 1980 Census of Population provides data on means of transportation to work. An index at the back of the book lists tables from these censuses which appear in previous editions of *Abstract.*

Employment and payroll figures for all modes of transportation except interstate railroads are supplied by the Florida Department of Labor and Employment Security. Interstate railroads are not included because their employees are not covered by the same unemployment law as workers in other industries.

Water transportation (SIC code 44) includes both the movement of vessels through Florida waterways and the volume of commodities shipped into and out of Florida ports. The authorities of the various ports in the state have supplied data on their activities.

Air transportation (SIC code 45) is represented by data showing exports and imports obtained from *U.S. Airborne Exports and General Imports*, published by the U.S. Bureau of the Census. Air traffic information comes from two sources developed by the Federal Aviation Administration of the U.S. Department of Transportation: *FAA Air Traffic Activity* and *Airport Activity Statistics of Certified Route Air Carriers.*

Unpublished data on miles of track in the state's rail system may be obtained from Department of Transportation, Office of Planning.

SECTION 14.00. COMMUNICATIONS

EXPLANATORY NOTES. Newspaper publishing and other print media (SIC code 27) are considered to be manufacturing by the U.S. Bureau of the Census as well as the Office of Management and Budget, which establishes the Standard Industrial Classification. Since newspapers, periodicals, and books compete with electronic media in providing communications, data are repeated in this section. Table 12.50 in Section 12.00 shows newspapers as a component of the manufacturing industry.

SOURCES. Also included in Section 14.00 are data on the U.S. Postal Service (SIC code 43), telephones (SIC code 481), telegraph (SIC code 482), and radio and television broadcasting (SIC code 483). The Florida Public Service Commission supplies data on telephone companies in Florida. Employment and payroll data are from the Florida Department of Labor and Employment Security, Bureau of Labor Market Information. (See discussion under Section 6.00 of this Appendix.)

A copyrighted source has been used with permission for newspaper circulation: Editor and Publisher Co., Inc., *Editor and Publisher International Yearbook.* This yearbook provides detailed information for individual daily, weekly, and special audience newspapers.

SECTION 15.00. POWER AND ENERGY

SOURCES. Data in this section have been selected to describe the status of the electric, gas, and sanitary service industries, and the consumption and production of electricity, gas, gasoline, fuel oil, and nuclear power. Energy infor-

676

mation is supplied by the Energy Information Administration, U.S. Department of Energy in its various publications.

A major source of data on electrical energy in Florida is *Statistics of the Florida Electric Utility Industry*, published by the Florida Public Service Commission. It supplies data on generating capacity, average consumption of electricity, electricity sales, and rates.

The Governor's Energy Office issues *Florida Energy Data*, which primarily covers energy consumption, but also contains pricing and production data.

The Bureau of Labor Market Information of the State Department of Labor and Employment Security supplies information on employment and payroll in the utility industry. (See discussion under Section 6.00 of this Appendix.)

Consumption of motor fuel data are obtained from the publication *Highway Statistics* of the Federal Highway Administration and from the Governor's Energy Office.

Information on consumer prices of energy as measured by the Consumer Price Index, is reported in Section 24.00.

SECTION 16.00. WHOLESALE TRADE AND RETAIL TRADE

EXPLANATORY NOTES. Data from the 1987 Censuses of Wholesale and Retail Trade comprise several tables in this section. (An index of census tables appearing in previous *Abstracts* is at the back of this edition.) Number of establishments, employment, payroll, and sales are presented both by kind of business and by county in which the establishments are located.

SOURCES. Covered employment and payroll information by kind of business and county come from the Bureau of Labor Market Information of the Florida Department of Labor and Employment Security. (See the discussion under Section 6.00 of this Appendix.) Since there are some differences in coverage and classification, these figures are not necessarily comparable with those from the economic censuses.

The Florida Department of Revenue is the source for information on sales reported by firms in connection with the sales and use tax laws. In addition to the tables present in this section, printouts of county gross and taxable sales by business category are available from the Bureau of Economic and Business Research on a subscription basis. These also vary in coverage and classification from either the census or the Florida Department of Commerce figures. Data on retail sales tax collections may be found in Table 23.43. A time series of gross and taxable sales is to be found in Table 24.30.

Health professionals who operate at the retail level and are required to have a license such as dispensing opticians or pharmacists are reported by the Florida Department of Professional Regulation. These data are reported in Section 20.00.

The Bureau of the Census conducts an economic census every five years. The census of wholesale and retail trade is part of this quinquennial census. The Bureau of the Census also publishes *Current Business Reports* which contains sales and other data.

SECTION 17.00. FINANCE, INSURANCE, AND REAL ESTATE

EXPLANATORY NOTES. Industries covered in this section are those SIC codes numbered 60 through 67, including banking and other credit agencies, establishments dealing in securities and commodities, insurance and real estate offices, and investment firms.

SOURCES. Summaries of banking data for Florida may be found in the *Annual Report of the Florida Division of Banking*, published by the Comptroller's Office. Another major source of banking data is the Federal Deposit Insurance Corporation, which issues an *Annual Report*, *Statistics on Banking*, and *Data Book Operating Banks and Branches*.

Figures on number of establishments, employment, and payroll for banking and credit, insurance, real estate and investment industries come from the Florida Department of Labor and Employment Security, Bureau of Labor Market Information. (See the discussion in Section 6.00 of this Appendix.)

Sources of information on savings institutions include the *Savings Institutions Sourcebook*, published by the U.S. League of Savings Institutions; the *SAIF-Insured Savings Associations: Summary of Savings Accounts by Geographic Area* and *Savings and Home Financing Source Book* issued by the Office of Thrift Supervision, U.S. Department of the Treasury. The Office of Thrift Supervision also provides unpublished mortgage activity of loans made for single-family houses. The mortgage loan activity data presented in Table 17.33 is by permission of TRW REDI Property Data, Inc. This firm collects loan activity data in forty counties and provides reports by subscription.

A basic source of information on activities of insurance companies in Florida is the *Annual Report* of the Florida Department of Insurance. A source of information on the United States and for individual states is *The Fact Book: Property/Casualty Insurance Facts*, published by the Insurance Information Institute. Data on life insurance are from the American Council of Life Insurance in its *Life Insurance Fact Book Update*.

Information on professional persons who handle real estate transactions and are required to have a license is reported by the Florida Department of Professional Regulation.

SECTION 18.00. PERSONAL AND BUSINESS SERVICES

EXPLANATORY NOTES. The Standard Industrial Classification System lists services from SIC code 70 to SIC code 89. In this section, tables based on the establishments covered by the unemployment insurance law cover personal services (SIC code 72), business services (SIC code 73), auto repair services and parking (SIC code 75), miscellaneous repair services (SIC code 76), engineering, accounting, research, management and related services (SIC code 87), and services not elsewhere classified (SIC code 89). Information about establishments with other service SIC codes are to be found in Sections 19.00, 20.00, and 22.00.

The United States Bureau of the Census has taken a census of services industries as part of the economic census every five years since 1967. In 1977, coverage of service industries broadened from "selected services" to "all services except religious organizations and private households."

Data on selected service industries from the 1987 Census of Service Industries are reported in Tables 18.01 and 18.02. An index of census tables appearing in previous *Abstracts* is at the back of this edition.

SOURCES. Data on establishments, employment, and payroll of service establishments whose employees are covered by the unemployment insurance law are provided by the Bureau of Labor Market Information of the Florida Department of Labor and Employment Security. (See the discussion under Section 6.00 of this Appendix.) Data for the same area and industry from the census of service industries are not necessarily comparable because of differences in procedures, definitions, and establishments covered.

Many service establishments are operated by professional individuals who are licensed by the state. Data on these professionals have been supplied from the Florida Department of Professional Regulation.

Information on health, educational, and cultural services is reported in Section 20.00.

SECTION 19.00. TOURISM AND RECREATION

SOURCES. The Division of Tourism of the Florida Department of Commerce issues quarterly and county reports of tourist information and an annual report, *Florida Visitor Study: An Executive Summary*. It also supplies the unpublished results of a survey of Florida's top festivals and events. Data on tourist facilities (hotels, motels, and food service establishments) which are regulated by the Division of Hotels and Restaurants of the Florida Department of Business Regulation are available from the Department's *Master File Statistics*. The Florida Department of Revenue provides information on the sales of tourist-related businesses. Some of these data are in section 16.00 and are repeated here. The Department of Revenue also provides information on the tourist-development or local option tax collected in several counties.

Data on employment in tourist and recreation-related industries come from the Bureau of Labor Market Information, Florida Department of Labor and Employment Security. (See discussion under Section 6.00 of this Appendix.)

Data on boats registered by county in Florida are provided by the Department of Natural Resources, Division of Recreation and Parks. This agency also issues information on the nature, size, and popularity of state parks. Data on national parks in Florida were abstracted from the *National Park Statistical Abstract*, published by the National Park Service of the U.S. Department of the Interior.

The Division of Transportation Planning of the Florida Department of Transportation records traffic counts at strategic highway locations around the state. Estimates of the number of tourists entering Florida by automobile are made by the Florida Division of Tourism using these traffic counts and information from welcome stations. Tourist arrivals by air are based on arrivals at major airports. Individual visitors are interviewed on a randomly selected basis about expenditures and length of stay. Sample results are expanded to the total visitor population.

SECTION 20.00. HEALTH, EDUCATION AND CULTURAL SERVICES

SOURCES. Data on health and educational service establishments from the 1987 Census of Service Industries are presented in Tables 20.01 and 20.02. An index of census tables appearing in previous *Abstracts* is at the back of this edition.

Data on employment are from the covered employment and payroll figures supplied by the Bureau of Labor Market Information of the Florida Department of Labor and Employment Security. (See discussion under Section 6.00 of this Appendix.)

Information on physicians, dentists, nurses, opticians, pharmacists, and other licensed health service practitioners and professionals comes from the Department of Professional Regulation, State of Florida.

Bed capacity of licensed hospitals and nursing homes is reported by the Office of Licensure and Certification in the Florida Department of Health and Rehabilitative Services.

Health, United States is an annual publication of the U.S. National Center for Health Statistics (NCHS) and contains national and some regional and state data on health facilities and services. The Health Insurance Association of America provides data on hospital costs and managed health care, Medicaid and public health expenditures in their publication *Source Book of Health Insurance Data*.

Educational establishment information comes from the Florida Department of Education: *Profiles of Florida School Districts*; the Division of Community Colleges, unpublished data; the Division of Public Schools, *MIS Statistical Briefs* and *MIS Statistical Reports*; and the Center for Educational Statistics of the U.S. Department of Education. In Section 23.00, Table 23.50 presents informtion on lottery revenues and appropriations for education.

Library information is supplied by the Division of Library Services of the Florida Department of State in *Florida Library Directory with Statistics*.

Data on veterans hospitals comes from the U.S. Veterans Administration, *Annual Report of the Secretary of Veterans Affairs*.

SECTION 21.00. GOVERNMENT AND ELECTIONS

SOURCES. Every five years since 1957, the U.S. Bureau of the Census conducts a census of governments. The census of governments covers four major subject areas: governmental organization, taxable property values, public employment, and governmental finances. Table 21.01 presents information from the 1987 census about governmental units by type in Florida and the United States. Table 21.07 is included to show numbers of local governments and elected officials in Florida by county and by type of government. An index of census tables appearing in previous *Abstracts* is at the back of this edition.

The Division of Elections in the Florida Department of State provides information on registered voters and numbers of votes cast in given elections. Current figures on voting-age population are released annually by the Bureau of Economic and Business Research (BEBR), University of Florida.

Several private sources have granted permission to include data in this section. The Joint Center for Political Studies provides information on black elected officials in the annual *Black Elected Officials: A National Roster*. The Elections Research Center publishes votes cast in major elections in the biennial *American Votes*. The Congressional Quarterly, Inc. publishes information on the composition of Congress in its *Weekly Report*. The Council of State Governments publishes information on the composition of state legislatures in the biennial *State Elected Officials and the Legislatures*.

SECTION 22.00. COURTS AND LAW ENFORCEMENT

EXPLANATORY NOTES. Data on criminal offenses are subject to certain limitations. Many crimes are not reported to law enforcement agencies and hence are not counted in preparing crime statistics. Victims may report crimes to prosecuting authorities rather than to law enforcement agencies or for various reasons may not report at all.

An additional factor to consider when studying crime rates in Florida is the presence of large numbers of tourists. The crime rates in this section are based on resident population. When adjustments are made for the tourist presence, the crime rate in Florida drops. *Crime in Florida* does not give modified crime rates for Florida counties; however, these data can be obtained from the Statistical Analysis Center (SAC) of the Florida Department of Law Enforcement.

SOURCES. The principal source of data on crimes and criminals in Florida is the annual report of the State Department of Law Enforcement, *Crime in Florida*. Other sources on the criminal justice system include publications of two divisions of the U.S. Department of Justice: the annual, *Crime in the United States*, from the Federal Bureau of Investigation; and reports and bulletins from the Bureau of Justice Statistics.

Data on legal services come from the Florida Bar and the Florida Department of Labor and Employment Security, Bureau of Labor Market Information.

Prison and prisoner information is made available by the Florida Department of Corrections in its *Annual Report*.

SECTION 23.00. GOVERNMENT FINANCE AND EMPLOYMENT

EXPLANATORY NOTES. A number of tables in the Health, Education and Cultural Services section (20.00) contain data on property valuations, revenue, expenditure, and taxes for education by public agencies. In Section 19.00, Table 19.54 provides figures on the tourist development/local option tax and Table 19.70 provides information about tax collections from tourist-related businesses.

Although the official records of the Comptroller are used by the Bureau of the Census in its compilations on state and local government finances, the Bureau of the Census has found it necessary at times to classify and present the government financial statistics in terms of its own system of uniform concepts and categories rather than according to the diverse terminology and structure of individual governments. This procedure explains the differences which may be found between similar data from the two sources.

SOURCES. The U.S. Bureau of the Census publishes a number of annual series, including *State Government Finances, City Government Finances, County Government Employment, Public Employment, Finances of Selected Public Employee Retirement Systems* (quarterly) and *Governmental Finances*. This edition contains data from the 1987 Census of Governments. (An index of census tables in previous *Abstracts* appears at the end of this book). The U.S. Bureau of the Census also releases annually *Federal Expenditure by State for Fiscal Year.*

Official records and reports of the Comptroller of the State of Florida comprise the basic source of information about government finances in Florida and are published in the *Florida Comprehensive Annual Financial Report* and *Annual Report of the Comptroller.* Other State of Florida sources of data on government finances and employment include the Department of Revenue, *Florida Ad Valorem Valuations and Tax Data;* the Department of Business Regulation, for data on pari-mutuel wagering and beverage licenses; Department of the Lottery, for ticket sales and appropriations for education; *The Report of the State Treasurer;* the Bureau of Labor Market Information on employment and payroll; the Division of Retirement, *Annual Report;* and the Florida Department of Banking and Finance, *Local Government Financial Report.*

SECTION 24.00. ECONOMIC INDICATORS AND PRICES

EXPLANATORY NOTES. Tables in the first twenty-three sections of *Abstract* are primarily cross-sectional or "snapshot" portrayals of a set of circumstances or a situation existing at any one time. Because many readers are interested in charting trends over time, most tables in Section 24.00 contain data over several years.

Consumer price indexes are developed by the Bureau of Labor Statistics (BLS) of the U.S. Department of Labor and appear in the monthly *CPI Detailed Report, Monthly Labor Review,* the annual *Handbook of Labor Statistics,* and the U.S. Department of Commerce monthly publications *Survey of Current Business.* The BLS publishes two indexes: one reflecting the buying habits of all urban households (CPI-U) and one reflecting the buying habits of urban wage earners and clerical workers (CPI-W). Both indexes are comparable with historical CPI figures; the index for all urban households is used in tables in this section (except for the entry of the CPI-W index in Table 24.73). The CPI-U is based on information reflecting the buying habits of about 80 percent of the U.S. population and represents all urban residents, including professional workers, the self-employed, the poor, the unemployed, and retired persons. Not included are persons living outside urban areas, farm families, persons in military services, and those in institutions. The Bureau of Labor Statistics issues a bi-monthly CPI for the Miami-Ft. Lauderdale CMSA and Tampa-St. Petersburg-Clearwater MSA. (See Table 24.74.)

The BLS introduced a revised CPI with the release of the January 1987 index. Both the CPI-U and the CPI-W use updated expenditure weights based on data tabulated from the consumer expenditure surveys. Also, the rental equivalence measures of home ownership costs in both the CPI-U and the CPI-W was improved to better represent both owners' and renters' shelter costs.

The series of producer prices appears in Tables 24.72 and 24.75. According to the BLS, the series measures the average changes in prices received in primary markets of the United States by producers of commodities in all stages of processing. The sample used for calculating the indexes contains nearly 2,800 commodities and about 10,000 quotations selected to represent the movement of prices of all commodities produced in the agriculture, forestry, fishing, mining, manufacturing, gas, electric, and all public utilities sectors.

The *Florida Price Level Index* (FPLI) is prepared and released by the State of Florida Office of the Governor. The FPLI measures relative price levels across counties. Items representative of the expenditure categories used by the BLS in the CPI are surveyed in each county. Table 24.79 shows the relative weights of selected items in the survey; Table 24.80 compares the index and subindexes for major items across counties.

Data on price trends in construction are in Section 11.00. Section 15.00 contains additional information on energy prices.

SOURCES. Extensive series of economic indicators for the United States, Florida and its counties are maintained in the BEBR Data Base, Bureau of Economic and Business Research, University of Florida.

The U.S. Department of Labor, Bureau of Labor Statistics prepares consumer and producer price indexes and publishes them in detailed monthly reports and the annual *Handbook of Labor Statistics*. The U.S. Department of Commerce also publishes indexes in the monthly *Survey of Current Business*.

The Department of Revenue of the State of Florida has data on sales and use tax collections.

The U.S. Department of Commerce, International Trade Administration reports building permit activity in the states in *Construction Review*. Table 24.20 presents data from current and previous editions of this publication back to 1975.

Data on new incorporations and failures of industrial and commercial establishments are available by permission from the copyrighted reports, *New Business Incorporations and Business Failure Record*, published by Dun and Bradstreet.

SECTION 25.00. STATE COMPARISONS

SOURCES. Both economic and noneconomic factors are listed in Table 25.01 to permit the reader to compare aspects of life in Florida with similar characteristics of living conditions in other Sunbelt and populous states. There are numerous sources to this table, most of which have been discussed in previous sections. The *U. S.. Abstract* published by the Bureau of the Census is a primary source for this table. Sources not previously mentioned are the Bureau of the Census, *State and Metropolitan Area Data Book* and the copyrighted reports: *Physicians Characteristics and Distributions in the U.S.* published by the American Medical Association, *Estimates of School Statistics* published by the National Education Association, and *American Votes* published by the Elections Research Center.

SUMMARY OF SOURCES

STATE SOURCES. Most of the state publications are available free of charge from the agency which issues the report. Supplies are frequently limited and sometimes requests cannot be honored unless they come from other state agencies. The state has a system of state depository libraries, coordinated by the Division of Library Services, Florida Department of State, R.A. Gray Building, Tallahassee. All state agency publications are supposed to be on file in depository libraries or available for interlibrary loan. The reference departments of most libraries are willing to answer questions about data in these publications if the requests are not too time-consuming. The Florida Division of State Library Services issues a monthly and annual summary of state agency publications called *Florida Public Documents*.

Depository libraries of the State of Florida include the public libraries of Bay, Broward, and Orange counties, Cocoa, Jacksonville, Miami Beach, Miami-Dade, Ocala, St. Petersburg, Tampa-Hillsborough, and West Palm Beach. University libraries designated as depositories are those at Central Florida, Florida Atlantic, Florida (Gainesville), Florida International, Florida State, Miami, North Florida,

South Florida, West Florida, Jacksonville, and Stetson universities. The State Library of Florida in the R.A. Gray Building in Tallahassee also is a depository.

FEDERAL SOURCES. Some federal reports are available without charge from the agency which issues the information, but most federal publications must be purchased from the Superintendent of Documents, U.S. Government Printing Office (GPO), Washington, D.D. 20402 (phone 202/783-3238) or from a local Government Printing Office bookstore. Publications purchased from the GPO must be paid for in advance. *The Statistical Abstract of the United States* is similar in purpose to the *Florida Statistical Abstract* and much more comprehensive. Readers who are interested in information about the nation, its regions, and states are referred to it.

The federal government also maintains a system of depository libraries in all 50 states, usually the same libraries as state depositories. The University of Florida is designated as a regional depository library and is required to receive and retain one copy of all depository government publications made available to depository libraries either in print or on microfiche. Many of the libraries listed above as state depositories are also federal depositories and some are not listed. Refer to the annual directory printed by the University of Florida Libraries, *Federal Document Depositories and Resource Information for Florida and Puerto Rico.*

PRIVATE SOURCES. A number of private agencies and associations issue publications or reports which have been used in this edition of *Abstract*. Some are copyrighted and have been used with permission. Several have additional information which can be obtained for a fee.

American Council of Life Insurance, Washington, D.C.
American Medical Association, Chicago, Illinois.
Congressional Quarterly, Inc., Washington, D.C.
Council of State Governments, Lexington, Kentucky.
Dun and Bradstreet Corporation, New York, New York
Editor and Publisher Company, Inc., New York, New York
Elections Research Center, Washington, D.C.
Federal Deposit Insurance Corporation, Washington, D.C.
Florida Associations of Homes for the Aging, Tallahassee, Florida
Health Insurance Association of America, Washington, D.C.
Insurance Information Institute, New York, New York
Joint Center for Political Studies, Washington, D.C.
National Education Association, Washington, D.C.
TRW REDI Property Data, Inc., Walnut Creek, California
U.S. League of Savings Associations, Chicago, Illinois

COMPUTER TAPES. The University of Florida Library in Gainesville maintains an extensive collection of information of and about Florida in books and files and on computer tapes. All the data from the population, housing and economic censuses can be accessed from their computer tapes. Data from the 1990 census is also available on CD-Rom.

BUREAU PUBLICATIONS. The Bureau of Economic and Business Research can supply a variety of detailed information about Florida:

Florida Estimates of Population. Intercensal estimates of the population of Florida, its counties, cities and unincorporated areas. Also includes components of population change and density figures. Published annually.

Florida Population: Census Summary 1990. Summary of census counts for the state, cities and counties. Provides state and county figures for components of population change, resident live births and deaths, and population per square mile. Published 1991.

Population Studies. Bulletins providing information on age, race and sex components of Florida's population, household numbers and average household size, projections of population, discussions of estimation and projection methodology and other topics related to population. Published 3-4 times a year.

Economic Leaflets. Data, analyses and background information on state and regional economic and business topics for those interested in economic trends and developments in Florida. Frequently contains current population, housing and personal income information. Published monthly.

Printouts of gross and taxable sales information. Printouts of sales information from the Florida Department of Revenue reports of gross and taxable sales for the sales and use taxes. Available by county and by kind-of-business category. Issued monthly and annually.

The Florida Outlook. Detailed quarterly forecasts of the Florida economy, incisive analyses of economic developments in Florida and the nation and the outlook for twenty of Florida's metropolitan areas. Published quarterly. Available only by subscription.

The Florida Long-term Economic Forecast. Long-range, ten-year economic forecast for the State of Florida and its Metropolitan Statistical Area (MSAs). Volume 1 of the six-volume set is a summary forecast of income, employment, construction and population for the state and all MSAs. Each additional volume concentrates on a specific region of the state (Northeast, Northwest, Central, Southeast, Southwest). May be purchased individually or as a set. Published annually.

BEBR monographs. In-depth analyses of topics relevant to an understanding of the Florida economic and business climate. Issued periodically, in handy paperback format. Current titles include *Population Projections What Do We Really Know?*; *Local Government Economic Analysis Using Microcomputers*; *Cuban Immigration and Immigrants in Florida and the United States: Implications for Immigration Policy*; *Urban Development Issues: What is Controversial in Urban Sprawl?*; and *Preparing the Economic Element of the Comprehensive Plan.*

Building Permit Activity in Florida. Monthly comparisons with year-to-date data, with an annual summary of the value and number of units permitted in the state, counties, cities and unincorporated areas of Florida.

BEBR Data Base. A computerized data management system which contains extensive economic data for the United States, Florida and all counties. Provides easy access to current and historical data for Florida, any of its counties and Metropolitan Statistical Areas and for the United States. Users can develop, edit, process and store their own data using BEBR Data Base software. Continuously updated. Available only by subscription.

County Profiles. Printouts of historical data for population, housing/ construction, employment by industry, gross and taxable sales and income and earnings from the BEBR Data Base. Continuously updated. Available for individual counties.

Florida Consumer Survey. Survey data on Florida consumers' confidence in the economy, predictions for mortgage rates, and inflation and special topics.

Special publications:
      Charlotte Harbor Fiscal Impact Model
      Energy Use and Water Supply in Florida
      Financial Alternatives for Capital Improvements
      Florida's Infrastructure Needs and Resources: A Preliminary Look
      Modeling Capital Needs for Local Governments
      1980 Census Handbook: Florida Counties
      Preparing the Capital Improvements Element
      The Economy of Florida
      The Fiscal Impact Model
      The Urbanization of Florida's Population: An Historical Perspective of
          County Growth, 1930-1970
      Understanding Impact Fees

For pricing and ordering information, please write or call:
      Bureau of Economic and Business Research
      221 Matherly Hall
      University of Florida
      Gainesville, Florida 32611-2017
      904/392-0171

GLOSSARY

ALIEN. Person who is not a citizen of the United States whether or not he/she is a resident, legally or illegally.

AMERICAN INDIANS, ESKIMOS, AND ALEUTS. See Race.

ANCESTRY. A person's nationality group, lineage, or the country in which the person or the person's parents or ancestors were born before their arrival in the U.S. Different from other indicators of ethnicity, such as country of birth and language spoken in home and is a separate characteristic from race.

ASIANS. See Race.

BLACK PERSONS. See Race.

BUSINESS ESTABLISHMENT. A commercial enterprise.

CENTRAL BUSINESS DISTRICT (CBD). Commercial center of a city. An area of high land valuation, high concentration of retail and service businesses, offices, hotels, theaters, and high traffic flow. For census enumeration, in a metropolitan central city or other city of greater than 50,000 population.

CHILDREN. Sons and daughters classified as "own child of householder," including stepchildren and adopted children, who have never been married and are under age 18.

CIVILIAN LABOR FORCE. See Labor Force.

CLASS OF WORKERS. Private wage and salary workers who work for a private employer for wages, salary, commission, tips, pay-in-kind, or at price rates. Private employers include churches and other nonprofit organizations. Also includes persons who consider themselves self-employed but who work for corporations where in most cases these persons own or are a part of a group that owns controlling interest in the corporation.
Government workers who work for governmental unit, regardless of the activity of the particular agency.
Self-employed workers who work for profit or fees in their own unincorporated business, profession, or trade, or who operate a farm. Includes owner-operators of large stores and manufacturing establishments, as well as small merchants, independent craft-persons and professionals, farmers, peddlers, and other persons who conduct enterprises of their own.
Unpaid family workers who work without pay on a farm or in a business operated by a person to whom they are related by blood or marriage.

COLLEGE STUDENTS. See Residency.

COMMUTE. Travel back and forth regularly, usually between place of residence and place of work.

CONSOLIDATED METROPOLITAN STATISTICAL AREA (CMSA). A large metroplitan complex in which individual metroplitan components, Primary Metropolitan Statistical Areas, (PMSAs) have been defined.

CONSUMER PRICE INDEX (CPI). A measure of the average level of prices over time in a fixed market collection of goods and services. The index is intended to represent prices of most items and services that people purchase in daily living, and is calculated to represent purchases by urban wage earners and clerical workers or by all urban consumers.

CONTRACT RENT. See Rent.

COUNTY. An administrative subdivison of a state; a local government organization and political jurisdiction which is authorized and designated by a state's constitution or statutes.

EARNINGS. Sum of wage and salary income and net income from farm and nonfarm self-employment. Reported before deductions for personal income taxes, social security, bond purchases, union dues, and other deductions.

EDUCATIONAL ATTAINMENT. Years of school completed.

EMPLOYED PERSONS. All civilians 16 years of age and over that work at all as paid employees for an employer or, in their own business or profession, on their own farm or who work 15 hours or more as unpaid workers in an enterprise operated by a family member and all those temporarily absent from their jobs due to such factors as illness or vacation (during a given reference week).

ENERGY. The ability to do work; can exist in many forms such as chemical, light, heat, etc.
Primary energy is energy available from conversion of original fuel rather than from a secondary form such as electricity.
Renewables are energy sources that can be used continuously or regenerated quickly such as wind, sunlight, wood and solid waste.

FAMILY. A householder and one or more other persons living in the same household who are related to the householder by birth, marriage, or adoption. All persons in a household who are related to the householder and are regarded as members of his or her family.

FAMILY INCOME. See Income.

FARM. Any place where $1,000 or more of agricultural products were sold in 1979 or normally would have been sold during the census year.

FARM POPULATION. See Rural farm population.

FIRM. A business organization or entity consisting of one or more establishment(s) under common ownership or control; a commercial partnership of two or more persons.

GROSS STATE PRODUCT (GSP). The gross market value of the goods and services attributable to labor and property located in a state.

GROUP QUARTERS. All institutions offering care or custody. Workers' dormitories, monasteries, convents, large rooming houses or boarding houses or communes having at least ten persons unrelated to the resident who maintains the living quarters. Certain living arrangements regardless of the number or relationship of the people in the unit such as military barracks, college dormitories, missions and flophouses. All persons not living in households are classified by the Bureau of the Census as living in group quarters.

HOUSEHOLD. The person or persons occupying a housing unit.

HOUSEHOLD INCOME. See Income.

HOUSEHOLDER. Person, or one of the persons, in whose name the home is owned or rented and who is listed in column one of the census questionnaire. If there is no such person in the household, any adult household member could be designated as "householder."
Family householder is a householder living with one or more persons related to him or her by birth, marriage, or adoption.
Nonfamily householder is a householder living alone or with nonrelatives only.

HOUSING UNIT. A house, an apartment, a group of rooms, or a single room occupied as a separate living quarters, or if vacant, intended for occupancy as a separate living quarters.
Occupied housing unit is the usual place of residence of the person or group of persons living there at the time of the census enumeration, or the unit from which the occupants are only temporarily absent (away on vacation, etc.).
Owner-occupied housing unit is one in which the owner or co-owner lives whether the unit is paid for or mortgaged.
Renter-occupied unit is any unit not classified as owner-occupied, including a unit rented for cash rent or one occupied without payment of cash rent.
Vacant housing unit has no one living in it at the time of census enumeration, unless the occupants are only temporarily absent. May be classified as "seasonal and migratory," or "year-round." Seasonal unit is intended for occupancy during only certain seasons of the year. Migratory unit is held for occupancy for migratory labor employed in farm work during crop season. Year-round vacant unit is available or intended for occupancy at any time of the year.
Year-round housing unit includes occupied and vacant units available or intended for year-round use. Excluded are vacant units intended for seasonal occupancy and/or held for migratory labor.

INCOME. The amount of money or monetary equivalent which is received during a specified time period in exchange for work performed, sale of goods or property, or from profits made on financial investments.
Adjusted gross income is a tax defined concept of income. Certain kinds of income such as some portion of capital gains, social security, and in-kind transfer payments are excluded and certain types of expenses such as some trade and business expenses, alimony payments, and contributions to individual retirement plans are deducted.
Family income is compiled by summing and treating as a single amount the income of all family members aged 15 and over.
Household income includes the income of the householder and all other persons age 15 and over in the household, whether related to the householder or not. Because many households consist of only one person, average household income is usually less than average family income.
Interest, dividend, or net rental income includes interest on savings or bonds, dividends from stockholdings or membership in associations, net royalties, and net income from rental of property to others and receipts from boarders or lodgers.
Labor income is an item generally used for various types of supplemental earnings in cash and in kind.
Mean income is the amount obtained by dividing the total income of a particular statistical universe by the number of units in that universe.
Median income is the amount which divides the income distribution into two equal groups; one having incomes above the median and the other having incomes below the median. For households, families, and unrelated

individuals the median income is based on the distribution of the total number of units including those with no income. The median for persons is based on persons with income.

Money income. The sum of amounts reported separately for wage and salary income; nonfarm net self-employment income; farm net self-employment income; interest, dividend, net royalty or rental income; social security or railroad retirement income; public assistance or welfare income; unemployment compensation; alimony; veterans payments; and all other income. Not included are monies received from the sale of property; the value of income "in-kind" from food stamps, public housing subsidies, medical care, employer contributions for pensions, etc.; withdrawal of bank deposits; money borrowed; tax refunds; exchanges of money between relatives living in the same household; gifts and lump-sum inheritances, insurance payments, and other types of lump-sum receipts.

Personal income is current income received by persons from all sources. Measured before deduction of personal contributions to social insurance programs and income and other personal taxes. Is reported in current dollars. Includes the following categories of earnings: private and governmental wages and salaries; labor income; farm and nonfarm proprietors income; property income; and government and business transfer payments, but excludes transfers among persons. (Also, includes some nonmonetary income such as estimated net rental values--to owner--of owner-occupied homes, and the value of services furnished without payment, and food and fuel produced and consumed on farms.)

Disposable personal income is personal income less personal tax and nontax payments. Personal taxes include income, estate, gift, personal property and license taxes. Nontax payments include fines and penalties, tuition and donations.

Property income is net rental income, dividends, and interest.

Proprietors income is net income of owners of unincorporated businesses (farm and nonfarm with the latter including the income of independent professionals).

Public assistance income includes three items: supplementary security income payments made by federal or state welfare agencies to low income persons who are aged (age 65 or over), blind, or disabled; and to families with dependent children; and general assistance. Separate payments received for hospital or other medical care are excluded.

Social security income includes social security pensions and survivors benefits and permanent disability insurance payments made by the Social Security Administration prior to deductions. Medicare reimbursements are not included.

INDUSTRIAL CLASSIFICATION SYSTEM, STANDARD. Industrial classification system for classifying establishments by type of economic activity. Developed and published in a manual by the Executive Office of the President, Office of Management and Budget, and recently revised and published in 1987 (which supersedes the 1972/77 edition). Major industries are assigned two-digit SIC codes: 01 through 99; subdivisions are classified by three- and four-digit codes. The major industry groups and their SIC codes are as follows:

Agriculture (01, 02, 07)
Forestry and fishing (08, 09)
Mining (10-14)
Construction (15-17)
Manufacturing (20-39)
Transportation, communications , electric, gas, and sanitary
    services (40-49)
Wholesale trade (50-51)
Retail trade (52-59)
Finance, insurance, and real estate (60-67)
Services (70-89)

Public administration (91-97)
Nonclassifiable establishments (99)
An example of SIC coding is the construction industry which is divided into major group, SIC 15, "building construction--general contractors and operative builders;" group SIC 16, "heavy construction other than building construction;" and group SIC 17, "construction--special trade contractors." Group 15 is in turn divided into group 152--"general building contractors, residential buildings," group 153--"operative builders," and 154--"general building contractors, nonresidential buildings." Finally group 152 is subdivided into 1521--"general contractors, single-family houses," and 1522--"general contractors, residential buildings, other than single-family."

INMATES OF INSTITUTIONS. See Group quarters.

INTEREST, DIVIDEND, OR NET RENTAL INCOME. See Income.

LABOR FORCE. Includes the civilian labor force which comprises all civilians in the noninstitutional population 16 years and over classified as "employed" or "unemployed" and members of the Armed Forces stationed in the United States.

MANUFACTURED HOUSING. Any prefabricated dwelling such as mobile home or modular housing.

MANUFACTURING ESTABLISHMENT. An enterprise usually consisting of a single physical location where raw materials are transformed into new products.

MARITAL STATUS. Classification refers to the status at the time of census enumeration. Separated persons are those living apart because of marital discord, with or without a legal separation. Persons in common-law marriages are classified as married; persons whose only marriage has been annulled are classified as never married; all persons under age 15 are classified as never married. Single persons are those classified as never married.

MARKET VALUE. Amount a seller reasonably expects to obtain in a market for commodities, merchandise, services or whatever is being sold.

MARRIED-COUPLE FAMILY. Family in which the householder and spouse are counted as members of the same household.

MEDICAID. In all states except Arizona, a jointly-funded state and federal health care program for low-income persons. States establish their own eligibility criteria and may set benefits above the minimum established by Federal law.

MEDICARE. Federal health insurance program for people aged 65 and over. Also, covers (since 1973) eligible disabled persons of any age and persons with chronic kidney disease.

METROPOLITAN POPULATION. Population living inside metropolitan statistical areas (MSAs) or consolidated metropolitan statistical areas (CMSAs).

METROPOLITAN STATISTICAL AREA (MSA). A geographic area with a large population nucleus together with adjacent communities which have a high degree of economic and social integration with the nucleus. An MSA may include entire counties and generally has a city of at least 50,000 population or an urbanized area of at least 50,000 with a total metropolitan population of at least 100,000. This term replaces the term Standard Metropolitan Statistical Area which was used prior to January 1983. See maps at front of the book for lists of counties in SMSAs and MSAs.

MOBILE HOME. Moveable dwelling, ten or more feet wide and thirty-five or more feet long (a moveable dwelling of less than these dimensions is considered to be a travel trailer or a motor home), designed to be towed on its own chassis, and without need of a permanent foundation.

MILITARY PERSONNEL. See Labor Force and Residency.

MILL. Unit of monetary value equal to 1/1000 of a U.S. dollar.

MILLAGE RATE. Tax rate stated in mills where one mill produces one dollar of tax for every $1,000 of taxable property.

MONEY INCOME. See Income.

MUNICIPALITY. Political subdivision within which a municipal corporation has been established to provide a general local government for a specific population concentration in a defined area. In Florida, municipalities may be called cities, towns, or villages and have been established either by special acts of the legislature or by general law.

NONFAMILY HOUSEHOLDER. See Householder.

NONMETROPOLITAN POPULATION. Population living outside of metropolitan areas (as defined by the U.S. Office of Management and Budget).

NONPERMANENT RESIDENTS. Persons who indicate on the census form that they are in a residence only temporarily and have a usual home elsewhere.

NONPUBLIC SCHOOL. See Private school.

NONRELATIVES. Any persons in the household not related to the householder by birth, marriage, or adoption. Includes roomers, boarders, partners, roommates, paid employees, wards, and foster children.

OCCUPATIONAL LICENSING. Required operational licenses for professional persons who operate at the retail level such as dispensing opticians or pharmacists.

OCCUPIED HOUSING UNIT. See Housing unit.

OWNER-OCCUPIED HOUSING UNIT. See Housing unit.

PER CAPITA. (per person) A per capita figure is defined by taking the total for some item (e.g. government expenditures, income) and dividing it by the number of persons in the specified population.

PERSONAL INCOME. See Income.

PERSONS PER FAMILY. Number of persons living in families divided by the number of families.

PERSONS PER HOUSEHOLD. Number of persons living in households divided by the number of households.

PLACE OF BIRTH. For census enumeration, the mother's usual state or country of residence at the time of birth. Native-born persons are those born in the U.S., Puerto Rico, or an outlying area of the U.S. Includes a small number of persons born at sea or in a foreign country but with at least one American parent. Foreign-born persons are those not classified as native born.

PLACE OF WORK. Geographic location at which workers carried out their occupational activities.

POVERTY STATUS. Defined by income levels determined by federal interagency committees which (depending on family or household size) describe a family or household as being in extreme want of necessities. Income cutoffs or poverty thresholds used by the Bureau of the Census to determine the poverty status of families and individuals are defined by family size and by presence and number of family members aged 18 and under. Unrelated individuals and two-person families are differentiated by age of householder. Poverty thresholds are revised annually to allow for changes in the cost of living as reflected in the Consumer Price Index and are computed on a national basis only.

POVERTY THRESHOLD. See Poverty status.

PRIMARY METROPOLITAN STATISTICAL AREA (PMSA). A metropolitan statistical area which is part of a larger urban complex with a population over one million and is designated as a Consolidated Metropolitan Statistical Area (CMSA).

PRIVATE SCHOOL. Any individual, association, co-partnership or corporation which designates itself an education center and which includes kindergarten or a higher grade below college level. Primarily supported by private funds.

PROPERTY INCOME. See Income.

PROPRIETORS' INCOME. See Income.

PUBLIC ASSISTANCE INCOME. See Income.

PUBLIC SCHOOL. Any school which is controlled and supported primarily by a local, state, or federal agency.

RACE. In census enumeration, reflects self-identification by respondents and does not necessarily denote a scientific definition of biological stock.
American Indians, Eskimos, and Aleuts includes persons who classified in one of these specific categories or who entered the name of a specific Indian tribe.
Asians and Pacific Islanders includes persons who indicated their race as Japanese (also Nipponese and Japanese American), Chinese (also Taiwanese and Cantonese), Filipino, Korean, Vietnamese, Asian Indian, Hawaiian, Guamanian, or Samoan.
Black persons includes those who indicated their race as Black or Negro, as well as persons who classified themselves as Jamaican, Black Puerto Rican, West Indian, Haitian, or Nigerian.
Other race category includes Asian and Pacific Islander groups not listed separately (Cambodian, Laotian, Pakestani, or Fiji Islander); persons who wrote in entries such as Cuban, Puerto Rican, Mexican, or Dominican; and persons who indicated other races not included in specific categories.
White persons includes those who indicated their race as "white," as well as persons who entered a response such as Canadian, German, Italian, Lebanese, or Polish.

RENT OR CONTRACT RENT. Monthly payments made for the temporary occupancy of a building, regardless of any furnishings, utilities, or services that may be included. The statistics on rent are tabulated for "specific renter-occupied" housing units and for "specified vacant for rent" housing units which include renter units except one-family houses on 10 or more acres. In census enumeration excludes any rent paid for additional units or for business premises. Renter units occupied without payment of cash rent are categorized separately as "no cash rent."

RENTER-OCCUPIED HOUSING UNIT. See Housing unit.

RESIDENCY. The place where a person lives and sleeps most of the time. The place may not be the person's legal or voting residence. College students are considered to be residents of the community in which they live while attending college. Military personnel (persons in the armed services) are counted as residents of the area in which their installations are located.

RETAIL TRADE. Businesses primarily engaged in selling merchandise for personal, household, or farm consumption.

RURAL FARM POPULATION. Only in rural areas and includes all persons living on places of one acre or more from which at least $1,000 worth of agricultural products were sold during 1979.

RURAL POPULATION. Population not classified as urban.

SCHOOL DISTRICT. A political organization and jurisdiction that supports and administers local public schools. There is an independent school district in each Florida county and there are 28 community college districts in the state.

SCHOOL ENROLLMENT. Cumulative number of students registered during a school year.

SEPARATE LIVING QUARTERS. Where occupants live and eat separately from other persons in the building and have direct access from the outside of the building or through a common hall.

SERVICE INDUSTRIES. Establishments primarily engaged in rendering a wide variety of services to individuals and to business establishments.

SIC. Abbreviation of Standard Industrial Classification. See Industrial Classification System, Standard.

SOCIAL SECURITY INCOME. See Income.

SPANISH OR HISPANIC ORIGIN. Persons who classified themselves in one of the Spanish origin categories listed on the census questionnaire--Mexican, Puerto Rican, Cuban, or other Spanish/Hispanic origin.

SPECIAL DISTRICT. A local government entity that has been established to provide one or more specific functions such as fire protection, public transit, water management, libraries, or hospitals. About one-third of Florida's special districts have taxing power.

STANDARD METROPOLITAN STATISTICAL AREAS (SMSAS). See Metropolitan Statistical Areas.

TENURE OF HOUSING UNIT. See Housing unit.

TRANSFER PAYMENTS. General disbursements to persons for which they do not render current services. These include payments by government and business to individuals and nonprofit institutions.

UNEMPLOYED PERSONS. All civilians 16 years of age and over who do not work and who actively seek employment, and who are available to work except for temporary illness (during a given reference week).

UNITS IN STRUCTURE. The number of occupied and vacant housing units in a "structure" or separate building.

UNRELATED INDIVIDUAL. Householder living alone or with nonrelatives or household member who is not related to the householder by blood, marriage, or adoption, or person living in group quarters who is not an inmate of an institution.

URBAN POPULATION. Comprises all persons living in urbanized areas and in places (incorporated and unincorporated) of 2,500 or more inhabitants outside urbanized areas.

URBANIZED AREA. Incorporated place and adjacent densely settled surrounding area that together have a minimum population of 50,000.

VACANT HOUSING UNIT. See Housing unit.

WHITE PERSONS. See Race.

WHOLESALE TRADE. Establishments primarily engaged in selling merchandise to retailers, to institutions, to industrial, commercial, and professional users, or to other wholesalers.

WORKERS. See Labor force and Class of workers.

WORKER'S COMPENSATION. State administered medical care payments and income maintenance. Benefits are granted for work caused disability, illness, injury or death.

YEAR-ROUND HOUSING UNIT. See Housing unit.

YEAR STRUCTURE BUILT. Refers to when the building was first constructed. For a houseboat, mobile home, or trailer, the manufacturer's model year.

ZIP CODE. Five digit code used by the post office to identify geographical postal zones. The first digit identifies one of ten postal national service areas. The second digit identifies a state, a portion of a large state or two smaller states. The third digit identifies a portion of a state--a "sectional center" or "zoned city." The fourth and fifth digits identify specific postal facilities. A sectional center is the hub city and surrounding areas; a zoned city is a large city where the city itself is the postal zone.

INDEX OF CENSUS TABLES

THE U.S. BUREAU OF THE CENSUS CONDUCTS VARIOUS CENSUSES AT REGULAR INTERVALS. THIS INDEX LISTS TABLES FROM PREVIOUS *FLORIDA STATISTICAL ABSTRACTS* WHICH INCLUDE DATA FROM THESE CENSUSES. ALL TABLES WITH DATA FROM THE CENSUS OF POPULATION AND HOUSING APPEARING IN PREVIOUS *ABSTRACTS* ARE INCLUDED HERE. FOR OTHER CENSUSES, ONLY THE ONE OR TWO MOST RECENT CENSUSES ARE INDEXED. NO TABLES IN THIS EDITION OF *ABSTRACT* ARE INCLUDED HERE.

CENSUS OF AGRICULTURE
(CONDUCTED APPROXIMATELY EVERY 5 YEARS)

CENSUS OF AGRICULTURE (CONTINUED)
(CONDUCTED APPROXIMATELY EVERY 5 YEARS)

AREA AND DEMOGRAPHIC CHARACTERISTIC INCLUDED	CENSUS YEAR	FLORIDA STATISTICAL ABSTRACT YEAR	TABLE
FLORIDA, STATE ONLY (CONTINUED)			
SPECIFIED CHARACTERISTICS	1978-1982	1985-1989	9.34
DO	1982-1987	1990	9.34
STATE AND COUNTIES			
CHARACTERISTICS OF FARMS	1974	1977	9.10
DO	1974	1978	9.09
DO	1974	1979	9.08
FARM ACREAGE BY USE	1974	1977	9.09
DO	1974	1978	9.08
DO	1978	1981	9.40
DO	1982	1984	9.35
DO	1982	1985-1989	9.36
DO	1987	1990	9.36
CHARACTERISTICS OF OPERATORS	1974	1978-1979	9.10
DO	1982	1984	9.36
DO	1982	1985-1988	9.37
DO	1982	1984-1989	9.38
DO	1987	1990	9.38
CHARACTERISTICS OF OPERATORS AND HIRED WORKERS	1978	1981	9.43
ESTABLISHMENTS, RECEIPTS, AND PAYROLL	1978	1981	9.03
FARMS, SIZE, VALUE, AND VALUE OF PRODUCTS SOLD	1978	1981-1983	9.39
DO	1978-1982	1984-1986	9.39
DO	1982-1987	1990	9.39
FARMS, SIZE AND VALUE OF LAND AND BUILDINGS	1978-1982	1984	9.34
DO	1978-1982	1985-1989	9.35
DO	1982-1987	1990	9.35
MARKET VALUE OF AGRICULTURAL PRODUCTS SOLD	1978-1982	1984	9.36
DO	1978-1982	1985-1989	9.37
DO	1982-1987	1990	9.37
FARM ACREAGE BY TYPE OF ORGANIZATION	1978-1982	1984	9.37

CENSUS OF CONSTRUCTION INDUSTRIES
(CONDUCTED APPROXIMATELY EVERY 5 YEARS)

AREA AND DEMOGRAPHIC CHARACTERISTIC INCLUDED	CENSUS YEAR	FLORIDA STATISTICAL ABSTRACT YEAR	TABLE
FLORIDA, STATE ONLY			
RECEIPTS BY LOCATION, CLASS, AND OWNERSHIP	1967-1977	1981	11.08
PAYROLL, RECEIPTS, AND VALUE ADDED BY SIC CODE	1977	1981	11.02
RECEIPTS AND EMPLOYMENT BY SIC CODE	1972-1977	1981	11.06
RECEIPTS BY TYPE OF CONSTRUCTION	1972-1977	1981	11.07
ESTABLISHMENTS WITH PAYROLL, CHARACTERISTICS	1967-1977	1981	11.09
DO	1967-1982	1985-1986	11.66
ESTABLISHMENTS BY RECEIPT SIZE CLASS	1977-1982	1985-1986	11.65
INDUSTRY RATIOS FOR SPECIFIC ESTABLISHMENTS WITH PAYROLL	1982	1985-1986	11.72

CENSUS OF GOVERNMENTS
(CONDUCTED APPROXIMATELY EVERY 5 YEARS)

AREA AND DEMOGRAPHIC CHARACTERISTIC INCLUDED	CENSUS YEAR	FLORIDA STATISTICAL ABSTRACT YEAR	TABLE
FLORIDA, SELECTED STATES, AND UNITED STATES			
SUMMARY OF FINANCES	1977	1980	23.02
DO	1977	1980	23.03
EMPLOYMENT BY LEVEL OF GOVERNMENT AND BY FUNCTION	1977	1980	23.04
FLORIDA AND UNITED STATES			
NUMBER OF GOVERNMENTAL UNITS BY TYPE	1982	1983-1988	21.01
DO	1987	1989-1990	21.01
REAL ESTATE SALES	1977	1979	23.86
TAX REVENUE	1977	1979	23.87
TAXES PER 1,000 OF PERSONAL INCOME	1977	1979	25.01
PER CAPITA REVENUE AND EXPENDITURE	1977	1980	23.01
ASSESSED REAL PROPERTIES BY TYPE	1977	1979	23.88
FLORIDA, STATE ONLY			
NUMBER OF GOVERNMENTAL UNITS	1977	1979	21.01
NUMBER AND CHARACTERISTICS	1972-1977	1979	21.03
NUMBER BY POPULATION SIZE	1972-1977	1979	21.05
SPECIAL DISTRICTS	1977	1978	21.03
DO	1977	1979	21.02
NUMBER OF SCHOOL SYSTEMS BY ENROLLMENT SIZE	1972-1977	1979	21.06
REGIONAL PLANNING AGENCIES	1977	1979	20.26
EMPLOYEE ORGANIZATION BY FUNCTION OF EMPLOYMENT	1977	1980	23.79
LABOR-MANAGEMENT AGREEMENTS BY TYPE OF GOVERNMENT	1977	1980	23.80
EMPLOYEE RETIREMENT SYSTEMS	1977	1979	23.61
DO	1977	1979	23.62
STATE AND COUNTIES			
SCHOOL SYSTEMS	1977	1979-1983	21.07
DO	1982	1984-1988	21.07
DO	1987	1989-1990	21.07
NUMBER OF UNITS AND ELECTED OFFICIALS	1977	1980	21.07
COUNTY GOVERNMENT EMPLOYMENT AND PAYROLL	1977	1979	23.68
NUMBER AND TYPE OF GOVERNMENT UNIT	1977	1979-1983	21.07
DO	1982	1984-1988	21.07
DO	1987	1989-1990	21.07
SMSAS AND COUNTIES			
SALES OF REAL PROPERTY	1972	1974	20.91
DO	1977	1979	23.89
MUNICIPALITIES WITH POPULATION OF 30,000 OR MORE			
EMPLOYMENT AND PAYROLL	1977	1979	23.69
STATE AND SMSAS			
NUMBER AND TYPE OF GOVERNMENT UNIT	1982	1985	21.06

CENSUS OF HOUSING
(CONDUCTED EVERY 10 YEARS)

AREA AND DEMOGRAPHIC CHARACTERISTIC INCLUDED	CENSUS YEAR	FLORIDA STATISTICAL ABSTRACT YEAR	TABLE
FLORIDA AND UNITED STATES			
PROVISIONAL HOUSING CHARACTERISTICS	1980	1982	1A.01
BY RACE	1980	1982	1A.02

AREA AND DEMOGRAPHIC CHARACTERISTIC INCLUDED	CENSUS YEAR	FLORIDA STATISTICAL ABSTRACT YEAR	TABLE
FLORIDA, SELECTED STATES, AND UNITED STATES			
OCCUPIED HOUSING UNITS	1970	1975	26.01
PERCENTAGE OWNER-OCCUPIED	1970	1975	26.01
FLORIDA, STATE ONLY			
VALUE OF OWNER-OCCUPIED HOUSING UNITS	1970	1972	8.621
PLUMBING CHARACTERISTICS	1970	1972	8.681
MOBILE HOMES BY TYPE OF OCCUPANT AND LOCATION	1970	1974	8.72
COOPERATIVES AND CONDOMINIUMS	1970	1974	8.84
HOUSING UNITS WILL ALL PLUMBING AND 1 OR MORE PERSONS PER ROOM	1970	1975	25.01
HOUSING UNITS LACKING SOME OR ALL PLUMBING FACILITIES	1970	1975	25.01
STATE AND COUNTIES			
YEAR ROUND HOUSING UNITS AND HOUSEHOLDS	1970	1974	8.58
DO	1970	1975-1978	2.05
DO	1980	1983-1990	2.01
TOTAL, YEAR ROUND, AND VACANT SEASONAL AND MIGRATORY HOUSING UNITS	1980	1983-1990	2.01
YEAR ROUND HOUSING UNITS VACANT BY REASON FOR VACANCY	1980	1982	2.07
OCCUPIED MOBILE HOMES	1970	1974	8.73
HOUSING UNITS BY TENURE AND RACE OF OWNER	1960-1970	1971	8.092
HOUSING UNITS BY YEAR OF CONSTRUCTION	1970	1972	8.522
HOUSING UNITS BY TYPE OF STRUCTURE AND MEDIAN NUMBER OF ROOMS	1960-1970	1971	8.262
OWNER-OCCUPIED HOUSING UNITS BY VALUE	1960-1970	1971	8.312
DO	1960-1970	1972	8.642
NONCONDOMINIUM	1980	1982	2.09
RENTER-OCCUPIED HOUSING UNITS BY AMOUNT OF RENT	1970	1971	8.322
DO	1970	1972	8.662
DO	1980	1982	2.25
HOUSEHOLDS OWNING A SECOND HOME	1970	1973	8.532
HOUSEHOLDS BY NUMBER OF AUTOMOBILES	1970	1974	8.62
HOUSING UNITS WITH TELEPHONES	1970	1971	14.412
STRUCTURAL CHARACTERISTICS OF HOUSING UNITS	1970	1973	8.672
SOURCE OF WATER; METHOD OF SEWAGE DISPOSAL	1970	1974	8.60
PLUMBING IN HOUSING UNITS BY RACE OF HEAD	1970	1972	8.692
DO	1970	1973	8.652
TYPE AND PURPOSE OF FUEL USED	1970	1973	8.692
DO	1980	1983	2.09
DO	1980	1983	2.10
HOUSING UNITS WITH SPECIFIED APPLIANCES	1970	1973	8.682
MOBILE HOMES BY TYPE OF OWNER BY SPECIFIED CHARACTERISTIC	1970	1974	8.74
MOBILE HOMES BY MODEL YEAR	1970	1974	8.75
MOBILE HOMES BY HOUSEHOLD COMPOSITION	1970	1974	8.78
COOPERATIVES AND CONDOMINIUMS	1970	1974	8.86
COOPERATIVES AND CONDOMINIUMS BY ECONOMIC CHARACTERISTICS OF OCCUPANTS	1970	1974	8.88
YEAR ROUND CONDOMINIUMS BY TENURE AND VACANCY STATUS	1980	1982	2.20
OCCUPIED HOUSING UNITS AND NUMBER AND PERCENTAGE RENTER-OCCUPIED	1980	1982	2.06
TOTAL PERSONS AND PERSONS 65 AND OVER BY HOUSEHOLD TYPE	1980	1982	2.15
NONPERMANENT RESIDENTS AND PERSONS IN NONPERMANENT HOUSEHOLDS BY AGE	1980	1982-1984	1.53

CENSUS OF HOUSING (CONTINUED)
(CONDUCTED EVERY 10 YEARS)

AREA AND DEMOGRAPHIC CHARACTERISTIC INCLUDED	CENSUS YEAR	FLORIDA STATISTICAL ABSTRACT	
		YEAR	TABLE
STATE AND COUNTIES (CONTINUED)			
PERSONS IN HOUSEHOLDS AND PERSONS IN HOUSEHOLDS LACKING COMPLETE PLUMBING FACILITIES BY HOUSEHOLD TYPE	1980	1982	2.16
HOUSEHOLDS AND AVERAGE HOUSEHOLD SIZE	1970-1980	1983-1990	2.05
OCCUPIED HOUSING UNITS BY NUMBER OF UNITS IN STRUCTURE	1980	1983	2.08
OCCUPIED HOUSING UNITS BY RACE OR SPANISH ORIGIN OF HOUSEHOLDER	1980	1983	2.07
DO	1980	1984-1986	2.07
COUNTIES AND CITIES			
NUMBER OF HOUSING UNITS	1970	1972-1973	8.154
SMSAS			
HOUSING UNITS LACKING PLUMBING FACILITIES OR DILAPIDATED	1970	1975	2.57
HOUSING UNITS IN CENTRAL CITIES	1970	1976-1978	25.02
HOUSING UNITS IN ONE-UNIT STRUCTURES	1970	1976-1978	25.02
MOBILE HOMES BY HOUSING CHARACTERISTICS	1980	1985-1986	2.35
SMSAS AND CITIES			
CHARACTERISTICS OF HOUSING UNITS	1970	1974	8.64
CHARACTERISTICS OF HOUSEHOLDS	1970	1974	8.66
HOUSEHOLDS BY TYPE OF FUEL USED	1970	1974	13.62
STATE AND CONGRESSIONAL DISTRICTS			
HOUSING UNITS	1970-1980	1981	2.02
CITIES OF 30,000 OR MORE			
YEAR ROUND HOUSING UNITS BY OCCUPANCY STATUS	1980	1982	2.08
OWNER-OCCUPIED NONCONDOMINIUM HOUSING UNITS BY VALUE	1980	1982	2.10
RENTER-OCCUPIED HOUSING UNITS BY TYPE AND AMOUNT OF RENT	1980	1982	2.26

CENSUS OF MANUFACTURES
(CONDUCTED APPROXIMATELY EVERY 5 YEARS)

AREA AND DEMOGRAPHIC CHARACTERISTIC INCLUDED	CENSUS YEAR	FLORIDA STATISTICAL ABSTRACT	
		YEAR	TABLE
FLORIDA AND UNITED STATES			
PURCHASED FUELS BY TYPE AND ELECTRIC ENERGY USED	1977	1981	15.05
FLORIDA, SELECTED STATES, AND UNITED STATES			
VALUE ADDED BY MANUFACTURE	1977	1980-1981	25.01
DO	1978	1982	25.01
ESTABLISHMENTS, EMPLOYEES, AND VALUE ADDED	1977	1980	12.02
BY INDUSTRY	1977	1980	12.01
DO	1977	1980	12.08
ENERGY COSTS	1982	1985-1986	24.75

CENSUS OF MANUFACTURES (CONTINUED)
(CONDUCTED APPROXIMATELY EVERY 5 YEARS)

AREA AND DEMOGRAPHIC CHARACTERISTIC INCLUDED	CENSUS YEAR	FLORIDA STATISTICAL ABSTRACT YEAR	TABLE
STATE AND SMSAS			
CHARACTERISTICS	1963-1977	1981	12.01
DO	1967-1982	1985	12.01
DO	1972-1986	1990	12.01
VALUE ADDED BY MANUFACTURE	1977	1981	25.02
DO	1972-1986	1990	12.01
STATE AND COUNTIES			
ESTABLISHMENTS, EMPLOYMENT, AND VALUE ADDED	1977	1983-1984	12.06
DO	1982	1985-1990	12.06
FLORIDA, STATE ONLY			
ESTABLISHMENTS, EMPLOYMENT, AND VALUE ADDED	1967-1977	1981-1982	12.02
DO	1977	1983	12.02
DO	1967-1977	1984	12.02
DO	1972-1982	1985-1986	12.02
CHARACTERISTICS BY SIC CODE	1977	1981	12.03
DO	1977	1981	12.08
SMSAS AND COUNTIES			
ESTABLISHMENTS, EMPLOYMENT, AND VALUE ADDED	1977	1980	12.04
EMPLOYMENT AND PAYROLL	1977	1980	12.05
VALUE ADDED, COST OF MATERIALS, CAPITAL EXPENDITURES	1977	1980	12.03
CHARACTERISTICS	1977	1981	12.07
BY INDUSTRY GROUP	1977	1981	12.09
ESTABLISHMENTS, EMPLOYMENT, VALUE ADDED, VALUE OF			
SHIPMENTS AND NEW CAPITAL EXPENDITURE	1977	1982-1984	12.06
DO	1982	1985-1990	12.06
SMSAS			
VALUE ADDED	1977	1980	25.02

CENSUS OF MINERAL INDUSTRIES
(CONDUCTED APPROXIMATELY EVERY 5 YEARS)

AREA AND DEMOGRAPHIC CHARACTERISTIC INCLUDED	CENSUS YEAR	FLORIDA STATISTICAL ABSTRACT YEAR	TABLE
FLORIDA, STATE ONLY			
CHARACTERISTICS OF ESTABLISHMENTS BY SIC CODE	1977	1981	10.02
STATE AND COUNTIES			
CHARACTERISTICS BY INDUSTRY GROUP	1977	1981	10.03
MINERAL ESTABLISHMENTS BY MAJOR GROUP AND			
EMPLOYMENT SIZE CLASS	1982	1985	10.73

699

CENSUS OF POPULATION
(CONDUCTED EVERY 10 YEARS)

AREA AND DEMOGRAPHIC CHARACTERISTIC INCLUDED	CENSUS YEAR	FLORIDA STATISTICAL ABSTRACT YEAR	TABLE
FLORIDA, SELECTED STATES, AND UNITED STATES			
LAND AND WATER AREAS	1970	1975-1976	8.01
TOTAL POPULATION	1880-1970	1971	2.030
DO	1880-1970	1973	2.030
DO	1970-1980	1981	1.11
DO	1980	1983-1990	1.12
POPULATION BY SEX	1950-1970	1971	2.080
DO	1970	1972	2.080
POPULATION BY RACE	1950-1970	1971	2.090
DO	1970	1972	2.090
POPULATION BY VOTING AGE	1970	1971	19.170
NET MIGRATION OF POPULATION 65 AND OVER	1970	1973	2.840
FAMILIES LIVING IN POVERTY	1970	1977	5.43
POPULATION 65 YEARS OLD AND OLDER	1970	1976	25.01
EDUCATIONAL ATTAINMENT	1970	1976	25.01
DO	1980	1982-1990	25.01
MEDIAN FAMILY INCOME	1970	1976	25.01
DO	1980	1982-1990	25.01
MEDIAN BLACK FAMILY INCOME	1970	1976	25.01
FAMILIES BELOW POVERTY LEVEL	1970	1976	25.01
PERCENTAGE OF	1970	1982	25.01
PERCENTAGE OF PERSONS BELOW POVERTY LEVEL	1980	1982-1990	25.01
POPULATION, RANK AMONG STATES, DENSITY, PERCENTAGE			
CHANGE, AND PERCENTAGE BLACK, OF SPANISH ORIGIN	1980	1981-1990	25.01
POPULATION AGED 65 AND OVER	1980	1981-1982	25.01
NONPERMANENT RESIDENTS AND PERSONS IN			
NONPERMANENT HOUSEHOLDS	1980	1982	1.50
BY STATE AND USUAL RESIDENCE	1980	1982	1.52
INMIGRANTS TO FLORIDA AND OUTMIGRANTS FROM			
FLORIDA, 1975-1980	1980	1983	1.49
FARM POPULATION	1970-1980	1983-1986	9.01
MOBILITY STATUS	1980	1984-1990	25.01
SPANISH ORIGIN	1980	1984-1990	25.01
LIVING ON FARMS	1980	1984-1990	25.01
PERSONS IN GROUP QUARTERS	1980	1985-1986	2.16
FLORIDA AND UNITED STATES			
POPULATION BY SEX, RACE, AND AGE	1980	1981	1.15
POPULATION IN CONGRESSIONAL DISTRICTS	1980	1981	1.05
FASTEST GROWING SMSAS	1970-1980	1981	1.12
PROVISIONAL SOCIAL AND ECONOMIC CHARACTERISTICS	1980	1982	1A.01
BY RACE	1980	1982	1A.02
FLORIDA, STATE ONLY			
TOTAL POPULATION	1830-1980	1982-1990	1.10
AGE, RACE, SEX	1960-1970	1971	2.241
DO	1980	1983-1990	1.34
DO	1980	1984-1990	1.37
URBAN AND RURAL POPULATION	1970	1972	2.111
DO	1970	1973	2.111
DO	1830-1980	1982-1990	1.10
POPULATION IN CORRECTIONAL INSTITUTIONS	1970	1975	1.81
POPULATION IN MENTAL INSTITUTIONS	1970	1975	1.82
POPULATION IN SCHOOLS FOR JUVENILE DELINQUENTS	1970	1975	1.86
POPULATION IN INSTITUTIONS FOR TUBERCULOSIS, CHRONIC			
DISEASE OR IN HOMES FOR THE AGED	1970	1975	1.83
RESIDENCE IN 1965 OF 1970 POPULATION BY RACE AND			
SPANISH LANGUAGE	1970	1974	2.29

AREA AND DEMOGRAPHIC CHARACTERISTIC INCLUDED	CENSUS YEAR	FLORIDA STATISTICAL ABSTRACT YEAR	TABLE
FLORIDA, STATE ONLY (CONTINUED)			
PERSONS 18 AND OVER BY TYPE OF VOCATIONAL TRAINING	1970	1974	4.62
POPULATION IN HOUSEHOLDS BY HOUSEHOLD RELATIONSHIPS	1940-1970	1971	2.291
FAMILIES WITH FARM SELF-EMPLOYMENT INCOME	1970	1974	10.22
NONPERMANENT RESIDENTS AND PERSONS IN NONPERMANENT			
HOUSEHOLDS BY AGE AND HOUSEHOLD COMPOSITION	1980	1982	1.51
POPULATION BY SPANISH ORIGIN	1980	1983-1984	1.40
BY RACE	1980	1983-1984	1.41
STATE AND SMSAS			
POPULATION AND PERCENTAGE CHANGE	1940-1980	1981	1.65
DO	1950-1980	1982	1.65
DO	1960-1980	1983-1990	1.65
POPULATION, LAND AREA IN 1970, DENSITY, AND PERCENTAGE			
CHANGE	1980	1981-1982	25.02
STATE AND COUNTIES			
TOTAL POPULATION	1960-1970	1971	2.112
DO	1960-1970	1972	2.202
DO	1960-1970	1973	2.222
DO	1960-1970	1975-1977	1.20
DO	1960-1970	1979-1980	1.20
DO	1970-1980	1981	1.20
DO	1970-1980	1983-1990	1.20
DO	1980	1981	1.24
POPULATION:			
BY AGE GROUP	1970	1971	2.252
DO	1980	1982-1983	1.35
DO	1980	1984	1.38
BY RACE	1960-1970	1971	2.142
DO	1980	1981	1.28
DO	1980	1982	1.26
DO	1980	1983-1984	1.42
BY SEX	1960-1970	1971	2.132
DO	1980	1983	1.35
BY SPANISH ORIGIN	1980	1981-1982	1.28
RURAL POPULATION BY FARM AND NONFARM	1970	1973	2.272
VETERANS	1970	1973	2.502
POPULATION DENSITY	1960-1970	1974	2.75
DO	1970	1975-1976	1.75
DO	1960-1970	1977-1981	1.75
COMPONENTS OF CHANGE: NATURAL INCREASE AND			
NET MIGRATION	1960-1970	1973	2.712
DO	1970-1980	1981	1.72
PERCENTAGE DISTRIBUTION, PERCENTAGE CHANGE, AND			
COUNTY RANKS	1960-1970	1976-1980	1.73
DO	1980	1981	1.73
RESIDENCE IN 1965 OF 1970 POPULATION	1970	1973	2.282
RESIDENCE IN 1975 OF 1980 POPULATION	1980	1983	1.48
VOTING-AGE POPULATION	1970	1971	19.292
DO	1980	1982-1990	21.25
POPULATION 65 AND OVER	1970	1971	2.312
DO	1970	1973	2.842
DO	1980	1982	1.27
DO	1980	1982	1.37
DO	1970-1980	1983	1.37
DO	1980	1983-1984	1.42
DO	1980	1983	2.13

AREA AND DEMOGRAPHIC CHARACTERISTIC INCLUDED	CENSUS YEAR	FLORIDA STATISTICAL ABSTRACT YEAR	TABLE
STATE AMD COUNTIES (CONTINUED)			
POPULATION 65 AND OVER (CONTINUED)			
DO	1980	1984	1.36
DO	1980	1984-1990	1.36
BY RACE	1980	1983-1984	1.42
EDUCATIONAL ATTAINMENT	1970	1973	4.602
DO	1970-1980	1983	4.30
DO	1980	1984-1986	4.30
POVERTY LEVEL	1970	1972	5.562
DO	1980	1983-1984	5.52
DO	1980	1983	5.53
FAMILIES/HOUSEHOLDS BY INCOME LEVEL	1970	1972	5.512
DO	1970-1980	1983-1990	5.50
DO	1970-1980	1983-1984	5.51
COMMUTING FLOWS	1970	1975	6.30
POPULATION IN HOUSEHOLDS	1970	1971	2.302
DO	1980	1982	2.15
DO	1980	1983	2.12
DO	1980	1983	2.13
DO	1980	1983	2.14
HOUSEHOLDS AND PERSONS PER HOUSEHOLD	1970-1980	1981	2.06
MEDIAN AGE	1980	1982	1.36
MARITAL STATUS	1980	1982	1.45
LAND AREA	1980	1982-1990	8.03
NONPERMANENT RESIDENTS AND PERSONS IN NONPERMANENT			
HOUSEHOLDS BY AGE	1980	1982	1.53
PERSONS IN GROUP QUARTERS	1980	1983-1986	2.15
LANGUAGE SPOKEN AT HOME	1980	1983	1.45
EMPLOYMENT	1980	1983	6.09
DO	1980	1983-1985	6.24
LABOR FORCE PARTICIPATION	1980	1983-1986	6.11
TRANSPORTATION TO WORK	1980	1983	13.01
STATE, PLANNING DISTRICTS, AND COUNTIES			
POPULATION BY AGE GROUP AND RACE	1970	1972	2.402
POPULATION BY VOTING AGE	1970	1972	19.122
POPULATION BY RACE AND SEX	1970	1972-1973	2.452
POPULATION IN HOUSEHOLDS BY RACE AND RELATIONSHIP	1970	1972	2.822
COMPONENTS OF CHANGE BY RACE	1960-1970	1972	2.712
RURAL POPULATION BY AGE GROUP AND RACE	1970	1972	2.262
MARITAL STATUS BY SEX	1970	1972	2.602
POPULATION 65 AND OVER BY RELATIONSHIP, QUARTERS,			
AND RACE	1970	1972	2.842
POPULATION 21 YEARS AND OVER BY AGE AND SEX	1970	1972	19.122
TOTAL POPULATION	1960-1980	1981	1.66
DO	1980	1981	1.23
DO	1970-1980	1982-1990	1.66
STATE, MARKET REGIONS, AND COUNTIES			
TOTAL POPULATION	1970	1974	2.25
DO	1970	1975-1979	1.25
DO	1960-1970	1980	1.25
DO	1960-1980	1981	1.25
DO	1970-1980	1982-1983	1.25
DO	1970-1980	1984-1989	1.68

AREA AND DEMOGRAPHIC CHARACTERISTIC INCLUDED	CENSUS YEAR	FLORIDA STATISTICAL ABSTRACT YEAR	TABLE
STATE HEALTH AND REHABILITATIVE SERVICES DISTRICTS, AND COUNTIES			
TOTAL POPULATION	1970-1980	1983-1990	1.67
SMSAS			
POPULATION ANNEXED TO CENTRAL CITIES	1960-1970	1973	2.203
POPULATION CHANGE	1960-1970	1976	1.74
DO	1960-1970	1977-1979	1.74
POPULATION BY NATIVITY AND RACE	1960-1970	1974	2.92
GENERAL CHARACTERISTICS	1970	1973	24.013
EDUCATIONAL ATTAINMENT	1970	1975-1978	25.02
MEDIAN SCHOOL YEAR COMPLETED	1970	1977	25.02
MEDIAN FAMILY INCOME	1970	1975-1978	25.02
MEDIAN BLACK FAMILY INCOME	1970	1976	25.02
FAMILIES WITH INCOMES BELOW POVERTY LEVEL	1970	1975-1978	25.02
LAND AREA	1970	1976-1980	25.02
EMPLOYED PERSONS BY OCCUPATION	1970	1973	9.153
WORKERS BY MEANS OF TRANSPORTATION	1970	1973	16.403
COMMUTING FLOWS	1980	1985	6.45
SMSAS AND PLACES OF 10,000 OR MORE			
TOTAL POPULATION	1970	1971	2.184
STATE, COUNTIES, CITIES, UNINCORPORATED AREAS			
TOTAL POPULATION	1970	1973	2.314
DO	1970	1974	2.31
DO	1970	1975-1980	1.31
DO	1970-1980	1981	1.31
DO	1980	1982-1990	1.31
HOUSING UNITS	1970-1980	1981	2.05
SPECIFIED CITIES			
TOTAL POPULATION	1970	1976-1979	1.29
MOST POPULOUS CITIES			
TOTAL POPULATION, RANK AND PERCENTAGE CHANGE	1970-1980	1981-1982	1.67
DO	1970-1980	1983	1.68
DO	1970-1980	1984-1990	1.69
TOTAL POPULATION AND RANK	1980	1984-1985	1.13
INCORPORATED PLACES OF 2,500 OR MORE			
POPULATION BY SEX AND AGE GROUP	1970	1972	2.304
PLACES OF 1,000 OR MORE INMATES			
POPULATION OF INSTITUTIONS	1970	1975	1.87
CITIES OF 25,000 OR MORE			
HOUSEHOLDS BY INCOME	1970	1974	5.38
CITIES OF 30,000 OR MORE			
POPULATION BY RACE AND SPANISH ORIGIN	1980	1982	1.28
POPULATION 65 AND OVER BY SEX	1980	1982	1.38
CITIES OF 100,000 OR MORE			
FOREIGN STOCK	1970	1974	2.87
DO	1970	1974	2.89

CENSUS OF POPULATION (CONTINUED)
(CONDUCTED EVERY 10 YEARS)

AREA AND DEMOGRAPHIC CHARACTERISTIC INCLUDED	CENSUS YEAR	FLORIDA STATISTICAL ABSTRACT YEAR	TABLE
STATE AND CONGRESSIONAL DISTRICTS			
TOTAL POPULATION	1970-1980	1981	1.06
POPULATION BY RACE AND SPANISH ORIGIN	1970-1980	1981	1.96

CENSUS OF RETAIL TRADE
(CONDUCTED APPROXIMATELY EVERY 5 YEARS)

AREA AND DEMOGRAPHIC CHARACTERISTIC INCLUDED	CENSUS YEAR	FLORIDA STATISTICAL ABSTRACT YEAR	TABLE
FLORIDA, SELECTED STATES, AND UNITED STATES			
RETAIL SALES PER CAPITA	1977	1981-1982	25.01
STATE AND COUNTIES			
WHOLESALE AND RETAIL TRADE, SALES	1977	1981-1984	16.06
DO	1982	1985-1989	16.06
DO	1987	1990	16.06
SALES, AND SALES PER ESTABLISHMENT	1939-1977	1981	16.11
ESTABLISHMENTS AND SALES BY KIND OF BUSINESS	1977	1981	16.12
STATE, SMSAS, AND COUNTIES			
ESTABLISHMENTS BY TYPE OF ORGANIZATION, PAYROLL AND PAID EMPLOYMENT	1977	1980	16.15
RETAIL SALES PER CAPITA	1977	1980	16.19
SALES BY KIND OF BUSINESS	1977	1980	16.17
ESTABLISHMENTS BY KIND OF BUSINESS	1977	1980	16.16
STATE AND SMSAS			
RETAIL SALES PER CAPITA	1977	1981-1982	25.02
SMSAS			
RETAIL SALES FOR CENTRAL BUSINESS DISTRICTS	1977-1982	1985-1986	16.10
FLORIDA, STATE ONLY			
ESTABLISHMENTS AND SALES BY KIND OF BUSINESS	1977	1982-1984	16.12
DO	1982	1985-1989	16.12
DO	1987	1990	16.12
ESTABLISHMENTS, SALES, AND SALES PER ESTABLISHMENT	1977	1980	16.11
DO	1939-1977	1982-1984	16.11
DO	1939-1982	1985-1989	16.11
DO	1939-1987	1990	16.11
RETAIL TRADE ESTABLISHMENTS, SALES AND SALES PER ESTABLISHMENT BY SPECIFIED KIND OF BUSINESS	1977	1980	16.14
FLORIDA, SPECIFIED STATES, AND UNITED STATES			
SALES PER CAPITA	1972	1978	25.01
DO	1977	1980	25.01

CENSUS OF SERVICE INDUSTRIES
(CONDUCTED APPROXIMATELY EVERY 5 YEARS)

AREA AND DEMOGRAPHIC CHARACTERISTIC INCLUDED	CENSUS YEAR	FLORIDA STATISTICAL ABSTRACT YEAR	TABLE
FLORIDA, STATE ONLY			
HOTELS, CAMPING FACILITIES, AMUSEMENT AND RECREATION SERVICES, ESTABLISHMENTS, RECEIPTS, PAYROLL, AND EMPLOYMENT BY KIND OF BUSINESS	1977	1980	19.74
ESTABLISHMENTS, RECEIPTS, PAYROLL, AND EMPLOYMENT BY KIND OF BUSINESS	1977	1980	18.06
AUTO REPAIR, SERVICES, AND GARAGES, ESTABLISHMENTS, RECEIPTS, PAYROLL, AND EMPLOYMENT BY KIND OF BUSINESS	1977	1980	18.08
MISCELLANEOUS REPAIR SERVICES, ESTABLISHMENTS, RECEIPTS, PAYROLL, AND EMPLOYMENT BY KIND OF BUSINESS	1977	1980	18.09
ARCHITECTURE AND ENGINEERING SERVICES, ESTABLISHMENTS RECEIPTS, PAYROLL, AND EMPLOYMENT BY KIND OF BUSINESS	1977	1980	18.12
ESTABLISHMENTS AND RECEIPTS BY SIC CODE	1977	1981-1984	18.02
ESTABLISHMENTS, RECEIPTS, AND RECEIPTS PER ESTABLISHMENT	1947-1977	1981	18.01
DO	1948-1977	1982-1984	18.01
LEGAL SERVICES, ESTABLISHMENTS, RECEIPTS, EMPLOYMENT, AND PAYROLL BY FORM OF ORGANIZATION	1977	1982	22.53
STATE AND COUNTIES			
ESTABLISHMENTS AND RECEIPTS	1977	1981-1984	18.03
SELECTED SERVICES, RECEIPTS AND PAYROLL	1977	1980	18.03
STATE AND SELECTED CITIES			
RECEIPTS, PAYROLL	1977	1980	18.04
STATE, SMSAS, AND COUNTIES			
AUTO AND MISCELLANEOUS REPAIR SERVICES, ESTABLISHMENTS, RECEIPTS, PAYROLL AND EMPLOYMENT	1977	1980	18.10
HOTELS, MOTELS, TRAILER PARKS, CAMPS, ESTABLISHMENTS, RECEIPTS, PAYROLL, AND EMPLOYMENT	1977	1980	18.05
LEGAL SERVICES, ESTABLISHMENTS, RECEIPTS, PAYROLL AND EMPLOYMENT	1977	1980	22.58
STATE, SMSAS, AND SELECTED COUNTIES			
ESTABLISHMENTS, RECEIPTS, PAYROLL, AND EMPLOYMENT	1977	1980	18.13
PERSONAL AND BUSINESS SERVICES, ESTABLISHMENTS, RECEIPTS, PAYROLL, AND EMPLOYMENT	1977	1980	18.07
SMSAS			
LEGAL SERVICES, ESTABLISHMENTS, RECEIPTS, AND NUMBER BY TYPE OF PRACTICE	1977	1982	22.54

CENSUS OF TRANSPORTATION
(CONDUCTED APPROXIMATELY EVERY 5 YEARS)

AREA AND DEMOGRAPHIC CHARACTERISTIC INCLUDED	CENSUS YEAR	FLORIDA STATISTICAL ABSTRACT YEAR	TABLE
FLORIDA, STATE ONLY			
CHARACTERISTICS OF TRAVEL TO AND THROUGH FLORIDA	1977	1980	19.28
DO	1977	1980	19.27
TRAVEL ORIGINATING IN FLORIDA	1977	1980	19.80
TRUCK INVENTORY AND USE	1977	1981	13.01
COMPARATIVE SUMMARY OF TRUCKS BY USAGE AND TYPE AS A PERCENTAGE OF TOTAL TRUCKS	1967-1982	1985-1986	13.01

CENSUS OF WHOLESALE TRADE
(CONDUCTED APPROXIMATELY EVERY 5 YEARS)

AREA AND DEMOGRAPHIC CHARACTERISTIC INCLUDED	CENSUS YEAR	FLORIDA STATISTICAL ABSTRACT YEAR	TABLE
FLORIDA, STATE ONLY			
ESTABLISHMENTS, SALES AND SALES PER ESTABLISHMENT	1977	1980	16.01
DO	1939-1977	1981	16.01
DO	1948-1977	1982-1984	16.01
DO	1948-1982	1985-1989	16.01
DO	1948-1987	1990	16.01
BY SIC CODE	1977	1981-1984	16.02
DO	1982	1985-1989	16.02
DO	1987	1990	16.02
ESTABLISHMENTS BY TYPE OF OPERATION	1972-1977	1980	16.02
ESTABLISHMENTS, SALES, SALES PER ESTABLISHMENT BY KIND OF BUSINESS	1972-1977	1980	16.03
DO	1977	1982-1984	16.02
DO	1982	1985-1989	16.02
DO	1987	1990	16.02
STATE AND COUNTIES			
WHOLESALE AND RETAIL TRADE, SALES	1977	1981-1984	16.06
DO	1982	1985-1989	16.06
DO	1987	1990	16.06

INDEX OF TABLES

O

Ocala. See City and Metroplitan area
    data.
Occupational therapists............20.36
Office equipment...................12.50
Office space.......................23.43
Ohio. See State data.
Oil (See also Fuel oil and
    Petroleum):
    Extraction................6.21, 10.72
    Production.....................15.09
    Required for electric utilities..15.27
Okaloosa County. See County and Metro-
    politan area data.
Okeechobee County. See County data.
Oklahoma. See State data.
Old-age assistance............7.15, 7.18
Old-age, survivors, disability, and
    health insurance (OASDI). See
    Social security.
Optical goods, manufacturing.......12.50
Opticians..........................20.38
Optometrists................20.05, 20.36
Orange County. See County and Metro-
    politan area data.
Oranges:
    Acreage....................9.52, 9.55
    Cash receipts..............9.25, 9.26
    Concentrate.....................9.56
    Juice sales.....................9.56
    Prices..........................9.53
    Production......9.51, 9.52, 9.53, 9.54
    Yield per acre..................9.52
Orchards (See also Fruit crops).....9.34
Orchestras.........................19.75
Organizations and associations.....20.30
                                   23.43
Orientals. See Asian population.
Orlando. See City and Metroplitan area
    data.
Osceola County. See County and Metro-
    politan area data.
Osteopathic physicians......20.01, 20.05
                                   20.33

P

Paint, glass, and wallpaper
    stores.........................16.43
Paints, manufacturing..............12.50
Palm Bay. See City and Metropolitan
    area data.
Palm Beach County. See County and
    Metropolitan area data.
Panama City. See City and Metropolitan
    area data.
Paper and allied products....6.21, 12.50
                         12.63, 16.02, 16.43
    Price index.....................24.75
Pari-mutuels................23.45, 23.54
    Tax revenue from...............23.35

Parks:
    Employment.........23.76, 23.77, 23.78
    National.......................19.53
    Special districts..............21.01
    State..........................19.52
Parole and probation........22.11, 22.12
                                   25.01
Parole and Probation Commission....23.41
Pasco County. See County and Metro-
    politan area data.
Pastureland.........................9.36
Patients. See Hospitals.
Pawn shops..................16.81, 23.43
Payroll (See also Earnings).........6.57
    Accounting, auditing, and book-
        keeping services...........18.25
    Advertising agencies and
        services...................18.22
    Agriculture..........9.15, 9.17, 9.27
    Amusement and recreation
        services..........19.75, 19.78
    Apparel stores.................16.43
    Automobile:
        Dealers....................16.43
        Rental.............18.21, 19.75
    Automotive services.......16.43, 18.02
                               18.21, 18.40
    Banks......................17.39, 17.40
    Barber and beauty shops.........18.20
    Broadcasting.............14.35, 14.36
    Building materials dealers.......16.43
    Business organizations.........20.30
    Business services..18.02, 18.22, 18.25
                               18.35, 18.51
    Chiropractors' offices.........20.05
    Communications...........14.35, 14.36
    Computer and data processing
        services...................18.22
    Construction.............11.71, 11.73
    Correctional institutions......22.50
                                   23.71
    Counties.........................6.22
    Credit agencies...........17.39, 17.41
    Credit reporting and collection
        services...................18.22
    Defense contracts..............23.15
    Dentists' offices.........20.05, 20.07
    Detective agencies........18.22, 22.50
    Drug stores....................16.43
    Eating and drinking places.......16.43
                                   19.73
    Economic programs..............23.71
    Education..........20.05, 20.27, 23.71
    Electric, gas, and sanitary
        services............15.15, 15.16
    Engineering, architectural, and
        surveying services....18.25, 18.51
    Environmental programs..........23.71
    Equipment rental...............18.22
    Finance, insurance, and real
        estate.....................17.39
    Fire protection..........22.50, 23.71
    Fishing industries.............10.71

R